Hardball Retrospective:

Evaluating Scouting and Development Outcomes for the Modern-Era Franchises

Derek Bain

Edited by Marianne Landrum

Foreword by Don Daglow

Photo Credits:

Cover photograph (Rod Carew, Minnesota Twins) –
NATIONAL BASEBALL HALL OF FAME LIBRARY
COOPERSTOWN, N.Y.

Hardball Retrospective: Evaluating Scouting and Development Outcomes for the Modern-Era Franchises [Print Edition]

Derek Bain (Author), Marianne Landrum (Editor)

Print Edition - First Release May 2015
Digital Edition - First Release January 2015

ISBN 9781508790990

Please direct all feedback and inquiries to: support@tuatarasoftware.com

Be sure to check out the enhanced digital version of **Hardball Retrospective**, which contains bonus content including a chapter on Sustained Excellence along with supplementary tables and charts!

Table of Contents

It is the phrase that launched a billion arguments and filled the infinite hours of sports fans' tedium.

"What if...?"

When I wrote my first computer baseball game in 1971 I was driven by a "What if?" I was heartbroken because when I was ten years old Bobby Richardson had caught Willie McCovey's line drive in the 9th inning of Game 7 and stolen the 1962 World Series from my San Francisco Giants.

With my computer program I could replay that series over and over again, and about half the time I could experience the joy -- albeit simulated joy -- of my Giants winning the championship. As the years went by and I developed Baseball games with Earl Weaver and Eddie Dombrower, and then for over 20 years with Tony La Russa, I always came back to re-playing that World Series.

And exploring the "What if...?"

Some arguments, however, don't lend themselves to such computer simulation. The old standard of, "Who would win a series between the 1927 Yankees and the Big Red Machine of the 1970's," is a prime example. We can play the two teams in a simulation game, but the athletes are separated in time by five decades, over two full generations. How do we account for the differences in nutrition, training, equipment and even culture?

The short answer is that we can guess the answers, but we can't know.

This leads to a central assumption of data analysis in sports: we can do a fabulous job analyzing today's stats, but the farther we go into the past, the murkier the comparisons become. And if we compare eras to each other we walk on an ice layer of credibility that grows perilously thin.

Happily, there are exceptions.

Derek Bain has proven that there are ways to do complex analysis of some important "What if" questions that hold water for 1915 data as well as they do for today's stats. With some ingenious statistical methods he has produced one of the finest Baseball research books I've seen in recent years, one that belongs in true fans' collections along with the works of long-time brilliant writers and researchers like John Thorn, Pete Palmer, Bill James, Mike Gershman and the pioneers who guided SABR before we ever had sabermetrics.

Bain's book is called Hardball Retrospective, and you're reading it right now.

In this volume he has answered one of the great what-if's of all time: if you subtract all of your favorite team's trades, both good and bad, how much better or worse would they have done? I had wondered about that issue for years, and Bain has answered all these questions for us. My theory that the Giants' poor trades in the 1960's took us out of the World Series instead of ushering us in?

Sustained by "Judge" Bain.

My theories about the Giants' trades of the late 1990's?

Disproven. Turns out I was wrong.

Many writers would have presented this data as a series of tables and given us a book of numbers. I'm delighted to report that Bain has done the opposite, and along with the clearly organized tables of data he has given us a lively narrative, team by team, of how this alternate history plays out in the win-loss records he calculates for each world view.

The front office of each club is not just responsible for trades: they are involved in scouting, drafting, signing, compensation and player development just as thoroughly as they decide on trades. What we are really doing in this analysis -- as Bain notes -- is separating out the impact of trades and retaining that of scouting, recruiting and teaching.

In fact, in the pages that follow, Bain also gives us a bonus analysis of the efficacy of teams' draft strategies since the creation of the Amateur Draft in Baseball in 1965. I was shocked to read how some teams have picked terribly over and over again in rounds 2 through 4, where talent should be more conspicuous, only to just as reliably make great choices in rounds 11 and higher, where players are not expected to make the big club.

Some of the patterns will shock you.

I've had great fun reading this book, and I've gained both valuable knowledge and interesting perspectives. I hope you enjoy it even more than I have.

– Don Daglow

Preface

Imagine the roster of your favorite baseball team from any particular year. Remove all of the players that your team acquired through trades and free agency. Would you be able to field a competitive team? All right, let us re-populate the roster with every player that the organization originally drafted and signed. Yes, we will include undrafted free agents and foreign players who signed with their first Major League team, as well. How does the team stack up now? Is the club better or worse than the squad that you imagined at first? Would the team make the playoffs if player X had not been traded?

I applied these criteria to every Major League Baseball franchise of the modern era (1901-present) in order to establish the proficiency of each organization with respect to scouting, development and performance.

Acknowledgments

Antonina, Michael, Brendan and Renée – the BEST family in the Cosmos!! Thank you for all of your love, patience and encouragement throughout this process.

Marianne Landrum – thank you for editing, proofreading and offering valuable writing insight. I am extremely grateful to have such a wonderful Aunt.

My amazing parents and grandparents - for instilling me with the values that I strive to teach my children today.

To all of my relatives – for your kindness and inspiration.

To all past, present and future members of the Dunellen Fantasy Baseball League- thanks for the competition. Our draft-day banter is always a blast!

Don Daglow, Eddie Dombrower and all of the ingenious talent that produced computer baseball games and simulations, past and present – your programming and artistic creativity spurred my imagination and motivated my compositions. Special thanks to Don Daglow for writing the Foreword!

Mike Lynch – thank you for granting me the opportunity to write for the Seamheads community.

Bill James, Pete Palmer, John Thorn, Craig Wright, Dave Smith, Sean Lahman, Tom Ruane, Clifford Blau for your inspired work in the field of Sabermetrics.

Dedicated to Vernon Peter "Pop-Pop" Corby

Methodology

I began my research by downloading the Baseball-Databank SQL database and the Retrosheet transaction file. I imported the files into MySQL and then executed multiple searches against the Retrosheet transaction file, looking for all players with the following transaction types:

Da - amateur draft pick
Df - first year draft pick
Fa - amateur free agent signing
Fb - amateur free agent "bonus baby" signing under the 1953-57 rule requiring player to stay on ML roster
Fo - free agent signing with first ML team
J - jumped teams
P - purchase

For the transaction types listed below, I also specified that the "from league" field could not be the American or National League:

C - conditional deal
D - rule 5 draft pick
Dm - minor league draft pick
M - obtained rights when entering into working agreement with minor league team
T - trade

After correcting any team-ID mismatches between the Baseball-Databank and Retrosheet files, I performed the following tasks:

- Execute 3 queries (batting, fielding, pitching) for each year (1901-2013) to extract single-season data for each player. I inserted a field that contained the team-ID for the player's original team as determined by the transaction queries.
- Export the results to individual Microsoft Excel files.
- Sort the results in ascending order on Franchise-ID, Player.
- Generate subtotals based on Franchise-ID for all counting categories (AB,R,H,etc.)

I copied the subtotals into another spreadsheet, sorted by year and league. The new spreadsheet contained columns with each team's "original" and "actual" won-loss record and winning percentage. The "original" won-loss record was calculated by normalizing the runs scored and runs allowed, against the league average for that season. This was necessary due to the distribution of plate appearances and innings pitched across the "original" teams (the variance is much closer between "actual" teams, assuming each team played the same number of games during a season). Using Bill James' Pythagorean record, I was able to generate a winning percentage for each "original" team and determine estimated wins and losses for each team. Adding another column to calculate the difference between their "original" and "actual" winning percentage allowed me to sort on this field and determine the highest and lowest differences between the "original" players versus the "actual" players. In addition, I calculated the "original" and "actual" WAR (Wins Above Replacement) and Win Shares for every team. The results of my findings can be found in the proceeding pages.

WAR - Wins Above Replacement
http://www.baseball-
reference.com/bullpen/Wins_Above_Replacement_Player?vm=r

The Baseball-Reference Bullpen has defined Wins Above Replacement as follows:

Wins Above Replacement Player, **or WARP, Is a statistic published in Baseball Prospectus that attempts to measure the "total value" of a player over a given season.**

WARP, intuitively, attempts to express the total number of wins that a given player adds to his team over the course of a season by comparing the player's performance with that of a fictitious "replacement player." A "replacement player" is assumed to be an average Triple-A callup who might appear in the majors only as replacement for an injured player, and whose hitting, fielding, and (if applicable) pitching skills are far below league average. According to Baseball Prospectus, a team consisting entirely of replacement-level players would likely be historically bad, winning only 20-25 games over a full 162-game season.

To compute WARP, Baseball Prospectus uses three other proprietary statistics: Batting Runs Above Replacement (BRAR), Fielding Runs Above Replacement (FRAR), and Pitching Runs Above Replacement (PRAR). The three numbers are added and divided by the number of runs per win that season (another proprietary number; in recent years, this number is around 10).

Most regular position players will accumulate 3-5 WARP over a season. A legitimate All-Star-caliber player may have over 7 WARP. Over 10 WARP is a strong MVP candidate, while over 15 WARP is a "one-for-the-ages" season. On the flip side, a player with -1 WARP or less is probably in danger of disappearing from baseball.

Teams can also be ranked by cumulative WARP. A team with a total of 30 WARP or less among all players would be a disastrous, certain last-place finisher. 50-60 WARP can be expected from a .500 team. 65-70 WARP is a playoff-caliber team while much more than that would be a strong World Series candidate.

The Baseball-Reference Bullpen has defined Win Shares as follows:

Win Shares **is a statistic developed by sabermetrician and author Bill James. The statistic is meant to assess a player's value in terms of his ability to help his team win games.**

To say as much as possible without taking away from the value of James' book (ISBN 1931584036), the concept of Win Shares is derived from Marginal Runs Scored and Marginal Runs Saved. The margin is defined as one half of the league average runs scored for hitters, and one and one half the league average runs allowed for pitchers.

For example: In 2004 the Chicago Cubs scored 789 runs and allowed 665 runs. The average amount of runs scored was 751 runs, the margin was 376 for hitters and 1127 for pitchers - 375.5625 and 1126.6875 to be exact. To calculate marginal runs, subtract the hitting runs margin from the amount of runs the Cubs actually scored (789-376) and subtract the total amount of runs allowed from the pitching runs margin (1127-665). This yields totals of 413 hitting runs and 462 pitching runs, which add up to 875.

Therefore, Cubs had 875 marginal runs. Dividing that amount by twice the amount of league average runs (1502) gives an expected winning percentage of 0.582, or 94 wins. Since the Cubs only won 89 games, all final totals are cut down by about 1.05%.

Figuring out how to allot marginal runs per player takes several pages and paragraphs to explain- it has a lot to do with Runs Created and some to do with sabermetric fielding analysis. It could be explained here, but that's why Mr. James sells books. That's the basics behind calculating Win Shares for a team.

Win Shares can be used to answer many questions, such as "who were Player X's teammates?", or to compile a list of managers and their players.

The Baseball-Reference Bullpen has defined Pythagorean Theorem of Baseball as follows:

> **The Pythagorean Theorem of Baseball is a creation of Bill James which relates the number of runs a team has scored and surrendered to its actual winning percentage, based on the idea that runs scored/runs allowed is a better indicator of a team's (future) performance than a team's actual winning percentage. This results in a formula which is referred to as Pythagorean Winning Percentage.**
>
> **The Formula**
>
> **There are two ways of calculating Pythagorean Winning Percentage (W%). The more commonly used and simpler version uses an exponent of 2 in the formula.**
>
> $$W\% = \frac{(Runs\ Scored)^2}{(Runs\ Scored)^2 + (Runs\ Allowed)^2}$$
>
> **More accurate versions of the formula use 1.81 or 1.83 as the exponent.**
>
> $$W\% = \frac{(Runs\ Scored)^{1.81}}{(Runs\ Scored)^{1.81} + (Runs\ Allowed)^{1.81}}$$
>
> **Expected W-L can then be obtained by multiplying W% by the team's total number of games played, then rounding off.**

oWAR ("Original" WAR) - **Wins Above Replacement for players on "original" teams**
aWAR ("Actual" WAR) - **Wins Above Replacement for players on "actual" teams**
oWS ("Original" WS) - **Win Shares for players on "original" teams**
aWS ("Actual" WS) - **Win Shares for players on "actual" teams**
oWAR+ ("Original" WAR+) - **WAR above league average for "original" teams**
aWAR+ ("Actual" WAR+) - **WAR above league average for "actual" teams**
oWS+ ("Original" WS+) - **Win Shares above league average for "original" teams**
aWS+ ("Actual" WS+) - **Win Shares above league average for "actual" teams**
oWARavg ("Original" WAR average) – **WAR divided by Player-Seasons**
oWSavg ("Original" WS average) - **Win Shares divided by Player-Seasons**
oPW% ("Original" Pythagorean W-L percentage) - **Pythagorean Won-Loss percentage for the "original" teams**
aPW% ("Actual" Pythagorean W-L percentage) - **Pythagorean Won-Loss percentage for the "actual" teams**
Player-Seasons - **# of years in which a player recorded at least one game played**
PS-Draft - **total player-seasons for a team divided by the team's total drafts**

The Amateur Draft

Major League Baseball implemented the Amateur Draft in 1965 to contend with the escalating costs of acquiring high school and college graduates. Individuals eligible for the draft include high school graduates, junior college students and 4-year college students* who are residents of the United States, Canada and U.S. Territories such as Puerto Rico. The draft order is determined by reversing the order of the standings from the previous season. Also known as the First Year Player Draft or "Rule 4" Draft, the process currently consists of 40 rounds. Additional information regarding the draft can be found on the Major League Baseball website (mlb.com).

http://mlb.mlb.com/mlb/history/draft/

http://mlb.mlb.com/mlb/draftday/rules.jsp

*- "4-year college students must complete their junior or senior years and be at least 21 years of age"

Prior to the Amateur Draft, amateur player acquisition options primarily consisted of free agent signings, purchases or trades with minor league franchises. Honus Wagner was purchased by the Louisville Colonels in July of 1897 from Paterson of the Atlantic League. The Red Sox purchased Babe Ruth, Ernie Shore and Ben Egan from Baltimore of the International League on July 9, 1914.

Players in foreign countries are generally acquired via purchase or free agency. The Yankees purchased Alfonso Soriano from the Hiroshima Toyo Carp of the Japan Central League on September 29, 1998. Seattle purchased Ichiro Suzuki on November 30, 2000 from Orix Blue Wave of the Japan Pacific League. The Dodgers signed free agent Hiroki Kuroda on December 16, 2007.

The Philadelphia Athletics traded $40,000 and three players to Milwaukee of the American Association in return for Al Simmons on December 15, 1923. The Yankees acquired Joe DiMaggio from the San Francisco Seals of the Pacific Coast League on November 21, 1934 in exchange for four players and $5,000. This form of transaction fell out of favor in the middle of the 1950's.

The players chosen by the Los Angeles Dodgers in the 1968 MLB Amateur Draft have outperformed every other team's selections by a significant margin. The total career Win Shares for the Dodgers' class of '68 (1613) exceeds the runner-up 1989 Cleveland Indians by more than 650. The squad also tops the Amateur Draft WAR leader boards with 188, besting the 1983 Red Sox by 13. Los Angeles' extraordinary group includes Steve Garvey, Ron Cey, Davey Lopes, Doyle Alexander, Joe Ferguson, Geoff Zahn and Bill Buckner. The Dodgers' front office consisted of Buzzie Bavasi, Fresco Thompson and Al Campanis.

The Boston Red Sox drafts of 1976, 1983 and 1989 placed in the top 25 for career WS and WAR with the 1968 draft earning the fifteenth position on the WS list. GM Dick O'Connell and Scouting Director Neil Mahoney grabbed Cecil Cooper, Ben Oglivie and Bill F. Lee in '68. O'Connell's selections in '76 (Wade Boggs, John Tudor and Bruce Hurst) accumulated the third-best career WS total (858). Haywood Sullivan and Eddie Kasko's choices in '83 (Roger Clemens and Ellis Burks) tallied the second-highest career WAR total (175). Lou Gorman and Kasko snagged Jeff Bagwell and Mo Vaughn in the '89 draft.

GM Hank Peters and the Cleveland Indians appear twice on the top 25 career WS register. The Tribe's selections in 1989 (Jim Thome, Brian S. Giles and Curt Leskanic) place second All-Time on the Amateur Draft career Win Shares list while finishing fifth on the WAR leader boards. Two year later Peters struck gold again with Manny Ramirez. He also presided over the Baltimore Orioles' 1978 draft which yielded Cal Ripken and Mike Boddicker and the 1987 selections of Steve Finley, Pete Harnisch and David Segui.

Jim Campbell and Bill LaJoie of the Detroit Tigers stockpiled talented ballplayers in the mid-Seventies. Lance Parrish and Mark "The Bird" Fidrych were chosen in the '74 draft with Lou Whitaker and Jason Thompson among those selected in the subsequent season. The crowning achievement comprised their selections of Alan Trammell, Jack Morris, Steve Kemp and Dan Petry in 1976. Cubs GM Dallas Green earns kudos for his consecutive draft successes in 1984-85. Greg Maddux and Jamie Moyer's draft class of '84 placed third-highest on the top 25 career WAR register while Rafael Palmeiro and Mark Grace rank thirteenth on the corresponding Win Share list.

The worst draft of All-Time belongs to the Charlie Finley and the 1979 Oakland Athletics (0 Win Shares). Bert Bradley was the lone player to reach the Major Leagues, receiving a "Cup of Coffee" in '83. Harry Dalton and Walter Shannon guided the 1973 California Angels to a runner-up finish on the draft failure list. Pat D. Kelly (7 AB in 1980) and Mike Overy (6.14 ERA) are featured in this nondescript group. Twins' owner Calvin Griffith opted for Bob Gorinski (.195 BA in '77) and Mark Wiley (6.06 ERA) with the top two picks in the 1970 draft. Ten years later Yankees' brain trust Gene Michael and Bobby Hofman managed to eke out 0.35 Win Shares from Tom Dodd, Ben Callahan and Clay Christiansen. Does anyone recall the quartet of Cubs' recruits, Ray Sadler, Steve Smyth, John Webb and Peter Zoccolillo, from Ed Lynch and Jim Hendry's dreadful effort in '99?

The Red Sox, Athletics and Dodgers top the overall rankings for the 50-year history of the MLB Amateur Draft. The Blue Jays lead the Expansion franchises based on average career WS and WAR per draft. The players drafted by the Chicago White Sox place last among the Turn of the Century franchises in average career Win Shares and WAR. The Pale Hose draft classes failed to compile at least 100 WS on 21 occasions (through 2003). The San Diego Padres fared worst among the Expansion franchises (excluding the Marlins, Rockies, Diamondbacks and Rays due to lack of data). The Friars posted 16 seasons below the 100 career WS mark (through 2003).

franchID	totalWS	exp	drafts	avgWS	franchID	totalWAR	exp	drafts	avgWAR
BOS	9,962.06		49	203.31	BOS	1305.51		49	26.64
OAK	9,812.82		49	200.26	OAK	1194.50		49	24.38
LAD	8,930.37		49	182.25	TOR	850.10	1977	37	22.98
TOR	6,661.17	1977	37	180.03	WSN	1000.21	1969	46	21.74
STL	8,815.32		49	179.90	LAD	996.16		49	20.33
ANA	8,762.58	1961	49	178.83	KCR	929.49	1969	46	20.21
TEX	8,608.82	1961	49	175.69	STL	971.20		49	19.82
WSN	8,075.90	1969	46	175.56	PIT	937.39		49	19.13
ATL	8,421.76		49	171.87	MIN	897.05		49	18.31
CIN	8,385.37		49	171.13	ATL	888.99		49	18.14
MIN	8,347.58		49	170.36	SEA	665.07	1977	37	17.97
KCR	7,791.14	1969	46	169.37	ANA	870.92	1961	49	17.77
PIT	8,125.37		49	165.82	TEX	861.68	1961	49	17.59
SEA	5,844.35	1977	37	157.96	CIN	843.35		49	17.21
SFG	7,726.50		49	157.68	MIL	783.00	1969	46	17.02
NYM	7,719.26	1962	49	157.54	CHC	819.32		49	16.72
MIL	7,222.87	1969	46	157.02	PHI	804.89		49	16.43
PHI	7,525.43		49	153.58	CLE	787.91		49	16.08
CHC	7,519.97		49	153.47	NYY	769.07		49	15.70
NYY	7,337.70		49	149.75	SFG	762.91		49	15.57
CLE	7,244.20		49	147.84	NYM	755.10	1962	49	15.41
DET	6,713.89		49	137.02	BAL	694.56		49	14.17
HOU	6,571.17	1962	49	134.11	HOU	675.53	1962	49	13.79
BAL	6,549.51		49	133.66	DET	666.55		49	13.60
SDP	5,996.89	1969	46	130.37	ARI	230.50	1998	17	13.56
CHW	6,040.66		49	123.28	COL	297.72	1993	22	13.53
COL	2,705.32	1993	22	122.97	CHW	629.13		49	12.84
ARI	2,029.49	1998	17	119.38	TBD	199.00	1998	17	11.71
TBD	1,879.99	1998	17	110.59	SDP	535.15	1969	46	11.63
FLA	1,768.03	1993	22	80.37	FLA	174.48	1993	22	7.93

Player Development

I examined the scouting and development of Major League baseball players from several perspectives, focusing on the Amateur Draft in order to provide a consistent method for player acquisition. Fundamentally, this places all teams on equal ground in terms of selecting from the same group of available players each year. All players eligible for the Draft are not equal with respect to monetary demands and all teams are not equal in terms of resources. Furthermore, teams may chose to pass on drafting a high school graduate who has already committed to a college. Using a half-century's worth of results from the Amateur Draft, I divided the players into four groups based on the round in which they were selected. I added the number of player-seasons for each range to determine the groupings (Round 1, 2-4, 5-10 and 11-89), omitting all players who were drafted but did not sign in a particular season.

The Player Development chart compares the Amateur Draft results for each team by dividing the total OWAR and OWS into total Player-Seasons for each grouping. The Graduation Rate chart represents the number of Player-Seasons per draft, relating how many ballplayers drafted by each team have "graduated" to the big leagues along with the number of seasons they have played.

Player Development (OWARavg and OWSavg compared to League Average)

DraftRoundGroup	OWAR	OWS	Player-Seasons	OWARavg	OWSavg
MLB-Round 1	8324	70591	9880	0.84	7.14
MLB-Round 2-4	6035	52956	9368	0.64	5.65
MLB-Round 5-10	3917	40227	7932	0.49	5.07
MLB-Round 11-89	4521	45322	9549	0.47	4.75
ANA-Round 1	356	3200	495	0.72	6.46
ANA-Round 2-4	235	2400	398	0.59	6.03
ANA-Round 5-10	213	2008	350	0.61	5.74
ANA-Round 11-89	67	1154	294	0.23	3.92
ARI-Round 1	79	627	85	0.93	7.37
ARI-Round 2-4	18	284	89	0.20	3.19
ARI-Round 5-10	70	460	96	0.72	4.80
ARI-Round 11-89	64	658	135	0.47	4.88
ATL-Round 1	255	2348	345	0.74	6.81
ATL-Round 2-4	273	2520	433	0.63	5.82
ATL-Round 5-10	135	1506	289	0.47	5.21
ATL-Round 11-89	225	2048	348	0.65	5.88
BAL-Round 1	315	2312	337	0.93	6.86
BAL-Round 2-4	202	1952	318	0.63	6.14
BAL-Round 5-10	83	959	260	0.32	3.69
BAL-Round 11-89	95	1326	320	0.30	4.14
BOS-Round 1	501	3502	422	1.19	8.30
BOS-Round 2-4	337	2326	338	1.00	6.88
BOS-Round 5-10	326	2790	362	0.90	7.71
BOS-Round 11-89	141	1344	292	0.48	4.60
CHC-Round 1	215	2093	333	0.65	6.28
CHC-Round 2-4	314	2441	409	0.77	5.97
CHC-Round 5-10	133	1411	342	0.39	4.12
CHC-Round 11-89	157	1576	353	0.45	4.46

CHW-Round 1	278	2395	372	0.75	6.44
CHW-Round 2-4	89	1373	374	0.24	3.67
CHW-Round 5-10	75	767	186	0.40	4.12
CHW-Round 11-89	187	1505	338	0.55	4.45
CIN-Round 1	238	2171	329	0.72	6.60
CIN-Round 2-4	251	2525	378	0.66	6.68
CIN-Round 5-10	226	2294	392	0.58	5.85
CIN-Round 11-89	129	1396	336	0.38	4.16
CLE-Round 1	235	2212	344	0.68	6.43
CLE-Round 2-4	178	1680	319	0.56	5.26
CLE-Round 5-10	109	1192	281	0.39	4.24
CLE-Round 11-89	266	2161	393	0.68	5.50
COL-Round 1	137	833	111	1.24	7.50
COL-Round 2-4	79	620	126	0.63	4.92
COL-Round 5-10	54	585	104	0.52	5.63
COL-Round 11-89	27	668	149	0.18	4.48
DET-Round 1	230	2218	371	0.62	5.98
DET-Round 2-4	154	1750	317	0.48	5.52
DET-Round 5-10	150	1334	268	0.56	4.98
DET-Round 11-89	133	1411	343	0.39	4.11
FLA-Round 1	114	803	107	1.06	7.51
FLA-Round 2-4	61	530	126	0.48	4.21
FLA-Round 5-10	-1	158	78	-0.01	2.03
FLA-Round 11-89	1	276	83	0.01	3.33
HOU-Round 1	248	2428	360	0.69	6.74
HOU-Round 2-4	143	1438	273	0.52	5.27
HOU-Round 5-10	101	1095	237	0.42	4.62
HOU-Round 11-89	185	1610	302	0.61	5.33
KCR-Round 1	248	2165	358	0.69	6.05
KCR-Round 2-4	397	2820	405	0.98	6.96
KCR-Round 5-10	115	1102	232	0.50	4.75
KCR-Round 11-89	169	1704	371	0.46	4.59
LAD-Round 1	265	2151	317	0.84	6.78
LAD-Round 2-4	208	2094	394	0.53	5.31
LAD-Round 5-10	245	2473	354	0.69	6.99
LAD-Round 11-89	278	2213	430	0.65	5.15
MIL-Round 1	455	3379	316	1.44	10.69
MIL-Round 2-4	129	1120	208	0.62	5.38
MIL-Round 5-10	108	1507	308	0.35	4.89
MIL-Round 11-89	91	1217	245	0.37	4.97
MIN-Round 1	274	2762	360	0.76	7.67
MIN-Round 2-4	397	2712	400	0.99	6.78
MIN-Round 5-10	96	1092	257	0.37	4.25
MIN-Round 11-89	130	1781	356	0.37	5.00

NYM-Round 1	332	3144	438	0.76	7.18
NYM-Round 2-4	167	1816	377	0.44	4.82
NYM-Round 5-10	74	960	258	0.29	3.72
NYM-Round 11-89	182	1799	397	0.46	4.53
NYY-Round 1	**220**	**1913**	**243**	**0.91**	**7.87**
NYY-Round 2-4	**161**	**1409**	**314**	**0.51**	**4.49**
NYY-Round 5-10	**134**	**1742**	**359**	**0.37**	**4.85**
NYY-Round 11-89	**254**	**2274**	**454**	**0.56**	**5.01**
OAK-Round 1	445	3820	494	0.90	7.73
OAK-Round 2-4	332	2315	356	0.93	6.50
OAK-Round 5-10	253	2150	347	0.73	6.19
OAK-Round 11-89	165	1528	307	0.54	4.98
PHI-Round 1	**249**	**2217**	**349**	**0.71**	**6.35**
PHI-Round 2-4	**330**	**2514**	**390**	**0.85**	**6.45**
PHI-Round 5-10	**122**	**1552**	**306**	**0.40**	**5.07**
PHI-Round 11-89	**104**	**1243**	**307**	**0.34**	**4.05**
PIT-Round 1	363	2531	280	1.30	9.04
PIT-Round 2-4	176	1598	312	0.57	5.12
PIT-Round 5-10	146	1497	278	0.53	5.38
PIT-Round 11-89	251	2500	484	0.52	5.17
SDP-Round 1	**215**	**2410**	**360**	**0.60**	**6.70**
SDP-Round 2-4	**157**	**1569**	**250**	**0.63**	**6.27**
SDP-Round 5-10	**51**	**835**	**237**	**0.22**	**3.52**
SDP-Round 11-89	**112**	**1183**	**316**	**0.35**	**3.74**
SEA-Round 1	357	2644	314	1.14	8.42
SEA-Round 2-4	110	1218	260	0.42	4.69
SEA-Round 5-10	137	1036	186	0.74	5.57
SEA-Round 11-89	61	947	249	0.24	3.80
SFG-Round 1	**312**	**2900**	**461**	**0.68**	**6.29**
SFG-Round 2-4	**178**	**1865**	**346**	**0.51**	**5.39**
SFG-Round 5-10	**106**	**1158**	**292**	**0.36**	**3.97**
SFG-Round 11-89	**168**	**1804**	**394**	**0.43**	**4.58**
STL-Round 1	328	2843	377	0.87	7.54
STL-Round 2-4	208	2059	383	0.54	5.37
STL-Round 5-10	132	1508	301	0.44	5.01
STL-Round 11-89	303	2406	449	0.67	5.36
TBD-Round 1	**81**	**630**	**64**	**1.27**	**9.85**
TBD-Round 2-4	**41**	**325**	**63**	**0.66**	**5.16**
TBD-Round 5-10	**35**	**453**	**89**	**0.39**	**5.10**
TBD-Round 11-89	**41**	**471**	**119**	**0.35**	**3.96**
TEX-Round 1	352	3068	486	0.72	6.31
TEX-Round 2-4	105	1476	354	0.30	4.17
TEX-Round 5-10	149	1675	320	0.46	5.23
TEX-Round 11-89	256	2390	445	0.57	5.37

TOR-Round 1	296	2172	276	1.07	7.87
TOR-Round 2-4	222	1644	278	0.80	5.91
TOR-Round 5-10	194	1480	261	0.74	5.67
TOR-Round 11-89	138	1365	291	0.48	4.69
WSN-Round 1	330	2699	376	0.88	7.18
WSN-Round 2-4	381	2563	380	1.00	6.74
WSN-Round 5-10	147	1448	302	0.49	4.80
WSN-Round 11-89	141	1366	249	0.57	5.48

Graduation Rates (# of Player-Seasons per Draft)

FranchID	OWAR	OWS	Player-Seasons	OWARavg	OWSavg	# Drafts	PS-Draft
TEX	862	8609	1605	0.54	5.36	49	32.76
ANA	871	8763	1537	0.57	5.70	49	31.37
STL	971	8815	1510	0.64	5.84	49	30.82
OAK	1194	9813	1504	0.79	6.52	49	30.69
LAD	996	8930	1495	0.67	5.97	49	30.51
SFG	763	7726	1493	0.51	5.18	49	30.47
KCR	930	7791	1366	0.68	5.70	45	30.36
NYM	755	7719	1470	0.51	5.25	49	30.00
TOR	850	6661	1106	0.77	6.02	37	29.89
CHC	819	7520	1437	0.57	5.23	49	29.33
CIN	843	8385	1435	0.59	5.84	49	29.29
WSN	1000	8076	1307	0.77	6.18	45	29.04
ATL	889	8422	1415	0.63	5.95	49	28.88
BOS	1305	9962	1414	0.92	7.05	49	28.86
MIN	897	8348	1373	0.65	6.08	49	28.02
NYY	769	7338	1370	0.56	5.36	49	27.96
PIT	937	8125	1354	0.69	6.00	49	27.63
PHI	805	7525	1352	0.60	5.57	49	27.59
CLE	788	7244	1337	0.59	5.42	49	27.29
SEA	665	5844	1009	0.66	5.79	37	27.27
DET	667	6714	1299	0.51	5.17	49	26.51
CHW	629	6041	1270	0.50	4.76	49	25.92
SDP	535	5997	1163	0.46	5.16	45	25.84
ARI	231	2029	405	0.57	5.01	16	25.31
BAL	695	6550	1235	0.56	5.30	49	25.20
MIL	783	7223	1077	0.73	6.71	45	23.93
HOU	676	6571	1172	0.58	5.61	49	23.92
COL	298	2705	490	0.61	5.52	21	23.33
TBD	199	1880	335	0.59	5.61	16	20.94
FLA	175	1768	394	0.44	4.49	21	18.76

The Angels record the second-highest graduation rate (31 player-seasons per Draft) while procuring the fifth-best OWSavg for rounds 5-10 in the Amateur Draft. Jim Edmonds (67 Career WAR, 319 Career WS) tops the list of mid-round recruits for the Halos, which also features Garret Anderson, Bruce Bochte, Wally Joyner, John Lackey, Carney Lansford, Mark McLemore, Gary Pettis, Tim Salmon, Jarrod Washburn and Devon White. Mike Trout is angling for the premier position in the Angels' blue-chip bunch, which is presently occupied by Tom Brunansky, Darin Erstad, Chuck Finley, Troy Glaus, Andy Messersmith, Frank Tanana and Jered Weaver. Seventeenth-round draftees Dante Bichette and Mike Napoli are the lone late-rounders of note as Los Angeles tallied the third-worst OWARavg in rounds 11-89.

Arizona's draft choices from rounds 2-4 rank last among the 30 ballclubs in OWARavg and OWSavg. On the other hand, the Diamondbacks' brass has chosen wisely in rounds 5-10 (5ᵗʰ in OWARavg). The D-Backs' first-round selections are headlined by Max Scherzer and Justin Upton while the returns from mid-round picks include Brad Penny, Dan Uggla (11ᵗʰ Round) and Brandon Webb.

Atlanta's late-round selections top the leader boards in OWSavg and place third in OWARavg, including the quintet of Dusty Baker (26ᵗʰ Round), Brett Butler (23ʳᵈ Round, 305 Career WS), Jermaine Dye, Glenn Hubbard and Kevin Millwood. Chipper Jones (69 Career WAR, 420 Career WS), Jeff Blauser, Dale Murphy and Adam Wainwright are among the notable first-round choices for the Braves. Ron Gant, Tom Glavine (82 Career WAR, 312 Career WS), David Justice, Ryan Klesko, Brian McCann, Mickey Rivers and Jason Schmidt complete Atlanta's upper-to-mid round draft picks.

Baltimore's draft record can be described as inconsistent. The blue-chip prospects score a ninth-place finish in OWARavg while the middle-to-late rounders settle near the bottom of the pack. Bobby Grich (327 Career WS) and Mike Mussina (82 Career WAR) headline a flock of first-round selections featuring Ben McDonald, Brian Roberts and Jayson Werth. In rounds 2-4 the Orioles system yields several treasures, Don Baylor, Doug DeCinces, Eddie Murray (58 Career WAR, 427 Career WS) and Cal Ripken, Jr. (66 Career WAR, 423 Career WS). Notable O's middle-to-late round picks include Mike Boddicker, Al Bumbry, Mike Flanagan and Steve Finley.

Boston wins the award for overall scouting and development specific to players selected in the Amateur Draft. The organization ranks fifth among first-round selections and outshines the competition in rounds 2-10, placing second in rounds 2-4 while nailing down the top spot for rounds 5-10. Roger Clemens leads all Sox draftees with 143 Career WAR and 437 Career WS). Boston blue-chippers Ellis Burks, Rick Burleson, Carlton Fisk (60 Career WAR, 364 Career WS), Nomar Garciaparra, Bruce Hurst, Jim Rice, Aaron Sele, Bob Stanley and Mo Vaughn are prominent, and mid-round prospects, including Jeff Bagwell, Wade Boggs, Dwight Evans, Fred Lynn, Amos Otis, Curt Schilling and John Tudor flourished under the direction of the Sox' coaching staff.

The Cubs' first-round draftees own the third-lowest marks in OWARavg and OWSavg while the organization rates seventh-worst overall in OWSavg. Chicago's foremost selections are a mixed bag consisting of Joe Carter, Jon Garland, Burt Hooton, Rafael Palmeiro (63 Career WAR, 401 Career WS) and Kerry Wood. The Cubbies claim the eighth-best OWARavg in rounds 2-4 on the shoulders of Greg Maddux (111 Career WAR, 404 Career WS) assisted by fellow hurlers Larry Gura, Ken Holtzman, Joe Niekro, Rick Reuschel and Lee Smith. Among the notable mid-to-late round products of the Cubs' farm system are Oscar Gamble, Mark Grace (24ᵗʰ Round), Kyle Lohse (29ᵗʰ Round), Jamie Moyer, Bill North and Steve Trachsel.

The White Sox rank worst overall among "Turn of the Century" franchises in OWARavg and OWSavg, placing next-to-last in rounds 2-4. Chicago's first-rounders grade slightly below average. Frank E. Thomas (70 Career WAR, 405 Career WS) stands out among the Sox selections, which encompass fellow number-one picks Harold Baines, Alex Fernandez, Jack McDowell and Robin Ventura. A short list of mid-to-late draftees for the Pale Hose includes Mark Buehrle, Mike Cameron, Doug Drabek, Ray Durham and Rich Gossage.

Cincinnati excels in the scouting and development of mid-round draft picks, scoring fifth (Rounds 2-4) and fourth (Rounds 5-10) in OWSavg. Featuring Johnny Bench (62 Career WAR, 365 Career WS), this gifted collection encompasses Eric Davis, Adam Dunn, Charlie Leibrandt, Hal McRae, Paul O'Neill, Reggie Sanders, Danny Tartabull and Joey Votto. Barry Larkin (67 Career WAR, 344 Career WS) outdistances the first-round recruits while Ken Griffey (29th Round) and Trevor Hoffman close out the endgame selections.

Despite the presence of Manny Ramirez amid the team's premier picks, Cleveland notches the fifth-worst record in OWARavg for first-rounders. Chris Chambliss, Charles Nagy, C.C. Sabathia and Greg Swindell round out the Tribes' blue-chippers. The club follows an unexceptional path through the middle rounds of the Amateur Draft, noting exemptions for Albert Belle, Dennis Eckersley and Von Hayes. The Indians' redemption occurs with the late-round draft picks as the franchise secured first place in OWARavg and a runner-up finish in OWSavg for rounds 11-89. Superb endgame selections consist of Buddy Bell, Brian S. Giles, Richie Sexson, and Jim Thome (391 Career WS).

The Rockies' blue-chip prospects place fourth in OWARavg, but struggle to develop late-round draftees, finishing second-to-last in OWARavg for players drafted in rounds 11-89. Todd Helton compiled 60 Career WAR and 315 Career WS, while fellow first-rounder Troy Tulowitzki continues to steadily climb the ranks. Matt Holliday leads the active mid-rounders with 219 Career WAR through 2013. Colorado ranks third-worst in Graduation Rate (23 player-seasons per Draft).

Detroit boasts the worst OWSavg and scores next-to-last in OWARavg among first-round draft picks while the franchise places 26th in overall OWARavg. Only five of the Tigers' top prospects amassed 20+ Career WAR – Travis Fryman, Kirk Gibson, Howard Johnson, Lance Parrish and current Tigers' ace Justin Verlander. Other distinguished members of Detroit's farm system include Curtis Granderson, Chris Hoiles, Jack Morris, John Smoltz (22nd Round, 72 Career WAR), Jason D. Thompson, Alan Trammell and Lou Whitaker (66 Career WAR, 346 Career WS).

The Marlins first-round draft choices rank eighth in OWARavg, but generally the team's scouting and development results are dreadful as the club ranks dead last overall in OWARavg, OWSavg and Graduation Rate (18 player-seasons per Draft). Prominent first-round selections for Miami include Josh Beckett, Jose D. Fernandez, Adrian Gonzalez, Charles Johnson and Mark Kotsay. Giancarlo Stanton (2nd Round) stands tall among the remaining Marlins' draftees in conjunction with Steve Cishek, Josh Johnson, Josh Willingham (17th Round) and Randy Winn.

Houston accrues the sixth-worst OWARavg rate among first-round selections and claims the fourth-lowest Graduation Rate (23 player-seasons per Draft). Lance Berkman and Craig Biggio (426 Career WS) co-star in the Astros' first-round rankings with Floyd Bannister, John Mayberry and Billy Wagner holding down supporting roles. Mid-round recruits consist of Ken Caminiti, Bill D. Doran, Luis E. Gonzalez, Shane Reynolds and Ben Zobrist. The 'Stros achieve the fifth-best OWARavg in rounds 11-89 based on the development and consistent production from Ken Forsch, Darryl Kile, Kenny Lofton, Roy Oswalt (23rd Round) and Johnny Ray.

Kansas City's first-round draft picks have collectively flopped as its second-worst OWSavg attests. Exceptions to the substandard results include Kevin Appier, Johnny Damon (302 Career WS), Alex Gordon, Zack Greinke and Willie Wilson. On the positive side, the Royals lead the Majors in OWSavg and place fourth in OWARavg for Amateur Draft rounds 2-4. George Brett (435 Career WS) highlights a star-studded cast consisting of Carlos Beltran (322 Career WS), David Cone, Cecil Fielder, Mark Gubicza, Ruppert Jones, Dennis Leonard and Jon Lieber. The organization's prized mid-to-late rounders are Jeff Conine (58th Round), Mark Ellis, Tom Gordon, Bret Saberhagen (19th Round), Kevin Seitzer and Mike Sweeney.

The Dodgers offset pedestrian results in the early rounds with tremendous scores in rounds 5-10 (2nd in OWSavg) and 11-89 (4th in OWARavg). Drafted in the 62nd Round, Mike

Piazza (324 Career WS) is a wonderful representative of late-round success. In addition the Los Angeles' endgame claims consist of Orel Hershiser (17th Round), Ted Lilly (23rd Round), Russell Martin (17th Round) and Dave Stewart (16th Round). Famous first-rounders for the Dodgers include Steve Garvey, Clayton Kershaw, Paul Konerko, Rick Rhoden, Mike Scioscia, Rick Sutcliffe and Bob Welch. Ron Cey tops a throng of mid-rounders which encompass Doyle Alexander, Bill Buckner, Joe Ferguson, Sid Fernandez, John Franco, Charlie Hough, Eric Karros, Matt Kemp, Davey Lopes, Bill Russell, Steve Sax, Shane Victorino, Steve Yeager and Eric Young.

Milwaukee's first round draft picks yield the top OWARavg and OWSavg among all Major League teams. Paul Molitor, Gary Sheffield and Robin Yount produced 60+ WAR and 400+ Win Shares in their careers. Other notable Brewers first-rounders include Ryan Braun, Prince Fielder, Darrell Porter, Ben Sheets, B.J. Surhoff, Gorman Thomas and Greg Vaughn. However the organization is deficient in the scouting and development of middle-to-late round talent. Second-rounder Chris Bosio and eleventh-rounder Jeff Cirillo pace the Brew Crew's Round 2+ group with 22 Career WAR while Mark Loretta accrued 178 Career WS.

Minnesota's draft picks in rounds 2-4 place third in OWARavg and OWSavg and the organization scores fifth overall in OWSavg. Headlined by Bert Blyleven (85 Career WAR, 341 Career WS) and Graig Nettles (317 Career WS), the round 2-4 group also counts Scott Erickson, Justin Morneau, Denny Neagle, A.J. Pierzynski and Frank Viola among its members. The Twins' blue-chip prospects, a group which encompasses Jay Bell, Michael Cuddyer, Gary Gaetti, Torii Hunter, Chuck Knoblauch, Joe Mauer and Kirby Puckett, attained the ninth-best OWSavg. Rick Dempsey, Kent Hrbek (17th Round) and Brad Radke are among the notable mid-to-late round selections.

The Mets rank third-worst in OWARavg for players selected in rounds 5-10 of the Amateur Draft. New York's scouting and development perform poorly overall, rating 25th in OWARavg and 23rd in OWSavg. The Metropolitans first-rounders, a collection including Hubie Brooks, Jeromy Burnitz, Dwight Gooden, Gregg Jefferies, Jon Matlack, Ken Singleton, Darryl Strawberry and David Wright, are somewhat better than the League in OWSavg. Twelfth-round selection Nolan Ryan (63 Career WAR, 339 Career WS) highlights the remaining Mets draftees along with A.J. Burnett, Lenny Dykstra and Mookie Wilson.

The Yankees' blue-chip prospects place sixth in OWSavg while players chosen in rounds 2-4 rank fifth-worst. Derek Jeter (407 Career WS) heads the first-round crew which includes Tim Belcher, Willie McGee and Thurman Munson. Ron Guidry and Al Leiter are the only Pinstripers of note that were drafted in the next three rounds. More than a few of the Bronx Bombers' mid-to-late round selections fashioned prolific careers including Brad Ausmus (48th Round), Greg Gagne, Mike Lowell (20th Round), Don Mattingly (19th Round), Fred McGriff, Andy Pettitte (22nd Round), Jorge Posada (24th Round) and J.T. Snow.

The Athletics earn a second-place overall finish in OWARavg for the Amateur Draft and secure a third-place ribbon in OWSavg. Oakland executed particularly well in rounds 2-4 (4th in OWARavg) and 5-10 (3rd in OWSavg). Reggie Jackson (74 Career WAR, 441 Career WS) headlines the Oakland first-rounders club, which also features Eric Chavez, Phil Garner, George Hendrick, Chet Lemon, Mark McGwire, Rick Monday, Mike Morgan, Nick Swisher and Barry Zito. Fourth-round selection Rickey Henderson (115 Career WAR, 543 Career WS) tops the A's mid-to-late round draftees. Other noteworthy products of the Oakland farm system include Sal Bando, Vida Blue, Jose Canseco, Darrell Evans, Jason Giambi, Tim Hudson, Dwayne Murphy, Terry Steinbach, Kevin Tapani, Gene Tenace (20th Round) and Mickey Tettleton.

Philadelphia rates highly in the scouting and development of players chosen in Amateur Draft rounds 2-4 with a sixth-place finish in OWARavg. On the other hand the team stumbles through the twilight rounds, ranking 25th out of 30 teams in OWARavg and OWSavg. The Phillies' first-rounders score in the bottom-third of the League, a class consisting of Pat Burrell, Cole Hamels, Greg Luzinski, Lonnie Smith and Chase Utley. Mike Schmidt (103 Career WAR, 463 Career WS) headlines the recruits from rounds 2-4 joined by fellow members Larry Hisle, Scott

Rolen, Jimmy Rollins and Randy Wolf. Mid-to-late round gems include Bob Boone, Darren Daulton (25th Round), Ryan Howard and Ryne Sandberg (20th Round).

The Pirates number-one draft picks score exceptionally well in OWARavg (2nd) and OWSavg (3rd) compared to the League average, due in large part to the contributions of Barry Bonds (156 Career WAR, 694 Career WS). Moises Alou, Richie Hebner, Jason Kendall and present-day center fielder Andrew McCutchen pay significant dividends for the Bucs. A number of Pittsburgh's mid-to-late round selections achieved stardom including Bronson Arroyo, Jose A. Bautista, Jay Buhner, John Candelaria, Gene Garber, Dave Parker (14th Round, 324 Career WS), Willie Randolph (55 Career WAR, 305 Career WS), Tim Wakefield and Richie Zisk.

The Padres' woeful performance in the Amateur Draft is underscored by the second-worst OWARavg and fourth-worst OWSavg overall. San Diego's premier picks rank last in OWARavg in spite of the presence of Andy Benes, Johnny Grubb, Derrek Lee, Kevin McReynolds and Dave Winfield (412 Career WS). Featuring Hall of Famers Tony Gwynn (386 Career WS) and Ozzie Smith (325 Career WS) along with John Kruk, the Friar's selections in rounds 2-4 provide a positive variance in the franchise record. Jake Peavy (15th Round) is the lone Padre drafted in the fifth round or later to register at least 20 Career WAR.

The Mariners excel in the drafting and development of first and mid-round selections. M's blue-chippers include Ken Griffey Jr. (402 Career WS), Dave Henderson, Tino Martinez, Mike Moore, Alex Rodriguez (94 Career WAR, 479 Career WS) and Jason Varitek. On the other hand, Seattle's late-round prospects place third-worst in OWSavg. An exception to the rule, Raul Ibanez (36th Round) tallied 209 Career WS. Bret Boone, Alvin Davis, Mike Hampton, Mark Langston and Derek Lowe highlight Seattle's mid-round picks.

The Giants furnish an atrocious record in the Amateur Draft, posting below-average results in all OWARavg and OWSavg categories along with the fourth-worst overall ranking. San Francisco's first-round selections place 27th out of 30 clubs. Buster Posey is steadily ascending the leader boards among the Giants' premier choices which include Matt Cain, Will Clark (320 Career WS), Royce Clayton, Dave Kingman, Tim Lincecum, Gary Matthews, Chris Speier, Robby Thompson and Matt D. Williams. The franchise cultivated a group of mid-to-late round picks comprised of Jim Barr, John Burkett, Jack Clark, Chili Davis, George Foster, Garry Maddox, Bill Mueller and Joe Nathan.

St. Louis sparkles in the scouting and development of late-rounders as the club's second-place finish in OWARavg for rounds 11-89 surely attests. Thirteenth-round selection Albert Pujols (92 Career WAR, 405 Career WS) leads the flock of Cardinals' success stories along with John Denny (29th Round), Jeff Fassero (22nd Round), Keith Hernandez (42nd Round) and Placido Polanco (19th Round). The organization achieves moderate results in the first round including J.D. Drew, Brian Jordan, Terry Kennedy, Ted Simmons, Garry Templeton and Andy Van Slyke. Noteworthy Cardinals' mid-rounders consist of Coco Crisp, Dan Haren, Lance Johnson, Ray Lankford, Yadier Molina, Jerry Mumphrey, Terry Pendleton, Jerry Reuss and Todd Zeile.

The Tampa Bay organization ranks second in OWSavg and third in OWARavg in terms of first-round Amateur Draft selections. The Rays count Josh Hamilton, Evan Longoria, David Price and B.J. Upton among the franchise's finest ballplayers. The farm system also bore middle-to-late rounders such as Carl Crawford, Aubrey Huff and James Shields (16th Round). Tampa Bay's Graduation Rate is an abysmal 20 player-seasons per Draft, the second-worst record in the League.

Texas yields the highest graduation rate (32 player-seasons per Draft) yet the club registers an unremarkable 24th place result for overall OWARavg. The Rangers' late-round jewels, comprising Rich Aurilia (24th Round), Travis Hafner, Mike Hargrove (25th Round), Ian Kinsler and Kenny Rogers (39th Round), manage a fourth-place showing in OWSavg. The organization's prized first-rounders include Kevin J. Brown, Jeff Burroughs, Rick Helling, Carlos Pena, Roy Smalley III, Jim Sundberg and Mark Teixeira. The club logs dismal outcomes in rounds 2-4 (third-worst in the Majors) and among the Rangers selected in rounds 2-10, only Ryan Dempster, Aaron Harang, Bill Madlock and Darren Oliver register at least 20 Career WAR.

Toronto's upper and middle-level draft choices prospered, particularly the ballplayers chosen in rounds 5-10 (2nd in OWARavg). Roy Halladay (64 Career WAR) heads the list of first-rounders developed in the Blue Jays' farm system together with Chris J. Carpenter, Shawn Green, Aaron Hill, Lloyd Moseby, Shannon Stewart, Todd Stottlemyre and Vernon Wells. Middle-to-late round selections Jeff Kent (20th Round), John Olerud, Dave Stieb and David Wells all post 50+ Career WAR. Other noteworthy Jays draftees include Jesse Barfield, Pat Hentgen, Orlando Hudson, Jimmy Key, Woddy Williams and Michael Young.

Washington posts the highest OWARavg in the Major Leagues for rounds 2-4 and finishes third in OWSavg for rounds 11-89. Bryce Harper and Stephen Strasburg should augment the Nationals' first-round scores which presently mirror League average rates. The Nats top selections include Delino DeShields, Cliff Floyd, Bill Gullickson, Tony Phillips, Steve Rogers, Tim Wallach, Rondell White and Ryan Zimmerman. Among the mid-to-late round choices, Gary Carter, Andre Dawson, Randy D. Johnson (101 Career WAR) and Tim Raines amassed 300+ Career Win Shares. The thriving farm system also produced Jason Bay (Round 22), Marquis Grissom, Mark Grudzielanek, Cliff P. Lee, Brandon Phillips, Scott Sanderson, Javier Vazquez and Jose Vidro.

Los Angeles / California / Anaheim Angels

Year/Team	OPW%	PW	PL	APW%	AW	AL	Diff+/-
1961 LAA	0.000 F	0	0	0.435	70	91	0.000
1962 LAA	0.000 F	0	0	0.531	86	76	0.000
1963 LAA	0.000 F	0	0	0.435	70	91	0.000
1964 LAA	0.000 F	0	0	0.506	82	80	0.000
1965 CAL	0.000 F	0	0	0.463	75	87	0.000
1966 CAL	0.000 F	0	0	0.494	80	82	0.000
1967 CAL	0.478 F	78	84	0.522	84	77	0.043
1968 CAL	0.491 F	80	82	0.414	67	95	-0.077
1969 CAL	0.429	69	93	0.438	71	91	0.010

franchID	OWAR	OWS	AWAR	AWS	WARdiff	WSdiff	P/D/W/F
1961 ANA	-22.877	106.482	35.289	209.997	-58.166	-103.514	F
1962 ANA	72.225	382.154	35.679	257.999	36.546	124.156	F
1963 ANA	4.331	154.942	28.385	210.002	-24.054	-55.060	F
1964 ANA	-30.254	139.092	32.169	245.991	-62.423	-106.899	F
1965 ANA	5.446	181.122	30.150	225.005	-24.704	-43.883	F
1966 ANA	20.512	243.164	30.631	240.002	-10.119	3.163	F
1967 ANA	19.340	201.556	31.620	252.006	-12.280	-50.450	F
1968 ANA	25.215	209.799	22.775	201.002	2.440	8.797	F
1969 ANA	24.798	202.342	25.179	212.998	-0.381	-10.657	

Legend: (P) = Pennant / Most Wins in League (D) = Division Winner (W) = Wild Card Winner (F) = Failed to Qualify

The Los Angeles Angels joined the American League in 1961 as the circuit expanded its membership to 10 teams. Halos' first basemen lead all expansion franchises with 47 WS>10 player-seasons including 12 appearances by Wally Joyner.

The scouting department endured a rough spell in the early years of the Angels' existence. The organization struggled to churn out talent that would provide a significant impact for the ball club until the tail end of the 1960's. In 1966 outfielder Rick Reichardt offered the first glimmer of hope, batting at a .288 clip with 16 homers in 89 games. Jim McGlothlin fashioned a 12-8 record with a 2.96 ERA. "Red" tied for the League lead with 6 shutouts. The 1969 "Original" Angels were the first to exceed the minimum 4000 PA and BFP standards*. Andy Messersmith topped the pitching staff with 16 wins and a 2.52 ERA while Ken Tatum anchored the bullpen with 22 saves.

Year/Team	OPW%	PW	PL	APW%	AW	AL	Diff+/-
1970 CAL	0.527	85	77	0.531	86	76	0.003
1971 CAL	0.478	77	85	0.469	76	86	-0.008
1972 CAL	0.475	77	85	0.484	75	80	0.009
1973 CAL	0.420	68	94	0.488	79	83	0.068
1974 CAL	0.451	73	89	0.420	68	94	-0.031
1975 CAL	0.474	77	85	0.447	72	89	-0.027
1976 CAL	0.480	78	84	0.469	76	86	-0.011
1977 CAL	0.458	74	88	0.457	74	88	-0.001
1978 CAL	0.488	79	83	0.537	87	75	0.049
1979 CAL	0.497 F	80	82	0.543 D	88	74	0.046

franchID	OWAR	OWS	AWAR	AWS	WARdiff	WSdiff	P/D/W/F
1970 ANA	24.092	205.548	31.637	257.998	-7.545	-52.450	
1971 ANA	32.267	206.240	25.913	228.006	6.355	-21.766	

Year/Team							
1972 ANA	22.451	173.311	25.543	225.001	-3.093	-51.690	
1973 ANA	12.910	148.814	32.309	236.997	-19.399	-88.183	
1974 ANA	19.508	163.800	33.109	204.001	-13.601	-40.201	
1975 ANA	23.209	189.312	29.683	216.002	-6.474	-26.690	
1976 ANA	27.501	205.582	27.833	227.991	-0.332	-22.408	
1977 ANA	22.866	176.357	36.396	222.002	-13.531	-45.644	
1978 ANA	22.980	204.310	36.192	260.998	-13.212	-56.689	
1979 ANA	29.988	224.747	49.505	264.004	-19.518	-39.257	F

The 1970 Halos posted the club's best record in the decade (85-77) on the mighty shoulders of the pitching staff. Clyde "Skeeter" Wright, coming off a 1-8 record in 1969, compiled 22 wins with a 2.83 ERA in '70. He finished sixth in the Cy Young balloting, and averaged 19 victories with a 2.93 ERA and a 1.180 WHIP from 1970-72. Staff ace Messersmith won 20 contests in 1971 and 1974 followed by a workhorse effort in 1975. "Bluto" twirled 321.2 innings and recorded 19 victories while furnishing career-bests in ERA (2.29) and WHIP (1.057). Marty "Bulldog" Pattin fashioned a 17-13 mark with a 3.24 ERA in '72. Tom Bradley yielded consecutive 200+ strikeout campaigns along with a 2.97 ERA (1971-72).

The Angels dipped below the .500 mark in 1971 and proceeded to wallow in mediocrity until 1981. California struggled to generate offense throughout the Seventies. The 1973 squad registered the franchise's low-water mark at 68-94. Bobby Darwin bashed 25 long balls and knocked in 94 runs in '74. Jerry Remy swiped 35 bases per season (1975-78). Tom Murphy enjoyed a one-year fling as the closer, posting a 1.90 ERA along with 10 wins and 20 saves in 1975. Dave LaRoche notched 20 saves per year (1975-78) along with a 2.72 ERA.

Frank Tanana paced the Junior Circuit in strikeouts in '75 (269), WHIP in '76 (0.988) and ERA in '77 (2.54). He completed 43 of 65 starts (1976-77) and placed third in the AL Cy Young voting in '76. Julio Cruz nabbed 59 bases in '78, and followed up with 49 in 1979. Bruce Bochte (.316/16/100) drilled 38 doubles and earned a trip to the All-Star game, while Ron D. Jackson delivered 40 two-baggers in '79. Sid Monge assumed the fireman role in '79, securing 12 wins and saving 19 games with a 2.40 ERA.

Win Shares > 20	Single-Season	1961-1979
Paul Schaal - 3B (ANA) Carney Lansford - 3B (ANA) x4	Rick Reichardt - LF (ANA) Andy Messersmith - SP (ANA) x3	Clyde Wright - SP (ANA) Frank Tanana - SP (ANA) x3 Sid Monge - RP (ANA)

Year/Team	OPW%	PW	PL	APW%	AW	AL	Diff+/-
1980 CAL	0.482	78	84	0.406	65	95	-0.076
1981 CAL	0.547	89	73	0.464	51	59	-0.083
1982 CAL	0.517	84	78	0.574 D	93	69	0.057
1983 CAL	0.485	78	84	0.432	70	92	-0.052
1984 CAL	0.462	75	87	0.500	81	81	0.038
1985 CAL	0.486 D	79	83	0.556	90	72	0.069
1986 CAL	0.480	78	84	0.568 D	92	70	0.088
1987 CAL	0.459	74	88	0.463	75	87	0.004
1988 CAL	0.476	77	85	0.463	75	87	-0.013
1989 CAL	0.506	82	80	0.562	91	71	0.056

franchID	OWAR	OWS	AWAR	AWS	WARdiff	WSdiff	P/D/W/F
1980 ANA	22.076	197.221	29.433	195.000	-7.357	2.221	
1981 ANA	19.801	142.764	25.516	152.999	-5.715	-10.235	
1982 ANA	30.944	214.819	**52.356**	279.002	-21.412	-64.182	
1983 ANA	30.298	224.473	29.511	209.999	0.787	14.474	
1984 ANA	26.268	206.431	32.222	242.992	-5.954	-36.561	

1985 ANA	32.144	220.726	36.589	270.004	-4.445	-49.278	D
1986 ANA	28.575	195.154	**48.379**	276.001	-19.804	-80.847	
1987 ANA	26.666	187.249	33.491	224.998	-6.826	-37.749	
1988 ANA	25.329	188.255	30.904	225.003	-5.575	-36.747	
1989 ANA	31.385	215.767	42.141	273.007	-10.756	-57.240	

Dave Collins delivered a .303 BA and ran wild at the top of the order, swiping 79 bases in '80. He led the League with 15 triples and nabbed 60 bags in 1984. The tide began to turn for California in 1981 as the "Original" Angels finished with an 89-73 record. Carney Lansford won the American League batting title with a .336 average. California topped the Major Leagues with 18 WS>10 player-seasons at the hot corner during the Eighties.

The Halos recorded 84 victories in 1982, falling two games short of the A's for the Western Division title. Tom Brunansky clobbered 26 long balls and knocked in 84 runs per season from 1983-89. Richard Dotson earned 22 victories in 1983 and Ken Schrom recorded 15 wins. California set a team record with 255 stolen bases in '83 and added 235 in '84. Alan Wiggins, Julio Cruz, Dickie Thon and Ken Landreaux all swiped at least 30 bases in 1983. Gary Pettis tore up the base paths with 48 steals in '84 and pilfered 56 bags in the subsequent season. The swift center fielder was rewarded with five Gold Glove Awards for his stellar defensive play.

Mike Witt delivered 15 victories in 1984 including a perfect game against Texas on the final day of the regular season. He delivered an 18-10 record with 208 strikeouts and a 2.84 ERA, placing third in the '86 Cy Young balloting. The Angels clinched the AL Western Division crown with 83 victories in 1985. Dennis Rasmussen registered 18 victories in '86, tying Witt for the team lead. Kirk McCaskill whiffed 202 batters en route to a 17-10 mark. He rebounded from two injury-plagued seasons to post a 15-10 record with a 2.93 ERA in 1989.

Wally "World" Joyner slammed 22 round-trippers, plated 100 baserunners and batted .290, capturing a second-place finish in the 1986 AL ROY voting. He increased his output with a .285 BA, 34 wallops and 117 ribbies in his sophomore season. Devon White put together a 20/30 campaign in his first full season in '87. "Devo" was honored with the first of seven Gold Glove Awards in 1988. Brian Harper earned a full-time gig at age 29 and supplied a .325 BA. Bryan Harvey saved 17 games with a 2.17 ERA in his rookie year (1988). Chuck Finley blossomed into the staff leader (16-9, 2.57) as the squad concluded the season one game above .500 (82-80) in 1989. GM Mike Port oversaw the Angels' finest draft class (1988) based on career Win Shares. He presided over six Amateur Drafts from 1985-1990 with an average yield of 345 WS.

Year/Team	OPW%	PW	PL	APW%	AW	AL	Diff+/-
1990 CAL	0.467	76	86	0.494	80	82	0.027
1991 CAL	0.480	78	84	0.500	81	81	0.020
1992 CAL	0.493	80	82	0.444	72	90	-0.048
1993 CAL	0.533	86	76	0.438	71	91	-0.095
1994 CAL	0.453	73	89	0.409	47	68	-0.044
1995 CAL	0.557 D	90	72	0.538	78	67	-0.019
1996 CAL	0.453	73	89	0.435	70	91	-0.019
1997 ANA	0.547 D	89	73	0.519	84	78	-0.028
1998 ANA	0.518	84	78	0.525	85	77	0.007
1999 ANA	0.458	74	88	0.432	70	92	-0.026

franchID	OWAR	OWS	AWAR	AWS	WARdiff	WSdiff	P/D/W/F
1990 ANA	26.077	199.923	39.527	240.003	-13.450	-40.080	
1991 ANA	30.107	224.031	32.524	242.997	-2.417	-18.966	
1992 ANA	30.106	245.010	20.027	215.995	10.079	29.015	
1993 ANA	39.314	277.748	27.875	212.994	11.439	64.754	
1994 ANA	18.920	166.075	17.134	140.995	1.785	25.080	
1995 ANA	38.897	263.948	39.515	234.005	-0.619	29.943	D

1996 ANA	34.976	274.172	26.822	210.001	8.154	64.171	
1997 ANA	40.312	313.101	34.362	251.994	5.950	61.106	D
1998 ANA	37.693	303.757	33.756	255.000	3.937	48.757	
1999 ANA	25.270	247.865	20.918	209.996	4.352	37.869	

Finley registered consecutive 18-9 records to begin the Nineties. He topped the circuit with 13 complete games in 1993 and surpassed the 200-strikeout mark three times. Jim Abbott (18-11, 2.89) placed third in the 1991 AL Cy Young voting and furnished a 2.77 ERA in the subsequent campaign. Harvey (1.60 ERA, 46 SV) whiffed 101 batters in 78.2 innings in '91. He locked down 45 contests in '93 after missing most of the previous season due to injury, posting a 1.70 ERA and 0.841 WHIP.

Joyner produced a .301 BA, 21 long balls and 96 ribbies for the '91 crew. White scored 108 runs, swiped 35 bases and slashed 36 two-base knocks per season (1991-93). Rookie outfielder Chad Curtis nabbed 43 bags in '92 and contributed a .285 BA with 48 steals in 1993. Joe Grahe (3.52, 21 SV) and Roberto Hernandez (1.65, 12 SV) filled in admirably for Harvey in '92. Hernandez compiled 38 saves with a 2.29 ERA in '93 and posted a 3.07 ERA with 32 saves per season during a seven-year span (1993-99).

The Angels promoted three talented batsmen to full-time status which thrust the club into pennant contention. California finished only 2 games behind the Rangers for the Western Division crown in 1993. Tim Salmon (.283/31/95) won the AL Rookie of the Year Award in '93. "Kingfish" walloped 30 circuit clouts and drove in 98 runs while supplying a .297 BA from 1993-98. Dante Bichette rocked 29 round-trippers, drove in 118 runs and averaged .316 from 1993-99. He led the League with 197 hits, 40 home runs, 128 RBI and a .620 SLG in '95, finishing runner-up in the MVP balloting. Paul Sorrento plastered 26 four-baggers and amassed 84 RBI per year from 1995-97.

The Halos overtook the Rangers in '95, winning the club's second division title with a 90-72 record. Garret Anderson (.321/16/69) placed second in the 1995 AL ROY voting and maintained a .300 BA in his first five seasons. Jim Edmonds (.290/33/107) provided stellar defense in center field. He achieved the first of eight Gold Glove Awards in '97 and averaged .298 with 28 quadruples, 86 ribbies and 98 runs scored over a four-year period (1995-98). Freshman reliever Troy Percival whiffed 94 batters in 62 innings (1.95 ERA) in '95. He assumed the closer's role and notched 34 saves per season (1996-99). Mike Fetters contributed 32 saves with a 3.38 ERA in 1996.

The team was renamed the Anaheim Angels in '97 and the club captured its third division title with 89 victories. Damion Easley clubbed 22 taters, pilfered 28 bases and registered 97 tallies. He received an All-Star nod in the following summer, batting .272 with 38 doubles, 27 four-baggers and 100 RBI. Lee Stevens posted a .300 BA with 21 clouts as a part-timer in '97. The Halos finished four games behind the Rangers in 1998, and then plunged into last place to close out the decade.

Year/Team	OPW%	PW	PL	APW%	AW	AL	Diff+/-
2000 ANA	0.503	81	81	0.506	82	80	0.003
2001 ANA	0.467	76	86	0.463	75	87	-0.004
2002 ANA	0.548 W	89	73	0.611 W	99	63	0.063
2003 ANA	0.529	86	76	0.475	77	85	-0.054
2004 ANA	0.478	77	85	0.568 D	92	70	0.090
2005 LAA	0.560 W	91	71	0.586 D	95	67	0.027
2006 LAA	0.503	82	80	0.549	89	73	0.046
2007 LAA	0.480	78	84	0.580 D	94	68	0.100
2008 LAA	0.504	82	80	0.617 P	100	62	0.113
2009 LAA	0.460	75	87	0.599 D	97	65	0.139
2010 LAA	0.464	75	87	0.494	80	82	0.030

2011 LAA	0.493	80	82	0.531	86	76	0.038
2012 LAA	0.504	82	80	0.549	89	73	0.046
2013 LAA	0.514	83	79	0.481	78	84	-0.032

franchID	OWAR	OWS	AWAR	AWS	WARdiff	WSdiff	P/D/W/F
2000 ANA	43.944	279.669	34.732	246.003	9.212	33.666	
2001 ANA	37.428	267.371	31.173	225.005	6.255	42.367	
2002 ANA	44.073	285.858	47.032	297.001	-2.959	-11.143	W
2003 ANA	39.926	266.117	33.515	231.010	6.411	35.107	
2004 ANA	44.596	267.174	45.309	276.002	-0.713	-8.828	
2005 ANA	**48.236**	**309.898**	43.572	284.998	4.664	24.900	W
2006 ANA	34.851	253.028	42.410	266.996	-7.559	-13.968	
2007 ANA	34.006	259.010	42.122	281.996	-8.116	-22.986	
2008 ANA	39.517	**302.263**	38.328	**300.004**	1.189	2.259	
2009 ANA	31.456	253.842	43.325	290.994	-11.869	-37.153	
2010 ANA	26.313	215.354	29.193	240.246	-2.880	-24.892	
2011 ANA	35.325	256.019	37.588	257.996	-2.263	-1.977	
2012 ANA	41.245	237.644	44.717	267.004	-3.472	-29.360	
2013 ANA	41.353	237.737	34.451	234.005	6.902	3.732	

Anaheim posted six winning seasons from 2000-2009 and the franchise achieved a .503 Win% for the decade (815-805). This corresponds with the stability and leadership at key positions in the organization, including manager, Mike Scioscia, the only manager during this period. Darin Erstad (.355/25/100/28) ignited the offense as he amassed 240 base hits and tallied 121 runs while earning the first of three Gold Glove Awards in 2000. Troy Glaus crossed the plate 120 times and launched 47 four-baggers. Glaus supplied 39 moon-shots, drove in 107 baserunners and scored 106 runs per season (2000-02). Edmonds paced the squad with 129 runs scored and added 42 bombs. He scored 100 runs, jacked 35 long balls and knocked in 98 runs per year from 2000-05.

Garret Anderson averaged .299 with 30 homers and 120 ribbies from 2000-03. He paced the circuit with 56 two-base hits in '02 and then duplicated the feat with 49 doubles in the ensuing campaign. Salmon swatted 34 big-flies and accrued 102 aces. Bengie Molina (.271/14/81) finished fourth in the 2000 AL ROY balloting. He knocked in 95 runs in '08 and belted a career-high 20 dingers in '09. Troy Percival averaged 35 saves per year from 2000-04 and closed out 40 contests with a 1.92 ERA in '02.

Anaheim earned the AL Wild Card entry in 2002 with an 89-73 record, placing 5 games behind the Oakland Athletics. Jarrod Washburn (18-6, 3.15) placed fourth in the 2002 AL Cy Young balloting. Ramon Ortiz contributed 15 victories while rookie right-hander John Lackey delivered 9 victories and a 3.66 ERA in 18 starts. Lackey received an All-Star invitation and placed third in the Cy Young voting in 2007, posting a 19-9 mark with a league-best 3.01 ERA.

The Halos registered 86 victories in 2003, but the Mariners triumphed by a ten-game margin. Shigetoshi Hasegawa enjoyed his finest season in '03, saving 16 games with a 1.48 ERA. Francisco J. Rodriguez whiffed 123 batters in 84 innings in '03 while Scot Shields added 109 in 60 relief appearances. "K-Rod" ascended to the closer's role in 2005 and began a string of four consecutive seasons with 40+ saves, culminating with an MLB-record 62 saves in '08.

The franchise was re-branded in 2005 as the Los Angeles Angels of Anaheim. Oakland won the AL West by one game as Los Angeles achieved its second Wild Card. The 2005 Angels recorded the highest pitWARnorm (26) and pitWSnorm (132) in team history. The Halos finished in third place with 82 victories in '06, only 3 games behind the Mariners for the division lead. Jered Weaver (11-2, 2.56) won his first 9 decisions in his inaugural season (2006). He paced the American League with 233 strikeouts in 2010 and earned in his first All-Star appearance. Weaver

(18-8, 2.41) placed runner-up in the 2011 AL Cy Young balloting then topped the circuit with 20 wins and a 1.018 WHIP in '12. Bobby Jenks delivered back-to-back 40+ save seasons in 2006-07.

Oakland won the AL West crown in 2008, with Los Angeles placing third, only two games behind. Ervin Santana yielded a 16-7 mark with a 3.49 ERA in 2008 and then fashioned a 17-10 mark in 2010. Joe Saunders supplied a 3.41 ERA and led the staff with a 17-7 mark in 2008. Kendry Morales seized the first base opening in 2009, mashing 34 homers and driving in 108 runs along with a .306 average. Mike Napoli set personal-bests with 30 jacks and a .320 BA in 2011. Jean Segura achieved All-Star status with a .294 BA and 44 stolen bases in '13.

Mike Trout (.326/30/83) delivered one of the finest performances by a rookie in MLB history. The "Millville Meteor" collected 2012 AL Rookie of the Year honors and placed second in the MVP balloting while leading the League with 129 runs scored and 49 stolen bases. Trout produced a .323 BA with 27 dingers, 33 steals and a franchise-best 39 Win Shares during his sophomore season, once more the runner-up in the MVP race.

Win Shares > 20	Single-Season	1980-2013
Wally Joyner - 1B (ANA) x5	Dante Bichette - LF (ANA)	Tim Salmon - RF (ANA) x6
Darin Erstad - 1B (ANA)	Darin Erstad - LF (ANA)	Tim Salmon - DH (ANA)
Kendry Morales - 1B (ANA)	Garret Anderson - LF (ANA) x2	Richard Dotson - SP (ANA)
Alan Wiggins - 2B (ANA)	Dave Collins - CF (ANA)	Mike Witt - SP (ANA)
Dickie Thon - SS (ANA) x2	Devon White - CF (ANA) x3	Chuck Finley - SP (ANA)
Erick Aybar - SS (ANA) x2	Jim Edmonds - CF (ANA) x9	Jim Abbott - SP (ANA)
Jean Segura – SS (ANA)	Mike Trout - CF (ANA) x2	John Lackey - SP (ANA)
Troy Glaus - 3B (ANA) x5	Tom Brunansky - RF (ANA)	Jered Weaver - SP (ANA)
Mike Napoli - C (ANA)		

Note: 4000 PA or BFP to qualify, except during strike-shortened seasons (1972 = 3800, 1981 & 1994 = 2700, 1995 = 3500) and 154-game schedule (3800)
- failed to qualify: 1961-68, 1979

Angels All-Time "Originals" Roster

Jim Abbott	Bobby Darwin	Hal King	Garrett Richards
Kyle Abbott	Doug R. Davis	Bob Kipper	Jerrod Riggan
Nick Adenhart	Jason Dickson	Ed Kirkpatrick	Aurelio Rodriguez
Willie Aikens	Frank Dimichele	Don Kirkwood	Fernando
Kim Allen	Gary DiSarcina	Michael Kohn	Rodriguez
Lloyd Allen	John M. Doherty	Casey Kotchman	Francisco J.
Bob Allietta	Tom Donohue	Gil Kubski	Rodriguez
Juan Alvarez	Jim Dorsey	Fred Kuhaulua	Francisco R.
Alexi Amarista	Richard Dotson	John Lackey	Rodriguez
Ruben Amaro, Jr.	Trent Durrington	Ken Landreaux	Rafael Rodriguez
Alfredo Amezaga	Damion Easley	Dick Lange	Sean Rodriguez
Brian J. Anderson	Steve Eddy	Carney Lansford	Ron Romanick
Garret Anderson	Ken Edenfield	Dave LaRoche	Andrew Romine
Jim Anderson	Jim Edmonds	Vic Larose	Bobby Rose
Kent Anderson	Tom Egan	Phil Leftwich	Michael Roth
Steve Andrade	Dave Engle	Scott A. Lewis	Jorge Rubio
Dan Ardell	Darin Erstad	Pedro Liriano	Tim Salmon
George Arias	Seth Etherton	Carlos Lopez	Freddy Sandoval
Jose Arredondo	Jorge Fabregas	Andrew Lorraine	Ervin Santana
Erick Aybar	Bob Ferris	Steve Lubratich	Tom Satriano
John Balaz	Mike Fetters	Urbano Lugo	Joe Saunders
Larry Barnes	Chuck Finley	Keith Luuloa	Paul Schaal
Del Bates	John Flannery	Dave Machemer	Jeff Schmidt
Justin Baughman	Kevin Flora	Tony Mack	Scott Schoeneweis

Trevor Bell	P.J. Forbes	Warner Madrigal	Dick C. Schofield
Erik Bennett	Willie Fraser	Martin Maldonado	Ken Schrom
Dusty Bergman	Miguel Garcia	Jeff Manto	Daryl Sconiers
Dante Bichette	Vern Geishert	Nick Maronde	Darryl Scott
Mike Bishop	Steve Geltz	Dave Marshall	Jean Segura
Bruce Bochte	Craig Gerber	Jeff Mathis	Harvey Shank
Danny Boone	Troy Glaus	Dallas McPherson	Scot Shields
Chris Bootcheck	Larry Gonzales	Rudy Meoli	Tom Silverio
Buddy Boshers	Miguel Angel Gonzalez	Andy Messersmith	Bill Simas
Thad Bosley	Danny Goodwin	Mike Miley	Dick Simpson
Ralph Botting	Nick Gorneault	Darrell Miller	Tyler Skaggs
Peter Bourjos	Joe Grahe	Norm Miller	Billy E. Smith
Tom Bradley	Steve Green	Alan Mills	Will Smith
Brian Brady	Todd Greene	Bengie Molina	John Snyder
Dan Briggs	Tom Gregorio	Sid Monge	Paul Sorrento
Mark Brouhard	Doug Griffin	Bill Mooneyham	Jim Spencer
Barret Browning	Aaron Guiel	Jeremy Moore	Rick Steirer
Curt Brown	Ryan Hancock	Marcus Moore	Lee Stevens
Matthew Brown	Brian Harper	Kendry Morales	Ed Sukla
Mike C. Brown	Bill Harrelson	Angel Moreno	Mark Sweeney
Randy Brown	John Harris	Rance Mulliniks	Paul Swingle
Steve Brown	Paul Hartzell	Tom Murphy	Frank Tanana
Tom Brunansky	Bryan Harvey	Tommy Murphy	Jarvis Tatum
T.R. Bryden	Shigetoshi Hasegawa	Mike Napoli	Ken Tatum
Gary Buckels	Andy Hassler	Cotton Nash	Andrew Taylor
Ryan Budde	Hilly Hathaway	Efren Navarro	Rich G. Thompson
Jamie Burke	Brad Havens	Morris Nettles	Dickie Thon
Kole Calhoun	Johnny Hellweg	Doug Nickle	Alex Torres
Alberto Callaspo	Bret Hemphill	Darren O'Day	Bobby Trevino
John Caneira	Joe Henderson	Ramon Ortiz	Mike Trout
David L. Carpenter	Matt Hensley	John Orton	Mark Trumbo
Alexi Casilla	Roberto Hernandez	Sean O'Sullivan	Chris Turner
Bobby Cassevah	David Herndon	Mike Overy	Ken Turner
Ray Chadwick	Jack Hiatt	Dennis Paepke	John Verhoeven
Dave Chalk	Chuck Hockenbery	Orlando Palmeiro	Jordan Walden
Tyler Chatwood	David Holdridge	Erik Pappas	Mike Walters
Anthony Chavez	Mike Holtz	Billy Parker	Dick Wantz
Robinson Checo	Mark Holzemer	Marty Pattin	Colby Ward
Bruce Christensen	Steve Hovley	Troy Percival	Jackie Warner
McKay Christensen	Doug Howard	Eduardo Perez	Greg Washburn
Bobby Clark	Jack Howell	Marty Perez	Jarrod Washburn
Pat Clements	Ron D. Jackson	Matt Perisho	Jered Weaver
Stan Cliburn	Bobby Jenks	Chris Pettit	Gary Wheelock
Pete Coachman	Doug Jennings	Gary Pettis	Devon White
Mike Colangelo	Kevin Jepsen	J.R. Phillips	Dan Whitmer
Dave Collins	Luis D. Jimenez	Gus Polidor	Alan Wiggins
Keith Comstock	Gary Johnson	Chuck Porter	Reggie Willits
Hank Conger	Jay Johnstone	Chris Pritchett	Shad Williams
Mike Cook	Greg Jones	Robb Quinlan	Bobby Wilson
Brian Cooper	Wally Joyner	Edwar Ramirez	Matt Wise
Sherman Corbett	Steve Kealey	Orlando Ramirez	Mike Witt
Patrick Corbin	Pat Keedy	Sap Randall	Brandon Wood
Terry Cox	Pat D. Kelly	Dennis Rasmussen	Jake Woods
Julio Cruz	Howie Kendrick	Floyd Rayford	Clyde Wright
Chad Curtis	Kirk McCaskill	Rick Reichardt	
Paul Dade	Jim McGlothlin	Jerry Remy	
Mark Dalesandro	Mark T. McLemore	Steven Shell	

Year/Team	OPW%	PW	PL	APW%	AW	AL	Diff+/-
1962 HOU	0.000 F	0	0	0.400	64	96	0.000
1963 HOU	0.000 F	0	0	0.407	66	96	0.000
1964 HOU	0.000 F	0	0	0.407	66	96	0.000
1965 HOU	0.474 F	77	85	0.401	65	97	-0.073
1966 HOU	0.462 F	75	87	0.444	72	90	-0.017
1967 HOU	0.435 F	70	92	0.426	69	93	-0.009
1968 HOU	0.418 F	68	94	0.444	72	90	0.026
1969 HOU	0.489	79	83	0.500	81	81	0.011

franchID	OWAR	OWS	AWAR	AWS	WARdiff	WSdiff	P/D/W/F
1962 HOU	19.040	28.313	32.426	191.992	-13.386	-163.680	F
1963 HOU	-10.226	188.602	21.187	198.004	-31.413	-9.401	F
1964 HOU	-26.842	131.880	20.872	197.997	-47.714	-66.117	F
1965 HOU	43.599	252.992	26.413	194.998	17.186	57.995	F
1966 HOU	43.002	276.931	33.480	216.001	9.522	60.929	F
1967 HOU	36.315	244.229	33.028	206.996	3.287	37.233	F
1968 HOU	31.770	226.441	28.132	215.999	3.638	10.442	F
1969 HOU	41.490	251.878	42.314	243.002	-0.825	8.877	

Legend: (P) = Pennant / Most Wins in League (D) = Division Winner (W) = Wild Card Winner (F) = Failed to Qualify

From the early days of Houston's expansion effort, the organization focused on the development of its farm system. The franchise leads all expansion teams with 30 WS>20 player-seasons (second basemen) and 25 WS>20 seasons (right fielders). Initially dubbed the Colt .45's, the club embraced the Astros moniker in 1965 as Joe L. Morgan ignited the offense. "Little Joe" placed second in the 1965 NL ROY voting, scoring 100 runs and swiping 20 bags. Sonny Jackson delivered a .292 average and 49 steals in '66. Rusty Staub led the League with 44 doubles in 1967 and posted a .333 BA. "Le Grande Orange" clubbed 29 moon-shots and batted .302 in '69. GM Paul Richards acquired Morgan, Staub and Bob Watson as amateur free agents during his four-year stint in the Colt .45's front office.

Dave Giusti won 15 games for the 1966 squad and Larry Dierker contributed 10 victories with a 3.18 ERA. Dierker recorded career-highs in '69 with 20 victories, 232 strikeouts, 20 complete games and a 2.23 ERA. Don Wilson's inaugural season in '67 included a 10-9 mark with a 2.79 ERA and 1.141 WHIP. Wilson registered 235 strikeouts and notched 16 wins. The 1969 "Original" Astros were the first to exceed the minimum 4000 PA and BFP standards*.

Year/Team	OPW%	PW	PL	APW%	AW	AL	Diff+/-
1970 HOU	0.510	83	79	0.488	79	83	-0.022
1971 HOU	0.520	84	78	0.488	79	83	-0.032
1972 HOU	0.536	87	75	0.549	84	69	0.013
1973 HOU	0.567 P	92	70	0.506	82	80	-0.060
1974 HOU	0.517	84	78	0.500	81	81	-0.017
1975 HOU	0.535	87	75	0.398	64	97	-0.137
1976 HOU	0.526	85	77	0.494	80	82	-0.032
1977 HOU	0.567 P	92	70	0.500	81	81	-0.067
1978 HOU	0.459	74	88	0.457	74	88	-0.002
1979 HOU	0.542 D	88	74	0.549	89	73	0.007

franchID	OWAR	OWS	AWAR	AWS	WARdiff	WSdiff	P/D/W/F
1970 HOU	36.446	273.539	36.786	236.999	-0.339	36.540	
1971 HOU	38.261	278.753	38.152	237.002	0.109	41.751	

1972 HOU	**54.732**	298.004	44.367	251.993	10.365	46.011	
1973 HOU	**54.877**	328.795	35.083	245.997	19.794	82.798	P
1974 HOU	47.425	284.183	37.989	243.001	9.436	41.182	
1975 HOU	**50.014**	291.176	28.737	192.002	21.277	99.175	
1976 HOU	**52.923**	**316.086**	31.137	240.002	21.786	76.084	
1977 HOU	**54.626**	306.086	38.910	242.996	15.716	63.090	P
1978 HOU	30.822	253.367	32.970	221.999	-2.148	31.368	
1979 HOU	46.949	314.221	33.128	266.996	13.821	47.225	D

The Astros took flight in 1970, blazing a vapor trail through eight consecutive winning seasons. Morgan fueled the offense with a .290 BA, 108 runs scored and 55 stolen bases per season from 1970-77. His superb production in 1975-76 was rewarded with back-to-back MVP honors. Morgan amassed the highest Win Shares total in the history of the franchise (43) while batting .327 with 67 steals and a league-best 132 walks in '75. For an encore he posted a .320 BA, 27 dingers, 111 RBI and 60 stolen bases in '76 while topping the circuit in OBP (.444) and SLG (.576). Morgan and Doug Rader captured five straight Gold Glove Awards for their defensive excellence.

Staub bashed a career-high 30 long balls in 1970 and plated 121 runs in '78. Larry Dierker retained his ace status with 16 wins and a 3.87 ERA in 1970. Wilson paced the hurlers with 16 wins and a 2.45 ERA in '71. Giusti successfully converted to the role of relief ace, saving 26 games with a 3.06 ERA. He teamed with Tom Burgmeier (9-7, 1.73) to save 47 contests in '71. Houston came up one game short in '71 as Cincinnati seized the NL West crown.

Cesar Cedeno finished sixth in the NL MVP voting in '72, batting .320 with 22 homers, 82 RBI, and 55 stolen bases. He stole 50+ bases in each season from 1972-77. John Mayberry (.298/25/100) became entrenched as the first baseman in 1972. Mayberry blasted 34 round-trippers and knocked in 106 runs in '75 en route to a runner-up finish in the MVP voting. Bob "Bull" Watson batted .305 from 1972-79, topping out at 22 homers and 110 RBI in '77. The Astros captured the franchise's first pennant in 1973, topping the National League in victories with a 92-70 mark.

The Astros paced the Senior Circuit in oWAR and oWS in '76 including the third-highest offWARnorm (33) of All-Time. J.R. Richard ascended to the role of staff ace in '76, reaching the 20-win plateau and striking out 214 batters. Richard joined the 300-strikeout club in 1978, adding another 18 victories to his impressive totals. He topped the National League with 313 strikeouts and a 2.71 ERA in '79.

Ken Forsch (19 SV, 2.15) earned a trip to the All-Star contest in '76. Forsch (10-6, 2.70) and Joe Sambito (11 SV, 3.07) secured the late innings during the '78 campaign. Sambito flourished in the fireman role, notching 22 saves while delivering a 1.77 ERA in '79. The 'Stros took control of the National League West, capturing the pennant in 1977 and taking the division crown in '79. GM Spec Richardson yielded substandard results in the Amateur Draft including five consecutive seasons below 100 Career Total Win Shares, contributing to the Astros talent shortage in the ensuing decade.

Win Shares > 20	Single-Season	1962-1979
Rusty Staub - 1B (HOU)	Cesar Cedeno - CF (HOU) x6	Larry Dierker - SP (HOU)
John Mayberry - 1B (HOU) x3	Terry Puhl - CF (HOU)	Don Wilson - SP (HOU)
Bob Watson - 1B (HOU) x3	Rusty Staub - RF (HOU) x7	Wayne Twitchell - SP (HOU)
Joe L. Morgan - 2B (HOU) x13	Greg Gross - RF (HOU)	J.R. Richard - SP (HOU)
Bob Watson - LF (HOU) x2	Terry Puhl - RF (HOU)	

Year/Team	OPW%	PW	PL	APW%	AW	AL	Diff+/-
1980 HOU	0.598 P	97	65	0.571 D	93	70	-0.027
1981 HOU	0.477	77	85	0.555 D	61	49	0.078
1982 HOU	0.450 F	73	89	0.475	77	85	0.025
1983 HOU	0.554 F	90	72	0.525	85	77	-0.029
1984 HOU	0.560 F	91	71	0.494	80	82	-0.067
1985 HOU	0.448 F	73	89	0.512	83	79	0.064
1986 HOU	0.449 F	73	89	0.593 D	96	66	0.144
1987 HOU	0.364 F	59	103	0.469	76	86	0.105
1988 HOU	0.496 F	80	82	0.506	82	80	0.010
1989 HOU	0.461 F	75	87	0.531	86	76	0.070

franchID	OWAR	OWS	AWAR	AWS	WARdiff	WSdiff	P/D/W/F
1980 HOU	63.901	352.700	47.710	278.994	16.191	73.706	P
1981 HOU	30.229	189.276	33.880	183.005	-3.651	6.271	
1982 HOU	41.983	301.759	31.124	231.004	10.859	70.756	F
1983 HOU	55.441	344.001	37.772	255.006	17.670	88.995	F
1984 HOU	55.288	339.989	40.556	239.999	14.732	99.989	F
1985 HOU	33.196	276.280	34.815	249.000	-1.619	27.280	F
1986 HOU	36.228	298.745	45.836	288.001	-9.608	10.744	F
1987 HOU	28.555	249.561	35.535	228.004	-6.981	21.558	F
1988 HOU	43.511	309.732	34.088	245.996	9.423	63.736	F
1989 HOU	37.392	339.866	30.611	258.002	6.781	81.864	F

The Astros were light-years ahead of the competition in 1980 as the Braves finished a distant 16 games back. However the organization failed to develop sufficient pitching talent. The moundsmen fell below the minimum BFP requirements for 14 consecutive seasons (1982-1995). J.R. Richard (10-4, 1.90) earned his first All-Star nod with a spectacular first half in 1980. Unfortunately he suffered a life-threatening massive blood clot later that month which effectively ended his career.

Mike Easler finally broke into the lineup in 1980 at age 29 and he took advantage of the opportunity. The "Hit Man" batted .338 and cleared the fence 21 times. In 1984 Easler bashed 27 bombs and drove in 91 runs, complimenting a .313 BA. Mayberry crushed 30 moon-shots while Cedeno hit .309 with 48 stolen bases in '80. Burgmeier (24 SV, 2.00), Sambito (17 SV, 2.19) and Dave S. Smith (10 SV, 1.93) protected the late-inning leads in 1980. Smith assumed the closer's role in '85, averaging 26 saves from 1985-1990 with a 2.38 ERA and a WHIP of 1.129.

Johnny Ray (.281/7/63) placed second in the 1982 NL ROY voting. Ray established personal-bests with 42 doubles and 83 RBI while earning his lone All-Star game appearance in '88. Floyd Bannister delivered 12 wins with a 3.43 ERA and 209 strikeouts in 1982; he posted a 16-10 record with a 3.35 ERA in the subsequent season. Glenn Davis blasted 20 long balls in his inaugural campaign (1985). He belted 31 big-flies and drove in 101 runs in his sophomore season, earning a runner-up finish in the 1986 NL MVP balloting. Davis supplied 30 round-trippers and 96 ribbies from 1986-89. Bill D. Doran (.283/16/79) pilfered 31 bases after swiping 42 bags in the previous year. Charlie Kerfeld fortified the relief corps, winning 11 games with a 2.69 ERA in '86.

Houston's front office attained success in three consecutive Amateur Drafts (1987-89) which provided the foundation for the Astros' sustained excellence from 1996-2008. Scouting Director Dan O'Brien Jr. teamed with GM Dick Wagner to select Craig Biggio and Darryl Kile in '87. O'Brien repeated the feat with Wagner's successor, Bill Wood, procuring Luis E. Gonzalez, Kenny Lofton ('88) and Shane Reynolds ('89).

Year/Team	OPW%	PW	PL	APW%	AW	AL	Diff+/-
1990 HOU	0.371 F	60	102	0.463	75	87	0.092
1991 HOU	0.389 F	63	99	0.401	65	97	0.013
1992 HOU	0.411 F	67	95	0.500	81	81	0.089
1993 HOU	0.554 F	90	72	0.525	85	77	-0.029
1994 HOU	0.520 F	84	78	0.574	66	49	0.054
1995 HOU	0.535 F	87	75	0.528	76	68	-0.008
1996 HOU	0.522	85	77	0.506	82	80	-0.016
1997 HOU	0.600 P	97	65	0.519 D	84	78	-0.081
1998 HOU	0.530 D	86	76	0.630 D	102	60	0.100
1999 HOU	0.593 P	96	66	0.599 D	97	65	0.006

franchID	OWAR	OWS	AWAR	AWS	WARdiff	WSdiff	P/D/W/F
1990 HOU	31.233	278.769	25.124	225.004	6.109	53.764	F
1991 HOU	17.546	206.103	22.403	194.996	-4.857	11.107	F
1992 HOU	28.471	279.035	31.412	242.998	-2.941	36.037	F
1993 HOU	41.709	277.203	45.625	255.000	-3.916	22.203	F
1994 HOU	24.968	176.034	34.319	198.006	-9.350	-21.972	F
1995 HOU	36.489	222.232	41.454	228.000	-4.965	-5.768	F
1996 HOU	37.172	241.341	34.547	245.999	2.625	-4.657	
1997 HOU	40.182	257.771	46.356	252.001	-6.174	5.771	P
1998 HOU	42.939	255.515	57.266	305.996	-14.327	-50.480	D
1999 HOU	50.391	269.030	52.636	291.003	-2.245	-21.973	P

The Houston organization decided to convert Craig Biggio from catcher to second baseman. The move paid immediate dividends in 1992 as he pilfered 38 bases and played in 162 games. Biggio (.309/22/81) nabbed 47 bags, led the League with 146 runs scored and tallied 35 Win Shares while placing fourth in the 1997 NL MVP balloting. He destroyed opposition pitching in '98, batting .325 with 51 doubles, 20 homers and 50 steals while scoring 123 runs and setting a career-high with 210 base hits. Fleet-footed center fielder Kenny Lofton sprinted into the lineup in '92. Over the next four seasons he averaged .316 with 62 stolen bases and 10 triples. Lofton batted .317 and led the League with 75 stolen bases in '96 while setting career-highs in at-bats, runs (132), hits (210) and doubles (35). The impeccable defender notched ten appearances on the Fielding WAR and WS leader boards.

A shortage of quality moundsmen remained the primary concern for the Astros. Darryl Kile emerged in 1993, earning 15 wins along with a 3.51 ERA and a trip to the All-Star game. He dominated the opposition in '97, capping a 19-7 season with 205 strikeouts and a 2.57 ERA. Houston settled into the National League Central after the divisions were realigned in 1994. Ken Caminiti (.302/26/94) enhanced his production in 1995 after averaging only 12 dingers and 69 ribbies during the previous six seasons. He crushed 40 bombs and knocked in 130 baserunners while batting .326, capturing 1996 NL MVP honors.

The Astros reappeared on the radar screen in 1996 as the squad finished just one game behind the Cubs. Shane Reynolds anchored the rotation, compiling a 3.65 ERA along with a 16-10 record. Two years later, he posted a 19-8 record with a 3.51 ERA and 209 strikeouts. The '97 crew captured the Central division flag, finishing 13 games ahead of the Pirates. Houston would not release its stranglehold on the Central until 2009, securing 12 consecutive titles in the process! In nine of the twelve seasons during this stretch, the Astros topped the National League in victories. GM Gerry Hunsicker presided over Houston's personnel moves for the bulk of this incredible period. Todd Jones settled into a late-inning role in the bullpen and registered 31 saves. Billy Wagner closed out 23 contests and struck out 106 batters in only 66.1 innings pitched in 1997, the first of three consecutive seasons in which he exceeded 14 strikeouts per 9 innings! Wagner whiffed 124 in only 74 innings in 1999, nailing down 39 saves with a 1.57 ERA in the process.

The Astros edged the Cubbies for the division crown by a single victory in 1998. Houston overwhelmed its division rivals in '99 as the club ended the season 13 games ahead of the Pirates. Luis E. Gonzalez elevated his game in 1999, topping the circuit with 206 base hits while producing a .335 BA with 26 jacks and 111 ribbies. Bobby Abreu matched Gonzalez in batting average and commenced an eight-year streak with at least 100 bases on balls (1999-2006). Freddy Antonio Garcia secured 17 victories during his rookie season (1999).

Year/Team	OPW%	PW	PL	APW%	AW	AL	Diff+/-
2000 HOU	0.531 P	86	76	0.444	72	90	-0.087
2001 HOU	0.591 P	96	66	0.574 P	93	69	-0.017
2002 HOU	0.582 D	94	68	0.519	84	78	-0.064
2003 HOU	0.566 P	92	70	0.537	87	75	-0.029
2004 HOU	0.601 P	97	65	0.568 W	92	70	-0.033
2005 HOU	0.564 P	91	71	0.549 W	89	73	-0.015
2006 HOU	0.565 P	92	70	0.506	82	80	-0.059
2007 HOU	0.528 D	86	76	0.451	73	89	-0.077
2008 HOU	0.549 P	89	73	0.534	86	75	-0.015
2009 HOU	0.488	79	83	0.457	74	88	-0.031
2010 HOU	0.485	79	83	0.469	76	86	-0.016
2011 HOU	0.466	76	86	0.346	56	106	-0.121
2012 HOU	0.389	63	99	0.340	55	107	-0.049
2013 HOU	0.427	69	93	0.315	51	111	-0.112

franchID	OWAR	OWS	AWAR	AWS	WARdiff	WSdiff	P/D/W/F
2000 HOU	39.845	233.179	39.966	216.004	-0.121	17.175	P
2001 HOU	42.408	263.649	44.716	279.003	-2.308	-15.354	P
2002 HOU	42.860	249.279	44.308	251.999	-1.448	-2.720	D
2003 HOU	48.364	260.850	44.142	261.000	4.222	-0.149	P
2004 HOU	51.354	291.852	47.327	276.000	4.026	15.852	P
2005 HOU	42.388	274.334	43.598	267.005	-1.211	7.329	P
2006 HOU	40.789	262.893	41.155	245.999	-0.366	16.894	P
2007 HOU	32.986	238.274	30.650	219.000	2.337	19.274	D
2008 HOU	42.147	273.666	32.367	258.000	9.780	15.666	P
2009 HOU	37.084	229.235	28.998	221.994	8.086	7.241	
2010 HOU	38.487	252.488	23.872	227.996	14.615	24.491	
2011 HOU	33.892	229.775	21.302	167.975	12.589	61.800	
2012 HOU	19.018	194.890	10.308	164.995	8.710	29.895	
2013 HOU	26.659	218.300	8.316	151.913	18.343	66.387	

Gonzalez (.311/31/114) continued his offensive assault against National League hurlers in 2000. Exceeding all expectations "Gonzo" launched 57 blasts and knocked in 142 runs in the subsequent season. He boasted .325 BA and scored 128 runs, finishing third in the 2001 NL MVP voting. Richard Hidalgo hammered 44 round-trippers and plated 122 baserunners to complement his .314 BA in 2000. Three years later he topped the Astros with a .309 BA and 28 home runs. Abreu posted a .299 BA with 41 doubles, 22 four-ply swats, 99 ribbies, 30 stolen bases and 100 runs scored from 2000-09. He topped the leader boards with 50 two-baggers in '02 and achieved 30-30 status twice.

Biggio dialed long-distance 20 times while scoring 118 runs. He collected his 3000th hit during his final campaign in 2007. Lance Berkman swatted 21 long balls during his freshman year (2000) and drilled a league-best 55 doubles in the ensuing season. "Big Puma" bashed 42 big-flies, drove in 128 baserunners and registered 106 tallies, placing third in the 2002 NL MVP balloting. In 2006 he earned another third place finish, batting .315 with 45 clouts and 136 ribbies. During the decade he averaged .300 with 31 home runs and 103 RBI. Jones assumed closing responsibilities in 2000, saving 42 games as Wagner suffered through an off-year. Jones nailed down 38 saves per year from 2005-07.

Kile topped the rotation with 20 victories in 2000, buttressed by Scott Elarton's 17-7 mark. He posted a 16-11 record with a 3.09 ERA in '01 while Garcia (18-6, 3.05) paced the League in ERA and finished third in the Cy Young voting. Two newcomers completed the starting rotation - Wade Miller (16-8, 3.40 in his first full season) and rookie Roy Oswalt (14-3, 2.73). Oswalt ascended to the role of staff ace, posting 19 wins and 208 strikeouts to go along with a 3.01 ERA in '02. Oswalt (20-10, 3.49) fanned 206 batsmen in '04 and tallied another 20-win season in the subsequent year. "The Wizard of Os" topped the circuit with a 2.98 ERA in 2006 and a league-best 1.025 WHIP in 2010.

The Astros out-paced the Cardinals by 8 games in '01 and finished 10 games ahead of the Redbirds in the next season. Wagner returned to form in 2001, dousing 39 late-inning fires. In 2003 he whiffed 105 batters in 86 innings, notching 44 saves in the process. Wagner delivered 35 saves per year with a 2.23 ERA from 2001-08. Phil Nevin garnered his lone All-Star selection in 2001, hitting .306 with 41 round-trippers and 126 RBI. Melvin Mora paced the club with a .340 BA in 2004 while posting a league-best .419 OBP. He set career-highs with 41 doubles, 27 round-trippers, 104 RBI and 111 runs scored.

Johan Santana (20-6, 2.49) earned Cy Young honors in '04, compiling a league-high 265 strikeouts and 0.921 WHIP. Santana brought home his second Cy Young Award in 2006, leading the League with a 19-6 record, 2.77 ERA, 0.997 WHIP and 245 whiffs. He paced the circuit with a 2.53 ERA in 2008. Fireballing right-hander Brad Lidge handled some of the late-inning workload in 2004. "Lights-Out" saved 29 games, while striking out 157 in 94.2 innings. Lidge was a perfect 41 of 41 in converting save opportunities in '09.

Houston posted 97 victories in '04 and outdistanced the Pirates by 14 games. The trend continued in 2005, with Pittsburgh finishing 11 games behind the 'Stros. Carlos Guillen supplied a .318 BA with 20 dingers and 97 RBI in 2004. He led the team with 100 runs scored and a .320 BA in '06, earning career-bests with 21 wallops and 102 RBI in the following campaign. Morgan Ensberg mashed 36 moon-shots and plated 101 baserunners as he achieved All-Star status in '05. Hunter Pence batted .322 with 17 long balls as he placed third in the 2007 NL ROY balloting. Houston finally lost its grip on the NL Central in 2009, falling 2 games short of another division title. Ben Zobrist pounded 27 long balls and knocked in 97 runs while batting .297 in '09. Wandy Rodriguez fashioned a 3.02 ERA and recorded 14 victories in '09.

Win Shares > 20	Single-Season	1980-2013
Glenn Davis - 1B (HOU) x3	Phil Nevin - 3B (HOU) x2	Bobby Abreu - RF (HOU) x11
Phil Nevin - 1B (HOU)	Melvin Mora - 3B (HOU) x2	Richard Hidalgo - RF (HOU)
Lance Berkman - 1B (HOU)	Morgan Ensberg - 3B (HOU)	Lance Berkman - RF (HOU)
x5	Craig Biggio - C (HOU)	x2
Bill D. Doran - 2B (HOU) x3	Mike Easler - LF (HOU)	Hunter Pence - RF (HOU) x2
Johnny Ray - 2B (HOU) x2	Luis E. Gonzalez - LF (HOU)	Ben Zobrist - RF (HOU)
Craig Biggio - 2B (HOU) x10	x6	Mike Easler - DH (HOU)
Ben Zobrist - 2B (HOU) x3	Lance Berkman - LF (HOU) x2	Darryl Kile - SP (HOU)
Carlos Guillen - SS (HOU) x2	Kenny Lofton - CF (HOU) x7	Johan Santana - SP (HOU) x4
Julio Lugo - SS (HOU)	Richard Hidalgo - CF (HOU)	Roy Oswalt - SP (HOU) x2
Ken Caminiti - 3B (HOU) x6	Lance Berkman - CF (HOU)	Brad Lidge - RP (HOU)

Note: 4000 PA or BFP to qualify, except during strike-shortened seasons
(1972 = 3800, 1981 & 1994 = 2700, 1995 = 3500) and 154-game schedule (3800)
-   failed to qualify: 1962-68, 1982-1995

Fernando Abad	Ernie Fazio	Doug Konieczny	Bert Roberge
Bobby Abreu	John Fishel	Keith Lampard	Jeriome Robertson
Ed Acosta	Ken Forsch	Jason Lane	Oscar Robles
Glenn Adams	Lou Frazier	Jack Lazorko	Wandy Rodriguez
Ricky Adams	Alejandro Freire	Brad Lidge	Wilfredo Rodriguez
Dave Adlesh	Tom Funk	Jack Lind	Dave Rohde
Troy Afenir	Ty Gainey	Kenny Lofton	Rodrigo Rosario
Matt Albers	Mike Gallo	Scott Loucks	Mike Rose
Jason Alfaro	Victor Garate	Julio Lugo	Mark Ross
Jose Altuve	Freddy Antonio Garcia	Jordan Lyles	Sean Runyan
Josh Anderson	Art Gardner	Rob Mallicoat	Kirk Saarloos
Eric Anthony	Chris Gardner	Tommy Manzella	Mark Saccomanno
Jose Arcia	Samuel Gervacio	J. D. Martinez	Joe Sambito
Don Arlich	Hector Gimenez	Dave Matranga	Chris Sampson
Ed Armbrister	Keith Ginter	John Mayberry	Roger Samuels
Don August	Dave Giusti	Edwin Maysonet	Luis Sanchez
Mark Bailey	Luis E. Gonzalez	Leon McFadden	Johan Santana
Jeff Baldwin	Jason Green	Tony McKnight	Pedro Santana
Reggie Baldwin	Bill Greif	Bo McLaughlin	Jay Schlueter
Jeff Ball	Tom Griffin	Mark S. McLemore	Todd Self
Floyd Bannister	Greg Gross	Louie Meadows	Carroll Sembera
Brandon Barnes	Jerry Grote	Dave Meads	Scott Servais
Manuel Barrios	Mike Grzanich	Donaldo Mendez	Tom Shearn
Jimmy Barthmaier	Carlos Guillen	Mike Mendoza	J. B. Shuck
Phil Barzilla	Juan Gutierrez	Hector Mercado	Paul Siebert
John Bateman	Dave Hajek	Ron Meridith	Brian Sikorski
Lance Berkman	John Halama	Brian Meyer	Dave Silvestri
Craig Biggio	Tim Hamulack	Aaron Miles	Mike Simms
Bruce Bochy	Devern Hansack	Wade Miller	Mark Small
Brian Bogusevic	Buddy Harris	John Mizerock	Billy L. Smith
Ryan Bowen	Chuck Harrison	Ray Montgomery	Chuck Smith
Eric Bruntlett	Roric Harrison	Melvin Mora	Dave S. Smith
John Buck	Dean Hartgraves	Joe L. Morgan	Julio Solano
Eric Bullock	Chris K. Hatcher	Alvin Morman	Jose Sosa
Tom Burgmeier	Jeff Heathcock	Andy Mota	Scipio Spinks
Chris Burke	Danny Heep	Tony Mounce	Fred Stanley
Mike Burns	Randy Hennis	James Mouton	Mike T. Stanton
Ray Busse	Oscar Henriquez	Ivan Murrell	Rusty Staub
Jeff Calhoun	Carlos Eduardo	Bry Nelson	Mel Stottlemyre, Jr.
Ken Caminiti	Hernandez	Phil Nevin	Drew Sutton
Joe Cannon	Carlos Enrique	Fernando Nieve	Mitch Talbot
Jason Castro	Hernandez	Bud Norris	Alex Taveras
Ramon Castro	Enzo Hernandez	Al Osuna	Derrel Thomas
Andujar Cedeno	Manny Hernandez	Roy Oswalt	Otis Thornton
Cesar Cedeno	Pedro J. Hernandez	John Paciorek	Tim Tolman
Raul Chavez	Jose C. Herrera	Jim Pankovits	J.R. Towles
Rich Chiles	Steve Hertz	Stan Papi	Chris Truby
Jose Cisnero	Richard Hidalgo	Troy Patton	Wayne Twitchell
Brooks Conrad	Jason Hirsh	Felipe Paulino	Glenn Vaughan
Danny Coombs	John Hoffman	Jailen Peguero	Henry Villar
Gary C. Cooper	Chris Holt	Bert Pena	Billy Wagner
Mike Cosgrove	D.J. Houlton	Hunter Pence	Jamie Walker
Jim Crawford	Larry Howard	Pat Perry	Donne Wall
Jay Dahl	Trenidad Hubbard	Roberto Petagine	Dan Walters
Brian Dallimore	Brian L. Hunter	Joe Pittman	Danny Walton
Pat Darcy	Blaise Ilsley	Gordie Pladson	Bob Watkins

Jeff Datz	Chuck Jackson	Aaron Pointer	Bob Watson
Brock Davis	Sonny Jackson	Colin Porter	Terry Wells
Glenn Davis	Al Javier	Terry Puhl	Barry Wesson
Ron E. Davis	Juan Jimenez	Luis Pujols	Ed Whited
Jesus de la Rosa	Charlton Jimerson	Chad Qualls	Tom Wiedenbauer
Ramon de los Santos	Chris Johnson	Doug Rader	Brian Williams
Larry Dierker	Cliff Johnson	Gary Rajsich	Rick Williams
Bill D. Doran	Mark J. Johnson	Santiago Ramirez	Walt Williams
Jim Dougherty	Russ Johnson	Edgar Ramos	Don Wilson
Cory Doyne	Chris D. Jones	Gene Ratliff	Gary S. Wilson
Cameron Drew	Todd Jones	Johnny Ray	Robbie Wine
Mike Easler	Jeff Juden	Larry Ray	Wally Wolf
Scott Elarton	Charlie Kerfeld	Tim Redding	Larry Yellen
Morgan Ensberg	Dallas Keuchel	Chad Reineke	Danny Young
Felix Escalona	Darryl Kile	Shane Reynolds	Larry Yount
Alvaro Espinoza	Alan Knicely	Karl Rhodes	Chris Zachary
Tony Eusebio	Mark Knudson	J.R. Richard	Ben Zobrist

Philadephia / Kansas City / Oakland Athletics

Year/Team	OPW%	PW	PL	APW%	AW	AL	Diff+/-
1901 PHA	0.674 P	92	44	0.544	74	62	-0.130
1902 PHA	0.679 F	92	44	0.610 P	83	53	-0.069
1903 PHA	0.631 P	88	52	0.556	75	60	-0.076
1904 PHA	0.553	85	69	0.536	81	70	-0.016
1905 PHA	0.634 P	98	56	0.622 P	92	56	-0.012
1906 PHA	0.533	82	72	0.538	78	67	0.004
1907 PHA	0.529	82	72	0.607	88	57	0.078
1908 PHA	0.566 P	87	67	0.444	68	85	-0.121
1909 PHA	0.642 P	99	55	0.621	95	58	-0.021

franchID	OWAR	OWS	AWAR	AWS	WARdiff	WSdiff	P/D/W/F
1901 PHA	7.359	50.964	32.058	221.996	-24.699	-171.032	P
1902 PHA	8.258	48.448	37.576	249.001	-29.318	-200.553	F
1903 PHA	6.295	48.777	37.561	225.000	-31.266	-176.223	P
1904 PHA	13.129	76.025	41.955	243.006	-28.826	-166.982	
1905 PHA	12.882	102.132	48.692	276.004	-35.810	-173.872	P
1906 PHA	15.285	114.550	38.923	234.002	-23.638	-119.451	
1907 PHA	16.631	123.948	45.341	264.007	-28.711	-140.059	
1908 PHA	20.908	141.547	28.316	204.003	-7.407	-62.456	P
1909 PHA	43.552	232.197	55.227	285.001	-11.675	-52.804	P

Legend: (P) = Pennant / Most Wins in League (D) = Division Winner (W) = Wild Card Winner (F) = Failed to Qualify

The Philadelphia Athletics commenced play in 1901 as one of the eight original members of the American League. The A's second basemen top the leader boards with the most WS>20 player-seasons (41) among the "Turn of the Century" franchises, led by Eddie Collins (16). The club's third basemen are knotted with the Braves and Giants at 35 WS>20 seasons apiece. The "Original" A's top the Junior Circuit in pennants (19) and playoff appearances (27).

The Athletics achieved 13 pennants under the steady guidance of owner / manager Connie Mack. The franchise secured five titles in its inaugural decade including the first American League title in 1901. Eddie Plank reeled off four consecutive seasons with 20+ victories following a 17-win debut in '01. "Gettysburg Eddie" fashioned a 2.42 ERA with a 1.110 WHIP while averaging 21 victories, 296 innings pitched and 29 complete games during the decade. The

White Sox placed a distant second behind Philadelphia as Chief Bender notched 17 victories in his rookie season (1903). Bender posted a 2.43 ERA with a WHIP of 1.079 while completing 21 contests per year from 1903-09.

The Athletics coasted to the title in 1905 as the Tribe trailed by 15 games at season's end. Andy Coakley contributed a record of 18-8 with a 1.84 ERA. "Sunny" Jim Dygert accrued 21 victories with a 2.34 ERA and a WHIP of 1.089 (all personal-bests) during the 1907 campaign as Philadelphia came up two games short of Detroit for the American League crown. Matty McIntyre sparked the lineup with a league-best 105 runs scored as the A's outlasted the Indians by two games in 1908 and commenced a run of four consecutive pennants. Eddie Collins posted a .347 BA with 104 aces in his first full season (1909) while rookie third-sacker Frank J. "Home Run" Baker paced the circuit with 19 triples. Mack acquired Plank, Collins and Stuffy McInnis as amateur free agents during his first decade of ownership. "The Tall Tactician" procured Baker and "Shoeless" Joe Jackson in separate minor-league deals during the '08 campaign.

Year/Team	OPW%	PW	PL	APW%	AW	AL	Diff+/-
1910 PHA	0.679 P	105	49	0.680 P	102	48	0.001
1911 PHA	0.657 P	101	53	0.669 P	101	50	0.011
1912 PHA	0.582	90	64	0.592	90	62	0.010
1913 PHA	0.626 P	96	58	0.627 P	96	57	0.001
1914 PHA	0.611 P	94	60	0.651 P	99	53	0.041
1915 PHA	0.368	57	97	0.283	43	109	-0.086
1916 PHA	0.384	59	95	0.235	36	117	-0.149
1917 PHA	0.500	77	77	0.359	55	98	-0.140
1918 PHA	0.410	52	76	0.406	52	76	-0.004
1919 PHA	0.381	53	87	0.257	36	104	-0.123

franchID	OWAR	OWS	AWAR	AWS	WARdiff	WSdiff	P/D/W/F
1910 PHA	50.924	274.987	58.878	305.996	-7.954	-31.010	P
1911 PHA	53.067	304.412	52.339	303.002	0.728	1.410	P
1912 PHA	46.395	289.380	42.452	269.994	3.942	19.386	
1913 PHA	46.882	282.386	48.880	287.995	-1.998	-5.609	P
1914 PHA	47.288	276.718	51.453	294.000	-4.165	-17.282	P
1915 PHA	17.684	174.612	2.168	129.001	15.516	45.611	
1916 PHA	29.137	178.007	8.554	108.001	20.584	70.006	
1917 PHA	36.515	223.047	22.873	165.002	13.642	58.045	
1918 PHA	23.361	181.710	10.491	155.999	12.869	25.711	
1919 PHA	33.314	224.448	9.061	107.996	24.253	116.451	

Athletics' second basemen led the Major Leagues with 33 WS>10 player-seasons from 1910-1929, with Collins achieving the feat 18 times. He furnished a .326 BA during the decade while registering 99 tallies and swiping 49 bags per year including a league-best 81 thefts in 1910. Collins paced the American League in runs scored for three straight seasons (1912-14). He merited MVP honors and recorded the highest Win Shares total in franchise history (42) during the 1914 campaign. Jack Coombs averaged 27 victories over a three-year stretch covering 1910-12. He topped the circuit with a 31-9 record and 13 shutouts in 1910 while posting a 1.30 ERA and a 1.028 WHIP. Bender established career-bests with 23 victories, a 1.58 ERA and a 0.916 WHIP in '10. Three years later he furnished 21 wins and saved 13 contests. Bender supplied an 18-6 record with a 2.15 ERA and a 1.109 WHIP per year from 1910-14.

Baker delivered four home run titles (1911-14) in succession and paced the AL in RBI during back-to-back seasons (1912-13). He accrued 38 Win Shares in 1912 while setting career-highs in batting average (.347), base hits (200), runs scored (116), RBI (130) and stolen bases (40). "Shoeless" Joe Jackson scorched the opposition with a .408 BA and topped the leader boards with a .468 OBP in his rookie season (1911). He also registered 38 Win Shares while establishing personal-bests with 233 safeties, 126 tallies, 45 doubles, 41 stolen bases and a .590 SLG. Jackson recorded the most hits in 1912-13, legged out 26 triples in 1912 and produced a .354 BA during the decade. Jackson placed second in the 1913 AL MVP race, batting .373 with a league-best .551 SLG. McIntyre ignited the offense with a career-best .323 BA while scoring 102 aces for the '11 squad.

Stuffy McInnis produced career-highs with a .327 BA, 101 ribbies and 27 steals in 1912. Philadelphia notched successive pennants in 1913-14. Amos "Lightning" Strunk bolted 30 two-base knocks and batted .316 for the Athletics during the 1916 campaign while Bob Shawkey established personal-bests with 24 victories, 8 saves, a 2.21 ERA and a 1.030 WHIP in multiple mound roles. Shawkey averaged 20 wins with a 3.02 ERA over a four-year period from 1919-1922. Stan Coveleski supplied a 2.35 ERA, 1.139 WHIP, 20 victories and 21 complete games per year from 1916-19 including 9 shutouts in '17. "Bullet" Joe Bush yielded a 2.38 ERA and completed 23 of 32 starts in a three-year span from 1916-18.

Win Shares > 20	Single-Season	1901-1919
Stuffy McInnis - 1B (OAK) x3	Joe Jackson - LF (OAK) x4	Chief Bender - SP (OAK) x3
Eddie Collins - 2B (OAK) x16	Amos Strunk - CF (OAK) x2	Jack Coombs - SP (OAK) x2
Morrie Rath - 2B (OAK) x2	Joe Jackson - RF (OAK) x3	Stan Coveleski - SP (OAK) x7
John Knight - SS (OAK)	Matty McIntyre - RF (OAK)	Joe Bush - SP (OAK) x5
Frank J. Baker - 3B (OAK) x8	Eddie Murphy - RF (OAK) x2	Bob Shawkey - SP (OAK) x3
Ed Lennox - 3B (OAK)	Eddie Plank - SP (OAK) x9	Jimmy Dygert - SW (OAK)
Matty McIntyre - LF (OAK)	Andy Coakley - SP (OAK)	Bob Shawkey - SW (OAK)
Bris Lord - LF (OAK)		

Year/Team	OPW%	PW	PL	APW%	AW	AL	Diff+/-
1920 PHA	0.468	72	82	0.312	48	106	-0.156
1921 PHA	0.430	66	88	0.346	53	100	-0.084
1922 PHA	0.441	68	86	0.422	65	89	-0.019
1923 PHA	0.549 P	84	70	0.454	69	83	-0.095
1924 PHA	0.496	76	78	0.467	71	81	-0.029
1925 PHA	0.562	87	67	0.579	88	64	0.017
1926 PHA	0.476	73	81	0.553	83	67	0.078
1927 PHA	0.480	74	80	0.591	91	63	0.111
1928 PHA	0.559 P	86	68	0.641	98	55	0.081
1929 PHA	0.605 P	93	61	0.693 P	104	46	0.088

franchID	OWAR	OWS	AWAR	AWS	WARdiff	WSdiff	P/D/W/F
1920 PHA	34.388	227.966	14.952	144.000	19.436	83.966	
1921 PHA	33.160	211.023	23.497	159.000	9.663	52.023	
1922 PHA	30.572	220.038	23.379	194.999	7.193	25.039	
1923 PHA	31.242	225.553	24.395	206.996	6.847	18.558	P
1924 PHA	34.298	234.430	25.851	212.991	8.447	21.439	
1925 PHA	44.353	263.705	44.802	264.000	-0.449	-0.295	
1926 PHA	41.528	249.701	41.809	249.002	-0.281	0.699	
1927 PHA	41.194	273.945	48.349	273.000	-7.155	0.944	
1928 PHA	48.115	296.547	51.994	294.001	-3.880	2.545	P
1929 PHA	49.574	300.264	53.067	311.995	-3.493	-11.732	P

Collins notched career-highs with a 372 BA, 224 base hits and 38 two-baggers in 1920. He topped the Junior Circuit in stolen bases and placed runner-up in the AL MVP balloting in successive seasons (1923-24). Collins delivered a .347 BA from 1920-27 and surpassed the 3000-hit plateau in '25. Jackson (.382/12/121) led the AL with 20 triples while producing personal-bests in home runs and RBI. Shawkey (20-13, 2.45) claimed the 1920 AL ERA crown. Coveleski duplicated his output from the previous season with 24 triumphs while pacing the AL with 133 whiffs and a 1.108 WHIP. "Covey" surpassed 20 victories for the fourth consecutive season in 1921 and later achieved ERA titles in '23 and '25. Steve O'Neill compiled a .318 BA and belted 29 two-base knocks per year from 1920-22. Whitey Witt batted .306 and tallied 100 runs per year from 1921-24.

Eddie Rommel topped the circuit in victories during the '22 and '25 seasons. Rommel (27-13, 3.28) and Bush (26-7, 3.31) finished second and fourth respectively in the 1922 AL MVP balloting. Herb Pennock delivered a 19-6 record as the A's edged the Tigers to secure the 1923 AL pennant. "The Squire of Kennett Square" placed third in the 1926 AL MVP race and averaged 19 victories with a 3.03 ERA during a six-year stretch (1923-28). First-sacker Charlie Grimm aka "Jolly Cholly" supplied personal-bests with a .345 BA, 194 base hits and 99 RBI for the '23 crew. Joe Hauser swatted 27 big-flies and plated 115 baserunners in 1924. Mack assembled a profusion of exceptional ballplayers in 1923-24 including Al Simmons, Lefty Grove, Jimmie Foxx and Mickey Cochrane.

Al Simmons commenced an 11-year streak with at least 100 RBI during his inaugural campaign in 1924. "Bucketfoot Al" registered 253 base hits and knocked in 129 runs, placing runner-up in the 1925 AL MVP race in his sophomore season. He batted .356 with 40 two-baggers and 119 ribbies per year from 1924-29. The Athletics and White Sox finished the 1925 season in a dead heat with the Senators. Washington seized the pennant by percentage points. Al Wingo conjured a .370 BA and scored 104 runs while Dick Burrus compiled 200 safeties and batted at a .340 clip.

Lefty Grove paced the Junior Circuit in strikeouts for seven consecutive seasons (1925-1931). He achieved his first of nine appearances atop the ERA leader board in '26 and fashioned a 25-8 record with 2.74 ERA per year from 1927-1933. Mickey Cochrane compiled a .314 BA through his first five seasons including a .331 mark in his rookie campaign. Max "Camera Eye" Bishop coaxed at least 100 walks for eight straight years (1926-33). The Athletics defeated the Yankees to earn back-to-back pennants in 1928-29, claiming both titles by a six-game margin. George Earnshaw (24-8, 3.29) topped the 20-win plateau in three successive seasons (1929-1931). Jimmie Foxx (.354/33/118) tallied 123 runs along with a league-best .463 OBP in '29.

Year/Team	OPW%	PW	PL	APW%	AW	AL	Diff+/-
1930 PHA	0.563	87	67	0.662 P	102	52	0.099
1931 PHA	0.569	88	66	0.704 P	107	45	0.135
1932 PHA	0.594 P	91	63	0.610	94	60	0.016
1933 PHA	0.485	75	79	0.523	79	72	0.038
1934 PHA	0.495	76	78	0.453	68	82	-0.041
1935 PHA	0.454	70	84	0.389	58	91	-0.065
1936 PHA	0.442	68	86	0.346	53	100	-0.096
1937 PHA	0.476	73	81	0.358	54	97	-0.118
1938 PHA	0.471	72	82	0.349	53	99	-0.122
1939 PHA	0.449	69	85	0.362	55	97	-0.087

franchID	OWAR	OWS	AWAR	AWS	WARdiff	WSdiff	P/D/W/F
1930 PHA	51.987	311.741	50.662	306.005	1.326	5.735	
1931 PHA	58.740	318.811	53.495	320.997	5.245	-2.186	
1932 PHA	54.672	294.335	53.738	282.001	0.935	12.335	P
1933 PHA	40.046	265.775	40.812	237.002	-0.766	28.772	
1934 PHA	35.992	231.672	29.518	204.003	6.474	27.669	
1935 PHA	33.093	208.630	26.321	174.004	6.772	34.626	
1936 PHA	25.317	194.795	11.423	158.997	13.894	35.797	
1937 PHA	29.182	210.210	25.081	162.002	4.101	48.208	
1938 PHA	33.276	225.507	22.078	159.000	11.198	66.507	
1939 PHA	30.422	231.059	16.737	165.001	13.685	66.058	

Grove dominated the Junior Circuit from 1930-33 with a cumulative record of 108-27. He achieved MVP status in 1931 with a 31-4 mark along with personal-bests in ERA (2.06), WHIP (1.077) and Win Shares (41). The six-time All-Star averaged 20 wins with a 2.91 ERA and 20 complete games per season during the decade. Simmons notched back-to-back batting titles in 1930-31 and pummeled rival moundsmen for a .351 BA with 34 two-baggers, 25 clouts, 118 runs scored, 204 base hits and 133 ribbies per season from 1930-34. Cochrane contributed a .327 BA from 1930-36 and established career-highs in home runs (23), RBI (112) and runs scored (118) during the 1932 campaign.

Foxx annihilated opposing hurlers throughout the decade as he averaged .336 with 42 moon-shots, 140 RBI and 124 runs scored per season! "Beast" accrued 40 Win Shares in '32 while earning MVP accolades with league-bests in home runs (58), RBI (169) and runs (151). Foxx (.356/48/163) seized the batting championship, claimed MVP honors and received the first of nine consecutive All-Star selections for an encore. He clubbed 50 round-trippers, knocked in 175 baserunners and collected another batting title en route to his third MVP trophy in 1938.

The A's accrued the highest pitWARnorm (29) and pitWSnorm (133) in franchise history during the 1931 season. Philadephia slipped past New York to secure the Junior Circuit title in '32. The organization endured a forty-year playoff drought as the Athletics failed to finish above .500 for 14 consecutive campaigns. Third-sacker Pinky Higgins eclipsed the century mark in RBI during successive seasons (1937-38). Bob L. Johnson walloped 27 moon-shots, drove in 107 baserunners and scored 102 runs per year from 1933-1941. "Indian Bob" earned seven All-Star selections in his career and established personal-bests with a .338 BA and 115 aces in '39.

Wally Moses delivered seven straight seasons with a batting average above .300 including a career-best .345 BA in 1935. Moses compiled 200+ base hits in back-to-back campaigns (1935-36). Left fielder Rip Radcliff set personal records with 207 safeties and 120 tallies while procuring his lone All-Star nomination in '36.

Win Shares > 20	Single-Season	1920-1939
Charlie Grimm - 1B (OAK) x2	Al Wingo - LF (OAK)	Tom Zachary - SP (OAK)
Joe Hauser - 1B (OAK) x2	Al Simmons - LF (OAK) x7	Slim Harriss - SP (OAK)
Dick Burrus - 1B (OAK)	Bob L. Johnson - LF (OAK) x7	Lefty Grove - SP (OAK) x11
Jimmie Foxx - 1B (OAK) x12	Rip Radcliff - LF (OAK) x2	Sam Gray - SP (OAK) x2
Max Bishop - 2B (OAK) x3	Whitey Witt - CF (OAK)	George Earnshaw - SP (OAK) x3
Jimmie Dykes - SS (OAK)	Al Simmons - CF (OAK) x3	
Jimmie Foxx - 3B (OAK)	Wally Moses - CF (OAK)	Socks Seibold - SP (OAK)
Pinky Higgins - 3B (OAK) x3	Bob L. Johnson - CF (OAK)	Eddie Rommel - SW (OAK) x2
Steve O'Neill - C (OAK)	Eddie Rommel - SP (OAK) x2	Lefty Grove - SW (OAK)
Wally Schang - C (OAK)	Herb Pennock - SP (OAK) x3	Jack F. Wilson - SW (OAK)
Mickey Cochrane - C (OAK)x9		

Year/Team	OPW%	PW	PL	APW%	AW	AL	Diff+/-
1940 PHA	0.443	68	86	0.351	54	100	-0.092
1941 PHA	0.489	75	79	0.416	64	90	-0.074
1942 PHA	0.394	61	93	0.357	55	99	-0.037
1943 PHA	0.431	66	88	0.318	49	105	-0.112
1944 PHA	0.439	68	86	0.468	72	82	0.028
1945 PHA	0.493	76	78	0.347	52	98	-0.146
1946 PHA	0.418	64	90	0.318	49	105	-0.100
1947 PHA	0.518	80	74	0.506	78	76	-0.011
1948 PHA	0.487	75	79	0.545	84	70	0.058
1949 PHA	0.542	84	70	0.526	81	73	-0.017

franchID	OWAR	OWS	AWAR	AWS	WARdiff	WSdiff	P/D/W/F
1940 PHA	30.147	214.113	20.398	161.998	9.750	52.115	
1941 PHA	30.632	225.951	22.568	191.999	8.064	33.952	
1942 PHA	26.337	204.470	14.154	165.004	12.184	39.466	
1943 PHA	31.962	232.171	10.483	147.002	21.479	85.169	
1944 PHA	37.708	265.362	28.470	216.006	9.238	49.356	
1945 PHA	32.593	232.405	18.276	156.006	14.317	76.399	
1946 PHA	25.980	194.457	20.877	146.999	5.103	47.458	
1947 PHA	29.620	235.374	29.981	233.998	-0.361	1.376	
1948 PHA	38.549	265.396	32.881	252.001	5.668	13.395	
1949 PHA	37.331	265.660	31.233	243.003	6.098	22.657	

Foxx (.297/36/119) claimed a runner-up finish in the 1940 AL MVP balloting while Radcliff delivered a career-best .342 BA and led the circuit with 200 hits. Bill Nicholson produced 27 long balls and drove in 105 baserunners per season from 1940-44. "Swish" paced the League in home runs and RBI during successive seasons (1943-44). Sam Chapman (.322/25/106) posted his highest batting average in 1941. Eddie Stanky paced the circuit with 128 runs scored and 148 bases on balls. "The Brat" coaxed more than 100 walks in every year from 1945 to 1951 except the 1948 season. Phil Marchildon registered 19 victories with a 3.22 ERA despite allowing a league-worst 141 walks in '47. Ferris Fain and Elmer Valo combined to draw 249 bases on balls in '49.

Year/Team	OPW%	PW	PL	APW%	AW	AL	Diff+/-
1950 PHA	0.408	63	91	0.338	52	102	-0.070
1951 PHA	0.496	76	78	0.455	70	84	-0.042
1952 PHA	0.498 F	77	77	0.513	79	75	0.015
1953 PHA	0.445 F	69	85	0.383	59	95	-0.062
1954 PHA	0.413 F	64	90	0.331	51	103	-0.082
1955 KCA	0.373 F	57	97	0.409	63	91	0.036
1956 KCA	0.452 F	70	84	0.338	52	102	-0.114
1957 KCA	0.568 F	87	67	0.386	59	94	-0.182
1958 KCA	0.513 F	79	75	0.474	73	81	-0.039
1959 KCA	0.470 F	72	82	0.429	66	88	-0.041

franchID	OWAR	OWS	AWAR	AWS	WARdiff	WSdiff	P/D/W/F
1950 OAK	33.225	211.211	20.916	156.005	12.309	55.206	
1951 OAK	40.561	235.936	35.240	210.004	5.321	25.932	
1952 OAK	39.690	245.996	31.107	236.998	8.583	8.998	F
1953 OAK	22.994	178.174	22.805	176.997	0.189	1.177	F
1954 OAK	26.765	203.347	16.033	188.998	10.732	14.349	F
1955 OAK	28.139	213.790	16.033	188.998	12.106	24.792	F
1956 OAK	26.869	182.195	17.788	155.997	9.081	26.198	F
1957 OAK	50.023	275.831	23.039	177.008	26.984	98.823	F
1958 OAK	34.671	205.946	27.776	218.993	6.895	-13.047	F
1959 OAK	48.077	250.755	30.604	198.001	17.473	52.753	F

A number of talented players came through the Athletics system in the 1950's, but the franchise mired in mediocrity until the mid-Sixties. Stanky (.300/8/51) led the League in walks (144) and OBP (.460), placing him third in the MVP balloting. Second-sacker Nellie Fox earned All-Star selections in 11 straight seasons, averaging .303 from 1951-1960 and leading the League in base hits four times. Fox was nearly impossible to fan; in fifteen full seasons (1950-1964) he never exceeded 18 whiffs! "Mighty Mite" registered eight appearances on the Fielding WAR and WS leader boards, placing second on the all-time list behind Bill Mazeroski and Frank White (tied with 9).

Ferris Fain achieved successive batting titles in 1951-52. Sam Chapman launched 23 long balls and knocked in 95 runs in 1950. Utilityman Hector Lopez belted 22 big-flies and drove in 93 runs in '59. Bobby Shantz (24-7, 2.48) won the 1952 AL MVP Award, posting a league-best 1.048 WHIP. The Athletics relocated to Kansas City prior to the start of the 1955 season. Arnie Portocarrero notched 15 victories in 1958 along with a 3.25 ERA. Art Ditmar (13-9, 2.90) topped the circuit with a 1.030 WHIP in '59.

Win Shares > 20	Single-Season	1940-1959
Nick Etten - 1B (OAK) x3	Elmer Valo - LF (OAK)	Eddie Smith - SP (OAK)
Ferris Fain - 1B (OAK) x2	Sam Chapman - CF (OAK) x2	Roger Wolff - SP (OAK)
Nellie Fox - 2B (OAK) x9	Wally Moses - RF (OAK) x4	Phil Marchildon - SP (OAK)
Eddie Stanky - 2B (OAK) x6	Bill Nicholson - RF (OAK) x5	Bobby Shantz - SP (OAK)
Eric Tipton - LF (OAK) x2	Ron Northey - RF (OAK) x2	

Year/Team	OPW%	PW	PL	APW%	AW	AL	Diff+/-
1960 KCA	0.509 F	78	76	0.377	58	96	-0.133
1961 KCA	0.422 F	68	94	0.379	61	100	-0.043
1962 KCA	0.420 F	68	94	0.444	72	90	0.024
1963 KCA	0.401 F	65	97	0.451	73	89	0.050
1964 KCA	0.370 F	60	102	0.352	57	105	-0.018
1965 KCA	0.484	78	84	0.364	59	103	-0.120
1966 KCA	0.507 F	82	80	0.463	74	86	-0.045
1967 KCA	0.458	74	88	0.385	62	99	-0.073
1968 OAK	0.559	90	72	0.506	82	80	-0.052
1969 OAK	0.521	84	78	0.543	88	74	0.023

franchID	OWAR	OWS	AWAR	AWS	WARdiff	WSdiff	P/D/W/F
1960 OAK	33.830	229.418	22.236	173.995	11.594	55.422	F
1961 OAK	11.514	162.824	18.823	182.996	-7.309	-20.172	F
1962 OAK	31.003	175.678	28.653	215.997	2.350	-40.319	F
1963 OAK	19.400	191.366	27.831	218.997	-8.431	-27.631	F
1964 OAK	17.308	157.713	22.117	170.999	-4.809	-13.286	F
1965 OAK	31.082	204.027	21.841	177.000	9.241	27.027	
1966 OAK	26.100	193.322	21.248	222.001	4.852	-28.679	F
1967 OAK	24.583	161.686	22.067	186.001	2.515	-24.315	
1968 OAK	34.888	221.355	39.514	246.001	-4.627	-24.646	
1969 OAK	33.091	225.229	38.925	263.993	-5.834	-38.764	

Kansas City stockpiled gifted ballplayers throughout the Sixties including amateur free agent Bert Campaneris ('61) and a talented trio consisting of Jim "Catfish" Hunter, Rollie Fingers and Joe Rudi ('64). General Managers Hank Bauer (1965) and Ed Lopat (1966-67) laid the groundwork for the A's dynasty in the Seventies with their selections in the Amateur Draft. (Sal Bando, Gene Tenace, Rick Monday, Reggie Jackson, Darrell Evans and Vida Blue)

Bert Campaneris swiped 50+ bases for 5 consecutive years (1965-69); "Campy" stole 62 bases in consecutive years (1968-69) and led the American League with 177 base hits in '68. Jim Nash fashioned a 12-1 record with a 2.06 ERA and 1.118 WHIP in his rookie campaign (1966). Nash added 13 wins and a team-best 2.28 ERA and 1.050 WHIP two years later. Jack Aker saved 32 games with a 1.99 ERA and 0.965 WHIP. Clete Boyer led the A's with 26 clouts and 96 RBI in '67. The fine-fielding Boyer placed fourth among third basemen with 7 seasons on the Fielding WAR and WS charts.

The franchise transferred to Oakland in 1968 and came within one victory of the American League pennant. Ken "Hawk" Harrelson (.275/35/109) made his lone All-Star appearance and finished third in the AL MVP voting. "Hawk" launched 30 moon-shots for the '69 squad. Jackson belted 29 round-trippers in his first full season; he then dialed long distance 47 times and plated 118 baserunners in the subsequent campaign while recording a career-high 39 Win Shares. George Brunet posted a 2.86 ERA and 1.056 WHIP while John "Blue Moon" Odom compiled 16 victories and a 2.45 ERA. Divisional play began in 1969, and Minnesota took the AL West crown by a mere two games over Oakland. Third-sacker Bando swatted 31 long balls and drove in 113 runs.

Year/Team	OPW%	PW	PL	APW%	AW	AL	Diff+/-
1970 OAK	0.502	81	81	0.549	89	73	0.047
1971 OAK	0.529	86	76	0.627 D	101	60	0.099
1972 OAK	0.554 D	90	72	0.600 P	93	62	0.046
1973 OAK	0.567 D	92	70	0.580 D	94	68	0.013
1974 OAK	0.613 P	99	63	0.556 D	90	72	-0.057
1975 OAK	0.582 P	94	68	0.605 P	98	64	0.023
1976 OAK	0.577 P	93	69	0.540	87	74	-0.036
1977 OAK	0.535	87	75	0.391	63	98	-0.143
1978 OAK	0.530	86	76	0.426	69	93	-0.104
1979 OAK	0.455	74	88	0.333	54	108	-0.122

franchID	OWAR	OWS	AWAR	AWS	WARdiff	WSdiff	P/D/W/F
1970 OAK	32.645	201.198	43.446	267.003	-10.801	-65.805	
1971 OAK	37.241	241.007	50.848	303.006	-13.607	-61.999	
1972 OAK	33.869	208.878	48.453	278.999	-14.584	-70.121	D
1973 OAK	37.876	234.422	46.999	281.993	-9.122	-47.571	D
1974 OAK	44.506	253.925	45.484	269.998	-0.978	-16.073	P
1975 OAK	42.604	262.242	50.476	294.001	-7.872	-31.759	P
1976 OAK	43.024	246.956	45.740	261.003	-2.716	-14.047	P
1977 OAK	33.610	222.023	19.591	189.007	14.018	33.016	
1978 OAK	39.434	242.251	22.344	206.997	17.090	35.254	
1979 OAK	32.315	211.949	7.816	161.996	24.499	49.952	

Oakland managed a .500 record in 1970, placing third behind Minnesota and California. Second baseman Felix Millan batted .310 and scored 100 runs. Campaneris bashed a career-high 22 dingers and pilfered 42 bags. Jack Aker (16 SV, 2.06), Paul Lindblad (8-2, 2.70) and Ken Sanders (13 SV, 1.75) quelled the late rallies, with Sanders (31 SV, 1.91) assuming the lion's share of the responsibilities during the subsequent season.

Jim "Catfish" Hunter ascended to elite status during a five-year period (1971-75) as he delivered at least 20 victories per year with a 2.65 ERA and a 1.027 WHIP. The eight-time All-Star collected the 1974 AL Cy Young Award after notching 25 wins and topping the circuit in ERA (2.49) and WHIP (0.986). "True" Blue fashioned a miniscule 1.82 ERA and 0.952 WHIP to complement his 24-8 record as he secured the 1971 AL MVP and Cy Young Awards. Blue also eclipsed the 20-win mark in '73 and '75. He posted an ERA of 2.87 along with a 1.164 WHIP over an eight-year stretch from 1971-78. The Athletics' offense struggled to keep pace with the mound crew's brilliant performances and the squad fell one game short of the division crown.

Oakland captured the club's first division title in 1972, overtaking the Twins by 5 games. Joe Rudi placed runner-up in the AL MVP balloting in '72 and '74. He topped the circuit with 191 base knocks and 9 triples in '72 and then drilled a league-high 39 doubles two years later. Odom posted a 15-6 record with a 2.50 ERA. The relief corps continued to excel as Rollie Fingers, Sanders, Aker and crew combined for 72 saves. Fingers fashioned a 2.63 ERA and a 1.092 WHIP while saving 24 contests per year from 1971-78. He topped the charts in consecutive seasons (1977-78), notching a personal-best 37 saves in '78.

The Athletics captured another division title with a comfortable eight-game margin over the Twins. Evans rocked 41 round-trippers and drove in 104 runs while leading the League with

124 bases on balls. Bando (.287/29/98) topped the AL with 32 two-base hits and 295 total bases. Tenace coaxed 104 walks per season from 1973-79. Jackson (.293/32/117) secured 1973 AL MVP honors, pacing the Junior Circuit in runs (99), home runs, RBI and SLG (.531). He belted a league-best 36 four-baggers for the '75 squad. "Mr. October" dialed long-distance 29 times and pilfered 18 bases per year during the Seventies.

The A's secured three successive pennants while pacing the American League in oWAR and oWS from 1974-76. Oakland triumphed in 99 contests in '74, overpowering Minnesota by 11 games. Claudell Washington (.308/10/77) swiped 40 bases for the '75 squad. Rick Monday supplied career-highs with 32 moon-shots and 107 aces in '76 while solid relief work by Skip Lockwood (10-7, 2.67, 19 SV) bolstered the bullpen.

Oakland's run ended in 1977 as Kansas City commenced a four-year streak atop the AL West. The Athletics nearly caught the Royals in '78, finishing only two games behind. Don "Full Pack" Stanhouse contributed 24 saves. The 1979 squad slumped to a 74-88 record. "Disco" Dan Ford knocked in 101 runners and added 21 circuit clouts. Chet Lemon (.318/17/86) drilled 44 doubles to lead the League. The pitching staff faltered as Matt Keough (2-17, 5.04), Mike Morgan (2-10, 5.94) and Blue (14-14, 5.01) suffered through miserable campaigns.

Win Shares > 20	Single-Season	1960-1979
Gene Tenace - 1B (OAK) x4	Sal Bando - 3B (OAK) x9	George Hendrick - CF (OAK)
Joe Rudi - 1B (OAK)	Darrell Evans - 3B (OAK) x7	Chet Lemon - CF (OAK) x5
Dick Green - 2B (OAK)	Gene Tenace - C (OAK) x3	Ken Harrelson - RF (OAK)
Felix Millan - 2B (OAK)	Joe Rudi - LF (OAK) x2	Reggie Jackson - RF (OAK)
Phil Garner - 2B (OAK) x2	Claudell Washington - LF	x12
Bert Campaneris - SS (OAK)	(OAK)	Vida Blue - SP (OAK) x3
x5	Rick Monday - CF (OAK) x5	Catfish Hunter - SP (OAK) x4
Clete Boyer - 3B (OAK)	Reggie Jackson - CF (OAK)	Ken Sanders - RP (OAK)

Year/Team	OPW%	PW	PL	APW%	AW	AL	Diff+/-
1980 OAK	0.567	92	70	0.512	83	79	-0.054
1981 OAK	0.630 P	102	60	0.587 P	64	45	-0.043
1982 OAK	0.529 D	86	76	0.420	68	94	-0.109
1983 OAK	0.498 D	81	81	0.457	74	88	-0.041
1984 OAK	0.532 D	86	76	0.475	77	85	-0.057
1985 OAK	0.510 F	83	79	0.475	77	85	-0.035
1986 OAK	0.538	87	75	0.469	76	86	-0.069
1987 OAK	0.501 F	81	81	0.500	81	81	-0.001
1988 OAK	0.523 F	85	77	0.642 P	104	58	0.119
1989 OAK	0.557 F	90	72	0.611 P	99	63	0.054

franchID	OWAR	OWS	AWAR	AWS	WARdiff	WSdiff	P/D/W/F
1980 OAK	45.955	268.302	35.567	249.001	10.388	19.300	
1981 OAK	30.334	186.902	26.102	192.002	4.232	-5.101	P
1982 OAK	32.905	241.519	19.431	204.003	13.474	37.516	D
1983 OAK	31.885	220.328	29.133	222.001	2.752	-1.673	D
1984 OAK	33.033	229.803	31.663	231.004	1.370	-1.201	D
1985 OAK	36.407	247.111	30.457	231.002	5.950	16.109	F
1986 OAK	40.097	246.255	29.324	228.000	10.773	18.255	
1987 OAK	39.990	260.649	41.469	243.000	-1.479	17.649	F
1988 OAK	45.152	294.453	51.599	311.997	-6.447	-17.544	F
1989 OAK	45.283	285.121	47.186	297.003	-1.903	-11.881	F

Oakland's lumber company produced an offensive barrage in 1980, vaulting the club back into contention. Rickey Henderson (.303/9/53) sparked the turnaround, scoring 111 runs and swiping 100 bases in 126 attempts! Henderson batted .319 while pacing the circuit in runs, hits and stolen bases during the strike-shortened campaign in '81. He finished second in the 1981 AL MVP voting and earned his lone Gold Glove Award. "The Man of Steal" captivated the A's faithful with his baserunning exploits, setting a Major League record with 130 stolen bases in 172 tries. Henderson (.314/24/82) took third place in the 1985 AL MVP vote, leading the League with 146 runs scored and 80 stolen bases.

Jackson was runner-up in the 1980 AL MVP voting, posting a .300 BA with 111 RBI and leading the circuit with 41 bombs. In 1982 he drove in 101 baserunners and tied for the league-lead with 39 four-baggers. George Hendrick (.302/25/109) delivered 33 doubles for the '80 crew and repeated the feat three years later while notching a personal-best .318 BA. Mike Norris (22-9, 2.53) placed second in the 1980 AL Cy Young voting. Keough (16-13, 2.92) and Blue (14-10, 2.97) rebounded nicely as Brian Kingman pitched respectably while managing to lose 20 games (8-20, 3.83).

The Athletics posted 102 victories and breezed to the 1981 American League pennant, finishing 13 games ahead of California. Fingers slammed the door on the opposition, saving 28 games with a 1.04 ERA and 0.872 WHIP as he captured AL MVP and Cy Young Awards. Steve McCatty placed second to Fingers in the AL Cy Young voting with a league-leading 14 wins and second-best 2.33 ERA in the strike-shortened season.

Oakland topped the American League Western Division for the next 3 seasons. The Athletics edged the Royals by a single victory in '82 as Dwayne Murphy left the yard 27 times, filched 26 bags and knocked in 94 runs. The six-time Gold Glove winner launched a career-high 33 blasts two years later. Ernie Camacho (2.43, 23 SV) reinforced the bullpen as the A's cruised to another division title, defeating the Royals by a 9-game margin. Evans augmented the attack, claiming the home run title with 40 bombs for the '85 squad.

The Oakland organization sustained a 5-year talent drought from 1985-89 resulting in the club failing to attain the 4000 BFP pre-requisite in every season except 1986. The A's fell one game short of Kansas City despite a career year from Mike Davis (.287/24/82). Jose Canseco injected new life into the lineup, bashing 33 homers and driving in 117 runs en route to the 1986 AL ROY Award. "The Chemist" achieved the first 40/40 season (40 home runs and 40 stolen bases) two years later, scoring 120 runs and batting .307 while registering 39 Win Shares in the process. Mark McGwire enhanced the offense in '87, launching 49 moon-shots and driving in 118 runs to capture the AL Rookie of the Year award. "Big Mac" blasted 36 long balls and knocked in 100 baserunners per year from 1987-1992. Defensive wizard Walt Weiss secured the A's third consecutive ROY award despite negligible contributions from the batter's box.

Year/Team	OPW%	PW	PL	APW%	AW	AL	Diff+/-
1990 OAK	0.508	82	80	0.636 P	103	59	0.127
1991 OAK	0.561	91	71	0.519	84	78	-0.043
1992 OAK	0.518	84	78	0.593 D	96	66	0.075
1993 OAK	0.476	77	85	0.420	68	94	-0.057
1994 OAK	0.490 D	79	83	0.447	51	63	-0.043
1995 OAK	0.494	80	82	0.465	67	77	-0.029
1996 OAK	0.463	75	87	0.481	78	84	0.018
1997 OAK	0.423	69	93	0.401	65	97	-0.022
1998 OAK	0.510	83	79	0.457	74	88	-0.054
1999 OAK	0.472 F	77	85	0.537	87	75	0.065

franchID	OWAR	OWS	AWAR	AWS	WARdiff	WSdiff	P/D/W/F
1990 OAK	43.352	271.057	47.879	308.993	-4.528	-37.935	
1991 OAK	43.815	272.896	31.063	252.000	12.752	20.897	
1992 OAK	47.853	280.475	43.856	287.995	3.998	-7.519	
1993 OAK	35.233	254.003	27.663	204.002	7.570	50.001	

41

1994 OAK	22.682	182.169	19.804	153.003	2.878	29.167	D
1995 OAK	34.004	239.075	32.684	200.996	1.320	38.079	
1996 OAK	29.079	241.483	32.565	233.997	-3.487	7.487	
1997 OAK	24.967	224.249	24.893	194.995	0.074	29.254	
1998 OAK	41.659	**306.850**	28.712	222.004	12.948	84.845	
1999 OAK	42.608	304.697	42.415	261.002	0.193	43.695	F

Seattle outpaced Oakland to claim the AL West by five games in '90. Henderson (.325/28/61) augmented his trophy case with the 1990 AL MVP Award. He compiled 40 Win Shares while topping the circuit in runs scored (119), stolen bases (65), OBP (.439) and OPS (1.016). Luis Polonia delivered a personal-best .335 BA in '90 and nabbed 51 bags per season from 1991-93. The A's finished 6 games behind the White Sox in '91 as Kevin Tapani (16-9, 2.99) and Mike Morgan (14-10, 2.78) bolstered the mound corps. Canseco (.266/44/122) scored 115 runs, swiped 26 bases and placed fourth in the 1991 AL MVP voting. Mickey Tettleton swatted 32 long balls and averaged 111 bases on balls per year from 1991-93 including a league-leading 122 free passes in '92. Felix Jose laced 40 two-base hits and batted .305.

The White Sox outlasted the A's again in 1992, taking the division by 5 games. Rod Beck (1.76, 0.837 WHIP, 17 SV) established his presence in the back-end of the bullpen. "Shooter" locked up the closer's role in the following campaign, converting 48 saves with a 2.16 ERA and 0.882 WHIP. Beck earned three All-Star nominations while averaging 36 saves with a 2.90 ERA and a 1.094 WHIP from 1992-98. Terry Steinbach belted 35 home runs and registered 100 RBI in 1996 after averaging 11 homers in his first nine seasons. McGwire clubbed 52 circuit clouts in 130 contests as he topped the AL in homers, OBP (.467) and SLG (.730). "Big Mac" pounded 58 moon-shots and drove in 123 runs as he prepared for his assault on the record books. McGwire and Sammy Sosa engaged in a summer-long assault on Roger Maris' single-season home run record in 1998. McGwire emerged with the title, bashing 70 big-flies and plating 147 baserunners en route to a runner-up finish in the MVP voting. For an encore he walloped 65 four-baggers and matched his RBI total from the previous year.

Oakland descended to last place in 1997, 20 games behind the Angels. Scott Brosius (.300/19/98) earned his lone all-star nod while Jason Giambi infused the lineup with a .295 average, 27 taters and 110 RBI in 1998. Giambi sustained his output with a .315 BA, 33 long balls and 123 ribbies in the next season. Ben Grieve (.288/18/79) clubbed 41 doubles and captured the 1998 AL ROY honors. The Athletics vaulted back into contention at 83-79, only 5 games behind the Rangers. In 1999 the pitching staff failed to reach the 4000 BFP pre-requisite. However, Tim Hudson (11-2, 3.23) was a beacon of hope for the troubled rotation. Tony Batista (.277/31/100) enrolled in the 30-homer club.

Year/Team	OPW%	PW	PL	APW%	AW	AL	Diff+/-
2000 OAK	0.513	83	79	0.565 D	91	70	0.052
2001 OAK	0.541 W	88	74	0.630 W	102	60	0.089
2002 OAK	0.578 P	94	68	0.636 D	103	59	0.058
2003 OAK	0.527	85	77	0.593 D	96	66	0.065
2004 OAK	0.474	77	85	0.562	91	71	0.088
2005 OAK	0.567 P	92	70	0.543	88	74	-0.024
2006 OAK	0.498	81	81	0.574 D	93	69	0.076
2007 OAK	0.477	77	85	0.469	76	86	-0.008
2008 OAK	0.519 D	84	78	0.466	75	86	-0.053
2009 OAK	0.507	82	80	0.463	75	87	-0.044
2010 OAK	0.483	78	84	0.500	81	81	0.017
2011 OAK	0.479	78	84	0.457	74	88	-0.022
2012 OAK	0.476	77	85	0.580 D	94	68	0.104
2013 OAK	0.439	71	91	0.593 D	96	66	0.154

franchID	OWAR	OWS	AWAR	AWS	WARdiff	WSdiff	P/D/W/F
2000 OAK	40.270	282.895	44.560	272.999	-4.290	9.897	
2001 OAK	44.124	287.895	53.715	306.003	-9.590	-18.108	W
2002 OAK	45.802	304.820	48.601	**309.004**	-2.799	-4.185	P
2003 OAK	44.382	280.236	42.729	287.995	1.653	-7.758	
2004 OAK	43.259	237.979	43.146	273.000	0.113	-35.021	
2005 OAK	38.892	265.707	41.031	264.000	-2.139	1.707	P
2006 OAK	38.488	263.016	35.690	279.001	2.798	-15.985	
2007 OAK	36.750	235.056	37.577	228.007	-0.827	7.049	
2008 OAK	35.378	250.244	28.574	225.003	6.804	25.241	D
2009 OAK	34.373	255.206	33.954	225.001	0.419	30.205	
2010 OAK	33.208	230.496	34.218	243.002	-1.010	-12.506	
2011 OAK	34.718	238.618	31.320	222.001	3.398	16.618	
2012 OAK	26.109	223.381	48.411	282.000	-22.302	-58.619	
2013 OAK	23.028	197.618	43.664	287.998	-20.636	-90.380	

Jason Giambi captured the 2000 AL MVP Award as he led the A's offensive barrage with a .333 BA, 43 homers and 137 RBI. The "Giambino" produced a .308 BA with 37 clouts and 120 ribbies over a six-year period beginning in 1998 and ending in 2003. Batista set career marks in 2000 with 41 jacks and 114 RBI. He delivered 31 long balls and drove in 100 baserunners per year from 1999-2004 in spite of a .249 BA. Miguel Tejada sported a .297 BA with 37 doubles, 29 round-trippers, 116 RBI and 102 runs scored per season from 2000-06. "Miggy" topped the circuit with 150 ribbies in '04 and blasted 50 two-base knocks during the following campaign. The slugging shortstop surpassed the 200-hit plateau three times and earned 2002 AL MVP honors.

Tim Hudson achieved 20 victories and placed runner-up in the 2000 AL Cy Young race in spite of a 4.14 ERA. Hudson delivered 18 victories in the following year; he then posted personal-bests with a 2.70 ERA and 1.075 WHIP in '03. Dave Veres briefly attained the closer's role, saving 29 games with a 2.85 ERA. Nevertheless, Seattle managed to outshine Oakland by 6 games. In 2001 the Athletics earned a trip to the playoffs as the Wild Card entry. Mark Mulder (21-8, 3.45) took his turn as staff ace while playing the role of bridesmaid in the Cy Young voting. Mulder produced an 18-8 record with a 3.65 ERA over five seasons from 2001 to 2005. Eric Chavez reeled off six consecutive Gold Glove Awards (2001-07) and dialed long distance 29 times per season over the same timeframe.

Barry Zito captured the 2002 AL Cy Young award with 23 wins and 2.75 ERA. The Athletics clinched the pennant with a record of 94-68. Angel Berroa (.287/17/73) secured 2003 AL ROY honors and fellow shortstop Bobby Crosby (.239/22/64) added the ROY hardware to his trophy case in '04. Huston Street (1.72, 23 SV) claimed the third consecutive ROY Award for the A's in 2005. In nine seasons Street fashioned a 2.98 ERA with a 1.036 WHIP while saving 26 contests per year. Oakland outlasted the Angels by a single game to attain the 2005 American League pennant.

The Athletics finished last in '06, only four games behind the front-running Mariners. Nick Swisher swatted 35 long balls and knocked in 95 baserunners (both career-bests) while Emil Brown drilled 41 doubles. Eric Byrnes cracked 26 home runs and swiped 25 bags. "Pigpen" scored 103 runs and pilfered 50 bases in the subsequent season. Oakland rebounded in 2008, taking the division crown after ending the season in a tie for first place with Seattle. Ryan Ludwick emerged as an offensive threat, batting .299 with 37 circuit clouts, 113 ribbies and 104 runs scored. Rich Harden was unhittable when healthy, delivering a 10-2 mark with a 2.07 ERA and striking out 181 batters in 148 innings. Andrew Bailey fashioned a 1.84 ERA and 0.876 WHIP in relief, earning the 2009 AL ROY Award. Andre Ethier established personal bests with 31 long balls and 106 ribbies. Yoenis Cespedes placed runner-up in the 2012 AL ROY balloting after batting at a .292 clip with 23 round-trippers in his inaugural campaign.

Win Shares > 20	Single-Season	1980-2013
Darrell Evans - 1B (OAK) x2	Rickey Henderson - LF (OAK) x11	Jose Canseco - RF (OAK) x3
George Hendrick - 1B (OAK)	Jose Canseco - LF (OAK)	Felix Jose - RF (OAK)
Mark McGwire - 1B (OAK) x8	Eric Byrnes - LF (OAK)	Ben Grieve - RF (OAK)
Mickey Tettleton - 1B (OAK)	Yoenis Cespedes - LF (OAK)	Andre Ethier - RF (OAK) x4
Jason Giambi - 1B (OAK) x7	Dwayne Murphy - CF (OAK) x4	Ryan Ludwick - RF (OAK)
Nick Swisher - 1B (OAK)	Rickey Henderson - CF (OAK) x2	Nick Swisher - RF (OAK) x2
Mike Bordick - 2B (OAK)	George Hendrick - RF (OAK)	Jason Giambi - DH (OAK)
Miguel Tejada - SS (OAK) x8	Mike Davis - RF (OAK)	Mike Norris - SP (OAK)
Scott Brosius - 3B (OAK)		Kevin Tapani - SP (OAK)
Eric Chavez - 3B (OAK) x4		Tim Hudson - SP (OAK) x2
Mickey Tettleton - C (OAK) x3		Barry Zito - SP (OAK)

Note: 4000 PA or BFP to qualify, except during strike-shortened seasons
(1972 = 3800, 1981 & 1994 = 2700, 1995 = 3500) and 154-game schedule (3800)
- failed to qualify: 1901-1903, 1905-1906, 1908, 1911-1912, 1950-1964, 1966, 1985, 1987-1989, 1999

Athletics All-Time "Originals" Roster

Glenn Abbott	Moxie Divis	Lew Krausse, Jr.	Arnie Portocarrero
Kurt Abbott	Chuck Dobson	Ian Krol	Landon Powell
Tal Abernathy	Ed V. Donnelly	Bill Krueger	Ike Powers
Mark Acre	Sean Doolittle	Ted Kubiak	Ariel Prieto
Dick Adams	Brian Dorsett	Tim Kubinski	Jim Pruett
Willie E. Adams	Carl Doyle	Bert Kuczynski	Danny Putnam
Dick Adkins	Larry Drake	John Kull	Tim Pyznarski
Jon Adkins	Kirk Dressendorfer	Mike Kume	Tad Quinn
Jack Aker	Michael Driscoll	Bob Lacey	Omar Quintanilla
Bob Allen	Eric DuBose	Marcel Lachemann	Rip Radcliff
Dana Allison	Joe Dugan	Rene Lachemann	Hal Raether
Wayne Ambler	Dave Duncan	Ed Lagger	Mario Ramos
Walter Ancker	Carl Duser	Gerald Laird	Morrie Rath
Dwain Anderson	Jimmy Dygert	Bill Landis	Carl Ray
Walter Anderson	Jimmie Dykes	Walt Lanfranconi	Anthony Recker
Elbert Andrews	George Earnshaw	Red Lanning	Howie Reed
Fred Applegate	Vallie Eaves	Jack Lapp	Al Reiss
Fred Archer	Harry Eccles	Ed Larkin	Jim Reninger
Danny Ardoin	Charlie Eckert	Tony LaRussa	Otto Rettig
Marcos Armas	Ralph Edwards	George Lauzerique	Todd Revenig
Harry Armbruster	Chester Emerson	Otis Lawry	Tommie Reynolds
George Armstrong	Mario Encarnacion	Steve Lawson	John Rheinecker
Howard Armstrong	Charlie Engle	Brett Laxton	Jack Richardson
Larry Arndt	Jim Eppard	Fred Lear	Ken Richardson
Orie Arntzen	Hank Erickson	Justin Lehr	Don Richmond
Joe Astroth	Larry Eschen	Dave Leiper	Harry Riconda
Keith Atherton	Andre Ethier	Dummy Leitner	Brad Rigby
Tommy Atkins	Nick Etten	Jack Lelivelt	Bob Rinker
Shooty Babitt	Darrell Evans	Chet Lemon	Connor Robertson
Eddie Bacon	Tommy Everidge	Ed Lennox	Ray Roberts
Benito Baez	Art Ewoldt	Elmer Leonard	Bruce Robinson
Andrew Bailey	Everett Fagan	John Leovich	Ben Rochefort
Gene Bailey	Frank Fahey	Brian Lesher	Ellie Rodriguez
Jeff Baisley	Howard Fahey	Allan Lewis	Henry Alberto Rodriguez
Frank J. Baker	Ferris Fain	Darren Lewis	
John Baker	Jim Fairbank	Dutch Lieber	Rick Rodriguez
Neal Baker	Ramon Fermin	Glenn I. Liebhardt	Roberto Rodriguez

Sal Bando
Everett Bankston
Dave Barbee
Mike Barlow
Babe Barna
Bill Barrett
Scotty Barr
Hardin Barry
Jack Barry
John Barthold
Irv Bartling
Harry Barton
Norm Bass
Charlie Bates
Dick Bates
Bill Bathe
Tony Batista
Chris Batton
Lou Bauer
Dave Beard
Bill Beckmann
Rod Beck
Mark Bellhorn
Chief Bender
Vern Benson
Al Benton
Johnny Berger
Angel Berroa
Charlie Berry
Jason Beverlin
Hank Biasatti
Lyle Bigbee
Bill Bishop
Max Bishop
Don Black
Lance Blankenship
Joe Blanton
Ray Blemker
Vida Blue
Chet Boak
Charlie Boardman
Warren Bogle
Pat Bohen
Joe Boley
Jeremy Bonderman
Dan Boone
Mike Bordick
Rich Bordi
Henry Bostick
Charlie Bowles
Joe Bowman
Clete Boyer
Dallas Braden
Bill Bradford
Bert Bradley
Dallas Bradshaw
Al Brancato

Bill Ferrazzi
Willy Fetzer
Pedro Figueroa
Eddie Files
Dana Fillingim
Rollie Fingers
Herman Fink
Lou Finney
Todd Fischer
Jack Flater
Lew Flick
Mort Flohr
Ron Flores
Stu Flythe
Dan Ford
Dick Fowler
Jack Fox
Nellie Fox
Jimmie Foxx
Harvey Freeman
Tony Freitas
Pat French
Walter French
Charlie Fritz
Harry Fritz
Ollie Fuhrman
Dot Fulghum
Mike Gallego
Chick Galloway
Joe Gantenbein
Santiago Casilla
Phil Garner
Brent Gates
Doc Gautreau
Bob Geary
Alex George
Steve Gerkin
Esteban German
Franklyn German
Jason Giambi
Charlie G. Gibson
Joe Giebel
Tom Glass
Sam Gray
Jeff M. Gray
Sonny Gray
Dick Green
Grant Green
Joe Green
Kevin Gregg
Bill Grevell
Ben Grieve
A. J. Griffin
Ivy Griffin
Lee Griffeth
Pug Griffin
Charlie Grimm

Bill Lillard
Lou Limmer
Paul Lindblad
Bob Lindemann
Axel Lindstrom
Winston Llenas
Skip Lockwood
Dario Lodigiani
Lep Long
Pete Loos
Hector Lopez
Bris Lord
Pete Lovrich
Sam Lowry
Hal Luby
Ryan Ludwick
Scott Lydy
Rick Lysander
Chris Mabeus
Earle Mack
Eric Mackenzie
Gordon Mackenzie
Felix Mackiewicz
Ed Madjeski
Al Mahon
Emil Mailho
Jim Mains
Ben Mallonee
Lew Malone
Frank Manush
Phil Marchildon
Johnny Marcum
Gonzalo Marquez
Doc Martin
Manny Martinez
Pat Martin
Wedo Martini
Damon Mashore
Len Matarazzo
Joe Mathes
Francisco Matos
Wid Matthews
Cloy Mattox
Harry Matuzak
Vin Mazzaro
Wickey McAvoy
Marcus McBeth
Bill McCahan
Emmett McCann
Steve McCatty
Sam F. McConnell
Les McCrabb
Frank McCue
Hank McDonald
Jason McDonald
Marshall McDougall
Lee McElwee

Dutch Romberger
Eddie Rommel
Buck Ross
Tyson Ross
Harland Rowe
Chuck Rowland
Emil Roy
Stan Royer
Al Rubeling
Joe Rudi
Joe Rullo
Lefty Russell
Mickey Rutner
Oscar Salazar
Roger Salmon
Gus Salve
John Sanders
Ken Sanders
Reggie J. Sanders
Tommy Sandt
Jose R. Santiago
Rusty Saunders
Bob Savage
Randy Scarbery
Wally Schang
Heinie Scheer
Carl Scheib
Jim Schelle
Red Schillings
Biff Schlitzer
Hack Schumann
Randy Schwartz
Jerry Schypinski
Socks Seibold
Justin Sellers
Bill Shanner
Billy Shantz
Bobby Shantz
Ralph Sharman
Jeff Shaver
Bob Shawkey
Dave Shean
Red Shea
Tom Sheehan
Scott Sheldon
Ed Sherling
Joe Sherman
Tex Shirley
Charlie Shoemaker
Bill Shores
Frank Sigafoos
Al Simmons
John Slappey
Joe Slusarski
Dave M. Smith
Eddie Smith
Red M. Smith

Dud Branom
Frank Brazill
Bill Breckinridge
Rube Bressler
George Brickley
John Briscoe
Lou Brissie
Jorge Brito
Bobby Brooks
Scott Brosius
Art Brouthers
Boardwalk Brown
Corey Brown
Emil Brown
Jeremy Brown
Norm Brown
Lou Bruce
Earle Brucker
Earle Brucker, Jr.
George Brunet
Billy Bryan
Derek Bryant
Travis Buck
Mark Budaska
Red Bullock
Bill Burgo
Dennis Burns
Todd Burns
John Burrows
Dick Burrus
Jared Burton
Don Buschhorn
Ed Busch
Joe Bush
Ralph Buxton
Freddie Bynum
Harry Byrd
Eric Byrnes
Jim Byrnes
Greg Cadaret
Trevor Cahill
Sugar Cain
Fred Caligiuri
Frank Callaway
Ernie Camacho
Bert Campaneris
Jose Canseco
Andrew Carignan
Doc Carroll
Nick Carter
Sol Carter
Joe Cascarella
George Caster
Jim Castiglia
Luis Castro
Jake Caulfield
Yoenis Cespedes

Lew Groh
Wayne Gross
Matt Grott
Lefty Grove
Roy Grover
Creighton Gubanich
Randy Gumpert
Johnny Guzman
Marcus Gwyn
Bruno Haas
Bill Haeffner
Fred Hahn
Irv Hall
Dave Hamilton
Tom Hamilton
Buddy Hancken
Jay Hankins
Jack Hannifin
Rich Harden
Jack Harper
Ken Harrelson
Slim Harrell
Bill Harrington
Lum Harris
Slim Harriss
Tom Harrison
Vic Harris
Jason Hart
Chad Harville
Joe Hassler
Gene Hasson
Bob Hasty
Gary Haught
Joe Hauser
Jack Hayden
Frankie Hayes
Nathan Haynes
Thomas Healy
Fred Heimach
Heinie Heitmuller
Eric Helfand
Scott Hemond
Rickey Henderson
George Hendrick
Weldon Henley
Gene Hermanski
Ramon J. Hernandez
Troy Herriage
George Hesselbacher
Pinky Higgins
Charlie High
Dave Hill
Donnie Hill
Ed Hilley
Red Hill
A.J. Hinch
Danny Hoffman

Conny McGeehan
Bill McGhee
John McGillen
Beauty McGowan
Mark McGwire
Stuffy McInnis
Matty McIntyre
Cody McKay
Tim McKeithan
Bob McKinney
Eric McNair
Bob McNamara
Bill McNulty
John McPherson
Jerry McQuaig
Bill Meehan
Roy Meeker
Kevin Melillo
Joe Mellana
Dave Melton
Henry Mercedes
Scott Meyer
Chris Michalak
Carl Miles
Felix Millan
Bill P. Miller
Rudy Miller
Billy Milligan
Bill Mills
Ray Miner
Craig Mitchell
Ralph Mitterling
Mike Mohler
Izzy Molina
Rick Monday
Agustin Montero
Aurelio Monteagudo
Bobby D. Moore
Ferdie Moore
Kelvin Moore
Roy Moore
Willie Morales
Herbie Moran
Juan Moreno
Dave Morey
Mike Morgan
Bill Morrisette
Doyt Morris
Bud Morse
Wally Moses
Charlie Moss
Mark Mulder
Jim Mullin
Jake Munch
Bill Murphy
Dwayne Murphy
Eddie Murphy

Syd Smith
Bernie Snyder
Scott Spiezio
Larry Stahl
Don Stanhouse
Eddie Stanky
Max Stassi
Irv Stein
Terry Steinbach
Bill Stellbauer
Phil Stephenson
Bill Stewart
Art Stokes
Mickey Storey
Dan Straily
Huston Street
John Strohmayer
Joe Strong
Amos Strunk
Dean Sturgis
Tanyon Sturtze
Lena Styles
Ken Suarez
Jim R. Sullivan
Champ Summers
Kurt Suzuki
Buck Sweeney
Nick Swisher
John Taff
Kevin Tapani
Arlas Taylor
Harry E. Taylor
Joe Taylor
Mark Teahen
Miguel Tejada
Gene Tenace
Mickey Tettleton
Dave Thies
Shag Thompson
Buck Thrasher
Lee Tinsley
Eric Tipton
Tom Tischinski
Pat Tobin
Jose Tolentino
Ron Tompkins
Rupe Toppin
Bob Trice
George Turbeville
Tink Turner
Jim Tyack
Woody Upchurch
Elmer Valo
Ozzie Van Brabant
Todd Van Poppel
Porter Vaughan
Roy Vaughn

Charlie Chant	Willie Hogan	Glenn Myatt	Al Veach
John Chapman	Chick Holmes	Elmer Myers	Dave Veres
Sam Chapman	Jim Holmes	Joseph Myers	Luis Vizcaino
Eric Chavez	Jim Holt	Jack Nabors	Hal Wagner
Scott Chiamparino	Red Holt	Bill Nagel	Johnny Walker
Steve Chitren	Alex Hooks	Pete Naktenis	Tom W. Walker
Michael Choice	Leon Hooten	Jim Nash	Jack Wallaesa
Ryan Christenson	Sam Hope	Rollie Naylor	Denny Walling
Ed Cihocki	Byron Houck	Mike Neill	Jimmy C. Walsh
Lou Ciola	Ben Houser	Rob Nelson	Bruce Walton
Frank Cipriani	Steve Howard	David Newhan	John Wasdin
Jim E. Clark	Dann Howitt	Skeeter Newsome	Claudell Washington
Gowell Claset	Dick Howser	Bill Nicholson	Herb Washington
Tom Clyde	Earl Huckleberry	Butch Nieman	Mule Watson
Andy Coakley	Tim Hudson	Pete Noonan	Harry Weaver
Mickey Cochrane	Hank Hulvey	Fred Norman	Ryan Webb
Ed Coleman	Catfish Hunter	Mike Norris	Ramon Webster
Joe P. Coleman	Carl Husta	Ron Northey	Jemile Weeks
Allan Collamore	Warren Huston	Charlie O'Brien	Walt Weiss
Eddie Collins	Joe Jackson	Blue Moon Odom	Frank Welch
Eddie Collins, Jr.	Reggie Jackson	Dave Odom	Don Wengert
Jesus Colome	Luis A. Jimenez	John E. O'Donoghue	Buzz Wetzel
Bob Cone	Miguel Jimenez	Alexi Ogando	Woody Wheaton
Bill Connelly	Bill L. Johnson	Curly Ogden	Don White
Steve Connelly	Bob L. Johnson	Miguel Olivo	Wally Whitehurst
Bill G. Conroy	Dan Johnson	Harry J. O'Neill	Walt Whittaker
Tim Conroy	Doug Johns	Harry M. O'Neill	Spider Wilhelm
Owen Conway	Jing Johnson	Steve O'Neill	Bobby Wilkins
Brent Cookson	Ken T. Johnson	Steve Ontiveros	Al Williams
Bobby Coombs	Paul Johnson	Don O'Riley	Dale Willis
Jack Coombs	Roy Johnson	Billy Orr	Dewey Williams
Ron Coomer	Hal Jones	Jose D. Ortiz	Dib Williams
Pat Cooper	Jeff A. Jones	Ossie Orwoll	Don R. Williams
Art Corcoran	John Jones	Bill Oster	George E. Williams
Rod Correia	Marcus Jones	Dave Otto	Lefty Willis
Ray Cosey	Felix Jose	Jack Owens	Marsh Williams
Neal Cotts	Bob Joyce	Doc Ozmer	Whitey Wilshere
Stan Coveleski	Dick Joyce	Sam Page	Jack F. Wilson
Steve Cox	Jeff Kaiser	Eddie Palmer	Jason Windsor
Toots Coyne	John Kalahan	Joe Palmisano	Al Wingo
Walt Craddock	Bill Kalfass	Jim Panther	Ed Wingo
George Craig	Teddy Kearns	Craig Paquette	Hank Winston
Doc Cramer	Dave Keefe	Tony Parisse	Ron Witmeyer
Sam Crane	Vic Keen	Ace Parker	Whitey Witt
D.T. Cromer	Jim Keesey	Rube Parnham	John Wojcik
Jim Cronin	Al Kellett	Joe Pate	Steve Wojciechowski
Bobby Crosby	Walt Kellner	Bronswell Patrick	Chuck Wolfe
Cap Crowell	Al Kellogg	Mike Patterson	Roger Wolff
Woody Crowson	Skeeter Kell	Bill Patton	Lefty Wolf
Press Cruthers	Bill Kelly	Jack Peerson	Darrell Woodard
Fausto Cruz	Ren Kelly	Monte Peffer	Mike Woodard
Dick Culler	Ed Kenna	Cliff Pennington	Doc Wood
Mike Cunningham	Vern Kennedy	Herb Pennock	Jason Wood
Jim Curry	Joe Keough	Bob Pepper	Mike Wood
Bert Daly	Matt Keough	Joel Peralta	Gary Woods
Jeff M. D'Amico	Bill Kern	Charlie Perkins	Fred Worden
Harry Damrau	Gus Ketchum	Cy Perkins	Weldon Wyckoff

Art Daney	Steve Kiefer	Jim Peterson	Keiichi Yabu
Dave Danforth	Evans Killeen	Rusty Peters	George Yankowski
Buck Danner	Lee E. King	Gregorio Petit	Rube Yarrison
Jack Daugherty	Brian Kingman	Dan Pfister	Tyler Yates
Jeff Davanon	Mike Kircher	Steve Phoenix	Carroll Yerkes
Claude Davidson	Bill Kirk	Adam Piatt	Lefty York
Chick Davies	Tom Kirk	Rob Picciolo	Elmer Yoter
Bob E. Davis	Ernie Kish	Val Picinich	Curt Young
Bud Davis	Lou Klimchock	Tony Pierce	Ernie Young
Crash Davis	Lou Knerr	William Pierson	Eddie Yount
Lefty Davis	John Knight	Squiz Pillion	Tom Zachary
Mike Davis	Bill Knowlton	Ed Pinnance	Joe Zapustas
Chubby Dean	Tom Knowlson	Eddie Plank	Bob Zick
Sam Demel	Pete Koegel	Don Plarski	Jimmy Zinn
Claud Derrick	Shane Komine	Luis Polonia	Barry Zito
Jimmie DeShong	Bruce Konopka	Jim Ralph Poole	Sam Zoldak
Bill Dietrich	Harry Krause	Ray Poole	
Art Ditmar	Lew Krausse	Odie Porter	

Toronto Blue Jays

Year/Team	OPW%	PW	PL	APW%	AW	AL	Diff+/-
1977 TOR	0.000 F	0	0	0.335	54	107	0.000
1978 TOR	0.000 F	0	0	0.366	59	102	0.000
1979 TOR	0.000 F	0	0	0.327	53	109	0.000
1980 TOR	0.000 F	0	0	0.414	67	95	0.000
1981 TOR	0.402 F	65	97	0.349	37	69	-0.053
1982 TOR	0.469 F	76	86	0.481	78	84	0.012
1983 TOR	0.603 F	98	64	0.549	89	73	-0.053
1984 TOR	0.612 F	99	63	0.549	89	73	-0.063
1985 TOR	0.665 F	108	54	0.615 P	99	62	-0.050
1986 TOR	0.623 F	101	61	0.531	86	76	-0.092
1987 TOR	0.613 F	99	63	0.593	96	66	-0.020
1988 TOR	0.514 F	83	79	0.537	87	75	0.023
1989 TOR	0.469	76	86	0.549 D	89	73	0.081

franchID	OWAR	OWS	AWAR	AWS	WARdiff	WSdiff	P/D/W/F
1977 TOR			15.687	161.998	-15.687	-161.998	F
1978 TOR	129.775	739.977	17.401	176.999	112.374	562.978	F
1979 TOR	3.770	120.031	12.694	159.002	-8.923	-38.971	F
1980 TOR	18.904	149.677	23.309	200.999	-4.405	-51.322	F
1981 TOR	15.350	116.334	9.010	110.994	6.340	5.341	F
1982 TOR	29.205	178.754	30.961	234.009	-1.756	-55.255	F
1983 TOR	37.572	210.456	45.656	267.002	-8.084	-56.545	F
1984 TOR	48.731	247.853	47.476	266.998	1.254	-19.146	F
1985 TOR	54.967	284.673	48.328	**296.999**	6.639	-12.326	F
1986 TOR	46.527	251.159	45.082	258.000	1.445	-6.841	F
1987 TOR	49.835	257.389	50.787	288.000	-0.953	-30.611	F
1988 TOR	32.883	194.477	44.859	261.009	-11.976	-66.532	F
1989 TOR	32.373	204.830	44.546	267.005	-12.173	-62.176	

Legend: (P) = Pennant / Most Wins in League (D) = Division Winner (W) = Wild Card Winner (F) = Failed to Qualify

The Toronto franchise joined the American League when the Junior Circuit expanded to 14 clubs in 1977. The Blue Jays developed the most first basemen and shortstops among the "Expansion" teams based on aggregate WS>20 player-seasons. Conversely the club's left fielders have failed to post a single WS>20 campaign.

Dave Stieb emerged as an All-Star in his second season, delivering a 3.29 ERA and 14 wins per year from 1980-1990. He placed fourth in the 1982 AL Cy Young vote and led the circuit with a 2.48 ERA in 1984. Lloyd Moseby busted loose in '83 with a .315 BA, 18 homers, 81 ribbies and 39 steals. Barfield bashed 27 big flies and brandished a cannon arm in right field. Barfield launched 40 moon-shots en route to the home run title and placed fifth in the 1986 AL MVP voting. Tony Fernandez seized the shortstop position in 1985 and established personal-bests with 213 base knocks and 91 aces during the '86 campaign. Fernandez earned four consecutive Gold Glove Awards (1986-89).

Jimmy Key earned a starting job after saving 10 games in 1984. Key locked up the ERA (2.76) and WHIP (1.057) titles, notched 17 victories and finished runner-up in the 1987 AL Cy Young balloting. Mark Eichhorn registered 14 relief wins, saved 10 contests and posted a 1.72 ERA for the '86 squad. His sidearm delivery perplexed batters, enabling Eichhorn to whiff 166 in 157 innings. Lefty reliever Jeff Musselman added 12 wins in 1987 while setting up for Eichhorn and Dale Mohorcic (2.99, 16 saves). The 1989 "Original" Blue Jays were the first to exceed the minimum 4000 PA and BFP standards*. Toronto concluded the season with 76 wins and finished 11 games behind Milwaukee. GM Pat Gillick procured Carlos Delgado as an amateur free agent in 1988 and then selected Jeff Kent and John Olerud in the 1989 Amateur Draft.

Year/Team	OPW%	PW	PL	APW%	AW	AL	Diff+/-
1990 TOR	0.537 P	87	75	0.531	86	76	-0.006
1991 TOR	0.473	77	85	0.562 D	91	71	0.089
1992 TOR	0.449	73	89	0.593 P	96	66	0.144
1993 TOR	0.479	78	84	0.586 P	95	67	0.107
1994 TOR	0.506	82	80	0.478	55	60	-0.028
1995 TOR	0.469	76	86	0.389	56	88	-0.080
1996 TOR	0.461	75	87	0.457	74	88	-0.004
1997 TOR	0.501	81	81	0.469	76	86	-0.032
1998 TOR	0.495	80	82	0.543	88	74	0.048
1999 TOR	0.492	80	82	0.519	84	78	0.026
franchID	OWAR	OWS	AWAR	AWS	WARdiff	WSdiff	P/D/W/F
1990 TOR	36.873	225.441	47.210	257.999	-10.337	-32.557	P
1991 TOR	29.419	219.330	43.965	273.003	-14.546	-53.673	
1992 TOR	26.214	206.934	**47.687**	**287.996**	-21.473	-81.063	
1993 TOR	39.254	239.018	**49.403**	**285.003**	-10.149	-45.985	
1994 TOR	29.763	187.821	26.632	164.993	3.131	22.828	
1995 TOR	27.167	208.686	25.408	168.001	1.760	40.685	
1996 TOR	36.934	244.077	34.660	222.002	2.273	22.076	
1997 TOR	37.701	251.125	33.269	227.997	4.432	23.128	
1998 TOR	45.214	266.675	44.709	263.995	0.505	2.681	
1999 TOR	38.060	253.634	40.096	252.008	-2.036	1.626	

The organization's player development strategy culminated with an American League pennant in 1990. Stieb delivered an 18-6 record with an ERA of 2.93 and he twirled a no-hitter in Cleveland on September 2, 1990. Eichhorn (3.08, 13 SV) handled the late-inning assignments. Eric Yelding pilfered 64 bases while Fernandez led the AL with 17 triples. Fernandez batted .321 with 36 doubles in '98 and followed with a .328 BA along with 41 two-baggers in the ensuing year.

Toronto finished below .500 from 1991-93. Key (16-12, 3.05), David "Boomer" Wells (15-10, 3.72) and Todd Stottlemyre (15-8, 3.78) anchored the rotation in '91 while Mike Timlin excelled in the setup role (11-6, 3.16). Key contributed 18 wins and a 3.00 ERA in 1993 and then placed second in the 1994 AL Cy Young vote after winning 17 of 21 decisions. Wells earned a trip to the All-Star game with a 16-8 record and a 3.21 ERA in 1995. He followed up with an 18-4 record with a league-best WHIP of 1.045 three years later. Timlin nailed down 31 contests after a promotion to the closer's role in '96.

Xavier Hernandez augmented the relief corps in 1992 with 9 victories, 7 saves and a 2.11 ERA. He collected 9 saves in the following season while striking out 101 batters in 96.2 innings pitched. Pat Hentgen (19-9, 3.87) boosted the formidable mound crew in '93 and achieved 1996 AL Cy Young honors as he furnished a 20-10 record with a 3.22 ERA while leading the circuit in innings pitched, complete games and shutouts.

Olerud highlighted a revitalized offense in 1993, capturing the AL batting crown with a .363 average along with 24 dingers and 107 RBI. He also led the League with 54 doubles and a .473 OBP while placing third in the MVP balloting and recording 36 Win Shares. Olerud blistered opposing hurlers with a .354 BA along with 22 taters and 93 ribbies in '98. "Hard-Hittin'" Mark Whiten jacked 25 round-trippers and knocked in 99 runs for the Jays in '93.

The Blue Jays flew under the radar for the balance the Nineties, barely soaring above .500 in '94 and '97. Jose Mesa locked down the fireman's role in 1995 after toiling through several uninspiring seasons in the starting rotation. Mesa (1.13, 46 SV) nearly won the MVP and Cy Young Awards with his dominant effort and then recorded 39 saves in the ensuing campaign. Derek Bell thrived in '95, posting a .334 BA with 86 ribbies and 27 stolen bases. He swiped a career-high 29 bags (in 32 attempts), slashed 40 doubles and drove in 113 runs in the subsequent campaign. Bell (.314/22/108) notched personal-bests in base hits (198), doubles (41), home runs and runs scored (111) during the 1998 season. Glenallen Hill earned full-time work, plastering 24 homers and swiping 25 bags for the 1995 crew.

Carlos Delgado commenced a 13-year stretch (1996-2008) during which he produced 36 two-base knocks, 35 wallops and 112 ribbies per season along with a .282 BA. Delgado dialed long-distance 44 times, crossed home plate 113 times and knocked in 134 runs for the '99 club. Geronimo Berroa belted 36 four-baggers, drove in 106 runs and registered 101 tallies while teammate Ed Sprague, Jr. crushed 36 long balls and plated 101 baserunners for the '96 brigade. Kent crushed 29 circuit clouts and registered 121 RBI, signifying an increase of 66 from the prior year! Kent (.297/31/128) recorded a career-high in ribbies during the '98 campaign.

Shawn Green prospered during his fourth full season, batting .278 with 35 bombs and 100 ribbies in 1998. He detonated 45 doubles and 42 big-flies while scoring 134 and driving in 123 runs in the following year. Shannon Stewart pilfered 51 bases in 1998 and began a streak of six consecutive seasons from 1999-2004 in which he achieved a batting average over .300. Timlin, Mesa and Billy Koch combined for 91 saves. Steve Karsay added a 10-2 mark in long relief.

Year/Team	OPW%	PW	PL	APW%	AW	AL	Diff+/-
2000 TOR	0.485	79	83	0.512	83	79	0.028
2001 TOR	0.547 D	89	73	0.494	80	82	-0.053
2002 TOR	0.572 D	93	69	0.481	78	84	-0.090
2003 TOR	0.557 D	90	72	0.531	86	76	-0.026
2004 TOR	0.519	84	78	0.416	67	94	-0.103
2005 TOR	0.551 D	89	73	0.494	80	82	-0.057
2006 TOR	0.527	85	77	0.537	87	75	0.010
2007 TOR	0.497	81	81	0.512	83	79	0.015
2008 TOR	0.499	81	81	0.531	86	76	0.032
2009 TOR	0.508	82	80	0.463	75	87	-0.045

2010 TOR	0.509	82	80	0.525	85	77	0.016
2011 TOR	0.544	88	74	0.500	81	81	-0.044
2012 TOR	0.465	75	87	0.451	73	89	-0.014
2013 TOR	0.401 F	65	97	0.457	74	88	0.056

franchID	OWAR	OWS	AWAR	AWS	WARdiff	WSdiff	P/D/W/F
2000 TOR	46.780	272.402	37.825	249.000	8.955	23.402	
2001 TOR	51.500	297.261	38.727	239.998	12.774	57.264	D
2002 TOR	51.472	312.267	34.214	234.011	17.258	78.256	D
2003 TOR	45.378	284.520	42.652	257.991	2.726	26.529	D
2004 TOR	38.084	268.643	27.112	200.993	10.972	67.649	
2005 TOR	43.422	279.321	37.516	239.999	5.905	39.322	D
2006 TOR	41.927	266.208	44.255	261.002	-2.328	5.207	
2007 TOR	33.110	238.856	38.597	248.995	-5.487	-10.140	
2008 TOR	36.879	247.770	43.231	258.003	-6.351	-10.232	
2009 TOR	42.446	252.607	41.468	224.995	0.977	27.611	
2010 TOR	31.410	223.208	43.434	255.002	-12.024	-31.794	
2011 TOR	35.036	230.647	33.824	242.994	1.212	-12.347	
2012 TOR	17.566	213.055	29.220	219.001	-11.654	-5.946	
2013 TOR	13.369	217.526	30.861	222.004	-17.492	-4.478	F

David Wells cruised to a 20-win season in 2000 albeit with 4.11 ERA. Steve Karsay successfully handled 20 save chances following a 10-2 record in relief during the prior campaign. Kent (.334/33/125) registered the highest Win Share mark in franchise history (36), captured the MVP award and set career-highs with 114 tallies. He supplied 40 two-baggers, 28 dingers and 110 ribbies per season from 1997-2005 while batting .296 and meriting five All-Star selections. Toronto second basemen topped the Majors with 24 WS>10 player-seasons from 2000-09.

Delgado (.344/41/137) mashed an AL-best 57 doubles and accrued 35 Win Shares in 2000. He walloped 42 round-trippers and paced the circuit with 145 RBI while placing second in the 2003 AL MVP voting. Koch averaged 36 saves per season over a four-year period (1999-2002) and closed out a career-high 44 contests while posting 11 victories in '02. Green led the Jays' offensive assault in 2001 with 49 blasts, 125 RBI, 121 runs and 20 stolen bases. He provided 37 doubles, 38 clouts, 112 ribbies and 114 tallies during a five-year stretch (1998-2002).

Olerud collected three Gold Glove Awards and surpassed the century mark In RBI twice from 2000-03 while Stewart delivered 42 doubles, 101 aces and a .311 BA during the same timeframe. Stewart recorded a career-best 202 hits while batting .316 with 103 runs scored. Toronto finally broke Boston's stranglehold on the AL East in 2001 as the Jays' moundsmen recorded the best pitWARnorm (29) and pitWSnorm (117) in franchise history. Mesa anchored the relief corps (2.34, 42 saves). The Blue Jays retained the division crown in 2002, finishing 9 games ahead of the Yankees.

Roy Halladay matched "Boomer" Wells with a 19-7 record, delivered a 2.93 ERA and earned his first All-Star nod in 2002. Halladay (22-7, 3.25) carved up the opposition with surgeon-like precision in 2003, meriting his first Cy Young Award while leading the AL in victories and complete games. "Doc" delivered a 20-11 record with a 2.78 ERA and placed runner-up in the 2008 AL Cy Young race, topping the leader boards with 9 complete games and a 1.053 WHIP. He achieved his second Cy Young trophy on the heels of a 21-win campaign in 2010; he then whiffed a career-best 220 batsmen in the subsequent season.

In a hard-fought battle for the division in '03, the Blue Jays managed to squeak by the Yankees to secure a third consecutive title. Woody G. Williams fashioned an 18-9 mark along with a 3.87 ERA. Vernon Wells (.317/33/117) claimed the League lead with 215 base hits and 49 two-base knocks while notching personal-bests in virtually all offensive categories including runs scored (118). Wells rapped at least 40 doubles and 30 long balls in 2006 and 2010.

Michael Young commenced a string of five straight seasons with at least 200 hits in 2003. The seven-time All-Star supplied a .311 BA with 202 safeties and 38 doubles from 2003-2011. Young (.331/24/91) prevailed in the AL batting race and tallied a league-leading 221 hits in '05. The Red Sox recouped the A.L. Eastern division title by three games over ornithological rivals (Blue Jays and Orioles). Seven members of the Toronto lumberjacks swatted at least 20 big-flies including Casey Blake (.271/28/88) and Craig A. Wilson (.264/29/82).

In 2005 the Blue Jays swooped past the Orioles, collecting another division crown. Gustavo Chacin notched 13 victories in his rookie campaign and Aaron Small posted a 10-0 record in 15 appearances! Timlin delivered a 2.24 ERA and 13 saves as the primary setup man. Chris J. Carpenter (21-5, 2.83) nailed down the 2005 AL Cy Young Award and led the Junior Circuit with a 1.069 WHIP during the ensuing season. Carpenter (17-4, 2.24) secured the ERA crown in 2009 and missed his second Cy Young Award by a whisker.

The Blue Jays fell one game shy of the AL Wild Card as Alex Rios scored 114 runs and smacked 24 big-flies in 2006. He established career-highs with 25 long balls, 91 ribbies and a .304 in 2012 and then pilfered 42 bags in the ensuing year. David Weathers saved 33 contests after accumulating 41 in his previous 16 seasons while Kelvim Escobar (18-7, 3.40) achieved personal-bests in victories and ERA. The Jays tied the Yankees for second place in '09, falling 4 games short of the Red Sox. Alfredo Aceves scavenged 10 relief wins. Adam Lind (.305/35/114) and Aaron Hill (.286/36/108) ended the season among the American League leaders in home runs and RBI.

Win Shares > 20	Single-Season	1977-2013
Carlos Delgado - 1B (TOR) x9	Michael Young - SS (TOR) x4	Michael Young - DH (TOR)
John Olerud - 1B (TOR) x8	Felipe Lopez - SS (TOR)	Dave Stieb - SP (TOR) x4
Jeff Kent - 2B (TOR) x8	Casey Blake - 3B (TOR)	Jimmy Key - SP (TOR) x2
Aaron Hill - 2B (TOR) x3	Lloyd Moseby - CF (TOR) x4	Pat Hentgen - SP (TOR)
Orlando Hudson - 2B (TOR) x2	Vernon Wells - CF (TOR) x3	Roy Halladay - SP (TOR) x6
Tony Fernandez - SS (TOR) x6	Jesse Barfield - RF (TOR) x2	Chris J. Carpenter - SP (TOR) x2
Cesar Izturis - SS (TOR)	Derek Bell - RF (TOR)	Mark Eichhorn - RP (TOR)
	Shawn Green - RF (TOR) x5	
	Alex Rios - RF (TOR) x3	

Note: 4000 PA or BFP to qualify, except during strike-shortened seasons
(1972 = 3800, 1981 & 1994 = 2700, 1995 = 3500) and 154-game schedule (3800)
- failed to qualify: 1977-88

Blue Jays All-Time "Originals" Roster

Brent Abernathy	Carlos Delgado	Ricardo Jordan	Andre Robertson
Alfredo Aceves	Jeff DeWillis	Steve Karsay	Ryan Roberts
Russ Adams	Carlos F. Diaz	Jeff Kent	Kenny Robinson
Danny Ainge	Jonathan Diaz	Jimmy Key	Jimmy Rogers
Carlos Almanzar	Robinzon Diaz	Randy Knorr	Mike Romano
Henderson Alvarez	Rob Ducey	Billy Koch	Davis Romero
Clayton Andrews	Sam Dyson	Erik Kratz	Ricky Romero
Luis Aquino	Mark Eichhorn	Joe Lawrence	Francisco Rosario
J. P. Arencibia	Brad Emaus	Brandon League	Mike Rouse
Dave Baker	Jose Escobar	Luis Leal	Marc Rzepczynski
John Bale	Kelvim Escobar	Adam Lind	Alex A. Sanchez
Josh Banks	Tom Evans	Doug Linton	Anthony Sanders
Travis Baptist	Danny Farquhar	Nelson Liriano	Steve Senteney
Jesse Barfield	Junior Felix	Jesse Litsch	Mike Sharperson

Kevin Batiste
Howard Battle
Derek Bell
Geronimo Berroa
Willie Blair
Casey Blake
Pat Borders
Denis Boucher
Brent Bowers
Brian Bowles
Tilson Brito
Scott Brow
Enrique Burgos
David Bush
Rich Butler
Rob Butler
Francisco Cabrera
Sil Campusano
Chris J. Carpenter
Giovanni Carrara
Joel Carreno
Kevin Cash
Scott Cassidy
Tony J. Castillo
Brett Cecil
Domingo Cedeno
John Cerutti
Gustavo Chacin
Vinnie Chulk
Stan Clarke
Pasqual Coco
Tim Collins
Mike Coolbaugh
David Cooper
Brad Cornett
Tim Crabtree
Rickey Cradle
Evan Crawford
Felipe Crespo
Steve Cummings
Joe Davenport
Tom Davey
Steve K. Davis
Dewon Day
Jordan De Jong
Francisco de la Rosa

Tony Fernandez
Bob File
Huck Flener
Matt Ford
Ryan Freel
Freddy Adrian Garcia
Webster Garrison
Dave Gassner
Ray Giannelli
Jay Gibbons
Gary Glover
Graham Godfrey
Tyrell Godwin
Ryan Goins
Yan Gomes
Alex S. Gonzalez
Franklyn Gracesqui
Beiker Graterol
Shawn Green
Gabe Gross
Roy Halladay
Darren Hall
Jeff Hearron
Adeiny Hechavarria
Mark Hendrickson
Pat Hentgen
Toby Hernandez
Xavier Hernandez
Jose R. Herrera
Aaron Hill
Glenallen Hill
Paul Hodgson
Vince Horsman
Orlando Hudson
Edwin Hurtado
Drew Hutchison
Tim Hyers
Alexis Infante
Cesar Izturis
Zach Jackson
Casey Janssen
Chad Jenkins
Shawn Jeter
Dane Johnson
Mike K. Johnson
Reed Johnson

Graeme Lloyd
Felipe Lopez
Luis Lopez
Aaron Loup
Mark Lukasiewicz
Brandon Lyon
Bob MacDonald
Jim Mann
Fred Manrique
Shaun Marcum
Jake Marisnick
Domingo Martinez
Sandy Martinez
Tom Mastny
Darin Mastroianni
Dustin McGowan
Adam Melhuse
Paul Menhart
Jose Mesa
Brad A. Mills
Brian Milner
Dale Mohorcic
Lloyd Moseby
Julio Mosquera
Pedro Munoz
Greg Myers
Jeff Musselman
Abraham O. Nunez
Greg O'Halloran
John Olerud
Tyler Pastornicky
Oswaldo Peraza
Luis Perez
Robert Perez
Jason Perry
Adam L. Peterson
Geno Petralli
Josh Phelps
Kevin Pillar
Charlie Puleo
David Purcey
Tom Quinlan
Guillermo Quiroz
Jeff Scott Richardson
Scott Richmond
Alexis Rios

Ron Shepherd
Dave Shipanoff
Moises Sierra
Jose Silva
Steve Sinclair
Aaron Small
Brian Smith
Mike A. Smith
Travis Snider
Luis Sojo
Paul Spoljaric
Ed Sprague, Jr.
Matt Stark
Todd Steverson
Shannon Stewart
Dave Stieb
Todd Stottlemyre
Chris Stynes
William Suero
Ken Takahashi
Eric Thames
Curtis Thigpen
Andy Thompson
Rich C. Thompson
Ryan Thompson
Mike Timlin
Dilson Torres
Eugenio Velez
Jamie Vermilyea
Dave Walsh
Steve Wapnick
Jeff Ware
Dave Weathers
Ben Weber
David Wells
Vernon Wells
Mark Whiten
Matt E. Williams
Woody G. Williams
Craig A. Wilson
Nigel Wilson
Kevin Witt
Chris Woodward
Eric Yelding
Michael Young
Eddie Zosky

Year/Team	OPW%	PW	PL	APW%	AW	AL	Diff+/-
1901 BSN	0.557 P	78	62	0.500	69	69	-0.057
1902 BSN	0.580	81	59	0.533	73	64	-0.048
1903 BSN	0.524 F	73	67	0.420	58	80	-0.104
1904 BSN	0.411	63	91	0.359	55	98	-0.052
1905 BSN	0.423	65	89	0.331	51	103	-0.092
1906 BSN	0.509 F	78	76	0.325	49	102	-0.185
1907 BSN	0.363 F	56	98	0.392	58	90	0.029
1908 BSN	0.490 F	76	78	0.409	63	91	-0.081
1909 BSN	0.369 F	57	97	0.294	45	108	-0.075

franchID	OWAR	OWS	AWAR	AWS	WARdiff	WSdiff	P/D/W/F
1901 BSN	28.268	266.500	21.996	206.997	6.272	59.503	P
1902 BSN	44.124	**314.396**	27.911	219.007	16.213	95.389	
1903 BSN	33.401	284.756	17.365	173.921	16.036	110.835	F
1904 BSN	29.548	251.512	12.382	164.998	17.165	86.514	
1905 BSN	30.130	261.326	11.379	152.984	18.750	108.343	
1906 BSN	17.388	240.024	10.013	147.002	7.374	93.022	F
1907 BSN	20.093	221.072	18.916	173.998	1.177	47.074	F
1908 BSN	25.050	239.238	20.319	189.001	4.730	50.237	F
1909 BSN	11.831	186.296	4.050	134.991	7.781	51.305	F

The Braves franchise has existed since 1876 under various nicknames (Red Caps, Beaneaters, Doves, Rustlers, Bees). The club played in Boston through 1952 and moved to Milwaukee, staying there from 1953-1965, before settling in Atlanta. Based on the WS>20 frame of reference, the organization has only developed 9 quality second basemen which ranks them next-to-last among the "Turn of the Century" franchises. The team's right fielders never finished in the top three WS>10 totals. The third basemen rate second-best with 35 WS>20 player-seasons which were led by Eddie Mathews (12) and Chipper Jones (9).

The Beaneaters earned the first National League pennant in the Modern Era by a lone game over the Phillies. Jimmy Collins produced a .332 BA and posted career-bests with 108 aces and 42 doubles while Chick Stahl contributed 105 runs scored. Stahl topped the charts with 19 three-base hits in '04. The 1902 crew hold the franchise records for offWARnorm (24) and offWSnorm (190) while topping the circuit in oWS. Vic Willis (27-20, 2.20) matched his career-high in victories while completing 45 of 46 starts and accruing 410 innings pitched. Willis notched at least 20 wins in four straight seasons (1906-09) and fashioned an ERA of 2.44 with a 1.167 WHIP from 1901-09. Kid Nichols tallied 21 victories with personal-bests in ERA (2.02) and WHIP (1.003) for the '04 squad. Otto Hess triumphed in 20 contests and furnished a 1.83 ERA with a 1.076 WHIP in 1906. Boston first basemen paced the Major Leagues with 27 WS>10 player-seasons from 1901-09 including 7 seasons apiece for Kitty Bransfield, Dan McGann, and Fred Tenney.

Year/Team	OPW%	PW	PL	APW%	AW	AL	Diff+/-
1910 BSN	0.335 F	52	102	0.346	53	100	0.012
1911 BSN	0.342 F	53	101	0.291	44	107	-0.050
1912 BSN	0.358	55	99	0.340	52	101	-0.018
1913 BSN	0.472 F	73	81	0.457	69	82	-0.015
1914 BSN	0.531 F	82	72	0.614 P	94	59	0.083
1915 BSN	0.504 F	78	76	0.546	83	69	0.042
1916 BSN	0.532 F	82	72	0.586	89	63	0.053
1917 BSN	0.529 F	82	72	0.471	72	81	-0.059

Year/Team							
1918 BSN	0.544	70	58	0.427	53	71	-0.117
1919 BSN	0.522 P	73	67	0.410	57	82	-0.112

franchID	OWAR	OWS	AWAR	AWS	WARdiff	WSdiff	P/D/W/F
1910 BSN	15.476	156.664	14.873	159.003	0.603	-2.339	F
1911 BSN	13.239	125.975	10.755	131.999	2.484	-6.024	F
1912 BSN	13.397	136.334	21.210	156.002	-7.813	-19.668	
1913 BSN	28.732	201.192	27.700	207.005	1.032	-5.813	F
1914 BSN	25.706	228.146	36.995	282.007	-11.288	-53.862	F
1915 BSN	22.843	223.109	39.384	249.004	-16.541	-25.895	F
1916 BSN	28.333	238.981	37.548	266.994	-9.214	-28.013	F
1917 BSN	35.724	225.462	36.673	215.996	-0.948	9.465	F
1918 BSN	26.696	177.942	21.287	158.999	5.409	18.943	
1919 BSN	**26.765**	164.982	23.987	171.002	2.778	-6.020	P

Bill L. James savored a 26-7 campaign in 1914 as he furnished a 1.90 ERA and a WHIP of 1.140. Rabbit Maranville rates among the top defensive shortstops of all-time, compiling 6 seasons on the Fielding WAR and WS charts. Lefty Tyler notched 15 wins per season with a 2.47 ERA and 1.180 WHIP from 1913-18. He secured personal-bests with a 19-8 record and 2.00 ERA in '18. Boston outlasted St. Louis to earn the pennant in 1919. Jesse Barnes topped the NL with 25 victories in 1919 while fashioning a 2.40 ERA and a 1.008 WHIP.

Win Shares > 20	Single-Season	1901-1919
Fred Tenney - 1B (ATL) x4	Les Mann - LF (ATL)	Togie Pittinger - SP (ATL) x2
Dan McGann - 1B (ATL) x2	Chick Stahl - CF (ATL) x3	Vic Willis - SP (ATL) x5
Rabbit Maranville - SS (ATL) x6	Johnny Bates - CF (ATL) x2	Irv Young - SP (ATL)
Jimmy Collins - 3B (ATL) x4	Patsy Donovan - RF (ATL)	Bill L. James - SP (ATL)
Milt Stock - 3B (ATL) x2	Tommy Griffith - RF (ATL)	Lefty Tyler - SP (ATL)
Bill Rariden - C (ATL)	Kid Nichols - SP (ATL) x2	Jesse Barnes - SP (ATL) x2

Year/Team	OPW%	PW	PL	APW%	AW	AL	Diff+/-
1920 BSN	0.517 P	80	74	0.408	62	90	-0.109
1921 BSN	0.536	83	71	0.516	79	74	-0.020
1922 BSN	0.533	82	72	0.346	53	100	-0.187
1923 BSN	0.490	75	79	0.351	54	100	-0.139
1924 BSN	0.389	60	94	0.346	53	100	-0.043
1925 BSN	0.509	78	76	0.458	70	83	-0.051
1926 BSN	0.447	69	85	0.434	66	86	-0.012
1927 BSN	0.442	68	86	0.390	60	94	-0.052
1928 BSN	0.458	71	83	0.327	50	103	-0.131
1929 BSN	0.404	62	92	0.364	56	98	-0.040

franchID	OWAR	OWS	AWAR	AWS	WARdiff	WSdiff	P/D/W/F
1920 BSN	26.118	180.631	18.155	185.997	7.963	-5.366	P
1921 BSN	27.778	193.721	31.003	236.999	-3.225	-43.278	
1922 BSN	27.071	195.413	12.018	158.999	15.052	36.414	
1923 BSN	29.462	196.552	20.555	162.000	8.907	34.552	
1924 BSN	14.795	151.181	11.249	158.999	3.546	-7.817	
1925 BSN	26.786	201.756	26.012	210.002	0.774	-8.246	
1926 BSN	20.445	150.982	24.773	198.004	-4.329	-47.022	
1927 BSN	21.949	146.539	22.465	180.003	-0.516	-33.464	
1928 BSN	29.002	191.260	16.160	149.999	12.842	41.260	
1929 BSN	19.231	156.589	15.597	167.996	3.634	-11.408	

The Braves captured the flag with 80 victories in 1920. Barnes compiled 20 wins along with a 2.64 ERA. Third-sacker Milt Stock eclipsed the .300 mark in four straight seasons (1919-1922) and registered 200+ base knocks in '20 and '25. Ray Powell tallied 114 runs and paced the NL with 18 triples in 1921. Maranville contributed career-bests with 198 safeties and 115 aces during the '22 campaign.

Dolf Luque (27-8, 1.93) recorded 38 Win Shares while topping the Senior Circuit in victories, ERA and shutouts (6) in 1923. "The Pride of Havana" merited another ERA title two years later and posted the best WHIP (1.172) in the National League. Red Lucas, aka "The Nashville Narcissus," delivered 19 wins during the 1929 season along with league-bests in complete games (28) and WHIP (1.204).

Year/Team	OPW%	PW	PL	APW%	AW	AL	Diff+/-
1930 BSN	0.447 F	69	85	0.455	70	84	0.008
1931 BSN	0.469 F	72	82	0.416	64	90	-0.053
1932 BSN	0.527 F	81	73	0.500	77	77	-0.027
1933 BSN	0.587 F	90	64	0.539	83	71	-0.048
1934 BSN	0.540 F	83	71	0.517	78	73	-0.024
1935 BSN	0.402 F	62	92	0.248	38	115	-0.154
1936 BSN	0.521 F	80	74	0.461	71	83	-0.060
1937 BSN	0.567 F	87	67	0.520	79	73	-0.047
1938 BSN	0.528 F	81	73	0.507	77	75	-0.022
1939 BSN	0.518 F	80	74	0.417	63	88	-0.100

franchID	OWAR	OWS	AWAR	AWS	WARdiff	WSdiff	P/D/W/F
1930 BSN	22.617	217.285	18.380	209.992	4.236	7.293	F
1931 BSN	31.565	231.519	17.067	192.000	14.498	39.518	F
1932 BSN	25.838	218.547	25.274	231.001	0.564	-12.454	F
1933 BSN	23.489	248.988	27.647	248.995	-4.159	-0.007	F
1934 BSN	26.198	238.903	26.589	234.002	-0.391	4.901	F
1935 BSN	12.071	154.434	11.617	113.994	0.454	40.440	F
1936 BSN	26.303	197.212	22.400	213.004	3.903	-15.792	F
1937 BSN	26.951	215.197	24.465	237.000	2.486	-21.803	F
1938 BSN	21.976	195.082	19.652	231.002	2.324	-35.920	F
1939 BSN	24.645	190.500	20.164	188.998	4.480	1.502	F

Wally Berger reveled in a fantastic rookie season as he clubbed 38 round-trippers, plated 119 baserunners and batted .310 for the '30 squad. He placed third in the 1933 NL MVP vote and then paced the circuit with 34 wallops and 130 ribbies in 1935. Berger produced a .305 BA with 34 two-baggers, 28 taters and 103 RBI per year from 1930-36. Lucas fashioned personal-bests with a 2.94 ERA and 1.099 WHIP while completing 28 of 31 starts in '32. Boston fell below the PA and/or BFP requirements for the entire decade.

"Milkman" Jim Turner (20-11, 2.38) placed fourth in the 1937 NL MVP race during his inaugural campaign, leading the NL in ERA, WHIP (1.091) and complete games (24). Fellow moundsman Lou Fette (20-10, 2.88) finished fifth in the voting and tied Turner for the League lead with 5 shutouts. Bucky Walters (27-11, 2.29) tallied 36 Win Shares and merited the 1939 NL MVP Award while pacing the circuit in victories, ERA, WHIP, complete games and innings pitched in successive seasons.

Win Shares > 20	Single-Season	1920-1939
Billy Urbanski - SS (ATL)	Dolf Luque - SP (ATL) x3	Lou Fette - SP (ATL)
Wally Berger - LF (ATL)	Garland Braxton - SP (ATL)	Jim Turner - SP (ATL)
Wally Berger - CF (ATL) x6	Ed Brandt - SP (ATL) x2	Bucky Walters - SP (ATL) x4
Vince DiMaggio - CF (ATL) x3		

Year/Team	OPW%	PW	PL	APW%	AW	AL	Diff+/-
1940 BSN	0.543	84	70	0.428	65	87	-0.115
1941 BSN	0.526	81	73	0.403	62	92	-0.123
1942 BSN	0.475	73	81	0.399	59	89	-0.077
1943 BSN	0.461 F	71	83	0.444	68	85	-0.017
1944 BSN	0.497 F	77	77	0.422	65	89	-0.075
1945 BSN	0.417 F	64	90	0.441	67	85	0.024
1946 BSN	0.452 F	70	84	0.529	81	72	0.078
1947 BSN	0.495 F	76	78	0.558	86	68	0.064
1948 BSN	0.506 F	78	76	0.595 P	91	62	0.089
1949 BSN	0.514 F	79	75	0.487	75	79	-0.027

franchID	OWAR	OWS	AWAR	AWS	WARdiff	WSdiff	P/D/W/F
1940 BSN	31.529	240.841	15.628	195.001	15.901	45.840	
1941 BSN	26.915	202.537	19.519	186.003	7.396	16.535	
1942 BSN	20.852	173.491	20.634	174.005	0.219	-0.513	
1943 BSN	31.350	242.523	19.428	203.999	11.922	38.524	F
1944 BSN	24.520	236.406	27.076	194.996	-2.556	41.410	F
1945 BSN	13.463	180.872	33.741	200.995	-20.278	-20.123	F
1946 BSN	20.298	181.316	37.305	243.000	-17.008	-61.684	F
1947 BSN	22.631	187.250	41.626	257.999	-18.995	-70.749	F
1948 BSN	25.978	177.487	51.261	272.991	-25.283	-95.504	F
1949 BSN	25.458	190.780	35.676	225.001	-10.218	-34.221	F

Walters delivered 20 victories and completed 26 games per season over a six-year span from 1939-1944 in addition to a 2.67 ERA and a 1.193 WHIP. Elbie Fletcher plated 104 runs for the Bees in 1940, led the NL for three consecutive years in OBP (1940-42) and coaxed 100+ bases on balls four times in his career. Vince DiMaggio knocked in 100 baserunners for the '41 club.

Warren Spahn paced the League in ERA, WHIP and shutouts while compiling 21 victories in his first full season (1947). Spahn led the NL in strikeouts during four straight seasons and thrice exceeded the 20-win mark from 1949-1952. Alvin Dark rapped 39 doubles and batted at a .322 clip as he earned the 1948 NL ROY Award. The Braves dipped below the PA and/or BFP requirements from 1943 through 1951.

Year/Team	OPW%	PW	PL	APW%	AW	AL	Diff+/-
1950 BSN	0.534 F	82	72	0.539	83	71	0.005
1951 BSN	0.589 F	91	63	0.494	76	78	-0.095
1952 BSN	0.505	78	76	0.418	64	89	-0.087
1953 ML1	0.664 P	102	52	0.597	92	62	-0.066
1954 ML1	0.624 P	96	58	0.578	89	65	-0.047
1955 ML1	0.595 P	92	62	0.552	85	69	-0.043
1956 ML1	0.599 P	92	62	0.597	92	62	-0.002
1957 ML1	0.617 P	95	59	0.617 P	95	59	0.000
1958 ML1	0.561 P	86	68	0.597 P	92	62	0.037
1959 ML1	0.590 P	91	63	0.551	86	70	-0.038

franchID	OWAR	OWS	AWAR	AWS	WARdiff	WSdiff	P/D/W/F
1950 BSN	29.625	197.827	35.776	248.999	-6.151	-51.173	F
1951 BSN	36.232	219.848	38.644	228.002	-2.412	-8.154	F
1952 BSN	29.658	213.570	24.772	192.004	4.886	21.566	
1953 ML1	52.223	300.727	42.705	275.994	9.518	24.732	P
1954 ML1	48.718	280.212	38.423	255.000	10.296	25.213	P

1955 ML1	**46.507**	**267.495**	38.423	255.000	8.085	12.495	P
1956 ML1	**47.512**	**266.896**	43.219	275.998	4.293	-9.102	P
1957 ML1	**46.812**	**271.879**	45.814	284.999	0.997	-13.121	P
1958 ML1	**43.641**	**266.553**	45.571	275.992	-1.930	-9.438	P
1959 ML1	**45.484**	**260.696**	44.340	257.999	1.145	2.697	P

GM John Quinn assembled a talented group of ballplayers who rewarded the organization by leading the circuit in oWAR and oWS while capturing 7 consecutive pennants (1953-1959). Quinn landed three future Hall of Famers as amateur free agents during his stint in the Braves' front office – Eddie Mathews (1949), Hank Aaron (1952) and Phil Niekro (1958).

Vern Bickford won 19 contests in 1950, topping the NL with 27 complete games in 39 starts and 311.2 innings pitched. Dark drilled a league-high 41 two-baggers in '51. "The Swamp Fox" tallied 126 runs while posting a .300 BA with 23 big-flies in '53. Earl Torgeson scored a league-leading 120 runs in 1950. "The Earl of Snohomish" dialed long distance 24 times and pilfered 20 bags in '51.

The '52 Braves finished 11 games behind the Dodgers. Relief ace Hoyt Wilhelm (15-3, 2.43, 11 saves) appeared in a 71 contests and garnered the ERA title in his rookie campaign, placing second in the NL ROY balloting. Wilhelm delivered 12 wins, 7 saves and a 2.10 ERA for the '54 squad. "Old Sarge" joined the starting rotation in 1959 and posted a 15-11 mark with a league-best 2.19 ERA, but he returned to full-time relief work two years later.

In March 1953 the Braves became the first franchise to relocate in 50 years (the Baltimore Orioles had transferred to New York in 1903). Milwaukee paced the National League with 102 victories in '53 as the Dodgers finished a distant 16 games behind. The club established defensive high-water marks with 8 fldWARnorm and 60 fldWSnorm during the 1953 season.

Spahn (23-7, 2.10) topped the circuit in wins, ERA and WHIP in 1953. He claimed Cy Young honors in '57 and placed runner-up three times in his career. Spahn fashioned a 2.92 ERA with a 1.180 WHIP and compiled 20 wins per season during the Fifties. Johnny Antonelli earned his first All-Star appearance and finished third in the 1954 NL MVP voting as he notched 21 victories while leading the League with a 2.30 ERA and 6 shutouts. Antonelli posted a 3.09 ERA with 16 wins per season during the Braves' triumphant run.

Mathews batted .302, crushed a league-best 47 long balls and drove in 135 baserunners in his sophomore season. He recorded 38 Win Shares and placed second in the 1953 NL MVP voting. The nine-time All-Star swatted 39 four-baggers, knocked in 103 runs and registered 106 tallies per year from 1953-59. Mathews paced the circuit with 46 big-flies in '59. Bill Bruton pilfered 26 bases in his inaugural year and topped the stolen base charts for three successive seasons (1953-55). Johnny Logan totaled 100 aces in '53 and then rapped 37 two-base knocks in '55. Milwaukee's shortstops paced the Majors with 18 WS>10 player-seasons as Dark and Logan accomplished the feat eight times apiece.

"Hammerin'" Hank Aaron debuted in 1954, placing fourth in the NL ROY vote. He pummeled opposing hurlers for the balance of the decade, producing a .329 BA with 201 base knocks, 36 two-baggers, 33 clouts and 110 ribbies per year while scoring 111 runs. Aaron (.322/44/132) posted league-bests in home runs, RBI and runs scored (118) to secure his lone MVP award in '57. The "Hammer" merited 21 consecutive All-Star selections (1955-1975) and collected batting titles in '56 (.328) and '59 (.355).

Gene Conley contributed a 14-9 record and 2.96 ERA as Milwaukee outlasted Philadelphia by an 11-game margin in 1954. The Braves tomahawked the opposition in 1955 and '56 as the Dodgers placed a distant second in both campaigns. Dick Donovan entered the rotation in '55 and delivered a 15-9 mark with a 3.32 ERA. He furnished a league-best 1.155 WHIP in 1956 then supplied a 16-6 record with a 2.77 ERA in the subsequent campaign.

George Crowe belted 31 circuit clouts and knocked in 92 runs as the '57 Braves bested the Dodgers by 10 games. The Pirates nearly ended the Braves' supremacy in '58 as the Buccos fell 2 games short of the pennant. Wes Covington supplied a .330 average with 24 jacks and 74 ribbies as a part-timer. Milwaukee cruised to the pennant in '59, posting another double-digit lead over the Dodgers as the season reached its conclusion. Don McMahon earned the closer's role, saving a league-best 15 games while achieving an ERA of 2.57.

Win Shares > 20	Single-Season	1940-1959
Elbie Fletcher - 1B (ATL) x4	Ray Mueller - C (ATL) x2	Warren Spahn - SP (ATL) x14
Earl Torgeson - 1B (ATL) x2	Del Crandall - C (ATL) x3	Ken Heintzelman - SP (ATL)
Alvin Dark - SS (ATL) x5	Bill Bruton - CF (ATL) x2	Johnny Antonelli - SP (ATL)
Johnny Logan - SS (ATL) x4	Chet Ross - LF (ATL)	x3
Eddie Mathews - 3B (ATL)	Hank Aaron - RF (ATL) x14	Hoyt Wilhelm - SP (ATL)
x12	Al Javery - SP (ATL)	

Year/Team	OPW%	PW	PL	APW%	AW	AL	Diff+/-
1960 ML1	0.519	80	74	0.571	88	66	0.052
1961 ML1	0.569 P	92	70	0.539	83	71	-0.030
1962 ML1	0.572	93	69	0.531	86	76	-0.041
1963 ML1	0.510	83	79	0.519	84	78	0.008
1964 ML1	0.473	77	85	0.543	88	74	0.071
1965 ML1	0.478	77	85	0.531	86	76	0.053
1966 ATL	0.493	80	82	0.525	85	77	0.032
1967 ATL	0.439	71	91	0.475	77	85	0.037
1968 ATL	0.517	84	78	0.500	81	81	-0.017
1969 ATL	0.462	75	87	0.574 D	93	69	0.112

franchID	OWAR	OWS	AWAR	AWS	WARdiff	WSdiff	P/D/W/F
1960 ML1	36.808	237.896	39.515	264.002	-2.707	-26.107	
1961 ML1	41.939	279.200	35.297	248.998	6.642	30.202	P
1962 ML1	48.550	287.384	41.171	258.000	7.379	29.383	
1963 ML1	45.629	275.551	37.294	251.997	8.335	23.554	
1964 ML1	42.226	271.976	42.095	263.998	0.131	7.979	
1965 ML1	39.578	253.089	44.365	258.000	-4.787	-4.911	
1966 ATL	46.604	273.244	51.157	255.000	-4.553	18.244	
1967 ATL	38.267	260.727	37.326	230.994	0.941	29.733	
1968 ATL	46.236	281.801	39.505	242.995	6.730	38.806	
1969 ATL	37.962	267.627	38.600	278.992	-0.638	-11.365	

A four-way scramble for the pennant ensued as the Braves finally returned to Earth in 1960. When the dust settled, the Dodgers emerged victorious, as the Cardinals, Pirates and Braves all finished within one game. Bruton sparkled at the top of the order, batting .286 with a league-best 112 runs and 13 three-baggers. He contributed 17 taters, 22 steals and 99 runs scored in the ensuing campaign. Chuck Estrada placed second in the Rookie of the Year balloting with an 18-11 record and a 3.58 ERA.

Aaron surpassed the century mark for runs scored in 13 consecutive seasons (1955-1967) and seized three home run and RBI titles during the decade. "Hammer" produced a .308 BA with 38 four-baggers, 111 RBI and 20 stolen bases per year in the Sixties. Aaron (.319/44/130) secured a personal-best with 40 Win Shares in 1963. Mathews belted 39 blasts and drove in 124 runs in 1960 and averaged 30 jacks with 93 ribbies from 1960-65. He paced the League with a .399 OBP in '63 and coaxed over 100 bases on balls five times in his career.

Spahn opened the decade with back-to-back consolation prizes in the Cy Young balloting. He topped the charts in '61 with a 3.02 ERA and 1.153 WHIP; he then matched his career-best with a 23-7 mark two years later. Spahn led the League in complete games for seven straight seasons (1957-1963) and averaged 21 victories from 1960-63.

Milwaukee claimed the squad's lone pennant in the Sixties by percentage points over San Francisco in '61. Donovan topped the circuit with a 2.40 ERA and 1.026 WHIP, and then recorded a career-high 20 wins in the ensuing season. Joey Jay posted 21 wins in successive seasons and earned an All-Star selection in '61. Wilhelm (2.30, 18 SV) reclaimed his relief ace role and provided a 1.99 ERA, 0.975 WHIP, saving 16 contests per year from 1961-69. Juan Pizarro initiated a four-year stretch in which he averaged 15 victories, a 2.93 ERA and a 1.198 WHIP counting a 19-9 record with a 2.56 ERA in '64.

The Braves secured 93 victories in '62 but finished second as the Giants secured the National League pennant. Terry Fox (1.71, 16 saves) shared closing assignments with Wilhelm. Ed "The Poet" Charles authored a .288 batting average, 17 dingers and 84 RBI while fellow rookie Manny Jimenez recorded a .301 average.

The Braves dipped below the .500 mark from 1964-67. Denis Menke (.283/20/65) settled in at shortstop while second-sacker Felix Mantilla crushed 30 long balls in '64 (besting his previous career-high by 19). Mantilla delivered 18 blasts and 92 RBI for an encore. Rico Carty placed runner-up in the 1964 NL ROY voting as he manufactured a .330 average with 22 clouts and 88 RBI. "Beeg Mon" delivered a .342 BA in merely 339 plate appearances in '69.

Joe Torre (.323/20/109) finished fifth in the 1964 NL MVP voting and went on to swat 27 dingers in the ensuing year. Torre launched a personal-best 36 long balls and drove in 101 baserunners while batting .315 in '66. Tony Cloninger tied for the team lead in '64 with 19 victories then compiled a record of 24-11 with a 3.29 ERA during the subsequent campaign. Mack Jones crushed 31 big-flies for the '65 crew. The Braves moved from Milwaukee to Atlanta following the 1965 season.

Second sacker Bobby Knoop earned an All-Star nod and the first of three straight Gold Glove awards, as he belted 11 three-baggers and 17 blasts in 1966. Wilhelm's protégé, Phil Niekro, enjoyed a breakthrough season in 1967 with 11 wins, 9 saves and a 1.87 ERA. "Knucksie" registered 23 victories with a 2.56 ERA and a 1.027 WHIP en route to a second-place finish in the 1969 NL Cy Young voting.

Atlanta climbed back into contention in '68 as the club placed third behind San Francisco. Clay Carroll (2.27, 17 SV), Cecil Upshaw (2.47, 13 SV) and Claude Raymond (2.83, 10 saves) combined with Wilhelm to form an exceptional relief quartet. Upshaw notched 27 saves with a 2.91 ERA in '69 while Ron Reed won a career-high 18 games, sharing late-inning assignments with Wilhelm.

Year/Team	OPW%	PW	PL	APW%	AW	AL	Diff+/-
1970 ATL	0.508	82	80	0.469	76	86	-0.039
1971 ATL	0.503	82	80	0.506	82	80	0.003
1972 ATL	0.428	69	93	0.455	70	84	0.027
1973 ATL	0.510	83	79	0.472	76	85	-0.038
1974 ATL	0.567 P	92	70	0.543	88	74	-0.024
1975 ATL	0.458	74	88	0.416	67	94	-0.042
1976 ATL	0.491	79	83	0.432	70	92	-0.059
1977 ATL	0.470	76	86	0.377	61	101	-0.094
1978 ATL	0.430	70	92	0.426	69	93	-0.004
1979 ATL	0.458	74	88	0.413	66	94	-0.045

franchID	OWAR	OWS	AWAR	AWS	WARdiff	WSdiff	P/D/W/F
1970 ATL	47.259	298.953	37.993	227.990	9.266	70.964	
1971 ATL	43.878	287.444	34.069	246.008	9.809	41.436	
1972 ATL	36.834	260.926	29.182	209.992	7.652	50.933	

1973 ATL	46.152	293.178	43.187	227.997	2.965	65.181	
1974 ATL	42.867	303.829	41.456	263.992	1.411	39.837	P
1975 ATL	35.123	265.447	22.405	201.001	12.719	64.447	
1976 ATL	44.843	294.843	27.432	210.003	17.411	84.840	
1977 ATL	40.553	283.514	19.948	182.999	20.605	100.515	
1978 ATL	28.293	252.046	24.654	207.000	3.639	45.046	
1979 ATL	28.880	231.889	27.716	198.002	1.164	33.887	

Aaron knocked in 118 baserunners in consecutive campaigns (1970-71) and delivered one of his finest seasons in 1971, posting career-highs with 47 blasts and a .669 SLG. "The Hammer" pounded 40 round-trippers in '73 as he approached Babe Ruth's career record of 714 home runs. Aaron surpassed "The Babe" when he cleared the fences on April 8, 1974. He retired after the 1976 season with MLB career-bests in home runs (755), RBI (2297) and total bases (6856).

Carty (.366/25/101) secured the batting title in 1970. Sandy "Iron Pony" Alomar pilfered 35 bags and earned an All-Star appearance. He then succeeded on 39 of 49 stolen base attempts in the ensuing year. Cito Gaston (.318/29/93) joined Alomar at the 1970 All-Star game, setting career-bests in batting average, home runs and RBI. Menke contributed personal-bests in batting average (.304) and RBI (92). Raymond, McMahon, Carroll and Wilhelm combined for 71 saves. Carl Morton garnered the 1970 NL ROY Award with an 18-11 record and 3.60 ERA despite conceding a league-worst 125 walks.

Torre supplied consecutive 200-hit seasons (1970-71) and collected the 1971 NL MVP hardware for his efforts. He led the Senior Circuit with a .363 BA, 137 RBI and 230 base hits while setting the Braves' franchise record with 41 Win Shares. Ron Hunt set a Major League record in 1971 as he reached base via HBP 50 times! Hunt led the League in HBP for seven straight seasons (1968-1974). Ralph Garr compiled a .343 BA with 219 hits while swiping 30 bases in his first full season. "Road Runner" prevailed in the NL batting race with a .353 average and paced the circuit with 214 hits and 17 triples in '74. Earl C. Williams belted 33 bombs and drove in 87 runs, earning the 1971 NL ROY Award.

The wheels fell off in 1972 as the Braves skidded to a 69-93 mark. "Knucksie" provided 16 wins along with a 3.06 ERA while Carroll saved 37 contests for an otherwise pedestrian pitching corps. Niekro (20-13, 2.38) placed third in the 1974 NL Cy Young vote, leading the League in wins, complete games (18) and innings pitched (302.1). He whiffed a league-leading 262 batsmen in '77 and averaged 19 victories, 23 complete games and 239 strikeouts over a three-year period (1977-79). Niekro exceeded the 300-inning threshold and led the NL in complete games during all 3 campaigns!

Dusty Baker supplied a .321 BA in his rookie campaign (1972) and then notched career-highs with 101 runs scored and 99 RBI during his sophomore year; he crushed 30 moon-shots for the '77 crew. The Braves captured the club's lone pennant of the decade by a 2-game margin over the Reds in '74. The bullpen tandem of Tom House (1.93, 11 SV) and Clay Carroll (12-5, 2.15) secured the late-inning leads.

The Braves added the blazing speed of Mickey Rivers to the starting lineup on a full-time basis in '75. "Mick The Quick" swiped a career-high 70 bases and legged out 13 triples after nabbing 30 bags in 118 games during his rookie season. Rivers (.312/8/67) earned his lone All-Star nod and placed third in the MVP voting in 1976. Atlanta endured back-to-back last place finishes in 1978-79. Bill Robinson knocked in 104 runs while blasting 26 dingers in '77. Bob Horner achieved 1978 NL ROY honors by crushing 23 four-ply swats in only 89 contests and then boosted his output to 33 taters and 98 ribbies in the ensuing year.

Win Shares > 20	Single-Season	1960-1979
Joe Torre - 1B (ATL)	Wayne Garrett - 3B (ATL)	Dusty Baker - CF (ATL) x2
Hank Aaron - 1B (ATL) x2	Joe Torre - C (ATL) x5	Mickey Rivers - CF (ATL) x4
Ron Hunt - 2B (ATL) x2	Rico Carty - LF (ATL) x3	Rico Carty - DH (ATL)
Denis Menke - 2B (ATL)	Ralph Garr - LF (ATL) x2	Joey Jay - SP (ATL)
Sandy Alomar - 2B (ATL)	Dusty Baker - LF (ATL) x3	Phil Niekro - SP (ATL) x8
Denis Menke - SS (ATL) x3	Hank Aaron - CF (ATL) x2	Carl Morton - SP (ATL)
Ed Charles - 3B (ATL)	Lee Maye - CF (ATL)	Hoyt Wilhelm - RP (ATL)
Joe Torre - 3B (ATL)	Cito Gaston - CF (ATL)	Phil Niekro - SW (ATL)
Hank Aaron - LF (ATL)		

Year/Team	OPW%	PW	PL	APW%	AW	AL	Diff+/-
1980 ATL	0.498	81	81	0.503	81	80	0.005
1981 ATL	0.526	85	77	0.472	50	56	-0.054
1982 ATL	0.540 D	87	75	0.549 D	89	73	0.010
1983 ATL	0.568 P	92	70	0.543	88	74	-0.025
1984 ATL	0.530 P	86	76	0.494	80	82	-0.036
1985 ATL	0.495	80	82	0.407	66	96	-0.087
1986 ATL	0.419	68	94	0.447	72	89	0.028
1987 ATL	0.481	78	84	0.429	69	92	-0.052
1988 ATL	0.468	76	86	0.338	54	106	-0.131
1989 ATL	0.443	72	90	0.394	63	97	-0.049

franchID	OWAR	OWS	AWAR	AWS	WARdiff	WSdiff	P/D/W/F
1980 ATL	40.401	302.102	26.824	242.990	13.576	59.112	
1981 ATL	31.196	206.536	20.112	150.007	11.084	56.529	
1982 ATL	46.472	298.663	37.173	266.998	9.299	31.665	D
1983 ATL	51.061	293.661	**44.072**	264.000	6.989	29.661	P
1984 ATL	37.406	271.754	29.657	240.005	7.749	31.749	P
1985 ATL	31.311	241.686	19.474	198.002	11.838	43.685	
1986 ATL	27.798	214.969	28.756	215.993	-0.958	-1.024	
1987 ATL	38.578	254.327	28.884	206.999	9.694	47.328	
1988 ATL	32.285	230.910	16.230	162.001	16.055	68.909	
1989 ATL	32.915	217.857	27.837	189.004	5.078	28.853	

Atlanta crawled back to respectability in 1980, reaching the .500 mark while finishing a distant second to Houston. Rivers posted career-bests with a .333 BA, 210 base hits and 96 runs scored while Horner launched a career-best 35 circuit clouts. Baker (.294/29/97) placed fourth in the 1980 NL MVP race and continued to roast opposing hurlers with a .320 BA in the subsequent campaign. The bullpen chores were shared between Rick Camp (1.91, 22 SV) and Frank LaCorte (2.82, 11 SV). Camp secured the closer's role in '81, notching 9 wins and 17 saves along with a 1.78 ERA. The Braves ended the season only three games behind the division-winning Dodgers in '81.

Dale Murphy carried the team to a division title in 1982 and back-to-back pennants in 1983-84. "Murph" captured consecutive NL MVP Awards (1982-83) as he crushed 36 long balls and led the League in RBI in both campaigns while becoming a member of the 30/30 club in '83. In a four-year stretch covering 1982-85 he pummeled the opposition with a .293 BA, 36 big-flies, 110 RBI, 20 stolen bases and 114 runs scored. Murphy (.295/44/105) set career-highs in home runs, walks (115), OBP (.417) and SLG (.580) during the 1987 season.

Niekro posted a 17-4 record while Ron Reed (2.66, 14 SV) and Steve "Bedrock" Bedrosian (2.42, 11 SV) anchored the relief corps. Bedrosian collected the NL Cy Young hardware in 1987, compiling 40 saves with a 2.83 ERA. Atlanta overtook Los Angeles by 3 games in '82. Craig McMurtry (15-9, 3.08) placed second in the NL Rookie of the Year voting in '83 and shared the team lead in victories with Larry McWilliams (15-8, 3.25). Second baseman Glenn Hubbard established career bests with 12 home runs and 70 RBI en route to his only All-Star selection.

Brett Butler swiped 39 bases and led the League with 13 three-base hits. He ran wild on the basepaths in '84, stealing 52 bags in 74 attempts; he then delivered a .311 BA with 47 stolen bases and 106 runs scored for the '85 squad. Butler contributed 40 thefts, 10 triples and 99 tallies per year from 1983-89. The Braves squeaked past the Dodgers to secure successive pennants in '83 and '84.

The Braves endured a six-year period in the N.L. West basement from 1985 to 1990, slumping to 94 losses in '86. The bullpen quartet of Brian Fisher (2.38, 14 SV), Ken Dayley (2.76, 11 SV), Jim Acker and Tom Waddell tallied 44 saves in 1985. Zane Smith won 15 contests while Terry Leach fashioned a record of 11-1 primarily in relief for the '87 staff. Jacoby batted .300 with 32 jacks but only managed to drive home 69 baserunners. Milt Thompson, Gerald Perry, Albert Hall and Butler swiped at least 30 bags. Tom Glavine furnished a 14-8 mark with a 3.68 ERA in 1989 after struggling to a 7-17 record in the previous campaign.

Year/Team	OPW%	PW	PL	APW%	AW	AL	Diff+/-
1990 ATL	0.483	78	84	0.401	65	97	-0.082
1991 ATL	0.561 P	91	71	0.580 D	94	68	0.019
1992 ATL	0.603 P	98	64	0.605 P	98	64	0.002
1993 ATL	0.584 P	95	67	0.642 P	104	58	0.058
1994 ATL	0.528	86	76	0.596 W	68	46	0.069
1995 ATL	0.487	79	83	0.625 P	90	54	0.138
1996 ATL	0.533 D	86	76	0.593 P	96	66	0.060
1997 ATL	0.524 W	85	77	0.623 P	101	61	0.100
1998 ATL	0.564 P	91	71	0.654 P	106	56	0.090
1999 ATL	0.540 D	87	75	0.636 P	103	59	0.096

franchID	OWAR	OWS	AWAR	AWS	WARdiff	WSdiff	P/D/W/F
1990 ATL	34.684	231.313	26.791	194.999	7.893	36.314	
1991 ATL	**47.555**	279.209	44.433	282.002	3.122	-2.793	P
1992 ATL	45.706	280.923	44.016	**294.002**	1.690	-13.079	P
1993 ATL	**45.068**	**277.654**	50.596	**312.000**	-5.528	-34.346	P
1994 ATL	25.978	176.849	34.999	204.000	-9.021	-27.151	
1995 ATL	28.607	221.069	41.666	**269.998**	-13.059	-48.929	
1996 ATL	35.918	**254.357**	52.504	287.997	-16.586	-33.640	D
1997 ATL	37.446	252.989	**55.402**	303.001	-17.956	-50.012	W
1998 ATL	33.978	236.597	**60.187**	318.002	-26.209	-81.405	P
1999 ATL	33.569	232.682	50.029	**308.999**	-16.460	-76.317	D

Butler batted .309 with 51 steals and 108 runs scored for the '90 squad. He compiled a .304 BA and swiped 38 bags per year from 1990-95. Ron Gant (.303/32/84) achieved consecutive seasons with at least 30 home runs and 30 stolen bases (1990-91). Gant placed fifth in the 1993 NL MVP race while establishing personal highs with 36 moon-shots, 117 ribbies and 113 runs scored. After missing the entire 1994 season due to a broken leg suffered in an ATV accident, he then rallied with 29 taters and 23 stolen bases in the following campaign. Atlanta led the Majors with 19 WS>10 player-seasons during the 1990's.

David Justice (.282/28/78) nabbed 1990 NL ROY accolades and finished third in the 1993 NL MVP race when he clubbed 40 big-flies and knocked in a career-best 120 runs. He merited his third All-Star selection, producing a .329 average with 33 jacks and 101 ribbies in '97. Zane Smith registered a 2.55 ERA in 1990 and notched 16 victories with a 3.20 ERA in the following campaign.

63

Bobby Cox was hired to manage the Braves in June 1990 and John Schuerholz accepted GM responsibilities in October. Together they created the blueprint that enabled Atlanta to reach the playoffs in 11 of the next 20 seasons. Patience with the pitching staff paid dividends in '91. Glavine (20-11, 2.55) earned the NL Cy Young Award, leading the League in victories and complete games while posting a career-best WHIP of 1.095. He registered 20+ victories in three straight seasons, coinciding with the Braves' pennant run. Glavine (20-8, 2.76) was runner-up in the 1992 NL Cy Young vote and placed third in '93 with a 22-6 record and 3.20 ERA. He collected his second NL Cy Young Award in '98, posting a record of 20-6 with a 2.47 ERA.

Avery recorded an 18-10 mark with a 3.38 ERA for the '91 crew then logged an 18-6 record and a 2.94 ERA two years later. Atlanta secured the first of three consecutive pennants, winning by six games over Cincinnati as Duane Ward (2.77, 23 SV) and Paul Assenmacher (3.24, 15 SV) shared the late-inning responsibilities. Ward notched 12 saves with a 1.95 ERA in '92. In the ensuing campaign he whiffed 97 batters while delivering a 2.13 ERA with 45 saves.

The Braves prevailed over the Padres by 2 games in '92 and sailed to the pennant by an 11-game margin over the Giants in the ensuing season. Tommy Greene collected several Cy Young votes with a 16-4 record and 3.42 ERA. Mike W. Stanton contributed 27 saves, albeit with a 4.67 ERA while fellow southpaw Derek Lilliquist fashioned a 2.25 ERA and saved 10 contests. Jeff Blauser (.305/15/73) earned an All-Star nod and crossed home plate 110 times.

Atlanta migrated to the National League East when divisional realignment was approved in 1994 and the team proceeded to fall one game short of the Phillies. The '95 Braves slumped to 79 wins, placing them 9 games behind the Expos. Mark Wohlers (2.09, 25 SV) emerged as the closer, whiffing 90 batters in 64.2 innings then recording 39 saves and punching out 100 batters in 77.1 innings. Chipper Jones (.265/23/86) finished second in the 1995 NL ROY balloting. He supplied a .301 BA with 108 runs scored, 33 doubles, 31 four-baggers and 105 RBI from 1995-99. Jones achieved 1999 NL MVP honors as he tomahawked 45 big-flies, plated 110 runners and batted at a .319 clip, also scoring 116 times and succeeding on 25 of 28 stolen base attempts.

Vinny Castilla swatted 30+ long balls in five consecutive seasons (1995-99). He achieved a rare feat when he produced identical batting averages (.304), home runs (40) and RBI (113) in back-to-back campaigns (1996-97). Castilla torched opposing pitchers for a .319 average, 46 moon-shots and 144 ribbies in 1998. The Braves turned the tables on the Expos in '96, taking the division title by a four-game margin. Ryan Klesko belted a career-high 34 dingers. Al Martin (.300/18/72) supplied personal bests in BA, doubles (40), stolen bases (38) and runs scored (101). Turk Wendell closed out 18 contests while furnishing an ERA of 2.84.

The Atlanta franchise clinched the Wild Card in '97. It then achieved the club's fourth pennant of the decade in '98. Kevin Millwood rendered a 17-8 record in his first full campaign; he then placed third in the 1999 NL Cy Young voting, winning 18 games and pacing the circuit with a 0.996 WHIP. Javy Lopez matured into a solid run producer, crushing 34 long balls and knocking in 106 runs.

Andruw Jones (.271/31/90) collected the first of ten consecutive Gold Gloves and pilfered 27 bags in 31 tries. Jones' 11 appearances on the Fielding WAR and WS charts are tied for second-place among outfielders. The Braves achieved back-to-back division titles in 1999 and 2000. Jermaine Dye (.294/27/119) earned a full-time gig and drilled 44 doubles. John Rocker seized the closer's job, saving 38 contests while striking out 104 batters in 72.1 innings pitched.

Year/Team	OPW%	PW	PL	APW%	AW	AL	Diff+/-
2000 ATL	0.530 D	86	76	0.586 D	95	67	0.056
2001 ATL	0.523	85	77	0.543 D	88	74	0.020
2002 ATL	0.490	79	83	0.631 P	101	59	0.142
2003 ATL	0.536 D	87	75	0.623 P	101	61	0.088
2004 ATL	0.532 D	86	76	0.593 D	96	66	0.061

2005 ATL	0.528	86	76	0.556 D	90	72	0.027
2006 ATL	0.525 D	85	77	0.488	79	83	-0.037
2007 ATL	0.424	69	93	0.519	84	78	0.095
2008 ATL	0.503	81	81	0.444	72	90	-0.058
2009 ATL	0.526	85	77	0.531	86	76	0.004
2010 ATL	0.481	78	84	0.562 W	91	71	0.081
2011 ATL	0.498	81	81	0.549	89	73	0.051
2012 ATL	0.521 W	84	78	0.580 W	94	68	0.059
2013 ATL	0.530	86	76	0.593 D	96	66	0.063

franchID	OWAR	OWS	AWAR	AWS	WARdiff	WSdiff	P/D/W/F
2000 ATL	**40.003**	**253.269**	44.532	285.009	-4.528	-31.739	D
2001 ATL	32.643	238.317	39.905	263.994	-7.262	-25.677	
2002 ATL	30.779	227.685	44.087	**302.997**	-13.307	-75.311	
2003 ATL	34.595	230.432	**50.921**	303.006	-16.325	-72.574	D
2004 ATL	35.366	231.270	45.166	287.999	-9.800	-56.728	D
2005 ATL	33.667	237.847	40.077	269.999	-6.410	-32.152	
2006 ATL	34.181	237.605	38.254	237.002	-4.073	0.603	D
2007 ATL	22.715	192.702	41.697	252.003	-18.982	-59.301	
2008 ATL	31.320	219.909	35.389	216.007	-4.069	3.902	
2009 ATL	34.061	236.084	46.820	258.001	-12.760	-21.917	
2010 ATL	38.044	248.972	45.713	273.001	-7.668	-24.029	
2011 ATL	36.586	259.492	41.130	266.995	-4.544	-7.503	
2012 ATL	40.195	258.182	38.960	281.999	1.235	-23.817	W
2013 ATL	**44.070**	254.324	44.993	283.361	-0.923	-29.037	

The Braves bashed the opposition and snatched a second straight NL East title in 2000. Justice jacked 41 gopher balls to lead the lumber company and tied Dye for the team lead with 118 RBI. Dye (.315/44/120) produced career-bests in home runs, RBI and SLG (.622) during the 2006 season. He tallied 27 bombs and 87 ribbies per season from 2000-2009. Rafael Furcal (.295, 40 SB) won the 2000 NL ROY Award and registered over 100 runs scored in four consecutive campaigns (2003-06) including 130 aces in '03. Rocker fashioned a 2.89 ERA and closed out 24 contests while Glavine (21-9, 3.40) was the runner-up in the NL Cy Young balloting.

Chipper Jones produced a .316 BA with 28 big-flies and 94 ribbies per year from 2000-08 and surpassed the century mark in RBI for eight straight seasons (1996-2003). He scorched opposition moundsmen at a .364 clip en route to the NL batting title in 2008. Andruw Jones logged career-bests with a .303 BA, 199 base knocks, 122 tallies and 36 two-baggers, earning the first of five All-Star selections in 2000. "The Curacao Kid" supplied 36 jacks, 108 RBI and 30 doubles per season covering an eight-year stretch (2000-07). He erupted for 51 circuit clouts and 128 RBI in 2005, leading the League in both categories and securing a second-place finish in the NL MVP voting.

Montreal overtook Atlanta in 2001 by 3 games in spite of the Braves' offense, as four Braves' batsmen knocked in over 100 runs apiece. Klesko (.286/30/113) established personal-bests in RBI and runs scored (105). Esteban Yan teamed with John Rocker to save 45 games. The Expos ran away from the pack in '02 and the Braves finished a distant third, 19 games behind. Odalis Perez contributed 15 wins, a 3.00 ERA and a miniscule 0.990 WHIP. Millwood tied Glavine for the team lead with 18 victories, then posted a league-best 2.86 ERA in 2005.

A tight three-way battle for the National League East ensued in 2003 with the Braves emerging victorious. Lopez achieved fifth place in the 2003 NL MVP voting as he bashed 43 four-ply swats, drove in 109 runs and batted .328 (all career-highs). Marcus Giles (.316/21/69) clocked 49 doubles and attained All-Star status, topping the 100-run mark twice in three seasons.

65

Jason Schmidt blossomed into the staff ace, registering a record of 17-5 while logging 208 strikeouts, a 2.34 ERA and a 0.953 WHIP on his way to a runner-up finish in the 2003 NL Cy Young balloting. Schmidt whiffed 251 opponents in 225 innings and posted an 18-7 record with a 3.20 ERA in the subsequent year. Castilla drilled 35 round-trippers and drove in a league-leading 131 runs as Atlanta outlasted Philadelphia by three games in 2004.

The Braves rebounded from a pedestrian effort to claim the NL East in 2006 with 85 victories as the rest of the division played .500 ball. Brian McCann (.333/24/93) made his first of six successive trips to the All-Star contest. McCann delivered a .295 BA with 37 two-base knocks, 22 taters and 92 ribbies per season from 2006-09. Adam LaRoche (.285/32/90) and Jeff "Frenchy" Francoeur (.260/29/103) augmented a stacked lineup. LaRoche plated 100 baserunners in 2010 and 2012 and established a personal-best with 33 moon-shots in '12. The mound crew received a collective thrashing in '07, yielding the worst pitWARnorm (7) and pitWSnorm (44) in club history as Atlanta plummeted to a 69-93 mark.

Mark DeRosa scored 103 runs while batting .285 with 21 jacks for the '08 crew. Joey Devine was lights-out in relief, fashioning a 0.59 ERA and a 0.832 WHIP. Atlanta won 85 games and placed second to Philadelphia in 2009. Adam Wainwright (19-7, 2.63) led the League in wins, games started and innings pitched, earning a third-place finish in the 2009 NL Cy Young race. He placed runner-up for the Cy Young Award in 2010 and 2012 and furnished a 2.95 ERA with a 1.140 WHIP from 2009-2013. Tommy Hanson enjoyed a successful debut, winning 11 of 15 decisions along with a 2.89 ERA. Rookie shortstop Elvis Andrus swiped 33 bases in 39 tries while fellow freshmen Garrett Jones bashed 21 long balls in only 82 games. Martin Prado posted a .307 BA in back-to-back seasons (2009-2010) and drilled 40 doubles while registering 100 tallies in '10.

Neftali Feliz (2.73, 40 SV) secured Rookie of the Year honors in 2010. Jason Heyward (.277/18/72) finished second in the 2010 NL ROY voting. Two years later he swatted 27 big-flies and collected a Gold Glove Award. Craig Kimbrel earned NL ROY honors in 2011 and notched 46 saves per year (2011-13), leading the League for three successive seasons. Through 2013 Kimbrel recorded a 1.39 ERA along with a 0.902 WHIP and a strikeout rate of 15.1 batters per 9 innings! Freddie Freeman placed second to Kimbrel in the battle for rookie accolades. He produced a .319 BA with 23 jacks and 109 ribbies en route to his first All-Star selection in 2013. Slick-fielding shortstop Andrelton Simmons belted 17 home runs and merited Gold Glove honors in his first full season (2013).

Win Shares > 20	Single-Season	1980-2013
Ryan Klesko - 1B (ATL) x3	Bob Horner - 3B (ATL)	Ron Gant - CF (ATL) x2
Garrett Jones - 1B (ATL)	Brook Jacoby - 3B (ATL) x3	Andruw Jones - CF (ATL) x9
Freddie Freeman – 1B (ATL)	Vinny Castilla - 3B (ATL)	Dale Murphy - RF (ATL)
Adam LaRoche - 1B (ATL)	Chipper Jones - 3B (ATL) x9	David Justice - RF (ATL) x3
Marcus Giles - 2B (ATL) x2	Javy Lopez - C (ATL) x3	Jermaine Dye - RF (ATL) x3
Mark DeRosa - 2B (ATL)	Brian McCann - C (ATL) x2	Jason Heyward - RF (ATL)
Kelly Johnson - 2B (ATL)	Ron Gant - LF (ATL)	Tom Glavine - SP (ATL) x6
Martin Prado - 2B (ATL)	Ryan Klesko - LF (ATL)	Steve Avery - SP (ATL)
Rafael Ramirez - SS (ATL)	David Justice - LF (ATL)	Kevin Millwood - SP (ATL)
Jeff Blauser - SS (ATL) x2	Chipper Jones - LF (ATL) x2	Jason Schmidt - SP (ATL)
Rafael Furcal - SS (ATL) x4	Martin Prado - LF (ATL)	Adam Wainwright - SP (ATL)
Yunel Escobar - SS (ATL)	Dale Murphy - CF (ATL) x6	x2
Andrelton Simmons -SS (ATL)	Brett Butler - CF (ATL) x10	

Note: 4000 PA or BFP to qualify, except during strike-shortened seasons
(1972 = 3800, 1981 & 1994 = 2700, 1995 = 3500) and 154-game schedule (3800)
- failed to qualify: 1903, 1906-1911, 1913-1917, 1930-1939, 1943-1951

Hank Aaron	Bob Dresser	Swede Larsen	John Rocker
Tommie Aaron	Jim Driscoll	Bill Lauterborn	Pat Rockett
Woody Abernathy	John Dudra	Al Lawson	Phil Roof
Winston Abreu	Oscar Dugey	Bob Lawson	George Rooks
Jim Acker	Taylor Duncan	Terry Leach	Bob Roselli
Luis Alcaraz	Bill Dunlap	Jack Leary	Larry Rosenthal
Cory Aldridge	Jermaine Dye	Wade Lefler	Bunny Roser
Sandy Alomar	Tom Earley	Denny Lemaster	Chet Ross
Jose L. Alvarez	Jamie Easterly	Mark Lemke	Bama Rowell
Bill Anderson	Gary Eave	Max Leon	Ed Rowen
Stan Andrews	Derrin Ebert	Don G. Leppert	Normie Roy
Elvis Andrus	Ox Eckhardt	Anthony Lerew	Chico M. Ruiz
Bill Annis	John Edelman	John Leroy	Paul Runge
Johnny Antonelli	Foster Edwards	Fred M. Lewis	Jarrod Saltalamacchia
Maurice Archdeacon	Dave Eilers	Ted Lewis	Clint Sammons
Jamie Arnold	Glenn Elliott	Don Liddle	Amado Samuel
Jose Ascanio	Rowdy Elliott	Derek Lilliquist	Mike Sandlock
Tom Asmussen	Bob Emmerich	Rufino Linares	Al Santorini
Brian Asselstine	John Ennis	Em Lindbeck	Rob Sasser
Paul Assenmacher	Dick Errickson	Ernie Lindemann	Johnny Scalzi
Luis Atilano	Yunel Escobar	Walt Linden	Hal Schacker
Harry Aubrey	Chuck Estrada	Carl Lindquist	Jordan Schafer
Steve Avery	Buck Etchison	Jeff Locke	Al Schellhase
Luis Avilan	Chick Evans	Johnny Logan	Jason Schmidt
Joe Ayrault	Kerby Farrell	Jack Lohrke	Dan Schneider
Bill Bagwell	Gus Felix	George Lombard	Ron Schueler
Fred Bailey	Neftali Feliz	Kevin Lomon	Jack Schulte
Harvey Bailey	Nanny Fernandez	Red Long	Joe Schultz
Dusty Baker	Lou Fette	Bruce Look	Carl Schutz
Mike Balas	Hank Fischer	Javy Lopez	Art Schwind
Lee Bales	Brian Fisher	Bobby Lowe	Chris Seelbach
Jim Ball	Tom C. Fisher	Fletcher Low	Rube Sellers
Bill Banks	Charlie Fitzberger	Mike Lum	Frank Sexton
Frank Barberich	Ed Fitzpatrick	Fernando Lunar	Joe Shannon
Brian Bark	Elbie Fletcher	Dolf Luque	Red Shannon
Jesse Barnes	Tyler Flowers	Alejandro Machado	Bud Sharpe
George Barnicle	Curry Foley	Mike Macha	Steve Shemo
Marty F. Barrett	Bill Ford	Ken Mackenzie	Jason Shiell
Red Barron	Gene M. Ford	Harry Macpherson	Vince Shupe
Kevin Barry	Hod Ford	Kid Madden	Oscar Siemer
Doc Bass	Wenty Ford	Tommy Madden	Andrelton Simmons
Joe Batchelder	John Foster	Jerry Maddox	Mike Simon
Johnny Bates	Leo Foster	Mickey Mahler	Randall Simon
Rafael Batista	John Fox	Rick Mahler	Matt Sinatro
Brandon Beachy	Terry Fox	Mike G. Mahoney	Hosea Siner
Mike Beard	Jeff Francoeur	Mike J. Mahoney	Sibby Sisti
Fred Beck	Freddie Freeman	Bobby Malkmus	Roe Skidmore
Howie Bedell	Jimmy Freeman	Marty Malloy	Lou Sleater
Steve Bedrosian	Charlie Frisbee	Charlie Maloney	Hank Small
Rick Behenna	Sam Frock	Jim H. Manning	Bob E. Smith
Matt Belisle	John Fuller	Les Mann	Bobby Smith
Mike A. Bell	Rafael Furcal	Don Manno	Edgar (AE) Smith
Rob Bell	Len G. Gabrielson	Felix Mantilla	Fred V. Smith
Bruce Benedict	Gil Gallagher	Dick Manville	Ken Smith
Marty Bergen	Daff Gammons	Paul Marak	Stub Smith
Wally Berger	Ron Gant	Georges Maranda	Tom Smith

Wilson Betemit	Adrian Garrett	Rabbit Maranville	Zane Smith
Christian Bethancourt	Wayne Garrett	Jason Marquis	Scott Sobkowiak
Vern Bickford	Ralph Garr	Luis Marquez	Bill Southworth
Ethan Blackaby	Jim Garry	Andy Marte	Bill Sowders
Al Blanche	Cito Gaston	Al Martin	Warren Spahn
Gregor Blanco	Evan Gattis	Billy G. Martin	Al Spangler
Kevin Blankenship	Cory Gearrin	Hector Martinez	Chet Spencer
Larvell Blanks	Pete Gebrian	Ray Martin	Ed Sperber
Wade Blasingame	Joe Genewich	Mike Massey	Tim Spooneybarger
Jeff Blauser	Sam Gentile	Roy Massey	Harry Spratt
Ray Boggs	George Gerberman	Eddie Mathews	Zeke Spruill
Jung Bong	Lefty Gervais	Pascual Matos	Chick Stahl
J. C. Boscan	Gus Getz	Al Mattern	Mike W. Stanton
Bob Botz	Bob Giggie	Joe Matthews	Fred Stem
Jake Boultes	Larry Gilbert	Rick Matula	Bill Stemmeyer
Micah Bowie	Rod Gilbreath	Larry Maxie	Adam Stern
Blaine Boyer	Marcus Giles	Darrell May	Joe Stewart
Buzz Boyle	Billy Ging	Lee Maye	Milt Stock
Larry Bradford	Ed Giovanola	Gene McAuliffe	George H. Stone
Foghorn Bradley	Roland Gladu	Macay McBride	Paul Strand
Bill Brady	Tom Glavine	Brian McCann	Oscar Streit
Bob Brady	Hal Goldsmith	Bill J. McCarthy	Allie Strobel
Ed Brandt	Mike A. Gonzalez	Bill T. McCarthy	Dutch Stryker
Kitty Bransfield	Gene Good	Roger McCardell	George Stultz
John Braun	Ralph Good	Jeff McCleskey	Jesus Sucre
Garland Braxton	Charlie Gorin	Hal McClure	Andy Sullivan
Buster Bray	Johnny Goryl	Ed McDonald	Billy Sullivan
Jim Breazeale	Philip Gosselin	Frank McElyea	Jim D. Sullivan
Hal Breeden	Tony Graffanino	Dan McGann	John L. Sullivan
Tony Brizzolara	Skinny K. Graham	Dan McGee	Butch Sutcliffe
Chris Brock	Sid Graves	Kevin McGlinchy	Pedro Swann
Steve Brodie	Nick Green	Joey McLaughlin	John Taber
Sig Broskie	Tommy Greene	Ralph McLeod	Roy Talcott
Andrew A. Brown	Buddy Gremp	Don McMahon	Chuck Tanner
Bob Brown	Tommy Griffith	Craig McMurtry	Tony Tarasco
Drummond Brown	George Grossart	Dinny McNamara	Pop Tate
Fred Brown	Skip Guinn	Tim McNamara	Aaron Taylor
Kevin D. Brown	Tom Gunning	Ed McNichol	Ed J. Taylor
Lew Brown	Bucky Guth	Mike McQueen	Hawk Taylor
Oscar Brown	Dick Gyselman	Hugh McQuillan	Sammy Taylor
Roosevelt Brown	Mert Hackett	Bill McTigue	Julio Teheran
Sam Brown	Dad Hale	Larry McWilliams	Fred Tenney
Bruce Brubaker	David Hale	Kris Medlen	Joey Terdoslavich
Bob Brush	Albert Hall	Denis Menke	Duane Theiss
Bill Bruton	Steve Hammond	Kent Mercker	Bert Thiel
Francisley Bueno	Vern Handrahan	Dan L. Meyer	Andres Thomas
Art Bues	Harry Hanebrink	Tom Miller	Charles Thomas
Charlie Buffinton	Preston Hanna	Art Mills	Herb Thomas
Joe Burg	Tommy Hanson	Kevin Millwood	Walt Thomas
Billy Burke	Dick H. Harley	Zach Miner	Fuller Thompson
Joe J, Burns	Terry Harper	Mike Minor	Milt Thompson
Adam Butler	Dave Harris	Keith Mitchell	Tommy R. Thompson
Art Butler	Joe Harrington	Junior Moore	Scott Thorman
Brett Butler	Matt Harrison	Hiker Moran	Bob R. Thorpe
Cecil Butler	Bob Hartman	Pat Moran	Andy Tomberlin
Bill Calhoun	Roy Hartsfield	Mike Mordecai	Earl Torgeson
Joe Callahan	Bill Hawes	Cy A. Morgan	Red Torphy

Jack Cameron	Scott Hawley	Joe M. Morgan	Frank Torre
Dave A. Campbell	Hal Haydel	Ed Moriarty	Joe Torre
Jorge Campillo	Bunny E. Hearn	Gene Moriarity	Pablo Torrealba
Rick Camp	Deunte Heath	Dan Morogiello	Steve Torrealba
Hugh Canavan	Ken Heintzelman	Jim Moroney	Clay Touchstone
Barbaro Canizares	Wes Helms	Guy Morrison	Ira Townsend
Rip Cannell	Heinie Heltzel	John Morrill	Leo Townsend
Jose Capellan	Bob Hendley	Carl Morton	Walt Tragesser
Pat Capri	Don Hendrickson	Charlie A. Morton	Sam Trott
Ramon Caraballo	Ellie Hendricks	Damian Moss	Bob Trowbridge
Ben Cardoni	Ron Henry	Joe Mowry	Greg Tubbs
Eddie Carnett	Al Hermann	Ray Mueller	Tommy Tucker
Pat Carney	Remy Hermoso	Joe Muich	Tom Tuckey
Clay Carroll	Diory Hernandez	Buzz Murphy	Jim Turner
Dixie Carroll	Luis Hernandez	Dave Murphy	Matt Turner
Rico Carty	Ed Herrmann	Dale Murphy	Fred Tyler
Vinny Castilla	Rick Herrscher	Frank Murphy	Johnnie Tyler
Ramon A. Castro	Earl Hersh	Amby Murray	Lefty Tyler
Rome Chambers	Frank Hershey	Matt Murray	Jim Tyng
Jaye Chapman	Mike Hessman	Joey Nation	Bob Uecker
Bill Chappelle	Jason Heyward	Tom Needham	Mike Ulisney
Ed Charles	Jim Hickey	Art Nehf	Arnold Umbach
Buster Chatham	Mike Hickey	Gary Neibauer	Jim Umbricht
Bruce Chen	Charlie Hickman	Tommy Neill	Cecil Upshaw
Lloyd Christenbury	Brandon Hicks	Joe Nelson	Billy Urbanski
Buzz Clarkson	Bill Higgins	Tommy Nelson	Luke Urban
Earl Clark	Garry Hill	Chet Nichols, Jr.	Merkin Valdez
Glen Clark	Oliver Hill	Kid Nichols	Bill Vargus
Marty Clary	Mike Hines	David Nied	Charlie Vaughan
Chet Clemens	John Hinton	Phil Niekro	Al Veigel
Paul Clemens	Herb Hippauf	Melvin Nieves	Jonny Venters
Tony Cloninger	Trey Hodges	Jake Northrop	Gene Verble
Brad Clontz	Ralph Hodgin	Don Nottebart	Tony Von Fricken
Gene Cocreham	George Hodson	Win Noyes	Brad Voyles
Jack Coffey	Stew Hofferth	Dizzy Nutter	Phil Voyles
Kevin Coffman	Shanty Hogan	Charlie Nyce	Tom Waddell
Ed Cogswell	Brad Hogg	Brett Oberholtzer	Terrell Wade
Dave Cole	Dutch Holland	Rowland Office	Adam Wainwright
Willie Collazo	Damon Hollins	Joe Ogrodowski	Lefty Wallace
Don Collins	Abie Hood	Kid O'Hara	Murray Wall
Jimmy Collins	J. J. Hoover	Chi-Chi Olivo	Bucky Walters
Wilson Collins	Bob Horner	Jess Orndorff	Duane Ward
Bill Collver	Sadie Houck	Frank O'Rourke	John Warner
Roman Colon	Pat House	John O'Rourke	Link Wasem
Clint Compton	Tom House	Tom O'Rourke	Chris Waters
Gene Conley	Tyler Houston	Pete Orr	Bert Weeden
Jocko Conlon	Walt Hriniak	Jimmy Osting	Roy Weir
Frank Connaughton	Glenn Hubbard	Larry Owen	Jimmy Welsh
John Connor	Otto Huber	Ernie Padgett	Turk Wendell
Rip Conway	Brian R. Hunter	James Parr	Stan Wentzel
Bill Cooney	Ron Hunt	Charlie Parsons	Johnny Werts
Johnny Cooney	Jerry J. Hurley	Gene Patton	Jim Wessinger
Gary N. Cooper	George Jackson	Mike Payne	Oscar Westerberg
David Cortes	Brook Jacoby	Brayan Pena	Frank West
Joe Coscarart	Bernie James	Tony Francisco Pena	Max E. West
Humberto Cota	Bill L. James	Henry Peploski	Al Weston
Ernie Courtney	Chuck James	Hub Perdue	Jeff Wetherby

Dee Cousineau
Wes Covington
Joe Cowley
Bill Coyle
Charlie Cozart
Del Crandall
Connie Creeden
Fred Crolius
Chris Cron
Ray Crone
Bill Cronin
George Crowe
Cal Crum
Dick Crutcher
Todd Cunningham
Sammy Curran
Bill Currie
Cliff Curtis
Jim Czajkowski
John Dagenhard
Bill Daley
Clay Dalrymple
Bill Dam
Jack Daniels
Alvin Dark
Mike Davey
Kyle Davies
Ken Dayley
Pat Deasley
Jeff Dedmon
Randall Delgado
John DeMerit
Drew Denson
Mark DeRosa
Rube Dessau
Ducky Detweiler
Adrian Devine
Joey Devine
Rex DeVogt
Scott Diamond
Bob Didier
George Diehl
Steve Dignan
Vince DiMaggio
Jack Dittmer
Cozy P. Dolan
Art Doll
Ed Donnelly
Bill Donovan
Dick Donovan
Patsy Donovan
Bill Dreesen

Al Javery
Joey Jay
Virgil Jester
German Jimenez
Manny Jimenez
Art H. Johnson
Ben F. Johnson
Ernie T. Johnson
Joe Johnson
Kelly Johnson
Andruw Jones
Bill Jones
Brandon Jones
Chipper Jones
Garrett Jones
Mack Jones
David Justice
Owen Kahn
Ike Kamp
Tom Kane
Kenshin Kawakami
Dick Kelley
Joe Kelley
Mike R. Kelly
Van Kelly
Art Kenney
Rick Kester
Hod Kibbie
Craig Kimbrel
Ryan Klesko
Fred Klobedanz
Billy Klusman
Bobby Knoop
Fritz Knothe
Joe Knotts
Brad Komminsk
George Kopacz
Joe Koppe
Brian Kowitz
Ben Kozlowski
Jimmy Kremers
Steve Kuczek
Frank LaCorte
Fred Lake
Frank LaManna
Henry Lampe
Hunter Lane
Jerry Lane
Ryan Langerhans
Johnny Lanning
Gene Lansing
Adam LaRoche

Eddie Perez
Odalis Perez
Gerald Perry
Eddie D. Phillips
Taylor Phillips
Ron Piche
Dave Pickett
Jack Pierce
Al Pierotti
Andy Pilney
Togie Pittinger
Juan Pizarro
Biff Pocoroba
Dale Polley
Bob Porter
Leo Posada
Mike Potts
Martin Prado
Billy Queen
Ruben Quevedo
Joe Quinn
Paul Radford
Horacio Ramirez
Max Ramirez
Rafael Ramirez
Merritt Ranew
Bill Rariden
Cory Rasmus
Curt Raydon
Irv Ray
Claude Raymond
Ron Reed
Earl Reid
Carlos Reyes
Jo-Jo Reyes
Armando Reynoso
Dennis Ribant
Rusty Richards
Lee Richmond
Art Rico
Jim J. Riley
Ray Rippelmeyer
Ben Rivera
Luis G. Rivera
Mickey Rivers
Mel Roach
Joe Roa
Mike Roarke
Curt Roberts
Skippy Roberge
Bill Robinson
Humberto Robinson

Bert Whaling
Bobby Wheelock
Tom Whelan
Larry Whisenton
Pete Whisenant
Bob Whitcher
George Whiteman
Gil Whitehouse
Jack W. White
Sam White
Sean White
Will White
Frank Whitney
Jim Whitney
Whitey Wietelmann
Claude Wilborn
Hoyt Wilhelm
Joe Wilhoit
Carl Willey
Ace Williams
Earl B. Williams
Earl C. Williams
Glenn Williams
Vic Willis
Charlie Wilson
Frank Wilson
Jimmie Wilson
Zeke Wilson
Joe Winkelsas
Nick Wise
Roy Witherup
Corky Withrow
Mark Wohlers
Sid Womack
Brad Woodall
Alex Wood
George Woodend
Woody Woodward
Red Worthington
Al Wright
Ed Wright
Ron Wright
Esteban Yan
George Yeager
Al Yeargin
Herman Young
Irv Young
Matt E. Young
Steve Ziem
Paul Zuvella

Year/Team	OPW%	PW	PL	APW%	AW	AL	Diff+/-
1969 SE1	0.000 F	0	0	0.395	64	98	0.000
1970 MIL	0.000 F	0	0	0.401	65	97	0.000
1971 MIL	0.000 F	0	0	0.429	69	92	0.000
1972 MIL	0.000 F	0	0	0.417	65	91	0.000
1973 MIL	0.490 F	79	83	0.457	74	88	-0.033
1974 MIL	0.493 F	80	82	0.469	76	86	-0.024
1975 MIL	0.494 F	80	82	0.420	68	94	-0.075
1976 MIL	0.482 F	78	84	0.410	66	95	-0.072
1977 MIL	0.407 F	66	96	0.414	67	95	0.006
1978 MIL	0.531	86	76	0.574	93	69	0.043
1979 MIL	0.554 D	90	72	0.590	95	66	0.036

franchID	OWAR	OWS	AWAR	AWS	WARdiff	WSdiff	P/D/W/F
1969 SE1	20.003	42.561	26.536	191.992	-6.532	-149.430	F
1970 MIL	-107.573	0.000	26.169	195.005	-133.742	-195.005	F
1971 MIL	11.699	135.054	23.681	206.998	-11.982	-71.944	F
1972 MIL	4.252	112.641	19.987	195.001	-15.735	-82.360	F
1973 MIL	21.299	162.556	31.326	221.998	-10.026	-59.441	F
1974 MIL	19.347	172.534	27.476	227.996	-8.129	-55.462	F
1975 MIL	20.223	178.764	23.386	203.999	-3.163	-25.235	F
1976 MIL	19.266	171.045	21.923	197.996	-2.658	-26.951	F
1977 MIL	18.523	156.281	23.192	200.995	-4.669	-44.714	F
1978 MIL	33.572	199.373	**49.491**	278.999	-15.919	-79.626	
1979 MIL	**43.663**	**251.384**	45.505	284.998	-1.842	-33.614	D

Legend: (P) = Pennant / Most Wins in League (D) = Division Winner (W) = Wild Card Winner (F) = Failed to Qualify

The Brewers franchise has existed since 1969. One of four expansion entries, the team joined the American League as the Seattle Pilots. On the heels of the club's lone season in Seattle, the team was sold to a group of investors from Milwaukee including Bud Selig. The club was relocated to Wisconsin and renamed the Brewers. When MLB expanded again in 1998, Selig decided to shift the Brewers to the National League in order to maintain an even number of teams in both leagues. The Brewers developed the second-most left fielders (based on WS>20 seasons) among the "Expansion" teams.

Bill Parsons placed second in the 1971 AL Rookie of the Year voting as he delivered 13 victories and a 3.20 ERA. Jim Slaton contributed 10 wins and a 3.78 ERA in '71 and then averaged 12 wins and a 3.81 ERA from 1973-77. Darrell Porter (.254/16/67) finished third in the AL ROY balloting in '73. Porter led the circuit with 121 bases on balls while posting a .290 BA with 20 jacks and 112 ribbies in 1979. Eighteen-year-old shortstop Robin Yount debuted in '74. "The Kid" drilled 34 doubles in 1977 and batted at a .293 clip during the following campaign. Bill Travers yielded a 15-16 record with a 2.81 ERA, earning a trip to the All-Star game in '76.

GM Harry Dalton presided over the most successful run in Brewers' history. Milwaukee achieved five playoff appearances during Dalton's tenure (1978-1991). Under the direction of Dalton and Scouting Director Dan Duquette, Milwaukee's draft choices in 1986 earned the highest Career Total Win Shares (750) and Career Total WAR (101) in team annals. On the other hand Dalton's draft picks failed to accumulate 100 Career Total Win Shares for three straight seasons (1988-1990).

The Indians edged out the Brewers for the American League Eastern division crown in '78. Paul "The Ignitor" Molitor batted .273 with 30 stolen bases and finished second in the 1978 AL ROY voting. Molitor sparked the offense with a .322 average, 16 triples and 33 stolen bases in

'79. Gorman Thomas crushed 32 round-trippers for the '78 squad and then clubbed 45 moon-shots while plating 123 baserunners in the ensuing year. Lary Sorensen posted an 18-12 record, 3.21 ERA and 1.165 WHIP, punching a ticket to his lone All-Star appearance. Bill Castro saved 8 games and fashioned a 1.81 ERA.

Milwaukee compiled 90 victories en route to its first division title in '79 as the Brew Crew outlasted the Red Sox by four games. Sixto Lezcano's breakout campaign included a Gold Glove Award along with personal-bests in batting average (.321), home runs (28) and RBI (101).

Year/Team	OPW%	PW	PL	APW%	AW	AL	Diff+/-
1980 MIL	0.576 D	93	69	0.531	86	76	-0.045
1981 MIL	0.510 F	83	79	0.569 D	62	47	0.059
1982 MIL	0.542	88	74	0.586 P	95	67	0.044
1983 MIL	0.543	88	74	0.537	87	75	-0.006
1984 MIL	0.428	69	93	0.416	67	94	-0.012
1985 MIL	0.477	77	85	0.441	71	90	-0.036
1986 MIL	0.466	75	87	0.478	77	84	0.012
1987 MIL	0.555 P	90	72	0.562	91	71	0.006
1988 MIL	0.528	86	76	0.537	87	75	0.009
1989 MIL	0.538 D	87	75	0.500	81	81	-0.038

franchID	OWAR	OWS	AWAR	AWS	WARdiff	WSdiff	P/D/W/F
1980 MIL	38.754	218.546	47.629	258.000	-8.875	-39.454	D
1981 MIL	24.807	165.921	25.300	186.001	-0.492	-20.081	F
1982 MIL	46.034	252.422	49.286	284.992	-3.252	-32.570	
1983 MIL	40.591	238.376	41.141	261.000	-0.550	-22.624	
1984 MIL	21.409	172.486	25.299	200.998	-3.891	-28.512	
1985 MIL	22.978	193.422	24.653	212.999	-1.675	-19.577	
1986 MIL	28.939	196.411	32.568	231.000	-3.629	-34.590	
1987 MIL	46.168	258.094	44.628	272.999	1.540	-14.904	P
1988 MIL	38.508	251.227	36.548	261.002	1.961	-9.775	
1989 MIL	41.332	262.923	34.979	243.006	6.353	19.917	D

The reigning AL East champions ran away with the crown in '80, besting the Tigers by eleven games. Moose Haas furnished a 3.10 ERA and 16 wins (both career-bests) along with a 1.197 WHIP. In 1983 Haas provided a record of 13-3 with a 3.27 ERA in 25 starts. Thomas belted 38 big-flies and surpassed the 100-RBI mark in 1980; he then dialed long-distance 39 times while plating 112 baserunners during the 1982 campaign.

Yount set a career-high with 49 doubles, scored 121 runs and made his first All-Star appearance in 1980. He collected his first MVP and Gold Glove Awards in 1982, establishing personal bests in batting average (.331), home runs (29) and RBI (114) while leading the League with 210 hits, 46 doubles and a .578 SLG. "The Kid" contributed a .312 BA with 21 jacks, 103 RBI and 19 steals in '87 and produced comparable numbers when he claimed 1989 AL MVP honors.

Milwaukee's moundsmen failed to reach the 2700 BFP requirement in 1981. The Brew Crew battled Baltimore for the AL East title in 1982 with the Orioles emerging victorious by a single game. Molitor (.302/19/71) scored 136 times, collected 201 base hits and pilfered 41 bases. He batted at a .353 clip, swiped 45 bags and led the League with 114 runs scored and 41 doubles while placing fifth in the 1987 AL MVP voting. Molitor (.312/13/60) scored 115 runs and pilfered 41 bags for the '88 squad.

The Brewers finished in second place, 10 games behind the Orioles in '83. Slaton won 14 games in relief while portsider Frank DiPino delivered 20 saves, a 2.65 ERA and a 1.009 WHIP as a rookie closer. Molitor missed all but 13 games in 1984 due to injury, contributing heavily to the Brewers' descent into last place.

Teddy Higuera (15-8, 3.90) placed second in the 1985 AL ROY voting. Higuera (20-11, 2.79) finished second in the 1986 AL Cy Young balloting. He struck out 240 batsmen and compiled 18 victories in '87 and during the subsequent campaign posted a 16-9 record with a 2.45 ERA while leading the League in WHIP (0.999). Dan Plesac bolstered the bullpen with 10 wins and 14 saves in his rookie year (1986); he then teamed with Chuck Crim to save 35 games in '87. Kevin Bass batted .311 with 20 blasts and 22 stolen bases.

The Brewers secured the franchise's first pennant in 1987. Dale Sveum belted 25 round-trippers and drove in 95 runs in his first full season but never approached those totals again in his 12-year career. Dion James supplied a .312 batting average along with 37 doubles. Milwaukee finished in third place, four games behind Boston in '88. Doug Jones (2.27, 37 SV) entered the late-inning mix while Plesac (2.41, 30 SV) continued to be effective from the left side. Jeff Parrett (12-4, 2.65) and Crim (2.91, 9 SV) added to the bullpen's success. The '89 Brewers claimed the AL East, concluding the season six games ahead of the Red Sox. Chris Bosio (15-10, 2.95) assumed the role of staff ace.

Year/Team	OPW%	PW	PL	APW%	AW	AL	Diff+/-
1990 MIL	0.516	84	78	0.457	74	88	-0.059
1991 MIL	0.574 D	93	69	0.512	83	79	-0.062
1992 MIL	0.587 P	95	67	0.568	92	70	-0.020
1993 MIL	0.504	82	80	0.426	69	93	-0.078
1994 MIL	0.496	80	82	0.461	53	62	-0.036
1995 MIL	0.533 W	86	76	0.451	65	79	-0.082
1996 MIL	0.525	85	77	0.494	80	82	-0.031
1997 MIL	0.448	73	89	0.484	78	83	0.036
1998 MIL	0.513	83	79	0.457	74	88	-0.056
1999 MIL	0.476	77	85	0.460	74	87	-0.017
franchID	OWAR	OWS	AWAR	AWS	WARdiff	WSdiff	P/D/W/F
1990 MIL	32.983	227.727	32.609	222.002	0.374	5.726	
1991 MIL	39.784	258.992	37.216	248.995	2.568	9.996	D
1992 MIL	48.297	290.782	42.871	275.994	5.426	14.788	P
1993 MIL	33.806	247.255	24.253	206.999	9.553	40.257	
1994 MIL	21.515	163.846	19.691	159.003	1.825	4.844	
1995 MIL	30.995	216.052	23.695	194.998	7.300	21.055	W
1996 MIL	38.040	271.487	31.682	240.005	6.358	31.482	
1997 MIL	34.358	271.020	28.555	234.005	5.802	37.015	
1998 MIL	30.901	238.180	27.048	222.005	3.853	16.175	
1999 MIL	34.490	235.598	31.530	221.998	2.960	13.600	

The Brew Crew chugged home in third place, 3 games behind the Blue Jays despite a career-high 43 saves from Doug Jones in 1990. Milwaukee seized the division crown in '91 by 8 games over Detroit despite the collapse at the back end of the bullpen. Jones and Plesac lost their mojo, opening the door for Doug Henry (1.00, 15 SV). Jones returned to form one year later, supplying 11 wins, 36 saves and a 1.85 ERA while Henry chipped in with 29 saves. Jones allowed only 9 bases on balls in '97 and compiled 36 saves with a 2.02 ERA and a 0.884 WHIP!

Molitor supplied a .325 BA and led the AL with 133 runs scored, 216 hits and 13 triples in '91. He finished second in the 1993 AL MVP race, batting .332 with 22 jacks, 111 ribbies and 121 runs while pacing the circuit with 211 base hits. Molitor (.341/9/113) topped the circuit with 225 base knocks in '96 and averaged .313 with 33 two-baggers from 1990-98.

The Brewers captured the AL pennant with 95 victories in 1992, finishing 8 games ahead of the Yankees. The rotation included Jaime Navarro (17-11, 3.33), Bosio (16-6, 3.62) and Bill Wegman (13-14, 3.20). Rookie hurler Cal Eldred achieved an 11-2 record with a microscopic 1.79

ERA and 0.987 WHIP in 14 starts. Pat Listach received 1992 AL ROY honors, batting .290 and nabbing 54 bags while Darryl Hamilton pilfered 41 bases.

Gary Sheffield (.330/33/100) earned a batting title and placed third in the 1992 AL MVP voting. "Sheff" supplied a .314 BA with 42 round-trippers and 120 RBI while drawing 142 free passes and topping the League with a .465 OBP. New York edged Milwaukee for the AL East title in '93. MLB increased the number of divisions per league and the Brewers became a member of the American League Central division in 1994. The Royals seized the Central by six games over the Brew Crew. Milwaukee won 86 contests and secured the Wild Card entry in 1995. Jaime Navarro produced a 14-6 record with a 3.28 ERA following two sub-par campaigns in which his combined ERA approached 6.00. B.J. Surhoff established a personal-best with a .320 BA. Surhoff (.308/28/107) set career-highs in home runs, RBI, hits (207) and runs (104) in '99.

The White Sox triumphed over the Brewers for the Wild Card in '96 by a single game. Aussie backstop Dave Nilsson provided a .331 BA with 84 RBI while John Jaha blasted 34 circuit clouts and plated 118 baserunners. Jaha belted 35 four-baggers and knocked in 111 runs in '99. Greg Vaughn swatted 41 quadruples and drove in 117 runs. He clouted 50 round-trippers and knocked in 119 baserunners en route to a fourth-place finish in the 1998 NL MVP balloting and then walloped 45 long balls and drove in 118 runs in the ensuing season. Vaughn crushed 30 round-trippers per season from 1991-99.

Jeff Cirillo produced a .317 BA with 40 two-base knocks per year from 1996-2001. The Brewers descended into the basement in the team's final season in the American League. Milwaukee became the first franchise to switch leagues in the modern era when the club was transferred to the National League Central division prior to the 1998 season. Milwaukee sunk to last place in the NL Central in 1999 as the moundsmen posted franchise-worsts in pitWARnorm (6) and pitWSnorm (40).

Year/Team	OPW%	PW	PL	APW%	AW	AL	Diff+/-
2000 MIL	0.519 W	84	78	0.451	73	89	-0.069
2001 MIL	0.463	75	87	0.420	68	94	-0.044
2002 MIL	0.350 F	57	105	0.346	56	106	-0.004
2003 MIL	0.474 F	77	85	0.420	68	94	-0.055
2004 MIL	0.510 F	83	79	0.416	67	94	-0.094
2005 MIL	0.572 F	93	69	0.500	81	81	-0.072
2006 MIL	0.492 F	80	82	0.463	75	87	-0.029
2007 MIL	0.616 F	100	62	0.512	83	79	-0.104
2008 MIL	0.560 F	91	71	0.556 W	90	72	-0.004
2009 MIL	0.536 F	87	75	0.494	80	82	-0.042
2010 MIL	0.561 F	91	71	0.475	77	85	-0.086
2011 MIL	0.630 F	102	60	0.593 D	96	66	-0.038
2012 MIL	0.572 F	93	69	0.512	83	79	-0.059
2013 MIL	0.477	77	85	0.457	74	88	-0.020

franchID	OWAR	OWS	AWAR	AWS	WARdiff	WSdiff	P/D/W/F
2000 MIL	38.866	247.860	24.014	219.004	14.852	28.856	W
2001 MIL	28.448	205.359	27.355	204.003	1.094	1.356	
2002 MIL	12.163	148.241	19.175	168.003	-7.011	-19.762	F
2003 MIL	39.856	241.849	28.085	204.002	11.771	37.847	F
2004 MIL	47.484	264.829	33.178	201.000	14.306	63.829	F
2005 MIL	47.078	296.047	40.025	243.000	7.054	53.046	F
2006 MIL	32.805	265.558	33.344	225.002	-0.539	40.556	F
2007 MIL	50.718	325.918	44.214	248.994	6.504	76.924	F
2008 MIL	37.487	261.180	42.001	270.001	-4.514	-8.821	F
2009 MIL	40.038	277.886	32.664	239.998	7.374	37.889	F
2010 MIL	42.827	278.207	39.697	231.000	3.130	47.207	F

2011 MIL	59.407	368.667	47.746	288.005	11.660	80.662	F
2012 MIL	51.383	304.862	31.522	248.994	19.861	55.867	F
2013 MIL	38.416	254.089	28.310	222.004	10.106	32.085	

The Brew Crew managed 84 victories in 2000 to clinch the NL Wild Card. Sheffield belted a career-best 43 home runs while batting .325 with 109 ribbies. He placed runner-up in the MVP voting in 2004 after finishing third in the prior season. "Sheff" averaged .304 with 36 round-trippers and 125 RBI from 2003-05. Cirillo posted his second consecutive .326 BA and set career marks with 53 doubles, 111 runs scored and 115 RBI. Geoff Jenkins jacked 34 big-flies and crossed home plate 100 times in 2000. From 2003-05 he averaged .283 with 27 quadruples and 91 RBI.

Steve W. Sparks harnessed his knuckler and delivered a 14-9 record with a 3.65 ERA in '01. The Brewers' offense fell short of the 4000 PA requirement in 2002. The mound crew tapped out and failed to reach 4000 BFP from 2003-2012. Ben Sheets struck out 264 batters in 237 innings and produced a stellar WHIP (0.983) to complement a 2.70 ERA in 2004. He posted 13 wins along with a 3.09 ERA and 1.150 WHIP in '08.

Mark Loretta batted .335 with 16 dingers and 76 ribbies while amassing 208 hits and scoring 108 runs in '04. Ron Belliard earned an All-Star nod in 2004, batting .282 with 48 doubles. He jacked 17 homers and knocked in 78 runs in '05. Bill Hall produced a career year in 2006, belting 35 round-trippers and scoring 101 runs. Prince Fielder blasted 28 long balls in his rookie season and then led the National League with a 50-homer campaign in '07. He pounded 46 four-baggers and knocked in 141 runs on the way to a third-place finish in the 2009 NL MVP race. Fielder produced 33 doubles, 35 big-flies and drove in 108 baserunners per season from 2006-2013.

Ryan J. Braun (.324/34/97) received NL Rookie of the Year honors in 2007 after leading the League with a .634 SLG. "The Hebrew Hammer" averaged .313 with 34 circuit clouts, 107 RBI and 21 stolen bases from 2007-2012 including a league-best 203 base hits in '09. Braun (.332/33/111) achieved MVP honors in 2011; he then paced the NL with 41 dingers and 108 runs scored in the ensuing season. J.J. Hardy walloped 50 home runs and Corey Hart provided consecutive 20-20 seasons over a two-year period (2007-08). Hart belted 31 four-ply swats and plated 102 runners while Rickie Weeks scored 112 runs and smacked 29 taters in 2010. Yovani Gallardo topped the 200-strikeout mark in four successive seasons (2009-2012).

Win Shares > 20	Single-Season	1969-2013
Prince Fielder - 1B (MIL) x5	Gary Sheffield - 3B (MIL)	Sixto Lezcano - RF (MIL) x2
Paul Molitor - 2B (MIL)	Jeff Cirillo - 3B (MIL) x3	Gorman Thomas - RF (MIL)
Jim Gantner - 2B (MIL)	Ryan J. Braun - 3B (MIL)	Kevin Bass - RF (MIL)
Mark Loretta - 2B (MIL) x2	Darrell Porter - C (MIL) x2	Gary Sheffield - RF (MIL) x7
Rickie Weeks - 2B (MIL)	Greg Vaughn - LF (MIL) x3	Geoff Jenkins - RF (MIL)
Robin Yount - SS (MIL) x5	Gary Sheffield - LF (MIL) x3	Corey Hart - RF (MIL) x3
Pat Listach - SS (MIL)	Geoff Jenkins - LF (MIL)	Paul Molitor - DH (MIL) x4
Bill Hall - SS (MIL)	Ryan J. Braun - LF (MIL) x5	John Jaha - DH (MIL)
J.J. Hardy - SS (MIL) x2	Gorman Thomas - CF (MIL) x3	Teddy Higuera - SP (MIL) x2
Paul Molitor - 3B (MIL) x5	Robin Yount - CF (MIL) x4	Ben Sheets - SP (MIL)

Note: 4000 PA or BFP to qualify, except during strike-shortened seasons
(1972 = 3800, 1981 & 1994 = 2700, 1995 = 3500) and 154-game schedule (3800)
- failed to qualify: 1969-1977, 1981, 2002-2009

Pilots / Brewers All-Time "Originals" Roster

Mike J. Adams	Alcides Escobar	Dave Krynzel	Ray Peters
Jay Aldrich	Horacio Estrada	Dave LaPoint	Dan Plesac
Drew Anderson	Dana Eveland	Matt LaPorta	Carlos Ponce

Larry Anderson
Norichika Aoki
Rick Auerbach
Jerry Augustine
Brian Banks
Kevin Barker
Chris Barnwell
Kevin Bass
Billy Bates
Gary Beare
Andy Beene
Ron Belliard
Jerry Bell
Tommy Bianco
Mike Birkbeck
Frank Bolick
Chris Bosio
Steve Bowling
Marshall Boze
Zach Braddock
Glenn Braggs
Michael Brantley
Ryan J. Braun
Craig Breslow
Hiram Burgos
Lorenzo Cain
George Canale
Robinson Cancel
Juan Castillo
Bill Castro
Jason Childers
Matt Childers
Mark Ciardi
Jeff Cirillo
Bryan Clutterbuck
Jaime Cocanower
Bob Coluccio
Carlos Corporan
Barry Cort
Callix Crabbe
Tim Crews
Chuck Crim
Jeff C. D'Amico
Dick Davis
Khris Davis
Valerio de los Santos
Edgar Diaz
Tim Dillard
Frank DiPino
Brian Drahman
Todd Dunn
Butch Edge
Cal Eldred
Rob Ellis
Narciso Elvira
Greg Erardi

Eric Farris
Mike Felder
Prince Fielder
Mike Fiers
Darren Ford
George Frazier
La Vel Freeman
Eric Fryer
Miguel Fuentes
Yovani Gallardo
Mat Gamel
Jim Gantner
Pedro Garcia
Scooter Gennett
Chris S. George
Bob L. Gibson
Cole Gillespie
Caleb Gindl
Fernando Gonzalez
David Green
Taylor Green
Tony Gwynn, Jr.
Moose Haas
Bill Hall
Sean Halton
Darryl Hamilton
Donovan Hand
Bob Hansen
J.J. Hardy
Corey Hart
Tom Hausman
Bert Heffernan
Ben Hendrickson
Doug Henry
Teddy Higuera
Sam Hinds
Gary Holle
Wilbur Howard
Bobby Hughes
Mike Ignasiak
Hernan Iribarren
Bucky Jacobsen
John Jaha
Dion James
Jeremy Jeffress
Geoff Jenkins
Bobby M. Jones
Doug Jones
Scott Karl
Rickey Keeton
Tom Kelly
Mark Kiefer
Mike Kinkade
Danny Klassen
Kevin Kobel
Erik Komatsu

Brett Lawrie
Allen Levrault
Sixto Lezcano
Pat Listach
Doug Loman
Mickey Lopez
Mark Loretta
Willie Lozado
Jonathan Lucroy
Lucas Luetge
Ruddy Lugo
Bill Lyons
Mike Madden
Alex Madrid
Brian Mallette
Sean Maloney
Oreste Marrero
Greg Martinez
Luis Martinez
Gary Martz
Mike Matheny
Mike McClendon
Russ McGinnis
Tom McGraw
Tim McIntosh
Sam Mejias
Joey Meyer
Roger Miller
Angel Miranda
Paul Molitor
Charlie Montoyo
Charlie Moore
Jim Morris
Willie Mueller
Greg Mullins
Dan Murphy
Jaime Navarro
Brad Nelson
Jimmy Nelson
Nick Neugebauer
Jose Nieves
Juan Nieves
Dave Nilsson
Takahito Nomura
Jake Odorizzi
Troy O'Leary
Jim Paciorek
Manny Parra
Jeff Parrett
Bill Parsons
Dave Pember
Hipolito Pena
Wily Peralta
Danny Perez
Jeff Peterek
Kyle Peterson

Darrell Porter
Josh Prince
Randy Ready
Ernest Riles
Sid Roberson
Billy Jo Robidoux
Eduardo Rodriguez
Mark Rogers
Ed Romero
Vinny Rottino
Jim Rushford
Chris Saenz
Lenn Sakata
Angel Salome
Dennis Sarfate
Logan Schafer
Bill Schroeder
Ben Sheets
Gary Sheffield
Bob Sheldon
Duane Singleton
Bob Skube
Jim Slaton
Travis Smith
Lary Sorensen
Steve W. Sparks
Bill Spiers
Dave E. Stapleton
Mitch Stetter
B.J. Surhoff
Dale Sveum
Ty Taubenheim
Joe Thatcher
Caleb Thielbar
Dan Thomas
Gorman Thomas
Tyler Thornburg
Brian Tollberg
Bill Travers
Tim Unroe
Ty Van Burkleo
Greg Vaughn
Jesus Vega
Carlos Velazquez
Randy Veres
Mark Watson
Rickie Weeks
Bill Wegman
Tom Wilhelmsen
Antone Williamson
Steve Woodard
Rob Wooten
Kelly Wunsch
Robin Yount

Year/Team	OPW%	PW	PL	APW%	AW	AL	Diff+/-
1901 STL	0.465 F	65	75	0.543	76	64	0.078
1902 STL	0.435	61	79	0.418	56	78	-0.017
1903 STL	0.415	58	82	0.314	43	94	-0.101
1904 STL	0.433	67	87	0.487	75	79	0.054
1905 STL	0.431	66	88	0.377	58	96	-0.054
1906 STL	0.572	88	66	0.347	52	98	-0.225
1907 STL	0.471	73	81	0.340	52	101	-0.131
1908 STL	0.375	58	96	0.318	49	105	-0.057
1909 STL	0.534	82	72	0.355	54	98	-0.179

franchID	OWAR	OWS	AWAR	AWS	WARdiff	WSdiff	P/D/W/F
1901 STL	33.187	245.266	33.734	227.990	-0.547	17.276	F
1902 STL	20.500	230.700	12.561	167.977	7.939	62.723	
1903 STL	22.025	198.780	10.346	128.995	11.679	69.785	
1904 STL	27.305	246.083	38.618	222.010	-11.313	24.073	
1905 STL	30.323	256.306	19.680	173.997	10.643	82.309	
1906 STL	27.066	244.970	16.363	155.993	10.703	88.977	
1907 STL	21.339	230.221	14.184	152.999	7.155	77.222	
1908 STL	29.224	247.717	13.512	146.996	15.712	100.720	
1909 STL	37.895	217.682	22.974	161.999	14.922	55.683	

Legend: (P) = Pennant / Most Wins in League (D) = Division Winner (W) = Wild Card Winner (F) = Failed to Qualify

The Cardinals franchise has existed since 1882. An original member of the American Association, the club was known as the Brown Stockings during its inaugural season. The team nickname was shortened to the Browns and the organization remained in the AA until the League folded after the 1891 campaign. The Browns entered the National League in the subsequent season and played under the "Perfectos" moniker for one year (1899) before settling on the Cardinals as the team's nickname.

St. Louis claimed 10 pennants from 1924-1948 with the talent that was scouted and honed primarily under the administration of Branch Rickey. The franchise yielded the most WS>20 player-seasons at first base (56) in MLB history. Johnny Mize (10), Albert Pujols (9), Keith Hernandez (8) and Stan Musial (7) demonstrate the Cardinals' wealth of talent at that position. The starting staff tied for third among the "Turn of the Century" clubs with 71 WS>20 player-seasons. The organization neglected the hot corner as it failed to place in the top 3 WS>10 player-seasons in any decade.

"Wee" Willie Sudhoff contributed 21 victories, a 2.27 ERA and a 1.083 WHIP for the '03 staff. "Turkey" Mike Donlin surpassed the century mark in runs scored on three occasions. Donlin tallied 124 aces to lead the National League in 1905 while recording personal bests in batting average (.356), base hits (216) and Win Shares (37). Mordecai Brown crafted a league-best 1.04 ERA for the 1906 squad while topping the charts in shutouts (9) and WHIP (0.934). "Three-Finger" eclipsed the 20-win mark in six consecutive seasons (1906-1911) and posted an ERA below 2.00 for the same duration with the exception of 1911. He led the National League with 27 victories, 32 complete games in 34 starts, 7 saves and 342.2 innings pitched while accruing 36 Win Shares in '09. Brown averaged 22 wins with a 1.51 ERA and a WHIP of 0.928 from 1904-09.

Year/Team	OPW%	PW	PL	APW%	AW	AL	Diff+/-
1910 STL	0.506	78	76	0.412	63	90	-0.095
1911 STL	0.451	69	85	0.503	75	74	0.052
1912 STL	0.422	65	89	0.412	63	90	-0.010
1913 STL	0.409	63	91	0.340	51	99	-0.069
1914 STL	0.468	72	82	0.529	81	72	0.061
1915 STL	0.399	61	93	0.471	72	81	0.071
1916 STL	0.433	67	87	0.392	60	93	-0.041
1917 STL	0.517	80	74	0.539	82	70	0.023
1918 STL	0.453	58	70	0.395	51	78	-0.057
1919 STL	0.516	72	68	0.394	54	83	-0.121

franchID	OWAR	OWS	AWAR	AWS	WARdiff	WSdiff	P/D/W/F
1910 STL	30.481	207.693	25.713	188.995	4.768	18.698	
1911 STL	24.705	185.867	22.018	225.004	2.687	-39.137	
1912 STL	27.132	180.909	21.509	189.002	5.623	-8.093	
1913 STL	20.762	158.351	13.069	152.992	7.693	5.358	
1914 STL	24.442	202.183	37.310	243.005	-12.869	-40.822	
1915 STL	22.093	160.512	33.566	215.995	-11.473	-55.483	
1916 STL	20.665	187.843	17.845	179.999	2.820	7.844	
1917 STL	29.083	231.070	30.145	245.999	-1.063	-14.929	
1918 STL	18.427	134.984	22.469	153.003	-4.042	-18.019	
1919 STL	23.626	169.531	19.850	162.003	3.776	7.528	

Brown fashioned a 25-14 record with a 1.86 ERA in 1910 and achieved 21 victories while saving 13 contests in the subsequent campaign. Bobby Byrne topped the circuit with 178 base knocks and 43 two-baggers in 1910. Babe Adams eclipsed the 20-win mark twice (1911, 1913) and led the League in WHIP on five occasions including a personal-best 0.896 in 1919. "Hickory" Bob Harmon added 23 victories in 1911 despite issuing an astounding 181 bases on balls!

Slim Sallee averaged 15 wins with a 2.47 ERA and a WHIP of 1.136 throughout the course of the decade. He posted career-bests with 21 wins and a 2.06 ERA for the '19 crew. Ed Konetchy and Keith Hernandez tied for second place among first basemen with 6 appearances on the Fielding WAR and WS charts. Konetchy paced the NL with 38 two-base knocks in 1911. Rogers Hornsby led the circuit with 17 triples and a .484 SLG while batting .327 in '17.

Win Shares > 20	Single-Season	1901-1919
Ed Konetchy - 1B (STL) x6	Homer Smoot - CF (STL) x2	Willie Sudhoff - SP (STL)
Freddy Parent - SS (STL) x4	Mike Donlin - CF (STL)	Mordecai Brown - SP (STL) x7
Rogers Hornsby - SS (STL)	Charlie Hemphill - CF (STL)	Babe Adams - SP (STL) x5
Bobby Byrne - 3B (STL) x2	x2	Bob Harmon - SP (STL)
Rogers Hornsby - 3B (STL) x2	Red Murray - CF (STL)	Art Fromme - SP (STL)
Frank Snyder - C (STL)	Walton Cruise - CF (STL)	Slim Sallee - SP (STL) x2
Mike Donlin - LF (STL) x2	Jack Smith - CF (STL)	Pol Perritt - SP (STL)
Spike Shannon - LF (STL)	Mike Donlin - RF (STL)	Mordecai Brown - SW (STL)
Al S. Shaw - LF (STL)	Red Murray - RF (STL)	Slim Sallee - SW (STL) x2
Possum Whitted - LF (STL)		

Year/Team	OPW%	PW	PL	APW%	AW	AL	Diff+/-
1920 STL	0.497	77	77	0.487	75	79	-0.010
1921 STL	0.558 F	86	68	0.569	87	66	0.010
1922 STL	0.557 F	86	68	0.552	85	69	-0.005
1923 STL	0.520	80	74	0.516	79	74	-0.004

Year/Team	OPW%	PW	PL	APW%	AW	AL	Diff+/-
1924 STL	0.548 P	84	70	0.422	65	89	-0.125
1925 STL	0.512	79	75	0.503	77	76	-0.008
1926 STL	0.527	81	73	0.578 P	89	65	0.051
1927 STL	0.566 P	87	67	0.601	92	61	0.035
1928 STL	0.592	91	63	0.617 P	95	59	0.024
1929 STL	0.536 F	82	72	0.513	78	74	-0.022

franchID	OWAR	OWS	AWAR	AWS	WARdiff	WSdiff	P/D/W/F
1920 STL	36.534	230.095	38.129	225.003	-1.595	5.091	
1921 STL	48.798	267.843	44.378	261.007	4.420	6.837	F
1922 STL	48.425	267.081	41.439	255.001	6.986	12.079	F
1923 STL	34.894	232.805	35.547	236.995	-0.653	-4.190	
1924 STL	34.375	215.659	30.672	194.998	3.703	20.662	P
1925 STL	38.468	233.160	37.569	231.000	0.899	2.160	
1926 STL	30.104	209.987	41.431	267.006	-11.327	-57.019	
1927 STL	32.484	244.801	39.630	276.002	-7.146	-31.201	P
1928 STL	38.670	248.755	46.151	285.002	-7.481	-36.247	
1929 STL	29.563	225.264	35.395	233.994	-5.833	-8.731	F

Hornsby crushed rival hurlers throughout the decade, claiming seven batting titles with a cumulative .382 average. "Rajah" supplied 25 round-trippers, 115 RBI, 120 runs, 40 doubles, 12 triples and 208 base hits per season during this stretch. Hornsby (.401/42/152) registered 250 base hits and 47 Win Shares while leading the circuit in virtually every major offensive category in 1922. He eclipsed the enchanted .400 mark three times and earned MVP honors in '25 and '29. St. Louis topped the NL in oWAR and oWS in 1920 but finished in a three-way tie for second place. Austin McHenry (.350/17/102) collected 201 safeties and drilled 37 two-base hits in 1921. "Sunny" Jim Bottomley furnished a .327 BA in the first ten seasons of his career and drove in 100+ baserunners for six straight years (1924-29). Bottomley (.325/31/126) secured 1928 NL MVP honors after leading the circuit in triples (20), homers and RBI. The Cardinals seized the franchise's first pennant by a one-game margin over the Pirates in 1924. Ray Blades tallied 112 aces while hitting at a .342 clip in '25.

The Cards tiptoed past the Giants and Pirates to claim another pennant in 1927. Pittsburgh claimed the title in '28 although St. Louis paced the National League in oWAR and oWS. Chick Hafey surpassed the .300 mark for seven consecutive campaigns (1927-1933), producing a .332 BA with 35 doubles per year, notching career-bests with 47 doubles, 29 four-ply swats and 125 ribbies in 1929. Taylor Douthit scored 100+ runs in three straight seasons (1928-1930) and established personal marks with 128 runs scored, 206 base hits, 42 doubles and a .336 BA in '29. Don Hurst contributed 31 jacks, 125 ribbies, 100 runs and a .304 BA.

Year/Team	OPW%	PW	PL	APW%	AW	AL	Diff+/-
1930 STL	0.549 P	85	69	0.597 P	92	62	0.048
1931 STL	0.556	86	68	0.656 P	101	53	0.099
1932 STL	0.502	77	77	0.468	72	82	-0.034
1933 STL	0.502	77	77	0.536	82	71	0.034
1934 STL	0.569 P	88	66	0.621 P	95	58	0.052
1935 STL	0.593	91	63	0.623	96	58	0.030
1936 STL	0.565 P	87	67	0.565	87	67	0.000
1937 STL	0.559 P	86	68	0.526	81	73	-0.033
1938 STL	0.543 P	84	70	0.470	71	80	-0.073
1939 STL	0.511	79	75	0.601	92	61	0.090

franchID	OWAR	OWS	AWAR	AWS	WARdiff	WSdiff	P/D/W/F
1930 STL	28.179	212.936	**48.243**	275.993	-20.064	-63.057	P
1931 STL	**36.477**	**255.773**	45.436	**302.997**	-8.959	-47.224	
1932 STL	**30.888**	202.341	34.293	215.994	-3.405	-13.654	
1933 STL	31.162	204.889	**40.460**	246.001	-9.298	-41.113	
1934 STL	34.690	226.310	**45.619**	285.007	-10.929	-58.697	P
1935 STL	33.079	233.527	45.410	287.999	-12.331	-54.471	
1936 STL	32.982	252.522	36.439	261.001	-3.456	-8.479	P
1937 STL	32.572	234.433	34.561	240.004	-1.989	-5.571	P
1938 STL	29.585	209.555	35.794	212.997	-6.209	-3.442	P
1939 STL	34.068	210.151	**48.836**	275.995	-14.767	-65.844	

Branch Rickey organized the Cardinals' farm system and supplemented it with amateur free agents such as Johnny Mize and Dizzy Dean (1930), Enos Slaughter (1935) and Stan Musial (1938). The Cardinals outlasted the Cubs and Giants en route to the first of five pennants in the 1930's. Hafey earned the 1930 NL batting crown with a .349 BA and finished fifth in the MVP balloting. Dizzy Dean topped the National League leader board in four straight seasons (1932-35) with 190+ strikeouts. He seized 1934 NL MVP honors and accrued 36 Win Shares after leading the circuit with a 30-7 record along with 7 shutouts. Dean posted successive runner-up finishes in the MVP tabulations as he notched 28 victories in '35 and added a league-high 11 saves to his 24-win total in '36.

Paul Derringer compiled an 18-8 record in his rookie season (1931) then toiled through a demoralizing campaign two years later as he posted a 7-27 mark despite an ERA of 3.30. "Duke" responded with four 20-win seasons later in his career, finishing third in the 1939 NL MVP voting with 25 victories and a 2.93 ERA. Hurst (.339/24/143) pummeled rival hurlers while seizing the NL RBI title in 1932. Pepper Martin posted a career-high .316 BA as he topped the circuit in runs scored (122) and stolen bases (28) during the 1933 campaign. "The Wild Horse of the Osage" earned four All-Star invites and thrice tallied 120+ aces.

Joe Medwick produced a .338 BA for the decade, averaging 208 base hits, 49 two-baggers, 20 clouts, 123 ribbies and 108 runs from 1934-39. A 10-time All-Star selection, Medwick laced 64 doubles to top the charts in '36. "Ducky" sizzled during his 1937 NL MVP campaign as he totaled 38 Win Shares while batting .374 with 31 jacks and 154 RBI along with 237 safeties, 56 doubles, 111 runs and a .641 SLG (all league-leading totals). Ripper Collins (.333/35/128) recorded 200 base hits while leading the circuit in home runs and SLG (.615) during the 1934 campaign. St. Louis squeaked past New York by a two-game margin. Paul "Daffy" Dean averaged 19 victories with a 3.40 ERA and a 1.179 WHIP in his freshman and sophomore seasons (1934-35). Bill C. Lee furnished a 20-6 record with a 2.96 ERA in '35. "Big Bill" placed runner-up in the 1938 NL MVP balloting as he topped the circuit with 22 victories, 9 shutouts and a 2.66 ERA. Ival Goodman slashed a league-best 18 three-baggers in his inaugural season (1935) and then walloped 30 long balls and tallied 103 aces in '38.

The Redbirds secured three successive pennants from 1936-38. Johnny Mize produced a .346 BA in his first four seasons along with 37 doubles, 11 triples, 25 clouts and 104 RBI. "The Big Cat" paced the League with a .349 BA and 28 moon-shots while earning a runner-up finish in the 1939 NL MVP balloting. Cardinals' first sackers topped the Major Leagues with 35 WS>10 player-seasons from 1930-1949. Johnny Rizzo (.301/23/111) finished sixth in the MVP race during his rookie campaign (1938). Enos "Country" Slaughter delivered a .320 BA while leading the NL with 52 two-base knocks in his sophomore year.

Win Shares > 20	Single-Season	1920-1939
Jim Bottomley - 1B (STL) x6	Pepper Martin - 3B (STL)	Ival Goodman - RF (STL) x2
Don Hurst - 1B (STL)	Austin McHenry - LF (STL)	Enos Slaughter - RF (STL) x6
Ripper Collins - 1B (STL) x2	Ray Blades - LF (STL)	Lee Meadows - SP (STL)
Johnny Mize - 1B (STL) x10	Chick Hafey - LF (STL) x5	Bill Sherdel - SP (STL)
Rogers Hornsby - 2B (STL) x10	Joe Medwick - LF (STL) x9	Bill Hallahan - SP (STL)
Sam Bohne - 2B (STL)	Johnny Rizzo - LF (STL)	Dizzy Dean - SP (STL) x5
Charlie Gelbert - SS (STL)	Taylor Douthit - CF (STL) x2	Paul Dean - SP (STL) x2
Billy Myers - SS (STL)	Chick Hafey - CF (STL)	Paul Derringer - SP (STL) x4
Les Bell - 3B (STL)	Pepper Martin - RF (STL)	Bill C. Lee - SP (STL) x2

Year/Team	OPW%	PW	PL	APW%	AW	AL	Diff+/-
1940 STL	0.471	73	81	0.549	84	69	0.078
1941 STL	0.536	83	71	0.634	97	56	0.098
1942 STL	0.601 P	93	61	0.688 P	106	48	0.088
1943 STL	0.543	84	70	0.682 P	105	49	0.139
1944 STL	0.609 P	94	60	0.682 P	105	49	0.072
1945 STL	0.549	85	69	0.617	95	59	0.068
1946 STL	0.573	88	66	0.628 P	98	58	0.055
1947 STL	0.544 P	84	70	0.578	89	65	0.034
1948 STL	0.522 P	80	74	0.552	85	69	0.030
1949 STL	0.526	81	73	0.623	96	58	0.097

franchID	OWAR	OWS	AWAR	AWS	WARdiff	WSdiff	P/D/W/F
1940 STL	30.786	205.036	41.569	252.000	-10.782	-46.964	
1941 STL	35.198	232.498	45.232	290.994	-10.034	-58.496	
1942 STL	40.208	244.502	57.478	318.004	-17.270	-73.501	P
1943 STL	35.928	218.532	57.928	315.005	-22.000	-96.473	
1944 STL	44.903	239.168	61.646	315.002	-16.743	-75.834	P
1945 STL	37.231	219.564	45.847	285.008	-8.616	-65.444	
1946 STL	39.184	235.283	47.547	293.994	-8.362	-56.963	
1947 STL	33.867	210.701	45.154	266.996	-11.287	-56.294	P
1948 STL	33.099	222.208	39.266	255.005	-6.167	-32.797	P
1949 STL	37.309	232.211	45.970	288.001	-8.661	-55.790	

Mize paced the League with 43 wallops and 137 RBI en route to a runner-up finish in the 1940 NL MVP balloting. He averaged .309 with 33 jacks, 113 ribbies and 99 runs scored from 1940-48 despite missing three seasons due to military service. Mize led the NL with 51 round-trippers, 138 RBI and 137 runs scored in 1947 and then swatted 40 big-flies in the ensuing campaign. Slaughter batted .312 for the decade and placed second in the 1942 NL MVP race when he posted league-bests in hits (188) and triples (17). The 10-time All-Star outfielder topped the charts with 130 RBI in '46.

"Pistol" Pete Reiser earned the batting crown with a .343 average and placed runner-up in the 1941 NL MVP balloting while topping the circuit in runs scored (117), doubles (39) and triples (17). Medwick delivered a .318 BA and tallied 100 runs scored. Smooth-fielding shortstop Marty Marion earned 7 All-Star selections and appeared six times on the Fielding WAR and WS charts. "Slats" led the League with 38 doubles in '42 and merited MVP honors in '44 based on his defensive dexterity. St. Louis achieved the pennant in '42 and '44 by double-digit margins over Chicago.

Stan "The Man" Musial scorched opposing hurlers with a .346 BA and notched three batting titles during the decade. The three-time MVP winner topped the charts five times in base hits and doubles along with four seasons atop the triples leader board in the 1940's. Musial established personal bests in batting average (.376), runs scored (135), hits (230), home runs (39), RBI (131) and Win Shares (46) in '48. Mort Cooper eclipsed the 20-win plateau in three straight seasons (1942-44), pacing the circuit with a 1.78 ERA, 0.987 WHIP and 10 shutouts and collecting the 1942 NL MVP award. Johnny Beazley contributed a record of 21-6 with a 2.13 ERA during his rookie campaign (1942). Whitey Kurowski produced a .323 BA in '45, and then set personal bests two years later with 27 big-flies, 104 ribbies and 108 runs scored. Howie Pollet topped the charts with 21 victories, 266 innings pitched and a 2.10 ERA while finishing fourth in the 1946 NL MVP race.

The Redbirds captured back-to-back pennants in 1947-48, outlasting the Giants and Dodgers respectively. Eight-time All-Star backstop Walker Cooper enjoyed a breakout campaign in 1947, slamming 35 round-trippers and driving in 122 baserunners. Red Schoendienst led the NL with 26 stolen bases during his rookie year (1945) and then tallied 102 runs in 1949.

Year/Team	OPW%	PW	PL	APW%	AW	AL	Diff+/-
1950 STL	0.518	80	74	0.510	78	75	-0.008
1951 STL	0.464	71	83	0.526	81	73	0.062
1952 STL	0.494	76	78	0.571	88	66	0.077
1953 STL	0.485	75	79	0.539	83	71	0.054
1954 STL	0.468	72	82	0.468	72	82	0.000
1955 STL	0.446	69	85	0.442	68	86	-0.004
1956 STL	0.483	74	80	0.494	76	78	0.011
1957 STL	0.532	82	72	0.565	87	67	0.033
1958 STL	0.499	77	77	0.468	72	82	-0.032
1959 STL	0.521	80	74	0.461	71	83	-0.060
franchID	OWAR	OWS	AWAR	AWS	WARdiff	WSdiff	P/D/W/F
1950 STL	36.474	230.150	33.222	233.996	3.252	-3.846	
1951 STL	31.629	217.633	34.096	242.999	-2.467	-25.366	
1952 STL	36.177	214.645	42.624	263.994	-6.447	-49.349	
1953 STL	34.180	213.554	42.096	249.005	-7.917	-35.451	
1954 STL	27.474	199.236	30.025	204.006	-2.551	-4.770	
1955 STL	27.193	197.197	30.025	204.006	-2.832	-6.809	
1956 STL	34.739	218.923	33.894	228.002	0.846	-9.079	
1957 STL	41.019	248.509	39.047	260.997	1.972	-12.487	
1958 STL	37.177	229.334	27.734	215.989	9.443	13.345	
1959 STL	38.750	236.672	33.245	212.999	5.506	23.672	

Musial yielded a .335 average with 38 doubles, 28 home runs, 103 RBI and 101 runs scored from 1950-58. He placed runner-up in the MVP balloting three times and topped the League batting average charts four times during the Fifties. Schoendienst drilled a league-high 43 doubles in '50, batted .342 with 107 runs scored in '53 and led the National League with 200 hits in '57. Slaughter topped the century mark in RBI in '50 and '52.

Preacher Roe compiled a 19-11 record with a 3.30 ERA in '50. Roe's sensational effort in 1951 included a 22-3 mark with a 3.04 ERA. Jim Hearn delivered an 11-4 mark with a 2.49 ERA and 0.955 WHIP in 16 starts in 1950; he then fashioned a 17-9 record with a 3.62 ERA in the subsequent campaign. The Cardinals placed second behind the "Whiz Kids" from Philadelphia in 1950. In the following year, the Redbirds slumped to a last-place finish and languished in the second division through the 1956 season.

Murry Dickson managed to win 20 games in spite of a 4.02 ERA in 1951. Gerry Staley provided an 18-12 record with a 3.62 ERA from 1951-53. Shifting to the bullpen in '57, Staley topped the NL in appearances (67) and saved 14 games with a 2.24 ERA in '59. Ken Raffensberger (17-13, 2.81) furnished a 2.81 ERA and tied for the League lead with 6 shutouts in 1952. Solly Hemus exceeded the century mark in runs scored during successive seasons (1952-53).

Harvey "Kitten" Haddix (20-9, 3.06) led the circuit with 6 shutouts, and finished second in the NL ROY balloting in 1953. Haddix spun a perfect game for 12 innings on May 26, 1959, only to lose the game in the 13th frame. Wally Moon (.304/12/76) scored 106 runs and received the 1954 NL ROY Award. Rip Repulski contributed 19 long balls, 39 doubles and scored 99 times. Ken Boyer (.306/26/98) made his first trip to the All-Star game in 1956 and went on to average .291 with 23 dingers and 81 RBI through his first five campaigns. Don "Blazer" Blasingame tallied 94 runs in his inaugural season (1956) and then crossed home plate 108 times and pilfered 21 bags in '57. St. Louis emerged from the basement in 1957, posting 82 victories to finish in third place. Stu Miller captured the NL ERA title in '58 with a 2.47 mark despite making only 20 starts in 41 games. Lindy McDaniel joined Staley in the bullpen, earning 15 saves and vulturing 14 wins in 1959. The Redbirds produced another third-place finish in '59, placing 11 games behind the Braves.

Win Shares > 20	Single-Season	1940-1959
Ray Sanders - 1B (STL)	Stan Musial - LF (STL) x3	Ernie White - SP (STL)
Johnny Hopp - 1B (STL)	Pete Reiser - LF (STL)	Mort Cooper - SP (STL) x3
Stan Musial - 1B (STL) x7	Enos Slaughter - LF (STL) x3	Ray Starr - SP (STL)
Lou Klein - 2B (STL)	Dick Sisler - LF (STL)	Nate Andrews - SP (STL)
Red Schoendienst - 2B (STL) x4	Wally Moon - LF (STL) x3	Max Lanier - SP (STL)
Don Blasingame - 2B (STL)	Terry Moore - CF (STL) x2	Nels Potter - SP (STL) x2
Marty Marion - SS (STL)	Pete Reiser - CF (STL) x2	Preacher Roe - SP (STL) x3
Eddie Lake - SS (STL)	Buster Adams - CF (STL) x2	Howie Pollet - SP (STL) x2
Solly Hemus - SS (STL) x2	Johnny Hopp - CF (STL)	Ken Raffensberger - SP (STL) x2
Jimmy Brown - 3B (STL)	Johnny Wyrostek - CF (STL)	Harvey Haddix - SP (STL)
Whitey Kurowski - 3B (STL) x4	Stan Musial - CF (STL)	Larry Jackson - SP (STL) x4
Ken Boyer - 3B (STL) x8	Wally Moon - CF (STL)	Johnny Beazley - SW (STL)
Walker Cooper - C (STL)	Stan Musial - RF (STL) x5	Ken Burkhart - SW (STL)
	Wally Moon - RF (STL)	

Year/Team	OPW%	PW	PL	APW%	AW	AL	Diff+/-
1960 STL	0.524	81	73	0.558	86	68	0.035
1961 STL	0.529	86	76	0.519	80	74	-0.010
1962 STL	0.451	73	89	0.519	84	78	0.067
1963 STL	0.531	86	76	0.574	93	69	0.043
1964 STL	0.487	79	83	0.574 P	93	69	0.087
1965 STL	0.488	79	83	0.497	80	81	0.009
1966 STL	0.454	74	88	0.512	83	79	0.058
1967 STL	0.460	75	87	0.627 P	101	60	0.167
1968 STL	0.473	77	85	0.599 P	97	65	0.126
1969 STL	0.382	62	100	0.537	87	75	0.155

franchID	OWAR	OWS	AWAR	AWS	WARdiff	WSdiff	P/D/W/F
1960 STL	39.965	265.344	36.209	258.004	3.755	7.340	
1961 STL	44.906	285.162	32.852	239.997	12.054	45.165	
1962 STL	39.126	242.062	41.358	252.001	-2.232	-9.939	
1963 STL	45.334	283.988	48.967	279.001	-3.633	4.987	
1964 STL	41.600	269.263	39.719	278.999	1.881	-9.735	

1965 STL	33.860	234.385	35.564	240.002	-1.704	-5.618
1966 STL	36.257	251.415	34.086	249.002	2.171	2.414
1967 STL	36.521	238.637	**48.581**	**302.997**	-12.060	-64.360
1968 STL	37.852	238.745	**46.289**	**290.997**	-8.437	-52.252
1969 STL	28.796	220.608	42.323	260.999	-13.526	-40.391

Los Angeles edged St. Louis for the division title in 1960. Larry Jackson tallied 16 wins and 13 complete games per season along with a 3.29 ERA and a 1.198 WHIP from 1960-68. Jackson (24-11, 3.14) topped the League in victories, delivered a career-best 1.085 WHIP and placed runner-up in the 1964 NL Cy Young race. Lindy McDaniel emerged as the bullpen ace with a league-leading 26 saves, a 12-4 record and a 2.09 ERA in '60. He placed third in the Cy Young vote and fifth in the MVP race. In 1963 McDaniel (13-7, 2.86) paced the circuit with 22 saves and 48 games finished. Staley swooped in for 13 relief wins, 10 saves and a 2.42 ERA, while Johnny Klippstein notched 14 saves with a 2.91 ERA in '60.

The Cardinals placed 6 games behind the Braves in '61. Bob Gibson averaged 18 wins, 222 strikeouts, 18 complete games, a 2.64 ERA and a 1.127 WHIP from 1961-69. Gibson captured the NL MVP and Cy Young Awards with a sensational effort, posting a miniscule 1.12 ERA, 0.853 WHIP, 22 victories and 268 whiffs. He completed 28 of 34 starts, and tossed 13 shutouts! Luis Arroyo (15-5, 2.19, 29 SV) and Stu Miller (14-5, 2.66, 17 SV) vaulted to the top of the relief corps in '61. Miller averaged 9 victories, 21 saves, a 2.69 ERA and 1.145 WHIP from 1961-66. Moon (.328/17/88) paced the circuit with a .434 OBP in '61.

The Cards ended the season with 86 wins and finished third in '63. Musial (.330/19/82) enjoyed his penultimate season in '62; however the offense had struggled mightily following his retirement after the 1963 campaign. John Wyatt provided 6 wins, 18 saves and a 3.26 ERA per year from 1963-67. Boyer assumed the leadership role, batting .301 with 26 four-baggers, 104 RBI and 96 runs scored per year from 1960-64. Boyer (.295/24/119) led the League in RBI and captured the National League MVP Award in '64. Ray Sadecki won 20 games in '64, and then whiffed 208 opposition batsmen in '68.

St. Louis descended into the depths of the National League in 1964. Despite the presence of Bob Gibson and Steve Carlton, the Redbirds finished below .500 in every season from '64 through '76. The ballclub reached a low point in '69, losing 100 games on the wings of an atrocious offense. Tim McCarver (.295/14/69) finished second in the NL MVP race while Dick Hughes (16-6, 2.67) placed runner-up in the NL ROY balloting in '67. Nelson Briles contributed 19 wins and a 2.81 ERA in '68. Steve "Lefty" Carlton (17-11, 2.17) joined Bob Gibson in the 200-strikeout club during the 1969 campaign. Wayne Granger saved 27 contests while appearing in a league-best 90 games.

Year/Team	OPW%	PW	PL	APW%	AW	AL	Diff+/-
1970 STL	0.426	69	93	0.469	76	86	0.044
1971 STL	0.496	80	82	0.556	90	72	0.060
1972 STL	0.474	77	85	0.481	75	81	0.007
1973 STL	0.446	72	90	0.500	81	81	0.054
1974 STL	0.458	74	88	0.534	86	75	0.077
1975 STL	0.463	75	87	0.506	82	80	0.043
1976 STL	0.456	74	88	0.444	72	90	-0.011
1977 STL	0.529 D	86	76	0.512	83	79	-0.017
1978 STL	0.452	73	89	0.426	69	93	-0.026
1979 STL	0.488	79	83	0.531	86	76	0.042

franchID	OWAR	OWS	AWAR	AWS	WARdiff	WSdiff	P/D/W/F
1970 STL	35.151	230.316	36.509	228.000	-1.358	2.316	
1971 STL	39.319	241.771	41.001	270.001	-1.682	-28.229	
1972 STL	43.173	253.885	33.893	224.999	9.280	28.886	
1973 STL	31.532	225.330	37.372	242.999	-5.840	-17.669	
1974 STL	33.482	236.118	38.345	258.002	-4.863	-21.884	
1975 STL	36.281	243.010	34.196	246.006	2.085	-2.996	
1976 STL	34.626	246.647	30.576	215.999	4.051	30.647	
1977 STL	43.799	305.041	30.841	248.992	12.959	56.049	D
1978 STL	36.811	276.141	25.964	207.001	10.847	69.140	
1979 STL	43.783	277.527	39.095	257.997	4.687	19.530	

The Cardinals continued to flutter aimlessly through the first half of the decade. Jim Hickman sparked the Cards' lineup in 1970, blasting 32 long balls and driving in 115 runs while hitting .315. Hickman was rewarded with his lone All-Star selection. Nate Colbert crushed 38 moon-shots in consecutive campaigns (1970-71) and set a career-high with 111 RBI in '71. Gibson (23-7, 3.12) received his second Cy Young Award, tallying a career-high 274 strikeouts in 1970. "Hoot" amassed 19 wins and whiffed 208 batsmen in '72 while fashioning an ERA of 2.46. Clay Kirby set career marks in '70 with 15 wins, 231 strikeouts, a 2.83 ERA and a 1.182 WHIP. Granger led the League with 35 saves while McDaniel closed out 29 contests.

The '71 Redbirds placed a respectable 6 games behind the Pirates, albeit with an 80-82 record. Willie Montanez belted 30 big-flies and delivered 99 ribbies en route to a runner-up finish in the 1971 NL Rookie of the Year balloting. Ted "Simba" Simmons appeared in six All-Star contests in the Seventies while producing a .300 BA with 32 two-baggers, 16 dingers and 89 RBI per year from 1971-79. GM Bing Devine and Scouting Director George Silvey struck paydirt in the '71 Amateur Draft. Selections including Keith Hernandez, Jerry Mumphrey and Larry Herndon combined for the highest Career Total Win Shares (718) in club history.

Carlton dominated the NL in '72, earning the Cy Young Award while setting personal bests with 27 victories, 41 starts, 30 complete games, a 1.97 ERA and a 0.993 WHIP! He struck out 310 batters in 346.1 innings, spun 8 shutouts and accrued 39 Win Shares. In 1977 "Lefty" collected another Cy Young trophy, winning 23 games with a 2.64 ERA. Carlton averaged 18 wins, 16 complete games, 210 strikeouts and a 3.18 ERA through the Seventies. Bake McBride batted .303 with 30 steals and captured Rookie of the Year honors in 1974. "Shake 'n Bake" swiped 26 bags per season while batting .313 in his first four campaigns. Chuck Taylor delivered a 2.17 ERA with 11 saves in '74. Mike Torrez enjoyed a 20-win season in '75 and yielded 16 wins and 12 complete games per year from 1972-79. Jerry Reuss chipped in with 18 victories and a 2.54 ERA in '75 as he merited his first All-Star selection. Al "The Mad Hungarian" Hrabosky earned a third-place finish in the 1975 NL Cy Young balloting, notching 22 saves and 13 relief wins while posting a 1.66 ERA.

Jose Cruz averaged .301 with 30 doubles and 36 stolen bases from 1976-79. Cruz led Cardinal outfielders with 7 appearances on the Fielding WAR and WS leader boards. John Denny fashioned a league-best 2.52 ERA in '76. The Cardinals finally re-surfaced in '77, taking the NL East by a lone game over the Phillies and Pirates. Garry Templeton (.322/8/79) tallied 200 base knocks and pilfered 28 bags in his first full season (1977). "Jumpsteady" led the NL with 211 safeties in '79 and topped the NL in triples for the third year in a row. Bob Forsch achieved a 20-7 mark with a 3.48 ERA in '77. Keith Hernandez (.344/11/105) topped the circuit in batting average, runs (116) and doubles (48) while sharing 1979 NL MVP honors with Willie Stargell.

Win Shares > 20	Single-Season	1960-1979
Joe Cunningham - 1B (STL)	Mike Shannon - 3B (STL)	Jose Cruz - RF (STL) x2
Jim Hickman - 1B (STL)	Tim McCarver - C (STL) x2	Bob Gibson - SP (STL) x8
Nate Colbert - 1B (STL)	Ted Simmons - C (STL) x9	Steve Carlton - SP (STL) x6
Keith Hernandez - 1B (STL)	Jose Cruz - LF (STL) x6	Lindy McDaniel - RP (STL)
x8	Jackie Brandt - CF (STL)	Luis Arroyo - RP (STL)
Garry Templeton - SS (STL)	Willie Montanez - CF (STL)	Stu Miller - RP (STL)
x4	Bake McBride - CF (STL)	

Year/Team	OPW%	PW	PL	APW%	AW	AL	Diff+/-
1980 STL	0.540 D	88	74	0.457	74	88	-0.083
1981 STL	0.555 P	90	72	0.578 D	59	43	0.023
1982 STL	0.552	89	73	0.568 P	92	70	0.016
1983 STL	0.517 D	84	78	0.488	79	83	-0.030
1984 STL	0.499 D	81	81	0.519	84	78	0.020
1985 STL	0.519	84	78	0.623 P	101	61	0.104
1986 STL	0.452	73	89	0.491	79	82	0.039
1987 STL	0.517	84	78	0.586 P	95	67	0.069
1988 STL	0.439	71	91	0.469	76	86	0.030
1989 STL	0.463	75	87	0.531	86	76	0.068

franchID	OWAR	OWS	AWAR	AWS	WARdiff	WSdiff	P/D/W/F
1980 STL	49.024	291.693	35.271	222.003	13.752	69.691	D
1981 STL	29.872	192.703	26.412	176.999	3.460	15.705	P
1982 STL	54.799	318.242	37.231	275.993	17.568	42.248	
1983 STL	54.815	310.452	36.155	237.001	18.660	73.451	D
1984 STL	42.319	317.505	33.549	252.007	8.770	65.498	D
1985 STL	39.416	306.622	50.084	303.000	-10.668	3.622	
1986 STL	29.868	277.500	25.317	236.995	4.551	40.505	
1987 STL	34.996	278.006	37.741	284.998	-2.745	-6.992	
1988 STL	19.887	234.419	31.161	227.997	-11.274	6.422	
1989 STL	25.967	240.401	39.801	257.993	-13.835	-17.592	

St. Louis achieved back-to-back pennants in 1980 and '81. The Redbirds won 88 games in '80, outlasting the Pirates and Expos by five games. Hernandez (.321/16/99) paced the circuit with 111 runs scored and a .408 OBP. "Mex" earned 11 Gold Glove Awards for his stellar play at first base during his career. Jerry Mumphrey swiped 52 bases in 57 attempts while Templeton batted .319 with 31 steals. Simmons hit .303 with 21 moon-shots and 98 ribbies. "Simba" (.308/13/108) clubbed 39 doubles in '83. Jose Cruz (.302/11/91) pilfered 36 bases and placed third in the 1980 NL MVP voting. Cruz averaged .310 with 30 doubles, 89 ribbies and 23 steals from 1983-85 while topping the NL with 192 base knocks in '83.

"Lefty" earned the Cy Young Award in 1980, pacing the NL in wins (24), games started (38), innings (304) and strikeouts (286). Carlton (23-10, 3.10) collected his fourth Cy Young trophy in '82. He completed 19 of 38 starts and paced the circuit in wins, shutouts (6), strikeouts (286) and innings pitched (295.2). Reuss (18-6, 2.51) finished runner-up to Carlton in the 1980 NL Cy Young balloting. He supplied a 10-4 mark with a 2.30 ERA during the strike-shortened 1981 campaign, and then amassed an 18-11 mark with a 3.11 ERA and 1.107 WHIP in '82. Bill Caudill posted a 2.19 ERA in 72 relief appearances in 1980. Caudill earned 12 relief wins and 26 saves while delivering a 2.35 ERA and 111 whiffs in '82; he then achieved All-Star status with a 36-save season in '84.

Leon "Bull" Durham (.312/22/90/28 SB) and Larry Herndon (.292/23/88) emerged as offensive threats in 1982. Herndon hit .302 with 20 dingers and 92 ribbies in '83 while Durham set a career-high with 96 RBI in '84. Terry Kennedy (.295/21/97) drilled 42 two-base knocks in '82 and plated 98 runners in 1983. Luis DeLeon (2.03, 15 SV) provided solid work in the setup role in 1982. John Denny (19-6, 2.37) received Cy Young honors in '83, giving the Cardinals three trophies in four years. St. Louis outlasted Montreal by a single game and claimed the NL East title in 1983.

Fleet-footed rookie outfielder Vince Coleman ran at will in 1985, swiping 110 bases in 135 attempts and taking home the NL Rookie of the Year Award. "Vincent Van Go" surpassed the 100-steal mark for three consecutive seasons and scored 121 runs in 1987. Tom Herr batted .302, swiped 31 bases in 34 attempts and drove in 110 runs despite swatting a mere 8 dingers while Danny Cox (18-9, 2.88) developed into a front-line starter for the '85 squad.

Todd Worrell received 1986 NL ROY honors, delivering a 2.08 ERA and saving 36 contests. Worrell notched 33 saves and struck out a career-best 92 batters in the subsequent season. Andy Van Slyke (.293/21/82/34 SB) and Terry Pendleton (.286/12/96) boosted the offense in 1987. Van Slyke batted .288 with 25 wallops, 100 ribbies and 101 runs scored along with an NL-best 13 triples in '88, earning him the first of five consecutive Gold Glove Awards.

Mike Dunne (13-6, 3.03) earned a runner-up finish in the 1987 NL ROY voting, while teammate Joe Magrane (9-7, 3.54) finished third. Magrane led the League with a 2.18 ERA in 24 starts in '88 and then furnished an 18-9 record with an ERA of 2.91 in the ensuing season. Jim Gott (3.49, 34 SV) reinvented himself as a closer in 1988 after spending 4 years as an ineffective starter. Joe Boever (3.94, 21 SV) split late-inning duties with Worrell in '89.

Year/Team	OPW%	PW	PL	APW%	AW	AL	Diff+/-
1990 STL	0.477 F	77	85	0.432	70	92	-0.045
1991 STL	0.532 F	86	76	0.519	84	78	-0.014
1992 STL	0.563 D	91	71	0.512	83	79	-0.051
1993 STL	0.536	87	75	0.537	87	75	0.001
1994 STL	0.478	77	85	0.465	53	61	-0.013
1995 STL	0.496	80	82	0.434	62	81	-0.062
1996 STL	0.495	80	82	0.543 D	88	74	0.048
1997 STL	0.509	82	80	0.451	73	89	-0.058
1998 STL	0.467	76	86	0.512	83	79	0.046
1999 STL	0.487	79	83	0.466	75	86	-0.021

franchID	OWAR	OWS	AWAR	AWS	WARdiff	WSdiff	P/D/W/F
1990 STL	32.821	269.804	31.868	210.003	0.953	59.801	F
1991 STL	37.092	288.527	32.096	252.003	4.996	36.525	F
1992 STL	47.819	286.817	40.029	248.998	7.791	37.819	D
1993 STL	33.817	247.123	34.973	261.001	-1.156	-13.878	
1994 STL	21.031	164.980	18.893	158.996	2.138	5.984	
1995 STL	27.290	195.401	19.520	185.997	7.770	9.404	
1996 STL	32.829	224.914	34.689	264.006	-1.860	-39.092	
1997 STL	36.372	221.177	37.217	219.009	-0.846	2.168	
1998 STL	30.455	197.991	42.221	248.995	-11.765	-51.004	
1999 STL	24.419	191.161	34.315	225.001	-9.896	-33.841	

Coleman pilfered 77 bags in '90 while protégé Alex Cole batted .300 with 40 stolen bases. Pendleton (.319/22/86) was awarded the 1991 NL MVP trophy as he paced the circuit in batting average and base knocks. He earned a runner-up finish in the MVP balloting during the subsequent campaign, hitting .311 with 21 clouts and 105 ribbies. Ray Lankford legged out a league-leading 15 triples and swiped 44 bases in his rookie year (1991). Lankford (.293/20/86) pilfered 42 bases and laced 40 doubles in the ensuing season. He delivered a .285 average with 36 doubles, 27 four-ply swats, 93 ribbies and 26 steals from 1995-98. The St. Louis pitching staff was unable to achieve the 4000 BFP requirement during the 1990 and 1991 seasons.

Stellar relief work returned St. Louis to the top of the NL East in '92 as the club took the division title by five games over Pittsburgh. Van Slyke hit .324 with a league-high 45 doubles, 89 RBI and 103 runs scored. Mike Perez (9-3, 1.84) enjoyed a solid rookie year in a setup role. Jeff Fassero delivered a 2.29 ERA and 12 wins in 1993, primarily in a relief capacity. He whiffed 222 batsmen and posted a 3.33 ERA with 15 victories in 1996. Gott resumed closing duties in '93, saving 25 games with a 2.32 ERA. Todd Zeile crushed 36 two-baggers and knocked in 103 runs in 1993 and belted 25 long balls with 95 ribbies per year from 1996-99. Bernard Gilkey furnished a .305 average and mashed 40 doubles in '93. Three years later Gilkey (.317/30/117) slapped 44 doubles and tallied 108 runs. Todd Worrell (2.02, 32 SV) resurrected his career in '95 after missing all of 1990-91 due to injury. He led the NL with 44 saves in 1996, earning his third All-Star selection along with a fifth place finish in the Cy Young voting.

Brian Jordan (.296/22/81) attained 20-20 status in 1995. He scored 100 runs, cranked 25 gopher balls and drove in 91 while hitting .316 in '98. Jordan (.283/23/115) achieved his sole All-Star selection and reached the century mark in RBI and runs scored in 1999. Lance "One Dog" Johnson (.333/9/69) received his lone All-Star nod in '96 as he paced the League with 227 hits and 21 three-base hits! He set career-highs in runs scored (117), stolen bases (50) and batting average. Johnson batted .297 with 14 triples and 36 steals per year from 1990-96. Dmitri Young laced 48 doubles while posting a .310 BA in '98 as the Redbirds descended into the cellar of the NL Central. GM Walt Jocketty and Scouting Director John Mozeliak's Amateur Draft class of 1999 (Albert Pujols and Coco Crisp primarily) top the team chronicles with 116 Career Total WAR.

Year/Team	OPW%	PW	PL	APW%	AW	AL	Diff+/-
2000 STL	0.503	81	81	0.586 D	95	67	0.083
2001 STL	0.546 W	88	74	0.574 W	93	69	0.029
2002 STL	0.516 W	84	78	0.599 D	97	65	0.083
2003 STL	0.540 W	88	74	0.525	85	77	-0.016
2004 STL	0.532 F	86	76	0.648 P	105	57	0.116
2005 STL	0.524 F	85	77	0.617 P	100	62	0.093
2006 STL	0.499 F	81	81	0.516 D	83	78	0.016
2007 STL	0.499	81	81	0.481	78	84	-0.017
2008 STL	0.525 F	85	77	0.531	86	76	0.006
2009 STL	0.502 D	81	81	0.562 D	91	71	0.059
2010 STL	0.556 P	90	72	0.531	86	76	-0.025
2011 STL	0.513 D	83	79	0.556 W	90	72	0.043
2012 STL	0.498	81	81	0.543 W	88	74	0.045
2013 STL	0.575 P	93	69	0.599 P	97	65	0.023

franchID	OWAR	OWS	AWAR	AWS	WARdiff	WSdiff	P/D/W/F
2000 STL	26.386	210.236	44.498	285.005	-18.112	-74.769	
2001 STL	36.072	255.988	41.074	278.999	-5.002	-23.010	W
2002 STL	33.700	239.832	44.171	290.992	-10.471	-51.160	W
2003 STL	38.289	248.497	41.313	254.999	-3.023	-6.502	W
2004 STL	45.993	291.800	50.133	315.003	-4.140	-23.203	F
2005 STL	41.911	273.617	43.359	300.000	-1.449	-26.383	F
2006 STL	31.845	245.012	33.523	249.006	-1.678	-3.994	F
2007 STL	37.948	266.540	26.233	234.000	11.716	32.540	
2008 STL	39.674	262.324	41.162	257.994	-1.488	4.330	F
2009 STL	40.453	266.037	43.190	272.995	-2.737	-6.958	D

2010 STL	45.873	**284.719**	40.837	257.999	5.036	26.720	P
2011 STL	38.055	262.263	43.252	270.001	-5.197	-7.738	D
2012 STL	34.043	268.103	43.159	264.002	-9.116	4.101	
2013 STL	37.277	284.324	41.891	**290.997**	-4.613	-6.672	P

Dmitri Young (.303/18/88) drilled 37 doubles in 2000 and then smacked 29 long balls and plated 85 runners in '03. "Da Meat Hook" swatted 38 two-baggers while batting .320 in 2007. Adam Kennedy rapped 33 doubles and nabbed 22 bags in 2000; he then posted a .312 BA with 32 two-base knocks in '02. Rick Ankiel (11-7, 3.50) registered a runner-up finish in the 2000 NL ROY race. After struggling mightily with his control over the next several seasons, Ankiel resurfaced as an outfielder and blasted 25 round-trippers in 2008.

Jose Jimenez moved to the bullpen in 2000 and saved 24 games with a 3.18 ERA. Jimenez managed 41 saves and a career-best 1.186 WHIP in '02, topping the NL with 69 games finished. Morris (22-8, 3.16) earned a third-place finish in the 2001 NL Cy Young balloting and made his first All-Star appearance. He delivered a 17-9 record with a 3.42 ERA in '02. Jordan jacked 25 gopher balls and batted in 97 runners in 2001 while J.D. Drew supplied a 323 BA along with 27 wallops and a career-high 1.027 OPS in only 109 games. He finished sixth in the 2004 NL MVP balloting following a productive year in which he batted .305 with 31 clouts, 118 runs scored, 118 walks and 1.006 OPS. Drew reached the century mark in RBI and drilled 34 doubles in '06.

Albert Pujols pummeled the opposition in his inaugural campaign, bashing 37 big-flies and driving in 130 runs while batting .329. "Prince Albert" received ROY honors and finished fourth in the 2001 NL MVP race. Pujols averaged .334 with 43 doubles, 41 circuit clouts, 124 RBI, 119 runs and a 1.055 OPS from 2001-2009! During that timeframe he collected three MVP Awards ('05, '08, '09), placed runner-up four times and compiled a personal-best 39 Win Shares in '09. The Cardinals earned the NL Wild Card from 2001 through 2003 as the Astros claimed the division titles for 3 consecutive years. Rheal Cormier was lights-out in a setup role, furnishing a record of 8-0 with a 1.70 ERA and a 0.933 WHIP in '03. Braden Looper (3.68, 28 SV) assumed the closer's role and followed up with 29 saves and a 2.70 ERA in '04. Shortstop Jack E. Wilson (.308/11/59) received his lone All-Star invitation in 2004, collecting 201 base knocks including 41 two-baggers and an NL-best 12 triples.

Coco Crisp crunched 42 doubles and batted .300 in 2005 and then paced the League with 49 stolen bases in 2011. Placido Polanco delivered a .331 BA in 2005, scorching opposing hurlers for a .341 average while amassing 200 hits and scoring 105 runs en route to his first All-Star appearance. The Cardinals suffered through another dry spell with the mound crew, failing to reach the BFP requirements from 2004-2008 with the exception of 2007. Dan Haren led the club with a 15-9 record, 3.07 ERA and 192 strikeouts in '07, notching 16 victories with a 3.33 ERA and 206 whiffs in the subsequent year. Haren posted 223 strikeouts and a league-best 1.003 WHIP in '09. St. Louis' hurlers posted franchise-worst marks in pitWARnorm (7) and pitWSnorm (46) during the 2007 season. Yadier Molina earned six straight Gold Glove Awards (2008-2013) and placed third in the 2013 NL MVP balloting. Molina appeared on the Fielding WAR and WS leader boards in seven of his nine full seasons (through 2013).

St. Louis secured 81 victories and clinched the NL Central title by a single game over Pittsburgh in '09. Allen Craig socked 35 doubles and 22 long balls while driving home 92 baserunners in 2012. He was rewarded with an All-Star selection in 2013, posting a .315 BA while plating 97 baserunners. Matt Carpenter (.318/11/78) topped the NL leader boards in 2013 with 199 safeties, 126 runs scored and 55 doubles while earning his first All-Star invitation and placing fourth in the NL MVP race.

Win Shares > 20	Single-Season	1980-2013
Leon Durham - 1B (STL)	Todd Zeile - 3B (STL) x2	Ray Lankford - CF (STL) x5
Albert Pujols - 1B (STL) x9	Albert Pujols - 3B (STL)	Lance Johnson - CF (STL)
Daric Barton - 1B (STL)	Terry Kennedy - C (STL) x2	Coco Crisp – CF (STL)
Allen Craig – 1B (STL)	Yadier Molina - C (STL) x2	Leon Durham - RF (STL)
Tom Herr - 2B (STL)	Larry Herndon - LF (STL)	Brian Jordan - RF (STL) x2
Placido Polanco - 2B (STL)	Vince Coleman - LF (STL)	J.D. Drew - RF (STL) x3
Matt Carpenter – 2B (STL)	Bernard Gilkey - LF (STL) x2	Jerry Reuss - SP (STL)
Jack E. Wilson - SS (STL)	Albert Pujols - LF (STL) x2	John Denny - SP (STL)
Terry Pendleton - 3B (STL) x3	Andy Van Slyke - CF (STL) x5	

Note: 4000 PA or BFP to qualify, except during strike-shortened seasons
(1972 = 3800, 1981 & 1994 = 2700, 1995 = 3500) and 154-game schedule (3800)
- failed to qualify: 1901, 1921-1922, 1929, 1990-1991, 2004-2006, 2008

Cardinals All-Time "Originals" Roster

Ody Abbott	Wheezer Dell	Wally Kimmick	Mike Potter
Babe Adams	Lee DeMontreville	Curtis King	Nels Potter
Buster Adams	Don Dennis	Jim King	Joe Presko
Joe Adams	John Denny	Lynn King	Mike Proly
Matt Adams	Paul Derringer	Nellie King	George Puccinelli
Jim D. Adduci	Joe DeSa	Billy Kinloch	Albert Pujols
Henry Adkinson	Daniel Descalso	Josh Kinney	Finners Quinlan
Cy Alberts	Matt DeWitt	Matt Kinzer	Roy Radebaugh
Eliezer Alfonzo	Brandon Dickson	Clay Kirby	Ken Raffensberger
Luis Alicea	Murry Dickson	Lou Klein	Brady Raggio
Armando Almanza	Chuck Diering	Nub Kleinke	John Raleigh
Tom Alston	Mike Difelice	Bob Klinger	Bill Ramsey
Walter Alston	Pat Dillard	Rudy Kling	Mike Jeffrey Ramsey
Ruben Amaro	Dutch Distel	Johnny Klippstein	Dick Rand
Bryan Anderson	Steve Dixon	Clyde Kluttz	Colby Rasmus
Craig Anderson	Tom Dixon	Jack Knight	Eric Rasmussen
John Andrews	George Dockins	Mike Knode	Britt Reames
Nate Andrews	She Donahue	Will Koenigsmark	Phil Redding
Pat Ankenman	Mike Donlin	Gary Kolb	Milt Reed
Rick Ankiel	Blix Donnelly	Ed Konetchy	Tom Reilly
John Antonelli	Jim Donohue	George Kopshaw	Art Reinhart
Scott Arnold	Gary Dotter	Pete Kozma	Pete Reiser
Rene Arocha	Klondike Douglass	Kurt Krieger	Jack Reis
Luis Arroyo	Taylor Douthit	Howie Krist	Ken Reitz
Rudy Arroyo	Dennis Dove	Chris Krug	Bob Repass
Dennis Aust	Dave Dowling	Ryan Kurosaki	Andy Replogle
Manuel Aybar	Jeff Doyle	Whitey Kurowski	Rip Repulski
Les Backman	Tom Dozier	Marty Kutyna	Jerry Reuss
Dave Bakenhaster	Clem Dreisewerd	Eddie Lake	Anthony Reyes
Scott Baker	Lee Dressen	Chris Lambert	Flint Rhem
Tom H. Baker	J.D. Drew	Tito Landrum	Charlie Rhodes
O.F. Baldwin	Charlie Duffee	Max Lanier	Del Rice
Art Ball	Bob Duliba	Ray Lankford	Hal Rice
Jimmy Bannon	Chris Duncan	Bob Larmore	Bill Richardson
Brian Barber	Wiley Dunham	Dan Larson	Chris Richard
George Barclay	Jack Dunleavy	Don Lassetter	Gordie Richardson
Ray Bare	Mike Dunne	Bill C. Lee	Dave Ricketts
Clyde Barfoot	Don Durham	Leron Lee	Dick Ricketts
Dick Barrett	Leon Durham	Jim Lentine	Elmer Rieger

Frank Barrett	Erv Dusak	(NULL) Leonard	Lew Riggs
Dave Bartosch	Jim Dwyer	Jose Leon	Andy Rincon
Daric Barton	Eddie Dyer	Dan Lewandowski	Tink Riviere
Allen Battle	Johnny Echols	Bill Lewis	Johnny Rizzo
Moose Baxter	Joe Edelen	Jim Lindeman	Jerry Robertson
Ralph Beard	Harry Elliott	Royce Lint	Skipper Roberts
Jim Beauchamp	Slim Emmerich	Carlisle Littlejohn	Kerry Robinson
Johnny Beazley	Bill Endicott	John Littlefield	Shane Robinson
Zinn Beck	Charlie Enwright	Harry Lochhead	Jose I. Rodriguez
Ed Biecher	Hal Epps	Jeoff Long	Preacher Roe
Clarence Beers	John Ericks	Braden Looper	Wally Roettger
Hi Bell	Chuck Essegian	Art Lopatka	Ray Rolling
Les Bell	Roy Evans	Joe Lotz	John Romonosky
Rigo Beltran	Terry Evans	John Lovett	Marc Ronan
Alan Benes	Bryan Eversgerd	Grover Lowdermilk	Gene Roof
Joe Benes	Reuben Ewing	Lou Lowdermilk	Jorge Roque
Pug Bennett	Fred Fagin	Sean Lowe	Santiago Rosario
Sid Benton	Harry Fanok	Bill Ludwig	Trevor Rosenthal
Jeff Berblinger	Jeff Fassero	Memo Luna	Sonny Ruberto
Augie Bergamo	Stan Ferens	Ernie Lush	Paul Russell
Jack Berly	Neil Fiala	Lance Lynn	Brendan Ryan
Joe Bernard	C. J. Fick	Red Lynn	Mike P. Ryan
Harry Berte	Bien Figueroa	George Lyons	Mike Ryba
Frank Betcher	Sam Fishburn	Hersh Lyons	Ray Sadecki
Bill Bethea	Mike P. Fitzgerald	Tyler Lyons	Bob Sadowski
Harry Betts	Tim Flood	Bob Mabe	Bob F. Sadowski
Bruno Betzel	Jake Flowers	John Mabry	Fernando Salas
Steve Bilko	Curt Ford	Lonnie Maclin	Mark Salas
Frank Bird	Bob Forsch	Max Macon	Slim Sallee
Charlie Bishop	Jesse Fowler	Lee Magee	Ike Samuels
George Bjorkman	Charlie Frank	Harl W. Maggert	Eduardo Sanchez
Ray Blades	Fred Frankhouse	Joe Magrane	Ray Sanders
Ed Blake	Herman Franks	Bob Mahoney	War Sanders
Coonie Blank	John Frascatore	Eddie Malone	Bill Sarni
Don Blasingame	Sam Freeman	Gus Mancuso	Luis Saturria
Buddy Blattner	Howard Freigau	Seth Maness	Jimmie Schaffer
Bob Blaylock	Art Fromme	Julio Manon	Bob Scheffing
Gary Blaylock	John Fulgham	Walt Marbet	Bill Schindler
Michael Blazek	Les Fusselman	Marty Marion	Freddy Schmidt
Jack Bliss	Phil Gagliano	Fred Marolewski	Willard Schmidt
Bud Bloomfield	Fred Gaiser	Eli Marrero	Red Schoendienst
Joe Boever	John Gall	Charlie Marshall	Dick Schofield
Mitchell Boggs	Jim Galloway	Max Marshall	Heinie Schuble
Sam Bohne	Joe Gannon	Fred Martin	Walt Schulz
Dick Bokelmann	Joe Garagiola	Pepper Martin	Skip Schumaker
Bill Bolden	Jaime Garcia	Stu Martin	Lou Scoffic
Don Bollweg	Glenn Gardner	Ernie Mason	George W. Scott
Pedro Borbon	Art Garibaldi	Tom Matchick	Ray Searage
Jim Bottomley	John Gast	Greg Mathews	Tom Seats
Weldon Bowlin	Gary Geiger	Joe Mather	Epp Sell
Bob J. Bowman	Charlie Gelbert	T.J. Mathews	Carey Selph
Cloyd Boyer	George Genovese	Harry Maupin	Walter Sessi
Ken Boyer	Rube Geyer	Dal Maxvill	Mike Shannon
Terry Bradshaw	Bob Gibson	Jakie May	Spike Shannon
Jackie Brandt	George Gilham	Jack McAdams	Wally Shannon

Roy Brashear	Frank Gilhooley	Bake McBride	Al S. Shaw
Joe Bratcher	Bernard Gilkey	Tim McCarver	Gerry Shea
Danny Breeden	Carden Gillenwater	Pat McCauley	Biff Sheehan
Herb Bremer	George Gillpatrick	Joe McClain	Ray Shepardson
Rod Brewer	Keith Glauber	Kyle McClellan	Bill Sherdel
Nelson Briles	Tommy Glaviano	Jim McCormick	Tim Sherrill
John Brock	Bill Gleason	Mike McCoy	Vince Shields
Brian Broderick	Bob Glenn	Harry McCurdy	Kevin Siegrist
Tony Brottem	Harry Glenn	Lindy McDaniel	Ted Simmons
Andrew M. Brown	Roy Golden	Von McDaniel	John Sipin
Buster Brown	Bill Goodenough	Keith McDonald	Dick Sisler
Cal Browning	Ival Goodman	Dewey McDougal	Enos Slaughter
Jim Brown	Reid Gorecki	Joe McEwing	Bill Smith
Jimmy Brown	Hank Gornicki	Guy McFadden	Bobby Gene Smith
Mordecai Brown	Julio Gotay	Chappie McFarland	Bud Smith
Duff Brumley	Jim Gott	Bill McGee	Hal R. Smith
Glenn Brummer	Al Grabowski	Dan McGeehan	Jack Smith
Justin Brunette	Wayne Granger	Jim McGinley	Wally Smith
Johnny Bucha	Mark Grater	Stoney McGlynn	Homer Smoot
Jerry Buchek	Bill Greason	Mark McGrillis	Esix Snead
Jim Bucher	Gene Green	Austin McHenry	Frank Snyder
Fritz Buelow	Scarborough Green	Otto McIvor	Donovan Solano
Kirk Bullinger	Tyler Greene	Jim McKnight	Ed Spiezio
Al Burch	Luke Gregerson	Ralph McLaurin	Ed Sprague
Bob Burda	Lee Gregory	Wayne McLeland	Jerry Staley
Tom Burgess	Tim Griesenbeck	Bob Meacham	Oscar Stanage
Ken Burkhart	John Grimes	Lee Meadows	Pete Standridge
Jack Barnett	Ross Grimsley	Joe Medwick	Harry Stanton
Ed Burns	Dan Griner	Luis Melendez	Ray Starr
Farmer Burns	Johnny Grodzicki	Steve Melter	Nick Stavinoha
Mike Busby	Mike Gulan	Rube Melton	Gene Stechschulte
Brent Butler	Don Gutteridge	Ted Menze	Bill Steele
Keith Butler	Santiago Guzman	John Mercer	Bob Steele
Bud Byerly	Bob Habenicht	Ed Mickelson	Bill Stein
Bill Byers	Jim Hackett	Mike Milchin	Blake Stein
Bobby Byrne	Harvey Haddix	Bob L. Miller	Justin Stein
Al Cabrera	Chick Hafey	Chuck Miller	Steve Stemle
Jack Calhoun	Kevin Hagen	Shelby Miller	Bob Stephenson
Carmen Cali	Joe Hague	Stu Miller	Ray Stephens
John Callahan	Ed Haigh	Buster Mills	Stuffy Stewart
Wesley Callahan	Bill Hallahan	Larry Milton	Tige Stone
Billy Campbell	Joe Hall	Johnny Mize	Allyn Stout
Cardell Camper	Russ Hall	Vinegar Bend Mizell	Da Rond Stovall
Sal Campisi	Jack Hamilton	Herb Moford	Johnny Stuart
Lew Camp	Mark Hamilton	Yadier Molina	Bobby Sturgeon
Chris Cannizzaro	Loy Hanning	Willie Montanez	Willie Sudhoff
Tex Carleton	Danny Haren	Steve Montgomery	Harry Sullivan
Steve Carlton	Bob Harmon	Wally Moon	Suter Sullivan
Duke Carmel	Ray Harrell	Terry Moore	Kid Summers
Cris Carpenter	Bo Hart	Bill L. Moran	Tom Sunkel
David D. Carpenter	Mike Hartley	Charlie Moran	Max Surkont
Matt Carpenter	Arnold Hauser	Forrest More	Charlie Swindells
Larry Carter	Bill Hawke	Eddie Morgan	So Taguchi
Bob Caruthers	Blake Hawksworth	Matt Morris	John Tamargo
Alex Castellanos	Pink Hawley	Walter Morris	Chuck Taylor

Bill Caudill	Doc Hazleton	Hap Morse	Ed R. Taylor
Adron Chambers	Bunny C. Hearn	Clayton Mortensen	Garry Templeton
Bill Chambers	Jim Hearn	Jason Motte	Greg Terlecky
Johnnie Chambers	Cliff Heathcote	Heinie C. Mueller	Dick Terwilliger
Ed Chapman	Tom Heintzelman	Heinie E. Mueller	Tommy Thevenow
Chappy Charles	Clarence Heise	Jerry Mumphrey	Jake Thielman
Tom Cheney	Charlie Hemphill	Bob Muncrief	Tom Thomas
Paul Chervinko	Solly Hemus	Red Munger	Brad Thompson
Pete Childs	Jeremy Hernandez	Simmy Murch	Bobby Tiefenauer
Nelson Chittum	Keith Hernandez	Tim Murchison	Jess Todd
Bob Chlupsa	Larry Herndon	Wilbur Murdoch	Specs Toporczer
Don Choate	Tom Herr	Howard Murphy	Angel Torres
Frank Cimorelli	Neal Hertweck	John Murphy	Mike Torrez
Ralph Citarella	Ed Heusser	Mike Murphy	Paul Toth
Stubby Clapp	Jim Hickman	Red Murray	Harry Trekell
Jim F. Clark	Eddie Higgins	Danny Murtaugh	Oscar Tuero
Mark Clark	Irv Higginbotham	Stan Musial	Tom Turner
Mike Clark	Palmer Hildebrand	Bert Myers	Art Twineham
Phil J. Clark	Tom Hilgendorf	Billy Myers	Mike Tyson
Terry Clark	Marc Hill	Lynn Myers	Tom Urbani
Dain Clay	Steven Hill	Sam W. Narron	John Urrea
Doug Clemens	Howard Hilton	Chris Narveson	Lon Ury
Reggie Cleveland	Jack Himes	Earl Naylor	Mike Vail
Ed Clough	Bruce Hitt	John Nelson	Benny Valenzuela
Nate Colbert	Ed Hock	Mel Nelson	John Vann
Alex Cole	Art Hoelskoetter	Rocky Nelson	Jay Van Noy
Dick Cole	Jarrett Hoffpauir	Charlie Niebergall	Andy Van Slyke
Percy Coleman	Aaron Holbert	Dick Niehaus	Ernie Vick
Vince Coleman	Ken Holcombe	Tom Nieto	Bob Vines
Walter Coleman	Ed Holly	Tom Niland	Michael Wacha
(NULL) Collins	Ducky Holmes	Howie Nunn	Bill Wakefield
Ripper Collins	Wattie Holm	Ken Oberkfell	Speed Walker
Jackie Collum	Buck Hopkins	Dan O'Brien	Brett Wallace
Charles Comiskey	Bill Hopper	Ken O'Dea	Ty Waller
Joe Connor	Johnny Hopp	Bruce Ogrodowski	Les Walrond
Ed Conwell	Rogers Hornsby	Tom O'Hara	P.J. Walters
Duff Cooley	Oscar Horstmann	Gene Oliver	Cy Warmoth
Mort Cooper	Ricky Horton	Al Olmsted	Ray Washburn
Walker Cooper	Earl Howard	Denny O'Neil	Steve Waterbury
Mays Copeland	Cal Howe	Jack O'Neill	George Watkins
Rheal Cormier	Roland Howell	Mike O'Neill	Allen Watson
Jim Cosman	Al Hrabosky	Joe Orengo	Milt Watson
John Costello	Jimmy Hudgens	Charlie O'Rourke	Art Weaver
Chip Coulter	Nat Hudson	Patsy O'Rourke	Skeeter Webb
Jack Coveney	Frank Huelsman	Ernie Orsatti	Dick Wheeler
Bill Cox	Dick Hughes	Bill Ortega	Jimmy Whelan
Danny Cox	Tom E. Hughes	Donovan Osborne	Jack Whillock
Allen Craig	Joel Hunt	Adam Ottavino	Abe White
Forrest Crawford	Randy Hunt	John Otten	Burgess Whitehead
Glenn Crawford	Bill Hurst	Mickey Owen	Ernie White
Doug Creek	Don Hurst	Pablo Ozuna	Possum Whitted
Jack Creel	Chad Hutchinson	Don Padgett	Bob Wicker
Bernie Creger	Pat Hynes	Matt Pagnozzi	Floyd Wicker
Creepy Crespi	Walt Irwin	Tom Pagnozzi	Ted Wieand
Coco Crisp	Larry Jackson	Al Papai	Fred Wigington

Tripp Cromer	Ryan C. Jackson	Freddy Parent	Del Wilber
Ed Crosby	Bert James	Kelly Paris	Randy Wiles
Jeff Cross	Charlie James	Mike Parisi	Denney Wilie
Rich Croushore	Larry Jaster	Harry Parker	Ted Wilks
Mike Crudale	Stan Javier	Roy Parker	Howie Williamson
Walton Cruise	Jon Jay	Harry Patton	Otto Williams
Gene Crumling	Jose Jimenez	Tom Patton	Ron Willis
Hector Cruz	Ben J. Johnson	Gil Paulsen	Steamboat Williams
Jose Cruz	Ken W. Johnson	George Paynter	Craig Wilson
Tommy Cruz	Keith Johns	Josh Pearce	Jack E. Wilson
Tony Cruz	Lance Johnson	Alex Pearson	Jim Winford
Victor Cruz	Tyler Johnson	Homer Peel	Ivey Wingo
Joe Cunningham	Gordon Jones	Charlie Peete	Jay Witasick
Ray Cunningham	Howie Jones	Heinie Peitz	Kolten Wong
Murphy Currie	Nippy Jones	Joe Peitz	Gene Woodburn
Jermaine Curtis	Tim W. Jones	Geronimo Pena	John Wood
Carl Dale	Brian Jordan	Terry Pendleton	Floyd Wooldridge
Gene Dale	Jimmy Journell	Ray Pepper	Mark Worrell
Jack Damaska	Oscar Judd	Audry Perez	Todd Worrell
Pete Daniels	Lyle Judy	Chris Perez	Roy Wright
Rolla Daringer	Al Jurisich	Mike Perez	John Wyatt
Jerry Davanon	Skip Jutze	Pol Perritt	Johnny Wyrostek
Otis Davis	Jason Karnuth	Shane Peterson	Ray Yochim
Spud Davis	Eddie Kazak	Steve Peters	Bobby Young
Boots Day	Bob Keely	Lee Pfund	Dmitri Young
Pea Ridge Day	Jeff Keener	Eddie H. Phillips	Don Young
Dizzy Dean	Frank Kellert	Charlie Pickett	J.B. Young
Paul Dean	John Kelleher	Cotton Pippen	George Zackert
Adam Debus	Mick Kelleher	Gaylen Pitts	Todd Zeile
Tony DeFate	Billy Kelly	Tim Plodinec	Bart Zeller
Rube DeGroff	John Kelly	Bill Plummer	Eddie Zimmerman
Joe Delahanty	Joe W. Kelly	Placido Polanco	Ed Zmich
Art Delaney	Adam Kennedy	Cliff Politte	George Zuverink
Bill DeLancey	Terry Kennedy	Howie Pollet	
Luis DeLeon	George Kernek	Stu Pomeranz	
Eddie Delker	Hal Kime	Bill Popp	

Year/Team	OPW%	PW	PL	APW%	AW	AL	Diff+/-
1901 CHC	0.420	59	81	0.381	53	86	-0.038
1902 CHC	0.527	74	66	0.496	68	69	-0.031
1903 CHC	0.524	73	67	0.594	82	56	0.071
1904 CHC	0.524	81	73	0.608	93	60	0.083
1905 CHC	0.505	78	76	0.601	92	61	0.096
1906 CHC	0.518	80	74	0.763 P	116	36	0.245
1907 CHC	0.564 P	87	67	0.704 P	107	45	0.140
1908 CHC	0.570	88	66	0.643 P	99	55	0.072
1909 CHC	0.536	83	71	0.680	104	49	0.144

franchID	OWAR	OWS	AWAR	AWS	WARdiff	WSdiff	P/D/W/F
1901 CHC	28.319	227.465	21.502	158.998	6.817	68.467	
1902 CHC	37.454	280.815	29.953	203.960	7.501	76.856	
1903 CHC	48.042	**304.156**	39.349	246.008	8.693	58.147	
1904 CHC	46.976	302.016	38.985	278.572	7.991	23.444	
1905 CHC	40.997	256.416	45.824	275.921	-4.826	-19.505	
1906 CHC	58.865	**362.820**	**59.017**	**344.999**	-0.152	17.821	
1907 CHC	40.745	271.726	48.625	**321.001**	-7.879	-49.275	P
1908 CHC	47.751	**315.317**	49.838	**297.001**	-2.087	18.316	
1909 CHC	33.640	253.822	53.230	311.999	-19.590	-58.177	

Legend: (P) = Pennant / Most Wins in League (D) = Division Winner (W) = Wild Card Winner (F) = Failed to Qualify

The Chicago White Stockings commenced play in 1876 as one of the original National League franchises. The club changed its nickname to the Colts (1890) and Orphans (1898) before settling on the "Cubs" in 1903. Based on the WS>20 frame of reference, it has developed the second-fewest quality center fielders (13) and third-fewest right fielders (16) among the "Turn of the Century" franchises. The relief corps has been a source of strength, delivering the most WS>10 player-seasons (63). Lee Smith leads the bullpen crew with 10 WS>10 seasons, followed by Bruce Sutter with 8. On the other hand, the franchise never placed in the top three WS>10 leaders at any outfield position.

Second-sacker Tom P. Daly socked a league-leading 38 two-baggers, drove in 90 baserunners and hit .315 for the Cubbies in 1901. Danny Green contributed a .311 BA from 1901-03. Bill Bradley scored 104 runs and delivered a .340 BA in '02. Jack W. Taylor white-washed the opposition 8 times while topping the circuit in ERA (1.29) and WHIP (0.953). Taylor surpassed the 20-win mark on four occasions and completed 279 of 287 career starts! Joe Tinker nabbed at least 20 bags during eleven consecutive seasons (1902-1912). His defensive proficiency at shortstop is reflected in 7 appearances on the Fielding WAR and WS leader boards (third-place All-Time).

Frank Chance posted a .318 average from 1903-06. "The Peerless Leader" twice topped the NL in stolen bases including a career-best 67 in '03. Chance contributed a .450 OBP during the '05 campaign and tallied 103 runs in the subsequent season (both league-bests). Johnny Evers swiped 32 bases per year (1903-1910). Chicago paced the Major Leagues with 34 WS>10 player-seasons at the keystone position from 1901-1919.

"Tornado" Jake Weimer eclipsed the 20-win mark in three out of four campaigns while fashioning a 2.16 ERA and a 1.158 WHIP from 1903-06. "Long" Tom Hughes supplied a 20-7 record with a 2.57 ERA in '03. Hughes established personal bests with a 2.21 ERA and 1.089 WHIP for the 1908 squad. Following a five-year absence, Buttons Briggs returned to the Major

Leagues where he compiled a 19-11 record with a 2.05 ERA and completed 28 of 30 starts for the '04 crew. Fred Glade added 18 victories with a 2.27 ERA and a 1.059 WHIP. Bill Dahlen knocked in a league-leading 80 runs. "Big" Ed Reulbach crafted a 1.72 ERA with a 1.048 WHIP from 1905-09. He topped the circuit in winning percentage for three straight campaigns (1906-08), posting a combined record of 60-15. Bob Rhoads averaged 18 wins with a 2.14 ERA and a 1.159 WHIP from 1905-08. "Dusty" won 22 contests and completed 31 of 34 starts spanning 315 innings pitched in '06.

The 1906 Cubs' pitching staff delivered the highest pitWSnorm (161) in MLB history. Chicago's moundsmen tied with Philadephia and Pittsburgh for the most WS>10 player-seasons during the decade. Carl Lundgren supplied career-bests with a 1.17 ERA, 1.072 WHIP and 18 victories in 1907. The Cubs claimed the franchise's first pennant by four games over the Giants and the Pirates. The team also led the National League in oWS during the '03, '06 and '08 campaigns.

Year/Team	OPW%	PW	PL	APW%	AW	AL	Diff+/-
1910 CHC	0.517	80	74	0.675 P	104	50	0.158
1911 CHC	0.487	75	79	0.597	92	62	0.111
1912 CHC	0.500	77	77	0.607	91	59	0.107
1913 CHC	0.551	85	69	0.575	88	65	0.025
1914 CHC	0.474	73	81	0.506	78	76	0.033
1915 CHC	0.506	78	76	0.477	73	80	-0.029
1916 CHC	0.508	78	76	0.438	67	86	-0.070
1917 CHC	0.500 F	77	77	0.481	74	80	-0.019
1918 CHC	0.477 F	61	67	0.651 P	84	45	0.174
1919 CHC	0.543 F	76	64	0.536	75	65	-0.007

franchID	OWAR	OWS	AWAR	AWS	WARdiff	WSdiff	P/D/W/F
1910 CHC	36.356	271.557	51.738	311.997	-15.381	-40.440	
1911 CHC	25.443	233.121	43.514	276.004	-18.071	-42.883	
1912 CHC	31.224	248.051	39.993	273.000	-8.768	-24.948	
1913 CHC	32.278	247.783	37.644	264.001	-5.365	-16.217	
1914 CHC	22.278	199.687	31.076	233.996	-8.798	-34.309	
1915 CHC	32.916	233.164	30.850	218.999	2.066	14.165	
1916 CHC	26.109	196.727	29.427	200.994	-3.317	-4.266	
1917 CHC	23.856	188.709	29.266	221.996	-5.410	-33.287	F
1918 CHC	25.955	183.389	42.425	252.002	-16.469	-68.613	F
1919 CHC	13.828	165.506	36.424	224.997	-22.596	-59.490	F

King Cole (20-4, 1.80) secured the NL ERA title in his rookie campaign (1910). Frank "Wildfire" Schulte (.300/21/107) merited NL MVP honors in 1911 after topping the charts in home runs, RBI and SLG (.534). Jim Delahanty hit .339 and knocked in 94 runs. Heinie Zimmerman (.372/14/99) topped the circuit in batting average, hits (207), doubles (41) and home runs as he compiled 34 Win Shares and slugged .571 in his most prominent season (1912). Johnny Evers (.341) and Bill John Sweeney (.344/1/100) delivered career-highs in batting average.

Larry Cheney tallied 26 victories in his inaugural season and eclipsed the 20-win plateau for three straight years (1912-14). Cheney saved 11 contests in 1913 and supplied personal bests with a 1.92 ERA and 1.119 WHIP during the 1916 campaign. Fred Toney amassed 24 victories while posting a 2.20 ERA in 1917. Toney delivered 17 wins with a 2.39 ERA and 1.132 WHIP from 1915-1921. Charlie Hollocher produced a .316 BA and paced the NL with 161 safeties as a rookie in 1918. Dutch Ruether (19-6, 1.82) furnished career-bests in ERA and WHIP (1.146) in '19. Chicago fell short of the PA and/or BFP requirements from 1917 to 1921.

Year/Team	OPW%	PW	PL	APW%	AW	AL	Diff+/-
1920 CHC	0.534 F	82	72	0.487	75	79	-0.047
1921 CHC	0.436 F	67	87	0.418	64	89	-0.017
1922 CHC	0.440	68	86	0.519	80	74	0.080
1923 CHC	0.497	76	78	0.539	83	71	0.042
1924 CHC	0.472	73	81	0.529	81	72	0.057
1925 CHC	0.473	73	81	0.442	68	86	-0.032
1926 CHC	0.510	79	75	0.532	82	72	0.023
1927 CHC	0.492	76	78	0.556	85	68	0.063
1928 CHC	0.560	86	68	0.591	91	63	0.031
1929 CHC	0.573	88	66	0.645 P	98	54	0.072

franchID	OWAR	OWS	AWAR	AWS	WARdiff	WSdiff	P/D/W/F
1920 CHC	23.889	210.531	30.671	224.999	-6.783	-14.468	F
1921 CHC	17.954	151.549	24.757	192.000	-6.803	-40.450	F
1922 CHC	24.954	184.576	32.276	239.993	-7.322	-55.418	
1923 CHC	35.262	224.382	36.481	249.003	-1.219	-24.622	
1924 CHC	25.490	223.234	26.800	242.996	-1.310	-19.762	
1925 CHC	27.551	200.357	25.690	204.002	1.861	-3.645	
1926 CHC	**33.302**	**219.413**	40.424	246.002	-7.122	-26.589	
1927 CHC	25.421	211.414	36.862	255.003	-11.441	-43.588	
1928 CHC	30.086	220.759	42.517	273.001	-12.431	-52.242	
1929 CHC	24.749	186.533	**49.043**	**294.000**	-24.294	-107.467	

Toney crafted a record of 21-11 with a 2.65 ERA for the 1920 crew. Hollocher compiled a .320 BA from 1920-1923, surpassing the 200-hit mark and batting .340 in '22. Cy Williams amassed four home run titles in his career and delivered a .320 BA from 1920-26; the center fielder bashed 41 four-ply swats and plated 114 baserunners in '23. Ruether contributed 21 victories during the 1922 season.

Bob O'Farrell supplied a .321 BA over two seasons (1922-23) while fellow backstop Bubbles Hargrave served up a .320 mark from 1922-27. Hargrave seized the batting crown in '26 with a .353 average. George "Boots" Grantham eclipsed the .300 BA plateau in eight successive years (1924-1931), posting a .315 mark during that stretch. Pat Malone compiled 18 victories in his rookie season (1928). He topped the circuit with 22 wins, 5 shutouts and 166 whiffs in his sophomore campaign. Chicago paced the National League in oWAR and oWS in '26.

Year/Team	OPW%	PW	PL	APW%	AW	AL	Diff+/-
1930 CHC	0.538	83	71	0.584	90	64	0.046
1931 CHC	0.493	76	78	0.545	84	70	0.052
1932 CHC	0.547 P	84	70	0.584 P	90	64	0.037
1933 CHC	0.489	75	79	0.558	86	68	0.069
1934 CHC	0.479	74	80	0.570	86	65	0.091
1935 CHC	0.595	92	62	0.649 P	100	54	0.054
1936 CHC	0.564 F	87	67	0.565	87	67	0.001
1937 CHC	0.514	79	75	0.604	93	61	0.090
1938 CHC	0.530 F	82	72	0.586 P	89	63	0.055
1939 CHC	0.538	83	71	0.545	84	70	0.007

franchID	OWAR	OWS	AWAR	AWS	WARdiff	WSdiff	P/D/W/F
1930 CHC	35.088	204.907	47.015	269.991	-11.926	-65.085	
1931 CHC	22.867	180.641	44.120	252.002	-21.253	-71.361	
1932 CHC	30.645	221.599	36.883	270.000	-6.237	-48.402	P
1933 CHC	29.816	203.417	39.919	258.004	-10.103	-54.586	
1934 CHC	30.576	202.457	40.600	258.005	-10.024	-55.548	
1935 CHC	42.070	271.574	49.918	300.008	-7.848	-28.435	
1936 CHC	44.329	269.657	43.102	260.999	1.227	8.658	F
1937 CHC	41.323	261.522	43.009	279.002	-1.686	-17.480	
1938 CHC	39.137	248.285	40.580	266.996	-1.443	-18.711	F
1939 CHC	31.455	239.754	37.154	252.002	-5.700	-12.248	

Woody English averaged 133 runs scored over a three-year period (1929-1931) including 152 aces in 1930. He surpassed the 200-hit mark in back-to-back campaigns (1930-31) and placed fourth in the 1931 NL MVP balloting. Grantham set personal bests with 120 runs scored, 18 dingers and 99 ribbies during the 1930 season. Malone led the League with 22 complete games and 20 wins. Gabby Hartnett crushed 37 long balls and plated 122 baserunners while hitting at a .339 clip. "Old Tomato Face" earned six straight All-Star selections (1933-38) and claimed MVP honors after producing a .344 BA in '35.

Chicago outlasted Pittsburgh to take the pennant in '32. Lon Warneke (22-6, 2.37) placed runner-up in the NL MVP race while leading the circuit in victories and ERA. "The Arkansas Hummingbird" fashioned a 3.18 career ERA, received five All-Star invitations and surpassed the 20-win plateau on three occasions. Billy Herman eclipsed the 200-hit mark three times including his rookie season (1932). The second-sacker batted .312 for the decade and topped the NL with 227 base hits and 57 doubles in '35. Guy Bush aka "The Mississippi Mudcat" established career-bests with 20 victories and a 2.75 ERA in '33. Augie Galan tallied 203 safeties including 41 doubles while leading the NL in runs scored (133) and stolen bases (22) in his first full season (1935). Stan Hack surpassed the century mark in runs scored for six successive years (1936-1941). "Smiling Stan" received his first All-Star nod in 1938 when he supplied a .320 BA with personal highs in base hits (195) and triples (11).

Johnny Moore compiled a .328 batting average from 1934-37. Moore drilled 35 doubles and knocked in 98 runs in '34. Frank Demaree delivered a .314 BA over a six-year period (1935-1940). An All-Star selection in back-to-back campaigns, Demaree tallied 212 safeties while batting .350 in '36 and then drove in 115 baserunners in the ensuing year. Dolph Camilli clubbed at least 23 round-trippers in 8 straight seasons (1935-1942). He averaged 27 jacks and 99 ribbies during this stretch and topped the NL with a .446 SLG in '37. Mike Kreevich totaled 99 runs scored in '36, led the League with 16 triples in '37 and batted at a .323 clip in '39.

Win Shares > 20	Single-Season	1920-1939
Dolph Camilli - 1B (CHC) x7	Gabby Hartnett - C (CHC) x7	Johnny Moore - RF (CHC)
George Grantham - 2B (CHC) x3	Stan Hack - 3B (CHC) x9	Frank Demaree - RF (CHC) x2
Sparky Adams - 2B (CHC)	Bob O'Farrell - C (CHC) x3	Pat Malone - SP (CHC) x3
Billy Herman - 2B (CHC) x8	Bubbles Hargrave - C (CHC)	Ed W. Morris - SP (CHC)
Woody English - SS (CHC)	Augie Galan - LF (CHC) x5	Lon Warneke - SP (CHC) x4
Bernie Friberg - 3B (CHC)	Cy Williams - CF (CHC) x2	Hugh Casey - SP (CHC)
Woody English - 3B (CHC)	Alex Metzler - CF (CHC)	Guy Bush - SW (CHC)
	Mike Kreevich - CF (CHC) x2	

Year/Team	OPW%	PW	PL	APW%	AW	AL	Diff+/-
1940 CHC	0.554	85	69	0.487	75	79	-0.067
1941 CHC	0.562	87	67	0.455	70	84	-0.108
1942 CHC	0.540	83	71	0.442	68	86	-0.098
1943 CHC	0.567 P	87	67	0.484	74	79	-0.083
1944 CHC	0.530	82	72	0.487	75	79	-0.043
1945 CHC	0.654 P	101	53	0.636 P	98	56	-0.018
1946 CHC	0.626 P	96	58	0.536	82	71	-0.090
1947 CHC	0.480	74	80	0.448	69	85	-0.032
1948 CHC	0.474	73	81	0.416	64	90	-0.058
1949 CHC	0.489	75	79	0.396	61	93	-0.093

franchID	OWAR	OWS	AWAR	AWS	WARdiff	WSdiff	P/D/W/F
1940 CHC	36.215	222.380	38.531	224.995	-2.315	-2.615	
1941 CHC	32.236	231.306	35.155	209.997	-2.919	21.309	
1942 CHC	33.048	233.675	33.607	204.002	-0.560	29.673	
1943 CHC	39.947	240.265	42.399	222.003	-2.452	18.262	P
1944 CHC	32.490	234.160	37.140	224.995	-4.650	9.165	
1945 CHC	48.464	298.327	53.177	293.996	-2.742	13.154	P
1946 CHC	34.158	234.775	37.752	245.996	-0.440	1.195	P
1947 CHC	25.590	199.649	23.907	206.996	1.683	-7.347	
1948 CHC	26.857	187.742	28.393	192.004	-1.536	-4.262	
1949 CHC	25.183	199.461	22.025	183.002	3.158	16.459	

Hack topped the League leader boards in base hits during consecutive seasons (1940-41). Camilli (.285/34/120) secured 1941 NL MVP honors as he led the circuit in home runs and RBI. Kirby Higbe posted a league-best 22-9 record despite issuing 132 free passes. Hugh Casey paced the NL with 13 saves in 1942 and repeated the feat when he successfully closed out 18 contests in 1947. The Cubs captured the NL pennant in '43 by three games over the Cardinals. Herman drove in 100 runs and supplied a .330 BA for the '43 squad. Galan accepted over 100 free passes for three successive years (1943-45) and tallied 114 aces in '45.

Chicago recorded 101 victories during the 1945 campaign to secure the club's second pennant in three years. The squad topped the opposition in oWS and oWAR while outlasting the Pirates by eight contests. Phil Cavarretta delivered the most hits in the NL during the '44 season. He seized 1945 NL MVP honors and claimed the batting crown with a .355 average. "Handy" Andy Pafko plated 110 baserunners in '45 and appeared in four consecutive All-Star games (1947-1950). Hank Wyse led the starting rotation with 22 victories along with a 2.68 ERA and a WHIP of 1.175. The Cubs repeated as National League champions in 1946 as the squad sustained an eight-game margin over the Cards. Harry "The Cat" Brecheen fashioned a 2.74 ERA with a 1.167 WHIP from 1943-49. Breechen notched 20 wins while leading the NL in strikeouts (149), shutouts (7), ERA (2.24) and WHIP (1.037) during the 1948 season. Hank Majeski drilled 41 two-base hits and knocked in 120 runs for the '48 crew.

Year/Team	OPW%	PW	PL	APW%	AW	AL	Diff+/-
1950 CHC	0.501	77	77	0.418	64	89	-0.083
1951 CHC	0.477 F	73	81	0.403	62	92	-0.075
1952 CHC	0.543 F	84	70	0.500	77	77	-0.043
1953 CHC	0.414	64	90	0.422	65	89	0.008
1954 CHC	0.477	73	81	0.416	64	90	-0.062
1955 CHC	0.449	69	85	0.471	72	81	0.022
1956 CHC	0.409 F	63	91	0.390	60	94	-0.019
1957 CHC	0.456	70	84	0.403	62	92	-0.053
1958 CHC	0.486 F	75	79	0.468	72	82	-0.019
1959 CHC	0.489 F	75	79	0.481	74	80	-0.008

franchID	OWAR	OWS	AWAR	AWS	WARdiff	WSdiff	P/D/W/F
1950 CHC	22.621	176.358	23.591	191.997	-0.970	-15.639	
1951 CHC	22.811	215.062	21.042	185.999	1.769	29.063	F
1952 CHC	36.166	248.810	34.478	230.992	1.688	17.818	F
1953 CHC	30.122	218.648	24.535	195.002	5.587	23.646	
1954 CHC	27.472	225.463	26.338	215.994	1.134	9.469	
1955 CHC	29.661	243.424	26.338	215.994	3.323	27.430	
1956 CHC	27.250	177.854	23.736	180.000	3.514	-2.146	F
1957 CHC	29.240	172.910	26.175	186.000	3.065	-13.089	
1958 CHC	36.685	200.270	36.334	215.998	0.351	-15.729	F
1959 CHC	36.994	210.405	32.617	222.000	4.377	-11.595	F

Ernie Banks made his debut in '53. He averaged .295 with 38 round-trippers and 109 RBI from 1954-1959. "Mr. Cub" slugged 40+ home runs five times including four consecutive campaigns (1957-1960) and earned back-to-back MVP Awards in '58 and '59. Banks led the NL with 47 home runs, 129 RBI and a .614 SLG while establishing career-highs in runs scored (119), hits (193) and batting average (.313) in 1958. For an encore he walloped 45 four-baggers, plated 147 baserunners and tallied 33 Win Shares.

Andy Pafko blasted 36 long balls and knocked in 92 runs in 1950. Smoky Burgess delivered his best season in 1955 (.301/21/78) and batted .298 for the decade. The Cubs failed to reach the PA requirements in '58 and '59. Bob Rush led the Cubbies rotation, averaging 12 wins with a 3.63 ERA and 1.272 WHIP from 1950 through 1958. Rush received an All-Star nod in '52, delivering a record of 17-13 with a 2.70 ERA and 1.142 WHIP. Warren Hacker (15-9, 2.58) also excelled in 1952, completing 12 of 20 starts. Frank T. Smith notched 20 saves with a 2.67 ERA in '54. The Cubs fell below the BFP requirements in '51, '52 and '56.

Win Shares > 20	Single-Season	1940-1959
Phil Cavarretta - 1B (CHC) x2	Andy Pafko - LF (CHC)	Kirby Higbe - SP (CHC) x2
Augie Galan - 1B (CHC)	Augie Galan - CF (CHC)	Hank Wyse - SP (CHC)
Ernie Banks - SS (CHC) x6	Andy Pafko - CF (CHC) x2	Harry Brecheen - SP (CHC)
Hank Majeski - 3B (CHC)	Phil Cavarretta - RF (CHC)	Bob Rush - SP (CHC)
Andy Pafko - 3B (CHC)		

Year/Team	OPW%	PW	PL	APW%	AW	AL	Diff+/-
1960 CHC	0.430 F	66	88	0.390	60	94	-0.041
1961 CHC	0.434	70	92	0.416	64	90	-0.019
1962 CHC	0.428	69	93	0.364	59	103	-0.064
1963 CHC	0.505	82	80	0.506	82	80	0.001
1964 CHC	0.461	75	87	0.469	76	86	0.008
1965 CHC	0.553 F	90	72	0.444	72	90	-0.109
1966 CHC	0.510	83	79	0.364	59	103	-0.146

Year/Team	OPW%	PW	PL	APW%	AW	AL	Diff+/-
1967 CHC	0.581	94	68	0.540	87	74	-0.041
1968 CHC	0.534	87	75	0.519	84	78	-0.016
1969 CHC	0.521	84	78	0.568	92	70	0.047

franchID	OWAR	OWS	AWAR	AWS	WARdiff	WSdiff	P/D/W/F
1960 CHC	29.331	193.051	20.002	180.003	9.328	13.048	F
1961 CHC	41.055	223.147	31.669	191.997	9.386	31.149	
1962 CHC	26.467	211.502	21.854	176.998	4.614	34.503	
1963 CHC	38.586	276.742	34.959	245.995	3.627	30.747	
1964 CHC	34.562	251.188	32.489	228.001	2.074	23.187	
1965 CHC	36.722	291.970	27.645	215.997	9.078	75.973	F
1966 CHC	43.356	235.299	27.129	176.997	16.227	58.303	
1967 CHC	41.962	279.000	39.193	260.997	2.769	18.003	
1968 CHC	39.275	269.331	34.477	251.998	4.798	17.333	
1969 CHC	36.860	252.346	45.290	275.996	-8.430	-23.649	

GM John Holland acquired the lumber crew that arrived in the early 1960's as Lou Brock, Billy L. Williams and Ron Santo joined Banks in the starting lineup. Banks averaged .263 with 27 jacks and 92 ribbies for the decade. Santo arrived in '60 and supplied 27 blasts and 99 RBI per season from 1961-1969. He posted the Cubs' highest Win Shares total (36) while placing fourth in the 1967 NL MVP balloting. Williams (.278/25/86) took home NL ROY honors in '61 and provided similar numbers through the course of the decade (.292/27/94). Brock averaged 48 stolen bases, 30 doubles and 96 runs scored from '62 through '69.

George Altman chipped in with 27 dingers and 96 RBI in '61. Second-sacker Ken Hubbs won the NL ROY and Gold Glove Awards in '62. Chicago finished above .500 in 1963, setting the stage for an excellent run at the end of the Sixties. Dick Ellsworth won 22 games and completed 19 contests while compiling an ERA of 2.11 for the '63 squad. Ron Perranoski headed the relief crew, averaging a 2.55 ERA and 15 saves per season during the decade. He placed fourth in the 1963 MVP voting with a 16-3 record, 1.67 ERA and 21 saves. Al Worthington delivered 15 saves per year with a 2.55 ERA from 1963-68. Chicago peaked with a 94-win season in 1967, falling 2 games short of the NL title. The Cubbies averaged 87 wins from '66 to '69. Pat Jarvis tallied 16 wins and a 2.60 ERA in '68. The Cubs fell short of the PA requirements in '60 and failed to meet the BFP requirements in '65.

Year/Team	OPW%	PW	PL	APW%	AW	AL	Diff+/-
1970 CHC	0.561 P	91	71	0.519	84	78	-0.042
1971 CHC	0.512	83	79	0.512	83	79	0.000
1972 CHC	0.559 P	91	71	0.548	85	70	-0.011
1973 CHC	0.505	82	80	0.478	77	84	-0.027
1974 CHC	0.460	75	87	0.407	66	96	-0.053
1975 CHC	0.536 D	87	75	0.463	75	87	-0.073
1976 CHC	0.499	81	81	0.463	75	87	-0.036
1977 CHC	0.499 F	81	81	0.500	81	81	0.001
1978 CHC	0.445 F	72	90	0.488	79	83	0.043
1979 CHC	0.497 F	81	81	0.494	80	82	-0.003

franchID	OWAR	OWS	AWAR	AWS	WARdiff	WSdiff	P/D/W/F
1970 CHC	39.722	234.366	46.068	252.005	-6.346	-17.639	P
1971 CHC	34.551	247.978	39.420	249.004	-4.870	-1.025	
1972 CHC	38.799	255.152	43.683	255.006	-4.885	0.146	P
1973 CHC	43.278	271.195	33.151	231.006	10.127	40.189	
1974 CHC	29.593	207.937	30.551	198.001	-0.958	9.936	
1975 CHC	38.738	237.698	31.189	225.000	7.550	12.698	D
1976 CHC	32.805	219.223	29.896	225.005	2.909	-5.782	

1977 CHC	44.110	255.867	37.657	242.993	6.453	12.874	F
1978 CHC	37.923	227.440	29.858	237.002	8.065	-9.562	F
1979 CHC	41.812	245.671	37.240	239.992	4.572	5.679	F

Banks retired in 1971 but Williams and Santo provided several outstanding seasons to begin the 1970's. Brock continued to produce throughout the decade, with an average of .298 and 55 steals per season. He pilfered 118 bases in 1974, finishing runner-up in the NL MVP balloting. Williams (.322/42/129) led the National League with 205 base hits and 137 runs scored in 1970. "Sweet Swingin' Billy" crushed 37 quadruples, knocked in 122 runs, and paced the NL with a .333 average in '72. Williams was the runner-up in the NL MVP voting in both campaigns. Santo smacked 26 long balls and drove in 114 runs in '70.

The Cubs captured the pennant in 1970 and 1972, defeating the Pirates by 6 games in both seasons. Perranoski saved 34 contests with a 2.43 ERA in '70. Jim Brewer assumed the closer role from '71 to '73, posting career-bests in ERA (1.26) and WHIP (0.843) in 1972. Ken Holtzman dominated the opposition from 1972-75, averaging 19 victories with a 2.92 ERA and 1.175 WHIP. Jim Colborn made his lone All-Star appearance in 1973 on the strength of a 20-12 record and 3.18 ERA. The Mets overtook the Cubbies by a single game in '73. Oscar Gamble and Billy North ignited the offense as Gamble slammed 31 four-baggers in 1977 while North swiped at least 50 bases on four occasions from 1973-1979. Chicago took the NL East title in 1975 by percentage points over Pittsburgh. The influx of batting talent from the farm ceased as the Cubs failed to meet the PA requirements from 1978 through 1986.

Rick Reuschel logged 20 victories and a 2.79 ERA in '77. Larry Gura fashioned a 16-4 mark with a 2.72 ERA and 1.096 WHIP in '78. Burt Hooton won 13 games per year with a 3.20 ERA from 1972-1979. He delivered his peak performance in 1978, amassing a record of 19-10 with a 2.71 ERA and 1.089 ERA and placing second in the NL Cy Young balloting. Knuckleballer Joe Niekro followed with another runner-up finish after achieving 21 victories with a 3.00 ERA in 1979. Bruce Sutter notched 31 saves with a 1.34 ERA and 0.857 WHIP in '77. He topped that effort with a league-leading 37 saves in '79, earning the Cy Young Award. Ron G. Davis stockpiled 14 wins in 1979 as the setup man.

Win Shares > 20	Single-Season	1960-1979
Don Kessinger - SS (CHC)	George Altman - RF (CHC)	Bill Stoneman - SP (CHC)
Ron Santo - 3B (CHC) x8	Billy L. Williams - RF (CHC) x2	Jim Colborn - SP (CHC)
Billy L. Williams - LF (CHC) x8	Dick Ellsworth - SP (CHC)	Rick Reuschel - SP (CHC)
Lou Brock - LF (CHC) x10	Ken Holtzman - SP (CHC)	Bruce Sutter - RP (CHC) x3
Billy North - CF (CHC) x3		

Year/Team	OPW%	PW	PL	APW%	AW	AL	Diff+/-
1980 CHC	0.520 F	84	78	0.395	64	98	-0.125
1981 CHC	0.498 F	81	81	0.369	38	65	-0.129
1982 CHC	0.461 F	75	87	0.451	73	89	-0.010
1983 CHC	0.461 F	75	87	0.438	71	91	-0.022
1984 CHC	0.490 F	79	83	0.596 P	96	65	0.107
1985 CHC	0.479 F	78	84	0.478	77	84	-0.001
1986 CHC	0.503 F	81	81	0.438	70	90	-0.066
1987 CHC	0.458	74	88	0.472	76	85	0.014
1988 CHC	0.538 D	87	75	0.475	77	85	-0.063
1989 CHC	0.611 P	99	63	0.574 P	93	69	-0.037

franchID	OWAR	OWS	AWAR	AWS	WARdiff	WSdiff	P/D/W/F
1980 CHC	35.126	195.592	25.380	192.001	9.747	3.591	F
1981 CHC	35.598	162.460	14.097	113.996	21.501	48.464	F
1982 CHC	42.340	232.953	29.460	218.996	12.880	13.957	F

1983 CHC	41.582	229.420	36.012	212.997	5.570	16.423	F
1984 CHC	38.636	259.331	44.862	**288.001**	-6.226	-28.670	F
1985 CHC	42.193	244.176	34.317	231.005	7.876	13.171	F
1986 CHC	37.808	253.491	32.232	210.000	5.576	43.491	F
1987 CHC	37.153	212.135	35.931	228.002	1.223	-15.867	
1988 CHC	39.673	268.668	33.919	231.000	5.754	37.667	D
1989 CHC	40.642	**308.119**	41.222	**279.000**	-0.580	29.120	P

Joe Niekro contributed a 20-12 record in 1980 and then supplied 17 wins with a 2.47 ERA in '82. Gura compiled 18 victories in '80 and '82. Joe Carter and Mel Hall emerged as offensive threats as the Cubs rebuilt during the 80's. Hall (.283/17/56) placed third in the 1983 NL ROY voting. Carter (.302/29/121) collected 200 base hits and led the League in RBI in 1986. He averaged 31 blasts and 108 RBI from 1986-1989.

GM Dallas Green's astute draft choices in 1984-85 (comprised of Greg Maddux, Jamie Moyer, Rafael Palmeiro and Mark Grace) returned 1467 Career Total Win Shares and 267 Career Total WAR. Conversely, Jim Frey's draft choices over a three-year period from 1988-1990 recorded a total of 21 Career Total Win Shares! Reuschel revived his career, winning 14 games per season with a 3.10 ERA from 1985-1989. "Big Daddy" topped the NL with 12 complete games and a 1.097 WHIP, earning a third-place finish in the Cy Young balloting in 1987. Mike Krukow (20-9, 3.05) completed 10 games with a 1.057 WHIP in '86. Shawon Dunston drilled 37 doubles and 17 dingers.

Greg Maddux toiled through his first season (6-14, 5.61). "Mad Dog" regrouped with an 18-8 record and a 3.18 ERA in '88. Maddux netted a third-place finish in the 1989 NL Cy Young race after posting a 19-12 mark with a 2.95 ERA. Billy Hatcher (.296/11/63) delivered career-highs in almost every category in 1987 including 53 stolen bases and 96 runs scored. Rafael Palmeiro received an All-Star nod in '88 after smacking 41 doubles and batting .307. Mark Grace batted .314 in '89 after placing second in the NL ROY voting in 1988. In 1988 Chicago sneaked past Pittsburgh to win the division. The club dominated the NL in '89 en route to another pennant, triumphing 99 times while the Mets finished a distant 11 games off the pace. Center fielder Jerome Walton earned 1989 NL ROY honors with a .293 average and 24 steals.

The Cubs' bullpen sustained their excellent performance throughout the Eighties. Sutter averaged 30 saves over six seasons (1980-1985) and finished fifth or higher in the Cy Young voting on three occasions. He notched a National League-record 45 saves in 1984 along with a 1.54 ERA. Lee Smith provided 29 saves per season from 1982-1989, along with a 2.91 ERA and more than a strikeout per inning. Dennis Lamp achieved a perfect 11-0 mark as a setup man in '85 while Donnie Moore secured 31 saves with a 1.92 ERA. Davis managed 26 saves per year from 1982-1985 albeit with a 3.99 ERA. Bill Landrum (1.67, 26 SV) and Craig Lefferts (2.69, 20 SV) entered the late-inning mix in 1989. Chicago earned playoff berths in eight out of eleven seasons from 1988-1998.

Year/Team	OPW%	PW	PL	APW%	AW	AL	Diff+/-
1990 CHC	0.493	80	82	0.475	77	85	-0.018
1991 CHC	0.525 D	85	77	0.481	77	83	-0.044
1992 CHC	0.492	80	82	0.481	78	84	-0.011
1993 CHC	0.548 D	89	73	0.519	84	78	-0.030
1994 CHC	0.548 W	89	73	0.434	49	64	-0.114
1995 CHC	0.534 W	86	76	0.507	73	71	-0.027
1996 CHC	0.530 D	86	76	0.469	76	86	-0.061
1997 CHC	0.471	76	86	0.420	68	94	-0.051
1998 CHC	0.523 W	85	77	0.552 W	90	73	0.030
1999 CHC	0.496	80	82	0.414	67	95	-0.083

franchID	OWAR	OWS	AWAR	AWS	WARdiff	WSdiff	P/D/W/F
1990 CHC	33.630	263.740	29.853	231.002	3.777	32.738	
1991 CHC	41.111	274.306	34.774	231.002	6.337	43.304	D
1992 CHC	28.797	253.484	28.823	233.997	-0.026	19.486	
1993 CHC	39.143	267.453	36.197	251.995	2.946	15.458	D
1994 CHC	23.606	162.676	20.382	147.001	3.224	15.675	W
1995 CHC	28.836	200.134	30.866	219.003	-2.031	-18.869	W
1996 CHC	32.463	222.313	28.108	228.001	4.355	-5.688	D
1997 CHC	22.555	194.311	25.186	204.000	-2.631	-9.689	
1998 CHC	35.323	215.295	40.315	270.000	-4.992	-54.705	W
1999 CHC	27.811	214.586	24.558	201.003	3.253	13.583	

Chicago reached the playoffs six times in the 1990's. Mark Grace batted .314 for the decade including a league-leading 51 doubles in 1995. Palmeiro swatted 33 four-baggers and drove in 107 runs per year, posting a .299 batting average in the Nineties. Carter launched 27 long balls and knocked in 102 runs per year from 1990-1998. The Cubs took the NL East crown in 1991 by one game over Philadelphia. Lee Smith was the runner-up in the '91 Cy Young balloting after leading the League with 47 saves. Smith managed 40 saves and a 2.92 ERA from 1990-1995.

Maddux received 4 consecutive NL Cy Young Awards during a dominant stretch from 1992-1995. He was practically untouchable in 1994-1995 as he posted a combined record of 35-8 with a 1.60 ERA and a 0.853 WHIP. Maddux averaged 18 wins with a 2.54 ERA and a 1.055 WHIP over the course of the decade. The Cubs outlasted the Cardinals by two games in '93. Backstop Rick Wilkins enjoyed a career year in '93, pounding 30 long balls while hitting .303.

The crew claimed consecutive NL Wild Cards in '94 and '95. The Cubs captured the NL Central flag by a single game over the Astros in 1996. Chicago descended into last place in '97 in spite of a 17-5 record from southpaw Jamie Moyer. The Cubbies rebounded to earn another Wild Card in '98. Kerry Wood achieved NL ROY honors, striking out 233 in only 166.2 innings. Doug Glanville (.325/11/73) eclipsed the 200-hit mark in '99 and successfully pilfered 34 bases in 36 attempts.

Year/Team	OPW%	PW	PL	APW%	AW	AL	Diff+/-
2000 CHC	0.468	76	86	0.401	65	97	-0.067
2001 CHC	0.516 F	84	78	0.543	88	74	0.027
2002 CHC	0.483	78	84	0.414	67	95	-0.070
2003 CHC	0.526 F	85	77	0.543 D	88	74	0.017
2004 CHC	0.434 F	70	92	0.549	89	73	0.115
2005 CHC	0.486 F	79	83	0.488	79	83	0.002
2006 CHC	0.442 F	72	90	0.407	66	96	-0.035
2007 CHC	0.450 F	73	89	0.525 D	85	77	0.075
2008 CHC	0.532 W	86	76	0.602 P	97	64	0.071
2009 CHC	0.421	68	94	0.516	83	78	0.095
2010 CHC	0.463	75	87	0.463	75	87	0.000
2011 CHC	0.454	74	88	0.438	71	91	-0.016
2012 CHC	0.471	76	86	0.377	61	101	-0.094
2013 CHC	0.430	70	92	0.407	66	96	-0.023

franchID	OWAR	OWS	AWAR	AWS	WARdiff	WSdiff	P/D/W/F
2000 CHC	26.387	184.619	27.085	195.004	-0.698	-10.385	
2001 CHC	36.790	203.443	44.953	264.002	-8.163	-60.559	F
2002 CHC	29.854	181.318	39.477	200.996	-9.623	-19.678	
2003 CHC	39.651	202.722	43.752	264.010	-4.100	-61.288	F

2004 CHC	27.853	161.320	**50.730**	267.011	-22.876	-105.691	F
2005 CHC	37.130	195.226	38.701	237.009	-1.571	-41.783	F
2006 CHC	29.587	153.944	28.259	198.003	1.328	-44.059	F
2007 CHC	32.535	169.235	40.230	255.010	-7.694	-85.775	F
2008 CHC	35.965	218.507	**52.230**	290.994	-16.265	-72.487	W
2009 CHC	28.603	184.496	38.531	248.994	-9.928	-64.498	
2010 CHC	28.104	213.885	30.865	224.996	-2.761	-11.111	
2011 CHC	25.969	208.111	28.950	213.004	-2.981	-4.893	
2012 CHC	25.228	208.638	13.628	182.998	11.600	25.640	
2013 CHC	27.109	193.227	26.431	197.993	0.678	-4.766	

Palmeiro walloped 42 circuit clouts and knocked in 115 runs per season from 2000 through 2003. Maddux continued to put up impressive numbers on a yearly basis, winning 15 games per season with a 3.70 ERA and 1.172 WHIP from 2000-2008. Unfortunately the organization was unable to achieve the PA requirements in any season from 2001-07 with the exception of 2002. Moyer compiled a 20-6 record with a 3.43 ERA in 2001. He made his only All-Star appearance in '03, registering a 21-7 mark with a 3.27 ERA. Cubs' starting pitchers paced the Major Leagues with 46 WS>10 player-seasons from 2000-09. Mark Prior received an All-Star invitation and finished third in the Cy Young balloting in 2002. He compiled an 18-6 record, 2.43 ERA, 1.103 WHIP, and struck out 245 batters. Wood topped the National League with 266 strikeouts in 2003 and surpassed 200 for three consecutive seasons (2001-2003). He resurrected his career as a reliever, notching 34 saves in '08.

Eric Hinske received the Rookie of the Year Award in 2002, scoring 99 runs and swatting 24 dingers. Dontrelle "D-Train" Willis (14-6, 3.30) garnered the 2003 NL ROY Award. He amassed 22 victories along with a 2.63 ERA in '05, earning a runner-up finish in the NL Cy Young voting. Carlos "El Toro" Zambrano delivered 15 wins per year along with a 3.39 ERA between 2003 and 2008. Corey Patterson slammed 24 home runs and stole 32 bases in '04. Jon Garland accrued 18 victories in '05 and '06. Geovany Soto (.285/23/86) achieved 2008 NL ROY honors. Chicago finished three games behind Houston in '08, clinching the NL Wild Card with 86 victories. The Cubbies plummeted into last place in '09, managing only 68 wins. Casey McGehee (.301/16/66) placed fifth in the '09 ROY voting. He mashed 38 doubles, 23 quadruples and knocked in 104 in 2010. Carlos Marmol saved 38 contests while striking out 16 batters per nine innings. Starlin Castro paced the NL with 207 base knocks and earned his first All-Star selection in 2011. Josh Donaldson merited a fourth-place finish in the 2013 MVP race as he clubbed 37 doubles and 24 circuit clouts.

Win Shares > 20	Single-Season	1980-2013
Mark Grace - 1B (CHC) x9	Rick Wilkins - C (CHC)	Rafael Palmeiro - DH (CHC)
Rafael Palmeiro - 1B (CHC) x10	Geovany Soto - C (CHC)	Larry Gura - SP (CHC)
Scott Fletcher - SS (CHC)	Carmelo Martinez - LF (CHC)	Joe Niekro - SP (CHC)
Starlin Castro - SS (CHC)	Joe Carter - CF (CHC)	Greg Maddux - SP (CHC) x8
Eric Hinske - 3B (CHC)	Doug Glanville - CF (CHC)	Mark Prior - SP (CHC)
Casey McGehee - 3B (CHC)	Joe Carter - RF (CHC) x3	Jon Garland - SP (CHC)
Josh Donaldson – 3B (CHC)	Oscar Gamble - DH (CHC)	Dontrelle Willis - SP (CHC)

Note: 4000 PA or BFP to qualify, except during strike-shortened seasons
(1972 = 3800, 1981 & 1994 = 2700, 1995 = 3500) and 154-game schedule (3800)
- failed to qualify: 1917-1921, 1936, 1938, 1951-1952, 1956, 1958-1960, 1965, 1977-1986, 2001, 2003-2007

Cliff Aberson	Paul Erickson	Ron Law	Don Robertson
Jimmy Adair	Frank Ernaga	Hal Leathers	Kevin Roberson
Red Adams	Uel Eubanks	Tom Lee	Dan Rohn
Sparky Adams	Bill Everitt	Craig Lefferts	Rolando Roomes
Terry Adams	Johnny Evers	Lou Legett	Dave Rosello
Al Alburquerque	Jim Fanning	Jon Leicester	Gary Ross
Dale Alderson	Kyle Farnsworth	DJ LeMahieu	Dave Rowe
Vic Aldridge	Duke Farrell	Dave Lemonds	Ken Rudolph
Matt Alexander	Darcy Fast	Roy Leslie	Dutch Ruether
Bob E. Allen	Vern Fear	Carlos Lezcano	Bob Rush
Milo Allison	Marv Felderman	Frankie Libran	Chris Rusin
George Altman	John Felske	Dave Liddell	James Russell
Rich Amaral	Charlie A. Ferguson	Fred Liese	Rip Russell
Vicente Amor	Howie Fitzgerald	Gene Lillard	Jason Ryan
Bob Anderson	Ryan Flaherty	Chang-Yong Lim	Jimmy Ryan
Jim Andrews	Scott Fletcher	Kyle Lohse	Jae Kuk Ryu
Fred Andrus	Jesse Flores	Vance Lovelace	Ray Sadler
Tom Angley	John Fluhrer	Peanuts Lowrey	Vic Saier
Alex Arias	George Flynn	Pat Luby	Jeff Samardzija
Mitch Atkins	Jocko Flynn	Fred Luderus	Felix Sanchez
Dick Aylward	Gene Fodge	Carl Lundgren	Ron Santo
Fred Baczewski	Jake Fox	Tom Lundstedt	Ed Sauer
Sweetbreads Bailey	Matt Franco	Henry Lynch	Germany Schaefer
Gene Baker	Ossie France	Mike J. Lynch	Joe Schaffernoth
Mark Baldwin	Buck V. Freeman	Tom Lynch	Hank Schenz
Tony Balsamo	Bernie Friberg	Dad Lytle	Morrie Schick
Ernie Banks	Danny Friend	Bill Mack	Larry Schlafly
Richie Barker	Oscar Fuhr	Steve Macko	Ed Schorr
Darwin Barney	Kyuji Fujikawa	Clarence Maddern	Paul Schramka
Cuno Barragan	Kosuke Fukudome	Len Madden	Buddy Schultz
Bob Barrett	Sam Fuld	Greg Maddux	Don Schulze
Vince Barton	Fred Fussell	Sal Madrid	Frank Schulte
Clyde Beck	Augie Galan	Willard Mains	Wes Schulmerich
Heinz Becker	Sean Gallagher	Hank Majeski	Jeff Schwarz
Fred Beebe	Oscar Gamble	Pat Malone	Rudy Schwenck
Jeff Beliveau	Bill Gannon	Garth Mann	Gary Scott
Francis Beltran	Jon Garland	Kelly Mann	Herman Segelke
Damon Berryhill	Cecil Garriott	Carlos Marmol	Kurt Seibert
Joe A. Berry	Charlie Gassaway	William Marriott	Mike Sember
Dick Bertell	Chippy Gaw	Fred Marsh	Al Severinsen
Rick Bladt	Dave Geisel	Sean Marshall	Tommy Sewell
Footsie Blair	Emil Geiss	Carmelo Martinez	Marty Shay
Jerry Blevins	Dave Gerard	Dave Martinez	Steve Shea
Cy Block	Robert Gibson	Javier Martinez	Clyde Shoun
Randy Bobb	Mark Gilbert	Joe Marty	Ed Sicking
John Boccabella	Hal Gilson	Randy Martz	Walter Signer
Bill Bonham	Joe Girardi	Gordon Massa	Duke Simpson
Chris Booker	Chris Gissell	Juan Mateo	Andrew Sisco
George Borchers	Fred Glade	Nelson Mathews	Cy Slapnicka
Bob Borkowski	Doug Glanville	Bobby Mattick	Sterling Slaughter
Shawn Boskie	Bob Glenalvin	Hal Mauck	Roy Smalley, Jr.
John Bottarini	John Goetz	Carmen Mauro	Dwight Smith
Pat Bourque	Walt Golvin	Jason Maxwell	Earl L. Smith
Bill Bowman	Pat Gomez	Derrick May	Frank T. Smith

Bill Bradley	Geremi Gonzalez	Bill McAfee	Greg A. Smith
Harvey Branch	Julio C. Gonzalez	Algie McBride	Harry W. Smith
Harry Brecheen	Marwin Gonzalez	Bill McCabe	Happy Smith
Herb Brett	Mike Gordon	Dutch McCall	Jason Smith
Jim Brewer	George Gore	Harry McChesney	Lee Smith
Buttons Briggs	Earl Grace	Bill McClellan	Steve Smyth
Lou Brock	Mark Grace	Monte McFarland	Ray Soff
Mandy Brooks	Hank Grampp	Casey McGehee	Marcelino Solis
Jim Brosnan	George Grantham	Gus McGinnis	Rudy Sommers
Brant Brown	Tom Grant	Jimmy McMath	Geovany Soto
Joe E. Brown	Joe Graves	Brian McNichol	Bob Speake
Jophery Brown	Adam Greenberg	Russ Meers	Justin Speier
Jumbo Brown	Danny Green	Adalberto Mendez	Rob Sperring
Pidge Browne	Frank Griffith	Bill Merritt	Bob Spicer
Ray Brown	Hank Griffin	Lennie Merullo	Carl Spongberg
Jacob Brumfield	Denver Grigsby	Steve Mesner	Charlie Sprague
Tod Brynan	Ernie Groth	Roger Metzger	Eddie Stack
Jim Bullinger	Ad Gumbert	Alex Metzler	Tuck Stainback
Nelson Burbrink	Larry Gura	Chad Meyers	Gale Staley
Freddie Burdette	Charlie Guth	Dutch Meyer	Tom Stanton
Smoky Burgess	Brandon Guyer	Ralph Michaels	Ed Stauffer
Tom Burns	Eddie Haas	Hank Miklos	John Stedronsky
Ray Burris	Warren Hacker	Doc Miller	Kennie Steenstra
Dick Burwell	Stan Hack	Dusty Miller	Morrie Steevens
Guy Bush	Rip Hagerman	George Milstead	Ed Stein
John Buzhardt	Johnny Halrston	Sergio Mitre	Red Steiner
Alex Cabrera	Drew Hall	Bill Moisan	Dave Stenhouse
Alberto Cabrera	Mel Hall	Jose Molina	Jake Stenzel
Marty Callaghan	Erik Hamren	Fritz Mollwitz	Earl Stephenson
Dolph Camilli	Frank Hankinson	Luis Montanez	Walter Stephenson
Tony Campana	Bill Hanlon	Al Montgomery	Dave Stevens
Gilly Campbell	Doug Hansen	George Moolic	Ace Stewart
Ron Campbell	Ollie Hanson	Charley Moore	Jimmy Stewart
Vin Campbell	Ed Hanyzewski	Donnie Moore	Mack Stewart
Frank Campos	Alex Hardy	Johnny Moore	Tuffy Stewart
Russ Canzler	Bubbles Hargrave	Vern Morgan	Bill Stoneman
Mike Capel	Mike Harkey	Moe Morhardt	Dean Stone
Esmailin Caridad	Brendan Harris	George Moriarty	Lou Stringer
Don Carlsen	Josh Harrison	Ed W. Morris	George Stueland
Bill Carney	Chuck Hartenstein	Mal Moss	Jim St.Vrain
Chris John Carpenter	J.C. Hartman	Curt Motton	Bill Sullivan
Al Carson	Gabby Hartnett	Jamie Moyer	Marty Sullivan
Joe Carter	Zaza Harvey	Billy Muffett	Billy Sunday
Hugh Casey	Billy Hatcher	Eddie Mulligan	Sy Sutcliffe
Andrew Cashner	Ryan Hawblitzel	Joe Munson	Bruce Sutter
Pedro Castellano	Bill Hayes	Danny F. Murphy	Dave Swartzbaugh
Frank Castillo	Mike Hechinger	Jim O. Murray	Bill John Sweeney
Welington Castillo	Roy Henshaw	Tony Murray	Jason Szuminski
Starlin Castro	Fred Herbert	Richie Myers	Jerry Tabb
Ted Cather	Billy Herman	Tom Nagle	Bob Talbot
Phil Cavarretta	Chico Hernandez	Lynn Nelson	Chink Taylor
Ronny Cedeno	Jesus Hernaiz	Joel Newkirk	Harry W. Taylor
Cliff Chambers	Tom Hernon	Art Nichols	Jack W. Taylor
Frank Chance	Leroy Herrmann	Hugh Nicol	Bud Teachout
Harry Chapman	John Hibbard	Al Niehaus	Patsy Tebeau

Ossie Chavarria	Eddie Hickey	Joe Niekro	Amaury Telemaco
Virgil Cheeves	Kirby Higbe	Ricky Nolasco	John Tener
Larry Cheney	R.E. Hillebrand	Billy North	Bob Terlecki
Rocky Cherry	Bobby Hill	Phil Norton	Wayne Terwilliger
Robinson Chirinos	Dave Hillman	Lou Novikoff	Nate Teut
Harry Chiti	Rich Hill	Rube Novotney	Ron Theobald
Hee Seop Choi	Eric Hinske	Rich Nye	Ryan Theriot
Len Church	Gene Hiser	Pete James O'Brien	Tom Thobe
John Churry	Glen Hobbie	Johnny O'Connor	Red Thomas
Dad Clarke	Larry Hoffman	Bob O'Farrell	Scot Thompson
Dad Clark	Micah Hoffpauir	Jim Oglesby	Walter Thornton
Sumpter Clarke	Ed Holley	Will Ohman	Bob J. Thorpe
Steve Clevenger	Jessie Hollins	Len Okrie	Ozzie Timmons
Buck Coats	John Hollison	Barney Olsen	Joe Tinker
Jim Colborn	Bobo Holloman	Vern Olsen	Bud Tinning
King Cole	Charlie Hollocher	Ryan O'Malley	Jim Todd
Casey Coleman	Billy Holm	Kevin Orie	Fred Toney
Phil Collins	Ken Holtzman	Bob Osborn	Steve Trachsel
Rip Collins	Marty Honan	Fred Osborn	Jim Tracy
Tyler Colvin	Burt Hooton	Tiny Osborne	Bill Traffley
Jorge Comellas	Trader Horne	Reggie Otero	Bill Tremel
Bunk Congalton	John Houseman	Billy Ott	Coaker Triplett
Fritzie Connally	Mike Hubbard	Ernie Ovitz	Harry Truby
Bill Connors	Ken Hubbs	Dave Owen	Pete Turgeon
Jim Connor	Joe Hughes	Andy Pafko	Ted Turner
Jim Cook	Terry Hughes	Karl Pagel	Babe Twombly
Jimmy J. Cooney	Tom J. Hughes	Rafael Palmeiro	Earl Tyree
Larry Corcoran	Ed Hutchinson	Blake Parker	Jim Tyrone
Mike Corcoran	Scotty Ingerton	Doc Parker	Wayne Tyrone
Frank Corridon	Charlie Irwin	Jiggs Parrott	Pedro Valdes
Hooks Cotter	Frank Isbell	Tom Parrott	Raul Valdes
Henry Cotto	Brett Jackson	Roy Partee	Andy Varga
Roscoe Coughlin	Darrin Jackson	Corey Patterson	Gary Varsho
Billy Cowan	Lou Jackson	Eric Patterson	Donald Veal
George Crosby	Randy Jackson	Dave Pavlas	Joe Vernon
Juan Cruz	Mike E. Jacobs	Ted Pawelek	Hector Villanueva
Charlie Cuellar	Ray Jacobs	George Pearce	Ismael Villegas
Bruce Cunningham	Tony Jacobs	Jim Pearce	Josh Vitters
Doc Curley	Pat Jacquez	Hal Peck	Otto Vogel
Jack Curtis	Jake Jaeckel	Les Peden	Eddie Waitkus
Bill Dahlen	Joe Jaeger	Chick Pedroes	Matt Walbeck
Tom P. Daly	Art Jahn	Jon Perlman	Rube Walker
Doug Dascenzo	Bill H. James	Ron Perranoski	Derek Wallace
Bill Davidson	Rick James	Chris Petersen	Jack Wallace
Ron G. Davis	Pat Jarvis	Billy Petrick	Joe Wallis
Steve M. Davis	Hal Jeffcoat	Bob Pettit	Tom Walsh
George Decker	Robin Jennings	Big Jeff Pfeffer	Jerome Walton
Joe Decker	Garry Jestadt	Bobby Pfeil	Chris Ward
Jim Delahanty	Abe Johnson	Bill Phyle	Dick Ward
Jim Delsing	Don S. Johnson	Jeff Pico	Jack D. Warner
Fred Demarais	Footer Johnson	Felix Pie	Lon Warneke
Frank Demaree	Roy Joiner	Andy Piercy	Logan Watkins
Harry DeMiller	Davy Jones	Ray Pierce	Doc Watson
Roger Denzer	Percy Jones	Chris Piersoll	Ken Weafer
Mike Diaz	Ryan Jorgensen	Carmen Pignatiello	Orlie Weaver

Lance Dickson
Pickles Dillhoefer
Alec Distaso
Tom Dolan
Rafael Dolis
Josh Donaldson
Frank Donnelly
Jack Doscher
Tom Downey
Darin Downs
Scott Downs
Moe Drabowsky
Sammy Drake
Solly Drake
Paddy Driscoll
Dick Drott
Keith Drumright
Jason Dubois
Hugh Duffy
Nick Dumovich
Courtney Duncan
Jim Dunegan
Sam Dungan
Shawon Dunston
Kid Durbin
Frank Dwyer
Don Eaddy
Bill Earley
Howard Earl
Mal Eason
Roy Easterwood
Charlie Eden
Ed Eiteljorge
Pete Elko
Allen Elliott
Carter Elliott
Jim Ellis
Dick Ellsworth
Don Elston
Steve Engel
Woody English

Billy Jurges
Al Kaiser
Don Kaiser
Jack Katoll
Tony Kaufmann
Greg Keatley
Bob Kelly
Joe J. Kelly
David Kelton
Snapper Kennedy
Ted Kennedy
Mel Kerr
Don Kessinger
Brooks Kieschnick
Newt Kimball
Jerry Kindall
Jim Kirby
Malachi Kittridge
Ted Kleinhans
Johnny Kling
Joe Klugmann
Hub Knolls
Cal Koonce
Joe Kraemer
Mike Kreevich
Mickey Kreitner
Gus Krock
Gene Krug
Mike Krukow
Emil Kush
Pete LaCock
Junior Lake
Blake Lalli
Pete Lamer
Dennis Lamp
Les Lancaster
Bill Landrum
Ced Landrum
Bill Lange
Al Lary
Jimmy Lavender

George Piktuzis
Renyel Pinto
Whitey Platt
Paul Popovich
Bo Porter
Mike Porzio
Phil Powers
Don Prince
Mark Prior
Ed Putman
John Pyecha
Jim Qualls
Frank C. Quinn
Wimpy Quinn
Steve Rain
Brooks Raley
Fernando Ramsey
Newt Randall
Clay Rapada
Jon Ratliff
Tommy Raub
Bob Raudman
Fred Raymer
Frank Reberger
Hal Reilly
Josh Reilly
Laurie Reis
Laddie Renfroe
Ed Reulbach
Paul Reuschel
Rick Reuschel
Jose A. Reyes
Archie Reynolds
Bob Rhoads
Dusty Rhodes
Fred Richards
Beryl Richmond
Reggie Richter
Marv Rickert
George Riley
Skel Roach

John Webb
Jake Weimer
Butch Weis
Johnny Welch
Todd Wellemeyer
Randy Wells
Kirby White
Charlie Wiedemeyer
Harry Wilke
Rick Wilkins
Bob Will
Art Williams
Billy L. Williams
Cy Williams
Dontrelle Willis
Jim Willis
Jim Williams
Randy Williams
Ed Winceniak
Kettle Wirts
Casey Wise
Harry Wolfe
Harry Wolverton
Kerry Wood
Jim Woods
Walt Woods
Al Worthington
Chuck Wortman
Bob Wright
Pat Wright
Rick Wrona
Michael Wuertz
Hank Wyse
George Yantz
Tony York
Gus Yost
Carlos Zambrano
Heinie Zimmerman
Pete Zoccolillo
Julio Zuleta

Year/Team	PW%	PW	PL	AW%	AW	AL	Diff+/-
1998 ARI	0.000 F	0	0	0.401	65	97	0.000
1999 ARI	0.000 F	0	0	0.617 D	100	62	0.000
2000 ARI	0.000 F	0	0	0.525	85	77	0.000
2001 ARI	0.000 F	0	0	0.568 D	92	70	0.000
2002 ARI	0.609 F	99	63	0.605 D	98	64	-0.004
2003 ARI	0.495 F	80	82	0.519	84	78	0.024
2004 ARI	0.364	59	103	0.315	51	111	-0.049
2005 ARI	0.444 F	72	90	0.475	77	85	0.031
2006 ARI	0.523 W	85	77	0.469	76	86	-0.054
2007 ARI	0.468	76	86	0.556 P	90	72	0.088
2008 ARI	0.521	84	78	0.506	82	80	-0.015
2009 ARI	0.503	82	80	0.432	70	92	-0.071
2010 ARI	0.529 D	86	76	0.401	65	97	-0.128
2011 ARI	0.478	77	85	0.580 D	94	68	0.103
2012 ARI	0.535 W	87	75	0.500	81	81	-0.035
2013 ARI	0.542 D	88	74	0.500	81	81	-0.042

franchID	OWAR	OWS	AWAR	AWS	WARdiff	WSdiff	P/D/W/F
1998 ARI	32.242	0.000	21.003	194.999	11.240	-194.999	F
1999 ARI	45.847	209.968	52.762	300.005	-6.915	-90.037	F
2000 ARI	29.704	173.100	41.615	255.004	-11.911	-81.904	F
2001 ARI	49.733	233.639	50.965	275.999	-1.232	-42.360	F
2002 ARI	44.737	290.293	51.047	294.001	-6.310	-3.708	F
2003 ARI	38.069	235.446	43.884	252.004	-5.815	-16.557	F
2004 ARI	15.365	169.439	17.730	152.995	-2.365	16.444	
2005 ARI	27.819	189.087	31.007	230.996	-3.188	-41.909	F
2006 ARI	40.435	213.324	38.753	228.002	1.682	-14.678	W
2007 ARI	29.745	217.008	33.670	269.997	-3.925	-52.989	
2008 ARI	38.345	240.063	42.597	245.992	-4.252	-5.929	
2009 ARI	32.632	221.171	35.190	210.002	-2.557	11.169	
2010 ARI	33.726	241.989	26.794	195.007	6.932	46.982	D
2011 ARI	32.428	258.582	38.388	282.001	-5.960	-23.419	
2012 ARI	34.258	267.906	35.821	243.003	-1.563	24.903	W
2013 ARI	37.306	274.212	30.996	243.000	6.309	31.212	D

Legend: (P) = Pennant / Most Wins in League (D) = Division Winner (W) = Wild Card Winner (F) = Failed to Qualify

The Diamondbacks attained National League membership in 1998. The franchise failed to claim a pennant or lead the Senior Circuit in oWAR or oWS through 2013. Junior Spivey batted .301/16/78 for the '02 crew while Byung-Hyun Kim excelled as the Snakes' sidewinding closer (8-3, 2.04, 36 SV). Vicente Padilla accrued 14 victories in back-to-back campaigns (2002-03). Brandon Webb produced a 2.84 ERA in 28 starts in his rookie year. Webb earned a Cy Young Award in 2006 (16-8, 3.10) followed by successive runner-up finishes. He delivered a record of 18-10 with a 3.01 ERA in '07 and boasted a 22-7 mark in '08. Oscar Villareal made 86 relief appearances, scavenging 10 "vulture" wins along with a 2.57 ERA in 2003. Alex Cintron (.317/13/51) teamed with Spivey to solidify the middle infield.

The 2004 Diamondbacks were the first to exceed the minimum 4000 PA and BFP standards. Erubiel Durazo (.321/22/88) and Lyle Overbay (.301/16/87) flourished in an otherwise lackluster offense. Overbay paced the circuit with 53 two-base knocks, and then contributed 22 jacks and 92 ribbies while batting .312 two years later. Chad Tracy (.308/27/72) and Rod Barajas (.254/21/60) contributed to the Rattlesnakes in 2005.

Arizona claimed the NL Wild Card in '06 with a record of 85 wins and 77 losses. The D-Backs' hurlers inflicted venom in the opposition, delivering franchise-bests in pitWARnorm (28) and pitWSnorm (108). Second-sacker Dan Uggla began a five-year streak with at least 25 home runs and 85 RBI in '06. Uggla blasted a career-high 36 round-trippers in 2011. The Snakes faded in the oppressive desert heat In 2007, slithering to a 76-86 record. Brad Penny (16-4, 3.03) placed third in the NL Cy Young balloting. Jose Valverde established himself as the relief ace, notching 47 saves to go along with a 2.66 ERA. "Papa Grande" nailed down 44 saves for the '09 crew and closed out a league-high 49 contests two years later.

The Diamondbacks regained their form in 2008, placing only two games behind the division-winning Dodgers. Carlos Quentin broke through with a .288/36/100 season. Jack Cust launched 33 bombs and Stephen Drew cranked 21. The '09 squad finished one game above .500, coming in third behind Colorado and Los Angeles. Mark Reynolds crushed 44 big-flies but whiffed an incredible 223 times! Justin Upton earned his first all-star nod in '09 (.300/26/86/20 SB). Upton swatted 31 circuit clouts, swiped 21 bags and finished fourth in the 2011 NL MVP race. Several pitchers emerged, including Jorge de la Rosa (16-9, 4.38), Brett Anderson (11-11, 4.06) and Ross Ohlendorf (11-10, 3.92).

Carlos Gonzalez (.336/34/117) claimed the batting title and topped the circuit with 197 hits as he finished third in the 2010 NL MVP race. Miguel Montero socked 36 two-base hits and earned his first All-Star selection in 2011. Paul Goldschmidt supplied 36 long balls and knocked in 125 runs en route to a runner-up finish in the 2013 NL MVP balloting.

Win Shares > 20	Single-Season	1998-2013
Chad Tracy - 1B (ARI)	Stephen Drew - SS (ARI) x2	Carlos Gonzalez - LF (ARI)
Paul Goldschmidt – 1B (ARI)	Mark Reynolds - 3B (ARI)	Justin Upton – LF (ARI)
Junior Spivey - 2B (ARI)	Miguel Montero - C (ARI) x2	Justin Upton - RF (ARI)
Dan Uggla - 2B (ARI) x6	Carlos Quentin - LF (ARI)	Brandon Webb - SP (ARI) x3

Note: 4000 PA or BFP to qualify, except during strike-shortened seasons
(1972 = 3800, 1981 & 1994 = 2700, 1995 = 3500) and 154-game schedule (3800)
- failed to qualify: 1998-2003, 2005

Diamondbacks All-Time "Originals" Roster

Hector Ambriz	Eury De La Rosa	Javier Lopez	Duaner Sanchez
Brett Anderson	Jorge de la Rosa	Scott Maine	Sergio Santos
Greg Aquino	Doug DeVore	Alfredo Marte	Max Scherzer
Bryan Augenstein	Stephen Drew	Brandon Medders	Daniel Schlereth
Rod Barajas	Erubiel Durazo	Wade Miley	Konrad Schmidt
Brian Barden	Adam C. Eaton	Garrett Mock	Mike A. Schultz
Trevor Bauer	Jake Elmore	Miguel Montero	Evan Scribner
Chad Beck	Barry Enright	Dustin Nippert	Leyson Septimo
Nick Bierbrodt	Jerry Gil	Jordan Norberto	Bryan Shaw
Emilio Bonifacio	Paul Goldschmidt	Abraham Nunez	Doug Slaten
Charles Brewer	Alberto Gonzalez	Vladimir Nunez	Greg T. Smith
Brian Bruney	Carlos Gonzalez	Ross Ohlendorf	Chris Snyder
Jason Bulger	Edgar G. Gonzalez	Tim Olson	Junior Spivey
Ron Calloway	Enrique Gonzalez	Lyle Overbay	Daniel Stange
Chris Capuano	Andrew Good	Chris Owings	Phil Stockman
Chris W. Carter	Brian Gordon	Micah Owings	Luis Terrero
Wilkin Castillo	Mike Gosling	Vicente Padilla	Chad Tracy
Matt Chico	Andy Green	Jarrod Parker	Dan Uggla

Alex Cintron	Scott Hairston	Gerardo Parra	Justin Upton
Pedro Ciriaco	Robby Hammock	Tony R. Pena	Cesar Valdez
J.D. Closser	John Hester	Brad Penny	Jose Valverde
Josh Collmenter	Conor Jackson	Beltran Perez	Esmerling Vasquez
Jason Conti	Steven Jackson	A. J. Pollock	Oscar Villarreal
Ryan Cook	Matt Kata	Bret Prinz	Zach Walters
Lance Cormier	Byung-Hyun Kim	Carlos Quentin	Brandon Webb
Collin Cowgill	Eric Knott	Mark Reynolds	Ryan Wheeler
Jack Cust	Mike Koplove	Danny Richar	Bill C. White
Casey Daigle	Marc Krauss	Rusty Ryal	Clay Zavada
Jamie D'Antona	Josh Kroeger	Rob Ryan	
Matt Davidson	Tommy Layne	Erik Sabel	

Brooklyn / Los Angeles Dodgers

Year/Team	OPW%	PW	PL	APW%	AW	AL	Diff+/-
1901 BRO	0.481	67	73	0.581	79	57	0.100
1902 BRO	0.396	55	85	0.543	75	63	0.147
1903 BRO	0.427	60	80	0.515	70	66	0.088
1904 BRO	0.498	77	77	0.366	56	97	-0.132
1905 BRO	0.406 F	63	91	0.316	48	104	-0.090
1906 BRO	0.407 F	63	91	0.434	66	86	0.027
1907 BRO	0.476	73	81	0.439	65	83	-0.037
1908 BRO	0.446	69	85	0.344	53	101	-0.102
1909 BRO	0.391 F	60	94	0.359	55	98	-0.032

franchID	OWAR	OWS	AWAR	AWS	WARdiff	WSdiff	P/D/W/F
1901 BRO	43.032	277.511	35.904	237.005	7.128	40.506	
1902 BRO	25.294	220.407	29.107	224.999	-3.813	-4.592	
1903 BRO	26.875	228.569	35.208	210.005	-8.333	18.563	
1904 BRO	36.267	250.970	21.597	167.997	14.670	82.973	
1905 BRO	35.860	258.483	13.691	144.000	22.169	114.483	F
1906 BRO	44.198	320.986	20.856	198.002	23.342	122.984	F
1907 BRO	42.515	276.763	20.755	194.999	21.760	81.764	
1908 BRO	28.520	234.364	15.716	158.998	12.804	75.366	
1909 BRO	18.422	169.051	15.103	165.000	3.319	4.052	F

Legend: (P) = Pennant / Most Wins in League (D) = Division Winner (W) = Wild Card Winner (F) = Failed to Qualify

The Brooklyn Atlantics played for six seasons in the American Association prior to entering the National League in 1890. The franchise assumed several names including the Grays, Bridegrooms, Superbas and Robins prior to settling on "Dodgers" in 1932. Based on the WS>20 frame of reference, the Dodgers have developed the fewest quality shortstops (7) among the "Turn of the Century" franchises.

The club has cultivated the second-most WS>20 seasons at catcher (23) and third-most among second basemen (32). Mike Piazza leads the backstops with 8 WS>20 seasons while Lonny Frey, Davey Lopes, Jackie Robinson and Jim Gilliam are tied with 5 WS>20 seasons apiece. Further, the Dodgers rank first with 116 WS>10 player-seasons at the keystone position. The "Original" Dodgers accrued 18 playoff appearances through 2013 versus 27 for the "Actual" Dodgers.

The Superbas paced the circuit in oWS in 1901 as Jimmy Sheckard (.354/11/104) tallied 116 runs and 33 Win Shares while leading the NL with 19 triples and a .534 SLG. The left fielder batted at a .332 clip and topped the leader boards with 9 big-flies and 67 stolen bases in '03. Fielder Jones contributed a .311 BA and 120 runs scored for the '01 crew. Harry Howell delivered 15 victories, a 2.02 ERA, 1.075 WHIP and 30 complete games per year from 1904-08. Harry Lumley led the League with 18 triples and 9 jacks in his rookie season (1904). The "Judge" served notice with a .477 SLG and 33 Win Shares during the '06 campaign. Nap Rucker fashioned a 2.13 ERA and a 1.153 WHIP while completing 28 of 33 starts per season from 1907-09.

Year/Team	OPW%	PW	PL	APW%	AW	AL	Diff+/-
1910 BRO	0.490	75	79	0.416	64	90	-0.074
1911 BRO	0.537	83	71	0.427	64	86	-0.110
1912 BRO	0.496 F	76	78	0.379	58	95	-0.117
1913 BRO	0.439 F	68	86	0.436	65	84	-0.003
1914 BRO	0.528 F	81	73	0.487	75	79	-0.041
1915 BRO	0.444 F	68	86	0.526	80	72	0.082
1916 BRO	0.468 F	72	82	0.610 P	94	60	0.143
1917 BRO	0.500 F	77	77	0.464	70	81	-0.036
1918 BRO	0.551 F	71	57	0.452	57	69	-0.099
1919 BRO	0.592 F	83	57	0.493	69	71	-0.099

franchID	OWAR	OWS	AWAR	AWS	WARdiff	WSdiff	P/D/W/F
1910 BRO	35.272	216.332	22.604	191.999	12.668	24.332	
1911 BRO	32.991	222.703	17.935	191.995	15.055	30.708	
1912 BRO	36.293	211.887	28.285	174.002	8.008	37.886	F
1913 BRO	38.670	216.634	34.796	195.000	3.874	21.633	F
1914 BRO	46.285	287.069	25.030	206.998	21.255	80.071	I
1915 BRO	20.710	265.031	19.630	239.998	1.080	25.033	F
1916 BRO	47.508	314.552	44.793	282.001	2.714	32.551	F
1917 BRO	36.561	261.874	26.998	209.999	9.563	51.874	F
1918 BRO	37.891	251.324	19.757	170.878	18.134	80.446	F
1919 BRO	30.266	227.527	29.093	207.001	1.173	20.526	F

Rucker led the League in shutouts (6), innings pitched (320.1), complete games (27) and games started (39) in 1910. The southpaw posted a 2.59 ERA and averaged 18 victories from 1910-13. Sheckard coaxed a staggering 147 bases on balls from opposition hurlers in 1911 and notched 122 walks in the subsequent season. He also led the circuit with 121 runs scored and a .434 OBP. Jake Daubert earned back-to-back batting crowns (1913-14) including a personal-best .350 BA in '13. Zack Wheat slugged .461 to lead the NL in '16 and collected a batting title with a .318 average two years later. Primarily known as the Robins during this period, the club failed to meet the BFP requirements for 22 consecutive seasons (1912-1933). Hy Myers paced the circuit with a .436 SLG, 14 three-base knocks and 73 ribbies in 1919.

Win Shares > 20	Single-Season	1901-1919
Jake Daubert - 1B (LAD) x4	Fielder Jones - CF (LAD) x7	Joe Yeager - SP (LAD)
Claude Ritchey - 2B (LAD) x3	Jimmy Sheckard - CF (LAD)	Oscar Jones - SP (LAD)
Red J. Smith - 3B (LAD) x4	Hy Myers - CF (LAD) x2	Harry Howell - SP (LAD) x3
Jimmy Sheckard - LF (LAD) x9	Fielder Jones - RF (LAD)	Nap Rucker - SP (LAD) x5
Zack Wheat - LF (LAD) x10	Harry Lumley - RF (LAD)	Lew Richie - SP (LAD)
Al Scheer - LF (LAD)	Benny Meyer - RF (LAD)	Elmer Knetzer - SP (LAD)
	Casey Stengel - RF (LAD)	Leon Cadore - SP (LAD)

Year/Team	OPW%	PW	PL	APW%	AW	AL	Diff+/-
1920 BRO	0.570 F	88	66	0.604 P	93	61	0.034
1921 BRO	0.453 F	70	84	0.507	77	75	0.053

Year/Team	OPW%	PW	PL	APW%	AW	AL	Diff+/-
1922 BRO	0.507 F	78	76	0.494	76	78	-0.013
1923 BRO	0.492 F	76	78	0.494	76	78	0.002
1924 BRO	0.532 F	82	72	0.597	92	62	0.066
1925 BRO	0.401 F	62	92	0.444	68	85	0.043
1926 BRO	0.420 F	65	89	0.464	71	82	0.044
1927 BRO	0.345 F	53	101	0.425	65	88	0.080
1928 BRO	0.389 F	60	94	0.503	77	76	0.115
1929 BRO	0.460 F	71	83	0.458	70	83	-0.003

franchID	OWAR	OWS	AWAR	AWS	WARdiff	WSdiff	P/D/W/F
1920 BRO	38.983	271.531	**42.671**	**279.001**	-3.687	-7.469	F
1921 BRO	15.637	187.902	30.203	231.000	-14.566	-43.098	F
1922 BRO	31.314	248.961	30.415	228.000	0.899	20.961	F
1923 BRO	21.573	234.572	33.605	227.994	-12.032	6.578	F
1924 BRO	34.359	302.957	40.630	275.998	-6.271	26.959	F
1925 BRO	24.004	182.441	31.829	204.001	-7.824	-21.560	F
1926 BRO	22.518	237.468	27.228	212.994	-4.710	24.474	F
1927 BRO	7.782	154.034	25.105	195.002	-17.324	-40.968	F
1928 BRO	13.707	188.546	36.584	231.009	-22.877	-42.463	F
1929 BRO	21.722	179.847	34.192	210.002	-12.470	-30.155	F

Wheat posted a .347 BA over a six year span covering 1920-25. "Buck" delivered career-highs with 16 swats and drove in 112 baserunners in '22. He batted at a .375 clip during the two successive campaigns and accrued 35 Win Shares in 1924. Wheat set personal bests in '25 with 221 base hits, 125 runs, 42 doubles and 14 triples. Daubert legged out 22 three-baggers and batted .336 with 114 tallies and 205 safeties for the '22 squad. Johnny Frederick (.328/24/75) supplied a league-leading 52 doubles while scoring 127 times and compiling 206 base knocks in his inaugural season.

Year/Team	OPW%	PW	PL	APW%	AW	AL	Diff+/-
1930 BRO	0.522 F	80	74	0.558	86	68	0.036
1931 BRO	0.458 F	71	83	0.520	79	73	0.062
1932 BRO	0.334 F	51	103	0.526	81	73	0.192
1933 BRO	0.424 F	65	89	0.425	65	88	0.001
1934 BRO	0.427	66	88	0.467	71	81	0.040
1935 BRO	0.438	68	86	0.458	70	83	0.019
1936 BRO	0.346	53	101	0.435	67	87	0.089
1937 BRO	0.453 F	70	84	0.405	62	91	-0.048
1938 BRO	0.476	73	81	0.463	69	80	-0.012
1939 BRO	0.467	72	82	0.549	84	69	0.082

franchID	OWAR	OWS	AWAR	AWS	WARdiff	WSdiff	P/D/W/F
1930 BRO	23.634	202.448	44.820	258.003	-21.186	-55.555	F
1931 BRO	19.492	190.226	35.847	237.007	-16.354	-46.781	F
1932 BRO	13.137	167.654	**38.127**	242.999	-24.990	-75.345	F
1933 BRO	24.309	191.855	28.687	195.001	-4.378	-3.147	F
1934 BRO	25.918	176.601	35.848	212.999	-9.929	-36.398	
1935 BRO	28.741	174.195	29.771	210.001	-1.029	-35.806	
1936 BRO	20.353	175.769	23.277	200.991	-2.924	-25.222	
1937 BRO	27.066	178.659	23.419	185.999	3.648	-7.339	F
1938 BRO	27.983	181.973	31.001	206.998	-3.017	-25.025	
1939 BRO	26.298	182.190	37.386	252.000	-11.088	-69.810	

Brooklyn suffered through 101 losses in 1936 in spite of Van Mungo's exploits on the mound. Mungo topped the leader boards with 238 whiffs. Dutch E. Leonard fashioned a league-best 1.227 WHIP for the '38 crew and then notched 20 victories in the ensuing season. Bobo Newsom eclipsed the 20-win plateau in successive campaigns (1938-39), completing a league-best 31 of 40 starts in '38. Ernie Lombardi (.342/19/95) captured the batting crown and merited 1938 NL MVP honors. "Schnozz" manufactured a .315 BA during the Thirties and earned 7 All-Star selections in his career. Johnny Vander Meer, aka "The Dutch Master," is the only pitcher in MLB history to twirl no-hitters in back-to-back outings, accomplishing the feat in June of 1938.

Win Shares > 20	Single-Season	1920-1939
Del Bissonette - 1B (LAD) Andy High - 2B (LAD) Lonny Frey - 2B (LAD) x5 Ernie Lombardi - C (LAD)	Johnny Frederick - CF (LAD) x2 Van Mungo - SP (LAD) x2	Bobo Newsom - SP (LAD) x5 Dutch E. Leonard - SP (LAD) x3

Year/Team	OPW%	PW	PL	APW%	AW	AL	Diff+/-
1940 BRO	0.453	70	84	0.575	88	65	0.122
1941 BRO	0.409 F	63	91	0.649 P	100	54	0.240
1942 BRO	0.449	69	85	0.675	104	50	0.226
1943 BRO	0.480	74	80	0.529	81	72	0.050
1944 BRO	0.431	66	88	0.409	63	91	-0.022
1945 BRO	0.515	79	75	0.565	87	67	0.050
1946 BRO	0.480	74	80	0.615	96	60	0.136
1947 BRO	0.503	78	76	0.610 P	94	60	0.107
1948 BRO	0.514	79	75	0.545	84	70	0.032
1949 BRO	0.539 P	83	71	0.630 P	97	57	0.091

franchID	OWAR	OWS	AWAR	AWS	WARdiff	WSdiff	P/D/W/F
1940 BRO	26.598	182.300	40.723	264.003	-14.125	-81.703	
1941 BRO	28.473	184.411	**52.894**	299.998	-24.421	-115.587	F
1942 BRO	29.596	179.437	50.107	311.994	-20.511	-132.557	
1943 BRO	25.668	194.441	37.118	243.000	-11.450	-48.559	
1944 BRO	16.435	162.994	22.719	189.004	-6.284	-26.011	
1945 BRO	36.291	224.848	42.018	261.005	-5.727	-36.157	
1946 BRO	26.080	190.384	45.931	287.992	-19.851	-97.608	
1947 BRO	27.671	194.112	45.059	**281.999**	-17.388	-87.887	
1948 BRO	26.533	196.503	37.792	252.004	-11.260	-55.500	
1949 BRO	35.279	216.043	**52.722**	290.975	-17.443	-74.932	P

Newsom secured a fourth-place finish in the MVP balloting with a 21-5 record and a 2.83 ERA for the '40 club. Lonny Frey pilfered 22 bags and crossed home plate 102 times in 1940. Vander Meer struck out the most batsmen in the National League for three consecutive campaigns (1941-43). Lombardi seized a second batting title with a .330 average in '42. George Kell cuffed opposing hurlers at a .324 clip from 1946-49 and collected a batting title with a .343 average in '49.

Jackie Robinson earned Rookie of the Year honors in 1947, scoring 125 runs and swiping 29 bases. Robinson (.342/16/124) secured the 1949 NL MVP Award along with the batting crown. He established career-highs in batting average, RBI, base hits (203), triples (12) and stolen bases (37). Ralph Branca furnished a 21-12 record with a 2.67 ERA in 1947 and procured three straight All-Star selections. Duke Snider slammed 23 moon-shots and drove in 92 baserunners while scoring 100 runs in his first full season (1949). Roy Campanella (.287/22/82), Gil Hodges (.285/23/115) and Carl Furillo (.322/18/106) provided extra thump to the productive Brooklyn lineup. Don Newcombe (17-8, 3.17) spun 5 shutouts en route to the 1949 NL Rookie of the Year Award.

Year/Team	OPW%	PW	PL	APW%	AW	AL	Diff+/-
1950 BRO	0.512	79	75	0.578	89	65	0.066
1951 BRO	0.537 P	83	71	0.618	97	60	0.081
1952 BRO	0.575 P	89	65	0.627 P	96	57	0.052
1953 BRO	0.558	86	68	0.682 P	105	49	0.124
1954 BRO	0.482	74	80	0.597	92	62	0.115
1955 BRO	0.508	78	76	0.641 P	98	55	0.133
1956 BRO	0.491	76	78	0.604 P	93	61	0.112
1957 BRO	0.552	85	69	0.545	84	70	-0.006
1958 LAD	0.484	75	79	0.461	71	83	-0.023
1959 LAD	0.527	81	73	0.564 P	88	68	0.037

franchID	OWAR	OWS	AWAR	AWS	WARdiff	WSdiff	P/D/W/F
1950 BRO	35.649	225.273	**47.408**	266.997	-11.759	-41.724	
1951 BRO	**38.743**	243.591	**50.778**	291.002	-12.035	-47.411	P
1952 BRO	37.211	247.118	**51.051**	**287.996**	-13.840	-40.878	P
1953 BRO	41.891	278.094	**58.778**	**315.007**	-16.887	-36.913	
1954 BRO	39.059	262.306	**52.865**	**293.997**	-13.806	-31.690	
1955 BRO	36.807	247.185	**52.865**	**293.997**	-16.057	-46.811	
1956 BRO	33.614	242.525	**45.666**	**278.996**	-12.052	-36.471	
1957 BRO	37.591	253.175	40.752	252.005	-3.160	1.170	
1958 LAD	28.830	232.370	28.331	212.994	0.499	19.377	
1959 LAD	32.582	254.305	41.404	**264.003**	-8.822	-9.697	

GM Branch Rickey acquired the majority of the talent that achieved three pennants for Brooklyn in four seasons (1949, 1951-52). Rickey's amateur free agent signings consisted of Snider and Hodges (1943), Robinson (1945), Campanella and Newcombe (1946). Campanella received three NL MVP Awards ('51, '53, '55). "Campy" averaged .318 and slammed 35 long balls with 119 RBI per year during his MVP campaigns. Hodges drove in 100+ runs for seven straight seasons (1949-1955) and blasted over 30 round-trippers from '50 through '54. Robinson batted .323 with 16 dingers and 96 tallies per year in the first half of the decade. Jethroe scored 100 runs and swiped 35 bases, picking up ROY honors in 1950, and Kell (.340/8/101) led the League in hits (218) and doubles (56).

Snider's typical output in the Fifties included a .308 batting average, 33 circuit clouts and 103 ribbies. He topped the NL with 199 safeties and in 1950 began a streak of seven straight All-Star selections. "The Silver Fox" paced the circuit in runs scored from 1953-55 and surpassed the 40-home run mark in five successive seasons (1953-57). Robinson (38 WS in '51) and Snider (38 WS in '54) tied with the highest single-season Win Shares total in team history.

Newcombe anchored the pitching staff in the Fifties. In spite of missing two seasons for military service, "Newk" averaged 21 victories over four seasons (1950-51 and 1955-56). Newcombe (27-7, 3.06) topped the League in wins and WHIP (0.989), meriting the 1956 NL MVP and Cy Young Awards. The Dodgers outlasted the Giants by four games in 1951. The crew captured its second consecutive pennant with 89 victories in '52, defeating the Phillies by 3 games.

Joe Black (15-4, 2.15) saved 15 games and earned NL Rookie of the Year honors in '52. Jim "Junior" Gilliam was named NL ROY after scoring 125 runs in '53. Carl Erskine reached the 20-victory plateau in 1953. "Skoonj" Furillo topped the NL with a .344 mark. Brooklyn earned 86 wins in '53 but finished a distant 16 games behind Milwaukee. Clem Labine delivered a 3.33 ERA and notched 47 saves from '55 to'57.

116

In the team's final season in Brooklyn (1957), the Dodgers again placed second to the Braves. Johnny Podres paced the NL with a 2.66 ERA, 1.082 WHIP and 6 shutouts in 1957. Don Drysdale entered the rotation in 1957, furnishing a 2.69 ERA along with a 17-9 record. He led the League with 242 strikeouts in 1959.

The inaugural year in Los Angeles yielded a 75-win season but the squad rebounded to finish in second place in '59. Cal "Buster" McLish emerged as a successful starting pitcher in 1958 at age 31, recording 16 victories and a 2.99 ERA. He fashioned a 19-8 record with a 3.63 ERA for the '59 squad. Charlie Neal scored 103 runs, drilled 30 doubles, 19 taters and led the League with 11 triples.

Win Shares > 20	Single-Season	1940-1959
Jackie Robinson - 1B (LAD)	George Kell - 3B (LAD) x4	Sam Jethroe - CF (LAD) x2
Gil Hodges - 1B (LAD) x9	Don Hoak - 3B (LAD) x3	Irv Noren - CF (LAD)
Jackie Robinson - 2B (LAD) x5	Jim Gilliam - 3B (LAD)	Carl Furillo - RF (LAD) x4
Jim Gilliam - 2B (LAD) x5	Roy Campanella - C (LAD) x6	Johnny Vander Meer - SP (LAD)
Charlie Neal - 2B (LAD)	Luis Olmo - LF (LAD)	Ralph Branca - SP (LAD)
Stan Rojek - SS (LAD)	Jackie Robinson - LF (LAD)	Don Newcombe - SP (LAD) x4
George Strickland - SS (LAD)	Irv Noren - LF (LAD)	Don Drysdale - SP (LAD) x7
Chico Carrasquel - SS (LAD)	Goody Rosen - CF (LAD)	
	Duke Snider - CF (LAD) x9	

Year/Team	OPW%	PW	PL	APW%	AW	AL	Diff+/-
1960 LAD	0.529 P	81	73	0.532	82	72	0.004
1961 LAD	0.500	81	81	0.578	89	65	0.078
1962 LAD	0.469	76	86	0.618	102	63	0.149
1963 LAD	0.476	77	85	0.611 P	99	63	0.135
1964 LAD	0.512	83	79	0.494	80	82	-0.018
1965 LAD	0.491	80	82	0.599 P	97	65	0.108
1966 LAD	0.525	85	77	0.586 P	95	67	0.061
1967 LAD	0.515	83	79	0.451	73	89	-0.064
1968 LAD	0.489	79	83	0.469	76	86	-0.020
1969 LAD	0.488	79	83	0.525	85	77	0.037
franchID	OWAR	OWS	AWAR	AWS	WARdiff	WSdiff	P/D/W/F
1960 LAD	41.381	259.591	41.799	215.995	-0.418	13.596	P
1961 LAD	42.733	291.622	43.194	266.999	-0.461	24.622	
1962 LAD	41.594	296.147	50.567	306.000	-8.973	-9.852	
1963 LAD	34.863	284.812	43.996	297.008	-9.133	-12.195	
1964 LAD	40.366	278.446	40.865	240.000	-0.499	38.446	
1965 LAD	39.697	299.811	41.830	291.001	-2.132	8.810	
1966 LAD	47.196	280.594	51.701	284.995	-4.504	-4.401	
1967 LAD	45.481	274.573	32.579	218.995	12.903	55.578	
1968 LAD	37.884	256.222	34.472	227.999	3.412	28.223	
1969 LAD	41.289	276.355	39.877	255.000	1.412	21.355	

The Dodgers emerged victorious in a four-way battle between the Cardinals, Braves, and Pirates to secure the National League pennant in 1960. Los Angeles then failed to reach the playoffs again until 1978. Roberto Clemente claimed 4 batting titles in the Sixties and batted .328 for the decade. He collected the NL MVP Award in 1966, batting .317 with career-bests in home runs (29) and runs batted in (119). Clemente accrued 35 Win Shares and supplied a career-high .357 BA in '67. Dodgers' right fielders combined to lead the Major Leagues with 39 WS>10 player-seasons from 1950-69.

"Diamond" Jim Gentile finished second in the ROY balloting in '60 with 21 blasts and 98 RBI. In the subsequent campaign Gentile belted 46 round-trippers and topped the League with 141 runs driven in. Frank "Hondo" Howard (.268/23/77) won the Rookie of the Year Award in '60 and two years later crushed 31 long balls and knocked in 119 runs. Howard accrued 37 Win Shares in '68 and walloped at least 44 big-flies while plating 100+ baserunners in three consecutive seasons (1968-1970).

Maury Wills took the NL MVP honors in '62, as he pilfered 104 bases and set career-highs in hits (208) and runs scored (130). Wills paced the NL in stolen bases for six consecutive seasons (1960-1965). Tommy H. Davis was the prime beneficiary of Wills' baserunning exploits as he led the League with 153 RBI, 230 hits and a .346 BA in '62. He reprised his role as National League batting champion with a .326 BA in 1963. Willie "3-Dog" Davis (.285/21/85) scored 103 runs and topped the charts with 10 triples in '62.

Sandy Koufax ascended to the top of the rotation and dominated the National League from 1962-66. After posting 18 wins and 269 whiffs in '61, Koufax averaged 22 victories, 289 strikeouts and 20 complete games with a 1.95 ERA and 0.926 WHIP over the next 5 campaigns. He earned three Cy Young Awards along with MVP honors in 1963. His 382 strikeouts in '65 and four career no-hitters were Major League records (both marks were surpassed by Nolan Ryan). Podres (18-5, 3.74) tied Koufax for the staff lead in victories in 1961. Drysdale posted 17 wins, 210 strikeouts and 15 complete games per season from 1960-68. He captured the Cy Young Award in '62, amassing 25 wins while leading the League in innings pitched and strikeouts. Los Angeles placed a distant second to San Francisco in '64, finishing 13 games back. Jim Lefebvre (.250/12/69) was awarded with NL Rookie of the Years honors in 1965. He bashed 24 quadruples and knocked in 74 runs in the subsequent season. Pete Richert received invitations to the All-Star contest in 1965-66. Richert delivered a 2.60 ERA and 15 victories in '65.

The Dodgers' draft class of 1966, including Charlie Hough, Bill Russell and Ted Sizemore, amassed 664 Career Total Win Shares. Yet this was only a precursor to the heist that the Los Angeles front office accomplished two years later. GM Buzzie Bavasi and his co-horts selected eight players during the '68 Amateur Draft who produced at least 100 Win Shares in their careers. The Los Angeles class of '68 holds the All-Time record for Career Total Win Shares (1613) and Career Total WAR (188). Bavasi secured a trove of amateur free agents during his 18-year stint with the Dodgers encompassing Wills ('51), Clemente, Drysdale, Koufax ('54), Willie Davis, Frank Howard ('58) and Sutton ('64).

Don "Black & Decker" Sutton furnished a 2.99 ERA with 209 strikeouts in his debut season (1966). Bill Singer supplied 15 wins per year (1967-69) along with a 2.60 ERA and 1.119 WHIP. "The Singer Throwing Machine" was rewarded with an All-Star nod in '69, hurling 16 complete games and winning 20 while striking out 247 batters.

Year/Team	OPW%	PW	PL	APW%	AW	AL	Diff+/-
1970 LAD	0.500	81	81	0.540	87	74	0.040
1971 LAD	0.476	77	85	0.549	89	73	0.073
1972 LAD	0.502	81	81	0.548	85	70	0.046
1973 LAD	0.552	89	73	0.590	95	66	0.038
1974 LAD	0.545	88	74	0.630 P	102	60	0.085
1975 LAD	0.508	82	80	0.543	88	74	0.035
1976 LAD	0.525	85	77	0.568	92	70	0.043
1977 LAD	0.497	80	82	0.605 D	98	64	0.108
1978 LAD	0.553 D	90	72	0.586 P	95	67	0.033
1979 LAD	0.490	79	83	0.488	79	83	-0.002

franchID	OWAR	OWS	AWAR	AWS	WARdiff	WSdiff	P/D/W/F
1970 LAD	44.826	294.111	37.956	261.004	6.871	33.107	
1971 LAD	37.577	256.717	43.934	267.002	-6.357	-10.284	
1972 LAD	44.327	279.939	44.037	255.002	0.290	24.937	
1973 LAD	45.996	308.907	**47.438**	284.993	-1.442	23.914	
1974 LAD	44.519	303.959	**59.790**	**305.993**	-15.272	-2.034	
1975 LAD	40.240	278.787	49.035	264.009	-8.795	14.778	
1976 LAD	35.320	299.517	37.509	275.995	-2.189	23.522	
1977 LAD	35.406	271.612	**55.285**	294.000	-19.878	-22.388	
1978 LAD	40.828	297.693	**52.175**	**285.002**	-11.347	12.691	D
1979 LAD	39.557	276.505	41.589	236.998	-2.033	39.507	

Clemente averaged .336 during his last three seasons and collected his 3000th hit before his untimely death in a plane crash on December 31, 1972. Howard crushed 44 round-trippers, knocked in 126 runs and amassed 132 bases on balls, while Willie Davis (.305/8/93) led the League with 16 triples in 1970. Davis is tied for second place among outfielders with 11 seasons on the Fielding WAR and WS leader boards. Wes "Mr. Steady" Parker (.305/10/111) paced the NL with 47 doubles.

Don Sutton yielded consistent results throughout the Seventies, including a 17-11 record with 12 complete games, 3.07 ERA and a 1.108 WHIP per season. He twirled nine shutouts and posted a 2.08 ERA with a 0.913 WHIP in '72. Jim Merritt (20-12, 4.08) finished fourth in the 1970 NL Cy Young balloting. Pete Richert (1.98, 13 SV) and Stan Williams (10-1, 1.99, 15 SV) shared the closer's role.

The Dodgers tallied 89 victories in 1973, falling 3 games short of the Astros for the NL West title. Los Angeles posted 88 wins in the subsequent season, finishing third as Atlanta grabbed the division crown. Bill Singer secured 20 wins and whiffed 241 opponents in '73. Jack Billingham won 19 games in successive seasons (1973-74), topping the NL with 7 shutouts and 40 games started in 1973. Doug Rau enjoyed a five-season run, yielding 15 wins and a 3.20 ERA from 1974-78.

Ron "Penguin" Cey debuted at the hot corner in 1973 and made 6 consecutive All-Star appearances (1974-79). He walloped 23 quadruples and batted in 90 runs per year in the Seventies. Steve Garvey produced 200 hits per season along with a .313 BA, 22 four-baggers and 104 RBI from 1974-79. The Dodgers' first sacker received MVP accolades in '74 and placed runner-up in '78. The 1974 Dodgers supplied the highest offWARnorm (24) and offWSnorm (184) in franchise history.

Davey Lopes swiped 53 bases per season (1973-79) including a league-best 77 steals in 1975. Los Angeles topped the Majors with 48 WS>10 seasons from 1970-1999 at the keystone position. Bill Buckner contributed a .314 average, 30 doubles and 31 stolen bases to the '74 squad. Ivan DeJesus pilfered 41 bags and scored 104 runs to lead the National League in '78, and in '79 Jerry Royster totaled 103 runs and stole 35 bases.

In 1976 knuckleballer Charlie Hough led the bullpen corps with a 12-6 record, 18 saves and a 2.21 ERA. In the following season Hough saved 22 contests and delivered a 3.32 ERA. Doyle Alexander (17-11, 3.65) and Rick Rhoden (16-10, 3.74) bolstered the staff in 1977. Geoff Zahn crafted a 3.03 ERA and supplied 14 wins in '78. Los Angeles finally ended its playoff drought, winning the NL West in '78 by four games over San Francisco. Rick Sutcliffe secured NL Rookie of the Year honors in 1979, winning 17 contests with a 3.46 ERA.

Win Shares > 20	Single-Season	1960-1979
Jim Gentile - 1B (LAD) x2	Ron Cey - 3B (LAD) x7	Roberto Clemente - RF (LAD) x12
Ron Fairly - 1B (LAD) x2	Johnny Roseboro - C (LAD) x2	Frank Howard - RF (LAD) x2
Wes Parker - 1B (LAD)	Joe Ferguson - C (LAD)	Ron Fairly - RF (LAD)
Steve Garvey - 1B (LAD) x7	Tommy H. Davis - LF (LAD) x2	Willie Crawford - RF (LAD)
Jim Lefebvre - 2B (LAD) x2	Frank Howard - LF (LAD) x7	Sandy Koufax - SP (LAD) x4
Davey Lopes - 2B (LAD) x5	Ron Fairly - LF (LAD)	Bill Singer - SP (LAD) x2
Maury Wills - SS (LAD) x4	Bill Buckner - LF (LAD) x2	Don Sutton - SP (LAD) x5
Don Demeter - 3B (LAD)	Willie Davis - CF (LAD) x9	Doug Rau - SP (LAD)
Ken McMullen - 3B (LAD) x4		
Billy Grabarkewitz - 3B (LAD)		

Year/Team	OPW%	PW	PL	APW%	AW	AL	Diff+/-
1980 LAD	0.463	75	87	0.564	92	71	0.102
1981 LAD	0.542 D	88	74	0.573	63	47	0.030
1982 LAD	0.519	84	78	0.543	88	74	0.024
1983 LAD	0.567	92	70	0.562 P	91	71	-0.005
1984 LAD	0.530	86	76	0.488	79	83	-0.042
1985 LAD	0.561 P	91	71	0.586 D	95	67	0.025
1986 LAD	0.518 D	84	78	0.451	73	89	-0.068
1987 LAD	0.515	83	79	0.451	73	89	-0.064
1988 LAD	0.485	78	84	0.584 D	94	67	0.099
1989 LAD	0.493	80	82	0.481	77	83	-0.011

franchID	OWAR	OWS	AWAR	AWS	WARdiff	WSdiff	P/D/W/F
1980 LAD	33.748	263.362	44.319	275.999	-10.571	-12.638	
1981 LAD	27.087	171.075	33.735	188.997	-6.647	-17.922	D
1982 LAD	41.766	270.963	**50.335**	263.993	-8.569	6.970	
1983 LAD	43.768	299.690	42.637	**273.002**	1.131	26.688	
1984 LAD	43.762	280.742	34.368	236.997	9.393	43.746	
1985 LAD	45.111	288.253	47.964	284.999	-2.853	3.253	P
1986 LAD	38.886	248.313	33.425	219.005	5.461	29.308	D
1987 LAD	36.885	251.177	29.290	218.999	7.595	32.178	
1988 LAD	31.212	243.924	39.601	282.000	-8.389	-38.076	
1989 LAD	35.489	220.460	38.294	231.000	-2.805	-10.540	

Garvey (.304/26/106) paced the NL in hits for the final time, delivering 200 base knocks in 1980. Buckner collected a batting title in '80, led the NL in doubles twice and knocked in 100+ runs in three seasons. Sutton paced the League with a 2.20 ERA and 0.989 WHIP in 1980. He extended his streak of consecutive seasons with 100+ strikeouts to 21 seasons (1966-1986).

Steve Howe earned 1980 NL Rookie of the Year honors, saving 17 games with a 2.66 ERA. He furnished a 2.17 ERA and 14 saves per season from 1980-83. Bob Welch supplied 14 wins, a 3.21 ERA and a 1.225 WHIP per year in the Eighties. Tom "Wimpy" Paciorek achieved his best seasons from 1981-83, batting .315 with 29 doubles per year. Los Angeles outlasted San Francisco by a single game to take the Western division crown in '81.

Fernando Valenzuela (13-7, 2.48) dominated the League in 1981, capturing the Cy Young and Rookie of the Year Awards. "El Toro" paced the NL in games started, complete games, innings pitched, shutouts (8) and strikeouts (180). He finished second in the Cy Young balloting in '86, recording career-bests with 21 wins, 20 complete games and 242 whiffs.

The Braves edged the Dodgers for the title in three straight campaigns (1982-84). Cey swatted 24 round-trippers and drove in 89 runs per year during that timeframe. Steve Sax captured NL Rookie of the Year honors in '82, amassed 200+ hits twice and pilfered over 40 bases five times during the decade. Geoff Zahn (18-8, 3.73) placed sixth in the 1982 Cy Young voting.

After moving to the starting rotation, Hough averaged 16 victories, 12 complete games and a 3.58 ERA from 1982-88. Sutcliffe produced a league-leading 2.96 ERA in '82. The "Red Baron" received Cy Young honors in 1984, posting a record of 20-6 with a 3.43 ERA and career-high 213 strikeouts. Tom Niedenfuer provided a right-handed compliment to Howe, securing 13 saves with a 3.01 ERA from 1982-88.

Rudy Law ran wild on the basepaths, swiping 77 bags in '83 and Doyle Alexander delivered back-to-back seasons with 17 wins (1983-84). Ron Kittle bashed 35 moon-shots and plated 100 runners, securing Rookie of the Year honors in '83. Jeffrey "Hack Man" Leonard drilled 21 homers in consecutive seasons ('83-'84) and added 24 jacks and 93 RBI in 1989. Right fielder Mike A. Marshall belted 28 circuit clouts and knocked in 95 runs in '84, while Alejandro Pena topped the NL with a 2.48 ERA in the same season.

Orel Hershiser (19-3, 2.03) placed third in the NL Cy Young balloting in 1985 after finishing third in the ROY balloting during the previous campaign. The "Bulldog" overmatched the opposition in 1988, hurling 59 scoreless innings to close out the season. He led the League with a 23-8 record, 15 complete games, 8 shutouts and 267 innings pitched while earning Cy Young honors.

Lopes succeeded on 47 of 51 stolen base attempts as a part-timer in 1985. Ted Power logged 27 saves in his lone season as the closer. Los Angeles squeaked past San Diego in 1985 to secure its first pennant in 25 years. The '86 squad followed up with a division title, defeating the Padres again by percentage points. Sid Fernandez whiffed 200 batters and fashioned a 16-6 record in '86. "El Sid" managed 13 wins per season with a 3.18 ERA and 1.138 WHIP from 1985-89. Dave Stewart notched three consecutive 20-win seasons (1987-89) but came up short in the Cy Young balloting in each campaign. John Franco averaged 7 wins, 29 saves and a 2.47 ERA while receiving three All-Star invitations from 1985-89.

Year/Team	OPW%	PW	PL	APW%	AW	AL	Diff+/-
1990 LAD	0.492	80	82	0.531	86	76	0.039
1991 LAD	0.469	76	86	0.574	93	69	0.105
1992 LAD	0.475	77	85	0.389	63	99	-0.086
1993 LAD	0.492	80	82	0.500	81	81	0.008
1994 LAD	0.440	71	91	0.509 D	58	56	0.069
1995 LAD	0.502	81	81	0.542 D	78	66	0.040
1996 LAD	0.577 P	94	68	0.556 W	90	72	-0.022
1997 LAD	0.536 D	87	75	0.543	88	74	0.008
1998 LAD	0.510	83	79	0.512	83	79	0.003
1999 LAD	0.558 D	90	72	0.475	77	85	-0.083

franchID	OWAR	OWS	AWAR	AWS	WARdiff	WSdiff	P/D/W/F
1990 LAD	34.545	243.882	39.568	257.999	-5.023	-14.117	
1991 LAD	30.111	216.835	44.205	279.000	-14.094	-62.164	
1992 LAD	30.120	216.503	28.605	188.997	1.515	27.506	
1993 LAD	27.208	210.831	38.805	242.995	-11.598	-32.165	
1994 LAD	20.296	147.340	28.131	174.002	-7.835	-26.662	
1995 LAD	35.768	205.753	38.013	233.998	-2.244	-28.245	
1996 LAD	41.068	248.492	39.496	269.997	1.572	-21.505	P
1997 LAD	38.197	232.754	42.876	263.996	-4.678	-31.242	D
1998 LAD	34.857	222.133	32.829	249.000	2.028	-26.867	
1999 LAD	37.573	220.504	36.594	230.997	0.979	-10.493	D

The Dodgers pitching staff remained well-stocked in the Nineties. Bob Welch fashioned a 2.95 ERA and amassed 27 wins, earning Cy Young honors. Dave Stewart delivered career-bests with 22 victories, a 2.56 ERA and a 1.157 WHIP in '90. Ramon J. Martinez (20-6, 2.92) struck out 223 batters and made his lone All-Star appearance en route to a runner-up finish in the 1990 NL Cy Young balloting. Juan Guzman (10-3, 2.99) placed second in the ROY voting in 1991. He combined for a 30-8 record during the next two seasons, and posted a league-best ERA of 2.93 in '96.

Veteran hurlers Sid Fernandez (14-11, 2.73 in '92) and Orel Hershiser (16-6, 3.87 in '95) bolstered the rotation. John Franco retained late-inning responsibilities throughout the decade, despite a poor WHIP (1.354). Franco's typical production included 27 saves and a 2.81 ERA. John Wetteland delivered 37 saves and a 2.53 ERA from 1992-99, earning three All-Star invitations.

Los Angeles suffered through seven straight losing seasons (1988-1994) until a succession of talented prospects returned the franchise to the "promised land." The Dodgers' offense in the early 90's included holdovers such as Sax (.304 with 31 SB in '91), Candy Maldonado (.273/22/95 in 1990) and Mike Devereaux (.276/24/107 in '92).

Eric Karros commenced the Rookie of the Year parade, blasting 20 round-trippers with 88 RBI in 1992. Karros delivered 31 homers, 104 RBI and a .284 average from 1995-99. Mike Piazza sizzled in '93, launching 35 long balls and batting .318 with 112 RBI. Piazza produced a .330 batting average, 34 home runs and 109 RBI from 1993-99, placing second in the MVP voting in '96 and '97. Raul Mondesi drilled 27 doubles and batted .306 in his inaugural campaign. He averaged 29 four-baggers, 90 ribbies and 25 stolen bases while batting .285 from 1995-97. After Hideo Nomo won the ROY Award in '95, Todd Hollandsworth (.291, 21 SB) gave the Dodgers five straight winners!

The Dodgers fell one game short of the division title in '95 as the Padres claimed victory with 82 wins. Nomo (13-6, 2.54) whiffed 236 batters in his inaugural year (1995). "The Tornado" yielded 234 strikeouts per season from 1995-97. On the basepaths Tom Goodwin swiped 50+ bags in 3 straight seasons (1995-97) while Eric Young achieved the feat in '96 and '99. Young (.324/8/74) was selected to the All-Star team in 1996 along with Henry A. Rodriguez (.276/36/103). Los Angeles cruised to the pennant, tallying 94 wins and overtaking San Diego by seven games.

Pedro J. Martinez (Ramon's younger brother) solidified his credentials with a superb season in 1997. Pedro paced the League with a 1.90 ERA, 13 complete games and a 0.932 WHIP while notching 305 strikeouts. He dominated the opposition in '99, tallying 23 victories, 313 strikeouts, a 2.07 ERA and 0.923 WHIP. Martinez received the Cy Young Award in both campaigns. Dodgers' starting pitchers compiled 41 WS>10 player-seasons during the Nineties (tops in the Major Leagues).

The club repeated as division winners in '97 and picked up another title in '99 by a 2-game margin over the Giants. Jose Offerman led the circuit in triples in '98 and '99 and scored 100+ runs. Roger Cedeno batted .313 and nabbed 66 bases in '99.

Year/Team	OPW%	PW	PL	APW%	AW	AL	Diff+/-
2000 LAD	0.512	83	79	0.531	86	76	0.019
2001 LAD	0.502	81	81	0.531	86	76	0.029
2002 LAD	0.493	80	82	0.568	92	70	0.074
2003 LAD	0.471 D	76	86	0.525	85	77	0.054
2004 LAD	0.429	70	92	0.574 D	93	69	0.145
2005 LAD	0.364	59	103	0.438	71	91	0.074
2006 LAD	0.546 D	88	74	0.543 W	88	74	-0.002
2007 LAD	0.522	85	77	0.506	82	80	-0.016

2008 LAD	0.532 D	86	76	0.519 D	84	78	-0.014
2009 LAD	0.556 W	90	72	0.586 P	95	67	0.030
2010 LAD	0.525	85	77	0.494	80	82	-0.032
2011 LAD	0.572 P	93	69	0.509	82	79	-0.062
2012 LAD	0.546 D	89	73	0.531	86	76	-0.016
2013 LAD	0.502 D	81	81	0.568 D	92	70	0.066

franchID	OWAR	OWS	AWAR	AWS	WARdiff	WSdiff	P/D/W/F
2000 LAD	34.531	225.615	42.064	258.005	-7.533	-32.390	
2001 LAD	28.545	203.976	38.827	258.007	-10.282	-54.030	
2002 LAD	28.454	214.597	38.054	275.997	-9.600	-61.400	
2003 LAD	26.975	206.268	37.750	255.006	-10.776	-48.738	D
2004 LAD	25.076	216.716	39.926	278.991	-14.850	-62.275	
2005 LAD	21.797	173.179	28.449	212.998	-6.652	-39.819	
2006 LAD	33.667	238.472	**46.988**	265.823	-13.321	-27.351	D
2007 LAD	38.051	259.278	41.231	246.004	-3.180	13.273	
2008 LAD	36.176	237.218	43.596	252.009	-7.420	-14.790	D
2009 LAD	44.000	260.551	**50.921**	**285.002**	-6.922	-24.451	W
2010 LAD	42.549	267.256	35.547	240.002	7.002	27.255	
2011 LAD	**46.168**	**285.889**	39.450	246.000	6.719	39.889	P
2012 LAD	47.171	289.726	34.519	257.993	12.651	31.733	D
2013 LAD	38.454	263.085	**47.243**	276.002	-8.789	-12.917	D

Los Angeles finished behind San Francisco for three consecutive years (2000-02), losing the division title by a single game in 2000. Piazza (.324/38/113) placed third in the NL MVP voting in 2000. He delivered 36 blasts and 102 ribbies from 2000-02. Karros swatted 31 long balls and knocked in 102 runs in '00 while Eric Young pilfered 54 bags in 61 attempts. Mondesi produced 25 big-flies and 22 steals per season (2000-03). Paul Konerko provided consistent power, walloping 30 four-baggers and driving in 94 runs per season from 2000-2012.

Pedro J. Martinez posted a .726 winning percentage from 2000-05, twice leading the League in strikeouts and three times in ERA. Martinez received his third Cy Young Award in 2000, going 18-6 with a miniscule 1.74 ERA and magnificent WHIP of 0.737! Chan Ho Park whiffed 200+ batters in back-to-back campaigns (2000-01), fashioning an 18-10 record with a 3.27 ERA in 2000. Nomo topped the charts with 220 whiffs and Paul LoDuca batted .320 with 25 clouts and 90 RBI in 2001.

Eric Gagne dominated the opposition in the late innings from 2002-04, notching 51 saves with a 1.79 ERA and 122 punch-outs per season. Gagne received the Cy Young Award in '03, posting 55 saves with a 1.20 ERA and 0.692 WHIP! The Dodgers backed into the playoffs in '03, edging the Padres despite a losing record. Adrian Beltre exploded in '04, pacing the NL with 48 long balls while batting .334 with 37 Win Shares. Beltre collected 200 hits, scored 104 runs and knocked in 121 en route to a runner-up in the MVP balloting.

The 2005 squad submitted the worst record in team history (59-103), but Los Angeles bounced back to win division titles in '06 and '08 along with the Wild Card in '09. Russell Martin received a Gold Glove Award for his work behind the plate in '07 while batting .293 with 19 homers and 87 runs batted in. Takashi Saito earned an All-Star invitation with 39 saves and a 1.40 ERA. Shane Victorino scored 102 runs in back-to-back seasons (2008-09). The "Flyin' Hawaiian" led the NL with 13 triples in '09. James Loney batted .331 in 96 games as a rookie in '07 while Matt Kemp hit .342 in 98 contests. Kemp belted 26 long balls and nabbed 34 bags in 2009. "The Bison" earned a runner-up finish in the 2011 NL MVP race, batting .324 with league-bests in home runs (39), RBI (126) and runs scored (115).

Chad Billingsley (16-10, 3.36) tallied 201 strikeouts in 2008, and in the same year Jonathan Broxton struck out 114 batters in 76 innings and amassed 36 saves. Joakim Soria supplied 38 saves and a 1.84 ERA per year from 2008-2010. Ted Lilly compiled 17 wins in '08 and followed with a 3.10 ERA and 1.056 WHIP in '09. Clayton Kershaw collected three consecutive ERA and WHIP titles (2011-13). "The Claw" topped the NL in strikeouts and earned Cy Young Awards in 2011 and 2013. Kenley Jansen averaged 14 strikeouts per 9 innings pitched from 2010-13 and ascended to the closer's role in 2012.

Win Shares > 20	Single-Season	1980-2013
Bill Buckner - 1B (LAD)	Jeffrey Leonard - LF (LAD)	Doyle Alexander - SP (LAD)
Eric Karros - 1B (LAD) x3	Rudy Law - CF (LAD)	Orel Hershiser - SP (LAD) x4
Paul Konerko - 1B (LAD) x4	Mitch Webster - CF (LAD)	Fernando Valenzuela - SP
Steve Sax - 2B (LAD) x4	Mike Devereaux - CF (LAD)	(LAD) x2
Jose Offerman - 2B (LAD)	Raul Mondesi - CF (LAD)	Dave Stewart - SP (LAD)
Adrian Beltre - 3B (LAD) x4	Shane Victorino - CF (LAD) x4	Pedro J. Martinez - SP (LAD)
Mike Scioscia - C (LAD)	Matt Kemp - CF (LAD) x3	x5
Mike Piazza - C (LAD) x8	Mike A. Marshall - RF (LAD)	Clayton Kershaw - SP (LAD)
Paul Lo Duca - C (LAD) x2	Mitch Webster - RF (LAD)	x2
Russell Martin - C (LAD)	Raul Mondesi - RF (LAD) x3	John Wetteland - RP (LAD)
A.J. Ellis - C (LAD)	Rick Sutcliffe - SP (LAD)	Eric Gagne - RP (LAD)
Carlos Santana – C (LAD)		

Note: 4000 PA or BFP to qualify, except during strike-shortened seasons
(1972 = 3800, 1981 & 1994 = 2700, 1995 = 3500) and 154-game schedule (3800)
- failed to qualify: 1905-1906, 1909, 1912-1933, 1937, 1941

Dodgers All-Time "Originals" Roster

Reggie Abercrombie	Al Ferrara	Bill Leard	Lew Richie
Cal Abrams	Sergio Ferrer	Hal Lee	Adam Riggs
Tony Abreu	Alfredo Figaro	Jim Lefebvre	Claude Ritchey
Ace Adams	Pembroke Finlayson	Ken Lehman	Lew Ritter
Raleigh Aitchison	Neal Finn	Larry LeJeune	German Rivera
Ed Albosta	William Fischer	Don LeJohn	Todd Rizzo
Doyle Alexander	Bob Fisher	Steve Lembo	Jim Roberts
Horace Allen	Tom Fitzsimmons	Bob Lennon	Earl Robinson
Luke Allen	Darrin Fletcher	Dutch E. Leonard	Jackie Robinson
Whitey Alperman	Sam Fletcher	Jeffrey Leonard	Trayvon Robinson
Orlando Alvarez	Dee Fondy	Dennis Lewallyn	Sergio Robles
Victor Alvarez	Alan Foster	Phil Lewis	Lou Rochelli
Ed Amelung	John Franco	Bob Lillis	Rich Rodas
Steve Ames	Jack Franklin	Ted Lilly	Felix Rodriguez
Sandy Amoros	Wayne Franklin	Josh Lindblom	Hector Rodriguez
Dave C. Anderson	Johnny Frederick	Paul Lo Duca	Henry A. Rodriguez
John J. Anderson	George Freese	Billy Loes	Ricardo Rodriguez
Sparky Anderson	Lonny Frey	Dick Loftus	Paco Rodriguez
Bill Antonello	Marion Fricano	Bob Logan	Ed Roebuck
Ed Appleton	Nig Fuller	Ernie Lombardi	Ron Roenicke
Billy Ashley	Carl Furillo	Vic Lombardi	Packy Rogers
Bob Aspromonte	Gabe Gabler	James Loney	Stan Rojek
Pedro Astacio	John Gaddy	Tom F. Long	Damian Rolls
Toby Atwell	Eric Gagne	Davey Lopes	Jim Romano
Willy Aybar	Bob Gallagher	Al Lopez	Johnny Roseboro
Johnny Babich	Phil Gallivan	Arturo Lopez	Goody Rosen
Jose Baez	Balvino Galvez	Luis A. Lopez	Max Rosenfeld
Tom C. Baker	John Gamble	Charlie Loudenslager	Bob Ross

Frank Baldwin	Karim Garcia	Turk Lown	Dave Ross
Dan Bankhead	Luis A. Garcia	Harry Lumley	Jean-Pierre Roy
Jack Banta	Onelki Garcia	Don Lund	Jerry Royster
Jim Barbieri	Daniel Garibay	Ed MacGamwell	Nap Rucker
Rex Barney	Steve Garvey	Keith Macwhorter	Ernie Rudolph
Bob Barr	Welcome Gaston	Morris Madden	Justin Ruggiano
Tony Barron	Sid Gautreaux	Matt Magill	Andy Rush
Boyd Bartley	Jim Gentile	George Magoon	Bill Russell
Monty Basgall	Ben Geraghty	Duster Mails	John A. Russell
Eddie Basinski	Bob Giallombardo	Charlie Malay	Johnny Rutherford
Emil Batch	Charlie Gilbert	Candy Maldonado	Hyun-jin Ryu
Jim Baxes	Wally Gilbert	Mal Mallette	Takashi Saito
Erve Beck	Geronimo Gil	Isidro Marquez	Manny Salvo
Joe Beckwith	Paul Gillespie	Mike A. Marshall	Romulo Sanchez
Hank Behrman	Jim Gilliam	Ethan Martin	Jerry Sands
Wayne Belardi	Roy Gleason	Pedro J. Martinez	Carlos Santana
George G. Bell	John Glenn	Ramon J. Martinez	Jack Savage
Josh Bell	John Gochnauer	Russell Martin	Dave Sax
Juan Bell	Chuck Goggin	Onan Masaoka	Steve Sax
Edwin Bellorin	Jose Gonzalez	Earl Mattingly	Art Schallock
Adrian Beltre	Tom Goodwin	Gene Mauch	Bill Schardt
Peter Bergeron	Greg Goossen	Ralph Mauriello	Al Scheer
Moe Berg	Glen Gorbous	Lucas May	Dutch Schliebner
Ray Berres	Ray Gordinier	Scott May	Henry Schmidt
Herman Besse	Dee Gordon	Jamie McAndrew	Steve Schmoll
Dann Bilardello	Rick Gorecki	Gene McCann	Charlie Schmutz
Chad Billingsley	Herb Gorman	Bill McCarren	Frank Schneiberg
Jack Billingham	Billy Grabarkewitz	Johnny McCarthy	Paul Schreiber
Del Bissonette	Dick Gray	Lew McCarty	Howie Schultz
Joe Black	Harvey Green	Jim McCloskey	Mike Scioscia
Rae Blaemire	Nelson Greene	Mike McCormack	Dick L. Scott
Henry Blanco	Hal Gregg	Walt McCredie	Tim Scott
Nate Bland	Bert Griffith	Terry McDermott	Larry See
Rafael Bournigal	Derrell Griffith	James McDonald	Elmer Sexauer
Gene Brabender	Connie Grob	Sandy McDougal	Greg Shanahan
Gibby Brack	Javy Guerra	Pryor McElveen	George Sharrott
Mark Bradley	Wilton Guerrero	Pat McGlothin	Ray Shearer
George Bradshaw	Brad Gulden	Harry McIntire	Jimmy Sheckard
Joe Bradshaw	Franklin Gutierrez	Kit McKenna	Jack Sheehan
Ralph Branca	Joel Guzman	Ed McLane	Red Sheridan
Sid Bream	Juan Guzman	Cal McLish	Vince Sherlock
William Brennan	Chris Gwynn	John McMakin	Larry Sherry
Tony Brewer	Bert Haas	Tommy McMillan	Norm Sherry
Rocky Bridges	John Hale	Ken McMullen	Zak Shinall
Greg Brock	Bill B. Hall	Jim McTamany	Craig Shipley
Matt Broderick	John Hall	Roberto Mejia	Bart Shirley
Jerry Brooks	Jeff Hamilton	Jonathan Meloan	Steve Shirley
John Brown	Bert Hamric	Jim Merritt	Harry Shriver
Lloyd Brown	Pat Hannifan	Mike Metcalfe	George Shuba
Tommy Brown	Joel Hanrahan	Benny Meyer	Dick Siebert
Jonathan Broxton	Dave Hansen	Leo Meyer	Joe Simpson
Mike T. Brumley	F.C. Hansford	Glenn Mickens	Bill Singer
Ralph Bryant	Charlie Hargreaves	Eddie Miksis	Ted Sizemore
Bill Buckner	Bill T. Harris	Don Miles	Frank Skaff
Cy Buker	Bill Hart	Fred Miller	Gordon Slade

Larry Burchart	Jeff Hartsock	Hack L. Miller	Lefty Sloat
Glenn Burke	Mickey Hatcher	Larry Miller	Aleck Smith
Sandy Burk	Ray Hathaway	Lemmie Miller	Charley Smith
Larry Burright	Joe Hatten	Otto Miller	Dick A. Smith
Paul Burris	Chris Haughey	Ralph D. Miller	Jack H. Smith
Moe Burtschy	Phil Haugstad	Rod Miller	Nate Smith
Mike Busch	George Hausmann	Walt Miller	Red J. Smith
Nick Buss	Ed Head	Bob Milliken	Clancy Smyres
Max Butcher	Hughie Hearne	Wally Millies	Red Smyth
Johnny Butler	Jake Hehl	Mike Mimbs	Duke Snider
Edgar Caceres	Harry Heitmann	Paul Minner	Jack Snyder
Leon Cadore	Lafayette Henion	Steve Mintz	Eddie Solomon
Miguel Cairo	Ubaldo Heredia	Bobby Van Mitchell	Andy Sommerville
Sam Calderone	Matt Herges	Russ Mitchell	Joakim Soria
Leo Callahan	Carlos A. Hernandez	Joe Moeller	Juan Sosa
Dick Calmus	Leo Hernandez	George Mohart	Karl Spooner
Doug Camilli	Elian Herrera	Raul Mondesi	Dennis Springer
Al Campanis	Marty Herrmann	Rafael Montalvo	George Stallings
Jim Campanis	Orel Hershiser	Cy Moore	George Staller
Roy Campanella	Greg Heydeman	Gary Moore	Jerry Standaert
Kevin Campbell	Jim Hibbs	Ray Moore	Joe Stanka
Guy Cantrell	Buddy Hicks	Bobby Morgan	Casey Stengel
Chico Carrasquel	Andy High	Bryan Morris	Ed Stevens
Marcos Carvajal	George Hildebrand	Walt Moryn	Dave Stewart
Braulio Castillo	Shawn Hillegas	Earl Mossor	Royle Stillman
Juan Castro	Koyie Hill	Ray Moss	Bob Stinson
Tom Catterson	Hunkey Hines	Glen Moulder	Ricky Stone
Art Ceccarelli	Don Hoak	Ray Mowe	George Strickland
Roger Cedeno	Oris Hockett	Van Mungo	Jim Strickland
Ron Cey	Gil Hodges	Les Munns	Franklin Stubbs
Ed Chandler	Jamie Hoffmann	Jose Munoz	Eric Stults
Glenn Chapman	Bert Hogg	Mike Munoz	Bill Sudakis
Chin-Feng Chen	Todd Hollandsworth	Noe Munoz	Rick Sutcliffe
Bob Chipman	Gary Holman	Jim F. Murray	Don Sutton
Walt Chipple	Darren Holmes	Hy Myers	Tommy Tatum
Larry Ciaffone	Brian Holton	Steve Nagy	Ben E. Taylor
Gino Cimoli	Wally Hood	Sam Nahem	Zack Taylor
George Cisar	Lefty Hopper	Norihiro Nakamura	Dick Teed
Moose Clabaugh	Charlie Hough	Shane Nance	Chuck Templeton
Roberto Clemente	Ed Householder	Charlie Neal	Joe Tepsic
Alta Cohen	Frank Howard	Ron Negray	Grant Thatcher
Chuck Coles	Matt Howard	Bernie Neis	Brad Thomas
Steve Colyer	Mike Howard	Jeff Nelson	Leo Thomas
Chuck Connors	Dixie H. Howell	Dick Nen	Ray Thomas
Alex Cora	Harry Howell	Don Newcombe	Tim Thompson
Claude Corbitt	Ken Howell	Bobo Newsom	Joe Thurston
Chuck Corgan	Steve Howe	Don Nicholas	Thad Tillotson
John Corriden	Chin-Lung Hu	Chris Nichting	Shawn Tolleson
Pete Coscarart	Ken Huckaby	Tom Niedenfuer	Steve Toole
Bobby Cox	Johnny Hudson	Otho Nitcholas	Bert Tooley
Dick Cox	Rex Hudson	Al Nixon	Jeff Torborg
Glenn Cox	Mike Huff	Hideo Nomo	Dick Tracewski
George Crable	Ed Hug	Irv Noren	Brian Traxler
Roger Craig	Mickey Hughes	Franklin Nunez	Nick Tremark
Willie Crawford	Eric Hull	Bob O'Brien	Overton Tremper

Pat Crisham	John Hummel	John O'Brien	Ramon Troncoso
Claude Crocker	Al Humphrey	Whitey Ock	Fred Underwood
Jack Cronin	Bernie Hungling	Danny O'Connell	Lino Urdaneta
Bubba Crosby	Billy Hunter	Jose Offerman	Ismael Valdez
Bill E. Crouch	George Hunter	Nate Oliver	Rene Valdez
Don Crow	Willard Hunter	Luis Olmo	Bobby Valentine
Francisco Cruceta	Joe Hutcheson	Ralph Onis	Fernando Valenzuela
Henry Cruz	Roy Hutson	Eddie Oropesa	Hector Valle
Bert Cunningham	Tom Hutton	Phil Ortega	Deacon Van Buren
George Cutshaw	Garey Ingram	Hector Ortiz	Sandy Vance
Omar Daal	Bert Inks	Charlie Osgood	Chris Van Cuyk
Jud Daley	Kazuhisa Ishii	Franquelis Osoria	Johnny Van Cuyk
Jack Dalton	Edwin Jackson	Johnny Ostrowski	Johnny Vander Meer
Fats Dantonio	Spook Jacobs	Antonio Osuna	Scott Van Slyke
Cliff Dapper	Cleo James	Willis Otanez	Max Venable
Bob Darnell	Mike James	Chink Outen	Dario Veras
Jake Daubert	Kenley Jansen	Tom Paciorek	Shane Victorino
Ray Daviault	Roy Jarvis	Erv Palica	Jose Vizcaino
Tommy H. Davis	George Jeffcoat	Ed Palmquist	Paul Wachtel
Willie Davis	Sam Jethroe	Chan Ho Park	Ben Wade
Lindsay Deal	Luis A. Jimenez	Wes Parker	Cory Wade
Tommy Dean	Fred Johnston	Art Parks	Gale Wade
Alejandro De Aza	Keith Johnson	Jose Parra	Bull Wagner
Art Decatur	Steve Johnson	Jay Partridge	Josh Wall
Artie Dede	Tim Johnson	Kevin Pasley	Stan Wall
Rod Dedeaux	Art Jones	Jim Pastorius	Preston Ward
Pat Deisel	Binky Jones	Daryl Patterson	Rube Ward
Ivan DeJesus	Fielder Jones	Dave Patterson	Tommy Warren
Ivan De Jesus	Oscar Jones	Jimmy Pattison	Carl Warwick
Rubby De La Rosa	Ross Jones	Xavier Paul	Fred Waters
Bert Delmas	Dutch Jordan	Harley Payne	Eric Weaver
Billy DeMars	Jimmy Jordan	Stu Pederson	Les Webber
Don Demeter	Spider Jorgensen	Alejandro Pena	Mitch Webster
Travis Denker	Von Joshua	Angel Pena	Gary Weiss
Eddie Dent	Eric Junge	Jim Pendleton	Bob Welch
Bob Detherage	Eric Karros	Jack Perconte	John Wells
Mike Devereaux	John Karst	George Pfister	Johnny Werhas
Blake DeWitt	Chick Keating	Ray Phelps	Wally Westlake
Jose Diaz	Chet Kehn	Mike Piazza	Max W. West
Juan C. Diaz	Mike Kekich	Jorge Piedra	John Wetteland
Victor Diaz	George Kell	Joe Pignatano	Mack Wheat
Leo Dickerman	Bill Kelso	Ed Pipgras	Zack Wheat
Ben Diggins	Matt Kemp	Norman Plitt	Ed L. Wheeler
Mike Dimmel	Brickyard Kennedy	Bud Podbielan	Barney White
Jose Dominguez	Maury Kent	Johnny Podres	Myron White
John Douglas	Clayton Kershaw	Nick Polly	Dick Whitman
Red Downey	Clyde King	Jim Richard Poole	Nick Willhite
Darren Dreifort	Fred Kipp	Bill Posedel	Dick Williams
Frank Drews	Wayne Kirby	Sam Post	Jeff Williams
Don Drysdale	Enos Kirkpatrick	Dykes Potter	Leon Williams
Jim Duckworth	Chris Kitsos	Dennis Powell	Reggie D. Williams
Clise Dudley	Ron Kittle	Ted Power	Stan Williams
John Duffie	Tom Klawitter	Scott Proctor	Todd Williams
Mariano Duncan	Stan Klopp	Luke Prokopec	Woody W. Williams
Jack Dunn	Elmer Knetzer	Yasiel Puig	Maury Wills

Joe Dunn	Barney Koch	John Purdin	Bob Wilson
Roberto Duran	Paul Konerko	Eddie Pye	Eddie Wilson
Bull Durham	Jim Korwan	Steve Rachunok	Tack Wilson
Rich Durning	Sandy Koufax	Marv Rackley	Tex Wilson
Red Durrett	Joe Koukalik	Jack Radtke	Lave Winham
Bruce Edwards	Clarence Kraft	Ed Rakow	Chris Withrow
Rube Ehrhardt	Jack Kraus	Bob Ramazzotti	George Witt
Harry Eisenstat	Abe Kruger	Willie Ramsdell	Tracy Woodson
Scott Elbert	Jeff Kubenka	Bob Randall	Gene Wright
Bruce Ellingsen	Hong-Chih Kuo	Gary Rath	Ricky Wright
A.J. Ellis	Hiroki Kuroda	Bob Rauch	Wesley Wright
Johnny Enzmann	Jul Kustus	Doug Rau	Frank Wurm
Nathan Eovaldi	Clem Labine	Lance Rautzhan	Ad Yale
Carl Erskine	Candy LaChance	Phil Reardon	Joe Yeager
Leon Everitt	Lee Lacy	Harry Redmond	Steve Yeager
Bunny Fabrique	Frank Lamanske	Bobby Reis	Delwyn Young
Jim Fairey	Andrew Lambo	Doc Reisling	Eric Young
Ron Fairly	Ray Lamb	Jason Repko	Zip Zabel
George Fallon	Rafael Landestoy	Dennys Reyes	Chink Zachary
Alex Farmer	Joe Landrum	Gilberto Reyes	Geoff Zahn
Jesus Feliciano	Norm Larker	R.J. Reynolds	Chad Zerbe
Pedro Feliciano	Andy LaRoche	Billy Rhiel	Bill Zimmerman
Joe Ferguson	Chris Latham	Rick Rhoden	Don Zimmer
Chico H. Fernandez	Rudy Law	Paul Richards	
Sid Fernandez	Brent Leach	Pete Richert	

Year/Team	OPW%	PW	PL	APW%	AW	AL	Diff+/-
1901 NYG	0.541 F	76	64	0.380	52	85	-0.161
1902 NYG	0.455 F	64	76	0.353	48	88	-0.102
1903 NYG	0.568 P	79	61	0.604	84	55	0.036
1904 NYG	0.617 P	95	59	0.693 P	106	47	0.076
1905 NYG	0.634 P	98	56	0.686 P	105	48	0.052
1906 NYG	0.591 P	91	63	0.632	96	56	0.040
1907 NYG	0.539	83	71	0.536	82	71	-0.003
1908 NYG	0.621 P	96	58	0.636	98	56	0.015
1909 NYG	0.582 P	90	64	0.601	92	61	0.019

franchID	OWAR	OWS	AWAR	AWS	WARdiff	WSdiff	P/D/W/F
1901 NYG	28.747	192.077	13.510	156.001	15.237	36.076	F
1902 NYG	24.612	209.562	14.732	143.999	9.879	65.563	F
1903 NYG	38.890	239.559	45.983	252.001	-7.094	-12.442	P
1904 NYG	68.531	349.699	60.981	317.997	7.550	31.702	P
1905 NYG	69.916	348.165	66.630	315.008	3.286	33.157	P
1906 NYG	65.965	361.065	50.899	287.986	15.066	73.079	P
1907 NYG	50.777	268.593	48.654	246.007	2.123	22.586	
1908 NYG	61.831	298.263	61.849	293.995	-0.018	4.268	P
1909 NYG	53.876	288.436	53.928	275.997	-0.051	12.439	P

Legend: (P) = Pennant / Most Wins in League (D) = Division Winner (W) = Wild Card Winner (F) = Failed to Qualify

The New York Gothams enlisted in the National League in 1883. Two years later the club amended its nickname to the Giants. The "Original" Giants claimed the most pennants (24) and playoff appearances (29) among all Major League teams through 2013. The Giants rank second among the "Turn of the Century" franchises at first base (52), third base (tied-35) and right field (52) based on WS>20 player-seasons. On the other hand, the organization has never placed in the top three WS>10 totals for starting pitchers.

Christy Mathewson furnished 26 victories with a 1.94 ERA and a 1.028 WHIP per season from 1901-09. "Big Six" completed 31 of 38 starts while striking out 198 batsmen per year during that timeframe. He posted the highest Win Shares total (39) for a Giants hurler as he paced the Senior Circuit with a 1.28 ERA and 0.933 WHIP during the the '05 campaign. Mathewson (37-11, 1.43) delivered personal bests in victories, innings pitched (390.2), shutouts (11) and WHIP (0.827) in 1908. In the ensuing season "Matty" fashioned the lowest ERA (1.14) of his career.

"Wee" Willie Keeler rapped at least 200 hits in 8 straight seasons (1894-1901) while batting .378 with 140 runs scored per year throughout the stretch. Red Donahue exceeded the 20-victory mark in back-to-back campaigns (1901-02) after previously floundering to a 17-60 record. New York captured 6 pennants from 1901-09 including four in a row (1903-06). The crew compiled the highest oWAR and oWS in the National League in successive seasons (1904-05).

Harry H. Davis claimed four consecutive home run titles (1904-07), while Dummy Taylor (21-15, 2.34) fashioned a 1.033 WHIP in '04. Cy Seymour (.377/8/121) accrued 40 Win Shares and topped the NL in batting average, RBI, hits (219), doubles (40) and triples (21) in 1905. Hooks Wiltse confounded rival batsmen, furnishing a 2.29 ERA and a 1.108 WHIP from 1904-09 and surpassing the 20-win mark in back-to-back campaigns (1908-09).

Year/Team	OPW%	PW	PL	APW%	AW	AL	Diff+/-
1910 NYG	0.585 P	90	64	0.591	91	63	0.006
1911 NYG	0.659 P	102	52	0.647 P	99	54	-0.012
1912 NYG	0.619	95	59	0.682 P	103	48	0.063
1913 NYG	0.590 P	91	63	0.664 P	101	51	0.075
1914 NYG	0.573 P	88	66	0.545	84	70	-0.027
1915 NYG	0.536	83	71	0.454	69	83	-0.082
1916 NYG	0.586 P	90	64	0.566	86	66	-0.021
1917 NYG	0.573 P	88	66	0.636 P	98	56	0.064
1918 NYG	0.539	69	59	0.573	71	53	0.034
1919 NYG	0.475	67	73	0.621	87	53	0.146

franchID	OWAR	OWS	AWAR	AWS	WARdiff	WSdiff	P/D/W/F
1910 NYG	53.090	274.454	59.493	272.998	-6.404	1.457	P
1911 NYG	61.390	310.202	63.209	296.996	-1.818	13.205	P
1912 NYG	52.590	290.540	56.783	308.997	-4.193	-18.457	
1913 NYG	48.369	276.217	55.195	302.999	-6.826	-26.782	P
1914 NYG	47.788	247.769	44.956	251.997	2.832	-4.228	P
1915 NYG	41.501	236.509	31.122	207.002	10.379	29.507	
1916 NYG	47.491	251.460	43.892	257.996	3.599	-6.536	P
1917 NYG	36.838	237.139	48.496	294.000	-11.658	-56.861	P
1918 NYG	27.794	185.667	32.480	213.002	-4.686	-27.336	
1919 NYG	26.547	186.135	38.127	261.004	-11.580	-74.868	

New York posted the highest oWAR in the National League for 10 consecutive seasons (1908-1917). In a dominant stretch covering 1913-17, the Giants seized four pennants (narrowly missing in '15) while leading the League in oWAR and oWS. The troops opened the decade with a first-place finish, outpacing the Reds by five games. The 1911 squad trounced the competition by a 17-game margin, becoming the first NL team to transcend the 100-victory mark.

"Matty" mystified the opposition, posting his fourth consecutive campaign with an ERA below 2.00 in 1911. He notched his fifth ERA title in '13 and concluded a twelve-year run with 20+ victories in '14. Rube Marquard contributed three straight seasons above the 20-win mark (1911-13) and netted the NL strikeout title with 237 whiffs in '12. Giants' moundsmen accounted for 123 WS>10 player-seasons across three decades spanning 1910 through 1939.

Danny F. Murphy established career marks with a .329 BA and 104 tallies in '11. Larry Doyle (.330/10/90) received MVP honors in 1912, following a third-place finish in the previous season. "Laughing Larry" topped the Senior Circuit with a .320 BA, 189 hits and 40 two-base knocks in 1915. Jeff Tesreau (17-7, 1.96) paced the NL in ERA during his debut season (1912). Tesreau compiled 26 wins in '14 and fashioned a career ERA of 2.43 along with a 1.145 WHIP in seven seasons.

Chief Meyers placed third in the 1912 NL MVP race as he batted .358 while pacing the circuit with a .441 OBP. George J. Burns topped the Senior Circuit five times apiece in runs scored and bases on balls. He nabbed 41 bags per season from 1913-19 and tallied 34 Win Shares in '17. Burns' glovework garnered five appearances on the Fielding WAR and WS leader boards. Dick Rudolph fashioned a 2.30 ERA and a WHIP of 1.032 over a three-year period from 1914-16, averaging 22 victories and 330 innings pitched while completing 29 of 39 starts during this span. Ernie Shore contributed a 19-8 record with a 1.64 ERA in '15. Heinie Groh accrued 35 Win Shares while topping the NL in hits (182), doubles (39) and OBP (.385) in 1917. Ferdie Schupp achieved his finest campaign with a 21-7 record, 1.95 ERA and a 1.000 WHIP. Ross Youngs hit .302 in his rookie season and paced the League with 31 two-baggers in his sophomore year.

Win Shares > 20	Single-Season	1901-1919
Harry H. Davis - 1B (SFG) x3	Chief Meyers - C (SFG)	Ross Youngs - RF (SFG) x7
Fred Merkle - 1B (SFG) x2	Art Wilson - C (SFG)	Red Donahue - SP (SFG) x2
Danny F. Murphy - 2B (SFG) x2	Josh Devore - LF (SFG)	Christy Mathewson - SP (SFG) x12
Larry Doyle - 2B (SFG) x6	George J. Burns - LF (SFG) x9	Dummy Taylor - SP (SFG)
Doc Crandall - 2B (SFG)	Claude Cooper - LF (SFG)	Hooks Wiltse - SP (SFG) x2
Art Fletcher - SS (SFG) x4	Cy Seymour - CF (SFG) x4	Rube Marquard - SP (SFG) x3
Buck Herzog - SS (SFG) x2	Fred Snodgrass - CF (SFG) x3	Jeff Tesreau - SP (SFG) x4
Art Devlin - 3B (SFG) x6	Willie Keeler - RF (SFG) x5	Dick Rudolph - SP (SFG) x3
Buck Herzog - 3B (SFG)	Danny F. Murphy - RF (SFG) x3	Doc Crandall - SP (SFG)
Tillie Shafer - 3B (SFG)	Steve Evans - RF (SFG) x2	Ernie Shore - SP (SFG)
Heinie Groh - 3B (SFG) x6	Dave Robertson - RF (SFG)	Ferdie Schupp - SP (SFG)

Year/Team	OPW%	PW	PL	APW%	AW	AL	Diff+/-
1920 NYG	0.420	65	89	0.558	86	68	0.139
1921 NYG	0.472	73	81	0.614 P	94	59	0.142
1922 NYG	0.452	70	84	0.604 P	93	61	0.152
1923 NYG	0.522	80	74	0.621 P	95	58	0.099
1924 NYG	0.528	81	73	0.608 P	93	60	0.080
1925 NYG	0.513	79	75	0.566	86	66	0.053
1926 NYG	0.508	78	76	0.490	74	77	-0.018
1927 NYG	0.559	86	68	0.597	92	62	0.038
1928 NYG	0.544	84	70	0.604	93	61	0.060
1929 NYG	0.581 P	90	64	0.556	84	67	-0.025

franchID	OWAR	OWS	AWAR	AWS	WARdiff	WSdiff	P/D/W/F
1920 NYG	26.918	208.020	40.193	258.001	-13.275	-49.981	
1921 NYG	31.213	195.207	**45.104**	**282.002**	-13.892	-86.795	
1922 NYG	27.104	186.919	**49.350**	278.995	-22.246	-92.075	
1923 NYG	34.235	228.825	**45.912**	285.002	-11.677	-56.177	
1924 NYG	**36.936**	**241.419**	49.547	278.998	-12.611	-37.579	
1925 NYG	30.190	221.282	36.199	258.001	-6.010	-36.719	
1926 NYG	31.332	208.779	31.707	222.009	-0.374	-13.230	
1927 NYG	**39.276**	239.548	42.258	276.005	-2.981	-36.456	
1928 NYG	32.036	219.356	**46.174**	279.002	-14.138	-59.646	
1929 NYG	**36.807**	223.305	43.666	251.999	-6.859	-28.693	P

The Giants finished below .500 in four consecutive seasons (1919-1922) before resurfacing as a contender in '23. Youngs compiled 204 base knocks and batted .351 during the 1920 campaign. He eclipsed the 200-hit mark again in 1923 and topped the League with 121 runs scored. Youngs posted a career-high .356 BA in the subsequent season. George "High Pockets" Kelly led the NL with 94 RBI in his first full season (1920) and averaged .307 with 31 two-baggers and 110 ribbies from 1920-25. Jigger Statz tallied 209 base knocks and 110 runs scored in '23.

Frankie Frisch led the League with 223 safeties in 1923. "The Fordham Flash" achieved 200+ base hits and nabbed the NL stolen base title three times while eclipsing the century mark in runs scored seven times in his career. Frisch produced a .329 BA with 104 runs per year from 1921-29 and accrued a personal-best 35 Win Shares in '27. Hack Wilson collected four home run titles including three in a row (1926-28). He slugged 30 round-trippers and knocked in 129 runs from 1926-29, batting .325 with 32 doubles and 110 tallies during the stretch.

St. Louis emerged with the National League title in 1927, ending the season only a single game ahead of Pittsburgh and New York. Waite Hoyt delivered successive years with 20+ victories in 1927-28. Bill Terry topped the century mark in runs scored and RBI for six straight years (1927-1932). He bested the 200-hit plateau for the first time in '29 and managed a .372 batting average. Freddie Lindstrom (.358/14/107) contributed 231 base hits (tops in the League) and finished runner-up in the 1928 NL MVP balloting. Lindstrom's teammate, Larry Benton (25-9, 2.73), placed fourth and led the circuit in victories and complete games (28).

New York secured its first pennant in twelve seasons by a two-game margin over Chicago in '29. Red Lucas (19-12, 3.60) paced the NL with a 1.204 WHIP and completed 28 of 32 starts. Bill Walker secured ERA titles in 1929 and 1931. New York right fielders placed among the top 3 WS>10 player-seasons in four continuous decades spanning 1901-1939. The fleet totaled 56 player-seasons led by Mel Ott with 9. "Master Melvin" dialed long distance 42 times, plated 151 baserunners and registered 138 runs scored while batting .328 with a league-leading 113 walks for the '29 squad.

Year/Team	OPW%	PW	PL	APW%	AW	AL	Diff+/-
1930 NYG	0.541	83	71	0.565	87	67	0.024
1931 NYG	0.569 P	88	66	0.572	87	65	0.003
1932 NYG	0.508	78	76	0.468	72	82	-0.041
1933 NYG	0.536 P	83	71	0.599 P	91	61	0.063
1934 NYG	0.562	86	68	0.608	93	60	0.046
1935 NYG	0.549	85	69	0.595	91	62	0.046
1936 NYG	0.525	81	73	0.597 P	92	62	0.072
1937 NYG	0.503	77	77	0.625 P	95	57	0.122
1938 NYG	0.522	80	74	0.553	83	67	0.031
1939 NYG	0.506 F	78	76	0.510	77	74	0.004

franchID	OWAR	OWS	AWAR	AWS	WARdiff	WSdiff	P/D/W/F
1930 NYG	**39.814**	**237.480**	44.431	261.001	-4.617	-23.520	
1931 NYG	36.084	225.026	**46.438**	260.997	-10.354	-35.971	P
1932 NYG	26.641	190.550	32.865	215.995	-6.224	-25.445	
1933 NYG	**33.980**	220.286	39.332	**273.006**	-5.353	-52.719	P
1934 NYG	**38.340**	**245.403**	41.272	279.000	-2.933	-33.597	
1935 NYG	31.569	214.401	42.258	273.001	-10.689	-58.600	
1936 NYG	27.626	210.452	39.732	**275.997**	-12.107	-65.545	
1937 NYG	31.592	202.892	**44.875**	284.995	-13.283	-82.104	
1938 NYG	28.659	192.618	39.562	249.001	-10.903	-56.383	
1939 NYG	32.044	202.446	32.780	231.002	-0.736	-28.556	F

Wilson set the MLB record with 191 RBI during the 1930 campaign. He topped the NL with 56 clouts, 105 walks and a .723 SLG while establishing personal bests in BA (.356), base hits (208) and runs scored (146). Terry (.401/23/129) seized his lone batting crown along with the National League record for hits in a single season (254). He topped the .300 mark in each of his final 10 seasons and averaged .350 with 207 hits, 35 doubles, 106 runs scored and 100 RBI from 1927-1935. Terry's defensive contributions at first base are documented by six appearances on the Fielding WAR and WS charts.

Over a ten-year period covering 1929-1938, Ott clubbed 32 round-trippers, scored 115 runs and knocked in 121 per season while maintaining a .315 batting average. He collected 6 home run titles and surpassed the century mark for bases on balls ten times! Ott received 11 straight All-Star nominations and amassed a career-high 37 Win Shares in 1934. Travis Jackson notched career-highs with a .339 BA in '30 and 101 RBI in '34. Lindstrom hit .379 with 127 tallies and Frisch (.346/10/114) tied his career-high with 121 runs scored for the '30 squad.

The Giants finished first in the oWAR and oWS leader boards for 1930 and 1934. However, New York ended both seasons in second place, two games behind St. Louis. Earl Webb delivered a .333 BA and set the MLB record with 67 triples in 1931. Lucas, aka "The Nashville Narcissus," fashioned a 2.94 ERA and a 1.099 WHIP (both career-bests) and completed 28 of 31 starts for the '32 crew. Rube Walberg added 20 victories and topped the NL with 291 innings pitched.

"Prince" Hal Schumacher averaged 20 wins per season along with a 2.76 ERA and a 1.194 WHIP from 1933-35. Ben Cantwell (20-10, 2.62) enjoyed his finest year in '33. Sam Leslie garnered personal bests with a .332 BA and 102 ribbies for the '34 crew. Jo-Jo Moore surpassed the century mark in runs scored for three successive seasons (1934-36). "The Gause Ghost" hit .331 with 37 two-base knocks, placing third in the 1934 NL MVP race. Moore followed with consecutive 200-hit campaigns and merited six All-Star selections in his career. Hank Leiber (.331/22/107) contributed career-highs in almost every major offensive category in 1935 including 203 base knocks and 110 runs. Cliff Melton burst on the scene with a 20-win campaign in his rookie year (1937). "Mountain Music" fashioned a 2.61 ERA and a 1.093 WHIP while completing 14 of 27 starts and topping the circuit with 7 saves.

Win Shares > 20	Single-Season	1920-1939
George Kelly - 1B (SFG) x3	Harry Danning - C (SFG) x2	Hack Wilson - RF (SFG)
Bill Terry - 1B (SFG) x9	Jo-Jo Moore - LF (SFG) x4	Waite Hoyt - SP (SFG) x5
Sam Leslie - 1B (SFG)	Jigger Statz - CF (SFG)	Red Lucas - SP (SFG) x3
Frankie Frisch - 2B (SFG) x10	Hack Wilson - CF (SFG) x5	Larry Benton - SP (SFG)
George Kelly - 2B (SFG)	Mel Ott - CF (SFG)	Rube Walberg - SP (SFG) x2
Travis Jackson - SS (SFG) x5	Freddie Lindstrom - CF (SFG)	Bill Walker - SP (SFG)
Frankie Frisch - 3B (SFG) x2	Len Koenecke - CF (SFG)	Ben Cantwell - SP (SFG)
Freddie Lindstrom - 3B (SFG) x3	Hank Leiber - CF (SFG) x2	Hal Schumacher - SP (SFG) x3
Mel Ott - 3B (SFG)	Mel Ott - RF (SFG) x14	Cliff Melton - SW (SFG)
	Earl Webb - RF (SFG)	

Year/Team	OPW%	PW	PL	APW%	AW	AL	Diff+/-
1940 NYG	0.565 P	87	67	0.474	72	80	-0.092
1941 NYG	0.593 P	91	63	0.484	74	79	-0.109
1942 NYG	0.551 F	85	69	0.559	85	67	0.008
1943 NYG	0.470	72	82	0.359	55	98	-0.110
1944 NYG	0.501 F	77	77	0.435	67	87	-0.066
1945 NYG	0.474 F	73	81	0.513	78	74	0.040
1946 NYG	0.458	71	83	0.396	61	93	-0.062
1947 NYG	0.519	80	74	0.526	81	73	0.007
1948 NYG	0.530 F	82	72	0.506	78	76	-0.023
1949 NYG	0.515	79	75	0.474	73	81	-0.041

franchID	OWAR	OWS	AWAR	AWS	WARdiff	WSdiff	P/D/W/F
1940 NYG	38.538	231.041	33.334	216.000	5.204	15.041	P
1941 NYG	34.881	215.205	33.862	222.000	1.020	-6.795	P
1942 NYG	29.959	204.274	36.873	254.998	-6.914	-50.725	F
1943 NYG	15.553	156.958	22.368	164.998	-6.815	-8.040	
1944 NYG	21.165	197.211	28.077	201.006	-6.912	-3.795	F
1945 NYG	33.255	222.443	38.230	234.001	-4.975	-11.559	F
1946 NYG	19.753	155.504	28.397	182.999	-8.644	-27.496	
1947 NYG	32.635	218.004	41.801	243.002	-9.165	-24.998	
1948 NYG	25.187	202.530	35.949	234.001	-10.762	-31.471	F
1949 NYG	38.625	200.406	37.748	215.997	0.877	-15.592	

The Giants secured back-to-back pennants in 1940-41. Ott walloped 30 four-baggers, scored 118 runs and drew 109 bases on balls in 1942 (all NL-bests) while placing third in the MVP race. Willard Marshall (.291/36/107) delivered career-highs in home runs, RBI and runs scored (102) for the '47 squad. Bobby Thomson slugged 29 long balls and tallied 105 runs in his rookie campaign (1947). "The Flying Scot" earned personal bests with a .309 BA, 198 base hits and 109 RBI in '49.

Whitey Lockman accrued 117 tallies while Sid Gordon (.299/30/107) scored 100 runs and finished fourth in the '48 MVP balloting. Gordon clubbed 25+ round-trippers in five straight seasons (1948-1952). New York failed to meet the PA and/or BFP requirements four times during the decade.

Year/Team	OPW%	PW	PL	APW%	AW	AL	Diff+/-
1950 NYG	0.441	68	86	0.558	86	68	0.117
1951 NYG	0.514	79	75	0.624 P	98	59	0.110
1952 NYG	0.508	78	76	0.597	92	62	0.089
1953 NYG	0.453	70	84	0.455	70	84	0.002
1954 NYG	0.537	83	71	0.630 P	97	57	0.093
1955 NYG	0.515 F	79	75	0.519	80	74	0.005
1956 NYG	0.492 F	76	78	0.435	67	87	-0.057
1957 NYG	0.436	67	87	0.448	69	85	0.012
1958 SFG	0.459	71	83	0.519	80	74	0.061
1959 SFG	0.479 F	74	80	0.539	83	71	0.060

franchID	OWAR	OWS	AWAR	AWS	WARdiff	WSdiff	P/D/W/F
1950 SFG	26.021	228.482	40.573	258.001	-14.552	-29.520	
1951 SFG	37.620	**261.045**	50.674	**294.001**	-13.054	-32.956	
1952 SFG	36.897	**261.146**	42.301	275.999	-5.404	-14.853	
1953 SFG	31.271	212.304	36.314	210.001	-5.043	2.303	
1954 SFG	30.198	226.520	37.956	239.999	-7.757	-13.478	
1955 SFG	31.545	236.623	37.956	239.999	-6.411	-3.376	F
1956 SFG	29.607	230.958	29.307	200.997	0.300	29.962	F
1957 SFG	25.608	209.830	31.782	207.001	-6.174	2.828	
1958 SFG	36.484	261.799	38.306	240.001	-1.822	21.799	
1959 SFG	38.748	259.558	41.567	248.995	-2.818	10.563	F

The Giants stormed back from a dismal last-place effort in 1950, finishing four games behind the Dodgers in '51. Gordon posted back-to-back 100+ RBI campaigns in 1950-51, and Bobby Thomson belted 32 round-trippers and produced 101 RBI in 1951, placing eighth in the MVP voting. The "Flying Scot" led the National League with 14 triples in '52 and received his third All-Star nod. He generated 20+ home runs and over 100 RBI for three straight seasons (1951-53). Monte Irvin batted .312 with 24 blasts and a league-best 121 runs batted in, earning third place in the 1951 NL MVP vote. Irvin delivered a .329 batting average with 21 long balls and 97 RBI in 1953.

Willie Mays bashed 20 moon-shots in his debut season and received NL ROY honors in 1951. Military obligations caused Mays to miss most of the 1952 season and all of 1953. "The Say Hey Kid" earned MVP honors upon his return in '54, crushing 41 four-baggers, driving in 110 runs and leading the League with a .345 average. Mays swatted 51 big-flies and knocked in 127 runs in '55. He averaged .328 with 38 homers, 103 RBI, 117 runs scored and 28 stolen bases from 1954-59. An outstanding center fielder, Mays collected the first of twelve consecutive Gold Glove Awards in 1957. He is the All-Time leader among outfielders with 13 seasons on the Fielding WAR and WS leader boards.

Orlando Cepeda batted .312 with 25 taters, 96 ribbies and league-high 38 doubles en route to the NL ROY Award in '58. The "Baby Bull" posted similar numbers in the subsequent season and added 23 stolen bases. Willie McCovey (.354/13/58) received the Rookie of the Year Award in 1959 despite playing only 52 games.

New York struggled to cultivate pitching talent in the Fifties. Jack Harshman delivered a record of 14-8 with a 2.95 ERA in his first season (1954). He tallied 15 victories in '56 and fashioned a 2.89 ERA with 17 complete games in 29 starts in 1958. Marv Grissom earned an All-Star invitation in 1954, notching 10 wins and saving 19 games with a 2.35 ERA. The Giants failed to attain the BFP requirements in 1955, 1956 and 1959. The franchise relocated to San Francisco prior to the '58 season.

Win Shares > 20	Single-Season	1940-1959
Phil Weintraub - 1B (SFG)	Wes Westrum - C (SFG)	Whitey Lockman - CF (SFG)
Whitey Lockman - 1B (SFG)	Sid Gordon - 3B (SFG)	Bobby Thomson - CF (SFG)
Orlando Cepeda - 1B (SFG) x8	Bobby Thomson - 3B (SFG)	Willie Mays - CF (SFG) x17
	Sid Gordon - LF (SFG) x3	Willard Marshall - RF (SFG)
Eddie Mayo - 2B (SFG) x2	Monte Irvin - LF (SFG)	Jack Harshman - SP (SFG)

Year/Team	OPW%	PW	PL	APW%	AW	AL	Diff+/-
1960 SFG	0.578 F	89	65	0.513	79	75	-0.065
1961 SFG	0.565	92	70	0.552	85	69	-0.013
1962 SFG	0.589 P	95	67	0.624 P	103	62	0.035
1963 SFG	0.561 P	91	71	0.543	88	74	-0.017
1964 SFG	0.594 P	96	66	0.556	90	72	0.038
1965 SFG	0.631 P	102	60	0.586	95	67	-0.045
1966 SFG	0.604 P	98	64	0.578	93	68	-0.026
1967 SFG	0.592 P	96	66	0.562	91	71	-0.030
1968 SFG	0.549 P	89	73	0.543	88	74	-0.005
1969 SFG	0.529	86	76	0.556	90	72	0.027
franchID	OWAR	OWS	AWAR	AWS	WARdiff	WSdiff	P/D/W/F
1960 SFG	43.629	306.116	37.121	237.001	6.509	69.114	F
1961 SFG	45.624	316.934	42.139	255.001	3.484	61.932	
1962 SFG	52.684	355.041	50.682	308.992	2.001	46.049	P
1963 SFG	54.073	333.547	45.592	263.996	8.480	69.550	P
1964 SFG	48.205	326.294	43.622	270.005	4.583	56.288	P
1965 SFG	54.428	341.009	44.556	284.992	9.872	56.017	P
1966 SFG	48.873	330.391	40.445	279.000	8.428	51.391	P
1967 SFG	46.755	326.669	44.018	272.998	2.737	53.671	P
1968 SFG	48.572	319.726	41.928	264.000	6.643	55.726	P
1969 SFG	41.571	306.293	42.520	270.001	-0.949	36.291	

Mays scored 100+ runs in 12 straight seasons (1954-1965). He delivered a .307 average, 42 big-flies and 114 RBI from 1960-66. Mays captured his second MVP Award in '65, belting 52 home runs to lead the NL. Orlando Cepeda supplied a .307 batting average, 34 four-ply swats and 109 RBI from 1960-64. "Cha Cha" earned a runner-up finish in the '61 MVP vote, pacing the NL with 46 moon-shots and 142 runs driven in. He took home the MVP Award in '67, batting .325 with 25 wallops and 111 RBI. Bill D. White collected 7 straight Gold Glove Awards for his slick fielding at first base while batting .296 with 21 swats and 94 RBI from 1960-66.

The Giants failed to reach the BFP requirements in 1960, but in spite of this setback, several hurlers emerged as aces in the Sixties and vaulted the team into contention on a yearly basis. Mike F. McCormick delivered a league-leading 2.70 ERA with 15 wins in 1960. He yielded 22 victories and a 2.85 ERA en route to a Cy Young Award in '67. Juan Marichal earned 8 consecutive All-Star appearances from 1962-69, averaging 22 wins per season with 23 complete games, 207 strikeouts, a 2.46 ERA and 1.027 WHIP! The "Dominican Dandy" paced the National League with 25 wins in '63, 26 wins with 30 complete games in '68, and a 2.10 ERA in '69. The squad edged the Braves by 2 games in '62 and generated its highest offWARnorm (33) and offWSnorm (218) in team history while fending off the Reds in '63. Gaylord Perry amassed 21 victories in 1966 and earned his first All-Star invitation; he led the League with 325.1 innings pitched in '69.

San Francisco's farm system teemed with outfield prospects. Willie Kirkland crushed 27 four-baggers and plated 95 runners in '61 as San Francisco finished in a virtual tie with Milwaukee. Leon "Daddy Wags" Wagner tagged 30 circuit clouts and drove in 91 runs per year from 1961-65. Felipe Alou played his way into a full-time role by 1962 and rewarded the Giants with an All-Star season including a .316 average, 25 taters and 98 ribbies. Alou paced the NL with 218 hits and 122 runs scored in 1966 and set career-highs in batting average (.327) and homers (31). He also led the League with 210 hits in 1968, the "Year of the Pitcher". Jose Cardenal nabbed 35+ bases three times. Matty Alou led the NL with a .342 average in '66 and posted league-bests with 231 hits and 41 doubles in '69. He batted .335 from 1966-69. Bobby Bonds bashed 32 moon-shots, swiped 45 bases and topped the League with 120 runs scored in his first full season (1969).

"Stretch" McCovey busted loose with 44 round-trippers and 102 ribbies in 1963 and then proceeded to pummel 37 long balls and knock in 102 runs per season from 1965-69. "Mac" garnered NL MVP honors in 1969 as he hit .320 with 45 blasts and 126 runs batted in. San Francisco pummeled the opposition in 1964 as Los Angeles finished a distant second, 13 games back. Jim Ray Hart batted .285 with 28 round-trippers and 89 RBI from 1964-68. The 1965 club notched a franchise-best 102 victories and then managed 98 wins in the following year. Eddie Fisher finished fourth in the MVP balloting in '65, winning 15 games and saving 24 with a 2.40 ERA. Frank Linzy furnished a 1.43 ERA and notched 21 saves in his rookie season (1965). Backstop Tom Haller cleared the fences 27 times in '66. Chicago made a strong run in 1967-68 but came up short in both campaigns. Bobby Bolin pitched primarily in relief, fashioning a 10-5 mark with a 1.99 ERA and 0.985 WHIP in '68, while Minnie Rojas collected 12 wins, 27 saves and a 2.51 ERA that same year. Bill Hands achieved 20 wins with a 2.49 ERA in 300 innings pitched as divisional play began in '69. San Francisco ceded the division crown to Cincinnati.

Chub Feeney was the General Manager for more than two decades including the period during the Giants' incredible run of 7 consecutive pennants from 1962-68. He amassed a gifted horde of athletes comprised of Mays ('50), McCovey and Cepeda ('55), Juan Marichal ('57), Gaylord Perry ('58) and Bobby Bonds ('64). Feeney directed the Giants' finest draft in 1968 (755 Career Total Win Shares), opting for the outfield trio of George Foster, Gary Matthews and Garry Maddox. Two years later his successor Horace Stoneham procured slugger Dave Kingman along with Chris Speier and Jim Barr.

Year/Team	OPW%	PW	PL	APW%	AW	AL	Diff+/-
1970 SFG	0.498	81	81	0.531	86	76	0.033
1971 SFG	0.484	78	84	0.556 D	90	72	0.072
1972 SFG	0.546	88	74	0.445	69	86	-0.101
1973 SFG	0.498	81	81	0.543	88	74	0.045
1974 SFG	0.476	77	85	0.444	72	90	-0.031
1975 SFG	0.478	77	85	0.497	80	81	0.019
1976 SFG	0.482	78	84	0.457	74	88	-0.025
1977 SFG	0.530	86	76	0.463	75	87	-0.067
1978 SFG	0.532	86	76	0.549	89	73	0.017
1979 SFG	0.476	77	85	0.438	71	91	-0.037

franchID	OWAR	OWS	AWAR	AWS	WARdiff	WSdiff	P/D/W/F
1970 SFG	39.678	277.398	41.243	257.997	-1.565	19.401	
1971 SFG	**44.975**	**302.926**	42.532	270.007	2.442	32.919	
1972 SFG	38.653	269.669	31.847	206.995	6.805	62.674	
1973 SFG	42.379	294.390	41.584	264.003	0.795	30.387	
1974 SFG	40.580	274.064	29.148	216.001	11.431	58.063	
1975 SFG	49.460	300.759	36.212	239.998	13.248	60.761	
1976 SFG	42.760	267.321	28.582	222.005	14.178	45.316	
1977 SFG	45.760	285.587	32.454	224.998	13.305	60.590	
1978 SFG	45.951	298.934	41.001	266.996	4.950	31.937	
1979 SFG	26.028	243.120	23.609	213.003	2.419	30.117	

The Giants fell into a deep slumber, failing to win a single division title from 1969 through 1997! San Francisco's offense hit on all cylinders in 1970. Mays blasted 28 round-trippers and subsequently led the League in walks (112) and OBP (.425) in '71. Matty Alou collected 201 hits in '70 and batted .304 from 1970-73. Cepeda belted 34 long balls and knocked in 111 runs. McCovey drilled 39 doubles and 39 moon-shots, plated 126 runners and led the League in walks (137) and SLG (.612). Dick Dietz earned his lone All-Star appearance, batting .300 with 36 doubles, 22 four-baggers, 107 RBI and 109 bases on balls. Ollie "Downtown" Brown set career-highs with 23 dingers, 89 ribbies and a .292 batting average.

Bobby Bonds eclipsed the .300 mark for the only time in his career (.302), posting career-bests with 200 hits, 134 runs, 36 doubles, 10 triples and 48 stolen bases in 1970. He averaged .274 with 28 bombs, 86 runs batted in, 102 runs scored and 38 steals over the course of the decade. Jose Cardenal hit .293 with 24 steals per season from 1970-76 including a .317 BA in '75. Ken Henderson established career-highs with 104 runs scored, 20 stolen bases and a .294 average in 1970. He batted .292 with 20 clouts and 95 RBI in '74.

Gaylord Perry flourished throughout the Seventies, exceeding the 20-win plateau four times. Perry collected Cy Young Awards in '72 and '78 and placed second in '70. He furnished a 1.92 ERA and 0.978 WHIP and amassed 24 wins in 1972. Perry averaged 18 victories, 20 complete games, 191 strikeouts and a 2.92 ERA for the decade. Hands tallied 18 wins with a 3.70 ERA in 1970.

Marichal fashioned an 18-11 record in '71 with a 2.94 ERA and a 1.075 WHIP as the Giants topped the circuit in oWAR and oWS. The club finished two games shy of the Reds in '72. Garry Maddox provided a .293 BA, 30 doubles and 24 steals per year from 1972-79 including a .330 average in '76. "The Secretary of Defense" was presented with 8 Gold Gloves for his stellar glovework as a center fielder and placed among the Fielding WAR and WS leaders 9 times in his career.

Dave May earned a trip to the 1973 All-Star classic, batting .303 with 25 home runs, 93 ribbies and leading the League with 295 total bases. Gary Matthews received the Rookie of the Year Award in '73, hitting .300 with 10 triples. "Sarge" produced a .289 average with 17 jacks and 14 steals from 1973-79. Ron Bryant compiled 24 wins in '73 and then proceeded to lose 15 of 18 decisions in the ensuing season. Elias Sosa finished third in the 1973 NL ROY balloting, saving 18 games and winning 10.

Jim Barr supplied a 2.74 ERA in 1974 and won 15 games with a 2.89 ERA in '76. Dave Kingman crushed 35 round-trippers and knocked in 89 runs per year from 1975-79. "Kong" swatted 48 big-flies and plated 115 runners in 1979. John Montefusco claimed the Rookie of the Year Award in 1975, posting a 15-8 record, 215 strikeouts and a 2.88 ERA. "The Count" amassed 16 wins and 6 shutouts in 1976.

George Foster (.306/29/121) placed runner-up in the 1976 MVP balloting. Foster erupted for 52 circuit clouts, 149 runs batted in, 124 runs scored and a .631 SLG (all NL-leading totals), earning the '77 NL MVP trophy. He paced the circuit with 40 bombs and 120 ribbies in 1978. Gary Lavelle assumed the closer's role, nailing down 20 saves in '77 and '79, and delivering a 2.66 ERA during his first six seasons. San Francisco posted consecutive second-place finishes in 1977-78. Jack Clark bashed 25 quadruples and drove home 98 runs while batting .306 for the '78 squad. Bob Knepper notched 17 wins with 16 complete games, 6 shutouts and a 2.63 ERA in 1978.

Win Shares > 20	Single-Season	1960-1979
Bill D. White - 1B (SFG) x5	Willie McCovey - LF (SFG)	Bobby Bonds - RF (SFG) x9
Felipe Alou - 1B (SFG) x2	Ken Henderson - LF (SFG) x2	Jack Clark - RF (SFG) x4
Willie McCovey - 1B (SFG) x8	Gary Matthews - LF (SFG) x4	Gary Matthews - RF (SFG)
Tony Taylor - 2B (SFG)	Jose Cardenal - LF (SFG)	Juan Marichal - SP (SFG) x6
Eddie Bressoud - SS (SFG) x2	George Foster - LF (SFG) x7	Gaylord Perry - SP (SFG) x7
Chris Speier - SS (SFG)	Dave Kingman - LF (SFG)	Mike F. McCormick - SP (SFG)
Jim Davenport - 3B (SFG)	Matty Alou - CF (SFG) x5	Bill Hands - SP (SFG) x2
Jim Ray Hart - 3B (SFG) x4	Jose Cardenal - CF (SFG) x2	Jim Barr - SP (SFG)
Tom Haller - C (SFG) x3	Felipe Alou - CF (SFG)	John Montefusco - SP (SFG)
Randy Hundley - C (SFG) x2	Garry Maddox - CF (SFG) x4	x2
Dick Dietz - C (SFG)	Dave May - CF (SFG)	Bob Knepper - SP (SFG)
Orlando Cepeda - LF (SFG)	Ken Henderson - CF (SFG)	Eddie Fisher - RP (SFG)
Leon Wagner - LF (SFG) x3	Felipe Alou - RF (SFG) x2	

Year/Team	OPW%	PW	PL	APW%	AW	AL	Diff+/-
1980 SFG	0.457	74	88	0.466	75	86	0.009
1981 SFG	0.534	87	75	0.505	56	55	-0.030
1982 SFG	0.446	72	90	0.537	87	75	0.091
1983 SFG	0.474	77	85	0.488	79	83	0.014
1984 SFG	0.508	82	80	0.407	66	96	-0.101
1985 SFG	0.424 F	69	93	0.383	62	100	-0.041
1986 SFG	0.594 F	96	66	0.512	83	79	-0.081
1987 SFG	0.544	88	74	0.556 D	90	72	0.012
1988 SFG	0.578 F	94	68	0.512	83	79	-0.066
1989 SFG	0.524	85	77	0.568 D	92	70	0.044

franchID	OWAR	OWS	AWAR	AWS	WARdiff	WSdiff	P/D/W/F
1980 SFG	28.052	221.883	25.256	224.990	2.797	-3.108	
1981 SFG	26.238	182.771	23.802	167.994	2.437	14.777	
1982 SFG	25.211	246.855	36.020	260.999	-10.809	-14.144	
1983 SFG	24.989	250.192	32.110	237.006	-7.121	13.186	
1984 SFG	42.939	294.610	27.794	198.000	15.145	96.610	
1985 SFG	37.941	300.508	24.596	186.000	13.345	114.508	F
1986 SFG	44.215	315.181	37.603	248.996	6.612	66.185	F
1987 SFG	51.163	334.220	44.647	270.002	6.517	64.217	
1988 SFG	44.505	311.636	40.985	249.002	3.520	62.634	F
1989 SFG	36.803	261.016	40.671	276.005	-3.868	-14.989	

Steve Stone earned the Cy Young Award in 1980, posting 25 victories with a 3.23 ERA. Kingman clouted 30+ moon-shots and plated over 90 runs in four of his last five campaigns. San Francisco triumphed in 87 contests in 1981, falling one game short of Los Angeles for the Western Division title. Knepper furnished a 2.18 ERA and 1.060 WHIP in '81 and went on to win 17 contests with a 3.14 ERA in 1986.

Jack Clark drilled 27 dingers and knocked in 103 runs in '82. "The Ripper" tore up the National League in '87, bashing 35 homers and leading the circuit in walks (136), OBP (.459) and

SLG (.597). Lavelle resumed the closer's role in '83, saving 20 games with a 2.59 ERA. Matthews scored 101 runs and topped the NL in walks (103) and OBP (.410) in '84. Chili Davis batted .315 with 21 four-ply swats while Dan Gladden sizzled with a .351 average and 31 steals in 86 games for the 1984 Giants.

Scott Garrelts delivered 10 wins, 12 saves and a 3.05 ERA from 1985-88, primarily as a reliever. Converted to a starting pitcher in 1989, Garrelts produced a 14-5 record with a league-leading 2.28 ERA.

Rob Deer walloped a career-best 33 quadruples in '86, and averaged 28 swats from 1986-89. Matt Nokes placed third in the Rookie of the Year voting in '87, belting 32 round-trippers and driving in 87 runs. The Giants' offense tied the output from the '51 and '98 clubs for the best OBP (.342) in club history while producing the top SLG (.442). DeWayne Buice (3.39, 17 SV) and Jeff D. Robinson (2.85, 14 SV) shared the late-inning assignments. San Francisco finished percentage points behind Cincinnati in '87.

Will Clark drilled 35 long balls and batted .308 in his sophomore campaign and then paced the NL with 109 RBI and 100 walks in 1988. "The Thrill" batted .333 with 38 doubles, 23 dingers, 111 runs batted in and a league-high 104 runs scored, placing runner-up in the 1989 NL MVP balloting. In 1989 the squad ended up in a second-place tie with the Padres, two games behind the Reds. The Giants failed to reach the BFP requirements in 1985, '86 and '88.

Year/Team	OPW%	PW	PL	APW%	AW	AL	Diff+/-
1990 SFG	0.525	85	77	0.525	85	77	0.000
1991 SFG	0.488	79	83	0.463	75	87	-0.025
1992 SFG	0.425	69	93	0.444	72	90	0.019
1993 SFG	0.520	84	78	0.636	103	59	0.116
1994 SFG	0.490	79	83	0.478	55	60	-0.012
1995 SFG	0.454	74	88	0.465	67	77	0.012
1996 SFG	0.460	75	87	0.420	68	94	-0.040
1997 SFG	0.400	65	97	0.556 D	90	72	0.156
1998 SFG	0.539 D	87	75	0.546	89	74	0.007
1999 SFG	0.542 W	88	74	0.531	86	76	-0.011

franchID	OWAR	OWS	AWAR	AWS	WARdiff	WSdiff	P/D/W/F
1990 SFG	34.936	259.692	34.957	255.005	-0.021	4.687	
1991 SFG	36.613	254.544	29.686	224.997	6.927	29.546	
1992 SFG	25.640	213.983	26.794	216.002	-1.154	-2.018	
1993 SFG	37.418	247.671	48.221	308.992	-10.803	-61.322	
1994 SFG	21.062	160.476	20.765	165.002	0.297	-4.525	
1995 SFG	21.020	184.260	19.875	200.997	1.146	-16.737	
1996 SFG	25.229	184.350	22.707	203.999	2.522	-19.649	
1997 SFG	23.977	190.622	35.954	270.000	-11.977	-79.379	
1998 SFG	34.893	223.852	45.067	266.993	-10.174	-43.140	D
1999 SFG	36.880	247.166	38.981	258.002	-2.101	-10.836	W

The Giants finished in second place, six games behind the Reds in 1990. Matt D. Williams paced the NL with 122 RBI in 1990, later topping the circuit with 43 wallops in '94. Williams delivered a .278 average with 30 swats and 96 ribbies in the Nineties. He was the runner-up in the 1994 MVP balloting and finished third in '99, producing a .303 average with 35 dingers and 142 RBI.

John Burkett managed 14 victories and a 3.79 ERA in his rookie season (1990). He paced the National League with 22 wins in '93, finishing fourth in the Cy Young balloting. Jeff Brantley (1.56, 19 SV) earned an All-Star nod in 1990; he supplied a league-high 44 saves with a 2.41

ERA in '96. Jack Clark received 104 walks in only 442 plate appearances in '90. Chili Davis posted a .282 average with 23 blasts and 86 RBI from 1990-97.

Will Clark (.301/29/116) led the League with a .536 SLG, earned a Gold Glove Award in 1991, and batted .302 for the decade. After descending into the cellar in '92, San Francisco rebounded to another second place effort. Terry Mulholland delivered a 16-win campaign in 1992, and proceeded to top the League with 12 complete games in '93. Charlie Hayes excelled in 1993, producing career-bests with 45 doubles, 25 four-baggers, 98 RBI and a .305 batting average. Despite finishing below .500, the '94 squad fell three games short of the Padres for the division title. The club collected its first Western Division crown in 1998, outlasting the Padres and Dodgers by four games.

The club earned a Wild Card title in '99, coming up two games behind Los Angeles. Marvin Benard busted out with 100 runs scored, 36 two-base hits, 27 stolen bases and a .290 average in '99. Chris Singleton batted .300 with 17 taters and 20 steals in his rookie season. Russ Ortiz posted an 18-9 record despite leading the NL with 125 bases on balls. Bobby Howry locked down 28 contests. Howry's relief efforts were complemented by Mike Remlinger (10-1, 2.37), Dennis Cook (10-5, 3.86) and Keith Foulke (2.22, 9 SV, 123 K's). In six consecutive draft classes from 1996-2001 (the last five under GM Brian Sabean's leadership) San Francisco fell short of 100 Career Total Win Shares.

Year/Team	OPW%	PW	PL	APW%	AW	AL	Diff+/-
2000 SFG	0.520 D	84	78	0.599 P	97	65	0.079
2001 SFG	0.509 D	83	79	0.556	90	72	0.046
2002 SFG	0.519 D	84	78	0.590 W	95	66	0.071
2003 SFG	0.468 F	76	86	0.621 D	100	61	0.153
2004 SFG	0.543 F	88	74	0.562	91	71	0.019
2005 SFG	0.482	78	84	0.463	75	87	-0.019
2006 SFG	0.447 F	72	90	0.472	76	85	0.025
2007 SFG	0.429 F	70	92	0.438	71	91	0.009
2008 SFG	0.461 F	75	87	0.444	72	90	-0.017
2009 SFG	0.483 F	78	84	0.543	88	74	0.060
2010 SFG	0.508 F	82	80	0.568 D	92	70	0.060
2011 SFG	0.458 F	74	88	0.531	86	76	0.072
2012 SFG	0.425	69	93	0.580 D	94	68	0.155
2013 SFG	0.439	71	91	0.469	76	86	0.030

franchID	OWAR	OWS	AWAR	AWS	WARdiff	WSdiff	P/D/W/F
2000 SFG	32.071	213.689	**52.354**	**290.995**	-20.283	-77.305	D
2001 SFG	29.281	192.083	46.994	270.000	-17.713	-77.917	D
2002 SFG	23.582	196.058	**51.809**	285.005	-28.227	-88.947	D
2003 SFG	28.802	207.904	43.507	300.000	-14.705	-92.096	F
2004 SFG	32.128	213.137	41.433	273.004	-9.305	-59.868	F
2005 SFG	30.008	207.194	25.098	224.999	4.910	-17.805	
2006 SFG	35.222	202.104	28.233	227.996	6.989	-25.892	F
2007 SFG	31.492	198.228	29.324	213.003	2.168	-14.775	F
2008 SFG	32.594	194.521	27.116	215.999	5.478	-21.478	F
2009 SFG	37.719	228.670	36.172	264.005	1.546	-35.335	F
2010 SFG	34.419	223.772	42.502	276.007	-8.083	-52.236	F
2011 SFG	35.656	219.236	35.779	257.991	-0.124	-38.755	F
2012 SFG	25.210	227.124	37.979	281.997	-12.769	-54.873	
2013 SFG	31.211	232.503	27.565	227.998	3.645	4.506	

The Giants edged the Dodgers by a single game for the NL West crown in 2000 and repeated as division champions in '01 and '02. Foulke provided a 2.42 ERA, 0.961 WHIP and 32 saves per season from 2000-04. He led the League with 43 saves and earned an All-Star selection in 2003. Benard scored 102 runs and pilfered 22 bags while Deivi Cruz drilled 46 doubles and hit .302 in 2000. Gil Heredia won 15 games in '00 while John Burkett fashioned a 3.04 ERA and struck out 187 batters in '01.

Bill R. Mueller (.326/19/85) socked 45 doubles and took home the batting crown in 2003. Russ Ortiz placed fourth in the NL Cy Young vote, posting a 21-7 mark despite yielding the most walks for the second time in his career. Joe Nathan saved 41 games per year from 2004-09 with a 1.87 ERA and 0.934 WHIP; he fashioned a 1.37 ERA with a 0.897 WHIP while notching 43 saves in 2013. Salomon Torres surfaced as a solid reliever, delivering a 3.34 ERA from 2004-08, topping the NL with 94 appearances in '06 and notching 28 saves in '08. The '05 squad stumbled to a 78-win season but finished only two games behind the Rockies.

Francisco Liriano (12-3, 2.16) earned an All-Star invitation and finished third in the Rookie of the Year voting in 2006. He whiffed 201 batters and accumulated 14 victories with a 3.62 ERA in 2010. Pedro Feliz cranked 22 round-trippers and knocked in 98 runs in '06. Jeremy Accardo enjoyed a 30-save campaign in '07 along with a 2.14 ERA. Brian Wilson averaged 42 saves with a 2.97 ERA from 2008-10, pacing the NL with 48 saves in 2010.

Tim Lincecum collected back-to-back Cy Young Awards in 2008-09. "The Freak" struck out over 260 batters in both seasons, combining for a 33-12 record. Matt Cain delivered a 14-9 mark with a 2.93 ERA and 1.096 WHIP from 2009-2012 and twirled a perfect game on June 13, 2012. Pablo Sandoval blasted 44 two-base hits, 25 moon-shots and plated 90 runners while batting .330 in his first full season (2009). David Aardsma broke into a late-inning role in '09, fashioning a 2.52 ERA and 38 saves.

Buster Posey (.305/18/67) merited NL Rookie of the Year honors in 2010. He batted .336 with 39 two-baggers, 24 clouts and 103 ribbies en route to the 2012 NL MVP Award. The talent-starved lineup failed to reach the PA requirements from 2003-09 excluding 2005.

Win Shares > 20	Single-Season	1980-2013
Jack Clark - 1B (SFG) x3	Matt D. Williams - 3B (SFG)	Marvin Benard - CF (SFG)
Will Clark - 1B (SFG) x6	x4	Chili Davis - RF (SFG)
Brandon Belt – 1B (SFG)	Pablo Sandoval - 3B (SFG) x2	Dave Kingman - DH (SFG)
Robby Thompson - 2B (SFG)	Bob Brenly - C (SFG) x2	Chili Davis - DH (SFG)
x3	Buster Posey - C (SFG) x2	Tim Lincecum - SP (SFG) x2
Bill R. Mueller - 3B (SFG)	Chili Davis - CF (SFG)	Keith Foulke - RP (SFG)

Note: 4000 PA or BFP to qualify, except during strike-shortened seasons
(1972 = 3800, 1981 & 1994 = 2700, 1995 = 3500) and 154-game schedule (3800)
- failed to qualify: 1901-1902, 1939, 1942, 1944-1945, 1948, 1955-1956, 1959-1960, 1985-1986, 1988, 2003-2004, 2006-2009

Giants All-Time "Originals" Roster

David Aardsma	Jesse English	Dick Lajeskie	Armando Rios
Jeremy Accardo	Eric Erickson	Hal Lanier	Jimmy Ripple
Tom Acker	Angel Escobar	Paul LaPalme	John Roach
Ehire Adrianza	Geno Espineli	Pat Larkin	Dave Robertson
Kurt Ainsworth	Dick Estelle	Tacks Latimer	Daryl Robertson
Ed Albrecht	Bobby Etheridge	Gary Lavelle	Rich P. Robertson
Mike Aldrete	Steve Evans	Les Layton	Jack W. Robinson
Gary Alexander	Joe Evers	Mike Lee	Jeff D. Robinson

Myron Allen	Pete Falcone	Roy Lee	Rafael Robles
Felipe Alou	Rikkert Faneyte	Al Lefevre	Andre Rodgers
Jesus Alou	Frank Fanovich	Hank Leiber	Eric Rodin
Matty Alou	Bob Farley	Johnnie LeMaster	Guillermo Rodriguez
Joey Amalfitano	Doc Farrell	Dick LeMay	Jose Rodriguez
Red Ames	Jim Faulkner	Mark Leonard	Kevin Rogers
Hub Andrews	Charlie Faust	Sam Leslie	Ryan Rohlinger
John Andre	Harry Feldman	Fred D. Lewis	Minnie Rojas
Jack Aragon	Harry Felix	Tim Lincecum	Sergio Romo
Chris Arnold	Pedro Feliz	Todd Linden	Jimmy Rosario
Jim Asbell	Bobby Fenwick	Freddie Lindstrom	Harry Rosenberg
Bill Ayers	George Ferguson	Scott Linebrink	Joe Rosselli
Charlie Babb	Osvaldo Fernandez	Frank Linzy	George Ross
Charlie Babington	Tom Ferrick	Francisco Liriano	Frank Rosso
Lore Bader	Steve Filipowicz	Dennis Littlejohn	Mike Rowland
Loren Bain	Bill Finley	Jeff Little	Johnny Rucker
Al Baird	Rube Fischer	Greg Litton	Dick Rudolph
Harry Baldwin	Don Fisher	Jake Livingstone	Tom Runnells
George Bamberger	Eddie Fisher	Whitey Lockman	Dan Runzler
Hal Bamberger	Leo Fishel	Lou Lombardo	Connie Ryan
Tom Bannon	John Fitzgerald	Thomas Loughran	Rosy Ryan
Lorenzo Barcelo	Matty Fitzgerald	Noah Lowry	Gary Ryerson
Curt Barclay	Freddie Fitzsimmons	Ray Lucas	Billy Sadler
Scott Barnes	Tom Fleming	Red Lucas	Ryan Sadowski
Virgil Barnes	Art Fletcher	Trey Lunsford	Jack Salveson
Francisco Barrios	Paul Florence	Waddy Macphee	Ed Samcoff
Jose Barrios	Ray Foley	Garry Maddox	Ron Samford
Jim Barr	Joe Fontenot	Chris Magruder	Hector Sanchez
Bob Barthelson	Chad Fonville	Freddie Maguire	Jonathan Sanchez
Bill Bartley	Jesse Foppert	Jack Maguire	Pablo Sandoval
Bob Barton	George Foster	Jim Mahady	Andres Santana
Larry Battam	Pop Foster	Bill Malarkey	Francisco Santos
Joe Bean	Reddy Foster	Joe Malay	Mackey Sasser
Desmond Beatty	Keith Foulke	Kirt Manwaring	Skeeter Scalzi
Marty Becker	Art Fowler	Joe Margoneri	Mort Scanlan
Roy Beecher	Alan Fowlkes	Juan Marichal	George Scharein
Ed Begley	Charlie Fox	Rube Marquard	Rube Schauer
Gene Begley	Kevin Frandsen	Doc E. Marshall	Mike Schemer
Clay Bellinger	Pepe Frias	Willard Marshall	Nate Schierholtz
Brandon Belt	Frankie Frisch	Barney Martin	Bob Schmidt
Marvin Benard	Tito Fuentes	Joe W. Martin	Bob Schroder
Mike Benjamin	Chick Fullis	Joe Martinez	Hal Schumacher
Larry Benton	Aaron Fultz	Shairon Martis	Ferdie Schupp
Curt Bernard	Frank Funk	Christy Mathewson	Wayne Schurr
Joe Berry, Jr.	Frank Gabler	Henry Mathewson	Doc Sechrist
Hi Bithorn	Al Gallagher	Osiris Matos	Dave Sells
Damaso Blanco	Al Gardella	Gary Matthews	Frank Seward
Ossie Blanco	Billy Gardner	Mike Mattimore	Cy Seymour
Marv Blaylock	Bob Garibaldi	Ernie Maun	Adam Shabala
Bob Blewett	Willie Garoni	Dave May	Tillie Shafer
Clint Blume	Greg Garrett	Buster Maynard	Jack Sharrott
Randy Bockus	Scott Garrelts	Eddie Mayo	Jim Sheehan
Brian Bocock	Gil Garrido	Willie Mays	Tommy Sheehan
Carl Boles	Alex Gaston	Randy McCament	Ralph Shinners
Bobby Bolin	Lloyd Gearhart	Paul McClellan	Joe Shipley

Bobby Bonds	Dinty Gearin	Mike F. McCormick	Ernie Shore
Hank Boney	Harvey Gentry	Moose McCormick	Seth Sigsby
Boof Bonser	Bill George	Willie McCovey	Al Sima
Ike Boone	Oscar Georgy	Malcolm McDonald	Chris Singleton
Bill Bordley	Les German	Kevin McGehee	Scottie Slayback
Andy Boswell	Charlie Gettig	Mickey McGowan	Bruce Sloan
Steve Bourgeois	Paul Giel	Alex McKinnon	Al J. Smith
Chris Bourjos	Tookie Gilbert	Art McLarney	Al K. Smith
Chick Bowen	Conor Gillaspie	Jack McMahon	Earl S. Smith
Cy Bowen	Dan Gladden	George McMillan	George A. Smith
John Bowker	Jim Gladd	Hugh McMullen	Harry J. Smith
Ernie Bowman	Randy Gomez	Jim McNamara	Mike Elwood Smith
Roger Bowman	Ed Goodson	Frank McPartlin	Red R. Smith
Jim Boyle	Jim Goodwin	Charlie Mead	Fred Snodgrass
Vic Bradford	Sid Gordon	Sammy Meeks	Colonel Snover
Fred Brainard	Tom D. Gorman	Cliff Melton	Steve Soderstrom
Jeff Brantley	Hank Gowdy	Fred Merkle	Mose Solomon
Bob Brenly	Moonlight Graham	John Merritt	Elias Sosa
Eddie Bressoud	Tyler Graham	Butch Metzger	Henry Sosa
Jack Brewer	Mark Grant	Chief Meyers	Horace Speed
Jamie Brewington	Mickey Grasso	Jim Middleton	Chris Speier
Marshall Bridges	Kent Greenfield	John Middleton	Daryl Spencer
Troy Brohawn	Sandy Griffin	Larry Miggins	George Spencer
Ken Brondell	Jason Grilli	Jim McCurdy Miller	Vern Spencer
Chris Brown	Roy Grimes	Whitey Miller	Al Spohrer
Eddie Brown	Marv Grissom	Willie Mills	Heinie Stafford
Jake Brown	Heinie Groh	Damon Minor	Al Stanek
Ollie Brown	Tom Grubbs	Doug Mirabelli	Steve Stanicek
William Brown	Ken Grundt	Patrick Misch	Jigger Statz
Greg Brummett	Juan Guerrero	Randy Moffitt	Jeff Stember
Ron Bryant	Harry Gumbert	Rinty Monahan	Joe Stephenson
Mike Budnick	Eric Gunderson	Johnny Monell	Glen Stewart
Charlie Buelow	Edwards Guzman	John Monroe	Steve Stone
De Wayne Buice	Tom Hafey	John Montefusco	Jim Stoops
Madison Bumgarner	Don Hahn	Ramon Monzant	Joe Strain
Nate Bump	Ed Halicki	Jim Mooney	Steve Stroughter
Frank Burke	Tom Haller	Al Moore	Guy Sularz
John P. Burke	Jim Hamby	Jo-Jo Moore	Eric Surkamp
John Burkett	Bill Hands	Jose M. Morales	Bill Swabach
George J. Burns	Andy Hansen	Howie Moss	Russ Swan
Pete Burnside	Scott Hardesty	Manny Mota	Ad Swigler
Brian Burres	Bud Hardin	Bill R. Mueller	Tim Talton
Buster Burrell	Red Hardy	Don Mueller	Kensuke Tanaka
Emmanuel Burriss	Alan Hargesheimer	Terry Mulholland	Jose Tartabull
Brian Buscher	John Harrell	Scott Munter	Jack Taschner
Frank Butler	Bob Harrison	Masanori Murakami	Stu Tate
Bob Cain	Gail Harris	Red Murff	Bill Taylor
Matt Cain	Jack Harshman	Bob Murphy	Bob Taylor
Jim Callahan	Jim Ray Hart	Danny F. Murphy	Dummy Taylor
Mark Calvert	Chick Hartley	Danny J. Murphy	Jack B. Taylor
Sal Campfield	Grover Hartley	Pat Murphy	Tony Taylor
Jay Canizaro	Clint Hartung	Yale Murphy	Jim Tennant
Ben Cantwell	Charlie Hayes	Calvin Murray	Bill Terry
Doug Capilla	Francis Healy	Rich Murray	Jeff Tesreau
John Carden	Dave Heaverlo	Jimmy Myers	Nick Testa

Jose Cardenal	Gorman Heimueller	Mike Myers	Greg Thayer
Roger Carey	Bud Heine	Philip Nastu	Henry Thielman
Jim Carlin	Heath Hembree	Joe Nathan	Fay Thomas
Dan Carlson	Ken Henderson	Julio Navarro	Gary Thomasson
Bob Carpenter	Ed Hendricks	Offa Neal	Robby Thompson
Bill Carrick	Jack Hendricks	Thomas Neal	Bobby Thomson
Don Carrithers	Gail Henley	Ray Nelson	Jim Thorpe
Blackie Carter	Butch Henline	Charlie Newman	Erick Threets
Mike Caruso	Brad Hennessey	Roy Nichols	Verle Tiefenthaler
Alberto Castillo	Clay Hensley	Lance Niekro	Mike Tiernan
Foster Castleman	Ron Herbel	Ray Noble	Clay Timpner
Slick Castleman	Gil Heredia	Matt Nokes	Tip Tobin
Red Causey	Rudy A. Hernandez	Nick Noonan	Andy Tomasic
Orlando Cepeda	Buck Herzog	Rafael Novoa	Tommy Toms
Bob Chance	Larry Hesterfer	Walter Ockey	Tony Torcato
Tiny Chaplin	Joe Heving	Jimmy O'Connell	Hector Torres
Frank Charles	Mahlon Higbee	Jack Ogden	Salomon Torres
Angel Chavez	Alex Hinshaw	Bill O'Hara	Yorvit Torrealba
Nestor Chavez	Bobby Hofman	Tom O'Malley	Kelvin Torve
Artie Clarke	Ed Hogan	John O'Neill	Red Tramback
Bill Clarkson	Walter Holke	Mickey O'Neil	Red Treadway
Dad Clarkson	Steve Holm	Tip O'Neill	Ken Trinkle
Doug Clark	Bob Hooper	Steve R. Ontiveros	Eddie Tucker
Jack Clark	Dick Hoover	John Orsino	Bob Tufts
Roy Clark	Brian Horwitz	Russ Ortiz	Earl Turner
Willie Clark	Steve Hosey	Daniel Ortmeier	Ty Tyson
Will Clark	Jim Howarth	Dan Otero	Carlos Valdez
Royce Clayton	Shorty Howe	Mel Ott	Carlos Valderrama
Alan Cockrell	Bobby Howry	Phil Ouellette	William Van
Andy Cohen	Waite Hoyt	Henry Oxley	Landingham
Craig Colbert	Bill Hubbell	Jose Pagan	Ike Van Zandt
Bill Collins	Al Huenke	Emilio Palmero	Freddie Velazquez
Ramon Conde	Phil Huffman	Matt Palmer	Ryan Verdugo
Joe Connell	Rick Huisman	Jay Parker	Johnny Vergez
Joe H. Connolly	Harry Hulihan	Roy Parmelee	Jose Vidal
Jim Constable	John Humphries	Casey Parsons	Carlos Villanueva
Dennis Cook	Randy Hundley	Jiggs Parson	Ken Vining
Claude Cooper	Herb Hunter	Joe Paterson	Ozzie Virgil
Mike Corkins	Walt Huntzinger	John A. Patterson	Ryan Vogelsong
Terry Cornutt	Adam Hyzdu	Pat Patterson	Bruce Von Hoff
Kevin Correia	Monte Irvin	Gene Paulette	Jason Waddell
Al Corwin	Travis Ishikawa	Francisco Peguero	Ham Wade
Pete Cote	Travis Jackson	Jim Pena	Heinie Wagner
Jon Coutlangus	Merwin Jacobson	Juan C. Perez	Leon Wagner
Dick Cramer	Skip James	Tony Perezchica	Rube Walberg
Doc Crandall	Bill Jennings	Bob Perry	Bill Walker
Brandon Crawford	Marcus Jensen	Gaylord Perry	Red Waller
Pat Crawford	Ryan Jensen	Cap Peterson	Joe Wall
Pete Cregan	Waldis Joaquin	Pretzel Pezzullo	Reggie Walton
Buddy Crump	Art G. Johnson	Monte Pfyl	Libe Washburn
Deivi Cruz	Elmer Johnson	Jack S. Phillips	Neal Watlington
Jacob Cruz	Erik Johnson	Mike Phillips	Earl Webb
Al Cuccinello	Fred Johnson	Urbane Pickering	Red Webb
Charlie Culberson	Frank Johnson	Mario Picone	Johnny Weekly
Jack Cummings	Greg Johnston	Sandy Piez	Phil Weintraub

Bill A. Cunningham	Jim B. Johnson	Jess Pike	Lew Wendell
Harry Curtis	John Henry Johnson	Brett Pill	Fred Wenz
Mike Cvengros	Stan Jok	Skip Pitlock	Huyler Westervelt
John D'Acquisto	Dax Jones	Emil Planeta	Wes Westrum
George Daly	Johnny Jones	Ed Plank	Don Wheeler
Harry Danning	Red Jones	Rance Pless	Zach Wheeler
Claude Davenport	Sherman Jones	Joe Poetz	Lew Whistler
Jim Davenport	Claude Jonnard	Hugh Poland	Bill D. White
Chili Davis	Buck Jordan	Ned Porter	Bernie Williams
Harry H. Davis	Kevin Joseph	Buster Posey	Davey Williams
Ira Davis	Rick Joseph	Lou Pote	Frank Williams
John H. Davis	Ray Katt	Alonzo Powell	Jerome Williams
Wayland Dean	Bob Kearney	Dante Powell	Keith Williams
Steve Decker	Willie Keeler	Willie Prall	Matt D. Williams
Dummy Deegan	Duke Kelleher	Johnny Pramesa	Reggie B. Williams
Rob Deer	George Kelly	Joe P. Price	Jim Willoughby
Charlie Dees	John I. Kennedy	Miguel Puente	Art Wilson
Bill DeKoning	Monte Kennedy	John Puhl	Brian Wilson
Al Demaree	Buddy Kerr	Luis Quintana	Hack Wilson
Mark Dempsey	Mike Kickham	John Rabb	Neil Wilson
Art Devlin	Roger Kieschnick	Dave Rader	Parke Wilson
Jim H. Devlin	Pete Kilduff	John Rainey	Trevor Wilson
Josh Devore	Eric King	Erasmo Ramirez	Hooks Wiltse
Mark Dewey	Dave Kingman	Cody Ransom	Gordie Windhorn
Felix Diaz	Bob Kinsella	Jeff Ransom	Jesse Winters
Walt Dickson	Bill Kinsler	Goldie Rapp	Alan Wirth
Dick Dietz	La Rue Kirby	Pat Rapp	Mickey Witek
Ed Doheny	Willie Kirkland	Steve Reed	Johnnie Wittig
Red Donahue	Al Klawitter	Randy Reese	Pete Woodruff
Matt Downs	Joe Klinger	Joe Regan	Ted Wood
Larry Doyle	Joe Kmak	Jessie Reid	Babe Young
Rob Dressler	Bob Knepper	Bill Reidy	Ross Youngs
Louis Drucke	Justin Knoedler	Mike Remlinger	Jeff Yurak
Andy Dunning	Pip Koehler	Nap Reyes	Sal Yvars
Jake Dunning	Len Koenecke	Bob Reynolds	Adrian Zabala
Ben Dyer	Alex Konikowski	Bobby Rhawn	Elmer Zacher
Hugh East	Wally Kopf	Frank Riccelli	Dom Zanni
MIke Eden	Dave Koslo	Antoan Richardson	Dave Zearfoss
Steve Edlefsen	Randy Kutcher	Danny Richardson	Walter Zink
Jason Ellison	Coco Laboy	Lance Richbourg	
Gil English	Joe Lafata	Bill Rigney	

Year/Team	OPW%	PW	PL	APW%	AW	AL	Diff+/-
1901 CLE	0.179 F	24	112	0.397	54	82	0.219
1902 CLE	0.495	67	69	0.507	69	67	0.013
1903 CLE	0.504	71	69	0.550	77	63	0.046
1904 CLE	0.568	88	66	0.570	86	65	0.001
1905 CLE	0.542	83	71	0.494	76	78	-0.048
1906 CLE	0.521	80	74	0.582	89	64	0.061
1907 CLE	0.507	78	76	0.559	85	67	0.053
1908 CLE	0.549	85	69	0.584	90	64	0.035
1909 CLE	0.463	71	83	0.464	71	82	0.001

franchID	OWAR	OWS	AWAR	AWS	WARdiff	WSdiff	P/D/W/F
1901 CLE	0.845	20.639	15.503	162.004	-14.658	-141.365	F
1902 CLE	6.219	38.144	34.015	207.003	-27.796	-168.859	
1903 CLE	9.901	55.197	36.728	231.001	-26.827	-175.804	
1904 CLE	9.129	70.634	46.706	257.997	-37.577	-187.363	
1905 CLE	13.093	100.522	33.477	228.003	-20.384	-127.481	
1906 CLE	15.855	101.907	52.350	267.010	-36.495	-165.103	
1907 CLE	17.403	118.981	36.193	254.989	-18.790	-136.008	
1908 CLE	21.929	148.351	40.554	269.997	-18.625	-121.647	
1909 CLE	20.920	165.439	27.808	213.001	-6.888	-47.562	

Legend: (P) = Pennant / Most Wins in League (D) = Division Winner (W) = Wild Card Winner (F) = Failed to Qualify

The Cleveland Blues enlisted as one of the eight original American League franchises in 1901. Based on the WS>20 frame of reference, Cleveland has developed the second-most quality left fielders (52) and starting pitchers (87) among the "Turn of the Century" franchises. Indians' left fielders rank first with 123 WS>10 seasons.

Cleveland's efforts to cultivate second basemen have been futile. The team places last among the "ToC" franchises at the keystone position with a mere 6 WS>20 player-seasons. Moreover, the organization's second basemen and center fielders never finished in the top three WS>10 totals for the "Turn of the Century" teams. The organization played under several nicknames including the "Blues" (1901), "Bronchos" (1902) and "Naps" (1903-1914) before settling on the "Indians" moniker in 1915. Cleveland posted the highest oWAR in the American League four times in the club's inaugural decade.

Addie Joss is the all-time Major League leader with a career WHIP of 0.968. He twirled a perfect game against the White Sox on October 2, 1908 and surpassed the 20-win plateau in four successive campaigns (1905-08), including a league-best 27 victories in '07. From 1902-09 he completed 28 of 31 starts per season and fashioned a 1.89 career ERA. Earl "Crossfire" Moore (20-8, 1.74) completed all of his 27 starts in 1903 and led the AL in ERA. Ed Killian compiled 23 victories in 1905 and then delivered career-bests with 25 wins and a 1.78 ERA in '07. Otto Hess contributed 20 victories with a 1.83 ERA during the 1906 campaign. The Naps finished only two games behind the Athletics for the American League pennant in '08.

Year/Team	OPW%	PW	PL	APW%	AW	AL	Diff+/-
1910 CLE	0.431	66	88	0.467	71	81	0.037
1911 CLE	0.465	72	82	0.523	80	73	0.057
1912 CLE	0.449	69	85	0.490	75	78	0.041
1913 CLE	0.487	75	79	0.566	86	66	0.079
1914 CLE	0.368	57	97	0.333	51	102	-0.035

Year/Team	OPW%	PW	PL	APW%	AW	AL	Diff+/-
1915 CLE	0.385	59	95	0.375	57	95	-0.010
1916 CLE	0.490 F	75	79	0.500	77	77	0.010
1917 CLE	0.451 F	69	85	0.571	88	66	0.121
1918 CLE	0.513	66	62	0.575	73	54	0.062
1919 CLE	0.535 F	75	65	0.604	84	55	0.069

franchID	OWAR	OWS	AWAR	AWS	WARdiff	WSdiff	P/D/W/F
1910 CLE	14.459	157.096	23.705	213.005	-9.245	-55.909	
1911 CLE	17.434	189.332	31.451	239.998	-14.017	-50.666	
1912 CLE	17.617	158.519	30.022	225.003	-12.405	-66.485	
1913 CLE	24.077	186.565	38.870	258.001	-14.793	-71.436	
1914 CLE	17.811	142.213	17.302	153.002	0.509	-10.789	
1915 CLE	22.475	171.892	25.554	171.006	-3.079	0.886	
1916 CLE	34.094	232.531	34.569	231.002	-0.475	1.529	F
1917 CLE	24.124	237.787	38.382	264.000	-14.258	-26.213	F
1918 CLE	31.761	**210.181**	**37.574**	218.997	-5.813	-8.816	
1919 CLE	34.909	275.268	40.240	252.005	-5.331	23.264	F

Moore notched 22 victories and topped the circuit with 6 shutouts and 185 whiffs in 1910. Vean Gregg (23-7, 1.80) paced the AL in ERA and WHIP (1.054) in his rookie year (1911) and exceeded the 20-win mark in three successive seasons (1911-13). Guy Morton (16-15, 2.14) established personal bests in ERA and WHIP (1.038) during the 1915 season. Excluding the 1918 season, the Indians fell short of the BFP requirements from 1916-1920. Jack Graney smoked 41 two-base hits, tallied 106 runs and coaxed 102 walks in '16. Tribe shortstops capped the Majors with 38 WS>10 player-seasons from 1910-1929. Ray Chapman set an MLB record for most sacrifice hits in a season (67) and pilfered 52 bags while batting .302 in 1917. Roger Peckinpaugh supplied a career-best .305 BA in '19.

Win Shares > 20	Single-Season	1901-1919
Claude Rossman - 1B (CLE)	Jack Graney - LF (CLE)	Vean Gregg - SP (CLE) x3
George Stovall - 1B (CLE)	Ed Killian - SP (CLE) x2	Gene Krapp - SP (CLE)
Ray Chapman - SS (CLE) x3	Otto Hess - SP (CLE)	Nick N. Cullop - SP (CLE)
Roger Peckinpaugh - SS (CLE) x5	Addie Joss - SP (CLE) x4	Guy Morton - SP (CLE)
George Perring - 3B (CLE)	Glenn J. Liebhardt - SP (CLE)	Willie Mitchell - SW (CLE)
	Earl Moore - SP (CLE) x3	

Year/Team	OPW%	PW	PL	APW%	AW	AL	Diff+/-
1920 CLE	0.518 F	80	74	0.636 P	98	56	0.118
1921 CLE	0.559 P	86	68	0.610	94	60	0.051
1922 CLE	0.473	73	81	0.506	78	76	0.033
1923 CLE	0.535	82	72	0.536	82	71	0.001
1924 CLE	0.444	68	86	0.438	67	86	-0.006
1925 CLE	0.474	73	81	0.455	70	84	-0.019
1926 CLE	0.546 P	84	70	0.571	88	66	0.026
1927 CLE	0.464	71	83	0.431	66	87	-0.033
1928 CLE	0.458	70	84	0.403	62	92	-0.055
1929 CLE	0.478	74	80	0.533	81	71	0.055

franchID	OWAR	OWS	AWAR	AWS	WARdiff	WSdiff	P/D/W/F
1920 CLE	31.328	254.942	**53.777**	**293.999**	-22.449	-39.057	F
1921 CLE	41.138	279.636	**51.817**	282.001	-10.678	-2.365	P
1922 CLE	28.410	229.030	36.295	233.996	-7.885	-4.966	
1923 CLE	**42.432**	**248.258**	47.113	245.986	-4.681	2.271	
1924 CLE	34.496	224.703	32.791	201.001	1.705	23.702	
1925 CLE	27.772	211.130	32.860	210.002	-5.088	1.129	

1926 CLE	41.872	**273.967**	37.550	263.998	4.322	9.969	P
1927 CLE	37.022	236.755	24.787	198.004	12.235	38.750	
1928 CLE	36.038	220.311	22.578	186.004	13.460	34.307	
1929 CLE	41.574	239.153	32.608	243.003	8.966	-3.850	

Chapman was batting .303 on August 16, 1920 when he was struck in the head by a Carl Mays' delivery. He died one day later, the only ballplayer to be fatally injured during a Major League game. Peckinpaugh transcended the 100-run mark in successive seasons (1920-21) and secured MVP honors in 1924 based principally on his proficient glovework. Elmer J. Smith notched career-highs with a .316 BA and 103 ribbies in '20.

Cleveland fought a tightly contested battle with Detroit in 1921 and emerged triumphant by a single game. Sam P. Jones realized his potential in '21, racking up 23 victories and twirling 5 shutouts. "Sad Sam" contributed 21 wins as the '23 Tribe paced the circuit in oWAR and oWS. Joe Sewell compiled a .322 BA during the Twenties. He posted career-bests with a .353 BA and 109 RBI in 1923 and led the AL with 45 doubles in the ensuing campaign. Sewell established the modern-day record as he struck out only 4 times out of 608 at-bats (covering 699 plate appearances) in '25.

George Uhle notched consecutive 20-win seasons (1922-23). "The Bull" topped the League with 26 victories and 357.2 innings pitched for the '23 squad. Uhle surpassed the 300-inning mark again in 1926 as he led the AL with a 27-11 record while completing 32 of 36 starts. Cleveland established its defensive aptitude in 1924 with a fldWARnorm of 9 and fldWSnorm of 62. In a three-way tussle with the White Sox and Yankees, the Indians seized the '26 pennant. Although relegated to part-time status through the first six seasons of his career, during the Twenties Riggs Stephenson maintained a .340 BA. Achieving full-time status in '27, "Old Hoss" hit .344, tallied 101 runs and smacked a league-best 46 doubles. Stephenson set career-highs in 1929 with 17 blasts and 110 ribbies. The '29 campaign featured impressive debuts by Earl H. Averill and Wes Ferrell. "The Earl of Snohomish" produced a .332 BA with 198 base knocks, 110 runs scored and 96 RBI. Ferrell notched the first of six 20-win seasons in his career while completing 18 of 25 starts.

Year/Team	OPW%	PW	PL	APW%	AW	AL	Diff+/-
1930 CLE	0.496	76	78	0.526	81	73	0.030
1931 CLE	0.558	86	68	0.506	78	76	-0.051
1932 CLE	0.542	84	70	0.572	87	65	0.030
1933 CLE	0.492	76	78	0.497	75	76	0.005
1934 CLE	0.541	83	71	0.552	85	69	0.011
1935 CLE	0.547	84	70	0.536	82	71	-0.011
1936 CLE	0.552	85	69	0.519	80	74	-0.032
1937 CLE	0.518	80	74	0.539	83	71	0.021
1938 CLE	0.533	82	72	0.566	86	66	0.033
1939 CLE	0.566	87	67	0.565	87	67	-0.001

franchID	OWAR	OWS	AWAR	AWS	WARdiff	WSdiff	P/D/W/F
1930 CLE	38.897	241.846	30.380	243.004	8.516	-1.159	
1931 CLE	43.344	245.205	37.082	233.999	6.262	11.206	
1932 CLE	43.291	257.027	41.130	261.002	2.161	-3.975	
1933 CLE	37.217	242.834	29.061	225.008	8.156	17.827	
1934 CLE	41.415	248.605	40.479	255.001	0.936	-6.395	
1935 CLE	43.169	253.793	41.223	245.997	1.946	7.796	
1936 CLE	41.342	231.820	45.848	239.997	-4.506	-8.176	
1937 CLE	42.012	243.905	41.760	249.005	0.252	-5.100	
1938 CLE	38.163	242.928	40.880	257.996	-2.717	-15.068	
1939 CLE	42.132	268.894	42.553	260.997	-0.421	7.897	

Earl Averill averaged .318 with 35 two-baggers, 22 circuit clouts, 105 RBI and 110 runs scored during the Thirties. He established personal bests with 140 runs and 143 RBI in '31 while slugging 32 round-trippers in successive seasons (1931-32). The six-time All-Star finished third in the 1936 AL MVP balloting as he paced the League in hits (232) and triples (15). Johnny Hodapp (.354/9/121) topped the AL with 225 base hits and 51 doubles while Ed Morgan (.349/26/136) tallied 122 runs, 204 base knocks and 47 doubles during the 1930 campaign. Left fielder Joe Vosmik batted .311 for the decade and plated 117 baserunners in his first full season (1931). He rapped a league-leading 216 hits, 47 two-baggers and 20 triples along with a career-high .348 BA en route to a third-place finish in the 1935 AL MVP vote. Vosmik's 201 safeties topped the leader boards in '38 and he tallied a personal best with 121 runs scored.

Indians' moundsmen registered the most WS>10 player-seasons (59) during the decade. Ferrell surpassed the 20-victory plateau in four successive years (1929-1932). He garnered 34 Win Shares and placed runner-up in the 1935 AL MVP balloting, furnishing a 25-14 record while completing 31 of 38 starts. Watty Clark compiled 20 wins along with a career-best WHIP of 1.212 for the '32 Tribe. Mel Harder (15-17, 2.95) claimed the ERA title in 1933. He delivered 20+ wins in back-to-back seasons (1934-35) and netted four straight All-Star selections commencing in '34. Odell Hale knocked in 100+ baserunners in successive years (1934-35) and produced career-bests with 126 runs scored, 50 doubles and a .316 BA in '36.

Hal Trosky's splendid rookie campaign featured a .330 BA, 206 base hits, 117 runs scored, 45 doubles, 35 round-trippers and 142 RBI. The Indians' first-sacker topped the circuit with 162 RBI while establishing personal bests in every major batting category in '36. Trosky supplied a .317 BA with 104 tallies, 30 jacks and 126 ribbies per season (1934-39), while Zeke Bonura contributed a .313 BA with 19 wallops and 106 RBI during the same interval.

The Tribe posted three consecutive second-place finishes (1937-39). Clint Brown twice led the League in appearances and notched 18 saves in '37 and '39. Clay Bryant (19-11, 3.10) managed to lead the League in walks and strikeouts in 1938, while Jeff Heath (.343/21/112) set career-highs in batting average and runs scored (104). Ken Keltner's defensive proficiency at the hot corner is substantiated by 5 appearances on the fielding WS and WAR charts. Keltner swatted 26 long balls and plated 113 baserunners in his inaugural season (1938) then batted .325 in his sophomore year.

Bob Feller earned his first of eight All-Star selections as he paced the AL with 240 strikeouts in 1938. "Rapid Robert" (24-9, 2.85) achieved "ace" status in '39, leading the League in wins, innings pitched (296.2), strikeouts (246) and complete games (24) while placing third in the AL MVP race. His streak of 7 successive years atop the leader boards for strikeouts was interrupted by 3+ years of military service during World War II. GM Cy Slapnicka presided over the acquisitions of Feller ('36), Keltner ('37), Lou Boudreau and Bob Lemon ('38).

Win Shares > 20	Single-Season	1920-1939
Ed Morgan - 1B (CLE) x2	Riggs Stephenson - LF (CLE) x4	Watty Clark - SP (CLE) x2
Hal Trosky - 1B (CLE) x6	Joe Vosmik - LF (CLE) x2	Willis Hudlin - SP (CLE) x2
Zeke Bonura - 1B (CLE) x2	Earl H. Averill - CF (CLE) x10	Wes Ferrell - SP (CLE) x5
Johnny Hodapp - 2B (CLE)	Elmer Smith - RF (CLE)	Ray Benge - SP (CLE)
Joe Sewell - SS (CLE) x8	Sam P. Jones - SP (CLE) x3	Clint Brown - SP (CLE)
Joe Sewell - 3B (CLE)	George Uhle - SP (CLE) x4	Mel Harder - SP (CLE) x5
Odell Hale - 3B (CLE) x2	Joe Shaute - SP (CLE)	Clay Bryant - SP (CLE)
Ken Keltner - 3B (CLE) x4	Jesse Petty - SP (CLE) x2	Bob Feller - SP (CLE) x6
Johnny Bassler - C (CLE)		Wes Ferrell - SW (CLE)
Jeff Heath - LF (CLE) x5		

Year/Team	OPW%	PW	PL	APW%	AW	AL	Diff+/-
1940 CLE	0.486	75	79	0.578	89	65	0.092
1941 CLE	0.545	84	70	0.487	75	79	-0.058
1942 CLE	0.475	73	81	0.487	75	79	0.012
1943 CLE	0.477	73	81	0.536	82	71	0.059
1944 CLE	0.496	76	78	0.468	72	82	-0.029
1945 CLE	0.574 P	88	66	0.503	73	72	-0.070
1946 CLE	0.493	76	78	0.442	68	86	-0.051
1947 CLE	0.574	88	66	0.519	80	74	-0.054
1948 CLE	0.606	93	61	0.626 P	97	58	0.020
1949 CLE	0.556	86	68	0.578	89	65	0.022

franchID	OWAR	OWS	AWAR	AWS	WARdiff	WSdiff	P/D/W/F
1940 CLE	42.932	268.698	42.376	266.996	0.555	1.702	
1941 CLE	43.074	267.373	34.966	225.004	8.108	42.369	
1942 CLE	34.444	218.837	29.097	224.999	5.347	-6.162	
1943 CLE	38.448	220.023	38.504	246.003	-0.056	-25.981	
1944 CLE	41.191	229.366	36.507	216.003	4.684	13.363	
1945 CLE	38.273	236.212	35.173	219.006	3.100	17.207	P
1946 CLE	39.276	235.470	31.320	203.996	7.957	31.474	
1947 CLE	45.491	255.613	39.371	240.003	6.120	15.610	P
1948 CLE	57.927	291.555	59.662	291.005	-1.736	0.550	P
1949 CLE	43.503	263.955	44.961	267.004	-1.458	-3.048	P

Feller (27-11, 2.61) placed runner-up in the 1940 AL MVP balloting as he led the circuit in every major pitching category. He compiled 25 victories and whiffed 260 opponents in '41. Feller enjoyed a sensational return to the diamond as he notched a career-best 35 Win Shares in '46 and topped the American League in every pitching category except ERA. He struck out a career-high 346 batsmen and completed 36 of 42 starts including 10 shutouts. Seven-time All-Star shortstop Lou Boudreau socked 46 two-base hits and drove in 101 runs in his first full season (1940). Boudreau (.355/18/106) garnered 1948 AL MVP honors as he established personal bests in batting average, runs scored (116), hits (199), home runs and RBI. "Old Shufflefoot" registered 34 Win Shares and coaxed 98 bases on balls while striking out only 9 times!

Thornton Lee (22-11, 2.37) completed 30 of 34 starts, paced the Junior Circuit in ERA and WHIP (1.165) and placed fourth in the '41 AL MVP vote. Jeff Heath (.340/24/123) achieved All-Star honors in 1941 while producing career-bests in hits (199), triples (20), home runs, RBI and stolen bases (18). Cleveland ended a 19-year drought, outlasting New York by a 3-game margin in 1945. The Tribe dominated the American League, claiming 10 pennants in a 15-year stretch covering 1945-1959.

The Indians achieved three successive pennants from 1947-49. Keltner bashed 31 moonshots, plated 119 baserunners and made his seventh All-Star appearance in '48. Tommy "Old Reliable" Henrich (.308/25/100) topped the circuit with 138 runs scored and 14 triples. Dale Mitchell supplied a .314 BA over the course of seven full seasons (1947-1953), exceeding the 200-hit mark in back-to-back campaigns (1948-49) and leading the circuit in base hits and triples (23) in '49.

Larry Doby became the first African-American to play in the American League in July, 1947. Doby batted .301 in his first full season (1948) and went on to clout 24 homers and score 106 runs in '49. Bob Lemon surpassed 20 victories on six different occasions beginning with the 1948 season. He twirled a league-high 10 shutouts, finished fifth in the MVP race, and commenced a streak of 7 consecutive All-Star appearances. Mike E. Garcia (14-5, 2.36) secured the ERA title and placed fourth in the 1949 AL ROY vote.

Year/Team	OPW%	PW	PL	APW%	AW	AL	Diff+/-
1950 CLE	0.554	85	69	0.597	92	62	0.043
1951 CLE	0.588 P	91	63	0.604	93	61	0.016
1952 CLE	0.631 P	97	57	0.604	93	61	-0.027
1953 CLE	0.588 P	91	63	0.597	92	62	0.009
1954 CLE	0.635 P	98	56	0.721 P	111	43	0.085
1955 CLE	0.545	84	70	0.604	93	61	0.059
1956 CLE	0.580 P	89	65	0.571	88	66	-0.009
1957 CLE	0.490	75	79	0.497	76	77	0.007
1958 CLE	0.527	81	73	0.503	77	76	-0.024
1959 CLE	0.503 P	77	77	0.578	89	65	0.075

franchID	OWAR	OWS	AWAR	AWS	WARdiff	WSdiff	P/D/W/F
1950 CLE	46.822	268.999	48.486	275.995	-1.664	-6.996	
1951 CLE	51.200	287.005	45.973	278.997	5.228	8.008	P
1952 CLE	54.950	295.508	50.261	278.999	4.688	16.509	P
1953 CLE	48.460	277.574	47.599	276.000	0.862	1.574	P
1954 CLE	47.466	265.862	52.132	279.005	-4.666	-13.143	P
1955 CLE	45.834	256.721	52.132	279.005	-6.298	-22.284	
1956 CLE	47.671	271.494	44.193	264.005	3.478	7.488	P
1957 CLE	36.296	245.826	32.486	227.996	3.810	17.830	
1958 CLE	36.995	232.647	37.099	231.005	-0.104	1.642	
1959 CLE	36.518	235.532	35.962	266.999	0.556	31.467	P

The Tribe flourished in the Fifties under the leadership of GM Hank Greenberg and manager Al Lopez. Boston outlasted Cleveland by a single contest in 1950. The Indians delivered a resounding victory in '51, winning the pennant by 14 games over the Red Sox. This initiated a run of four consecutive pennants for the Tribe in which the club outpaced the opposition by at least ten games. Cleveland moundsmen topped the WS>10 charts with 43 player-seasons.

Doby knocked in 100+ runs five times, batting .284 with 27 circuit clouts from 1950-56. He placed second in the 1956 AL MVP balloting after leading the League with 32 home runs and 126 RBI and led all Cleveland outfielders with 6 appearances on the fielding WS and WAR leader boards. Luke Easter mashed 29 long balls and drove in 102 runs per season from 1950-52. The Tribe battered opposition hurlers in 1952, producing the highest offWARnorm (29) and offWSnorm (168) in club annals.

Al Rosen collected the MVP Award in 1953, batting .336 with league-bests in home runs (43), RBI (145), runs scored (115) and SLG (.613). He yielded the highest Win Share total (43) in team history as he averaged 31 round-trippers and 114 RBI from 1950-54. Gus Zernial topped the AL with 33 moon-shots and 129 RBI. "Ozark Ike" crushed 42 quadruples in '53 and supplied 33 homers and 108 ribbies per season from 1950-53 while Eddie Robinson batted .279 with 24 taters and 102 RBI in the same span.

Bob Lemon amassed a league-best 23 victories in 1950 and '54 while pacing the circuit in complete games on four occasions from 1950-56. Lemon averaged 21 wins, a 3.24 ERA and 20 complete games during this stretch. Sal Maglie hurled 5 shutouts and produced a 2.71 ERA in '50. "The Barber" won 23 contests with a 2.93 ERA and 1.141 WHIP in the subsequent season, placing fourth in the MVP voting.

Minnie Minoso (.326/10/76) earned a runner-up finish in the 1951 AL ROY voting, pacing the circuit with 14 triples and 31 stolen bases. The "Cuban Comet" scored 100 runs per season for the decade, batting .306 with 16 homers and 88 ribbies. Minoso finished fourth in the MVP balloting in 3 campaigns. Cleveland left fielders dominated the WS>10 leader boards with 60 player-seasons from 1930-1959.

Feller led the American League with a 22-8 record in 1951. Allie Reynolds (20-8, 2.06) topped the League with 6 shutouts, 160 strikeouts and earned a runner-up finish in the '52 AL MVP balloting. Satchel Paige won 12 games in relief and saved 10 contests in 1952. Ray Boone belted 23 long balls and drove in 99 runs per year while batting .295 (1953-56) including a league-leading 116 RBI in '55.

The 1954 Indians posted the best record in franchise history (98-56). Bobby Avila won the batting title with a .341 average in 1954, while Garcia (19-8, 2.64) captured the League ERA title. "The Big Bear" posted a 20-10 mark with a 2.84 ERA and completed 17 contests per year from 1951-54. Al "Fuzzy" Smith topped the American League with 123 runs scored, batted .306 and placed third in the 1955 AL MVP balloting. After a runner-up finish in '55 Cleveland delivered another title in 1956.

Herb Score whiffed 245 batters en route to the AL Rookie of the Year Award in '55. He followed up with a 20-9 record, 2.53 ERA, and 263 strikeouts in 1956. Brooks Lawrence notched 19 victories in '56. Harry "Suitcase" Simpson legged out 11 three-base hits, slugged 21 homers and drove in 105 runs. Jim Lemon tied Simpson for the League lead in triples and pounded 27 big-flies in '56 and went on to plate 100 runners and swat 33 blasts in 1959.

Rocky Colavito (.276/21/65) finished second in the 1956 AL ROY balloting. He clubbed 40+ moon-shots and drove in 100+ runs in successive years (1958-59). Colavito paced the AL with a .620 SLG in '58 (.620) and 42 home runs in '59, placing in the top 4 in the MVP voting in both campaigns. Don Mossi saved 11 games in '56 and produced a 17-9 mark with a 3.36 ERA and 1.136 WHIP in 1959.

The best of a mediocre lot in '59, the Tribe played .500 ball yet managed to capture the American League flag by one game. Sam "Toothpick" Jones (21-15, 2.83) placed second in the Cy Young voting in 1959, leading the circuit in wins, ERA and shutouts. Jim Perry (12-10, 2.65) was the runner-up in the 1959 AL ROY balloting. The Indians would fail to win another division title until 1978 and spent the next 36 years in pursuit of its next pennant.

Win Shares > 20	Single-Season	1940-1959
Eddie Robinson - 1B (CLE)	Gus Zernial - LF (CLE) x2	Bob Lemon - SP (CLE) x7
Bobby Avila - 2B (CLE) x4	Al E. Smith - LF (CLE)	Johnny Schmitz - SP (CLE)
Lou Boudreau - SS (CLE) x8	Jim Gleeson - CF (CLE)	Mike E. Garcia - SP (CLE) x3
Oscar Grimes - 3B (CLE)	Larry Doby - CF (CLE) x8	Sal Maglie - SP (CLE)
Al Rosen - 3B (CLE) x5	Jeff Heath - RF (CLE)	Allie Reynolds - SP (CLE)
Minnie Minoso - 3B (CLE)	Tommy Henrich - RF (CLE) x5	Herb Score - SP (CLE)
Ray Boone - 3B (CLE) x3	Hank Edwards - RF (CLE)	Brooks Lawrence - SP (CLE)
Sherm Lollar - C (CLE) x3	Al E. Smith - RF (CLE) x2	Sam P. Jones - SP (CLE) x2
Dale Mitchell - LF (CLE) x3	Rocky Colavito - RF (CLE) x4	Mike E. Garcia - SW (CLE)
Minnie Minoso - LF (CLE) x9	Thornton Lee - SP (CLE)	Sal Maglie - SW (CLE)
Gene Woodling - LF (CLE) x4	Steve Gromek - SP (CLE) x2	

Year/Team	OPW%	PW	PL	APW%	AW	AL	Diff+/-
1960 CLE	0.498	77	77	0.494	76	78	-0.004
1961 CLE	0.536	87	75	0.484	78	83	-0.052
1962 CLE	0.487	79	83	0.494	80	82	0.007
1963 CLE	0.496	80	82	0.488	79	83	-0.009
1964 CLE	0.494	80	82	0.488	79	83	-0.006
1965 CLE	0.498	81	81	0.537	87	75	0.039
1966 CLE	0.505	82	80	0.500	81	81	-0.005
1967 CLE	0.492	80	82	0.463	75	87	-0.029
1968 CLE	0.493	80	82	0.534	86	75	0.041
1969 CLE	0.427	69	93	0.385	62	99	-0.042

franchID	OWAR	OWS	AWAR	AWS	WARdiff	WSdiff	P/D/W/F
1960 CLE	34.718	218.614	32.272	227.997	2.446	-9.383	
1961 CLE	33.509	226.193	34.917	233.996	-1.408	-7.802	
1962 CLE	34.594	233.486	28.135	239.996	6.459	-6.510	
1963 CLE	29.427	213.039	34.846	236.997	-5.419	-23.959	
1964 CLE	28.137	198.466	38.647	237.001	-10.510	-38.535	
1965 CLE	39.404	215.290	**50.832**	260.996	-11.427	-45.706	
1966 CLE	**37.665**	216.411	39.650	242.993	-1.985	-26.582	
1967 CLE	35.876	204.968	38.574	225.006	-2.698	-20.038	
1968 CLE	34.962	209.212	41.936	257.998	-6.974	-48.787	
1969 CLE	29.970	185.371	25.656	185.998	4.314	-0.628	

Roger Maris earned consecutive MVP Awards in 1960-61. He belted 39 long balls while leading the American League in RBI (112) and SLG (.581) in 1960. Maris eclipsed Babe Ruth's home run record with 61 four-baggers in '61, plating 142 baserunners and scoring a league-best 132 runs while accruing 35 Win Shares. Colavito blasted 33 round-trippers and drove in 102 runs per year from 1960-66; he paced the AL with 108 RBI and 93 bases on balls in '65. Jim Lemon (.269/38/100) made his lone All-Star appearance in '60 while Minoso (.311/20/105) led the American League with 184 hits and captured his third Gold Glove Award. Al E. Smith batted .315 in '60 and set career-bests in home runs (28) and RBI (93) in 1961.

Jim Perry started and finished the decade with a bang. Perry's 18 victories topped the American League in '60 and in 1969 he fashioned a 20-6 record with a 2.82 ERA. "Toothpick" Sam Jones tallied 18 wins with a 3.19 ERA in 1960, and Gordy Coleman delivered a .282 average with 27 dingers and 86 ribbies from 1961-62. Cleveland posted 87 victories in 1961, coming up three games short of New York. With the exception of its 82-80 season in '66, the Tribe finished at or below .500 for the remainder of the decade. Billy Moran (.282/17/74) received an All-Star invitation in 1962. Floyd Robinson led the League with 45 doubles in '62 along with a .312 batting average, 11 taters and 109 RBI. Hank Aguirre (16-8, 2.21) furnished a league-best ERA and joined Moran on the All-Star team. Bill Dailey notched 21 saves with a 1.99 ERA in 1963. Mudcat Grant (21-7, 3.30) amassed the most victories and shutouts in '65.

"Sudden" Sam McDowell was effectively wild. Although he allowed 100+ bases on balls in eight consecutive seasons (1964-71), McDowell led the League with a 2.18 ERA and 325 strikeouts in 1965. He delivered a 1.81 ERA in '68 and struck out 200+ batters in 6 straight years (1965-70). Tommy John fashioned a 2.71 ERA with a 1.172 WHIP in his first five campaigns (1965-69). John (10-5, 1.98) received an All-Star invite in 1968. Tommie Agee (.273/22/86) won the Rookie of the Year Award in 1966. After two off-years Agee rebounded with a .271 average, 26 four-baggers and 97 runs scored in '69. Sonny Siebert produced consecutive 16-8 records in 1965-66, earning an All-Star invite in '66. Steve Hargan (14-13, 2.62) posted 6 shutouts in '67 and was rewarded with a trip to the Mid-Summer Classic.

Luis Tiant (21-9, 1.60) delivered career-bests in ERA, shutouts (9), strikeouts (264) and WHIP (0.871) in 1968. "El Tiante" appeared in his first All-Star game and finished fifth in the AL MVP voting. The League caught up to Tiant in '69 as he posted a 9-20 record while yielding the most home runs (37) and bases on balls (129). Ron Taylor (2.70, 13 SV), Steve Hamilton (2.13, 11 SV) and Vicente Romo (1.60, 12 SV) solidified the bullpen in '68. Lou Piniella (.282/11/68) secured 1969 AL ROY honors; nevertheless Cleveland slumped to a 69-93 record.

Year/Team	OPW%	PW	PL	APW%	AW	AL	Diff+/-
1970 CLE	0.494	80	82	0.469	76	86	-0.025
1971 CLE	0.377	61	101	0.370	60	102	-0.006
1972 CLE	0.460	74	88	0.462	72	84	0.002
1973 CLE	0.435	70	92	0.438	71	91	0.003
1974 CLE	0.485	79	83	0.475	77	85	-0.009

1975 CLE	0.430	70	92	0.497	79	80	0.067
1976 CLE	0.514	83	79	0.509	81	78	-0.004
1977 CLE	0.484	78	84	0.441	71	90	-0.043
1978 CLE	0.531 D	86	76	0.434	69	90	-0.097
1979 CLE	0.510	83	79	0.503	81	80	-0.007

franchID	OWAR	OWS	AWAR	AWS	WARdiff	WSdiff	P/D/W/F
1970 CLE	**38.631**	211.289	37.323	228.000	1.308	-16.711	
1971 CLE	19.102	156.406	18.354	180.000	0.748	-23.594	
1972 CLE	23.435	171.941	26.651	216.000	-3.216	-44.059	
1973 CLE	26.441	176.806	27.440	213.007	-0.999	-36.201	
1974 CLE	22.337	178.896	26.500	230.996	-4.163	-52.101	
1975 CLE	18.848	166.802	34.654	236.998	-15.807	-70.196	
1976 CLE	33.544	218.250	39.499	243.002	-5.955	-24.752	
1977 CLE	29.361	192.276	33.643	213.000	-4.282	-20.724	
1978 CLE	29.497	209.596	32.046	207.004	-2.550	2.592	D
1979 CLE	35.695	232.583	35.045	243.002	0.650	-10.419	

Agee (.286/24/75) set career-bests in runs scored (107), hits (182) and doubles (30) in 1970. He pilfered 31 bags and won his second Gold Glove Award. Ray Fosse (.307/18/61) earned All-Star invitations in 1970 and '71. Jim Perry (24-12, 3.04) earned the 1970 AL Cy Young Award, completing 13 of 40 starts with a 1.130 WHIP and amassed 17 victories with a 2.96 ERA in 1974.

McDowell (20-12, 2.92) placed third in the Cy Young balloting in '70 as he led the circuit with 305 innings pitched, 131 bases on balls and 304 strikeouts. Siebert averaged a 16-9 mark with a 3.16 ERA and 1.194 WHIP from 1970-71. Mudcat Grant assumed the closer's role in 1970, saving 24 games with a 1.86 ERA.

Chris Chambliss (.275/9/48) won the AL Rookie of the Year Award in 1971. Chambliss batted .293 and drove in 96 runs, placing fifth in the MVP balloting in '76. Mike Hedlund posted a 15-9 record with a 2.71 ERA in 1971. Cleveland labored to a 61-101 mark in 1971, and tied for the worst record in Tribe history since 1950. The Tribe remained in the American League East basement through '73.

Lou Piniella clubbed 33 two-base hits and batted .312 in '72 and produced a .330 BA as a part-timer in '77. Dick Tidrow accumulated 14 victories with a 2.77 ERA in '72. Luis Tiant paced the American League with a 1.91 ERA in 1972. "El Tiante" rendered a 20-13 mark with a 3.31 ERA and 1.185 WHIP from 1973-76. Dave Nelson swiped 94 bases from 1972-73 and John Lowenstein nabbed 36 bags in '74.

The Indians posted 83 victories in '76, finishing only two games behind the Orioles for the division title. Jim Kern received a promotion to late-inning work in '76 and provided 10 wins and 19 saves per year from 1976-79. Kern (13-5, 1.57) saved 29 games and placed fourth in the '79 Cy Young balloting. Tommy John (20-7, 2.78) placed runner-up in the Cy Young balloting in '77 and repeated the feat in '79 with a record of 21-9 and a 2.96 ERA.

In 1978 the Tribe amassed 86 victories, edging the Brew Crew for the AL East crown. Dennis Eckersley (20-8, 2.99) finished fourth in the 1978 AL Cy Young voting. Buddy Bell (.299/18/101) delivered 200 base hits, 42 doubles and earned the first of six consecutive Gold Gloves in '79. Nine seasons on the fielding WS and WAR leader boards (second all-time behind Brooks Robinson) validate Bell's superior defense as a third baseman. Alfredo Griffin was rewarded with the 1979 AL ROY hardware after hitting .287 with 10 triples and 21 stolen bases. Phil Seghi held the title of Indians' GM for 12 years (1973-1985). Cleveland's draft selections during Seghi's administration averaged only 70 Career Total Win Shares.

Win Shares > 20	Single-Season	1960-1979
Chris Chambliss - 1B (CLE) x2	Floyd Robinson - LF (CLE)	Jim Perry - SP (CLE) x2
Billy Moran - 2B (CLE)	Lou Piniella - LF (CLE)	Sonny Siebert - SP (CLE)
Max Alvis - 3B (CLE)	Tommie Agee - CF (CLE) x3	Dennis Eckersley - SP (CLE)
Buddy Bell - 3B (CLE) x6	Roger Maris - RF (CLE) x4	x2
Ray Fosse - C (CLE)	Floyd Robinson - RF (CLE) x3	Tommy John - SP (CLE)
Jim Lemon - LF (CLE)	Sam McDowell - SP (CLE) x4	Hank Aguirre - SW (CLE)
Rocky Colavito - LF (CLE) x3	Luis Tiant - SP (CLE) x4	Jim Kern - RP (CLE)

Year/Team	OPW%	PW	PL	APW%	AW	AL	Diff+/-
1980 CLE	0.475	77	85	0.494	79	81	0.019
1981 CLE	0.400 F	65	97	0.505	52	51	0.105
1982 CLE	0.458	74	88	0.481	78	84	0.023
1983 CLE	0.407 F	66	96	0.432	70	92	0.025
1984 CLE	0.475 F	77	85	0.463	75	87	-0.012
1985 CLE	0.376 F	61	101	0.370	60	102	-0.006
1986 CLE	0.469 F	76	86	0.519	84	78	0.050
1987 CLE	0.497 F	80	82	0.377	61	101	-0.120
1988 CLE	0.461	75	87	0.481	78	84	0.020
1989 CLE	0.487	79	83	0.451	73	89	-0.036

franchID	OWAR	OWS	AWAR	AWS	WARdiff	WSdiff	P/D/W/F
1980 CLE	37.655	235.713	36.848	237.000	0.807	-1.286	
1981 CLE	22.673	149.801	25.531	155.999	-2.859	-6.198	F
1982 CLE	38.464	231.523	38.359	233.994	0.105	-2.471	
1983 CLE	28.382	219.053	32.263	209.998	-3.881	9.056	F
1984 CLE	30.196	218.671	35.288	224.995	-5.092	-6.324	F
1985 CLE	27.470	195.219	21.848	179.999	5.622	15.220	F
1986 CLE	32.205	236.809	33.916	252.006	-1.711	-15.197	F
1987 CLE	34.480	236.774	22.372	182.994	12.108	53.780	F
1988 CLE	37.134	246.097	32.913	233.996	4.221	12.101	
1989 CLE	34.089	230.590	32.364	218.992	1.725	11.598	

Cleveland was mired in the American League East basement for the entire decade of the Eighties, unable to attain the .500 mark. The club's best effort was a third place finish in 1989 (79-83). The Indians failed to reach the BFP requirements from 1981-87 excluding the 1982 season. John (22-9, 3.43) led the League with 6 shutouts and placed fourth in the 1980 AL Cy Young balloting. Bell (.329/17/83) supplied his highest BA while backstops Rick Cerone (.277/14/85) and Ron Hassey (.318/8/65) enjoyed career years. Ed Farmer saved 30 contests and posted a 3.34 ERA. Tidrow made a league-high 84 relief appearances in '80 after vulturing 13 relief wins during the previous year. In 1982 Lowenstein belted 24 long balls and batted .320 in a platoon role.

Pedro Guerrero finished fourth or better in the MVP balloting 4 times in the Eighties. Guerrero (.320/33/87) topped the circuit in OBP (.422) and SLG (.577) in 1985 and smashed a league-leading 42 doubles while knocking in 117 runs in '89. Von Hayes pilfered 48 bases in 1984 and paced the League with 107 runs and 46 two-baggers in 1986. Cory Snyder (.272/24/69) placed fourth in the 1986 AL Rookie of the Year voting. Greg Swindell amassed 18 victories and completed 12 games with a 3.20 ERA in 1988, earning his lone All-Star appearance in the following campaign. Eckersley was converted to relief pitching in 1987. In '88 "Eck" led the circuit with 45 saves and placed runner-up in the Cy Young voting. He saved 33 contests with a 1.56 ERA and 0.607 WHIP in '89, walking only 3 batters in 57 2/3 innings! GM Hank Peters and Scouting Director Chet Montgomery rewarded the Indians' faithful with a tremendous harvest in the 1989 Amateur Draft. Jim Thome and Brian S. Giles attained superstar status and the group yielded 957 Career Total Win Shares and 142 Career Total WAR.

Year/Team	OPW%	PW	PL	APW%	AW	AL	Diff+/-
1990 CLE	0.421 F	68	94	0.475	77	85	0.054
1991 CLE	0.401 F	65	97	0.352	57	105	-0.049
1992 CLE	0.519 F	84	78	0.469	76	86	-0.050
1993 CLE	0.475 F	77	85	0.469	76	86	-0.006
1994 CLE	0.544 F	88	74	0.584 W	66	47	0.040
1995 CLE	0.580 P	94	68	0.694 P	100	44	0.114
1996 CLE	0.553 F	90	72	0.615 P	99	62	0.062
1997 CLE	0.532 D	86	76	0.534 D	86	75	0.002
1998 CLE	0.542 D	88	74	0.549 D	89	73	0.007
1999 CLE	0.555 P	90	72	0.599 D	97	65	0.043

franchID	OWAR	OWS	AWAR	AWS	WARdiff	WSdiff	P/D/W/F
1990 CLE	26.443	212.422	30.686	231.001	-4.243	-18.580	F
1991 CLE	35.038	216.551	25.279	170.997	9.759	45.554	F
1992 CLE	31.492	231.303	31.492	228.001	0.000	3.302	F
1993 CLE	26.829	219.120	32.300	227.998	-5.471	-8.878	F
1994 CLE	34.751	195.982	35.931	197.994	-1.179	-2.012	F
1995 CLE	**57.589**	**287.401**	**52.841**	**300.003**	4.748	-12.602	P
1996 CLE	55.086	289.949	**53.307**	**297.001**	1.780	-7.052	F
1997 CLE	49.645	264.974	43.262	258.003	6.383	6.971	D
1998 CLE	49.122	289.082	42.317	267.003	6.805	22.079	D
1999 CLE	53.273	**308.505**	49.140	290.996	4.133	17.509	P

Cleveland suffered through a talent drought in the first half of the Nineties. The Tribe failed to reach the PA (1990-94, 1996) and BFP (1992, 1994) requirements. Kelly Gruber (.274/31/118) earned a Gold Glove at the hot corner in 1990 and placed fourth in the AL MVP voting. Eckersley posted a miniscule 0.61 ERA and a 0.614 WHIP along with 48 saves in 1990. "Eck" received American League MVP and Cy Young honors for his performance in 1992 which included a 7-1 record with a 1.91 ERA and 51 saves.

Charles Nagy anchored the Indians' rotation and received invitations to three All-Star contests in the Nineties. Nagy won 17 games and delivered career-bests in ERA (2.96), WHIP (1.198) and complete games (10) in 1992. He averaged 16 victories per season from 1995-99 despite a 4.46 ERA. Steve Olin notched 29 saves with a 2.34 ERA in '92, and the following year Greg McMichael placed runner-up in the Rookie of the Year race, nailing down 19 saves with a 2.06 ERA in '93.

Albert Belle appeared in 5 consecutive All-Star games from 1993-97. Belle produced a .302 average with 39 doubles, 40 circuit clouts, 125 ribbies and 102 runs scored. He topped the League three times in RBI and placed in the top three in the AL MVP balloting from 1994-96. Belle blasted 52 doubles and 50 home runs in '95 and compiled personal bests with 200 hits, 152 RBI and 37 Win Shares.

The curse finally lifted in 1995 as the Indians bashed their way to the pennant by an eight game margin over the Brewers in the new American League Central division. The Indians' lumberjacks feasted on AL pitching in the latter half of the decade, posting franchise records in batting average (.285), OBP (.375) and SLG (.490) in 1995. Manny Ramirez placed third in the 1999 AL MVP balloting as he led the circuit with 165 RBI and a .613 SLG. He mashed 36 doubles, 36 round-trippers and drove in 123 runs per season from 1995-99 while batting .314 with 103 runs scored. In the same timeframe, Jim Thome batted .296 with 33 big-flies, 97 ribbies and 102 runs.

The Tribe took the division title in '97 by six games over the Pale Hose, repeating the feat in 1998. Jeff Shaw topped the circuit with 42 saves in 1997 and followed up with a 2.12 ERA, 48 saves and his first All-Star appearance in '98. Bartolo Colon (14-9, 3.71) appeared in his first

Midsummer Classic in '98 and provided an 18-5 record with a 3.95 ERA in the subsequent season. Cleveland achieved their second pennant of the decade in 1999. Sean Casey (.322/25/99), Brian S. Giles (.315/39/115) and Richie Sexson (.255/31/116) all exceeded the 25-homer plateau for the first time in their careers. Danny Graves compiled 8 wins and saved 27 contests.

Year/Team	OPW%	PW	PL	APW%	AW	AL	Diff+/-
2000 CLE	0.525 D	85	77	0.556	90	72	0.031
2001 CLE	0.527 D	85	77	0.562 D	91	71	0.035
2002 CLE	0.495	80	82	0.457	74	88	-0.038
2003 CLE	0.502	81	81	0.420	68	94	-0.083
2004 CLE	0.553 P	90	72	0.494	80	82	-0.059
2005 CLE	0.516 D	84	78	0.574	93	69	0.058
2006 CLE	0.501	81	81	0.481	78	84	-0.020
2007 CLE	0.504	82	80	0.593 D	96	66	0.089
2008 CLE	0.504	82	80	0.500	81	81	-0.004
2009 CLE	0.439	71	91	0.401	65	97	-0.038
2010 CLE	0.483	78	84	0.426	69	93	-0.057
2011 CLE	0.450	73	89	0.494	80	82	0.044
2012 CLE	0.423 F	68	94	0.420	68	94	-0.003
2013 CLE	0.469 F	76	86	0.568 W	92	70	0.099

franchID	OWAR	OWS	AWAR	AWS	WARdiff	WSdiff	P/D/W/F
2000 CLE	49.110	289.713	**53.650**	270.002	-4.540	19.711	D
2001 CLE	46.178	277.492	49.758	272.996	-3.580	4.496	D
2002 CLE	43.406	259.196	29.503	221.997	13.904	37.199	
2003 CLE	41.685	262.595	26.747	203.998	14.938	58.597	
2004 CLE	**49.872**	**296.142**	40.332	240.000	9.540	56.142	P
2005 CLE	47.764	300.279	**52.125**	279.009	-4.361	21.270	D
2006 CLE	44.020	272.579	42.751	234.003	1.269	38.576	
2007 CLE	42.468	273.877	45.967	288.005	-3.499	-14.129	
2008 CLE	37.418	250.782	38.747	243.000	-1.329	7.782	
2009 CLE	27.898	204.756	28.263	194.998	-0.364	9.758	
2010 CLE	31.141	222.767	24.465	206.959	6.675	15.808	
2011 CLE	36.358	224.834	31.018	239.994	5.341	-15.160	
2012 CLE	25.528	184.059	18.733	203.997	6.795	-19.938	F
2013 CLE	28.049	211.349	39.038	276.005	-10.989	-64.655	F

The Tribe outlasted the Pale Hose by a single game in 2000, taking the division for the fourth year in a row. Ramirez hit .319 with 37 four-ply swats and 116 RBI from 2000-08. "Man-Ram" paced the League with a .349 BA in '02 and 43 home runs in '04. Thome averaged .280 with 45 clouts, 117 ribbies, 103 runs scored and 113 bases on balls from 2000-04. He walloped a career-high 52 big-flies in '02 and tied Belle for second highest Win Shares total in team history (37).

Sexson belted 33 long balls and knocked in 99 runs per season from 2000-06. Giles blasted 37 two-baggers and 37 round-trippers per year (2000-02) while batting .308 with 107 RBI and 107 runs scored. Graves saved 31 games per year from 2000-2002 and collected 41 saves in 2004.

In 2001 the squad earned its fifth straight Central Division title. C.C. Sabathia (17-5, 4.39) placed runner-up in the 2001 AL ROY balloting and produced 19 victories, leading the League with 241 innings pitched en route to a Cy Young Award in 2007. From 2007-10, Sabathia averaged a record of 19-8 with 214 whiffs, 3.11 ERA and a 1.148 WHIP. Shaw posted 43 saves with a 1.085 WHIP in 2001, earning his second All-Star invitation.

Colon delivered a 20-8 record with a 2.93 ERA in 2002 after striking out 200+ batters in the previous two campaigns. He was crowned AL Cy Young winner in 2005, tallying 21 victories with a career-best WHIP of 1.159. Paul Byrd (17-11, 3.90) enjoyed his best season in 2002, posting his best WHIP (1.147).

Chicago edged Cleveland and Minnesota in '03. The Indians stormed back in 2004, winning the American League pennant with 90 victories. Sean Casey (.324/24/99) hammered 44 doubles and scored 101 runs in 2004, and Jaret Wright (15-8, 3.28) achieved short-term success the same year. Victor Martinez provided additional thump, batting .302 with 37 doubles, 21 dingers and 99 RBI from 2004-07.

The Tribe survived a battle with the Twins to take the Central crown in '05. Danys Baez accumulated 32 saves per season in a three-year stretch from 2003-05, topping out at 41 saves in '05. Roberto H. Hernandez, playing under the assumed name of Fausto Carmona, rebounded from a miserable rookie campaign to place fourth in the 2007 AL Cy Young voting. Hernandez compiled a 19-8 mark with a 3.06 ERA.

Jhonny Peralta (.276/23/89) set career highs with 42 doubles and 104 runs scored in 2008 while Willy Taveras topped the leaderboards with 68 stolen bases. Cleveland descended to the depths of the division in 2009, limping home with 71 wins. Inept mound work was the chief culprit as the staff compiled a franchise-worst ERA of 4.87.

Win Shares > 20	Single-Season	1980-2013
Von Hayes - 1B (CLE) x2	Victor Martinez - C (CLE) x2	Manny Ramirez - RF (CLE) x6
Pedro Guerrero - 1B (CLE)	John Lowenstein - LF (CLE)	Albert Belle - RF (CLE)
Jim Thome - 1B (CLE) x8	Pedro Guerrero - LF (CLE) x2	Brian S. Giles - RF (CLE) x3
Sean Casey - 1B (CLE) x2	Albert Belle - LF (CLE) x5	Manny Ramirez - DH (CLE)
Richie Sexson - 1B (CLE) x2	Brian S. Giles - LF (CLE) x2	Jim Thome - DH (CLE)
Jason Kipnis – 2B (CLE)	Manny Ramirez - LF (CLE) x5	Victor Martinez - DH (CLE)
Jhonny Peralta - SS (CLE) x4	Von Hayes - CF (CLE)	Charles Nagy - SP (CLE)
Pedro Guerrero - 3B (CLE) x2	Brian S. Giles - CF (CLE) x2	Roberto H. Hernandez - SP (CLE)
Kelly Gruber - 3B (CLE) x2	Pedro Guerrero - RF (CLE)	C.C. Sabathia - SP (CLE)
Jim Thome - 3B (CLE) x2	Von Hayes - RF (CLE)	
Rick Cerone - C (CLE)		

Note: 4000 PA or BFP to qualify, except during strike-shortened seasons
(1972 = 3800, 1981 & 1994 = 2700, 1995 = 3500) and 154-game schedule (3800)
- failed to qualify: 1901, 1916-1917, 1919-1920, 1981, 1983-1987, 1990-1994, 1996

Indians All-Time "Originals" Roster

Fred Abbott	Harry Eells	Larry Kopf	Jose Ramirez
Al Aber	Bruce Egloff	Kevin Kouzmanoff	Manny Ramirez
Bill Abernathie	Hack Eibel	Tom Kramer	Ken Ramos
Bert Adams	Ike Eichrodt	Gene Krapp	Rudy Regalado
Tommie Agee	George Ellison	Ernie Krueger	Herman Reich
Hank Aguirre	Alan Embree	Jack Kubiszyn	Duke Reilley
Vic Albury	Red Embree	Bub Kuhn	Art Reinholz
Hugh Alexander	Luis Encarnacion	Kenny Kuhn	Bugs Reisigl
Andy Allanson	Jim Eschen	Duane Kuiper	Ken Retzer
Bob Gray Allen	Ferd Eunick	Hal Kurtz	Argenis Reyes
Cody Allen	Joe Evans	Bob Kuzava	Allie Reynolds
Beau Allred	Tony Faeth	Guy Lacy	Kevin Rhomberg
Joe Altobelli	Jerry Fahr	Doyle Lade	Paul Rigdon
Max Alvis	Harry Fanwell	Aaron Laffey	David Riske

Larry Andersen	Ed Farmer	Otis Lambeth	Reggie Ritter
Chris Archer	John E. Farrell	Tom Lampkin	Jim Rittwage
Alan Ashby	Bob Feller	Grover Land	Roberto Rivera
Michael Aubrey	Wes Ferrell	Matt Langwell	Eddie Robinson
Rick Austin	Jack Fimple	Juan Lara	Floyd Robinson
Bruce Aven	Gus Fisher	Bill Lattimore	Bill K. Rodgers
Earl D. Averill	Paul Fitzke	Brooks Lawrence	Josh Rodriguez
Earl H. Averill	Ray Flanigan	Jim Lawrence	Jose Roman
Bobby Avila	Ted Ford	Roxie Lawson	Niuman Romero
Mike Joseph Bacsik	Jerry Fosnow	Emil Leber	Ramon Romero
Danys Baez	Ray Fosse	Gene Leek	Vicente Romo
Steve Bailey	Ed Foster	Thornton Lee	Hector Rondon
Bock Baker	Ben Francisco	Norm Lehr	Al Rosen
Frank Baker	Joe Frazier	Nemo Leibold	Claude Rossman
Howard Baker	Vern Freiburger	Bob Lemon	Bob Rothel
Mark Ballinger	Jim Fridley	Jim Lemon	Luther Roy
Chris Bando	Buck Frierson	Eddie Leon	Dick Rozek
Walter Barbare	Johnson Fry	Curt Leskanic	Lloyd Russell
Jap Barbeau	Vern Fuller	Jesse Levis	Hank Ruszkowski
Jeff Barkley	Ralph Gagliano	Dutch Levsen	Jim Rutherford
Les Barnhart	Steve Gajkowski	Jensen Lewis	Buddy Ryan
Brian Barton	Milt Galatzer	Mark Lewis	Jack Ryan
Jim Baskette	Denny Galehouse	Scott E. Lewis	C.C. Sabathia
Johnny Bassler	Dave Gallagher	Glenn J. Liebhardt	Danny Salazar
Ray Bates	Jackie Gallagher	Carl Lind	Jose G. Santiago
Johnny Beall	Shorty Gallagher	Bill Lindsay	Rick Sawyer
Belve Bean	Bob Garbark	Jim Lindsey	Richie Scheinblum
Kevin Bearse	Mike E. Garcia	Fred Link	Johnny Schmitz
Chris Beasley	Ray Gardner	Pete Lister	Dave Schuler
Joe Becker	Ryan Garko	Paddy Livingston	Bill Schwartz
Gene Bedford	Clarence Garrett	Bobby Locke	Herb Score
Phil Bedgood	John Gaub	Stu Locklin	Luke Scott
Buddy Bell	Greek George	Sherm Lollar	Marco Scutaro
David Bell	George Gerken	Albie Lopez	Rudy Seanez
Albert Belle	Brian S. Giles	Ramon Lopez	Bob Seeds
Gary Bell	Johnny Gill	John Lowenstein	Pat Seerey
Rob Belloir	Chris Gimenez	Hector Luna	Ted Sepkowski
Harry Bemis	Tinsley Ginn	Jack Lundbom	Joe Sewell
Ray Benge	Luke Glavenich	Gordy Lund	Luke Sewell
Henry Benn	Mike Glavine	Harry Lunte	Richie Sexson
Boze Berger	Jim Gleeson	Al Luplow	Wally Shaner
Heinie Berger	Sal Gliatto	Rube Lutzke	Joe Shaute
Al Bergman	Jonah Goldman	Russ Lyon	Jeff Shaw
Josh A. Billings	Stan Goletz	Chuck Machemehl	Danny Shay
Steve Biras	Jeanmar Gomez	Ray Mack	Pete Shields
Joe Birmingham	Luis A. Gonzalez	Ever Magallanes	Jim Shilling
Lloyd Bishop	Orlando Gonzalez	Sal Maglie	Ginger Shinault
Fred Blanding	Lee Gooch	Harry Malmberg	Bill Shipke
Johnny Blatnik	Al Gould	Rick Manning	Milt Shoffner
John Bohnet	Rod Graber	Cliff Mapes	Paul Shuey
Cecil Bolton	Peaches Graham	Roger Maris	Sonny Siebert
Walt Bond	Tommy Gramly	J.D. Martin	Harry Simpson
Juan Bonilla	Jack Graney	Tony Martinez	Duke Sims
Bill Bonness	Eddie Grant	Victor Martinez	Tony Sipp
Zeke Bonura	Mudcat Grant	Willie Martinez	Carl Sitton

Red Booles	Danny Graves	Phil Masi	Joe Skalski
Ray Boone	Dave Gregg	Carl Mathias	Brian Slocum
Lou Boudreau	Vean Gregg	Julius Matos	Al E. Smith
Abe Bowman	Alfredo Griffin	Mike Matthews	Charlie E. Smith
Gary Boyd	Oscar Grimes	Matt McBride	Clay Smith
Jack Bracken	Steve Gromek	Ralph McCabe	Elmer Smith
Jack Bradley	Lee Gronkiewicz	Mike W. McCormick	Tommy Smith
Dick Braggins	Ernest Groth	Frank McCrea	Brad Snyder
Russell Branyan	Harvey Grubb	Jim McDonnell	Cory Snyder
Bert Brenner	Kelly Gruber	John Joseph	Bill Sodd
Tom Brennan	Pedro Guerrero	McDonald	Zach Sorensen
Lynn Brenton	Lou Guisto	Sam McDowell	Chick Sorrells
Bernardo Brito	Tom Gulley	T. J. McFarland	Billy Southworth
Jack Brohamer	Red Gunkel	Jim McGuire	Jeremy Sowers
Herman Bronkie	Jeremy Guthrie	Archie McKain	Joe Sprinz
Clint Brown	Odell Hale	Hal McKain	Freddy Spurgeon
Dick Brown	John Halla	Greg McMichael	Jason Stanford
Jamie Brown	Doc Hamann	Tom McMillan	Dolly Stark
Jordan Brown	Steve Hamilton	Harry McNeal	George Starnagle
Larry Brown	Jack Hammond	Pat McNulty	Bill Steen
Jim Bruske	Garry Hancock	Luis Medina	Bryan Stephens
Clay Bryant	Rich Hand	Moxie Meixell	Riggs Stephenson
Mark Budzinski	Mel Harder	Mitch Meluskey	Dick Stigman
Johnny Burnett	Jason Hardtke	Brett Merriman	Kelly Stinnett
Cory Burns	Carroll Hardy	Bud Messenger	George Stovall
Hank Butcher	Jack D. Hardy	Dewey Metivier	Jesse Stovall
Paul Byrd	Steve Hargan	Jake W. Miller	Jake Striker
Fernando Cabrera	Spec Harkness	Ray Miller	Floyd Stromme
Jose Cabrera	Billy Harrell	Frank Mills	Charley Suche
Joe Caffie	Billy Harris	Jack Mills	Lefty Sullivan
Ben Caffyn	Pep Harris	Al Milnar	Steve Sundra
Wayne Cage	Oscar Harstad	Pete Milne	Greg Swindell
Bruce Caldwell	Bruce Hartford	Don Minnick	Kazuhito Tadano
Dave Callahan	Luther Harvel	Minnie Minoso	Brian Tallet
Paul Calvert	Ron Hassey	Dale Mitchell	Julian Tavarez
Lou Camilli	Arthur Hauger	Willie Mitchell	Willy Taveras
Soup Campbell	Wynn Hawkins	Dave Mlicki	Dwight Taylor
Willie Canate	Howie Haworth	Dustan Mohr	Pete Taylor
Kit Carson	Von Hayes	Blas Monaco	Ron Taylor
Paul Carter	Jerad Head	Ed Montague	Al Tedrow
Paul Casanova	Fran Healy	Leo Moon	J.J. Thobe
Sean Casey	Jeff Heath	Earl Moore	Art Thomason
Pete Center	Neal Heaton	Jim Moore	Carl Thomas
Ed Cermak	Mike Hedlund	Billy Moran	Fred Thomas
Rick Cerone	Jim Hegan	Ed Morgan	Jim Thome
Chris Chambliss	Jack Heidemann	Jeff Moronko	Derek Thompson
Ray Chapman	Rick Heiserman	Guy Morton	Rich N. Thompson
Lonnie Chisenhall	Hank Helf	Don Mossi	Jack Thoney
Ryan Church	Bernie Henderson	Gordie Mueller	Luis Tiant
Al Cihocki	Tim Hendryx	Edward Mujica	Dick Tidrow
Uke Clanton	Phil Hennigan	Oscar Munoz	Joe Tipton
Bob Clark	Tommy Henrich	Ray Murray	Chick Tolson
Dave Clark	Earl Henry	Jeff Mutis	Dick Tomanek
Ginger Clark	Fernando Hernandez	Lou Nagelsen	Josh Tomlin
Nig Clarke	Jackie Hernandez	Russ Nagelson	Wyatt Toregas

Watty Clark	Roberto H. Hernandez	Charles Nagy	Red Torkelson
Ty Cline	Alex Herrera	Hal Naragon	Eider Torres
Rocky Colavito	Frank Herrmann	Ray Narleski	Hal Trosky
Vince Colbert	Otto Hess	Ken Nash	Quincy Trouppe
Ed Cole	Jack Hickey	Mike Naymick	Eddie Turchin
Gordy Coleman	Bob Higgins	Troy Neel	Dave Tyriver
Hap Collard	Mark Higgins	Jim Neher	George Uhle
Bartolo Colon	Oral Hildebrand	Dave Nelson	Willie Underhill
Bruce Connatser	Chuck Hiller	Milo Netzel	Jerry Upp
Jose Constanza	Herbert Hill	Jeff Newman	Bill Upton
Jack Conway	Hugh Hill	Dolan Nichols	Dutch Ussat
Herb Conyers	Harry Hinchman	Rod Nichols	Al Van Camp
Vic Correll	Tommy Hinzo	Milt Nielsen	Jonathan Van Every
Tim Costo	Johnny Hodapp	Russ Nixon	Roberto Vargas
Howard Craghead	Gomer Hodge	Junior Noboa	Dike Varney
Carlos Crawford	Tex Hoffman	Jim Norris	Cal Vasbinder
Bill Cristall	Harry Hogan	Jon Nunnally	Dave Vineyard
Frank Cross	Eddie Hohnhorst	Ivan Ochoa	Rube Vinson
Jim Crowell	Joe Horgan	Paul O'Dea	Joe Vosmik
Trevor Crowe	Dave Hoskins	Ted Odenwald	Neil Wagner
Eric Crozier	Dixie M. Howell	Chad Ogea	Howard Wakefield
Nick N. Cullop	Dave Hudgens	Steve Olin	Ed Walker
Al Cypert	Willis Hudlin	Dave Oliver	Mike C. Walker
Bill Dailey	David Huff	Ivy Olson	Roy Walker
Bud Daley	Roy Hughes	Dan Osinski	Norm Wallen
Lee Dashner	Johnny Humphries	Harry Ostdiek	Bill Wambsganss
Homer Davidson	Bill Hunter	Harry Otis	Frank Wayenberg
Bill Davis	James Hurst	Johnny Oulliber	Roy Weatherly
Jason Davis	Joe Inglett	Pat Paige	Floyd Weaver
Joe Dawson	Happy Iott	Satchel Paige	Jim B. Weaver
Hank DeBerry	Tommy Irwin	Sam Parrilla	Ray Webster
Mike de la Hoz	Hank Izquierdo	Ben Paschal	Ralph Weigel
Roland de la Maza	Maicer Izturis	Mike Paul	Elmer Weingartner
Ben Demott	Damian Jackson	Stan Pawloski	Ollie Welf
Kyle Denney	Art Jacobs	Monte Pearson	Bill Wertz
Otto Denning	Lefty James	Roger Peckinpaugh	Hi West
Sean Depaula	Tex Jeanes	Ken Penner	Lee Wheat
Shorty Desjardien	Mike Jeffcoat	Jhonny Peralta	Ed R. Wheeler
George DeTore	Dan Jessee	Luis Perdomo	Alex White
Jim R. Devlin	Larry Johnson	Rafael Perez	Elder White
Einar Diaz	Rankin Johnson	Bill Perrin	Hal White
George Dickerson	Tommy John	George Perring	Larry White
Paul Dicken	Sam Jones	Chan Perry	Matt White
Don Dillard	Sam P. Jones	Herb Perry	Mike White
Harley Dillinger	Sheldon Jones	Jim Perry	Darrell Whitmore
Jerry Dipoto	Scott Jordan	Robert Person	Kevin Wickander
Walt Doan	Addie Joss	Vinnie Pestano	Sandy Wihtol
Joe Dobson	Josh Judy	Jesse Petty	Eric Wilkins
Larry Doby	Ken Jungels	Larry Pezold	Roy Wilkinson
Mike Donovan	Ike Kahdot	Cord Phelps	Billy Williams
Tom Donovan	George Kahler	Doug Piatt	Les Willis
Bill J. Doran	Nick Kahl	Horacio Pina	Matt T. Williams
Red Dorman	Bob Kaiser	Lou Piniella	Papa Williams
Gus Dorner	Paul Kardow	Stan Pitula	Artie Wilson
Cal Dorsett		Ray Poat	Jim G. Wilson

Logan Drake	Tom Kelley	Lou Polchow	Fred Winchell
Tom Drake	Ken Keltner	Drew Pomeranz	Scott Winchester
Ryan Drese	Jim Kern	Dave Pope	Ralph Winegarner
Tim Drew	Jack Kibble	Dick Porter	Ernie Wolf
Travis Driskill	Ed Killian	Nellie Pott	Gene Woodling
George Dunlop	Dennis Kinney	Bill Pounds	Chuck Workman
Steve Dunning	Jason Kipnis	Mike Powers	Ab Wright
Jerry Dybzinski	Harry Kirsch	Tot Pressnell	Jaret Wright
Luke Easter	Billy Klaus	Jackie Price	Lucky Wright
Ted Easterly	Hal Kleine	Zach Putnam	Joe Wyatt
Dennis Eckersley	Steve James Kline	Frankie Pytlak	Earl Yingling
Eddie Edmonson	Cotton Knaupp	Joe Rabbitt	George Young
George Edmondson	Bill Knickerbocker	Tom Raftery	Carl Yowell
Doc Edwards	Ray Knode	Eric Raich	Oscar Zamora
Hank Edwards	Masahide Kobayashi	Larry Raines	Gus Zernial
Jim Joe Edwards	Elmer Koestner	Jason Rakers	Bill Zuber
Mike D. Edwards	Dick Kokos	Alex Ramirez	

Year/Team	OPW%	PW	PL	APW%	AW	AL	Diff+/-
1977 SEA	0.000 F	0	0	0.395	64	98	0.000
1978 SEA	0.000 F	0	0	0.350	56	104	0.000
1979 SEA	0.000 F	0	0	0.414	67	95	0.000
1980 SEA	0.000 F	0	0	0.361	59	103	0.000
1981 SEA	0.000 F	0	0	0.404	44	65	0.000
1982 SEA	0.463 F	75	87	0.469	76	86	0.006
1983 SEA	0.402 F	65	97	0.370	60	102	-0.031
1984 SEA	0.465 F	75	87	0.457	74	88	-0.009
1985 SEA	0.506 F	82	80	0.457	74	88	-0.049
1986 SEA	0.461	75	87	0.414	67	95	-0.048
1987 SEA	0.487	79	83	0.481	78	84	-0.005
1988 SEA	0.468	76	86	0.422	68	93	-0.046
1989 SEA	0.543	88	74	0.451	73	89	-0.092

franchID	OWAR	OWS	AWAR	AWS	WARdiff	WSdiff	P/D/W/F
1977 SEA	77.409	343.098	19.256	191.997	58.154	151.100	F
1978 SEA	60.307	249.956	20.123	168.005	40.184	81.952	F
1979 SEA	54.673	226.071	33.098	201.000	21.575	25.071	F
1980 SEA	32.173	182.546	19.888	177.001	12.285	5.545	F
1981 SEA	-1.287	94.783	22.509	131.999	-23.795	-37.216	F
1982 SEA	24.938	170.781	34.061	228.005	-9.124	-57.224	F
1983 SEA	19.035	154.278	22.935	180.002	-3.900	-25.725	F
1984 SEA	33.809	188.590	32.703	222.008	1.107	-33.418	F
1985 SEA	36.829	206.603	33.769	222.002	3.060	-15.400	F
1986 SEA	26.876	181.218	28.997	200.997	-2.121	-19.779	
1987 SEA	33.942	219.881	38.105	234.001	-4.162	-14.121	
1988 SEA	35.622	212.476	35.021	204.005	0.601	8.471	
1989 SEA	35.853	242.665	33.895	219.002	1.958	23.663	

Legend: (P) = Pennant / Most Wins in League (D) = Division Winner (W) = Wild Card Winner (F) = Failed to Qualify

The Junior Circuit expanded to 14 clubs in 1977 as the Seattle Mariners and Toronto Blue Jays entered the League. The Mariners boast the greatest number of designated hitters based on WS>20 (11) and WS>10 (19) seasons among expansion franchises. Seattle center fielders maintain a three-way tie for the lead with 16 WS>20 seasons while the club's shortstops place second with 11.

Enrique Romo notched 10 wins and 10 saves per season with a 3.15 ERA from 1977-79. Bud H. Black and Mike Moore joined the rotation in '82. Black established career-highs with 17 wins, a 3.12 ERA and a 1.128 WHIP in 1984. Moore collected 17 victories and 14 complete games in 1985 along with a 3.46 ERA. He placed third in the 1989 AL Cy Young balloting, posting 19 wins with a 2.61 ERA. Ed Vande Berg (9-4, 2.37) finished fourth in the 1982 AL ROY voting and paced the League with 78 appearances.

The 1983 "Original" Mariners were the first to exceed the minimum 4000 BFP standards, while the offense failed to meet the minimum PA requirements until 1986*. Matt J. Young (11-15, 3.27) earned an All-Star nod in '83. Alvin Davis (.284/27/116) captured the American League Rookie of the Year Award in 1984 and received his only All-Star invite. Davis delivered a .290 average along with 22 long balls and 88 ribbies from 1984-89. Phil Bradley batted .302 over his first four seasons (1984-87), producing his best output in 1985. Bradley crushed 26 round-trippers, pilfered 22 bases and scored 100 runs while hitting at a .300 clip. He swiped 40 bags and crossed home plate 101 times in '87.

Mark Langston (17-10, 3.40) placed runner-up in the 1984 AL Rookie of the Year balloting with a league-high 204 strikeouts. Langston also posted the most whiffs in '86 and '87, averaging 16 victories, 10 complete games, 244 strikeouts and a 3.68 ERA from 1986-89. Jim Presley (.265/27/107) achieved an All-Star appearance in 1986. Second-sacker Harold Reynolds stole 60 bases in '87 and delivered a .300 batting average in 1989. Ivan Calderon blasted 28 wallops and drove in 83 runs in 1987. Scouting director Roger Jongewaard deserves credit for four of Seattle's top five Amateur Drafts (1987, 1991-93). Jongewaard along with GM Dick Balderson selected Ken Griffey Jr. with the first pick of the '87 draft.

Dave Henderson (.304/24/94) posted career-bests in batting average, doubles (38), RBI and runs scored (100) in '88. "Hendu" appeared on the fielding WS and WAR leader boards on five occasions, one fewer than fellow center fielder Ken Griffey Jr. The M's hurlers produced the club's best ERA (3.39) and WHIP (1.287) in 1989. Mike Schooler saved 33 contests and fashioned a 2.81 ERA in '89. Seattle finished above .500 for the first time in '89, finishing only one game behind Kansas City for the division title.

Year/Team	OPW%	PW	PL	APW%	AW	AL	Diff+/-
1990 SEA	0.534 D	87	75	0.475	77	85	-0.059
1991 SEA	0.494	80	82	0.512	83	79	0.018
1992 SEA	0.448	73	89	0.395	64	98	-0.053
1993 SEA	0.484	78	84	0.506	82	80	0.022
1994 SEA	0.433	70	92	0.438	49	63	0.005
1995 SEA	0.472	76	86	0.545 D	79	66	0.073
1996 SEA	0.556 W	90	72	0.528	85	76	-0.028
1997 SEA	0.503	82	80	0.556 D	90	72	0.052
1998 SEA	0.491	80	82	0.472	76	85	-0.019
1999 SEA	0.549 D	89	73	0.488	79	83	-0.062

franchID	OWAR	OWS	AWAR	AWS	WARdiff	WSdiff	P/D/W/F
1990 SEA	40.816	236.478	38.781	231.004	2.035	5.474	D
1991 SEA	39.949	238.406	37.125	248.997	2.824	-10.590	
1992 SEA	32.057	181.962	30.889	192.002	1.168	-10.040	
1993 SEA	36.519	222.994	41.073	246.000	-4.554	-23.006	
1994 SEA	18.498	141.031	24.646	147.002	-6.148	-5.971	
1995 SEA	37.665	209.269	41.265	237.003	-3.600	-27.734	
1996 SEA	44.565	249.517	45.752	255.000	-1.187	-5.484	W
1997 SEA	42.600	262.799	49.551	269.995	-6.951	-7.196	
1998 SEA	41.393	259.859	44.560	228.003	-3.167	31.856	
1999 SEA	46.483	295.865	33.750	237.001	12.733	58.864	D

Griffey Jr. received a Gold Glove Award and an All-Star nod in every season during the Nineties. "Junior" batted .302 with 38 moon-shots, 109 RBI and 100 runs scored per season over the course of the decade. He cranked 56 long balls and knocked in 147 runs in 1997, amassing 33 Win Shares while earning American League MVP honors. Calderon drilled 44 doubles in 1990 and swiped 30+ bases in consecutive seasons (1990-91). Erik Hanson furnished an 18-9 mark with 211 strikeouts, 3.24 ERA and a 1.157 WHIP in his first full season (1990). Lee Guetterman matched his career high in victories (11) while Schooler saved 30 games with a 2.25 ERA. Seattle celebrated its first division title in 1990.

Mark Langston tallied 19 victories with a 3.00 ERA in '91 and collected 5 consecutive Gold Glove Awards (1991-95). Mike Moore compiled a 17-8 record with a 2.96 ERA in 1991 and Bill C. Swift manufactured a 1.99 ERA and saved 17 games. Swift moved to the rotation and promptly led the League with a 2.04 ERA in 22 starts. In 1993 he placed second in the Cy Young balloting after winning 21 contests with a 2.82 ERA and a career-best WHIP of 1.074.

Edgar Martinez paced the League in batting average in 1992 (.343) and 1995 (.356). Martinez crushed 52 doubles and scored a league-high 121 runs en route to a third-place finish in the '95 AL MVP voting. From 1995-99 he tallied a .334 average with 44 doubles, 27 round-trippers, 102 RBI and 104 runs scored. Dave Fleming (17-10, 3.38) finished third in the 1992 AL ROY voting. Bret Boone produced a .320 BA in 1994 and then plated 95 runs in '98. Tino Martinez supplied 31 wallops and 119 RBI from 1995-99. The "Bamtino" blasted 44 quadruples, knocked in 141 runners and placed runner-up in the 1997 AL MVP balloting.

Omar Vizquel pilfered 37 bases per year from 1995-99. "Little O" scored 112 runs and hit .333 in his best offensive campaign (1999). Known primarily for his defense, Vizquel collected 11 Gold Glove Awards in his career. Alex Rodriguez (.358/36/123) finished second in the '96 American League MVP voting. He collected 215 hits, and led the League in batting average, runs (141) and doubles (58). "A-Rod" paced the circuit with 213 hits in 1998, and swatted 40+ circuit clouts in '98 and '99. Seattle shortstops delivered the most WS>10 seasons (15) in the Major Leagues during the Nineties.

The Mariners' front office achieved inferior results in six of the seven Amateur Drafts from 1996-2002, as the draft classes averaged only 61 Career Total Win Shares during this period. In the wake of five losing seasons, Seattle rebounded with 90 victories and earned the AL Wild Card entry in '96. Jose L. Cruz tagged 26 long balls and logged second-place in the '97 AL ROY campaign, while Shawn Estes (19-5, 3.18) earned his lone All-Star nod in the same year despite leading the League with 100 bases on balls. Kerry Ligtenberg nailed down 30 contests with a 2.71 ERA and 1.027 WHIP In '98 and Matt Mantei tallied 32 saves in the subsequent season. Mike Hampton amassed a record of 22-4 with a 2.90 ERA in '99 en route to a runner-up placement in the Cy Young balloting. The M's captured the Western division crown with a six game cushion over Texas in 1999.

Year/Team	OPW%	PW	PL	APW%	AW	AL	Diff+/-
2000 SEA	0.551 D	89	73	0.562 W	91	71	0.011
2001 SEA	0.567 P	92	70	0.716 P	116	46	0.149
2002 SEA	0.528	86	76	0.574	93	69	0.046
2003 SEA	0.594 P	96	66	0.574	93	69	-0.020
2004 SEA	0.436	71	91	0.389	63	99	-0.047
2005 SEA	0.514	83	79	0.426	69	93	-0.088
2006 SEA	0.524 D	85	77	0.481	78	84	-0.042
2007 SEA	0.591 P	96	66	0.543	88	74	-0.047
2008 SEA	0.519	84	78	0.377	61	101	-0.142
2009 SEA	0.527	85	77	0.525	85	77	-0.002
2010 SEA	0.462	75	87	0.377	61	101	-0.086
2011 SEA	0.466	76	86	0.414	67	95	-0.053
2012 SEA	0.574 D	93	69	0.463	75	87	-0.111
2013 SEA	0.520 D	84	78	0.438	71	91	-0.081

franchID	OWAR	OWS	AWAR	AWS	WARdiff	WSdiff	P/D/W/F
2000 SEA	47.787	296.644	45.169	272.992	2.617	23.651	D
2001 SEA	59.116	326.214	60.246	348.002	-1.130	-21.788	P
2002 SEA	49.153	280.615	48.516	278.998	0.637	1.616	
2003 SEA	48.876	290.442	45.808	279.006	3.068	11.436	P
2004 SEA	36.569	234.024	28.142	188.995	8.428	45.029	
2005 SEA	40.939	268.242	25.809	207.000	15.129	61.242	
2006 SEA	42.765	273.674	30.888	233.999	11.877	39.675	D
2007 SEA	55.168	317.269	33.710	263.995	21.458	53.273	P

2008 SEA	40.994	250.537	21.313	182.999	19.682	67.539	
2009 SEA	43.873	**277.152**	29.030	255.003	14.844	22.148	
2010 SEA	33.060	244.855	18.030	182.998	15.030	61.857	
2011 SEA	35.519	236.170	23.768	201.006	11.751	35.163	
2012 SEA	37.047	**273.940**	32.319	224.998	4.728	48.942	D
2013 SEA	37.416	**254.123**	23.136	213.005	14.279	41.118	D

Seattle conquered the Western Division during the first decade of the 21st century. The Mariners captured the flag in 2000 and 2006 and took home the American League pennant on three occasions (2001, 2003 and 2007). The M's posted the most victories in team history in '03 and repeated the feat in '07. Alex Rodriguez earned three AL MVP Awards ('03, '05, '07) and bashed his way to five home run titles during the 2000's. "A-Rod" hit .304 with 44 moon-shots, 124 RBI and 18 stolen bases from 2000-09. Rodriguez holds the Mariners record with 38 Win Shares in 2005. Griffey Jr. clouted 40 quadruples and knocked in 118 runs in 2000. Edgar Martinez (.324/37/145) topped the circuit in RBI.

Derek Lowe (2.56, 42 SV) paced the American League in saves in 2000. He joined the rotation in 2002 and proceeded to win 21 games with a 2.58 ERA, placing third in the Cy Young balloting. Kazuhiro Sasaki provided 40 saves per season with a 2.98 ERA and 1.032 WHIP during his three seasons as the closer (2000-02). Cruz submitted a 30-30 campaign while Tino Martinez crushed 34 round-trippers and plated 113 runners in '01. Boone (.331/37/141) scored 118 runs, supplied 206 hits and paced the League in RBI while notching the second-highest Win Shares score in club annals. In a three-year span from 2001-03 he averaged .301 with 32 four-baggers, 112 RBI and 106 runs scored. The 2001 squad produced the fourth-best offWARnorm (32) in MLB history along with the franchise-best offWSnorm (188).

Ichiro Suzuki (.350/8/69) topped the American League in batting average, hits (242) and stolen bases (56) as he secured the MVP and ROY Awards in 2001. Suzuki led the AL in base hits in seven seasons and collected 200+ hits in 10 straight campaigns. He batted .372 with a MLB-record 262 base knocks in 2004 and achieved Gold Glove status in every season of his career. Joe Mays (17-13, 3.16) supplied a 1.151 WHIP and earned an All-Star nod in 2001. Raul Ibanez delivered a .294 average with 24 dingers and 103 ribbies in his first full season (2002). From 2006-2009 Ibanez blasted 36 doubles, 28 home runs and knocked in 108 runs per year. Jason Varitek whacked 31 doubles and 25 four-ply swats in 2003. Mantei closed out 29 games in '03 while lefty Damaso Marte added 11 saves and a 1.58 ERA.

David Ortiz placed fourth or better in the AL MVP balloting from 2004-07, batting .304 with 42 doubles, 44 circuit clouts, 135 RBI and 111 runs scored. "Big Papi" topped the leader-boards with 54 moon-shots and 137 ribbies in 2006 after driving in 148 in the previous campaign. The M's designated hitters outshined the competition, posting 13 WS>10 seasons from 2000-09. Brian Fuentes posted 30 saves per year from 2005-10 with a 3.14 ERA and 1.186 WHIP. "T-Rex" paced the circuit with 48 saves in 2009. J.J. Putz dominated opposing batsmen in '07, notching 40 saves with a 1.38 ERA and a miniscule WHIP of 0.698! Jose Lopez thumped 25 long balls and knocked in 96 runs in '09. Shin-Soo Choo pounded 38 doubles in 2009 and delivered consecutive 20-20 campaigns in 2009-10. He established career-highs with 107 runs, 112 bases on balls and a .423 OBP in '13.

Felix Hernandez (19-5, 2.49) led the League in victories, garnering a runner-up finish in the 2009 Cy Young voting. "King Felix" captured the ERA crown and Cy Young Award in 2010 with a 13-12 record, 1.057 WHIP and league-best 2.27 ERA. Ryan Franklin (1.92, 38 SV) received an All-Star invitation in 2009 while port-sider George Sherrill added 21 saves with a 1.70 ERA. Rafael Soriano topped the AL with 45 saves in 2010 while fashioning a 1.73 ERA and 0.802 WHIP. Asdrubal Cabrera swatted 25 big-flies and drove in 92 runs while earning his first All-Star appearance in 2011. Adam Jones collected his third Gold Glove Award and set personal-bests with 33 jacks and 108 ribbies in 2013.

Win Shares > 20	Single-Season	1977-2013
Alvin Davis - 1B (SEA) x4	Phil Bradley - LF (SEA) x3	Ichiro Suzuki - RF (SEA) x8
Tino Martinez - 1B (SEA) x3	Ivan Calderon - LF (SEA)	Shin-Soo Choo - RF (SEA) x3
Harold Reynolds - 2B (SEA)	Raul Ibanez - LF (SEA) x2	Edgar Martinez - DH (SEA) x7
Bret Boone - 2B (SEA) x3	Dave Henderson - CF (SEA)	David Ortiz - DH (SEA) x5
Alex Rodriguez - SS (SEA) x8	x3	Bud H. Black - SP (SEA)
Omar Vizquel - SS (SEA) x2	Ken Griffey, Jr. - CF (SEA)	Mark Langston - SP (SEA) x3
Asdrubal Cabrera - SS (SEA)	x11	Mike Hampton - SP (SEA)
Edgar Martinez - 3B (SEA) x2	Ichiro Suzuki - CF (SEA)	Joe Mays - SP (SEA)
Alex Rodriguez - 3B (SEA) x7	Adam Jones - CF (SEA) x2	Derek Lowe - SP (SEA)
Kyle Seager - 3B (SEA) x2	Shin-Soo Choo - CF (SEA)	Felix Hernandez - SP (SEA) x2
Jason Varitek - C (SEA)	Ivan Calderon - RF (SEA)	J.J. Putz - RP (SEA)
Kenji Johjima - C (SEA)		

Note: 4000 PA or BFP to qualify, except during strike-shortened seasons
(1972 = 3800, 1981 & 1994 = 2700, 1995 = 3500) and 154-game schedule (3800)
- failed to qualify: 1977-1985

Mariners All-Time "Originals" Roster

Dustin Ackley	Josh David Fields	Derek Lowe	Enrique Romo
Nathan Adcock	Dan Firova	Mark Lowe	Ryan Rowland-Smith
Darrel Akerfelds	Doug Fister	Rick Luecken	Roger Salkeld
Jamie Allen	Brian Fitzgerald	Carlos L. Maldonado	Marino Santana
Bud Anderson	Dave Fleming	Jim Maler	Kazuhiro Sasaki
Scott Atchison	Tim Fortugno	Matt Mangini	Michael Saunders
Phillippe Aumont	Eric Fox	Matt Mantei	Aaron Scheffer
Cha Seung Baek	Nick Franklin	Damaso Marte	Mike Schooler
Wladimir Balentien	Ryan Franklin	Edgar Martinez	Kyle Seager
Brandon Bantz	Emiliano Fruto	Tino Martinez	Paul Serna
Terry Bell	Brian Fuentes	Julio Mateo	Andy Sheets
Karl Best	Mike Gardiner	Joe Mays	George Sherrill
Yuniesky Betancourt	Charles Gipson	Bill McGuire	Allan Simpson
Bud H. Black	George Glinatsis	Vance McHenry	Terrmel Sledge
Travis Blackley	Jerry Goff	Rusty McNealy	Brick Smith
Willie Bloomquist	Ken Griffey, Jr.	Chris Mears	Roy W. Smith
T.J. Bohn	Kevin Gryboski	Gil Meche	Chris Snelling
Bret Boone	Lee Guetterman	Jim Mecir	Brian Snyder
Jim Bowie	Giomar Guevara	Yoervis Medina	Rafael Soriano
Phil Bradley	Jesus Guzman	Orlando Mercado	Sean Spencer
Darren Bragg	Mike Hampton	Kameron Mickolio	Dennis Stark
Mickey Brantley	Lee Hancock	Brad Miller	Bob Stoddard
Lesli Brea	Todd Haney	Shane Monahan	Jamal Strong
Greg Briley	Erik Hanson	Adam Moore	Ichiro Suzuki
Jaime Bubela	Tim Harikkala	Mike Moore	Mac Suzuki
Dave Burba	Mike L. Hart	Trey Moore	Brian Sweeney
Asdrubal Cabrera	Dave Henderson	Brandon Morrow	Bill C. Swift
Ivan Calderon	Dave Hengel	John Moses	Jesus Tavarez
Mike Campbell	Felix Hernandez	Ron Musselman	Scott M. Taylor
Carter Capps	Brett Hinchliffe	Clint Nageotte	Terry Taylor
Rafael Carmona	John Hobbs	Oswaldo Navarro	Wade Taylor
Troy Cate	Chris H. Howard	Ricky Nelson	Justin Thomas
Al Chambers	Raul Ibanez	Marc Newfield	Matt Thornton
Shin-Soo Choo	Hisashi Iwakuma	Scott Nielsen	Chris Tillman
Jermaine Clark	Chris Jakubauskas	Donell Nixon	Carlos Triunfel

Jeff Clement	Cesar Jimenez	Edwin Nunez	Matt Tuiasosopo
Ken Cloude	Kenji Johjima	Eric O'Flaherty	Brian Turang
Darnell Coles	Rob Johnson	David Ortiz	Luis Valbuena
Jim Converse	Adam Jones	Spike Owen	Dave Valle
Rod Craig	Calvin Jones	Clay Parker	Ed Vande Berg
Dean Crow	Munenori Kawasaki	Scott Patterson	Andy Van Hekken
Jose L. Cruz	Justin Kaye	James Paxton	Jason Varitek
John Cummings	Shawn Kelley	Carlos Peguero	Anthony Varvaro
Jeff Darwin	Steve Kent	Michael Pineda	Ramon Vazquez
Alvin Davis	Kevin King	Joel Pineiro	Ron Villone
Tim Davis	Bobby LaFromboise	Greg Pirkl	Omar Vizquel
Wilson Delgado	Bryan LaHair	Arquimedez Pozo	Matt Wagner
Rich DeLucia	Mark Langston	Jim Presley	Dusty Wathan
Carlos A. Diaz	Patrick Lennon	Stephen Pryor	Chris Widger
Eddy Diaz	Justin Leone	J.J. Putz	Bill Wilkinson
Juan H. Diaz	Jim M. Lewis	Erasmo J. Ramirez	Mike L. Wilson
Mario Diaz	Alex Liddi	J. C. Ramirez	Bob Wolcott
Greg Dobbs	Kerry Ligtenberg	Desi Relaford	Kerry Woodson
Dave Edler	Bobby Livingston	Harold Reynolds	Matt J. Young
Shawn Estes	Aaron Looper	Pat Rice	Clint Zavaras
Jeff Farnsworth	Aquilino Lopez	Rene Rivera	Jordan Zimmerman
Ryan Feierabend	Jose Lopez	Alex Rodriguez	Mike Zunino

Florida / Miami Marlins

Year/Team	OPW%	PW	PL	APW%	AW	AL	Diff+/-
1993 FLA	0.000 F	0	0	0.395	64	98	0.000
1994 FLA	0.000 F	0	0	0.443	51	64	0.000
1995 FLA	0.000 F	0	0	0.469	67	76	0.000
1996 FLA	0.000 F	0	0	0.494	80	82	0.000
1997 FLA	0.451 F	73	89	0.568 W	92	70	0.117
1998 FLA	0.398 F	64	98	0.333	54	108	-0.064
1999 FLA	0.408 F	66	96	0.395	64	98	-0.013

franchID	OWAR	OWS	AWAR	AWS	WARdiff	WSdiff	P/D/W/F
1994 FLA	174.618	633.987	16.742	153.002	157.876	480.986	F
1995 FLA	52.749	302.145	31.369	201.001	21.379	101.144	F
1996 FLA	30.117	253.963	36.029	240.000	-5.911	13.963	F
1997 FLA	35.315	218.632	41.075	276.002	-5.760	-57.370	F
1998 FLA	15.407	152.352	12.691	162.000	2.716	-9.649	F
1999 FLA	14.299	172.756	21.056	191.998	-6.757	-19.242	F

Legend: (P) = Pennant / Most Wins in League (D) = Division Winner (W) = Wild Card Winner (F) = Failed to Qualify

The Florida Marlins joined the National League as MLB expanded to 28 teams in 1993. The 1999 "Original" Marlins were the first to exceed the minimum 4000 PA standards, while the pitching staff failed to meet the minimum BFP requirements until 2003*. Florida has failed to reach the post-season or lead the League in oWAR or oWS (through 2013).

Charles Johnson collected four consecutive Gold Gloves from 1995-98 and his stellar defense behind the dish resulted in five seasons on the fielding WS and WAR leader boards. Edgar Renteria hit .309 with 16 steals and placed runner-up in the '96 NL ROY balloting. Luis Castillo nabbed 50 bags while batting .302 for the 1999 squad.

Year/Team	OPW%	PW	PL	APW%	AW	AL	Diff+/-
2000 FLA	0.495 F	80	82	0.491	79	82	-0.004
2001 FLA	0.400 F	65	97	0.469	76	86	0.070
2002 FLA	0.476 F	77	85	0.488	79	83	0.012
2003 FLA	0.522	85	77	0.562 W	91	71	0.040
2004 FLA	0.465	75	87	0.512	83	79	0.047
2005 FLA	0.505	82	80	0.512	83	79	0.007
2006 FLA	0.502	81	81	0.481	78	84	-0.020
2007 FLA	0.455	74	88	0.438	71	91	-0.017
2008 FLA	0.467	76	86	0.522	84	77	0.055
2009 FLA	0.477	77	85	0.537	87	75	0.060
2010 FLA	0.449	73	89	0.494	80	82	0.045
2011 FLA	0.510 W	83	79	0.444	72	90	-0.066
2012 FLA	0.478	77	85	0.426	69	93	-0.052
2013 FLA	0.468	76	86	0.383	62	100	-0.085

franchID	OWAR	OWS	AWAR	AWS	WARdiff	WSdiff	P/D/W/F
2000 FLA	29.984	227.731	31.175	236.999	-1.191	-9.268	F
2001 FLA	27.376	217.585	36.291	227.998	-8.915	-10.413	F
2002 FLA	37.091	241.384	35.565	236.997	1.526	4.387	F
2003 FLA	43.871	260.130	46.076	272.991	-2.204	-12.861	
2004 FLA	32.663	222.483	36.926	248.998	-4.263	-26.515	
2005 FLA	33.553	228.778	41.973	249.005	-8.420	-20.227	
2006 FLA	33.787	237.718	34.610	233.999	-0.822	3.719	
2007 FLA	29.720	232.508	34.075	213.001	-4.355	19.507	
2008 FLA	23.007	200.653	36.605	251.997	-13.598	-51.344	
2009 FLA	31.566	230.543	40.280	261.000	-8.714	-30.457	
2010 FLA	36.261	237.115	36.767	239.995	-0.505	-2.881	
2011 FLA	39.805	254.047	35.685	215.998	4.120	38.050	W
2012 FLA	28.328	236.192	17.973	207.002	10.356	29.189	
2013 FLA	33.003	255.788	18.576	185.997	14.427	69.790	

GM Dave Dombrowski and Scouting Director Alex Avila presided over the Marlins top draft (based on Career Total Win Shares) in 2000. Their selections included Adrian Gonzalez and Josh Willingham. Livan Hernandez accrued 17 victories in 2000. Hernandez (15-10, 3.20) delivered a career-best ERA along with the lone WS>20 season by a Marlins' hurler in 2003. Castillo paced the circuit with 62 stolen bases along with a .334 BA and 101 runs scored in 2000. Johnson produced career-highs in batting (.304), home runs (31) and RBI (91) during the 2000 campaign.

Kevin Millar batted at a .314 clip in '01 and bashed 25 long balls while plating 96 baserunners in 2003. Edgar Renteria received consecutive Gold Glove Awards in 2002-03. He drilled 47 doubles and knocked in 100 runs while batting .330 in 2003. Renteria scored 100 times in back-to-back campaigns (2005-06) and achieved a career-best .332 BA in '07. The Marlins and Expos tied for second place in the NL East in '03, only two games behind the Braves. Randy Winn crossed home plate 103 times in '03 and in 2005 supplied a .306 average with 47 doubles and 20 quadruples. Mark Kotsay delivered 37 doubles and a .314 BA in '04.

Miguel Cabrera produced a .324 BA with 35 circuit clouts and 120 RBI from 2004-2013. Cabrera (.330/44/139) seized the Triple Crown in 2012, earned consecutive MVP Awards (2012-13) and secured three straight batting titles (2011-13). He surpassed the 30-Win Share plateau four successive campaigns and holds the Marlins' record with 35 Win Shares in '11. Adrian Gonzalez pummeled opposing hurlers since establishing full-time status in 2006. Gonzalez averaged 31 moon-shots and 103 ribbies from 2006-2011 and hit .338 with a league-leading 213 hits in '11. Gonzalez slugged 40 round-trippers and compiled 33 Win Shares in '09. Josh Willingham swatted 26 big-flies in his rookie season (2006). He walloped 29 dingers while driving home 98 runs in '11, and then set personal-bests with 35 round-trippers and 110 ribbies in the following campaign.

Josh Beckett (20-7, 3.27) finished second in the 2007 Cy Young balloting. Beckett posted career-bests in ERA (2.89) and WHIP (1.026) in 2011. The 2007 squad delivered the highest batting average (.281), OBP (.347) and SLG (.436) in team history. Chris Coghlan received the 2009 NL ROY Award after posting a .321 mark with 31 doubles, while Ronald Belisario provided effective relief work in the same year, fashioning an ERA of 2.04 along with a 1.146 WHIP. In 2010, Josh Johnson (11-6, 2.30) paced the circuit in ERA and Alexander Gonzalez smacked 42 doubles, belted 23 four-baggers and plated 88 runners. The franchise amended its name to the Miami Marlins for the 2012 season. Giancarlo Stanton dialed long-distance 37 times and topped the Senior Circuit with a .608 SLG. Jose D. Fernandez (12-6, 2.19) burst onto the scene as a 20-year old. The freshman hurler won the 2013 NL Rookie of the Year Award and placed third in the Cy Young balloting.

Win Shares > 20	Single-Season	1993-2013
Adrian Gonzalez - 1B (FLA) x6	Charles Johnson - C (FLA)	Randy Winn - CF (FLA)
Miguel Cabrera - 1B (FLA) x4	Miguel Cabrera - LF (FLA)	Miguel Cabrera - RF (FLA)
Luis Castillo - 2B (FLA) x3	Chris Coghlan - LF (FLA)	Randy Winn - RF (FLA)
Edgar Renteria - SS (FLA) x3	Josh Willingham - LF (FLA)	Giancarlo Stanton - RF (FLA)
Alex Gonzalez - SS (FLA)	Mark Kotsay - CF (FLA) x2	Livan Hernandez - SP (FLA)
Miguel Cabrera - 3B (FLA) x4		

Note: 4000 PA or BFP to qualify, except during strike-shortened seasons
(1972 = 3800, 1981 & 1994 = 2700, 1995 = 3500) and 154-game schedule (3800)
- failed to qualify: 1993-2002

Marlins All-Time "Originals" Roster

Jim C. Adduci	Mike Duvall	Christopher Leroux	John Roskos
Chris Aguila	Matt Erickson	Jhan Marinez	Alex Sanabia
Hector Almonte	Jose D. Fernandez	Carlos M. Martinez	Gaby Sanchez
Chip Ambres	Jeff Fulchino	Osvaldo Martinez	Tony Saunders
Robert Andino	Amaury Garcia	Kevin Mattison	Brett Sinkbeil
Jeff Bailey	Harvey Garcia	Billy McMillon	Kyle Skipworth
Daniel Barone	Jose Garcia	Brian Meadows	Rob Stanifer
Denny Bautista	Ross Gload	Randy Messenger	Giancarlo Stanton
Yorman Bazardo	Adrian Gonzalez	Kevin Millar	Taylor Tankersley
Josh Beckett	Alex Gonzalez	Jai Miller	Graham Taylor
Ronald Belisario	Gabe Gonzalez	Ralph Milliard	Michael Tejera
Dave Berg	Brad Hand	Logan Morrison	Aaron Thompson
Brent Billingsley	Brandon Harper	Blaine Neal	Ryan Tucker
Josh Booty	Chris D. Hatcher	Edgar Olmos	Luis Ugueto
Jay Buente	Brett Hayes	Kevin Olsen	Marc Valdes
Miguel Cabrera	Felix Heredia	Scott Olsen	Rick VandenHurk
Arquimedes Caminero	Jeremy Hermida	Marcell Ozuna	Claudio Vargas
Brett Carroll	Livan Hernandez	Jason Pearson	Jason Vargas
Luis Castillo	Kevin Hooper	Bryan Petersen	Elih Villanueva
Travis Chick	Hansel Izquierdo	Julio Ramirez	Chris Volstad
Steve Cishek	Ryan D. Jackson	A. J. Ramos	Bryan Ward
Chris Clapinski	Dan Jennings	John Raynor	Sean West
Chris Coghlan	Charles Johnson	Mike Redmond	Josh Willingham
Scott Cousins	Josh Johnson	Eric Reed	Josh Wilson
Will Cunnane	Logan Kensing	Edgar Renteria	Randy Winn

Vic Darensbourg	Gary Knotts	Chris Resop	Ross Wolf
Brad Davis	Tom Koehler	Nate Robertson	Tim Wood
Matt Dominguez	Mark Kotsay	Nate Rolison	Christian Yelich
Todd Dunwoody	Andy Larkin	Sandy Rosario	Mauro Zarate

New York Mets

Year/Team	OPW%	PW	PL	APW%	AW	AL	Diff+/-
1962 NYM	0.000 F	0	0	0.250	40	120	0.000
1963 NYM	0.000 F	0	0	0.315	51	111	0.000
1964 NYM	0.000 F	0	0	0.327	53	109	0.000
1965 NYM	0.376 F	61	101	0.309	50	112	-0.067
1966 NYM	0.438 F	71	91	0.410	66	95	-0.028
1967 NYM	0.483 F	78	84	0.377	61	101	-0.107
1968 NYM	0.560 F	91	71	0.451	73	89	-0.110
1969 NYM	0.537 D	87	75	0.617 P	100	62	0.080

franchID	OWAR	OWS	AWAR	AWS	WARdiff	WSdiff	P/D/W/F
1962 NYM	-113.007	26.379	15.948	120.002	-128.954	-93.623	F
1963 NYM	11.345	146.028	5.329	153.003	6.016	-6.975	F
1964 NYM	4.455	183.423	13.473	159.001	-9.018	24.421	F
1965 NYM	0.839	195.554	7.111	149.999	-6.271	45.555	F
1966 NYM	9.494	242.068	13.166	197.995	-3.671	44.073	F
1967 NYM	39.057	260.301	16.654	182.997	22.403	77.304	F
1968 NYM	34.561	231.830	32.399	219.009	2.163	12.822	F
1969 NYM	44.960	286.940	39.877	300.006	5.083	-13.066	D

Legend: (P) = Pennant / Most Wins in League (D) = Division Winner (W) = Wild Card Winner (F) = Failed to Qualify

National League baseball returned to New York in 1962 in the wake of the departure of the Dodgers and Giants four years earlier. The Metropolitans produced the most starting pitchers (based on WS>10 and WS>20 seasons), center fielders and relievers (WS>10) among the "Expansion" teams. The club has a poor track record with respect to developing first basemen, managing merely 3 WS>20 seasons in sixty years.

Tom Seaver emerged as the first superstar for the Metropolitans. "Tom Terrific" (16-13, 2.76) took home NL Rookie of the Year honors in 1967 and followed up with 16 wins and a 2.20 ERA in '68. Seaver merited his first Cy Young Award with a 25-7 mark, 2.21 ERA and 31 Win Shares in 1969. Paul Blair led the League with 12 triples in 1967 and collected his first of eight Gold Glove Awards. "Motormouth" scored 102 runs in '69 while batting .285 with 26 round-trippers. Blair and Kenny Lofton are tied with the most seasons (10) in the top 15 for fielding WAR and Win Shares among expansion era outfielders.

Jerry Koosman (19-12, 2.08) and Jim Hardin (18-13, 2.51) joined Seaver in the Mets' rotation in 1968. Koosman placed runner-up in the ROY balloting and posted a record of 17-9 with a 2.28 ERA and career-best WHIP of 1.058. The 1968 "Original" Mets were the first to exceed the minimum 4000 BFP standards and the offense met the PA requirements in 1969*. The club achieved its first division title in '69, taking the East by 3 games over the Cubs. Cleon Jones produced a .340 batting average and made his lone All-Star appearance in 1969.

GM George Weiss orchestrated the Mets' finest outcome in the Amateur Draft. The class of '65 which included Nolan Ryan, Steve Renko, Ken Boswell and Jim McAndrew totaled 578 Career Total Win Shares. Prior to the implementation of the Draft, Weiss procured Blair ('61), Koosman ('64) and Seaver ('66) as amateur free agents. Subsequent to Weiss' departure from the front office, the New York draft classes from 1969-1975 underachieved, averaging only 59

Career Total Win Shares. The front office during this timeframe comprised primarily of GM Bob Scheffing and Scouting Director Nelson Burbrink.

Year/Team	OPW%	PW	PL	APW%	AW	AL	Diff+/-
1970 NYM	0.478	77	85	0.512	83	79	0.035
1971 NYM	0.510	83	79	0.512	83	79	0.003
1972 NYM	0.424	69	93	0.532	83	73	0.108
1973 NYM	0.512 D	83	79	0.509 D	82	79	-0.002
1974 NYM	0.492	80	82	0.438	71	91	-0.054
1975 NYM	0.479	78	84	0.506	82	80	0.027
1976 NYM	0.449	73	89	0.531	86	76	0.082
1977 NYM	0.457	74	88	0.395	64	98	-0.062
1978 NYM	0.451	73	89	0.407	66	96	-0.043
1979 NYM	0.479	78	84	0.389	63	99	-0.090

franchID	OWAR	OWS	AWAR	AWS	WARdiff	WSdiff	P/D/W/F
1970 NYM	44.549	238.172	43.173	248.993	1.376	-10.820	
1971 NYM	42.370	242.049	46.422	249.001	-4.052	-6.952	
1972 NYM	29.193	231.499	33.311	248.999	-4.118	-17.500	
1973 NYM	43.292	250.624	35.368	246.004	7.924	4.620	D
1974 NYM	43.756	236.801	31.599	212.997	12.156	23.804	
1975 NYM	41.139	234.688	37.731	245.996	3.408	-11.308	
1976 NYM	40.806	241.444	45.354	258.002	-4.548	-16.558	
1977 NYM	49.721	264.692	27.959	191.999	21.762	72.693	
1978 NYM	37.731	225.124	26.719	197.996	11.012	27.127	
1979 NYM	50.780	262.505	24.827	188.998	25.954	73.506	

Tug McGraw tallied 132 saves during the Seventies and posted a 3.02 ERA. He furnished a 1.70 ERA in back-to-back seasons (1971-72) and saved 27 games in 1972. Dick Selma nailed down 22 contests in 1970. The Metropolitans delivered 83 victories and finished three games behind the Pirates in '71. Nolan Ryan racked up 300+ strikeouts in every year from 1972-77 with the exception of 1975. "The Ryan Express" averaged 17 wins, 20 complete games and 302 strikeouts per season from 1972-79. Ryan set a Major League record with 383 whiffs in 1973 and earned a runner-up finish in the Cy Young balloting. Jon Matlack captured the NL Rookie of the Year Award in 1972, furnishing a 15-10 record with a 2.32 ERA. He posted career-bests with 17 victories in '76 and a 2.27 ERA in '78. Jerry Johnson notched 12 wins and 18 saves with a 2.97 ERA in '72.

New York rebounded from the worst record in franchise history (69-93), taking the division crown by one game over the Cubs in 1973. Tom Seaver flourished as the staff ace, receiving the Cy Young Award in '73 and '75 and finishing as runner-up after posting a 1.76 ERA in 1971. He eclipsed 20 victories in 4 campaigns and struck out 200+ batters in 9 consecutive seasons. During the Seventies, Seaver delivered 18 wins, 230 strikeouts, a 2.61 ERA and 1.073 WHIP per season. The Metropolitans' starting pitchers delivered the most WS>10 seasons (54) in the decade, counting 10 from Seaver.

Ken Singleton (.302/23/103) paced the National League with a .425 OBP and set career-bests with 123 bases on balls and 100 runs scored in '73. He compiled 35 Win Shares and finished third in the 1977 MVP balloting with a .328 average and 99 RBI. Singleton placed runner-up in the '79 voting after launching 35 long balls and driving in 111 runs. Steve Renko amassed 15 wins and fashioned a 2.81 ERA in '73. Buzz Capra led the League with a 2.28 ERA while tallying 16 wins in 1974. Ed Figueroa delivered 18 wins and a 3.12 ERA per year from 1974-77, culminating in a 20-win campaign in 1977.

Jerry Morales knocked in 91 runs in 1975 and then drilled 34 doubles and batted .290 to earn an All-Star berth in '77. Jerry Koosman (21-10, 2.69) placed second in the NL Cy Young balloting in 1976 and managed another 20-win campaign in '79. Leroy Stanton slammed 27 four-baggers and delivered 90 RBI in 1977. Craig Swan topped the leader board with a 2.43 ERA in 1978, and the following year Lee Mazzilli supplied a .303 average with 34 two-base knocks and swiped 34 bags en route to his lone All-Star invitation.

Win Shares > 20	Single-Season	1962-1979
Cleon Jones - LF (NYM) x2	Jerry Koosman - SP (NYM) x3	Steve Renko - SP (NYM)
Ken Singleton - LF (NYM)	Tom Seaver - SP (NYM) x8	Buzz Capra - SP (NYM)
Paul Blair - CF (NYM) x4	Jon Matlack - SP (NYM) x3	Dick Selma - RP (NYM)
Lee Mazzilli - CF (NYM) x2	Nolan Ryan - SP (NYM) x4	Tug McGraw - RP (NYM)
Ken Singleton - RF (NYM) x6		

Year/Team	OPW%	PW	PL	APW%	AW	AL	Diff+/-
1980 NYM	0.476	77	85	0.414	67	95	-0.062
1981 NYM	0.464	75	87	0.398	41	62	-0.066
1982 NYM	0.427	69	93	0.401	65	97	-0.026
1983 NYM	0.427	69	93	0.420	68	94	-0.007
1984 NYM	0.447	72	90	0.556	90	72	0.108
1985 NYM	0.524	85	77	0.605	98	64	0.081
1986 NYM	0.589 P	95	67	0.667 P	108	54	0.078
1987 NYM	0.544 D	88	74	0.568	92	70	0.024
1988 NYM	0.510	83	79	0.625 P	100	60	0.115
1989 NYM	0.541	88	74	0.537	87	75	-0.004

franchID	OWAR	OWS	AWAR	AWS	WARdiff	WSdiff	P/D/W/F
1980 NYM	41.185	242.012	25.220	200.999	15.966	41.013	
1981 NYM	28.375	166.164	17.426	123.002	10.949	43.163	
1982 NYM	28.742	229.650	19.318	195.001	9.424	34.649	
1983 NYM	23.515	219.415	19.270	204.000	4.245	15.415	
1984 NYM	41.814	267.114	36.755	270.001	5.059	-2.887	
1985 NYM	44.715	256.242	49.024	293.997	-4.309	-37.755	
1986 NYM	59.311	299.730	56.605	323.994	2.706	-24.264	P
1987 NYM	47.001	267.430	50.600	275.997	-3.600	-8.567	D
1988 NYM	47.868	276.796	60.484	299.999	12.615	-23.203	
1989 NYM	47.808	297.412	46.509	260.993	1.299	36.418	

The Metropolitans languished in the cellar from 1980 to 1984, winning only 69 games in '82 and '83. However GM Frank Cashen and Scouting Director Joe McIlvane reveled in their success at the draft table. The Mets' draft classes averaged 424 Career Total Win Shares from 1980-83 and formed the foundation of the pennant-winning '86 squad. Mazzilli pilfered 41 bags while Singleton swatted 24 home runs and batted in 104 runs for the 1980 club. Jim Bibby (19-6, 3.32) placed third in the 1980 NL Cy Young balloting and received his first All-Star nod at age 35. Neil Allen delivered 20 saves with a 3.31 ERA per year from 1980-82. Tug McGraw (1.46, 20 SV) earned a fifth-place finish in the 1980 NL Cy Young balloting.

Hubie Brooks hit .307 and finished third in the NL ROY balloting in 1981. He plated 100 runs in '85 and then batted .340 in an injury-shortened 1986 campaign. Tom Seaver paced the circuit with a 14-2 record during the abbreviated 1981 season while Nolan Ryan led the way with a 1.69 ERA. The "Ryan Express" continued to rack up strikeout victims as he posted league-leading totals in 4 consecutive seasons (1987-90). Ryan whiffed 301 batters in 1989 at age 42! Mookie Wilson swiped 53 bases and tallied 90 runs scored per year from 1982-84.

Darryl Strawberry captured the 1983 NL Rookie of the Year Award, slugging 26 round-trippers and stealing 19 bases. He averaged 31 circuit clouts and 25 stolen bases during the Eighties and entered the 30-30 club in 1987. Strawberry led the League with a .545 SLG while clubbing 39 four-baggers, swiping 29 bags and finishing second in the 1988 NL MVP race. Jody Davis bashed 24 long balls in '83 and went on to knock in a career-high 94 runs in 1984.

Dwight Gooden achieved Rookie of the Year honors in 1984 after leading the National League in strikeouts (276) and WHIP (1.073). For an encore "Doc" earned the Cy Young Award in '85, pacing the NL with a 24-4 record, 1.53 ERA and 268 K's. Gooden delivered 18 victories, 213 strikeouts, a 2.62 ERA and 1.102 WHIP per season during his first five campaigns. Doug Sisk fashioned a 2.09 ERA and saved 15 contests in '84 despite a high WHIP (1.429).

Mike Scott developed into an ace after learning the split-fingered fastball. Scott fashioned a 17-10 mark with 208 strikeouts, a 2.93 ERA and a 1.059 WHIP from 1985-89. He claimed Cy Young honors in 1986, topping the circuit with a 2.22 ERA and 306 whiffs. Jeff Reardon led the League with 41 saves in 1985. "The Terminator" notched 31 saves per year with a 3.22 ERA from 1982-89. Roger McDowell averaged 21 saves and a 2.91 ERA in his first five seasons. The '85 squad emerged from the depths, posting 85 victories and finishing second to Montreal.

The Mets dominated the National League in 1986, achieving the club's first pennant with a 13-game cushion over the runner-up Phillies. The pitching staff delivered the highest pitWARnorm of All-Time (38) along with the second-best pitWSnorm (157). Greg A. Harris posted a career-best 20 saves in '86. The squad took the division title in '87 by mere percentage points and then placed third in 1988. Gerald Young pilfered 65 stolen bases. Tim Leary supplied 17 wins with a 2.91 ERA while Randy Myers (1.72, 26 SV) furnished his best WHIP (0.912) in 1988. Kevin Mitchell was crowned MVP in 1989 after he paced the National League with 47 home runs, 125 RBI and a .635 SLG. "World" recorded the highest single-season Win Share total in franchise history (38). The '89 Mets registered 88 wins but were no match for the Cubs.

Year/Team	OPW%	PW	PL	APW%	AW	AL	Diff+/-
1990 NYM	0.551	89	73	0.562	91	71	0.010
1991 NYM	0.486	79	83	0.478	77	84	-0.007
1992 NYM	0.452	73	89	0.444	72	90	-0.007
1993 NYM	0.481	78	84	0.364	59	103	-0.116
1994 NYM	0.478	77	85	0.487	55	58	0.008
1995 NYM	0.516	84	78	0.479	69	75	-0.037
1996 NYM	0.484	78	84	0.438	71	91	-0.045
1997 NYM	0.474	77	85	0.543	88	74	0.070
1998 NYM	0.472	77	85	0.543	88	74	0.071
1999 NYM	0.481	78	84	0.595 W	97	66	0.114

franchID	OWAR	OWS	AWAR	AWS	WARdiff	WSdiff	P/D/W/F
1990 NYM	49.233	294.815	53.587	273.005	-4.354	21.811	
1991 NYM	37.729	260.302	40.291	231.001	-2.561	29.301	
1992 NYM	29.888	218.343	32.167	216.002	-2.278	2.341	
1993 NYM	33.221	194.518	26.184	177.005	7.037	17.513	
1994 NYM	23.075	151.083	18.939	165.002	4.136	-13.919	
1995 NYM	27.536	199.041	32.753	207.001	-5.217	-7.960	
1996 NYM	27.288	202.324	30.533	213.001	-3.245	-10.677	
1997 NYM	26.425	237.865	33.318	264.004	-6.893	-26.139	
1998 NYM	24.652	222.086	36.776	264.001	-12.124	-41.915	
1999 NYM	32.959	230.352	49.322	290.997	-16.363	-60.645	

New York battled Pittsburgh for NL East supremacy in 1990. The Pirates claimed victory by a lone game though the Mets topped the circuit in oWAR and oWS. Lenny Dykstra paced the

NL with 192 hits and a .418 OBP while batting .325 with 106 runs scored and 33 stolen bases in 1990. "Nails" placed runner-up in the 1993 NL MVP race, topping the League with 143 runs scored, 194 base hits and 129 bases on balls. Dykstra accrued 35 Win Shares and contributed career-highs in all key offensive categories except batting average.

Dave Magadan contributed a .328 average in '90 while Gregg Jefferies drilled a league-leading 40 doubles. Jefferies (.342/16/83) produced career-highs in batting average and stolen bases (46) in 1993 and batted at a .325 clip in '94. Mitchell thumped 35 moon-shots in '90 and added 30 jacks in '94. Strawberry walloped 37 four-baggers and plated 108 runners, taking third place in the 1990 NL MVP balloting. "Doc" Gooden racked up 223 strikeout victims en route to a 19-7 campaign in 1990. Ryan led the League in WHIP in 1990-91, collected a league-high 232 whiffs in '90 and extended his Major League record as he twirled a seventh no-hitter in 1991. Rick Aguilera settled into the closer's role in 1990. He posted 40+ saves in consecutive seasons (1991-92) and delivered 28 saves per year with a 3.51 ERA and 1.178 WHIP during the Nineties. Jeff Reardon nailed down 40 contests in 1991. The Metropolitans endured consecutive last-place finishes in 1991-92.

Randy Myers led the League in saves on three occasions including 53 in 1993. In addition to four career All-Star appearances, Myers (1.51, 45 SV) finished fourth in the MVP and Cy Young balloting in 1997. Southpaw Pete Schourek fashioned an 18-7 mark with a 3.22 ERA and placed runner-up in the 1995 NL Cy Young balloting. Heathcliff Slocumb notched 30+ saves in back-to-back years (1995-96). Second-sacker Quilvio Veras filched 56 bags in '95. Todd Hundley busted loose with 41 swats and 112 RBI in '96, clubbed 30 long balls in 1997 and received All-Star nods in both campaigns. Kevin Elster enjoyed a career-year in '96, knocking 32 doubles, 24 home runs and driving in 99. Jeromy Burnitz blasted 33 circuit clouts and amassed 104 RBI per season (1997-99). Bobby J. Jones earned a trip to the '97 All-Star game with a 15-9 record and a 3.63 ERA. Fernando Vina delivered a .311 batting average with 198 hits and 101 runs scored in 1998. Edgardo Alfonzo (.304/27/108) scored 123 runs and smashed 41 two-base hits in 1999 while Preston Wilson (.280/26/71) placed second in the Rookie of the Year balloting.

Year/Team	OPW%	PW	PL	APW%	AW	AL	Diff+/-
2000 NYM	0.448	73	89	0.580 W	94	68	0.132
2001 NYM	0.464	75	87	0.506	82	80	0.042
2002 NYM	0.496	80	82	0.466	75	86	-0.030
2003 NYM	0.470	76	86	0.410	66	95	-0.061
2004 NYM	0.506	82	80	0.438	71	91	-0.068
2005 NYM	0.564 D	91	71	0.512	83	79	-0.052
2006 NYM	0.495	80	82	0.599 P	97	65	0.104
2007 NYM	0.560 P	91	71	0.543	88	74	-0.017
2008 NYM	0.526 D	85	77	0.549	89	73	0.024
2009 NYM	0.460	75	87	0.432	70	92	-0.028
2010 NYM	0.470	76	86	0.488	79	83	0.017
2011 NYM	0.484	78	84	0.475	77	85	-0.009
2012 NYM	0.492	80	82	0.457	74	88	-0.035
2013 NYM	0.514	83	79	0.457	74	88	-0.057

franchID	OWAR	OWS	AWAR	AWS	WARdiff	WSdiff	P/D/W/F
2000 NYM	33.008	236.691	43.210	281.997	-10.203	-45.306	
2001 NYM	28.125	210.622	34.251	245.997	-6.126	-35.375	
2002 NYM	29.754	222.595	30.149	225.001	-0.395	-2.406	
2003 NYM	21.039	209.219	18.836	197.995	2.203	11.224	
2004 NYM	25.047	231.764	28.254	212.998	-3.208	18.766	
2005 NYM	32.768	227.785	40.784	249.007	-8.015	-21.222	D
2006 NYM	29.348	241.738	44.481	**290.994**	-15.132	-49.255	
2007 NYM	39.772	247.256	42.786	264.001	-3.013	-16.745	P

2008 NYM	36.966	243.258	42.656	267.000	-5.690	-23.742	D
2009 NYM	28.639	194.226	27.318	209.994	1.321	-15.768	
2010 NYM	30.629	228.976	33.101	236.997	-2.472	-8.021	
2011 NYM	36.752	237.453	35.654	231.002	1.097	6.451	
2012 NYM	27.700	262.324	24.110	221.996	3.590	40.329	
2013 NYM	36.890	251.612	20.944	221.997	15.945	29.615	

New York experienced four consecutive sub .500 seasons (2000-03). Burnitz surpassed 30 home runs in four out of five seasons (2000-04). Alfonzo (.324/25/94) cracked 40 doubles, scored 109 runs and made his lone All-Star appearance in 2000. Terrence Long (.288/18/80) crossed home plate 104 times and finished runner-up in the 2000 Rookie of the Year vote. Preston Wilson entered the 30-30 club, smacking 31 long balls and swiping 36 bags in '00. He received an All-Star invite in 2003, blasting 36 round-trippers and driving in 141 runs.

Jason Isringhausen notched 30+ saves in seven of eight campaigns (2000-07), averaging 34 saves with a 2.81 ERA and a 1.171 WHIP. Octavio Dotel sizzled as a late-inning reliever, striking out 12 batters per 9 IP in '01. Dotel posted a 1.85 ERA and 0.873 WHIP in 2002 and graduated to the closer's role. He accumulated 36 saves in '03 before returning to middle relief during the following year.Fernando Vina collected a pair of Gold Gloves and batted .303 with 95 runs scored in 2001. Jay Payton belted 28 four-baggers and knocked in 89 runs while reliever Guillermo Mota excelled in the setup role, fashioning a 1.97 ERA with a 0.990 WHIP in '03.

The Mets delivered 91 wins, claiming the division title over the Nationals in 2005. Jose B. Reyes sizzled on the base-paths, leading the League with 60+ stolen bases for three straight seasons (2005-07). Reyes supplied 204 hits and 19 three-base knocks in 2008 and secured the NL batting crown three years later with a .337 BA. David Wright supplied 42 doubles, 29 quadruples, 22 steals, 112 RBI and 106 runs scored while batting .311 from 2005-08. "Captain America" notched 34 Win Shares with a career-best .325 BA while placing fourth in the NL MVP balloting in '07.

The club returned to the top of the heap after a mediocre effort in '06, capturing the second National League pennant in 2007. Scott Kazmir topped the League leader boards with 239 strikeouts while Heath Bell furnished a 2.02 ERA and 0.961 ERA in '07. Bell averaged 44 saves with a 2.36 ERA from 2009-2011. A.J. Burnett whiffed 231 batters and compiled 18 victories in 2008. Nelson R. Cruz clobbered 33 long balls and bagged 20 steals while Mike J. Jacobs whacked 32 wallops and drove in 93 runs. The Metropolitans and Phillies played to a virtual tie in '08 with the New Yorkers emerging as the champions. Carlos Gomez belted 24 long balls, nabbed 40 bags and merited Gold Glove honors in 2013.

Win Shares > 20	Single-Season	1980-2013
Lee Mazzilli - 1B (NYM)	Daniel Murphy – 2B (NYM)	Lenny Dykstra - CF (NYM) x3
Dave Magadan - 1B (NYM)	Jose B. Reyes - SS (NYM) x5	Angel Pagan - CF (NYM) x2
Gregg Jefferies - 1B (NYM)	Hubie Brooks - 3B (NYM)	Carlos Gomez – CF (NYM)
Jose Oquendo - 2B (NYM)	Edgardo Alfonzo - 3B (NYM)	Darryl Strawberry - RF (NYM)
Gregg Jefferies - 2B (NYM)	x2	x7
Quilvio Veras - 2B (NYM)	David Wright - 3B (NYM) x7	Jeromy Burnitz - RF (NYM) x3
Fernando Vina - 2B (NYM) x2	Todd Hundley - C (NYM) x2	Dwight Gooden - SP (NYM)
Edgardo Alfonzo - 2B (NYM)	Kevin Mitchell - LF (NYM) x2	Mike Scott - SP (NYM)
x2	Mookie Wilson - CF (NYM)	

Note: 4000 PA or BFP to qualify, except during strike-shortened seasons
(1972 = 3800, 1981 & 1994 = 2700, 1995 = 3500) and 154-game schedule (3800)
- failed to qualify: 1962-1968

Shawn Abner	Ed Figueroa	Barry Lyons	Josh Satin
Benny Agbayani	Nelson Figueroa	Evan MacLane	Scott Sauerbeck
Rick Aguilera	Mike Fiore	Dave Magadan	Doug Saunders
Edgardo Alfonzo	Mike R. Fitzgerald	Robert Manuel	Calvin Schiraldi
Neil Allen	Shaun Fitzmaurice	Alfredo Martinez	Al Schmelz
Rick A. Anderson	Jesus Flores	Fernando Martinez	Dave Schneck
Bob Apodaca	Wilmer Flores	Jose M. Martinez	Pete Schourek
Benny Ayala	Tim Foli	Ted Martinez	Chris Schwinden
Wally Backman	Rich Folkers	Jon Matlack	Mike Scott
Kevin Baez	Brook Fordyce	Kazuo Matsui	Kim Seaman
Rick Baldwin	Micah Franklin	Lee Mazzilli	Tom Seaver
Brian Bannister	Danny Frisella	Ernie McAnally	Dick Selma
Lute Barnes	Larry Fritz	Jim McAndrew	Jae Weong Seo
Chris Basak	Brent Gaff	Lloyd McClendon	Don Shaw
Jose J. Bautista	Daniel Garcia	Terry McDaniel	Tsuyoshi Shinjo
Billy Beane	Guillermo Garcia	Allen McDill	Ken Singleton
Larry Bearnarth	Ron Gardenhire	Roger McDowell	Doug Sisk
Heath Bell	Jeff Gardner	Tug McGraw	Heathcliff Slocumb
Butch Benton	Wes Gardner	Collin McHugh	Bernie Smith
Juan Berenguer	Rod Gaspar	Jeff McKnight	Dave W. Smith
Dwight Bernard	Dillon Gee	Jenrry Mejia	Joe M. Smith
Jim Bethke	Gary Gentry	Carlos Mendoza	Earl Snyder
Jeff Bettendorf	Gonzalez Germen	Keith A. Miller	Alay Soler
Jim Bibby	John Gibbons	Lastings Milledge	Cliff Speck
Jeff Bittiger	Brian J. Giles	Randy Milligan	Steve Springer
Paul Blair	Brian Givens	John Milner	Roy Staiger
Terry Blocker	Carlos Gomez	Kevin Mitchell	Leroy Stanton
Tim Bogar	Dicky Gonzalez	Joe Moock	John Stephenson
Bruce Boisclair	Dwight Gooden	Tommy Moore	Randy Sterling
Ken Boswell	Mauro Gozzo	Jerry Morales	Josh Stinson
Marshall Brant	Jeremy Griffiths	Guillermo Mota	Tobi Stoner
Craig Brazell	Kip Gross	Kevin Mulvey	Pat Strange
Hubie Brooks	Rich Hacker	Carlos Muniz	Darryl Strawberry
Terry Bross	Ike Hampton	Daniel Murphy	Brent Strom
Curtis Brown	Jim Hardin	Dan Murray	Craig Swan
Mike Bruhert	Bud Harrelson	Dennis Musgraves	Ron Swoboda
A.J. Burnett	Denny Harriger	Neal Musser	Hisanori Takahashi
Jeromy Burnitz	Greg A. Harris	Randy Myers	Jeff Tam
Drew Butera	Greg Harts	Bob Myrick	La Schelle Tarver
Craig Cacek	Matt Harvey	Danny Napoleon	Randy Tate
Eric Cammack	Aaron Heilman	Tito Navarro	Ramon Tatis
Joe Campbell	Bob Heise	Jamie Nelson	Ruben Tejada
Buzz Capra	Joe Hietpas	Jonathon Niese	Dave Telgheder
Mike Carp	Erik Hiljus	Kirk Nieuwenhuis	George Theodore
Hector Carrasco	Eric Hillman	Joe Nolan	Josh Thole
Ezequiel Carrera	Ron Hodges	Jose Antonio Nunez	Mike Thomas
Mark Carreon	Scott Holman	Greg Olson	Lou Thornton
Robert Carson	Pat Howell	Jose Oquendo	Jay Tibbs
Raul Casanova	Justin Huber	Rey Ordonez	Rusty Tillman
Alberto T. Castillo	Charlie Hudson	Brian Ostrosser	Jorge Toca
Juan F. Castillo	Jesse Hudson	Ricky Otero	Jackson Todd
Manny Castillo	Philip Humber	Rick Ownbey	Wilfredo Tovar
Juan Centeno	Todd Hundley	John Pacella	Billy Traber
Jaime Cerda	Butch Huskey	Angel Pagan	Alex Trevino

Juan Cerros	Ryota Igarashi	Bobby Parnell	Jason Tyner
Kelvin Chapman	Jeff Innis	Jarrod Patterson	Jordany Valdespin
Endy Chavez	Jason Isringhausen	Jay Payton	Julio Valera
John Christensen	Roy Lee Jackson	Al Pedrique	Yohanny Valera
Maikel Cleto	Mike J. Jacobs	Mike Pelfrey	De Wayne Vaughn
Dave Cochrane	Jason Jacome	Brock Pemberton	Gil Velazquez
Kevin Collins	Gregg Jefferies	Wily Mo Pena	Quilvio Veras
Archie Corbin	Stan Jefferson	Timo Perez	Brandon Villafuerte
Tim H. Corcoran	Bob D. Johnson	Yusmeiro Petit	Fernando Vina
Mardie Cornejo	Jerry Johnson	Jason L. Phillips	Joe Vitko
Joe Crawford	John Johnstone	Grover Powell	Dave Von Ohlen
Cesar Crespo	Randy G. Johnson	Curtis Pride	Pete Walker
Enrique Cruz	Bobby J. Jones	Rich Puig	Tyler Walker
Nelson R. Cruz	Cleon Jones	Bill Pulsipher	Hank Webb
Brian Daubach	Mike Jorgensen	Jose Quintana	Mike Welch
Ike B. Davis	Takashi Kashiwada	Elvin Ramirez	David West
Jody Davis	Scott Kazmir	Hector Ramirez	Mickey Weston
Mark DeJohn	Bobby Keppel	Mario Ramirez	Ty Wigginton
Matt den Dekker	Jay Kleven	Barry Raziano	Charlie Williams
Bill Denehy	Joe Klink	Jeff Reardon	Eddie Williams
Alex Diaz	Satoru Komiyama	Joe Redfield	Paul Wilmet
Lenny DiNardo	Dae-Sung Koo	Prentice Redman	Mookie Wilson
Chris Donnels	Jerry Koosman	Steve Renko	Paul Wilson
Octavio Dotel	Ed Kranepool	Jose B. Reyes	Preston Wilson
D.J. Dozier	Marc Kroon	Ronn Reynolds	Vance Wilson
Lucas Duda	Eddie Kunz	Juan Rios	Herm Winningham
Jeff Duncan	Juan Lagares	Jason Roach	David Wright
Duffy Dyer	Bill Latham	Grant Roberts	Billy Wynne
Lenny Dykstra	Marcus Lawton	Tom Robson	Ed Yarnall
Bill Edgerton	Tim Leary	Rich Rodriguez	Al Yates
Josh Edgin	Aaron Ledesma	Les Rohr	Masato Yoshii
Kevin Elster	Manuel Lee	Rafael Roque	Ned Yost
Alex Escobar	Matt Lindstrom	Luis Rosado	Floyd Youmans
Nino Espinosa	Scott Little	Don Rose	Anthony Young
Frank Estrada	Ron Locke	Dick Rusteck	Gerald Young
Leo Estrella	Terrence Long	Nolan Ryan	Alan Zinter
Nick Evans	Eric Ludwick	Jesus Sanchez	
Jeurys Familia	Zach Lutz	Orlando Sanchez	

Year/Team	OPW%	PW	PL	APW%	AW	AL	Diff+/-
1969 MON	0.000 F	0	0	0.321	52	110	0.000
1970 MON	0.000 F	0	0	0.451	73	89	0.000
1971 MON	0.000 F	0	0	0.441	71	90	0.000
1972 MON	0.000 F	0	0	0.449	70	86	0.000
1973 MON	0.000 F	0	0	0.488	79	83	0.000
1974 MON	0.522 F	85	77	0.491	79	82	-0.031
1975 MON	0.503 F	81	81	0.463	75	87	-0.040
1976 MON	0.447 F	72	90	0.340	55	107	-0.108
1977 MON	0.479 F	78	84	0.463	75	87	-0.016
1978 MON	0.553	90	72	0.469	76	86	-0.083
1979 MON	0.572 P	93	69	0.594	95	65	0.022

franchID	OWAR	OWS	AWAR	AWS	WARdiff	WSdiff	P/D/W/F
1969 MON			20.005	156.004	-20.005	-156.004	F
1970 MON	-31.909	14.666	23.670	218.994	-55.579	-204.328	F
1971 MON	-84.203	160.581	21.764	213.003	-105.967	-52.421	F
1972 MON	26.865	169.249	23.744	210.007	3.121	-40.759	F
1973 MON	32.808	196.332	32.187	236.997	0.621	-40.664	F
1974 MON	46.505	258.034	37.543	237.002	8.962	21.032	F
1975 MON	28.366	263.097	26.156	224.998	2.210	38.100	F
1976 MON	24.192	207.374	17.230	164.977	6.962	42.397	F
1977 MON	47.034	306.571	33.390	225.001	13.644	81.570	F
1978 MON	47.071	282.663	28.719	228.006	18.352	54.656	
1979 MON	**53.985**	**327.938**	41.402	285.001	12.584	42.938	P

Legend: (P) = Pennant / Most Wins in League (D) = Division Winner (W) = Wild Card Winner (F) = Failed to Qualify

Canada's inaugural entry in the Major Leagues, the Montreal Expos, began play in 1969 as one of four expansion teams. The franchise produced the most WS>20 player-seasons in left field among the "Expansion" clubs and tops the leader boards in WS>10 player-seasons in right field. Moreover, the team also ranks in second place in terms of WS>20 player-seasons at third base and catcher. The 1977 "Original" Expos were the first to exceed the minimum 4000 PA standards while the pitching staff met the BFP requirements in 1978*.

Steve Rogers (10-5, 1.54) placed runner-up in the 1973 NL Rookie of the Year balloting. He surpassed 300 innings pitched and provided a 17-16 mark with a 3.10 ERA and 17 complete games in 1977 and delivered a 2.47 ERA and 13 victories in the subsequent campaign. Freshman hurler Dennis Blair collected 11 wins and posted a 3.27 ERA in '74 while rookie reliever Dale Murray posted a miniscule 1.03 ERA with a 0.990 WHIP in 32 games. Murray compiled 15 relief wins in 1975 and the following year saved 13 contests while ranking first in the League with 81 appearances.

Gary Carter thumped 17 round-trippers and placed second in the 1975 NL Rookie of the Year balloting. The "Kid" blasted 31 four-baggers and drove in 84 runs in 1977. Carter ranks second among expansion era catchers with eight seasons in the top five for fielding WAR and Win Shares. Warren Cromartie ripped 41 doubles in his first full season (1977) and eclipsed that mark with 46 two-base knocks in '79. Andre Dawson received ROY honors in 1977, hitting .282 with 19 home runs and 21 stolen bases. "The Hawk" delivered 25 circuit clouts, 92 ribbies and 35 steals in 1979.

GM Charlie Fox and Scouting Director Danny Menendez selected Tim Raines, Scott Sanderson and Bill Gullickson in the 1977 Amateur Draft. The group tallied the highest Career Total Win Shares (651) in franchise history. Ellis Valentine cracked 25 long balls in consecutive seasons (1977-78) and earned a Gold Glove in 1978. Montreal battled Pittsburgh for the NL Eastern division title in '78, falling one game short. Larry Parrish crushed 30 quadruples, batted .307 and finished fourth in the 1979 NL MVP voting. Tony Scott pilfered 37 bases and Gary Roenicke blasted 25 four-baggers as a part-timer in '79. Dan Schatzeder fashioned a 2.83 ERA with a 10-5 record while David Palmer vultured 10 wins and posted 2.64 ERA in long relief during the '79 season. The Expos claimed the franchise's first pennant in 1979, amassing 93 victories and finishing 10 games ahead of the Phillies.

Year/Team	OPW%	PW	PL	APW%	AW	AL	Diff+/-
1980 MON	0.513	83	79	0.556	90	72	0.042
1981 MON	0.533	86	76	0.556	60	48	0.022
1982 MON	0.581 P	94	68	0.531	86	76	-0.050
1983 MON	0.513	83	79	0.506	82	80	-0.006
1984 MON	0.481	78	84	0.484	78	83	0.004
1985 MON	0.556 D	90	72	0.522	84	77	-0.034
1986 MON	0.496	80	82	0.484	78	83	-0.011
1987 MON	0.494	80	82	0.562	91	71	0.067
1988 MON	0.436	71	91	0.500	81	81	0.064
1989 MON	0.438	71	91	0.500	81	81	0.062

franchID	OWAR	OWS	AWAR	AWS	WARdiff	WSdiff	P/D/W/F
1980 MON	45.032	285.414	42.283	270.004	2.749	15.410	
1981 MON	35.766	208.564	28.952	179.998	6.814	28.567	
1982 MON	52.837	297.169	46.740	257.998	6.097	39.171	P
1983 MON	49.209	277.497	41.451	245.996	7.757	31.501	
1984 MON	45.679	273.721	35.424	233.998	10.255	39.723	
1985 MON	55.837	320.951	37.539	252.000	18.299	68.951	D
1986 MON	44.176	293.454	36.582	234.001	7.594	59.453	
1987 MON	34.095	282.874	39.965	273.004	-5.869	9.870	
1988 MON	26.006	239.071	36.069	242.988	-10.064	-3.917	
1989 MON	32.525	224.694	38.344	243.007	-5.819	-18.313	

Carter produced 24 home runs and 92 RBI per season from 1980-87. "Kid" (.264/29/101) placed second in the 1980 NL MVP balloting and won the first of three consecutive Gold Glove Awards. He led the League with 106 RBI in '84 and finished third in the '86 NL MVP voting after knocking in 105 runs. Dawson batted .285 and supplied 25 long balls, 90 ribbies and 20 steals per season during the Eighties. "Hawk" was the runner-up in the '81 and '83 MVP races. He captured the award in 1987, leading the circuit with 49 round-trippers and 137 runs driven in.

Scott Sanderson notched 16 wins with a 3.11 ERA for the 1980 squad, and followed up with a 2.95 ERA in '81. Bill Gullickson posted a 10-5 record with a 3.00 ERA, finished second in the 1980 NL ROY campaign and earned 17 wins in '83. The Expos posted 86 victories in 1981, placing four games behind the Cardinals. Montreal's Amateur Draft classes averaged a mere 76 Career Total Win Shares during GM John McHale's tenure (1980-84). However, McHale secured the services of amateur free agents Andres Galarraga ('79) and Larry Walker ('84).

Tim Raines swiped 71 bases in his rookie campaign, finishing second in the 1981 NL ROY battle. "Rock" received All-Star invites for seven straight seasons (1981-87), batting .310 with 103 runs scored and 72 stolen bases during that period. Raines paced the League with 70+ steals in four consecutive years (1981-84) and topped the leader board with a .334 batting average in 1986.

The club overtook St. Louis by five games in '82 en route to its second pennant. Tim Wallach belted a career-high 28 homers in 1982 and twice led the National League with 42 doubles. In 1987 he placed fourth in the MVP vote, swatting 26 four-baggers and plating 123 runners. The hurlers for the '82 Expos fashioned the best ERA (3.47) and WHIP (1.256) in team annals. Steve Rogers amassed 19 victories, led the senior circuit with a 2.40 ERA and placed runner-up in the Cy Young vote.

The Cardinals rebounded in 1983 and took the division title by a single victory. Charlie Lea (15-10, 2.89) received an All-Star invitation in 1984 after posting similar numbers in '83 (16-11, 3.12). The Expos captured the NL East crown in '85, concluding the season five games ahead of the Mets as Raines (35 WS) and Carter (33 WS) yielded the highest single-season Win Share totals in team history. Joe Hesketh (10-5, 2.49) enjoyed success as a starter in 1985 and notched 9 saves with a 2.85 ERA as a reliever in '88. Bob James fashioned a 2.13 ERA and saved 32 contests in '85.

Pete Incaviglia tattooed 30 moon-shots in his freshman year (1986). Larry Parrish earned his second All-Star invitation in '87, slugging 32 round-trippers and driving in 100 runs. Andres Galarraga (.302/29/92) was the NL leader with 184 hits and 42 two-base knocks in 1988. The '88 Expos posted the lowest OBP (.302) in franchise history. John Dopson forged a 3.04 ERA despite a 3-11 record in 1988. Montreal suffered consecutive last-place finishes, compiling a franchise-worst 71-91 mark in 1988-89.

Year/Team	OPW%	PW	PL	APW%	AW	AL	Diff+/-
1990 MON	0.514	83	79	0.525	85	77	0.011
1991 MON	0.487	79	83	0.441	71	90	-0.046
1992 MON	0.510	83	79	0.537	87	75	0.027
1993 MON	0.470	76	86	0.580	94	68	0.110
1994 MON	0.480	78	84	0.649 P	74	40	0.170
1995 MON	0.544 P	88	74	0.458	66	78	-0.086
1996 MON	0.508	82	80	0.543	88	74	0.035
1997 MON	0.543 D	88	74	0.481	78	84	-0.062
1998 MON	0.521	84	78	0.401	65	97	-0.119
1999 MON	0.500	81	81	0.420	68	94	-0.080

franchID	OWAR	OWS	AWAR	AWS	WARdiff	WSdiff	P/D/W/F
1990 MON	34.967	247.710	41.564	255.012	-6.597	-7.302	
1991 MON	32.885	228.405	29.295	212.998	3.590	15.407	
1992 MON	37.385	255.975	39.882	260.999	-2.498	-5.024	
1993 MON	36.075	233.252	38.158	281.991	-2.084	-48.739	
1994 MON	25.933	170.041	**38.534**	**221.999**	-12.601	-51.958	
1995 MON	29.960	209.983	29.201	197.990	0.759	11.993	P
1996 MON	29.748	248.625	40.245	263.999	-10.497	-15.374	
1997 MON	36.240	242.812	35.278	233.998	0.962	8.815	D
1998 MON	29.788	222.003	23.966	195.002	5.821	27.001	
1999 MON	31.975	215.850	28.647	203.994	3.328	11.856	

"Hawk" clubbed 27 round-trippers and knocked in 100 runs while posting a career-high .310 batting average in 1990. Andre Dawson (.272/31/104) made his 8th All-Star appearance in '91. Delino DeShields placed second in the 1990 NL ROY balloting, batting .289 and swiping 42 bags. He averaged 42 stolen bases per year from 1990-98 and topped the League with 14 triples in '97. The club compiled a Major League-best 43 WS>10 seasons from 1990-2009 at the keystone position, capped by 10 from DeShields.

Super-utilityman Tony Phillips developed into one of the best leadoff batters, averaging 104 runs scored and 107 bases on balls from 1990-97 while setting a career-high with 27 dingers in '95. Raines contributed 45+ steals in three straight seasons (1990-92) and scored 102 runs in back-to-back campaigns (1991-92). Scott Sanderson amassed a career-high 17 victories in 1990 and Bill Gullickson followed suit in '91, reaching the 20-win plateau. Marquis Grissom outstripped the competition, swiping 76 bases in '91 and 78 in the ensuing year. Grissom tallied a career-best 30 Win Shares in 1993 and then scored 106 runs while amassing 207 base knocks in '96. Grissom and Dawson achieved seven seasons in the top five for fielding WAR and Win Shares. Norm Charlton (2.99, 26 SV) received an All-Star invite in 1992, while Mel Rojas fashioned a 1.43 ERA with 10 saves. Rojas tallied 36 saves in 1996.

Larry Walker earned his first All-Star invitation in 1992, batting .301 with 23 home runs. He rapped 44 doubles to pace the National League in '94 and belted 36 long balls in '95. Walker (.366/49/130) compiled 32 Win Shares and achieved MVP honors in 1997. He scored 143 runs, collected 208 hits, swiped 33 bases and led the circuit in home runs, OBP (.452) and SLG (.720). Walker repeated as batting champion in 1998 (.363) and 1999 (.379). Gene Harris notched 23 saves in '93, and in the same year Galarraga scorched the opposition, collecting the batting crown with a .370 average. The "Big Cat" pounced again in 1996, leading the League with 47 home runs and 150 RBI. From 1996-98 Galarraga delivered a .309 average with 44 quadruples and 137 runs driven in.

Randy D. Johnson harnessed his electric stuff in 1993. After leading the League with over 100 bases on balls for three consecutive seasons, Johnson posted a 19-8 record, 3.24 ERA and a league-high 308 strikeouts. The "Big Unit" collected the Cy Young Award in 1995, amassing an 18-2 mark while topping the circuit in ERA (2.48), WHIP (1.045) and strikeouts (294). Johnson produced 16 wins, 268 strikeouts and a 2.86 ERA per season from 1993-99. Montreal secured the pennant with 88 victories in '95 and took the division title by three games over Atlanta in '97.

Vladimir Guerrero (.324/38/109) tallied 202 in his first full season (1998). "Vlad the Impaler" drilled 42 moon-shots and drove in 131 runs in '99. Guerrero eclipsed the .300 mark in batting average in every season from 1997-2008. Matt Stairs cranked 26 four-baggers and knocked in 106 runs in '98 and set a career-high with 38 wallops in 1999. Ugueth Urbina (1.30, 34 SV) earned a trip to the 1998 Mid-Summer Classic and paced the National League with 41 saves in '99. Kent Bottenfield won 18 games in his first full season in the starting rotation (1999).

Year/Team	OPW%	PW	PL	APW%	AW	AL	Diff+/-
2000 MON	0.512	83	79	0.414	67	95	-0.099
2001 MON	0.541 D	88	74	0.420	68	94	-0.121
2002 MON	0.602 P	98	64	0.512	83	79	-0.090
2003 MON	0.522	85	77	0.512	83	79	-0.009
2004 MON	0.495	80	82	0.414	67	95	-0.081
2005 WSN	0.539 W	87	75	0.500	81	81	-0.039
2006 WSN	0.500	81	81	0.438	71	91	-0.062
2007 WSN	0.524 W	85	77	0.451	73	89	-0.073
2008 WSN	0.503	81	81	0.366	59	102	-0.136
2009 WSN	0.522	85	77	0.364	59	103	-0.158
2010 WSN	0.486	79	83	0.426	69	93	-0.060
2011 WSN	0.538 D	87	75	0.497	80	81	-0.042
2012 WSN	0.578 D	94	68	0.605 P	98	64	0.027
2013 WSN	0.524	85	77	0.531	86	76	0.007

franchID	OWAR	OWS	AWAR	AWS	WARdiff	WSdiff	P/D/W/F
2000 MON	29.476	233.484	27.233	200.999	2.243	32.485	
2001 MON	34.481	241.663	25.373	204.004	9.108	37.659	D
2002 MON	46.171	285.357	38.361	249.002	7.811	36.355	P

Year								
2003 MON	41.074	**277.942**	33.613	248.998	7.461	28.944	
2004 MON	36.386	237.834	23.554	201.000	12.832	36.834	
2005 WSN	**46.200**	**287.812**	30.011	242.997	16.189	44.815	W
2006 WSN	36.609	249.632	25.934	212.995	10.675	36.637	
2007 WSN	38.290	**277.790**	21.461	219.003	16.829	58.787	W
2008 WSN	37.239	243.311	18.384	177.003	18.856	66.308	
2009 WSN	35.246	214.390	22.151	177.002	13.095	37.388	
2010 WSN	31.921	221.031	29.681	207.000	2.240	14.031	
2011 WSN	31.087	231.624	32.563	239.993	-1.476	-8.370	D
2012 WSN	**47.859**	262.023	45.115	**294.004**	2.744	-31.981	D
2013 WSN	31.853	254.724	31.368	258.004	0.485	-3.280	

Vladimir Guerrero delivered excellent results, averaging .326 with 33 wallops and 110 RBI from 2000-08. "Vladdy" batted .345 in 2000 and achieved 30-30 status in back-to-back seasons (2001-02). He led the League with 206 hits in '02 and garnered MVP honors when he batted .337 with 39 swats, 126 RBI and 124 runs scored in 2004. Delino DeShields (.296/10/86) swiped 37 bags and set career-highs in batting average and RBI in 2000. Brad Fullmer (.295/32/104) and John Vander Wal (.299/24/94) enjoyed career years.

Johnson collected four consecutive Cy Young Awards from 1999-2002, amassing over 300 strikeouts in each campaign. He also paced the League with 24 wins in '02 and submitted the lowest ERA (2001 and 2002). Antonio Alfonseca led the League with 45 saves in 2000. Gabe White added 11 victories with a 0.940 WHIP in the setup role. Jose Vidro (.330/24/99) tallied 200 hits with 101 runs scored in 2000 and batted .318 from 2000-03. Orlando Cabrera drove in 96 runs in '00 and earned the first of two Gold Glove Awards. "O.C." supplied career-bests with a .301 average and 101 runs scored in 2007.

Montreal collected a division title in 2001 and amassed a franchise-best 98 wins en route to the 2002 NL pennant. Floyd scored 123 runs with 31 circuit clouts and 103 ribbies while batting .317 in '01. He clubbed 34 big-flies in 2005. Walker (.350/38/123) collected his third batting title in 2001. Urbina returned to the closer's role after missing most of 2000 due to injury. He notched 40 saves and earned an All-Star nod in 2002. Kirk Rueter fashioned a 14-8 mark with a 3.23 ERA in 2002. Jorge Julio (1.99, 22 SV) placed third in the ROY balloting in '02 and amassed 36 saves in the subsequent season. Jason Bay received the 2004 NL ROY Award, belting 26 moon-shots with 82 runs driven in. He swatted 30 four-baggers and knocked in 99 runs per year from 2004-09. Brad Wilkerson crossed home plate 112 times and slugged 32 home runs in '04.

The team moved to Washington D.C. in 2005 and changed its name to the Nationals. The club promptly claimed the NL Wild Card entry in 2005 and 2007. Cliff P. Lee furnished an 18-5 record in 2005. After suffering through a miserable season in '07, he rebounded with a masterful effort in 2008. Lee dominated the League with a 22-3 record and 2.54 ERA en route to the Cy Young Award. Three years later he notched a third-place finish while fashioning a career-best 2.40 ERA. Chad Cordero tallied 47 saves with a 1.82 ERA and 0.969 ERA, finishing fifth in the 2005 NL Cy Young balloting. "The Chief" averaged 38 saves from 2005-07.

Grady Sizemore merited three consecutive All-Star nods from 2006-08. He paced the circuit with 134 runs scored and 53 doubles in '06 and joined the 30-30 club in 2008. Ryan Zimmerman drilled 47 doubles and drove in 110 runs en route to a second-place finish in the 2006 NL ROY balloting. Zimmerman (.292/33/106) scored 110 runs and earned his first trip to the Mid-Summer Classic in 2009. Brandon Phillips scored 107 runs and produced a 30-30 campaign in '07. Milton Bradley (.321/22/77) delivered a league-best .436 OBP in '08. Javier Vazquez (15-10, 2.89) posted a career-best ERA and WHIP (1.026) in 2009, placing fourth in the NL Cy Young vote. He supplied 200 whiffs per season (2000-09). Washington right fielders

183

topped the Major Leagues with 22 WS>10 seasons while the left fielders (17) tied Cleveland for the top spot in the decade. Bryce Harper (.270/22/59) tallied 98 runs and claimed 2012 NL ROY honors. Ian Desmond registered consecutive campaigns with at least 20 home runs and 20 stolen bases (2012-13).

Win Shares > 20	Single-Season	1969-2013
Andres Galarraga - 1B (WSN) x5	Tim Wallach - 3B (WSN) x3	Ellis Valentine - RF (WSN)
Tony Bernazard - 2B (WSN)	Gary Carter - C (WSN) x9	Andre Dawson - RF (WSN) x3
Tony Phillips - 2B (WSN)	Tim Raines - LF (WSN) x7	Larry Walker - RF (WSN) x8
Delino DeShields - 2B (WSN)	Gary Roenicke - LF (WSN)	Vladimir Guerrero - RF (WSN) x10
Mike Lansing - 2B (WSN)	Tony Phillips - LF (WSN)	Matt Stairs - RF (WSN)
Jose Vidro - 2B (WSN) x2	Cliff Floyd - LF (WSN) x2	Matt Stairs - DH (WSN)
Brandon Phillips - 2B (WSN)	Jason Bay - LF (WSN) x3	Milton Bradley - DH (WSN)
Orlando Cabrera - SS (WSN) x4	Andre Dawson - CF (WSN) x6	Steve Rogers - SP (WSN) x2
Ian Desmond - SS (WSN) x2	Tim Raines - CF (WSN)	Randy D. Johnson - SP (WSN) x8
Larry Parrish - 3B (WSN)	Marquis Grissom - CF (WSN) x3	Javier Vazquez - SP (WSN)
Tony Phillips - 3B (WSN) x2	Grady Sizemore - CF (WSN) x4	Cliff P. Lee - SP (WSN) x2
Ryan Zimmerman - 3B (WSN) x6	Bryce Harper - CF (WSN)	Bob James - RP (WSN)

Note: 4000 PA or BFP to qualify, except during strike-shortened seasons
(1972 = 3800, 1981 & 1994 = 2700, 1995 = 3500) and 154-game schedule (3800)
- failed to qualify: 1969-1977

Expos / Nationals All-Time "Originals" Roster

Israel Alcantara	Nate Field	Sandy Leon	Wilkin Ruan
Antonio Alfonseca	Jeff Fischer	Richie Lewis	Kirk Rueter
Tavo Alvarez	Cliff Floyd	Larry Lintz	Carl Sadler
Shane Andrews	Barry Foote	Bryan Little	Angel Salazar
Bill Atkinson	Scott Forster	Steve Lombardozzi,	Scott Sanderson
Derek Aucoin	Kevin Foster	Jr.	F.P. Santangelo
Collin Balester	Kris Foster	Brian Looney	Nelson Santovenia
Bret Barberie	Terry Francona	Jose Macias	Pat Scanlon
Greg Bargar	Jerry Fry	Quinn Mack	Dan Schatzeder
Brian Barnes	Mike Fuentes	Pepe Mangual	Curt Schmidt
Michael Barrett	Brad Fullmer	Chris Marrero	Brian Schneider
Tim Barrett	Andres Galarraga	Michael Martinez	Chris Schroder
Jeff Barry	Armando Galarraga	Henry Mateo	Tony Scott
Miguel Batista	Mark Gardner	Troy Mattes	Phil Seibel
Jason Bay	Mike Gates	Justin Maxwell	Jimmy Serrano
Esteban Beltre	Joe Gilbert	Yunesky Maya	Atahualpa Severino
Yamil Benitez	Rene Gonzales	Byron McLaughlin	Razor Shines
Chad Bentz	Tom P. Gorman	Brad J. Mills	Joe Siddall
Jay Bergmann	Rick Grapenthin	Tommy Milone	Grady Sizemore
Roger Bernadina	Marquis Grissom	Nate Minchey	J.D. Smart
Tony Bernazard	Mark Grudzielanek	Craig Minetto	Jhonatan Solano
Dennis Blair	Vladimir Guerrero	Luke Montz	Stan Spencer
Matt Blank	Bill Gullickson	Balor Moore	Matt Stairs
Mike Blowers	Geraldo Guzman	Bill R. Moore	Craig Stammen
Geoff Blum	Chris Haney	Tyler Moore	Randy St. Claire
Hiram Bocachica	Gerry Hannahs	Andres Mora	Mike Stenhouse
Doug Bochtler	Bryce Harper	David Moraga	Drew Storen
Kent Bottenfield	Gene Harris	Dale Murray	Chris Stowers

Milton Bradley	Mike J. Hart	Glenn Murray	Stephen Strasburg
Bill Bray	Heath Haynes	Chris Nabholz	Scott Strickland
Billy Brewer	Bryan Hebson	Bob Natal	Everett Stull
Jolbert Cabrera	Jim Henderson	Al Newman	Jeff Tabaka
Orlando Cabrera	Rod Henderson	Derek Norris	Daryl Thompson
Brett Campbell	Bob Henley	Talmadge Nunnari	Mike Thurman
Casey Candaele	Cesar D. Hernandez	Jack O'Connor	Andy Tracy
Jamey Carroll	Joe Hesketh	Mike O'Connor	John Trautwein
Gary Carter	Shawn Hill	Jerry Owens	T.J. Tucker
Jeff Carter	Mike Hinckley	Alex Pacheco	Ugueth Urbina
Craig Caskey	Brian Holman	David Palmer	Sergio Valdez
Kory Casto	Don Hopkins	Jose Paniagua	Wilson Valdez
Matt Cepicky	Dave Hostetler	Christian Parker	Ellis Valentine
Norm Charlton	Terry Humphrey	Larry Parrish	John Vander Wal
Archi Cianfrocco	Jim Hunter	Val Pascucci	Ben Van Ryn
Greg Colbrunn	Jeff Huson	Bob Pate	Javier Vazquez
Trace Coquillette	Pete Incaviglia	John H. Patterson	Jose Vidro
Roy Corcoran	Tim Ireland	Brad Peacock	Dave Wainhouse
Chad Cordero	Bob James	Carlos Perez	Larry Walker
Wil Cordero	Randy D. Johnson	Eury Perez	Tim Wallach
Reid Cornelius	Roy E. Johnson	Tomas Perez	Dan Warthen
Jim Cox	Tony Johnson	Joe Pettini	Brandon Watson
Warren Cromartie	Wallace Johnson	Tommy Phelps	Matt Watson
Nelson Cruz	Taylor Jordan	Brandon Phillips	Gary Wayne
Scott Davison	Jorge Julio	Tony Phillips	Justin Wayne
Andre Dawson	Nate Karns	Simon Pond	Neil Weber
Rick DeHart	Joe Keener	Jeremy Powell	Derrick White
Tomas de la Rosa	Joe Kerrigan	Tim Raines	Gabe White
Delino DeShields	Cole Kimball	Bobby Ramos	Jerry White
Ian Desmond	Jeff Kobernus	Darrell Rasner	Josh Whitesell
Ross Detwiler	Josh Labandeira	Steve Ratzer	Rondell White
John Dopson	Pete LaForest	Shane Rawley	Tom Wieghaus
Hal Dues	Tim Laker	Bob Reece	Brad Wilkerson
Jayson Durocher	Larry Landreth	Anthony Rendon	Darrin Winston
Rick Engle	Chip Lang	Al Reyes	Cliff Young
Danny Espinosa	John Lannan	Bombo Rivera	Pete Young
Marco Estrada	Mike Lansing	Luis A. Rivera	Tim Young
Steve Falteisek	Yovanny Lara	Gary Roenicke	Jordan Zimmermann
Howard Farmer	Charlie Lea	Steve Rogers	Ryan Zimmerman
Jose M. Fernandez	Cliff P. Lee	Mel Rojas	
Anthony Ferrari	Danilo Leon	Pat Rooney	

Year/Team	OPW%	PW	PL	APW%	AW	AL	Diff+/-
1901 SLB	0.000 F	0	0	0.350	48	89	0.350
1902 SLB	0.391 F	53	83	0.574	78	58	0.182
1903 SLB	0.463 F	65	75	0.468	65	74	0.005
1904 SLB	0.511 F	79	75	0.428	65	87	-0.084
1905 SLB	0.476	73	81	0.353	54	99	-0.123
1906 SLB	0.562 F	86	68	0.510	76	73	-0.052
1907 SLB	0.528	81	73	0.454	69	83	-0.074
1908 SLB	0.444	68	86	0.546	83	69	0.102
1909 SLB	0.378	58	96	0.407	61	89	0.029

franchID	OWAR	OWS	AWAR	AWS	WARdiff	WSdiff	P/D/W/F
1901 SLB	2.869	46.833	19.878	143.998	-17.010	-97.165	F
1902 SLB	2.598	51.184	31.082	230.990	-28.483	-179.806	F
1903 SLB	7.272	84.639	22.771	194.999	-15.499	-110.359	F
1904 SLB	5.296	81.330	21.115	195.008	-15.819	-113.678	F
1905 SLB	11.968	96.628	21.016	161.997	-9.049	-65.369	
1906 SLB	7.047	116.735	36.926	228.004	-29.880	-111.269	F
1907 SLB	12.986	126.868	33.654	207.003	-20.668	-80.135	
1908 SLB	11.270	144.513	36.480	248.999	-25.210	-104.486	
1909 SLB	13.674	154.636	19.283	182.998	-5.608	-28.362	

Legend: (P) = Pennant / Most Wins in League (D) = Division Winner (W) = Wild Card Winner (F) = Failed to Qualify

The St. Louis Browns joined the Major Leagues in 1901 as one of the eight original American League franchises. The team originally entered the League as the Milwaukee Brewers, but fled to St. Louis after a singular campaign in Wisconsin. The franchise's futile efforts concluded with the failure to secure a single pennant during its tenure in St. Louis. The Browns relocated to Baltimore in 1954 and changed the team nickname to the Orioles.

Based on the WS>20 frame of reference, the franchise has developed the fewest quality catchers (2), left fielders (12), center fielders (12) and right fielders (6) among the "Turn of the Century" franchises. The organization also places second-to-last in starting pitcher development. The club's first basemen, outfielders, starting and relief pitchers never finished in the top three WS>10 totals for the "Turn of the Century" teams.

Barney Pelty anchored the rotation as he delivered a 2.39 ERA and averaged 23 complete games from 1904-09. "The Yiddish Curver" perplexed opposition batsmen, posting a record of 16-11 with a 1.59 ERA and 0.951 WHIP in '06.

Year/Team	OPW%	PW	PL	APW%	AW	AL	Diff+/-
1910 SLB	0.355	55	99	0.437	66	85	0.082
1911 SLB	0.355	55	99	0.296	45	107	-0.059
1912 SLB	0.365	56	98	0.344	53	101	-0.021
1913 SLB	0.394	61	93	0.373	57	96	-0.021
1914 SLB	0.472	73	81	0.464	71	82	-0.008
1915 SLB	0.414	64	90	0.409	63	91	-0.005
1916 SLB	0.550	85	69	0.513	79	75	-0.037
1917 SLB	0.289	45	109	0.370	57	97	0.081
1918 SLB	0.492	63	65	0.475	58	64	-0.017
1919 SLB	0.396	55	85	0.482	67	72	0.086

franchID	OWAR	OWS	AWAR	AWS	WARdiff	WSdiff	P/D/W/F
1910 SLB	-1.479	133.499	1.329	141.003	-2.807	-7.504	
1911 SLB	2.893	129.202	4.497	135.000	-1.605	-5.798	
1912 SLB	18.833	165.389	18.714	158.997	0.119	6.391	
1913 SLB	17.456	173.239	17.219	170.998	0.237	2.241	
1914 SLB	24.122	216.735	22.615	212.995	1.497	3.741	
1915 SLB	26.687	212.163	23.819	189.002	2.868	23.161	
1916 SLB	41.424	266.377	37.700	236.996	3.724	29.381	
1917 SLB	21.997	189.141	20.483	170.998	1.514	18.143	
1918 SLB	29.783	203.787	27.868	174.001	1.915	29.787	
1919 SLB	28.950	209.189	27.448	200.996	1.502	8.193	

Cy R. Morgan fashioned an ERA of 2.08 over four campaigns (1908-1911). He recorded 18 victories and a 1.55 ERA in 1910. Burt Shotton swiped 40+ bases in four consecutive years (1913-16). Carl Weilman manufactured 17 victories with a 2.19 ERA and a 1.126 WHIP over a three-year period covering 1914-16 and in the same timeframe, Jeff Pfeffer racked up 22 victories and completed 28 games per season with a 1.99 ERA. Pfeffer (25-11, 1.92) accrued 30 Win Shares in 1916 while establishing career-bests in wins, ERA, complete games, innings pitched and WHIP. Second sacker Del Pratt drove in 103 runs as the Browns won 85 contests and finished only two games behind Detroit.

George Sisler compiled a .337 BA over a four-year stretch from 1916 through 1919 and claimed the stolen base crown with 45 swipes in '18. Scott Perry (20-19, 1.98) paced the circuit in complete games (30), games started (36) and innings pitched (332.1). Allen Sothoron set personal bests In ERA (1.94) and WHIP (1.048) during the 1918 season and furnished a 20-win effort during the subsequent campaign.

Win Shares > 20	Single-Season	1901-1919
George Sisler - 1B (BAL) x7	Burt Shotton - CF (BAL) x2	Jeff Pfeffer - SP (BAL) x4
Del Pratt - 2B (BAL) x6	Barney Pelty - SP (BAL)	Carl Weilman - SP (BAL)
Wid Conroy - 3B (BAL)	Cy R. Morgan - SP (BAL)	Scott Perry - SP (BAL)
Burt Shotton - LF (BAL) x2	Earl Hamilton - SP (BAL)	Allen Sothoron - SP (BAL)

Year/Team	OPW%	PW	PL	APW%	AW	AL	Diff+/-
1920 SLB	0.483	74	80	0.497	76	77	0.014
1921 SLB	0.439	68	86	0.526	81	73	0.087
1922 SLB	0.532	82	72	0.604	93	61	0.072
1923 SLB	0.455 F	70	84	0.487	74	78	0.032
1924 SLB	0.467	72	82	0.487	74	78	0.020
1925 SLB	0.463 F	71	83	0.536	82	71	0.073
1926 SLB	0.465	72	82	0.403	62	92	-0.063
1927 SLB	0.473	73	81	0.386	59	94	-0.088
1928 SLB	0.468	72	82	0.532	82	72	0.064
1929 SLB	0.480	74	80	0.520	79	73	0.040

franchID	OWAR	OWS	AWAR	AWS	WARdiff	WSdiff	P/D/W/F
1920 SLB	**39.068**	223.288	39.640	227.996	-0.572	-4.708	
1921 SLB	30.668	232.388	34.296	243.001	-3.628	-10.612	
1922 SLB	**45.836**	247.491	**55.191**	278.999	-9.355	-31.507	
1923 SLB	29.572	200.658	34.977	222.002	-5.405	-21.343	F
1924 SLB	27.553	194.709	32.389	221.995	-4.836	-27.286	
1925 SLB	23.626	229.191	30.483	245.997	-6.856	-16.806	F
1926 SLB	30.067	231.559	18.892	185.999	11.175	45.560	

1927 SLB	29.248	194.447	19.004	176.997	10.244	17.450
1928 SLB	33.171	223.656	34.443	246.001	-1.272	-22.345
1929 SLB	35.463	249.770	31.778	237.001	3.685	12.769

Sisler established the Major League record with 257 base hits in 1920, a record which stood for 84 seasons until Ichiro Suzuki collected 262 safeties in 2004. He batted .407 en route to his first batting crown and set personal bests with 137 runs, 49 doubles, 19 dingers, 122 ribbies, and 33 Win Shares. Pratt averaged .311 with 33 doubles and 80 RBI from 1920-24.

St. Louis led the American League in oWAR during the 1920 and 1922 seasons. The Browns posted a record of 82-72 and placed second behind the White Sox in '22. Sisler (.420/8/105) earned the MVP award while collecting his second batting title. He topped the circuit in hits (246), runs (134), stolen bases (51) and swatted 18 triples for the third straight season. Pfeffer and Elam Vangilder contributed 19 victories apiece for the 1922 crew while Marty McManus plated 109 runners and legged out 11 three-base hits. McManus delivered a .317 BA with 31 two-base hits and 94 RBI over three campaigns (1922-24).

Sisler manufactured 211 hits per season along with a .347 BA during the Twenties. Browns' backstop Muddy Ruel furnished a .303 batting average over a 5-year span covering 1923-27. Charley Root garnered 18 victories with a 2.82 ERA for the '26 staff. "Chinski" topped the League with 26 wins, 48 appearances and 309 innings pitched in 1927 despite issuing 117 free passes. He placed fourth in the MVP balloting. Root won 19 contests with a 3.47 ERA in '29. Shortstop Red Kress (.305/9/107) surpassed the 100-RBI plateau in three consecutive seasons (1929-1931).

Year/Team	OPW%	PW	PL	APW%	AW	AL	Diff+/-
1930 SLB	0.388	60	94	0.416	64	90	0.028
1931 SLB	0.437	67	87	0.409	63	91	-0.028
1932 SLB	0.441	68	86	0.409	63	91	-0.032
1933 SLB	0.423	65	89	0.364	55	96	-0.059
1934 SLB	0.414 F	64	90	0.441	67	85	0.027
1935 SLB	0.399 F	62	92	0.428	65	87	0.028
1936 SLB	0.428 F	66	88	0.375	57	95	-0.053
1937 SLB	0.373 F	58	96	0.299	46	108	-0.075
1938 SLB	0.465 F	72	82	0.362	55	97	-0.103
1939 SLB	0.384	59	95	0.279	43	111	-0.104

franchID	OWAR	OWS	AWAR	AWS	WARdiff	WSdiff	P/D/W/F
1930 SLB	28.246	212.334	20.780	192.006	7.465	20.327	
1931 SLB	22.928	188.943	25.971	189.000	-3.043	-0.057	
1932 SLB	24.577	191.088	27.328	188.995	-2.751	2.093	
1933 SLB	17.589	172.835	23.509	165.001	-5.920	7.834	
1934 SLB	12.097	194.633	22.601	201.006	-10.504	-6.373	F
1935 SLB	15.604	188.078	22.880	195.000	-7.276	-6.923	F
1936 SLB	19.494	204.505	22.146	171.005	-2.652	33.500	F
1937 SLB	24.271	178.270	18.945	138.003	5.326	40.267	F
1938 SLB	39.017	230.880	26.322	165.005	12.695	65.875	F
1939 SLB	22.389	167.604	14.499	128.996	7.890	38.607	

Kress produced a mirror image of his offensive output in '30 and '31. In 1930 he delivered a .313 BA with 43 doubles, 8 triples, 16 home runs and 112 RBI. He matched his totals for three-base hits and round-trippers while clubbing 46 doubles, driving in 114 runs and hitting .311 in the subsequent season. McManus supplied a .320 batting average and topped the American League by swiping 23 bags.

Heinie Meine aka "The Count of Luxemborg" led the League with 19 victories and 284 innings pitched while posting an ERA of 2.98 and completing 22 of 35 starts. Fred Schulte supplied a .297 BA while scoring 101 runs per season from 1931-33. Harlond Clift tallied 108 runs per year from 1936-1942, registering a career-high with 145 in '36. Clift plated 118 baserunners in consecutive seasons (1937-38) and dialed long distance 34 times for the '38 crew. The influx of gifted players was reduced to a trickle as St. Louis failed to meet the minimum PA and/or BFP requirements for 25 seasons (1934-1959) with the exception of 1939.

Win Shares > 20	Single-Season	1920-1939
Marty McManus - 2B (BAL) x2	Harlond Clift - 3B (BAL) x6	Elam Vangilder - SP (BAL) x2
Red Kress - SS (BAL) x2	Muddy Ruel - C (BAL)	Charley Root - SP (BAL) x3
Marty McManus - 3B (BAL)	Fred Schulte - CF (BAL)	Heinie Meine - SP (BAL)

Year/Team	OPW%	PW	PL	APW%	AW	AL	Diff+/-
1940 SLB	0.477 F	73	81	0.435	67	87	-0.042
1941 SLB	0.443 F	68	86	0.455	70	84	0.011
1942 SLB	0.504 F	78	76	0.543	82	69	0.039
1943 SLB	0.471 F	73	81	0.474	72	80	0.002
1944 SLB	0.535 F	82	72	0.578 P	89	65	0.043
1945 SLB	0.505 F	78	76	0.536	81	70	0.031
1946 SLB	0.483 F	74	80	0.429	66	88	-0.054
1947 SLB	0.376 F	58	96	0.383	59	95	0.008
1948 SLB	0.493 F	76	78	0.386	59	94	-0.108
1949 SLB	0.427 F	66	88	0.344	53	101	-0.083

franchID	OWAR	OWS	AWAR	AWS	WARdiff	WSdiff	P/D/W/F
1940 SLB	25.906	223.246	24.445	200.998	1.461	22.248	F
1941 SLB	24.993	189.116	36.177	210.001	-11.184	-20.885	F
1942 SLB	35.171	237.123	42.061	246.000	-6.891	-8.877	F
1943 SLB	32.883	256.449	35.605	216.011	-2.722	40.438	F
1944 SLB	44.322	280.457	37.620	267.003	6.702	13.454	F
1945 SLB	37.863	275.164	32.008	243.001	5.855	32.163	F
1946 SLB	21.998	258.703	23.545	197.996	-1.547	60.707	F
1947 SLB	17.178	208.312	21.051	177.007	-3.873	31.305	F
1948 SLB	36.713	235.220	26.030	177.000	10.683	58.220	F
1949 SLB	30.577	243.039	20.537	159.002	10.040	84.036	F

Vern Stephens recorded the second highest Win Share total in team annals (34), placed third in the 1944 AL MVP balloting and drove in a league-leading 109 runs. "Junior" produced a .288 BA with 22 taters and 103 ribbies per year (1942-1949). Stephens' run production peaked during a three-year stretch from 1948-1950 as he delivered 117 runs scored, 33 jacks and 147 RBI per season. Jim Russell batted .312 and crossed home plate 109 times for the '44 squad. Jack Kramer contributed a 17-13 record with an ERA of 2.49.

Year/Team	OPW%	PW	PL	APW%	AW	AL	Diff+/-
1950 SLB	0.531 F	82	72	0.377	58	96	-0.155
1951 SLB	0.431 F	66	88	0.338	52	102	-0.093
1952 SLB	0.355 F	55	99	0.416	64	90	0.061
1953 SLB	0.480 F	74	80	0.351	54	100	-0.130
1954 BAL	0.493 F	76	78	0.351	54	100	-0.143
1955 BAL	0.523 F	80	74	0.370	57	97	-0.152
1956 BAL	0.556 F	86	68	0.448	69	85	-0.107

franchID							
1957 BAL	0.564 F	87	67	0.500	76	76	-0.064
1958 BAL	0.493 F	76	78	0.484	74	79	-0.009
1959 BAL	0.554 F	85	69	0.481	74	80	-0.073

franchID	OWAR	OWS	AWAR	AWS	WARdiff	WSdiff	P/D/W/F
1950 BAL	30.801	258.978	18.278	174.004	12.523	84.974	F
1951 BAL	16.915	204.451	11.534	156.002	5.382	48.449	F
1952 BAL	16.707	203.870	25.755	191.997	-9.048	11.873	F
1953 BAL	36.145	193.659	22.036	161.996	14.108	31.663	F
1954 BAL	22.411	165.957	14.215	170.999	8.196	-5.042	F
1955 BAL	27.710	205.192	14.215	170.999	13.495	34.193	F
1956 BAL	14.246	203.103	27.077	207.001	-12.831	-3.898	F
1957 BAL	33.786	220.906	37.492	228.003	-3.706	-7.097	F
1958 BAL	31.727	205.809	32.174	222.004	-0.447	-16.196	F
1959 BAL	35.176	221.327	30.846	222.003	4.330	-0.676	F

The Browns' inept offense failed to exceed the minimum PA standards from 1952-59 while the incompetent mound corps fell short of the BFP requirements from 1950-57. Stephens thumped 30 round-trippers and paced the circuit with 144 RBI while Al Zarilla scorched opposing hurlers for a .325 average in 1950. Hank Thompson drove in 91 runs in '50 and then belted 26 long balls for the '54 squad. Ned Garver (20-12, 3.73) completed 24 of 33 starts, made his only appearance in the All-Star contest and placed second in the 1951 AL MVP balloting.

The franchise relocated to Baltimore in 1954 and changed its nickname to the Orioles. Roy Sievers produced 30 four-baggers and knocked in 96 runs per year from 1954-59. "Squirrel" finished third in the 1957 AL MVP balloting, batting .301 with a league-best 42 bombs and 114 RBI. He delivered 39 jacks and 108 ribbies during the subsequent campaign. Dave Jolly vultured 11 wins and saved 10 games while posting a 2.43 ERA in '54.

Bob Turley led the American League with 185 strikeouts in 1954 although he also issued the most free passes (181)! "Bullet Bob" tallied 17 wins with a 3.06 ERA in '55. Turley paced the AL with 21 wins and 19 complete games en route to Cy Young honors in 1958. Billy O'Dell posted a 2.93 ERA, won 14 games and earned his first All-Star invite in '58.

Milt Pappas attained 15 victories with a 3.27 ERA in 1959. Tito Francona enjoyed a stellar season, supplying a .363 batting average along with 20 dingers. The organization was unable to produce any WS>10 seasons among its catchers, first basemen or second basemen during the Fifties. GM Paul Richards signed Brooks Robinson, Ron Hansen and Pappas as amateur free agents during his brief stint in the O's front office. Lee MacPhail succeeded Richards and acquired a bevy of prospects including Boog Powell, Jim Palmer and Sparky Lyle.

Win Shares > 20	Single-Season	1940-1959
Vern Stephens - SS (BAL) x8	Jim Russell - LF (BAL) x2	Jack Kramer - SP (BAL)
Hank Thompson - 3B (BAL) x2	Roy Sievers - LF (BAL) x3	Ned Garver - SP (BAL) x3
	Tito Francona - CF (BAL)	Billy O'Dell - SP (BAL)

Year/Team	OPW%	PW	PL	APW%	AW	AL	Diff+/-
1960 BAL	0.573 P	88	66	0.578	89	65	0.005
1961 BAL	0.473	77	85	0.586	95	67	0.114
1962 BAL	0.478	77	85	0.475	77	85	-0.003
1963 BAL	0.483	78	84	0.531	86	76	0.048
1964 BAL	0.549	89	73	0.599	97	65	0.050
1965 BAL	0.457	74	88	0.580	94	68	0.123
1966 BAL	0.497	80	82	0.606 P	97	63	0.110

franchID							
1967 BAL	0.433	70	92	0.472	76	85	0.039
1968 BAL	0.484	78	84	0.562	91	71	0.078
1969 BAL	0.498	81	81	0.673 P	109	53	0.175

franchID	OWAR	OWS	AWAR	AWS	WARdiff	WSdiff	P/D/W/F
1960 BAL	**37.594**	242.660	40.938	266.998	-3.344	-24.338	P
1961 BAL	29.756	205.746	46.330	285.002	-16.574	-79.255	
1962 BAL	24.545	191.499	36.209	230.999	-11.664	-39.500	
1963 BAL	27.538	201.025	39.713	257.999	-12.176	-56.974	
1964 BAL	42.061	256.550	44.621	291.003	-2.561	-34.454	
1965 BAL	28.616	211.004	39.876	282.005	-11.260	-71.001	
1966 BAL	30.935	203.484	**53.811**	**290.992**	-22.877	-87.509	
1967 BAL	25.799	185.620	44.735	227.996	-18.936	-42.376	
1968 BAL	35.685	208.923	47.742	273.001	-12.058	-64.078	
1969 BAL	34.205	217.768	**61.183**	**327.006**	-26.978	-109.238	

The Orioles captured the franchise's first pennant in 1960, ending the year 11 games ahead of the Indians. Ron Hansen earned the 1960 AL ROY award and placed fifth in the MVP voting after swatting 22 four-baggers and knocking in 86 runs. Brooks Robinson began a string of 15 consecutive All-Star appearances in 1960 and collected 16 straight Gold Glove awards. Known as the "Vacuum Cleaner" for his fielding prowess at the hot corner, Robinson received AL MVP honors in 1964. He batted .317 with 28 home runs, accrued 33 Win Shares and led the League with 118 RBI.

Dean Chance (14-10, 2.96) finished third in the 1962 AL ROY balloting. Chance topped the circuit in victories (20), ERA (1.65), complete games (15), shutouts (11) and innings pitched en route to achieving Cy Young honors in 1964. He amassed 20 wins in 1967 along with a 2.73 ERA and league-high 18 complete games. Billy O'Dell delivered career-bests with 19 wins and 20 complete games in 1962. Three years later he collected 10 victories and 18 saves with a 2.18 ERA.

Pete Ward (.295/22/84) placed second in the 1963 AL ROY voting while Steve D. Barber fashioned a 20-13 mark with a 2.75 ERA in the same season. Barber averaged 13 wins with a 3.07 ERA from 1960-66. Boog Powell crushed 39 moon-shots and topped the League with a .606 SLG in 1964 and went on to finish third in the 1966 AL MVP balloting, thumping 34 round-trippers and driving in 109 runs. The slugging lefty set career-highs with a .304 average and 121 RBI and placed runner-up in the '69 MVP race.

Baltimore posted 89 victories in '64 and finished in third place, three games behind the Yankees. Pappas posted a 16-7 record with a 2.97 ERA in '64. "Gimpy" supplied a 14-10 mark with a 3.34 ERA from 1960-68. Wally Bunker (19-5, 2.69) placed second in the 1964 AL ROY balloting. GM Harry Dalton and Scouting Director Walter Shannon executed the greatest Amateur Draft in Baltimore history based on Career Total Win Shares (654) and Career Total WAR (96) owing principally to contributions from Bobby Grich and Don Baylor.

Dave McNally amassed 20+ victories in four consecutive seasons (1968-71) and led the League with a 0.895 WHIP in 1968. Tom Phoebus added 15 victories with a 2.62 ERA for the '68 staff. Mike Epstein mashed 30 taters for the 1969 crew and in the same year Jim Palmer managed a 16-4 record with a 2.34 ERA. Down in the bullpen, Darold Knowles collected 9 wins and 13 saves along with a 2.24 ERA, earning his only trip to the All-Star game in 1969. Sparky Lyle achieved 8 wins and 17 saves while Eddie Watt notched 16 saves with a 1.65 ERA. The 1969 O's delivered the worst WSdiff (-109) and WARdiff (-26) vs. the output of the "Actual" Orioles from the same year.

Year/Team	OPW%	PW	PL	APW%	AW	AL	Diff+/-
1970 BAL	0.532	86	76	0.667 P	108	54	0.135
1971 BAL	0.508	82	80	0.639 P	101	57	0.131
1972 BAL	0.568 P	92	70	0.519	80	74	-0.049
1973 BAL	0.599 P	97	65	0.599 P	97	65	0.000
1974 BAL	0.492	80	82	0.562 P	91	71	0.069
1975 BAL	0.459	74	88	0.566	90	69	0.107
1976 BAL	0.524 D	85	77	0.543	88	74	0.019
1977 BAL	0.510	83	79	0.602	97	64	0.092
1978 BAL	0.517	84	78	0.559	90	71	0.042
1979 BAL	0.503	82	80	0.642 P	102	57	0.138

franchID	OWAR	OWS	AWAR	AWS	WARdiff	WSdiff	P/D/W/F
1970 BAL	37.545	239.188	56.806	324.001	-19.261	-84.813	
1971 BAL	38.820	252.713	54.954	303.005	-16.134	-50.293	
1972 BAL	41.861	249.587	40.264	240.000	1.597	9.587	P
1973 BAL	41.123	237.530	50.140	290.992	-9.017	-53.462	P
1974 BAL	32.479	219.207	40.396	273.003	-7.917	-53.796	
1975 BAL	37.474	214.727	43.947	269.999	-6.472	-55.272	
1976 BAL	30.292	232.697	37.037	264.004	-6.745	-31.307	D
1977 BAL	32.556	216.858	39.859	290.998	-7.303	-74.139	
1978 BAL	29.040	199.663	43.082	269.994	-14.041	-70.330	
1979 BAL	32.532	211.557	50.233	305.997	-17.701	-94.440	

Jim Palmer collected at least 20 wins in eight seasons during the Seventies. For the decade "Cakes" averaged a 19-10 record with 18 complete games and a 2.54 ERA. Palmer earned three Cy Young awards ('73, '75, '76), leading the circuit with a 2.40 ERA in 1973 and a 2.09 ERA in 1975. Boog Powell (.297/35/114) captured the 1970 AL MVP award. Robinson drove in 90+ runs in 1970-71 and finished fourth in the 1971 AL MVP race.

Baltimore led the American League in oWS in back-to-back campaigns (1970-71) and placed second in the AL East in '70, three games behind New York. Dave McNally paced the League with 24 wins and placed second in the 1970 AL Cy Young voting. Knowles saved 27 contests in 1970 and fashioned a 2.04 ERA and baffled the opposition in '72, delivering a miniscule 1.37 ERA along with 11 saves. Pappas notched 17 wins in back-to-back seasons (1971-72) and pitched a near-perfect game in September 1972.

The Orioles' front office fared poorly in the Amateur Draft over the 16-year period from 1971-1986. Primarily under the direction of GM Hank Peters and Scouting Director Tom Giordano, Baltimore's draft classes averaged only 57 Career Total Win Shares excluding the '73 and '78 drafts. Peters and Giordano deserve credit for the selections of Cal Ripken Jr. and Mike Boddicker in 1978 (610 Career Total Win Shares) while GM Frank Cashen and Scouting Director David Ritterpusch chose Eddie Murray and Mike Flanagan five years prior.

The "O's" delivered consecutive pennants in 1972-73, leading the League in oWAR while surpassing the 90-win plateau in both seasons. Lyle provided a league-high 35 saves in '72 and finished third in the MVP balloting. He was rewarded with Cy Young honors in 1977 after supplying 13 victories, 26 saves and a 2.17 ERA. Baltimore posted the lowest ERA in franchise history (2.70) in 1972.

Don Baylor added a power-speed combination to the Orioles lineup in 1972. Baylor averaged 30 stolen bases per season (1972-79) including 52 thefts in '76. After crushing 34 long balls in the previous campaign, Baylor collected AL MVP honors in 1979. He topped the circuit with 139 RBI and 120 runs scored, as well as smashing 36 round-trippers en route to his lone All-Star appearance.

Second-sacker Davey Johnson slugged 43 circuit clouts and plated 99 runners in 1973. Bobby Grich earned four consecutive Gold Gloves awards (1973-76) and in 1979 he belted 30 home runs and knocked in 101 runs. Al Bumbry claimed the 1973 AL ROY award, stinging the opposition with a .337 average and league-high 11 triples. "The Bee" nabbed 42 bags in '76 and batted .317 in 1977.

Baltimore took the AL Eastern division title by two games over Cleveland in '76. Wayne Garland tallied 20 victories with a 2.67 ERA in '76 and completed 21 contests in the following season. Enos Cabell posted career-highs in 1977 with 36 doubles, 16 homers, 101 runs scored and 42 stolen bases. Eddie Murray received the 1977 AL ROY award, blasting 27 home runs and driving in 88 runs. The Orioles placed second in 1977 behind the Red Sox and subsequently fell two games short in the ensuing year.

Doug DeCinces drilled 37 two-base hits and 28 wallops for the '78 squad. Mike Flanagan amassed 19 victories in 1978 and went on to win the AL Cy Young award in '79, posting a 23-9 mark with a 3.08 ERA and a career-low 1.186 WHIP. Dennis Martinez hurled a league-high 18 complete games in 1979 and collected 15 wins.

Win Shares > 20	Single-Season	1960-1979
Roy Sievers - 1B (BAL) x2	Brooks Robinson - 3B (BAL) x10	Merv Rettenmund - RF (BAL)
Boog Powell - 1B (BAL) x5	Pete Ward - 3B (BAL) x2	Eddie Murray - DH (BAL)
Mike Epstein - 1B (BAL) x2	Doug DeCinces - 3B (BAL) x3	Don Baylor - DH (BAL) x2
Eddie Murray - 1B (BAL) x10	Tito Francona - LF (BAL) x2	Dean Chance - SP (BAL) x3
Davey Johnson - 2B (BAL) x3	Boog Powell - LF (BAL)	Dave McNally - SP (BAL) x2
Bobby Grich - 2B (BAL) x9	Don Baylor - LF (BAL) x2	Jim Palmer - SP (BAL) x8
Ron Hansen - SS (BAL) x2	Lenny Green - CF (BAL)	Milt Pappas - SP (BAL)
Wayne Causey - SS (BAL)	Al Bumbry - CF (BAL) x2	Wayne Garland - SP (BAL)
Mark Belanger - SS (BAL) x2	Fred Valentine - RF (BAL)	Mike Flanagan - SP (BAL)
Bobby Grich - SS (BAL)		Sparky Lyle - RP (BAL)
Enos Cabell - 3B (BAL)		

Year/Team	OPW%	PW	PL	APW%	AW	AL	Diff+/-
1980 BAL	0.489	79	83	0.617	100	62	0.128
1981 BAL	0.495	80	82	0.562	59	46	0.067
1982 BAL	0.551 P	89	73	0.580	94	68	0.029
1983 BAL	0.604 P	98	64	0.605 D	98	64	0.001
1984 BAL	0.564 P	91	71	0.525	85	77	-0.040
1985 BAL	0.546	89	73	0.516	83	78	-0.031
1986 BAL	0.452	73	89	0.451	73	89	-0.002
1987 BAL	0.453	73	89	0.414	67	95	-0.039
1988 BAL	0.446	72	90	0.335	54	107	-0.111
1989 BAL	0.435 F	70	92	0.537	87	75	0.102

franchID	OWAR	OWS	AWAR	AWS	WARdiff	WSdiff	P/D/W/F
1980 BAL	30.514	211.743	49.124	300.007	-18.610	-88.264	
1981 BAL	22.349	147.139	24.179	176.997	-1.830	-29.858	
1982 BAL	32.583	227.315	46.342	282.000	-13.759	-54.685	P
1983 BAL	42.650	255.462	49.026	294.002	-6.376	-38.540	P
1984 BAL	39.426	256.693	35.292	255.002	4.134	1.691	P
1985 BAL	35.336	220.161	41.006	249.002	-5.670	-28.840	
1986 BAL	30.213	195.004	34.104	219.002	-3.890	-23.997	
1987 BAL	29.051	191.144	26.449	201.000	2.602	-9.856	
1988 BAL	19.457	179.413	16.728	162.000	2.729	17.413	
1989 BAL	22.766	199.651	32.376	260.997	-9.610	-61.345	F

Eddie Murray slugged 27 long balls and knocked in 100 runs per season during the Eighties. "Steady Eddie" placed in the top five in the MVP voting in each season from 1981-85, including runner-up finishes in 1982-83. Murray accrued 33 Win Shares, led the American League with a .410 OBP and collected his third consecutive Gold Glove Award in '84. Al Bumbry received an All-Star invitation in 1980 and totaled 32 Win Shares while batting .318 with 205 hits, 118 runs scored and 44 stolen bases.

Bobby Grich tied for the League lead with 22 homers during the strike-shortened campaign in '81 and topped the circuit with a .543 SLG. Sammy Stewart logged an ERA of 2.32 as a long reliever while Dennis Martinez (14-5, 3.31) led the circuit in victories in 1981. Martinez averaged 14 wins with a 3.03 ERA from 1987-89. Palmer (15-5, 3.13) paced the League with a 1.137 WHIP and earned a runner-up finish in the 1982 AL Cy Young voting. DeCinces (.301/30/97) posted his best single-season statistics across the board in 1982 and finished third in the MVP race. In 1986 he belted 26 round-trippers and plated 96 runs. Baltimore scored three consecutive pennants in the Eighties (1982-84). The Orioles outlasted the Brewers by a single game in '82.

Cal Ripken Jr. won the 1982 AL ROY award after belting 28 circuit clouts and knocking in 93 runs. He also began his streak of 2,632 consecutive games played during his inaugural campaign. Ripken (.318/27/102) received MVP honors during the ensuing season as he paced the League with 211 hits, 121 runs and 47 doubles. The "Iron Man" played in 19 consecutive All-Star games and averaged 26 home runs and 93 RBI from 1982-89. Ripken posted the highest total in franchise history when he registered 37 Win Shares in '84. Baltimore compiled a franchise-best 98 victories and defeated Milwaukee by a ten-game margin in 1983. Mike Boddicker placed third in the 1983 AL ROY race, posting a 16-8 record with career-bests in ERA (2.77) and WHIP (1.078). In 1984, he topped the American League with 20 victories and a 2.79 ERA, earning his only trip to the Mid-Summer Classic. Baylor supplied a career-high .303 BA in 1983 and blasted 31 long balls with 94 ribbies in '86.

The '84 squad outdistanced the Red Sox by seven games and accrued franchise-bests in offWARnorm (21) and offWSnorm (139). Storm Davis yielded a 3.12 ERA in 1984 and amassed 19 victories in '89. Mike D. Young walloped 28 moon-shots in 1985. Bryn Smith fashioned an 18-5 record with a 2.91 ERA. The O's managed to win 89 contests in 1985, coming up three games behind Boston for the division title. The club fell on hard times in 1986, finishing in the AL East basement for three straight seasons. Larry Sheets busted out with a .316 average, 31 four-baggers and 94 ribbies in '87. Gregg Olson (1.69, 27 SV) received the AL ROY award in 1989. Jeff Ballard achieved an 18-8 mark. The offense failed to meet the minimum PA requirements in 1989.

Year/Team	OPW%	PW	PL	APW%	AW	AL	Diff+/-
1990 BAL	0.465	75	87	0.472	76	85	0.007
1991 BAL	0.496 F	80	82	0.414	67	95	-0.082
1992 BAL	0.478	77	85	0.549	89	73	0.071
1993 BAL	0.475	77	85	0.525	85	77	0.050
1994 BAL	0.538 W	87	75	0.563	63	49	0.024
1995 BAL	0.538 D	87	75	0.493	71	73	-0.045
1996 BAL	0.461	75	87	0.543 W	88	74	0.082
1997 BAL	0.499	81	81	0.605 P	98	64	0.106
1998 BAL	0.462	75	87	0.488	79	83	0.026
1999 BAL	0.496	80	82	0.481	78	84	-0.015
franchID	OWAR	OWS	AWAR	AWS	WARdiff	WSdiff	P/D/W/F
1990 BAL	32.888	209.199	30.513	228.001	2.374	-18.802	
1991 BAL	40.558	206.960	33.909	201.000	6.649	5.960	F
1992 BAL	39.013	221.485	46.443	267.004	-7.430	-45.519	F

Year	OWAR	OWS	AWAR	AWS	WARdiff	WSdiff	P/D/W/F
1993 BAL	29.900	211.168	39.857	255.001	-9.957	-43.834	
1994 BAL	28.300	172.223	32.438	189.004	-4.138	-16.781	W
1995 BAL	35.396	211.505	38.339	213.000	-2.943	-1.495	D
1996 BAL	25.557	201.104	43.166	264.002	-17.610	-62.898	
1997 BAL	36.941	240.550	46.903	**293.992**	-9.963	-53.442	
1998 BAL	30.645	221.725	43.837	237.000	-13.192	-15.275	
1999 BAL	39.025	256.085	39.434	234.003	-0.410	22.082	

Dennis Martinez posted a 3.02 ERA from 1990-95, leading the circuit with a 2.39 ERA in 1991. Boddicker (17-8, 3.36) received a Gold Glove Award in 1990. Gregg Olson saved 33 games per season from 1990-1993 with a 2.41 ERA. The "Otter" regained the closer's role and saved 30 games in '98. Eddie Murray (.330/26/95) added a batting crown to his trophy case in 1990 and placed fifth in the MVP balloting. Pete Harnisch fashioned a 2.70 ERA in 1991 and received an All-Star invitation. He amassed 16 wins with a 2.98 ERA in '93. Ripken (.323/34/114) achieved American League MVP honors in '91. The offense failed to meet the minimum PA requirements in 1991 and 1992.

Steve Finley pilfered 44 bags in 1992 and topped the League with 13 triples in '93. He smacked 45 doubles and scored 126 runs in 1996 and launched 34 long balls with a career-high 103 ribbies in '99. Mike Mussina furnished an 18-5 record with a 2.54 ERA in his first full season (1992) and finished fourth in the AL Cy Young voting. "Moose" paced the League with 19 victories in '95, posting 16 wins with a 3.53 ERA and a 1.177 WHIP from 1992-99. Baltimore earned the 1994 AL Wild Card entry with 87 wins. An identical victory total netted a division title for the Orioles in the subsequent campaign. David Segui delivered a .301 average from 1995-99. Arthur Rhodes captured 10 wins in '97, and Mark Leiter closed out 23 games in 1998. Armando Benitez struck out 128 batters in 78 innings and saved 22 contests in 1999.

Year/Team	OPW%	PW	PL	APW%	AW	AL	Diff+/-
2000 BAL	0.515	83	79	0.457	74	88	-0.058
2001 BAL	0.436	71	91	0.391	63	98	-0.045
2002 BAL	0.440 F	71	91	0.414	67	95	-0.027
2003 BAL	0.488 F	79	83	0.438	71	91	-0.050
2004 BAL	0.519	84	78	0.481	78	84	-0.038
2005 BAL	0.500	81	81	0.457	74	88	-0.043
2006 BAL	0.506 F	82	80	0.432	70	92	-0.074
2007 BAL	0.493 F	80	82	0.426	69	93	-0.067
2008 BAL	0.512	83	79	0.422	68	93	-0.090
2009 BAL	0.451	73	89	0.395	64	98	-0.056
2010 BAL	0.456	74	88	0.407	66	96	-0.049
2011 BAL	0.399	65	97	0.426	69	93	0.027
2012 BAL	0.448 F	73	89	0.574 W	93	69	0.126
2013 BAL	0.521	84	78	0.525	85	77	0.004

franchID	OWAR	OWS	AWAR	AWS	WARdiff	WSdiff	P/D/W/F
2000 BAL	35.175	241.342	30.223	222.007	4.952	19.334	
2001 BAL	25.773	215.087	19.529	188.993	6.244	26.094	
2002 BAL	31.177	232.348	26.340	200.996	4.837	31.352	F
2003 BAL	39.553	238.747	28.061	212.996	11.492	25.751	F
2004 BAL	30.361	221.612	39.535	234.001	-9.175	-12.389	
2005 BAL	35.352	223.908	34.301	222.000	1.051	1.908	
2006 BAL	36.720	210.477	27.229	210.002	9.491	0.475	F
2007 BAL	36.026	204.932	28.812	207.002	7.214	-2.070	F
2008 BAL	39.263	238.669	25.966	204.008	13.296	34.661	
2009 BAL	30.031	222.937	24.418	192.000	5.613	30.938	

2010 BAL	39.126	252.836	21.630	197.996	17.495	54.840	
2011 BAL	29.646	217.103	24.918	206.998	4.727	10.105	
2012 BAL	21.250	229.447	36.059	267.113	-14.810	-37.666	F
2013 BAL	28.712	243.411	34.892	247.856	-6.180	-4.446	

Finley belted 35 home runs and drove in 96 runs in 2000 and set a career-best with 36 wallops and collected his fifth Gold Glove award in '04. Jeffrey Hammonds (.335/20/106) earned an All-Star nod in 2000 while Segui (.334/19/103) produced career-highs in batting average, RBI, runs scored (93) and doubles (42). Mussina averaged 15 wins with a 3.87 ERA and 1.209 WHIP from 2000-08. In his final season "Moose" reached the 20-win plateau and received Gold Glove honors for the seventh time in his career. Brian Roberts drilled a league-leading 50 doubles in 2004 and went on to hammer 56 two-baggers in '09. Roberts averaged 46 doubles and 35 steals from 2004-09, leading the American League with 50 swipes in 2007.

Armando Benitez saved 40+ games in three seasons from 2000-04, pacing the circuit with 47 saves in 2004. David Dellucci scored 97 runs and blasted 29 round-trippers in 2005. Chris Ray ascended to the closer's role in 2006 and notched 33 saves with a 2.73 ERA. Erik Bedard (13-5, 3.16) struck out 221 batters and placed fifth in the 2007 AL Cy Young voting. Nick Markakis batted .300 with 23 circuit clouts and 112 ribbies in his sophomore season and delivered 45 two-base hits per year from 2007-2010. Jayson Werth jacked 36 round-trippers and drove in 99 runs in 2009. "Werewolf" paced the League with 46 doubles in the subsequent season.

Jim R. Johnson topped the 50-save plateau in back-to-back campaigns (2012-13). Koji Uehara (1.09 ERA, 21 SV) posted a phenomenal 0.565 WHIP as a short reliever in 2013. Matt Wieters swatted 20+ big-flies in three successive seasons (2011-13). Manny Machado drilled 51 doubles to lead the Junior Circuit and flashed Gold Glove-caliber leather at the hot corner during his sophomore campaign (2013).

Win Shares > 20	Single-Season	1980-2013
Brian Roberts - 2B (BAL) x3	Matt Wieters - C (BAL)	Jayson Werth - RF (BAL) x3
Cal Ripken - SS (BAL) x10	Steve Finley - CF (BAL) x5	Mike Boddicker - SP (BAL)
Manny Machado – 3B (BAL)	Nick Markakis - RF (BAL) x2	Mike Mussina - SP (BAL) x2

Note: 4000 PA or BFP to qualify, except during strike-shortened seasons (1972 = 3800, 1981 & 1994 = 2700, 1995 = 3500) and 154-game schedule (3800)
- failed to qualify: 1901-04, 1906, 1923, 1925, 1934-1938, 1940-1959, 1989, 1991-1992, 2002-2003, 2006-2007

Browns / Orioles All-Time "Originals" Roster

Harry Ables	Sean Douglass	Billy Lee	Cal Ripken
Jerry Adair	Brian Dubois	Dud Lee	Sendy Rleal
Mike Adamson	Jim Duggan	Jim Lehew	Brian Roberts
Ryan Adams	Ron Dunn	Paul Lehner	Dave L. Roberts
Willie J. Adams	Ryne Duren	Mark Leiter	Gene Robertson
Sam Agnew	Joe Durham	Don Lenhardt	Brooks Robinson
George Aiton	Cedric Durst	Dave Leonhard	Jack Roche
Manny Alexander	Radhames Dykhoff	Hod Leverette	Ike Rockenfield
Walt Alexander	Marshall Edwards	Walt Leverenz	Eddy Rodriguez
Sled Allen	George Elder	Jim Levey	Vic Rodriguez
Mack Allison	Jumbo Elliott	Rommie Lewis	Ed Roetz
Andy Anderson	Verdo Elmore	Nig Lipscomb	Eddie Rogers
Kim Andrew	Jack Enzenroth	Radhames Liz	Tom Rogers
Rob Andrews	Mike Epstein	Chuck Locke	Gilberto Rondon
Matt Angle	Vaughn Eshelman	Adam Loewen	Charley Root

Hank Arft	Oscar Estrada	Johnny Lucadello	Chuck Rose
Tony Arnold	Andy Etchebarren	Dick Luebke	Pete Rose, Jr.
Jake Arrieta	Homer Ezzell	Joe Lutz	Rico Rossy
Xavier Avery	Brandon Fahey	Sparky Lyle	Dave Rowan
Art Bader	Chet Falk	Adrian Lynch	Willie Royster
Red Badgro	Brian Falkenborg	Manny Machado	Muddy Ruel
Grover Baichley	Cliff Fannin	Calvin Maduro	William Rumler
Bill F. Bailey	Bill Fincher	Joe Mahoney	Jim Russell
Bob Bailor	Steve Finley	John Maine	Frank Sacka
Floyd Baker	Jeff Fiorentino	George Maisel	Brian Sackinsky
Bobby Balcena	Jack Fisher	Val Majewski	Marino Salas
Jeff Ballard	Red Fisher	Alex Malloy	Dee Sanders
Steve D. Barber	Tom G. Fisher	Billy Maloney	Charlie Sands
Ray Barker	Charlie Flannigan	Frank Mancuso	Fred Sanford
Red Barkley	Mike Flanagan	Ernie Manning	Frank Saucier
Edgar Barnhart	John Flinn	Rolla Mapel	Bob Saverine
Ed Barnowski	Gil Flores	Nick Markakis	Ollie Sax
Kimera Bartee	Pedro Florimon	Duke Markell	Jeff Schaefer
Rick Bauer	Bobby Floyd	Roger Marquis	Art Scharein
George Baumgardner	Mike Fontenot	Babe Martin	Joe Schepner
Don Baylor	Dave Ford	Dennis Martinez	Dutch Schirick
Bill Bayne	Tito Francona	Tom Martin	Ray Schmandt
Charlie Beamon	Roger Freed	John Matias	Pete Schmidt
Lew Beasley	Bill Friel	Luis Matos	Hank Schmulbach
Pedro Beato	Owen Friend	Brian Matusz	Jonathan Schoop
Blaine Beatty	Jim Fuller	Mel Mazzera	Erik Schullstrom
Steve Bechler	Chris Fussell	Bill McAllester	Fred Schulte
Boom-Boom Beck	Eddie Gaedel	George McBride	Johnny Schulte
Erik Bedard	Bob Galasso	Tim McCabe	Len Schulte
Fred Beene	Eddy Garabito	Larry McCall	Blackie Schwamb
Ollie Bejma	Chico Garcia	Jerry McCarthy	Al Schweitzer
Mark Belanger	Jesse Garcia	Scott McClain	Hal Schwenk
Beau Bell	Kiko Garcia	Bill McCorry	Don Secrist
Eric Bell	Wayne Garland	Bob McCrory	David Segui
Armando Benitez	Debs Garms	Ben McDonald	Doc Shanley
Fred Bennett	Ned Garver	Darnell McDonald	Owen Shannon
Herschel Bennett	Tom Gastall	Joe McDonald	Larry Sheets
Johnny Berardino	Kevin Gausman	Bill McGill	John Shelby
Brad Bergesen	Lefty George	Mickey McGuire	Barry Shetrone
Jason Berken	Ken Gerhart	Reeve McKay	Ray Shore
Frank Bertaina	Lou Gertenrich	Jim McLaughlin	Rick Short
Fred Besana	Charlie E. Gibson	Marty McManus	Burt Shotton
Larry Bettencourt	Billy Gilbert	Dave McNally	Roy Sievers
Larry Bigbie	Jack Gilligan	Glenn McQuillen	Eddie Silber
Pete Bigler	Paul Gilliford	Tommy Mee	Syl Simon
Jim Bilbrey	Tony Giuliani	Heinie Meine	Pete Sims
Emil Bildilli	Leo Gomez	Walt Meinert	George Sisler
Kurt Birkins	Curtis Goodwin	Miguel Mejia	Dave Skaggs
Frank Biscan	Claude Gouzzie	Ski Melillo	Tod Sloan
Bud C. Black	Joe Grace	Jose Mercedes	Bryn Smith
John Black	Fred Graf	Luis Mercedes	Ed Smith
George Blaeholder	Bert Graham	Bob Milacki	Jim Smith
Bert Blue	Bill Grahame	Larry Milbourne	Mark C. Smith
Mike Boddicker	George Grant	Bill F. Miller	Mark E. Smith
Charlie Bold	Pete Gray	Charlie Miller	Wib Smith

Stew Bolen	Lenny Green	Ed Miller	Henry Smoyer
George Bone	Howie Gregory	John E. Miller	Charlie Snell
Julio Bonetti	Bobby Grich	Ox Miller	Nate Snell
Luther Bonin	Art Griggs	Randy Miller	Brandon Snyder
Bobby Bonner	Ed Grimes	Lefty Mills	Jim Snyder
Benny Bowcock	Sig Gryska	Ryan Minor	Allen Sothoron
Tim Bowden	Tedd Gullic	Paul Mitchell	Clyde Southwick
Sam Bowens	Ernie Gust	Roy Mitchell	Nate Spears
Ray Boyd	Ricky Gutierrez	Bill Mizeur	Hack Spencer
George Bradley	John Habyan	Ron Moeller	Tubby Spencer
Otis Brannan	Hal Haid	Gabe Molina	Paul Speraw
Marv Breeding	Jerry Hairston, Jr.	Vince Molyneaux	Hal Spindel
Bunny Brief	Bob Hale	John Montague	Brad Springer
Leon Brinkopf	George Hale	Scrappy Moore	Jay Spurgeon
Chris Britton	Ed Hallinan	Cy R. Morgan	Pete Stanicek
Jim Britton	Marc Hall	Bugs Morris	Buck Stanton
Zach Britton	Bill H. Hallman	Les Moss	Charlie Starr
Bill Brown	Earl Hamilton	Allie Moulton	Herman Starrette
Bobby L. Brown	Jeffrey Hammonds	Billy Mullen	John Stefero
Curly Brown	Larry Haney	Ed Murray	Randy Stein
Elmer Brown	Ron Hansen	Eddie Murray	Garrett Stephenson
Leon Brown	Larry Harlow	Mike Mussina	Jim Stephens
Mark Brown	Chuck Harmon	Buddy Napier	John Stephens
Walter Brown	Pete Harnisch	Al Naples	Vern Stephens
Willard Brown	Bill Harper	Buster Narum	Chuck Stevens
Ed Bruyette	Candy Harris	Bob Neighbors	Sammy Stewart
Jim Buchanan	Willie Harris	Red Nelson	Fred Stiely
Damon Buford	Sam Harshany	Tex Nelson	Rollie Stiles
Al Bumbry	Kevin Hart	Otto Neu	Wes Stock
Dylan Bundy	Roy Hartzell	Ernie Nevers	Dwight Stone
Wally Bunker	Ed Hawk	Maury Newlin	Ron Stone
Chris Burkam	Jimmy Haynes	Patrick Newnam	Lin Storti
Leo Burke	Red Hayworth	Carl Nichols	Alan Strange
Pat Burke	Drungo Hazewood	Dave Nicholson	Ed Strelecki
Jack I. Burns	Jay Heard	Harry Niles	Phil Stremmel
Bill Burwell	Tommy Heath	Tim Nordbrook	Bill Strickland
Chris Bushing	Wally Hebert	Lou Nordyke	Luke Stuart
John Butler	Al Heist	Hub Northen	Marlin Stuart
Kid Butler	Mel Held	Johnny Oates	Guy Sturdy
Milt Byrnes	Ed Hemingway	George O'Brien	Gordie Sundin
Enos Cabell	George Hennessey	Alex Ochoa	Bill Swaggerty
Daniel Cabrera	Dutch Henry	Billy O'Dell	Pinky Swander
Tom Cafego	David Hernandez	George O'Donnell	Bud Swartz
Napoleon Calzado	Bobby Herrera	John P. O'Donoghue	Josh Swindell
Paul Carey	Johnnie Heving	Chuck Oertel	Jeff Tackett
Tom Carey	Hunter Hill	Augie Ojeda	Willie Tasby
D.J. Carrasco	Chuck Hinton	Francisco Oliveras	Anthony Telford
Carlos Casimiro	L. J. Hoes	Garrett Olson	Tom Tennant
Wayne Causey	James Hoey	Gregg Olson	Frank Tepedino
Dean Chance	Cal Hogue	Mike Oquist	Bud J. Thomas
Wei-Yin Chen	Herm Holshouser	Frankie Pack	Frank Thompson
Tony Chevez	Don Hood	Jim Palmer	Hank Thompson
Tom Chism	John Hoover	John Papa	Sloppy Thurston
Bobby Chouinard	Ivan Howard	Milt Pappas	Johnny Tillman
Darryl Cias	Hal Hudson	Al Pardo	George Tomer

Al Clancy	Kyle Hudson	Pat Parker	Lou Tost
Cap Clark	Ben Huffman	Jim Park	Josh Towers
Howie Clark	Steve Huntz	Chad Paronto	Jim Traber
Bob Clemens	Dave Huppert	John Parrish	Bill Trotter
Verne Clemons	Herb Hutson	Mike Parrott	Frank Truesdale
Harlond Clift	Hooks Iott	Ham Patterson	Bob Turley
Herb Cobb	Sig Jakucki	Barney Pelty	Koji Uehara
Ivanon Coffie	Ray Jansen	Hayden Penn	Henry Urrutia
Rich Coggins	Heinie Jantzen	Brad Pennington	Harry Vahrenhorst
Ray Coleman	Jesse Jefferson	Kewpie Pennington	Fred Valentine
Pat Collins	Joe Jenkins	Parson Perryman	Elam Vangilder
Dick Colpaert	Chet Johnson	Scott Perry	Jack Voigt
Pete Compton	Darrell Johnson	Sid Peterson	Ollie Voigt
Wid Conroy	Davey Johnson	Jeff Pfeffer	Frank Waddey
Rollin Cook	Dave C. Johnson	Tom Phillips	Fred Walden
Bob Cooney	Jim R. Johnson	Tom Phoebus	Irv Waldron
Rocky Coppinger	Johnny Johnston	Calvin Pickering	Ernie Walker
Mark M. Corey	Dave Jolly	Jim Pisoni	Jerry Walker
Red Corriden	Earl Jones	Lou Polli	Tom R. Walker
Chuck Cottier	Ricky Jones	Sidney Ponson	Jim E. Walkup
Sam Covington	Stacy Jones	Boog Powell	Don Wallace
Jake Crawford	Harry Kane	Jack Powell	Dee Walsh
Tony Criscola	Eddie Kasko	Jay Powell	Pete Ward
Joe Crisp	Dick Kauffman	Carl Powis	Buzzy Wares
Dode Criss	Junior Kennedy	Del Pratt	Hal Warnock
Ned Crompton	Ray Kennedy	Earl Pruess	B.J. Waszgis
Frank Crossin	Keith Kessinger	Hub Pruett	Eddie Watt
Bill H. Crouch	Phil Ketter	Jim Pyburn	Mike Wegener
Jack Crouch	Bill Killefer	Ewald Pyle	Carl Weilman
Terry Crowley	Harry Kimberlin	Art Quirk	Don Welchel
Perry Currin	Chad Kimsey	Mike Raczka	George Werley
George Curry	Wes Kingdon	Tim Raines, Jr.	Jayson Werth
Angelo Dagres	Gene Kingsale	Aaron Rakers	Lefty West
John Daley	Scott Klingenbeck	Allan Ramirez	Dutch Wetzel
Bill Dalrymple	Nap Kloza	Milt Ramirez	Bill Whaley
Mike E. Darr	Jack Knott	Ribs Raney	Charlie White
Rich Dauer	Darold Knowles	Chris Ray	Eli Whiteside
Blake Davis	Ben Koehler	Farmer Ray	Fuzz White
Mike Davison	Ryan Kohlmeier	Jim Ray	Matt Wieters
Storm Davis	Ray Kolp	Keith Reed	Dallas Williams
Tommy J. Davis	Ernie Koob	Tony Rego	Gus Williams
Joey Dawley	Jack Kramer	Nolan Reimold	Joe Willis
Joe DeBerry	Wayne Krenchicki	Mike Reinbach	Mike Willis
Doug DeCinces	Red Kress	Merv Rettenmund	Terry Wilshusen
Jim Dedrick	Paul Krichell	Arthur Rhodes	Ernie Wingard
Shorty Dee	Rick Krivda	Chuck Ricci	Jerry Witte
David Dellucci	Ed Kusel	Harry Rice	Ken Wood
Cesar Devarez	Joe Kutina	Scott Rice	Craig Worthington
Walt DeVoy	Steve Lake	Tom Richardson	Jim Wright
Gordon Dillard	Al LaMacchia	Ray Richmond	Rasty Wright
Bob Dillinger	David Lamb	Fred Rico	Mike Young
Bill Dillman	Lyman Lamb	Jim N. Riley	Russ Young
Ken Dixon	Don Larsen	Matt Riley	Al Zarilla
Leo Dixon	Bill Lasley	Jeff Rineer	Gregg Zaun
Len Dondero	Doc Lavan	Billy Ripken	Frank Zupo

Year/Team	OPW%	PW	PL	APW%	AW	AL	Diff+/-
1969 SDP	0.000 F	0	0	0.321	52	110	0.000
1970 SDP	0.000 F	0	0	0.389	63	99	0.000
1971 SDP	0.000 F	0	0	0.379	61	100	0.000
1972 SDP	0.000 F	0	0	0.379	58	95	0.000
1973 SDP	0.425 F	69	93	0.370	60	102	-0.055
1974 SDP	0.352 F	57	105	0.370	60	102	0.018
1975 SDP	0.421 F	68	94	0.438	71	91	0.017
1976 SDP	0.489 F	79	83	0.451	73	89	-0.038
1977 SDP	0.439	71	91	0.426	69	93	-0.013
1978 SDP	0.509	82	80	0.519	84	78	0.009
1979 SDP	0.508	82	80	0.422	68	93	-0.086

franchID	OWAR	OWS	AWAR	AWS	WARdiff	WSdiff	P/D/W/F
1969 SDP			6.827	155.998	-6.827	-155.998	F
1970 SDP	130.285	555.583	24.968	188.998	105.316	366.585	F
1971 SDP	18.734	375.888	23.660	183.006	-4.926	192.881	F
1972 SDP	11.677	133.684	16.553	174.000	-4.876	-40.316	F
1973 SDP	42.482	276.597	16.388	180.001	26.094	96.596	F
1974 SDP	18.410	197.881	11.800	179.999	6.610	17.882	F
1975 SDP	25.975	212.236	22.261	212.999	3.714	-0.763	F
1976 SDP	39.205	255.906	24.309	218.997	14.896	36.910	F
1977 SDP	9.966	199.452	20.682	207.001	-10.717	-7.549	
1978 SDP	46.670	307.174	36.294	251.999	10.376	55.175	
1979 SDP	35.982	260.449	24.457	203.995	11.525	56.454	

Legend: (P) = Pennant / Most Wins in League (D) = Division Winner (W) = Wild Card Winner (F) = Failed to Qualify

The San Diego Padres debuted in 1969 along with the Montreal Expos, as the National League expanded to 12 teams. San Diego is tied for the most WS>20 player-seasons at second base among the "Expansion" clubs and tops the leader boards in WS>10 player-seasons at shortstop. On the other hand, the franchise has yet to capture the National League pennant in 40 years of existence. The 1977 "Original" Padres were the first to exceed the minimum 4000 PA and BFP standards*.

Dave Winfield joined the Padres' lineup in 1973, jumping directly from college to the big leagues. Winfield (.308/34/118) topped the RBI leader board in '79, accumulating 32 Win Shares and finishing third in the NL MVP balloting. He received an invitation to the Mid-Summer Classic for 12 consecutive seasons (1977-1988). Johnny Grubb batted .311 in his rookie campaign (1973) and bashed 36 two-baggers in '75. Mike Caldwell fashioned a 14-5 record with a 2.95 ERA in 1974.

Randy Jones ascended to the top of the rotation, delivering 20 victories with a league-best 2.24 ERA and placing runner-up in the 1975 NL Cy Young vote. Jones claimed the award in 1976, leading the National League in wins (22), games started (40), innings pitched (315.1) and WHIP (1.027). Gene Richards pilfered 56 bases and placed third in the 1977 NL ROY voting.

The Padres enjoyed the club's first winning season in 1978. Caldwell managed a 22-9 mark, completing 23 starts and placing second in the Cy Young race. Ozzie Smith swiped 40 bases and finished second in the 1978 NL Rookie of the Year balloting. Mike Ivie established career-highs with 27 long balls and 89 RBI in '79.

Year/Team	OPW%	PW	PL	APW%	AW	AL	Diff+/-
1980 SDP	0.444	72	90	0.451	73	89	0.007
1981 SDP	0.467	76	86	0.373	41	69	-0.094
1982 SDP	0.480	78	84	0.500	81	81	0.020
1983 SDP	0.466 F	75	87	0.500	81	81	0.034
1984 SDP	0.544 F	88	74	0.568 D	92	70	0.024
1985 SDP	0.561	91	71	0.512	83	79	-0.049
1986 SDP	0.518	84	78	0.457	74	88	-0.061
1987 SDP	0.510	83	79	0.401	65	97	-0.109
1988 SDP	0.490	79	83	0.516	83	78	0.025
1989 SDP	0.527	85	77	0.549	89	73	0.022

franchID	OWAR	OWS	AWAR	AWS	WARdiff	WSdiff	P/D/W/F
1980 SDP	24.498	217.128	29.303	219.002	-4.806	-1.874	
1981 SDP	23.048	152.781	14.911	122.998	8.137	29.783	
1982 SDP	29.177	250.747	27.933	242.999	1.244	7.747	
1983 SDP	26.720	231.300	27.391	242.999	-0.671	-11.698	F
1984 SDP	45.703	293.306	32.313	275.998	13.390	17.308	F
1985 SDP	41.642	284.467	34.664	248.994	6.978	35.473	
1986 SDP	47.683	298.810	29.279	222.001	18.404	76.808	
1987 SDP	40.580	269.373	26.810	195.001	13.770	74.371	
1988 SDP	47.071	**291.467**	35.252	248.997	11.820	42.470	
1989 SDP	46.434	303.790	37.508	266.997	8.926	36.794	

Dave Winfield delivered 25 round-trippers and 100 RBI per season (1980-88). He established career-bests with 37 home runs in 1982 and a .340 batting average in 1984. Gene Richards hit .301 with 61 steals in 1980 and paced the National League with 12 triples in '81. Ozzie Smith set career-highs with a .303 BA, 75 RBI, 104 runs scored, 40 doubles and 31 Win Shares in 1987. "The Wizard of Oz" collected 13 consecutive Gold Glove awards for his superb skills at shortstop. The Padres delivered consecutive last-place finishes in 1980 and 1981.

GM Jack McKeon and Scouting Director Bob Fontaine achieved the highest Career Total Win Shares (785) and Career Total WAR (94) in Padres' history with the selections of Tony Gwynn, Kevin McReynolds and John Kruk in the '81 Amateur Draft. In addition, McKeon excelled with the signing of amateur free agents including Benito Santiago ('82), Roberto Alomar ('85) and Jose Valentin ('86).

Mike Caldwell led the staff with 17 wins in '82. Eric Show posted consecutive 15-win campaigns (1983-84) and furnished a 16-11 mark with a 3.26 ERA and 1.082 WHIP in '88. Mark Thurmond achieved a 14-8 record with a 2.97 ERA in 1984. Gary Lucas and Dan Spillner shared the high-leverage relief assignments for the Padres in the first half of the decade. Lucas averaged 15 saves with a 2.72 ERA from 1981-83. Spillner excelled in 1982, amassing 12 wins and 21 saves along with a 2.49 ERA. San Diego failed to exceed the minimum PA standards in 1983-84.

Tony Gwynn achieved four batting titles in the Eighties, averaging .336 with 201 hits and 34 steals per season from 1984-89. Gwynn batted .351 while compiling 35 Win Shares and placing third in the 1984 NL MVP race and went on to lead the League with 200+ base hits in four campaigns, and runs scored (107) in 1986. Ozzie Guillen received ROY honors in 1985 and pilfered 36 bags in '89. Andy Hawkins tallied 18 victories with a 3.15 ERA for the '85 squad. San Diego fell short of consecutive division titles by percentage points to the Dodgers. The '86 Friars posted the best WSdiff (+76) and WARdiff (+18) vs. the output of the "Actual" Padres from the same year.

Kevin McReynolds produced 27 four-baggers and 97 ribbies per season from 1986-88. Benito Santiago (.300/18/79) captured the 1987 NL ROY award and set career marks with 33 doubles and 21 stolen bases while John Kruk supplied a .313 BA with 20 dingers and 91 RBI in the same year. Roberto Alomar batted .295 with 42 steals in '89. Mark Williamson collected 10 wins and 9 saves, setting up for Mitch "Wild Thing" Williams (2.76, 36 SV). The 1989 club ended the season two games behind the Reds.

Year/Team	OPW%	PW	PL	APW%	AW	AL	Diff+/-
1990 SDP	0.494	80	82	0.463	75	87	-0.031
1991 SDP	0.513	83	79	0.519	84	78	0.006
1992 SDP	0.595	96	66	0.506	82	80	-0.089
1993 SDP	0.477	77	85	0.377	61	101	-0.100
1994 SDP	0.508 D	82	80	0.402	47	70	-0.106
1995 SDP	0.508 D	82	80	0.486	70	74	-0.022
1996 SDP	0.537 W	87	75	0.562 D	91	71	0.024
1997 SDP	0.484	78	84	0.469	76	86	-0.015
1998 SDP	0.515	83	79	0.605 D	98	64	0.090
1999 SDP	0.467	76	86	0.457	74	88	-0.010

franchID	OWAR	OWS	AWAR	AWS	WARdiff	WSdiff	P/D/W/F
1990 SDP	38.949	272.062	35.041	224.993	3.907	47.070	
1991 SDP	40.679	289.486	33.040	252.003	7.640	37.482	
1992 SDP	52.682	324.283	37.385	246.004	15.298	78.279	
1993 SDP	34.824	252.479	28.381	183.001	6.444	69.478	
1994 SDP	28.589	161.208	27.159	140.998	1.430	20.210	D
1995 SDP	29.071	192.292	31.878	210.007	-2.807	-17.715	D
1996 SDP	33.685	218.172	45.767	273.003	-12.082	-54.831	W
1997 SDP	34.538	219.365	30.134	227.995	4.404	-8.631	
1998 SDP	27.229	199.889	47.499	294.004	-20.270	-94.115	
1999 SDP	29.469	188.222	30.280	221.999	-0.811	-33.778	

Roberto Alomar produced a .308 batting average with 32 doubles, 95 runs scored and 31 doubles per year during the Nineties. The perennial All-Star placed third in the 1999 MVP voting, setting career-bests with 24 home runs, 120 ribbies and a league-leading 138 runs scored. Sandy Alomar Jr. received ROY honors in 1990 and busted out with his best offensive campaign in '97, belting 21 long balls and plating 83 runners while hitting .324.

Winfield clouted 24 round-trippers per year (1990-93) and knocked in 108 runs in 1992. After managing 8 wins, 9 saves and a 2.30 ERA as a reliever in 1990, the Padres inserted Greg W. Harris into the starting rotation. Harris yielded a 9-5 record with an ERA of 2.23. Williams averaged 34 saves with a 3.11 ERA from 1991-93, albeit with a 1.517 WHIP.

Tony Gwynn collected four consecutive batting titles (1994-97), yielding a .344 average for the decade. "Mr. Padre" hit .394 during the abbreviated '94 season. Gwynn (.372/17/119) tallied 220 hits en route to a sixth-place finish in the 1997 NL MVP vote. Shane Mack achieved a .309 batting average from 1990-94. The San Diego offense generated the highest offWARnorm total (35) in Major League history in 1992.

Carlos Baerga eclipsed the 200-hit and 100 RBI plateaus in successive seasons (1992-93). Baerga averaged .315 with 19 dingers per year from 1992-95. Dave Hollins established himself at the hot corner in 1992, blasting 27 round-trippers and knocking in 93 runs. He earned an All-Star nod in '93 and scored 104 runs in back-to-back campaigns (1992-93). San Diego tallied 96 victories in 1992 (representing a 13-win increase from '91) while pacing the circuit in oWAR and oWS. Unfortunately, Atlanta amassed 98 wins and won the National League Western Division crown.

The Friars melted down in '93, compiling only 77 wins; however, the squad rebounded with back-to-back division titles in 1994-95 and earned a Wild Card entry in 1996. Andy Benes anchored the Friars' rotation and topped the National League with 189 strikeouts in 1994. Benes (18-10, 3.83) placed third in the 1998 NL Cy Young balloting. Joey Hamilton fashioned a 9-6 record with a 2.98 ERA in his rookie campaign (1994) and won 15 contests in 1996. The Padres' brass (chiefly GM Randy Smith and later Kevin Towers) averaged a mere 55 Career Total Win Shares with their Amateur Draft picks spanning a five-year period (1994-98).

Jose Valentin jacked 24 long balls and plated 95 runners in '96 while Santiago smacked a career-high 30 quadruples. Bob Patterson posted a 0.961 WHIP in relief while Rich Loiselle saved 29 games with a 3.10 ERA in 1997. Joey Cora (.300/11/54) drilled 40 doubles with 105 runs scored en route to his lone All-Star appearance in '97. Dustin Hermanson tallied 14 victories with a 3.13 ERA and 1.171 WHIP in '98. The '98 squad placed four games behind the front-running Giants. Homer Bush supplied a .320 BA with 32 stolen bases in 1999.

Year/Team	OPW%	PW	PL	APW%	AW	AL	Diff+/-
2000 SDP	0.461	75	87	0.469	76	86	0.008
2001 SDP	0.390	63	99	0.488	79	83	0.097
2002 SDP	0.485	79	83	0.407	66	96	-0.078
2003 SDP	0.467	76	86	0.395	64	98	-0.072
2004 SDP	0.533 D	86	76	0.537	87	75	0.004
2005 SDP	0.463 F	75	87	0.506 D	82	80	0.043
2006 SDP	0.475 F	77	85	0.543 D	88	74	0.069
2007 SDP	0.538 F	87	75	0.546	89	74	0.008
2008 SDP	0.447 F	72	90	0.389	63	99	-0.058
2009 SDP	0.462 F	75	87	0.463	75	87	0.001
2010 SDP	0.496	80	82	0.556	90	72	0.060
2011 SDP	0.479	78	84	0.438	71	91	-0.040
2012 SDP	0.458 F	74	88	0.469	76	86	0.012
2013 SDP	0.412	67	95	0.469	76	86	0.057

franchID	OWAR	OWS	AWAR	AWS	WARdiff	WSdiff	P/D/W/F
2000 SDP	26.354	181.464	27.982	228.007	-1.627	-46.543	
2001 SDP	23.060	177.673	30.326	236.996	-7.266	-59.323	
2002 SDP	34.447	192.559	22.416	197.997	12.031	-5.438	
2003 SDP	25.366	200.134	24.412	192.004	0.953	8.129	
2004 SDP	39.964	233.695	41.507	261.004	-1.542	-27.309	D
2005 SDP	36.066	202.030	38.649	245.995	-2.583	-43.965	F
2006 SDP	38.362	234.952	43.036	263.995	-4.675	-29.043	F
2007 SDP	38.148	237.544	**45.578**	266.997	-7.431	-29.453	F
2008 SDP	25.817	216.159	27.638	189.004	-1.821	27.156	F
2009 SDP	29.544	230.304	26.717	224.997	2.827	5.307	F
2010 SDP	26.003	215.411	39.109	270.005	-13.107	-54.595	
2011 SDP	34.102	210.664	29.603	212.996	4.499	-2.332	
2012 SDP	31.007	232.498	27.447	228.003	3.560	4.495	F
2013 SDP	19.994	220.563	23.452	227.998	-3.458	-7.435	

Roberto Alomar swiped 39 bags and scored 111 runs while batting .310 in 2000. He collected his 10th Gold Glove award and finished fourth in the 2001 MVP race. Alomar delivered a .336 average, 20 homers, 100 ribbies and 113 runs while accruing the highest Win Share total in franchise history (35). Derrek Lee produced 31 clouts and 88 RBI from 2000-05. Lee placed third in the 2005 NL MVP balloting, pacing the circuit with 199 hits, 50 doubles, a .335 batting average and .662 SLG. He also crushed 46 long balls and knocked in 107 runs while compiling the third-highest Win Share total in team history (34). "D-Lee" swatted 35 home runs and drove in a career-high 111 runs in '09.

Jose Valentin averaged 27 big-flies from 2000-04 and scored 107 times in 2000. The 2001 Friars posted the worst won-loss record (63-99) in team annals. Rodrigo Lopez (15-9, 3.57) finished second in the ROY balloting in 2002 while fellow right-hander Matt Clement whiffed 215 batters. Tim Worrell emerged as a late-inning relief candidate in 2002 with an 8-2 record, 2.25 ERA and 1.181 WHIP. Thrust into the closer's role in the following season, Worrell delivered a 2.87 ERA and saved 38 contests.

San Diego took the division title by a single game over Colorado in 2004 as the pitching staff delivered the best pitWARnorm (28) and pitWSnorm (123) in team history. Jake Peavy paced the circuit with a 2.27 ERA in 2004. He earned the 2007 NL Cy Young award, posting a 19-6 mark while topping the League with a 2.54 ERA, 240 strikeouts and a 1.061 WHIP. Oliver Perez fashioned a 2.98 ERA and struck out 239 opposing batsmen in '04. Akinori Otsuka (7-2, 1.75) finished third in the ROY vote, striking out 87 batters in 77.1 innings and tallied 32 saves with a 2.11 ERA in 2006.

Khalil Greene (.273/15/65) slapped 31 doubles and placed runner-up in the 2004 NL ROY voting. Greene pounded 44 doubles and 27 bombs while driving home 97 runs in '07. Dustin Hermanson posted a 2.04 ERA with a 1.099 WHIP and 34 saves in 2005. Gary Matthews Jr. (.313/19/79) made his lone All-Star appearance in '06, collecting 194 base hits and scoring 102 runs and in the following season Xavier Nady set career-highs across the board, batting .305 with 37 two-baggers, 25 wallops and 97 ribbies.

Shortstop Jason Bartlett supplied 30 steals and a .320 batting average in 2009. Mat Latos delivered 14 wins, a 2.92 ERA and a 1.083 WHIP in his first full season (2010). The Padres' offense failed to exceed the minimum PA standards in 2005-07 and the mound crew was unable to attain the BFP requirements from 2007-09. Chase Headley (.286/31/115) topped the Senior Circuit in RBI, placed fifth in NL MVP balloting and captured a Gold Glove Award in 2012.

Win Shares > 20	Single-Season	1969-2013
Mike Ivie - 1B (SDP)	Dave Hollins - 3B (SDP)	Tony Gwynn - CF (SDP)
John Kruk - 1B (SDP) x3	Chase Headley - 3B (SDP)	Gary Matthews, Jr. - CF (SDP)
Derrek Lee - 1B (SDP) x5	Gene Richards - LF (SDP) x3	Dave Winfield - RF (SDP) x8
Roberto Alomar - 2B (SDP) x10	Dave Winfield - LF (SDP) x2	Tony Gwynn - RF (SDP) x7
Carlos Baerga - 2B (SDP) x3	Kevin McReynolds - LF (SDP) x3	Dave Winfield - DH (SDP)
Ozzie Smith - SS (SDP) x7	Shane Mack - LF (SDP)	Randy Jones - SP (SDP) x2
Jose Valentin - SS (SDP)	Johnny Grubb - CF (SDP)	Mike Caldwell - SP (SDP)
Khalil Greene - SS (SDP)	Kevin McReynolds - CF (SDP) x2	Jake Peavy - SP (SDP)
Jason Bartlett - SS (SDP)		Dan Spillner - RP (SDP)

Note: 4000 PA or BFP to qualify, except during strike-shortened seasons
(1972 = 3800, 1981 & 1994 = 2700, 1995 = 3500) and 154-game schedule (3800)
- failed to qualify: 1969-1976, 1983-1984, 2005-2009

Padres All-Time "Originals" Roster

Dusty Allen	Steve Fireovid	Jody Lansford	Gene Richards
Bill Almon	Tim Flannery	Greg LaRocca	Nikco Riesgo
Roberto Alomar	Bryce Florie	Mat Latos	Dave W. Roberts
Sandy Alomar, Jr.	Logan Forsythe	Brian Lawrence	Dave Robinson

Gabe Alvarez	Jay Franklin	Wade LeBlanc	Leo Rosales
Matt Antonelli	Scott Fredrickson	Derrek Lee	Mel Rosario
Tucker Ashford	David Freese	Mark L. Lee	A.J. Sager
Jim Austin	Nate Freiman	Jim S. Lewis	Scott Sanders
Dylan Axelrod	Dave Freisleben	Rod Lindsey	Benito Santiago
Carlos Baerga	Ernesto Frieri	Jon Link	Bobby Scales
Chuck Baker	J.J. Furmaniak	Jose Lobaton	John Scott
Josh Barfield	Jay Gainer	Rich Loiselle	Wascar Serrano
Jason Bartlett	Ralph Garcia	Bill Long	Darrell Sherman
Cliff Bartosh	Josh Geer	Joey Long	Bob Shirley
Anthony Bass	Bob Geren	Luis M. Lopez	Eric Show
Mike Baxter	Rusty Gerhardt	Rodrigo Lopez	Candy Sierra
Robbie Beckett	Justin Germano	Gary Lucas	Walter Silva
Andy Benes	Joe Goddard	Cory Luebke	Steve Simpson
Victor Bernal	Brandon Gomes	Drew Macias	Burch Smith
Jim Beswick	Charlie Greene	Shane Mack	Ozzie Smith
Joe Bitker	Gary Green	Luis M. Martinez	Roger Smithberg
Kyle Blanks	Khalil Greene	Mike Martin	Frank Snook
Ricky Bones	Brian Greer	Pablo Martinez	Eric Sogard
Eddie Bonine	Johnny Grubb	Pedro A. Martinez	Ali Solis
Greg Booker	Ozzie Guillen	Gary Matthews, Jr.	Josh Spence
Brad Brach	Domingo Guzman	Dave Maurer	Dan Spillner
Doug Brocail	Freddy Guzman	Matt Maysey	George Stablein
Greg Burke	Doug Gwosdz	Paul McAnulty	Dave Staton
Sean Burroughs	Tony Gwynn	Rodney McCray	Tim Stauffer
Homer Bush	Jedd Gyorko	Ray McDavid	Jim Steels
Randy Byers	Joey Hamilton	Joe McIntosh	Craig Stimac
Mike Bynum	Larry Hardy	Kevin McReynolds	Rick Sweet
Cam Cairncross	Greg W. Harris	Tommy Medica	Jim Tatum
Mike Caldwell	Andy Hawkins	Juan Melo	Blake Tekotte
Shawn Camp	Dirk Hayhurst	Jason Middlebrook	Tom Tellmann
Cesar Carrillo	Ray Hayward	Matt Mieske	Dale Thayer
Jack Cassel	Chase Headley	Miles Mikolas	Jason M. Thompson
Tony Castillo	Jeremy Hefner	Colt Morton	Mike P. Thompson
Simon Castro	Dustin Hermanson	Sean Mulligan	Mark Thurmond
Jose Ceda	Pedro M. Hernandez	Steve Mura	Ron Tingley
Mike Champion	Junior Herndon	Heath Murray	Rich Troedson
Floyd Chiffer	Kevin Higgins	Xavier Nady	J.J. Trujillo
Jerald Clark	Dave Hilton	Warren Newson	Jerry Turner
Matt Clement	George Hinshaw	Kevin Nicholson	Efrain Valdez
Clay Condrey	Ray Holbert	Wil Nieves	Rafael Valdez
Joey Cora	Dave Hollins	Paul Noce	Jose Valentin
Mike Couchee	Ben Howard	Eric Nolte	Guillermo Velasquez
Eric Cyr	Thomas Howard	Omar Olivares	Will Venable
James Darnell	Jon Huber	Akinori Otsuka	Nick Vincent
Ben Davis	Chad Huffman	Bob Owchinko	Ed Vosberg
Bob J. Davis	Mike Humphreys	Chris Oxspring	Kevin Walker
Erik Davis	Nick Hundley	Lance Painter	Gene Walter
Gerry Davis	Cedric Hunter	Mark Parent	Mark Wasinger
Roger Deago	Colt Hynes	Andy Parrino	Steve Watkins
Jaff Decker	Hideki Irabu	Bob Patterson	Dave Wehrmeister
Steve Delabar	Mike Ivie	David Pauley	Jared Wells
Glenn Dishman	Jimmy Jones	Jake Peavy	Andrew Werner
Mike Dupree	Randy Jones	Alex Pelaez	Jim Wilhelm
Luis Durango	Sean Kazmar	Oliver Perez	Mark Williamson

Juan Eichelberger	Greg Keagle	Broderick Perkins	Mitch Williams
Michael Ekstrom	Brandon Kintzler	Chris Prieto	Dave Winfield
Randy Elliott	Corey Kluber	Luis Quinones	Tim Worrell
Todd Erdos	Jon Knott	Ramon A. Ramirez	Lance Zawadzki
Barry Evans	Brandon Kolb	Cesar Ramos	
Paul Faries	George Kottaras	Kevin Reese	
Jeremy Fikac	John Kruk	Don Reynolds	

Philadelphia Phillies

Year/Team	OPW%	PW	PL	APW%	AW	AL	Diff+/-
1901 PHI	0.549	77	63	0.593	83	57	0.044
1902 PHI	0.501	70	70	0.409	56	81	-0.092
1903 PHI	0.509	71	69	0.363	49	86	-0.146
1904 PHI	0.478	74	80	0.342	52	100	-0.136
1905 PHI	0.617	95	59	0.546	83	69	-0.071
1906 PHI	0.506	78	76	0.464	71	82	-0.042
1907 PHI	0.527	81	73	0.565	83	64	0.038
1908 PHI	0.542	83	71	0.539	83	71	-0.003
1909 PHI	0.525	81	73	0.484	74	79	-0.042

franchID	OWAR	OWS	AWAR	AWS	WARdiff	WSdiff	P/D/W/F
1901 PHI	**46.276**	266.535	36.783	248.992	9.493	17.544	
1902 PHI	37.859	224.506	13.518	167.995	24.341	56.511	
1903 PHI	39.253	232.401	18.439	147.005	20.814	85.396	
1904 PHI	45.387	293.709	18.627	156.000	26.760	137.708	
1905 PHI	51.374	329.655	35.937	248.996	15.437	80.658	
1906 PHI	54.876	327.260	28.814	213.005	26.062	114.255	
1907 PHI	**56.230**	**349.904**	31.087	249.009	25.143	100.895	
1908 PHI	47.782	295.282	40.197	249.000	7.585	46.281	
1909 PHI	39.034	258.197	34.392	222.004	4.642	36.193	

Legend: (P) = Pennant / Most Wins in League (D) = Division Winner (W) = Wild Card Winner (F) = Failed to Qualify

The Philadephia Quakers entered the National League in 1883. The team adopted the "Phillies" moniker for the 1890 season. The "Original" Phillies lone pennant was achieved in 1950 and the team has the fewest playoff appearances (4) among the 16 "Turn of the Century" franchises. Based on the WS>20 frame of reference, the club has also developed the fewest quality first basemen (12) among the "Turn of the Century" teams and using WS>10 seasons, Philadelphia rates worst among first basemen (41) and center fielders (56). The organization's first basemen and relief pitchers have never finished in the top three WS>10 totals.

On a positive note, Phillies' second basemen placed runner-up for the most WS>20 player-seasons, led by Nap Lajoie and Ryne Sandberg. Lajoie made his Major League debut in 1896 and topped the leader boards with 127 RBI in back-to-back campaigns (1897-98). Lajoie (.426/14/125) captured the Triple Crown and paced the circuit in most offensive categories in 1901. He fashioned a .338 career BA including five batting titles.

"Big" Ed Delahanty thrice eclipsed the .400 mark in batting average during the 1890's. A three-time League leader in RBI, Delahanty accrued 32 Win Shares in '01 and collected his second batting crown with a .376 BA in 1902. Elmer Flick (.367/11/110) managed 200 base knocks in 1900 while leading the circuit in RBI. He collected the batting title in '05 and paced the League in triples for three consecutive years (1905-07).

The Phillies ended the '01 season one game behind the Braves and topped the National League in oWAR. Center fielder Roy A. Thomas led the National League in bases on balls on seven occasions. Philadelphia nearly won its first pennant in 1905, posting 95 victories and falling three games short of the New York Giants. John Titus contributed a .308 BA and 99 tallies. Tully Sparks supplied three consecutive seasons with an ERA below 2.20 from 1905-07.

Al Orth (27-17, 2.34) topped the charts in victories and innings pitched while completing 36 of 39 starts in 1906. "The Curveless Wonder" amassed 33 Win Shares while fellow portsider Doc White led the League in ERA (1.52) and WHIP (0.903). White accumulated 27 victories and Sparks contributed 22 wins as the 1907 Phillies basked atop the oWAR and oWS leader boards. Phillies' left fielders collected 20 WS>10 player-seasons during the first decade of the Twentieth Century. Sam Mertes clubbed a league-high 32 two-base hits and plated 104 runners in '03. Sherry Magee (.328/4/85) accounted for 37 Win Shares for the '07 crew. Philadelphia's offense provided the highest offWSnorm (204) in club history.

Year/Team	OPW%	PW	PL	APW%	AW	AL	Diff+/-
1910 PHI	0.515	79	75	0.510	78	75	-0.006
1911 PHI	0.457	70	84	0.520	79	73	0.062
1912 PHI	0.469 F	72	82	0.480	73	79	0.011
1913 PHI	0.495 F	76	78	0.583	88	63	0.088
1914 PHI	0.448 F	69	85	0.481	74	80	0.032
1915 PHI	0.525 F	81	73	0.592 P	90	62	0.067
1916 PHI	0.459 F	71	83	0.595	91	62	0.136
1917 PHI	0.522 F	80	74	0.572	87	65	0.050
1918 PHI	0.394 F	50	78	0.447	55	68	0.053
1919 PHI	0.398 F	56	84	0.343	47	90	-0.055

franchID	OWAR	OWS	AWAR	AWS	WARdiff	WSdiff	P/D/W/F
1910 PHI	42.912	272.158	37.452	233.997	5.459	38.161	
1911 PHI	39.944	243.527	32.707	236.974	7.237	6.553	
1912 PHI	32.028	208.582	31.112	219.001	0.915	-10.419	F
1913 PHI	37.207	215.737	40.666	263.996	-3.459	-48.259	F
1914 PHI	34.561	155.396	38.578	221.998	-4.017	-66.602	F
1915 PHI	41.068	217.861	44.790	270.005	-3.722	-52.145	F
1916 PHI	37.283	199.470	41.971	273.002	-4.688	-73.532	F
1917 PHI	39.303	195.383	40.236	261.000	-0.933	-65.617	F
1918 PHI	11.178	134.538	16.943	165.002	-5.765	-30.463	F
1919 PHI	17.214	108.314	13.854	141.001	3.359	-32.687	F

Philadelphia failed to meet the minimum PA and/or BFP requirements from 1912-1949 with the exception of two campaigns, the first in 1928 and the second ten years later in 1938. Lajoie produced the Phillies' highest Win Share total (46) while pacing the circuit with a .384 BA, 227 hits and 51 doubles in 1910. Magee posted career-bests in batting average (.331), runs scored (110) and RBI (123).

Pete Alexander dazzled opposing batsmen with his electric repertoire throughout his career, as he surpassed the 20-win mark in nine seasons including 28 victories during his rookie campaign (1911). The five-time ERA and WHIP champion posted earned run averages under 2.00 in every season from 1915-1920. "Old Pete" twirled 16 shutouts and completed 38 of 45 starts while compiling 42 Win Shares for the 1916 staff. Harry Coveleski's fleeting excellence lasted only the three seasons from 1914-16. "The Giant Killer" averaged 22 victories while furnishing an ERA of 2.30 along with a 1.117 WHIP. Eppa Rixey compiled a 22-10 record and established personal bests in ERA (1.85) and WHIP (1.091) in '16.

Win Shares > 20	Single-Season	1901-1919
Nap Lajoie - 2B (PHI) x11	Roy A. Thomas - CF (PHI) x7	George McQuillan - SP (PHI)
Sam Mertes - 2B (PHI)	Elmer Flick - CF (PHI)	Pete Alexander - SP (PHI) x12
Ed Abbaticchio - 2B (PHI) x2	Doc White - CF (PHI)	Tom Seaton - SP (PHI) x2
Kid Elberfeld - SS (PHI) x2	Sherry Magee - CF (PHI)	Harry Coveleski - SP (PHI) x3
Mickey Doolin - SS (PHI)	Elmer Flick - RF (PHI) x5	Erskine Mayer - SP (PHI)
Dave Bancroft - SS (PHI) x6	George Browne - RF (PHI)	Eppa Rixey - SP (PHI) x8
Ed Delahanty - LF (PHI) x2	John Titus - RF (PHI) x5	Bill Duggleby - SP (PHI)
Sam Mertes - LF (PHI) x3	Nixey Callahan - SP (PHI)	Al Orth - SP (PHI) x2
John Titus - LF (PHI)	Bill Bernhard - SP (PHI)	Doc White - SP (PHI) x5
Sherry Magee - LF (PHI) x7	Tully Sparks - SP (PHI) x2	

Year/Team	OPW%	PW	PL	APW%	AW	AL	Diff+/-
1920 PHI	0.471 F	73	81	0.405	62	91	-0.066
1921 PHI	0.500 F	77	77	0.331	51	103	-0.168
1922 PHI	0.475 F	73	81	0.373	57	96	-0.102
1923 PHI	0.418 F	64	90	0.325	50	104	-0.094
1924 PHI	0.492 F	76	78	0.364	55	96	-0.128
1925 PHI	0.528 F	81	73	0.444	68	85	-0.083
1926 PHI	0.503 F	78	76	0.384	58	93	-0.119
1927 PHI	0.482 F	74	80	0.331	51	103	-0.151
1928 PHI	0.385	59	95	0.283	43	109	-0.102
1929 PHI	0.460 F	71	83	0.464	71	82	0.004

franchID	OWAR	OWS	AWAR	AWS	WARdiff	WSdiff	P/D/W/F
1920 PHI	20.130	159.102	20.422	186.003	7.714	-26.901	F
1921 PHI	26.249	167.572	16.813	152.997	9.436	14.575	F
1922 PHI	30.833	167.137	27.498	171.000	3.334	-3.863	F
1923 PHI	25.165	149.439	19.921	149.998	5.244	-0.559	F
1924 PHI	27.141	188.447	20.649	164.999	6.492	23.448	F
1925 PHI	39.712	222.649	28.223	204.000	11.489	18.650	F
1926 PHI	26.822	176.726	21.489	174.001	5.333	2.725	F
1927 PHI	21.922	167.425	18.726	152.998	3.196	14.427	F
1928 PHI	17.030	134.655	13.923	129.001	3.106	5.654	
1929 PHI	27.461	183.225	30.496	212.995	-3.035	-29.771	F

Alexander (27-14, 1.91) topped the National League in victories, ERA, innings pitched and strikeouts while completing 33 of 40 starts in 1920. Rixey established career-bests as he tallied 25 wins with 313.1 innings pitched and 26 complete games in '22. Shortstop Dave Bancroft scored over 100 times in three straight years (1920-22) and forged a .309 BA during a seven-year stretch from 1920-26.

Chuck Klein made an immediate impact on the Phillies' offense, hitting at a .360 clip in his rookie year (1928) and blasting a league-leading 43 long balls while driving in 145 baserunners during his sophomore season. Klein accrued 200+ base hits and 100+ ribbies in five consecutive campaigns (1929-1933). Pinky Whitney initiated his career with three straight seasons of 100+ RBI. The Phillies' third sacker collected 200 base knocks and batted .327 for the '29 crew.

Year/Team	OPW%	PW	PL	APW%	AW	AL	Diff+/-
1930 PHI	0.423 F	65	89	0.338	52	102	-0.086
1931 PHI	0.439 F	68	86	0.429	66	88	-0.011
1932 PHI	0.626 F	96	58	0.506	78	76	-0.120

Year/Team	OPW%	PW	PL	APW%	AW	AL	Diff+/-
1933 PHI	0.481 F	74	80	0.395	60	92	-0.087
1934 PHI	0.444 F	68	86	0.376	56	93	-0.069
1935 PHI	0.391 F	60	94	0.418	64	89	0.028
1936 PHI	0.396 F	61	93	0.351	54	100	-0.045
1937 PHI	0.454 F	70	84	0.399	61	92	-0.056
1938 PHI	0.381	59	95	0.300	45	105	-0.081
1939 PHI	0.417 F	64	90	0.298	45	106	-0.119

franchID	OWAR	OWS	AWAR	AWS	WARdiff	WSdiff	P/D/W/F
1930 PHI	17.234	133.975	21.266	155.996	-4.033	-22.021	F
1931 PHI	20.991	166.035	25.044	197.997	-4.053	-31.963	F
1932 PHI	31.029	209.114	36.305	234.004	-5.276	-24.890	F
1933 PHI	33.473	190.826	19.917	179.999	13.556	10.826	F
1934 PHI	18.776	170.702	20.608	167.992	-1.832	2.710	F
1935 PHI	14.533	151.888	19.685	191.994	-5.152	-40.106	F
1936 PHI	12.464	159.615	23.489	161.988	-11.025	-2.374	F
1937 PHI	17.105	181.546	24.409	182.995	-7.304	-1.449	F
1938 PHI	12.342	146.160	8.811	134.998	3.531	11.163	
1939 PHI	17.558	156.462	7.402	134.999	10.156	21.462	F

Klein continued his assault on opposition hurlers as he slammed 40 circuit clouts while establishing career marks in batting average (.386), RBI (170), runs (158), and doubles (59) in 1930. He produced 250 hits yet failed to lead the National League, placing second to Bill Terry (254). Klein (.348/38/137) merited MVP honors in '32 after a runner-up finish in the prior campaign. He contributed a personal best in Win Shares (31) and notched three straight home run titles (1931-33). Pinky Whitney set career-highs with 207 hits along with a .342 BA in 1930 then knocked in 124 runners in '32. Curt Davis (22-16, 3.63) earned his second All-Star nod and finished fifth in the 1939 NL MVP balloting.

Win Shares > 20	Single-Season	1920-1939
Pinky Whitney - 3B (PHI) Chuck Klein - LF (PHI)	Chuck Klein - RF (PHI) x4	Curt Davis - SP (PHI) x3

Year/Team	OPW%	PW	PL	APW%	AW	AL	Diff+/-
1940 PHI	0.232 F	36	118	0.327	50	103	0.095
1941 PHI	0.335 F	52	102	0.279	43	111	-0.056
1942 PHI	0.397 F	61	93	0.278	42	109	-0.119
1943 PHI	0.440 F	68	86	0.416	64	90	-0.024
1944 PHI	0.408 F	63	91	0.399	61	92	-0.009
1945 PHI	0.324 F	50	104	0.299	46	108	-0.026
1946 PHI	0.482 F	74	80	0.448	69	85	-0.034
1947 PHI	0.524 F	81	73	0.403	62	92	-0.121
1948 PHI	0.468 F	72	82	0.429	66	88	-0.040
1949 PHI	0.473 F	73	81	0.526	81	73	0.053

franchID	OWAR	OWS	AWAR	AWS	WARdiff	WSdiff	P/D/W/F
1940 PHI	7.141	113.121	12.054	149.999	-4.913	-36.878	F
1941 PHI	15.541	119.845	13.626	129.001	1.915	-9.156	F
1942 PHI	17.552	147.032	8.417	125.999	9.135	21.032	F
1943 PHI	18.684	154.882	24.607	191.998	-5.923	-37.116	F
1944 PHI	19.885	182.451	29.289	182.999	-9.404	-0.547	F
1945 PHI	6.940	118.727	11.938	137.998	-4.998	-19.271	F
1946 PHI	28.476	190.438	26.024	207.004	2.452	-16.566	F

Del Ennis delivered a .313 batting average and earned an invitation to the All-Star game in his rookie season (1946). Harry "The Hat" Walker captured the batting crown with a .363 average and led the National League with 16 triples and a .436 OBP in '47. Richie Ashburn swiped a league-high 32 bags and hit .333 in his inaugural campaign (1948). Gene Bearden (20-7, 2.43) collected the ERA title and finished second in the Rookie of the Year balloting in '48.

Year/Team	OPW%	PW	PL	APW%	AW	AL	Diff+/-
1950 PHI	0.562 P	87	67	0.591 P	91	63	0.029
1951 PHI	0.508 F	78	76	0.474	73	81	-0.034
1952 PHI	0.557	86	68	0.565	87	67	0.008
1953 PHI	0.543	84	70	0.539	83	71	-0.004
1954 PHI	0.554	85	69	0.487	75	79	-0.067
1955 PHI	0.495 F	76	78	0.500	77	77	0.005
1956 PHI	0.474	73	81	0.461	71	83	-0.013
1957 PHI	0.479	74	80	0.500	77	77	0.021
1958 PHI	0.430	66	88	0.448	69	85	0.019
1959 PHI	0.438 F	67	87	0.416	64	90	-0.022

franchID	OWAR	OWS	AWAR	AWS	WARdiff	WSdiff	P/D/W/F
1950 PHI	35.159	**249.729**	38.276	**273.002**	-3.117	-23.273	P
1951 PHI	40.843	232.415	35.701	218.997	5.142	13.418	F
1952 PHI	**38.233**	245.301	45.778	261.004	-7.545	-15.703	
1953 PHI	38.820	238.795	40.090	249.000	-1.270	-10.205	
1954 PHI	48.608	250.717	37.952	231.000	10.656	19.717	
1955 PHI	46.050	237.523	37.952	231.000	8.098	6.523	F
1956 PHI	34.030	206.364	30.278	213.000	3.752	-6.636	
1957 PHI	37.985	239.009	35.818	230.998	2.167	8.011	
1958 PHI	37.503	197.283	37.132	207.004	0.372	-9.720	
1959 PHI	25.117	194.929	21.290	192.001	3.827	2.929	F

Philadelphia captured its lone pennant in 1950, beating the Cardinals by a seven-game margin and pacing the circuit in oWS. Ashburn ignited the top of the order, hitting .318 from 1950-58 while scoring 96 runs per season. "Whitey" surpassed the 200-hit mark on three occasions including 221 base knocks in '51. He collected two batting titles (.338 in '55 and .350 in '58) and paced the circuit three times in OBP. Ennis placed fourth in the 1950 NL MVP race, topping the League with 126 RBI while batting .311 with 31 round-trippers. Ennis produced 26 four-baggers and plated 112 runners per year from 1952-57.

Curt Simmons yielded a 17-8 mark with a 3.40 ERA in 1950 and topped the League with 6 shutouts in the subsequent season. Willie "Puddin' Head" Jones earned his first All-Star nod, swatting 25 long balls and scoring 100 runs. Robin Roberts dominated the circuit between 1950-55, averaging 23 victories and 27 complete games per season. Roberts posted a 2.93 ERA and 1.094 WHIP during this period, eclipsing 300 innings pitched in each campaign and finished second in the 1952 NL MVP race with a 28-7 record and a 2.59 ERA. Roberts registered a career-high 34 Win Shares in '53. Brooklyn outpaced Philly by three victories in '52.

Middle infielder Granny Hamner supplied career-highs in '53 with 21 home runs and 92 RBI. He followed with his best overall offensive season, batting .299 with 39 doubles, 13 dingers and 89 runs driven in. The 1954 squad finished a distant second to the Milwaukee Braves. Stan

Lopata crushed 32 round-trippers and knocked in 95 runs for the '56 squad. Harry "The Horse" Anderson hit .301 with 23 homers and 97 RBI in '58.

Jack S. Sanford (19-8, 3.08) received the 1957 NL ROY Award and paced the circuit with 188 strikeouts. Roy Face led the League with 20 saves in '58 and managed an 18-1 record in 57 relief appearances in 1959. By 1958, the Fightin' Phillies slumped to a 66-88 mark en route to a last-place finish in the National League. Philadelphia failed to reach the minimum PA requirements in '51, '55 and '59 while falling short of the BFP requirements in 1951.

Win Shares > 20	Single-Season	1940-1959
Ed Bouchee - 1B (PHI)	Harry Walker - CF (PHI)	Robin Roberts - SP (PHI) x6
Willie Jones - 3B (PHI) x3	Richie Ashburn - CF (PHI) x11	Curt Simmons - SP (PHI)
Stan Lopata - C (PHI)	Del Ennis - RF (PHI) x2	Jack S. Sanford - SP (PHI) x2
Del Ennis - LF (PHI) x4	Gene Bearden - SP (PHI)	

Year/Team	OPW%	PW	PL	APW%	AW	AL	Diff+/-
1960 PHI	0.415 F	64	90	0.383	59	95	-0.032
1961 PHI	0.401 F	65	97	0.305	47	107	-0.095
1962 PHI	0.388 F	63	99	0.503	81	80	0.115
1963 PHI	0.385 F	62	100	0.537	87	75	0.152
1964 PHI	0.483 F	78	84	0.568	92	70	0.085
1965 PHI	0.494	80	82	0.528	85	76	0.034
1966 PHI	0.496 F	80	82	0.537	87	75	0.041
1967 PHI	0.518	84	78	0.506	82	80	-0.012
1968 PHI	0.497	80	82	0.469	76	86	-0.028
1969 PHI	0.482	78	84	0.389	63	99	-0.093

franchID	OWAR	OWS	AWAR	AWS	WARdiff	WSdiff	P/D/W/F
1960 PHI	29.246	195.133	19.216	176.996	10.031	18.137	F
1961 PHI	32.654	167.932	17.549	140.998	15.105	26.934	F
1962 PHI	41.677	216.169	31.572	243.000	10.106	-26.831	F
1963 PHI	32.246	185.805	41.189	261.003	-8.943	-75.197	F
1964 PHI	32.073	212.079	43.098	275.997	-11.025	-63.917	F
1965 PHI	34.899	213.797	42.473	254.992	-7.574	-41.195	
1966 PHI	32.998	204.835	39.975	261.001	-6.977	-56.166	F
1967 PHI	38.066	242.386	42.614	245.995	-4.548	-3.609	
1968 PHI	39.274	232.916	28.870	227.998	10.404	4.918	
1969 PHI	32.603	200.595	27.794	189.001	4.809	11.594	

Ashburn led the National League with 116 walks and a .415 OBP, scoring 99 times for the '60 squad. Turk Farrell added 10 wins and 11 saves. Art Mahaffey tallied 19 victories and completed 20 of 39 starts in 1962. Sanford (24-7, 3.43) placed second in the 1962 NL Cy Young balloting. Face topped the circuit with 28 saves and fashioned a career-best ERA of 1.88. Philadelphia failed to meet the minimum PA requirements from 1960-64 and 1966. During GM John Quinn's tenure in the Philadephia front office, the organization drafted Mike Schmidt in 1971 and acquired amateur free agents Dick Allen (1960), Ferguson Jenkins (1962) and Toby Harrah (1966).

Ray Culp (14-11, 2.97) finished third in the 1963 NL ROY voting. Curt Simmons fashioned a 2.48 ERA along with a 15-9 record and compiled an 18-9 record in the following year. Hal Woodeshick earned a trip to the Mid-Summer Classic in 1963, notching 11 wins, 10 saves and a 1.97 ERA. In 1964 he topped the National League with 23 saves.

Dick Allen (.318/29/91) won the 1964 NL ROY Award, pacing the circuit with 125 runs scored and 13 triples. The "Wampum Walloper" supplied a .300 batting average with 30 bombs and 90 RBI from 1964-69, finishing fourth in the 1966 NL MVP race, crushing 40 long balls and knocking in 110 runs while leading the League with a .632 SLG. Chris Short averaged 17 wins and 188 strikeouts per season (1964-68) with a 2.82 ERA and a 1.154 WHIP. Turk Farrell contributed 10 wins, 12 saves and a 2.34 ERA for the '67 crew.

Fergie Jenkins reeled off six consecutive seasons of 20 or more victories from 1967-72. "Fly" delivered a 2.88 ERA and a 1.087 WHIP from 1967-69 and topped the League with 273 whiffs in '69. Alex Johnson posted a .312 BA with 32 doubles in '68 and in the following campaign plated 88 runs and hit .315. Culp furnished a 16-6 record with a 2.91 ERA in 1968 and notched 17 wins in '69. Philadelphia's starting pitchers topped the Majors with 37 WS>10 seasons in the Sixties.

Year/Team	OPW%	PW	PL	APW%	AW	AL	Diff+/-
1970 PHI	0.446	72	90	0.453	73	88	0.008
1971 PHI	0.440	71	91	0.414	67	95	-0.027
1972 PHI	0.451	73	89	0.378	59	97	-0.073
1973 PHI	0.488	79	83	0.438	71	91	-0.050
1974 PHI	0.533 D	86	76	0.494	80	82	-0.039
1975 PHI	0.497	80	82	0.531	86	76	0.034
1976 PHI	0.502	81	81	0.623 D	101	61	0.121
1977 PHI	0.527	85	77	0.623 P	101	61	0.096
1978 PHI	0.547	89	73	0.556 D	90	72	0.009
1979 PHI	0.515	83	79	0.519	84	78	0.003

franchID	OWAR	OWS	AWAR	AWS	WARdiff	WSdiff	P/D/W/F
1970 PHI	38.704	229.782	28.789	219.005	9.914	10.777	
1971 PHI	32.675	210.713	25.457	201.002	7.217	9.711	
1972 PHI	38.285	233.213	28.114	176.995	10.172	56.218	
1973 PHI	33.855	252.322	29.642	213.005	4.213	39.317	
1974 PHI	43.854	285.523	32.543	240.008	11.310	45.515	D
1975 PHI	47.410	289.900	47.902	258.004	-0.492	31.897	
1976 PHI	44.719	278.198	56.996	302.997	-12.276	-24.799	
1977 PHI	53.063	315.494	54.004	303.003	-0.941	12.491	
1978 PHI	57.742	320.607	47.194	270.003	10.548	50.604	
1979 PHI	41.865	297.078	38.879	251.993	2.986	45.085	

Alex Johnson collected 202 hits en route to a batting title in 1970. He delivered a .329 BA and earned his lone All-Star invite. Fergie Jenkins cemented his status as staff ace, posting a 3.19 ERA, 1.072 WHIP and 21 victories per season from 1970-74. "Fly" established a personal best with 35 Win Shares while earning Cy Young honors in 1971 (24-13, 2.77, 30 CG). He finished among the top three vote-getters on three other occasions. Jenkins paced the circuit with a 1.038 WHIP in '70 and recorded 25 victories with 29 complete games in '74.

Ray Culp compiled 17 wins with a 3.04 ERA in '70. Dave A. Roberts furnished a 2.10 ERA and 1.109 ERA, placing sixth in the 1971 NL Cy Young balloting. Rick Wise contributed a 17-14 record with a 2.88 ERA in '71 and won 19 contests during the 1975 season. Mike G. Marshall settled in as the closer in '71 and he established iron-man relief records shortly thereafter. Marshall made 92 relief appearances in 1973 then set the Major League record with 106 in the subsequent season! He led the League in saves three times including 32 in 1979, when he also relieved in 90 contests.

The Fightin' Phils descended into last place in 1971. Dick Allen received MVP honors in 1972 as he led the circuit with 37 home runs, 113 RBI and 99 walks along with a .420 OBP and a .603 SLG, producing a career-high 40 Win Shares. Greg Luzinski slammed 29 moon-shots and knocked in 97 runs in '73. "The Bull" placed runner-up in the MVP balloting in 1975 (.300/34/120) and 1977 (.309/39/130).

Phillies' shortstops tied for the most WS>10 seasons during the Seventies due to the emerging talents of Larry Bowa and Toby Harrah. Bowa legged out 13 triples in '72, pilfered 39 bags in '74 and hit .305 for the 1975 squad. Harrah provided a power/speed package, averaging 19 blasts and 21 steals from 1974-79. He topped the League with 109 walks in '77 and scored 99 runs in 1979.

The team rebounded to take the NL East division title in '74, placing two games ahead of the Pirates. After laboring through his rookie campaign, Mike Schmidt became entrenched at the hot corner. He collected 10 Gold Gloves for his defensive prowess and provided exceptional offensive production including a career-high 38 Win Shares in '74. Schmidt averaged 36 circuit clouts, 102 RBI, 105 runs scored and 18 stolen bases per year (1974-79). He led the National League in home runs for three straight seasons (1974-76) and tallied 120 bases on balls in '79.

In a three-way battle for the crown in '77, St. Louis emerged victorious by a single game over Philadelphia and Pittsburgh. Larry Christenson managed 19 victories. Larry Hisle secured consecutive All-Star appearances in 1977-78. He batted .302 with 28 clouts and a league-best 119 ribbies. Hisle crushed 34 long balls and knocked in 115 runs during the '78 campaign.

Bob Boone received Gold Glove Awards in 1978-79 while fellow backstop John Stearns nabbed 25 bags. Andre Thornton slugged 33 four-baggers and drove in 105 runs for the '78 squad. The '78 team posted its highest win total since 1905 but ended the year in third place behind the Pirates and Expos. Grant Jackson added 8 wins and 14 saves and Mark Clear (11-5, 14 SV) finished third in the ROY balloting for the '79 crew.

Win Shares > 20	Single-Season	1960-1979
Dick Allen - 1B (PHI) x3	John Stearns - C (PHI)	Chris Short - SP (PHI) x2
Andre Thornton - 1B (PHI) x2	Dick Allen - LF (PHI)	Fergie Jenkins - SP (PHI) x8
Dick Allen - 3B (PHI) x5	Alex Johnson - LF (PHI)	Dave A. Roberts - SP (PHI) x2
Toby Harrah - SS (PHI) x3	Greg Luzinski - LF (PHI) x5	Rick Wise - SP (PHI)
Larry Bowa - SS (PHI)	Johnny Briggs - LF (PHI)	Mike G. Marshall - RP (PHI)
Mike Schmidt - 3B (PHI) x13	Larry Hisle - LF (PHI) x2	x4
Toby Harrah - 3B (PHI) x4	Adolfo Phillips - CF (PHI)	

Year/Team	OPW%	PW	PL	APW%	AW	AL	Diff+/-
1980 PHI	0.500	81	81	0.562 D	91	71	0.061
1981 PHI	0.467	76	86	0.551	59	48	0.084
1982 PHI	0.504	82	80	0.549	89	73	0.045
1983 PHI	0.498	81	81	0.556 D	90	72	0.058
1984 PHI	0.489	79	83	0.500	81	81	0.011
1985 PHI	0.482	78	84	0.463	75	87	-0.019
1986 PHI	0.505	82	80	0.534	86	75	0.029
1987 PHI	0.541	88	74	0.494	80	82	-0.047
1988 PHI	0.460	75	87	0.404	65	96	-0.057
1989 PHI	0.463	75	87	0.414	67	95	-0.049

franchID	OWAR	OWS	AWAR	AWS	WARdiff	WSdiff	P/D/W/F
1980 PHI	44.548	279.951	44.014	272.995	0.534	6.956	
1981 PHI	20.779	169.888	28.277	177.001	-7.498	-7.113	
1982 PHI	44.347	304.436	42.252	266.996	2.095	37.441	

1983 PHI	44.543	275.280	43.623	269.994	0.920	5.286
1984 PHI	43.353	302.499	**46.988**	242.998	-3.634	59.501
1985 PHI	39.972	281.405	32.083	225.005	7.890	56.400
1986 PHI	38.650	288.979	37.409	258.009	1.241	30.969
1987 PHI	42.011	276.383	30.304	239.997	11.707	36.385
1988 PHI	31.961	247.489	19.814	195.002	12.147	52.487
1989 PHI	32.402	238.474	26.586	200.999	5.816	37.475

Schmidt collected three NL MVP Awards during the Eighties including back-to-back awards in 1980-81. He paced the circuit in home runs, RBI and SLG in all three campaigns, blasting 48 four-ply swats in '80. Schmidt also earned MVP honors in 1986 after hammering 37 long balls and knocking in 119 runs. From 1980-87 Schmidt slugged .559 and his average output consisted of 37 wallops and 105 ribbies. Lonnie Smith batted .339 with 33 stolen bases and placed third in the 1980 NL ROY balloting. Nicknamed "Skates" due to his mis-adventures in the outfield, Smith received his lone All-Star nod and earned a runner-up finish in the 1982 NL MVP race. He led the circuit with 120 runs scored while batting .307 with a career-best 68 steals. Smith averaged 53 steals from 1982-85 and enjoyed a bounce-back campaign in 1989.

Toby Harrah topped the 100-run plateau in '80 and '82 and earned his fourth All-Star invite with a .304 average and 25 dingers in 1982. Joe Charboneau (.289/23/87) received ROY honors in 1980 but struggled mightily thereafter and was out of the Majors by '82. Dick Ruthven posted 17 victories for the '80 squad. Luzinski plated 102 runs with 37 doubles in '82 and slammed 32 moon shots in 1983. Clear amassed 14 wins and 14 saves in '82 and delivered a 2.20 ERA with 16 saves in 1986. Bob Dernier delivered 38 stolen bases per year (1982-85) and was presented with a Gold Glove Award in 1984. Thornton (.273/32/116) attended the Mid-Summer Classic in '82 and returned in '84 after slugging a career-high 33 long balls.

The Phillies' farm system restocked its supply of infielders during the early Eighties. Ryne Sandberg scored 103 runs and pilfered 32 bags during his freshman year in '82. "Ryno" collected 9 consecutive Gold Glove Awards (1983-91) and received the 1984 NL MVP Award as he tallied 200 hits and 38 Win Shares while pacing the League with 19 triples and 114 runs. Julio Franco nabbed 32 bags and plated 80 runs en route to a runner-up finish in the ROY balloting in 1983. He produced a .310 batting average from 1986-89 and knocked in 92 runs in 1989. Juan Samuel swiped 72 bases and led the League with 19 triples, earning a second-place finish in the 1984 NL ROY vote. He eclipsed the 100-run mark three times and averaged 46 steals from 1984-89. Samuel swatted 28 homers, 15 triples and drove in 100 runs in 1987. Philadelphia accrued 35 WS>10 seasons at the keystone position from 1980-1999.

Willie Hernandez (1.92, 32 SV) dominated the opposition in 1984, earning MVP and Cy Young honors. Hernandez saved 31 contests and furnished a 0.900 WHIP during the subsequent season. George A. Bell delivered consistently on offense, averaging .292 with 34 doubles, 29 four-baggers and 104 RBI from 1984-89. Bell (.308/47/134) received MVP honors in 1987, pacing the League in RBI while scoring 111 times. Kevin Gross tallied 15 victories in 1985 and received an All-Star nod with 12 wins and a 3.69 ERA in '88. First-sacker Greg Walker drove in 90+ runs twice and Keith Moreland batted .307 with 106 ribbies in '85.

Ozzie Virgil, Jr. belted 27 long balls in 1987 and received two All-Star invitations. Bob Walk fashioned a 12-10 mark with a 2.71 ERA and 1.166 WHIP in 1988. Mark W. Davis ascended to the closer's role and tallied 28 saves with a 2.01 ERA. In 1989, Davis captured the Cy Young Award with 44 saves and a 1.85 ERA.

Despite a solid offense and three amazing seasons from the team's closers, the Phillies failed to win a division title in the Eighties primarily due to the starting rotation. Philadelphia fell two games short in 1984 as the Cardinals scraped by with 81 wins. The 1987 squad missed the playoffs by percentage points as the Mets emerged victorious.

Year/Team	OPW%	PW	PL	APW%	AW	AL	Diff+/-
1990 PHI	0.481	78	84	0.475	77	85	-0.005
1991 PHI	0.519	84	78	0.481	78	84	-0.037
1992 PHI	0.494	80	82	0.432	70	92	-0.062
1993 PHI	0.468	76	86	0.599 D	97	65	0.131
1994 PHI	0.537 D	87	75	0.470	54	61	-0.067
1995 PHI	0.381 F	62	100	0.479	69	75	0.099
1996 PHI	0.398	64	98	0.414	67	95	0.016
1997 PHI	0.459	74	88	0.420	68	94	-0.039
1998 PHI	0.520 F	84	78	0.463	75	87	-0.057
1999 PHI	0.476 F	77	85	0.475	77	85	-0.001

franchID	OWAR	OWS	AWAR	AWS	WARdiff	WSdiff	P/D/W/F
1990 PHI	33.256	237.206	27.565	231.003	5.690	6.203	
1991 PHI	44.270	263.855	27.309	233.998	16.961	29.857	
1992 PHI	33.126	237.499	31.436	210.000	1.690	27.499	
1993 PHI	30.629	242.015	51.695	291.007	-21.066	-48.992	
1994 PHI	28.732	159.720	23.349	162.000	5.384	-2.280	D
1995 PHI	27.147	165.096	29.332	207.006	-2.184	-41.910	F
1996 PHI	24.680	176.759	29.831	200.998	-5.150	-24.239	
1997 PHI	33.085	206.658	25.057	204.001	8.028	2.657	
1998 PHI	36.193	208.419	30.349	225.001	5.844	-16.581	F
1999 PHI	32.708	197.553	34.400	231.009	-1.692	-33.457	F

The Phillies bounced back from a last-place effort in 1990, finishing only one game behind the Cubs for the division title in '91. Sandberg paced the Senior Circuit with 40 quadruples and 116 runs in 1990. "Ryno" drove in 100 runs in '90 and '91 while concluding a run of 10 successive All-Star appearances in 1993. Franco (.341/15/78) collected a batting title in 1991 and established career-highs with 201 base hits, 108 runs scored and 36 stolen bases. In 1995 he hit .319 with 20 round-trippers and 98 ribbies. Todd Frohwirth (7-3, 1.87) and Chuck McElroy (6-2, 1.95) excelled as setup men in '91.

Bell knocked in 112 runs and Darren "Dutch" Daulton belted 27 round-trippers and plated 109 runners in 1992. Philadelphia outlasted Atlanta in 1994, taking the NL East crown by a one-game margin and leading the circuit in oWAR. Andy Ashby posted a 2.94 ERA in 1995 and delivered a 17-9 record with a 3.34 ERA en route to his first All-Star nod in '98. Bruce Ruffin worked the late innings from 1994-96, amassing 24 saves in 1996. Ricky Bottalico assumed Ruffin's role and rang up 34 saves in back-to-back seasons (1996-97).

Scott Rolen (.283/21/92) earned the 1997 NL ROY Award. He received his first of eight Gold Glove Awards in '98 and boosted the Phillies' offense with 31 four-baggers and 110 runs driven in. Mike R. Jackson ascended to full-time closer status in '98, saving 40 contests with a 1.55 ERA and 0.875 WHIP. He contributed 39 saves in the following campaign. Mike Lieberthal thumped 31 long balls and amassed 96 RBI. Philadelphia fell short of the minimum PA requirements in 1995 and from 1998-2001.

Year/Team	OPW%	PW	PL	APW%	AW	AL	Diff+/-
2000 PHI	0.435 F	71	91	0.401	65	97	-0.034
2001 PHI	0.500 F	81	81	0.531	86	76	0.031
2002 PHI	0.485	79	83	0.497	80	81	0.012
2003 PHI	0.475	77	85	0.531	86	76	0.056
2004 PHI	0.515	83	79	0.531	86	76	0.016

2005 PHI	0.488	79	83	0.543	88	74	0.055
2006 PHI	0.494	80	82	0.525	85	77	0.031
2007 PHI	0.511	83	79	0.549 D	89	73	0.038
2008 PHI	0.522	85	77	0.568 D	92	70	0.046
2009 PHI	0.547 D	89	73	0.574 D	93	69	0.027
2010 PHI	0.543 D	88	74	0.599 P	97	65	0.056
2011 PHI	0.495	80	82	0.630 P	102	60	0.134
2012 PHI	0.465	75	87	0.500	81	81	0.035
2013 PHI	0.468	76	86	0.451	73	89	-0.017

franchID	OWAR	OWS	AWAR	AWS	WARdiff	WSdiff	P/D/W/F
2000 PHI	33.902	202.392	27.645	194.997	6.257	7.395	F
2001 PHI	33.565	231.215	37.701	257.999	-4.137	-26.784	F
2002 PHI	29.911	205.471	41.517	240.003	-11.606	-34.532	
2003 PHI	31.878	196.917	44.343	257.999	-12.465	-61.082	
2004 PHI	35.003	227.724	42.241	257.998	-7.237	-30.274	
2005 PHI	36.293	248.775	45.094	263.997	-8.801	-15.222	
2006 PHI	37.716	227.599	44.858	254.996	-7.143	-27.397	
2007 PHI	39.427	245.403	44.783	266.997	-5.356	-21.594	
2008 PHI	37.963	237.276	43.857	276.004	-5.894	-38.729	
2009 PHI	43.028	259.568	45.546	279.003	-2.518	-19.435	D
2010 PHI	43.749	270.102	46.480	290.998	-2.731	-20.896	D
2011 PHI	40.497	238.975	52.996	305.997	-12.499	-67.021	
2012 PHI	27.827	218.114	30.264	242.996	-2.437	-24.881	
2013 PHI	32.021	256.709	16.991	217.936	15.029	38.773	

Scott Rolen produced a .290 batting average with 29 round-trippers, 107 RBI and 96 runs scored per year (2000-04). He placed fourth in the 2004 NL MVP race, bashing 34 bombs and driving in 124 runs while batting .314. Pat "The Bat" Burrell crushed 29 long balls and knocked in 94 runs per season (2001-08). He drilled 39 doubles and swatted 37 four-baggers while plating 116 runners in '02. Burrell (.281/32/117) placed seventh in the 2005 NL MVP vote. Jimmy Rollins paced the League with 12 triples and 46 stolen bases, earning a third-place finish in the 2001 NL ROY campaign. "J-Roll" delivered 39 doubles, 36 stolen bases and 104 runs scored from 2001-09. Rollins received the MVP Award in 2007 after topping the circuit with 139 runs scored and 20 three-base hits while blasting 30 moon-shots.

Chase Utley scored a league-best 131 runs in 2006. From 2005-09, Utley posted seasonal averages of .301 with 39 doubles, 29 circuit clouts, 101 RBI and 111 runs scored. Ryan Howard (.288/22/63) delivered outstanding power numbers in only 88 games, earning the 2005 NL ROY Award. Howard hit .313 while leading the NL with 58 four-ply swats and 149 runs driven in as he collected the MVP Award in '06. He paced the League again in 2008 with 48 home runs and 146 RBI whil averaging 44 wallops and 133 ribbies per season from 2006-2011. Fleet-footed outfielder Michael Bourn led the League in stolen bases for three consecutive seasons (2009-11), eclipsing 50 stolen bases in each year.

Randy Wolf tallied 16 wins and earned an All-Star invite in 2003. Cole Hamels furnished a 13-9 record with a 3.31 ERA and 1.127 WHIP per season (2007-11). Hamels led the League with 1.082 WHIP in '08. Gavin Floyd amassed 17 victories in 2008 and delivered a 1.162 WHIP for the 2011 squad. J.A. Happ (12-4, 2.93) placed runner-up in the 2009 NL ROY vote. Brett Myers fashioned a 3.14 ERA along with 14 wins in 2010. Mike Williams surpassed the 20-save mark from 2000-03. He made the All-Star team in 2002, posting a 2.93 ERA and saving 46 contests. Derrick Turnbow garnered 39 saves with a 1.74 ERA in '05.

The Phillies placed three games behind the Braves in '04 and posted consecutive last-place finishes. With the lumber company battering opposition hurlers, Philadelphia ended the 2008 season in a virtual tie with New York. The Phillies claimed back-to-back division titles in 2009-2010. Carlos "Chooch" Ruiz established career-highs in several offensive categories including a .325 BA, earning a trip to the 2012 Mid-Summer Classic.

Win Shares > 20	Single-Season	1980-2013
Mike Schmidt - 1B (PHI)	Jimmy Rollins - SS (PHI) x8	Pat Burrell - LF (PHI) x3
Ryan Howard - 1B (PHI) x5	Scott Rolen - 3B (PHI) x7	Michael Bourn - CF (PHI) x2
Ryne Sandberg - 2B (PHI) x7	Darren Daulton - C (PHI) x3	Marlon Byrd - CF (PHI)
Juan Samuel - 2B (PHI) x3	Mike Lieberthal - C (PHI)	Marlon Byrd – RF (PHI)
Julio Franco - 2B (PHI) x4	Carlos Ruiz - C (PHI)	Greg Luzinski - DH (PHI)
Mickey Morandini - 2B (PHI)	Lonnie Smith - LF (PHI) x2	Andre Thornton - DH (PHI) x2
Chase Utley - 2B (PHI) x7	George A. Bell - LF (PHI) x3	Willie Hernandez - RP (PHI)

Note: 4000 PA or BFP to qualify, except during strike-shortened seasons
(1972 = 3800, 1981 & 1994 = 2700, 1995 = 3500) and 154-game schedule (3800)
- failed to qualify: 1912-1927, 1929-1937, 1939-1949, 1951, 1955, 1959-1964, 1966, 1995, 1998-2001

Phillies All-Time "Originals" Roster

Ed Abbaticchio	Jerry Donovan	Bobby Korecky	Steve Ridzik
Johnny Abrego	Red Dooin	Fred Koster	Lee Riley
Bob A. Adams	Mickey Doolin	Joe Kracher	Frank Ringo
Joel Adamson	David Doster	Gary Kroll	Charlie Ripple
Luis Aguayo	Ken Dowell	Mike Krsnich	Wally Ritchie
Jack Albright	Dave Downs	Rocky Krsnich	Hank Ritter
Pete Alexander	Kelly Downs	Henry Krug	Eppa Rixey
Bob Gilman Allen	Conny Doyle	Nap Lajoie	Chris Roberson
Dick Allen	Denny Doyle	Jack Lamabe	Dave A. Roberts
Hank Allen	Kyle Drabek	Gene Lambert	Robin Roberts
Hezekiah Allen	Brandon Duckworth	Don Landrum	Craig Robinson
Ron Allen	Bill Duggleby	Tom Lanning	Mike Rogodzinski
Porfi Altamirano	Vern Duncan	Andy Lapihuska	Tony Roig
Dave S. Anderson	Lee Dunham	Ralph LaPointe	Scott Rolen
Harry Anderson	Davey Dunkle	Tommy Lasorda	Jimmy Rollins
John C. Anderson	George Durning	Billy Lauder	B. J. Rosenberg
Marlon Anderson	John Easton	Mike LaValliere	Frank Roth
Mike A. Anderson	Adam T. Eaton	Freddy Leach	Gene Rounsaville
Ed Andrews	Kid Elberfeld	Dan Leahy	Charlie Roy
Fred Andrews	Lee Elia	Bevo LeBourveau	Dutch Rudolph
Joe Antolick	Donnie Elliott	Greg Legg	Darin Ruf
Buzz Arlett	Hal Elliott	Clarence Lehr	Rudy Rufer
Steve Arlin	Ben Ellis	Ed Lennon	Bruce Ruffin
Morrie Arnovich	Cal Emery	Izzy Leon	Carlos Ruiz
Cody Asche	Spoke Emery	Randy Lerch	Cameron Rupp
Miguel Asencio	Del Ennis	Walt Lerian	John W. Russell
Richie Ashburn	Terry Enyart	Barry Lersch	Dick Ruthven
Andy Ashby	Don Erickson	Charlie Letchas	Bill Salisbury
Ezequiel Astacio	Sergio Escalona	Jesse Levan	Juan Samuel
Dick Attreau	Jim Essian	Bert Lewis	Alejandro Sanchez
Bill Atwood	Bobby M. Estalella	Mike Lieberthal	Ryne Sandberg
Bob Ayrault	Johnny Estrada	Doug Lindsey	Ben Sanders
Ed Baecht	George Eyrich	Angelo Lipetri	Heinie Sand
Dave Baldwin	Roy Face	Tom Lipp	Jack S. Sanford

Henry Baldwin	Rags Faircloth	Bob Lipski	Ed Sanicki
Jay Baller	Ed Fallenstein	Joe Lis	Kevin Saucier
Dave Bancroft	Mike Farmer	Danny Litwhiler	Jimmie Savage
Alan Bannister	Sid Farrar	Mike Loan	Ted Savage
Tom Barry	Turk Farrell	Carlton Loewer	Joe Savery
Shawn Barton	Eddie Feinberg	Bill Lohrman	Carl Sawatski
Walt Bashore	Charlie J. Ferguson	Joe Lonnett	Phil Saylor
Antonio Bastardo	Don Ferrarese	Stan Lopata	Bob Scanlan
Bud Bates	John Fick	Marcelino Lopez	Frank Scanlan
Kim Batiste	Jack Fifield	Carlton Lord	Mac Scarce
Russ Bauers	Frank Figgemeier	Larry Loughlin	Steve Scarsone
Stan Baumgartner	Sam File	Lynn Lovenguth	Gene Schall
Bob Beall	Bob Finley	Jay Loviglio	Charley Schanz
Ernie Beam	Happy Finneran	Fred Lucas	Danny Schell
Gene Bearden	Tony Fiore	Al Lukens	Dutch Schesler
Bob Becker	Newt Fisher	Johnny Lush	Lou Schettler
George Beck	Frank Fletcher	Greg Luzinski	Brian Schlitter
Matt Beech	Paul Fletcher	Harry Lyons	Mike Schmidt
Petie Behan	Elmer Flick	Terry Lyons	Jeff Schneider
George A. Bell	Hilly Flitcraft	Harvey MacDonald	Barney Schultz
Art Benedict	Jose Flores	Andy Machado	John Schultze
Stan Benjamin	Bubba Floyd	Julio Machado	Rick Schu
Dave Bennett	Gavin Floyd	Jean Machi	Michael Schwimer
Dennis Bennett	Jim Fogarty	Mike Maddux	Lefty Scott
Gary Bennett	Gary Fortune	Art Madison	Tom Seaton
Joe Bennett	Bill Foxen	Ryan Madson	Duke Sedgwick
Rabbit Benton	Henry Fox	Sherry Magee	Kevin Sefcik
Bill Bernhard	Julio Franco	Wendell Magee	Zack Segovia
Joe Berry	Ed Freed	Tom Magrann	Jose Segura
Quintin Berry	Marvin Freeman	Art Mahaffey	Ray Semproch
Lefty Bertrand	Fred Frink	Frank Mahar	Paul Sentell
Huck Betts	Ben Froelich	Tom Maher	Manny Seoane
Charlie Bicknell	Todd Frohwirth	Jim Mahoney	Scott Service
Steve Bieser	Charlie Frye	Cy Malis	Nap Shea
Joseph Bisenius	Dave Fultz	Les Mallon	Chuck Sheerin
Jim Bishop	William Gallagher	Chuck Malone	Monk Sherlock
Jim Bivin	Freddy Galvis	Matt Maloney	Costen Shockley
Ron Blazier	Bob Gandy	George Mangus	Chris Short
Dan Boitano	Art Gardiner	Harry Marnie	Toots Shultz
Ed Boland	Ned Garvin	Doc W. Marshall	Anthony Shumaker
Jack Bolling	Geoff Geary	Mike G. Marshall	Dwight Siebler
Barry Bonnell	Phil Geier	Rube Marshall	Tripp Sigman
Bob Boone	Tony Ghelfi	Tom Marsh	Carlos Silva
John Boozer	Norm Gigon	Lou Marson	Curt Simmons
Toby Borland	Charlie Girard	Doc Martel	Alfredo Simon
Rick Bosetti	Buck Gladman	Buck Martinez	John Singleton
Derek Botelho	Kid Gleason	Hersh Martin	Pete Sivess
Ricky Bottalico	Bill Glynn	Jerry Martin	Ed Sixsmith
Ed Bouchee	Billy Goeckel	Hank Mason	Barney Slaughter
Michael Bourn	Jim Golden	Paul Masterson	Jake Smith
Larry Bowa	Mike Goliat	Scott Mathieson	Lonnie Smith
Bob L. Bowman	Greg Golson	Eddie Matteson	Pete J. Smith
Sumner Bowman	Wayne Gomes	Dale Matthewson	Roy P. Smith
Jason Boyd	Chile Gomez	Len Matuszek	Lefty Smoll
Jack Boyle	Howie Gorman	Dick Mauney	Harry Smythe

John Brackenridge
King Brady
Bobby Bragan
Art Bramhall
Cliff Brantley
Alonzo Breitenstein
John Briggs
Johnny Briggs
Bill Brinker
Brad Brink
Eude Brito
Jack Brittin
Frank Brooks
Domonic Brown
George Browne
Jackie Brown
Paul Brown
Frank Bruggy
Tyson Brummett
Roy Bruner
Warren Brusstar
Taylor Buchholz
Fred Burchell
Bill Burich
Elmer Burkart
Eddie Burke
Mack Burk
Pat Burrell
Al Burris
Paul Busby
Joe Buskey
Charlie Butler
Marlon Byrd
Marty Bystrom
Putsy Caballero
John Cahill
Earl Caldwell
Ralph Caldwell
Nixey Callahan
Jim Robert Campbell
Adrian Cardenas
Don Cardwell
Don Carman
Andrew Carpenter
Carlos Carrasco
Andy Carter
Ed Cassian
Carmen Castillo
Lendy Castillo
John Castle
Danny Cater
John Cavanaugh
Jose Cecena
Bob Chakales
George Chalmers

Joe Gormley
Anthony Gose
Tuffy Gosewisch
Nick Goulish
Reggie Grabowski
Mike J. Grace
Mike Grady
Wayne Graham
Jim Grant
Lou Grasmick
Don Grate
Lew Graulich
Jeff E. Gray
Bob Greenwood
Dallas Green
June Greene
Paddy Greene
Tyler Green
Bill Gray
John Grim
Jason Grimsley
Kevin Gross
Jeff Grotewold
Art Hagan
Jim Haislip
Bert Hall
Bob P. Hall
Bill W. Hallman
Cole Hamels
Garvin Hamner
Granny Hamner
Ray Hamrick
Snipe Hansen
J.A. Happ
Lou Hardie
Tim Harkness
Dick J. Harley
Bill Harman
Brad Harman
Terry Harmon
George J. Harper
Toby Harrah
Herb Harris
Mickey Harrington
Ray Hartranft
Don Hasenmayer
Mickey Haslin
Ralph Head
Ed Hearn
Bill Heath
Bronson Heflin
Hardie Henderson
Fritz Henrich
Snake Henry
Cesar A. Hernandez

Tim Mauser
Ed H. Mayer
Erskine Mayer
Paddy Mayes
Jackie Mayo
George McAvoy
Greg McCarthy
John McCloskey
Don McCormack
Lance McCullers
Ed McDonough
Chuck McElroy
Jim McElroy
Jack McFetridge
Patsy McGaffigan
Rogers McKee
Warren McLaughlin
George McQuillan
Francisco Melendez
Sam Mertes
Lenny Metz
Jack Meyer
Mickey Micelotta
Jason Michaels
Bob J. Miller
Dyar Miller
Elmer J. Miller
Hughie Miller
Joe Millette
Keith N. Miller
Ralph J. Miller
Red Miller
Russ Miller
John Milligan
Rudy Minarcin
Larry Mitchell
Fred Mollenkamp
Alex Monchak
Brad Moore
Euel Moore
Mickey Morandini
Seth Morehead
Harry Morelock
Keith Moreland
Jose Moreno
Jim Morrison
John W. Morris
Sparrow Morton
Walter Moser
Bitsy Mott
Frank Motz
Ron Mrozinski
Hugh Mulcahy
Moon Mullen
Manny Muniz

Gene Snyder
Bill Sorrell
Denny Sothern
Dick Spalding
Tully Sparks
Stan Sperry
Jim Spotts
Homer Spragins
Jack Spring
Charlie Sproull
Buck Stanley
John Stearns
Gene Steinbrenner
Dummy Stephenson
Bobby Stevens
Neb Stewart
Kevin Stocker
Gene Stone
Jeff Stone
Ray Stoviak
Mike Strahler
John Strike
Paul Stuffel
Michael Stutes
George Stutz
Ernie Sulik
Tom A. Sullivan
Rick Surhoff
George C. Susce
Steve Susdorf
Darrell Sutherland
Gary Sutherland
Les Sweetland
Lefty Taber
Lee Tate
Michael Taylor
Reggie Taylor
Wilfredo Tejada
Robinson Tejeda
Dick Thoenen
Bill Thomas
Erskine Thomason
Roy A. Thomas
Roy J. Thomas
Andre Thornton
John Thornton
Ben Tincup
Cannonball Titcomb
John Titus
Al Todd
Happy Townsend
Manny Trillo
Ricky Trlicek
Derrick Turnbow
Tuck Turner

Bill Champion	Willie Hernandez	Scott Munninghoff	Turkey Tyson
Travis Chapman	Yoel Hernandez	Red Munson	Dutch Ulrich
Joe Charboneau	Pancho Herrera	Con Murphy	Tom Underwood
Harry Cheek	John Herrnstein	Dummy Murphy	John Upham
Mitch Chetkovich	Jesse Hickman	Ed James Murphy	Chase Utley
Cupid Childs	Bill Higdon	Ed Joseph Murphy	Gene Vadeboncoeur
Rocky Childress	John Hiland	Pat Murray	Eric Valent
Pearce Chiles	Pat Hilly	Tom Murray	Fred Van Dusen
Dino Chiozza	Charlie Hilsey	Barney Mussill	Ben Van Dyke
Lou Chiozza	Larry Hisle	Brett Myers	Jim Vatcher
Larry Christenson	Harry Hoch	Bill Nahorodny	Joe Verbanic
Bubba Church	Bert Hodge	Al Neiger	Al Verdel
Ted Cieslak	Lefty Hoerst	Tom Newell	Tom Vickery
Mel Clark	Bill Hoffman	Frank Nicholson	Jonathan Villar
Ron Clark	Bill Hohman	Dickie Noles	Bill Vinton
Bill Clay	Joe Holden	Jerry Nops	Ozzie Virgil, Jr.
Mark Clear	Stan Hollmig	Leo Norris	Cy Vorhees
Wally Clement	Jim Holloway	Ryan Nye	George Vukovich
Tyler Cloyd	Marty Hopkins	Prince Oana	John Vukovich
Dave Coble	Del Howard	Dink O'Brien	Woody Wagenhorst
Dave Coggin	Ryan Howard	Frank O'Connor	Gary Wagner
Jimmie Coker	Red Howell	Harry O'Donnell	Ed Walczak
John F. Coleman	Dan Howley	Joe Oeschger	Bob Walk
John W. Coleman	Charles Hudson	Jim Olander	Greg Walker
Larry Colton	Keith Hughes	Ed Olivares	Harry Walker
Pat Combs	Tommy O. Hughes	Skinny O'Neal	Marty Walker
Jim Command	Billy Hulen	John O'Neil	Dave Wallace
Mike Compton	Bert Humphries	Joe O'Rourke	Doc Wallace
Bob Conley	Rich Hunter	Al Orth	Huck Wallace
Bert Conn	Harry Huston	Josh Outman	Mike Wallace
Gene Connell	Ham Iburg	Jim Owens	Augie Walsh
Jerry Connors	Doc Imlay	Red Owens	Jimmy M. Walsh
Bill Conway	Dane Iorg	Jorge Padilla	John Walsh
Paul Cook	Hal Irelan	Phil Paine	Walt Walsh
Gene Corbett	Orlando Isales	Lowell Palmer	Joe Ward
Pat Corrales	Fred Jacklitsch	Stan Palys	Kevin Ward
Mike Costanzo	Grant Jackson	Johnny Paredes	Piggy Ward
Dick Cotter	John Jackson	Dixie Parker	Buck Washer
Ed Cotter	Ken Jackson	Rick Parker	Ed Watkins
Harry Coveleski	Mike R. Jackson	Frank Parkinson	Frank Watt
Chet Covington	Mike W. Jackson	Steve Parris	Bill F. Webb
Larry Cox	Elmer Jacobs	Mike Pasquella	Lefty Weinert
Larry Crawford	Tom Jacquez	Jeff Patterson	Bud Weiser
Jack Crimian	Chris James	Frank Pearce	Harry Welchonce
Ches Crist	Jeff James	Harry Pearce	Bob Wells
Leo Cristante	Jason Jaramillo	Ike Pearson	Jim Westlake
John Crowley	Greg Jelks	Paul Penson	Gus Weyhing
Todd Cruz	Steve Jeltz	Bill Peterman	George L. Wheeler
Wil Culmer	Fergie Jenkins	Jonathan Pettibone	Matt Whisenant
Benny Culp	Alex Johnson	Adolfo Phillips	C.B. White
Bill Culp	Bill C. Johnson	Buz Phillips	Deke White
Ray Culp	Charlie Johnson	Wiley Piatt	Doc White
John Cumberland	John Johnson	Nick Picciuto	Jesse Whiting
Tony Curry	Youngy Johnson	Clarence Pickrel	Pinky Whitney
Jack Cusick	Broadway Jones	Ty Pickup	Jerry Willard

Sam Dailey

Ed Daily

Tony Daniels

Travis d'Arnaud

George Darrow

Darren Daulton

Curt Davis

Jacke Davis

Mark W. Davis

Bill Day

Marty Decker

Justin De Fratus

Bill Deitrick

Ed Delahanty

Tom Delahanty

Garton Del Savio

Tod Dennehey

Mike DePangher

Bob Dernier

Mickey Devine

Jake Diekman

Ron Diorio

Robert Dodd

John Dodge

Andy Dominique

Deacon Donahue

Jason Donald

Joe Donohue

Clarence Jones

Dale Jones

Ron Jones

Willie Jones

Charlie Jordan

Niles Jordan

Ricky Jordan

Orville Jorgens

George Jumonville

Joe Kappel

Ted Kazanski

Ed Keegan

Jimmie Keenan

Harry Keener

Hal Kelleher

Charlie Kelly

Mike J. Kelly

Al Kenders

Kyle Kendrick

Jason Kershner

Thornton Kipper

Garland Kiser

Chuck Klein

Bill Kling

Austin Knickerbocker

Joe Knight

George Knothe

Dick Koecher

Lerton Pinto

Jim Pirie

Alex Pitko

Walter Plock

Johnny Podgajny

John Poff

Al Porto

Lou Possehl

Troy Puckett

Nick Punto

Jesse Purnell

Shadow Pyle

Tom Qualters

John Quinn

Al Raffo

Pete Rambo

Elizardo Ramirez

Earl Rapp

Lou Raymond

Art Rebel

Billy Reed

Jerry Reed

Scott Reid

Tommy Reis

Butch Rementer

Marshall Renfroe

Ken Reynolds

Bob Rice

George Williams

Mike Williams

Claude Willoughby

Bill H. Wilson

Max Wilson

Bobby Wine

Rick Wise

Frank Withrow

Andy Woehr

Ed Wojna

Bill Wolff

Randy Wolf

Abe Wolstenholme

Hal Woodeshick

Frank Woodward

Vance Worley

Jim L. Wright

Russ Wrightstone

Rusty Yarnall

Bert Yeabsley

Charles Yingling

Del E. Young

Dick Young

Mike Zagurski

Brad Ziegler

Jon Zuber

Year/Team	OPW%	PW	PL	APW%	AW	AL	Diff+/-
1901 PIT	0.507	71	69	0.647 P	90	49	0.141
1902 PIT	0.522	73	67	0.741 P	103	36	0.219
1903 PIT	0.505	71	69	0.650 P	91	49	0.145
1904 PIT	0.509	78	76	0.569	87	66	0.059
1905 PIT	0.456	70	84	0.627	96	57	0.171
1906 PIT	0.562	86	68	0.608	93	60	0.046
1907 PIT	0.538	83	71	0.591	91	63	0.053
1908 PIT	0.461	71	83	0.636	98	56	0.175
1909 PIT	0.501	77	77	0.724 P	110	42	0.223

franchID	OWAR	OWS	AWAR	AWS	WARdiff	WSdiff	P/D/W/F
1901 PIT	33.704	237.138	**46.725**	**270.004**	-13.021	-32.866	
1902 PIT	35.384	242.628	**57.030**	**305.997**	-21.647	-63.369	
1903 PIT	32.829	256.224	43.391	**272.767**	-10.562	-16.543	
1904 PIT	39.919	290.428	37.901	260.998	2.018	29.430	
1905 PIT	34.797	257.436	40.228	287.995	-5.431	-30.560	
1906 PIT	41.834	257.137	44.779	279.003	-2.945	-21.865	
1907 PIT	38.926	251.908	43.065	273.004	-4.139	-21.097	
1908 PIT	28.729	228.405	42.756	294.009	-14.027	-65.605	
1909 PIT	29.711	239.907	**55.088**	**330.006**	-25.377	-90.099	

Legend: (P) = Pennant / Most Wins in League (D) = Division Winner (W) = Wild Card Winner (F) = Failed to Qualify

The Pittsburgh Alleghenys, one of eight charter members of the American Association, commenced play in 1882. The franchise aligned with the National League in 1891 and assumed the Pirates' nickname. The franchise has generated the most quality shortstops (42 WS>20 and 116 WS>10 seasons) and third basemen (38 WS>20 and 121 WS>10 seasons) among the "Turn of the Century" clubs. Arky Vaughan, Pee Wee Reese and Joe Cronin head the Pittsburgh shortstop contingent while Pie Traynor anchors the hot corner. The Bucs' left fielders top the WS>20 charts with 60 player-seasons, 19 of which can be attributed to Barry Bonds.

The Pirates, Cubs and Phillies' starting pitchers tied with 46 WS>10 seasons during the first decade of the 1900's. Jack Chesbro established himself as the staff workhorse, averaging 22 victories, 310 innings pitched and 28 complete games with a 2.44 ERA over 8 seasons (1901-08). "Happy Jack" owns the modern-day Major League record with 41 victories during the 1904 campaign. He notched his lowest ERA (1.82) and WHIP (0.937) while completing 48 of 51 starts and twirling 454.2 innings.

Sam Leever (25-7, 2.06) topped the National League leader boards in ERA while hurling 7 shutouts in 1903. "The Goshen Schoolmaster" doled out 18 victories per season with a 2.27 ERA and 1.106 WHIP from 1901-08. Jack "The Giant Killer" Pfiester stifled the opposition as he fashioned a league-best 1.15 ERA in '07. Howie Camnitz managed 18 victories per season with a 2.44 ERA from 1907-1913. Red fashioned a 1.56 ERA in '08 and then delivered a 25-6 record with a 1.62 ERA and 0.972 WHIP for an encore.

Ginger Beaumont tallied 31 WS and captured the batting crown with a .357 BA in 1902. The Bucs' center fielder led the League with 209 base hits, 137 runs scored, and 272 total bases while hitting .341 in the following year. Jimmy T. Williams thrice led the League in three-base hits and third-sacker Hans Lobert notched 31 Win Shares in 1908. The '09 squad produced the worst WSdiff (-90) and WARdiff (-25) vs. the "Actual" Pirates in franchise history.

Year/Team	OPW%	PW	PL	APW%	AW	AL	Diff+/-
1910 PIT	0.502	77	77	0.562	86	67	0.060
1911 PIT	0.549	85	69	0.552	85	69	0.003
1912 PIT	0.630 P	97	57	0.616	93	58	-0.014
1913 PIT	0.572	88	66	0.523	78	71	-0.048
1914 PIT	0.485	75	79	0.448	69	85	-0.037
1915 PIT	0.542	83	71	0.474	73	81	-0.068
1916 PIT	0.504	78	76	0.422	65	89	-0.081
1917 PIT	0.399	61	93	0.331	51	103	-0.068
1918 PIT	0.558 P	71	57	0.520	65	60	-0.038
1919 PIT	0.496	69	71	0.511	71	68	0.015

franchID	OWAR	OWS	AWAR	AWS	WARdiff	WSdiff	P/D/W/F
1910 PIT	31.704	227.233	38.054	257.999	-6.350	-30.766	
1911 PIT	31.318	223.246	46.182	254.998	-14.864	-31.752	
1912 PIT	39.622	275.570	47.749	279.009	-8.127	-3.439	P
1913 PIT	31.156	244.095	38.092	233.997	-6.936	10.098	
1914 PIT	23.691	224.191	25.030	206.998	-1.339	17.193	
1915 PIT	33.054	219.078	36.864	218.995	-3.810	0.082	
1916 PIT	22.794	192.782	24.815	195.004	-2.021	-2.221	
1917 PIT	20.523	161.169	21.708	153.004	-1.185	8.165	
1918 PIT	**30.867**	184.303	32.011	194.999	-1.143	-10.696	P
1919 PIT	16.261	138.119	30.694	213.003	-14.433	-74.884	

Max Carey averaged 45 stolen bases over fifteen seasons (1911-1925) and led the National League 10 times. Camnitz notched 20-win campaigns in back-to-back seasons (1911-12). Pittsburgh earned its first pennant by a two-game margin over the New York Giants in 1912. Claude Hendrix produced a 24-9 mark and topped the club with 27 Win Shares. Cy Falkenberg furnished a 23-10 record with a 2.22 ERA in 1913 and two years later Red Faber registered 24 victories with a 2.55 ERA. Wilbur Cooper baffled the opposition batsmen in 1916 with a career-best 1.87 ERA and averaged 20 wins per year from 1917-1924. The Pirates earned another pennant in 1918 by a single game over the Braves. Hendrix surpassed the 20-win plateau and Burleigh Grimes (19-9, 2.13) dazzled his adversaries while posting the lowest WHIP of his career (1.059).

Win Shares > 20	Single-Season	1901-1919
Jake Beckley - 1B (PIT)	Beals Becker - LF (PIT)	Sam Leever - SP (PIT) x3
Jiggs Donahue - 1B (PIT) x2	Ward Miller - LF (PIT)	Jack Pfiester - SP (PIT)
Dots Miller - 1B (PIT)	Ginger Beaumont - CF (PIT) x5	Ed Karger - SP (PIT)
Jimmy T. Williams - 2B (PIT) x3	George Van Haltren - CF (PIT)	Nick Maddox - SP (PIT)
Dots Miller - 2B (PIT)	Jimmy Slagle - CF (PIT) x2	Kaiser Wilhelm - SP (PIT)
Jim Viox - 2B (PIT)	Solly Hofman - CF (PIT) x2	Howie Camnitz - SP (PIT) x2
Solly Hofman - 2B (PIT)	Chief Wilson - CF (PIT)	Lefty Leifield - SP (PIT)
Terry Turner - SS (PIT)	Max Carey - CF (PIT) x9	Claude Hendrix - SP (PIT) x2
Hans Lobert - 3B (PIT) x2	Chief Wilson - RF (PIT)	Cy Falkenberg - SP (PIT) x2
Bill McKechnie - 3B (PIT)	Danny Moeller - RF (PIT)	Al Mamaux - SP (PIT)
George Gibson - C (PIT)	Jim Kelly - RF (PIT)	Wilbur Cooper - SP (PIT) x8
Jimmy Slagle - LF (PIT) x2	Jack Chesbro - SP (PIT) x6	Burleigh Grimes - SP (PIT) x7
Max Carey - LF (PIT) x2		Red Faber - SW (PIT)

Year/Team	OPW%	PW	PL	APW%	AW	AL	Diff+/-
1920 PIT	0.500	77	77	0.513	79	75	0.013
1921 PIT	0.548 P	84	70	0.588	90	63	0.040
1922 PIT	0.555 P	85	69	0.552	85	69	-0.003
1923 PIT	0.580 P	89	65	0.565	87	67	-0.015
1924 PIT	0.542	83	71	0.588	90	63	0.046
1925 PIT	0.570 P	88	66	0.621 P	95	58	0.051
1926 PIT	0.571 P	88	66	0.549	84	69	-0.022
1927 PIT	0.558	86	68	0.610 P	94	60	0.053
1928 PIT	0.602 P	93	61	0.559	85	67	-0.043
1929 PIT	0.567	87	67	0.575	88	65	0.008

franchID	OWAR	OWS	AWAR	AWS	WARdiff	WSdiff	P/D/W/F
1920 PIT	30.899	195.640	31.825	237.006	-0.926	-41.366	
1921 PIT	**32.010**	**207.486**	40.525	269.999	-8.515	-62.513	P
1922 PIT	**37.420**	**205.636**	47.408	254.997	-9.988	-49.361	P
1923 PIT	**39.133**	224.307	40.590	261.002	-1.457	-36.695	P
1924 PIT	34.920	207.780	40.634	270.004	-5.714	-62.224	
1925 PIT	**38.718**	218.545	**45.259**	**284.999**	-6.541	-66.453	P
1926 PIT	29.142	202.565	33.772	252.004	-4.630	-49.439	P
1927 PIT	29.591	208.055	**42.460**	**281.996**	-12.870	-73.941	
1928 PIT	33.218	226.424	37.904	254.994	-4.686	-28.570	P
1929 PIT	34.231	222.125	38.088	263.988	-3.857	-41.863	

The Pirates topped the Majors with 30 WS>10 seasons at the hot corner from 1910-1929. Pie Traynor eclipsed the 100-RBI mark on 7 occasions and placed sixth in the 1928 NL MVP balloting. Pittsburgh moundsmen registered 62 WS>10 seasons to lead the Majors during the 1920's. Faber posted 20+ victories in three consecutive campaigns (1920-22) and registered 36 Win Shares for the 1921 squad. He paced the League in ERA and WHIP in '21 and '22. The Bucs bettered the club's counterparts in oWAR and oWS while seizing the National League pennant in both seasons.

Cooper transcended the 20-win mark four times in five seasons (1920-24), failing only in 1923. "Jughandle" Johnny Morrison picked up the slack as he compiled a 25-13 record. Dazzy Vance sat atop the NL leader board in strikeouts for seven consecutive seasons (1922-28). Vance (28-6, 2.16) notched 35 Win Shares as he secured MVP honors in 1924 and led the League in victories, ERA, WHIP (1.022), complete games (30) and strikeouts (262). Carson Bigbee surpassed the 200-hit plateau and scored over 100 runs in back-to-back seasons (1921-22). During the 1922 campaign "Skeeter" manufactured a .350 BA and plated 99 runs while compiling 23 Win Shares. Max Carey set career-highs with 207 base hits and 140 runs scored during the '22 season and then led the squad with 29 Win Shares as the team earned its third consecutive pennant in 1923. "Scoops" established a personal best with a .343 BA in 1925.

Following several cups of coffee in the early 1920's, Kiki Cuyler burst on the scene with a vengeance, hitting at a .354 clip in his rookie year. Cuyler (.357/18/102) amassed a team-best 33 Win Shares while topping the NL with 144 runs scored and 26 triples. He delivered 220 base knocks and pilfered 41 bags en route to a runner-up finish in the 1925 NL MVP balloting. The Bucs sought retribution after missing the playoffs by one game in 1924, rallying to achieve three pennants in four seasons. The swashbuckling crew also fell short by a lone contest in the '27 season. Glenn "Buckshot" Wright knocked in 111 runners in his inaugural year (1924) and eclipsed the 100-RBI mark four times in his career. Pirates' shortstops posted 102 WS>10 player-seasons from 1920-1979 and finished third or better in six straight decades!

Paul Waner produced a .336 BA with a league-high 22 three-base hits during his rookie campaign (1926). "Big Poison" tallied 35 Win Shares and collected the NL MVP Award in 1927. Waner paced the circuit with a .380 BA, 237 hits, 18 triples, 131 RBI, and 342 total bases. Batting .333 for his career, Waner surpassed the .300 mark in 12 straight seasons (1926-1937). His brother Lloyd bested the 200-hit mark in four of his first five campaigns and topped the leader boards with 133 runs scored as a rookie in '27.

Ray Kremer garnered the ERA crown in back-to-back seasons (1926-27) and placed third in the 1926 NL MVP balloting. Vance topped the leader boards in ERA (2.09) and WHIP (1.063) during the '28 campaign. Grimes (25-14, 2.99) completed 28 of 37 starts and finished third in the MVP race. "Ol' Stubblebeard" delivered 19 wins per year for the duration of the decade, surpassing the 20-win plateau on five occasions.

Year/Team	OPW%	PW	PL	APW%	AW	AL	Diff+/-
1930 PIT	0.521	80	74	0.519	80	74	-0.002
1931 PIT	0.523	80	74	0.487	75	79	-0.036
1932 PIT	0.513	79	75	0.558	86	68	0.046
1933 PIT	0.518	80	74	0.565	87	67	0.047
1934 PIT	0.519	80	74	0.493	74	76	-0.026
1935 PIT	0.620 P	96	58	0.562	86	67	-0.058
1936 PIT	0.555	85	69	0.545	84	70	-0.009
1937 PIT	0.472	73	81	0.558	86	68	0.086
1938 PIT	0.525	81	73	0.573	86	64	0.048
1939 PIT	0.561 P	86	68	0.444	68	85	-0.116

franchID	OWAR	OWS	AWAR	AWS	WARdiff	WSdiff	P/D/W/F
1930 PIT	32.024	212.384	29.239	239.998	2.784	-27.615	
1931 PIT	28.427	214.675	23.612	225.004	4.816	-10.329	
1932 PIT	32.133	**230.129**	30.524	257.999	1.609	-27.870	
1933 PIT	33.062	**222.972**	40.229	260.997	-7.168	-38.026	
1934 PIT	36.729	231.102	34.546	221.995	2.183	9.108	
1935 PIT	42.006	262.479	42.929	257.991	-0.923	4.488	P
1936 PIT	**42.442**	**261.002**	40.548	252.003	1.893	8.999	
1937 PIT	32.401	225.907	38.410	258.008	-6.009	-32.101	
1938 PIT	**38.459**	**243.142**	**41.532**	258.002	-3.074	-14.859	
1939 PIT	**37.123**	226.598	31.347	204.005	5.776	22.593	P

Vance notched his third ERA and WHIP titles for the 1930 squad. Cuyler nabbed his fourth stolen base crown and delivered career-bests in hits (228), runs (155), doubles (50) and RBI (134). Wright (.321/22/126) offered personal bests in the triple-crown categories. Joe Cronin plated 126 baserunners in successive seasons (1930-31) and recorded 34 Win Shares in '31. Cronin topped the 100-RBI mark eight times in his career. Paul Waner mashed 62 doubles in 1932 and secured batting titles in '34 and '36. Dick "Shortwave" Bartell added 48 two-base knocks and scored 118 runs.

The Pirates overpowered the Cubs in '35, taking the pennant by a four-game margin. Arky Vaughan (.385/19/99) accumulated the third-highest Win Share total in Pirates' history and paced the League in OBP (.491), SLG (.607) and batting average. The 9-time All-Star established career-bests with 122 runs scored and 118 bases on balls during the ensuing year. Pittsburgh led the National League in oWAR and oWS in 1936 and 1938. First-sacker Gus Suhr achieved 100+ RBI three times and registered 111 tallies in '36. The 1939 Bucs registered the tenth pennant in team history and subsequently failed to capture another flag until 1971.

Win Shares > 20	Single-Season	1920-1939
Gus Suhr - 1B (PIT) x2	Carson Bigbee - LF (PIT) x2	Whitey Glazner - SP (PIT)
Glenn Wright - SS (PIT) x3	Kiki Cuyler - LF (PIT)	Johnny Morrison - SP (PIT) x2
Joe Cronin - SS (PIT) x9	Adam Comorosky - LF (PIT)	Ray Kremer - SP (PIT) x3
Dick Bartell - SS (PIT) x3	Kiki Cuyler - CF (PIT) x3	Dazzy Vance - SP (PIT) x5
Arky Vaughan - SS (PIT) x10	Mule Haas - CF (PIT)	Jack Scott - SP (PIT)
Tony Boeckel - 3B (PIT)	Kiki Cuyler - RF (PIT) x4	Hal Carlson - SP (PIT)
Pie Traynor - 3B (PIT) x9	Paul Waner - RF (PIT) x12	Carmen Hill - SP (PIT)
Cookie Lavagetto - 3B (PIT)	Red Faber - SP (PIT) x3	Sheriff Blake - SP (PIT)
Pat Duncan - LF (PIT) x2	Cy Blanton - SP (PIT)	Larry French - SP (PIT) x2
Lloyd Waner - CF (PIT) x5		

Year/Team	OPW%	PW	PL	APW%	AW	AL	Diff+/-
1940 PIT	0.636 F	98	56	0.506	78	76	-0.129
1941 PIT	0.529 F	81	73	0.526	81	73	-0.003
1942 PIT	0.588 F	91	63	0.449	66	81	-0.139
1943 PIT	0.596 F	92	62	0.519	80	74	-0.077
1944 PIT	0.548 F	84	70	0.588	90	63	0.040
1945 PIT	0.602 F	93	61	0.532	82	72	-0.070
1946 PIT	0.476 F	73	81	0.409	63	91	-0.067
1947 PIT	0.462 F	71	83	0.403	62	92	-0.060
1948 PIT	0.566 F	87	67	0.539	83	71	-0.027
1949 PIT	0.477 F	73	81	0.461	71	83	-0.016

franchID	OWAR	OWS	AWAR	AWS	WARdiff	WSdiff	P/D/W/F
1940 PIT	38.833	249.597	35.291	233.998	3.542	15.599	F
1941 PIT	30.922	225.571	32.234	243.000	-1.312	-17.429	F
1942 PIT	30.141	246.489	25.697	198.002	4.444	48.486	F
1943 PIT	43.895	263.104	38.587	239.998	5.308	23.106	F
1944 PIT	37.556	256.245	40.510	270.005	-2.954	-13.760	F
1945 PIT	44.286	281.334	41.656	246.000	2.630	35.334	F
1946 PIT	29.521	225.403	26.312	188.999	3.209	36.404	F
1947 PIT	54.093	298.187	31.228	186.004	22.865	112.183	F
1948 PIT	49.628	297.933	32.332	249.003	17.296	48.930	F
1949 PIT	45.902	275.894	29.371	212.999	16.531	62.894	F

The Pirates failed to meet the minimum BFP requirements from 1940-1955. Vaughan paced the 1940 Bucs with 15 triples and 113 runs scored while Cronin swatted a career-high 24 round-trippers. Claude Passeau notched 20 victories and fashioned an ERA of 2.50 along with a career-best WHIP of 1.133.

Bob Elliott (.317/22/113) earned NL MVP honors in '47 and led the League with 131 walks in the ensuing season. Ten-time All-Star shortstop Pee Wee Reese tallied a league-leading 132 runs and amassed 32 Win Shares during the '49 campaign. Ralph Kiner collected seven consecutive home run titles (1946-1952) and averaged 41 circuit clouts and 111 RBI during his first eight seasons. Kiner (.310/54/127) accrued 36 Win Shares and topped the League with a .658 SLG as he placed fourth in the National League MVP balloting.

Year/Team	OPW%	PW	PL	APW%	AW	AL	Diff+/-
1950 PIT	0.452 F	70	84	0.373	57	96	-0.079
1951 PIT	0.432 F	67	87	0.416	64	90	-0.016
1952 PIT	0.367 F	56	98	0.273	42	112	-0.094
1953 PIT	0.415 F	64	90	0.325	50	104	-0.091

1954 PIT	0.409 F	63	91	0.344	53	101	-0.065
1955 PIT	0.445 F	69	85	0.390	60	94	-0.056
1956 PIT	0.475	73	81	0.429	66	88	-0.046
1957 PIT	0.456	70	84	0.403	62	92	-0.054
1958 PIT	0.545	84	70	0.545	84	70	0.001
1959 PIT	0.461	71	83	0.506	78	76	0.045

franchID	OWAR	OWS	AWAR	AWS	WARdiff	WSdiff	P/D/W/F
1950 PIT	35.107	242.830	26.619	171.000	8.487	71.829	F
1951 PIT	37.590	251.483	24.990	192.001	12.600	59.482	F
1952 PIT	10.240	169.639	10.337	126.000	-0.097	43.639	F
1953 PIT	22.451	246.323	14.556	150.005	7.895	96.318	F
1954 PIT	25.582	226.269	16.575	180.000	9.008	46.270	F
1955 PIT	25.524	225.756	16.575	180.000	8.950	45.756	F
1956 PIT	23.837	208.086	24.637	197.995	-0.799	10.091	
1957 PIT	23.195	198.173	25.907	186.000	-2.712	12.174	
1958 PIT	35.985	261.035	34.890	252.007	1.095	9.028	
1959 PIT	24.099	207.549	30.565	233.996	-6.466	-26.447	

Kiner crushed 47 long balls and placed fifth in the NL MVP race in 1950. He paced the circuit with 124 runs scored, a .452 OBP and .627 SLG while batting .309 with 42 round-trippers in 1951. Elliott socked 24 dingers and drove in 107 runs in '50. Reese paced the League with 30 stolen bases in 1952 and batted .309 in '54. Andy Seminick tied his personal bests with 24 home runs and 68 RBI in 1950.

Gus Bell slashed a league-leading 12 triples in '51 and two years later earned his first All-Star invite, batting .300 with 30 four-baggers and 105 ribbies. Bell surpassed the 100-run plateau in 1953-54 and delivered a career-high .308 batting average in '55. Frank J. Thomas cranked 20+ homers for six consecutive seasons (1953-58), plated 102 runs in '53, and finished fourth in the 1958 NL MVP race. Dick Groat supplied a .315 batting average in '57, and the following year Bill Mazeroski won his first of eight Gold Glove Awards and walloped 19 homers. Dick Stuart launched 27 long balls during the '59 campaign.

Bob Friend (14-9, 2.83) captured the NL ERA title in 1955 and led the league in innings pitched in the two subsequent seasons. Friend tallied 22 victories and placed third in the 1958 NL Cy Young balloting. In 1958 Bob Purkey earned an All-Star nod with 17 wins and a 3.60 ERA. The Bucs ended the '58 season in second place, only two games behind the Braves. This was the franchise's lone campaign above the .500 mark during the decade of the Fifties. Vern Law compiled an 18-9 record with a 2.98 ERA and 1.120 WHIP along with 20 complete games for the '59 squad.

Based on Career Total Win Shares and Career Total WAR, GM Joe Brown participated in three of the top four drafts in Pittsburgh's history. Following a 21-year career as the Pirates GM from 1956-1976, he briefly served as interim GM and selected Barry Bonds with the sixth pick of the '85 Amateur Draft. Brown also signed Willie Stargell (1958) and Al Oliver (1964) as amateur free agents.

Win Shares > 20	Single-Season	1940-1959
Bill Mazeroski - 2B (PIT) x4	Johnny Dickshot - LF (PIT)	Johnny Barrett - RF (PIT)
Pee Wee Reese - SS (PIT) x10	Ralph Kiner - LF (PIT) x5	Claude Passeau - SP (PIT) x2
Bob Elliott - 3B (PIT) x7	Bob Skinner - LF (PIT) x2	Bob Friend - SP (PIT) x4
Andy Seminick - C (PIT)	Gus Bell - CF (PIT) x3	Vern Law - SP (PIT) x3
	Frank J. Thomas - CF (PIT)	

Year/Team	OPW%	PW	PL	APW%	AW	AL	Diff+/-
1960 PIT	0.520	80	74	0.617 P	95	59	0.097
1961 PIT	0.506	82	80	0.487	75	79	-0.019
1962 PIT	0.525	85	77	0.578	93	68	0.052
1963 PIT	0.468	76	86	0.457	74	88	-0.012
1964 PIT	0.506	82	80	0.494	80	82	-0.012
1965 PIT	0.461	75	87	0.556	90	72	0.094
1966 PIT	0.485	79	83	0.568	92	70	0.083
1967 PIT	0.386	62	100	0.500	81	81	0.114
1968 PIT	0.453	73	89	0.494	80	82	0.041
1969 PIT	0.476	77	85	0.543	88	74	0.067

franchID	OWAR	OWS	AWAR	AWS	WARdiff	WSdiff	P/D/W/F
1960 PIT	29.772	222.696	47.680	285.005	-17.908	-62.309	
1961 PIT	37.517	242.193	37.282	224.999	0.235	17.194	
1962 PIT	39.789	260.351	39.890	278.994	-0.101	-18.643	
1963 PIT	35.158	234.173	34.704	222.007	0.455	12.167	
1964 PIT	37.724	251.318	39.960	240.004	-2.236	11.314	
1965 PIT	32.128	226.133	44.062	269.999	-11.934	-43.866	
1966 PIT	38.718	240.888	48.294	275.996	-9.576	-35.108	
1967 PIT	24.444	195.797	33.947	243.003	-9.503	-47.206	
1968 PIT	28.474	202.718	38.144	240.000	-9.670	-37.282	
1969 PIT	40.944	248.355	50.496	264.002	-9.553	-15.647	

The Pirates engaged in a four-way battle for the National League crown in 1960, falling one game short of the Dodgers. Dick Groat received the 1960 NL MVP Award as he delivered a .325 average. Dick Stuart slammed 30 long balls and drove in 98 runs per season from 1960-65. Vern Law (20-9, 3.08) paced the League with 18 complete games and collected the NL Cy Young Award in 1960. "Deacon" delivered 17 victories with a 2.15 ERA and 0.998 WHIP for the '65 squad. Bob Friend averaged 15 wins and a 3.12 ERA from 1960-65.

Mazeroski earned 7 Gold Gloves Awards for his fielding excellence at second base during the Sixties. The Bucs' keystone corps led the Major Leagues with 36 WS>10 seasons from 1960-1979. Thomas connected for 34 round-trippers and plated 94 runners in '62. Dick Hall fashioned a 2.75 ERA and a 1.000 WHIP in various relief roles from 1962-69. Stuart crushed 42 four-ply swats and topped the League with 118 RBI during the 1963 campaign while swingman Al McBean delivered a 13-3 mark. He posted a 1.91 ERA with 22 saves during the subsequent season. Purkey (23-5, 2.81) placed third in the 1963 NL Cy Young balloting.

Groat tallied 201 base hits including 43 doubles and a .319 batting average en route to a runner-up finish in the 1964 NL MVP balloting. Bob Veale averaged 16 wins, 108 walks, 220 strikeouts and a 2.89 ERA from 1964-69. He topped the National League with 124 bases on balls and 250 strikeouts in '64 while Dave Wickersham notched 19 victories with a 3.44. Bob Lee supplied a 1.51 ERA and collected 19 saves in his rookie campaign (1964). He achieved All-Star status in his sophomore season, amassing 23 saves along with a 1.92 ERA.

Fred Whitfield slugged 26 circuit clouts, knocked in 90 runs and batted .293 to pace the Redbirds' offense in '65. Ron Kline saved a league-best 29 contests. First-sacker Donn Clendenon established career bests during the 1966 campaign, launching 28 four-baggers while knocking in 98 runs. Willie Stargell produced a .280 BA with 26 circuit clouts and 86 ribbies from 1964-69. Following last-place efforts in '63 and '65, the franchise reached its low point as the '67 squad tallied 100 losses. Dick Bosman captured the ERA crown in '69 with a 2.19 mark while swingman Bob Moose managed a 14-3 mark. Bobby Tolan drilled 21 quadruples and drove in 93 runs while scoring 104 times in '69.

Year/Team	OPW%	PW	PL	APW%	AW	AL	Diff+/-
1970 PIT	0.528	85	77	0.549 D	89	73	0.022
1971 PIT	0.530 P	86	76	0.599 P	97	65	0.069
1972 PIT	0.524	85	77	0.619 P	96	59	0.095
1973 PIT	0.444	72	90	0.494	80	82	0.050
1974 PIT	0.516	84	78	0.543 D	88	74	0.027
1975 PIT	0.534	87	75	0.571 D	92	69	0.037
1976 PIT	0.566 P	92	70	0.568	92	70	0.002
1977 PIT	0.524	85	77	0.593	96	66	0.068
1978 PIT	0.559 P	91	71	0.547	88	73	-0.012
1979 PIT	0.490	79	83	0.605 P	98	64	0.115

franchID	OWAR	OWS	AWAR	AWS	WARdiff	WSdiff	P/D/W/F
1970 PIT	39.505	278.954	42.125	266.996	-2.620	11.958	
1971 PIT	43.208	288.134	**50.994**	**291.003**	-7.787	-2.868	P
1972 PIT	44.672	287.420	**50.516**	**287.992**	-5.844	-0.572	
1973 PIT	36.988	282.402	37.161	240.004	-0.173	42.398	
1974 PIT	50.713	323.541	42.147	264.001	8.565	59.540	
1975 PIT	45.238	302.351	44.462	275.996	0.777	26.355	
1976 PIT	46.124	306.920	42.357	276.005	3.767	30.915	P
1977 PIT	53.697	**347.737**	44.009	288.001	9.688	59.736	
1978 PIT	49.081	**345.711**	40.084	263.997	8.998	81.714	P
1979 PIT	34.469	271.808	**48.562**	**294.006**	-14.092	-22.197	

Stargell delivered a .296 average, 42 round-trippers and 119 RBI from 1971-73, placing third or better in the MVP balloting in each of those campaigns. "Pops" paced the NL with 48 wallops in '71 while driving in 125 runs. He earned 35 Win Shares and topped the circuit in home runs and RBI during the 1973 season. Stargell shared NL MVP honors with Keith Hernandez in '79. Donn Clendenon and Bob Oliver knocked in 90+ runs while Tolan pilfered 57 bags, scored 112 runs, and batted .316 for the 1970 squad. Bucs backstop Manny Sanguillen excelled at the dish, finishing third in the batting races in 1970 (.325) and 1975 (.328). Dick Bosman amassed 16 wins with a 3.00 ERA in 1970. Dock Ellis averaged 14 wins with a 3.22 ERA from 1970-77. Ellis (19-9, 3.06) earned his lone All-Star nod and finished fourth in the 1971 NL Cy Young balloting. Blass (19-8, 2.49) placed runner-up in the Cy Young vote.

Pittsburgh overtook Chicago and won the pennant in 1971 after a runner-up finish in the prior campaign. The Cubbies returned the favor in '72. Al Oliver supplied 99 ribbies in '73 and batted over .300 in 9 consecutive campaigns (1976-84). The Pirates slumped to 72 wins in 1973, rebounding to finish only two games behind the Phillies in '74. Dave Cash appeared in three straight All-Star contests (1974-76) and led the circuit with 213 base hits in 1975. He also scored 111 runs, laced 40 doubles and batted .305. Richie Zisk reached the 100-RBI plateau in '74 and '77, crushing 30 four-ply swats in the latter campaign. The Bucs' batsmen registered the finest offWARnorm (26) and offWSnorm (201) output in franchise annals.

The Bucs ended the '75 season in a dead heat with the Cubs, with Chicago declared the winner. The Pirates captured another pennant in 1976, posting 92 victories. After ending the '77 season one game behind the Cardinals, Pittsburgh achieved its third pennant of the Seventies. The '78 crew managed the best WSdiff (+81) vs. the output of the "Actual" Pirates from the same year as the team defeated the Expos by a lone game. Dave Parker (.308/25/101) led the League with a .541 SLG and placed third in the 1975 NL MVP race. "Cobra" earned another third-place finish in '77, leading the NL in batting (.338), hits (215) and doubles (44). Parker took home the MVP Award in 1978, pacing the NL with a .334 batting average and .585 SLG while launching 30 long balls, 117 RBI and a career-high 36 Win Shares.

Several speedsters surfaced from the Pirates' farm system during the Seventies. Freddie Patek swiped 49 bases and topped the League with 11 triples in '71. "The Flea" averaged 41 steals from 1971-78, capturing the stolen base crown with 53 steals in '77. Frank Taveras nabbed 70 bags to lead the NL in '77 while Mitchell Page produced 21 homers and 42 stolen bases in his rookie campaign. Omar Moreno pilfered 70+ bags in each of the next two seasons, leading the League on both occasions while scoring 110 runs in 1979. Willie Randolph tallied 98 runs and 33 steals in '79.

John Candelaria furnished a 20-5 record and topped the NL with a 2.34 ERA for the 1977 squad. Ramon G. Hernandez fashioned a 1.67 ERA and notched 14 saves for the '72 Bucs. Gene Garber vultured 10 wins while leading the League in relief appearances (71) and games finished in 1975 and posted 25 saves with a 2.35 ERA and a WHIP of 0.923 in '78. Kent Tekulve earned back-to-back fifth place finishes in the Cy Young balloting (1978-79). "Teke" saved 31 contests in both campaigns and paced the circuit with 90+ relief appearances. Doug Bair supplied 28 saves with a 1.97 ERA for the 1978 squad.

Win Shares > 20	Single-Season	1960-1979
Donn Clendenon - 1B (PIT) x2	Gene Alley - SS (PIT)	Bobby Tolan - CF (PIT) x3
Bob Robertson - 1B (PIT)	Freddie Patek - SS (PIT)	Al Oliver - CF (PIT) x5
Bob Oliver - 1B (PIT)	Bob Bailey - 3B (PIT) x3	Omar Moreno - CF (PIT)
Willie Stargell - 1B (PIT) x3	Don Money - 3B (PIT) x2	Joe Christopher - RF (PIT)
Dave Cash - 2B (PIT) x3	Richie Hebner - 3B (PIT) x3	Richie Zisk - RF (PIT) x2
Rennie Stennett - 2B (PIT)	Manny Sanguillen - C (PIT) x4	Dave Parker - RF (PIT) x6
Don Money - 2B (PIT)	Willie Stargell - LF (PIT) x6	Bob Purkey - SP (PIT)
Willie Randolph - 2B (PIT) x7	Richie Zisk - LF (PIT) x2	Bob Veale - SP (PIT)
Dick Groat - SS (PIT) x4	Al Oliver - LF (PIT) x3	John Candelaria - SP (PIT)
	Mitchell Page - LF (PIT) x2	

Year/Team	OPW%	PW	PL	APW%	AW	AL	Diff+/-
1980 PIT	0.514	83	79	0.512	83	79	-0.001
1981 PIT	0.465	75	87	0.451	46	56	-0.014
1982 PIT	0.535	87	75	0.519	84	78	-0.017
1983 PIT	0.478	77	85	0.519	84	78	0.040
1984 PIT	0.496	80	82	0.463	75	87	-0.033
1985 PIT	0.455	74	88	0.354	57	104	-0.101
1986 PIT	0.473	77	85	0.395	64	98	-0.078
1987 PIT	0.476	77	85	0.494	80	82	0.018
1988 PIT	0.537	87	75	0.531	85	75	-0.006
1989 PIT	0.508	82	80	0.457	74	88	-0.051

franchID	OWAR	OWS	AWAR	AWS	WARdiff	WSdiff	P/D/W/F
1980 PIT	40.224	286.277	38.436	248.998	1.787	37.279	
1981 PIT	21.633	162.733	21.834	138.006	-0.201	24.727	
1982 PIT	45.524	288.221	42.459	252.001	3.065	36.220	
1983 PIT	37.007	245.043	43.270	251.999	-6.263	-6.956	
1984 PIT	39.926	252.814	37.602	225.002	2.324	27.813	
1985 PIT	39.999	230.191	26.045	170.998	13.954	59.193	
1986 PIT	36.003	238.900	29.207	192.000	6.796	46.901	
1987 PIT	35.806	238.989	33.077	239.994	2.729	-1.005	
1988 PIT	45.187	269.015	35.713	255.004	9.475	14.011	
1989 PIT	40.537	254.129	29.421	222.001	11.117	32.128	

The Pirates tied for second place with the Expos in 1980, five games behind the Cardinals. Miguel Dilone swiped 61 bags and delivered a .341 batting average while fellow outfielder Moreno pilfered 96 bases and led the National League with 13 triples. Randolph topped the leader boards with 119 bases on balls and scored 99 runs in 1980. Tony R. Armas slammed 35 four-baggers and knocked in 109 runs in 1980. He tied for the League lead with 22 dingers during the strike-shortened season in '81 and finished fourth in the MVP balloting. Armas paced the circuit with 43 jacks and 123 RBI in 1984.

Rick Langford completed a league-high 28 of 33 starts in 1980, while posting a 19-12 record with a 3.26 ERA and a 1.172 WHIP. He completed 18 of 24 starts in '81 and fashioned a 2.99 ERA. Woodie Fryman saved 17 games with a 2.25 ERA following 13 sesasons as a member of the starting rotation. Al Oliver (.319/19/117) set career-bests with 209 hits and 117 RBI. "Scoop" placed third in the 1982 NL MVP vote as he paced the circuit with a .331 batting average, 204 hits, 43 doubles and 109 RBI. Garber tallied 30 saves with a 2.34 ERA and Rod Scurry posted 14 saves with a 1.79 ERA for the '82 staff. Pittsburgh tallied 87 victories in '82, earning a third-place finish.

Tony Pena made five All-Star appearances and accumulated four Gold Glove Awards. Rick Honeycutt (16-11, 3.03), Dave Dravecky (14-8, 3.58) and Pascual Perez (15-8, 3.43) earned invitations to the 1983 All-Star game. Al Holland (2.26, 25 SV) finished sixth in the 1983 NL Cy Young balloting and notched 29 saves in the ensuing year. Pittsburgh hurlers fashioned the best pitWARnorm (29) in club history along with the seventh-highest pitWSnorm (139) totals of All-Time! Ed Whitson contributed a 14-8 record with a 3.24 ERA during the 1984 campaign and tallied a career-high 16 victories with a 2.66 ERA and 1.084 WHIP five years later. Candelaria fashioned a 2.72 ERA as the 1984 Bucs ended the season below .500 (80-82), but fell just one game short of the NL East title.

Parker (.312/34/125) earned a runner-up finish in the 1985 NL MVP race, topping the League in RBI and doubles (42). "Cobra" crushed 31 round-trippers and drove in 116 runners during the subsequent season. Pittsburgh replenished its farm system with the selections of Moises Alou, Jeff King, Rick Reed and Stan Belinda in the '86 Amateur Draft under the guidance of GM Syd Thrift and Scouting Director Elmer Gray. Barry Bonds filched 36 bags as a rookie in 1986 and scored 99 runs in his sophomore season. Bobby Bonilla hit .300 in '87 and the next year launched 24 long balls and drove in 100 runs. Tekulve topped the League with 85+ appearances in '82 and '87. Tim Burke (7-0, 1.19) recorded 18 saves with a 0.890 WHIP in '87.

Pittsburgh continued to finish below .500 until 1988 when the club collected 87 wins en route to a second-place finish behind Chicago. Perez topped the League with a WHIP of 0.941 and Steve Farr collected 20 saves with a 2.50 ERA in '88. Jose DeLeon whiffed 200+ opposition batsmen in consecutive seasons (1988-89). Mike Bielecki tallied an 18-7 record with a 3.14 ERA for the '89 squad.

Year/Team	OPW%	PW	PL	APW%	AW	AL	Diff+/-
1990 PIT	0.557 D	90	72	0.586 P	95	67	0.029
1991 PIT	0.511	83	79	0.605 P	98	64	0.094
1992 PIT	0.529	86	76	0.593 D	96	66	0.064
1993 PIT	0.438	71	91	0.463	75	87	0.024
1994 PIT	0.442	72	90	0.465	53	61	0.023
1995 PIT	0.492	80	82	0.403	58	86	-0.089
1996 PIT	0.503	82	80	0.451	73	89	-0.053
1997 PIT	0.519	84	78	0.488	79	83	-0.031
1998 PIT	0.522	85	77	0.426	69	93	-0.096
1999 PIT	0.510	83	79	0.484	78	83	-0.025

franchID	OWAR	OWS	AWAR	AWS	WARdiff	WSdiff	P/D/W/F
1990 PIT	44.423	265.761	45.197	**284.999**	-0.774	-19.238	D
1991 PIT	36.714	259.512	**51.540**	293.998	-14.826	-34.486	
1992 PIT	40.546	274.185	41.799	288.000	-1.254	-13.815	
1993 PIT	33.302	232.975	30.144	224.994	3.159	7.982	
1994 PIT	19.341	154.784	14.434	159.007	4.908	-4.223	
1995 PIT	30.093	211.763	23.168	174.002	6.925	37.761	
1996 PIT	32.696	233.456	31.043	218.992	1.653	14.463	
1997 PIT	35.086	241.115	33.921	237.001	1.166	4.115	
1998 PIT	33.673	230.719	30.282	206.995	3.391	23.723	
1999 PIT	27.902	189.514	34.682	233.999	-6.780	-44.485	

Bonds produced a .302 average with 36 circuit clouts, 108 RBI, 34 stolen bases and 109 runs scored per season during the Nineties. He won three NL MVP Awards ('90, '92, '93) along with a runner-up finish in 1991 and received Gold Glove honors eight times. In 1993 Bonds paced the League in home runs (46), RBI (123), OBP (.458) and SLG (.677) while scoring 129 runs. Bonilla supplied 24 clouts and 94 ribbies per season from 1990-97. "Bobby-Bo" scored 112 runs, launched 32 long balls and knocked in 120 runs as he earned a runner-up finish in the 1990 NL MVP voting. He placed third during the following campaign with a league-high 44 doubles, 100 RBI and a .302 batting average. Bonilla (.329/28/99) made his sixth All-Star appearance in the 1995 season.

Pittsburgh squeaked past New York to collect the division crown in 1990. Bip Roberts belted 36 doubles, swiped 46 bags and scored 104 runs while batting .309 in 1990. He delivered a career-best .323 average with 44 steals in 1992 and enjoyed his lone appearance in the All-Star game. Whitson furnished a 14-9 record with a career-best ERA of 2.60. Burke delivered a 2.52 ERA and saved 20 contests while Farr vultured 13 wins along with a 1.98 ERA. Farr averaged 26 saves with a 2.52 ERA from 1991-93.

The Bucs finished in third place in '91, only two games behind Chicago and came up short again in '92. Jay Buhner pounded 32 big-flies and drove in 99 runs per year (1991-97). Buhner crushed 40+ home runs in three consecutive seasons (1995-97) and earned an All-Star invite with 44 taters and 138 ribbies in 1996. John Smiley (20-8, 3.08) led the League in wins and placed third in the 1991 NL Cy Young vote. Tim Wakefield (8-1, 2.15) finished third in the 1992 NL ROY race and posted 16 wins with a 2.95 ERA in '95. Stan Belinda saved 18 games per season from 1991-93.

In the franchise's final year in the NL East, the Pirates sank to the bottom of the division, tallying a mere 71 victories during the 1993 campaign. Jeff King hit .295 and plated 98 runs in '93. In 1996-97, he averaged 29 wallops and 112 RBI. Moises Alou (.339/22/78) finished third in the 1994 NL MVP race. He drove in 115 runs in '97 and just fell short of MVP status in 1998 when he hit .312 with 104 runs scored, 38 home runs and a career-high 124 RBI.

Willie Greene blasted 26 long balls and knocked in 91 runs during the 1997 season. Tony Womack paced the NL in stolen bases in three straight campaigns (1997-99), swiping at least 58 bags per season. Jason Kendall batted .300 in his rookie season and received an All-Star invitation. He pilfered 26 bags, scored 95 runs and hit .327 in '98. Rick Reed managed 13 wins with a 2.89 ERA and 1.042 WHIP in '97. He received an All-Star invitation during the following campaign when he contributed 16 victories along with a 3.48 ERA. The '98 squad tangled in a fierce four-team battle for the NL Central crown. The Astros emerged victorious and the Cubs captured the Wild Card by percentage points over the Pirates. Kevin Young established career-highs with 27 dingers and 108 ribbies in 1998. Young (.298/26/106) drilled 41 doubles, scored 103 runs and stole 22 bases in the subsequent season.

232

Year/Team	OPW%	PW	PL	APW%	AW	AL	Diff+/-
2000 PIT	0.495	80	82	0.426	69	93	-0.070
2001 PIT	0.485	79	83	0.383	62	100	-0.103
2002 PIT	0.460	75	87	0.447	72	89	-0.013
2003 PIT	0.507	82	80	0.463	75	87	-0.044
2004 PIT	0.512	83	79	0.447	72	89	-0.065
2005 PIT	0.494	80	82	0.414	67	95	-0.081
2006 PIT	0.485	79	83	0.414	67	95	-0.071
2007 PIT	0.489	79	83	0.420	68	94	-0.069
2008 PIT	0.472	76	86	0.414	67	95	-0.058
2009 PIT	0.493	80	82	0.385	62	99	-0.108
2010 PIT	0.451	73	89	0.352	57	105	-0.099
2011 PIT	0.473	77	85	0.444	72	90	-0.029
2012 PIT	0.597 P	97	65	0.488	79	83	-0.109
2013 PIT	0.552 W	89	73	0.580 W	94	68	0.028

franchID	OWAR	OWS	AWAR	AWS	WARdiff	WSdiff	P/D/W/F
2000 PIT	34.414	209.242	31.257	207.000	3.158	2.243	
2001 PIT	32.770	220.991	15.728	185.995	17.042	34.996	
2002 PIT	27.253	212.359	22.395	216.001	4.858	-3.642	
2003 PIT	40.560	244.534	33.173	225.000	7.387	19.535	
2004 PIT	42.149	238.575	30.207	216.000	11.942	22.575	
2005 PIT	31.230	197.954	25.325	201.005	5.904	-3.051	
2006 PIT	33.081	211.008	26.193	201.002	6.888	10.006	
2007 PIT	35.561	220.520	26.795	203.997	8.767	16.523	
2008 PIT	27.065	205.085	19.937	201.003	7.129	4.081	
2009 PIT	26.851	208.307	22.048	186.000	4.803	22.307	
2010 PIT	30.130	248.982	12.409	170.997	17.721	77.985	
2011 PIT	35.142	260.608	20.514	215.997	14.627	44.611	
2012 PIT	46.182	**303.685**	24.273	236.997	21.909	66.688	P
2013 PIT	43.887	**285.875**	42.840	281.993	1.047	3.882	W

Barry Bonds elevated his game to super-human levels, batting .339 with 52 home runs, 123 runs scored and 174 walks from 2000-04. After placing runner-up in 2000, Bonds collected MVP honors in four consecutive campaigns. He earned 50 Win Shares while setting the Major League record with 73 round-trippers in 2001 and amassed an incredible 232 walks in '04. Alou set career-highs with a .355 batting average in 2000 and 39 home runs in 2004. Kendall scored 112 runs and batted .320 in 2000. Aramis Ramirez crushed 40 doubles and 34 moon-shots while batting .300 and driving in 112 runs during the 2001 season. Ramirez averaged .289 with 35 two-baggers, 30 home runs, and 102 RBI from 2001-08 and earned two All-Star selections. In 2012 he topped the League with 50 two-baggers.

Esteban Loaiza (21-9, 2.90) was the lone bright spot in the rotation as he led the League with 207 strikeouts and earning a runner-up finish in the 2003 Cy Young balloting. Jose Guillen slammed 31 circuit clouts and batted a career-best .311 in 2003 and delivered 27 dingers with 104 RBI for an encore. Kendall contributed a .325 BA in '03 and batted .319 in the subsequent season. Pittsburgh established the highest batting average (.284), OBP (.364) and SLG (.454) in team history during the 2004 season. Mike V. Gonzalez saved 24 contests in '06 while posting an ERA of 2.17. Matt Capps collected 21 saves with a WHIP of 0.969 in 2008. Nate McLouth paced the NL with 46 doubles while scoring 113 runs, swiping 23 bags and blasting 26 long balls en route to his first All-Star appearance in '08. Juan Oviedo, working under the alias of Leo Nunez, garnered 26 saves for the '09 club. The Bucs failed to make the playoffs in the decade, falling short by a single game to the Cardinals in 2009.

233

In the wake of six ordinary seasons, Joey A. Bautista erupted with a league-best 54 big-flies while driving in 124 runs in 2010. "Joey Bats" repeated the feat, blasting 43 round-trippers, drawing 132 bases on balls and slugging .608. He tallied 38 Win Shares and placed third in the MVP balloting in '11. Neil Walker posted a .296 BA during his rookie campaign (2010). Andrew McCutchen (.327/31/96) earned his first Gold Glove Award and led the NL with 194 hits in 2012. McCutchen batted .317 with 38 doubles and collected MVP honors in '13.

Win Shares > 20	Single-Season	1980-2013
Al Oliver - 1B (PIT)	Jason Kendall - C (PIT) x5	Tony R. Armas - RF (PIT)
Jeff King - 1B (PIT)	Miguel Dilone - LF (PIT)	Bobby Bonilla - RF (PIT) x2
Kevin Young - 1B (PIT)	Barry Bonds - LF (PIT) x19	Jay Buhner - RF (PIT)
Vance Law - 2B (PIT)	Bip Roberts - LF (PIT) x2	Moises Alou - RF (PIT)
Jeff Keppinger - 2B (PIT)	Moises Alou - LF (PIT) x5	Jose A. Bautista - RF (PIT) x2
Neil Walker - 2B (PIT)	Tony R. Armas - CF (PIT)	Esteban Loaiza - SP (PIT)
Bobby Bonilla - 3B (PIT) x3	Nate McLouth - CF (PIT)	Bronson Arroyo - SP (PIT)
Aramis Ramirez - 3B (PIT) x6	Andrew McCutchen - CF (PIT)	
Tony Pena - C (PIT) x2	x4	

Note: 4000 PA or BFP to qualify, except during strike-shortened seasons
(1972 = 3800, 1981 & 1994 = 2700, 1995 = 3500) and 154-game schedule (3800)
- failed to qualify: 1940-1955

Pirates All-Time "Originals" Roster

Bill Abstein	Truck Eagan	Steven Lerud	Chick Robitaille
Spencer Adams	Eddie Eayrs	Brent Lillibridge	Bill S. Rodgers
Gibson Alba	Stump Edington	Brad Lincoln	Ruben Rodriguez
Jonathan Albaladejo	Mike L. Edwards	Vive Lindaman	Billy Rohr
Butch Alberts	Brad Eldred	Jose Lind	Ray Rohwer
Jermaine Allensworth	Bob Elliott	Dick Lines	Mandy Romero
Gene Alley	Larry Elliot	Bob Linton	Zeke Rosebraugh
Gair Allie	Dock Ellis	Larry Littleton	Jack Rothfuss
Moises Alou	Angelo Encarnacion	Abel Lizotte	Phil Routcliffe
Jesse Altenburg	Jewel Ens	Esteban Loaiza	Don Rowe
Pedro Alvarez	Aubrey Epps	Hans Lobert	Vic Roznovsky
Tony Alvarez	Ralph Erickson	Alberto Lois	Matt Ruebel
Alf Anderson	Bill J. Evans	Bob Long	Scott Ruskin
Goat Anderson	Red Faber	Tony Longmire	Jim Sadowski
Jimmy Anderson	Hector Fajardo	Tom Lovelace	Tom Saffell
Jimmy Archer	Cy Falkenberg	Frank Luce	Freddy Sale
Tony R. Armas	Pete Falsey	Wild Bill Luhrsen	Ed Sales
Bronson Arroyo	Stan Fansler	Del Lundgren	Bill Salkeld
Rich Aude	Bill Farmer	Danny Lynch	Bill Sampen
Dave Augustine	Jack Farmer	Mike Joseph Lynch	Tony Sanchez
Joe Ausanio	Steve Farr	Ken Macha	Chance Sanford
Bob Babcock	Felix Fermin	Rob Mackowiak	Manny Sanguillen
Ed Bahr	Ed Fernandes	Gene Madden	Ben Sankey
Bob Bailey	Jack Ferry	Nick Maddox	Rich Sauveur
Scott Bailes	Jocko Fields	Harl V. Maggert	Doc Scanlan
Doug Baird	Luis Figueroa	Roy Mahaffey	Bobby Schang
Doug Bair	Hal Finney	Paul Maholm	Fritz Scheeren
Kirtley Baker	Harry Fisher	Tony Malinosky	John Scheneberg
Jeff Banister	Wilbur Fisher	Al Mamaux	Crazy Schmit
Eppie Barnes	Ed Fitz Gerald	Jim Mangan	Walter Schmidt
Clyde Barnhart	Steamer Flanagan	Angel Mangual	Joe Schultz, Jr.

Vic Barnhart	Don Flinn	Lou Manske	Bill Schuster
Dick Barone	John Flynn	Ravelo Manzanillo	Jack Scott
Bob Barr	Lee Fohl	Lou Marone	Rod Scurry
Johnny Barrett	Brownie Foreman	Joe Marshall	Jimmy Sebring
Dick Bartell	Larry Foss	Starling Marte	Andy Seminick
Les Bartholomew	Roy Foster	Jose Martinez	Sonny Senerchia
Tony Bartirome	Earl Francis	Paul Martin	Jimmy Sexton
Bill Batsch	Gene Freese	Silvio Martinez	Ralph Shafer
Ed Bauta	Larry French	Jim Mattox	Dick Sharon
Jose A. Bautista	Bob Friend	Bert Maxwell	Josh Sharpless
Alex Beam	Doug Frobel	Buckshot May	Ben Shaw
Trey Beamon	Woodie Fryman	Jerry May	Hunky Shaw
Ted Beard	Ken Gables	Milt May	Ben Shelton
Ginger Beaumont	Bob Ganley	Bill Mazeroskl	Chris Shelton
Beals Becker	Gussie Gannon	Dixie McArthur	Jack Shepard
Jake Beckley	John Ganzel	Ike McAuley	Keith Shepherd
Andy Bednar	Bob Garber	Al McBean	Tommy Shields
Ed Beecher	Gene Garber	Alex McCarthy	Brian Shouse
Joe Beimel	Carlos Garcia	Pete McClanahan	John Shovlin
Bo Belinsky	Harry Gardner	Sam J. McConnell	Harry Shuman
Stan Belinda	Jim Gardner	Jeff McCurry	Paddy Siglin
Bill Bell	Bill Garfield	Andrew McCutchen	Greg Sims
Fern Bell	Huck Geary	Orlando McFarlane	Tommie Sisk
Gus Bell	Johnny Gee	Frank McGinn	Bill Skiff
Rafael Belliard	John Gelnar	Irish McIlveen	Bob Skinner
Jeff Bennett	Wally Gerber	Bill McKechnie	Joel Skinner
Kris Benson	Joe Gibbon	Jim McKee	Jimmy Slagle
Clarence Berger	George Gibson	Nate McLouth	Phil Slattery
Tun Berger	Brett Gideon	Tom McNamara	Ron Slocum
Carlos Bernier	Harry Gilbert	Kyle McPherson	John Smiley
Dale Berra	John Gilbert	Pete McShannic	Bull Smith
Hal Bevan	Sam Gillen	Johnny Meador	Dick H. Smith
Mike Bielecki	Warren Gill	Dutch Meier	Earl C. Smith
Carson Bigbee	Len Gilmore	Roman Mejias	Harry T. Smith
Ralph Birkofer	Al Gionfriddo	Jose Melendez	Hal L. Smith
Rivington Bisland	Tommy Giordano	Mario Mendoza	Paul L. Smith
Brian Bixler	Whitey Glazner	Jock Menefee	Red W. Smith
Earl Blackburn	Billy Gleason	Ed Mensor	Sherry Smith
Fred Blackwell	Jot Goar	Jack Mercer	Vinnie Smith
Ron Blackburn	Denny Gonzalez	Jordy Mercer	Willie E. Smith
Vic Black	Mike V. Gonzalez	Mark Mercer	Frank Smykal
Sheriff Blake	Wiki Gonzalez	Orlando Merced	Ian Snell
Cy Blanton	Johnny Gooch	Art Merewether	Don Songer
Steve Blass	Tom Gorzelanny	George Merritt	Steve L. Sparks
Tony Boeckel	Howie Goss	Gene Michael	Glenn Spencer
Barry Bonds	John Grabow	Bill A. Miller	Roy Spencer
Bobby Bonilla	Milt Graff	Dots Miller	George Spriggs
Everett Booe	Charlie Gray	Jake G. Miller	Ed Spurney
Buddy Booker	Chummy Gray	Kurt Miller	Harry Staley
Frank Bork	Stan Gray	Paul Miller	Tom Stankard
Don Bosch	Chris Green	Ward Miller	Craig Stansberry
Dick Bosman	Fred Green	Blas Minor	Willie Stargell
Doe Boyland	Willie Greene	Jim Minshall	Ebba St. Claire
Erv Brame	Tommy Gregg	Danny Moeller	Gene Steere
Bill Brandt	Reddy Grey	Johnny Mokan	Bill Steinecke

Bucky Brandon
Chick Brandom
Ron Brand
Fred Breining
Sam Brenegan
Bill Brenzel
Fred Brickell
Gil Britton
Frank Brosseau
Adrian Brown
Byron Browne
Earl Browne
Mace Brown
Myrl Brown
Bill Brubaker
Jay Buhner
Scott Bullett
Bryan Bullington
Tim Burke
Sean Burnett
Ellis Burton
Tom Butters
Fred Cambria
Hank Camelli
Harry Camnitz
Howie Camnitz
Hutch Campbell
Jim R. Campbell
Kid Camp
John Candelaria
Matt Capps
Ralph Capron
Max Carey
Bobby Cargo
Fred Carisch
Hal Carlson
Paul Carpenter
Matias Carrillo
Lew Carr
Steve Carter
Dave Cash
Harry Cassady
Jose Castillo
Pete Castiglione
Howdy Caton
Leon Chagnon
Wes Chamberlain
Jack Chesbro
Bob Chesnes
Jason Christiansen
Joe Christopher
Chuck Churn
Bill Clancy
Bryan Clark
Stu Clarke

Burleigh Grimes
Dick Groat
Howdy Groskloss
Robbie Grossman
Al Grunwald
Cecilio Guante
Jose Guillen
Ben Guintini
Billy Gumbert
Frankie Gustine
Cesar Gutierrez
Yamid Haad
Mule Haas
Matt Hague
Bill L. Hall
Dick Hall
Newt Halliday
Ken Hamlin
Gene Handley
Gary Hargis
Bubba Harris
Fred Hartman
Fred Hayner
Charlie Heard
Richie Hebner
Rollie Hemsley
Claude Hendrix
Chad Hermansen
Alex Hernandez
Ramon G. Hernandez
Yoslan Herrera
Jake Hewitt
Carmen Hill
Homer Hillebrand
Jerry Hinsley
Jesse Hoffmeister
Solly Hofman
Al Holland
Bonnie Hollingsworth
Shawn Holman
Brock Holt
Rick Honeycutt
John Hope
Mike Hopkins
Jim Hopper
Elmer Horton
J.R. House
Lee Howard
Art Howe
Bill Hughes
Jared Hughes
Newt Hunter
Bert Husting
Ham Hyatt
Mel Ingram

Don Money
Felipe Montemayor
Eddie Moore
George Moore
Gene Moore
Bob Moose
Sam Moran
Ramon Morel
Lew Moren
Omar Moreno
Nyjer Morgan
John Morlan
Johnny Morrison
Phil Morrison
Charlie H. Morton
Daniel Moskos
Jim Mosolf
Walter Mueller
Joe Muir
Leo Murphy
Judge Nagle
Pete Naton
Jim Nealon
Ron Necciai
Jim Neidlinger
Cy Neighbors
Jim Nelson
John Newell
Chet Nichols
Ovid Nicholson
Sam Nichol
Steve Nicosia
Bill Niles
Red Nonnenkamp
Nelson Norman
Roberto Novoa
Eddie O'Brien
Jack J. O'Brien
Johnny O'Brien
Ray O'Brien
Tom O'Brien
Tommy O'Brien
Brian O'Connor
John O'Connell
Paddy O'Connor
Miguel Ojeda
Al Oliver
Bob Oliver
Tony Ordenana
Joe Orsulak
Junior Ortiz
Fred Osborne
Wayne Osborne
Keith Osik
Marty O'Toole

Ray Steineder
Rennie Stennett
R.C. Stevens
Bud Stewart
Arnie Stone
Alan Storke
Jim Stroner
Steamboat Struss
Bill Stuart
Dick Stuart
Moose Stubing
John Stuper
Joe Sugden
Gus Suhr
Homer Summa
Harry Swacina
Red Swanson
Hank Sweeney
Steve Swetonic
Bill V. Swift
Oad Swigart
Al Tate
Walt Tauscher
Frank Taveras
Carl Taylor
Dorn Taylor
Kent Tekulve
Jake Thies
Frank J. Thomas
Valmy Thomas
Fresco Thompson
Gus Thompson
Will Thompson
Cotton Tierney
Jack Tising
Bobby Tolan
Randy Tomlin
Pie Traynor
Fred Truax
Lee Tunnell
Terry Turner
Elmer Tutwiler
Dixie Upright
Bob Vail
Luis Valdez
John Van Benschoten
Dazzy Vance
George Van Haltren
Maurice Van Robays
Eddie Vargas
Rafael Vasquez
Arky Vaughan
Bob Veale
Bucky Veil
Jim Viox

Bill Clemensen	Phil Irwin	Bill Otey	Joe Vitelli
Ed Clements	Al Jackson	Ed Ott	Charlie Wacker
Donn Clendenon	Vic Janowicz	Juan Oviedo	Bill Wagner
Stew Cliburn	Julian Javier	Henry Owens	Paul Wagner
Gene Clines	Woody Jensen	Dick Padden	Tim Wakefield
Danny Clyburn	Johnny Jeter	Tom Padden	Mike A. Walker
Otis Clymer	Dave W. Johnson	Mitchell Page	Neil Walker
Tom Colcolough	Jason Johnson	Dave Parker	Jim Wallace
Gerrit Cole	Lloyd Johnson	Tom Parsons	Lee Walls
Bob Coleman	Mark P. Johnson	Claude Passeau	Connie Walsh
Lou Collier	Mike Johnston	Freddie Patek	Junior Walsh
Zip Collins	Rex Johnston	Ronny Paulino	Bernie Walter
Frank Colman	Alex Jones	Steven Pearce	Lloyd Waner
Adam Comorosky	Barry Jones	Red Peery	Paul Waner
Joe Conzelman	Cobe Jones	Julio Peguero	Chuck Ward
Dale Coogan	Henry Jones	Jesus Pena	Ed Warner
Steve Cooke	Odell Jones	Ramon Pena	Hooks Warner
Wilbur Cooper	Tim B. Jones	Roberto Pena	Bennie Warren
John Corcoran	Harry Jordan	Tony Pena	Bill Warwick
Francisco Cordova	Mike Jordan	Will Pennyfeather	Rico Washington
Chris Coste	Red Juelich	Laurin Pepper	Gary Waslewski
Ensign Cottrell	Jack Kading	George Perez	Tony Watson
Billy R. Cox	Jake Kafora	Pascual Perez	Jim Waugh
Joe Cronin	Frank Kalin	Chris Peters	Bill J. Webb
Michael Crotta	Jim Kane	Hardy Peterson	Lefty Webb
Cookie Cuccurullo	Erv Kantlehner	Paul Pettit	John Wehner
Bud Culloton	Ed Karger	Jack Pfiester	Bob Wellman
Brandon Cumpton	Bill Keen	Ed Phelps	Greg Wells
Lafayette Currence	Mickey Keliher	Bill C. Phillips	Bill Werle
Gene Curtis	Herb Kelly	Jason C. Phillips	Rip Wheeler
Harvey Cushman	Jim Kelly	Kevin Pickford	Rick White
Kiki Cuyler	Joe H. Kelly	Bill Pierro	Fred Whitfield
Bruce Dal Canton	Billy Kelsey	Tony Piet	Ed Whitson
Bennie Daniels	John Kelty	Marc Pisciotta	Dave Wickersham
Ike Danning	Jason Kendall	Jake Pitler	Kaiser Wilhelm
Chase d'Arnaud	Jeff Keppinger	Elmo Plaskett	Lefty Wilkie
Harry Daubert	Sam Khalifa	Kevin Polcovich	Marc Wilkins
Dave Davidson	Pat Kilhullen	Elmer Ponder	Albert J. Williams
Brandy Davis	Ralph Kiner	Ed Poole	Dave A. Williams
J.J. Davis	Jeff King	Bill Powell	Don F. Williams
Kane Davis	Lee Edward King	John Pregenzer	Jimmy T. Williams
Rajai Davis	Ed Kinsella	Mel Preibisch	Bill G. Wilson
Tod Davis	Bruce Kison	Bobby Prescott	Chief Wilson
Trench Davis	Ron Kline	Alex Presley	Gary M. Wilson
Cot Deal	Otto Knabe	Jim Price	Justin Wilson
Kory DeHaan	Phil Knell	Bob Priddy	Mike S. Wilson
Jose DeLeon	Cliff Knox	Tom Prince	Snake Wiltse
Bobby Del Greco	Nick Koback	Buddy Pritchard	Bill Windle
Miguel del Toro	Fred Kommers	Alfonso Pulido	Jim Winn
Chris Demaria	Dennis Konuszewski	Bob Purkey	Roy Wise
Larry Demery	Bill Koski	Drew Rader	Jack Wisner
Gene DeMontreville	Lou Koupal	Jack Rafter	Dave Wissman
Con Dempsey	Danny Kravitz	Pep Rambert	Ed Wolfe
Mike Derrick	Ray Krawczyk	Aramis Ramirez	Tony Womack
Elmer Dessens	Ray Kremer	Roberto Ramirez	Fred Woodcock

Tom Dettore	Al Krumm	Willie Randolph	Roy Wood
Jim Dickson	Charlie Kuhns	Tike Redman	Spades Wood
Johnny Dickshot	Earl Kunz	Todd Redmond	Ron Woods
Ernie Diehl	Masumi Kuwata	Rick Reed	Ron Wotus
Pop Dillon	Hi Ladd	Pee Wee Reese	Dave Wright
Miguel Dilone	Dan Lally	Wally Rehg	Glenn Wright
Benny Distefano	Wayne LaMaster	Arch Reilly	Henry Yaik
Ona Dodd	John Lamb	Rich Renteria	Emil Yde
Jiggs Donahue	Rick Lancellotti	Xavier Rescigno	Chief Yellow Horse
Lino Donoso	Rick Langford	Dino Restelli	Len Yochim
Jerry Dorsey	Marty Lang	Craig Reynolds	Shane Youman
Whammy Douglas	Rimp Lanier	Hal Rhyne	Chris R. Young
Ryan Doumit	Cookie Lavagetto	Joe Rickert	Harley Young
Skip Dowd	Sean Lawrence	Denny Riddleberger	Henry Youngman
Dave Dravecky	Vance Law	Culley Rikard	Kevin Young
Tim Drummond	Vern Law	Ricardo Rincon	Pep Young
Jim Duffalo	Bill Laxton	Jim Ritz	Walter Young
Matt Duff	Herman Layne	Carlos Rivera	Frankie Zak
Bernie Duffy	Tom Leahy	Fred Roat	Jeff Zaske
Chris Duffy	Bob Lee	Bip Roberts	George Ziegler
Gus Dugas	Cliff W. Lee	Bob Robertson	Richie Zisk
Zach Duke	Sam Leever	Rich W. Robertson	Billy Zitzmann
Pat Duncan	Lefty Leifield	Don Robinson	
Jim Dunn	Joe Leonard	Hank Robinson	

Year/Team	OPW%	PW	PL	APW%	AW	AL	Diff+/-
1961 WSA	0.000 F	0	0	0.379	61	100	0.000
1962 WSA	0.000 F	0	0	0.373	60	101	0.000
1963 WSA	0.000 F	0	0	0.346	56	106	0.000
1964 WSA	0.000 F	0	0	0.383	62	100	0.000
1965 WSA	0.000 F	0	0	0.432	70	92	0.000
1966 WSA	0.000 F	0	0	0.447	71	88	0.000
1967 WSA	0.000 F	0	0	0.472	76	85	0.000
1968 WSA	0.351 F	57	105	0.404	65	96	0.052
1969 WSA	0.545 F	88	74	0.531	86	76	-0.014

franchID	OWAR	OWS	AWAR	AWS	WARdiff	WSdiff	P/D/W/F
1961 WS2	-81.068	19.151	22.596	182.992	-103.664	-163.842	F
1962 WS2	-27.529	66.918	26.377	180.000	-53.907	-113.082	F
1963 WS2	-17.022	107.561	14.425	168.006	-31.447	-60.445	F
1964 WS2	-4.144	154.246	18.078	186.000	-22.222	-31.755	F
1965 WS2	-11.403	177.359	21.685	210.000	-33.088	-32.641	F
1966 WS2	-6.951	154.250	26.120	213.002	-33.071	-58.752	F
1967 WS2	-5.817	90.587	25.187	228.002	-31.005	-137.414	F
1968 WS2	-1.783	108.442	21.081	194.998	-22.864	-86.557	F
1969 WS2	27.199	220.003	36.434	257.994	-9.235	-37.991	F

Legend: (P) = Pennant / Most Wins in League (D) = Division Winner (W) = Wild Card Winner (F) = Failed to Qualify

The Washington Senators moved to Minnesota following the 1960 season. The American League expanded to 10 teams, with one franchise awarded to the vacated D.C. area. The expansion Senators (aka Senators II) struggled to construct the new ball club. One of the lone bright spots during its first decade was Del Unser who led the League with 8 triples and batted .286 in 1969. Joe H. Coleman posted consecutive campaigns with 12 wins and a 3.27 ERA (1968-69).

The 1975 "Original" Rangers were the first to exceed the minimum 4000 PA and BFP standards*. The Rangers developed the most catchers (based on WS>10 and WS>20 seasons) and third basemen (WS>10) among the "Expansion" teams. However, the franchise failed to lead the American League in WARnorm or WSnorm in any season through 2013.

Year/Team	OPW%	PW	PL	APW%	AW	AL	Diff+/-
1970 WSA	0.390 F	63	99	0.432	70	92	0.042
1971 WSA	0.462 F	75	87	0.396	63	96	-0.066
1972 TEX	0.339 F	55	107	0.351	54	100	0.012
1973 TEX	0.413 F	67	95	0.352	57	105	-0.061
1974 TEX	0.448 F	73	89	0.525	84	76	0.077
1975 TEX	0.437	71	91	0.488	79	83	0.051
1976 TEX	0.471	76	86	0.469	76	86	-0.002
1977 TEX	0.478 F	77	85	0.580	94	68	0.103
1978 TEX	0.458	74	88	0.537	87	75	0.079
1979 TEX	0.445	72	90	0.512	83	79	0.068

franchID	OWAR	OWS	AWAR	AWS	WARdiff	WSdiff	P/D/W/F
1970 WS2	10.749	141.467	29.557	210.005	-18.808	-68.538	F
1971 WS2	24.149	185.255	19.703	189.004	4.446	-3.749	F
1972 TEX	5.565	133.043	11.938	162.000	-6.373	-28.956	F

							P/D/W/F
1973 TEX	17.198	168.451	19.299	170.997	-2.101	-2.546	F
1974 TEX	31.683	240.865	39.706	249.003	-8.023	-8.138	F
1975 TEX	24.410	209.704	35.212	236.995	-10.802	-27.291	
1976 TEX	22.704	208.795	31.828	228.000	-9.124	-19.205	
1977 TEX	31.282	223.561	48.205	281.999	-16.922	-58.439	F
1978 TEX	34.576	209.338	45.303	260.997	-10.727	-51.659	
1979 TEX	31.896	215.923	40.356	249.006	-8.460	-33.083	

Joe H. Coleman anchored the staff in the early seventies. He was especially dominant from 1971-73, supplying 21 wins per season with a 3.16 ERA, 1.216 WHIP and 220 strikeouts. Jeff Burroughs slugged 30 circuit clouts in his first full campaign (1973). He paced the league with 118 RBI, tallied 32 Win Shares and batted .301 with 25 long balls en route to the 1974 AL MVP award. Burroughs set a career-high with 41 clouts in '77 and tallied a league-best 117 walks in the subsequent season.

Mike Hargrove (.323/4/66) received AL Rookie of the Year honors in 1974. Known as "The Human Rain Delay" for his routine in the batter's box, Hargrove led the League in bases on balls in '76 and '78. Bill Madlock delivered a .320 batting average from 1973-79 and collected back-to-back batting titles in 1975-76. "Mad Dog" earned an All-Star nod in '75 while hitting at a .354 clip. The Rangers posted last-place finishes in the American League West division in '75, '78 and '79. Jim Sundberg collected six consecutive Gold Glove Awards (1976-81). Len Randle supplied career-bests with a .304 batting average and 33 stolen bases in 1977. Bump Wills (.287/9/62) placed third in the 1977 AL ROY balloting and pilfered 52 bases the following year. The Rangers failed to exceed the minimum 4000 BFP standards in 1977. Rick Waits furnished a 3.20 ERA, 13 victories and 15 complete games in '78. Roy Smalley III clubbed 24 long balls, knocked in 95 runs and made his lone All-Star appearance while Steve Comer tallied 17 wins with a 3.68 ERA in 1979.

Win Shares > 20	Single-Season	1961-1979
Mike Hargrove - 1B (TEX) x3	Bill Madlock - 3B (TEX) x3	Del Unser - CF (TEX)
Bump Wills - 2B (TEX)	Jim Sundberg - C (TEX) x2	Jeff Burroughs - RF (TEX) x3
Bill Madlock - 2B (TEX)	Mike Hargrove - LF (TEX)	Joe H. Coleman - SP (TEX) x2
Roy Smalley III - SS (TEX) x2	Jeff Burroughs - LF (TEX)	

Year/Team	OPW%	PW	PL	APW%	AW	AL	Diff+/-
1980 TEX	0.453	73	89	0.472	76	85	0.019
1981 TEX	0.479	78	84	0.543	57	48	0.064
1982 TEX	0.473	77	85	0.395	64	98	-0.078
1983 TEX	0.461	75	87	0.475	77	85	0.014
1984 TEX	0.391	63	99	0.429	69	92	0.037
1985 TEX	0.424	69	93	0.385	62	99	-0.039
1986 TEX	0.481	78	84	0.537	87	75	0.056
1987 TEX	0.520 D	84	78	0.463	75	87	-0.057
1988 TEX	0.469	76	86	0.435	70	91	-0.035
1989 TEX	0.472	76	86	0.512	83	79	0.040

franchID	OWAR	OWS	AWAR	AWS	WARdiff	WSdiff	P/D/W/F
1980 TEX	31.038	214.806	43.218	227.999	-12.180	-13.193	
1981 TEX	22.115	130.430	25.932	170.998	-3.816	-40.568	
1982 TEX	31.428	202.518	21.703	191.998	9.725	10.520	
1983 TEX	32.529	197.212	35.189	230.999	-2.659	-33.788	
1984 TEX	18.160	154.317	27.430	206.994	-9.270	-52.677	
1985 TEX	22.857	172.387	28.825	185.995	-5.968	-13.609	

1986 TEX	33.124	208.917	39.312	260.999	-6.188	-52.082	
1987 TEX	32.726	189.973	33.315	224.991	-0.589	-35.018	D
1988 TEX	29.038	181.812	28.380	209.999	0.658	-28.187	
1989 TEX	30.314	181.952	39.048	248.969	-8.734	-67.017	

Len Barker totaled 19 victories in 1980 and led the League in strikeouts in back-to-back seasons (1980-81). He hurled a perfect game on May 15, 1981. Hargrove established career-bests with 85 RBI and 111 bases on balls during the 1980 campaign and topped the American League with a .424 OBP in '81. Wills scored 102 runs and swiped 34 bags for the 1980 squad. Danny Darwin yielded 13 wins and 8 saves with a 2.63 ERA for the 1980 bullpen crew. "Dr. Death" vultured 11 wins and posted an ERA of 2.36 in '89.

Dave Righetti (8-4, 2.05) earned 1981 AL ROY honors and pitched a no-hitter against Boston on July 4, 1983. He assumed the closer's role in 1984 and averaged 31 saves with a 2.90 ERA (1984-89). "Rags" set the Major League record in 1986 with 46 saves. Madlock earned batting titles in '81 and '83 and supplied his best slugging output (19 home runs and 95 RBI) in 1982. Jim Clancy won 16 games and topped the AL with 40 games started in 1982. Bill Sample nabbed 44 bags and Wayne Tolleson added 33 stolen bases in '83. The Rangers' farm system struggled to cultivate left fielders as Burroughs ('80) and Sample ('83) posted the lone WS>10 seasons during the decade.

The Rangers hit rock-bottom in 1984, collecting a mere 63 victories while posting franchise-worsts in offWARnorm (-2.3) and offWSnorm (43). Pete M. O'Brien delivered a .282 average with 22 dingers and 88 ribbies from 1984-87. Dave J. Schmidt notched 12 saves with a 2.56 ERA during the 1984 campaign. Oodibe McDowell averaged 28 stolen bases from 1985-89 and scored 105 times during the 1986 season. Ron Darling (16-6, 2.90) received his lone All-Star invite in 1985 and won a career-high 17 games in 1988. GM Tom Grieve and Scouting Director Sandy Johnson replenished the farm system with amateur free agents from Latin America. Their acquisitions include Sammy Sosa ('85), Juan Gonzalez, Wilson Alvarez ('86) and Ivan Rodriguez ('88).

Texas finally delivered its first winning season in 1987, capturing the division crown by four games over the Royals. Tom Henke led the American League in '87 with 34 saves and whiffed 128 batters in 94 innings. "The Terminator" averaged 26 saves from 1986-89. Walt Terrell amassed 17 victories in 1987 despite a 4.05 ERA. Ruben Sierra belted 34 doubles, 27 home runs and drove in 106 runs per season (1987-89). "El Caballo" (.306/29/119) amassed 33 Win Shares, and placed runner-up in the 1989 AL MVP vote, pacing the circuit in RBI, triples (14) and SLG (.543).

Year/Team	OPW%	PW	PL	APW%	AW	AL	Diff+/-
1990 TEX	0.488	79	83	0.512	83	79	0.024
1991 TEX	0.446	72	90	0.525	85	77	0.078
1992 TEX	0.433	70	92	0.475	77	85	0.042
1993 TEX	0.542 P	88	74	0.531	86	76	-0.011
1994 TEX	0.457	74	88	0.456 D	52	62	-0.001
1995 TEX	0.502	81	81	0.514	74	70	0.012
1996 TEX	0.575 P	93	69	0.556 D	90	72	-0.019
1997 TEX	0.503	81	81	0.475	77	85	-0.027
1998 TEX	0.544 D	88	74	0.543 D	88	74	-0.001
1999 TEX	0.512 W	83	79	0.586 D	95	67	0.074

franchID	OWAR	OWS	AWAR	AWS	WARdiff	WSdiff	P/D/W/F
1990 TEX	26.474	198.409	36.631	249.001	-10.158	-50.592	
1991 TEX	25.333	188.084	42.896	254.998	-17.564	-66.914	
1992 TEX	32.596	201.211	39.233	230.995	-6.637	-29.784	
1993 TEX	39.806	250.862	39.051	258.001	0.755	-7.139	P
1994 TEX	26.011	172.528	22.144	156.000	3.866	16.528	
1995 TEX	35.239	225.766	29.503	222.002	5.736	3.764	
1996 TEX	47.221	277.118	47.230	270.002	-0.009	7.116	P
1997 TEX	35.874	228.851	32.603	231.003	3.271	-2.152	
1998 TEX	46.336	278.847	43.402	264.002	2.934	14.845	D
1999 TEX	50.446	284.386	46.675	284.996	3.771	-0.610	W

Texas' player development peaked in the 1990's as it placed in the top three WS>10 leaders in third basemen, right fielders, starting pitchers, and swingmen. The Rangers topped the League with 13 WS>10 player-seasons at catcher. Ivan Rodriguez eclipsed the mark on eight occasions while Mike Stanley accomplished it four times. Shuttling between rotation and relief work, Danny Darwin paced the circuit with a 2.21 ERA and a 1.027 WHIP in '90. He fashioned a 15-11 mark with a 3.26 ERA and a league-best 1.068 WHIP as a full-time starter in '93. Henke saved 32 games per season with a 2.49 ERA from 1990-95. Dave Righetti collected 36 saves for the 1990 relief corps, while Kenny Rogers tallied 15 and Jerry Don Gleaton added 13 from the portside.

Texas suffered through back-to-back last place finishes in 1991-92, managing a mere 70 victories in 1992. Ruben Sierra (.307/25/116) achieved career-bests in batting average, runs scored (110) and hits (203) during the 1991 campaign. Juan Gonzalez topped the American League with 40+ home runs in back-to-back seasons (1992-93) and slugged a league-best .632 on the way to a fourth-place finish in the 1993 AL MVP voting. From 1996-99 "Juan Gone" delivered a .314 average with 43 wallops, 140 ribbies and 100 runs scored. He earned MVP honors in '96 and '98, pacing the league with 50 doubles and 157 RBI during the 1998 campaign.

Kevin J. Brown assumed the role of ace in the Rangers' rotation, accumulating 21 victories with a 3.32 ERA while making his first All-Star appearance in 1992. Brown placed runner-up in the Cy Young balloting while posting a league-best 1.89 ERA and 0.944 WHIP in '96. From 1996-99, he averaged 17 wins, a 2.50 ERA and a WHIP of 1.065 along with 210 strikeouts. Ivan Rodriguez earned 10 consecutive Gold Glove Awards and made an All-Star appearance in every season from 1992-2001. "Pudge" captured the 1999 AL MVP award, batting .332 with 35 circuit clouts, 113 RBI, 116 runs scored and 25 stolen bases. Jose Guzman notched a career-high 16 victories while Ron Darling tallied 15 wins in 1992. Rogers led the League with 81 appearances in '92 and moved to the rotation in the subsequent season. "The Gambler" spun a perfect game against the California Angels on July 28, 1994 and earned his first All-Star invitation with a 17-7 record in '95.

The Rangers rebounded with 88 wins in '93 and captured the franchise's first pennant. Stanley slugged 26 moon-shots and batted .305 for the 1993 squad. Despite issuing 122 free passes in '93, Wilson Alvarez managed to deliver a 2.95 ERA with a 15-8 record in '93. "Slammin" Sammy Sosa belted 43 round-trippers and plated 114 runners per season in addition to 22 steals from 1993-99. Sosa bashed 66 four-baggers and paced the League with 154 RBI and 138 runs scored en route to winning the 1998 NL MVP award and for an encore hit 63 long balls and knocked in 141 runs.

Dean Palmer eclipsed the 30-homer plateau on four occasions and received an All-Star invitation in 1998. Robb Nen produced a 2.84 ERA and saved 34 contests per year (1995-99). He made consecutive All-Star appearances in 1998-99, posting a 1.52 ERA with 40 saves and 110 strikeouts during the '98 season. Following two sub-par campaigns, Texas scored another pennant in 1996 while accruing 93 victories. Rusty Greer produced a .315 batting average with 39 doubles, 20 dingers, 99 RBI and 106 runs scored during the 1996-99 seasons. Billy Taylor entered the late-inning mix in '96 and tallied 33 saves in 1998. The Rangers' pitching staff accrued the top pitWARnorm (30) and pitWSnorm (139) in team history. Rick Helling achieved 20 wins in 1998 in spite of a 4.41 earned run average. The '98 squad took the AL West division title by four games over Anaheim. In 1999, the Rangers earned the Wild Card entry as Fernando Tatis established career-highs with 34 taters, 107 RBI and 104 runs. Jeff Zimmerman (9-3, 2.36) delivered a 0.833 WHIP and earned a trip to the 1999 All-Star Game during his rookie season.

Year/Team	OPW%	PW	PL	APW%	AW	AL	Diff+/-
2000 TEX	0.482	78	84	0.438	71	91	-0.043
2001 TEX	0.513	83	79	0.451	73	89	-0.062
2002 TEX	0.521	84	78	0.444	72	90	-0.076
2003 TEX	0.471	76	86	0.438	71	91	-0.032
2004 TEX	0.526 D	85	77	0.549	89	73	0.023
2005 TEX	0.535	87	75	0.488	79	83	-0.047
2006 TEX	0.522	85	77	0.494	80	82	-0.028
2007 TEX	0.496	80	82	0.463	75	87	-0.033
2008 TEX	0.480	78	84	0.488	79	83	0.008
2009 TEX	0.571 P	93	69	0.537	87	75	-0.034
2010 TEX	0.505 D	82	80	0.556 D	90	72	0.051
2011 TEX	0.511 D	83	79	0.593 D	96	66	0.082
2012 TEX	0.493	80	82	0.574 W	93	69	0.081
2013 TEX	0.517	84	78	0.558	91	72	0.041

franchID	OWAR	OWS	AWAR	AWS	WARdiff	WSdiff	P/D/W/F
2000 TEX	45.009	266.731	28.246	212.999	16.763	53.732	
2001 TEX	48.403	278.730	34.294	218.999	14.108	59.731	
2002 TEX	36.584	242.856	35.183	215.997	1.401	26.859	
2003 TEX	25.846	229.399	31.584	213.000	-5.738	16.400	
2004 TEX	43.315	274.596	37.701	267.005	5.614	7.591	D
2005 TEX	39.219	246.558	40.624	237.003	-1.406	9.555	
2006 TEX	40.563	252.999	38.242	239.996	2.321	13.003	
2007 TEX	36.956	249.176	27.868	224.999	9.089	24.177	
2008 TEX	38.243	238.986	36.936	236.997	1.307	1.989	
2009 TEX	35.867	247.794	36.833	261.004	-0.966	-13.210	P
2010 TEX	36.142	216.585	42.410	270.009	-6.267	-53.423	D
2011 TEX	37.587	219.945	51.601	288.006	-14.014	-68.061	D
2012 TEX	29.155	201.006	47.890	278.998	-18.735	-77.992	
2013 TEX	28.859	199.099	48.522	271.251	-19.663	-72.152	

Ivan Rodriguez produced a .309 BA from 2000-06. Rodriguez batted .347 with 27 round-trippers in 2000 and hit .334 during the 2004 season. Palmer knocked in 102 runs and thumped 29 long balls in 2000. Sosa averaged 54 home runs, 135 ribbies, 125 runs scored and 103 bases on balls from 2000-02. He walloped 64 quadruples, led the League in RBI (160) and runs scored (146) and accrued a franchise-best 44 Win Shares in '01. Sosa finished runner-up in the MVP balloting. Kevin J. Brown topped the League with a 2.58 ERA and 0.991 WHIP in 2000. Brown posted a 14-9 record with a 2.39 ERA and made his sixth appearance in the Midsummer Classic in '03. Ryan Dempster whiffed 209 opposition batsmen in 2000 and won 17 contests with a 2.96 ERA in '08. Nen closed out his career with three consecutive seasons with 40+ saves including a league-best 45 in 2001. He furnished a microscopic 0.848 WHIP along with a 1.50 ERA in 2000.

The 2001 Rangers produced the highest offWARnorm (20) and fldWARnorm (6) in team history. Gonzalez supplied a .325 BA with 35 clouts and 140 RBI in '01. Rich Aurilia (.324/37/97) merited his lone All-Star appearance in 2001 as he scored 114 runs and paced the League with 206 base hits. Zimmerman saved 28 contests with a 2.40 ERA and 0.897 WHIP. Hank Blalock clubbed 29 big-flies, plated 97 runs per season (2003-05) and surpassed the century mark in runs and RBI during the '04 campaign. Mark Teixeira socked 26 four-baggers in his rookie season (2003). From 2004-11 "Tex" produced a .284 BAwith 37 doubles, 36 homers, 117 RBI and 101 runs scored per year. The 5-time Gold Glove Award winner topped the circuit with 39 blasts and 122 ribbies while placing runner-up in the 2009 AL MVP race.

Scott Podsednik (.314/9/58) energized the Rangers' offense from the leadoff spot, swiping 43 bases and scoring 100 runs en route to a runner-up finish in the 2003 ROY balloting. "The Podfather" paced the circuit with 70 stolen bases in '04 and tallied 59 during the subsequent season. Danny Kolb emerged as a late-inning relief candidate with a 1.96 ERA and 21 saves in '03, and the following year notched 39 saves and received an invitation to the All-Star contest. Texas took the AL West division crown in 2004 and finished only a few percentage points behind Seattle in '06. Travis Hafner produced a .296 average with 35 doubles, 32 round-trippers and 108 RBI per season (2004-07). "Pronk" swatted 42 long balls, scored 100 runs and led the circuit with a .659 SLG in '06. Rogers amassed 18 wins in '04, 17 in '06 and collected 5 Gold Glove Awards during the decade.

Aaron Harang paced the circuit with 16 victories and 216 strikeouts in 2006. Carlos Pena established career-bests across the board in 2007 including 46 four-baggers, 121 RBI and 99 runs scored. Pena led the League with 39 moon-shots in 2009. Edinson Volquez (17-6, 3.21) struck out 206 batters and earned an All-Star nod during his inaugural season (2008). Ian Kinsler delivered a .319 BA with 41 doubles and earned his first All-Star nod in '08. He achieved 30/30 campaigns in 2009 and 2011. Bouncing back from a last-place finish in 2008, the Rangers registered 93 victories on the way to the division title in '09. Edwin Encarnacion powered the offense with 42 clouts and 110 ribbies in 2012. Chris Davis crushed a league-leading 53 round-trippers and plated 138 baserunners to earn a third-place finish in the 2013 AL MVP balloting.

Win Shares > 20	Single-Season	1980-2013
Pete M. O'Brien - 1B (TEX)	Fernando Tatis - 3B (TEX)	Sammy Sosa - RF (TEX) x7
Mark Teixeira - 1B (TEX) x6	Hank Blalock - 3B (TEX)	Juan Gonzalez - RF (TEX) x4
Carlos Pena - 1B (TEX) x2	Mike Stanley - C (TEX)	Travis Hafner - DH (TEX) x3
Chris Davis – 1B (TEX)	Ivan Rodriguez - C (TEX) x7	Edwin Encarnacion - DH
Edwin Encarnacion – 1B	Juan Gonzalez - LF (TEX)	(TEX)
(TEX)	Rusty Greer - LF (TEX) x3	Kenny Rogers - SP (TEX)
Ian Kinsler - 2B (TEX) x3	Oddibe McDowell - CF (TEX)	Kevin J. Brown - SP (TEX) x5
Rich Aurilia - SS (TEX)	Ruben Sierra - RF (TEX) x2	Dave Righetti - RP (TEX)

Note: 4000 PA or BFP to qualify, except during strike-shortened seasons
(1972 = 3800, 1981 & 1994 = 2700, 1995 = 3500) and 154-game schedule (3800)
- failed to qualify: 1961-1974, 1977

Senators (II) / Rangers All-Time "Originals" Roster

Jose Alberro	Jan Dukes	Kerry Lacy	John Poloni
Gerald Alexander	Tom Dunbar	Mike Lamb	Andy Pratt
Brian Allard	Dan Duran	Stephen Larkin	Jurickson Profar
Wilson Alvarez	German Duran	Corey Lee	Ron Pruitt
Scott Anderson	Joey Eischen	Colby Lewis	Greg Pryor
Randy Asadoor	Dave Elder	Rick Lisi	Pat Putnam
Doug Ault	Edwin Encarnacion	Mark Little	Tom Ragland
Rich Aurilia	Cody Eppley	Wes Littleton	Ramon S. Ramirez
Mike James Bacsik	Robbie Erlin	Kameron Loe	Len Randle

Bob Baird	Scott Eyre	Don Loun	Evan Reed
John Barfield	Bill Fahey	Joe Lovitto	Nick Regilio
Andy Barkett	Monty Fariss	Terrell Lowery	Kevin Reimer
Len Barker	Jim Farr	Mike Loynd	Kevin Richardson
Blake Beavan	Scott Feldman	Josh Lueke	Mike Richardt
Kevin Belcher	Ray Fontenot	Ed Lynch	Dave Righetti
Mike J. Bell	Wilmer Font	Pete Mackanin	Tanner Roark
Joaquin Benoit	Tony Fossas	Bill Madlock	Ivan Rodriguez
Larry Biittner	Steve Foucault	Kevin Mahar	Kenny Rogers
Dick Billings	Jim French	Greg Mahlberg	Jason Romano
Hank Blalock	Hanley Frias	Bob W. Malloy	Wayne Rosenthal
Terry Bogener	Jeff Frye	David Manning	Robbie Ross
Brandon Boggs	Kazuo Fukumori	Barry Manuel	Marc Sagmoen
Tommy Boggs	Leury Garcia	Sam Marsonek	Bill Sample
Brian Bohanon	Reynaldo Garcia	Gene Martin	Rey Sanchez
Julio Borbon	Craig Gentry	Leonys Martin	Julio Santana
Jason Botts	Jim Gideon	Don Mason	Tanner Scheppers
Carl Bouldin	Benji Gil	Jim Mason	Dave J. Schmidt
Jason Bourgeois	Jerry Don Gleaton	Mike Mason	Gerry Schoen
Mark Brandenburg	Ryan Glynn	Nick Masset	Donnie Scott
Ed Brinkman	Bill Gogolewski	Ruben Mateo	Tony Scruggs
Pete Broberg	Mauro Gomez	Terry Mathews	Bob Sebra
Ike Brookens	Juan Gonzalez	Doug Mathis	Jon Shave
Bob Brower	Jason Grabowski	Rob Maurer	Ruben Sierra
Jim Brower	Gary Gray	John Mayberry, Jr.	Roy Smalley III
Jerry Browne	Rusty Greer	Oddibe McDowell	Chris W. Smith
Kevin J. Brown	Tom Grieve	Kevin Mench	Daryl Smith
Kevin L. Brown	Mike Griffin	Travis Metcalf	Dan C. Smith
Tom W. Brown	Justin Grimm	Drew Meyer	Dan S. Smith
Cliff Brumbaugh	Jose Guzman	Gary Mielke	Dick K. Smith
Kevin Buckley	Travis Hafner	Jim Miles	Keith L. Smith
Steve Buechele	Aaron Harang	Eddie L. Miller	Justin Smoak
Jeff Burroughs	Mike Hargrove	Matt J. Miller	Sammy Sosa
Terry Burrows	Donald Harris	Paul Mirabella	Mike Stanley
John Butcher	Bill Haselman	Kevin Mmahat	Rick Stelmaszek
Joey Butler	Bill Haywood	Dave Moates	Scott Stewart
Jeff Byrd	Roy Heiser	Craig Monroe	Ron Stillwell
Nick Capra	Rick Helling	Eric Moody	Dick Such
Don Castle	Tom Henke	Barry Moore	Jim Sundberg
Mike Cather	Rick Henninger	Jose Morban	John Sutton
Andy Cavazos	Dwayne Henry	Mitch Moreland	Greg Tabor
Jesse Chavez	Bill Hepler	Edwin Moreno	Yoshinori Tateyama
Jim Clancy	Wilson Heredia	Warren Morris	Fernando Tatis
Cody Clark	Jose Hernandez	A.J. Murray	Billy Taylor
David Clyde	Danny Herrera	Sam F. Narron	Taylor Teagarden
Frank Coggins	Derek Holland	Gene Nelson	Mark Teixeira
Joe H. Coleman	Roy Howell	Robb Nen	Nick Tepesch
Cris Colon	Travis Hughes	Mike Nickeas	Jeff Terpko
Steve Comer	Tug Hulett	Ramon Nivar	Walt Terrell
Wayne Comer	David Hulse	Laynce Nix	Stan Thomas
Glen Cook	Tommy Hunter	Dick Nold	Bobby Thompson
Scott Coolbaugh	Eric Hurley	Pete M. O'Brien	Mike W. Thompson
Dave Criscione	Jonathan Hurst	Jose Oliva	Wayne Tolleson
Mike Cubbage	Jack Jenkins	Darren Oliver	Jim Umbarger
Bobby Cuellar	Kelvin Jimenez	Mike Olt	Del Unser

John Danks	Bob E. Johnson	Javier Ortiz	Mike Venafro
Ron Darling	Jonathan Johnson	Joe Ortiz	Edinson Volquez
Yu Darvish	Bob O. Jones	Dean Palmer	Rick Waits
Danny Darwin	Jason Jones	Ken Pape	La Rue Washington
Chris Davis	Don Kainer	Danny Patterson	Len Whitehouse
Doug Davis	John E. Kennedy	Roger Pavlik	Matt Whiteside
Odie Davis	Paul Kilgus	Dan Peltier	Joe Wieland
Ryan Dempster	Ian Kinsler	Carlos Pena	Curtis Wilkerson
John Dettmer	Michael Kirkman	Shannon Penn	Bump Wills
Thomas Diamond	Brandon Knight	Martin Perez	C.J. Wilson
Edwin Diaz	Danny Kolb	Mark Petkovsek	Desi Wilson
R.A. Dickey	Randy Kramer	Jay Pettibone	Steve Wilson
Juan Dominguez	Jim Kremmel	Zach Phillips	Bobby Witt
Brian Doyle	Chad Kreuter	Manny Pina	John Wockenfuss
Kelly Dransfeldt	Jeff Kunkel	Luis Pineda	George Wright
Steve Dreyer	Al Lachowicz	Scott Podsednik	Jeff Zimmerman

Year/Team	OPW%	PW	PL	APW%	AW	AL	Diff+/-
1998 TBD	0.000 F	0	0	0.389	63	99	0.000
1999 TBD	0.000 F	0	0	0.426	69	93	0.000
2000 TBD	0.000 F	0	0	0.429	69	92	0.000
2001 TBD	0.000 F	0	0	0.383	62	100	0.000
2002 TBD	0.419 F	68	94	0.342	55	106	-0.078
2003 TBD	0.382 F	62	100	0.389	63	99	0.006
2004 TBD	0.506 F	82	80	0.435	70	91	-0.071
2005 TBD	0.404 F	65	97	0.414	67	95	0.010
2006 TBD	0.423 F	68	94	0.377	61	101	-0.046
2007 TBD	0.469	76	86	0.407	66	96	-0.062
2008 TBD	0.528 W	86	76	0.599 D	97	65	0.070
2009 TBD	0.467	76	86	0.519	84	78	0.051
2010 TBD	0.573 P	93	69	0.593 P	96	66	0.019
2011 TBD	0.513	83	79	0.562 W	91	71	0.049
2012 TBD	0.607 P	98	64	0.556	90	72	-0.051
2013 TBD	0.541 W	88	74	0.564 W	92	71	0.024

franchID	OWAR	OWS	AWAR	AWS	WARdiff	WSdiff	P/D/W/F
1998 TBD	46.512	257.211	24.334	189.010	22.178	68.201	F
1999 TBD	31.212	146.579	27.313	207.001	3.898	-60.422	F
2000 TBD	20.013	107.386	25.463	207.005	-5.451	-99.619	F
2001 TBD	20.078	155.184	17.588	185.996	2.490	-30.812	F
2002 TBD	27.634	191.067	13.550	164.996	14.083	26.071	F
2003 TBD	28.095	201.227	21.789	188.994	6.305	12.234	F
2004 TBD	30.957	249.422	23.518	210.009	7.439	39.413	F
2005 TBD	23.691	208.086	24.999	201.002	-1.308	7.085	F
2006 TBD	25.836	217.588	22.676	181.176	3.160	36.413	F
2007 TBD	34.993	221.479	32.138	197.999	2.855	23.480	
2008 TBD	39.490	276.109	46.519	291.006	-7.029	-14.897	W
2009 TBD	30.476	224.508	43.695	251.996	-13.219	-27.488	
2010 TBD	**44.636**	**274.729**	46.465	**288.001**	-1.828	-13.272	P
2011 TBD	30.120	224.156	42.749	272.998	-12.629	-48.842	
2012 TBD	**46.470**	254.721	46.724	269.991	-0.254	-15.270	P
2013 TBD	29.548	226.227	41.110	276.000	-11.563	-49.773	W

Legend: (P) = Pennant / Most Wins in League (D) = Division Winner (W) = Wild Card Winner (F) = Failed to Qualify

Tampa Bay entered the American League as an expansion entry in 1998. The Rays have not produced any starting pitchers who have exceeded 20 Win Shares in a single-season through 2013. Furthermore, none of the Rays' shortstops have surpassed 10 Win Shares. In its first five seasons of existence, the Devil Rays' minor league system yielded few players of note. Aubrey Huff slugged 34 long balls and knocked in 107 runs while batting .311 in '03. Huff delivered a .288 BA with 26 four-baggers and 92 RBI from 2003-08. Rolando Arrojo (14-12, 3.56) earned an All-Star nod and finished second in the AL ROY balloting during the Rays' inaugural campaign.

A pair of talented outfielders joined Huff in the Rays' lineup by 2003. Carl Crawford swiped over 50 bases on five occasions and collected four stolen base titles. "The Perfect Storm" thrice led the League in triples and surpassed the .300 batting average plateau four times from 2003-09. In 2010, Crawford (.307/19/90) was a first-time All-Star and Gold Glove winner. Rocco

Baldelli (.289/11/78) pilfered 27 bases and placed third in the 2003 AL ROY vote. Alex Sanchez boosted 52 bases in '03, and hit at a .322 clip as a part-timer in 2004.

Jorge Cantu hammered 40 doubles and 28 long balls while driving in 117 runs for the '05 squad. Following two sub-par seasons, Cantu rebounded with consecutive seasons of 40+ doubles and 95+ RBI. B.J. Upton delivered a .300 BA with 24 dingers and 22 swipes in his first full campaign (2007) and went on to nab at least 42 bags in three straight seasons (2008-10). Delmon Young (.288/13/93) drilled 38 two-baggers and placed runner-up in the 2007 AL ROY voting. Josh Hamilton earned a starting spot in the Rays' outfield and responded with a .304 average, 32 round-trippers and 130 ribbies in 2008. Hamilton rocked 40 two-base hits, 32 homers, drove in 100 runs and hit at a .359 clip en route to the 2010 AL MVP award. Evan Longoria (.272/27/85) received the AL ROY award in '08. "Longo" supplied 37 doubles, 28 four-baggers and 100 RBI in his first four seasons.

James Shields posted a 1.107 WHIP in 2007 but his breakout season came in 2011. Shields delivered a 16-12 record, 2.82 ERA and 1.043 WHIP along with a league-best 11 complete games. He struck out 225 batters, appeared in his first All-Star game and placed third in the Cy Young voting. David Price (19-6, 2.72) supplied a 1.193 WHIP and finished runner-up in the 2010 AL Cy Young balloting. Price (20-5, 2.56) merited Cy Young honors in 2012, leading the League in ERA and victories. Jeremy Hellickson (13-10, 2.95) received the 2011 AL ROY award. Dan Wheeler collected 13 saves in '08 and managed a WHIP of 0.867 in the subsequent season. The 2007 "Original" Rays were the first to exceed the minimum 4000 PA and BFP standards. Tampa Bay tallied 86 victories in 2008, earning the AL Wild Card entry. The '08 Rays posted franchise-bests in all WAR and Win Share categories with the exception of pitWARnorm. Longoria (33 WS), Crawford (31 WS) and Hamilton (30 WS) accrued at least 30 Win Shares in 2010.

Win Shares > 20	Single-Season	1998-2013
Aubrey Huff - 1B (TBD)	Carl Crawford - LF (TBD) x4	B.J. Upton - CF (TBD) x3
Akinori Iwamura - 2B (TBD)	Josh Hamilton - LF (TBD)	Aubrey Huff - RF (TBD)
Aubrey Huff - 3B (TBD)	Josh Hamilton - CF (TBD) x2	Aubrey Huff - DH (TBD)
Evan Longoria - 3B (TBD) x5		

Note: 4000 PA or BFP to qualify, except during strike-shortened seasons
(1972 = 3800, 1981 & 1994 = 2700, 1995 = 3500) and 154-game schedule (3800)
- failed to qualify: 1998-2006

(Devil) Rays All-Time "Originals" Roster

Rolando Arrojo	Elijah Dukes	Elliot Johnson	Ryan Rupe
Brandon Backe	Trevor Enders	Kenny Kelly	Juan Salas
Rocco Baldelli	Bartolome Fortunato	Joe Kennedy	Alex Sanchez
Wes Bankston	Lee Gardner	Kevin Kiermaier	Jared Sandberg
Tim Beckham	Joey Gathright	Evan Longoria	Travis Schlichting
Todd Belitz	Chad Gaudin	Hector Luna	Chris Seddon
Cedrick Bowers	Jonny Gomes	Mark Malaska	James Shields
Dewon Brazelton	Edgar V. Gonzalez	Seth McClung	Andy Sonnanstine
Reid Brignac	Toby Hall	Jake McGee	Jason Standridge
Josh Butler	Josh Hamilton	Matt Moore	Brian Stokes
Mickey Callaway	Jason Hammel	Jeff Niemann	Jon Switzer
Jorge Cantu	Jeremy Hellickson	Chad Orvella	B.J. Upton
Alex Cobb	Paul Hoover	Fernando Perez	Jose Veras
Alex Colome	Aubrey Huff	Travis Phelps	Stephen Vogt
Fernando Cortez	Rhyne Hughes	David Price	Doug Waechter
Carl Crawford	Akinori Iwamura	Jason Pridie	Dan Wheeler
Wade Davis	Delvin James	Ryan Reid	Delmon Young
Yurendell DeCaster	John Jaso	Jeff Ridgway	

| Matt Diaz | Desmond Jennings | Shawn Riggans |
| Derek Dietrich | Jason Jimenez | Zac Rosscup |

Cincinnati Reds

Year/Team	OPW%	PW	PL	APW%	AW	AL	Diff+/-
1901 CIN	0.483	68	72	0.374	52	87	-0.109
1902 CIN	0.598 P	84	56	0.500	70	70	-0.098
1903 CIN	0.523	73	67	0.532	74	65	0.009
1904 CIN	0.545	84	70	0.575	88	65	0.030
1905 CIN	0.529	81	73	0.516	79	74	-0.012
1906 CIN	0.362 F	56	98	0.424	64	87	0.062
1907 CIN	0.527	81	73	0.431	66	87	-0.095
1908 CIN	0.486	75	79	0.474	73	81	-0.012
1909 CIN	0.538	83	71	0.503	77	76	-0.035
franchID	OWAR	OWS	AWAR	AWS	WARdiff	WSdiff	P/D/W/F
1901 CIN	30.263	220.830	13.892	155.997	16.371	64.834	
1902 CIN	45.416	282.225	30.749	210.008	14.667	72.217	P
1903 CIN	49.070	298.541	37.800	222.001	11.270	76.540	
1904 CIN	42.216	318.135	39.166	263.995	3.050	54.140	
1905 CIN	36.974	284.589	33.972	237.005	3.001	47.584	
1906 CIN	39.392	313.736	24.735	191.994	14.658	121.742	F
1907 CIN	39.991	275.331	30.384	198.001	9.607	77.330	
1908 CIN	42.431	289.824	22.831	218.994	19.600	70.830	
1909 CIN	42.932	298.521	38.388	230.995	4.544	67.526	

Legend: (P) = Pennant / Most Wins in League (D) = Division Winner (W) = Wild Card Winner (F) = Failed to Qualify

The Cincinnati Reds entered the National League in 1890 after spending eight seasons in the American Association as the "Red Stockings." The Redlegs yielded the best results in terms of developing right fielders based on WS>20 (54) and WS>10 (134) among the "Turn of the Century" franchises. The Redlegs' All-Time right field brigade features Sam Crawford and Frank Robinson. Conversely, the organization has never placed in the top three WS>10 totals for starting pitchers, ranking third-worst among the "Turn of the Century" teams.

The Cincinnati Reds captured the National League pennant in 1902 and went on to suffer through a 67-year dry spell before returning to glory. Crawford (.330/16/104) topped the home run leader boards in his first full season (1901) and then proceeded to pace the circuit with 20+ triples in back-to-back campaigns. "Wahoo Sam" carried a .310 BA and slashed 17 three-baggers per season from 1901-09. In addition to Crawford, the outfield included Socks Seybold who topped the home run charts with 16 in '02. Patsy Dougherty delivered a .342 BA in his rookie season (1902) and led the League in runs scored in consecutive campaigns. Jimmy Barrett paced the Senior Circuit with a .407 OBP in '03.

Jesse Tannehill posted a league-best 2.18 ERA in 1901 and followed with a 1.95 ERA and a 20-6 mark for the '02 crew. "Powder" fashioned a 2.38 ERA and a WHIP of 1.083 while averaging 19 victories from 1901-05. Noodles Hahn notched at least 20 victories in three straight seasons (1901-03) and struck out a league-high 239 batsmen in '01. "Long" Bob Ewing amassed 20 victories and completed 30 of 34 starts for the 1905 club. Harry Steinfeldt manned the hot corner, ripping a league-best 32 doubles for the '03 squad. He posted a .327 BA in 1906, leading the circuit in hits and RBI. Second-sacker Miller Huggins tallied 117 runs and paced the League with 103 free passes in '05. Orval Overall (23-7, 1.68) twirled 8 shutouts in '07 and accrued 31 Win Shares. He led the League with 9 shutouts and 205 whiffs in 1909 and fashioned his lowest

ERA (1.42) and WHIP (0.996). Mike Mitchell averaged 19 three-base hits from 1909-1911. The Reds tied for second place in '09, seven games behind the Giants.

Year/Team	OPW%	PW	PL	APW%	AW	AL	Diff+/-
1910 CIN	0.554	85	69	0.487	75	79	-0.067
1911 CIN	0.534 F	82	72	0.458	70	83	-0.077
1912 CIN	0.519	80	74	0.490	75	78	-0.029
1913 CIN	0.481	74	80	0.418	64	89	-0.063
1914 CIN	0.487	75	79	0.390	60	94	-0.098
1915 CIN	0.544 P	84	70	0.461	71	83	-0.083
1916 CIN	0.512	79	75	0.392	60	93	-0.120
1917 CIN	0.458	70	84	0.506	78	76	0.049
1918 CIN	0.494	63	65	0.531	68	60	0.037
1919 CIN	0.465 F	65	75	0.686 P	96	44	0.221

franchID	OWAR	OWS	AWAR	AWS	WARdiff	WSdiff	P/D/W/F
1910 CIN	36.205	282.007	30.041	225.003	6.164	57.004	
1911 CIN	33.120	280.244	34.383	209.999	-1.262	70.244	F
1912 CIN	29.722	245.577	27.011	225.002	2.711	20.575	
1913 CIN	30.213	218.716	26.465	191.996	3.747	26.720	
1914 CIN	27.357	220.223	21.358	179.999	6.000	40.224	
1915 CIN	26.052	211.040	29.968	213.001	-3.916	-1.961	P
1916 CIN	28.653	203.061	25.651	179.998	3.002	23.063	
1917 CIN	22.431	174.580	34.339	234.000	-11.908	-59.421	
1918 CIN	18.265	121.613	33.070	203.998	-14.805	-82.385	
1919 CIN	21.008	145.810	40.793	287.998	-19.785	-142.188	F

Cincinnati began the decade with another second-place finish, coming in five games behind New York. Crawford topped the leader boards with 19 triples and 120 RBI in 1910 and set personal bests with a .378 BA, 217 base hits and 109 runs during the next season. He averaged .320 with 20 triples and 107 ribbies from 1910-15 and still remains the career leader in three-base hits with 309. Crawford transcended the WS>10 mark in every season from 1901 through 1916.

The Redlegs cornered the market on outfielders, topping the Major Leagues with 107 WS>10 seasons from 1901-1919. Dode Paskert eclipsed the WS>10 mark in 9 consecutive campaigns (1910-18). "Honey Boy" delivered a .315 BA with 102 tallies while Bob Bescher collected four successive stolen base titles (1909-1912) and scored a league-leading 120 runs in 1912. "Spittin'" Bill Doak (19-6, 1.72) collected the ERA crown in 1914. The Reds outlasted the Pirates and Giants and clinched the NL pennant by a single game in 1915. Bill Hinchman supplied a .315 BA and legged out a league-high 16 triples for the '16 crew. Jim Bagby (23-13, 1.99) set personal bests in ERA and WHIP (1.091) during his sophomore campaign. Hod Eller (19-9, 2.39) furnished a 1.071 WHIP for the '19 staff.

Win Shares > 20	Single-Season	1901-1919
Dick Hoblitzel - 1B (CIN)	Dode Paskert - CF (CIN) x4	Jesse Tannehill - SP (CIN) x4
Miller Huggins - 2B (CIN) x4	Rebel Oakes - CF (CIN)	Bob Ewing - SP (CIN) x3
Al Bridwell - SS (CIN) x3	Sam Crawford - RF (CIN) x11	Orval Overall - SP (CIN) x2
Jimmy Esmond - SS (CIN)	Socks Seybold - RF (CIN) x5	Bill Doak - SP (CIN)
Harry Steinfeldt - 3B (CIN) x4	Mike Mitchell - RF (CIN) x2	Dave Davenport - SP (CIN)
Mike Mowrey - 3B (CIN) x2	Harry Wolter - RF (CIN)	Gene Packard - SP (CIN)
Patsy Dougherty - LF (CIN) x4	Al Wickland - RF (CIN)	Hod Eller - SP (CIN)
Bob Bescher - LF (CIN) x2	Bill Hinchman - RF (CIN) x2	Jim Bagby - SP (CIN) x3
	Noodles Hahn - SP (CIN) x4	Rube Vickers - SW (CIN)

Year/Team	OPW%	PW	PL	APW%	AW	AL	Diff+/-
1920 CIN	0.497	77	77	0.536	82	71	0.039
1921 CIN	0.499	77	77	0.458	70	83	-0.042
1922 CIN	0.480 F	74	80	0.558	86	68	0.078
1923 CIN	0.476 F	73	81	0.591	91	63	0.115
1924 CIN	0.486 F	75	79	0.542	83	70	0.057
1925 CIN	0.501 F	77	77	0.523	80	73	0.022
1926 CIN	0.507 F	78	76	0.565	87	67	0.058
1927 CIN	0.553 F	85	69	0.490	75	78	-0.062
1928 CIN	0.469 F	72	82	0.513	78	74	0.044
1929 CIN	0.422 F	65	89	0.429	66	88	0.007

franchID	OWAR	OWS	AWAR	AWS	WARdiff	WSdiff	P/D/W/F
1920 CIN	24.295	169.501	34.758	245.998	-10.463	-76.496	
1921 CIN	22.372	166.264	30.973	210.011	-8.601	-43.746	
1922 CIN	31.401	183.323	39.151	258.004	-7.750	-74.681	F
1923 CIN	35.729	197.515	42.294	273.001	-6.565	-75.486	F
1924 CIN	33.730	197.340	42.397	248.999	-8.667	-51.659	F
1925 CIN	31.546	204.504	37.464	240.007	-5.918	-35.503	F
1926 CIN	28.660	190.353	45.490	260.996	-16.831	-70.643	F
1927 CIN	28.667	218.570	33.371	224.996	-4.704	-6.426	F
1928 CIN	21.569	184.155	28.214	234.003	-6.646	-49.849	F
1929 CIN	19.112	189.435	27.388	197.995	-8.276	-8.560	F

Cincinnati endured a talent famine as the organization failed to meet the PA and/or BFP requirements from 1922 through 1935. Jim Bagby accrued 33 Win Shares and topped the circuit with 31 wins, 30 complete games and 339.2 innings pitched in '20. Ken Williams (.332/39/155) provided the first 30/30 season in the history of the Major Leagues in 1922. He paced the League in home runs and RBI and averaged .339 with 27 jacks, 110 ribbies, 21 stolen bases and 102 runs scored from 1921-25. Pete Donohue enjoyed a five-year stint atop the Reds' rotation. He won 19 games per season with an aggregate ERA of 3.30 from 1922-26. Jesse Haines surpassed the 20-win plateau on three occasions during the "Roaring Twenties." "Pop" fashioned a record of 24-10 with a 2.72 ERA and led the NL with 25 complete games and 6 shutouts. Lew Fonseca eclipsed the .300 mark in four consecutive campaigns and claimed the batting title with a .369 average in '29.

Year/Team	OPW%	PW	PL	APW%	AW	AL	Diff+/-
1930 CIN	0.468 F	72	82	0.383	59	95	-0.085
1931 CIN	0.503 F	77	77	0.377	58	96	-0.126
1932 CIN	0.440 F	68	86	0.390	60	94	-0.050
1933 CIN	0.472 F	73	81	0.382	58	94	-0.090
1934 CIN	0.461 F	71	83	0.344	52	99	-0.117
1935 CIN	0.412 F	63	91	0.444	68	85	0.032
1936 CIN	0.518	80	74	0.481	74	80	-0.037
1937 CIN	0.484	74	80	0.364	56	98	-0.120
1938 CIN	0.484 F	75	79	0.547	82	68	0.063
1939 CIN	0.483 F	74	80	0.630 P	97	57	0.147

franchID	OWAR	OWS	AWAR	AWS	WARdiff	WSdiff	P/D/W/F
1930 CIN	19.198	162.251	22.855	177.001	-3.657	-14.751	F
1931 CIN	27.586	198.721	17.924	173.998	9.662	24.723	F
1932 CIN	18.354	176.863	24.203	180.007	-5.849	-3.144	F

1933 CIN	15.547	181.626	14.898	174.001	0.649	7.625	F
1934 CIN	18.656	179.146	16.782	155.996	1.874	23.150	F
1935 CIN	20.574	166.903	26.188	203.999	-5.615	-37.095	F
1936 CIN	32.901	218.356	29.092	222.002	3.809	-3.646	
1937 CIN	23.585	175.734	24.346	168.001	-0.761	7.733	
1938 CIN	25.415	193.371	37.349	246.004	-11.934	-52.633	F
1939 CIN	20.627	193.779	45.110	**291.010**	-24.483	-97.231	F

Second-sacker Tony "Cooch" Cuccinello sparked the Reds' lineup with a .313 BA and 30 doubles in 1930-31. Frank McCormick produced a league-leading 209 hits in each of his first two seasons (1938-39). "Buck" paced the National League with 128 RBI while batting .332 in his sophomore year. Cincinnati failed to develop any notable talent on the mound during the 1930's.

Win Shares > 20	Single-Season	1920-1939
Lew Fonseca - 1B (CIN) Frank McCormick - 1B (CIN) x3 Tony Cuccinello - 2B (CIN) x4	Chuck Dressen - 3B (CIN) Ken Williams - LF (CIN) x4 Gene Moore, Jr. - RF (CIN) x2 Dixie Davis - SP (CIN)	Herman Pillette - SP (CIN) Jimmy Ring - SP (CIN) Pete Donohue - SP (CIN) x2 Jesse Haines - SP (CIN)

Year/Team	OPW%	PW	PL	APW%	AW	AL	Diff+/-
1940 CIN	0.537 F	83	71	0.654 P	100	53	0.117
1941 CIN	0.494	76	78	0.571	88	66	0.078
1942 CIN	0.380 F	59	95	0.500	76	76	0.120
1943 CIN	0.444 F	68	86	0.565	87	67	0.121
1944 CIN	0.469	72	82	0.578	89	65	0.109
1945 CIN	0.453	70	84	0.396	61	93	-0.057
1946 CIN	0.447 F	69	85	0.435	67	87	-0.012
1947 CIN	0.474	73	81	0.474	73	81	0.000
1948 CIN	0.413	64	90	0.418	64	89	0.005
1949 CIN	0.471	73	81	0.403	62	92	-0.069

franchID	OWAR	OWS	AWAR	AWS	WARdiff	WSdiff	P/D/W/F
1940 CIN	23.749	215.472	**43.221**	**300.007**	-19.472	-84.535	F
1941 CIN	29.625	215.636	31.972	264.001	-2.347	-48.364	
1942 CIN	16.620	157.937	31.979	228.001	-15.359	-70.064	F
1943 CIN	23.998	203.665	34.719	260.995	-10.722	-57.330	F
1944 CIN	18.195	192.305	31.908	267.004	-13.713	-74.699	
1945 CIN	24.339	207.038	19.725	182.999	4.614	24.039	
1946 CIN	20.274	190.025	30.521	200.999	-10.247	-10.974	F
1947 CIN	26.932	190.153	33.201	219.001	-6.269	-28.848	
1948 CIN	20.990	169.061	22.751	191.997	-1.761	-22.936	
1949 CIN	23.640	183.118	21.298	186.001	2.342	-2.884	

McCormick (.309/19/127) garnered NL MVP honors in 1940 after topping the charts with 191 safeties and 44 two-base knocks. Elmer Riddle (19-4, 2.24) posted the best ERA in the National League in '41, following brief appearances on the Cincinnati roster during the previous two seasons. Eddie Joost displayed a keen batting eye, walking over 100 times in every season from 1947-1952 and scoring 128 runs for the '49 squad. Ewell Blackwell (22-8, 2.47) struck out a league-high 193 batsmen in '47. "The Whip" paced the NL in victories and complete games (23).

Year/Team	OPW%	PW	PL	APW%	AW	AL	Diff+/-
1950 CIN	0.493	76	78	0.431	66	87	-0.061
1951 CIN	0.491	76	78	0.442	68	86	-0.049

Year	OPW%	PW	PL	APW%	AW	AL	Diff+/-
1952 CIN	0.473	73	81	0.448	69	85	-0.025
1953 CIN	0.478	74	80	0.442	68	86	-0.037
1954 CIN	0.477	73	81	0.481	74	80	0.004
1955 CIN	0.540 F	83	71	0.487	75	79	-0.053
1956 CIN	0.573 F	88	66	0.591	91	63	0.018
1957 CIN	0.470 F	72	82	0.519	80	74	0.049
1958 CIN	0.541 F	83	71	0.494	76	78	-0.047
1959 CIN	0.499 F	77	77	0.481	74	80	-0.018

franchID	OWAR	OWS	AWAR	AWS	WARdiff	WSdiff	P/D/W/F
1950 CIN	27.684	189.999	26.440	197.998	1.244	-7.998	
1951 CIN	26.657	207.282	23.083	204.002	3.575	3.280	
1952 CIN	30.096	217.824	26.235	207.002	3.862	10.822	
1953 CIN	31.293	226.158	24.867	204.001	6.427	22.157	
1954 CIN	37.888	226.710	42.119	224.998	-4.231	1.712	
1955 CIN	42.934	256.903	42.119	224.998	0.815	31.905	F
1956 CIN	49.036	312.653	45.588	272.997	3.448	39.656	F
1957 CIN	42.371	274.923	39.290	239.997	3.080	34.926	F
1958 CIN	45.282	294.544	38.762	228.001	6.520	66.543	F
1959 CIN	47.185	278.057	38.319	221.999	8.866	56.058	F

Jim Konstanty (16-7, 2.66) saved 22 contests and topped the circuit with 74 appearances en route to a stunning victory in the 1950 NL MVP race. The Redlegs' first sackers paced the Majors with 17 WS>10 seasons during the Fifties. Ted Kluszewski (.326/49/141) secured the home run and RBI titles in '54, tallying 33 Win Shares and placing second in the NL MVP balloting. "Big Klu" batted .315 with 43 clouts and 116 ribbies from 1953-56. Furthermore, he displayed tremendous plate discipline by limiting his strikeouts to 35 per year!

GM Gabe Paul assembled a stellar squad via amateur free agency during his eight-year stint in the Cincinnati front office. Paul's acquisitions encompassed Frank Robinson ('53), Curt Flood, Vada Pinson ('56), Claude Osteen, Mike Cuellar ('57), Jim Maloney ('59), Pete Rose and Tony Perez ('60). Wally Post (.309/40/109) established career highs in batting average, home runs, RBI and runs scored (116) for the Redlegs in 1955. Joe Adcock slammed 38 round-trippers and knocked in 103 runs during the 1956 season. Frank Robinson slugged 38 long balls and scored a league-best 122 runs, meriting NL ROY honors in '56. Vada Pinson led all National Leaguers with 131 runs scored and 47 doubles in his first full season (1959). Johnny Temple contributed a .311 average and tallied 102 runs.

Win Shares > 20	Single-Season	1940-1959
Ted Kluszewski - 1B (CIN) x5	Roy McMillan - SS (CIN)	Wally Post - RF (CIN)
Joe Adcock - 1B (CIN) x4	Grady Hatton - 3B (CIN)	Elmer Riddle - SP (CIN) x2
Frank Robinson - 1B (CIN) x2	Ed Bailey - C (CIN)	Red Barrett - SP (CIN)
Johnny Temple - 2B (CIN) x2	Bob Nieman - LF (CIN)	Ewell Blackwell - SP (CIN) x2
Eddie R. Miller - SS (CIN) x2	Frank Robinson - LF (CIN) x3	Jim Konstanty - RP (CIN)
Eddie Joost - SS (CIN) x5	Vada Pinson - CF (CIN) x8	

Year/Team	OPW%	PW	PL	APW%	AW	AL	Diff+/-
1960 CIN	0.482 F	74	80	0.435	67	87	-0.047
1961 CIN	0.498 F	81	81	0.604 P	93	61	0.106
1962 CIN	0.560	91	71	0.605	98	64	0.044
1963 CIN	0.543	88	74	0.531	86	76	-0.012
1964 CIN	0.492	80	82	0.568	92	70	0.076
1965 CIN	0.548	89	73	0.549	89	73	0.001

1966 CIN	0.537	87	75	0.475	76	84	-0.062	
1967 CIN	0.580	94	68	0.537	87	75	-0.043	
1968 CIN	0.507	82	80	0.512	83	79	0.005	
1969 CIN	0.619 P	100	62	0.549	89	73	-0.069	

franchID	OWAR	OWS	AWAR	AWS	WARdiff	WSdiff	P/D/W/F
1960 CIN	39.778	255.184	33.215	201.005	6.564	54.179	F
1961 CIN	50.778	325.575	38.256	278.995	12.522	46.579	F
1962 CIN	56.066	335.808	43.913	293.995	12.153	41.813	
1963 CIN	55.007	327.211	42.754	257.995	12.253	69.216	
1964 CIN	44.206	291.413	46.861	275.997	-2.475	15.416	
1965 CIN	54.993	299.539	56.046	266.991	-1.053	32.548	
1966 CIN	48.323	285.814	36.568	227.998	11.755	57.816	
1967 CIN	54.039	316.409	39.885	261.014	14.034	55.061	
1968 CIN	51.138	326.679	37.742	249.005	14.154	81.674	
1969 CIN	59.085	355.256	37.483	267.000	21.602	88.256	P

Robinson delivered a .303 BA, 32 doubles, 32 homers, 101 RBI and 104 runs scored per year from 1956-1965. In 1962, "The Judge" accrued 41 Win Shares and was named NL MVP after hitting .342 with 39 moon-shots and 136 RBI. He established personal bests in batting average, hits (208), runs (134), doubles (51) and RBI. Adcock clubbed 35 four-baggers and drove in a career-best 108 runs in 1961. The 1962 Reds posted the highest oWAR and finished in third place, only four games behind the Giants.

The Reds dwarfed the other organizations in terms of developing center fielders, producing 36 WS>10 seasons during the Sixties. Pinson set a personal best with a .343 BA, led the League with 208 base knocks and secured a third-place finish in the NL MVP voting. He paced the circuit with 14 triples and 204 hits in '63. Curt Flood eclipsed the 200-hit mark in back-to-back seasons (1963-64) and posted a .335 BA in 1967. Flood earned 7 consecutive Gold Gloves for his defensive excellence in center field. Cincinnati won 88 contests in 1963 and finished second, only three games behind San Francisco. Pete Rose scored 101 runs and clinched the NL ROY Award. Rose topped the charts with 209 hits in 1965 while Tommy Harper paced the League with 126 runs scored. The Reds finished second to the Giants in three straight campaigns (1965-67).

On the hill, Ernie Broglio (21-9, 2.74) placed third in the Cy Young balloting and topped the leader boards in victories in 1960. Jim O'Toole furnished 17 wins per season, along with a 3.05 ERA and a 1.190 WHIP from 1961-64. Jim Maloney notched 23 victories and whiffed 265 batsmen for the '63 squad and manufactured a record of 18-8 with 235 strikeouts per year from 1963-66. Sammy Ellis contributed 22 victories to the Reds' efforts in 1965. GM Bill DeWitt set the wheels of the Big Red Machine in motion with the selections of Johnny Bench, Hal McRae and Bernie Carbo in the initial Amateur Draft. The Reds' class of 1965 posted the highest Career Total Win Shares (707) and Career Total WAR (105).

Frank Robinson (.316/49/122) achieved the Triple Crown and secured MVP honors in 1966 while leading the League in runs (122), OBP (.410) and SLG (.637). Jimmy Wynn, aka "The Toy Cannon," blasted 37 round-trippers and batted in 107 runs in '67. Johnny Bench achieved ROY honors and the first of 10 consecutive Gold Glove awards in '68. Rose collected batting crowns in consecutive seasons (1968-69) and placed runner-up in the MVP race in '68 after knocking 210 base hits. In the "Year of the Pitcher" Cincinnati tallied the highest offWSnorm total of All-Time (221).

Bridesmaids for 66 straight seasons, the Reds finally achieved the pennant in 1969 by a 13-game margin. Robinson (.308/32/100) placed third in the MVP balloting, surpassing the 100-run mark for the eighth time in his career. Harper topped the NL with 73 stolen bases. Tony

Perez bolstered the lineup with 37 circuit clouts and 122 ribbies. Lee May hammered 38 long balls and knocked in 110 runs.

Mike Cuellar (23-11, 2.38) collected the Cy Young award. From 1966-1975, Cuellar fashioned a record of 18-11 with a 2.97 ERA and 1.157 ERA while completing nearly half of his starts. Claude Osteen (20-15, 2.66) established career-bests with 16 complete games, 7 shutouts and a 1.143 WHIP.

Year/Team	OPW%	PW	PL	APW%	AW	AL	Diff+/-
1970 CIN	0.533 D	86	76	0.630 P	102	60	0.097
1971 CIN	0.527 D	85	77	0.488	79	83	-0.040
1972 CIN	0.555 D	90	72	0.617 D	95	59	0.062
1973 CIN	0.551	89	73	0.611 P	99	63	0.060
1974 CIN	0.557	90	72	0.605	98	64	0.048
1975 CIN	0.575 P	93	69	0.667 P	108	54	0.092
1976 CIN	0.562 D	91	71	0.630 P	102	60	0.068
1977 CIN	0.473	77	85	0.543	88	74	0.071
1978 CIN	0.502	81	81	0.571	92	69	0.069
1979 CIN	0.488	79	83	0.559 D	90	71	0.071

franchID	OWAR	OWS	AWAR	AWS	WARdiff	WSdiff	P/D/W/F
1970 CIN	48.644	329.777	46.745	306.002	1.899	23.775	D
1971 CIN	36.703	275.798	31.722	237.001	4.982	38.797	D
1972 CIN	46.007	315.529	47.317	284.995	-1.310	30.534	D
1973 CIN	45.994	345.449	45.085	297.003	0.909	48.446	
1974 CIN	52.647	336.816	52.734	294.003	-0.086	42.813	
1975 CIN	46.577	312.470	55.267	324.004	-8.690	-11.534	P
1976 CIN	51.709	302.042	65.283	306.001	-13.575	-3.959	D
1977 CIN	37.084	263.382	47.840	263.997	-10.755	-0.615	
1978 CIN	34.727	285.888	42.093	276.002	-7.366	9.886	
1979 CIN	39.490	289.976	44.758	269.999	-5.268	19.977	

The Big Red Machine streamrolled through the 70's as Cincinnati enjoyed the finest decade in franchise history. The Reds reaped the benefits of excellent scouting and development throughout the 1960's, as the team finished among the decade WS>10 leaders at five positions (catchers, first basemen, shortstops, left fielders and right fielders.) The Reds secured 3 consecutive division titles (1970-72). The 1970 squad topped the oWAR and oWS charts. Bench (.293/45/148) paced the League in home runs and RBI and claimed NL MVP honors. Harper became a member of the 30/30 club and accrued 33 Win Shares. Cesar Tovar tallied 120 runs and led the League with 36 doubles and 13 triples. Perez contributed personal bests with a .317 batting average, 40 circuit clouts, 129 RBI and 107 runs scored. The "Big Dog" placed third in the NL MVP balloting and notched 34 Win Shares. Rose hit .316 with 120 runs scored and a league-best 205 base hits. Cuellar (24-8, 3.48) topped the charts in victories and complete games (21).

The NL West battle went down to the wire in 1971 with Cincinnati emerging as the victor by a single game over Houston. Tovar supplied his best batting average (.311) and topped the charts with 204 base hits. The Reds fended off strong challenges from the Giants and Astros in '72. Bench (.270/40/125) accumulated 40 Win Shares and earned his second MVP award. Osteen fashioned a 20-11 record with a 2.64 ERA. Rose secured the MVP trophy in 1973 as he delivered his third batting title (.338) and established a personal best with 230 hits. "Charlie Hustle" eclipsed the .300 mark in 14 of 16 seasons from 1965-1980 and during that span he averaged .314 with 105 runs, 38 doubles and 203 base hits per year.

Harper nabbed 54 bags to lead the League in '73. Wynn dialed long-distance 32 times and drove in 108 runs in '74. Dave Concepcion swiped 41 bases and collected the first of five Gold Glove awards. Cincinnati shortstops (predominantly Concepion and Barry Larkin) placed in the top three WS>10 leaders for the Seventies, Eighties, and Nineties. Rose began a three-year stint atop the leader boards for doubles and runs scored, setting a personal best with 130 runs in 1976. Bench led the League with 129 RBI and set an individual best with 108 runs for the '74 crew. From 1970-75, the "Little General" walloped 33 big-flies and plated 113 baserunners per season. The Reds topped the Senior Circuit in oWS and secured the pennant with 93 victories in 1975. Ken Griffey posted career-bests with a .336 BA and 34 stolen bases in 1976. Lee May knocked in a league-leading 109 runs. The "Big Bopper" produced 28 four-baggers and 96 ribbies per season from 1968-1978. Hal McRae led the League with a .407 OBP and produced his highest batting average (.332). Rawly Eastwick secured late-inning leads as he notched 11 wins and 26 saves with a 2.09 ERA.

Griffey tallied 117 runs scored in 1977. Rose slapped 51 two-baggers for the '78 squad and Ross Grimsley, Jr. earned his lone All-Star appearance with a record of 20-11 and a 3.05 ERA. The Big Red Machine veered off-course toward the end of decade as the Redlegs stumbled to finish below the .500 mark in 1977 and 1979. GM Dick Wagner achieved a succession of prosperous Amateur Drafts during his term in the Reds' front office (1978-1983). Wagner's draft classes averaged 351 Career Total Win Shares and paved the way for the franchise's success from 1987-1995 including four pennants and two division titles.

Win Shares > 20	Single-Season	1960-1979
Lee May - 1B (CIN) x4	Johnny Bench - C (CIN) x10	Frank Robinson - RF (CIN) x10
Tony Perez - 1B (CIN) x2	Tony Gonzalez - LF (CIN)	
Pete Rose - 1B (CIN)	Pete Rose - LF (CIN) x4	Pete Rose - RF (CIN) x4
Pete Rose - 2B (CIN) x2	Bernie Carbo - LF (CIN)	Jimmy Wynn - RF (CIN)
Leo Cardenas - SS (CIN) x4	Cesar Tovar - LF (CIN)	Frank Robinson - DH (CIN)
Dave Concepcion - SS (CIN) x5	Tommy Harper - LF (CIN)	Hal McRae - DH (CIN) x4
Tony Perez - 3B (CIN) x5	Curt Flood - CF (CIN) x6	Jim O'Toole - SP (CIN)
Cesar Tovar - 3B (CIN) x2	Tony Gonzalez - CF (CIN) x2	Jim Maloney - SP (CIN) x2
Tommy Harper - 3B (CIN)	Jimmy Wynn - CF (CIN) x7	Mike Cuellar - SP (CIN)
Pete Rose - 3B (CIN) x4	Cesar Tovar - CF (CIN) x3	Claude Osteen - SP (CIN) x2
Ray Knight - 3B (CIN)	Tommy Harper - CF (CIN)	Ross Grimsley, Jr. - SP (CIN)
	Ken Griffey - RF (CIN) x4	Ernie Broglio - SW (CIN)

Year/Team	OPW%	PW	PL	APW%	AW	AL	Diff+/-
1980 CIN	0.483	78	84	0.549	89	73	0.067
1981 CIN	0.472	77	85	0.611 P	66	42	0.139
1982 CIN	0.495	80	82	0.377	61	101	-0.119
1983 CIN	0.472	76	86	0.457	74	88	-0.015
1984 CIN	0.414	67	95	0.432	70	92	0.018
1985 CIN	0.500	81	81	0.553	89	72	0.053
1986 CIN	0.491	80	82	0.531	86	76	0.040
1987 CIN	0.544 P	88	74	0.519	84	78	-0.026
1988 CIN	0.557 P	90	72	0.540	87	74	-0.017
1989 CIN	0.537 D	87	75	0.463	75	87	-0.074

franchID	OWAR	OWS	AWAR	AWS	WARdiff	WSdiff	P/D/W/F
1980 CIN	34.474	260.424	42.016	267.000	-7.542	-6.576	
1981 CIN	22.746	183.221	28.562	197.998	-5.816	-14.777	
1982 CIN	35.598	243.755	29.841	182.997	5.757	60.758	
1983 CIN	33.260	266.013	24.826	222.005	8.434	44.007	
1984 CIN	30.275	215.868	27.222	210.003	3.053	5.865	

1985 CIN	31.092	261.662	35.718	266.993	-4.626	-5.331	
1986 CIN	37.954	272.987	36.853	257.998	1.101	14.989	
1987 CIN	39.731	273.167	38.375	252.004	1.356	21.163	P
1988 CIN	44.051	290.293	37.549	260.996	6.502	29.297	P
1989 CIN	44.505	298.096	31.601	225.006	12.904	73.090	D

The Reds remained below the .500 mark through 1984 as the club endured 95 losses. Tom Hume managed 8 wins and 18 saves per season along with a 2.86 ERA over a four-year stretch (1979-82). Mario Soto anchored the rotation from 1981-85, posting a 15-11 record with a 3.16 ERA, 1.121 WHIP and 213 strikeouts per season. He secured a second-place finish in the Cy Young vote in '83 and topped the NL with 18 complete games. McRae (.308/27/133) paced the circuit in RBI and doubles (46) for the '82 crew.

The Reds' farm system produced a trio of fleet-footed outfielders in the middle of the decade. Eddie Milner nabbed 41 bags for the '83 squad. Gary Redus averaged 42 steals per year from 1983-87. Eric Davis pilfered 80 bases and blasted 27 long balls in his first full season (1986). Joaquin Andujar placed fourth in the NL Cy Young race during back-to-back campaigns (1984-85). He surpassed the 20-win mark in both seasons. Tom Browning (20-9, 3.55) finished second in the 1985 NL ROY balloting and Charlie Leibrandt earned a fifth-place finish in the Cy Young voting with 17 victories and a 2.69 ERA in '85.

Cincinnati developed a throng of closer candidates in the 1980's, including Jay Howell, Jeff Montgomery and Jeff Russell. Howell notched 29 saves in '85 and closed out 28 contests with a 1.58 ERA for the '89 staff. Montgomery added 18 saves while posting career-bests in ERA (1.37) and WHIP (0.989). Russell fashioned an ERA of 1.98 and a WHIP of 0.950 while pacing the circuit with 38 saves. Rob Dibble whiffed 141 batters in 99 innings as a setup man in '89.

The Redlegs notched back-to-back pennants in 1987-88. Davis (.293/37/100) entered the 30/30 club in '87. "Eric the Red" established career-highs in home runs, RBI and runs scored (120). Kal Daniels produced a .334 BA with 26 jacks as a part-timer. Danny Tartabull slugged 28 round-trippers and knocked in 100 runs per year during a three-year span (1986-88). Browning (18-5, 3.41) delivered a career-best 1.073 WHIP and twirled a perfect game in 1988. Chris Sabo slapped 40 two-base knocks and pilfered 40 bags, earning the 1988 NL ROY award while Nick Esasky walloped 30 moon-shots and knocked in 108 runs, as the Reds took the division title in '89.

Year/Team	OPW%	PW	PL	APW%	AW	AL	Diff+/-
1990 CIN	0.559 P	91	71	0.562 D	91	71	0.003
1991 CIN	0.523	85	77	0.457	74	88	-0.067
1992 CIN	0.454	74	88	0.556	90	72	0.101
1993 CIN	0.439	71	91	0.451	73	89	0.011
1994 CIN	0.558 P	90	72	0.579 D	66	48	0.021
1995 CIN	0.536 D	87	75	0.590 D	85	59	0.054
1996 CIN	0.458 F	74	88	0.500	81	81	0.042
1997 CIN	0.543 F	88	74	0.469	76	86	-0.074
1998 CIN	0.477 F	77	85	0.475	77	85	-0.002
1999 CIN	0.494 F	80	82	0.589	96	67	0.095
franchID	**OWAR**	**OWS**	**AWAR**	**AWS**	**WARdiff**	**WSdiff**	**P/D/W/F**
1990 CIN	47.512	288.853	45.960	273.007	1.552	15.846	P
1991 CIN	46.620	273.609	41.732	221.998	4.888	51.610	
1992 CIN	35.683	253.312	**45.485**	270.002	-9.802	-16.690	
1993 CIN	28.236	213.147	33.301	219.000	-5.065	-5.853	
1994 CIN	27.366	**188.934**	36.184	198.002	-8.818	-9.068	P

1995 CIN	**36.244**	**244.029**	**44.132**	255.004	-7.888	-10.975	D
1996 CIN	43.165	290.468	36.306	243.007	6.859	47.461	F
1997 CIN	43.416	271.598	30.002	228.001	13.413	43.596	F
1998 CIN	43.074	259.838	35.380	231.009	7.694	28.829	F
1999 CIN	38.776	258.562	44.208	288.007	-5.432	-29.445	F

Sabo supplied 25 round-trippers and swiped 25 bases as the Reds claimed the pennant in '90. Daniels set personal bests with 27 long balls and 94 ribbies. Tartabull (.316/31/100) paced the circuit with a .593 SLG in 1991. Dibble saved 22 contests and averaged 13.3 K's per 9 innings from 1990-92. Montgomery secured three All-Star invitations while saving 32 contests per season with a 2.91 ERA and a 1.189 WHIP from 1990-96. Russell notched 30+ saves in three consecutive campaigns (1991-93) and fashioned a career-best ERA of 1.63 in '92.

Cincinnati outlasted Chicago by one game to secure the pennant in '94. Paul O'Neill captured the batting crown with a .359 average. "The Warrior" surpassed the .300 mark in every campaign between 1993-98, posting a .317 BA with 34 doubles and 21 four-baggers per year. The Reds followed up with an NL Central division title in 1995. Reggie L. Sanders (.306/28/99) swiped 36 bags and earned his lone All-Star invite. Barry Larkin claimed the NL MVP award after he swiped 51 bases in 56 attempts and produced a .319 BA. In the subsequent campaign, he entered the 30/30 club and amassed 31 Win Shares.

With the exception of 2004, the Redlegs failed to meet the BFP requirements in every season from 1996-2009. O'Neill achieved career-bests with 42 doubles and 117 RBI in '97. Davis enjoyed a comeback season in 1998, delivering a career-best .327 BA along with 28 jacks and 89 ribbies. Led by Montgomery and Trevor Hoffman, the Reds registered the most WS>10 seasons by relief pitchers in the Nineties. Hoffman (1.48, 53 SV) posted career-bests in ERA, WHIP (0.849) and saves en route to a runner-up finish in the 1998 NL Cy Young balloting. He delivered a 2.62 ERA, 1.016 WHIP and 39 saves per season from 1994-2002. Scott Williamson (12-7, 2.41) saved 19 contests and claimed the 1999 NL ROY award.

Year/Team	OPW%	PW	PL	APW%	AW	AL	Diff+/-
2000 CIN	0.475 F	77	85	0.525	85	77	0.049
2001 CIN	0.534 F	87	75	0.407	66	96	-0.127
2002 CIN	0.499 F	81	81	0.481	78	84	-0.018
2003 CIN	0.500 F	81	81	0.426	69	93	-0.074
2004 CIN	0.492	80	82	0.469	76	86	-0.023
2005 CIN	0.489 F	79	83	0.451	73	89	-0.038
2006 CIN	0.495 F	80	82	0.494	80	82	-0.001
2007 CIN	0.438 F	71	91	0.444	72	90	0.006
2008 CIN	0.425 F	69	93	0.457	74	88	0.032
2009 CIN	0.458 F	74	88	0.481	78	84	0.024
2010 CIN	0.526 W	85	77	0.562 D	91	71	0.036
2011 CIN	0.507	82	80	0.488	79	83	-0.019
2012 CIN	0.515	83	79	0.599 D	97	65	0.084
2013 CIN	0.564 W	91	71	0.556 W	90	72	-0.008

franchID	OWAR	OWS	AWAR	AWS	WARdiff	WSdiff	P/D/W/F
2000 CIN	30.755	233.986	38.647	254.997	-7.892	-21.011	F
2001 CIN	26.412	210.014	25.622	198.001	0.791	12.013	F
2002 CIN	34.490	248.669	32.276	233.996	2.214	14.674	F
2003 CIN	28.919	221.850	20.633	206.999	8.286	14.850	F
2004 CIN	38.776	250.231	24.058	227.999	14.718	22.233	
2005 CIN	40.329	257.277	34.579	218.999	5.751	38.277	F

2006 CIN	26.972	245.209	37.711	240.002	-10.739	5.207	F
2007 CIN	29.413	210.524	36.505	216.003	-7.091	-5.479	F
2008 CIN	22.150	227.393	31.200	221.724	-9.049	5.669	F
2009 CIN	33.065	260.048	28.965	234.000	4.100	26.048	F
2010 CIN	46.226	271.008	46.808	272.998	-0.581	-1.990	W
2011 CIN	30.929	215.269	35.702	236.997	-4.773	-21.728	
2012 CIN	43.591	295.259	45.480	290.994	-1.889	4.265	
2013 CIN	42.902	279.385	43.851	270.001	-0.949	9.384	W

Sanders blasted a career-high 33 circuit clouts in 2001. Aaron Boone drove in 96 runs for the '03 squad. Adam Dunn (.266/46/102) accumulated 31 Win Shares in 2004. The "Big Donkey" slugged at least 40 round-trippers in 5 consecutive seasons (2004-08). Joey Votto (.297/24/84) placed second in the 2008 NL ROY balloting. He delivered a .324 BA with 37 swats and 113 ribbies en route to an MVP award in 2010. Hoffman continued his success in the closer's role, delivering a 2.77 ERA and 1.043 WHIP while averaging 40 saves per season for the decade (omitting the 2003 season, during which Hoffman only appeared in 9 games due to injury). He paced the circuit with 46 saves and earned another runner-up finish in the 2006 NL Cy Young balloting. B.J. Ryan notched 35 saves per season (2005-06, 2008) and fashioned an ERA of 2.41.

Cincinnati's farm system failed to bear any noteworthy starting pitchers from 2000-09 as Brett Tomko (11-7, 4.04) in 2004 was the lone hurler to surpass 10 Win Shares. Johnny Cueto (19-9, 2.78) placed fourth in the 2012 NL Cy Young balloting. Aroldis Chapman struck out 15.6 batters per nine innings and notched 38 saves in each of his first two seasons in the closer's role (2012-13). Jay Bruce rapped 32 circuit clouts and knocked in 102 baserunners per season from 2011-13.

Win Shares > 20	Single-Season	1980-2013
Dan Driessen - 1B (CIN)	Eric Davis - LF (CIN)	Jay Bruce - RF (CIN) x2
Ray Knight - 1B (CIN)	Kal Daniels - LF (CIN) x3	Joaquin Andujar - SP (CIN)
Nick Esasky - 1B (CIN)	Adam Dunn - LF (CIN) x3	Mario Soto - SP (CIN)
Adam Dunn - 1B (CIN) x2	Eric Davis - CF (CIN) x4	Charlie Leibrandt - SP (CIN)
Joey Votto - 1B (CIN) x5	Brady Clark - CF (CIN)	x2
Ron Oester - 2B (CIN)	Danny Tartabull - RF (CIN) x4	Johnny Cueto - SP (CIN)
Barry Larkin - SS (CIN) x8	Paul O'Neill - RF (CIN) x4	Jeff Montgomery - RP (CIN)
Chris Sabo - 3B (CIN) x2	Reggie L. Sanders - RF (CIN)	

Note: 4000 PA or BFP to qualify, except during strike-shortened seasons
(1972 = 3800, 1981 & 1994 = 2700, 1995 = 3500) and 154-game schedule (3800)
- failed to qualify: 1906, 1911, 1919, 1922-1935, 1938-1940, 1942-1943, 1946, 1955-1961, 1996-2003, 2005-2009

Reds All-Time "Originals" Roster

George Abrams	Bobby Durnbaugh	Chuck Kress	Billy Rhines
Joe Abreu	Jesse Duryea	Art Kruger	Len Rice
Jose Acevedo	Double Joe Dwyer	Johnny Kucab	Duane Richards
Bobby H. Adams	Billy Earle	Andy Kyle	Jeff S. Richardson
Karl Adams	Rawly Eastwick	Mike LaCoss	Elmer Riddle
Joe Adcock	Al Eckert	Jeff Lahti	John Riedling
Santo Alcala	Johnny Edwards	Al Lakeman	Jimmy Ring
Chuck Aleno	Sherman Edwards	Ray Lamanno	Bill Risley
Ethan Allen	Dick J. Egan	Clayton Lambert	Tony Robello
Rafael Almeida	Jake Eisenhart	Hobie Landrith	Dick Robertson
Yonder Alonso	Roy Ellam	Don Lang	Frank Robinson
Rogelio Alvarez	Hod Eller	Barry Larkin	Ron Robinson

Brant Alyea	Claude Elliott	Harry LaRoss	Eddy Rodriguez
Mike J. Anderson	Rube Ellis	Brandon Larson	Henry Alejandro
Wingo Anderson	Sammy Ellis	Jason LaRue	Rodriguez
Joaquin Andujar	Frank Emmer	Garland Lawing	Rosario Rodriguez
Pete Appleton	Eddie Erautt	Tom Lawless	Josh Roenicke
Jack Armstrong	Hal Erickson	Mike Leake	Mike Roesler
Mike Armstrong	Nick Esasky	King Lear	Cookie Rojas
Justin Atchley	Jimmy Esmond	Frank Leary	John Roper
Chick W. Autry	Bill Essick	John Leary	Adam Rosales
Jay Avrea	Bob Ewing	Sam LeCure	Pete Rose
Bobby Ayala	Pete Fahrer	Terry Lee	Cliff Ross
Joe Azcue	Buck Fausett	Charlie Leibrandt	Joe Rossi
Jim Bagby	Bob Ferguson	Brad Lesley	Larry Rothschild
Ed Bailey	Hobe Ferris	Al Libke	Chico G. Ruiz
Homer Bailey	Carlos Fisher	Buddy Lively	Randy Ruiz
Jim Bailey	Maurice Fisher	Wes Livengood	Jeff Russell
King Bailey	Paul Fittery	Keith Lockhart	B.J. Ryan
Bill Baker	Ray Fitzgerald	Gene Locklear	Chris Sabo
Ernie Baker	Wally Flager	James Lofton	Brad Salmon
Paul Bako	John Flavin	Howard Lohr	Gus Sandberg
Jack Baldschun	Curt Flood	Dale Long	Reggie L. Sanders
Mike Balenti	Carney Flynn	George Lowe	Roy G. Sanders
Junie Barnes	Doug Flynn	Larry Luebbers	Mo Sanford
Skeeter Barnes	Tom Foley	Eddie Lukon	Rafael Santo
Jimmy Barrett	Lew Fonseca	Donald Lutz	Domingo
Red Barrett	Steve Foster	Red Lutz	Dave Sappelt
Frank Baumholtz	Henry Fournier	Curt Lyons	Dane Sardinha
Harry Bay	Boob Fowler	Joe Mack	Manny Sarmiento
Dick Bayless	Chad Fox	Scott MacRae	Ralph Savidge
Ollie Beard	Howie Fox	Bobby Madritsch	Moe Savransky
Jim Beckman	Juan Francisco	Dan Mahoney	Pat Scantlebury
Jodie Beeler	Mike Frank	Danny Mahoney	Les Scarsella
Jim Begley	Todd Frazier	Bob P. Malloy	Bill Scherrer
Mel Behney	Justin Freeman	Jim Maloney	Admiral Schlei
Tim Belk	Benny Frey	Lefty Marr	George Schmees
Freddie Benavides	Emil Frisk	Armando Marsans	Karl Schnell
Johnny Bench	Joe Gaines	Clyde Mashore	Pete Schneider
Rube Benton	Lee Gamble	Bill Massey	Gene Schott
Bruce Berenyi	Harry Gaspar	Marcos Mateo	Barney Schreiber
Bill Bergen	Paul Gehrman	Lee May	Mike W. Schultz
William Bergolla	Frank Genins	Swat McCabe	Dick A. Scott
Bob Bescher	Ed Gerner	Jack McCarthy	Ed Scott
Kurt Bevacqua	Steve Gibralter	Tom P. McCarthy	Scott Scudder
Ewell Blackwell	Paul Gibson	Harry McCluskey	Charlie See
Jim Blackburn	Buddy Gilbert	Billy McCool	Diego Segui
Linc Blakely	Gus Gil	Frank McCormick	Hank Severeid
Cliff Blankenship	Duke Gillespie	Tex McDonald	Chris Sexton
Fred Blank	Haddie Gill	Will McEnaney	Socks Seybold
Jack Blott	Martin Glendon	Barney McFadden	Art Shamsky
Otto Bluege	Norm Glockson	Bill McGilvray	Eddie Shokes
Len Boehmer	Al Glossop	Dan McGinn	Johnny Siegle
Jim Bolger	Danny Godby	Howard McGraner	Al Silvera
Nino Bongiovanni	Lonnie Goldstein	Terry McGriff	Wayne Simpson
Aaron Boone	Jesse Gonder	(NULL) McGuire	Bert Sincock
Mel Bosser	Tony Gonzalez	Limb McKenry	Dick Sipek

Brad Boxberger	Keith Gordon	Kid McLaughlin	Dave Skaugstad
Jeff Branson	Mike L. Grace	Joe McManus	Walt Slagle
Ad Brennan	Tiny Graham	Roy McMillan	Chick Smith
Charlie Brewster	Yasmani Grandal	Herb McQuaid	Fred Smith
Al Bridwell	Didi Gregorius	Hal McRae	Jordan Smith
Gus Brittain	Frank Gregory	Rufus Meadows	Jud Smith
Ernie Broglio	Ken Griffey	Ray Medeiros	Milt Smith
Ben Broussard	Pat Griffin	Bob Meinke	Mike A. Smith
Joe Brovia	Ross Grimsley, Jr.	Karl Meister	Mike A. Smith
Keith Brown	Lee Grissom	Dutch Mele	Mike Elmer Smith
Marty Brown	Don Gross	Minnie Mendoza	Paul S. Smith
Scott Brown	Marv Gudat	Lloyd Merriman	Pop Smith
Tom Browning	Whitey Guese	Devin Mesoraco	Stephen Smitherman
Jay Bruce	Carlos Guevara	Ezra Midkiff	Ryan Snare
Will Brunson	Lefty Guise	Corky Miller	Mario Soto
Bob Buchanan	Don Gullett	Eddie R. Miller	Neftali Soto
Joseph Burns	Emil Haberer	Elmer Miller	Bob Spade
George Burpo	Leo Hafford	Eddie Milner	Jeff Sparks
Jack Bushelman	Noodles Hahn	Cotton Minahan	Tom Spencer
Ray Callahan	Jesse Haines	Steve Mingori	Harry Spies
Tom Cantwell	Charley Hall	Gino Minutelli	Harry Spilman
Bernie Carbo	Josh Hall	Mike Mitchell	Jerry Spradlin
Leo Cardenas	Billy Hamilton	Mike Modak	Harry Steinfeldt
Buddy Carlyle	Chris Hammond	Manny Montejo	Ben Stephens
Chet Carmichael	Lee Handley	Jeff Montgomery	Jeff Stevens
Chuck Carr	Ryan Hanigan	Dee Moore	Mark Stewart
Tom M. Carroll	Tommy Harper	Gene Moore, Jr.	Zach Stewart
Arnold Carter	Andy F. Harrington	Whitey Moore	Kurt Stillwell
Howie Carter	Jerry Harrington	Bob Moorhead	Archie Stimmel
Charlie Case	Bill M. Harris	Jake Mooty	Rocky Stone
Jack Cassini	Earl Harrist	Danny Morejon	Les Straker
Keefe Cato	Lenny Harris	Bill Moriarty	Gabby Street
Ike Caveney	Frank Harter	Jack Morrissey	Joe Stripp
Elio Chacon	Grady Hatton	Jo-Jo Morrissey	Drew Stubbs
Darrel Chaney	Lefty Hayden	Dustin Moseley	Clyde Sukeforth
Aroldis Chapman	Ben Hayes	Arnie Moser	Scott Sullivan
Calvin Chapman	Bob Hazle	Paul Moskau	Tom B. Sullivan
Charlie Chech	Mickey Heath	Chad Mottola	Glenn Sutko
Harry Chozen	Chink Heileman	Mike Mowrey	Evar Swanson
Cuckoo Christensen	Chris Heisey	Connie Murphy	Stan Swanson
Nick Christiani	Crese Heismann	Dick Murphy	Monty Swartz
Steve Christmas	Tommy Helms	Rob Murphy	Len Swormstedt
Tony Cingrani	Steve Henderson	Greasy Neale	Joe Szekely
Brady Clark	Bobby Henrich	Emmett Nelson	Jesse Tannehill
Lefty Clarke	Butch Henry	Mike Neu	Ted Tappe
Tommy Clarke	George Henry	Doc Newton	Danny Tartabull
Billy Clingman	Ernie Herbert	Bert Niehoff	Craig Tatum
Goat Cochran	Johnny Hetki	Bob Nieman	Eddie Taubensee
Robert Coello	Whitey Hilcher	Jack Niemes	Ben H. Taylor
Todd Coffey	Milt Hill	C.J. Nitkowski	Bruce Taylor
Geoff Combe	Bill Hinchman	Gary Nolan	George Tebeau
Jack Compton	Roy Hitt	John Noriega	Johnny Temple
Dave Concepcion	Bill Hobbs	Dan Norman	Scott Terry
Nardi Contreras	Dick Hoblitzel	Joe Nuxhall	Jack Theis
Cliff Cook	Mel Hoderlein	Rebel Oakes	Junior Thompson

Earl Cook	Trevor Hoffman	Pete J. O'Brien	Tug Thompson
Mickey Corcoran	Kenny Hogan	Fred Odwell	Paul Thormodsgard
Mark F. Corey	Marty Hogan	Ron Oester	Eddie Tiemeyer
Pop Corkhill	George Hogriever	John Oldham	Brett Tomko
Bob Coulson	Mul Holland	Joe Oliver	Dave Tomlin
John Courtright	Al Hollingsworth	Diomedes Olivo	Chuck Tompkins
Casey Cox	Chris Hook	Ray Olmedo	Felix Torres
Darron Cox	Buck Hooker	Logan Ondrusek	Cesar Tovar
Zack Cozart	Jay Hook	Paul O'Neill	Bill Tozer
Estel Crabtree	Hanson Horsey	Peaches O'Neill	Jeff Treadway
Harry Craft	Jeremy Horst	Luis Ordaz	Joe Trimble
Bill Cramer	Paul Householder	Ozzie Osborn	Justin Turner
Sam Crawford	Lefty Houtz	Pat Osburn	Twink Twining
Walker Cress	Jay Howell	Claude Osteen	George Twombly
Hughie Critz	Miller Huggins	Darrell Osteen	Maury Uhler
Lem Cross	Tom Hume	Jim O'Toole	Bob Usher
Tony Cuccinello	Eddie Hunter	Jimmy Outlaw	Chris Valaika
Mike Cuellar	Ken R. Hunt	Orval Overall	Corky Valentine
Johnny Cueto	Jerry Hurley	Eric Owens	Dave Van Gorder
Clarence Currie	Johnny Hutchings	Pat Pacillo	Farmer Vaughn
Ervin Curtis	Bob Ingersoll	Gene Packard	Emil Verban
Tom Daley	Larry Jacobus	Curtis Partch	Rube Vickers
Bill Dammann	Paul Janish	Dode Paskert	Pedro Villarreal
Kal Daniels	Kevin Jarvis	Frank Pastore	Pedro Viola
George Darby	Reggie Jefferson	Clare Patterson	Clyde Vollmer
Frank Dasso	Chief Johnson	Harry Pattee	Fritz Von Kolnitz
Dan Daub	Doc Johnston	Si Pauxtis	Joey Votto
Vic Davalillo	Mike N. Johnson	Don Pavletich	Rip Vowinkel
Dave Davenport	Ollie Johns	Bunny Pearce	Joe Wagner
Ted Davidson	Si Johnson	Jose Pena	Ryan Wagner
Dixie Davis	Bumpus Jones	Orlando Pena	Kermit Wahl
Eric Davis	Chris C. Jones	Antonio Perez	Don Wakamatsu
Lance Davis	Jeff R. Jones	Miguel Perez	Duane Walker
Peaches Davis	Lynn Jones	Tony Perez	Mysterious Walker
Wiley Davis	Tracy Jones	Harry Perkowski	Tony Walker
Travis Dawkins	Eddie Joost	Kent Peterson	Pat Watkins
Bill Dawley	Pinky Jorgensen	Ted Petoskey	Herm Wehmeier
Snake Deal	Frank Jude	Bill Pfann	Podge Weihe
Charlie DeArmond	Joe Just	Art Phelan	Don Werner
Arturo DeFreitas	Herb Juul	Denis Phipps	Dick West
Tommy de la Cruz	Mike Kahoe	Eddie Pick	George H. Wheeler
Enerio Del Rosario	Alex Kampouris	Ricky Pickett	Jack P. White
Chris Denorfia	John F. Kane	Herman Pillette	Al Wickland
Rob Dibble	Bob Katz	Vada Pinson	Jimmy Wiggs
Pedro Dibut	Austin Kearns	Ken Polivka	Milt Wilcox
Chris Dickerson	Cactus Keck	Harlin Pool	Denny Williams
Dutch Dietz	Alex Kellner	Scott Pose	Ken Williams
Bill Doak	Bill Kellogg	Wally Post	Scott Williamson
John Dobbs	Dutch Kemner	Ross Powell	Dan Wilson
Cozy J. Dolan	Fred Kendall	Jim Prendergast	Dewayne Wise
John Dolan	Kurt Kepshire	Joe W. Price	Whitey Wistert
Ed Donalds	Dan Kerwin	Eddie Priest	Ray Wolf
Pete Donohue	Ray King	Bill Prough	Harry Wolter
Dutch Dotterer	Ed Kippert	Tim Pugh	Bob Wood
Patsy Dougherty	Bobby Klaus	Harlan Pyle	Harry Wood

Astyanax Douglass	Ollie Klee	Mel D. Queen	Sam Woodruff
Jim Doyle	Ed Klieman	Charlie Rabe	Travis Wood
Chuck Dressen	Ted Kluszewski	Pat Ragan	Jimmy Wynn
Dan Driessen	Ray Knight	Chucho Ramos	Biff Wysong
Carl Druhot	Pete Knisely	Mike James Ramsey	Del J. Young
Jean Dubuc	Brian Koelling	Johnny Rawlings	Joel Youngblood
Frank Duffy	Mike Konnick	Rip Ragan	Pat Zachry
Dan Dumoulin	Jim Konstanty	Gary Redus	Benny Zientara
Grant Dunlap	John Koronka	Pokey Reese	
Adam Dunn	Mike Kosman	Mike Regan	
Scott Dunn	Charlie Krause	Dave Revering	

Boston Red Sox

Year/Team	OPW%	PW	PL	APW%	AW	AL	Diff+/-
1901 BOS	0.473 F	64	72	0.581	79	57	0.107
1902 BOS	0.418 F	57	79	0.562	77	60	0.144
1903 BOS	0.423 F	59	81	0.659 P	91	47	0.237
1904 BOS	0.486	75	79	0.617 P	95	59	0.131
1905 BOS	0.475	73	81	0.513	78	74	0.038
1906 BOS	0.344	53	101	0.318	49	105	-0.026
1907 BOS	0.443	68	86	0.396	59	90	-0.047
1908 BOS	0.544	84	70	0.487	75	79	-0.057
1909 BOS	0.557	86	68	0.583	88	63	0.025

franchID	OWAR	OWS	AWAR	AWS	WARdiff	WSdiff	P/D/W/F
1901 BOS	2.335	32.024	40.901	237.007	-38.566	-204.983	F
1902 BOS	2.271	29.529	38.734	231.002	-36.463	-201.473	F
1903 BOS	1.887	34.027	43.664	273.000	-41.777	-238.973	F
1904 BOS	6.354	75.513	41.874	284.995	-35.521	-209.483	
1905 BOS	10.993	98.662	33.893	233.999	-22.900	-135.337	
1906 BOS	11.324	107.579	15.815	147.000	-4.492	-39.420	
1907 BOS	20.054	115.044	25.717	176.996	-5.662	-61.953	
1908 BOS	24.902	174.278	36.007	224.994	-11.105	-50.716	
1909 BOS	36.690	244.326	37.418	264.003	-0.728	-19.677	

Legend: (P) = Pennant / Most Wins in League (D) = Division Winner (W) = Wild Card Winner (F) = Failed to Qualify

The Boston Americans joined the Major Leagues in 1901 as one of the eight original American League franchises. The team changed its moniker to the Red Sox in 1908. Based on the WS>20 frame of reference, the franchise has developed the second-most quality center fielders (56) and shortstops (34) and third-most quality left fielders (50) among the "Turn of the Century" franchises. The Red Sox leaders at those positions include Tris Speaker, Jim Fregosi and Ted Williams, respectively.

Boston has been ineffective in the development of its catchers. Carlton Fisk accounts for all of the WS>20 seasons for Red Sox backstops, save for a solo appearance by Rich Gedman. The team failed to produce any catchers of note until the Seventies. Furthermore, the organization's second basemen and starting pitchers never finished in the top three WS>10 totals for the "Turn of the Century" teams.

The Boston Americans endured losing records through the first seven seasons of its existence. The franchise's first winning record coincided with the changing of the team's nickname. The Red Sox accrued 84 victories in '08 and finished three games shy of the league-leading Athletics. Boston recorded 86 wins in the following year, but the squad was no match for

Philadelphia's 99-55 mark. George R. Stone collected the first batting title in team history as he delivered a .358 BA with 208 base knocks in 1906. Stone tallied 39 Win Shares and led the circuit in OBP (.417) and SLG (.501). Tris Speaker eclipsed the .300 mark in 10 straight seasons, batting .345 with 36 doubles, 96 runs scored and 36 steals per year from 1909-1918.

Year/Team	OPW%	PW	PL	APW%	AW	AL	Diff+/-
1910 BOS	0.545 F	84	70	0.529	81	72	-0.015
1911 BOS	0.597	92	62	0.510	78	75	-0.087
1912 BOS	0.667 P	103	51	0.691 P	105	47	0.024
1913 BOS	0.498	77	77	0.527	79	71	0.028
1914 BOS	0.541	83	71	0.595	91	62	0.054
1915 BOS	0.592	91	63	0.669 P	101	50	0.077
1916 BOS	0.547	84	70	0.591P	91	63	0.044
1917 BOS	0.631 P	97	57	0.592	90	62	-0.039
1918 BOS	0.539 F	69	59	0.595 P	75	51	0.057
1919 BOS	0.530 F	74	66	0.482	66	71	-0.048

franchID	OWAR	OWS	AWAR	AWS	WARdiff	WSdiff	P/D/W/F
1910 BOS	41.605	251.014	46.539	242.998	-4.934	8.016	F
1911 BOS	47.412	264.777	41.511	233.994	5.901	30.783	
1912 BOS	51.009	324.136	52.304	315.003	-1.295	9.132	P
1913 BOS	43.290	257.050	42.955	237.005	0.335	20.045	
1914 BOS	48.815	291.975	41.049	272.999	7.767	18.976	
1915 BOS	52.563	323.425	46.533	303.004	6.031	20.421	
1916 BOS	49.167	313.181	38.423	273.007	10.743	40.174	
1917 BOS	54.197	326.662	39.260	270.001	14.937	56.661	P
1918 BOS	43.400	286.947	31.631	224.997	11.769	61.950	F
1919 BOS	46.863	301.420	29.295	198.001	17.568	103.419	F

Boston boosted its win total to 92 games in 1911, but Philadelphia claimed its fourth consecutive pennant with a record of 101-53. The Sox finally overtook the A's in 1912 on the strength of 103 victories in conjunction with magnificent efforts from Tris Speaker and mound ace "Smokey" Joe Wood. Speaker (.383/10/90) earned MVP honors after leading the circuit in home runs, doubles (53), and OBP (.464) in 1912. The "Grey Eagle" amassed 52 Win Shares while batting .383 with 222 hits. Wood (34-5, 1.91), a 23-game winner in '11, topped the AL with 34 victories, 35 complete games in 38 starts and 10 shutouts. He tallied 44 Win Shares and placed fifth in the MVP voting. Dutch H. Leonard accrued 19 victories and fashioned an immaculate ERA of 0.96 along with a 0.886 WHIP for the '14 squad. Gavvy Cravath achieved three consecutive home run titles and hit .309 with 21 four-baggers and 114 ribbies from 1913-15. "Cactus Gavvy" (.341/19/128) placed runner-up in the 1913 MVP balloting. Boston lost the 1915 pennant to Detroit by a lone contest. Wood paced the League with 1.49 ERA, but his right arm could not withstand the rigors of pitching a full season. He was repurposed as an outfielder in 1918 and batted .366 as a part-time player in 1921.

Babe Ruth posted a record of 18-8 with a 2.44 ERA in his rookie year (1915). The southpaw hurled 9 shutouts and paced the circuit with a 1.75 ERA, winning 23 contests for the 1916 squad and the following season achieved personal bests with 24 wins and 35 complete games. The batting prowess of the "Bambino" was too great to ignore, so he split the next two seasons between the mound and the outfield. Excelling on the hill and in the batter's box, Ruth led the League in home runs as a part-time outfielder in 1918 and 1919, while completing 30 of 34 starts during this period. Speaker topped the leader boards in batting average (.386), OBP (.470), SLG (.502), hits (211), and doubles (41) in '16. The Red Sox were outdistanced by the Tigers, but the Beantowners redeemed themselves in 1917, overtaking Detroit by 5 games for its third pennant of the decade. With Ruth and Wood moving from the rotation to the outfield, the pitching staff was unable to meet the BFP requirements from 1918-1926.

Year/Team	OPW%	PW	PL	APW%	AW	AL	Diff+/-
1920 BOS	0.479 F	74	80	0.471	72	81	-0.009
1921 BOS	0.615 F	95	59	0.487	75	79	-0.128
1922 BOS	0.479 F	74	80	0.396	61	93	-0.083
1923 BOS	0.465 F	72	82	0.401	61	91	-0.063
1924 BOS	0.506 F	78	76	0.431	66	87	-0.075
1925 BOS	0.410 F	63	91	0.309	47	105	-0.101
1926 BOS	0.456 F	70	84	0.301	46	107	-0.155
1927 BOS	0.463	71	83	0.331	51	103	-0.132
1928 BOS	0.504	78	76	0.373	57	96	-0.132
1929 BOS	0.463	71	83	0.377	58	96	-0.086

franchID	OWAR	OWS	AWAR	AWS	WARdiff	WSdiff	P/D/W/F
1920 BOS	69.361	392.093	32.710	215.998	36.651	176.095	F
1921 BOS	63.169	374.969	26.492	225.005	36.678	149.964	F
1922 BOS	46.267	334.419	14.655	183.009	31.612	151.410	F
1923 BOS	65.105	374.123	13.481	183.000	51.624	191.123	F
1924 BOS	60.559	355.844	31.217	201.001	29.342	154.843	F
1925 BOS	33.035	234.633	12.678	141.004	20.357	93.628	F
1926 BOS	38.915	258.553	12.614	137.999	26.301	120.554	F
1927 BOS	32.643	230.713	13.744	153.000	18.899	77.713	
1928 BOS	29.777	218.346	19.138	171.000	10.638	47.346	
1929 BOS	30.091	226.404	17.875	173.995	12.216	52.409	

Tris Speaker continued his mastery of opposing hurlers throughout the first half of the "Roaring Twenties," supplying a .373 BA with 47 doubles and 106 runs scored per year from 1920-25. He paced the League in two-base hits over four consecutive seasons (1920-23) and established career-bests with 59 doubles, 130 RBI and a .610 SLG during the 1923 season.

Ruth blasted 54 long balls and batted .373 in his first full season as an outfielder in 1920. For an encore, the "Sultan of Swat" walloped 59 round-trippers and established individual marks for RBI (171) and runs scored (177). He won the MVP Award and tallied his highest Win Shares total (54) in '23, setting personal bests with 205 base hits, 45 doubles, 170 walks and a .393 batting average. The slugger collected a batting title in the subsequent season with a .378 mark.

Larry Gardner knocked in 100+ runs and eclipsed the .300 mark in back-to-back seasons (1920-21). Ray "Bummer" Grimes posted a .354 BA and drove in 99 runs for the '22 team. In a three-year stretch covering 1923-25, Jack Fournier contributed a .345 BA, 24 jacks and 116 ribbies per season. Boston and Cleveland finished in a tie for last-place in 1927 despite Ruth's majestic 60-homer campaign. The "Bambino" supplied a .355 BA, 47 home runs, 134 RBI, 136 runs scored and 124 bases on balls per season during the 1920's. He surpassed 50 home runs in a season on four occasions.

Year/Team	OPW%	PW	PL	APW%	AW	AL	Diff+/-
1930 BOS	0.466	72	82	0.338	52	102	-0.128
1931 BOS	0.471	73	81	0.408	62	90	-0.063
1932 BOS	0.413	64	90	0.279	43	111	-0.134
1933 BOS	0.500 F	77	77	0.423	63	86	-0.077
1934 BOS	0.565 F	87	67	0.500	76	76	-0.065
1935 BOS	0.489 F	75	79	0.510	78	75	0.020
1936 BOS	0.459 F	71	83	0.481	74	80	0.021
1937 BOS	0.501 F	77	77	0.526	80	72	0.025
1938 BOS	0.479	74	80	0.591	88	61	0.111
1939 BOS	0.511	79	75	0.589	89	62	0.078

franchID	OWAR	OWS	AWAR	AWS	WARdiff	WSdiff	P/D/W/F
1930 BOS	33.762	209.073	13.794	155.997	19.968	53.075	
1931 BOS	32.501	230.903	19.105	185.996	13.396	44.907	
1932 BOS	28.555	204.367	11.482	129.001	17.074	75.366	
1933 BOS	51.691	256.830	29.180	189.000	22.510	67.830	F
1934 BOS	39.082	251.168	31.827	227.998	7.255	23.170	F
1935 BOS	30.205	222.463	34.832	233.997	-4.626	-11.534	F
1936 BOS	21.626	193.321	36.346	221.998	-14.720	-28.677	F
1937 BOS	28.293	234.869	38.226	240.001	-9.933	-5.132	F
1938 BOS	32.805	222.853	43.252	263.995	-10.447	-41.142	
1939 BOS	29.183	241.660	42.173	266.999	-12.990	-25.339	

Ruth achieved his twelfth home run title in 1931, batting .373 with 199 hits and 46 circuit clouts while driving in 163 runs. The Sox suffered through another talent drought in the mid-1930's. Moose Solters enjoyed a three-year run during which he averaged .311 with 44 two-base knocks and 118 ribbies. Red Ruffing was the lone beacon of hope on the mound, executing four consecutive 20-win campaigns (1936-39), furnishing a 3.29 ERA and placing in the top-five MVP vote getters in '38 and '39. Boston finally managed to surpass the .500 mark in 1939, which coincided with the arrival of Ted Williams. "The Kid" delivered a .327 BA with 31 clouts and drove in a record-setting 145 runs during his rookie campaign. He drew 107 bases on balls, scored 131 runs and finished fourth in the MVP balloting. Bobby Doerr contributed a .318 BA in his second season as a full-timer.

Win Shares > 20	Single-Season	1920-1939
Ray Grimes - 1B (BOS) x2	Babe Ruth - RF (BOS) x11	Red Ruffing - SP (BOS) x6
Billy Rogell - SS (BOS) x3	Ted Williams - RF (BOS)	Danny MacFayden - SP (BOS)
Moose Solters - LF (BOS)	George Pipgras - SP (BOS)	

Year/Team	OPW%	PW	PL	APW%	AW	AL	Diff+/-
1940 BOS	0.518	80	74	0.532	82	72	0.014
1941 BOS	0.572 P	88	66	0.545	84	70	-0.027
1942 BOS	0.623 P	96	58	0.612	93	59	-0.011
1943 BOS	0.438	68	86	0.447	68	84	0.009
1944 BOS	0.528	81	73	0.500	77	77	-0.028
1945 BOS	0.437	67	87	0.461	71	83	0.024
1946 BOS	0.610 P	94	60	0.675 P	104	50	0.066
1947 BOS	0.528	81	73	0.539	83	71	0.011
1948 BOS	0.550	85	69	0.619	96	59	0.069
1949 BOS	0.549	84	70	0.623	96	58	0.075

franchID	OWAR	OWS	AWAR	AWS	WARdiff	WSdiff	P/D/W/F
1940 BOS	33.180	240.954	40.922	245.997	-7.742	-5.043	
1941 BOS	52.304	274.892	46.044	249.001	6.260	25.890	P

Year/Team							
1942 BOS	52.133	302.712	49.580	278.994	2.554	23.718	P
1943 BOS	29.297	208.873	27.605	203.998	1.693	4.875	
1944 BOS	41.309	231.744	38.218	230.999	3.091	0.745	
1945 BOS	26.376	186.551	26.968	212.997	-0.592	-26.446	
1946 BOS	56.132	313.743	51.043	312.005	5.089	1.738	P
1947 BOS	46.452	269.194	39.982	248.996	6.470	20.199	
1948 BOS	36.813	265.615	47.833	288.001	-11.020	-22.385	
1949 BOS	39.556	248.411	53.811	287.999	-14.255	-39.588	

The Red Sox earned consecutive pennants in 1941-42, outlasting the Yankees by two games in both instances. Ted Williams, also known as "The Splendid Splinter" and "Teddy Ballgame," destroyed American League pitching in '41, becoming the last player to bat over .400 for a single-season through 2013. He paced the junior circuit with a .406 BA, 37 round-trippers, 135 runs scored and 147 bases on balls, while collecting the first of six batting titles. In 1942, Williams captured the Triple Crown with a .356 BA, 36 moon-shots, and 137 RBI. Despite his tremendous offensive output, Williams came up short in the MVP balloting.

Johnny Pesky delivered a .331 BA and topped the charts with 205 hits in his rookie campaign ('42). He placed third in the MVP balloting and went on to serve in the Navy through 1945. Stan Spence set career-highs with a .323 BA and 203 base hits, and paced the circuit with 15 triples. Tex Hughson (22-6, 2.59) led the League in wins and complete games (22). Bill Voiselle tallied 21 victories and a league-best 161 strikeouts for the '44 crew, but the Sox were relegated to second-division status while Williams and Pesky served in the military.Boston executed a 27-win turnaround in the standings after the war ended. The Sox clinched the club's third pennant of the decade by a two-game margin over Detroit. On the mound, Dave "Boo" Ferriss notched 25 victories, while Hughson collected 20 wins and completed 21 of 35 starts in 1946. Williams (.342/38/123) finally claimed MVP honors, as he amassed 50 Win Shares. Doerr drove in 116 runs and placed third in the MVP race.

Pesky led the League with 200+ base hits in back-to-back seasons (1946-47). From 1942-1951, "The Needle" averaged .315 with 109 runs scored. Larry Jansen (21-5, 3.16) merited a runner-up position in the 1947 ROY voting. Dom DiMaggio supplied a .304 average with 34 doubles and 124 runs scored from 1948-1951. "The Little Professor" coaxed 101 walks and scored 127 times, but the Sox ended the season eight games behind the Tribe in '48. Mel Parnell (25-7, 2.77) topped the League leader board in victories and complete games (27) and finished fourth in the AL MVP race. Williams produced back-to-back batting titles in 1947-48 and earned his second MVP Award in '49 with a .343 BA, 43 long balls and 159 ribbies. He pummelled AL hurlers during the 1940's, hitting .356 with 39 two-baggers, 33 homers, 128 RBI, 136 runs scored and 142 walks per year. The Red Sox and Athletics tied for second place in '49, both only two games behind the Indians.

Year/Team	OPW%	PW	PL	APW%	AW	AL	Diff+/-
1950 BOS	0.558 P	86	68	0.610	94	60	0.053
1951 BOS	0.498	77	77	0.565	87	67	0.067
1952 BOS	0.481	74	80	0.494	76	78	0.013
1953 BOS	0.477	73	81	0.549	84	69	0.072
1954 BOS	0.446	69	85	0.448	69	85	0.002
1955 BOS	0.490	75	79	0.545	84	70	0.056
1956 BOS	0.485	75	79	0.545	84	70	0.061
1957 BOS	0.458	71	83	0.532	82	72	0.074
1958 BOS	0.433	67	87	0.513	79	75	0.080
1959 BOS	0.432	67	87	0.487	75	79	0.055

franchID	OWAR	OWS	AWAR	AWS	WARdiff	WSdiff	P/D/W/F
1950 BOS	41.018	251.097	50.245	282.005	-9.226	-30.909	P
1951 BOS	34.692	214.744	43.569	260.998	-8.877	-46.254	
1952 BOS	25.934	198.868	31.688	227.997	-5.754	-29.129	
1953 BOS	28.482	210.886	36.350	251.994	-7.868	-41.108	
1954 BOS	34.099	205.846	42.691	252.008	-8.592	-46.162	
1955 BOS	32.030	193.357	42.691	252.008	-10.661	-58.651	
1956 BOS	35.502	211.091	42.353	252.003	-6.850	-40.912	
1957 BOS	32.028	197.188	39.500	245.996	-7.472	-48.808	
1958 BOS	25.029	187.489	36.942	236.998	-11.913	-49.509	
1959 BOS	28.474	194.075	35.391	224.999	-6.917	-30.924	

The Sox squeaked past the Indians by a single game to take the American League pennant in 1950. Boston endured a pennant drought that lasted for 34 seasons, winning only four division titles in that span. Walt Dropo enjoyed a fine rookie season, setting the bar with 144 RBI as a first-year player. "Moose" batted .322 with 34 jacks and 101 runs scored and received his lone All-Star invitation. DiMaggio led the circuit with 131 runs scored and achieved a personal best with a .328 batting average. Doerr (.294/27/120) tied DiMaggio for the League lead in triples (11), tied his career-best with 27 dingers and set individual records for runs scored (103) and RBI (120).

Jansen accrued 21 victories for the '51 squad after posting a league-best 1.065 WHIP during the previous season. Williams missed most of the '52 and '53 seasons due to military service in the Korean War. Frank Sullivan posted league-leading totals with 18 wins and 260 innings pitched in '55 and topped the charts with a 1.055 WHIP in '57. The "Olde Towne Team" suffered four consecutive last-place finishes (1956-59). Charlie Maxwell supplied a .326 BA with 28 dingers in '56 and went on to set personal bests with 31 homers and 95 ribbies during the 1959 season. Tom Brewer chipped in with 19 wins for the '56 crew.

Williams swatted 38 long balls and threatened the .400 mark again in 1957 before settling for a .388 average and his fifth batting crown. In the subsequent year, "Thumper" earned his final title with a .328 BA. The Red Sox experienced a high turnover rate in the front office with four General Managers holding the position from 1958-1962. In spite of the instability, the Boston executives managed to acquire Carl Yastrzemski (1958), Jim Fregosi, Wilbur Wood (1960) and Rico Petrocelli (1961) as amateur free agents.

Win Shares > 20	Single-Season	1940-1959
Walt Dropo - 1B (BOS)	Dom DiMaggio - CF (BOS) x7	Dave Ferriss - SP (BOS) x2
Bobby Doerr - 2B (BOS) x8	Stan Spence - CF (BOS) x5	Larry Jansen - SP (BOS) x3
George Myatt - 2B (BOS)	Jim Piersall - CF (BOS) x2	Mel Parnell - SP (BOS) x4
Johnny Pesky - SS (BOS) x4	Jim Bagby Jr. - SP (BOS)	Mickey McDermott - SP (BOS)
Johnny Pesky - 3B (BOS) x2	Tex Hughson - SP (BOS) x2	Frank Sullivan - SP (BOS) x2
Ted Williams - LF (BOS) x14	Bill Voiselle - SP (BOS)	Tom Brewer - SP (BOS)
Charlie Maxwell - LF (BOS) x2		

Year/Team	OPW%	PW	PL	APW%	AW	AL	Diff+/-
1960 BOS	0.442	68	86	0.422	65	89	-0.020
1961 BOS	0.440	71	91	0.469	76	86	0.029
1962 BOS	0.471	76	86	0.475	76	84	0.004
1963 BOS	0.446	72	90	0.472	76	85	0.026
1964 BOS	0.441	71	91	0.444	72	90	0.004
1965 BOS	0.420	68	94	0.383	62	100	-0.037
1966 BOS	0.415	67	95	0.444	72	90	0.030
1967 BOS	0.535	87	75	0.568 P	92	70	0.033

1968 BOS	0.515	83	79	0.531	86	76	0.016
1969 BOS	0.514 D	83	79	0.537	87	75	0.023

franchID	OWAR	OWS	AWAR	AWS	WARdiff	WSdiff	P/D/W/F
1960 BOS	30.197	186.338	32.536	195.002	-2.340	-8.664	
1961 BOS	24.428	171.555	28.900	227.997	-4.472	-56.441	
1962 BOS	24.120	178.602	34.986	228.001	-10.866	-49.400	
1963 BOS	28.468	176.742	38.759	227.998	-10.290	-51.256	
1964 BOS	32.144	179.511	35.222	216.001	-3.078	-36.490	
1965 BOS	34.475	180.990	37.734	185.997	-3.259	-5.007	
1966 BOS	25.955	195.249	31.628	216.000	-5.673	-20.750	
1967 BOS	43.455	276.923	46.157	276.002	-2.703	0.922	
1968 BOS	30.128	235.410	37.550	257.999	-7.422	-22.589	
1969 BOS	31.375	234.495	40.808	260.997	-9.433	-26.502	D

The Red Sox continued to wallow in the second division as the franchise flopped through six straight last-place finishes (1961-66). Dick Radatz topped the circuit in saves twice and posted a 2.57 ERA and 1.111 WHIP from 1962-65. Albie Pearson batted .304 and earned his lone All-Star invitation in 1963 after scoring 115 runs during the previous campaign. Tony Conigliaro slugged a league-high 32 moon-shots in '65 while George C. Scott swatted 27 big-flies in his rookie season (1966).

Carl Yastrzemski collected the first of three batting titles in 1963, pacing the AL with a .321 BA, .418 OBP, 180 hits, 40 doubles and 95 walks. "Yaz" accomplished the Triple Crown in '67, delivering a .326 BA with 44 round-trippers and 121 RBI. He also accrued 42 Win Shares and led the League in hits, runs, OBP, and SLG en route to the MVP Award. Jim Lonborg (22-9, 3.16) received the Cy Young Award after pacing the circuit in wins and strikeouts (246). The Red Sox reversed the franchise's fortunes and settled for second place, seven games behind the Twins.

GM Dick O'Connell orchestrated four of the top six Amateur Drafts in the history of the franchise (based on Career Total Win Shares and Career Total WAR). His draft choices included Carlton Fisk ('67), Cecil Cooper ('68), Dwight Evans ('69), Jim Rice ('71), Fred Lynn ('73) and Wade Boggs ('76). Jim Fregosi topped the League with 13 triples, and Glenn Beckert scored 98 runs for the '68 squad. Wilbur Wood led the AL in relief appearances for three consecutive years and notched 13 wins and 16 saves with a 1.87 ERA. Boston emerged victorious from a four-way battle for the AL Eastern division title in 1969. Rico Petrocelli clubbed 40 circuit clouts and plated 97 runs while amassing 36 Win Shares. "Yaz" matched Petrocelli's home run output and knocked in 111 runs.

Year/Team	OPW%	PW	PL	APW%	AW	AL	Diff+/-
1970 BOS	0.528	85	77	0.537	87	75	0.009
1971 BOS	0.512	83	79	0.525	85	77	0.013
1972 BOS	0.547	89	73	0.548	85	70	0.001
1973 BOS	0.513	83	79	0.549	89	73	0.036
1974 BOS	0.545 D	88	74	0.519	84	78	-0.026
1975 BOS	0.576 D	93	69	0.594 D	95	65	0.018
1976 BOS	0.494	80	82	0.512	83	79	0.019
1977 BOS	0.554 D	90	72	0.602	97	64	0.048
1978 BOS	0.489	79	83	0.607	99	64	0.118
1979 BOS	0.533	86	76	0.569	91	69	0.036

franchID	OWAR	OWS	AWAR	AWS	WARdiff	WSdiff	P/D/W/F
1970 BOS	34.609	232.899	44.331	261.004	-9.722	-28.105	
1971 BOS	33.010	234.648	40.086	254.997	-7.076	-20.349	
1972 BOS	31.056	218.404	40.277	254.995	-9.221	-36.591	
1973 BOS	30.668	198.097	42.057	267.008	-11.389	-68.911	

1974 BOS	33.062	217.914	37.555	252.008	-4.493	-34.094	D
1975 BOS	34.424	233.886	41.970	285.004	-7.546	-51.118	D
1976 BOS	33.008	214.099	40.839	249.000	-7.831	-34.902	
1977 BOS	32.757	219.701	50.158	291.000	-17.401	-71.299	D
1978 BOS	33.630	217.214	46.258	296.996	-12.628	-79.782	
1979 BOS	36.005	218.895	48.239	272.996	-12.235	-54.101	

Yastrzemski (.329/40/102) set individual marks in batting average, runs scored (125) and stolen bases (23) as he earned a fourth-place finish in the 1970 AL MVP race. Fregosi produced career-highs with 33 two-baggers, 22 taters, 82 ribbies and 95 runs scored. Conigliaro established personal bests with 36 moon-shots and 116 RBI, while Amos Otis chipped in with a league-leading 36 doubles. Despite the fireworks on offense, the Sox finished in third place, four games behind the Yankees. Otis paced the circuit with 52 stolen bases and supplied a career-best .301 BA for the '71 BoSox. Wood earned top-5 finishes in the Cy Young balloting for three straight seasons. From 1971-75, "Wilbah" delivered 21 wins, 20 complete games, 45 starts, 336 innings pitched, a 3.08 ERA and 1.184 WHIP per year. Carlton Fisk legged out a league-high 9 triples and cranked 22 big-flies en route to the 1972 AL ROY Award. The Orioles outlasted the Red Sox by three games for the American League Eastern division crown. Bill "Spaceman" Lee (17-11, 2.75) merited his lone All-Star selection in '73 and accrued 17 victories in three successive seasons (1973-75).

Boston earned three division titles in four years (1974-77), yielding the flag to Baltimore in 1976. Fred Lynn (.331/21/105) merited MVP and ROY honors in 1975, topping the charts with 47 two-base knocks, 103 runs scored and a .566 SLG. Jim Rice (.309/22/102) placed runner-up for the ROY Award. Scott led the League with 36 home runs and 109 RBI. Otis paced the circuit with 40 doubles in '76. Fisk (.315/26/102) supplied personal-bests in batting average and runs scored (106) for the '77 crew. Rice topped the home run charts in back-to-back campaigns (1977-78) and earned the MVP Award in '78, pacing the circuit with 15 triples, 46 four-baggers, 139 RBI and 213 base hits. Bob Stanley vultured 15 relief wins and fashioned a career-best 2.60 ERA. Boston suffered through a losing campaign and posted the worst WSdiff (-86) in team history.

Lynn (.333/39/122) notched his lone batting title while leading the AL in OBP (.423) and SLG (.637). He accumulated 34 Win Shares, crossed home plate 116 times and placed fourth in the MVP balloting. Otis accomplished 12 successive seasons above 10 Win Shares while Lynn achieved the feat 11 times as the Red Sox center fielders totaled 36 WS>10 campaigns from 1970-1989. Cecil Cooper averaged .320 with 37 doubles, 25 round-trippers and 107 RBI per season from 1979-1983. Rice (.325/39/130) continued to mash the opposition, but the Brew Crew outdistanced the Sox by four games in 1979.

Win Shares > 20	Single-Season	1960-1979
George C. Scott - 1B (BOS) x4	Carlton Fisk - C (BOS) x6	Tony Conigliaro - RF (BOS)
Carl Yastrzemski - 1B (BOS) x3	Carl Yastrzemski - LF (BOS) x9	Jim Rice - DH (BOS)
Cecil Cooper - 1B (BOS) x5	Jim Rice - LF (BOS) x6	Wilbur Wood - SP (BOS) x3
Mike Andrews - 2B (BOS) x2	Albie Pearson - CF (BOS) x2	Bill F. Lee - SP (BOS)
Glenn Beckert - 2B (BOS)	Carl Yastrzemski - CF (BOS)	Jim Lonborg - SP (BOS)
Rico Petrocelli - 3B (BOS) x2	Amos Otis - CF (BOS) x8	Lynn McGlothen - SP (BOS)
	Fred Lynn - CF (BOS) x5	Dick Radatz - RP (BOS) x3

Year/Team	OPW%	PW	PL	APW%	AW	AL	Diff+/-
1980 BOS	0.495	80	82	0.519	83	77	0.023
1981 BOS	0.516	84	78	0.546	59	49	0.030
1982 BOS	0.517	84	78	0.549	89	73	0.032
1983 BOS	0.522	85	77	0.481	78	84	-0.041

Year/Team							
1984 BOS	0.519	84	78	0.531	86	76	0.012
1985 BOS	0.569 P	92	70	0.500	81	81	-0.069
1986 BOS	0.499	81	81	0.590 P	95	66	0.091
1987 BOS	0.471	76	86	0.481	78	84	0.011
1988 BOS	0.557 P	90	72	0.549 D	89	73	-0.008
1989 BOS	0.497	81	81	0.512	83	79	0.015

franchID	OWAR	OWS	AWAR	AWS	WARdiff	WSdiff	P/D/W/F
1980 BOS	35.088	224.029	43.376	249.004	-8.288	-24.975	
1981 BOS	25.540	164.832	29.090	177.002	-3.550	-12.170	
1982 BOS	36.303	249.627	40.291	266.998	-3.988	-17.371	
1983 BOS	39.809	254.070	33.581	233.992	6.228	20.078	
1984 BOS	35.654	215.156	44.156	258.003	-8.503	-42.846	
1985 BOS	48.209	242.836	48.593	243.000	-0.384	-0.163	P
1986 BOS	38.999	254.355	45.466	285.001	-6.468	-30.645	
1987 BOS	36.456	217.811	42.394	234.002	-5.937	-16.191	
1988 BOS	43.799	235.592	54.008	266.998	-10.208	-31.406	P
1989 BOS	33.323	220.148	47.563	249.006	-14.240	-28.858	

Ben Oglivie dialed long distance 41 times, topping the American League in 1980. He also set personal records with a .304 average, 118 RBI and 94 runs. Cooper posted individual bests with a .352 BA and 219 base knocks and topped the AL with 122 RBI in '80. Dwight Evans tied for the League lead with 22 homers in '81. "Dewey" supplied 30 doubles, 26 homers, 93 ribbies, 95 walks and 98 runs per year from 1981-89. Cooper launched 32 moon-shots in 1982 and drove in 126 runs in the following season. Lynn drilled 38 doubles and batted .299 in '82. He competed in his ninth straight All-Star game in the subsequent season. Rice produced a .304 BA with 29 home runs and 106 ribbies from 1975-1986. He led the American League with 39 four-baggers and 126 RBI during the 1983 season.

Wade Boggs accumulated five batting titles in the Eighties, hitting .357 or better in each campaign. The "Chicken Man" began a streak of seven consecutive seasons with 200+ base hits in 1983 and led the League in OBP for each season except '84. His single-season batting averages remained above .300 until he struggled through an off-year in '92. During a ten-year span beginning in 1982, Boggs batted at a .345 clip with 40 doubles and 100 runs scored per year. He delivered his highest batting average (.368) and hit total (240), guiding the Red Sox to the pennant in 1985. John Tudor (21-8, 1.93) earned a runner-up finish in the Cy Young balloting and topped the charts with 10 shutouts and a 0.938 WHIP. Dwight Evans garnered his eighth Gold Glove Award and topped the circuit with 114 walks. Carlton Fisk slugged a career-best 37 long balls and knocked in 107 runs. Boston cultivated four legitimate catchers (Fisk, Ernie Whitt, Rich Gedman and Bo Diaz), leading the Majors with 24 WS>10 seasons in the 1980's.

Roger Clemens (24-4, 2.48) swept the 1986 AL MVP and Cy Young balloting. "Rocket" topped the chart in victories, ERA and WHIP (0.969). Don Aase delivered a 2.98 ERA with 34 saves and received his lone All-Star invitation. Clemens garnered another Cy Young Award in 1987 as he led the League with 20 wins, 18 complete games, and 7 shutouts. Mike "Gator" Greenwell furnished a .328 BA in his inaugural campaign. The Sox seized the team's second pennant of the decade by one win over the Yankees in '88. Boggs posted a .366 BA and scored a career-high 128 runs. Greenwell (.325/22/119) rapped 39 two-base knocks and placed runner-up in the MVP balloting. Clemens hurled 8 shutouts and whiffed 291 batters.

Year/Team	OPW%	PW	PL	APW%	AW	AL	Diff+/-
1990 BOS	0.532	86	76	0.543 D	88	74	0.011
1991 BOS	0.482	78	84	0.519	84	78	0.037
1992 BOS	0.491	80	82	0.451	73	89	-0.040
1993 BOS	0.486	79	83	0.494	80	82	0.008

1994 BOS	0.576 P	93	69	0.470	54	61	-0.106
1995 BOS	0.511 F	83	79	0.597 D	86	58	0.087
1996 BOS	0.533 D	86	76	0.525	85	77	-0.008
1997 BOS	0.583 P	94	68	0.481	78	84	-0.102
1998 BOS	0.560 P	91	71	0.568 W	92	70	0.008
1999 BOS	0.538 D	87	75	0.580 W	94	68	0.042

franchID	OWAR	OWS	AWAR	AWS	WARdiff	WSdiff	P/D/W/F
1990 BOS	40.059	245.962	45.283	263.997	-5.224	-18.035	
1991 BOS	35.894	233.589	41.720	251.998	-5.826	-18.409	
1992 BOS	38.359	245.402	30.645	219.005	7.715	26.397	
1993 BOS	**46.725**	**281.952**	36.077	240.007	10.649	41.946	
1994 BOS	**40.667**	**239.370**	23.617	162.004	17.050	77.366	P
1995 BOS	42.139	275.458	44.109	258.002	-1.970	17.456	F
1996 BOS	**56.035**	**317.675**	40.848	254.999	15.187	62.676	D
1997 BOS	**63.795**	**317.766**	41.418	234.001	22.377	83.765	P
1998 BOS	**58.555**	292.788	46.160	275.994	12.394	16.794	P
1999 BOS	**55.500**	298.980	49.180	282.008	6.321	16.972	D

Boston clashed with Toronto late in the 1990 season, with the Blue Jays emerging as the AL Eastern division champions by a single victory. Clemens (21-6, 1.93) topped the ERA charts and earned a runner-up finish in the Cy Young race. Jeff Bagwell earned the ROY Award in '91 and produced a .320 BA two years later. The 1992 squad featured Brady Anderson (53 SB and 100 runs) and Curt Schilling (2.35 ERA and 0.990 WHIP). The Red Sox paced the American League in oWAR and oWS in every season from 1993-97 with the exception of 1995 when the Boston pitching staff failed to meet the BFP requirements. Bagwell (.368/39/116) merited MVP honors as he paced the circuit in RBI, runs scored (104) and SLG (.750) in 1994. Boston took the American League pennant by six games over Baltimore. John Valentin supplied individual bests with 27 dingers, 102 RBI and 20 steals in '95. Mo Vaughn claimed the AL MVP hardware after leading the circuit with 126 RBI.

Ellis Burks (.344/40/128) enjoyed a banner year in '96, placing third in the MVP voting. He established personal bests in every major offensive category, scored a league-leading 142 runs and slugged at a .639 clip. Anderson belted 50 round-trippers, knocked in 110 runs and scored 117 times. Vaughn (.326/44/143) established career highs in home runs, RBI, hits (207) and runs (118). The "Hit Dog" produced a .305 BA with 35 blasts and 111 ribbies from 1993-2000. The Red Sox claimed the division title by a six-game cushion over the Yankees. Clemens reveled in his career resurgence after several sub-par seasons in the mid-1990's. "Rocket" collected back-to-back Cy Young Awards in 1997-98 and led the League in strikeouts and ERA in both campaigns. Bagwell joined the "40/30" club, plated a career-high 135 runners and placed third in the MVP balloting. Valentin batted .306 and led the junior circuit with 47 two-base knocks. Nomar Garciaparra (.306/30/98) led the League with 209 hits and 11 triples, en route to winning the 1997 AL ROY Award.

Boston surpassed 90 wins and accomplished back-to-back pennants in 1997-98. Schilling whiffed at least 300 opposing batsmen in both seasons. "Nomah" batted .323 and set individual records with 35 circuit clouts and 122 ribbies during the 1998 season. Vaughn delivered his best batting average (.337) along with 205 hits and 40 jacks. In 1999 Bagwell (.304/42/126) topped the charts with 143 runs and 149 bases on balls, and swiped 30 bags. He produced a .301 BA with 36 doubles, 37 home runs, 116 RBI, 116 runs scored and 107 walks per year from 1994-2003. Garciaparra delivered consecutive batting titles in 1999-2000, hitting at a .357 clip in '99.

Year/Team	OPW%	PW	PL	APW%	AW	AL	Diff+/-
2000 BOS	0.576 P	93	69	0.525	85	77	-0.051
2001 BOS	0.527	85	77	0.509	82	79	-0.017
2002 BOS	0.507	82	80	0.574	93	69	0.067
2003 BOS	0.529	86	76	0.586 W	95	67	0.057
2004 BOS	0.537 D	87	75	0.605 W	98	64	0.068
2005 BOS	0.462	75	87	0.586 W	95	67	0.125
2006 BOS	0.551 P	89	73	0.531	86	76	-0.020
2007 BOS	0.510 W	83	79	0.593 P	96	66	0.082
2008 BOS	0.560 P	91	71	0.586 W	95	67	0.026
2009 BOS	0.529 D	86	76	0.586 W	95	67	0.058
2010 BOS	0.552	90	72	0.549	89	73	-0.003
2011 BOS	0.568 W	92	70	0.556	90	72	-0.012
2012 BOS	0.472	77	85	0.426	69	93	-0.047
2013 BOS	0.571 P	92	70	0.599 P	97	65	0.028

franchID	OWAR	OWS	AWAR	AWS	WARdiff	WSdiff	P/D/W/F
2000 BOS	50.358	278.596	41.134	254.994	9.224	23.602	P
2001 BOS	38.612	236.725	44.270	245.991	-5.659	-9.266	
2002 BOS	44.511	250.418	54.357	279.001	-9.846	-28.583	
2003 BOS	42.195	229.434	59.525	284.997	-17.330	-55.563	
2004 BOS	39.572	225.448	56.009	294.000	-16.438	-68.552	D
2005 BOS	31.985	220.133	47.271	284.998	-15.286	-64.865	
2006 BOS	43.300	268.792	39.188	258.014	4.112	10.778	P
2007 BOS	38.511	262.704	53.368	288.006	-14.856	-25.302	W
2008 BOS	47.361	264.550	52.600	284.999	-5.239	-20.449	P
2009 BOS	41.133	263.647	48.796	285.004	-7.663	-21.358	D
2010 BOS	42.852	234.380	42.248	247.459	0.604	-13.079	
2011 BOS	47.129	253.089	47.894	254.606	-0.765	-1.517	W
2012 BOS	32.425	213.861	26.245	204.236	6.180	9.625	
2013 BOS	42.852	246.854	56.132	290.998	-13.280	-44.144	P

Boston maintained its success into the first decade of the 2000's, making six playoff appearances and leading the AL in oWAR on two occasions. The Red Sox paced the Major Leagues in player development at first base (20 WS>10 seasons) and shortstop (19 WS>10 seasons). Bagwell set career bests with 152 runs scored and 47 four-baggers. Garciaparra drilled 51 doubles and paced the circuit with a .372 batting average. The Sox secured another pennant as the Orioles trailed by ten games in the final standings. Schilling placed runner-up in the Cy Young balloting in '01, '02, and '04. "Schill" averaged 22 victories, 271 strikeouts, a 3.15 ERA and a 1.034 WHIP in those campaigns. Clemens achieved Cy Young honors after posting a 20-3 record in 2001. David Eckstein swiped 29 bags in his rookie year (2001) and tallied 107 runs scored in his sophomore season. Bagwell (.288/39/130) exceeded 100 runs scored and 100 RBI for the sixth straight year (1996-2001).

Garciaparra whacked a league-leading 56 doubles and drove in 120 runs in '02. Clemens (18-4, 2.98) was honored with his seventh Cy Young Award in 2004. Boston returned to the playoffs with a division title in '04, holding off Toronto and Baltimore by a three-game margin. The "Olde Towne Team" earned playoff berths in four consecutive seasons (2006-09), including two pennants ('06 and '08), a wild card entry in '07 and a division title in 2009. Hanley Ramirez nabbed 51 bags and scored 119 times, securing the ROY Award in '06. Freddy Sanchez rapped 200 hits including a league-best 53 doubles as he earned the batting crown. Jonathan Papelbon confounded the opposition in his inaugural campaign, posting a miniscule 0.92 ERA and 0.776 WHIP along with 35 saves. In seven full seasons covering 2006-2012, the five-time All-Star averaged 37 saves with a 2.32 ERA and a 0.991 WHIP.

Dustin Pedroia slapped 39 doubles and batted .317 en route to the 2007 AL ROY Award. The "Laser Show" merited MVP honors in '08 as he hit .326 with a league-high 54 doubles, 213 base hits and 118 runs. Rafael Betancourt delivered a 1.47 ERA and a WHIP of 0.756 in a setup role. Ramirez scored 125 runs in successive seasons (2007-08) and entered the 30/30 club in 2008. "HanRam" secured a batting title with a .342 average and placed second in the MVP race in '09. "El Niño" supplied a .313 BA with 40 two-baggers, 25 jacks, 39 steals and 112 runs scored per year during a five-year stretch from 2006-2010.

Kevin Youkilis (.312/29/115) hammered 43 two-base hits and placed third in the AL MVP race in '08. Jacoby Ellsbury stole 50 bases in his inaugural season and topped the leader boards with 70 swipes during the 2009 campaign. He joined the 30/30 club in 2011, knocking 212 base hits and tallying 119 runs as he placed second in the MVP vote. Jed Lowrie rapped 45 doubles and supplied a .290 BA in 2013.

Win Shares > 20	Single-Season	1980-2013
Dwight Evans - 1B (BOS)	Nomar Garciaparra - SS (BOS) x6	Brady Anderson - CF (BOS) x3
Jeff Bagwell - 1B (BOS) x13	Hanley Ramirez - SS (BOS) x6	Jacoby Ellsbury - CF (BOS) x3
Mo Vaughn - 1B (BOS) x4	Jed Lowrie – SS (BOS)	Dwight Evans - RF (BOS) x6
Kevin Youkilis - 1B (BOS) x2	Wade Boggs - 3B (BOS) x9	Fred Lynn - RF (BOS)
Marty G. Barrett - 2B (BOS)	Freddy Sanchez - 3B (BOS)	Ellis Burks - RF (BOS)
Jody Reed - 2B (BOS)	Rich Gedman - C (BOS)	Trot Nixon - RF (BOS) x2
John Valentin - 2B (BOS)	Ben Oglivie - LF (BOS) x2	Ellis Burks - DH (BOS)
Dustin Pedroia - 2B (BOS) x5	Mike Greenwell - LF (BOS)	John Tudor - SP (BOS)
Jim Fregosi - SS (BOS) x8	Brady Anderson - LF (BOS)	Roger Clemens - SP (BOS) x9
Rico Petrocelli - SS (BOS) x3	Ellis Burks - LF (BOS)	Curt Schilling - SP (BOS) x5
Rick Burleson - SS (BOS) x2	Ellis Burks - CF (BOS) x2	Bob Stanley - RP (BOS) x2
John Valentin - SS (BOS)		
David Eckstein - SS (BOS) x2		

Note: 4000 PA or BFP to qualify, except during strike-shortened seasons
(1972 = 3800, 1981 & 1994 = 2700, 1995 = 3500) and 154-game schedule (3800)
- failed to qualify: 1901-1903, 1910, 1918-1926, 1933-1937, 1995

Red Sox All-Time "Originals" Roster

Don Aase	Brian Esposito	Steve Lomasney	Bill Regan
Andy Abad	George Estock	Jim Lonborg	Dick Reichle
Bob B. Adams	Dwight Evans	Walter Lonergan	Chris Reitsma
Doc Adkins	Adam Everett	Harry Lord	Win Remmerswaal
Harry Agganis	Luis Exposito	Jed Lowrie	Jim Rice
Juan Agosto	Carmen Fanzone	Johnny Lucas	Dustin Richardson
Joe Albanese	Jack Faszholz	Lou Lucier	Al Richter
Gary Allenson	Tim Federowicz	Tony Lupien	Woody Rich
Mel Almada	Jared Fernandez	Walt Lynch	Joe Riggert
Abe Alvarez	Dave Ferriss	Fred Lynn	Allen Ripley
Jose R. Alvarez	Stephen Fife	Steve Lyons	Walt Ripley
Luis Alvarado	Joel Finch	Danny MacFayden	Pop Rising
Brady Anderson	Tommy Fine	Billy Macleod	Jay Ritchie
Fred Anderson	Gar Finnvold	Bunny Madden	Anthony Rizzo
Lars Anderson	Carlton Fisk	Art Mahan	Jack E. Robinson
Ernie Andres	John Flaherty	Ron Mahay	Mike Rochford
Mike Andrews	Al Flair	Chris Mahoney	Frank Rodriguez
Luis Aponte	Bill Fleming	Jose Malave	Steve Rodriguez
Frank Arellanes	Don Florence	Jerry Mallett	Tony Rodriguez
Charlie Armbruster	Ben Flowers	Paul Maloy	Billy Rogell
Casper Asbjornson	Wes Flowers	Frank Malzone	Lee Rogers

Ken Aspromonte	Lew Ford	Josias Manzanillo	Red Rollings
James Atkins	Casey Fossum	Mike Maroth	Kevin Romine
Leslie Aulds	Rube Foster	Ollie Marquardt	Victor Rosario
Ramon Aviles	Jack Fournier	Bill Marshall	Brian Rose
Jim Bagby, Jr.	Frank Francisco	Anastacio Martinez	Si Rosenthal
Jeff Bagwell	Hersh Freeman	Carlos E. Martinez	Buster Ross
Cory Bailey	John Freeman	John Marzano	Jack Rothrock
Al Baker	Jim Fregosi	Justin Masterson	Red Ruffing
Jack Baker	Charlie French	Daisuke Matsuzaka	Rich Rundles
Tracy Baker	Reymond Fuentes	William Matthews	Jack Russell
Dick Baney	Curt Fullerton	Charlie Maxwell	Babe Ruth
Daniel Bard	Kason Gabbard	Ed D. Mayer	Jack F. Ryan
Brian Barkley	Fabian Gaffke	Chick Maynard	Ken Ryan
John Barnes	Dan Gakeler	Ken McBride	Mike J. Ryan
Marty G. Barrett	Ed Gallagher	Tom McBride	Gene Rye
Steve Barr	Jim Galvin	Dick McCabe	Donnie Sadler
Ed Barry	Nomar Garciaparra	Windy McCall	Ed Sadowski
Aaron Bates	Larry Gardner	Tom M. McCarthy	Anibal Sanchez
Matt Batts	Mike Garman	Amby McConnell	Freddy Sanchez
Frank Baumann	Cliff Garrison	Mickey McDermott	Angel Santos
Glenn Beckert	Ford Garrison	Jim McDonald	Bill Sayles
Hugh Bedient	Rich Gedman	Eddie McGah	Russ Scarritt
Engel Beltre	Dick Gernert	Lynn McGlothen	Sid Schacht
Juan Beniquez	Chappie Geygan	Art McGovern	Mark Schaeffer
Frank Bennett	Joe Giannini	Chris McGuiness	Bob Scherbarth
Joel Bennett	Norwood Gibson	Ryan McGuire	Chuck Schilling
Shayne Bennett	Russ Gibson	Jim McHale	Curt Schilling
Todd Benzinger	Dan Giese	Marty McHale	Bill Schlesinger
Rafael Betancourt	Andy Gilbert	Walt McKeel	Dave F. Schmidt
Ben Beville	Don Gile	Jud McLaughlin	Ted Schreiber
Tim Blackwell	Ralph Glaze	Larry McLean	Al Schroll
Tony Blanco	Harry Gleason	Marty McLeary	Don Schwall
Steve Blateric	John Godwin	Doc McMahon	Everett Scott
Clarence Blethen	Eusebio Gonzalez	Mike McNally	George C. Scott
Greg Blosser	Joe Gonzales	Gordon McNaughton	Bill Selby
Red Bluhm	Billy Goodman	Jeff McNeely	Aaron Sele
Larry Boerner	Jim Gosger	Norm McNeil	Jeff Sellers
Xander Bogaerts	Charlie Graham	Bill McWilliams	Merle Settlemire
Wade Boggs	Lee Graham	Irv Medlinger	Danny Sheaffer
Milt Bolling	Skinny A. Graham	Sam Mele	John Shea
Tom Bolton	Dave Gray	Luis Mendoza	Bud Sheely
Mark Bomback	Eli Grba	Mike Meola	Neill Sheridan
Tom Borland	Mike Greenwell	Andy Merchant	Steve Shields
Michael Bowden	Pumpsie Green	Cla Meredith	Strick Shofner
Sam Bowen	Marty Griffin	Spike Merena	Kelly Shoppach
Stew Bowers	Guido Grilli	Lou Merloni	Chick Shorten
Ted Bowsfield	Ray Grimes	Bart Miadich	Pat Simmons
Oil Can Boyd	Myron Grimshaw	John Michaels	Dave Sisler
Herb Bradley	Turkey Gross	Will Middlebrooks	Craig Skok
Hugh Bradley	Bobby Guindon	Dick Midkiff	Jack Slattery
Jackie Bradley	Hy Gunning	Rick Miller	Steve Slayton
Cliff Brady	Jackie Gutierrez	Dick Mills	Charlie Small
Al Brazle	Nick Hagadone	Bobby Vance Mitchell	Bob G. Smith
Ken Brett	Casey Hageman	Charlie Mitchell	Bob W. Smith
Tom Brewer	Ray Haley	Fred Mitchell	Chris M. Smith

275

Ralph Brickner	Josh Hancock	John Mitchell	Doug Smith
Drake Britton	Jim Hannan	Bill Monbouquette	John M. Smith
Dick Brodowski	Craig Hansen	Freddie Moncewicz	Mike Smithson
Dusty Brown	Greg Hansell	Bob Montgomery	Paddy Smith
Hal Brown	Travis Harper	Al Montreuil	Pete L. Smith
Mike G. Brown	Joe L. Harris	Bill H. Moore	Wally Snell
Mike A. Brumley	Mickey Harris	Al Moran	Miguel Socolovich
Clay Buchholz	Reggie Harris	Bill C. Moran	Moose Solters
Don Buddin	Charlie Hartman	Dave Morehead	Bill Sommers
Steve Burke	Herb Hash	Roger Moret	Bill Spanswick
Morgan Burkhart	Fred Hatfield	Red Morgan	Tris Speaker
Ellis Burks	Scott Hatteberg	Frank Morrissey	Stan Spence
Rick Burleson	John Hattig	Guy Morton, Jr.	Andy Spognardi
Jim Burton	Ed Hearne	Kevin Morton	Bobby Sprowl
Dennis Burtt	Bob Heffner	Earl Moseley	Jake Stahl
Frank Bushey	Randy Heflin	Jerry Moses	Tracy Stallard
Bill Butland	Harvey Hendrick	Doc Moskiman	Virgil Stallcup
Jim Byrd	Olaf Henriksen	Brandon Moss	Bob Stanley
Hick Cady	Bill R. Henry	Freddie Muller	Jack Stansbury
Paul Campbell	Jim Henry	Joe Mulligan	Dave L. Stapleton
Walter Carlisle	Mike Herrera	Frank Mulroney	Elmer Steele
Swede Carlstrom	Tom Herrin	Bill Mundy	Ben Steiner
Cleo Carlyle	Eric Hetzel	Peter Munro	Dernell Stenson
Bill Carrigan	Hob Hiller	David Murphy	Gene Stephens
Ed Carroll	Shea Hillenbrand	Walter Murphy	Jerry Stephenson
Jerry Casale	Gordie Hinkle	Matt Murton	Carl Stimson
Rex Cecil	Paul Hinson	Tony Muser	Chuck Stobbs
Chet Chadbourne	Harley Hisner	Alex Mustaikis	Al Stokes
Jim Chamblee	Butch Hobson	George Myatt	George R. Stone
Esty Chaney	George Hockette	Hap Myers	Howie Storie
Ed Chaplin	Eli Hodkey	Tim Naehring	George Stumpf
Pete Charton	Jack Hoey	Mike Nagy	Jim Suchecki
Jin Ho Cho	Glenn Hoffman	Bill Narleski	Frank Sullivan
Loyd Christopher	Harry Hooper	Daniel Nava	Haywood Sullivan
Neil Chrisley	Sam Horn	Yamaico Navarro	Marc Sullivan
Joe Cicero	Tony Horton	Kristopher Negron	Carl Sumner
Galen Cisco	Tommy Hottovy	Ernie Neitzke	Jeff Suppan
Otey Clark	Paul Howard	Hal Neubauer	George D. Susce
Roger Clemens	Les Howe	Don Newhauser	Bill Swanson
Tex Clevenger	Bill Howerton	Fred Newman	R.J. Swindle
Lou Clinton	Peter Hoy	Dick Newsome	Jim Tabor
Bill Clowers	Joe Hudson	Reid Nichols	Doug Taitt
George Cochran	Ed Hughes	Al Niemiec	Dennis Tankersley
Dave Coleman	Tex Hughson	Al Nipper	Arlie Tarbert
Michael Coleman	Bill Humphrey	Merlin Nippert	Scott R. Taylor
Chris Coletta	Ben Hunt	Trot Nixon	Junichi Tazawa
Ray Collins	Buddy Hunter	Willard Nixon	Yank Terry
Merl Combs	Bruce Hurst	Chet Nourse	Blaine Thomas
Billy Conigliaro	Jim Hutto	Les Nunamaker	Pinch Thomas
Tony Conigliaro	Jose Iglesias	Frank Oberlin	Don Thompson
Bud Connolly	Daryl Irvine	Mike O'Berry	Jocko Thompson
Ed Connolly	Ray Jablonski	Buck O'Brien	Faye Throneberry
Ed Connolly, Jr.	Lefty Jamerson	Syd O'Brien	Bob Tillman
Billy Consolo	Jerry Janeski	Ben Oglivie	Jackie Tobin
Jimmy E. Cooney	Larry Jansen	Tomokazu Ohka	Phil Todt

Cecil Cooper	Hal Janvrin	Bob Ojeda	Tony Tonneman
Scott Cooper	Ray Jarvis	Hideki Okajima	John Tudor
Marlan Coughtry	Tom Jenkins	Tom Oliver	Tom Umphlett
Fritz Coumbe	Earl Johnson	Hank Olmsted	Tex Vache
Ted Cox	Kris Johnson	Karl Olson	Julio Valdez
Gavvy Cravath	Rontrez Johnson	Marv Olson	John Valentin
Paxton Crawford	Vic Johnson	Ted Olson	Hy Vandenberg
Steve Crawford	Charlie Jones	Bill O'Neill	Tim Van Egmond
Pat Creeden	Dalton Jones	Emmett O'Neill	Mo Vaughn
Bob Cremins	Hunter Jones	George Orme	Wilton Veras
Jack Cressend	Rick Jones	Luis Ortiz	Bill Voiselle
Zach Crouch	Ed Jurak	Fritz Ostermueller	Jake Volz
Luis Cruz	Ryan Kalish	Joe Ostrowski	Charlie Wagner
Leon Culberson	Andy Karl	Amos Otis	Chico Walker
Tim Cullen	Marty Karow	Frank Owens	Luke Walker
Steve Curry	Benn Karr	Mike Page	Joe P. Walsh
John Curtis	Red Kellett	Jim Pagliaroni	Fred Walters
Babe Dahlgren	Win Kellum	Mike Palm	Rabbit Warstler
Pete Daley	Casey Kelly	Larry Pape	Eric Wedge
Dom Dallessandro	Ed Kelly	Jonathan Papelbon	Kyle Weiland
Mike Dalton	Russ Kemmerer	Mel Parnell	Herb Welch
Babe Danzig	Marty Keough	Stan Partenheimer	Tony Welzer
Bob Daughters	Bill Kerksieck	Hank Patterson	Sammy White
Jim Davis	Dana Kiecker	Carl Pavano	Ernie Whitt
Pep Deininger	Leo Kiely	Mike Paxton	Al Widmar
Manny Delcarmen	Jack Killilay	Johnny Peacock	Dana Williams
Alex Delgado	Sun-Woo Kim	Albie Pearson	Dave O. Williams
Jesus Delgado	Matt Kinney	Dustin Pedroia	Jimy Williams
Puchy Delgado	Walt Kinney	Eddie Pellagrini	Rip Williams
Ike Delock	Ron Klimkowski	Juan Pena	Ted Williams
Joe DeMaestri	Bob Kline	Juan P. Perez	Ted Wills
Brian Denman	Hal Kolstad	John Perrin	Duane Wilson
Sam Dente	Al Kozar	Bill Pertica	Earl Wilson
Joe DePastino	Rick Kreuger	Johnny Pesky	Gary J. Wilson
Mel Deutsch	Frank Kreutzer	Bob Peterson	George Wilson
Hal Deviney	Rube Kroh	Rico Petrocelli	Grady Wilson
Argenis Diaz	John Kroner	Ed Phillips	Jim A. Wilson
Bo Diaz	Marty Krug	Jim Piersall	John S. Wilson
George Dickey	Bill Kunkel	Stolmy Pimentel	Les Wilson
Emerson Dickman	Pete Ladd	George Pipgras	Hal Wiltse
Steve Dillard	Ty LaForest	Pinky Pittenger	George Winn
Dom DiMaggio	Roger LaFrancois	Erik Plantenberg	Tom Winsett
Vance Dinges	Joe Lahoud	Phil Plantier	Clarence Winters
Bob DiPietro	Sam Langford	Jeff Plympton	George Winter
Ray Dobens	John LaRose	Tom Poholsky	Joe Wood
Sam Dodge	Ryan Lavarnway	Jennings Poindexter	Joe F. Wood
Pat Dodson	Pete Laydon	Dick Pole	John Woods
Bobby Doerr	Johnny Lazor	Ralph Pond	Pinky Woods
John Donahue	Wilfredo Ledezma	Ken Poulsen	Wilbur Wood
Pat Donahue	Bill F. Lee	John Powers	Rob Woodward
Tom Doran	Sang-Hoon Lee	Larry Pratt	Brandon Workman
Harry Dorish	Bill Lefebvre	Todd Pratt	Hoge Workman
Melvin Dorta	Regis Leheny	George Prentiss	Jim C. Wright
Felix Doubront	John Leister	Ryan Pressly	Ken Wright
Danny Doyle	Dutch H. Leonard	Tex Pruiett	Tom Wright

Walt Dropo	Ted Lepcio	Paul Quantrill	Carl Yastrzemski
Justin Duchscherer	Dutch Lerchen	Frank W. Quinn	Steve Yerkes
Phil Dumatrait	Jon Lester	Rey Quinones	Kevin Youkilis
Ed Durham	Duffy Lewis	Carlos Quintana	Kevin Youkilis
Arnold Earley	Jack Lewis	Dick Radatz	Eduardo Zambrano
David Eckstein	John Lickert	Chuck Rainey	Norm Zauchin
Ben Egan	Che-Hsuan Lin	Hanley Ramirez	Matt Zieser
Elmer Eggert	Cole Liniak	Robert Ramsay	Jerry Zimmerman
Jacoby Ellsbury	Dick Littlefield	Josh Reddick	Charlie Zink
Steve Ellsworth	Jack Littrell	Johnny Reder	Bob Zupcic
Al Epperly	George Loepp	Jody Reed	

Colorado Rockies

Year/Team	OPW%	PW	PL	APW%	AW	AL	Diff+/-
1993 COL	0.000 F	0	0	0.414	67	95	0.000
1994 COL	0.000 F	0	0	0.453	53	64	0.000
1995 COL	0.000 F	0	0	0.535 W	77	67	0.000
1996 COL	0.000 F	0	0	0.512	83	79	0.000
1997 COL	0.487 F	79	83	0.512	83	79	0.025
1998 COL	0.433 F	70	92	0.475	77	85	0.043
1999 COL	0.482 F	78	84	0.444	72	90	-0.038

franchID	OWAR	OWS	AWAR	AWS	WARdiff	WSdiff	P/D/W/F
1993 COL			20.222	201.007			F
1994 COL	-45.120	0.000	20.218	159.005	-65.339	-159.005	F
1995 COL	20.960	125.724	35.000	230.998	-14.040	-105.274	F
1996 COL	6.697	118.232	33.014	249.002	-26.316	-130.770	F
1997 COL	20.360	163.113	35.894	249.001	-15.534	-85.888	F
1998 COL	25.108	195.691	35.745	231.007	-10.637	-35.315	F
1999 COL	13.278	169.321	29.771	216.002	-16.493	-46.681	F

Legend: (P) = Pennant / Most Wins in League (D) = Division Winner (W) = Wild Card Winner (F) = Failed to Qualify

The Colorado Rockies entered the Major Leagues in 1993 as an expansion franchise. The "Original" Rockies earned four playoff berths from 2004 to 2009 primarily on the strength of its offense. In its short history the Rockies have assembled a talented batting crew while failing miserably in the acquisition and development of a pitching staff. Ubaldo Jimenez is the lone pitcher to rise above the 20 Win Share plateau with his stellar performance in 2010. Based on the WS>20 frame of reference, the organization failed to develop stars at second base or right field.

Year/Team	OPW%	PW	PL	APW%	AW	AL	Diff+/-
2000 COL	0.583 F	94	68	0.506	82	80	-0.076
2001 COL	0.542 F	88	74	0.451	73	89	-0.092
2002 COL	0.463 F	75	87	0.451	73	89	-0.012
2003 COL	0.454	74	88	0.457	74	88	0.003
2004 COL	0.526 W	85	77	0.420	68	94	-0.106
2005 COL	0.495 D	80	82	0.414	67	95	-0.081
2006 COL	0.507	82	80	0.469	76	86	-0.038
2007 COL	0.546 D	88	74	0.552 W	90	73	0.006
2008 COL	0.462	75	87	0.457	74	88	-0.005
2009 COL	0.561 P	91	71	0.568 W	92	70	0.007
2010 COL	0.476	77	85	0.512	83	79	0.037
2011 COL	0.442	72	90	0.451	73	89	0.008
2012 COL	0.466	76	86	0.395	64	98	-0.071
2013 COL	0.499	81	81	0.457	74	88	-0.042

franchID	OWAR	OWS	AWAR	AWS	WARdiff	WSdiff	P/D/W/F
2000 COL	28.771	235.007	38.076	245.994	-9.305	-10.987	F
2001 COL	30.357	184.435	39.926	218.994	-9.570	-34.560	F
2002 COL	18.867	190.981	23.850	218.997	-4.983	-28.016	F
2003 COL	29.882	191.325	29.751	222.003	0.131	-30.678	
2004 COL	33.545	225.731	27.524	204.002	6.021	21.728	W
2005 COL	27.072	215.555	23.606	200.995	3.466	14.560	D
2006 COL	28.429	208.821	36.241	228.000	-7.812	-19.179	

Year							
2007 COL	**42.049**	264.226	43.781	**269.999**	-1.732	-5.774	D
2008 COL	33.514	221.834	36.337	221.997	-2.823	-0.163	
2009 COL	**44.474**	**297.212**	45.891	275.998	-1.417	21.213	P
2010 COL	32.057	232.498	45.775	248.997	-13.717	-16.499	
2011 COL	22.713	193.280	33.880	218.992	-11.167	-25.712	
2012 COL	27.808	217.691	23.697	191.997	4.111	25.694	
2013 COL	32.939	242.061	32.031	221.997	0.908	20.064	

The "Original" Rockies attained the team's first playoff berth in 2004, claiming the National League wild card entry. Colorado achieved the best WSdiff (+22) and WARdiff (+6) vs. the output of the "Actual" Rockies from the same season. Todd Helton (31 WS) appeared in five consecutive All-Star contests (2000-04), set the team record with 33 WS in '03 and collected a batting crown with a .372 mark in 2000. From 1998-2007 Helton delivered a .332 BA, 30 round-trippers, 108 RBI and 109 runs scored per season. Juan Pierre (23 WS) topped the League with 221 base knocks and 12 triples in 2004 and averaged 49 stolen bases from 2001-2012.

Colorado earned its first division title in '05 as Chone Figgins sparked the offense with 62 stolen bases and 113 runs. Garrett Atkins (.329/29/120) registered 117 tallies and drilled 48 two-baggers during his first full season in 2006. The organization placed third in the Majors with 12 WS>10 seasons at the hot corner from 2000-2009. The Rockies hit a speed bump during the '06 campaign, finishing last in the League in oWAR and oWS.

The Rockies rebounded with another division title in 2007. The team led the circuit in oWAR and three players exceeded 20 Win Shares (Matt Holliday 28, Troy Tulowitzki 25, Helton 23). Holliday topped the leader boards with a .340 BA, 216 hits, 50 doubles and 137 RBI, achieving career-bests with 120 runs scored and 36 dingers. Tulowitzki (.291/24/99) placed runner-up in the 2007 NL Rookie of the Year balloting.

The 2009 Rockies tore through the National League en route to the first pennant, leading the senior circuit in oWAR and oWS. Figgins, Holliday and Tulowitzki each tallied 26 Win Shares while Helton amassed 23. Jimenez assumed the role of staff ace, posting an ERA of 3.47 and racking up 198 strikeouts to go with 15 victories. He notched 19 victories with a 2.88 ERA and placed third in the 2010 NL Cy Young race.

Win Shares > 20	Single-Season	1993-2013
Todd Helton - 1B (COL) x8	Chone Figgins - 3B (COL) x2	Juan Pierre - CF (COL) x2
Troy Tulowitzki - SS (COL) x5	Matt Holliday - LF (COL) x7	Ubaldo Jimenez - SP (COL)
Garrett Atkins – 3B (COL)		

Note: 4000 PA or BFP to qualify, except during strike-shortened seasons
(1972 = 3800, 1981 & 1994 = 2700, 1995 = 3500) and 154-game schedule (3800)
- failed to qualify: 1993-2002

Rockies All-Time "Originals" Roster

Juan Acevedo	Sam Deduno	Ubaldo Jimenez	Chaz Roe
Garvin Alston	Jorge DePaula	Alan Johnson	Esmil Rogers
Nolan Arenado	Corey Dickerson	Terry Jones	Matt Roney
Alberto Arias	Mark DiFelice	Joe Koshansky	Wilin Rosario
Garrett Atkins	Scott Dohmann	David Lee	Josh Rutledge
Luis Ayala	Angel Echevarria	John Lindsey	Mike Saipe
Roger Bailey	Edgmer Escalona	Matt Macri	Jeff Salazar
Jeff Baker	Mike Esposito	Ryan Mattheus	Rob Scahill
Josh Bard	Thomas Field	Quinton McCracken	Todd Sears
Sean Barker	Chone Figgins	Michael McKenry	Alex Serrano

Clint Barmes	Dexter Fowler	Justin Miller	Ryan Shealy
Jason Bates	Jeff Francis	Jim Matthew Miller	Seth Smith
Doug Bernier	Choo Freeman	Franklin Morales	Jorge Sosa
Chad Bettis	Christian Friedrich	Juan Morillo	Ryan Speier
Bruce Billings	Cole Garner	Chris Nelson	Ryan Spilborghs
Charlie Blackmon	Jody Gerut	Josh Newman	Ian Stewart
Rex Brothers	Derrick Gibson	Juan Nicasio	Mark Strittmatter
Mark Brownson	Hector Gomez	Jayson Nix	Pedro Strop
John C. Burke	Lariel Gonzalez	Rafael Ortega	Cory Sullivan
Everth Cabrera	Sean Green	Jordan Pacheco	John Thomson
Edwar Cabrera	Luther Hackman	David Patton	Mark Thompson
Xavier Cedeno	Justin Hampson	Elvis Pena	Chin-Hui Tsao
Jhoulys Chacin	Will Harris	Neifi Perez	Troy Tulowitzki
Shawn Chacon	Brad Hawpe	Ben Petrick	Juan Uribe
Tim Christman	Todd Helton	Juan Pierre	Jermaine Van Buren
Darren Clarke	Jonathan Herrera	Scott Randall	Cory Vance
Edgard Clemente	Matt Holliday	Steven Register	Eduardo Villacis
Alvin Colina	Craig House	Bryan Rekar	Jake Westbrook
Aaron Cook	Luke Hudson	Rene Reyes	Jamey Wright
Manuel Corpas	Justin Huisman	Greg Reynolds	Eric Young, Jr.
Craig Counsell	Chris Iannetta	Matt Reynolds	Jason Young
Matt Daley	Jason Jennings	Aneury Rodriguez	

Kansas City Royals

Year/Team	OPW%	PW	PL	APW%	AW	AL	Diff+/-
1969 KCR	0.000	0	0	0.426	69	93	0.000
1970 KCR	0.000	0	0	0.401	65	97	0.000
1971 KCR	0.000	0	0	0.528	85	76	0.000
1972 KCR	0.000	0	0	0.494	76	78	0.000
1973 KCR	0.000	0	0	0.543	88	74	0.000
1974 KCR	0.456	74	88	0.475	77	85	0.019
1975 KCR	0.604	98	64	0.562	91	71	-0.042
1976 KCR	0.537	87	75	0.556 D	90	72	0.019
1977 KCR	0.598 P	97	65	0.630 P	102	60	0.032
1978 KCR	0.543 P	88	74	0.568 D	92	70	0.025
1979 KCR	0.564 P	91	71	0.525	85	77	-0.039

franchID	OWAR	OWS	AWAR	AWS	WARdiff	WSdiff	P/D/W/F
1969 KCR			25.431	206.989	-25.431	-206.989	F
1970 KCR	-5.741	97.035	23.207	194.991	-28.948	-97.957	F
1971 KCR	56.967	189.840	37.628	254.996	19.339	-65.156	F
1972 KCR	33.296	128.335	41.765	228.004	-8.469	-99.669	F
1973 KCR	28.994	168.348	32.979	263.993	-3.985	-95.646	F
1974 KCR	18.636	160.949	36.826	231.007	-18.190	-70.058	F
1975 KCR	38.191	226.285	45.347	273.000	-7.156	-46.715	F
1976 KCR	30.859	208.121	42.572	269.995	-11.713	-61.874	F
1977 KCR	**40.323**	**246.708**	**51.768**	**306.005**	-11.445	-59.297	P
1978 KCR	29.747	196.637	43.217	275.998	-13.469	-79.361	P
1979 KCR	34.956	224.194	37.276	254.994	-2.319	-30.801	P

Legend: (P) = Pennant / Most Wins in League (D) = Division Winner (W) = Wild Card Winner (F) = Failed to Qualify

Kansas City was awarded a new franchise to fill the void created by the Athletics' move to Oakland following the 1967 season. The Royals organization relied heavily on its scouting department and achieved four consecutive pennants once the "Original" Royals exceeded the PA and BFP requirements in 1977. Based on the WS>20 frame of reference, the club has failed to develop a shortstop of star quality since the inception of the franchise. The Royals top the WS>20 leader boards among the expansion teams at third base and relief pitcher and are tied with the Astros and Mariners in center field.

Steve Busby accomplished the Royals' first 20 Win Share season, posting a 22-14 record with a 3.39 ERA and 198 strikeouts in 1974. Doug Bird (2.99 ERA, 20 SV in '73) and Mark Littell (2.08 ERA, 16 SV in '76) anchored the late innings. George Brett, a second-round draft pick in 1971, emerged as a superstar at the hot corner with 195 base hits and a .308 BA in '75. Brett collected the first of three batting titles and placed runner-up in the 1976 AL MVP voting. Under the direction of Joe Burke, Kansas City endured substandard results in four consecutive Amateur Drafts as the draft classes from 1975 through 1978 fell short of 100 Career Total Win Shares.

The Royals captured the club's first pennant in '77 as four teammates surpassed the 20 Win Shares plateau (George Brett 29, Al Cowens 27, Dennis Leonard 23 and Ruppert Jones 23). The squad also led the League in oWAR and oWS. Cowens (.312/23/112) finished second in the 1977 AL MVP balloting and delivered career-highs in the triple-crown categories along with hits, runs scored and triples. Leonard bested the twenty victory mark in three of the four pennant-winning seasons and placed fourth in the 1977 AL Cy Young vote.

The K.C. crew repeated as pennant winners in '78 but compiled the worst WSdiff (-79) and WARdiff (-13) vs. the output of the "Actual" Royals from the same season. On the '79 club Brett hit .329 while topping the circuit with 212 base knocks and 20 triples. Willie Wilson, the Royals first-round pick in the 1974 draft, batted at a .315 clip, pilfered 83 bags and tallied 113 runs scored. Aurelio Lopez was promoted to the closer's role and responded with 21 saves in consecutive seasons (1979-80). "Señor Smoke" posted 10+ relief wins in both seasons and fashioned a 10-1 mark in 1984.

Year/Team	OPW%	PW	PL	APW%	AW	AL	Diff+/-
1980 KCR	0.596 P	97	65	0.599 D	97	65	0.003
1981 KCR	0.498	81	81	0.485	50	53	-0.012
1982 KCR	0.526	85	77	0.556	90	72	0.029
1983 KCR	0.479	78	84	0.488	79	83	0.009
1984 KCR	0.477	77	85	0.519 D	84	78	0.041
1985 KCR	0.486	79	83	0.562 D	91	71	0.076
1986 KCR	0.542 P	88	74	0.469	76	86	-0.072
1987 KCR	0.494	80	82	0.512	83	79	0.018
1988 KCR	0.554 D	90	72	0.522	84	77	-0.032
1989 KCR	0.551 P	89	73	0.568	92	70	0.017

franchID	OWAR	OWS	AWAR	AWS	WARdiff	WSdiff	P/D/W/F
1980 KCR	42.677	272.227	44.396	291.003	-1.719	-18.776	P
1981 KCR	20.598	135.793	24.918	150.006	-4.320	-14.213	
1982 KCR	31.848	206.678	39.962	270.004	-8.115	-63.326	
1983 KCR	23.726	195.884	28.784	236.998	-5.058	-41.114	
1984 KCR	31.422	212.353	33.928	251.999	-2.506	-39.646	
1985 KCR	29.581	212.278	41.119	272.997	-11.538	-60.719	
1986 KCR	37.454	219.020	34.879	228.006	2.574	-8.986	P
1987 KCR	32.823	210.175	37.157	249.002	-4.333	-38.827	
1988 KCR	42.876	225.871	40.455	252.001	2.421	-26.130	D
1989 KCR	42.328	227.794	44.647	276.000	-2.319	-48.205	P

Brett (36 WS) made a run at the magical .400 mark in the summer of 1980 before settling for a .390 BA. "Mullet" received the AL MVP award and led the League in OBP and SLG while driving in a career-best 118 runs. Wilson (32 WS) contributed a .326 BA with 79 stolen bases and paced the League in runs scored (133), hits (230) and triples (15). Dan Quisenberry (3.09 ERA, 33 SV) protected late-inning leads along with Doug Corbett (1.98 ERA, 23 SV) who tallied 24 Win Shares in his rookie year. Kansas City secured its fourth straight pennant in 1980 while leading the League in oWS.

Over the next half-decade the "Original" Royals failed to reach the playoffs. However, three teammates contributed spectacular single-season accomplishments. "Quiz" surpassed 20 Win Shares and topped the American League in saves for 4 straight seasons (1982-85). He averaged 40 saves and finished third or better in the Cy Young balloting in each season during that timeframe. Brett (.335/30/112) attained the highest Win Share mark in Royals history (37) in 1985. Bret Saberhagen (20-6, 2.87) fashioned a league-best 1.058 WHIP and earned his first Cy Young award at age 21. The '83 Royals registered the worst oWAR (24) and oWS (196) in team history, excluding strike-shortened seasons.

Greg "Moon Man" Minton saved 22 contests per season over a five-year period (1980-84). Eight-time Gold Glove winner Frank White led the crew to its fifth pennant in 1986, and in the following year Kevin Seitzer (.323/15/83) paced the American League with 207 base hits en route to a runner-up finish in the 1987 AL ROY campaign. Four Royals exceeded the 20 Win Shares level (George Brett 27, Mark Gubicza 24, Danny Jackson 22, Kevin Seitzer 22), as the squad earned a division title in '88. Gubicza (20-8, 2.70), Jackson (23-8, 2.73) and David Cone (20-3, 2.22) provided fierce competition for the top slot in the rotation.

Kansas City secured its sixth pennant and led the League in oWAR in 1989. Saberhagen (23-6, 2.16) dominated the opposition on the road to his second Cy Young award, leading the circuit in wins, ERA, WHIP (0.961), innings pitched and complete games. Bo Jackson justified his lone All-Star nod with 32 circuit clouts and 105 ribbies.

Year/Team	OPW%	PW	PL	APW%	AW	AL	Diff+/-
1990 KCR	0.512	83	79	0.466	75	86	-0.046
1991 KCR	0.505	82	80	0.506	82	80	0.001
1992 KCR	0.471	76	86	0.444	72	90	-0.027
1993 KCR	0.517	84	78	0.519	84	78	0.002
1994 KCR	0.533 D	86	76	0.557	64	51	0.023
1995 KCR	0.450	73	89	0.486	70	74	0.036
1996 KCR	0.460	75	87	0.466	75	86	0.006
1997 KCR	0.472	76	86	0.416	67	94	-0.056
1998 KCR	0.407	66	96	0.447	72	89	0.040
1999 KCR	0.508	82	80	0.398	64	97	-0.111

franchID	OWAR	OWS	AWAR	AWS	WARdiff	WSdiff	P/D/W/F
1990 KCR	39.919	210.369	37.641	225.009	2.277	-14.640	
1991 KCR	34.808	211.985	39.964	246.006	-5.156	-34.021	
1992 KCR	31.958	200.937	31.074	216.007	0.884	-15.069	
1993 KCR	42.799	244.449	34.952	252.003	7.848	-7.554	
1994 KCR	37.410	193.905	28.105	192.006	9.305	1.899	D
1995 KCR	33.109	210.979	26.895	210.000	6.213	0.979	
1996 KCR	37.293	249.978	33.046	224.998	4.246	24.981	
1997 KCR	35.378	227.628	30.351	200.999	5.027	26.629	
1998 KCR	36.016	244.294	23.842	216.001	12.174	28.293	
1999 KCR	38.882	244.390	27.273	191.997	11.608	52.393	

Cecil Fielder bolstered the Royals' offense, amassing 30 Win Shares in 1990. "Big Daddy" slugged 51 long balls in '90 and placed runner-up in back-to-back seasons (1990-91) for AL MVP honors. Brett seized his third batting title with a .329 BA and topped the charts with 45 two-baggers. Kevin Appier posted ERA's below 3.00 in 1992-93 and Cone (16-5, 2.94) cooled off the opposition with a Cy Young effort in '94 as the Royals delivered another division title. Cone (20-7, 3.55) reached the 200 strikeout plateau for the sixth time in his career during the 1998 campaign, while Tom "Flash" Gordon topped the leader boards with 46 saves. The 1993 staff produced the best pitWARnorm (32) and pitWSnorm (128) totals in team history. The starting rotation finished second in the Majors with 40 WS>10 seasons from 1990-99.

A new wave of talented prospects emerged in the Kansas City outfield during the Nineties. Brian McRae nabbed 37 bags and tallied 111 runs scored in 1996. Johnny Damon scored at least 100 runs in 9 consecutive seasons (1998-2006). Carlos Beltran (.293/22/108) stole 27 bases and won the AL ROY award in 1999. However, the Royals vulnerabilities in the middle infield and bullpen were exposed as the team placed last in the Majors in WS>10 seasons for second basemen, shortstops, and relief pitchers.

Year/Team	OPW%	PW	PL	APW%	AW	AL	Diff+/-
2000 KCR	0.507	82	80	0.475	77	85	-0.032
2001 KCR	0.475	77	85	0.401	65	97	-0.074
2002 KCR	0.482	78	84	0.383	62	100	-0.100
2003 KCR	0.467	76	86	0.512	83	79	0.045
2004 KCR	0.483	78	84	0.358	58	104	-0.125
2005 KCR	0.495	80	82	0.346	56	106	-0.150
2006 KCR	0.435	70	92	0.383	62	100	-0.052
2007 KCR	0.457	74	88	0.426	69	93	-0.031
2008 KCR	0.499	81	81	0.463	75	87	-0.036
2009 KCR	0.544 D	88	74	0.401	65	97	-0.143
2010 KCR	0.437 F	71	91	0.414	67	95	-0.023
2011 KCR	0.506	82	80	0.438	71	91	-0.068
2012 KCR	0.552 D	89	73	0.444	72	90	-0.108
2013 KCR	0.677 F	110	52	0.531	86	76	-0.146

franchID	OWAR	OWS	AWAR	AWS	WARdiff	WSdiff	P/D/W/F
2000 KCR	34.920	235.243	26.839	231.001	8.081	4.242	
2001 KCR	30.715	228.263	21.345	195.004	9.370	33.259	
2002 KCR	34.593	223.922	21.946	185.996	12.647	37.927	
2003 KCR	26.189	234.273	28.871	249.002	-2.682	-14.729	
2004 KCR	40.426	264.716	16.878	173.997	23.548	90.720	
2005 KCR	37.989	237.502	16.942	167.998	21.046	69.504	
2006 KCR	32.386	234.758	17.022	185.999	15.364	48.759	
2007 KCR	30.035	223.043	23.780	206.999	6.255	16.044	
2008 KCR	42.609	261.593	27.864	224.995	14.745	36.598	
2009 KCR	45.745	268.388	25.304	194.994	20.441	73.394	D
2010 KCR	33.717	233.800	24.897	201.004	8.820	32.796	F
2011 KCR	38.420	237.947	33.435	213.003	4.985	24.944	
2012 KCR	39.112	246.344	30.128	215.993	8.984	30.350	D
2013 KCR	54.835	323.513	39.243	257.997	15.593	65.515	F

The Royals' center fielders led the Majors with 19 WS>10 seasons. Beltran continued his assault on opposition pitchers as he averaged 29 home runs, 104 RBI, 29 stolen bases and 108 runs scored from 2001-09. Damon registered 214 base knocks and led the circuit with 136 runs and 46 stolen bases in 2000. First sacker Mike Sweeney swatted 29 round-trippers and drove in

144 runs for the same squad. In 2004, Kansas City achieved the best WSdiff (+91) and WARdiff (+24) vs. the output of the "Actual" Royals from the same season. Zack Greinke (16-8, 2.16) earned Cy Young honors and led the team to the division title in 2009.

Billy Butler ripped 51 doubles and walloped 21 blasts in '09. "Country Breakfast" merited his first All-Star appearance three years later as he established personal-bests in home runs (29) and RBI (107). Alex Gordon set career-highs with a .303 BA, 23 dingers, 87 ribbies and 101 runs scored in 2011. He earned three consecutive Gold Glove Awards (2011-13) and led the circuit with 51 two-baggers in 2012. Greg Holland whiffed 103 batsmen in 67 innings and recorded 47 saves while posting a miniscule 1.21 ERA for the 2013 squad. Eric Hosmer whacked 34 two-base knocks and delivered a .302 BA.

Win Shares > 20	Single-Season	1969-2013
George Brett - 1B (KCR) x2	Alex Gordon - LF (KCR) x3	Bret Saberhagen - SP (KCR) x3
Cecil Fielder - 1B (KCR) x2	Ruppert Jones - CF (KCR) x2	
Mike Sweeney - 1B (KCR)	Willie Wilson - CF (KCR)	Mark Gubicza - SP (KCR)
Jeff Conine - 1B (KCR)	Brian McRae - CF (KCR) x2	Danny Jackson - SP (KCR)
Billy Butler - 1B (KCR)	Johnny Damon - CF (KCR) x5	Kevin Appier - SP (KCR) x2
Eric Hosmer - 1B (KCR)	Carlos Beltran - CF (KCR) x6	David Cone - SP (KCR)
Mark Ellis - 2B (KCR) x2	Al Cowens - RF (KCR)	Zack Greinke - SP (KCR)
George Brett - 3B (KCR) x9	Carlos Beltran - RF (KCR)	Doug Corbett - RP (KCR)
Kevin Seitzer - 3B (KCR) x4	Billy Butler - DH (KCR)	Dan Quisenberry - RP (KCR) x4
Willie Wilson - LF (KCR) x3	Steve Busby - SP (KCR) x2	
Johnny Damon - LF (KCR)	Dennis Leonard - SP (KCR)	

Note: 4000 PA or BFP to qualify, except during strike-shortened seasons
(1972 = 3800, 1981 & 1994 = 2700, 1995 = 3500) and 154-game schedule (3800)
- failed to qualify: 1969-1976

Royals All-Time "Originals" Roster

Juan Abreu	Danny Duffy	Bill Laskey	Clint Robinson
Jeremy Affeldt	Chad Durbin	Dave Leeper	Derrick Robinson
Norm Angelini	Jarrod Dyson	Dennis Leonard	Tom Romano
Kevin Appier	Craig Eaton	Jon Lieber	Carlos Rosa
Jeff Austin	Chris Eddy	Mark Littell	Jose Rosado
Al Autry	Tom Edens	Ryan Long	Glendon Rusch
Mike Aviles	Mark Ellis	Aurello Lopez	Mark Ryal
Scott Bankhead	Bart Evans	Mendy Lopez	Bret Saberhagen
German Barranca	Irving Falu	David Lough	Luis Salazar
Brian Bass	Sal Fasano	Devon Lowery	Angel Sanchez
Jonah Bayliss	Carlos Febles	Ed Lucas	Brian Sanches
Charlie Beamon, Jr.	Tony Ferreira	Mike MacDougal	Israel Sanchez
Carlos Beltran	Cecil Fielder	Mike Macfarlane	Chad Santos
Brandon Berger	Mike Fyhrie	Mike Magnante	Jose Rafael Santiago
Sean Berry	Rich Gale	Mitch Maier	Jeff Schattlnger
Andres Berumen	Danny Garcia	Carlos C. Maldonado	Jeff Schulz
Brian Bevil	Joe Gates	Sheldon Mallory	Rodney Scott
Buddy Biancalana	Jim Gaudet	Keith Marshall	Jim Scranton
Jeff Bianchi	Chris C. George	Chito Martinez	Shawn Sedlacek
Doug Bird	Byron Gettis	Felix Martinez	Kevin Seitzer
Andres Blanco	Jeremy Giambi	Renie Martin	Brian Shackelford
Jaime Bluma	Johnny Giavotella	Ramon E. Martinez	Pat Sheridan
Mike Bovee	Jason Gilfillan	Victor Marte	Steve Shifflett
Roy Branch	Jimmy Gobble	Brent Mayne	Terry Shumpert
Ryan Z. Braun	Alexis Gomez	Bob McClure	Luis Silverio

George Brett	Raul Gonzalez	Zach McClellan	Jason Simontacchi
Mike Brewer	Alex Gordon	Randy McGilberry	Steve Sisco
Juan Brito	Tom Gordon	Brian McRae	Don Slaught
Dee Brown	Ruben Gotay	Carlos Mendez	Van Snider
Tom D. Brown	Jeff Granger	Dan Miceli	Kyle Snyder
Tom Bruno	Zack Greinke	Greg Minton	Mark Souza
Billy Buckner	Mark Gubicza	Dennis Moeller	Tim Spehr
Ryan Bukvich	Angel Guzman	Monty Montgomery	Paul Splittorff
Melvin Bunch	Shane Halter	Bobby V. Moore	Steve Staggs
Ambiorix Burgos	Bob Hamelin	Kerwin Moore	Andy Stewart
Steve Busby	Atlee Hammaker	Orber Moreno	Mel Stocker
Mike Butcher	Jed Hansen	John D. Morris	Larry Sutton
Billy Butler	Ken Harvey	Darryl Motley	Mike Sweeney
Tim Byrdak	Kelly Heath	Mike Moustakas	Everett Teaford
Kiko Calero	Bob Hegman	Scott Mullen	George Throop
Jim M. Campbell	Runelvys Hernandez	Donnie Murphy	Corey Thurman
Tom Candiotti	Kelvin Herrera	Rodney Myers	Gary Thurman
Lance Carter	Phil Hiatt	Rod Myers	Mike Tonis
Bobby Castillo	Greg Hibbard	Wil Myers	Matt Treanor
Craig Chamberlain	Jeremy Hill	Les Norman	Michael Tucker
Scott Chiasson	Luke Hochevar	Jose Nunez	Matt Tupman
Lance Clemons	Kevin Hodges	Wes Obermueller	Jeff Twitty
Tony Cogan	Greg Holland	Frank Ortenzio	Jorge Vasquez
Louis Coleman	Brad Holman	Bill Paschall	Joe Vitiello
Stu Cole	Norris Hopper	Cliff Pastornicky	Hector Wagner
Victor Cole	Eric Hosmer	Bill Pecota	Jeff Wallace
Onix Concepcion	David Howard	Jorge Pedre	Ron Washington
David Cone	J.P. Howell	Kit Pellow	U L Washington
Jeff Conine	Dusty Hughes	Melido Perez	John Wathan
Doug Corbett	Mark Huismann	Salvador Perez	Brad Wellman
Jeff Cornell	Clint Hurdle	Ken Phelps	Frank White
Shane Costa	Bo Jackson	Paul Phillips	Frank Wills
Al Cowens	Danny Jackson	Hipolito Pichardo	Mark Williams
Jeff Cox	Chris Jelic	Ed Pierce	Kris Wilson
Keith Creel	Joel Johnston	Jim Pittsley	Willie Wilson
Dave Cripe	Ron Johnson	Tom Poquette	Jim Wohlford
Aaron Crow	Rondin Johnson	Alex Prieto	Blake Wood
Johnny Damon	Mike Jones	Harvey Pulliam	Marvell Wynne
Butch Davis	Ruppert Jones	Mark Quinn	Yasuhiko Yabuta
John K. Davis	Kila Ka'aihue	Jamie Quirk	Jim York
David DeJesus	Matt Karchner	Dan Quisenberry	Joe Zdeb
Jose DeJesus	Mike Kingery	Joe Randa	
Luis M. de los Santos	Kevin Koslofski	Ken Ray	
Joe Dillon	Gary Lance	Dan Reichert	

Year/Team	OPW%	PW	PL	APW%	AW	AL	Diff+/-
1901 DET	0.456	62	74	0.548	74	61	0.092
1902 DET	0.502 P	68	68	0.385	52	83	-0.117
1903 DET	0.457	64	76	0.478	65	71	0.021
1904 DET	0.506 F	78	76	0.408	62	90	-0.098
1905 DET	0.487	75	79	0.516	79	74	0.029
1906 DET	0.473	73	81	0.477	71	78	0.004
1907 DET	0.546 P	84	70	0.613 P	92	58	0.067
1908 DET	0.546	84	70	0.588 P	90	63	0.043
1909 DET	0.629	97	57	0.645 P	98	54	0.016

franchID	OWAR	OWS	AWAR	AWS	WARdiff	WSdiff	P/D/W/F
1901 DET	5.999	40.666	32.630	219.000	-26.630	-178.334	
1902 DET	4.850	32.148	17.116	156.001	-12.267	-123.853	P
1903 DET	7.318	45.554	31.878	194.996	-24.560	-149.442	
1904 DET	9.037	70.476	12.889	186.007	-3.852	-115.531	F
1905 DET	6.642	93.441	23.715	237.004	-17.073	-143.563	
1906 DET	10.826	110.695	20.128	212.999	-9.302	-102.304	
1907 DET	19.362	**143.163**	38.710	**276.004**	-19.348	-132.842	P
1908 DET	23.317	144.321	**42.517**	269.997	-19.199	-125.676	
1909 DET	33.046	194.939	46.493	**293.955**	-13.447	-99.016	

Legend: (P) = Pennant / Most Wins in League (D) = Division Winner (W) = Wild Card Winner (F) = Failed to Qualify

Detroit attained Major League status as one of the eight original American League franchises in 1901. Based on the WS>20 frame of reference, it has developed the fewest quality third basemen (14) among the "Turn of the Century" franchises. Howard Johnson leads the way with five seasons above 20 Win Shares. The Tigers are tied for third-best in the WS>20 leader boards for right fielders (44), paced by Harry Heilmann and Al Kaline (8 seasons above 20 Win Shares apiece).

The starting rotation has been rock solid throughout the years as the moundsmen delivered the most WS>20 (93) and WS>10 (353) seasons. Conversely, the franchise produced the fewest relief pitcher WS>10 seasons (30) among the "Turn of the Century" clubs and never placed in the top three WS>10 leaders at second base or shortstop.

The Tigers snared two pennants in the club's opening decade. Ed Siever furnished a league-leading 1.91 ERA for the '02 squad. Frank Owen averaged 21 wins with a 2.12 ERA from 1904-06. Ty Cobb tallied 40 Win Shares in his first full season (1907). "The Georgia Peach" collected the first of 11 batting titles while leading the League with 119 RBI and 53 stolen bases. Right-hander George Mullin fashioned a 2.71 ERA and posted 20 victories per year from 1902-1911. He compiled 29 wins for the Tigers in 1909. The Athletics outlasted the Tigers, snaring the 1909 pennant by a meager 2-game cushion.

Year/Team	OPW%	PW	PL	APW%	AW	AL	Diff+/-
1910 DET	0.533	82	72	0.558	86	68	0.025
1911 DET	0.522	80	74	0.578	89	65	0.056
1912 DET	0.509	78	76	0.451	69	84	-0.058
1913 DET	0.457	70	84	0.431	66	87	-0.026
1914 DET	0.531	82	72	0.523	80	73	-0.008
1915 DET	0.598 P	92	62	0.649	100	54	0.052

Year/Team	OPW%	PW	PL	APW%	AW	AL	Diff+/-
1916 DET	0.565 P	87	67	0.565	87	67	0.000
1917 DET	0.599	92	62	0.510	78	75	-0.089
1918 DET	0.507	65	63	0.437	55	71	-0.070
1919 DET	0.597 P	84	56	0.571	80	60	-0.026

franchID	OWAR	OWS	AWAR	AWS	WARdiff	WSdiff	P/D/W/F
1910 DET	30.267	193.061	35.661	257.995	-5.394	-64.933	
1911 DET	33.347	215.667	35.596	267.006	-2.249	-51.339	
1912 DET	26.990	190.054	27.560	206.944	-0.570	-16.890	
1913 DET	25.629	181.958	28.376	197.999	-2.746	-16.040	
1914 DET	36.928	241.550	34.876	239.997	2.052	1.553	
1915 DET	52.451	299.013	50.256	300.005	2.195	-0.992	P
1916 DET	36.143	268.498	37.190	261.010	-1.048	7.489	P
1917 DET	43.290	258.656	38.262	234.002	5.028	24.655	
1918 DET	33.063	197.103	22.684	165.002	10.379	32.101	
1919 DET	48.731	282.396	34.181	239.997	14.550	42.399	P

Cobb obliterated the competition in 1911, batting .420 while topping the junior circuit with 248 hits, 147 runs, 47 doubles, 24 triples, 127 RBI and 83 stolen bases. He followed up with a .409 campaign and amassed 51 Win Shares in 1915 (the most WS in Tigers' history). Cobb failed to win the batting title in 1916, despite hitting at a .371 clip. Detroit captured successive pennants in 1915-16 behind the firepower generated by Cobb and Bobby Veach (.319/8/103 in '16). Eddie Cicotte notched 28 victories and fashioned a league-best 1.53 ERA and 0.912 WHIP in 1917. Carl Mays contributed 22 wins and a 1.74 ERA. Known as "Sub" due to his under-handed pitching motion, Mays delivered a 21-13 mark with 8 shutouts in the following campaign. The 1919 Tigers led the League in oWAR and oWS, procuring the team's fourth pennant in the process. Cicotte won 29 contests while completing 30 of 35 starts. Cobb (32 WS), Cicotte (32 WS) and Veach (31 WS) surpassed the 30 Win Shares plateau. Veach batted .355, pacing the circuit with 191 hits, 45 doubles, and 17 triples while Cobb collected his final batting title and batted an incredible .387 for the decade!

Win Shares > 20	Single-Season	1901-1919
George H. Burns - 1B (DET) x3	Doc Gessler - RF (DET)	Eddie Cicotte - SP (DET) x4
Harry Heilmann - 1B (DET)	Roscoe Miller - SP (DET)	Ed Lafitte - SP (DET)
Donie Bush - SS (DET) x5	Ed Siever - SP (DET)	Frank Allen - SP (DET)
Eddie Foster - 3B (DET) x3	George Mullin - SP (DET) x7	Hooks Dauss - SP (DET) x2
Ossie Vitt - 3B (DET) x2	Frank Owen - SP (DET) x2	Carl Mays - SP (DET) x5
Bobby Veach - LF (DET) x7	Bugs Raymond - SP (DET)	Lefty Williams - SP (DET)
Ty Cobb - CF (DET) x15	Ed Summers - SP (DET) x2	Eddie Cicotte - SW (DET)
Ty Cobb - RF (DET) x4	George Suggs - SP (DET) x2	Carl Mays - SW (DET)

Year/Team	OPW%	PW	PL	APW%	AW	AL	Diff+/-
1920 DET	0.506	78	76	0.396	61	93	-0.110
1921 DET	0.553	85	69	0.464	71	82	-0.089
1922 DET	0.527	81	73	0.513	79	75	-0.014
1923 DET	0.547	84	70	0.539	83	71	-0.008
1924 DET	0.530	82	72	0.558	86	68	0.028
1925 DET	0.518	80	74	0.526	81	73	0.008
1926 DET	0.480	74	80	0.513	79	75	0.033
1927 DET	0.542	83	71	0.536	82	71	-0.006
1928 DET	0.511	79	75	0.442	68	86	-0.070
1929 DET	0.543	84	70	0.455	70	84	-0.089

franchID	OWAR	OWS	AWAR	AWS	WARdiff	WSdiff	P/D/W/F
1920 DET	30.797	**236.583**	21.634	183.004	9.162	53.579	
1921 DET	**49.311**	**289.572**	40.443	212.999	8.868	76.573	
1922 DET	39.393	**266.641**	39.064	237.001	0.330	29.639	
1923 DET	36.404	248.232	43.338	249.001	-6.934	-0.769	
1924 DET	42.051	259.036	42.773	257.997	-0.722	1.039	
1925 DET	34.508	240.889	39.333	242.962	-4.825	-2.073	
1926 DET	40.341	263.185	36.348	237.005	3.993	26.180	
1927 DET	41.210	281.465	36.906	246.000	4.304	35.465	
1928 DET	39.168	259.372	28.379	203.999	10.789	55.373	
1929 DET	40.425	248.055	34.500	210.000	5.925	38.056	

The Motor City crew roared into the Twenties with three consecutive seasons atop the oWS leader board. The 1921 squad attained its best WSdiff (+77) vs. the output of the "Actual" Tigers from the same campaign. Mays (34 WS) mystified rival batsmen as he compiled a record of 27-9 with 7 saves. Harry Heilmann (.394/19/139) scored his first batting crown and rapped 237 hits. Cobb (.401/4/99) eclipsed the .400 plateau in 1922, but yielded the title to George Sisler (.420 BA). Captained by Cobb and Heilmann, Detroit outfielders compiled 58 WS>10 seasons from 1920-29. Moreover, the Tigers' left fielders continued this trend through 1949.

Heilmann (35 WS) paced the League with a .403 batting average en route to a third-place finish in the 1923 AL MVP balloting. "Slug" supplied a .364 BA for the decade along with 40 doubles and 113 ribbies per season. Heinie Manush earned a batting title with a .378 BA in '26 and went on to enjoy his finest year in 1928 (34 WS), leading the circuit with 241 base knocks and 47 two-baggers. Charlie Gehringer (.339/13/106) and Babe Herman (.381/21/113) supplied the thunder in the '29 Tigers lineup. Gehringer topped the charts with 215 hits, 131 runs scored, 45 doubles, 19 triples, and 27 steals.

Year/Team	OPW%	PW	PL	APW%	AW	AL	Diff+/-
1930 DET	0.516	79	75	0.487	75	79	-0.028
1931 DET	0.470	72	82	0.396	61	93	-0.074
1932 DET	0.516	79	75	0.503	76	75	-0.013
1933 DET	0.547	84	70	0.487	75	79	-0.060
1934 DET	0.578 P	89	65	0.656 P	101	53	0.077
1935 DET	0.582 P	90	64	0.616 P	93	58	0.034
1936 DET	0.568	87	67	0.539	83	71	-0.029
1937 DET	0.509	78	76	0.578	89	65	0.069
1938 DET	0.494	76	78	0.545	84	70	0.052
1939 DET	0.523	81	73	0.526	81	73	0.003

franchID	OWAR	OWS	AWAR	AWS	WARdiff	WSdiff	P/D/W/F
1930 DET	36.525	255.306	30.099	224.992	6.426	30.314	
1931 DET	32.213	228.521	23.975	182.998	8.238	45.523	
1932 DET	44.729	255.911	31.314	228.005	13.416	27.906	
1933 DET	41.283	255.355	35.108	224.998	6.175	30.357	
1934 DET	**49.000**	**282.854**	52.440	**303.003**	-3.440	-20.149	P
1935 DET	**49.872**	272.301	**51.017**	**278.998**	-1.145	-6.697	P
1936 DET	48.024	260.871	43.089	249.001	4.934	11.869	
1937 DET	42.963	258.144	40.607	266.993	2.356	-8.849	
1938 DET	37.906	255.920	34.791	252.001	3.116	3.919	
1939 DET	41.559	241.882	42.474	243.000	-0.915	-1.118	

Herman (32 WS) swatted 35 long balls and knocked in 130 runs while batting .393 during the 1930 campaign. Carl Hubbell's rapid ascension as ace of the Tigers' rotation culminated with MVP honors in '33. "Meal Ticket" posted league-bests in wins (23), innings pitched, shutouts, ERA (1.92), and WHIP (0.982). Detroit secured pennants in back-to-back seasons (1934-35). The '34 squad finished first in oWAR and oWS, with Gehringer (37 WS), Hubbell (32 WS), and Hank Greenberg (31 WS) exceeding the 30 Win Shares mark. Gehringer drilled 50 doubles and batted .356 while leading the League with 214 hits and 134 runs scored. Greenberg belted 63 two-base hits and drove in 139 runs, along with a .339 BA. Schoolboy Rowe yielded 24 wins with a 3.45 ERA.

Greenberg followed up with his first MVP award in 1935 and topped the leader boards with 36 round-trippers and 170 ribbies. Hubbell (26-6, 2.31) received his second MVP award in 1936, pacing the circuit in wins, ERA, and WHIP. Tommy Bridges surpassed the 20-win level in 3 consecutive campaigns (1934-36), including a league-best 23 victories in 1936. Gehringer slapped 60 doubles and achieved career-highs with 227 base hits and 144 runs in '36. "The Mechanical Man" secured MVP honors and the batting crown after hitting .371 during the '37 season. Greenberg made up for lost time after missing all but 12 games in 1936. "Hammerin' Hank" clouted 40 homers and drove in 183 runs in 1937 and then bashed 58 moon-shots in the subsequent season. Hubbell and Bridges led the influx of hurlers as the Tigers' starting staff posted 142 WS>10 seasons from 1930-1959.

Win Shares > 20	Single-Season	1920-1939
Wally Pipp - 1B (DET)	Heinie Manush - LF (DET) x5	Pete Fox - RF (DET)
Babe Herman - 1B (DET)	John Stone - LF (DET) x2	Gee Walker - RF (DET)
Lu Blue - 1B (DET) x3	Gee Walker - LF (DET)	John Stone - RF (DET)
Dale Alexander - 1B (DET)	Baby Doll Jacobson - CF	Lefty Stewart - SP (DET)
Hank Greenberg - 1B (DET)	(DET) x4	Carl Hubbell - SP (DET) x6
x6	Ray Powell - CF (DET)	Earl Whitehill - SP (DET)
Charlie Gehringer - 2B (DET)	Heinie Manush - CF (DET)	Tommy Bridges - SP (DET) x2
x10	Barney McCosky - CF (DET)	Schoolboy Rowe - SP (DET)
Topper Rigney - SS (DET)	x2	x2
Marv Owen - 3B (DET)	Harry Heilmann - RF (DET) x8	Elden Auker - SP (DET) x2
Rudy York - C (DET)	George W. Harper - RF (DET)	Luke Hamlin - SP (DET)
Bob Fothergill - LF (DET)	Babe Herman - RF (DET) x5	

Year/Team	OPW%	PW	PL	APW%	AW	AL	Diff+/-
1940 DET	0.552	85	69	0.584 P	90	64	0.033
1941 DET	0.473	73	81	0.487	75	79	0.014
1942 DET	0.464	71	83	0.474	73	81	0.010
1943 DET	0.536	83	71	0.506	78	76	-0.030
1944 DET	0.549 P	85	69	0.571	88	66	0.022
1945 DET	0.499	77	77	0.575 P	88	65	0.076
1946 DET	0.599	92	62	0.597	92	62	-0.002
1947 DET	0.519	80	74	0.552	85	69	0.033
1948 DET	0.525	81	73	0.506	78	76	-0.018
1949 DET	0.520	80	74	0.565	87	67	0.045

franchID	OWAR	OWS	AWAR	AWS	WARdiff	WSdiff	P/D/W/F
1940 DET	45.539	253.261	51.904	269.997	-6.365	-16.736	
1941 DET	36.773	228.322	35.130	224.994	1.643	3.327	
1942 DET	36.922	226.871	32.579	218.996	4.343	7.875	
1943 DET	40.103	246.747	39.859	233.999	0.244	12.748	
1944 DET	42.123	268.013	40.320	264.004	1.804	4.008	P
1945 DET	33.171	249.397	38.376	264.000	-5.204	-14.603	

1946 DET	**58.372**	303.604	49.857	275.999	8.514	27.605
1947 DET	47.206	266.259	44.081	255.003	3.125	11.256
1948 DET	47.057	266.011	40.634	233.999	6.423	32.012
1949 DET	42.264	232.585	43.409	260.996	-1.145	-28.411

Hank Greenberg (.340/41/150) continued his assault on American League hurlers, notching his second MVP award in 1940. Rudy York (.316/33/134) established career-bests in all of the major batting categories with the exception of triples and home runs. Whit Wyatt (22-10, 2.34) finished third in the MVP balloting in 1941 as he topped the charts in wins and WHIP (1.058).

The Tigers turned in a trio of twenty-game winners in '44 on the way to another pennant. Rip Sewell (23 WS) tallied 21 victories and completed 25 starts. Dizzy Trout (40 WS) fashioned a record of 27-9 and paced the circuit with a 2.12 ERA and 33 complete games. Trout finished runner-up for MVP honors behind teammate Hal Newhouser, winner of 29 contests with an ERA of 2.22. "Prince Hal" amassed 37 Win Shares in '45 en route to consecutive MVP awards and paced the League in wins (25), complete games (29), innings pitched, and ERA (1.81). Newhouser (26-9, 1.94) enjoyed his third consecutive season above the 25-win plateau and finished second in the 1946 AL MVP race. Detroit hurlers delivered the highest pitWARnorm (33) and pitWSnorm (133) totals in the history of the franchise.

In his first full season after returning from combat in World War II, Greenberg clubbed 44 moon-shots and drove in 127 runs for the '46 Tigers. Johnny Sain (20-14, 2.21) initiated three straight campaigns with at least 20 victories. Sain (28 WS) posted a runner-up finish in the 1948 MVP vote as he accrued 24 wins and completed 28 contests. Virgil Trucks (28 WS) fashioned a record of 19-11 with a 2.81 ERA, and Vic Wertz plated 133 runs after securing a full-time gig in '49.

Year/Team	OPW%	PW	PL	APW%	AW	AL	Diff+/-
1950 DET	0.541	83	71	0.617	95	59	0.076
1951 DET	0.462	71	83	0.474	73	81	0.012
1952 DET	0.425	65	89	0.325	50	104	-0.100
1953 DET	0.440	68	86	0.390	60	94	-0.051
1954 DET	0.433	67	87	0.442	68	86	0.009
1955 DET	0.578 P	89	65	0.513	79	75	-0.065
1956 DET	0.515	79	75	0.532	82	72	0.017
1957 DET	0.521 P	80	74	0.506	78	76	-0.015
1958 DET	0.557 P	86	68	0.500	77	77	-0.057
1959 DET	0.485	75	79	0.494	76	78	0.009

franchID	OWAR	OWS	AWAR	AWS	WARdiff	WSdiff	P/D/W/F
1950 DET	41.049	244.312	46.468	284.999	-5.418	-40.686	
1951 DET	33.270	204.667	33.891	218.998	-0.621	-14.331	
1952 DET	31.618	175.226	25.062	150.001	6.556	25.225	
1953 DET	27.813	162.054	23.783	180.000	4.031	-17.946	
1954 DET	41.703	226.462	42.884	237.002	-1.181	-10.540	
1955 DET	39.551	214.777	42.884	237.002	-3.333	-22.225	P
1956 DET	36.684	214.645	45.575	246.003	-8.891	-31.357	
1957 DET	36.311	233.016	35.908	234.002	0.404	-0.985	P
1958 DET	**37.965**	213.753	40.144	231.001	-2.179	-17.249	P
1959 DET	30.360	199.898	40.501	228.003	-10.142	-28.106	

Hoot Evers (26 WS) produced a .323 BA with 21 dingers, 103 ribbies, and a league-high 11 triples during the 1950 season. Harvey Kuenn (.308/2/48) merited Rookie of the Year honors after pacing the circuit with 209 hits in '52. With the exception of 1956, Detroit seized the pennant in each season from 1955-58. Al Kaline (31 WS) collected 200 hits and his lone batting title (.340 BA) on the way to a runner-up finish in the 1955 AL MVP balloting while Billy Pierce topped the charts with a 1.97 ERA and 1.099 WHIP.

Frank Lary (21-13, 3.15) headed a trio of Tigers who surpassed the 20-win mark in '56. Kaline finished third in the MVP race, and set a career-high with 128 RBI. Wertz blasted 32 round-trippers and then earned his fourth All-Star selection with a .282 batting average, 28 homers, and 105 RBI in 1957. Jim Bunning (20-8, 2.69) led the American League in victories and innings pitched during his first full season in '57. Kuenn won the batting crown with a .353 BA in 1959.

Win Shares > 20	Single-Season	1940-1959
Rudy York - 1B (DET) x4	Johnny Groth - CF (DET)	Dizzy Trout - SP (DET) x3
Les Fleming - 1B (DET)	Harvey Kuenn - CF (DET)	Hal Newhouser - SP (DET) x6
Roy Cullenbine - 1B (DET)	Al Kaline - CF (DET) x2	Johnny Sain - SP (DET) x3
Vic Wertz - 1B (DET) x2	Chet Laabs - RF (DET)	Fred Hutchinson - SP (DET)
Frank Bolling - 2B (DET)	Roy Cullenbine - RF (DET) x4	x2
Harvey Kuenn - SS (DET) x2	Pat Mullin - RF (DET)	Virgil Trucks - SP (DET) x2
Mark Christman - 3B (DET)	Vic Wertz - RF (DET) x3	Art Houtteman - SP (DET)
Hank Greenberg - LF (DET)	Al Kaline - RF (DET) x8	Billy Pierce - SP (DET) x5
Roy Cullenbine - LF (DET)	Harvey Kuenn - RF (DET)	Jim Bunning - SP (DET) x7
Dick Wakefield - LF (DET) x2	Whit Wyatt - SP (DET)	Frank Lary - SP (DET) x2
Barney McCosky - LF (DET)	Rip Sewell - SP (DET) x2	Bob Shaw - SW (DET)
Hoot Evers - LF (DET)		

Year/Team	OPW%	PW	PL	APW%	AW	AL	Diff+/-
1960 DET	0.429	66	88	0.461	71	83	0.032
1961 DET	0.515	83	79	0.623	101	61	0.109
1962 DET	0.513	83	79	0.528	85	76	0.015
1963 DET	0.478	77	85	0.488	79	83	0.010
1964 DET	0.486	79	83	0.525	85	77	0.039
1965 DET	0.490	79	83	0.549	89	73	0.059
1966 DET	0.482	78	84	0.543	88	74	0.061
1967 DET	0.527	85	77	0.562	91	71	0.034
1968 DET	0.560 P	91	71	0.636 P	103	59	0.076
1969 DET	0.508	82	80	0.556	90	72	0.047

franchID	OWAR	OWS	AWAR	AWS	WARdiff	WSdiff	P/D/W/F
1960 DET	27.895	175.296	39.013	213.003	-11.117	-37.707	
1961 DET	27.520	192.803	**54.068**	303.002	-26.549	-110.199	
1962 DET	28.879	195.485	42.964	255.005	-14.085	-59.520	
1963 DET	25.000	180.152	37.801	237.004	-12.800	-56.851	
1964 DET	33.526	216.343	40.803	254.998	-7.277	-38.655	
1965 DET	33.188	210.676	44.408	267.004	-11.220	-56.328	
1966 DET	34.751	232.450	43.158	264.001	-8.407	-31.552	
1967 DET	42.258	238.057	**49.030**	273.007	-6.772	-34.950	
1968 DET	**37.928**	255.984	56.858	**309.004**	-18.930	-53.019	P
1969 DET	**37.464**	223.204	45.996	270.005	-8.532	-46.801	

Detroit tallied its worst WSdiff (-110) and WARdiff (-27) vs. the output of the "Actual" Tigers during the 1961 campaign in spite of Al Kaline's efforts. He earned 30 Win Shares, bashed a league-leading 41 doubles and scored 116 runs while batting .324. Bill Freehan (.300/18/80) commenced a run of 10 consecutive All-Star appearances in 1964. On the mound, Bunning won 19 games in each season from 1964-66 and averaged 246 strikeouts with a 2.54 ERA during that timeframe.

Phil Regan earned his nickname, "The Vulture," after picking up 14 victories in relief appearances. Regan fashioned a 1.62 ERA, 0.934 WHIP and saved 21 contests for the '66 squad. Kaline made his 13th consecutive All-Star appearance and secured his tenth Gold Glove award in 1967, batting .308 with 25 jacks. The Tigers outlasted the Athletics in '68, taking the pennant by a single victory while leading the AL in oWAR and oWS. Freehan set career-highs with 25 circuit clouts and 84 ribbies and finished second in the MVP race. Willie Horton led the club with 36 long balls, and Jim Northrup drove in 90 runs.

GM Jim Campbell supervised 19 Amateur Drafts during his 21-year tenure in Detroit. Eleven of his draft classes accrued less than 100 Career Total Win Shares, and yet in the midst of this inferior run and possibly due to Scouting Director Bill Lajoie's acumen, the Tigers' draftees averaged 606 Career Total Win Shares and 93 Career Total WAR from 1974-76.

Year/Team	OPW%	PW	PL	APW%	AW	AL	Diff+/-
1970 DET	0.458	74	88	0.488	79	83	0.030
1971 DET	0.536	87	75	0.562	91	71	0.025
1972 DET	0.538	87	75	0.551 D	86	70	0.013
1973 DET	0.507	82	80	0.525	85	77	0.018
1974 DET	0.513	83	79	0.444	72	90	-0.069
1975 DET	0.426	69	93	0.358	57	102	-0.067
1976 DET	0.525 F	85	77	0.460	74	87	-0.065
1977 DET	0.482	78	84	0.457	74	88	-0.025
1978 DET	0.511	83	79	0.531	86	76	0.020
1979 DET	0.471	76	86	0.528	85	76	0.057

franchID	OWAR	OWS	AWAR	AWS	WARdiff	WSdiff	P/D/W/F
1970 DET	25.231	186.338	35.209	237.001	-9.978	-50.663	
1971 DET	36.201	222.732	47.530	272.999	-11.329	-50.267	
1972 DET	28.826	194.360	38.900	258.002	-10.074	-63.642	
1973 DET	33.657	215.707	36.853	254.999	-3.195	-39.292	
1974 DET	30.728	207.677	20.604	215.997	10.124	-8.319	
1975 DET	22.415	166.157	19.161	170.999	3.254	-4.842	
1976 DET	28.366	201.864	26.631	222.002	1.736	-20.137	F
1977 DET	22.017	170.257	33.612	221.997	-11.595	-51.741	
1978 DET	29.817	202.553	41.551	257.999	-11.735	-55.446	
1979 DET	30.641	197.924	40.810	251.995	-10.169	-54.071	

Mickey Lolich (25-14, 2.92) topped the American League in wins, games started, complete games, innings pitched, and strikeouts in 1971. Vida Blue edged Lolich for the Cy Young Award. John Hiller (10-5, 1.44) finished fourth in the MVP and Cy Young balloting in '73, topping the circuit with 38 saves and posting the highest Win Shares total in MLB history for a relief pitcher (30.8).

Baseball fans were entertained by the mound antics of Mark Fidyrch in 1976. "The Bird" merited Rookie of the Year honors and placed runner-up in the Cy Young balloting. He furnished a record of 19-9 with a league-best 2.34 ERA. Ron LeFlore provided a spark plug at the top of the lineup, generating a .300 BA and averaging 99 runs scored and 54 steals per season (1975-

79). Lerrin LaGrow delivered a 2.46 ERA and notched 25 saves for the '77 crew. Steve Kemp (.318/26/105) posted career-highs in the Triple Crown categories, and received his lone All-Star invitation in 1979.

Win Shares > 20	Single-Season	1960-1979
Bill Freehan - 1B (DET)	Lance Parrish - C (DET) x5	Leon Roberts - RF (DET)
Jason D. Thompson - 1B (DET) x2	Willie Horton - LF (DET) x2	Mickey Lolich - SP (DET) x3
Dick McAuliffe - 2B (DET) x2	Steve Kemp - LF (DET) x2	Jim Rooker - SP (DET)
Dick McAuliffe - SS (DET)	Jim Northrup - CF (DET)	Mark Fidrych - SP (DET)
Don Wert - 3B (DET)	Elliott Maddox - CF (DET)	Phil Regan - RP (DET)
Bill Freehan - C (DET) x4	Ron LeFlore - CF (DET) x4	John Hiller - RP (DET) x2
	Jim Northrup - RF (DET)	

Year/Team	OPW%	PW	PL	APW%	AW	AL	Diff+/-
1980 DET	0.507	82	80	0.519	84	78	0.012
1981 DET	0.531 D	86	76	0.550	60	49	0.019
1982 DET	0.510	83	79	0.512	83	79	0.002
1983 DET	0.481	78	84	0.568	92	70	0.087
1984 DET	0.504	82	80	0.642 P	104	58	0.138
1985 DET	0.464	75	87	0.522	84	77	0.057
1986 DET	0.524 D	85	77	0.537	87	75	0.013
1987 DET	0.515 F	83	79	0.605 P	98	64	0.090
1988 DET	0.510	83	79	0.543	88	74	0.033
1989 DET	0.451	73	89	0.364	59	103	-0.087

franchID	OWAR	OWS	AWAR	AWS	WARdiff	WSdiff	P/D/W/F
1980 DET	30.161	201.799	41.188	252.001	-11.027	-50.202	
1981 DET	24.179	151.177	26.300	180.004	-2.121	-28.826	D
1982 DET	34.036	220.370	38.997	249.004	-4.961	-28.634	
1983 DET	29.373	201.159	46.661	276.005	-17.288	-74.847	
1984 DET	36.417	230.082	57.261	311.996	-20.844	-81.915	
1985 DET	33.241	202.995	45.574	252.006	-12.333	-49.010	
1986 DET	42.418	235.710	43.416	261.004	-0.998	-25.294	D
1987 DET	40.079	251.409	51.218	294.003	-11.139	-42.594	F
1988 DET	34.271	248.159	36.186	263.999	-1.914	-15.840	
1989 DET	33.361	205.719	17.397	177.000	15.964	28.719	

LeFlore paced the American League with 97 stolen bases in 1980. The Tigers outlasted the Red Sox for the club's first division title in 1981 by a two-game margin. Jack Morris led the League in wins and placed third in the Cy Young balloting. Jason D. Thompson (.284/31/101) matched his career-best in home runs and drew 101 bases on balls for the '82 crew. Lou Whitaker (29 WS) established career-highs with a .320 BA, 206 hits, and 40 doubles in 1983 and Lance Parrish slugged 30 four-baggers and knocked in 99 runs per year (1982-85).

Detroit won 85 contests and topped the League in oWAR, seizing the AL Eastern Division title by four games in 1986. Morris anchored the pitching corps with a record of 21-8. Alan Trammell (.343/28/105) set career marks in batting average, runs (109), hits (205), home runs, and RBI. He tallied 35 Win Shares and finished runner-up in the 1987 MVP race. Howard Johnson earned a full-time job at the hot corner. "HoJo" proceeded to go on a five-year tear, slugging 31 long balls and swiping 32 bags per season (1987-91). Kirk Gibson never led the League in any offensive category and he never received an All-Star invitation despite averaging 27 homers, 30 steals, and 95 runs scored from 1984-88. Gibson's efforts were rewarded in 1988 when he received MVP honors after scoring 106 runs and netting 33 Win Shares. Mike Henneman earned 10+ victories in relief on three occasions and eclipsed the 20-save mark seven times in his career. The pitching staff endured a prolonged malaise in '89 (Morris and Ken Hill combined for a 13-29 record), and the Tigers ended the season in the AL East basement.

Year/Team	OPW%	PW	PL	APW%	AW	AL	Diff+/-
1990 DET	0.480	78	84	0.488	79	83	0.008
1991 DET	0.522	85	77	0.519	84	78	-0.004
1992 DET	0.520 F	84	78	0.463	75	87	-0.057
1993 DET	0.495	80	82	0.525	85	77	0.030
1994 DET	0.422	68	94	0.461	53	62	0.039
1995 DET	0.436	71	91	0.417	60	84	-0.019
1996 DET	0.422	68	94	0.327	53	109	-0.094
1997 DET	0.491	80	82	0.488	79	83	-0.004
1998 DET	0.476	77	85	0.401	65	97	-0.075
1999 DET	0.467	76	86	0.429	69	92	-0.038

franchID	OWAR	OWS	AWAR	AWS	WARdiff	WSdiff	P/D/W/F
1990 DET	39.399	221.568	33.891	236.975	5.507	-15.407	
1991 DET	40.705	237.438	36.660	252.001	4.044	-14.563	
1992 DET	44.635	224.347	34.207	225.000	10.427	-0.653	F
1993 DET	45.280	253.931	42.938	255.000	2.343	-1.069	
1994 DET	19.304	153.096	22.971	158.998	-3.668	-5.903	
1995 DET	29.385	209.395	19.417	180.003	9.968	29.392	
1996 DET	38.156	216.911	12.101	159.003	26.055	57.909	
1997 DET	35.532	236.748	33.714	236.999	1.818	-0.250	
1998 DET	39.277	240.474	26.369	194.995	12.908	45.478	
1999 DET	30.865	209.541	28.733	206.994	2.132	2.547	

During the 1991 season, Johnson achieved "30/30" status for the third time in five years, pacing the circuit with 38 moon-shots and 117 ribbies and scoring a career-high 108 runs. Hill contributed a record of 16-5 and placed second in the '94 Cy Young vote. John Smoltz (24-8, 2.94) achieved Cy Young status in 1996, topping the leader boards in victories, innings pitched, and strikeouts (276). The Tigers finished in the AL East cellar for 4 consecutive seasons (1994-97). The "Actual" 1996 squad put forth such a putrid effort that the basement-dwelling "Originals" scored the best WARdiff (+26) in team history. MLB realigned the divisions in '98 and Detroit was relocated to the AL Central.

Year/Team	OPW%	PW	PL	APW%	AW	AL	Diff+/-
2000 DET	0.395	64	98	0.488	79	83	0.092
2001 DET	0.422	68	94	0.407	66	96	-0.015
2002 DET	0.379 F	61	101	0.342	55	106	-0.037
2003 DET	0.400	65	97	0.265	43	119	-0.135
2004 DET	0.467	76	86	0.444	72	90	-0.023
2005 DET	0.429	69	93	0.438	71	91	0.010
2006 DET	0.485	79	83	0.586 W	95	67	0.102
2007 DET	0.527 D	85	77	0.543	88	74	0.016
2008 DET	0.470	76	86	0.457	74	88	-0.014
2009 DET	0.506	82	80	0.528	86	77	0.021
2010 DET	0.469	76	86	0.500	81	81	0.031
2011 DET	0.569 D	92	70	0.586 D	95	67	0.017
2012 DET	0.510 W	83	79	0.543 D	88	74	0.033
2013 DET	0.504 D	82	80	0.574 D	93	69	0.070

franchID	OWAR	OWS	AWAR	AWS	WARdiff	WSdiff	P/D/W/F
2000 DET	25.777	212.864	37.807	236.997	-12.030	-24.132	
2001 DET	24.872	247.265	19.665	198.002	5.208	49.263	
2002 DET	23.197	240.967	12.984	165.002	10.213	75.965	F
2003 DET	14.806	195.132	7.174	129.001	7.631	66.132	
2004 DET	27.453	238.621	36.609	215.995	-9.156	22.626	
2005 DET	30.181	221.187	30.858	213.002	-0.677	8.185	
2006 DET	35.092	241.979	39.790	285.006	-4.698	-43.027	
2007 DET	39.992	242.749	41.585	264.000	-1.593	-21.250	D
2008 DET	33.982	223.819	32.577	222.002	1.404	1.816	
2009 DET	39.307	244.018	33.423	257.997	5.885	-13.979	
2010 DET	36.613	238.643	38.512	242.999	-1.899	-4.356	
2011 DET	**47.774**	**285.458**	44.806	284.996	2.969	0.462	D
2012 DET	30.559	234.260	41.392	264.005	-10.834	-29.744	W
2013 DET	24.898	216.833	55.027	278.996	-30.129	-62.163	D

Travis Fryman established career-bests with a .321 batting average, 38 doubles, and 106 RBI during the 2000 season. Bobby Higginson (.300/30/102) bolstered the lineup with his greatest single-season production including 44 doubles and 104 runs scored. Francisco Cordero tallied 49 saves in 2004 and averaged 38 saves with a 3.01 ERA from 2004-2011. Justin Verlander (17-9, 3.63) received the AL Rookie of the Year honors in '06. Nevertheless, Detroit failed to crack the .500 mark from 1993-2006.

The curse was finally broken in 2007 as Detroit claimed its third division title, edging Chicago and Cleveland in a tight race. Curtis Granderson legged out 23 triples, and Verlander fashioned an 18-6 record. Granderson eclipsed the 40-home run mark in back-to-back seasons (2011-12) and paced the circuit with 136 runs scored and 119 RBI in 2011. Andres Torres cracked 43 two-base knocks and purloined 26 bags in 2010.

Verlander (24-5, 2.40) amassed 27 Win Shares and garnered the AL MVP and Cy Young trophies with a stellar season in 2011. He topped the leader boards ir wins, ERA, WHIP (0.920), innings pitched and strikeouts (250). Alex Avila (.295/19/82) established career-highs in every major offensive category and earned an All-Star invitation in 2011. Fernando Rodney flummoxed the opposition in 2012, posting 48 saves with a miniscule 0.60 ERA and 0.777 WHIP.

Win Shares > 20	Single-Season	1980-2013
Tony Clark - 1B (DET)	Alex Avila - C (DET)	Kirk Gibson - RF (DET) x2
Lou Whitaker - 2B (DET) x7	Kirk Gibson - LF (DET) x2	Jack Morris - SP (DET) x2
Alan Trammell - SS (DET) x7	Bobby Higginson - LF (DET)	Ken Hill - SP (DET)
Travis Fryman - SS (DET) x2	x3	John Smoltz - SP (DET) x2
Howard Johnson - 3B (DET)	Curtis Granderson - CF (DET)	Justin Thompson - SP (DET)
x5	x6	Justin Verlander - SP (DET)
Travis Fryman - 3B (DET)	Andres Torres - CF (DET)	x3
Chris Hoiles - C (DET)		

Note: 4000 PA or BFP to qualify, except during strike-shortened seasons
(1972 = 3800, 1981 & 1994 = 2700, 1995 = 3500) and 154-game schedule (3800)
- failed to qualify: 1904, 1976, 1987, 1992, 2002

Tigers All-Time "Originals" Roster

Bob M. Adams	Gene W. Ford	Dave Lemanczyk	Willis Roberts
Mike R. Adams	Eddie Foster	Mark Lemongello	Chris Robinson
Pat Ahearne	Larry Foster	Pete LePine	Jeff M. Robinson
Bill Akers	Bob Fothergill	George Lerchen	Mauricio Robles

Scott Aldred	Pete Fox	Don Leshnock	Mickey Rocco
Dale Alexander	Paul Foytack	Johnny Lewis	Buck Rodgers
Frank Allen	Moe Franklin	Jose Lima	Fernando Rodney
Ernie Alten	Jason Frasor	Chris Lindsay	Joe Rogalski
George Alusik	Jeff Frazier	Carl Linhart	Brian Rogers
Matt Anderson	Bill Freehan	Johnny Lipon	Bill Roman
George Archie	Luke French	Felipe Lira	Bruce Rondon
Harry Arndt	Cy Fried	Jack Lively	Jim Rooker
Fernando Arroyo	Bill Froats	Scott Livingstone	Cody Ross
Elden Auker	Travis Fryman	Nook Logan	Don Ross
Alex Avila	Charlie Fuchs	Mickey Lolich	Jack Rowan
Burke Badenhop	Frank Fuller	Lefty Lorenzen	Ken Rowe
Howard Bailey	Charlie Furbush	Art Loudell	Schoolboy Rowe
Del Baker	Chick Gagnon	Shane Loux	Rich Rowland
Doug Baker	Eddie Gaillard	Torey Lovullo	Dave Rozema
Steve Baker	Del Gainer	Dwight Lowry	Art Ruble
Billy Baldwin	Doug Gallagher	Willie Ludolph	Dave Rucker
Glen Barker	Barbaro Garbey	Scott Lusader	Chance Ruffin
Frank S. Barnes	Alex Garbowski	Duke Maas	Vern Ruhle
Sam Barnes	Avisail Garcia	Frank MacCormack	Dusty Ryan
Al Baschang	Luis R. Garcia	Bill MacDonald	Johnny Sain
Paddy Baumann	Mike R. Garcia	Elliott Maddox	Joe Samuels
Harry Baumgartner	Danny Gardella	Billy Maharg	Humberto Sanchez
John Baumgartner	Aubrey Gatewood	Bob Maier	Ramon Santiago
Danny Bautista	Charlie Gehringer	Alex Main	Victor Santos
Bill Bean	Rufe Gentry	Tom Makowski	Joe Sargent
Heinie Beckendorf	Doc Gessler	Herm Malloy	Dennis Saunders
Duane Below	Tony Giarratano	Hal Manders	Jay Sborz
Sean Bergman	Frank Gibson	Clyde Manion	Biff Schaller
Adam Bernero	Kirk Gibson	Phil Mankowski	Lou Schiappacasse
Johnny Bero	Sam Gibson	Jerry Manuel	Boss Schmidt
Neil Berry	Floyd Giebell	Heinie Manush	Mike Schwabe
Reno Bertoia	Bill Gilbreth	Leo Marentette	Chuck Scrivener
Randor Bierd	Bob Gillespie	Gene Markland	Steve Searcy
Josh H. Billings	George Gill	Dick Marlowe	Frank Secory
Babe Birrer	Joe Ginsberg	Buck Marrow	Chuck Seelbach
Ike Blessitt	Fred Gladding	Luis Marte	Bill Serena
Ben Blomdahl	John Glaiser	Cristhian Martinez	Rip Sewell
Lu Blue	Norman Glaser	John Martin	Gordon Seyfried
George Boehler	Ed Glynn	Roger Mason	Al L. Shaw
Brennan Boesch	Greg Gohr	Ron Mathis	Bob Shaw
John Bogart	Izzy Goldstein	Bob Mavis	Merv Shea
Bernie Boland	Purnal Goldy	Brian Maxcy	Hugh Shelley
Frank Bolling	Chris Gomez	Cameron Maybin	Jimmy Shevlin
Dave Borkowski	Dan Gonzales	Carl Mays	Ivcy Shiver
Red Borom	Don Gordon	Dick McAuliffe	Ron Shoop
Steve Boros	Johnny Gorsica	Arch McCarthy	Ed Siever
Jim Brady	Bill Graham	Barney McCosky	Hack Simmons
Rob Brantly	Curtis Granderson	Benny McCoy	Nelson Simmons
Tommy Bridges	Ted Gray	Ed McCreery	Scott Sizemore
Tarrik Brock	Al Greene	Red McDermott	Dave Skeels
Rico Brogna	Hank Greenberg	Dan McGarvey	Matt Skrmetta
Tom Brookens	Rick Greene	Jim McGarr	Bill Slayback
Louis Brower	Seth Greisinger	Pat McGehee	Jim Small
Alton Brown	Steve Grilli	John McHale	George C. Smith

Darrell Brown	Johnny Groth	Pat McLaughlin	George S. Smith
Frank Browning	Charlie Grover	Jim McManus	Jack J. Smith
Gates Brown	Joe Grzenda	Fred McMullin	Mayo Smith
Ike Brown	Glenn Gulliver	Carl McNabb	Rufus Smith
Lindsay Brown	Dave Gumpert	Norm McRae	Willie Smith
Bob Bruce	Dave Haas	Rusty Meacham	John Smoltz
Andy Bruckmiller	Kent Hadley	Vincent Maney	Drew Smyly
Arlo Brunsberg	Sammy Hale	Scott Medvin	Clint Sodowsky
Don Bryant	Bob L. Hall	Phil Meeler	Vic Sorrell
George Bullard	Herb Hall	Bob Melvin	Joe Sparma
Jim Bunning	Luke Hamlin	Herm Merritt	Kid Speer
Les Burke	Fred Haney	Catfish Metkovich	Bob Sprout
George H. Burns	Don Hankins	Charlie Metro	Mickey Stanley
Jack J. Burns	Jack Hannahan	Dan T. Meyer	Joe Staton
Sheldon Burnside	Charlie Harding	Ed Mierkowicz	Dave Stegman
Donie Bush	Shawn Hare	Andrew Miller	Lefty Stewart
Bill F. Butler	George W. Harper	Bob G. Miller	Phil Stidham
Les Cain	Andy M. Harrington	Hack J. Miller	John Stone
Dave W. Campbell	Bob Harris	Matt L. Miller	Lil Stoner
George Cappuzzello	Ned Harris	Otis Miller	Max St. Pierre
Conrad Cardinal	Clyde Hatter	Roscoe Miller	Bob Strampe
Javier Cardona	Ray Hayworth	Trever Miller	Doug Strange
Luke Carlin	Harry Heilmann	Clarence Mitchell	Walt Streuli
Jesse Carlson	Don Heinkel	Brian Moehler	Sailor Stroud
Ownie Carroll	Les Hennessey	John Mohardt	Jim Stump
Frank Carswell	Mike Henneman	Bob Molinaro	George Suggs
Chuck Cary	Chuck Hensley	Rich Monteleone	Charlie Sullivan
Joe Casey	Ray Herbert	Anse Moore	Jackie Sullivan
Ron Cash	Babe Herman	Bill C. Moore	Joe Sullivan
Nick Castellanos	Anderson Hernandez	Jackie Moore	John E. Sullivan
Marty Castillo	Gorkys Hernandez	Scott Moore	John Peter Sullivan
Frank Catalanotto	Art Herring	Harry Moran	Russ Sullivan
Pug Cavet	Gus Hetling	Chet Morgan	Ed Summers
Gary Christenson	Bobby Higginson	Kevin Morgan	Suds Sutherland
Mark Christman	Ed High	Jack Morris	Bill Joseph Sweeney
Mike Chris	Hugh High	Bubba Morton	Bob Swift
Eddie Cicotte	John Hiller	Guillermo Moscoso	Bob Sykes
Anthony Claggett	Ken Hill	Les Mueller	Ken Szotkiewicz
Davey Claire	Paul Hinrichs	George Mullin	Jordan Tata
Danny Clark	Billy Hoeft	Pat Mullin	Jackie Tavener
Phil B. Clark	Chief Hogsett	Eric Munson	Gary Taylor
Rickey Clark	Bobby Hogue	Jack Ness	Wiley Taylor
Rufe Clarke	Chris Hoiles	Johnny Neun	Birdie Tebbetts
Tony Clark	Bryan Holaday	Hal Newhouser	John Terry
Al Clauss	Fred Holdsworth	Ray Newman	Clete Thomas
Brent Clevlen	Carl Holling	Fred Nicholson	Frosty Thomas
Flea Clifton	Mike Hollimon	Simon Nicholls	George Thomas
Joe Cobb	Ken Holloway	Fu-Te Ni	Jason D. Thompson
Ty Cobb	Vern Holtgrave	Ron Nischwitz	Justin Thompson
Chris Codiroli	Joe Hoover	Jim Northrup	Tom Timmermann
Slick Coffman	Willie Horton	Lou North	Dave Tobik
Bert Cole	Tim Hosley	Randy Nosek	Andres Torres
Orlin Collier	Chuck Hostetler	Frank Okrie	Alan Trammell
Ralph Comstock	Gene Host	Red Oldham	Bubba Trammell
Clint Conatser	Fred House	Charley O'Leary	Allan Travers

Dick Conger
Allen Conkwright
Tim M. Corcoran
Francisco Cordero
Bryan Corey
Nate Cornejo
Johnny Couch
Tex Covington
Red Cox
Pete Craig
Davey Crockett
Casey Crosby
Frank Croucher
Roy Crumpler
Ivan Cruz
Rhiner Cruz
Roy Cullenbine
George Cunningham
Milt Cuyler
Chuck Daniel
Mike C. Darr
Doc Daugherty
Hooks Dauss
Jerry Davie
Harry A. Davis
Woody Davis
Charlie Deal
Dennis DeBarr
John Deering
Eulogio De La Cruz
Steve Demeter
Gene Desautels
John DeSilva
Jack Dilauro
Andy Dirks
George Disch
Brent Dlugach
Pat Dobson
John H. Doherty
Frank Doljack
Freddy Dolsi
Snooks Dowd
Red Downs
Jess Doyle
Paul Doyle
Dick Drago
Delos Drake
Bob Dustal
Scott Earl
Paul Easterling
Zeb Eaton
Eric Eckenstahler
Brian Edmondson
Dick W. Egan
Wish Egan

Frank House
Wayne Housie
Art Houtteman
Carl Hubbell
Clarence Huber
Tom F. Hughes
Bob Humphreys
Fred Hutchinson
Gary Ignasiak
Omar Infante
Brandon Inge
Riccardo Ingram
Ed Irvin
Herbert Jackson
Baby Doll Jacobson
Charlie Jaeger
Art James
Paul Jata
Frank Jelincich
Willie Jensen
Augie Johns
Bob W. Johnson
Howard Johnson
Roy C. Johnson
Syl Johnson
Bob W. Jones
Deacon C. Jones
Elijah Jones
Ken Jones
Milt Jordan
Matthew Joyce
Jair Jurrjens
Walt Justis
Al Kaline
Rudy Kallio
Gabe Kapler
Marty Kavanagh
Kris Keller
Bryan Kelly
Don Kelly
Steve Kemp
Russ Kerns
John Kerr
Masao Kida
John Kiely
Mike Kilkenny
Red Killefer
Chick King
Jay Kirke
Rube Kisinger
Rudy Kneisch
John Knox
Kurt Knudsen
Alan Koch
Brad Kocher

Andy Oliver
Lester Oliveros
Ole Olsen
Ollie O'Mara
Randy O'Neal
Eddie Onslow
Jack Onslow
Joe Orrell
Jose Ortega
Bobo Osborne
Stubby Overmire
Frank Owen
Marv Owen
Ray Oyler
Phil Page
Rey Palacios
Salty Parker
Slicker Parks
Lance Parrish
Dixie Parsons
Steve Partenheimer
Johnny Pasek
Larry Pashnick
Bob Patrick
Fred Payne
Terry Pearson
Marv Peasley
Steve Pegues
Rudy Pemberton
Gene Pentz
Pepper Peploski
Don Pepper
Hernan Perez
Santiago Perez
Hub Pernoll
Boyd Perry
Clay Perry
Hank Perry
Ryan Perry
John Peters
Rick Peters
Dan Petry
Adam Pettyjohn
Bubba Phillips
Red Phillips
Billy Pierce
Wally Pipp
Chris Pittaro
Al Platte
Boots Poffenberger
Rick Porcello
Lew Post
Brian Powell
Ray Powell
Jim Proctor

Mike Tresh
Dizzy Trout
Bun Troy
Virgil Trucks
John Tsitouris
Jacob Turner
Bill Tuttle
Guy Tutwiler
Jerry Ujdur
Pat Underwood
Al Unser
Virgil Vasquez
Bobby Veach
Coot Veal
Lou Vedder
Jorge Velandia
Justin Verlander
Tom Veryzer
George Vico
Brayan Villarreal
Ossie Vitt
Bill Voss
Jake Wade
Mark Wagner
Dick Wakefield
Chris Wakeland
Jim Walewander
Frank Walker
Gee Walker
Hub Walker
Jim H. Walkup
Jim Walsh
Ken Walters
Colin Ward
Daryle Ward
Jon Warden
Hap Ward
Jack R. Warner
Mike Warren
Dave Watkins
Johnny Watson
Jeff Weaver
Roger Weaver
Thad Weber
Milt Welch
Casper Wells
Ed Wells
Don Wert
Vic Wertz
Charlie Wheatley
Lou Whitaker
Earl Whitehill
Jo-Jo White
Sean Whiteside
Adam Wilk

Heinie Elder	Graham Koonce	Augie Prudhomme	Ed Willett
Babe Ellison	Howie Koplitz	Luke Putkonen	Carl Willis
Juan Encarnacion	George Korince	George Quellich	Johnnie Williams
Joe Erautt	Andy Kosco	Mike Rabelo	Lefty Williams
Tex Erwin	Clem Koshorek	Ryan Raburn	Glenn Wilson
Mark Ettles	Frank Kostro	Wilkin Ramirez	Icehouse Wilson
John Eubank	Lou Kretlow	Bugs Raymond	Mutt Wilson
Hoot Evers	Harvey Kuenn	Wayne Redmond	Squanto Wilson
Bill Faul	Chet Laabs	Bob Reed	Walter Wilson
Al Federoff	Ed Lafitte	Rich Reese	Hughie Wise
Jack Feller	Mike Laga	Phil Regan	Shannon Withem
Chico L. Fernandez	Lerrin LaGrow	Frank Reiber	Larry Woodall
Rick Ferrell	Gene Lamont	Alex Remneas	Jake Wood
Cy Ferry	Marvin Lane	Erwin Renfer	Joe P. Wood
Robert Fick	Jeff Larish	Tony Rensa	Mark Woodyard
Mark Fidrych	Steve Larkin	Ross Reynolds	Shawn Wooten
Bruce Fields	Frank Lary	Will Rhymes	Ralph Works
Casey Fien	Chick Lathers	Nolen Richardson	Danny Worth
Danny Fife	Charley Lau	Rob Richie	Yats Wuestling
Ed Fisher	Bill Lawrence	Hank Riebe	Whit Wyatt
Fritz Fisher	Rick Leach	Ron Rightnowar	Archie Yelle
Ira Flagstead	Razor Ledbetter	Topper Rigney	Tom Yewcic
Les Fleming	Don Lee	Kevin Ritz	Rudy York
Tom Fletcher	Mark O. Lee	Mike Rivera	John Young
Van Fletcher	Ron LeFlore	Bruce Robbins	Kip Young
Brian Flynn	Bill Leinhauser	Dave R. Roberts	Carl Zamloch
Jim Foor	Bill Lelivelt	Leon Roberts	Joel Zumaya

Washington Senators (I) / Minnesota Twins

Year/Team	OPW%	PW	PL	APW%	AW	AL	Diff+/-
1901 WS1	0.573	78	58	0.459	61	72	-0.114
1902 WS1	0.494	67	69	0.449	61	75	-0.045
1903 WS1	0.526	74	66	0.314	43	94	-0.212
1904 WS1	0.429	66	88	0.252	38	113	-0.177
1905 WS1	0.467 F	72	82	0.424	64	87	-0.043
1906 WS1	0.544 F	84	70	0.367	55	95	-0.177
1907 WS1	0.407	63	91	0.325	49	102	-0.082
1908 WS1	0.471	72	82	0.441	67	85	-0.030
1909 WS1	0.357	55	99	0.276	42	110	-0.080

franchID	OWAR	OWS	AWAR	AWS	WARdiff	WSdiff	P/D/W/F
1901 WS1	6.365	37.275	26.466	182.994	-20.100	-145.718	
1902 WS1	3.606	40.708	27.327	182.995	-23.722	-142.287	
1903 WS1	4.471	52.543	7.819	129.005	-3.348	-76.462	
1904 WS1	5.695	62.486	5.058	113.998	0.637	-51.512	
1905 WS1	3.269	76.052	15.934	191.996	-12.665	-115.945	F
1906 WS1	18.099	124.132	18.794	165.001	-0.695	-40.869	F
1907 WS1	11.459	92.102	29.675	147.005	-18.217	-54.903	
1908 WS1	18.441	126.544	33.681	200.999	-15.240	-74.454	
1909 WS1	19.735	122.652	12.388	126.004	7.347	-3.352	

Legend: (P) = Pennant / Most Wins in League (D) = Division Winner (W) = Wild Card Winner (F) = Failed to Qualify

Washington entered the Major Leagues as one of the eight original American League franchises in 1901. Based on the WS>20 frame of reference, the club developed the second-fewest quality catchers (6) and shortstops (9) among the "Turn of the Century" franchises. The organization's scouting and player development finished last among the ToC teams with 38 WS>10 seasons at shortstop. Joe Mauer accounts for all of the team's WS>20 seasons for backstops, therefore the team failed to produce any superstar catchers in its first century of existence! The Senators and Twins' right fielders, starting and relief pitchers never placed in the top three of the WS>10 leader boards.

The franchise ace, Walter Johnson, made his Major League debut in 1907. He completed 11 of 12 starts and fashioned an ERA of 1.88, commencing arguably the finest pitching career in the history of baseball. Johnson delivered a 1.65 ERA and 0.964 WHIP along with 14 wins in his first full season (1908). With minimal offensive support from his teammates, Johnson suffered through a 13-25 season in '09 and the Senators placed last in the American League with 99 losses.

Year/Team	OPW%	PW	PL	APW%	AW	AL	Diff+/-
1910 WS1	0.465 F	72	82	0.305	47	107	-0.160
1911 WS1	0.410 F	63	91	0.416	64	90	0.005
1912 WS1	0.582 F	90	64	0.599	91	61	0.017
1913 WS1	0.570 F	88	66	0.584	90	64	0.015
1914 WS1	0.563	87	67	0.526	81	73	-0.037
1915 WS1	0.565	87	67	0.556	85	68	-0.010
1916 WS1	0.489	75	79	0.497	76	77	0.008
1917 WS1	0.478	74	80	0.484	74	79	0.006
1918 WS1	0.491	63	65	0.563	72	56	0.071
1919 WS1	0.472	66	74	0.400	56	84	-0.072

franchID	OWAR	OWS	AWAR	AWS	WARdiff	WSdiff	P/D/W/F
1910 WS1	33.404	165.556	31.148	198.004	2.255	-32.448	F
1911 WS1	23.177	157.731	23.996	192.001	-0.819	-34.270	F
1912 WS1	44.210	258.792	39.294	273.000	4.916	-14.208	F
1913 WS1	45.013	275.572	38.377	270.003	6.635	5.569	F
1914 WS1	46.140	256.050	37.479	243.005	8.661	13.046	
1915 WS1	49.125	272.154	41.977	254.992	7.148	17.463	
1916 WS1	36.031	224.169	37.599	228.000	-1.568	-3.831	
1917 WS1	34.725	214.760	33.721	221.995	1.005	-7.234	
1918 WS1	26.160	188.581	35.366	215.999	-9.205	-27.418	
1919 WS1	33.616	194.938	31.056	168.000	2.559	26.937	

Johnson exceeded 30 Win Shares in a season on eight occasions and surpassed the 20-win plateau in every year from 1910-1919. "Big Train" topped the AL leader boards in '10 with 38 complete games in 42 starts, 370 innings pitched and 313 whiffs. The Senators' plodding offense received a boost from Clyde Milan who pilfered 44 bags. "Deerfoot" slapped 194 hits, scored 109 runs and swiped 58 bases during the next year.

The "Big Train" steamrolled the competition in 1912, amassing 33 wins along with his first ERA title (1.39). Johnson's efforts culminated with an MVP award in '13. He conquered the opposition batsmen, posting a 36-7 record with 11 shutouts while fashioning a miniscule ERA (1.14) and WHIP (0.780). Bob Groom (24-13, 2.62) gave the rotation a lift in 1912. Milan topped the stolen base charts with 88 steals in '12, and 75 swipes in '13. The 1915 Senators' moundsmen posted the highest pitWARnorm (28) and pitWSnorm (126) totals in team annals.

Sam Rice filched 35 bases and batted .302 in his first full season (1917). Over the course of the decade, Johnson's incredible yearly averages included 26 wins, 33 complete games, 222 strikeouts, a 1.59 ERA and a WHIP of 0.953. He surpassed 300 IP in every season except in 1919 (290 IP) and delivered an ERA under 2.00 in all seasons aside from 1917 (2.21).

Win Shares > 20	Single-Season	1901-1919
Tim Jordan - 1B (MIN) x2	Tilly Walker - LF (MIN) x2	Walter Johnson - SP (MIN)
Ray Morgan - 2B (MIN)	Clyde Milan - CF (MIN) x6	x14
Bill Kenworthy - 2B (MIN) x2	Sam Rice - RF (MIN) x6	Bert Gallia - SP (MIN)
Joe F. Connolly - LF (MIN)	Bob Groom - SP (MIN)	Joe Boehling - SW (MIN)

Year/Team	OPW%	PW	PL	APW%	AW	AL	Diff+/-
1920 WS1	0.470	72	82	0.447	68	84	-0.023
1921 WS1	0.492 F	76	78	0.523	80	73	0.031
1922 WS1	0.548 F	84	70	0.448	69	85	-0.100
1923 WS1	0.513 F	79	75	0.490	75	78	-0.023
1924 WS1	0.615 P	95	59	0.597 P	92	62	-0.018
1925 WS1	0.565 P	87	67	0.636 P	96	55	0.071
1926 WS1	0.507	78	76	0.540	81	69	0.033
1927 WS1	0.523	80	74	0.552	85	69	0.029
1928 WS1	0.511	79	75	0.487	75	79	-0.024
1929 WS1	0.474	73	81	0.467	71	81	-0.007

franchID	OWAR	OWS	AWAR	AWS	WARdiff	WSdiff	P/D/W/F
1920 WS1	27.020	215.647	29.048	204.006	-2.028	11.641	
1921 WS1	42.886	308.087	31.562	239.998	11.323	68.089	F
1922 WS1	35.747	290.732	25.285	206.997	10.462	83.735	F
1923 WS1	31.987	262.476	29.062	225.000	2.924	37.476	F
1924 WS1	**43.125**	**287.500**	**44.551**	**276.001**	-1.426	11.500	P
1925 WS1	39.892	**267.134**	**45.091**	**287.995**	-5.199	-20.861	P
1926 WS1	34.200	269.441	34.610	243.001	-0.410	26.440	
1927 WS1	36.577	253.883	37.817	254.999	-1.241	-1.116	
1928 WS1	40.488	273.032	37.172	225.000	3.316	48.033	
1929 WS1	30.760	245.104	30.379	212.997	0.381	32.106	

Rice contributed 211 base knocks and a .338 BA while pacing the junior circuit with 63 stolen bases in 1920. Irish Meusel produced a .320 batting average and 104 RBI per season from 1920-25. He drove in 132 runs in '22 and topped the charts with 125 ribbies in the subsequent season. In 1922 Tilly Walker thumped 37 taters and scored 111 runs (both career-bests) in his penultimate season.

Goose Goslin cracked the starting lineup in '23 and led the League with 18 triples, while in the same year Charlie Jamieson contributed a league-high 222 hits and batted .345 with 130 runs scored for the Washington ballclub. "Cuckoo" posted a career-best .359 BA in the ensuing campaign and hit at a .317 clip from 1920-1930. Jamieson, Goslin and Meusel lifted the Senators' left field contingent to a Major League-leading 31 WS>10 seasons during the 1920's.

Washington finally conquered the opposition, achieving consecutive pennants in 1924-25. Johnson (23-7, 2.72) received MVP accolades for his pitching exploits in '24. Goslin (.344/12/129) topped the circuit in RBI, while Rice supplied 216 hits. Washington led the League in oWAR and oWS in 1924. The Senators played the Athletics and White Sox to a virtual tie in '25. Rice, a .322 career hitter, established personal bests with 227 base knocks and a .350 batting average during the 1925 campaign.

Firpo Marberry pioneered the "relief ace" role, setting career-bests with 22 saves and 59 relief appearances in '26. Rice finished fourth in the 1926 AL MVP balloting after pacing the League with 216 base hits. Goslin averaged .348 with 99 runs scored and 114 RBI from 1924-28 and seized the batting crown after hitting at a .379 clip in 1928. Alvin "General" Crowder delivered a 21-5 record in '28 and posted 21 victories per season from 1928-33.

Year/Team	OPW%	PW	PL	APW%	AW	AL	Diff+/-
1930 WS1	0.569 P	88	66	0.610	94	60	0.042
1931 WS1	0.560	86	68	0.597	92	62	0.037
1932 WS1	0.512	79	75	0.604	93	61	0.092
1933 WS1	0.569 P	88	66	0.651 P	99	53	0.083
1934 WS1	0.476	73	81	0.434	66	86	-0.041
1935 WS1	0.450	69	85	0.438	67	86	-0.012
1936 WS1	0.518	80	74	0.536	82	71	0.018
1937 WS1	0.413	64	90	0.477	73	80	0.064
1938 WS1	0.495	76	78	0.497	75	76	0.001
1939 WS1	0.478	74	80	0.428	65	87	-0.050

franchID	OWAR	OWS	AWAR	AWS	WARdiff	WSdiff	P/D/W/F
1930 WS1	38.176	285.545	44.761	282.003	-6.585	3.542	P
1931 WS1	42.607	276.489	42.991	276.003	-0.384	0.486	
1932 WS1	36.755	265.995	40.665	279.004	-3.909	-13.009	
1933 WS1	38.885	263.448	47.484	**297.000**	-8.599	-33.553	P
1934 WS1	28.616	206.555	29.897	197.996	-1.281	8.559	
1935 WS1	30.019	216.691	26.617	201.000	3.402	15.691	
1936 WS1	39.028	259.921	36.818	245.993	2.210	13.927	
1937 WS1	26.883	215.259	26.925	219.001	-0.042	-3.742	
1938 WS1	37.530	246.722	34.704	225.006	2.826	21.716	
1939 WS1	32.980	238.081	31.325	195.003	1.654	43.078	

The Senators claimed the American League pennant in 1930 by a single game over the Athletics. Sam Rice topped the 200-hit mark for the sixth time in his career, batted at a .349 clip and scored a personal-best 121 runs. Goose Goslin established individual marks with 37 round-trippers and 138 RBI. Alvin Crowder (26-13, 3.33) led the League in wins and innings pitched for the '32 club. "General" followed up with a 24-win season as Washington outlasted New York for the League title in 1933. Joe Kuhel propelled the offense with a .322 BA and 107 ribbies.

The D.C. crew suffered last-place finishes in 1934-35. Buddy Myer (32 WS) procured the batting crown with a .349 average and collected 215 hits en route to a fourth-place finish in the 1935 AL MVP race. The Senators endured another miserable campaign in '37 in spite of Cecil Travis (.344 BA) and Buddy Lewis who batted .314 with 210 base knocks and 107 runs. Lewis supplied a .306 average with 30 doubles and 102 runs scored during a six-year stretch (1936-41). George Case nabbed the stolen base title in 5 consecutive seasons, averaging 45 thefts and 102 runs scored from 1939-1943.

Win Shares > 20	Single-Season	1920-1939
Joe Judge - 1B (MIN)	Irish Meusel - LF (MIN) x2	Bing Miller - RF (MIN)
Joe Kuhel - 1B (MIN) x4	Goose Goslin - LF (MIN) x10	Goose Goslin - RF (MIN)
Buddy Myer - 2B (MIN) x5	Charlie Jamieson - LF (MIN)	Alvin Crowder - SP (MIN) x4
Cecil Travis - SS (MIN) x3	Sam Rice - CF (MIN) x3	Bump Hadley - SP (MIN) x2
Howie Shanks - 3B (MIN)	Bing Miller - CF (MIN)	Firpo Marberry - SW (MIN)
Buddy Lewis - 3B (MIN) x2	Sam West - CF (MIN)	

Year/Team	OPW%	PW	PL	APW%	AW	AL	Diff+/-
1940 WS1	0.412	63	91	0.416	64	90	0.004
1941 WS1	0.470	72	82	0.455	70	84	-0.015
1942 WS1	0.423	65	89	0.411	62	89	-0.012
1943 WS1	0.490	75	79	0.549	84	69	0.059
1944 WS1	0.471 F	73	81	0.416	64	90	-0.055
1945 WS1	0.452	70	84	0.565	87	67	0.113
1946 WS1	0.391	60	94	0.494	76	78	0.102
1947 WS1	0.434	67	87	0.416	64	90	-0.019
1948 WS1	0.398	61	93	0.366	56	97	-0.032
1949 WS1	0.361	56	98	0.325	50	104	-0.036

franchID	OWAR	OWS	AWAR	AWS	WARdiff	WSdiff	P/D/W/F
1940 WS1	30.223	222.529	26.028	192.001	4.195	30.528	
1941 WS1	32.188	255.613	29.697	210.006	2.492	45.607	
1942 WS1	24.915	221.317	26.420	186.003	-1.505	35.313	
1943 WS1	29.278	233.799	40.527	251.993	-11.249	-18.194	
1944 WS1	22.779	211.179	30.010	192.007	-7.231	19.172	F
1945 WS1	33.277	240.404	40.643	261.009	-7.366	-20.604	
1946 WS1	17.150	208.480	27.373	227.993	-10.223	-19.513	
1947 WS1	20.055	217.685	18.222	192.002	1.833	25.683	
1948 WS1	14.236	181.387	13.115	167.997	1.121	13.390	
1949 WS1	20.878	169.014	15.493	150.003	5.385	19.011	

Travis (.359/7/101) paced the junior circuit with 218 base hits and tallied 34 Win Shares in 1941. Taffy Wright posted a .328 through his first five seasons (1938-42). Mickey Vernon (33 WS) earned his first All-Star invitation and collected his first batting title with a .353 average in '46. Vernon walloped a league-high 51 doubles and 207 hits while placing fifth in the AL MVP balloting.

Year/Team	OPW%	PW	PL	APW%	AW	AL	Diff+/-
1950 WS1	0.437 F	67	87	0.435	67	87	-0.002
1951 WS1	0.547 F	84	70	0.403	62	92	-0.144
1952 WS1	0.510 F	79	75	0.506	78	76	-0.003
1953 WS1	0.586 F	90	64	0.500	76	76	-0.086
1954 WS1	0.555 F	86	68	0.429	66	88	-0.127
1955 WS1	0.442	68	86	0.344	53	101	-0.098
1956 WS1	0.406 F	62	92	0.383	59	95	-0.022
1957 WS1	0.341 F	53	101	0.357	55	99	0.016
1958 WS1	0.463 F	71	83	0.396	61	93	-0.067
1959 WS1	0.565 F	87	67	0.409	63	91	-0.156

franchID	OWAR	OWS	AWAR	AWS	WARdiff	WSdiff	P/D/W/F
1950 MIN	30.897	189.919	25.218	201.000	5.680	-11.081	F
1951 MIN	35.705	211.967	21.674	185.998	14.031	25.969	F
1952 MIN	29.360	207.301	25.630	234.000	3.730	-26.699	F
1953 MIN	32.810	196.753	32.268	227.997	0.542	-31.244	F
1954 MIN	29.609	197.625	18.605	159.001	11.004	38.624	F
1955 MIN	28.329	189.083	18.605	159.001	9.724	30.082	
1956 MIN	24.762	162.469	18.236	177.001	6.526	-14.532	F
1957 MIN	18.870	125.405	17.886	164.998	0.984	-39.593	F
1958 MIN	25.788	174.005	18.895	183.002	6.892	-8.996	F
1959 MIN	48.383	240.586	28.790	188.994	19.593	51.593	F

After four consecutive last-place finishes from 1946-49, Washington suffered through a long dry spell, failing to meet the PA minimums in every year from 1950-1961 except in 1955 when the club finished in the American League basement. Early Wynn fashioned an 18-8 record and topped all hurlers with a 3.20 ERA and 1.250 WHIP in '50. Wynn exceeded 20 victories in five separate campaigns during the 1950's.

Mickey Vernon (.337/15/115) garnered his second batting crown and finished third in the 1953 AL MVP vote. Eddie Yost coaxed 100 bases on balls eight times during his career and led the League on six occasions. "The Walking Man" posted a .406 OBP and tallied 119 walks per year from 1950-1960. Calvin Griffith assumed ownership of the Senators upon his father Clark's passing in October 1955. Griffith, also serving as the club's GM, obtained a veratible All-Star squad via amateur free agency including Camilo Pascual ('52), Harmon Killebrew ('54), Bob Allison ('55), Jim Kaat ('57), Tony Oliva ('61), Reggie Smith ('63) and Rod Carew ('64).

Pete Runnels scored 103 runs and batted .322 for the '58 squad. Dick Hyde delivered 10 victories, 18 saves, and a 1.75 ERA. Wynn (22-10, 3.17) received the Cy Young Award and placed third in the 1959 AL MVP balloting. Harmon Killebrew walloped a league-best 42 big-flies upon earning a full-time job at the hot corner in 1959. Bob Allison thumped 30 moon-shots and prevailed in the AL Rookie of the Year vote.

Win Shares > 20	Single-Season	1940-1959
Mickey Vernon - 1B (MIN) x7	Harmon Killebrew - 3B (MIN) x4	George Case - RF (MIN)
Pete Runnels - 2B (MIN) x2		Ken Chase - SP (MIN)
Pete Runnels - SS (MIN)	George Case - LF (MIN) x2	Walt Masterson - SP (MIN)
Cecil Travis - 3B (MIN)	Buddy Lewis - RF (MIN) x3	Early Wynn - SP (MIN) x6
Eddie Yost - 3B (MIN) x6	Taffy Wright - RF (MIN) x2	Camilo Pascual - SP (MIN) x3

Year/Team	OPW%	PW	PL	APW%	AW	AL	Diff+/-
1960 WS1	0.529 F	81	73	0.474	73	81	-0.055
1961 MIN	0.486 F	79	83	0.438	70	90	-0.049
1962 MIN	0.576 P	93	69	0.562	91	71	-0.014
1963 MIN	0.608 P	99	63	0.565	91	70	-0.043
1964 MIN	0.557	90	72	0.488	79	83	-0.070
1965 MIN	0.644 P	104	58	0.630 P	102	60	-0.014
1966 MIN	0.526	85	77	0.549	89	73	0.023
1967 MIN	0.582 P	94	68	0.562	91	71	-0.020
1968 MIN	0.511	83	79	0.488	79	83	-0.023
1969 MIN	0.529 P	86	76	0.599 D	97	65	0.070

franchID	OWAR	OWS	AWAR	AWS	WARdiff	WSdiff	P/D/W/F
1960 MIN	37.650	214.025	34.783	218.994	2.866	-4.970	F
1961 MIN	35.021	182.417	34.350	210.001	0.671	-27.584	F
1962 MIN	39.713	216.620	47.711	272.997	-7.998	-56.377	P
1963 MIN	42.128	244.742	51.410	272.999	-9.282	-28.257	P
1964 MIN	46.025	210.127	46.238	236.996	-0.213	-26.869	
1965 MIN	43.814	275.591	45.782	306.003	0.273	-25.158	P
1966 MIN	35.081	228.186	45.133	267.002	-10.052	-38.816	
1967 MIN	43.726	271.095	46.713	272.999	-2.987	-1.904	P
1968 MIN	34.833	234.130	41.742	237.001	-6.909	-2.871	
1969 MIN	35.925	223.233	54.854	290.997	-18.929	-67.764	P

Pete Runnels procured batting crowns in 1960 (.320) and 1962 (.326). Killebrew clubbed 47 jacks and drove in 114 runs per year while Allison contributed 31 dingers and 94 RBI from 1961-64. The Senators abandoned Washington D.C. in favor of Minnesota following the 1960 campaign and the team was re-branded as the Twins.

Minnesota fans were immediately rewarded with the finest production in franchise history as the Twins produced back-to-back pennants in 1962-63. "Killer" paced the circuit with 48 home runs and 126 RBI and finished third in the 1962 AL MVP race. Camilo Pascual led the AL in strikeouts for three straight seasons (1961-63) and reached the 20-win mark in '62 and '63. Jim "Kitty" Kaat chipped in 18 victories and collected the first of 16 Gold Glove awards. Jimmie Hall belted 33 long balls in his rookie year ('63).

Tony Oliva (.323/32/94) collected a batting title and ROY honors in his initial season (1964), topping the leader boards with 217 base hits, 109 runs scored and 43 doubles. Falling merely two games short of a three-peat in '64, the Twins responded by seizing the club's third pennant of the 1960's by a 17-game margin over the Indians. Zoilo Versalles (32 WS) led the American League with 126 runs scored, 45 doubles, 12 triples, and 308 total bases. Versalles earned the MVP award and teammate Oliva placed runner-up after nabbing his second batting title with a .321 average.

Kaat (25-13, 2.75) led the American League in victories, games started, complete games and innings pitched in '66. Minnesota garnered its fourth pennant of the decade in 1967. Killebrew (38 WS) bashed 44 homers, drew 131 walks and finished second in the AL MVP balloting. Ted Abernathy furnished a 1.27 ERA and a 0.978 WHIP along with a league-leading 28 saves. Rod Carew achieved ROY honors on the strength of his .292 batting average and in 1969 he earned the first of seven batting titles and stole home seven times, one short of Ty Cobb's record. "Killer" received the MVP award after pacing the circuit with 49 long balls, 140 RBI and 145 bases on balls. The Twins outlasted the Athletics by two games for the American League pennant but registered the worst WSdiff (-65) and WARdiff (-18) in team history.

Year/Team	OPW%	PW	PL	APW%	AW	AL	Diff+/-
1970 MIN	0.540 D	87	75	0.605 D	98	64	0.065
1971 MIN	0.535 D	87	75	0.463	74	86	-0.073
1972 MIN	0.526	85	77	0.500	77	77	-0.026
1973 MIN	0.516	84	78	0.500	81	81	-0.016
1974 MIN	0.545	88	74	0.506	82	80	-0.039
1975 MIN	0.515	84	78	0.478	76	83	-0.038
1976 MIN	0.510	83	79	0.525	85	77	0.015
1977 MIN	0.587	95	67	0.522	84	77	-0.065
1978 MIN	0.481	78	84	0.451	73	89	-0.030
1979 MIN	0.513	83	79	0.506	82	80	-0.007

franchID	OWAR	OWS	AWAR	AWS	WARdiff	WSdiff	P/D/W/F
1970 MIN	35.589	230.474	45.446	294.002	-9.857	-63.528	D
1971 MIN	39.726	243.341	33.626	222.002	6.100	21.339	D
1972 MIN	30.177	213.176	33.426	231.010	-3.249	-17.834	
1973 MIN	41.045	215.089	43.992	243.001	-2.947	-27.912	
1974 MIN	42.441	234.451	42.328	245.999	0.112	-11.548	
1975 MIN	36.696	211.455	37.594	228.004	-0.898	-16.549	
1976 MIN	34.877	207.152	41.239	255.006	-6.362	-47.854	
1977 MIN	40.288	242.466	40.670	251.998	-0.382	-9.532	
1978 MIN	31.127	191.576	39.679	218.999	-8.552	-27.423	
1979 MIN	34.126	210.729	42.318	246.001	-8.192	-35.272	

Minnesota began the Seventies on a high note, scoring back-to-back division titles by the narrowest of margins. In 1970 the upstart Angels nearly upset the Twins, ending the season only two games behind the juggernaut. The scenario repeated itself in '71, with Oakland coming up just one game short in the Western division battle. The Twins remained competitive through the remainder of the decade but the club ultimately failed in its quest to return to the playoffs for 37 years.

Oliva (.325/23/107) led the League in hits for the fifth time in his career and finished runner-up in the 1970 AL MVP race. Killebrew cracked the 40-homer mark for the eighth time in '70 and topped the circuit with 119 RBI in '71. Reggie Smith launched 30 bombs and paced the AL with 33 doubles and 302 total bases in 1971. Carew reeled off four consecutive batting titles (1972-75), surpassing the 200-hit mark in '73 and '74.

The Twins posted six successive runner-up finishes from 1972-77 as the Athletics and the Royals ascended to the top of the AL West. Bert Blyleven established career-highs with 20 wins, 25 complete games, 9 shutouts and 258 strikeouts in 325 innings pitched. Kaat topped the 20-win mark in '74 and '75, placing fourth in the 1975 AL Cy Young balloting. Graig Nettles whacked 32 long balls to lead the AL in 1976 and earned his first Gold Glove award. Relief ace Bill "Soup" Campbell vultured 17 wins and saved 20 contests.

Carew flirted with a .400 batting average before ending his phenomenal 1977 campaign at .388. The AL MVP tallied 38 Win Shares and paced the circuit with 239 base hits, 128 runs scored, 16 triples and a .449 OBP. Carew completed the decade with a .343 BA and 6 batting crowns. Reggie Smith posted consecutive fourth-place finishes in the MVP races (1977-78) and achieved his best home run output with 32 jacks in '77.

Minnesota accrued 95 victories in '77, narrowly conceding the division title to Kansas City. Lyman Bostock batted .336 with 199 base hits and 104 runs scored. Nettles blasted 37 circuit clouts and drove in 107 runs, while Dave Goltz's 20 victories led the League and Campbell delivered 13 wins with a chart-topping 31 saves.

Win Shares > 20	Single-Season	1960-1979
Harmon Killebrew - 1B (MIN) x4	Graig Nettles - 3B (MIN) x7	Bob Allison - RF (MIN) x2
Pete Runnels - 1B (MIN)	Eric Soderholm - 3B (MIN)	Tony Oliva - RF (MIN) x8
Bob Allison - 1B (MIN)	Harmon Killebrew - LF (MIN) x3	Reggie Smith - RF (MIN) x5
Rod Carew - 1B (MIN) x4	Bob Allison - LF (MIN) x2	Jim Kaat - SP (MIN) x4
Rod Carew - 2B (MIN) x5	Jimmie Hall - CF (MIN) x2	Bert Blyleven - SP (MIN) x6
Zoilo Versalles - SS (MIN)	Reggie Smith - CF (MIN) x5	Dave Goltz - SP (MIN)
Rich Rollins - 3B (MIN)	Lyman Bostock - CF (MIN)	Ted W. Abernathy - RP (MIN)
Joe Foy - 3B (MIN)		Bill R. Campbell - RP (MIN)

Year/Team	OPW%	PW	PL	APW%	AW	AL	Diff+/-
1980 MIN	0.506	82	80	0.478	77	84	-0.027
1981 MIN	0.449	73	89	0.376	41	68	-0.072
1982 MIN	0.436	71	91	0.370	60	102	-0.066
1983 MIN	0.418 F	68	94	0.432	70	92	0.014
1984 MIN	0.544 F	88	74	0.500	81	81	-0.044
1985 MIN	0.485 F	79	83	0.475	77	85	-0.010
1986 MIN	0.488	79	83	0.438	71	91	-0.049
1987 MIN	0.500 F	81	81	0.525 D	85	77	0.024
1988 MIN	0.534	86	76	0.562	91	71	0.028
1989 MIN	0.516	84	78	0.494	80	82	-0.022

franchID	OWAR	OWS	AWAR	AWS	WARdiff	WSdiff	P/D/W/F
1980 MIN	37.759	239.480	30.583	231.004	7.176	8.476	
1981 MIN	18.557	128.834	10.915	122.998	7.642	5.836	
1982 MIN	31.277	190.672	23.815	179.998	7.462	10.675	
1983 MIN	34.813	230.711	24.998	210.000	9.815	20.711	F
1984 MIN	40.037	263.042	27.742	243.003	12.295	20.039	F
1985 MIN	36.725	239.372	32.813	230.993	3.913	8.379	F
1986 MIN	38.870	237.987	33.149	212.999	5.720	24.988	
1987 MIN	24.220	239.681	33.534	255.003	-9.314	-15.322	F
1988 MIN	42.407	**255.911**	47.802	273.000	-5.394	-17.089	
1989 MIN	39.050	241.725	37.908	239.999	1.142	1.726	

Minnesota experienced a rapid decline following the club's tremendous success in the previous 20-year period. The Twins posted consecutive last-place efforts in 1981-82 and subsequently failed to meet the minimum BFP requirements in 1983-85, and again in '87. Frank Viola endured an 11-25 record with a 5.38 ERA in two seasons after reaching the big leagues in '82. "Sweet Music" changed his tune in 1984, yielding 18 wins with a 3.21 ERA. Kent Hrbek slammed 23 big-flies and hit .301 in his inaugural campaign, securing a runner-up finish in the 1982 AL ROY race. Jesse Orosco notched 13 victories and 17 saves while posting a career-best 1.47 ERA in '83 and closed out 31 contests in the following season.

Blyleven placed third in the AL Cy Young race in consecutive years (1984-85). He fashioned a record of 19-7 with a 2.87 ERA in '84 and the following year topped the leader boards with 24 complete games, 293.2 innings pitched and 206 strikeouts. Hrbek batted .311 with 27 dingers and a career-best 107 RBI, garnering second place in the 1984 AL MVP balloting. Kirby Puckett exploded for 31 round-trippers in 1986 after combining to hit only 4 home runs in his freshman and sophomore seasons. Falling one hit shy of 200 in '85, Puckett surpassed the mark in each of the next four campaigns, batting at a .339 clip during this period. Gary Gaetti swatted 34 circuit clouts and notched the first of four consecutive Gold Glove awards in '86. Nettles and Gaetti contributed heavily to the 32 WS>10 seasons achieved by Minnesota third basemen from 1970-1989.

Viola (24-7, 2.64) procured Cy Young honors as the Twins returned to contention in '88. Minnesota finished the year in second place, four games behind Kansas City and led the League in oWS. Puckett (.356/24/121) amassed 31 Win Shares, paced the circuit with 234 base hits and finished third in the AL MVP vote for the second straight year. GM Andy MacPhail conducted the top three Amateur Drafts in club history (based on Career Total Win Shares). MacPhail procured Chuck Knoblauch, Denny Neagle, Scott Erickson in the '89 draft.

Year/Team	OPW%	PW	PL	APW%	AW	AL	Diff+/-
1990 MIN	0.479	78	84	0.457	74	88	-0.022
1991 MIN	0.482	78	84	0.586 P	95	67	0.104
1992 MIN	0.509	83	79	0.556	90	72	0.046
1993 MIN	0.458	74	88	0.438	71	91	-0.020
1994 MIN	0.453	73	89	0.469	53	60	0.016
1995 MIN	0.458	74	88	0.389	56	88	-0.069
1996 MIN	0.507	82	80	0.481	78	84	-0.025
1997 MIN	0.490	79	83	0.420	68	94	-0.070
1998 MIN	0.498	81	81	0.432	70	92	-0.066
1999 MIN	0.453	73	89	0.394	63	97	-0.059
franchID	OWAR	OWS	AWAR	AWS	WARdiff	WSdiff	P/D/W/F
1990 MIN	33.021	218.050	31.903	222.000	1.119	-3.950	
1991 MIN	32.542	233.610	**45.574**	**284.997**	-13.032	-51.387	

Year						
1992 MIN	34.544	236.377	45.705	270.001	-11.160	-33.624
1993 MIN	31.063	226.044	26.634	212.996	4.430	13.048
1994 MIN	19.174	159.832	18.817	158.999	0.357	0.832
1995 MIN	33.303	210.265	20.941	168.002	12.363	42.263
1996 MIN	41.609	264.657	32.662	233.997	8.947	30.660
1997 MIN	42.301	250.472	30.106	203.998	12.195	46.473
1998 MIN	39.972	257.042	25.960	210.003	14.011	47.038
1999 MIN	27.978	226.534	21.881	189.008	6.097	37.526

Viola produced a 20-12 record with a 2.67 ERA for the '90 crew. Second-sacker Chuck Knoblauch nabbed rookie honors with a .285 BA and 25 steals in 1991. Following a pair of losing seasons, the Twins rebounded in '92, finishing only six games behind the White Sox. Puckett earned his sixth Gold Glove Award and placed runner-up in the 1992 AL MVP race after leading the League with 210 base hits.

Jay Bell collected a Gold Glove award in '93 for his smooth fielding at shortstop while batting .310 with 102 runs scored. Minnesota floundered through the next three seasons, averaging 74 wins per year along with two last-place finishes. Knoblauch drilled a league-leading 45 doubles, swiped 35 bags and hit .312 for the '94 squad. He tallied 31 Win Shares in 1996, capping a banner year with 140 runs, 14 triples and a .341 average.

On the hill, port-sider Denny Neagle reveled in his finest season, contributing a 20-5 record with a 2.97 ERA and 1.084 WHIP. Knoblauch delivered a .298 BA, 106 runs scored, 30 doubles and 37 stolen bases per year during the 1990's and in 1997 set a career-high with 62 steals. Bell received his second All-Star invitation in '99, thumping 38 four-baggers and plating 112 runs.

Year/Team	OPW%	PW	PL	APW%	AW	AL	Diff+/-
2000 MIN	0.461	75	87	0.426	69	93	-0.035
2001 MIN	0.474	77	85	0.525	85	77	0.051
2002 MIN	0.487	79	83	0.584 D	94	67	0.097
2003 MIN	0.499	81	81	0.556 D	90	72	0.057
2004 MIN	0.455	74	88	0.568 D	92	70	0.113
2005 MIN	0.512	83	79	0.512	83	79	0.000
2006 MIN	0.470	76	86	0.593 D	96	66	0.122
2007 MIN	0.475	77	85	0.488	79	83	0.012
2008 MIN	0.548 D	89	73	0.540	88	75	-0.008
2009 MIN	0.540 W	87	75	0.534 D	87	76	-0.006
2010 MIN	0.506	82	80	0.580 D	94	68	0.074
2011 MIN	0.428	69	93	0.389	63	99	-0.039
2012 MIN	0.487	79	83	0.407	66	96	-0.080
2013 MIN	0.472 F	76	86	0.407	66	96	-0.064

franchID	OWAR	OWS	AWAR	AWS	WARdiff	WSdiff	P/D/W/F
2000 MIN	32.744	235.115	28.959	206.999	3.785	28.116	
2001 MIN	36.193	261.328	36.660	254.993	-0.467	6.335	
2002 MIN	40.867	272.649	42.066	281.995	-1.199	-9.346	
2003 MIN	40.355	274.369	41.751	270.004	-1.396	4.365	
2004 MIN	34.156	261.933	44.915	276.001	-10.760	-14.069	
2005 MIN	35.300	267.153	36.377	249.003	-1.077	18.150	
2006 MIN	38.149	269.287	45.923	288.001	-7.774	-18.714	
2007 MIN	36.925	254.513	32.492	237.002	4.433	17.511	
2008 MIN	43.153	275.544	37.238	264.000	5.914	11.545	D

309

2009 MIN	**48.383**	275.684	39.601	260.997	8.783	14.687	W
2010 MIN	38.260	252.950	44.243	282.002	-5.984	-29.053	
2011 MIN	26.641	223.354	13.867	189.000	12.773	34.353	
2012 MIN	30.626	240.389	24.162	197.905	6.464	42.484	
2013 MIN	33.516	261.595	19.830	198.002	13.686	63.593	F

Corey Koskie (.276/26/103) set career-bests in RBI and runs scored (100) during the 2001 season. Torii Hunter collected nine consecutive Gold Glove Awards (2001-09) for his superb defense in center field. "Everyday" Eddie Guardado paced the AL with 45 saves in '02 and tallied 35 saves per year with a 2.84 ERA from 2002-05. LaTroy Hawkins furnished a 2.22 ERA from 2002-04 and collected 25 saves for the '04 staff. Justin Morneau (.321/34/130) scored the MVP award in 2006, posting individual bests in the Triple Crown categories along with 190 hits, while that same year Joe Mauer achieved his first batting title with a .347 BA. Mauer, A.J. Pierzynski and Damian Miller accrued 20 WS>10 seasons as the Twins' farm system finally generated capable backstops.

Minnesota cruised to the AL Central division title in '08, taking Cleveland by seven games. Morneau (.300/23/129) yielded a runner-up finish in the 2008 AL MVP race and Mauer batted .328 en route to his second batting crown. Hunter tallied 25 taters and 89 ribbies per season from 2001-09. The Twins battled the Royals for the Central Division crown in 2009. The team earned the AL Wild Card entry as Kansas City seized the title by a single game. Mauer (.365/28/96) accrued 34 Win Shares and led the circuit in batting average, OBP (.444) and SLG (.587). Glen Perkins saved 36 contests while fashioning a 2.30 ERA and a 0.926 WHIP in 2013.

Win Shares > 20	Single-Season	1980-2013
Kent Hrbek - 1B (MIN) x3	Jay Bell - SS (MIN) x4	Torii Hunter - CF (MIN) x5
Doug Mientkiewicz - 1B (MIN)	Gary Gaetti - 3B (MIN) x2	Denard Span - CF (MIN)
Justin Morneau - 1B (MIN) x3	Corey Koskie - 3B (MIN) x2	Matt Lawton - RF (MIN)
John Castino - 2B (MIN)	Joe Mauer - C (MIN) x7	Michael Cuddyer - RF (MIN)
Chuck Knoblauch - 2B (MIN) x6	Gary Ward - LF (MIN)	Torii Hunter - RF (MIN)
	Jacque Jones - LF (MIN)	Frank Viola - SP (MIN) x4
Jay Bell - 2B (MIN)	Gary Ward - CF (MIN)	Denny Neagle - SP (MIN)
Todd Walker - 2B (MIN)	Kirby Puckett - CF (MIN) x7	

Note: 4000 PA or BFP to qualify, except during strike-shortened seasons
(1972 = 3800, 1981 & 1994 = 2700, 1995 = 3500) and 154-game schedule (3800)
- failed to qualify: 1905-1906, 1910-1913, 1921-1923, 1944, 1950-1954, 1956-1961, 1983-1985, 1987

Senators / Twins All-Time "Originals" Roster

Paul Abbott	Bobby Estalella	Frank Loftus	Bobby Reeves
Ted W. Abernathy	Frank Eufemia	Steve Lombardozzi	Rick Renick
Jose Acosta	Al Evans	Tom A. Long	Michael Restovich
Merito Acosta	Willie Eyre	Slim Love	Ben Revere
Rick Adams	Lenny Faedo	Steve Luebber	Sam Rice
Morrie Aderholt	John S. Farrell	Ralph Lumenti	Juan Rincon
Dewey Adkins	Terry Felton	Charlie Luskey	Todd Ritchie
Joe Agler	Mark Filley	Lyle Luttrell	Luis Rivas
Eddie Ainsmith	Carl Fischer	Jim Lyle	Saul Rivera
Jerry Akers	Clarence Fisher	Jerry Lynn	Red Roberts
Bernie Allen	Showboat Fisher	Ed Lyons	Sherry Robertson
Chad Allen	Angel Fleitas	Scotti Madison	Tyler Robertson
Bob Allison	Bill Forman	Hector Maestri	Rabbit Robinson
Luis Aloma	Mike Fornieles	Pete Magrini	Armando Roche
Dave Altizer	George Foss	Pat Mahomes	Freddy Rodriguez

Ossie Alvarez
Allan Anderson
Red Anderson
Bill Andrus
Oswaldo Arcia
Orville Armbrust
Lefty Atkinson
Jake Atz
Doc Ayers
Jesse Baker
Scott T. Baker
Grant Balfour
Pelham Ballenger
Win Ballou
Eddie Bane
Willie Banks
Red Barbary
Steve L. Barber
Turner Barber
Bruce Barmes
Red Barnes
Frank Barron
Dick Bass
Randy Bass
Charlie Becker
Rich Becker
Julio Becquer
Jay Bell
Allen Benson
Joe Benson
Jack Bentley
Bob Berman
Lou Bevil
Harry Biemiller
Elliot Bigelow
George Binks
Red Bird
Nick Blackburn
Bruno Block
Jimmy Bloodworth
Ossie Bluege
Bert Blyleven
Joe Boehling
Bob Boken
Joe Bokina
Cliff Bolton
Joe Bonikowski
Gus Bono
Rod Booker
Al Bool
Glenn Borgmann
Harley Boss
Lyman Bostock
Dave Boswell
Rob Bowen

Joe Foy
Ray Francis
Kevin Frederick
Jerry Freeman
Skipper Friday
Bob Friedrichs
Mark Funderburk
Gary Gaetti
Nemo Gaines
Stan Galle
Bert Gallia
Gus Gandarillas
Babe Ganzel
Rich Garces
Ramon Garcia
Rob Gardner
Jerry Garvin
Matt Garza
Bob Gebhard
Elmer Gedeon
Joe Gedeon
Henry Gehring
Patsy Gharrity
Shawn Gilbert
Ed Gill
Grant Gillis
Joe Gleason
Ed Goebel
Dave Goltz
Luis Gomez
Preston Gomez
Ruben Gomez
German Gonzalez
Julio E. Gonzalez
Vince Gonzales
Charlie Gooch
Clyde Goodwin
Marv Goodwin
Ray Goolsby
Bob Gorinski
Goose Goslin
Dan Graham
Oscar Graham
Dolly Gray
Milt Gray
Hal Griggs
Bob Groom
Harley Grossman
Eddie Guardado
Mike Guerra
Mark Guthrie
Bump Hadley
Mickey Haefner
Dick Hahn
Chip Hale

Jim Mallory
Jim B. Manning
Jeff Manship
Charlie Manuel
Moxie Manuel
Howard Maple
Firpo Marberry
Red Marion
Connie Marrero
Joe S. Martin
Joe Martina
Marty Martinez
Rogelio Martinez
Del Mason
Dan Masteller
Walt Masters
Walt Masterson
Frank Mata
Joe Mauer
Sam Mayer
Rudy May
Luis Maza
Tom McAvoy
Joe McCabe
David McCarty
Alex McColl
Paul McCullough
Phil McCullough
John J. McDonald
Howie McFarland
Frank McGee
Slim McGrew
Vance McIlree
Dave McKay
Al McLean
Jim McLeod
George McNamara
Earl McNeely
Pat Meares
Evan Meek
Dave Meier
Jack Merson
Jim Mertz
Irish Meusel
Doug Mientkiewicz
John Mihalic
Jose Mijares
Clyde Milan
Horace Milan
Dee Miles
Bing Miller
Damian Miller
Jason Miller
Ralph H. Miller
Ronnie Miller

Luis Rodriguez
Clay Roe
Buck Rogers
Garry Roggenburk
Saul Rogovin
Jim Roland
Rich Rollins
Alex Romero
J.C. Romero
Henri Rondeau
Claude Rothgeb
Pete Runnels
Michael Ryan
Alex Sabo
Mike Sadek
Ted Sadowski
Chico Salmon
Benj Sampson
Raul Sanchez
Jack D. Sanford
Don Savidge
Carl Sawyer
Ray Scarborough
Al Schacht
Owen Scheetz
Lefty Schegg
Fred Schemanske
Fred Scherman
Jerry Schoonmaker
Le Grant Scott
Pete Scott
Johnnie Seale
Dan Serafini
Gary Serum
John Sevcik
Howie Shanks
Warren Shanabrook
Shag Shaughnessy
Jim Shaw
Bert Shepard
Fred Sherry
Garland Shifflett
Duke Shirey
Mule Shirley
Danny Silva
Doug Simons
Fred Sington
Kevin Slowey
Carr Smith
Ray Smith
Reggie Smith
Tony Smith
Bill Snyder
Eric Soderholm
Rick Sofield

Shane Bowers	Jimmie Hall	Travis Miller	Jock Somerlott
Elmer Bowman	Tom Hall	Warren Miller	Denard Span
Travis Bowyer	Greg Halman	Willy Miranda	By Speece
Steve Braun	Pete Hamm	Mike Misuraca	Levale Speigner
Brent Brede	Roy Hansen	Monroe Mitchell	Ben Spencer
Jim Brillheart	Harry Hardy	George Mitterwald	Scott Stahoviak
Jeff Bronkey	Pinky Hargrave	Chad Moeller	Kevin Stanfield
Frank Brower	Harry Harper	Rene Monteagudo	Lee Stange
Jarvis Brown	Ben Harrison	Dan Monzon	Con Starkel
Fred Bruckbauer	Bucky Harris	Carlos Moore	Bill Starr
J.T. Bruett	Jeff Harris	Jose G. Morales	Buzz Stephen
Steve Brye	Roy Hawes	Charles Moran	Jim Stevens
Garland Buckeye	LaTroy Hawkins	Roy Moran	Bunky Stewart
Bud Bulling	Jackie Hayes	Julio Moreno	Dick Stone
Bobby Burke	Jim Hayes	Ray Morgan	Luis Suarez
Alex Burnett	Joe Haynes	Mike Moriarty	Denny Sullivan
Bill Burns	Harry Hedgpeth	Bill Morley	John Paul Sullivan
Randy Bush	Jim Heise	Justin Morneau	Pete Susko
Sal Butera	Liam Hendriks	Bill Morrell	Dizzy Sutherland
Ed Butka	John P. Henry	Danny Morris	Anthony Swarzak
Jack Calvo	Phil Hensiek	Ed Moyer	Bennie Tate
Kevin Cameron	Evelio Hernandez	Peter Moylan	Hughie Tate
Bill R. Campbell	Walt Herrell	Dick Mulligan	Danny Taylor
John Campbell	Herb Herring	Bill Murray	Fred Taylor
Rod Carew	Chris Herrmann	Bobby Murray	Kerry Taylor
Leon Carlson	Bryan Hickerson	Danny Musser	Tommy Taylor
Roy Carlyle	Aaron Hicks	Paul Musser	Jerry Terrell
Lew Carpenter	Herman Hill	Buddy Myer	Tim Teufel
Alex Carrasquel	Dutch Hinrichs	Mike Nakamura	Jug Thesenga
Scott Cary	Jim Hitchcock	Cholly Naranjo	Bud L. Thomas
George Case	Lloyd Hittle	Dan Naulty	Claude Thomas
Carl Cashion	Dennis Hocking	Denny Neagle	Lefty Thomas
Larry Casian	Ed Hodge	Doug Neff	Danny Thompson
Joe Cassidy	Izzy Hoffman	Pat Neshek	Forrest Thompson
John Castino	Ray Hoffman	Graig Nettles	Harry Thompson
Eli Cates	Wally Holborow	Jim Nettles	Lou Thuman
Hardin Cathey	Sammy Holbrook	Alan Newman	Terry Tiffee
Fred Chapman	Bill Hollahan	Chuck Nieson	Hal Toenes
Ken Chase	Bill Holland	Rabbit Nill	Matt Tolbert
Harry Child	Paul Hopkins	Tsuyoshi Nishioka	Steven Tolleson
Pete Cimino	Ed Hovlik	Tom Norton	Doc Tonkin
Doug Clarey	Joe Hovlik	Willie Norwood	Gil Torres
Jim Clark	Dave Howard	Joe Nossek	Ricardo Torres
Webbo Clarke	Kent Hrbek	Jim Obradovich	Rene Tosoni
Ellis Clary	Sid Hudson	Bryan Oelkers	Cecil Travis
Danny Clay	Jim M. Hughes	Trent Oeltjen	Ray Treadaway
Joe Cleary	Luke Hughes	Joe Ohl	Frank Trechock
Gil Coan	Torii Hunter	Kevin Ohme	Mike Trombley
Dick Coffman	Dick Hyde	Bob Oldis	George Tsamis
Syd Cohen	Darrell Jackson	Tony Oliva	Ollie Tucker
Chris Colabello	Beany Jacobson	Jim O'Neill	Lucas Turk
Choo Choo Coleman	Bucky Jacobs	Ernie Oravetz	Jimmy Uchrinscko
Joe F. Connolly	Jake Jacobs	Jesse Orosco	Ted Uhlaender
Tom Connolly	Charlie Jamieson	Baby Ortiz	Scott Ullger
Bill F. Conroy	Houston Jimenez	Roberto Ortiz	Sandy Ullrich

Sandy Consuegra	Adam Johnson	Champ Osteen	Roy Valdes
Charlie Conway	Ed Johnson	Jayhawk Owens	Sandy Valdespino
Jerry Conway	Tom Johnson	Juan Padilla	Jose Valdivielso
Cal Cooper	Walter Johnson	Vance Page	Danny Valencia
Henry Coppola	Dick Jones	Mike Palagyi	Javier Valentin
Ray Corbin	Jacque Jones	Derek Parks	Clay Van Alstyne
Marty Cordova	Steve Jones	Chris Parmelee	Buck Varner
Harry Courtney	Tim Jordan	Carlos Pascual	Fred Vaughn
Molly Craft	Terry Jorgensen	Camilo Pascual	Vince Ventura
Jesse Crain	Ralph Judd	Case Patten	Mickey Vernon
Jerry Cram	Joe Judge	Carlos Paula	Zoilo Versalles
Jerry Crider	Jim Kaat	Yorkis Perez	Bob Veselic
Herb Crompton	Bob Kahle	Dan Perkins	Frank Viola
Tom Crooke	Bill Kay	Glen Perkins	Rip Wade
Alvin Crowder	Burt Keeley	Sam Perlozzo	Doc Waldbauer
Ed Crowley	Harry Kelley	Nig Perrine	Kyle Waldrop
Michael Cuddyer	Hal Keller	Brock Peterson	Dixie E. Walker
Bert Cueto	Ron Keller	Leon Pettit	Tilly Walker
Midre Cummings	Frank Kelliher	Marty Pevey	Todd Walker
Bill J. Cunningham	Pat H. Kelly	Bill Phebus	Charlie Walters
Vern Curtis	Speed Kelly	Babe Phelps	Gary Ward
Jake Daniel	Eddie Kenna	Dick Phillips	Curt Wardle
Yo-Yo Davalillo	Bill G. Kennedy	Kyle Phillips	Jimmy Wasdell
Andre David	Bill Kenworthy	Charlie Pick	Scott Watkins
Cleatus Davidson	Bobby Kielty	Marino Pieretti	Tommy Watkins
Mark Davidson	Harmon Killebrew	A.J. Pierzynski	Allie Watt
Ike M. Davis	Dick Kimble	Josmil Pinto	Jim D. Weaver
Rex Dawson	Mike Kinnunen	Bill Pleis	Jim F. Weaver
Harry Dean	Bobby Kline	Trevor Plouffe	Monte Weaver
Buddy Dear	Elmer Klumpp	Mike Poepping	Lenny Webster
Juan Delis	Chuck Knoblauch	Jimmy Pofahl	Dick Weik
Rick Dempsey	Punch Knoll	Dan Porter	Johnny Welaj
Julio DePaula	Joe Kohlman	Mark Portugal	Dick Welteroth
Cole De Vries	Merlin Kopp	Squire Potter	Sam West
Roy Dietzel	Steve Korcheck	Hosken Powell	Bill Whitby
Reese Diggs	Corey Koskie	Jake Powell	Steve White
Brian Dinkelman	Joe Krakauskas	Paul Powell	Mark Wiley
Sonny Dixon	Jason Kubel	Bob Prichard	Rob Wilfong
Dan Dobbek	Joe Kuhel	Ray Prim	Mutt Williams
John Donaldson	Craig Kusick	Jake Propst	Enrique Wilson
Brian Dozier	Al Kvasnak	Doc Prothro	John N. Wilson
Buzz Dozier	Bobby LaMotte	Kirby Puckett	Tom G. Wilson
Lew Drill	Dick Lanahan	Brandon Puffer	Willy Wilson
Tom Drohan	Doc Land	Carlos Pulido	Ed Wineapple
Brian Duensing	Sam Lanford	Spencer Pumpelly	Ted Wingfield
Pat Duff	Pete Lapan	Hal Quick	Brian Wolfe
George Dumont	Gene Larkin	Frank Quilici	Larry Wolfe
Steve Dunn	Fred Lasher	Brian Raabe	Al Woods
Mike Durant	Tim Laudner	Josh Rabe	Dick Woodson
J.D. Durbin	Matt Lawton	Brad Radke	Junior Wooten
Mike Dyer	Hillis Layne	Rob Radlosky	Taffy Wright
Jake Early	Matt LeCroy	Ryan Radmanovich	Butch Wynegar
Carl East	Travis Lee	Frank Ragland	Early Wynn
Ed Edelen	Watty Lee	Doc Ralston	Rich Yett
Bob Edmondson	Ed Leip	Pedro Ramos	Bill Yohe

Sam Edmonston	Scott Leius	Wilson Ramos	Eddie Yost
Dave Edwards	Buddy Lewis	Fred Rath, Jr.	Chief Youngblood
Jim Eisenreich	Cory Lidle	Paul Ratliff	Paul Zahniser
Frank Ellerbe	Mike Lincoln	Jeff Reboulet	Jose Zardon
Joe Engel	Ed Linke	Pete Redfern	Bill Zepp
Russ Ennis	Hod Lisenbee	Mark Redman	Bill Zinser
Roger Erickson	Ad Liska	Jack Redmond	
Scott Erickson	Mickey Livingston	Jeff Reed	
Cal Ermer	Bob Loane	Stan Rees	

Chicago White Sox

Year/Team	OPW%	PW	PL	APW%	AW	AL	Diff+/-
1901 CHW	0.598 F	81	55	0.610 P	83	53	0.013
1902 CHW	0.629 F	86	50	0.552	74	60	-0.077
1903 CHW	0.544	76	64	0.438	60	77	-0.106
1904 CHW	0.629 P	97	57	0.578	89	65	-0.051
1905 CHW	0.422 F	65	89	0.605	92	60	0.184
1906 CHW	0.433 F	67	87	0.616 P	93	58	0.183
1907 CHW	0.576 F	89	65	0.576	87	64	0.000
1908 CHW	0.589 F	91	63	0.579	88	64	-0.010
1909 CHW	0.485 F	75	79	0.513	78	74	0.028

franchID	OWAR	OWS	AWAR	AWS	WARdiff	WSdiff	P/D/W/F
1901 CHW	5.269	35.576	43.659	249.003	-38.390	-213.427	F
1902 CHW	7.277	41.871	33.640	222.003	-26.363	-180.132	F
1903 CHW	1.511	49.839	15.852	179.999	-14.342	-130.160	
1904 CHW	16.337	108.010	37.422	266.999	-21.084	-158.988	P
1905 CHW	14.525	90.109	42.851	276.005	-28.326	-185.896	F
1906 CHW	19.219	116.296	37.751	279.013	-18.532	-162.717	F
1907 CHW	22.296	130.161	39.181	261.006	-16.886	-130.844	F
1908 CHW	37.554	153.873	40.609	263.997	-3.055	-110.124	F
1909 CHW	30.355	165.024	34.254	234.003	-3.899	-68.980	F

Legend: (P) = Pennant / Most Wins in League (D) = Division Winner (W) = Wild Card Winner (F) = Failed to Qualify

The Chicago White Sox gained entry to the major leagues as one of the eight original American League franchises in 1901. Based on the WS>20 frame of reference, the Sox have developed the fewest quality starting pitchers (31) among the "Turn of the Century" franchises. Ted Lyons and Ed A. Walsh are tied with five seasons above 20 Win Shares. The White Sox have cultivated the second-fewest WS>20 seasons at second base (11), left field (16) and right field (13).

Chicago ranks third-worst among "Turn of the Century" franchises for playoff appearances and the team has an abysmal track record for scouting and developing its talent, as it failed to meet the PA and/or BFP minimums in 54 seasons (out of 109). During a pathetic spell from 1934-1994, the Pale Hose were unable to meet the requirements in 45 of 61 seasons! The White Sox finished with the fewest WS>10 seasons amongst the "ToC" clubs for second basemen (46), third basemen (63), left fielders (39) and starting pitchers (193). Furthermore, the organization never placed in the top three of the WS>10 leader boards for left fielders, right fielders and starting pitchers. On a positive note, Chicago's designated hitters have produced the most WS>20 (7) and WS>10 (29) seasons among the 16 teams in existence since 1901.

Chicago garnered its first pennant in 1904 on the shoulders of Frank E. Smith. "Piano Mover" completed 22 of 23 starts in his inaugural year, yielding a 2.09 ERA and a 1.063 WHIP along with 16 victories and went on to compile 19 wins with a 2.13 ERA in his sophomore season. Ed A. Walsh delivered an ERA under 2.00 in five successive campaigns (1906-1910). "Big Ed" paced the American League with a 1.60 ERA, 37 complete games in 46 starts and 422.1 innings pitched in 1907.

Walsh (40-15, 1.42) accrued 45 Win Shares in 1908 and dominated the AL leader boards in virtually all major pitching categories. He completed 42 of 49 starts, pitched 464 innings and whiffed 269 opposing batsmen. The workload took a toll on Walsh's right arm as his innings pitched were reduced to 230.1 in the subsequent season. Smith picked up the slack in '09, completing 37 of 40 starts and winning 25 contests with an ERA of 1.80. He worked a league-high 365 innings and struck out 177.

Year/Team	OPW%	PW	PL	APW%	AW	AL	Diff+/-
1910 CHW	0.459	71	83	0.444	68	85	-0.015
1911 CHW	0.500 F	77	77	0.510	77	74	0.010
1912 CHW	0.490	75	79	0.506	78	76	0.017
1913 CHW	0.484	75	79	0.513	78	74	0.029
1914 CHW	0.373	57	97	0.455	70	84	0.081
1915 CHW	0.570	88	66	0.604	93	61	0.034
1916 CHW	0.521	80	74	0.578	89	65	0.057
1917 CHW	0.510	79	75	0.649 P	100	54	0.140
1918 CHW	0.507	65	63	0.460	57	67	-0.048
1919 CHW	0.542	76	64	0.629 P	88	52	0.087

franchID	OWAR	OWS	AWAR	AWS	WARdiff	WSdiff	P/D/W/F
1910 CHW	27.779	183.292	25.057	204.006	2.722	-20.714	
1911 CHW	36.141	185.669	40.993	230.999	-4.852	-45.330	F
1912 CHW	33.069	226.974	33.250	234.005	-0.181	-7.031	
1913 CHW	28.726	249.052	29.462	234.006	-0.736	15.047	
1914 CHW	23.314	201.595	29.932	210.007	-6.618	-8.412	
1915 CHW	46.579	243.902	59.484	279.002	-12.905	-35.101	
1916 CHW	37.326	244.549	48.783	266.995	-11.457	-22.446	
1917 CHW	45.546	284.106	51.571	299.996	-6.025	-15.890	
1918 CHW	32.263	209.873	31.114	171.003	1.150	38.870	
1919 CHW	39.769	276.482	46.473	264.000	-6.704	12.483	

Walsh continued to stand out among American League hurlers, leading the League with career-bests in ERA (1.27) and WHIP (0.820) during the 1910 season. The staff ace achieved consecutive runner-up finishes in the AL MVP races of '11 and '12, notching 27 victories in both years. Reb Russell (22-16, 1.90) tallied 31 Win Shares in his rookie campaign. Jim Scott managed a 20-21 record, albeit with an ERA of 1.90.

The White Sox muddled through the 1914 season, losing 95 matches on the way to a last-place finish. Chicago bounced back with an 84-70 record in 1915 bolstered by Scott's 24-11 record. Happy Felsch amassed 30 Win Shares in '17, hitting at a .308 clip and knocking in 102 runs. Edd Roush collected his first batting crown after pacing the circuit with a .341 average and from 1917-27, Roush surpassed the .300 mark in every season and batted .335 during that period. Chicago finished in third place, only 4 games behind New York for the AL pennant in '18. Roush batted .333 and led the League with a .455 slugging percentage and seized his second batting title in 1919 as the Pale Hose ended the year in a second-place tie with the Yankees. The smooth-fielding Sox supplied the best fldWARnorm (9) and fldWSnorm (62) totals in club history.

Year/Team	OPW%	PW	PL	APW%	AW	AL	Diff+/-
1920 CHW	0.510 F	79	75	0.623	96	58	0.113
1921 CHW	0.391	60	94	0.403	62	92	0.012
1922 CHW	0.558 P	86	68	0.500	77	77	-0.058
1923 CHW	0.499	77	77	0.448	69	85	-0.051
1924 CHW	0.440	68	86	0.435	67	87	-0.005
1925 CHW	0.562	87	67	0.513	79	75	-0.049
1926 CHW	0.541	83	71	0.529	81	72	-0.011
1927 CHW	0.504	78	76	0.458	70	83	-0.046
1928 CHW	0.461	71	83	0.468	72	82	0.007
1929 CHW	0.385	59	95	0.388	59	93	0.003

franchID	OWAR	OWS	AWAR	AWS	WARdiff	WSdiff	P/D/W/F
1920 CHW	48.533	322.212	46.312	287.992	2.221	34.220	F
1921 CHW	22.749	214.455	22.291	185.996	0.458	28.459	
1922 CHW	31.744	251.772	30.662	230.997	1.082	20.775	P
1923 CHW	29.378	226.303	33.679	207.002	-4.301	19.301	
1924 CHW	32.177	218.426	31.020	198.002	1.156	20.424	
1925 CHW	37.130	266.510	36.812	237.000	0.318	29.510	
1926 CHW	42.198	262.706	42.683	242.997	-0.485	19.709	
1927 CHW	31.062	221.356	30.682	210.002	0.380	11.354	
1928 CHW	25.277	216.797	23.707	216.003	1.570	0.794	
1929 CHW	20.666	195.309	16.739	176.995	3.927	18.314	

Buck Weaver batted at a .331 clip, accumulating 208 base knocks and scoring 102 runs for the 1920 squad while Felsch contributed a .338 BA and 115 RBI. Roush accrued 33 Win Shares and set individual marks with 196 hits, 90 RBI, and 36 steals. At the hot corner, Jimmy Johnston eclipsed .300 in three straight seasons, batting a collective .323 with 108 runs per year. He tallied 203 hits in 1921 and 1923. The Sox ascended from a last-place finish in 1921, clinching the '22 pennant by four games over the Browns. Ray Schalk's defensive prowess behind the plate factored heavily in his third-place finish in the AL MVP vote. Bibb Falk surpassed the .300 plateau in four straight years (1924-27), averaging .330 with 97 RBI during the span.

After concluding 1924 in the cellar, Chicago ended the '25 season in a three-way tie for first place. The Senators were awarded the pennant by .003 percentage points. Ted Lyons topped the leader boards with 21 victories and 5 shutouts while Johnny Mostil paced the circuit in runs (135), bases on balls (90) and stolen bases (43). "Bananas" delivered a .325 average with 120 runs scored and 35 steals and earned a runner-up finish in the '26 AL MVP race. The Pale Hose engaged in another three-team battle in 1926 with the Indians emerging victorious by a single game. Tommy Thomas (19-16, 2.98) tied with Lyons for the most innings pitched in '27 and completed 24 starts in three consecutive campaigns (1927-29). Lyons completed 30 of 34 starts and paced the AL with 22 victories. The Sox crashed in 1929, winning a mere 59 contests on the road to another last-place effort.

Year/Team	OPW%	PW	PL	APW%	AW	AL	Diff+/-
1930 CHW	0.445	69	85	0.403	62	92	-0.043
1931 CHW	0.354	55	99	0.366	56	97	0.012
1932 CHW	0.380	58	96	0.325	49	102	-0.055
1933 CHW	0.418	64	90	0.447	67	83	0.029
1934 CHW	0.398 F	61	93	0.349	53	99	-0.049
1935 CHW	0.510 F	79	75	0.487	74	78	-0.023
1936 CHW	0.451 F	69	85	0.536	81	70	0.086
1937 CHW	0.541 F	83	71	0.558	86	68	0.018
1938 CHW	0.486 F	75	79	0.439	65	83	-0.046
1939 CHW	0.484 F	75	79	0.552	85	69	0.068

franchID	OWAR	OWS	AWAR	AWS	WARdiff	WSdiff	P/D/W/F
1930 CHW	31.388	233.382	25.122	186.000	6.266	47.382	
1931 CHW	7.640	172.284	13.875	167.997	-6.235	4.288	
1932 CHW	21.515	205.372	17.043	146.998	4.472	58.374	
1933 CHW	26.449	210.683	28.718	201.002	-2.269	9.681	
1934 CHW	15.869	183.508	15.645	159.002	0.224	24.506	F
1935 CHW	28.853	242.156	29.167	222.005	-0.314	20.151	F
1936 CHW	32.392	197.703	33.933	242.995	-1.541	-45.292	F
1937 CHW	34.447	245.991	33.902	257.994	0.545	-12.003	F
1938 CHW	34.222	231.327	26.975	194.993	7.248	36.334	F
1939 CHW	42.620	243.372	36.540	255.002	6.080	-11.631	F

Chicago endured a seventh-place finish in 1930 followed by three straight years at the bottom of the standings. The Sox fell off the grid from 1934-1961 when the team failed to meet the PA and/or BFP minimums in every season with the exception of 1947 and 1954. Luke Appling was the lone superstar to emerge within the White Sox system during this dismal period. Appling's breakthrough season came in 1933 when the shortstop managed to bat .322 while driving in 85 runs. "Old Aches and Pains" batted over .300 for 9 straight years (1933-41) with an aggregate .325 BA. He collected his first batting title on the strength of a .388 average, knocked in 112 runs and placed second in the 1936 AL MVP race.

Win Shares > 20	Single-Season	1920-1939
Jimmy Johnston - 2B (CHW)	Bibb Falk - LF (CHW) x3	Ted Lyons - SP (CHW) x5
Luke Appling - SS (CHW) x10	Johnny Mostil - CF (CHW) x3	Tommy Thomas - SP (CHW) x2
Jimmy Johnston - 3B (CHW) x2	Carl Reynolds - CF (CHW)	Ted Blankenship - SW (CHW)
Willie Kamm - 3B (CHW) x4	Randy Moore - RF (CHW)	
	George Mogridge - SP (CHW)	

Year/Team	OPW%	PW	PL	APW%	AW	AL	Diff+/-
1940 CHW	0.566 F	87	67	0.532	82	72	-0.034
1941 CHW	0.454 F	70	84	0.500	77	77	0.046
1942 CHW	0.510 F	78	76	0.446	66	82	-0.064
1943 CHW	0.627 F	97	57	0.532	82	72	-0.094
1944 CHW	0.447 F	69	85	0.461	71	83	0.014
1945 CHW	0.490 F	75	79	0.477	71	78	-0.013
1946 CHW	0.493 F	76	78	0.481	74	80	-0.013
1947 CHW	0.506	78	76	0.455	70	84	-0.052
1948 CHW	0.408 F	63	91	0.336	51	101	-0.072
1949 CHW	0.517 F	80	74	0.409	63	91	-0.108

franchID	OWAR	OWS	AWAR	AWS	WARdiff	WSdiff	P/D/W/F
1940 CHW	49.686	277.301	35.631	245.999	14.055	31.302	F
1941 CHW	36.629	247.219	28.250	231.004	8.379	16.215	F
1942 CHW	33.373	259.978	22.920	198.007	10.453	61.971	F
1943 CHW	54.698	371.792	29.861	245.998	24.836	125.793	F
1944 CHW	28.286	247.559	20.332	212.995	7.954	34.564	F
1945 CHW	22.357	194.013	25.063	213.004	-2.706	-18.991	F
1946 CHW	35.557	246.836	26.303	221.998	9.254	24.838	F
1947 CHW	27.216	250.449	24.598	210.006	2.618	40.443	
1948 CHW	23.542	193.245	13.468	153.000	10.074	40.245	F
1949 CHW	27.652	242.950	26.733	188.995	0.918	53.955	F

Lyons (14-6, 2.10), in the twilight of his career, notched the League ERA title and completed all of his 20 starts in 1942. Appling amassed 40 Win Shares, topped the League in batting average (.328) and OBP (.419) and merited another runner-up finish in the '43 AL MVP race.

Year/Team	OPW%	PW	PL	APW%	AW	AL	Diff+/-
1950 CHW	0.442 F	68	86	0.390	60	94	-0.053
1951 CHW	0.495 F	76	78	0.526	81	73	0.031
1952 CHW	0.576 F	89	65	0.526	81	73	-0.050
1953 CHW	0.458 F	71	83	0.578	89	65	0.119
1954 CHW	0.482	74	80	0.610	94	60	0.128
1955 CHW	0.516 F	80	74	0.591	91	63	0.075
1956 CHW	0.472 F	73	81	0.552	85	69	0.080
1957 CHW	0.560 F	86	68	0.584	90	64	0.025
1958 CHW	0.492 F	76	78	0.532	82	72	0.040
1959 CHW	0.501 F	77	77	0.610 P	94	60	0.109

franchID	OWAR	OWS	AWAR	AWS	WARdiff	WSdiff	P/D/W/F
1950 CHW	13.853	186.427	24.721	179.999	-10.868	6.428	F
1951 CHW	25.598	182.478	44.037	243.001	-18.439	-60.523	F
1952 CHW	20.730	213.680	40.650	243.000	-19.920	-29.319	F
1953 CHW	31.455	214.421	37.459	267.000	-6.005	-52.579	F
1954 CHW	16.096	171.747	47.132	273.011	-31.036	-101.264	
1955 CHW	18.749	200.054	47.132	273.011	-28.383	-72.957	F
1956 CHW	26.102	202.670	46.921	255.000	-20.820	-52.329	F
1957 CHW	29.922	230.877	44.856	270.000	-14.934	-39.123	F
1958 CHW	34.665	253.862	34.037	246.002	0.628	7.860	F
1959 CHW	23.871	224.748	38.964	**281.997**	-15.093	-57.248	F

Ed Lopat won 21 contests and posted a league-best WHIP of 1.193 during the '51 season. In 1953 the southpaw topped the charts with a 2.42 ERA and 1.127 WHIP. Jim Busby led the Sox with a .312 batting average and "Jungle" Jim Rivera laced 16 triples. The '54 squad compiled the worst WSdiff (-101) and WARdiff (-31) vs. the output of the "Actual" White Sox during the same year.

Slick-fielding shortstop Luis Aparicio garnered the AL Rookie of the Year Award after pilfering 21 bases in '56. "Little Louie" nabbed the stolen base crown in 9 consecutive seasons averaging 41 swipes per year. He stole 56 bags in 69 attempts and placed runner-up in the 1959 AL MVP campaign.

Year/Team	OPW%	PW	PL	APW%	AW	AL	Diff+/-
1960 CHW	0.562 F	87	67	0.565	87	67	0.003
1961 CHW	0.568 F	92	70	0.531	86	76	-0.037
1962 CHW	0.531	86	76	0.525	85	77	-0.006
1963 CHW	0.550	89	73	0.580	94	68	0.030
1964 CHW	0.547	89	73	0.605	98	64	0.058
1965 CHW	0.490	79	83	0.586	95	67	0.097
1966 CHW	0.586 P	95	67	0.512	83	79	-0.073
1967 CHW	0.534	86	76	0.549	89	73	0.016
1968 CHW	0.505	82	80	0.414	67	95	-0.091
1969 CHW	0.513	83	79	0.420	68	94	-0.093

franchID	OWAR	OWS	AWAR	AWS	WARdiff	WSdiff	P/D/W/F
1960 CHW	40.380	252.541	44.612	260.998	-4.231	-8.458	F
1961 CHW	38.263	254.260	41.057	258.001	-2.795	-3.741	F
1962 CHW	34.570	222.079	40.869	254.998	-6.298	-32.920	
1963 CHW	42.954	243.678	50.803	281.998	-7.849	-38.320	
1964 CHW	36.570	235.552	45.469	293.998	-8.899	-58.446	
1965 CHW	38.075	246.201	44.551	284.992	-6.476	-38.791	
1966 CHW	35.453	243.456	36.649	248.998	-1.195	-5.543	P
1967 CHW	29.479	227.260	35.894	267.003	-6.415	-39.743	
1968 CHW	36.093	222.081	26.098	201.000	9.995	21.080	
1969 CHW	33.079	215.766	29.216	204.004	3.863	11.762	

Norm Cash slugged 41 round-trippers, knocked in 132 runs and scored 119 times during his breakout season in '61. He collected his lone batting title with a .361 average and led the American League with 193 hits and .487 OBP while finishing fourth in the MVP race. Cash clubbed 39 long balls in the following campaign but his average plummeted to .243. Johnny Romano supplied a .299 BA with 21 dingers in 1961 and slammed 25 four-baggers in the subsequent year. Romano and Earl Battey propelled the White Sox catching corps into a three-way tie for the league-lead with 15 WS>10 seasons during the 1960's.

Johnny Callison thumped a league-best 10 triples and scored 107 runs in '62. The Pale Hose posted runner-up finishes in back-to-back seasons (1962-63), falling victim to the Twins in both instances. Battey set individual bests with 26 taters and 84 ribbies in 1963 and Gary Peters (19-8, 2.33) collected the League ERA title and earned Rookie of the Year honors. Chicago ended the 1964 season in a third-place tie with Baltimore, only 3 games behind the Yankees. Callison (.274/31/104) ranked second in the MVP balloting. Peters topped AL hurlers with 20 victories and received his first All-Star invite. Aparicio set a personal-best with 57 stolen bases.

The '66 White Sox captured the team's first pennant in 44 years by a 10-game margin over the Twins. Callison pounded 40 two-base hits, Cash rocked 32 homers and Don Buford swiped 51 bags. Peters paced the circuit with a 1.98 ERA and a 0.982 WHIP. Relief ace Joe Hoerner provided a 2.16 and 13 saves per year from 1966-1971. Joe Horlen supplied a 19-7 record along with a league-best ERA of 2.06 in '67 as Chicago managed a third-place finish, eight games behind Minnesota.

Denny McLain accomplished a marvelous feat in 1968, amassing 31 wins, 336 innings and completing 28 of 41 contests. He fashioned a 1.96 ERA and 0.905 WHIP and swept the AL

MVP and Cy Young races. Through 2013 McLain was the last pitcher to surpass 30 wins in a single season. Chicago failed to capitalize on McLain's efforts, ending the year with a frustrating sixth-place finish. The Sox rebounded with a third-place effort as divisional play began in 1969. McLain topped the charts with 24 victories, 325 innings and 9 shutouts, repeating as the AL Cy Young Award winner. Buford scored 99 times in three straight campaigns (1969-1971).

Year/Team	OPW%	PW	PL	APW%	AW	AL	Diff+/-
1970 CHW	0.480	78	84	0.346	56	106	-0.135
1971 CHW	0.494	80	82	0.488	79	83	-0.006
1972 CHW	0.452	73	89	0.565	87	67	0.113
1973 CHW	0.499 F	81	81	0.475	77	85	-0.023
1974 CHW	0.514 F	83	79	0.500	80	80	-0.014
1975 CHW	0.474 F	77	85	0.466	75	86	-0.009
1976 CHW	0.382	62	100	0.398	64	97	0.015
1977 CHW	0.435 F	70	92	0.556	90	72	0.120
1978 CHW	0.454 F	74	88	0.441	71	90	-0.013
1979 CHW	0.466 F	76	86	0.456	73	87	-0.010

franchID	OWAR	OWS	AWAR	AWS	WARdiff	WSdiff	P/D/W/F
1970 CHW	24.641	205.270	20.457	167.999	4.184	37.271	
1971 CHW	33.764	227.742	46.929	237.001	-13.165	-9.258	
1972 CHW	30.277	222.511	40.060	260.995	-9.783	-38.485	
1973 CHW	25.417	231.625	32.893	230.998	-7.475	0.627	F
1974 CHW	32.439	212.892	39.717	239.998	-7.277	-27.106	F
1975 CHW	28.663	221.275	32.270	225.000	-3.608	-3.725	F
1976 CHW	16.110	154.182	27.718	192.004	-11.608	-37.822	
1977 CHW	27.337	174.903	45.944	269.998	-18.607	-95.096	F
1978 CHW	32.567	201.690	24.574	212.989	7.994	-11.299	F
1979 CHW	29.697	176.189	31.030	219.002	-1.333	-42.813	F

Chicago suffered through two miserable seasons in 1970 and 1972 and then, apart from a dreadful 100-loss season in 1976, proceeded to disappear from the radar until 1991. The franchise failed to produce enough talent on offense to meet the minimum PA requirements from 1977-1990. Brian Downing and Harold Baines were the only batsmen to achieve anything of note during this dismal period. GM Roland Hemond (1974-1984) and the White Sox front office floundered through the Amateur Draft process and Hemond's draftees, excluding Harold Baines and the class of '77, yielded only 87 Career Total Win Shares per season.

The slick-fielding Luis Aparicio batted .313 and collected his ninth Gold Glove Award in '70. "Beltin'" Bill Melton swatted 33 circuit clouts in consecutive years (1970-71). Carlos May supplied a .308 BA in '72 and drove in 96 runs in the subsequent campaign. Terry Forster furnished a 2.25 ERA and saved 29 contests for the '72 Sox and led the League with 24 saves in 1974. Bob Locker contributed 10 wins and 18 saves in '73 and maintained a 2.75 ERA for his career. Jorge Orta established personal bests with a .316 BA and 31 doubles in '74.

Rich Gossage flourished in the closer's role, saving a league-high 26 contests along with a 1.84 ERA in '75. "Goose" notched 151 strikeouts in 133 innings and posted a 1.62 ERA with 11 wins and 26 saves in 1977. Brian Downing earned his sole All-Star appearance as a backstop, setting personal bests with a .326 BA and .418 OBP in 1979.

Win Shares > 20	Single-Season	1960-1979
Norm Cash - 1B (CHW) x8	Johnny Romano - C (CHW) x2	Johnny Callison - RF (CHW) x4
Don Mincher - 1B (CHW)	Earl Battey - C (CHW) x2	
Don Buford - 2B (CHW) x2	Brian Downing - C (CHW)	Gary Peters - SP (CHW) x2

Jorge Orta - 2B (CHW) x2 Luis Aparicio - SS (CHW) x3 Don Buford - 3B (CHW) Bill Melton - 3B (CHW) x2	Don Buford - LF (CHW) x3 Carlos May - LF (CHW) Ken Berry - CF (CHW)	Joe Horlen - SP (CHW) Denny McLain - SP (CHW) x2 Rich Gossage - RP (CHW) x3

Year/Team	OPW%	PW	PL	APW%	AW	AL	Diff+/-
1980 CHW	0.396 F	64	98	0.438	70	90	0.041
1981 CHW	0.567 F	92	70	0.509	54	52	-0.057
1982 CHW	0.523 F	85	77	0.537	87	75	0.014
1983 CHW	0.548 F	89	73	0.611 P	99	63	0.063
1984 CHW	0.514 F	83	79	0.457	74	88	-0.057
1985 CHW	0.485 F	79	83	0.525	85	77	0.040
1986 CHW	0.514 F	83	79	0.444	72	90	-0.069
1987 CHW	0.487 F	79	83	0.475	77	85	-0.012
1988 CHW	0.410 F	66	96	0.441	71	90	0.031
1989 CHW	0.518 F	84	78	0.429	69	92	-0.090

franchID	OWAR	OWS	AWAR	AWS	WARdiff	WSdiff	P/D/W/F
1980 CHW	24.063	179.938	23.086	210.006	0.977	-30.068	F
1981 CHW	19.104	121.000	30.047	161.995	-10.943	-40.995	F
1982 CHW	30.021	194.358	46.678	261.003	-16.657	-66.645	F
1983 CHW	27.283	211.608	47.505	297.001	-20.223	-85.393	F
1984 CHW	38.083	249.902	33.970	222.001	4.113	27.901	F
1985 CHW	28.917	206.851	35.575	255.000	-6.658	-48.148	F
1986 CHW	33.255	213.323	25.894	216.004	7.361	-2.680	F
1987 CHW	29.247	213.495	29.337	230.996	-0.090	-17.500	F
1988 CHW	16.011	172.722	20.210	212.995	-4.199	-40.274	F
1989 CHW	31.685	239.165	28.537	207.005	3.148	32.160	F

Britt Burns delivered 15 victories with a 2.84 ERA and a career-best 1.160 WHIP during his inaugural season (1980). Harold Baines, the first selection in the 1977 amateur draft, belted 25 long balls and knocked in 105 runs in his third season (1982). Downing moved to left field and played error-free ball while contributing 109 runs and 28 blasts. Baines swatted a career-high 29 round-trippers and led the AL with a .541 SLG in '84 and in the subsequent season amassed 198 hits and 113 RBI. Burns contributed 18 wins in '85 before an injured hip forced him into early retirement. Downing established personal bests in home runs (29) and runs scored (110) while pacing the circuit with 106 walks in '87. The ChiSox designated hitters topped the Majors with 27 WS>10 seasons spanning from 1980 through 2009. GM Larry Himes thrived in the Amateur Draft during his brief tenure (1987-1990). His draft acquisitions comprised of Jack McDowell (1987), Robin Ventura (1988) and Frank E. Thomas (1989) in conjunction with Ray Durham, Bob Wickman and Alex Fernandez in 1990.

Year/Team	OPW%	PW	PL	APW%	AW	AL	Diff+/-
1990 CHW	0.556 F	90	72	0.580	94	68	0.024
1991 CHW	0.599 P	97	65	0.537	87	75	-0.062
1992 CHW	0.547 D	89	73	0.531	86	76	-0.017
1993 CHW	0.569 F	92	70	0.580 D	94	68	0.011
1994 CHW	0.615 F	100	62	0.593 D	67	46	-0.022
1995 CHW	0.489	79	83	0.472	68	76	-0.016
1996 CHW	0.532 D	86	76	0.525	85	77	-0.007
1997 CHW	0.493	80	82	0.497	80	81	0.004
1998 CHW	0.460	75	87	0.494	80	82	0.034
1999 CHW	0.504	82	80	0.466	75	86	-0.038

franchID	OWAR	OWS	AWAR	AWS	WARdiff	WSdiff	P/D/W/F
1990 CHW	36.238	258.357	35.732	281.998	0.505	-23.641	F
1991 CHW	45.646	278.919	39.134	260.992	6.512	17.927	P
1992 CHW	48.770	278.530	39.662	257.992	9.108	20.537	D
1993 CHW	50.062	270.668	44.999	282.001	5.062	-11.333	F
1994 CHW	44.136	208.397	38.510	201.003	5.627	7.394	F
1995 CHW	39.126	209.750	33.979	204.003	5.147	5.747	
1996 CHW	48.492	246.680	46.145	255.001	2.347	-8.321	D
1997 CHW	32.783	241.113	30.577	240.003	2.206	1.110	
1998 CHW	26.952	224.720	28.838	239.997	-1.886	-15.277	
1999 CHW	45.117	289.088	28.552	225.001	16.566	64.088	

Bobby Thigpen eclipsed Dave Righetti's single-season saves record when he successfully closed out 57 contests in 1990. He posted a 1.83 ERA and led the League with 77 appearances while earning top-5 finishes in the MVP and Cy Young balloting. Frank E. Thomas (.318/32/109) placed third in the 1991 AL MVP race, topping the leader boards with 132 bases on balls and a .453 OBP. Robin Ventura collected the first of 6 Gold Glove Awards and plated 100 runners in his sophomore season.

Chicago celebrated its return to relevance, taking the AL pennant for the first time in 25 seasons. The '91 team topped the leader boards in oWAR and oWS. Jack McDowell notched 17 wins and led the League with 15 complete games. The Sox seized the Western division title in '92, ending the year with a 5-game cushion over the A's. Thomas drilled a league-leading 46 doubles and Ventura added 38 two-base knocks, while McDowell (20-10, 3.18) placed runner-up finish in the Cy Young race.

Thomas procured back-to-back MVP Awards in '93 and '94. "The Big Hurt" slammed 41 four-baggers and tallied 128 ribbies during the 1993 season. McDowell merited Cy Young honors after pacing the circuit with 22 victories and 4 shutouts. Fellow hurler Alex Fernandez set individual marks with a record of 18-9, 3.13 ERA and 1.164 WHIP. Chicago dipped below the minimum PA requirements in 1993-94. The Pale Hose achieved the AL Central division title by a single game over the Brew Crew in '96. Ventura belted a career-high 34 round-trippers and batted in 105 baserunners. Thomas clubbed 40 moon-shots and amassed 134 ribbies and in the following year attained the batting crown (.347) and topped the OBP charts (.456) while placing third in the 1997 AL MVP balloting.

In 1998, for the eighth consecutive season, Thomas surpassed 100 runs, RBI, and bases on balls. Ray Durham added a spark to the top of the lineup, swiping 36 bags and scoring 126 runs. Ventura (.301/32/120) set individual marks in batting average and RBI and garnered his highest placement in the MVP voting (sixth) in 1999. Magglio Ordonez earned his first All-Star invitation with a .301 BA, 30 jacks, and 117 ribbies.

Year/Team	OPW%	PW	PL	APW%	AW	AL	Diff+/-
2000 CHW	0.520 W	84	78	0.586 P	95	67	0.067
2001 CHW	0.493	80	82	0.512	83	79	0.019
2002 CHW	0.532 D	86	76	0.500	81	81	-0.032
2003 CHW	0.506 D	82	80	0.531	86	76	0.025
2004 CHW	0.533 W	86	76	0.512	83	79	-0.020
2005 CHW	0.501	81	81	0.611 P	99	63	0.111
2006 CHW	0.533 D	86	76	0.556	90	72	0.022
2007 CHW	0.507	82	80	0.444	72	90	-0.063
2008 CHW	0.378	61	101	0.546 D	89	74	0.168
2009 CHW	0.451	73	89	0.488	79	83	0.037

2010 CHW	0.525 D	85	77	0.543	88	74	0.018
2011 CHW	0.506	82	80	0.488	79	83	-0.018
2012 CHW	0.492	80	82	0.525	85	77	0.033
2013 CHW	0.402	65	97	0.389	63	99	-0.013

franchID	OWAR	OWS	AWAR	AWS	WARdiff	WSdiff	P/D/W/F
2000 CHW	41.715	284.283	44.747	284.995	-3.032	-0.712	W
2001 CHW	43.881	265.808	36.765	248.999	7.116	16.809	
2002 CHW	41.990	253.545	40.629	243.003	1.361	10.542	D
2003 CHW	42.527	283.164	44.264	257.997	-1.737	25.167	D
2004 CHW	39.604	265.983	36.515	248.997	3.089	16.986	W
2005 CHW	35.927	256.555	43.287	297.005	-7.360	-40.450	
2006 CHW	45.039	293.984	42.405	270.009	2.634	23.975	D
2007 CHW	35.364	267.413	24.798	215.996	10.566	51.416	
2008 CHW	32.177	243.379	45.007	267.003	-12.830	-23.625	
2009 CHW	30.224	249.423	35.449	236.995	-5.225	12.428	
2010 CHW	32.264	238.397	41.424	264.132	-9.160	-25.735	D
2011 CHW	32.429	237.946	37.136	237.002	-4.707	0.944	
2012 CHW	34.667	210.753	43.002	246.094	-8.335	-35.340	
2013 CHW	18.894	176.118	24.075	188.990	-5.181	-12.871	

The White Sox initiated the club's most productive decade (2000-2009) with a wild card berth, falling one game short of the Central division title. Frank E. Thomas set individual records with 43 home runs, 143 RBI and 115 runs scored, placing runner-up in the MVP vote. Durham added 121 runs scored and Ordonez hit .315 with 32 dingers and 126 RBI. Mike Cameron (.267/25/110) established career bests in RBI and runs (99) and merited the first of three Gold Glove Awards in 2001. Mark Buehrle (16-8, 3.29) led the AL with a 1.066 WHIP in his sophomore season, while Bob Wickman (2.39 ERA, 32 SV) saved 28 contests per year over the final 10 seasons of his career.

Chicago claimed consecutive division titles in 2002-03. Ordonez thumped 38 four-baggers and plated 135 baserunners while batting .320, Buehrle posted a career-best 19 victories and Thomas surpassed the 40-home run plateau for the fifth time in his career during the 2003 campaign. Carlos Lee delivered 31 long balls and knocked in 113 runs. "El Caballo" dialed long distance at least 30 times in five straight seasons and averaged 112 RBI from 2003-07. Joe Borowski posted 33 saves and set individual marks with a 2.63 ERA and 1.054 WHIP for the '03 staff. The Sox earned a wild card entry in '04, placing four games behind the Tribe. Aaron Rowand smacked 38 doubles, 24 homers and hit .310 following a promotion to a full-time role in center field. Buehrle fashioned a career-best ERA of 3.12 along with 16 wins and placed fifth in the 2005 AL Cy Young race and Wickman paced the junior circuit with 45 saves.

The White Sox led the League in oWAR and oWS in '06 and attained another division crown. Thomas walloped 39 home runs and knocked in 114 runs while Durham established individual bests with 26 dingers and 93 ribbies. Ordonez (.363/28/139) amassed 31 Win Shares in '07, claiming the batting crown and leading the circuit with 54 two-base knocks. He placed second in his bid for MVP honors. Rowand (.309/27/89) received an All-Star nod and the Gold Glove Award. Chris B. Young belted 32 big-flies en route to a fourth-place finish in the ROY balloting. Three years later he set career-highs with 94 runs scored, 91 RBI and 28 stolen bases while earning his first All-Star nod. Mike Morse batted .303, clubbed 31 round-trippers and drove in 95 baserunners for the Pale Hose in 2011.

Win Shares > 20	Single-Season	1980-2013
Frank E. Thomas - 1B (CHW) x6	Mike Cameron - CF (CHW) x5	Frank E. Thomas - DH (CHW) x5
Mike Morse - 1B (CHW)	Aaron Rowand - CF (CHW) x2	Britt Burns - SP (CHW)
Ray Durham - 2B (CHW) x5	Chris B. Young - CF (CHW)	Alex Fernandez - SP (CHW)
Alexei Ramirez - SS (CHW)	Harold Baines - RF (CHW) x2	Jack McDowell - SP (CHW)
Robin Ventura - 3B (CHW) x7	Magglio Ordonez - RF (CHW) x5	Mark Buehrle - SP (CHW)
Brian Downing - LF (CHW) x4	Brian Downing - DH (CHW)	Bobby Thigpen - RP (CHW)
Carlos Lee - LF (CHW) x3	Harold Baines - DH (CHW)	

Note: 4000 PA or BFP to qualify, except during strike-shortened seasons
(1972 = 3800, 1981 & 1994 = 2700, 1995 = 3500) and 154-game schedule (3800)
- failed to qualify: 1901-1902, 1905-1909, 1911, 1920, 1934-1946, 1948-1953, 1955-1961, 1973-1975, 1977-1990, 1993-1994

White Sox All-Time "Originals" Roster

Jeff Abbott	Roy Elsh	Walt Kuhn	Danny Reynolds
Fritz Ackley	John Ely	Rusty Kuntz	Clayton Richard
Cy Acosta	Slim Embrey	Art Kusnyer	Lee Richard
Doug Adams	Charlie English	Jerry Kutzler	Branch Rickey
Herb Adams	George Enright	Fred Lamline	Johnny Riddle
Grady Adkins	Mutz Ens	Ken Landenberger	Johnny Rigney
Scotty Alcock	Chico Escarrega	Jim Landis	Royce Ring
Brandon Allen	Eduardo Escobar	Jesse Landrum	Swede Risberg
Rod Allen	Sammy Esposito	Dick Lane	Jim Rivera
Edwin Almonte	Cecil Espy	Frank Lange	Charlie Robertson
Clemente Alvarez	Mark Esser	Bill Lathrop	Mike Robertson
Brian N. Anderson	Art Evans	Barry Latman	Dewey Robinson
Hal Anderson	Bill L. Evans	Bob Lawrence	Les Rock
Luis Andujar	Red Evans	Danny Lazar	Liu Rodriguez
Luis Aparicio	Sam Ewing	Carlos Lee	Nerio Rodriguez
Luke Appling	Bibb Falk	Derek Lee	Dan Rohrmeier
Rudy Arias	Bob Fallon	George Lees	Johnny Romano
Gerry Arrigo	Joe Fautsch	Elmer Leifer	Lou Rosenberg
Ken Ash	Dutch Fehring	Rudy Leopold	Marv Rotblatt
Harold Baines	Happy Felsch	Dixie Leverett	Braggo Roth
Jeff Bajenaru	Hod Fenner	Alan Levine	Edd Roush
Jesse O. Baker	Alex Fernandez	Jeff Liefer	Aaron Rowand
James Baldwin	Clarence Fieber	Lyman Linde	Wade Rowdon
Charlie Barnabe	Josh Dean Fields	Chuck Lindstrom	Don Rudolph
Bob Barnes	Lou Fiene	Bob Locker	Scott Ruffcorn
Rich Barnes	Bill Fischer	Boone Logan	Johnny Ruffin
Salome Barojas	Al Fitzmorris	Ron Lolich	Josh Rupe
Cuke Barrows	Tom Flanigan	Jimmie Long	Adam Russell
Earl Battey	Roy Flaskamper	Dean Look	Reb Russell
Jim Battle	Josh Fogg	Ed Lopat	Blondy Ryan
Jim Baumer	Marv Foley	Pedro Lopez	Olmedo Saenz
Ross Baumgarten	Tom Fordham	Mem Lovett	Chris Sale
Gordon Beckham	Happy Foreman	Donny Lucy	David Sanders
Kevin Beirne	Terry Forster	Rob Lukachyk	Danny Sandoval
Kevin Bell	Ken Frailing	David Lundquist	Hector Santiago
Ralph Bell	Vic Frazier	Byrd Lynn	Johnny Schaive
Joe Benz	Jake Freeze	Ted Lyons	Ray Schalk
Jason Bere	Dave Frost	Robert Machado	Norm Schlueter
Joe Berger	Chick Gandil	Frank Mack	Brian Schmack

Marty Berghammer
Dennis Berran
Claude Berry
Ken Berry
Mike Bertotti
Rocky Biddle
Charlie Biggs
John Bischoff
Bill Black
George Blackerby
Lena Blackburne
Homer Blankenship
Ted Blankenship
Mike Blyzka
Milt Bocek
Ping Bodie
Brian Boehringer
Greg Bollo
Rodney Bolton
Pedro F. Borbon
Joe Borchard
Frenchy Bordagaray
Joe Borowski
Babe Borton
Daryl Boston
Billy Bowers
Emmett Bowles
Grant Bowler
Red Bowser
Bob Boyd
Harry Boyles
Don Bradey
Buddy Bradford
Chad Bradford
Doug Brady
Dave Brain
Fred Bratschi
Angel Bravo
Jim Breton
Alan Brice
Chuck Brinkman
Lance Broadway
Delos Brown
Joe H. Brown
Jack Bruner
Hal Bubser
Mark Buehrle
Don Buford
Bob Buhl
Britt Burns
Joe F. Burns
Jim Busby
Mike Buskey
Jerry Byrne
George Caithamer

Leo Garcia
Luis C. Garcia
Ramon A. Garcia
Lou Garland
Hank Garrity
Jim Geddes
Johnny Gerlach
Chris Getz
George Gick
Claral Gillenwater
Matt Ginter
Gordon Goldsberry
Andy Gonzalez
Gio Gonzalez
Miguel Antonio
Gonzalez
John Goodell
Rich Gossage
Dick Gossett
Johnny Grabowski
Roy Graham
Alex Grammas
Jimmy Grant
Lorenzo Gray
Craig Grebeck
Paul Gregory
Buddy Groom
Orval Grove
Frank Grube
Matt Guerrier
Charlie Haeger
Bud Hafey
Jerry Hairston
Sammy Hairston
Chet Hajduk
Jack Hallett
Ralph Hamner
Fred Hancock
Don Hanski
John Happenny
Pat Hardgrove
Jack G. Hardy
Lucas Harrell
Spencer Harris
Hub Hart
Ziggy Hasbrook
Mike Heathcott
Spencer Heath
Val Heim
Chris Heintz
Russ Heman
Frank Hemphill
Fernando Hernandez
Rudy Hernandez
Mike Hershberger

Jim Magnuson
Gary Majewski
Mike Maksudian
Jule Mallonee
Gordon Maltzberger
Carl Manda
Leo Mangum
Johnny Mann
Jay Marshall
Jim Marshall
J.C. Martin
Morrie Martin
Norberto Martin
Speed Martin
Wally Mattick
Mark Mauldin
Carlos May
Wally Mayer
Jack McAleese
Jim McAnany
Pryor McBee
Brian McCall
Brandon McCarthy
Harvey McClellan
Tommy McCraw
Jack McDowell
Ed McGhee
Stover McIlwain
Joel McKeon
Rich McKinney
Denny McLain
Polly McLarry
Sam McMackin
Jerry McNertney
Doug McWeeny
Paul Meloan
Bill Melton
Frank Menechino
Tony Menendez
Matt Merullo
Bobby Messenger
Scat Metha
William Metzig
Billy Meyer
George Meyer
Russ Meyer
Cass Michaels
John Michaelson
Bruce Miller
Frank Miller
Don Mincher
George Mogridge
Gustavo Molina
Richie Moloney
Larry Monroe

Hank Schreiber
Steve Schrenk
Bob Schultz
Webb Schultz
Jim Scoggins
Jim Scott
Bobby Seay
Ricky Seilheimer
Marcus Semien
Rich Severson
Bill Sharp
Earl Sheely
Frank Shellenback
Art Shires
Ray Shook
Dave Short
Ken Silvestri
Brian Simmons
Mel Simons
Mike Sirotka
Jim Siwy
Bud Sketchley
John Skopec
Craig Smajstrla
Joe Smaza
Art Smith
Bob A. Smith
Ernie Smith
Frank E. Smith
Harry M. Smith
Pop-Boy Smith
Roxy Snipes
Chris Snopek
Floyd Speer
Bob Spence
Mike Squires
Marv Staehle
Milt Steengrafe
Hank Steinbacher
Chris Stewart
Frank Stewart
Josh Stewart
Lee Stine
Tim Stoddard
John Stoneham
Dick Strahs
Monty Stratton
Elmer Stricklett
Ed Stroud
Billy Sullivan, Jr.
John J. Sullivan
Harry Suter
Leo Sutherland
Karl Swanson
Ryan Sweeney

Johnny Callison	Kevin Hickey	Jimmy Moore	Augie Swentor
Mike Cameron	Jim Hicks	Randy Moore	Steve Swisher
Bruce Campbell	Joe Hicks	Rich Morales	Shingo Takatsu
John Cangelosi	Dennis Higgins	Ray Morehart	Fred Talbot
Pat Caraway	Rich Hinton	Brent Morel	Leo Tankersley
Cisco Carlos	Ed Hobaugh	Russ Morman	Bruce Tanner
Cam Carreon	Shovel Hodge	Mike Morse	Lee Tannehill
Chris V. Carter	Joe Hoerner	Johnny Mostil	Fred Tauby
Norm Cash	Dutch Hoffman	Jose Mota	Harry J. Taylor
Carlos Castillo	Guy Hoffman	Bill L. Mueller	Leo Taylor
Vince Castino	Jeff Holly	Charlie Mullen	Zeb Terry
Paul Castner	David Holmberg	Greg Mulleavy	Kanekoa Texeira
Fabio Castro	Gail Hopkins	Fran Mullins	Bobby Thigpen
Bill Chamberlain	Joe Horlen	Dominic Mulrenan	Frank E. Thomas
Joe Chamberlain	Dwayne Hosey	Arnie Munoz	Larry Thomas
Harry Chappas	Ken Hottman	Aaron Myette	Tommy Thomas
Larry Chappell	Bruce Howard	Frank Naleway	Lee Thompson
Italo Chelini	Fred Howard	Andy Nelson	Les Tietje
Felix Chouinard	John Hudek	Roger Nelson	Kevin Tolar
Chief Chouneau	Daniel Hudson	Dan Neumeier	Carlos Torres
Bill Cissell	Jim R. Hughes	Bill Norman	Babe Towne
Bud Clancy	Tim Hulett	Scott Northey	Sean Tracey
Grey Clarke	Tim Hummel	Greg Norton	Chris Tremie
Pep Clark	Bill Hunnefield	Chris Nyman	Hal Trosky, Jr.
Chris Clemons	Tom Hurd	Jerry Nyman	Steve Trout
Mike Colbern	Jimmy Hurst	Nyls Nyman	Mike Trujillo
Willis Cole	Ira Hutchinson	Fred Olmstead	Thurman Tucker
Shano Collins	Tadahito Iguchi	Brian Omogrosso	Cy Twombly
Jocko Conlan	Charlie Jackson	Magglio Ordonez	Frenchy Uhalt
Sarge Connally	Ron H. Jackson	Jorge Orta	Bob Uhl
Merv Connors	Otto Jacobs	Jose L. Ortiz	Charlie Uhlir
Cecil Coombs	Hi Jasper	Red Ostergard	Mario Valdez
Ed Corey	Domingo Jean	Dennis O'Toole	Joe Valentine
Roy Corhan	Irv Jeffries	Jim Otten	Vito Valentinetti
Ed Correa	John Jenkins	Del Paddock	Joe Vance
Jess Cortazzo	Bart Johnson	Vicente Palacios	Pete Varney
Ernie Cox	Connie Johnson	Donn Pall	Randy Velarde
George Cox	Ernie R. Johnson	Frank Papish	Pat Veltman
Les Cox	Jimmy Johnston	Jim Parque	Robin Ventura
Roy Crabb	Lamar Johnson	Reggie Patterson	Dayan Viciedo
Joe Crede	Mark L. Johnson	Roy Patterson	Pete Vuckovich
Buck Crouse	Pete Johns	Josh Paul	Ed A. Walsh
Aaron Cunningham	Rankin Johnson, Jr.	John Pawlowski	Ed Arthur Walsh
Guy Curtright	Randy S. Johnson	George Payne	George Washington
Pete Daglia	Stan Johnson	Elmer Pence	Ehren Wassermann
Jerry Dahlke	Walt Johnson	Rusty Pence	Johnny Watwood
Tom D. Daly	Smead Jolley	John Perkovich	Bob Way
Pat Daneker	Al Jones	Len Perme	Buck Weaver
Jordan Danks	Deacon G. Jones	Stan Perzanowski	Biggs Wehde
Wally Dashiell	Jake Jones	Adam C. Peterson	Bob Weiland
Lum Davenport	Nate Jones	Buddy Peterson	Ed Weiland
Joel Davis	Tex Jones	Gary Peters	Al Weis
Mark A. Davis	Bubber Jonnard	Rube Peters	Mike Welday
Dave DeBusschere	Rip Jordan	Josh Phegley	Kip Wells
Mike Degerick	Tom Jordan	Dave Philley	Leo Wells

Flame Delhi	Duane Josephson	Damon Phillips	Ed White
Jason Dellaero	Ted Jourdan	Heath Phillips	John Whitehead
Fautino De Los Santos	Mike Joyce	Jeff Pierce	Frank Whitman
	Howie Judson	Babe Pinelli	Bob Wickman
Bucky Dent	Willie Kamm	John Pomorski	Jack Wieneke
Jim Derrington	John Francis Kane	Aaron Poreda	Al Williamson
Bernie DeViveiros	Ron Karkovice	Irv Porter	Hugh Willingham
Al DeVormer	Charlie Kavanagh	Jay Porter	Kenny Williams
John Dobb	Red Kelly	Bob Poser	Kid Willson
Jess Dobernic	Bob Kennedy	Leroy Powell	Bill D. Wilson
Brendan Donnelly	Dick Kenworthy	Frank Pratt	Craig F. Wilson
Charlie Dorman	Gus Keriazakos	Red Proctor	Red Wilson
Tom Dougherty	Dickey Kerr	Pid Purdy	Roy Wilson
Phil Douglas	Brian Keyser	Billy Purtell	Archie Wise
Brian Downing	Joe Kiefer	Lee Quillen	Pete Wojey
Doug Drabek	Bruce Kimm	Humberto Quintero	Polly Wolfe
Tom Drees	Harry Kinzy	Don Rader	Mellie Wolfgang
Larry Duff	Joe Kirrene	Scott Radinsky	Rich Wortham
Dan Dugan	Hugo Klaerner	Alexei Ramirez	Cy Wright
Gus Dundon	Fred Klages	Fred Rath	Dan Wright
Frank Dupee	Brent Knackert	Jon Rauch	Hugh Yancy
John Durham	Chris Knapp	Buck Redfern	Yam Yaryan
Ray Durham	Don Kolloway	Glenn Redmon	Chris B. Young
Don Eddy	Fabian Kowalik	Addison Reed	Rollie Zeider
Paul Edmondson	Jack Kralick	Bill Reeder	Dutch Zwilling
Wayne Edwards	Ken Kravec	Jeremy Reed	
Jack Egbert	Ralph Kreitz	Barney Reilly	
Robert Ellis	Jack Kucek	Carl Reynolds	

New York Yankees

Year/Team	OPW%	PW	PL	APW%	AW	AL	Diff+/-
1901 NYY	0.487 F	66	70	0.511	68	65	0.024
1902 NYY	0.401	55	81	0.362	50	88	-0.039
1903 NYY	0.453 F	63	77	0.537	72	62	0.085
1904 NYY	0.338 F	52	102	0.609	92	59	0.271
1905 NYY	0.498	77	77	0.477	71	78	-0.022
1906 NYY	0.593 P	91	63	0.596	90	61	0.003
1907 NYY	0.484	75	79	0.473	70	78	-0.011
1908 NYY	0.315	48	106	0.331	51	103	0.016
1909 NYY	0.467	72	82	0.490	74	77	0.023

franchID	OWAR	OWS	AWAR	AWS	WARdiff	WSdiff	P/D/W/F
1901 NYY	0.279	38.185	32.651	204.004	-32.373	-165.819	F
1902 NYY	1.114	18.134	29.296	149.894	-28.183	-131.760	
1903 NYY	4.654	47.472	27.402	216.002	-22.748	-168.530	F
1904 NYY	4.776	58.229	41.973	275.995	-37.197	-217.766	F
1905 NYY	8.882	90.238	31.452	213.007	-22.570	-122.769	
1906 NYY	14.351	**151.869**	37.273	269.987	-22.922	-118.118	P
1907 NYY	11.318	140.935	23.029	209.989	-11.711	-69.054	
1908 NYY	6.355	112.493	14.014	153.004	-7.659	-40.511	
1909 NYY	21.221	184.605	26.158	221.997	-4.937	-37.391	

Legend: (P) = Pennant / Most Wins in League (D) = Division Winner (W) = Wild Card Winner (F) = Failed to Qualify

The New York Yankees began as the Baltimore Orioles as one of the charter members of the American League in 1901. In order to establish competition with the National League, the team relocated to New York in 1903 and changed its name to the Highlanders. The organization assumed the "Yankees" moniker in 1913.

The most successful franchise in baseball history through 2013, the "Actual" Yankees have captured the most pennants based on winning percentage (40), Win Shares (40) and WAR (38). The "Original" Yankees have the largest differential, collecting "only" 15 pennants based on PW%, 25 Win Shares, and 13 WAR. A significant portion of this disparity can be attributed to the absence of Babe Ruth and Eddie Lopat from the "Original" Yankees. The Pinstripers earned 12 pennants with Ruth and Lopat but merely tallied three "Original" pennants during the same timeframe.

The Yankees' franchise produced the most catchers (33 WS>20 and 103 WS>10 seasons). New York has consistently yielded superstar backstops, including Bill Dickey, Yogi Berra, Elston Howard, Thurman Munson and Jorge Posada. Another dominant position throughout Yankees' history is center field, topping the "Turn of the Century" charts with 64 WS>20 and 153 WS>10 seasons. The legends covering the vast green pastures of Yankee Stadium include Earle Combs, Joe DiMaggio, Mickey Mantle, and Bernie F. Williams. The organization's first basemen generated 168 WS>10 seasons, surpassing all teams in the modern era.

Conversely, the Yankees have faced difficulties in regards to the scouting and development of superstars at the hot corner. Detroit is the only "Turn of the Century" franchise to churn out fewer WS>20 seasons among third basemen. Mike Lowell and Red Rolfe managed to exceed this threshold four times apiece.

In the first twenty years of the club's existence, the Orioles/Highlanders/Yankees did not have a great deal about which they could brag. The team's National League counterparts, the "Original" Giants, ruled both Leagues with 13 Pythagorean WPCT pennants. Meanwhile, the Yanks tallied a mere 2 pennants in 1906 and 1918. The notorious leader of the '06 squad was first sacker "Prince" Hal Chase (.323/0/76/28) whose career was undermined by frequent allegations of cheating or throwing games.

Year/Team	OPW%	PW	PL	APW%	AW	AL	Diff+/-
1910 NYY	0.536	83	71	0.583	88	63	0.047
1911 NYY	0.480	74	80	0.500	76	76	0.020
1912 NYY	0.375	58	96	0.329	50	102	-0.046
1913 NYY	0.475	73	81	0.377	57	94	-0.098
1914 NYY	0.535	82	72	0.455	70	84	-0.081
1915 NYY	0.530	82	72	0.454	69	83	-0.076
1916 NYY	0.463	71	83	0.519	80	74	0.057
1917 NYY	0.560	86	68	0.464	71	82	-0.096
1918 NYY	0.541 P	69	59	0.488	60	63	-0.054
1919 NYY	0.540	76	64	0.576	80	59	0.036

franchID	OWAR	OWS	AWAR	AWS	WARdiff	WSdiff	P/D/W/F
1910 NYY	33.269	210.108	42.065	264.000	-8.796	-53.892	
1911 NYY	34.227	209.515	37.263	227.999	-3.036	-18.483	
1912 NYY	20.726	146.326	21.742	149.995	-1.016	-3.670	
1913 NYY	29.133	197.925	17.747	171.005	11.386	26.920	
1914 NYY	29.601	231.667	30.461	210.001	-0.859	21.665	
1915 NYY	32.939	212.363	30.977	207.004	1.962	5.359	

Year/Team	OWAR	OWS	AWAR	AWS	WARdiff	WSdiff	P/D/W/F
1916 NYY	30.371	210.410	36.927	240.003	-6.556	-29.593	
1917 NYY	41.032	250.336	33.450	213.006	7.582	37.330	
1918 NYY	31.239	194.210	25.567	179.997	5.672	14.213	P
1919 NYY	33.318	230.864	33.314	240.002	0.004	-9.138	

Russ Ford (26-6, 1.65 in 1910) and Hippo Vaughn anchored the rotation. Vaughn averaged 20 victories with 24 complete games, a 2.14 ERA and a 1.143 WHIP from 1914-1920 and lifted the Yankees to the pennant in 1918, posting league-bests in wins, strikeouts, innings pitched and ERA (1.74). Chase captured a batting crown in 1916 with a .339 average while Benny Kauff pilfered 40 bags.

Win Shares > 20	Single-Season	1901-1919
Hal Chase - 1B (NYY) x3	Rube Oldring - CF (NYY)	Jack Quinn - SP (NYY) x2
Baldy Louden - 2B (NYY)	Benny Kauff - CF (NYY) x4	Hippo Vaughn - SP (NYY) x6
Baldy Louden - SS (NYY)	Ed Hahn - RF (NYY)	Ray Fisher - SP (NYY)
Clyde Engle - LF (NYY)	Wilbur Good - RF (NYY)	George McConnell - SP (NYY)
Birdie Cree - LF (NYY)	Benny Kauff - RF (NYY)	Al Schulz - SP (NYY)
Rube Oldring - LF (NYY)	Russ Ford - SP (NYY) x3	Ray Caldwell - SW (NYY)
Birdie Cree - CF (NYY)	Ray Caldwell - SP (NYY) x2	Tom L. Hughes - SW (NYY)

Year/Team	OPW%	PW	PL	APW%	AW	AL	Diff+/-
1920 NYY	0.571 P	88	66	0.617	95	59	0.045
1921 NYY	0.499 F	77	77	0.641 P	98	55	0.141
1922 NYY	0.443	68	86	0.610 P	94	60	0.167
1923 NYY	0.435	67	87	0.645 P	98	54	0.209
1924 NYY	0.507	78	76	0.586	89	63	0.079
1925 NYY	0.456	70	84	0.448	69	85	-0.008
1926 NYY	0.533	82	72	0.591 P	91	63	0.058
1927 NYY	0.545 P	84	70	0.714 P	110	44	0.169
1928 NYY	0.522	80	74	0.656 P	101	53	0.134
1929 NYY	0.565	87	67	0.571	88	66	0.007

franchID	OWAR	OWS	AWAR	AWS	WARdiff	WSdiff	P/D/W/F
1920 NYY	38.160	226.601	48.875	284.996	-10.714	-58.395	P
1921 NYY	34.028	217.814	51.080	294.007	-17.052	-76.194	F
1922 NYY	32.995	230.640	41.573	282.002	-8.578	-51.362	
1923 NYY	27.661	208.935	46.445	293.999	-18.784	-85.064	
1924 NYY	32.826	219.655	43.167	266.997	-10.341	-47.341	
1925 NYY	27.834	211.476	34.052	207.005	-6.218	4.471	
1926 NYY	35.214	243.379	49.449	273.003	-14.235	-29.624	
1927 NYY	53.117	290.546	66.514	329.993	-13.397	-39.447	P
1928 NYY	45.894	291.195	52.421	303.002	-6.527	-11.807	
1929 NYY	48.765	316.393	46.521	264.002	2.244	52.391	

New York's hurlers delivered the highest pitWARnorm (28) and pitWSnorm (133) totals in the history of the franchise. Urban Shocker led the mound corps from 1920-27 and posted at least 20 victories in four consecutive campaigns, including a 27-win season in 1921. Ed Barrow served as the club's Business Manager from 1921-1945 and teamed with head scout Paul Krichell to replenish the Bombers roster with gifted athletes. Barrow and Krichell secured the services of Lou Gehrig ('23), Joe Gordon ('36), Charlie Keller, Phil Rizzuto, Tommy Holmes ('37) and Yogi Berra ('43) via amateur free agency. They consummated minor league trades for Earle Combs ('24), Tony Lazzeri ('25) and Joe DiMaggio ('34) while purchasing the contracts of Bill Dickey ('28), Lefty Gomez ('29) and Dixie F. Walker ('30).

For the first time in club history, the 1927 "Original" Yankees led the American League in oPW, oWAR and oWS. The starting lineup, nicknamed "Murderer's Row," included Earle Combs, Tony Lazzeri, Bob Meusel and Lou Gehrig. Wilcy Moore paced the League with a 2.28 ERA and 13 saves as he accrued 19 victories, working primarily in relief. Gehrig's streak of 2,130 consecutive games played from 1925-1939 earned him the well-deserved nickname "The Iron Horse." In the thirteen campaigns where he played every game, Gehrig batted at a .343 clip, cranked out 36 home runs and averaged 147 runs batted in per season! He tallied 43 Win Shares in '27, hitting at a .373 clip while leading the AL with 52 doubles and 175 RBI.

"Poosh 'Em Up" Lazzeri hit .297 and drove in 99 runs per year, covering the first 11 seasons of his career. Combs, "The Kentucky Colonel," contributed a .325 career batting average and led the circuit with 20+ triples on three occasions. Meusel captured the home run and RBI titles in '25. Lefty O'Doul provided additional thump to the already stacked lineup when he made a successful transition from pitcher to outfielder in 1928. He placed second in the MVP voting and led the League with 254 hits and a .398 average in '29.

Year/Team	OPW%	PW	PL	APW%	AW	AL	Diff+/-
1930 NYY	0.546	84	70	0.558	86	68	0.012
1931 NYY	0.582 P	90	64	0.614	94	59	0.033
1932 NYY	0.588	91	63	0.695 P	107	47	0.106
1933 NYY	0.562	86	68	0.607	91	59	0.045
1934 NYY	0.535	82	72	0.610	94	60	0.076
1935 NYY	0.571	88	66	0.597	89	60	0.026
1936 NYY	0.580 P	89	65	0.667 P	102	51	0.087
1937 NYY	0.670 P	103	51	0.662 P	102	52	-0.007
1938 NYY	0.575 P	89	65	0.651 P	99	53	0.076
1939 NYY	0.607 P	94	60	0.702 P	106	45	0.095

franchID	OWAR	OWS	AWAR	AWS	WARdiff	WSdiff	P/D/W/F
1930 NYY	44.505	280.917	52.064	257.995	-7.559	22.921	
1931 NYY	58.185	308.338	65.642	282.001	-7.456	26.337	P
1932 NYY	58.761	340.753	61.645	321.005	-2.884	19.747	
1933 NYY	53.321	286.581	56.655	272.998	-3.334	13.583	
1934 NYY	45.825	279.959	53.273	282.003	-7.449	-2.044	
1935 NYY	49.136	294.364	46.789	266.999	2.346	27.365	
1936 NYY	55.536	305.509	59.685	306.007	-4.149	-0.497	P
1937 NYY	57.614	339.863	57.223	305.995	0.391	33.868	P
1938 NYY	50.287	310.104	52.768	297.000	-2.481	13.104	P
1939 NYY	60.803	345.561	60.482	318.007	0.321	27.555	P

The "Original" Yankees overpowered American League opponents during the 1930's, achieving 5 pennants. Gehrig captured the batting crown with a .363 BA in 1934 and topped the charts in home runs and RBI on three occasions during the 1930's. "Biscuit Pants" earned MVP honors in 1936, batting .354 with 49 circuit clouts, 152 RBI, and 167 runs scored! Lefty Gomez fashioned a record of 26-5 and earned a third-place finish in the 1934 AL MVP race. "Goofy" twice led the League with a 2.33 ERA. Bill Dickey plated 133 runs during the 1937 campaign, and earned a runner-up finish in the '38 AL MVP balloting while batting .313 for his career.

Joe DiMaggio delivered a .323 average, 29 blasts, and 125 RBI in his debut season (1936). In his sophomore campaign, he paced the American League with 151 runs and 46 round-trippers along with career-bests in hits (215) and RBI (167). "Joltin' Joe" claimed the AL batting title (.381) and the MVP award in '39.

New York produced 39 WS>10 seasons at third base from 1930-1959, led by consistent output from Billy Werber and Red Rolfe. Werber scored 129 runs in '34 and led the League in stolen bases in three campaigns. Rolfe contributed a .329 batting average with a league-best 213 hits, 46 doubles and 139 runs scored in 1939. The Bronx Bombers closed out the decade with 4 consecutive pennants (1936-39), besting opponents in oWS and oWAR in all four seasons. The '39 squad featured the highest All-Time fldWARnorm (12) along with the top offWARnorm (32), offWSnorm (215) and fldWSnorm (69) totals in team annals.

Win Shares > 20	Single-Season	1920-1939
Lou Gehrig - 1B (NYY) x13	Bob Meusel - LF (NYY)	Curt Walker - RF (NYY) x2
Aaron Ward - 2B (NYY) x2	Lefty O'Doul - LF (NYY) x3	Ben Chapman - RF (NYY) x2
Tony Lazzeri - 2B (NYY) x5	Earle Combs - LF (NYY)	George Selkirk - RF (NYY)
Joe Gordon - 2B (NYY) x7	Ben Chapman - LF (NYY)	Dixie F. Walker - RF (NYY) x7
Mark Koenig - SS (NYY)	Joe DiMaggio - LF (NYY)	Charlie Keller - RF (NYY) x2
Lyn Lary - SS (NYY) x2	George Selkirk - LF (NYY)	Urban Shocker - SP (NYY) x5
Frankie Crosetti - SS (NYY) x2	Earle Combs - CF (NYY) x5	Lefty Gomez - SP (NYY) x4
Billy Werber - 3B (NYY) x3	Ben Chapman - CF (NYY)	Johnny Allen - SP (NYY) x2
Red Rolfe - 3B (NYY) x4	Joe DiMaggio - CF (NYY) x11	Wilcy Moore - SW (NYY)
Bill Dickey - C (NYY) x6	Bob Meusel - RF (NYY) x2	Ivy Andrews - SW (NYY)
Joe Harris - LF (NYY)		

Year/Team	OPW%	PW	PL	APW%	AW	AL	Diff+/-
1940 NYY	0.560 P	86	68	0.571	88	66	0.011
1941 NYY	0.560	86	68	0.656 P	101	53	0.095
1942 NYY	0.609	94	60	0.669 P	103	51	0.060
1943 NYY	0.545 P	84	70	0.636 P	98	56	0.091
1944 NYY	0.533	82	72	0.539	83	71	0.006
1945 NYY	0.550	85	69	0.533	81	71	-0.017
1946 NYY	0.510	79	75	0.565	87	67	0.055
1947 NYY	0.545	84	70	0.630 P	97	57	0.085
1948 NYY	0.523	81	73	0.610	94	60	0.088
1949 NYY	0.538	83	71	0.630 P	97	57	0.091

franchID	OWAR	OWS	AWAR	AWS	WARdiff	WSdiff	P/D/W/F
1940 NYY	43.551	298.437	43.246	264.004	0.305	34.432	P
1941 NYY	43.022	287.700	51.332	303.000	-8.311	-15.300	
1942 NYY	48.896	296.661	59.397	308.997	-10.501	-12.336	
1943 NYY	49.706	284.756	52.424	293.995	-2.719	-9.239	P
1944 NYY	42.402	240.822	41.007	248.996	1.396	-8.174	
1945 NYY	40.503	223.617	41.655	242.996	-1.152	-19.379	
1946 NYY	47.289	267.259	46.596	260.995	0.694	6.263	
1947 NYY	49.728	283.464	51.027	291.004	-1.299	-7.539	
1948 NYY	48.516	281.574	50.714	282.010	-2.198	-0.436	
1949 NYY	39.427	269.388	45.229	291.003	-5.802	-21.615	

New York returned to the pack in the junior circuit in the 1940's, clinching only 2 pennants. DiMaggio set the Major League record for consecutive games with at least one hit (56 games in 1941). "The Yankee Clipper" won 3 MVP awards, and achieved a .325 career batting average while clouting 28 home runs and knocking in 118 runs per year. The lineup was bolstered by the addition of second sacker Joe Gordon. "Flash" received the AL MVP award in 1942 (.322/18/103) and belted 32 long balls for the '48 squad. Gordon sustained the Yankees' superb reputation for cultivating second basemen as the club produced 58 WS>10 seasons at the keystone position from 1930-1969.

Spud Chandler (20-4, 1.64) received the AL MVP award in 1943, leading the circuit in victories, ERA, complete games (20), shutouts (5), and WHIP (0.992). Snuffy Stirnweiss topped the circuit in hits, runs, triples and stolen bases in consecutive campaigns (1944-45). Tommy Holmes (.352/28/117) claimed runner-up status in the MVP balloting in 1945, smacking 47 doubles and 224 base hits in the process. Dixie F. Walker collected a batting title in 1944 with a .357 average, an RBI title with 124 in '45 and posted a career batting average of .306. DiMaggio led the League in home runs (39) and RBI (155) during the 1948 season. "Fireman" Joe Page finished third in the 1949 AL MVP race after posting 13 relief wins and 27 saves with a 2.59 ERA. Ellis "Old Folks" Kinder fashioned a 23-6 record with a 3.36 ERA.

Year/Team	OPW%	PW	PL	APW%	AW	AL	Diff+/-
1950 NYY	0.520	80	74	0.636 P	98	56	0.116
1951 NYY	0.487	75	79	0.636 P	98	56	0.149
1952 NYY	0.545	84	70	0.617 P	95	59	0.071
1953 NYY	0.523	80	74	0.656 P	99	52	0.133
1954 NYY	0.543	84	70	0.669	103	51	0.126
1955 NYY	0.537	83	71	0.623 P	96	58	0.086
1956 NYY	0.549	85	69	0.630 P	97	57	0.081
1957 NYY	0.504	78	76	0.636 P	98	56	0.132
1958 NYY	0.520	80	74	0.597 P	92	62	0.077
1959 NYY	0.492	76	78	0.513	79	75	0.021

franchID	OWAR	OWS	AWAR	AWS	WARdiff	WSdiff	P/D/W/F
1950 NYY	40.797	259.495	51.444	294.000	-10.647	-34.505	
1951 NYY	36.856	247.643	51.250	294.003	-14.394	-46.360	
1952 NYY	42.349	256.725	50.379	284.996	-8.029	-28.271	
1953 NYY	34.622	240.927	54.434	296.998	-19.812	-56.071	
1954 NYY	38.671	258.211	49.015	288.006	-10.344	-29.795	
1955 NYY	38.749	258.731	49.015	288.006	-10.266	-29.275	
1956 NYY	41.148	268.238	50.279	290.998	-9.131	-22.760	
1957 NYY	38.680	254.952	49.789	294.004	-11.110	-39.052	
1958 NYY	37.890	258.351	48.268	275.992	-10.378	-17.642	
1959 NYY	36.328	236.978	41.812	237.002	-5.484	-0.024	

The "Original" Yankees suffered through a 17-year pennant drought from 1944-1960, while the "Actual" Yankees hoisted 11 flags during that timeframe. However, other than in 1956, the team paced the circuit in oWS from 1955-1960. Phil Rizzuto garnered MVP honors in 1950 after placing runner-up in the year prior. "Scooter" established individual bests with a .324 batting average, 125 runs scored, 200 hits and 36 doubles. DiMaggio belted 32 round-trippers, knocked in 122 runs and led the AL with a .585 SLG.

Yogi Berra (.322/28/124) placed third in the 1950 AL MVP balloting and set personal highs in batting average and runs scored (116). The 3-time MVP furnished a .295 average with 27 circuit clouts and 108 RBI from 1950-56 and never finished lower than fourth in the MVP balloting. Gil McDougald (.306/14/63) secured Rookie of the Year honors in '51, and the following year Hank Sauer swatted 37 homers and plated 121 baserunners en route to an MVP award in '52. In a five-year span from 1950-54, Sauer delivered 32 taters and 95 ribbies per season.

Mickey Mantle stepped into the void created by DiMaggio's retirement after the '51 season. "The Mick" supplied a .311 BA with 23 clouts in his first full year (1952) and averaged .314 with 33 blasts, 97 RBI, 117 runs scored and 106 free passes from 1952-59. DiMaggio and Mantle, along with Bill Virdon, accounted for 36 of 75 WS>10 seasons attributed to Yankees' center fielders during a 40-year span covering 1930-1969.

Whitey Ford missed two seasons due to military service after posting a 9-1 record in his rookie season (1950). The "Chairman of the Board" furnished a 16-7 record with a 2.64 ERA from 1953-59 and claimed ERA titles in '56 and '58. New York logged three consecutive second-place finishes from 1952-54 as Cleveland overpowered the junior circuit. Kinder anchored the bullpen, notching a league-leading 27 saves with a 1.85 ERA for the '53 squad. Virdon claimed ROY honors in 1955 and posted a career-high .319 BA in the ensuing campaign.

The Yankees pulled within 4 games of the Indians in '56 and ended the 1957 campaign only two games behind the Tigers. Mantle (.353/52/130) earned the Triple Crown in 1956 and collected back-to-back MVP awards in 1956-57. "The Commerce Comet" amassed the most Win Shares in Yankees history with 51 in 1957 and set career-highs with a .365 BA and 146 walks. From 1954-59 Jensen smacked 26 four-baggers and knocked in 111 runs per season, meriting MVP honors in 1958 with 35 jacks and 122 ribbies. Vic Power, the smooth-fielding first sacker, batted .312 and collected his first of seven Gold Glove awards. Bob Cerv slugged 38 moon-shots and received his lone All-Star nod.

Win Shares > 20	Single-Season	1940-1959
George McQuinn - 1B (NYY) x2	Yogi Berra - C (NYY) x11	Jackie Jensen - RF (NYY) x4
Vic Power - 1B (NYY)	Charlie Keller - LF (NYY) x4	Hank Sauer - RF (NYY)
Bill Skowron - 1B (NYY) x2	Hank Sauer - LF (NYY)	Tiny Bonham - SP (NYY)
Snuffy Stirnweiss - 2B (NYY) x2	Bob Cerv - LF (NYY)	Spud Chandler - SP (NYY) x2
Jerry Priddy - 2B (NYY) x2	Norm Siebern - LF (NYY) x2	Jim Tobin - SP (NYY) x2
Gil McDougald - 2B (NYY)	Wally Judnich - CF (NYY) x2	Hank Borowy - SP (NYY)
Phil Rizzuto - SS (NYY) x7	Dixie F. Walker - CF (NYY)	Bill Bevens - SP (NYY)
Gil McDougald - SS (NYY) x2	Tommy Holmes - CF (NYY) x3	Ellis Kinder - SP (NYY)
Billy Johnson - 3B (NYY)	Johnny Lindell - CF (NYY)	Whitey Ford - SP (NYY) x5
Gil McDougald - 3B (NYY) x2	Mickey Mantle - CF (NYY) x12	Lew Burdette - SP (NYY)
	Tommy Holmes - RF (NYY) x3	Ellis Kinder - RP (NYY)
	Hank Bauer - RF (NYY) x2	

Year/Team	OPW%	PW	PL	APW%	AW	AL	Diff+/-
1960 NYY	0.457	70	84	0.630 P	97	57	0.173
1961 NYY	0.557 P	90	72	0.673 P	109	53	0.115
1962 NYY	0.518	84	78	0.593 P	96	66	0.075
1963 NYY	0.537	87	75	0.646 P	104	57	0.109
1964 NYY	0.569 P	92	70	0.611 P	99	63	0.042
1965 NYY	0.496	80	82	0.475	77	85	-0.021
1966 NYY	0.488	79	83	0.440	70	89	-0.047
1967 NYY	0.456	74	88	0.444	72	90	-0.011
1968 NYY	0.532	86	76	0.512	83	79	-0.020
1969 NYY	0.501	81	81	0.497	80	81	-0.004

franchID	OWAR	OWS	AWAR	AWS	WARdiff	WSdiff	P/D/W/F
1960 NYY	35.419	250.073	44.609	291.000	-9.190	-40.927	
1961 NYY	37.578	252.541	53.194	327.002	-15.616	-74.461	P
1962 NYY	33.679	239.176	50.207	288.002	-16.529	-48.826	
1963 NYY	36.634	256.435	50.487	311.992	-13.853	-55.557	
1964 NYY	35.092	259.430	46.265	296.999	-11.173	-37.568	P
1965 NYY	31.936	228.496	36.648	230.989	-4.712	-2.493	
1966 NYY	30.350	213.434	35.088	210.000	-4.737	3.434	
1967 NYY	28.346	216.866	26.490	215.992	1.857	0.874	
1968 NYY	26.009	226.954	32.135	249.002	-6.126	-22.048	
1969 NYY	29.701	218.839	32.769	240.000	-3.068	-21.161	

New York returned to peak status in 1961, overtaking Cleveland by three games and leading the League in oWAR and oWS. Elston Howard supplied a .348 BA with 21 taters. Ford (25-4, 3.21) topped the leader boards in victories and innings pitched and merited Cy Young honors. "Slick" achieved similar results in 1963, notching 24 wins with a 2.74 ERA. Mantle posted consecutive runner-up finishes in the MVP balloting (1960-61). "Muscles" topped the charts with 40 blasts and 119 runs scored in '60 and slugged 54 long balls in the summer of '61. Tom Tresh (.286/20/93) received the AL Rookie of the Year award in 1962. Norm Siebern set individual bests with 25 clouts, 117 RBI, 114 runs scored and a .308 batting average. Howard thumped a career-high 28 four-baggers and earned the AL MVP award in 1963.

The Yanks yielded consecutive third-place finishes before overtaking the Twins for the pennant in 1964. Howard accrued 33 Win Shares, batted at a .313 clip, and garnered his second Gold Glove award. Curt Blefary whacked 22 long balls and coaxed 88 walks, earning the 1965 AL Rookie of the Year honors. Mel Stottlemyre (20-9, 2.63) paced the junior circuit with 291 innings pitched and 18 complete games. The Bronx Bombers endured three straight losing seasons before finishing five games behind Detroit in '68. Stottlemyre surpassed the 20-win mark in back-to-back campaigns (1968-69) and led the League with 24 complete games in '69.

Year/Team	OPW%	PW	PL	APW%	AW	AL	Diff+/-
1970 NYY	0.551 P	89	73	0.574	93	69	0.023
1971 NYY	0.560 P	91	71	0.506	82	80	-0.054
1972 NYY	0.535	87	75	0.510	79	76	-0.025
1973 NYY	0.540	87	75	0.494	80	82	-0.046
1974 NYY	0.448	73	89	0.549	89	73	0.102
1975 NYY	0.520	84	78	0.519	83	77	-0.001
1976 NYY	0.502 F	81	81	0.610 P	97	62	0.108
1977 NYY	0.458	74	88	0.617 D	100	62	0.159
1978 NYY	0.458	74	88	0.613 P	100	63	0.156
1979 NYY	0.486	79	83	0.556	89	71	0.070

franchID	OWAR	OWS	AWAR	AWS	WARdiff	WSdiff	P/D/W/F
1970 NYY	34.403	238.748	38.483	279.000	-4.079	-40.252	P
1971 NYY	39.354	239.864	36.462	242.999	2.892	-3.135	P
1972 NYY	31.281	199.461	37.095	236.994	-5.814	-37.533	
1973 NYY	28.647	202.511	35.980	239.998	-7.333	-37.487	
1974 NYY	22.556	192.508	39.295	267.000	-16.739	-74.492	
1975 NYY	33.696	215.487	42.540	249.001	-8.844	-33.514	
1976 NYY	40.044	249.812	**48.209**	**290.997**	-8.165	-41.185	F
1977 NYY	26.634	182.080	51.433	299.989	-24.798	-117.909	
1978 NYY	25.370	195.075	49.358	**299.996**	-23.988	-104.921	
1979 NYY	27.840	199.258	42.180	266.999	-14.340	-67.741	

New York collected back-to-back pennants in 1970-71. The "Actual" Yankees have accumulated 11 pennants since '71, relying heavily on free agents and trades to bridge the talent gap. The "Original" Yankees have been competitive in the same timeframe (6 playoff appearances, no pennants) but not nearly as dominant.

Thurman Munson provided a .302 batting average and earned the 1970 AL Rookie of the Year honors. Roy White (.296/22/94) scored 109 runs and swiped 24 bags. Bobby Murcer (.331/25/94) topped the charts with a .427 OBP, amassing 37 Win Shares in '71. The Yankees slumped to a last-place finish in '74 but rebounded with a second-place finish in the AL East in 1975. Munson collected three consecutive Gold Glove awards (1973-75). "Tugboat" (.302/17/105) claimed MVP honors in '76.

Ron Guidry (25-3, 1.74) tallied 31 Win Shares and paced the American League in wins, ERA and WHIP (0.978) in 1978. "Louisiana Lightning" whiffed 248 opposition batsmen, hurled a league-high 9 shutouts, and secured the Cy Young award. Guidry followed up with another ERA title in 1979.

Win Shares > 20	Single-Season	1960-1979
Norm Siebern - 1B (NYY) x2	Deron Johnson - 3B (NYY)	Curt Blefary - RF (NYY)
Lee Thomas - 1B (NYY)	Elston Howard - C (NYY) x4	Bobby Murcer - RF (NYY) x2
Mickey Mantle - 1B (NYY) x2	Thurman Munson - C (NYY)	Ralph Terry - SP (NYY)
Deron Johnson - 1B (NYY)	x7	Jim Bouton - SP (NYY)
Bobby Richardson - 2B (NYY)	Tom Tresh - LF (NYY)	Mel Stottlemyre - SP (NYY) x3
Horace Clarke - 2B (NYY) x2	Roy White - LF (NYY) x7	Stan Bahnsen - SP (NYY)
Woodie Held - SS (NYY) x3	Don Lock - CF (NYY) x2	Fritz Peterson - SP (NYY)
Tony Kubek - SS (NYY)	Tom Tresh - CF (NYY) x2	Ron Guidry - SP (NYY) x2
Tom Tresh - SS (NYY)	Bobby Murcer - CF (NYY) x4	

Year/Team	OPW%	PW	PL	APW%	AW	AL	Diff+/-
1980 NYY	0.442	72	90	0.636 P	103	59	0.194
1981 NYY	0.440	71	91	0.551	59	48	0.111
1982 NYY	0.472	77	85	0.488	79	83	0.015
1983 NYY	0.529	86	76	0.562	91	71	0.033
1984 NYY	0.501	81	81	0.537	87	75	0.036
1985 NYY	0.517	84	78	0.602	97	64	0.086
1986 NYY	0.457	74	88	0.556	90	72	0.098
1987 NYY	0.453 F	73	89	0.549	89	73	0.097
1988 NYY	0.549	89	73	0.528	85	76	-0.021
1989 NYY	0.458	74	88	0.460	74	87	0.002

franchID	OWAR	OWS	AWAR	AWS	WARdiff	WSdiff	P/D/W/F
1980 NYY	23.676	177.633	**55.899**	**309.005**	-32.224	-131.372	
1981 NYY	15.155	113.871	**36.293**	177.001	-21.138	-63.130	
1982 NYY	26.348	172.930	44.756	236.996	-18.408	-64.065	
1983 NYY	34.238	215.460	48.379	273.001	-14.140	-57.541	
1984 NYY	29.957	206.600	49.628	261.000	-19.671	-54.399	
1985 NYY	29.828	216.569	**53.440**	291.006	-23.612	-74.437	
1986 NYY	24.318	196.435	46.716	269.996	-22.399	-73.561	
1987 NYY	28.517	234.188	37.860	266.996	-9.342	-32.808	F
1988 NYY	30.748	226.031	39.867	254.997	-9.120	-28.966	
1989 NYY	30.832	220.214	30.760	221.997	0.073	-1.783	

The 1980 "Original" Yankees posted the worst WARdiff (-32) and WSdiff (-131) in team history despite a 20-win campaign from Scott McGregor. New York muddled through consecutive last-place finishes in 1980-81. Guidry merited 5 consecutive Gold Glove awards (1982-86). "Gator" paced the circuit with a WHIP of 0.992 in 1981 and 21 complete games in '83. He transcended the 20-win plateau in '83 and '85.

GM Gene Michael atoned for the worst Amateur Draft in team history (1980) by choosing Fred McGriff, Bob Tewksbury, Mike Pagliarulo and Eric Plunk in the ensuing draft. He also selected Derek Jeter in his second tour of duty (1992). Tippy Martinez fashioned a 2.35 ERA and a 1.094 WHIP while saving 21 games in '83. Willie Upshaw (.306/27/104) rendered individual bests in batting average, home runs, and RBI. Willie McGee (.353/10/82) earned MVP honors and collected a batting title in 1985. He attained career-highs with 56 stolen bases and 114 runs scored while topping the League in hits (216) and triples (18). Andy McGaffigan delivered a 21-7 mark with a 2.59 ERA in a three-year span (1986-88), working primarily in relief.

Don Mattingly eclipsed the .300 mark in batting average in every season from 1984-89. During that span "Donnie Baseball" fashioned a .327 BA with 43 doubles, 27 circuit clouts, 114 RBI and 203 hits per year. The nine-time Gold Glover collected a batting crown with a .343 average in '84 and the following year secured MVP honors after driving in a league-leading 145 runs and set a personal best with 35 four-baggers. Mattingly accrued 34 Win Shares in 1986, and topped the charts with 238 hits, 53 two-base knocks, and a .573 SLG.

The Bronx Bombers fell one game short of the Red Sox for the AL Eastern division title in 1988. Jose Rijo split the season between the rotation and the bullpen, posting a 2.39 ERA and 13 victories. Fred McGriff began a streak of 7 straight seasons with 30+ homers. "Crime Dog" slugged a league-high 36 round-trippers in '89, and established a personal best with 119 bases on balls. The New York first sackers' paced the majors with 51 WS>10 seasons from 1980-1999.

Year/Team	OPW%	PW	PL	APW%	AW	AL	Diff+/-
1990 NYY	0.505	82	80	0.414	67	95	-0.091
1991 NYY	0.463	75	87	0.438	71	91	-0.025
1992 NYY	0.539	87	75	0.469	76	86	-0.070
1993 NYY	0.505 D	82	80	0.543	88	74	0.038
1994 NYY	0.494	80	82	0.619 P	70	43	0.126
1995 NYY	0.512	83	79	0.549 W	79	65	0.037
1996 NYY	0.495	80	82	0.568 D	92	70	0.073
1997 NYY	0.520 W	84	78	0.593 W	96	66	0.073
1998 NYY	0.531 W	86	76	0.704 P	114	48	0.172
1999 NYY	0.489	79	83	0.605 P	98	64	0.116

franchID	OWAR	OWS	AWAR	AWS	WARdiff	WSdiff	P/D/W/F
1990 NYY	29.759	239.472	21.664	200.999	8.096	38.473	
1991 NYY	26.503	213.467	33.247	213.000	-6.744	0.467	
1992 NYY	33.018	236.673	37.612	227.996	-4.594	8.676	
1993 NYY	37.742	256.092	44.346	263.997	-6.604	-7.905	D
1994 NYY	26.781	178.909	37.190	210.000	-10.409	-31.091	
1995 NYY	32.132	241.346	37.550	237.005	-5.418	4.341	
1996 NYY	39.276	271.001	47.774	276.001	-8.498	-5.001	
1997 NYY	39.112	270.519	54.749	287.996	-15.637	-17.477	W
1998 NYY	40.900	281.123	57.949	342.010	-17.049	-60.887	W
1999 NYY	42.592	283.117	51.754	294.007	-9.161	-10.890	

GM Harding Peterson and Scouting Director Brian Sabean delivered the finest Amateur Draft results in the history of the Bronx Bombers. The 1990 draft class featuring Jorge Posada, Andy Pettitte and Carl Everett accrued 752 Career Total Win Shares and 120 Career Total WAR. Rijo (15-6, 2.51) fashioned a league-best 1.077 WHIP and finished fourth in the Cy Young balloting in '91 and paced the circuit with 227 strikeouts in 1993. New York secured the division title in '93 by percentage points over Milwaukee after falling 8 games short in the previous season. McGriff blasted a career-high 37 moon-shots and scored 111 runs, earning a fourth-place finish in the MVP balloting.

Bernie F. Williams batted over .300 in 8 consecutive campaigns (1995-2002) and scored at least 100 runs in every year during that stretch, excluding '95. He contributed 32 two-base knocks, 24 round-trippers, 102 ribbies and sustained a .321 BA. J.T. Snow received 6 straight Gold Glove Awards (1995-2000). Andy Pettitte paced the circuit with 21 victories in his sophomore season and finished second in the AL Cy Young race. New York achieved runner-up status in 1995-96 but failed to make the playoffs.

Derek Jeter (.314/10/78) garnered AL Rookie of the Year honors in '96. In 17 full seasons from 1996-2012, "Captain Clutch" supplied a .313 BA with 110 runs scored, 194 base hits and 20 stolen bases per year. He earned 5 Gold Glove Awards, made 13 All-Star appearances, and surpassed the 200-hit plateau on 8 occasions. The Yankees secured back-to-back Wild Card entries in 1997-98. Mariano Rivera achieved "closer" status in '97 after performing exceptional work in the setup role during the prior season. "Sandman" delivered 40 saves per year along with a 2.01 ERA and a WHIP of 0.966 from 1997-2011. The MLB career leader with 652 saves, "Mo" paced the circuit with 45 saves and placed third in the 1999 AL Cy Young race.

Snow delivered personal bests with 36 doubles, 28 dingers, and 104 ribbies in '97. Williams collected a batting title with a .339 mark in '98. Jeter (.349/24/102) tallied 34 Win Shares and led the League with 219 base hits in 1999, while establishing career-highs in batting average, home runs, RBI, runs (134), and hits. Williams (.342/25/115) accrued 32 WS and set personal marks in batting average, runs scored (116), and walks (100). The Yankees' draft classes under the administration of GM Brian Cashman and Scouting Director Lin Garrett covering the period of 1998-2004 averaged only 31 Career Total Win Shares and 1 Career Total WAR.

Year/Team	OPW%	PW	PL	APW%	AW	AL	Diff+/-
2000 NYY	0.477	77	85	0.540 D	87	74	0.063
2001 NYY	0.511	83	79	0.594 D	95	65	0.083
2002 NYY	0.518	84	78	0.640 P	103	58	0.121
2003 NYY	0.556 W	90	72	0.623 P	101	61	0.068
2004 NYY	0.513	83	79	0.623 P	101	61	0.111
2005 NYY	0.468	76	86	0.586 D	95	67	0.119
2006 NYY	0.528 W	86	76	0.599 P	97	65	0.070
2007 NYY	0.518 D	84	78	0.580 W	94	68	0.063
2008 NYY	0.487	79	83	0.549	89	73	0.062
2009 NYY	0.507	82	80	0.636 P	103	59	0.128
2010 NYY	0.564 W	91	71	0.586 W	95	67	0.022
2011 NYY	0.573 P	93	69	0.599 P	97	65	0.025
2012 NYY	0.505 W	82	80	0.586 P	95	67	0.081
2013 NYY	0.539 W	87	75	0.525	85	77	-0.014

franchID	OWAR	OWS	AWAR	AWS	WARdiff	WSdiff	P/D/W/F
2000 NYY	41.010	277.637	42.637	260.997	-1.628	16.640	
2001 NYY	46.590	295.823	50.610	285.011	-4.020	10.812	
2002 NYY	43.916	281.132	58.546	308.996	-14.630	-27.864	
2003 NYY	45.047	301.904	59.067	303.002	-14.020	-1.098	W
2004 NYY	38.358	283.186	49.486	303.008	-11.129	-19.823	
2005 NYY	34.019	242.281	48.835	284.999	-14.815	-42.718	
2006 NYY	43.791	274.115	51.400	290.996	-7.609	-16.881	W
2007 NYY	46.952	263.799	52.170	281.997	-5.218	-18.199	D
2008 NYY	39.131	264.051	44.531	266.998	-5.400	-2.947	
2009 NYY	40.721	272.919	56.210	309.006	-15.489	-36.086	
2010 NYY	39.820	265.182	49.391	285.001	-9.571	-19.819	W
2011 NYY	40.410	268.450	53.707	291.008	-13.297	-22.557	P
2012 NYY	28.156	237.751	52.429	284.997	-24.273	-47.246	W
2013 NYY	32.584	249.014	30.910	253.496	1.674	-4.482	W

Williams posted career-bests with 30 wallops and 121 RBI in 2000. Alfonso Soriano drilled 34 doubles and swiped 43 bases, earning a third-place finish in the 2001 AL ROY race. He placed third in the MVP voting in the subsequent season, batting .300 with 39 jacks and 102 RBI while pacing the circuit with 209 hits, 128 runs scored and 41 stolen bases. He joined the 40/40 club (46 home runs, 41 stolen bases) in '06.

Jorge Posada (.281/30/101) finished third in the 2003 AL MVP balloting as the Yankees claimed the AL Wild Card and topped the League in oWS. Mike Lowell belted 32 homers and plated 105 runs. Hideki Matsui bolstered the Bombers' lineup with 42 doubles and 106 RBI en route to a second-place finish in the AL Rookie of the Year balloting. "Godzilla" delivered a .297 BA with 23 blasts, 110 RBI and 100 runs scored per season from 2003-05.

Jeter merited a runner-up finish in the '06 MVP race on the strength of his .343 batting average, 118 runs and career-best 34 stolen bases (in 39 attempts). "The Captain" produced a .334 BA with 212 hits, 107 runs scored and 30 steals, placing third in the 2009 AL MVP race and in 2012, he paced the Junior Circuit with 216 safeties while hitting .316. Robinson Cano yielded a .342 BA and received his first All-Star invitation in '06. The Bronx Bombers fell short of the Red Sox in the divisional race but earned the Wild Card entry with 86 wins.

Posada supplied personal bests with a .338 BA and 42 two-base knocks in '07. Lowell set individual marks in batting (.324) and RBI (120) and finished fifth in the MVP balloting. Cano (.319/29/109) accrued 35 Win Shares in 2010 and averaged .314 with 46 doubles, 29 home runs, 102 RBI, and 104 runs scored from 2009-2012. The Bronx Bombers secured the pennant by a lone victory over the runner-up Red Sox in 2011. Ian Kennedy (21-4, 2.88) topped the League in victories and placed fourth in the 2011 Cy Young balloting. John Axford contributed a league-leading 46 saves with a 1.95 ERA and Melky Cabrera eclipsed the 200-hit plateau and tallied 102 aces in 2011. The "Melk Man" delivered a .346 BA in the following campaign. Austin Jackson averaged 99 runs scored and 10 triples in his first four seasons (2010-13).

Win Shares > 20	Single-Season	1980-2013
Willie Upshaw - 1B (NYY)	Mike Lowell - 3B (NYY) x4	Carl Everett - CF (NYY) x2
Don Mattingly - 1B (NYY) x6	Jorge Posada - C (NYY) x5	Austin Jackson - CF (NYY)
Fred McGriff - 1B (NYY) x9	Hideki Matsui - LF (NYY) x2	Scott McGregor - SP (NYY)
J.T. Snow - 1B (NYY)	Alfonso Soriano - LF (NYY) x2	Bob Tewksbury - SP (NYY)
Nick Johnson - 1B (NYY)	Melky Cabrera - LF (NYY)	Jose Rijo - SP (NYY)
Damaso Garcia - 2B (NYY)	Willie McGee - CF (NYY) x2	Andy Pettitte - SP (NYY) x2
Alfonso Soriano - 2B (NYY) x2	Roberto Kelly - CF (NYY)	Al Leiter - SP (NYY)
Robinson Cano - 2B (NYY) x6	Bernie F. Williams - CF (NYY)	Ian Kennedy - SP (NYY)
Derek Jeter - SS (NYY) x13	x8	

Note: 4000 PA or BFP to qualify, except during strike-shortened seasons
(1972 = 3800, 1981 & 1994 = 2700, 1995 = 3500) and 154-game schedule (3800)
- failed to qualify: 1901, 1903-1904, 1921, 1976, 1987

Yankees All-Time "Originals" Roster

Manny Acosta	Craig Dingman	Steve Kraly	Brian Reith
David Adams	Tom Dodd	Zach Kroenke	Hal Reniff
Bob Addis	Atley Donald	Dick Kryhoski	Bill Renna
Steve Adkins	John Dowd	Tony Kubek	Roger Repoz
Bob Alexander	Al Downing	Johnny Kucks	Bill Reynolds
Johnny Allen	Slow Joe Doyle	Brandon Laird	Gordon Rhodes
Abraham Almonte	Mike Draper	Joe Lake	Bobby Richardson
Erick Almonte	Bill Drescher	Bill Lamar	Jose Rijo
Zoilo Almonte	Karl Drews	Frank Lankford	Danny Rios
Dell Alston	Monk Dubiel	Frank LaPorte	Juan Rivera
Ferrell Anderson	Tom Dukes	Lyn Lary	Mariano Rivera
Jason Anderson	Matt Dunbar	Tim Layana	Ruben Rivera
Rick L. Anderson	Shelley Duncan	Gene Layden	Phil Rizzuto

Ivy Andrews	Mike Dunn	Tony Lazzeri	Roxey Roach
Angel Aragon	Leo Durocher	Jalal Leach	Jake Robbins
Jim Archer	Jim Dyck	Ricky Ledee	Dale Roberts
Rugger Ardizoia	Logan Easley	Joe Lefebvre	David Robertson
Joaquin Arias	Robert Eenhoorn	Al Leiter	Jim Robertson
Tony J. Armas	Dave Eiland	Frank Leja	Aaron Robinson
Brad Arnsberg	Darrell Einertson	Don E. Leppert	Carlos Rodriguez
Brad Ausmus	Gene Elliott	Louis Leroy	Edwin Rodriguez
Jimmy Austin	John Ellis	Ed Levy	John Rodriguez
Chick M. Autry	Clyde Engle	Jim Leyritz	Oscar Roettger
John Axford	Jack Enright	Terry Ley	Jay Rogers
Oscar Azocar	Nino Escalera	Johnny Lindell	George Rohe
Loren Babe	Juan Espino	Bill Lindsey	Red Rolfe
Stan Bahnsen	Carl Everett	Phil Linz	Austin Romine
Bill H. Bailey	Charlie Fallon	Jack Little	Buddy Rosar
Frank W. Baker	Alex Ferguson	Clem Llewellyn	Steve Rosenberg
Steve Balboni	Frank Fernandez	Don Lock	Steve Roser
Neal Ball	Mike Ferraro	Tim Lollar	Ernie Ross
George Banks	Chick Fewster	Phil Lombardi	Allen Russell
Cy Barger	Mike Figga	Art Lopez	Kevin Russo
Ed Barney	Jesus Figueroa	Wilton Lopez	Marius Russo
Frank Barnes	Tom Filer	Baldy Louden	Jack Saltzgaver
Honey Barnes	Pete Filson	Mike Lowell	Celerino Sanchez
Tom Barrett	Jim Finigan	Joe Lucey	Deion Sanders
Rich Barry	Mike Fischlin	Roy Luebbe	Roy L. Sanders
Rich Batchelor	Ray Fisher	Matt Luke	Rafael Santana
George Batten	Mike J. Fitzgerald	Jerry Lumpe	Omir Santos
Hank Bauer	Randy Flores	Mitch Lyden	Bronson Sardinha
Mike Baxes	Hank Foiles	Jerry Lynch	Hank Sauer
Walter Beall	Ben Ford	Al Lyons	Don Savage
T.J. Beam	Russ Ford	Jim Lyttle	Jerry Scala
Colter Bean	Whitey Ford	Kevin Maas	Harry Schaeffer
Jim Beattie	Frank Foutz	John Mackinson	Roy Schalk
Rich Beck	Andy Fox	Dave Madison	Rich Scheid
Joe Beggs	Mark Freeman	Stubby Magner	Butch Schmidt
Tim Belcher	Ray French	Woody Main	Al Schulz
Zeke Bella	Steve Frey	Oswaldo Mairena	Art Schult
Rudy Bell	John Frill	Fritz Maisel	Ham Schulte
Benny Bengough	Bill Fulton	Frank Makosky	Pi Schwert
Lou Berberet	Liz Funk	Pat Maloney	Dick E. Scott
Justin Berg	John Gabler	Charlie Manning	Mickey Scott
Dave Bergman	Len H. Gabrielson	Rube Manning	Scott Seabol
Juan Bernhardt	Greg Gagne	Ramon Manon	Ken Sears
Walter Bernhardt	Joe Gallagher	Mickey Mantle	Kal Segrist
Yogi Berra	Keith Garagozzo	Cliff Markle	Fernando Seguignol
Don Bessent	Mike Garbark	Bob Marquis	George Selkirk
Bill Bevens	Anderson Garcia	Jeff Marquez	Frank Seminara
Monte Beville	Christian Garcia	Jim Marquis	Al Shealy
Harry Billiard	Damaso Garcia	Cuddles Marshall	George Shears
Tim Birtsas	Rosman Garcia	Billy A. Martin	Spec Shea
Buddy Blair	Brett Gardner	Carlos A. Martinez	Rollie Sheldon
Walter Blair	Earle Gardner	Jack Martin	Jim Shellenback
Gil Blanco	Milt Gaston	Tippy Martinez	Skeeter Shelton
Johnny Blanchard	Mike Gazella	Bob Martyn	Roy Sherid
Curt Blefary	Lou Gehrig	Victor Mata	Dennis Sherrill

Elmer Bliss	Al Gerheauser	Jimmy Mathison	Ben Shields
Ron Blomberg	Cesar Geronimo	Hideki Matsui	Charlie Shields
Eddie Bockman	Al Gettel	Don Mattingly	Urban Shocker
Tiny Bonham	Joe Giard	Pinky May	Tom Shopay
Lute Boone	Jake Gibbs	Zach McAllister	Bill Short
Paul Boris	Tom Gilles	Joe McCarthy	Norm Siebern
Hank Borowy	Frank Gleich	Larry McClure	Charlie Silvera
Jim Bouton	Joe Glenn	George McConnell	John Simmons
Fred Bradley	Lefty Gomez	Clyde McCullough	Elmer Singleton
Ryan Bradley	Pedro Gonzalez	Daniel McCutchen	Camp Skinner
Scott Bradley	Art Goodwin	Danny McDevitt	Lou Skizas
Neal Brady	Wilbur Good	Dave McDonald	Bill Skowron
Norm Branch	Joe Gordon	Donzell McDonald	Roger Slagle
Yhency Brazoban	Tom A. Gorman	Gil McDougald	Walt Smallwood
Don Brennan	Ted Goulait	Lou McEvoy	Hal W. Smith
Jim Brenneman	Larry Gowell	Andy McGaffigan	Joe S. Smith
Marv Breuer	Jack Graham	Willie McGee	Keith P. Smith
Fritz Brickell	Alex Graman	Bob McGraw	Klondike Smith
Jim Brideweser	Johnny Gray	Scott McGregor	Matt Smith
Harry Bright	Jim Greengrass	Fred McGriff	Chappie Snodgrass
Johnny Broaca	Kenny Greer	Red McKee	J.T. Snow
Lew Brockett	John-Ford Griffin	Jack McMahan	Jerry Snyder
Jim Bronstad	Bob Grim	Norm McMillan	Russ Snyder
Bobby W. Brown	Mario Guerrero	George McQuinn	Tony Solaita
Brian Buchanan	Ron Guidry	Charlie Meara	Alfonso Soriano
Jess Buckles	Cristian Guzman	Doc Medich	Steve Souchock
Mike Buddie	Eric Hacker	Rafael Medina	Shane Spencer
Bill Burbach	Ed Hahn	Mark Melancon	Charlie Spikes
Lew Burdette	Hinkey Haines	Bill Mellor	Russ Springer
Wally Burnette	George Halas	Ramiro Mendoza	Chris Spurling
C.B. Burns	Brad Halsey	Lloyd Merritt	Bill Stafford
Alex Burr	Roger Hambright	Melky Mesa	Charley Stanceu
Tom Buskey	Mike Handiboe	Tom Metcalf	Andy Stankiewicz
Ike Butler	Jim Hanley	Bud Metheny	Dick Starr
Joe Buzas	Truck Hannah	Hensley Meulens	Dutch Sterrett
Sammy Byrd	Harry Hanson	Bob Meusel	Snuffy Stirnweiss
Tommy Byrne	Joe Harris	Bob Meyer	Mel Stottlemyre
Melky Cabrera	Burt Hart	Pete Mikkelsen	Hal Stowe
Charlie Caldwell	Chris Hartje	Sam Militello	Nick Strincevich
Ray Caldwell	Buddy Hassett	John A. Miller	Bill Stumpf
Ben Callahan	Clem Hausmann	Orlando Miller	Tom Sturdivant
Archie Campbell	Chicken Hawks	Mike Milosevich	Johnny Sturm
Howie Camp	Mike Heath	Eric Milton	Pete Suder
Milo Candini	Don Heffner	Juan Miranda	Ed Sweeney
Andy Cannizaro	Mike Hegan	D. J. Mitchell	Jose Tabata
Jose Cano	Woodie Held	Johnny Mitchell	Pat Tabler
Robinson Cano	Bill Henderson	Fenton Mole	Vito Tamulis
Ozzie Canseco	Sean Henn	Carlos Monasterios	El Tappe
Mike Cantwell	Bill F. Henry	Ed Monroe	Don Taussig
Andy Carey	Drew Henson	Zach Monroe	Ralph Terry
Bubba Carpenter	Adrian Hernandez	Jesus Montero	Jay Tessmer
Frank Carpin	Michel Hernandez	Archie Moore	Dick Tettelbach
Amalio Carreno	Orlando Hernandez	Wilcy Moore	Bob Tewksbury
Dick Carroll	Willard Hershberger	Tom Morgan	Moe Thacker
Tom E. Carroll	Whitey Herzog	Hal Morris	Marcus Thames

Matt Carson	Frank Hiller	Ross Moschitto	Ira Thomas
Roy Castleton	Mack Hillis	Danny Mota	Kite Thomas
Bernie Castro	Jesse Hill	Lyle Mouton	Lee Thomas
Bob Cerv	Billy Hitchcock	Phil Mudrock	Myles Thomas
Francisco Cervelli	Sterling Hitchcock	Bobby Munoz	Homer Thompson
Mike Cervenak	Myril Hoag	Thurman Munson	Kevin Thompson
Joba Chamberlain	Chet Hoff	Bobby Murcer	Tommy C. Thompson
Spud Chandler	Fred Hofmann	Billy Murphy	Hank Thormahlen
Les Channell	Bill Hogg	Johnny Murphy	Marv Throneberry
Darrin Chapin	Bill Holden	J. R. Murphy	Bob Thurman
Ben Chapman	Fred Holmes	George Murray	Ray Tift
Mike Chartak	Tommy Holmes	Joe Murray	Gary Timberlake
Hal Chase	Roger Holt	Larry Murray	Dan Tipple
Dave Cheadle	Wally Hood, Jr.	Brian Myrow	Jim Tobin
Randy Choate	Shags Horan	Jerry Narron	Freddie Toliver
Bob Christian	Ralph Houk	Dioner Navarro	Rusty Torres
Clay Christiansen	Chris Howard	Cal Neeman	Tom Tresh
Justin Christian	Elston Howard	Bots Nekola	Gus Triandos
Mike Christopher	Tex Hoyle	Luke Nelson	Shane Turner
Russ Christopher	La Marr Hoyt	Tex Neuer	Bob Unglaub
Al Cicotte	Rex Hudler	Ernie Nevel	Willie Upshaw
Preston Claiborne	Phil Hughes	Floyd Newkirk	Tom Upton
Allie Clark	Tom L. Hughes	Gus Niarhos	Jack Urban
George Clark	Ken L. Hunt	Jerry Nielsen	Jose Uribe
Horace Clarke	Mark Hutton	Randy Niemann	Jose Valdez
Walter Clarkson	Kei Igawa	Johnny Niggeling	Russ Van Atta
Brandon Claussen	Garth Iorg	Otis Nixon	Bobby Vaughn
Ken Clay	Austin Jackson	Hector Noesi	Hippo Vaughn
Tyler Clippard	Jim Jackson	Wayne Nordhagen	Otto Velez
Al Closter	Johnny James	Ivan Nova	Mike Vento
Jim Coates	Marty Janzen	Eduardo Nunez	Frank Verdi
Jim Cockman	Jackie Jensen	Sherman Obando	Sammy Vick
Hy Cohen	Mike Jerzembeck	Andy O'Connor	Charlie Vinson
Phil Coke	Derek Jeter	Heinie Odom	Bill Virdon
Curt Coleman	D'Angelo Jimenez	Lefty O'Doul	Arodys Vizcaino
Jerry Coleman	Elvio Jimenez	Kirt Ojala	Curt Walker
Rip Coleman	Brett Jodie	Rube Oldring	Dixie F. Walker
Joe Collins	Billy Johnson	Jim Ollom	Joe F. Walsh
Orth Collins	Brian Johnson	Ed Olwine	Roxy Walters
Rip Collins	Deron Johnson	Queenie O'Rourke	Chien-Ming Wang
Loyd Colson	Don R. Johnson	Bill Otis	Jack Wanner
Earle Combs	Hank Johnson	Andy Oyler	Pee-Wee Wanninger
Tom Connelly	Jeff Johnson	Joe Pactwa	Aaron Ward
Jose Contreras	Johnny Johnson	Dave Pagan	Jay Ward
Andy Cook	Lou Johnson	Joe Page	Turner Ward
Doc Cook	Nick Johnson	Mike Pagliarulo	Jack Warhop
Dusty Cooke	Otis Johnson	Jimmy Paredes	Adam Warren
Ron Cook	Darryl Jones	Dan Pasqua	George Washburn
Phil Cooney	Gary Jones	Gil Patterson	Chris Welsh
Don Cooper	Mitch Jones	Ken Patterson	Butch Wensloff
Guy Cooper	Tom Jones	Mike Pazik	Julie Wera
Jim Corsi	Kevin Jordan	Steve Peek	Billy Werber
Dan Costello	Slats Jordan	Ramiro Pena	Dennis Werth
Clint Courtney	Art Jorgens	Lance Pendleton	Stefan Wever
Birdie Cree	Corban Joseph	Joe Pepitone	Steve Whitaker

Ken Crosby
Frankie Crosetti
Darwin Cubillan
Jack Cullen
Nick H. Cullop
George Culver
Colin Curtis
Fred Curtis
Pete Dalena
Bert Daniels
Bob Davidson
George Davis
Kiddo Davis
Russ Davis
Brian Dayett
Zach Day
Jim Deidel
Mike Dejan
Mike DeJean
Frank Delahanty
Dane De La Rosa
Luis de los Santos
Ray Demmitt
Don Demola
Tony DePhillips
Russ Derry
Matt DeSalvo
Jim Deshaies
Orestes Destrade
Charlie Devens
Bill Dickey
Jay Difani
Steve Dillon
Joe DiMaggio
Kerry Dineen

Mike Judd
Wally Judnich
Mike Jurewicz
Scott Kamieniecki
Bob Kammeyer
Rod Kanehl
Bill Karlon
Bill Karns
Herb Karpel
Ryan Karp
Jeff Karstens
Benny Kauff
Curt Kaufman
Eddie Kearse
Ray Keating
Bobby Keefe
Bob Keegan
Randy Keisler
Charlie Keller
Frankie Kelleher
Pat F. Kelly
Roberto Kelly
Bill A. Kennedy
Ian Kennedy
Jerry Kenney
Jim Kennedy
Ellis Kinder
Harry Kingman
Red Kleinow
Ed Klepfer
Steve Jack Kline
Mickey Klutts
Mark Koenig
George Kontos
Ernie Koy

Luis Peraza
Cecil Perkins
Fritz Peterson
Andy Pettitte
David Phelps
Andy Phillips
Jack D. Phillips
Al Piechota
Cy Pieh
Bill Piercy
Al Pilarcik
Duane Pillette
Gerry Pirtle
Herb Plews
Eric Plunk
Bob Porterfield
Jorge Posada
Les Powers
Vic Power
Jerry Priddy
Johnny Priest
Ambrose Puttmann
Mel J. Queen
Eddie Quick
Jack Quinn
Rafael Quirico
Dave Rajsich
Domingo Ramos
John Ramos
Stephen Randolph
Vic Raschi
Leroy Reams
Darren Reed
Jack Reed
Jimmie Reese

Roy White
Terry Whitfield
Kemp Wicker
Bob Wiesler
Scott Wiggins
Bill Wight
Ted Wilborn
Dean Wilkins
Ed Wilkinson
Bernie F. Williams
Bob Williams
Gerald Williams
Harry Williams
Archie Wilson
Pete Wilson
Tom L. Wilson
Matt Winters
Barney Wolfe
Dooley Womack
Hank Workman
Chase Wright
Mel Wright
Stan Yerkes
Mike York
Ralph Young
Eddie Yuhas
Jack Zalusky
Victor Zambrano
George Zeber
Roy Zimmerman
Guy Zinn
Bud Zipfel

TOTAL Pennants, Division Titles, Wild Cards
(Original vs. Actual, 1901-2013)

	OrigPen	OrigDiv	OrigWC	OrigTot		ActPen	ActDiv	ActWC	ActTot
BAL	6	2	1	9	BAL	9	1	2	12
BOS	15	8	2	25	BOS	11	4	7	22
CHW	4	6	2	12	CHW	8	3	0	11
CLE	15	6	0	21	CLE	5	5	2	12
DET	12	5	1	18	DET	10	4	1	15
KCR	6	4	0	10	KCR	1	5	0	6
LAA	0	3	2	5	LAA	1	7	1	9
MIL(AL)	2	4	1	7	MIL(AL)	1	1	0	2
MIN	9	3	1	13	MIN	5	9	0	14
NYY	16	2	7	25	NYY	42	5	4	51
OAK	19	7	1	27	OAK	15	10	1	26
SEA	3	6	1	10	SEA	1	2	1	4
TBA	2	0	2	4	TBA	1	1	2	4
TEX	3	5	1	9	TEX	0	6	1	7
TOR	1	4	0	5	TOR	3	2	0	5
	113	65	22	200		113	65	22	200
ARI	0	2	2	4	ARI	1	4	0	5
ATL	18	7	2	27	ATL	13	8	3	24
CHC	8	5	4	17	CHC	13	2	1	16
CIN	8	6	2	16	CIN	9	7	1	17
COL	1	2	1	4	COL	0	0	3	3
FLA	0	0	1	1	FLA	0	0	2	2
HOU	12	4	0	16	HOU	2	4	2	8
LAD	7	10	1	18	LAD	17	8	2	27
MIL(NL)	0	0	1	1	MIL(NL)	0	1	1	2
NYM	2	5	0	7	NYM	4	1	2	7
PHI	1	4	0	5	PHI	5	8	0	13
PIT	14	1	1	16	PIT	12	4	1	17
SDP	0	3	1	4	SDP	0	5	0	5
SFG	24	4	1	29	SFG	17	7	1	25
STL	14	7	3	24	STL	18	6	3	27
WSH	4	5	2	11	WSH	2	0	0	2
	113	65	22	200		113	65	22	200

TOTAL PW, WAR, WS Pennants (Original vs. Actual)

	oPw	oWAR	oWS	aPw	aWAR	aWS	oAVG	aAVG
BAL	6	7	6	9	8	7	6.33	8.00
BOS	15	16	15	11	12	11	15.33	11.33
CHW	4	8	4	8	7	9	5.33	8.00
CLE	15	20	14	5	14	5	16.33	8.00
DET	12	11	10	10	8	10	11.00	9.33
KCR	6	2	2	1	1	1	3.33	1.00
LAA	0	1	2	1	2	1	1.00	1.33
MIL (AL)	2	3	5	1	1	1	3.33	1.00
MIN	9	9	5	5	4	5	7.67	4.67
NYY	16	13	25	42	41	42	18.00	41.67
OAK	19	17	17	15	12	16	17.67	14.33
SEA	3	3	6	1	1	1	4.00	1.00
TBA	2	2	1	1	0	1	1.67	0.67
TEX	3	0	0	0	0	0	1.00	0.00
TOR	1	1	1	3	2	3	1.00	2.67
	113	113	113	113	113	113		
ARI	0	0	0	1	1	0	0.00	0.67
ATL	18	12	12	13	9	13	14.00	11.67
CHC	8	5	10	13	8	13	7.67	11.33
CIN	8	11	11	9	12	10	10.33	10.33
COL	1	2	1	0	0	1	1.33	0.33
FLA	0	0	0	0	0	0	0.00	0.00
HOU	12	14	9	2	3	2	11.67	2.33
LAD	7	4	2	17	22	18	4.33	19.00
MIL (NL)	0	0	0	0	0	0	0.00	0.00
NYM	2	4	2	4	5	4	2.67	4.33
PHI	1	5	2	5	5	5	2.67	5.00
PIT	14	8	10	12	12	12	10.67	12.00
SDP	0	1	3	0	1	0	1.33	0.33
SFG	24	26	27	17	21	16	25.67	18.00
STL	14	13	17	18	13	17	14.67	16.00
WSH	4	7	7	2	1	2	6.00	1.67
	113	113	113	113	113	113		

Pythagorean Win Percentage – Standings (1901-2013)

Franchise	League	OPW%	PW	PL	APW%	AW	AL	Diff(+/-)
1901 PHA	AL	0.674 P	92	44	0.544	74	62	-0.130
1901 CHW	AL	0.598 F	81	55	0.610 P	83	53	0.013
1901 WS1	AL	0.573	78	58	0.459	61	72	-0.114
1901 NYY	AL	0.487 F	66	70	0.511	68	65	0.024
1901 BOS	AL	0.473 F	64	72	0.581	79	57	0.107
1901 DET	AL	0.456	62	74	0.548	74	61	0.092
1901 CLE	AL	0.179 F	24	112	0.397	54	82	0.219
1901 SLB	AL	0.000 F	0	0	0.350	48	89	0.350
			468	484		541	541	
1901 BSN	NL	0.557 P	78	62	0.500	69	69	-0.057
1901 PHI	NL	0.549	77	63	0.593	83	57	0.044
1901 NYG	NL	0.541 F	76	64	0.380	52	85	-0.161
1901 PIT	NL	0.507	71	69	0.647 P	90	49	0.141
1901 CIN	NL	0.483	68	72	0.374	52	87	-0.109
1901 BRO	NL	0.481	67	73	0.581	79	57	0.100
1901 STL	NL	0.465 F	65	75	0.543	76	64	0.078
1901 CHC	NL	0.420	59	81	0.381	53	86	-0.038
			560	560		554	554	
			1028	1044				

Franchise	League	OPW%	PW	PL	APW%	AW	AL	Diff(+/-)
1902 PHA	AL	0.679 F	92	44	0.610 P	83	53	-0.069
1902 CHW	AL	0.629 F	86	50	0.552	74	60	-0.077
1902 DET	AL	0.502 P	68	68	0.385	52	83	-0.117
1902 CLE	AL	0.495	67	69	0.507	69	67	0.013
1902 WS1	AL	0.494	67	69	0.449	61	75	-0.045
1902 BOS	AL	0.418 F	57	79	0.562	77	60	0.144
1902 NYY	AL	0.401	55	81	0.362	50	88	-0.039
1902 SLB	AL	0.391 F	53	83	0.574	78	58	0.182
			545	543		544	544	
1902 CIN	NL	0.598 P	84	56	0.500	70	70	-0.098
1902 BSN	NL	0.580	81	59	0.533	73	64	-0.048
1902 CHC	NL	0.527	74	66	0.496	68	69	-0.031
1902 PIT	NL	0.522	73	67	0.741 P	103	36	0.219
1902 PHI	NL	0.501	70	70	0.409	56	81	-0.092
1902 NYG	NL	0.455 F	64	76	0.353	48	88	-0.102
1902 STL	NL	0.435	61	79	0.418	56	78	-0.017
1902 BRO	NL	0.396	55	85	0.543	75	63	0.147
			562	558		549	549	
			1107	1101				

Franchise	League	OPW%	PW	PL	APW%	AW	AL	Diff(+/-)
1903 PHA	AL	0.631 P	88	52	0.556	75	60	-0.076
1903 CHW	AL	0.544	76	64	0.438	60	77	-0.106
1903 WS1	AL	0.526	74	66	0.314	43	94	-0.212
1903 CLE	AL	0.504	71	69	0.550	77	63	0.046
1903 SLB	AL	0.463 F	65	75	0.468	65	74	0.005
1903 DET	AL	0.457	64	76	0.478	65	71	0.021
1903 NYY	AL	0.453 F	63	77	0.537	72	62	0.085
1903 BOS	AL	0.423 F	59	81	0.659 P	91	47	0.237

			560	560		548	548	
1903 NYG	NL	0.568 P	79	61	0.604	84	55	0.036
1903 BSN	NL	0.524 F	73	67	0.420	58	80	-0.104
1903 CHC	NL	0.524	73	67	0.594	82	56	0.071
1903 CIN	NL	0.523	73	67	0.532	74	65	0.009
1903 PHI	NL	0.509	71	69	0.363	49	86	-0.146
1903 PIT	NL	0.505	71	69	0.650 P	91	49	0.145
1903 BRO	NL	0.427	60	80	0.515	70	66	0.088
1903 STL	NL	0.415	58	82	0.314	43	94	-0.101
			559	561		551	551	
			1119	1121				

Franchise	League	OPW%	PW	PL	APW%	AW	AL	Diff(+/-)
1904 CHW	AL	0.629 P	97	57	0.578	89	65	-0.051
1904 CLE	AL	0.568	88	66	0.570	86	65	0.001
1904 PHA	AL	0.553	85	69	0.536	81	70	-0.016
1904 SLB	AL	0.511 F	79	75	0.428	65	87	-0.084
1904 DET	AL	0.506 F	78	76	0.408	62	90	-0.098
1904 BOS	AL	0.486	75	79	0.617 P	95	59	0.131
1904 WS1	AL	0.429	66	88	0.252	38	113	-0.177
1904 NYY	AL	0.338 F	52	102	0.609	92	59	0.271
			619	613		608	608	
1904 NYG	NL	0.617 P	95	59	0.693 P	106	47	0.076
1904 CIN	NL	0.545	84	70	0.575	88	65	0.030
1904 CHC	NL	0.524	81	73	0.608	93	60	0.083
1904 PIT	NL	0.509	78	76	0.569	87	66	0.059
1904 BRO	NL	0.498	77	77	0.366	56	97	-0.132
1904 PHI	NL	0.478	74	80	0.342	52	100	-0.136
1904 STL	NL	0.433	67	87	0.487	75	79	0.054
1904 BSN	NL	0.411	63	91	0.359	55	98	-0.052
			618	614		612	612	
			1237	1227				

Franchise	League	OPW%	PW	PL	APW%	AW	AL	Diff(+/-)
1905 PHA	AL	0.634 P	98	56	0.622 P	92	56	-0.012
1905 CLE	AL	0.542	83	71	0.494	76	78	-0.048
1905 NYY	AL	0.498	77	77	0.477	71	78	-0.022
1905 DET	AL	0.487	75	79	0.516	79	74	0.029
1905 SLB	AL	0.476	73	81	0.353	54	99	-0.123
1905 BOS	AL	0.475	73	81	0.513	78	74	0.038
1905 WS1	AL	0.467 F	72	82	0.424	64	87	-0.043
1905 CHW	AL	0.422 F	65	89	0.605	92	60	0.184
			616	616		606	606	
1905 NYG	NL	0.634 P	98	56	0.686 P	105	48	0.052
1905 PHI	NL	0.617	95	59	0.546	83	69	-0.071
1905 CIN	NL	0.529	81	73	0.516	79	74	-0.012
1905 CHC	NL	0.505	78	76	0.601	92	61	0.096
1905 PIT	NL	0.456	70	84	0.627	96	57	0.171
1905 STL	NL	0.431	66	88	0.377	58	96	-0.054
1905 BSN	NL	0.423	65	89	0.331	51	103	-0.092
1905 BRO	NL	0.406 F	63	91	0.316	48	104	-0.090

| | | | 616 | 616 | | 612 | 612 | |
| | | | 1232 | 1232 | | | | |

Franchise	League	OPW%	PW	PL	APW%	AW	AL	Diff(+/-)
1906 NYY	AL	0.593 P	91	63	0.596	90	61	0.003
1906 SLB	AL	0.562 F	86	68	0.510	76	73	-0.052
1906 WS1	AL	0.544 F	84	70	0.367	55	95	-0.177
1906 PHA	AL	0.533	82	72	0.538	78	67	0.004
1906 CLE	AL	0.521	80	74	0.582	89	64	0.061
1906 DET	AL	0.473	73	81	0.477	71	78	0.004
1906 CHW	AL	0.433 F	67	87	0.616 P	93	58	0.183
1906 BOS	AL	0.344	53	101	0.318	49	105	-0.026
			616	616		601	601	
1906 NYG	NL	0.591 P	91	63	0.632	96	56	0.040
1906 STL	NL	0.572	88	66	0.347	52	98	-0.225
1906 PIT	NL	0.562	86	68	0.608	93	60	0.046
1906 CHC	NL	0.518	80	74	0.763 P	116	36	0.245
1906 BSN	NL	0.509 F	78	76	0.325	49	102	-0.185
1906 PHI	NL	0.506	78	76	0.464	71	82	-0.042
1906 BRO	NL	0.407 F	63	91	0.434	66	86	0.027
1906 CIN	NL	0.362 F	56	98	0.424	64	87	0.062
			620	612		607	607	
			1236	1228				

Franchise	League	OPW%	PW	PL	APW%	AW	AL	Diff(+/-)
1907 CHW	AL	0.576 F	89	65	0.576	87	64	0.000
1907 DET	AL	0.546 P	84	70	0.613 P	92	58	0.067
1907 PHA	AL	0.529	82	72	0.607	88	57	0.078
1907 SLB	AL	0.528	81	73	0.454	69	83	-0.074
1907 CLE	AL	0.507	78	76	0.559	85	67	0.053
1907 NYY	AL	0.484	75	79	0.473	70	78	-0.011
1907 BOS	AL	0.443	68	86	0.396	59	90	-0.047
1907 WS1	AL	0.407	63	91	0.325	49	102	-0.082
			619	613		599	599	
1907 CHC	NL	0.564 P	87	67	0.704 P	107	45	0.140
1907 NYG	NL	0.539	83	71	0.536	82	71	-0.003
1907 PIT	NL	0.538	83	71	0.591	91	63	0.053
1907 PHI	NL	0.527	81	73	0.565	83	64	0.038
1907 CIN	NL	0.527	81	73	0.431	66	87	-0.095
1907 BRO	NL	0.476	73	81	0.439	65	83	-0.037
1907 STL	NL	0.471	73	81	0.340	52	101	-0.131
1907 BSN	NL	0.363 F	56	98	0.392	58	90	0.029
			617	615		604	604	
			1236	1228				

Franchise	League	OPW%	PW	PL	APW%	AW	AL	Diff(+/-)
1908 CHW	AL	0.589 F	91	63	0.579	88	64	-0.010
1908 PHA	AL	0.566 P	87	67	0.444	68	85	-0.121
1908 CLE	AL	0.549	85	69	0.584	90	64	0.035
1908 DET	AL	0.546	84	70	0.588 P	90	63	0.043
1908 BOS	AL	0.544	84	70	0.487	75	79	-0.057

Franchise	League	OPW%	PW	PL	APW%	AW	AL	Diff(+/-)
1908 WS1	AL	0.471	72	82	0.441	67	85	-0.030
1908 SLB	AL	0.444	68	86	0.546	83	69	0.102
1908 NYY	AL	0.315	48	106	0.331	51	103	0.016
			620	612		612	612	
1908 NYG	NL	0.621 P	96	58	0.636	98	56	0.015
1908 CHC	NL	0.570	88	66	0.643 P	99	55	0.072
1908 PHI	NL	0.542	83	71	0.539	83	71	-0.003
1908 BSN	NL	0.490 F	76	78	0.409	63	91	-0.081
1908 CIN	NL	0.486	75	79	0.474	73	81	-0.012
1908 PIT	NL	0.461	71	83	0.636	98	56	0.175
1908 BRO	NL	0.446	69	85	0.344	53	101	-0.102
1908 STL	NL	0.375	58	96	0.318	49	105	-0.057
			615	617		616	616	
			1234	1230				

Franchise	League	OPW%	PW	PL	APW%	AW	AL	Diff(+/-)
1909 PHA	AL	0.642 P	99	55	0.621	95	58	-0.021
1909 DET	AL	0.629	97	57	0.645 P	98	54	0.016
1909 BOS	AL	0.557	86	68	0.583	88	63	0.025
1909 CHW	AL	0.485 F	75	79	0.513	78	74	0.028
1909 NYY	AL	0.467	72	82	0.490	74	77	0.023
1909 CLE	AL	0.463	71	83	0.464	71	82	0.001
1909 SLB	AL	0.378	58	96	0.407	61	89	0.029
1909 WS1	AL	0.357	55	99	0.276	42	110	-0.080
			613	619		607	607	
1909 NYG	NL	0.582 P	90	64	0.601	92	61	0.019
1909 CIN	NL	0.538	83	71	0.503	77	76	-0.035
1909 CHC	NL	0.536	83	71	0.680	104	49	0.144
1909 STL	NL	0.534	82	72	0.355	54	98	-0.179
1909 PHI	NL	0.525	81	73	0.484	74	79	-0.042
1909 PIT	NL	0.501	77	77	0.724 P	110	42	0.223
1909 BRO	NL	0.391 F	60	94	0.359	55	98	-0.032
1909 BSN	NL	0.369 F	57	97	0.294	45	108	-0.075
			613	619		611	611	
			1225	1239				

Franchise	League	OPW%	PW	PL	APW%	AW	AL	Diff(+/-)
1910 PHA	AL	0.679 P	105	49	0.680 P	102	48	0.001
1910 BOS	AL	0.545 F	84	70	0.529	81	72	-0.015
1910 NYY	AL	0.536	83	71	0.583	88	63	0.047
1910 DET	AL	0.533	82	72	0.558	86	68	0.025
1910 WS1	AL	0.465 F	72	82	0.305	47	107	-0.160
1910 CHW	AL	0.459	71	83	0.444	68	85	-0.015
1910 CLE	AL	0.431	66	88	0.467	71	81	0.037
1910 SLB	AL	0.355	55	99	0.437	66	85	0.082
			617	615		609	609	
1910 NYG	NL	0.585 P	90	64	0.591	91	63	0.006
1910 CIN	NL	0.554	85	69	0.487	75	79	-0.067
1910 CHC	NL	0.517	80	74	0.675 P	104	50	0.158
1910 PHI	NL	0.515	79	75	0.510	78	75	-0.006
1910 STL	NL	0.506	78	76	0.412	63	90	-0.095

Franchise	League	OPW%	PW	PL	APW%	AW	AL	Diff(+/-)
1910 PIT	NL	0.502	77	77	0.562	86	67	0.060
1910 BRO	NL	0.490	75	79	0.416	64	90	-0.074
1910 BSN	NL	0.335 F	52	102	0.346	53	100	0.012
			616	616		614	614	
			1233	1231				

Franchise	League	OPW%	PW	PL	APW%	AW	AL	Diff(+/-)
1911 PHA	AL	0.657 P	101	53	0.669 P	101	50	0.011
1911 BOS	AL	0.597	92	62	0.510	78	75	-0.087
1911 DET	AL	0.522	80	74	0.578	89	65	0.056
1911 CHW	AL	0.500 F	77	77	0.510	77	74	0.010
1911 NYY	AL	0.480	74	80	0.500	76	76	0.020
1911 CLE	AL	0.465	72	82	0.523	80	73	0.057
1911 WS1	AL	0.410 F	63	91	0.416	64	90	0.005
1911 SLB	AL	0.355	55	99	0.296	45	107	-0.059
			614	618		610	610	
1911 NYG	NL	0.659 P	102	52	0.647 P	99	54	-0.012
1911 PIT	NL	0.549	85	69	0.552	85	69	0.003
1911 BRO	NL	0.537	83	71	0.427	64	86	-0.110
1911 CIN	NL	0.534 F	82	72	0.458	70	83	-0.077
1911 CHC	NL	0.487	75	79	0.597	92	62	0.111
1911 PHI	NL	0.457	70	84	0.520	79	73	0.062
1911 STL	NL	0.451	69	85	0.503	75	74	0.052
1911 BSN	NL	0.342 F	53	101	0.291	44	107	-0.050
			618	614		608	608	
			1232	1232				

Franchise	League	OPW%	PW	PL	APW%	AW	AL	Diff(+/-)
1912 BOS	AL	0.667 P	103	51	0.691 P	105	47	0.024
1912 PHA	AL	0.582	90	64	0.592	90	62	0.010
1912 WS1	AL	0.582 F	90	64	0.599	91	61	0.017
1912 DET	AL	0.509	78	76	0.451	69	84	-0.058
1912 CHW	AL	0.490	75	79	0.506	78	76	0.017
1912 CLE	AL	0.449	69	85	0.490	75	78	0.041
1912 NYY	AL	0.375	58	96	0.329	50	102	-0.046
1912 SLB	AL	0.365	56	98	0.344	53	101	-0.021
			619	613		611	611	
1912 PIT	NL	0.630 P	97	57	0.616	93	58	-0.014
1912 NYG	NL	0.619	95	59	0.682 P	103	48	0.063
1912 CIN	NL	0.519	80	74	0.490	75	78	-0.029
1912 CHC	NL	0.500	77	77	0.607	91	59	0.107
1912 BRO	NL	0.496 F	76	78	0.379	58	95	-0.117
1912 PHI	NL	0.469 F	72	82	0.480	73	79	0.011
1912 STL	NL	0.422	65	89	0.412	63	90	-0.010
1912 BSN	NL	0.358	55	99	0.340	52	101	-0.018
			618	614		608	608	
			1237	1227				

Franchise	League	OPW%	PW	PL	APW%	AW	AL	Diff(+/-)
1913 PHA	AL	0.626 P	96	58	0.627 P	96	57	0.001
1913 WS1	AL	0.570 F	88	66	0.584	90	64	0.015

349

Franchise	League	OPW%	PW	PL	APW%	AW	AL	Diff(+/-)
1913 BOS	AL	0.498	77	77	0.527	79	71	0.028
1913 CLE	AL	0.487	75	79	0.566	86	66	0.079
1913 CHW	AL	0.484	75	79	0.513	78	74	0.029
1913 NYY	AL	0.475	73	81	0.377	57	94	-0.098
1913 DET	AL	0.457	70	84	0.431	66	87	-0.026
1913 SLB	AL	0.394	61	93	0.373	57	96	-0.021
			615	617		609	609	
1913 NYG	NL	0.590 P	91	63	0.664 P	101	51	0.075
1913 PIT	NL	0.572	88	66	0.523	78	71	-0.048
1913 CHC	NL	0.551	85	69	0.575	88	65	0.025
1913 PHI	NL	0.495 F	76	78	0.583	88	63	0.088
1913 CIN	NL	0.481	74	80	0.418	64	89	-0.063
1913 BSN	NL	0.472 F	73	81	0.457	69	82	-0.015
1913 BRO	NL	0.439 F	68	86	0.436	65	84	-0.003
1913 STL	NL	0.409	63	91	0.340	51	99	-0.069
			617	615		604	604	
			1232	1232				

Franchise	League	OPW%	PW	PL	APW%	AW	AL	Diff(+/-)
1914 PHA	AL	0.611 P	94	60	0.651 P	99	53	0.041
1914 WS1	AL	0.563	87	67	0.526	81	73	-0.037
1914 BOS	AL	0.541	83	71	0.595	91	62	0.054
1914 NYY	AL	0.535	82	72	0.455	70	84	-0.081
1914 DET	AL	0.531	82	72	0.523	80	73	-0.008
1914 SLB	AL	0.472	73	81	0.464	71	82	-0.008
1914 CHW	AL	0.373	57	97	0.455	70	84	0.081
1914 CLE	AL	0.368	57	97	0.333	51	102	-0.035
			615	617		613	613	
1914 NYG	NL	0.573 P	88	66	0.545	84	70	-0.027
1914 BSN	NL	0.531 F	82	72	0.614 P	94	59	0.083
1914 BRO	NL	0.528 F	81	73	0.487	75	79	-0.041
1914 CIN	NL	0.487	75	79	0.390	60	94	-0.098
1914 PIT	NL	0.485	75	79	0.448	69	85	-0.037
1914 CHC	NL	0.474	73	81	0.506	78	76	0.033
1914 STL	NL	0.468	72	82	0.529	81	72	0.061
1914 PHI	NL	0.448 F	69	85	0.481	74	80	0.032
			615	617		615	615	
			1230	1234				

Franchise	League	OPW%	PW	PL	APW%	AW	AL	Diff(+/-)
1915 DET	AL	0.598 P	92	62	0.649	100	54	0.052
1915 BOS	AL	0.592	91	63	0.669 P	101	50	0.077
1915 CHW	AL	0.570	88	66	0.604	93	61	0.034
1915 WS1	AL	0.565	87	67	0.556	85	68	-0.010
1915 NYY	AL	0.530	82	72	0.454	69	83	-0.076
1915 SLB	AL	0.414	64	90	0.409	63	91	-0.005
1915 CLE	AL	0.385	59	95	0.375	57	95	-0.010
1915 PHA	AL	0.368	57	97	0.283	43	109	-0.086
			620	612		611	611	
1915 CIN	NL	0.544 P	84	70	0.461	71	83	-0.083
1915 PIT	NL	0.542	83	71	0.474	73	81	-0.068

350

Franchise	League	OPW%	PW	PL	APW%	AW	AL	Diff(+/-)
1915 NYG	NL	0.536	83	71	0.454	69	83	-0.082
1915 PHI	NL	0.525 F	81	73	0.592 P	90	62	0.067
1915 CHC	NL	0.506	78	76	0.477	73	80	-0.029
1915 BSN	NL	0.504 F	78	76	0.546	83	69	0.042
1915 BRO	NL	0.444 F	68	86	0.526	80	72	0.082
1915 STL	NL	0.399	61	93	0.471	72	81	0.071
			616	616		611	611	
			1236	1228				

Franchise	League	OPW%	PW	PL	APW%	AW	AL	Diff(+/-)
1916 DET	AL	0.565 P	87	67	0.565	87	67	0.000
1916 SLB	AL	0.550	85	69	0.513	79	75	-0.037
1916 BOS	AL	0.547	84	70	0.591 P	91	63	0.044
1916 CHW	AL	0.521	80	74	0.578	89	65	0.057
1916 CLE	AL	0.490 F	75	79	0.500	77	77	0.010
1916 WS1	AL	0.489	75	79	0.497	76	77	0.008
1916 NYY	AL	0.463	71	83	0.519	80	74	0.057
1916 PHA	AL	0.384	59	95	0.235	36	117	-0.149
			617	615		615	615	
1916 NYG	NL	0.586 P	90	64	0.566	86	66	-0.021
1916 BSN	NL	0.532 F	82	72	0.586	89	63	0.053
1916 CIN	NL	0.512	79	75	0.392	60	93	-0.120
1916 CHC	NL	0.508	78	76	0.438	67	86	-0.070
1916 PIT	NL	0.504	78	76	0.422	65	89	-0.081
1916 BRO	NL	0.468 F	72	82	0.610 P	94	60	0.143
1916 PHI	NL	0.459 F	71	83	0.595	91	62	0.136
1916 STL	NL	0.433	67	87	0.392	60	93	-0.041
			616	616		612	612	
			1234	1230				

Franchise	League	OPW%	PW	PL	APW%	AW	AL	Diff(+/-)
1917 BOS	AL	0.631 P	97	57	0.592	90	62	-0.039
1917 DET	AL	0.599	92	62	0.510	78	75	-0.089
1917 NYY	AL	0.560	86	68	0.464	71	82	-0.096
1917 CHW	AL	0.510	79	75	0.649 P	100	54	0.140
1917 PHA	AL	0.500	77	77	0.359	55	98	-0.140
1917 WS1	AL	0.478	74	80	0.484	74	79	0.006
1917 CLE	AL	0.451 F	69	85	0.571	88	66	0.121
1917 SLB	AL	0.289	45	109	0.370	57	97	0.081
			619	613		613	613	
1917 NYG	NL	0.573 P	88	66	0.636 P	98	56	0.064
1917 BSN	NL	0.529 F	82	72	0.471	72	81	-0.059
1917 PHI	NL	0.522 F	80	74	0.572	87	65	0.050
1917 STL	NL	0.517	80	74	0.539	82	70	0.023
1917 BRO	NL	0.500 F	77	77	0.464	70	81	-0.036
1917 CHC	NL	0.500 F	77	77	0.481	74	80	-0.019
1917 CIN	NL	0.458	70	84	0.506	78	76	0.049
1917 PIT	NL	0.399	61	93	0.331	51	103	-0.068
			616	616		612	612	
			1234	1230				

Franchise	League	OPW%	PW	PL	APW%	AW	AL	Diff(+/-)
1918 NYY	AL	0.541 P	69	59	0.488	60	63	-0.054
1918 BOS	AL	0.539 F	69	59	0.595 P	75	51	0.057
1918 CLE	AL	0.513	66	62	0.575	73	54	0.062
1918 CHW	AL	0.507	65	63	0.460	57	67	-0.048
1918 DET	AL	0.507	65	63	0.437	55	71	-0.070
1918 SLB	AL	0.492	63	65	0.475	58	64	-0.017
1918 WS1	AL	0.491	63	65	0.563	72	56	0.071
1918 PHA	AL	0.410	52	76	0.406	52	76	-0.004
			512	512		502	502	
1918 PIT	NL	0.558 P	71	57	0.520	65	60	-0.038
1918 BRO	NL	0.551 F	71	57	0.452	57	69	-0.099
1918 BSN	NL	0.544	70	58	0.427	53	71	-0.117
1918 NYG	NL	0.539	69	59	0.573	71	53	0.034
1918 CIN	NL	0.494	63	65	0.531	68	60	0.037
1918 CHC	NL	0.477 F	61	67	0.651 P	84	45	0.174
1918 STL	NL	0.453	58	70	0.395	51	78	-0.057
1918 PHI	NL	0.394 F	50	78	0.447	55	68	0.053
			513	511		504	504	
			1025	1023				

Franchise	League	OPW%	PW	PL	APW%	AW	AL	Diff(+/-)
1919 DET	AL	0.597 P	84	56	0.571	80	60	-0.026
1919 CHW	AL	0.542	76	64	0.629 P	88	52	0.087
1919 NYY	AL	0.540	76	64	0.576	80	59	0.036
1919 CLE	AL	0.535 F	75	65	0.604	84	55	0.069
1919 BOS	AL	0.530 F	74	66	0.482	66	71	-0.048
1919 WS1	AL	0.472	66	74	0.400	56	84	-0.072
1919 SLB	AL	0.396	55	85	0.482	67	72	0.086
1919 PHA	AL	0.381	53	87	0.257	36	104	-0.123
			559	561		557	557	
1919 BRO	NL	0.592 F	83	57	0.493	69	71	-0.099
1919 CHC	NL	0.543 F	76	64	0.536	75	65	-0.007
1919 BSN	NL	0.522 P	73	67	0.410	57	82	-0.112
1919 STL	NL	0.516	72	68	0.394	54	83	-0.121
1919 PIT	NL	0.496	69	71	0.511	71	68	0.015
1919 NYG	NL	0.475	67	73	0.621	87	53	0.146
1919 CIN	NL	0.465 F	65	75	0.686 P	96	44	0.221
1919 PHI	NL	0.398 F	56	84	0.343	47	90	-0.055
			561	559		556	556	
			1120	1120				

Franchise	League	OPW%	PW	PL	APW%	AW	AL	Diff(+/-)
1920 NYY	AL	0.571 P	88	66	0.617	95	59	0.045
1920 CLE	AL	0.518 F	80	74	0.636 P	98	56	0.118
1920 CHW	AL	0.510 F	79	75	0.623	96	58	0.113
1920 DET	AL	0.506	78	76	0.396	61	93	-0.110
1920 SLB	AL	0.483	74	80	0.497	76	77	0.014
1920 BOS	AL	0.479 F	74	80	0.471	72	81	-0.009
1920 WS1	AL	0.470	72	82	0.447	68	84	-0.023
1920 PHA	AL	0.468	72	82	0.312	48	106	-0.156

			617	615		614	614	
1920 BRO	NL	0.570 F	88	66	0.604 P	93	61	0.034
1920 CHC	NL	0.534 F	82	72	0.487	75	79	-0.047
1920 BSN	NL	0.517 P	80	74	0.408	62	90	-0.109
1920 PIT	NL	0.500	77	77	0.513	79	75	0.013
1920 STL	NL	0.497	77	77	0.487	75	79	-0.010
1920 CIN	NL	0.497	77	77	0.536	82	71	0.039
1920 PHI	NL	0.471 F	73	81	0.405	62	91	-0.066
1920 NYG	NL	0.420	65	89	0.558	86	68	0.139
			617	615		614	614	
			1234	1230				

Franchise	League	OPW%	PW	PL	APW%	AW	AL	Diff(+/-)
1921 BOS	AL	0.615 F	95	59	0.487	75	79	-0.128
1921 CLE	AL	0.559 P	86	68	0.610	94	60	0.051
1921 DET	AL	0.553	85	69	0.464	71	82	-0.089
1921 NYY	AL	0.499 F	77	77	0.641 P	98	55	0.141
1921 WS1	AL	0.492 F	76	78	0.523	80	73	0.031
1921 SLB	AL	0.439	68	86	0.526	81	73	0.087
1921 PHA	AL	0.430	66	88	0.346	53	100	-0.084
1921 CHW	AL	0.391	60	94	0.403	62	92	0.012
			613	619		614	614	
1921 STL	NL	0.558 F	86	68	0.569	87	66	0.010
1921 PIT	NL	0.548 P	84	70	0.588	90	63	0.040
1921 BSN	NL	0.536	83	71	0.516	79	74	-0.020
1921 PHI	NL	0.500 F	77	77	0.331	51	103	-0.168
1921 CIN	NL	0.499	77	77	0.458	70	83	-0.042
1921 NYG	NL	0.472	73	81	0.614 P	94	59	0.142
1921 BRO	NL	0.453 F	70	84	0.507	77	75	0.053
1921 CHC	NL	0.436 F	67	87	0.418	64	89	-0.017
			616	616		612	612	
			1229	1235				

Franchise	League	OPW%	PW	PL	APW%	AW	AL	Diff(+/-)
1922 CHW	AL	0.558 P	86	68	0.500	77	77	-0.058
1922 WS1	AL	0.548 F	84	70	0.448	69	85	-0.100
1922 SLB	AL	0.532	82	72	0.604	93	61	0.072
1922 DET	AL	0.527	81	73	0.513	79	75	-0.014
1922 BOS	AL	0.479 F	74	80	0.396	61	93	-0.083
1922 CLE	AL	0.473	73	81	0.506	78	76	0.033
1922 NYY	AL	0.443	68	86	0.610 P	94	60	0.167
1922 PHA	AL	0.441	68	86	0.422	65	89	-0.019
			616	616		616	616	
1922 STL	NL	0.557 F	86	68	0.552	85	69	-0.005
1922 PIT	NL	0.555 P	85	69	0.552	85	69	-0.003
1922 BSN	NL	0.533	82	72	0.346	53	100	-0.187
1922 BRO	NL	0.507 F	78	76	0.494	76	78	-0.013
1922 CIN	NL	0.480 F	74	80	0.558	86	68	0.078
1922 PHI	NL	0.475 F	73	81	0.373	57	96	-0.102
1922 NYG	NL	0.452	70	84	0.604 P	93	61	0.152
1922 CHC	NL	0.440	68	86	0.519	80	74	0.080

353

		616	616		615	615	
		1232	1232				

Franchise	League	OPW%	PW	PL	APW%	AW	AL	Diff(+/-)
1923 PHA	AL	0.549 P	84	70	0.454	69	83	-0.095
1923 DET	AL	0.547	84	70	0.539	83	71	-0.008
1923 CLE	AL	0.535	82	72	0.536	82	71	0.001
1923 WS1	AL	0.513 F	79	75	0.490	75	78	-0.023
1923 CHW	AL	0.499	77	77	0.448	69	85	-0.051
1923 BOS	AL	0.465 F	72	82	0.401	61	91	-0.063
1923 SLB	AL	0.455 F	70	84	0.487	74	78	0.032
1923 NYY	AL	0.435	67	87	0.645 P	98	54	0.209
		616	616		611	611	
1923 PIT	NL	0.580 P	89	65	0.565	87	67	-0.015
1923 NYG	NL	0.522	80	74	0.621 P	95	58	0.099
1923 STL	NL	0.520	80	74	0.516	79	74	-0.004
1923 CHC	NL	0.497	76	78	0.539	83	71	0.042
1923 BRO	NL	0.492 F	76	78	0.494	76	78	0.002
1923 BSN	NL	0.490	75	79	0.351	54	100	-0.139
1923 CIN	NL	0.476 F	73	81	0.591	91	63	0.115
1923 PHI	NL	0.418 F	64	90	0.325	50	104	-0.094
		615	617		615	615	
		1231	1233				

Franchise	League	OPW%	PW	PL	APW%	AW	AL	Diff(+/-)
1924 WS1	AL	0.615 P	95	59	0.597 P	92	62	-0.018
1924 DET	AL	0.530	82	72	0.558	86	68	0.028
1924 NYY	AL	0.507	78	76	0.586	89	63	0.079
1924 BOS	AL	0.506 F	78	76	0.431	66	87	-0.075
1924 PHA	AL	0.496	76	78	0.467	71	81	-0.029
1924 SLB	AL	0.467	72	82	0.487	74	78	0.020
1924 CLE	AL	0.444	68	86	0.438	67	86	-0.006
1924 CHW	AL	0.440	68	86	0.435	67	87	-0.005
		617	615		612	612	
1924 STL	NL	0.548 P	84	70	0.422	65	89	-0.125
1924 PIT	NL	0.542	83	71	0.588	90	63	0.046
1924 BRO	NL	0.532 F	82	72	0.597	92	62	0.066
1924 NYG	NL	0.528	81	73	0.608 P	93	60	0.080
1924 PHI	NL	0.492 F	76	78	0.364	55	96	-0.128
1924 CIN	NL	0.486 F	75	79	0.542	83	70	0.057
1924 CHC	NL	0.472	73	81	0.529	81	72	0.057
1924 BSN	NL	0.389	60	94	0.346	53	100	-0.043
		614	618		612	612	
		1231	1233				

Franchise	League	OPW%	PW	PL	APW%	AW	AL	Diff(+/-)
1925 WS1	AL	0.565 P	87	67	0.636 P	96	55	0.071
1925 PHA	AL	0.562	87	67	0.579	88	64	0.017
1925 CHW	AL	0.562	87	67	0.513	79	75	-0.049
1925 DET	AL	0.518	80	74	0.526	81	73	0.008
1925 CLE	AL	0.474	73	81	0.455	70	84	-0.019

354

1925 SLB	**AL**	0.463 F	71	83	0.536	82	71	0.073
1925 NYY	**AL**	0.456	70	84	0.448	69	85	-0.008
1925 BOS	**AL**	0.410 F	63	91	0.309	47	105	-0.101
			618	614		612	612	
1925 PIT	**NL**	0.570 P	88	66	0.621 P	95	58	0.051
1925 PHI	**NL**	0.528 F	81	73	0.444	68	85	-0.083
1925 NYG	**NL**	0.513	79	75	0.566	86	66	0.053
1925 STL	**NL**	0.512	79	75	0.503	77	76	-0.008
1925 BSN	**NL**	0.509	78	76	0.458	70	83	-0.051
1925 CIN	**NL**	0.501 F	77	77	0.523	80	73	0.022
1925 CHC	**NL**	0.473	73	81	0.442	68	86	-0.032
1925 BRO	**NL**	0.401 F	62	92	0.444	68	85	0.043
			617	615		612	612	
			1234	1230				

Franchise	League	OPW%	PW	PL	APW%	AW	AL	Diff(+/-)
1926 CLE	**AL**	0.546 P	84	70	0.571	88	66	0.026
1926 CHW	**AL**	0.541	83	71	0.529	81	72	-0.011
1926 NYY	**AL**	0.533	82	72	0.591 P	91	63	0.058
1926 WS1	**AL**	0.507	78	76	0.540	81	69	0.033
1926 DET	**AL**	0.480	74	80	0.513	79	75	0.033
1926 PHA	**AL**	0.476	73	81	0.553	83	67	0.078
1926 SLB	**AL**	0.465	72	82	0.403	62	92	-0.063
1926 BOS	**AL**	0.456 F	70	84	0.301	46	107	-0.155
			616	616		611	611	
1926 PIT	**NL**	0.571 P	88	66	0.549	84	69	-0.022
1926 STL	**NL**	0.527	81	73	0.578 P	89	65	0.051
1926 CHC	**NL**	0.510	79	75	0.532	82	72	0.023
1926 NYG	**NL**	0.508	78	76	0.490	74	77	-0.018
1926 CIN	**NL**	0.507 F	78	76	0.565	87	67	0.058
1926 PHI	**NL**	0.503 F	78	76	0.384	58	93	-0.119
1926 BSN	**NL**	0.447	69	85	0.434	66	86	-0.012
1926 BRO	**NL**	0.420 F	65	89	0.464	71	82	0.044
			615	617		611	611	
			1231	1233				

Franchise	League	OPW%	PW	PL	APW%	AW	AL	Diff(+/-)
1927 NYY	**AL**	0.545 P	84	70	0.714 P	110	44	0.169
1927 DET	**AL**	0.542	83	71	0.536	82	71	-0.006
1927 WS1	**AL**	0.523	80	74	0.552	85	69	0.029
1927 CHW	**AL**	0.504	78	76	0.458	70	83	-0.046
1927 PHA	**AL**	0.480	74	80	0.591	91	63	0.111
1927 SLB	**AL**	0.473	73	81	0.386	59	94	-0.088
1927 CLE	**AL**	0.464	71	83	0.431	66	87	-0.033
1927 BOS	**AL**	0.463	71	83	0.331	51	103	-0.132
			615	617		614	614	
1927 STL	**NL**	0.566 P	87	67	0.601	92	61	0.035
1927 NYG	**NL**	0.559	86	68	0.597	92	62	0.038
1927 PIT	**NL**	0.558	86	68	0.610 P	94	60	0.053
1927 CIN	**NL**	0.553 F	85	69	0.490	75	78	-0.062
1927 CHC	**NL**	0.492	76	78	0.556	85	68	0.063

Franchise	League	OPW%	PW	PL	APW%	AW	AL	Diff(+/-)
1927 PHI	NL	0.482 F	74	80	0.331	51	103	-0.151
1927 BSN	NL	0.442	68	86	0.390	60	94	-0.052
1927 BRO	NL	0.345 F	53	101	0.425	65	88	0.080
			616	616		614	614	
			1231	1233				

Franchise	League	OPW%	PW	PL	APW%	AW	AL	Diff(+/-)
1928 PHA	AL	0.559 P	86	68	0.641	98	55	0.081
1928 NYY	AL	0.522	80	74	0.656 P	101	53	0.134
1928 DET	AL	0.511	79	75	0.442	68	86	-0.070
1928 WS1	AL	0.511	79	75	0.487	75	79	-0.024
1928 BOS	AL	0.504	78	76	0.373	57	96	-0.132
1928 SLB	AL	0.468	72	82	0.532	82	72	0.064
1928 CHW	AL	0.461	71	83	0.468	72	82	0.007
1928 CLE	AL	0.458	70	84	0.403	62	92	-0.055
			615	617		615	615	
1928 PIT	NL	0.602 P	93	61	0.559	85	67	-0.043
1928 STL	NL	0.592	91	63	0.617 P	95	59	0.024
1928 CHC	NL	0.560	86	68	0.591	91	63	0.031
1928 NYG	NL	0.544	84	70	0.604	93	61	0.060
1928 CIN	NL	0.469 F	72	82	0.513	78	74	0.044
1928 BSN	NL	0.458	71	83	0.327	50	103	-0.131
1928 BRO	NL	0.389 F	60	94	0.503	77	76	0.115
1928 PHI	NL	0.385	59	95	0.283	43	109	-0.102
			616	616		612	612	
			1231	1233				

Franchise	League	OPW%	PW	PL	APW%	AW	AL	Diff(+/-)
1929 PHA	AL	0.605 P	93	61	0.693 P	104	46	0.088
1929 NYY	AL	0.565	87	67	0.571	88	66	0.007
1929 DET	AL	0.543	84	70	0.455	70	84	-0.089
1929 SLB	AL	0.480	74	80	0.520	79	73	0.040
1929 CLE	AL	0.478	74	80	0.533	81	71	0.055
1929 WS1	AL	0.474	73	81	0.467	71	81	-0.007
1929 BOS	AL	0.463	71	83	0.377	58	96	-0.086
1929 CHW	AL	0.385	59	95	0.388	59	93	0.003
			615	617		610	610	
1929 NYG	NL	0.581 P	90	64	0.556	84	67	-0.025
1929 CHC	NL	0.573	88	66	0.645 P	98	54	0.072
1929 PIT	NL	0.567	87	67	0.575	88	65	0.008
1929 STL	NL	0.536 F	82	72	0.513	78	74	-0.022
1929 BRO	NL	0.460 F	71	83	0.458	70	83	-0.003
1929 PHI	NL	0.460 F	71	83	0.464	71	82	0.004
1929 CIN	NL	0.422 F	65	89	0.429	66	88	0.007
1929 BSN	NL	0.404	62	92	0.364	56	98	-0.040
			616	616		611	611	
			1231	1233				

Franchise	League	OPW%	PW	PL	APW%	AW	AL	Diff(+/-)
1930 WS1	AL	0.569 P	88	66	0.610	94	60	0.042
1930 PHA	AL	0.563	87	67	0.662 P	102	52	0.099

356

Franchise	League	OPW%	PW	PL	APW%	AW	AL	Diff(+/-)
1930 NYY	AL	0.546	84	70	0.558	86	68	0.012
1930 DET	AL	0.516	79	75	0.487	75	79	-0.028
1930 CLE	AL	0.496	76	78	0.526	81	73	0.030
1930 BOS	AL	0.466	72	82	0.338	52	102	-0.128
1930 CHW	AL	0.445	69	85	0.403	62	92	-0.043
1930 SLB	AL	0.388	60	94	0.416	64	90	0.028
			614	618		616	616	
1930 STL	NL	0.549 P	85	69	0.597 P	92	62	0.048
1930 NYG	NL	0.541	83	71	0.565	87	67	0.024
1930 CHC	NL	0.538	83	71	0.584	90	64	0.046
1930 BRO	NL	0.522 F	80	74	0.558	86	68	0.036
1930 PIT	NL	0.521	80	74	0.519	80	74	-0.002
1930 CIN	NL	0.468 F	72	82	0.383	59	95	-0.085
1930 BSN	NL	0.447 F	69	85	0.455	70	84	0.008
1930 PHI	NL	0.423 F	65	89	0.338	52	102	-0.086
			618	614		616	616	
			1232	1232				

Franchise	League	OPW%	PW	PL	APW%	AW	AL	Diff(+/-)
1931 NYY	AL	0.582 P	90	64	0.614	94	59	0.033
1931 PHA	AL	0.569	88	66	0.704 P	107	45	0.135
1931 WS1	AL	0.560	86	68	0.597	92	62	0.037
1931 CLE	AL	0.558	86	68	0.506	78	76	-0.051
1931 BOS	AL	0.471	73	81	0.408	62	90	-0.063
1931 DET	AL	0.470	72	82	0.396	61	93	-0.074
1931 SLB	AL	0.437	67	87	0.409	63	91	-0.028
1931 CHW	AL	0.354	55	99	0.366	56	97	0.012
			616	616		613	613	
1931 NYG	NL	0.569 P	88	66	0.572	87	65	0.003
1931 STL	NL	0.556	86	68	0.656 P	101	53	0.099
1931 PIT	NL	0.523	80	74	0.487	75	79	-0.036
1931 CIN	NL	0.503 F	77	77	0.377	58	96	-0.126
1931 CHC	NL	0.493	76	78	0.545	84	70	0.052
1931 BSN	NL	0.469 F	72	82	0.416	64	90	-0.053
1931 BRO	NL	0.458 F	71	83	0.520	79	73	0.062
1931 PHI	NL	0.439 F	68	86	0.429	66	88	-0.011
			618	614		614	614	
			1234	1230				

Franchise	League	OPW%	PW	PL	APW%	AW	AL	Diff(+/-)
1932 PHA	AL	0.594 P	91	63	0.610	94	60	0.016
1932 NYY	AL	0.588	91	63	0.695 P	107	47	0.106
1932 CLE	AL	0.542	84	70	0.572	87	65	0.030
1932 DET	AL	0.516	79	75	0.503	76	75	-0.013
1932 WS1	AL	0.512	79	75	0.604	93	61	0.092
1932 SLB	AL	0.441	68	86	0.409	63	91	-0.032
1932 BOS	AL	0.413	64	90	0.279	43	111	-0.134
1932 CHW	AL	0.380	58	96	0.325	49	102	-0.055
			614	618		612	612	
1932 PHI	NL	0.626 F	96	58	0.506	78	76	-0.120
1932 CHC	NL	0.547 P	84	70	0.584 P	90	64	0.037

357

Franchise	League	OPW%	PW	PL	APW%	AW	AL	Diff(+/-)
1932 BSN	NL	0.527 F	81	73	0.500	77	77	-0.027
1932 PIT	NL	0.513	79	75	0.558	86	68	0.046
1932 NYG	NL	0.508	78	76	0.468	72	82	-0.041
1932 STL	NL	0.502	77	77	0.468	72	82	-0.034
1932 CIN	NL	0.440 F	68	86	0.390	60	94	-0.050
1932 BRO	NL	0.334 F	51	103	0.526	81	73	0.192
			615	617		616	616	
			1229	1235				

Franchise	League	OPW%	PW	PL	APW%	AW	AL	Diff(+/-)
1933 WS1	AL	0.569 P	88	66	0.651 P	99	53	0.083
1933 NYY	AL	0.562	86	68	0.607	91	59	0.045
1933 DET	AL	0.547	84	70	0.487	75	79	-0.060
1933 BOS	AL	0.500 F	77	77	0.423	63	86	-0.077
1933 CLE	AL	0.492	76	78	0.497	75	76	0.005
1933 PHA	AL	0.485	75	79	0.523	79	72	0.038
1933 SLB	AL	0.423	65	89	0.364	55	96	-0.059
1933 CHW	AL	0.418	64	90	0.447	67	83	0.029
			615	617		604	604	
1933 BSN	NL	0.587 F	90	64	0.539	83	71	-0.048
1933 NYG	NL	0.536 P	83	71	0.599 P	91	61	0.063
1933 PIT	NL	0.518	80	74	0.565	87	67	0.047
1933 STL	NL	0.502	77	77	0.536	82	71	0.034
1933 CHC	NL	0.489	75	79	0.558	86	68	0.069
1933 PHI	NL	0.481 F	74	80	0.395	60	92	-0.087
1933 CIN	NL	0.472 F	73	81	0.382	58	94	-0.090
1933 BRO	NL	0.424 F	65	89	0.425	65	88	0.001
			617	615		612	612	
			1232	1232				

Franchise	League	OPW%	PW	PL	APW%	AW	AL	Diff(+/-)
1934 DET	AL	0.578 P	89	65	0.656 P	101	53	0.077
1934 BOS	AL	0.565 F	87	67	0.500	76	76	-0.065
1934 CLE	AL	0.541	83	71	0.552	85	69	0.011
1934 NYY	AL	0.535	82	72	0.610	94	60	0.076
1934 PHA	AL	0.495	76	78	0.453	68	82	-0.041
1934 WS1	AL	0.476	73	81	0.434	66	86	-0.041
1934 SLB	AL	0.414 F	64	90	0.441	67	85	0.027
1934 CHW	AL	0.398 F	61	93	0.349	53	99	-0.049
			616	616		610	610	
1934 STL	NL	0.569 P	88	66	0.621 P	95	58	0.052
1934 NYG	NL	0.562	86	68	0.608	93	60	0.046
1934 BSN	NL	0.540 F	83	71	0.517	78	73	-0.024
1934 PIT	NL	0.519	80	74	0.493	74	76	-0.026
1934 CHC	NL	0.479	74	80	0.570	86	65	0.091
1934 CIN	NL	0.461 F	71	83	0.344	52	99	-0.117
1934 PHI	NL	0.444 F	68	86	0.376	56	93	-0.069
1934 BRO	NL	0.427	66	88	0.467	71	81	0.040
			616	616		605	605	
			1232	1232				

358

Franchise	League	OPW%	PW	PL	APW%	AW	AL	Diff(+/-)
1935 DET	AL	0.582 P	90	64	0.616 P	93	58	0.034
1935 NYY	AL	0.571	88	66	0.597	89	60	0.026
1935 CLE	AL	0.547	84	70	0.536	82	71	-0.011
1935 CHW	AL	0.510 F	79	75	0.487	74	78	-0.023
1935 BOS	AL	0.489 F	75	79	0.510	78	75	0.020
1935 PHA	AL	0.454	70	84	0.389	58	91	-0.065
1935 WS1	AL	0.450	69	85	0.438	67	86	-0.012
1935 SLB	AL	0.399 F	62	92	0.428	65	87	0.028
			616	616		606	606	
1935 PIT	NL	0.620 P	96	58	0.562	86	67	-0.058
1935 CHC	NL	0.595	92	62	0.649 P	100	54	0.054
1935 STL	NL	0.593	91	63	0.623	96	58	0.030
1935 NYG	NL	0.549	85	69	0.595	91	62	0.046
1935 BRO	NL	0.438	68	86	0.458	70	83	0.019
1935 CIN	NL	0.412 F	63	91	0.444	68	85	0.032
1935 BSN	NL	0.402 F	62	92	0.248	38	115	-0.154
1935 PHI	NL	0.391 F	60	94	0.418	64	89	0.028
			616	616		613	613	
			1233	1231				

Franchise	League	OPW%	PW	PL	APW%	AW	AL	Diff(+/-)
1936 NYY	AL	0.580 P	89	65	0.667 P	102	51	0.087
1936 DET	AL	0.568	87	67	0.539	83	71	-0.029
1936 CLE	AL	0.552	85	69	0.519	80	74	-0.032
1936 WS1	AL	0.518	80	74	0.536	82	71	0.018
1936 BOS	AL	0.459 F	71	83	0.481	74	80	0.021
1936 CHW	AL	0.451 F	69	85	0.536	81	70	0.086
1936 PHA	AL	0.442	68	86	0.346	53	100	-0.096
1936 SLB	AL	0.428 F	66	88	0.375	57	95	-0.053
			616	616		612	612	
1936 STL	NL	0.565 P	87	67	0.565	87	67	0.000
1936 CHC	NL	0.564 F	87	67	0.565	87	67	0.001
1936 PIT	NL	0.555	85	69	0.545	84	70	-0.009
1936 NYG	NL	0.525	81	73	0.597 P	92	62	0.072
1936 BSN	NL	0.521 F	80	74	0.461	71	83	-0.060
1936 CIN	NL	0.518	80	74	0.481	74	80	-0.037
1936 PHI	NL	0.396 F	61	93	0.351	54	100	-0.045
1936 BRO	NL	0.346	53	101	0.435	67	87	0.089
			614	618		616	616	
			1230	1234				

Franchise	League	OPW%	PW	PL	APW%	AW	AL	Diff(+/-)
1937 NYY	AL	0.670 P	103	51	0.662 P	102	52	-0.007
1937 CHW	AL	0.541 F	83	71	0.558	86	68	0.018
1937 CLE	AL	0.518	80	74	0.539	83	71	0.021
1937 DET	AL	0.509	78	76	0.578	89	65	0.069
1937 BOS	AL	0.501 F	77	77	0.526	80	72	0.025
1937 PHA	AL	0.476	73	81	0.358	54	97	-0.118
1937 WS1	AL	0.413	64	90	0.477	73	80	0.064
1937 SLB	AL	0.373 F	58	96	0.299	46	108	-0.075

			616	616		613	613	
1937 BSN	NL	0.567 F	87	67	0.520	79	73	-0.047
1937 STL	NL	0.559 P	86	68	0.526	81	73	-0.033
1937 CHC	NL	0.514	79	75	0.604	93	61	0.090
1937 NYG	NL	0.503	77	77	0.625 P	95	57	0.122
1937 CIN	NL	0.484	74	80	0.364	56	98	-0.120
1937 PIT	NL	0.472	73	81	0.558	86	68	0.086
1937 PHI	NL	0.454 F	70	84	0.399	61	92	-0.056
1937 BRO	NL	0.453 F	70	84	0.405	62	91	-0.048
			617	615		613	613	
			1233	1231				

Franchise	League	OPW%	PW	PL	APW%	AW	AL	Diff(+/-)
1938 NYY	AL	0.575 P	89	65	0.651 P	99	53	0.076
1938 CLE	AL	0.533	82	72	0.566	86	66	0.033
1938 WS1	AL	0.495	76	78	0.497	75	76	0.001
1938 DET	AL	0.494	76	78	0.545	84	70	0.052
1938 CHW	AL	0.486 F	75	79	0.439	65	83	-0.046
1938 BOS	AL	0.479	74	80	0.591	88	61	0.111
1938 PHA	AL	0.471	72	82	0.349	53	99	-0.122
1938 SLB	AL	0.465 F	72	82	0.362	55	97	-0.103
			616	616		605	605	
1938 STL	NL	0.543 P	84	70	0.470	71	80	-0.073
1938 CHC	NL	0.530 F	82	72	0.586 P	89	63	0.055
1938 BSN	NL	0.528 F	81	73	0.507	77	75	-0.022
1938 PIT	NL	0.525	81	73	0.573	86	64	0.048
1938 NYG	NL	0.522	80	74	0.553	83	67	0.031
1938 CIN	NL	0.484 F	75	79	0.547	82	68	0.063
1938 BRO	NL	0.476	73	81	0.463	69	80	-0.012
1938 PHI	NL	0.381	59	95	0.300	45	105	-0.081
			614	618		602	602	
			1230	1234				

Franchise	League	OPW%	PW	PL	APW%	AW	AL	Diff(+/-)
1939 NYY	AL	0.607 P	94	60	0.702 P	106	45	0.095
1939 CLE	AL	0.566	87	67	0.565	87	67	-0.001
1939 DET	AL	0.523	81	73	0.526	81	73	0.003
1939 BOS	AL	0.511	79	75	0.589	89	62	0.078
1939 CHW	AL	0.484 F	75	79	0.552	85	69	0.068
1939 WS1	AL	0.478	74	80	0.428	65	87	-0.050
1939 PHA	AL	0.449	69	85	0.362	55	97	-0.087
1939 SLB	AL	0.384	59	95	0.279	43	111	-0.104
			616	616		611	611	
1939 PIT	NL	0.561 P	86	68	0.444	68	85	-0.116
1939 CHC	NL	0.538	83	71	0.545	84	70	0.007
1939 BSN	NL	0.518 F	80	74	0.417	63	88	-0.100
1939 STL	NL	0.511	79	75	0.601	92	61	0.090
1939 NYG	NL	0.506 F	78	76	0.510	77	74	0.004
1939 CIN	NL	0.483 F	74	80	0.630 P	97	57	0.147
1939 BRO	NL	0.467	72	82	0.549	84	69	0.082
1939 PHI	NL	0.417 F	64	90	0.298	45	106	-0.119

Franchise	League	OPW%	PW	PL	APW%	AW	AL	Diff(+/-)
1940 CHW	AL	0.566 F	87	67	0.532	82	72	-0.034
1940 NYY	AL	0.560 P	86	68	0.571	88	66	0.011
1940 DET	AL	0.552	85	69	0.584 P	90	64	0.033
1940 BOS	AL	0.518	80	74	0.532	82	72	0.014
1940 CLE	AL	0.486	75	79	0.578	89	65	0.092
1940 SLB	AL	0.477 F	73	81	0.435	67	87	-0.042
1940 PHA	AL	0.443	68	86	0.351	54	100	-0.092
1940 WS1	AL	0.412	63	91	0.416	64	90	0.004
			618	614		610	616	
1940 PIT	NL	0.636 F	98	56	0.506	78	76	-0.129
1940 NYG	NL	0.565 P	87	67	0.474	72	80	-0.092
1940 CHC	NL	0.554	85	69	0.487	75	79	-0.067
1940 BSN	NL	0.543	84	70	0.428	65	87	-0.115
1940 CIN	NL	0.537 F	83	71	0.654 P	100	53	0.117
1940 STL	NL	0.471	73	81	0.549	84	69	0.078
1940 BRO	NL	0.453	70	84	0.575	88	65	0.122
1940 PHI	NL	0.232 F	36	118	0.327	50	103	0.095
			614	618		612	612	
			1233	1231				

Franchise	League	OPW%	PW	PL	APW%	AW	AL	Diff(+/-)
1941 BOS	AL	0.572 P	88	66	0.545	84	70	-0.027
1941 NYY	AL	0.560	86	68	0.656 P	101	53	0.095
1941 CLE	AL	0.545	84	70	0.487	75	79	-0.058
1941 PHA	AL	0.489	75	79	0.416	64	90	-0.074
1941 DET	AL	0.473	73	81	0.487	75	79	0.014
1941 WS1	AL	0.470	72	82	0.455	70	84	-0.015
1941 CHW	AL	0.454 F	70	84	0.500	77	77	0.046
1941 SLB	AL	0.443 F	68	86	0.455	70	84	0.011
			617	615		616	616	
1941 NYG	NL	0.593 P	91	63	0.484	74	79	-0.109
1941 CHC	NL	0.562	87	67	0.455	70	84	-0.108
1941 STL	NL	0.536	83	71	0.634	97	56	0.098
1941 PIT	NL	0.529 F	81	73	0.526	81	73	-0.003
1941 BSN	NL	0.526	81	73	0.403	62	92	-0.123
1941 CIN	NL	0.494	76	78	0.571	88	66	0.078
1941 BRO	NL	0.409 F	63	91	0.649 P	100	54	0.240
1941 PHI	NL	0.335 F	52	102	0.279	43	111	-0.056
			614	618		615	615	
			1231	1233				

Franchise	League	OPW%	PW	PL	APW%	AW	AL	Diff(+/-)
1942 BOS	AL	0.623 P	96	58	0.612	93	59	-0.011
1942 NYY	AL	0.609	94	60	0.669 P	103	51	0.060
1942 CHW	AL	0.510 F	78	76	0.446	66	82	-0.064
1942 SLB	AL	0.504 F	78	76	0.543	82	69	0.039
1942 CLE	AL	0.475	73	81	0.487	75	79	0.012

1942 DET	**AL**	0.464	71	83	0.474	73	81	0.010
1942 WS1	**AL**	0.423	65	89	0.411	62	89	-0.012
1942 PHA	**AL**	0.394	61	93	0.357	55	99	-0.037
			616	616		609	609	
1942 STL	**NL**	0.601 P	93	61	0.688 P	106	48	0.088
1942 PIT	**NL**	0.588 F	91	63	0.449	66	81	-0.139
1942 NYG	**NL**	0.551 F	85	69	0.559	85	67	0.008
1942 CHC	**NL**	0.540	83	71	0.442	68	86	-0.098
1942 BSN	**NL**	0.475	73	81	0.399	59	89	-0.077
1942 BRO	**NL**	0.449	69	85	0.675	104	50	0.226
1942 PHI	**NL**	0.397 F	61	93	0.278	42	109	-0.119
1942 CIN	**NL**	0.380 F	59	95	0.500	76	76	0.120
			613	619		606	606	
			1229	1235				

Franchise	League	OPW%	PW	PL	APW%	AW	AL	Diff(+/-)
1943 CHW	**AL**	0.627 F	97	57	0.532	82	72	-0.094
1943 NYY	**AL**	0.545 P	84	70	0.636 P	98	56	0.091
1943 DET	**AL**	0.536	83	71	0.506	78	76	-0.030
1943 WS1	**AL**	0.490	75	79	0.549	84	69	0.059
1943 CLE	**AL**	0.477	73	81	0.536	82	71	0.059
1943 SLB	**AL**	0.471 F	73	81	0.474	72	80	0.002
1943 BOS	**AL**	0.438	68	86	0.447	68	84	0.009
1943 PHA	**AL**	0.431	66	88	0.318	49	105	-0.112
			618	614		613	613	
1943 PIT	**NL**	0.596 F	92	62	0.519	80	74	-0.077
1943 CHC	**NL**	0.567 P	87	67	0.484	74	79	-0.083
1943 STL	**NL**	0.543	84	70	0.682 P	105	49	0.139
1943 BRO	**NL**	0.480	74	80	0.529	81	72	0.050
1943 NYG	**NL**	0.470	72	82	0.359	55	98	-0.110
1943 BSN	**NL**	0.461 F	71	83	0.444	68	85	-0.017
1943 CIN	**NL**	0.444 F	68	86	0.565	87	67	0.121
1943 PHI	**NL**	0.440 F	68	86	0.416	64	90	-0.024
			616	616		614	614	
			1234	1230				

Franchise	League	OPW%	PW	PL	APW%	AW	AL	Diff(+/-)
1944 DET	**AL**	0.549 P	85	69	0.571	88	66	0.022
1944 SLB	**AL**	0.535 F	82	72	0.578 P	89	65	0.043
1944 NYY	**AL**	0.533	82	72	0.539	83	71	0.006
1944 BOS	**AL**	0.528	81	73	0.500	77	77	-0.028
1944 CLE	**AL**	0.496	76	78	0.468	72	82	-0.029
1944 WS1	**AL**	0.471 F	73	81	0.416	64	90	-0.055
1944 CHW	**AL**	0.447 F	69	85	0.461	71	83	0.014
1944 PHA	**AL**	0.439	68	86	0.468	72	82	0.028
			616	616		616	616	
1944 STL	**NL**	0.609 P	94	60	0.682 P	105	49	0.072
1944 PIT	**NL**	0.548 F	84	70	0.588	90	63	0.040
1944 CHC	**NL**	0.530	82	72	0.487	75	79	-0.043
1944 NYG	**NL**	0.501	77	77	0.435	67	87	-0.066
1944 BSN	**NL**	0.497 F	77	77	0.422	65	89	-0.075

Franchise	League							
1944 CIN	NL	0.469 F	72	82	0.578	89	65	0.109
1944 BRO	NL	0.431	66	88	0.409	63	91	-0.022
1944 PHI	NL	0.408 F	63	91	0.399	61	92	-0.009
			615	617		615	615	
			1230	1234				

Franchise	League	OPW%	PW	PL	APW%	AW	AL	Diff(+/-)
1945 CLE	AL	0.574 P	88	66	0.503	73	72	-0.070
1945 NYY	AL	0.550	85	69	0.533	81	71	-0.017
1945 SLB	AL	0.505 F	78	76	0.536	81	70	0.031
1945 DET	AL	0.499	77	77	0.575 P	88	65	0.076
1945 PHA	AL	0.493	76	78	0.347	52	98	-0.146
1945 CHW	AL	0.490 F	75	79	0.477	71	78	-0.013
1945 WS1	AL	0.452	70	84	0.565	87	67	0.113
1945 BOS	AL	0.437	67	87	0.461	71	83	0.024
			616	616		604	604	
1945 CHC	NL	0.654 P	101	53	0.636 P	98	56	-0.018
1945 PIT	NL	0.602	93	61	0.532	82	72	-0.070
1945 STL	NL	0.549	85	69	0.617	95	59	0.068
1945 BRO	NL	0.515	79	75	0.565	87	67	0.050
1945 NYG	NL	0.474	73	81	0.513	78	74	0.040
1945 CIN	NL	0.453	70	84	0.396	61	93	-0.057
1945 BSN	NL	0.417	64	90	0.441	67	85	0.024
1945 PHI	NL	0.324 F	50	104	0.299	46	108	-0.026
			614	618		614	614	
			1230	1234				

Franchise	League	OPW%	PW	PL	APW%	AW	AL	Diff(+/-)
1946 BOS	AL	0.610 P	94	60	0.675 P	104	50	0.066
1946 DET	AL	0.599	92	62	0.597	92	62	-0.002
1946 NYY	AL	0.510	79	75	0.565	87	67	0.055
1946 CHW	AL	0.493 F	76	78	0.481	74	80	-0.013
1946 CLE	AL	0.493	76	78	0.442	68	86	-0.051
1946 SLB	AL	0.483 F	74	80	0.429	66	88	-0.054
1946 PHA	AL	0.418	64	90	0.318	49	105	-0.100
1946 WS1	AL	0.391	60	94	0.494	76	78	0.102
			616	616		616	616	
1946 CHC	NL	0.626 P	96	58	0.536	82	71	-0.090
1946 STL	NL	0.573	88	66	0.628 P	98	58	0.055
1946 PHI	NL	0.482 F	74	80	0.448	69	85	-0.034
1946 BRO	NL	0.480	74	80	0.615	96	60	0.136
1946 PIT	NL	0.476 F	73	81	0.409	63	91	-0.067
1946 NYG	NL	0.458	71	83	0.396	61	93	-0.062
1946 BSN	NL	0.452 F	70	84	0.529	81	72	0.078
1946 CIN	NL	0.447 F	69	85	0.435	67	87	-0.012
			615	617		617	617	
			1231	1233				

Franchise	League	OPW%	PW	PL	APW%	AW	AL	Diff(+/-)
1947 CLE	AL	0.574 P	88	66	0.519	80	74	-0.054
1947 NYY	AL	0.545	84	70	0.630 P	97	57	0.085

Franchise	League	OPW%	PW	PL	APW%	AW	AL	Diff(+/-)
1947 BOS	AL	0.528	81	73	0.539	83	71	0.011
1947 DET	AL	0.519	80	74	0.552	85	69	0.033
1947 PHA	AL	0.518	80	74	0.506	78	76	-0.011
1947 CHW	AL	0.506	78	76	0.455	70	84	-0.052
1947 WS1	AL	0.434	67	87	0.416	64	90	-0.019
1947 SLB	AL	0.376 F	58	96	0.383	59	95	0.008
			616	616		616	616	
1947 STL	NL	0.544 P	84	70	0.578	89	65	0.034
1947 PHI	NL	0.524 F	81	73	0.403	62	92	-0.121
1947 NYG	NL	0.519	80	74	0.526	81	73	0.007
1947 BRO	NL	0.503	78	76	0.610 P	94	60	0.107
1947 BSN	NL	0.495 F	76	78	0.558	86	68	0.064
1947 CHC	NL	0.480	74	80	0.448	69	85	-0.032
1947 CIN	NL	0.474	73	81	0.474	73	81	0.000
1947 PIT	NL	0.462 F	71	83	0.403	62	92	-0.060
			616	616		616	616	
			1232	1232				

Franchise	League	OPW%	PW	PL	APW%	AW	AL	Diff(+/-)
1948 CLE	AL	0.606 P	93	61	0.626 P	97	58	0.020
1948 BOS	AL	0.550	85	69	0.619	96	59	0.069
1948 DET	AL	0.525	81	73	0.506	78	76	-0.018
1948 NYY	AL	0.523	81	73	0.610	94	60	0.088
1948 SLB	AL	0.493 F	76	78	0.386	59	94	-0.108
1948 PHA	AL	0.487	75	79	0.545	84	70	0.058
1948 CHW	AL	0.408 F	63	91	0.336	51	101	-0.072
1948 WS1	AL	0.398	61	93	0.366	56	97	-0.032
			614	618		615	615	
1948 PIT	NL	0.566 F	87	67	0.539	83	71	-0.027
1948 NYG	NL	0.530 F	82	72	0.506	78	76	-0.023
1948 STL	NL	0.522 P	80	74	0.552	85	69	0.030
1948 BRO	NL	0.514	79	75	0.545	84	70	0.032
1948 BSN	NL	0.506 F	78	76	0.595 P	91	62	0.089
1948 CHC	NL	0.474	73	81	0.416	64	90	-0.058
1948 PHI	NL	0.468 F	72	82	0.429	66	88	-0.040
1948 CIN	NL	0.413	64	90	0.418	64	89	0.005
			615	617		615	615	
			1229	1235				

Franchise	League	OPW%	PW	PL	APW%	AW	AL	Diff(+/-)
1949 CLE	AL	0.556 P	86	68	0.578	89	65	0.022
1949 BOS	AL	0.549	84	70	0.623	96	58	0.075
1949 PHA	AL	0.542	84	70	0.526	81	73	-0.017
1949 NYY	AL	0.538	83	71	0.630 P	97	57	0.091
1949 DET	AL	0.520	80	74	0.565	87	67	0.045
1949 CHW	AL	0.517 F	80	74	0.409	63	91	-0.108
1949 SLB	AL	0.427 F	66	88	0.344	53	101	-0.083
1949 WS1	AL	0.361	56	98	0.325	50	104	-0.036
			618	614		616	616	
1949 BRO	NL	0.539 P	83	71	0.630 P	97	57	0.091
1949 STL	NL	0.526	81	73	0.623	96	58	0.097

Franchise	League	OPW%	PW	PL	APW%	AW	AL	Diff(+/-)
1949 NYG	NL	0.515	79	75	0.474	73	81	-0.041
1949 BSN	NL	0.514 F	79	75	0.487	75	79	-0.027
1949 CHC	NL	0.489	75	79	0.396	61	93	-0.093
1949 PIT	NL	0.477 F	73	81	0.461	71	83	-0.016
1949 PHI	NL	0.473 F	73	81	0.526	81	73	0.053
1949 CIN	NL	0.471	73	81	0.403	62	92	-0.069
			617	615		616	616	
			1234	1230				

Franchise	League	OPW%	PW	PL	APW%	AW	AL	Diff(+/-)
1950 BOS	AL	0.558 P	86	68	0.610	94	60	0.053
1950 CLE	AL	0.554	85	69	0.597	92	62	0.043
1950 DET	AL	0.541	83	71	0.617	95	59	0.076
1950 SLB	AL	0.531 F	82	72	0.377	58	96	-0.155
1950 NYY	AL	0.520	80	74	0.636 P	98	56	0.116
1950 CHW	AL	0.442 F	68	86	0.390	60	94	-0.053
1950 WSH	AL	0.437 F	67	87	0.435	67	87	-0.002
1950 PHA	AL	0.408 F	63	91	0.338	52	102	-0.070
			614	618		616	616	
1950 PHI	NL	0.562 P	87	67	0.591 P	91	63	0.029
1950 BSN	NL	0.534 F	82	72	0.539	83	71	0.005
1950 STL	NL	0.518	80	74	0.510	78	75	-0.008
1950 BRO	NL	0.512	79	75	0.578	89	65	0.066
1950 CHC	NL	0.501	77	77	0.418	64	89	-0.083
1950 CIN	NL	0.493	76	78	0.431	66	87	-0.061
1950 PIT	NL	0.452 F	70	84	0.373	57	96	-0.079
1950 NYG	NL	0.441	68	86	0.558	86	68	0.117
			618	614		614	614	
			1232	1232				

Franchise	League	OPW%	PW	PL	APW%	AW	AL	Diff(+/-)
1951 CLE	AL	0.588 P	91	63	0.604	93	61	0.016
1951 WSH	AL	0.547 F	84	70	0.403	62	92	-0.144
1951 BOS	AL	0.498	77	77	0.565	87	67	0.067
1951 PHA	AL	0.496 F	76	78	0.455	70	84	-0.042
1951 CHW	AL	0.495 F	76	78	0.526	81	73	0.031
1951 NYY	AL	0.487	75	79	0.636 P	98	56	0.149
1951 DET	AL	0.462	71	83	0.474	73	81	0.012
1951 SLB	AL	0.431 F	66	88	0.338	52	102	-0.093
			616	616		616	616	
1951 BSN	NL	0.589 F	91	63	0.494	76	78	-0.095
1951 BRO	NL	0.537 P	83	71	0.618	97	60	0.081
1951 NYG	NL	0.514	79	75	0.624 P	98	59	0.110
1951 PHI	NL	0.508 F	78	76	0.474	73	81	-0.034
1951 CIN	NL	0.491	76	78	0.442	68	86	-0.049
1951 CHC	NL	0.477 F	73	81	0.403	62	92	-0.075
1951 STL	NL	0.464	71	83	0.526	81	73	0.062
1951 PIT	NL	0.432 F	67	87	0.416	64	90	-0.016
			618	614		619	619	
			1234	1230				

Franchise	League	OPW%	PW	PL	APW%	AW	AL	Diff(+/-)

Franchise	League	OPW%	PW	PL	APW%	AW	AL	Diff(+/-)
1952 CLE	AL	0.631 P	97	57	0.604	93	61	-0.027
1952 CHW	AL	0.576 F	89	65	0.526	81	73	-0.050
1952 NYY	AL	0.545	84	70	0.617 P	95	59	0.071
1952 WSH	AL	0.510 F	79	75	0.506	78	76	-0.003
1952 PHA	AL	0.498 F	77	77	0.513	79	75	0.015
1952 BOS	AL	0.481	74	80	0.494	76	78	0.013
1952 DET	AL	0.425	65	89	0.325	50	104	-0.100
1952 SLB	AL	0.355 F	55	99	0.416	64	90	0.061
			619	613		616	616	
1952 BRO	NL	0.575 P	89	65	0.627 P	96	57	0.052
1952 PHI	NL	0.557	86	68	0.565	87	67	0.008
1952 CHC	NL	0.543 F	84	70	0.500	77	77	-0.043
1952 NYG	NL	0.508	78	76	0.597	92	62	0.089
1952 BSN	NL	0.505	78	76	0.418	64	89	-0.087
1952 STL	NL	0.494	76	78	0.571	88	66	0.077
1952 CIN	NL	0.473	73	81	0.448	69	85	-0.025
1952 PIT	NL	0.367 F	56	98	0.273	42	112	-0.094
			619	613		615	615	
			1239	1225				

Franchise	League	OPW%	PW	PL	APW%	AW	AL	Diff(+/-)
1953 CLE	AL	0.588 P	91	63	0.597	92	62	0.009
1953 WSH	AL	0.586 F	90	64	0.500	76	76	-0.086
1953 NYY	AL	0.523	80	74	0.656 P	99	52	0.133
1953 SLB	AL	0.480 F	74	80	0.351	54	100	-0.130
1953 BOS	AL	0.477	73	81	0.549	84	69	0.072
1953 CHW	AL	0.458 F	71	83	0.578	89	65	0.119
1953 PHA	AL	0.445 F	69	85	0.383	59	95	-0.062
1953 DET	AL	0.440	68	86	0.390	60	94	-0.051
			616	616		613	613	
1953 ML1	NL	0.664 P	102	52	0.597	92	62	-0.066
1953 BRO	NL	0.558	86	68	0.682 P	105	49	0.124
1953 PHI	NL	0.543	84	70	0.539	83	71	-0.004
1953 STL	NL	0.485	75	79	0.539	83	71	0.054
1953 CIN	NL	0.478	74	80	0.442	68	86	-0.037
1953 NYG	NL	0.453	70	84	0.455	70	84	0.002
1953 PIT	NL	0.415 F	64	90	0.325	50	104	-0.091
1953 CHC	NL	0.414	64	90	0.422	65	89	0.008
			618	614		616	616	
			1233	1231				

Franchise	League	OPW%	PW	PL	APW%	AW	AL	Diff(+/-)
1954 CLE	AL	0.635 P	98	56	0.721 P	111	43	0.085
1954 WSH	AL	0.555 F	86	68	0.429	66	88	-0.127
1954 NYY	AL	0.543	84	70	0.669	103	51	0.126
1954 BAL	AL	0.493 F	76	78	0.351	54	100	-0.143
1954 CHW	AL	0.482	74	80	0.610	94	60	0.128
1954 BOS	AL	0.446	69	85	0.448	69	85	0.002
1954 DET	AL	0.433	67	87	0.442	68	86	0.009
1954 PHA	AL	0.413 F	64	90	0.331	51	103	-0.082
			616	616		616	616	

Franchise	League	OPW%	PW	PL	APW%	AW	AL	Diff(+/-)
1954 ML1	NL	0.624 P	96	58	0.578	89	65	-0.047
1954 PHI	NL	0.554	85	69	0.487	75	79	-0.067
1954 NYG	NL	0.537	83	71	0.630 P	97	57	0.093
1954 BRO	NL	0.482	74	80	0.597	92	62	0.115
1954 CHC	NL	0.477	73	81	0.416	64	90	-0.062
1954 CIN	NL	0.477	73	81	0.481	74	80	0.004
1954 STL	NL	0.468	72	82	0.468	72	82	0.000
1954 PIT	NL	0.409 F	63	91	0.344	53	101	-0.065
			620	612		616	616	
			1236	1228				

Franchise	League	OPW%	PW	PL	APW%	AW	AL	Diff(+/-)
1955 DET	AL	0.578 P	89	65	0.513	79	75	-0.065
1955 CLE	AL	0.545	84	70	0.604	93	61	0.059
1955 NYY	AL	0.537	83	71	0.623 P	96	58	0.086
1955 BAL	AL	0.523 F	80	74	0.370	57	97	-0.152
1955 CHW	AL	0.516 F	80	74	0.591	91	63	0.075
1955 BOS	AL	0.490	75	79	0.545	84	70	0.056
1955 WSH	AL	0.442	68	86	0.344	53	101	-0.098
1955 KCA	AL	0.373 F	57	97	0.409	63	91	0.036
			617	615		616	616	
1955 ML1	NL	0.595 P	92	62	0.552	85	69	-0.043
1955 CIN	NL	0.540 F	83	71	0.487	75	79	-0.053
1955 NYG	NL	0.515 F	79	75	0.519	80	74	0.005
1955 BRO	NL	0.508	78	76	0.641 P	98	55	0.133
1955 PHI	NL	0.495 F	76	78	0.500	77	77	0.005
1955 CHC	NL	0.449	69	85	0.471	72	81	0.022
1955 STL	NL	0.446	69	85	0.442	68	86	-0.004
1955 PIT	NL	0.445 F	69	85	0.390	60	94	-0.056
			615	617		615	615	
			1231	1233				

Franchise	League	OPW%	PW	PL	APW%	AW	AL	Diff(+/-)
1956 CLE	AL	0.580 P	89	65	0.571	88	66	-0.009
1956 BAL	AL	0.556 F	86	68	0.448	69	85	-0.107
1956 NYY	AL	0.549	85	69	0.630 P	97	57	0.081
1956 DET	AL	0.515	79	75	0.532	82	72	0.017
1956 BOS	AL	0.485	75	79	0.545	84	70	0.061
1956 CHW	AL	0.472 F	73	81	0.552	85	69	0.080
1956 KCA	AL	0.452 F	70	84	0.338	52	102	-0.114
1956 WSH	AL	0.406 F	62	92	0.383	59	95	-0.022
			618	614		616	616	
1956 ML1	NL	0.599 P	92	62	0.597	92	62	-0.002
1956 CIN	NL	0.573 F	88	66	0.591	91	63	0.018
1956 NYG	NL	0.492 F	76	78	0.435	67	87	-0.057
1956 BRO	NL	0.491	76	78	0.604 P	93	61	0.112
1956 STL	NL	0.483	74	80	0.494	76	78	0.011
1956 PIT	NL	0.475	73	81	0.429	66	88	-0.046
1956 PHI	NL	0.474	73	81	0.461	71	83	-0.013
1956 CHC	NL	0.409 F	63	91	0.390	60	94	-0.019
			615	617		616	616	
			1233	1231				

Franchise	League	OPW%	PW	PL	APW%	AW	AL	Diff(+/-)
1957 KCA	AL	0.568 F	87	67	0.386	59	94	-0.182
1957 BAL	AL	0.564 F	87	67	0.500	76	76	-0.064
1957 CHW	AL	0.560 F	86	68	0.584	90	64	0.025
1957 DET	AL	0.521 P	80	74	0.506	78	76	-0.015
1957 NYY	AL	0.504	78	76	0.636 P	98	56	0.132
1957 CLE	AL	0.490	75	79	0.497	76	77	0.007
1957 BOS	AL	0.458	71	83	0.532	82	72	0.074
1957 WSH	AL	0.341 F	53	101	0.357	55	99	0.016
			617	615		614	614	
1957 ML1	NL	0.617 P	95	59	0.617 P	95	59	0.000
1957 BRO	NL	0.552	85	69	0.545	84	70	-0.006
1957 STL	NL	0.532	82	72	0.565	87	67	0.033
1957 PHI	NL	0.479	74	80	0.500	77	77	0.021
1957 CIN	NL	0.470 F	72	82	0.519	80	74	0.049
1957 PIT	NL	0.456	70	84	0.403	62	92	-0.054
1957 CHC	NL	0.456	70	84	0.403	62	92	-0.053
1957 NYG	NL	0.436	67	87	0.448	69	85	0.012
			616	616		616	616	
			1233	1231				

Franchise	League	OPW%	PW	PL	APW%	AW	AL	Diff(+/-)
1958 DET	AL	0.557 P	86	68	0.500	77	77	-0.057
1958 CLE	AL	0.527	81	73	0.503	77	76	-0.024
1958 NYY	AL	0.520	80	74	0.597 P	92	62	0.077
1958 KCA	AL	0.513 F	79	75	0.474	73	81	-0.039
1958 BAL	AL	0.493 F	76	78	0.484	74	79	-0.009
1958 CHW	AL	0.492 F	76	78	0.532	82	72	0.040
1958 WSH	AL	0.463 F	71	83	0.396	61	93	-0.067
1958 BOS	AL	0.433	67	87	0.513	79	75	0.080
			616	616		615	615	
1958 ML1	NL	0.561 P	86	68	0.597 P	92	62	0.037
1958 PIT	NL	0.545	84	70	0.545	84	70	0.001
1958 CIN	NL	0.541 F	83	71	0.494	76	78	-0.047
1958 STL	NL	0.499	77	77	0.468	72	82	-0.032
1958 CHC	NL	0.486 F	75	79	0.468	72	82	-0.019
1958 LAD	NL	0.484	75	79	0.461	71	83	-0.023
1958 SFG	NL	0.459	71	83	0.519	80	74	0.061
1958 PHI	NL	0.430	66	88	0.448	69	85	0.019
			617	615		616	616	
			1233	1231				

Franchise	League	OPW%	PW	PL	APW%	AW	AL	Diff(+/-)
1959 WSH	AL	0.565 F	87	67	0.409	63	91	-0.156
1959 BAL	AL	0.554 F	85	69	0.481	74	80	-0.073
1959 CLE	AL	0.503 P	77	77	0.578	89	65	0.075
1959 CHW	AL	0.501 F	77	77	0.610 P	94	60	0.109
1959 NYY	AL	0.492	76	78	0.513	79	75	0.021
1959 DET	AL	0.485	75	79	0.494	76	78	0.009
1959 KCA	AL	0.470 F	72	82	0.429	66	88	-0.041
1959 BOS	AL	0.432	67	87	0.487	75	79	0.055

				616	616			616	616	
1959 ML1	NL	0.590 P	91	63	0.551	86	70	-0.038
1959 LAD	NL	0.527	81	73	0.564 P	88	68	0.037
1959 STL	NL	0.521	80	74	0.461	71	83	-0.060
1959 CIN	NL	0.499 F	77	77	0.481	74	80	-0.018
1959 CHC	NL	0.489 F	75	79	0.481	74	80	-0.008
1959 SFG	NL	0.479 F	74	80	0.539	83	71	0.060
1959 PIT	NL	0.461	71	83	0.506	78	76	0.045
1959 PHI	NL	0.438 F	67	87	0.416	64	90	-0.022
			617	615		618	618	
			1233	1231				

Franchise	League	OPW%	PW	PL	APW%	AW	AL	Diff(+/-)
1960 BAL	AL	0.573 P	88	66	0.578	89	65	0.005
1960 CHW	AL	0.562 F	87	67	0.565	87	67	0.003
1960 WSH	AL	0.529 F	81	73	0.474	73	81	-0.055
1960 KCA	AL	0.509 F	78	76	0.377	58	96	-0.133
1960 CLE	AL	0.498	77	77	0.494	76	78	-0.004
1960 NYY	AL	0.457	70	84	0.630 P	97	57	0.173
1960 BOS	AL	0.442	68	86	0.422	65	89	-0.020
1960 DET	AL	0.429	66	88	0.461	71	83	0.032
			616	616		616	616	
1960 SFG	NL	0.578 F	89	65	0.513	79	75	-0.065
1960 LAD	NL	0.529 P	81	73	0.532	82	72	0.004
1960 STL	NL	0.524	81	73	0.558	86	68	0.035
1960 PIT	NL	0.520	80	74	0.617 P	95	59	0.097
1960 ML1	NL	0.519	80	74	0.571	88	66	0.052
1960 CIN	NL	0.482 F	74	80	0.435	67	87	-0.047
1960 CHC	NL	0.430 F	66	88	0.390	60	94	-0.041
1960 PHI	NL	0.415 F	64	90	0.383	59	95	-0.032
			616	616		616	616	
			1231	1233				

Franchise	League	OPW%	PW	PL	APW%	AW	AL	Diff(+/-)
1961 CHW	AL	0.568 F	92	70	0.531	86	76	-0.037
1961 NYY	AL	0.557 P	90	72	0.673 P	109	53	0.115
1961 CLE	AL	0.536	87	75	0.484	78	83	-0.052
1961 DET	AL	0.515	83	79	0.623	101	61	0.109
1961 MIN	AL	0.486 F	79	83	0.438	70	90	-0.049
1961 BAL	AL	0.473	77	85	0.586	95	67	0.114
1961 BOS	AL	0.440	71	91	0.469	76	86	0.029
1961 KCA	AL	0.422 F	68	94	0.379	61	100	-0.043
1961 LAA	AL	0.000 F	0	0	0.435	70	91	0.000
1961 WS1	AL	0.000 F	0	0	0.379	61	100	0.000
			648	648		807	807	
1961 ML1	NL	0.569 P	92	70	0.539	83	71	-0.030
1961 SFG	NL	0.565	92	70	0.552	85	69	-0.013
1961 STL	NL	0.529	86	76	0.519	80	74	-0.010
1961 PIT	NL	0.506	82	80	0.487	75	79	-0.019
1961 LAD	NL	0.500	81	81	0.578	89	65	0.078
1961 CIN	NL	0.498 F	81	81	0.604 P	93	61	0.106
1961 CHC	NL	0.434	70	92	0.416	64	90	-0.019

369

1961 PHI	NL	0.401 F	65	97	0.305	47	107	-0.095
			648	648		616	616
			1296	1296			

Franchise	League	OPW%	PW	PL	APW%	AW	AL	Diff(+/-)
1962 MIN	AL	0.576 P	93	69	0.562	91	71	-0.014
1962 CHW	AL	0.531	86	76	0.525	85	77	-0.006
1962 NYY	AL	0.518	84	78	0.593 P	96	66	0.075
1962 DET	AL	0.513	83	79	0.528	85	76	0.015
1962 CLE	AL	0.487	79	83	0.494	80	82	0.007
1962 BAL	AL	0.478	77	85	0.475	77	85	-0.003
1962 BOS	AL	0.471	76	86	0.475	76	84	0.004
1962 KCA	AL	0.420 F	68	94	0.444	72	90	0.024
1962 LAA	AL	0.000 F	0	0	0.531	86	76	0.000
1962 WS1	AL	0.000 F	0	0	0.373	60	101	0.000
			647	649		808	808
1962 SFG	NL	0.589 P	95	67	0.624 P	103	62	0.035
1962 ML1	NL	0.572	93	69	0.531	86	76	-0.041
1962 CIN	NL	0.560	91	71	0.605	98	64	0.044
1962 PIT	NL	0.525	85	77	0.578	93	68	0.052
1962 LAD	NL	0.469	76	86	0.618	102	63	0.149
1962 STL	NL	0.451	73	89	0.519	84	78	0.067
1962 CHC	NL	0.428	69	93	0.364	59	103	-0.064
1962 PHI	NL	0.388 F	63	99	0.503	81	80	0.115
1962 HOU	NL	0.000 F	0	0	0.400	64	96	0.000
1962 NYM	NL	0.000 F	0	0	0.250	40	120	0.000
			645	651		810	810
			1292	1300			

Franchise	League	OPW%	PW	PL	APW%	AW	AL	Diff(+/-)
1963 MIN	AL	0.608 P	99	63	0.565	91	70	-0.043
1963 CHW	AL	0.550	89	73	0.580	94	68	0.030
1963 NYY	AL	0.537	87	75	0.646 P	104	57	0.109
1963 CLE	AL	0.496	80	82	0.488	79	83	-0.009
1963 BAL	AL	0.483	78	84	0.531	86	76	0.048
1963 DET	AL	0.478	77	85	0.488	79	83	0.010
1963 BOS	AL	0.446	72	90	0.472	76	85	0.026
1963 KCA	AL	0.401 F	65	97	0.451	73	89	0.050
1963 LAA	AL	0.000 F	0	0	0.435	70	91	0.000
1963 WS1	AL	0.000 F	0	0	0.346	56	106	0.000
			648	648		808	808
1963 SFG	NL	0.561 P	91	71	0.543	88	74	-0.017
1963 CIN	NL	0.543	88	74	0.531	86	76	-0.012
1963 STL	NL	0.531	86	76	0.574	93	69	0.043
1963 ML1	NL	0.510	83	79	0.519	84	78	0.008
1963 CHC	NL	0.505	82	80	0.506	82	80	0.001
1963 LAD	NL	0.476	77	85	0.611 P	99	63	0.135
1963 PIT	NL	0.468	76	86	0.457	74	88	-0.012
1963 PHI	NL	0.385 F	62	100	0.537	87	75	0.152
1963 HOU	NL	0.000 F	0	0	0.407	66	96	0.000
1963 NYM	NL	0.000 F	0	0	0.315	51	111	0.000
			645	651		810	810

Franchise	League	OPW%	PW	PL	APW%	AW	AL	Diff(+/-)
1964 NYY	AL	0.569 P	92	70	0.611 P	99	63	0.042
1964 MIN	AL	0.557	90	72	0.488	79	83	-0.070
1964 BAL	AL	0.549	89	73	0.599	97	65	0.050
1964 CHW	AL	0.547	89	73	0.605	98	64	0.058
1964 CLE	AL	0.494	80	82	0.488	79	83	-0.006
1964 DET	AL	0.486	79	83	0.525	85	77	0.039
1964 BOS	AL	0.441	71	91	0.444	72	90	0.004
1964 KCA	AL	0.370 F	60	102	0.352	57	105	-0.018
1964 LAA	AL	0.000 F	0	0	0.506	82	80	0.000
1964 WS1	AL	0.000 F	0	0	0.383	62	100	0.000
			650	646		810	810	
1964 SFG	NL	0.594 P	96	66	0.556	90	72	-0.038
1964 LAD	NL	0.512	83	79	0.494	80	82	-0.018
1964 PIT	NL	0.506	82	80	0.494	80	82	-0.012
1964 CIN	NL	0.492	80	82	0.568	92	70	0.076
1964 STL	NL	0.487	79	83	0.574 P	93	69	0.087
1964 PHI	NL	0.483 F	78	84	0.568	92	70	0.085
1964 ML1	NL	0.473	77	85	0.543	88	74	0.071
1964 CHC	NL	0.461	75	87	0.469	76	86	0.008
1964 HOU	NL	0.000 F	0	0	0.407	66	96	0.000
1964 NYM	NL	0.000 F	0	0	0.327	53	109	0.000
			649	647		810	810	
			1299	1293				

Franchise	League	OPW%	PW	PL	APW%	AW	AL	Diff(+/-)
1965 MIN	AL	0.644 P	104	58	0.630 P	102	60	-0.014
1965 CLE	AL	0.498	81	81	0.537	87	75	0.039
1965 NYY	AL	0.496	80	82	0.475	77	85	-0.021
1965 DET	AL	0.490	79	83	0.549	89	73	0.059
1965 CHW	AL	0.490	79	83	0.586	95	67	0.097
1965 KCA	AL	0.484	78	84	0.364	59	103	-0.120
1965 BAL	AL	0.457	74	88	0.580	94	68	0.123
1965 BOS	AL	0.420	68	94	0.383	62	100	-0.037
1965 CAL	AL	0.000 F	0	0	0.463	75	87	0.000
1965 WS1	AL	0.000 F	0	0	0.432	70	92	0.000
			644	652		810	810	
1965 SFG	NL	0.631 P	102	60	0.586	95	67	-0.045
1965 CHC	NL	0.553 F	90	72	0.444	72	90	-0.109
1965 CIN	NL	0.548	89	73	0.549	89	73	0.001
1965 PHI	NL	0.494	80	82	0.528	85	76	0.034
1965 LAD	NL	0.491	80	82	0.599 P	97	65	0.108
1965 STL	NL	0.488	79	83	0.497	80	81	0.009
1965 ML1	NL	0.478	77	85	0.531	86	76	0.053
1965 HOU	NL	0.474 F	77	85	0.401	65	97	-0.073
1965 PIT	NL	0.461	75	87	0.556	90	72	0.094
1965 NYM	NL	0.376 F	61	101	0.309	50	112	-0.067
			809	811		809	809	
			1454	1462				

Franchise	League	OPW%	PW	PL	APW%	AW	AL	Diff(+/-)
1966 CHW	AL	0.586 P	95	67	0.512	83	79	-0.073
1966 MIN	AL	0.526	85	77	0.549	89	73	0.023
1966 KCA	AL	0.507 F	82	80	0.463	74	86	-0.045
1966 CLE	AL	0.505	82	80	0.500	81	81	-0.005
1966 BAL	AL	0.497	80	82	0.606 P	97	63	0.110
1966 NYY	AL	0.488	79	83	0.440	70	89	-0.047
1966 DET	AL	0.482	78	84	0.543	88	74	0.061
1966 BOS	AL	0.415	67	95	0.444	72	90	0.030
1966 CAL	AL	0.000 F	0	0	0.494	80	82	0.000
1966 WS1	AL	0.000 F	0	0	0.447	71	88	0.000
			649	647		805	805	
1966 SFG	NL	0.604 P	98	64	0.578	93	68	-0.026
1966 CIN	NL	0.537	87	75	0.475	76	84	-0.062
1966 LAD	NL	0.525	85	77	0.586 P	95	67	0.061
1966 CHC	NL	0.510	83	79	0.364	59	103	-0.146
1966 PHI	NL	0.496 F	80	82	0.537	87	75	0.041
1966 ATL	NL	0.493	80	82	0.525	85	77	0.032
1966 PIT	NL	0.485	79	83	0.568	92	70	0.083
1966 HOU	NL	0.462 F	75	87	0.444	72	90	-0.017
1966 STL	NL	0.454	74	88	0.512	83	79	0.058
1966 NYM	NL	0.438 F	71	91	0.410	66	95	-0.028
			811	809		808	808	
			1459	1457				

Franchise	League	OPW%	PW	PL	APW%	AW	AL	Diff(+/-)
1967 MIN	AL	0.582 P	94	68	0.562	91	71	-0.020
1967 BOS	AL	0.535	87	75	0.568 P	92	70	0.033
1967 CHW	AL	0.534	86	76	0.549	89	73	0.016
1967 DET	AL	0.527	85	77	0.562	91	71	0.034
1967 CLE	AL	0.492	80	82	0.463	75	87	-0.029
1967 CAL	AL	0.478 F	78	84	0.522	84	77	0.043
1967 KCA	AL	0.458	74	88	0.385	62	99	-0.073
1967 NYY	AL	0.456	74	88	0.444	72	90	-0.011
1967 BAL	AL	0.433	70	92	0.472	76	85	0.039
1967 WS1	AL	0.000 F	0	0	0.472	76	85	0.000
			728	730		808	808	
1967 SFG	NL	0.592 P	96	66	0.562	91	71	-0.030
1967 CHC	NL	0.581	94	68	0.540	87	74	-0.041
1967 CIN	NL	0.580	94	68	0.537	87	75	-0.043
1967 PHI	NL	0.518	84	78	0.506	82	80	-0.012
1967 LAD	NL	0.515	83	79	0.451	73	89	-0.064
1967 NYM	NL	0.483 F	78	84	0.377	61	101	-0.107
1967 STL	NL	0.460	75	87	0.627 P	101	60	0.167
1967 ATL	NL	0.439	71	91	0.475	77	85	0.037
1967 HOU	NL	0.435 F	70	92	0.426	69	93	-0.009
1967 PIT	NL	0.386	62	100	0.500	81	81	0.114
			808	812		809	809	
			1537	1541				

Franchise	League	OPW%	PW	PL	APW%	AW	AL	Diff(+/-)

Franchise	League/Div.	OPW%	PW	PL	APW%	AW	AL	Diff(+/-)
1968 DET	AL	0.560 P	91	71	0.636 P	103	59	0.076
1968 OAK	AL	0.559	90	72	0.506	82	80	-0.052
1968 NYY	AL	0.532	86	76	0.512	83	79	-0.020
1968 BOS	AL	0.515	83	79	0.531	86	76	0.016
1968 MIN	AL	0.511	83	79	0.488	79	83	-0.023
1968 CHW	AL	0.505	82	80	0.414	67	95	-0.091
1968 CLE	AL	0.493	80	82	0.534	86	75	0.041
1968 CAL	AL	0.491 F	80	82	0.414	67	95	-0.077
1968 BAL	AL	0.484	78	84	0.562	91	71	0.078
1968 WS1	AL	0.351 F	57	105	0.404	65	96	0.052
			810	810		809	809	
1968 NYM	NL	0.560 F	91	71	0.451	73	89	-0.110
1968 SFG	NL	0.549 P	89	73	0.543	88	74	-0.005
1968 CHC	NL	0.534	87	75	0.519	84	78	-0.016
1968 ATL	NL	0.517	84	78	0.500	81	81	-0.017
1968 CIN	NL	0.507	82	80	0.512	83	79	0.005
1968 PHI	NL	0.497	80	82	0.469	76	86	-0.028
1968 LAD	NL	0.489	79	83	0.469	76	86	-0.020
1968 STL	NL	0.473	77	85	0.599 P	97	65	0.126
1968 PIT	NL	0.453	73	89	0.494	80	82	0.041
1968 HOU	NL	0.418 F	68	94	0.444	72	90	0.026
			809	811		810	810	
			1619	1621				

Franchise	League/Div.	OPW%	PW	PL	APW%	AW	AL	Diff(+/-)
1969 WS1	AL East	0.545 F	88	74	0.531	86	76	-0.014
1969 BOS	AL East	0.514 D	83	79	0.537	87	75	0.023
1969 DET	AL East	0.508	82	80	0.556	90	72	0.047
1969 NYY	AL East	0.501	81	81	0.497	80	81	-0.004
1969 BAL	AL East	0.498	81	81	0.673 P	109	53	0.175
1969 CLE	AL East	0.427	69	93	0.385	62	99	-0.042
1969 MIN	AL West	0.529 P	86	76	0.599 D	97	65	0.070
1969 OAK	AL West	0.521	84	78	0.543	88	74	0.023
1969 CHW	AL West	0.513	83	79	0.420	68	94	-0.093
1969 CAL	AL West	0.429	69	93	0.438	71	91	0.010
1969 KCR	AL West	0.000 F	0	0	0.426	69	93	0.000
1969 SE1	AL West	0.000 F	0	0	0.395	64	98	0.000
			807	813		971	971	
1969 NYM	NL East	0.537 D	87	75	0.617 P	100	62	0.080
1969 CHC	NL East	0.521	84	78	0.568	92	70	0.047
1969 PHI	NL East	0.482	78	84	0.389	63	99	-0.093
1969 PIT	NL East	0.476	77	85	0.543	88	74	0.067
1969 STL	NL East	0.382	62	100	0.537	87	75	0.155
1969 MON	NL East	0.000 F	0	0	0.321	52	110	0.000
1969 CIN	NL West	0.619 P	100	62	0.549	89	73	-0.069
1969 SFG	NL West	0.529	86	76	0.556	90	72	0.027
1969 HOU	NL West	0.489	79	83	0.500	81	81	0.011
1969 LAD	NL West	0.488	79	83	0.525	85	77	0.037
1969 ATL	NL West	0.462	75	87	0.574 D	93	69	0.112
1969 SDP	NL West	0.000 F	0	0	0.321	52	110	0.000
			807	813		972	972	

373

Franchise	League/Div.	OPW%	PW	PL	APW%	AW	AL	Diff(+/-)
1970 NYY	AL East	0.551 P	89	73	0.574	93	69	0.023
1970 BAL	AL East	0.532	86	76	0.667 P	108	54	0.135
1970 BOS	AL East	0.528	85	77	0.537	87	75	0.009
1970 CLE	AL East	0.494	80	82	0.469	76	86	-0.025
1970 DET	AL East	0.458	74	88	0.488	79	83	0.030
1970 WS1	AL East	0.390 F	63	99	0.432	70	92	0.042
1970 MIN	AL West	0.540 D	87	75	0.605 D	98	64	0.065
1970 CAL	AL West	0.527	85	77	0.531	86	76	0.003
1970 OAK	AL West	0.502	81	81	0.549	89	73	0.047
1970 CHW	AL West	0.480	78	84	0.346	56	106	-0.135
1970 KCR	AL West	0.000 F	0	0	0.401	65	97	0.000
1970 MIL	AL West	0.000 F	0	0	0.401	65	97	0.000
			810	810		972	972	
1970 CHC	NL East	0.561 P	91	71	0.519	84	78	-0.042
1970 PIT	NL East	0.528	85	77	0.549 D	89	73	0.022
1970 NYM	NL East	0.478	77	85	0.512	83	79	0.035
1970 PHI	NL East	0.446	72	90	0.453	73	88	0.008
1970 STL	NL East	0.426	69	93	0.469	76	86	0.044
1970 MON	NL East	0.000 F	0	0	0.451	73	89	0.000
1970 CIN	NL West	0.533 D	86	76	0.630 P	102	60	0.097
1970 HOU	NL West	0.510	83	79	0.488	79	83	-0.022
1970 ATL	NL West	0.508	82	80	0.469	76	86	-0.039
1970 LAD	NL West	0.500	81	81	0.540	87	74	0.040
1970 SFG	NL West	0.498	81	81	0.531	86	76	0.033
1970 SDP	NL West	0.000 F	0	0	0.389	63	99	0.000
			808	812		971	971	
			1618	1622				

Franchise	League/Div.	OPW%	PW	PL	APW%	AW	AL	Diff(+/-)
1971 NYY	AL East	0.560 P	91	71	0.506	82	80	-0.054
1971 DET	AL East	0.536	87	75	0.562	91	71	0.025
1971 BOS	AL East	0.512	83	79	0.525	85	77	0.013
1971 BAL	AL East	0.508	82	80	0.639 P	101	57	0.131
1971 WS1	AL East	0.462 F	75	87	0.396	63	96	-0.066
1971 CLE	AL East	0.377	61	101	0.370	60	102	-0.006
1971 MIN	AL West	0.535 D	87	75	0.463	74	86	-0.073
1971 OAK	AL West	0.529	86	76	0.627 D	101	60	0.099
1971 CHW	AL West	0.494	80	82	0.488	79	83	-0.006
1971 CAL	AL West	0.478	77	85	0.469	76	86	-0.008
1971 KCR	AL West	0.000 F	0	0	0.528	85	76	0.000
1971 MIL	AL West	0.000 F	0	0	0.429	69	92	0.000
			808	812		966	966	
1971 PIT	NL East	0.530 P	86	76	0.599 P	97	65	0.069
1971 CHC	NL East	0.512	83	79	0.512	83	79	0.000
1971 NYM	NL East	0.510	83	79	0.512	83	79	0.003
1971 STL	NL East	0.496	80	82	0.556	90	72	0.060
1971 PHI	NL East	0.440	71	91	0.414	67	95	-0.027
1971 MON	NL East	0.000 F	0	0	0.379	61	100	0.000

Franchise	League/Div.	OPW%	PW	PL	APW%	AW	AL	Diff(+/-)
1971 CIN	NL West	0.527 D	85	77	0.488	79	83	-0.040
1971 HOU	NL West	0.520	84	78	0.488	79	83	-0.032
1971 ATL	NL West	0.503	82	80	0.506	82	80	0.003
1971 SFG	NL West	0.484	78	84	0.556 D	90	72	0.072
1971 LAD	NL West	0.476	77	85	0.549	89	73	0.073
1971 SDP	NL West	0.000 F	0	0	0.441	71	90	0.000
			810	810		971	971	
			1618	1622				

Franchise	League/Div.	OPW%	PW	PL	APW%	AW	AL	Diff(+/-)
1972 BAL	AL East	0.568 P	92	70	0.519	80	74	-0.049
1972 BOS	AL East	0.547	89	73	0.548	85	70	0.001
1972 DET	AL East	0.538	87	75	0.551 D	86	70	0.013
1972 NYY	AL East	0.535	87	75	0.510	79	76	-0.025
1972 CLE	AL East	0.460	74	88	0.462	72	84	0.002
1972 MIL	AL East	0.000 F	0	0	0.417	65	91	0.000
1972 OAK	AL West	0.554 D	90	72	0.600 P	93	62	0.046
1972 MIN	AL West	0.526	85	77	0.500	77	77	-0.026
1972 CAL	AL West	0.475	77	85	0.484	75	80	0.009
1972 CHW	AL West	0.452	73	89	0.565	87	67	0.113
1972 TEX	AL West	0.339 F	55	107	0.351	54	100	0.012
1972 KCR	AL West	0.000 F	0	0	0.494	76	78	0.000
			809	811		929	929	
1972 CHC	NL East	0.559 P	91	71	0.548	85	70	-0.011
1972 PIT	NL East	0.524	85	77	0.619 P	96	59	0.095
1972 STL	NL East	0.474	77	85	0.481	75	81	0.007
1972 PHI	NL East	0.451	73	89	0.378	59	97	-0.073
1972 NYM	NL East	0.424	69	93	0.532	83	73	0.108
1972 MON	NL East	0.000 F	0	0	0.379	58	95	0.000
1972 CIN	NL West	0.555 D	90	72	0.617 D	95	59	0.062
1972 SFG	NL West	0.546	88	74	0.445	69	86	-0.101
1972 HOU	NL West	0.536	87	75	0.549	84	69	0.013
1972 LAD	NL West	0.502	81	81	0.548	85	70	0.046
1972 ATL	NL West	0.428	69	93	0.455	70	84	0.027
1972 SDP	NL West	0.000 F	0	0	0.449	70	86	0.000
			810	810		929	929	
			1619	1621				

Franchise	League/Div.	OPW%	PW	PL	APW%	AW	AL	Diff(+/-)
1973 BAL	AL East	0.599 P	97	65	0.599 P	97	65	0.000
1973 NYY	AL East	0.540	87	75	0.494	80	82	-0.046
1973 BOS	AL East	0.513	83	79	0.549	89	73	0.036
1973 DET	AL East	0.507	82	80	0.525	85	77	0.018
1973 MIL	AL East	0.490 F	79	83	0.457	74	88	-0.033
1973 CLE	AL East	0.435	70	92	0.438	71	91	0.003
1973 OAK	AL West	0.567 D	92	70	0.580 D	94	68	0.013
1973 MIN	AL West	0.516	84	78	0.500	81	81	-0.016
1973 CHW	AL West	0.499 F	81	81	0.475	77	85	-0.023
1973 CAL	AL West	0.420	68	94	0.488	79	83	0.068
1973 TEX	AL West	0.413 F	67	95	0.352	57	105	-0.061
1973 KCR	AL West	0.000 F	0	0	0.543	88	74	0.000
			891	891		972	972	

Franchise	League/Div.	OPW%	PW	PL	APW%	AW	AL	Diff(+/-)
1973 NYM	NL East	0.512 D	83	79	0.509 D	82	79	-0.002
1973 CHC	NL East	0.505	82	80	0.478	77	84	-0.027
1973 PHI	NL East	0.488	79	83	0.438	71	91	-0.050
1973 STL	NL East	0.446	72	90	0.500	81	81	0.054
1973 PIT	NL East	0.444	72	90	0.494	80	82	0.050
1973 MON	NL East	0.000 F	0	0	0.488	79	83	0.000
1973 HOU	NL West	0.567 P	92	70	0.506	82	80	-0.060
1973 LAD	NL West	0.552	89	73	0.590	95	66	0.038
1973 CIN	NL West	0.551	89	73	0.611 P	99	63	0.060
1973 ATL	NL West	0.510	83	79	0.472	76	85	-0.038
1973 SFG	NL West	0.498	81	81	0.543	88	74	0.045
1973 SDP	NL West	0.425 F	69	93	0.370	60	102	-0.055
			891	891		970	970	
			1782	1782				

Franchise	League/Div.	OPW%	PW	PL	APW%	AW	AL	Diff(+/-)
1974 BOS	AL East	0.545 D	88	74	0.519	84	78	-0.026
1974 DET	AL East	0.513	83	79	0.444	72	90	-0.069
1974 MIL	AL East	0.493 F	80	82	0.469	76	86	-0.024
1974 BAL	AL East	0.492	80	82	0.562 P	91	71	0.069
1974 CLE	AL East	0.485	79	83	0.475	77	85	-0.009
1974 NYY	AL East	0.448	73	89	0.549	89	73	0.102
1974 OAK	AL West	0.613 P	99	63	0.556 D	90	72	-0.057
1974 MIN	AL West	0.545	88	74	0.506	82	80	-0.039
1974 CHW	AL West	0.514 F	83	79	0.500	80	80	-0.014
1974 KCR	AL West	0.456 F	74	88	0.475	77	85	0.019
1974 CAL	AL West	0.451	73	89	0.420	68	94	-0.031
1974 TEX	AL West	0.448 F	73	89	0.525	84	76	0.077
			972	972		970	970	
1974 PHI	NL East	0.533 D	86	76	0.494	80	82	-0.039
1974 MON	NL East	0.522 F	85	77	0.491	79	82	-0.031
1974 PIT	NL East	0.516	84	78	0.543 D	88	74	0.027
1974 NYM	NL East	0.492	80	82	0.438	71	91	-0.054
1974 CHC	NL East	0.460	75	87	0.407	66	96	-0.053
1974 STL	NL East	0.458	74	88	0.534	86	75	0.077
1974 ATL	NL West	0.567 P	92	70	0.543	88	74	-0.024
1974 CIN	NL West	0.557	90	72	0.605	98	64	0.048
1974 LAD	NL West	0.545	88	74	0.630 P	102	60	0.085
1974 HOU	NL West	0.517	84	78	0.500	81	81	-0.017
1974 SFG	NL West	0.476	77	85	0.444	72	90	-0.031
1974 SDP	NL West	0.352 F	57	105	0.370	60	102	0.018
			971	973		971	971	
			1943	1945				

Franchise	League/Div.	OPW%	PW	PL	APW%	AW	AL	Diff(+/-)
1975 BOS	AL East	0.576 D	93	69	0.594 D	95	65	0.018
1975 NYY	AL East	0.520	84	78	0.519	83	77	-0.001
1975 MIL	AL East	0.494 F	80	82	0.420	68	94	-0.075
1975 BAL	AL East	0.459	74	88	0.566	90	69	0.107
1975 CLE	AL East	0.430	70	92	0.497	79	80	0.067
1975 DET	AL East	0.426	69	93	0.358	57	102	-0.067

Franchise	League/Div.	OPW%	PW	PL	APW%	AW	AL	Diff(+/-)
1975 KCR	AL West	0.604 F	98	64	0.562	91	71	-0.042
1975 OAK	AL West	0.582 P	94	68	0.605 P	98	64	0.023
1975 MIN	AL West	0.515	84	78	0.478	76	83	-0.038
1975 CHW	AL West	0.474 F	77	85	0.466	75	86	-0.009
1975 CAL	AL West	0.474	77	85	0.447	72	89	-0.027
1975 TEX	AL West	0.437	71	91	0.488	79	83	0.051
			971	973		963	963	
1975 CHC	NL East	0.536 D	87	75	0.463	75	87	-0.073
1975 PIT	NL East	0.534	87	75	0.571 D	92	69	0.037
1975 MON	NL East	0.503 F	81	81	0.463	75	87	-0.040
1975 PHI	NL East	0.497	80	82	0.531	86	76	0.034
1975 NYM	NL East	0.479	78	84	0.506	82	80	0.027
1975 STL	NL East	0.463	75	87	0.506	82	80	0.043
1975 CIN	NL West	0.575 P	93	69	0.667 P	108	54	0.092
1975 HOU	NL West	0.535	87	75	0.398	64	97	-0.137
1975 LAD	NL West	0.508	82	80	0.543	88	74	0.035
1975 SFG	NL West	0.478	77	85	0.497	80	81	0.019
1975 ATL	NL West	0.458	74	88	0.416	67	94	-0.042
1975 SDP	NL West	0.421 F	68	94	0.438	71	91	0.017
			970	974		970	970	
			1940	1948				

Franchise	League/Div.	OPW%	PW	PL	APW%	AW	AL	Diff(+/-)
1976 DET	AL East	0.525 F	85	77	0.460	74	87	-0.065
1976 BAL	AL East	0.524 D	85	77	0.543	88	74	0.019
1976 CLE	AL East	0.514	83	79	0.509	81	78	-0.004
1976 NYY	AL East	0.502 F	81	81	0.610 P	97	62	0.108
1976 BOS	AL East	0.494	80	82	0.512	83	79	0.019
1976 MIL	AL East	0.482 F	78	84	0.410	66	95	-0.072
1976 OAK	AL West	0.577 P	93	69	0.540	87	74	-0.036
1976 KCR	AL West	0.537 F	87	75	0.556 D	90	72	0.019
1976 MIN	AL West	0.510	83	79	0.525	85	77	0.015
1976 CAL	AL West	0.480	78	84	0.469	76	86	-0.011
1976 TEX	AL West	0.471	76	86	0.469	76	86	-0.002
1976 CHW	AL West	0.382	62	100	0.398	64	97	0.015
			972	972		967	967	
1976 PIT	NL East	0.566 P	92	70	0.568	92	70	0.002
1976 PHI	NL East	0.502	81	81	0.623 D	101	61	0.121
1976 CHC	NL East	0.499	81	81	0.463	75	87	-0.036
1976 STL	NL East	0.456	74	88	0.444	72	90	-0.011
1976 NYM	NL East	0.449	73	89	0.531	86	76	0.082
1976 MON	NL East	0.447 F	72	90	0.340	55	107	-0.108
1976 CIN	NL West	0.562 D	91	71	0.630 P	102	60	0.068
1976 HOU	NL West	0.526	85	77	0.494	80	82	-0.032
1976 LAD	NL West	0.525	85	77	0.568	92	70	0.043
1976 ATL	NL West	0.491	79	83	0.432	70	92	-0.059
1976 SDP	NL West	0.489 F	79	83	0.451	73	89	-0.038
1976 SFG	NL West	0.482	78	84	0.457	74	88	-0.025
			971	973		972	972	
			1942	1946				

Franchise	League/Div.	OPW%	PW	PL	APW%	AW	AL	Diff(+/-)
1977 BOS	AL East	0.554 D	90	72	0.602	97	64	0.048
1977 BAL	AL East	0.510	83	79	0.602	97	64	0.092
1977 CLE	AL East	0.484	78	84	0.441	71	90	-0.043
1977 DET	AL East	0.482	78	84	0.457	74	88	-0.025
1977 NYY	AL East	0.458	74	88	0.617 D	100	62	0.159
1977 MIL	AL East	0.407 F	66	96	0.414	67	95	0.006
1977 TOR	AL East	0.000 F	0	0	0.335	54	107	0.000
1977 KCR	AL West	0.598 P	97	65	0.630 P	102	60	0.032
1977 MIN	AL West	0.587	95	67	0.522	84	77	-0.065
1977 OAK	AL West	0.535	87	75	0.391	63	98	-0.143
1977 TEX	AL West	0.478 F	77	85	0.580	94	68	0.103
1977 CAL	AL West	0.458	74	88	0.457	74	88	-0.001
1977 CHW	AL West	0.435 F	70	92	0.556	90	72	0.120
1977 SEA	AL West	0.000 F	0	0	0.395	64	98	0.000
			970	974		1131	1131	
1977 STL	NL East	0.529 D	86	76	0.512	83	79	-0.017
1977 PHI	NL East	0.527	85	77	0.623 P	101	61	0.096
1977 PIT	NL East	0.524	85	77	0.593	96	66	0.068
1977 CHC	NL East	0.499 F	81	81	0.500	81	81	0.001
1977 MON	NL East	0.479 F	78	84	0.463	75	87	-0.016
1977 NYM	NL East	0.457	74	88	0.395	64	98	-0.062
1977 HOU	NL West	0.567 P	92	70	0.500	81	81	-0.067
1977 SFG	NL West	0.530	86	76	0.463	75	87	-0.067
1977 LAD	NL West	0.497	80	82	0.605 D	98	64	0.108
1977 CIN	NL West	0.473	77	85	0.543	88	74	0.071
1977 ATL	NL West	0.470	76	86	0.377	61	101	-0.094
1977 SDP	NL West	0.439	71	91	0.426	69	93	-0.013
			971	973		972	972	
			1940	1948				

Franchise	League/Div.	OPW%	PW	PL	APW%	AW	AL	Diff(+/-)
1978 CLE	AL East	0.531 D	86	76	0.434	69	90	-0.097
1978 MIL	AL East	0.531	86	76	0.574	93	69	0.043
1978 BAL	AL East	0.517	84	78	0.559	90	71	0.042
1978 DET	AL East	0.511	83	79	0.531	86	76	0.020
1978 BOS	AL East	0.489	79	83	0.607	99	64	0.118
1978 NYY	AL East	0.458	74	88	0.613 P	100	63	0.156
1978 TOR	AL East	0.000 F	0	0	0.366	59	102	0.000
1978 KCR	AL West	0.543 P	88	74	0.568 D	92	70	0.025
1978 OAK	AL West	0.530	86	76	0.426	69	93	-0.104
1978 CAL	AL West	0.488	79	83	0.537	87	75	0.049
1978 MIN	AL West	0.481	78	84	0.451	73	89	-0.030
1978 TEX	AL West	0.458	74	88	0.537	87	75	0.079
1978 CHW	AL West	0.454 F	74	88	0.441	71	90	-0.013
1978 SEA	AL West	0.000 F	0	0	0.350	56	104	0.000
			971	973		1131	1131	
1978 PIT	NL East	0.559 P	91	71	0.547	88	73	-0.012
1978 MON	NL East	0.553	90	72	0.469	76	86	-0.083
1978 PHI	NL East	0.547	89	73	0.556 D	90	72	0.009
1978 STL	NL East	0.452	73	89	0.426	69	93	-0.026

378

Franchise	League/Div.	OPW%	PW	PL	APW%	AW	AL	Diff(+/-)
1978 NYM	**NL East**	0.451	73	89	0.407	66	96	-0.043
1978 CHC	**NL East**	0.445 F	72	90	0.488	79	83	0.043
1978 LAD	**NL West**	0.553 D	90	72	0.586 P	95	67	0.033
1978 SFG	**NL West**	0.532	86	76	0.549	89	73	0.017
1978 SDP	**NL West**	0.509	82	80	0.519	84	78	0.009
1978 CIN	**NL West**	0.502	81	81	0.571	92	69	0.069
1978 HOU	**NL West**	0.459	74	88	0.457	74	88	-0.002
1978 ATL	**NL West**	0.430	70	92	0.426	69	93	-0.004
			971	973		971	971	
			1941	1947				

Franchise	League/Div.	OPW%	PW	PL	APW%	AW	AL	Diff(+/-)
1979 MIL	**AL East**	0.554 D	90	72	0.590	95	66	0.036
1979 BOS	**AL East**	0.533	86	76	0.569	91	69	0.036
1979 CLE	**AL East**	0.510	83	79	0.503	81	80	-0.007
1979 BAL	**AL East**	0.503	82	80	0.642 P	102	57	0.138
1979 NYY	**AL East**	0.486	79	83	0.556	89	71	0.070
1979 DET	**AL East**	0.471	76	86	0.528	85	76	0.057
1979 TOR	**AL East**	0.000 F	0	0	0.327	53	109	0.000
1979 KCR	**AL West**	0.564 P	91	71	0.525	85	77	-0.039
1979 MIN	**AL West**	0.513	83	79	0.506	82	80	-0.007
1979 CAL	**AL West**	0.497 F	80	82	0.543 D	88	74	0.046
1979 CHW	**AL West**	0.466 F	76	86	0.456	73	87	-0.010
1979 OAK	**AL West**	0.455	74	88	0.333	54	108	-0.122
1979 TEX	**AL West**	0.445	72	90	0.512	83	79	0.068
1979 SEA	**AL West**	0.000 F	0	0	0.414	67	95	0.000
			972	972		1128	1128	
1979 MON	**NL East**	0.572 P	93	69	0.594	95	65	0.022
1979 PHI	**NL East**	0.515	83	79	0.519	84	78	0.003
1979 CHC	**NL East**	0.497 F	81	81	0.494	80	82	-0.003
1979 PIT	**NL East**	0.490	79	83	0.605 P	98	64	0.115
1979 STL	**NL East**	0.488	79	83	0.531	86	76	0.042
1979 NYM	**NL East**	0.479	78	84	0.389	63	99	-0.090
1979 HOU	**NL West**	0.542 D	88	74	0.549	89	73	0.007
1979 SDP	**NL West**	0.508	82	80	0.422	68	93	-0.086
1979 LAD	**NL West**	0.490	79	83	0.488	79	83	-0.002
1979 CIN	**NL West**	0.488	79	83	0.559 D	90	71	0.071
1979 SFG	**NL West**	0.476	77	85	0.438	71	91	-0.037
1979 ATL	**NL West**	0.458	74	88	0.413	66	94	-0.045
			972	972		969	969	
			1944	1944				

Franchise	League/Div.	OPW%	PW	PL	APW%	AW	AL	Diff(+/-)
1980 MIL	**AL East**	0.576 D	93	69	0.531	86	76	-0.045
1980 DET	**AL East**	0.507	82	80	0.519	84	78	0.012
1980 BOS	**AL East**	0.495	80	82	0.519	83	77	0.023
1980 BAL	**AL East**	0.489	79	83	0.617	100	62	0.128
1980 CLE	**AL East**	0.475	77	85	0.494	79	81	0.019
1980 NYY	**AL East**	0.442	72	90	0.636 P	103	59	0.194
1980 TOR	**AL East**	0.000 F	0	0	0.414	67	95	0.000
1980 KCR	**AL West**	0.596 P	97	65	0.599 D	97	65	0.003

Franchise	League/Div.	OPW%	PW	PL	APW%	AW	AL	Diff(+/-)
1980 OAK	AL West	0.567	92	70	0.512	83	79	-0.054
1980 MIN	AL West	0.506	82	80	0.478	77	84	-0.027
1980 ANA	AL West	0.482	78	84	0.406	65	95	-0.076
1980 TEX	AL West	0.453	73	89	0.472	76	85	0.019
1980 CHW	AL West	0.396 F	64	98	0.438	70	90	0.041
1980 SEA	AL West	0.000 F	0	0	0.364	59	103	0.000
			969	975		1129	1129	
1980 STL	NL East	0.540 D	88	74	0.457	74	88	-0.083
1980 CHC	NL East	0.520 F	84	78	0.395	64	98	-0.125
1980 PIT	NL East	0.514	83	79	0.512	83	79	-0.001
1980 MON	NL East	0.513	83	79	0.556	90	72	0.042
1980 PHI	NL East	0.500	81	81	0.562 D	91	71	0.061
1980 NYM	NL East	0.476	77	85	0.414	67	95	-0.062
1980 HOU	NL West	0.598 P	97	65	0.571 P	93	70	-0.027
1980 ATL	NL West	0.498	81	81	0.503	81	80	0.005
1980 CIN	NL West	0.483	78	84	0.549	89	73	0.067
1980 LAD	NL West	0.463	75	87	0.564	92	71	0.102
1980 SFG	NL West	0.457	74	88	0.466	75	86	0.009
1980 SDP	NL West	0.444	72	90	0.451	73	89	0.007
			973	971		972	972	
			1876	1688				

Franchise	League/Div.	OPW%	PW	PL	APW%	AW	AL	Diff(+/-)
1981 DET	AL East	0.531 D	86	76	0.550	60	49	0.019
1981 BOS	AL East	0.516	84	78	0.546	59	49	0.030
1981 MIL	AL East	0.510 F	83	79	0.569 D	62	47	0.059
1981 BAL	AL East	0.495	80	82	0.562	59	46	0.067
1981 NYY	AL East	0.440	71	91	0.551	59	48	0.111
1981 TOR	AL East	0.402 F	65	97	0.349	37	69	-0.053
1981 CLE	AL East	0.400 F	65	97	0.505	52	51	0.105
1981 OAK	AL West	0.630 P	102	60	0.587 P	64	45	-0.043
1981 CHW	AL West	0.567 F	92	70	0.509	54	52	-0.057
1981 CAL	AL West	0.547	89	73	0.464	51	59	-0.083
1981 KCR	AL West	0.498	81	81	0.485	50	53	-0.012
1981 TEX	AL West	0.479	78	84	0.543	57	48	0.064
1981 MIN	AL West	0.449	73	89	0.376	41	68	-0.072
1981 SEA	AL West	0.000 F	0	0	0.404	44	65	0.000
			1047	1059		749	749	
1981 STL	NL East	0.555 P	90	72	0.578 D	59	43	0.023
1981 MON	NL East	0.533	86	76	0.556	60	48	0.022
1981 CHC	NL East	0.498 F	81	81	0.369	38	65	-0.129
1981 PHI	NL East	0.467	76	86	0.551	59	48	0.084
1981 PIT	NL East	0.465	75	87	0.451	46	56	-0.014
1981 NYM	NL East	0.464	75	87	0.398	41	62	-0.066
1981 LAD	NL West	0.542 D	88	74	0.573	63	47	0.030
1981 SFG	NL West	0.534	87	75	0.505	56	55	-0.030
1981 ATL	NL West	0.526	85	77	0.472	50	56	-0.054
1981 HOU	NL West	0.477	77	85	0.555	61	49	0.078
1981 CIN	NL West	0.472	77	85	0.611 P	66	42	0.139
1981 SDP	NL West	0.467	76	86	0.373	41	69	-0.094
			972	972		640	640	

Franchise	League/Div.	OPW%	PW	PL	APW%	AW	AL	Diff(+/-)
1982 BAL	AL East	0.551 P	89	73	0.580	94	68	0.029
1982 MIL	AL East	0.542	88	74	0.586 P	95	67	0.044
1982 BOS	AL East	0.517	84	78	0.549	89	73	0.032
1982 DET	AL East	0.510	83	79	0.512	83	79	0.002
1982 NYY	AL East	0.472	77	85	0.488	79	83	0.015
1982 TOR	AL East	0.469 F	76	86	0.481	78	84	0.012
1982 CLE	AL East	0.458	74	88	0.481	78	84	0.023
1982 OAK	AL West	0.529 D	86	76	0.420	68	94	-0.109
1982 KCR	AL West	0.526	85	77	0.556	90	72	0.029
1982 CHW	AL West	0.523 F	85	77	0.537	87	75	0.014
1982 CAL	AL West	0.517	84	78	0.574 D	93	69	0.057
1982 TEX	AL West	0.473	77	85	0.395	64	98	-0.078
1982 SEA	AL West	0.463 F	75	87	0.469	76	86	0.006
1982 MIN	AL West	0.436	71	91	0.370	60	102	-0.066
			1132	1136		1134	1134	
1982 MON	NL East	0.581 P	94	68	0.531	86	76	-0.050
1982 STL	NL East	0.552	89	73	0.568 P	92	70	0.016
1982 PIT	NL East	0.535	87	75	0.519	84	78	-0.017
1982 PHI	NL East	0.504	82	80	0.549	89	73	0.045
1982 CHC	NL East	0.461 F	75	87	0.451	73	89	-0.010
1982 NYM	NL East	0.427	69	93	0.401	65	97	-0.026
1982 ATL	NL West	0.540 D	87	75	0.549 D	89	73	0.010
1982 LAD	NL West	0.519	84	78	0.543	88	74	0.024
1982 CIN	NL West	0.495	80	82	0.377	61	101	-0.119
1982 SDP	NL West	0.480	78	84	0.500	81	81	0.020
1982 HOU	NL West	0.450 F	73	89	0.475	77	85	0.025
1982 SFG	NL West	0.446	72	90	0.537	87	75	0.091
			970	974		972	972	
			2102	2110				

Franchise	League/Div.	OPW%	PW	PL	APW%	AW	AL	Diff(+/-)
1983 BAL	AL East	0.604 P	98	64	0.605 D	98	64	0.001
1983 TOR	AL East	0.603 F	98	64	0.549	89	73	-0.053
1983 MIL	AL East	0.543	88	74	0.537	87	75	-0.006
1983 NYY	AL East	0.529	86	76	0.562	91	71	0.033
1983 BOS	AL East	0.522	85	77	0.481	78	84	-0.041
1983 DET	AL East	0.481	78	84	0.568	92	70	0.087
1983 CLE	AL East	0.407 F	66	96	0.432	70	92	0.025
1983 CHW	AL West	0.548 F	89	73	0.611 P	99	63	0.063
1983 OAK	AL West	0.498 D	81	81	0.457	74	88	-0.041
1983 CAL	AL West	0.485	78	84	0.432	70	92	-0.052
1983 KCR	AL West	0.479	78	84	0.488	79	83	0.009
1983 TEX	AL West	0.461	75	87	0.475	77	85	0.014
1983 MIN	AL West	0.418 F	68	94	0.432	70	92	0.014
1983 SEA	AL West	0.402 F	65	97	0.370	60	102	-0.031
			1131	1137		1134	1134	
1983 STL	NL East	0.517 D	84	78	0.488	79	83	-0.030
1983 MON	NL East	0.513	83	79	0.506	82	80	-0.006

Franchise	League/Div.	OPW%	PW	PL	APW%	AW	AL	Diff(+/-)
1983 PHI	NL East	0.498	81	81	0.556 D	90	72	0.058
1983 PIT	NL East	0.478	77	85	0.519	84	78	0.040
1983 CHC	NL East	0.461 F	75	87	0.438	71	91	-0.022
1983 NYM	NL East	0.427	69	93	0.420	68	94	-0.007
1983 ATL	NL West	0.568 P	92	70	0.543	88	74	-0.025
1983 LAD	NL West	0.567	92	70	0.562 P	91	71	-0.005
1983 HOU	NL West	0.554 F	90	72	0.525	85	77	-0.029
1983 SFG	NL West	0.474	77	85	0.488	79	83	0.014
1983 CIN	NL West	0.472	76	86	0.457	74	88	-0.015
1983 SDP	NL West	0.466 F	75	87	0.500	81	81	0.034
			971	973		972	972	
			2101	2111				

Franchise	League/Div.	OPW%	PW	PL	APW%	AW	AL	Diff(+/-)
1984 TOR	AL East	0.612 F	99	63	0.549	89	73	-0.063
1984 BAL	AL East	0.564 P	91	71	0.525	85	77	-0.040
1984 BOS	AL East	0.519	84	78	0.531	86	76	0.012
1984 DET	AL East	0.504	82	80	0.642 P	104	58	0.138
1984 NYY	AL East	0.501	81	81	0.537	87	75	0.036
1984 CLE	AL East	0.475 F	77	85	0.463	75	87	-0.012
1984 MIL	AL East	0.428	69	93	0.416	67	94	-0.012
1984 MIN	AL West	0.544 F	88	74	0.500	81	81	-0.044
1984 OAK	AL West	0.532 D	86	76	0.475	77	85	-0.057
1984 CHW	AL West	0.514 F	83	79	0.457	74	88	-0.057
1984 KCR	AL West	0.477	77	85	0.519 D	84	78	0.041
1984 SEA	AL West	0.465 F	75	87	0.457	74	88	-0.009
1984 CAL	AL West	0.462	75	87	0.500	81	81	0.038
1984 TEX	AL West	0.391	63	99	0.429	69	92	0.037
			1132	1136		1133	1133	
1984 STL	NL East	0.499 D	81	81	0.519	84	78	0.020
1984 PIT	NL East	0.496	80	82	0.463	75	87	-0.033
1984 CHC	NL East	0.490 F	79	83	0.596 P	96	65	0.107
1984 PHI	NL East	0.489	79	83	0.500	81	81	0.011
1984 MON	NL East	0.481	78	84	0.484	78	83	0.004
1984 NYM	NL East	0.447	72	90	0.556	90	72	0.108
1984 HOU	NL West	0.560 F	91	71	0.494	80	82	-0.067
1984 SDP	NL West	0.544 F	88	74	0.568 D	92	70	0.024
1984 ATL	NL West	0.530 P	86	76	0.494	80	82	-0.036
1984 LAD	NL West	0.530	86	76	0.488	79	83	-0.042
1984 SFG	NL West	0.508	82	80	0.407	66	96	-0.101
1984 CIN	NL West	0.414	67	95	0.432	70	92	0.018
			970	974		971	971	
			2103	2109				

Franchise	League/Div.	OPW%	PW	PL	APW%	AW	AL	Diff(+/-)
1985 TOR	AL East	0.665 F	108	54	0.615 P	99	62	-0.050
1985 BOS	AL East	0.569 P	92	70	0.500	81	81	-0.069
1985 BAL	AL East	0.546	89	73	0.516	83	78	-0.031
1985 NYY	AL East	0.517	84	78	0.602	97	64	0.086
1985 MIL	AL East	0.477	77	85	0.441	71	90	-0.036
1985 DET	AL East	0.464	75	87	0.522	84	77	0.057

Franchise	League/Div.	OPW%	PW	PL	APW%	AW	AL	Diff(+/-)
1985 CLE	AL East	0.376 F	61	101	0.370	60	102	-0.006
1985 OAK	AL West	0.510 F	83	79	0.475	77	85	-0.035
1985 SEA	AL West	0.506 F	82	80	0.457	74	88	-0.049
1985 CAL	AL West	0.486 D	79	83	0.556	90	72	0.069
1985 KCR	AL West	0.486	79	83	0.562 D	91	71	0.076
1985 MIN	AL West	0.485 F	79	83	0.475	77	85	-0.010
1985 CHW	AL West	0.485 F	79	83	0.525	85	77	0.040
1985 TEX	AL West	0.424	69	93	0.385	62	99	-0.039
			1134	1134		1131	1131	
1985 MON	NL East	0.556 D	90	72	0.522	84	77	-0.034
1985 NYM	NL East	0.524	85	77	0.605	98	64	0.081
1985 STL	NL East	0.519	84	78	0.623 P	101	61	0.104
1985 PHI	NL East	0.482	78	84	0.463	75	87	-0.019
1985 CHC	NL East	0.479 F	78	84	0.478	77	84	-0.001
1985 PIT	NL East	0.455	74	88	0.354	57	104	-0.101
1985 LAD	NL West	0.561 P	91	71	0.586 D	95	67	0.025
1985 SDP	NL West	0.561	91	71	0.512	83	79	-0.049
1985 CIN	NL West	0.500	81	81	0.553	89	72	0.053
1985 ATL	NL West	0.495	80	82	0.407	66	96	-0.087
1985 HOU	NL West	0.448 F	73	89	0.512	83	79	0.064
1985 SFG	NL West	0.424 F	69	93	0.383	62	100	-0.041
			973	971		970	970	
			2106	2106				

Franchise	League/Div.	OPW%	PW	PL	APW%	AW	AL	Diff(+/-)
1986 TOR	AL East	0.623 F	101	61	0.531	86	76	-0.092
1986 DET	AL East	0.524 D	85	77	0.537	87	75	0.013
1986 BOS	AL East	0.499	81	81	0.590 P	95	66	0.091
1986 CLE	AL East	0.469 F	76	86	0.519	84	78	0.050
1986 MIL	AL East	0.466	75	87	0.478	77	84	0.012
1986 NYY	AL East	0.457	74	88	0.556	90	72	0.098
1986 BAL	AL East	0.452	73	89	0.451	73	89	-0.002
1986 KCR	AL West	0.542 P	88	74	0.469	76	86	-0.072
1986 OAK	AL West	0.538	87	75	0.469	76	86	-0.069
1986 CHW	AL West	0.514 F	83	79	0.444	72	90	-0.069
1986 MIN	AL West	0.488	79	83	0.438	71	91	-0.049
1986 TEX	AL West	0.481	78	84	0.537	87	75	0.056
1986 CAL	AL West	0.480	78	84	0.568 D	92	70	0.088
1986 SEA	AL West	0.461	75	87	0.414	67	95	-0.048
			1133	1135		1133	1133	
1986 NYM	NL East	0.589 P	95	67	0.667 P	108	54	0.078
1986 PHI	NL East	0.505	82	80	0.534	86	75	0.029
1986 CHC	NL East	0.503 F	81	81	0.438	70	90	-0.066
1986 MON	NL East	0.496	80	82	0.484	78	83	-0.011
1986 PIT	NL East	0.473	77	85	0.395	64	98	-0.078
1986 STL	NL East	0.452	73	89	0.491	79	82	0.039
1986 SFG	NL West	0.594 F	96	66	0.512	83	79	-0.081
1986 LAD	NL West	0.518 D	84	78	0.451	73	89	-0.068
1986 SDP	NL West	0.518	84	78	0.457	74	88	-0.061
1986 CIN	NL West	0.491	80	82	0.531	86	76	0.040
1986 HOU	NL West	0.449 F	73	89	0.593 D	96	66	0.144

1986 ATL	NL West	0.419	68	94	0.447	72	89	0.028
			973	971		969	969	
			2106	2106				

Franchise	League/Div.	OPW%	PW	PL	APW%	AW	AL	Diff(+/-)
1987 TOR	AL East	0.613 F	99	63	0.593	96	66	-0.020
1987 MIL	AL East	0.555 P	90	72	0.562	91	71	0.006
1987 DET	AL East	0.515 F	83	79	0.605 P	98	64	0.090
1987 CLE	AL East	0.497 F	80	82	0.377	61	101	-0.120
1987 BOS	AL East	0.471	76	86	0.481	78	84	0.011
1987 NYY	AL East	0.453 F	73	89	0.549	89	73	0.097
1987 BAL	AL East	0.453	73	89	0.414	67	95	-0.039
1987 TEX	AL West	0.520 D	84	78	0.463	75	87	-0.057
1987 OAK	AL West	0.501 F	81	81	0.500	81	81	-0.001
1987 MIN	AL West	0.500 F	81	81	0.525 D	85	77	0.024
1987 KCR	AL West	0.494	80	82	0.512	83	79	0.018
1987 CHW	AL West	0.487 F	79	83	0.475	77	85	-0.012
1987 SEA	AL West	0.487	79	83	0.481	78	84	-0.005
1987 CAL	AL West	0.459	74	88	0.463	75	87	0.004
			1135	1133		1134	1134	
1987 NYM	NL East	0.544 D	88	74	0.568	92	70	0.024
1987 PHI	NL East	0.541	88	74	0.494	80	82	-0.047
1987 STL	NL East	0.517	84	78	0.586 P	95	67	0.069
1987 MON	NL East	0.494	80	82	0.562	91	71	0.067
1987 PIT	NL East	0.476	77	85	0.494	80	82	0.018
1987 CHC	NL East	0.458	74	88	0.472	76	85	0.014
1987 CIN	NL West	0.544 P	88	74	0.519	84	78	-0.026
1987 SFG	NL West	0.544	88	74	0.556 D	90	72	0.012
1987 LAD	NL West	0.515	83	79	0.451	73	89	-0.064
1987 SDP	NL West	0.510	83	79	0.401	65	97	-0.109
1987 ATL	NL West	0.481	78	84	0.429	69	92	-0.052
1987 HOU	NL West	0.364 F	59	103	0.469	76	86	0.105
			970	974		971	971	
			2105	2107				

Franchise	League/Div.	OPW%	PW	PL	APW%	AW	AL	Diff(+/-)
1988 BOS	AL East	0.557 P	90	72	0.549 D	89	73	-0.008
1988 NYY	AL East	0.549	89	73	0.528	85	76	-0.021
1988 MIL	AL East	0.528	86	76	0.537	87	75	0.009
1988 TOR	AL East	0.514 F	83	79	0.537	87	75	0.023
1988 DET	AL East	0.510	83	79	0.543	88	74	0.033
1988 CLE	AL East	0.461	75	87	0.481	78	84	0.020
1988 BAL	AL East	0.446	72	90	0.335	54	107	-0.111
1988 KCR	AL West	0.554 D	90	72	0.522	84	77	-0.032
1988 MIN	AL West	0.534	86	76	0.562	91	71	0.028
1988 OAK	AL West	0.523 F	85	77	0.642 P	104	58	0.119
1988 CAL	AL West	0.476	77	85	0.463	75	87	-0.013
1988 TEX	AL West	0.469	76	86	0.435	70	91	-0.035
1988 SEA	AL West	0.468	76	86	0.422	68	93	-0.046
1988 CHW	AL West	0.410 F	66	96	0.441	71	90	0.031
			1134	1134		1131	1131	

1988 CHC	NL East	0.538 D	87	75	0.475	77	85	-0.063
1988 PIT	NL East	0.537	87	75	0.531	85	75	-0.006
1988 NYM	NL East	0.510	83	79	0.625 P	100	60	0.115
1988 PHI	NL East	0.460	75	87	0.404	65	96	-0.057
1988 STL	NL East	0.439	71	91	0.469	76	86	0.030
1988 MON	NL East	0.436	71	91	0.500	81	81	0.064
1988 SFG	NL West	0.578 F	94	68	0.512	83	79	-0.066
1988 CIN	NL West	0.557 P	90	72	0.540	87	74	-0.017
1988 HOU	NL West	0.496 F	80	82	0.506	82	80	0.010
1988 SDP	NL West	0.490	79	83	0.516	83	78	0.025
1988 LAD	NL West	0.485	78	84	0.584 D	94	67	0.099
1988 ATL	NL West	0.468	76	86	0.338	54	106	-0.131
			971	973		967	967	
			2105	2107				

Franchise	League/Div.	OPW%	PW	PL	APW%	AW	AL	Diff(+/-)
1989 MIL	AL East	0.538 D	87	75	0.500	81	81	-0.038
1989 BOS	AL East	0.497	81	81	0.512	83	79	0.015
1989 CLE	AL East	0.487	79	83	0.451	73	89	-0.036
1989 TOR	AL East	0.469	76	86	0.549 D	89	73	0.081
1989 NYY	AL East	0.458	74	88	0.460	74	87	0.002
1989 DET	AL East	0.451	73	89	0.364	59	103	-0.087
1989 BAL	AL East	0.435 F	70	92	0.537	87	75	0.102
1989 OAK	AL West	0.557 F	90	72	0.611 P	99	63	0.054
1989 KCR	AL West	0.551 P	89	73	0.568	92	70	0.017
1989 SEA	AL West	0.543	88	74	0.451	73	89	-0.092
1989 CHW	AL West	0.518 F	84	78	0.429	69	92	-0.090
1989 MIN	AL West	0.516	84	78	0.494	80	82	-0.022
1989 CAL	AL West	0.506	82	80	0.562	91	71	0.056
1989 TEX	AL West	0.472	76	86	0.512	83	79	0.040
			1134	1134		1133	1133	
1989 CHC	NL East	0.611 P	99	63	0.574 P	93	69	-0.037
1989 NYM	NL East	0.541	88	74	0.537	87	75	-0.004
1989 PIT	NL East	0.508	82	80	0.457	74	88	-0.051
1989 STL	NL East	0.463	75	87	0.531	86	76	0.068
1989 PHI	NL East	0.463	75	87	0.414	67	95	-0.049
1989 MON	NL East	0.438	71	91	0.500	81	81	0.062
1989 CIN	NL West	0.537 D	87	75	0.463	75	87	-0.074
1989 SDP	NL West	0.527	85	77	0.549	89	73	0.022
1989 SFG	NL West	0.524	85	77	0.568 D	92	70	0.044
1989 LAD	NL West	0.493	80	82	0.481	77	83	-0.011
1989 HOU	NL West	0.461 F	75	87	0.531	86	76	0.070
1989 ATL	NL West	0.443	72	90	0.394	63	97	-0.049
			973	971		970	970	
			2107	2105				

Franchise	League/Div.	OPW%	PW	PL	APW%	AW	AL	Diff(+/-)
1990 TOR	AL East	0.537 P	87	75	0.531	86	76	-0.006
1990 BOS	AL East	0.532	86	76	0.543 D	88	74	0.011
1990 MIL	AL East	0.516	84	78	0.457	74	88	-0.059
1990 NYY	AL East	0.505	82	80	0.414	67	95	-0.091

1990 DET	AL East	0.480	78	84	0.488	79	83	0.008
1990 BAL	AL East	0.465	75	87	0.472	76	85	0.007
1990 CLE	AL East	0.421 F	68	94	0.475	77	85	0.054
1990 CHW	AL West	0.556 F	90	72	0.580	94	68	0.024
1990 SEA	AL West	0.534 D	87	75	0.475	77	85	-0.059
1990 KCR	AL West	0.512	83	79	0.466	75	86	-0.046
1990 OAK	AL West	0.508	82	80	0.636 P	103	59	0.127
1990 TEX	AL West	0.488	79	83	0.512	83	79	0.024
1990 MIN	AL West	0.479	78	84	0.457	74	88	-0.022
1990 CAL	AL West	0.467	76	86	0.494	80	82	0.027
			1134	1134		1133	1133	
1990 PIT	NL East	0.557 D	90	72	0.586 P	95	67	0.029
1990 NYM	NL East	0.551	89	73	0.562	91	71	0.010
1990 MON	NL East	0.514	83	79	0.525	85	77	0.011
1990 CHC	NL East	0.493	80	82	0.475	77	85	-0.018
1990 PHI	NL East	0.481	78	84	0.475	77	85	-0.005
1990 STL	NL East	0.477 F	77	85	0.432	70	92	-0.045
1990 CIN	NL West	0.559 P	91	71	0.562 D	91	71	0.003
1990 SFG	NL West	0.525	85	77	0.525	85	77	0.000
1990 SDP	NL West	0.494	80	82	0.463	75	87	-0.031
1990 LAD	NL West	0.492	80	82	0.531	86	76	0.039
1990 ATL	NL West	0.483	78	84	0.401	65	97	-0.082
1990 HOU	NL West	0.371 F	60	102	0.463	75	87	0.092
			972	972		972	972	
			2105	2107				

Franchise	League/Div.	OPW%	PW	PL	APW%	AW	AL	Diff(+/-)
1991 MIL	AL East	0.574 D	93	69	0.512	83	79	-0.062
1991 DET	AL East	0.522	85	77	0.519	84	78	-0.004
1991 BAL	AL East	0.496 F	80	82	0.414	67	95	-0.082
1991 BOS	AL East	0.482	78	84	0.519	84	78	0.037
1991 TOR	AL East	0.473	77	85	0.562 D	91	71	0.089
1991 NYY	AL East	0.463	75	87	0.438	71	91	-0.025
1991 CLE	AL East	0.401 F	65	97	0.352	57	105	-0.049
1991 CHW	AL West	0.599 P	97	65	0.537	87	75	-0.062
1991 OAK	AL West	0.561	91	71	0.519	84	78	-0.043
1991 KCR	AL West	0.505	82	80	0.506	82	80	0.001
1991 SEA	AL West	0.494	80	82	0.512	83	79	0.018
1991 MIN	AL West	0.482	78	84	0.586 P	95	67	0.104
1991 CAL	AL West	0.480	78	84	0.500	81	81	0.020
1991 TEX	AL West	0.446	72	90	0.525	85	77	0.078
			1131	1137		1134	1134	
1991 STL	NL East	0.532 F	86	76	0.519	84	78	-0.014
1991 CHC	NL East	0.525 D	85	77	0.481	77	83	-0.044
1991 PHI	NL East	0.519	84	78	0.481	78	84	-0.037
1991 PIT	NL East	0.511	83	79	0.605 P	98	64	0.094
1991 MON	NL East	0.487	79	83	0.441	71	90	-0.046
1991 NYM	NL East	0.486	79	83	0.478	77	84	-0.007
1991 ATL	NL West	0.561 P	91	71	0.580 D	94	68	0.019
1991 CIN	NL West	0.523	85	77	0.457	74	88	-0.067
1991 SDP	NL West	0.513	83	79	0.519	84	78	0.006

Franchise	League/Div.	OPW%	PW	PL	APW%	AW	AL	Diff(+/-)
1991 SFG	NL West	0.488	79	83	0.463	75	87	-0.025
1991 LAD	NL West	0.469	76	86	0.574	93	69	0.105
1991 HOU	NL West	0.389 F	63	99	0.401	65	97	0.013
			973	971		970	970	
			2103	2109				

Franchise	League/Div.	OPW%	PW	PL	APW%	AW	AL	Diff(+/-)
1992 MIL	AL East	0.587 P	95	67	0.568	92	70	-0.020
1992 NYY	AL East	0.539	87	75	0.469	76	86	-0.070
1992 DET	AL East	0.520 F	84	78	0.463	75	87	-0.057
1992 CLE	AL East	0.519 F	84	78	0.469	76	86	-0.050
1992 BOS	AL East	0.491	80	82	0.451	73	89	-0.040
1992 BAL	AL East	0.478 F	77	85	0.549	89	73	0.071
1992 TOR	AL East	0.449	73	89	0.593 P	96	66	0.144
1992 CHW	AL West	0.547 D	89	73	0.531	86	76	-0.017
1992 OAK	AL West	0.518	84	78	0.593 D	96	66	0.075
1992 MIN	AL West	0.509	83	79	0.556	90	72	0.046
1992 CAL	AL West	0.493	80	82	0.444	72	90	-0.048
1992 KCR	AL West	0.471	76	86	0.444	72	90	-0.027
1992 SEA	AL West	0.448	73	89	0.395	64	98	-0.053
1992 TEX	AL West	0.433	70	92	0.475	77	85	0.042
			1134	1134		1134	1134	
1992 STL	NL East	0.563 D	91	71	0.512	83	79	-0.051
1992 PIT	NL East	0.529	86	76	0.593 D	96	66	0.064
1992 MON	NL East	0.510	83	79	0.537	87	75	0.027
1992 PHI	NL East	0.494	80	82	0.432	70	92	-0.062
1992 CHC	NL East	0.492	80	82	0.481	78	84	-0.011
1992 NYM	NL East	0.452	73	89	0.444	72	90	-0.007
1992 ATL	NL West	0.603 P	98	64	0.605 P	98	64	0.002
1992 SDP	NL West	0.595	96	66	0.506	82	80	-0.089
1992 LAD	NL West	0.475	77	85	0.389	63	99	-0.086
1992 CIN	NL West	0.454	74	88	0.556	90	72	0.101
1992 SFG	NL West	0.425	69	93	0.444	72	90	0.019
1992 HOU	NL West	0.411 F	67	95	0.500	81	81	0.089
			973	971		972	972	
			2107	2105				

Franchise	League/Div.	OPW%	PW	PL	APW%	AW	AL	Diff(+/-)
1993 NYY	AL East	0.505 D	82	80	0.543	88	74	0.038
1993 MIL	AL East	0.504	82	80	0.426	69	93	-0.078
1993 DET	AL East	0.495	80	82	0.525	85	77	0.030
1993 BOS	AL East	0.486	79	83	0.494	80	82	0.008
1993 TOR	AL East	0.479	78	84	0.586 P	95	67	0.107
1993 BAL	AL East	0.475	77	85	0.525	85	77	0.050
1993 CLE	AL East	0.475 F	77	85	0.469	76	86	-0.006
1993 CHW	AL West	0.569 F	92	70	0.580 D	94	68	0.011
1993 TEX	AL West	0.542 P	88	74	0.531	86	76	-0.011
1993 CAL	AL West	0.533	86	76	0.438	71	91	-0.095
1993 KCR	AL West	0.517	84	78	0.519	84	78	0.002
1993 SEA	AL West	0.484	78	84	0.506	82	80	0.022
1993 OAK	AL West	0.476	77	85	0.420	68	94	-0.057

Franchise	League/Div.	OPW%	PW	PL	APW%	AW	AL	Diff(+/-)
1993 MIN	AL West	0.458	74	88	0.438	71	91	-0.020
			1134	1134		1134	1134	
1993 CHC	NL East	0.548 D	89	73	0.519	84	78	-0.030
1993 STL	NL East	0.536	87	75	0.537	87	75	0.001
1993 NYM	NL East	0.481	78	84	0.364	59	103	-0.116
1993 MON	NL East	0.470	76	86	0.580	94	68	0.110
1993 PHI	NL East	0.468	76	86	0.599 D	97	65	0.131
1993 PIT	NL East	0.438	71	91	0.463	75	87	0.024
1993 FLA	NL East	0.000 F	0	0	0.395	64	98	0.000
1993 ATL	NL West	0.584 P	95	67	0.642 P	104	58	0.058
1993 HOU	NL West	0.554 F	90	72	0.525	85	77	-0.029
1993 SFG	NL West	0.520	84	78	0.636	103	59	0.116
1993 LAD	NL West	0.492	80	82	0.500	81	81	0.008
1993 SDP	NL West	0.477	77	85	0.377	61	101	-0.100
1993 CIN	NL West	0.439	71	91	0.451	73	89	0.011
1993 COL	NL West	0.000 F	0	0	0.414	67	95	0.000
			973	971		1134	1134	
			2107	2105				

Franchise	League/Div.	OPW%	PW	PL	APW%	AW	AL	Diff(+/-)
1994 BOS	AL East	0.576 P	93	69	0.470	54	61	-0.106
1994 BAL	AL East	0.538 w	87	75	0.563	63	49	0.024
1994 TOR	AL East	0.506	82	80	0.478	55	60	-0.028
1994 NYY	AL East	0.494	80	82	0.619 P	70	43	0.126
1994 DET	AL East	0.422	68	94	0.461	53	62	0.039
1994 CHW	AL Central	0.615 F	100	62	0.593 D	67	46	-0.022
1994 CLE	AL Central	0.544 F	88	74	0.584 w	66	47	0.040
1994 KCR	AL Central	0.533 D	86	76	0.557	64	51	0.023
1994 MIL	AL Central	0.496	80	82	0.461	53	62	-0.036
1994 MIN	AL Central	0.453	73	89	0.469	53	60	0.016
1994 OAK	AL West	0.490 D	79	83	0.447	51	63	-0.043
1994 TEX	AL West	0.457	74	88	0.456 D	52	62	-0.001
1994 CAL	AL West	0.453	73	89	0.409	47	68	-0.044
1994 SEA	AL West	0.433	70	92	0.438	49	63	0.005
			1136	1132		797	797	
1994 PHI	NL East	0.537 D	87	75	0.470	54	61	-0.067
1994 ATL	NL East	0.528	86	76	0.596 w	68	46	0.069
1994 MON	NL East	0.480	78	84	0.649 P	74	40	0.170
1994 NYM	NL East	0.478	77	85	0.487	55	58	0.008
1994 FLA	NL East	0.000 F	0	0	0.443	51	64	0.000
1994 CIN	NL Central	0.558 P	90	72	0.579 D	66	48	0.021
1994 CHC	NL Central	0.548 w	89	73	0.434	49	64	-0.114
1994 HOU	NL Central	0.520 F	84	78	0.574	66	49	0.054
1994 STL	NL Central	0.478	77	85	0.465	53	61	-0.013
1994 PIT	NL Central	0.442	72	90	0.465	53	61	0.023
1994 SDP	NL West	0.508 D	82	80	0.402	47	70	-0.106
1994 SFG	NL West	0.490	79	83	0.478	55	60	-0.012
1994 LAD	NL West	0.440	71	91	0.509 D	58	56	0.069
1994 COL	NL West	0.000 F	0	0	0.453	53	64	0.000
			973	971		802	802	
			2109	2103				

Franchise	League/Div.	OPW%	PW	PL	APW%	AW	AL	Diff(+/-)
1995 BAL	AL East	0.538 D	87	75	0.493	71	73	-0.045
1995 NYY	AL East	0.512	83	79	0.549 w	79	65	0.037
1995 BOS	AL East	0.511 F	83	79	0.597 D	86	58	0.087
1995 TOR	AL East	0.469	76	86	0.389	56	88	-0.080
1995 DET	AL East	0.436	71	91	0.417	60	84	-0.019
1995 CLE	AL Central	0.580 P	94	68	0.694 P	100	44	0.114
1995 MIL	AL Central	0.533 w	86	76	0.451	65	79	-0.082
1995 CHW	AL Central	0.489	79	83	0.472	68	76	-0.016
1995 MIN	AL Central	0.458	74	88	0.389	56	88	-0.069
1995 KCR	AL Central	0.450	73	89	0.486	70	74	0.036
1995 CAL	AL West	0.557 D	90	72	0.538	78	67	-0.019
1995 TEX	AL West	0.502	81	81	0.514	74	70	0.012
1995 OAK	AL West	0.494	80	82	0.465	67	77	-0.029
1995 SEA	AL West	0.472	76	86	0.545 D	79	66	0.073
			1134	1134		1009	1009	
1995 MON	NL East	0.544 P	88	74	0.458	66	78	-0.086
1995 NYM	NL East	0.516	84	78	0.479	69	75	-0.037
1995 ATL	NL East	0.487	79	83	0.625 P	90	54	0.138
1995 PHI	NL East	0.381 F	62	100	0.479	69	75	0.099
1995 FLA	NL East	0.000 F	0	0	0.469	67	76	0.000
1995 CIN	NL Central	0.536 D	87	75	0.590 D	85	59	0.054
1995 HOU	NL Central	0.535 F	87	75	0.528	76	68	-0.008
1995 CHC	NL Central	0.534 w	86	76	0.507	73	71	0.027
1995 STL	NL Central	0.496	80	82	0.434	62	81	-0.062
1995 PIT	NL Central	0.492	80	82	0.403	58	86	-0.089
1995 SDP	NL West	0.508 D	82	80	0.486	70	74	-0.022
1995 LAD	NL West	0.502	81	81	0.542 D	78	66	0.040
1995 SFG	NL West	0.454	74	88	0.465	67	77	0.012
1995 COL	NL West	0.000 F	0	0	0.535 w	77	67	0.000
			970	974		1007	1007	
			2104	2108				

Franchise	League/Div.	OPW%	PW	PL	APW%	AW	AL	Diff(+/-)
1996 BOS	AL East	0.533 D	86	76	0.525	85	77	-0.008
1996 NYY	AL East	0.495	80	82	0.568 D	92	70	0.073
1996 BAL	AL East	0.461	75	87	0.543 w	88	74	0.082
1996 TOR	AL East	0.461	75	87	0.457	74	88	-0.004
1996 DET	AL East	0.422	68	94	0.327	53	109	-0.094
1996 CLE	AL Central	0.553 F	90	72	0.615 P	99	62	0.062
1996 CHW	AL Central	0.532 D	86	76	0.525	85	77	-0.007
1996 MIL	AL Central	0.525	85	77	0.494	80	82	-0.031
1996 MIN	AL Central	0.507	82	80	0.481	78	84	-0.025
1996 KCR	AL Central	0.460	75	87	0.466	75	86	0.006
1996 TEX	AL West	0.575 P	93	69	0.556 D	90	72	-0.019
1996 SEA	AL West	0.556 w	90	72	0.528	85	76	-0.028
1996 OAK	AL West	0.463	75	87	0.481	78	84	0.018
1996 CAL	AL West	0.453	73	89	0.435	70	91	-0.019
			1133	1135		1132	1132	
1996 ATL	NL East	0.533 D	86	76	0.593 P	96	66	0.060
1996 MON	NL East	0.508	82	80	0.543	88	74	0.035

Franchise	League/Div.	OPW%	PW	PL	APW%	AW	AL	Diff(+/-)
1996 NYM	NL East	0.484	78	84	0.438	71	91	-0.045
1996 PHI	NL East	0.398	64	98	0.414	67	95	0.016
1996 FLA	NL East	0.000 F	0	0	0.494	80	82	0.000
1996 CHC	NL Central	0.530 D	86	76	0.469	76	86	-0.061
1996 HOU	NL Central	0.522	85	77	0.506	82	80	-0.016
1996 PIT	NL Central	0.503	82	80	0.451	73	89	-0.053
1996 STL	NL Central	0.495	80	82	0.543 D	88	74	0.048
1996 CIN	NL Central	0.458 F	74	88	0.500	81	81	0.042
1996 LAD	NL West	0.577 P	94	68	0.556 w	90	72	-0.022
1996 SDP	NL West	0.537 w	87	75	0.562 D	91	71	0.024
1996 SFG	NL West	0.460	75	87	0.420	68	94	-0.040
1996 COL	NL West	0.000 F	0	0	0.512	83	79	0.000
			973	971		1134	1134	
			2106	2106				

Franchise	League/Div.	OPW%	PW	PL	APW%	AW	AL	Diff(+/-)
1997 BOS	AL East	0.583 P	94	68	0.481	78	84	-0.102
1997 NYY	AL East	0.520 w	84	78	0.593 w	96	66	0.073
1997 TOR	AL East	0.501	81	81	0.469	76	86	-0.032
1997 BAL	AL East	0.499	81	81	0.605 P	98	64	0.106
1997 DET	AL East	0.491	80	82	0.488	79	83	-0.004
1997 CLE	AL Central	0.532 D	86	76	0.534 D	86	75	0.002
1997 CHW	AL Central	0.493	80	82	0.497	80	81	0.004
1997 MIN	AL Central	0.490	79	83	0.420	68	94	-0.070
1997 KCR	AL Central	0.472	76	86	0.416	67	94	-0.056
1997 MIL	AL Central	0.448	73	89	0.484	78	83	0.036
1997 ANA	AL West	0.547 D	89	73	0.519	84	78	-0.028
1997 SEA	AL West	0.503	82	80	0.556 D	90	72	0.052
1997 TEX	AL West	0.503	81	81	0.475	77	85	-0.027
1997 OAK	AL West	0.423	69	93	0.401	65	97	-0.022
			1135	1133		1122	1142	
1997 MON	NL East	0.543 D	88	74	0.481	78	84	-0.062
1997 ATL	NL East	0.524 w	85	77	0.623 P	101	61	0.100
1997 NYM	NL East	0.474	77	85	0.543	88	74	0.070
1997 PHI	NL East	0.459	74	88	0.420	68	94	-0.039
1997 FLA	NL East	0.451 F	73	89	0.568 w	92	70	0.117
1997 HOU	NL Central	0.600 P	97	65	0.519 D	84	78	-0.081
1997 CIN	NL Central	0.543 F	88	74	0.469	76	86	-0.074
1997 PIT	NL Central	0.519	84	78	0.488	79	83	-0.031
1997 STL	NL Central	0.509	82	80	0.451	73	89	-0.058
1997 CHC	NL Central	0.471	76	86	0.420	68	94	-0.051
1997 LAD	NL West	0.536 D	87	75	0.543	88	74	0.008
1997 COL	NL West	0.487 F	79	83	0.512	83	79	0.025
1997 SDP	NL West	0.484	78	84	0.469	76	86	-0.015
1997 SFG	NL West	0.400	65	97	0.556 D	90	72	0.156
			948	996		1144	1124	
			2083	2129		2266	2266	

Franchise	League/Div.	OPW%	PW	PL	APW%	AW	AL	Diff(+/-)
1998 BOS	AL East	0.560 P	91	71	0.568 w	92	70	0.008
1998 NYY	AL East	0.531 w	86	76	0.704 P	114	48	0.172

390

Franchise	League/Div.	OPW%	PW	PL	APW%	AW	AL	Diff(+/-)
1998 TOR	AL East	0.495	80	82	0.543	88	74	0.048
1998 BAL	AL East	0.462	75	87	0.488	79	83	0.026
1998 TBD	AL East	0.000 F	0	0	0.389	63	99	0.000
1998 CLE	AL Central	0.542 D	88	74	0.549 D	89	73	0.007
1998 MIN	AL Central	0.498	81	81	0.432	70	92	-0.066
1998 DET	AL Central	0.476	77	85	0.401	65	97	-0.075
1998 CHW	AL Central	0.460	75	87	0.494	80	82	0.034
1998 KCR	AL Central	0.407	66	96	0.447	72	89	0.040
1998 TEX	AL West	0.544 D	88	74	0.543 D	88	74	-0.001
1998 ANA	AL West	0.518	84	78	0.525	85	77	0.007
1998 OAK	AL West	0.510	83	79	0.457	74	88	-0.054
1998 SEA	AL West	0.491	80	82	0.472	76	85	-0.019
			1052	1054		1135	1131	
1998 ATL	NL East	0.564 P	91	71	0.654 P	106	56	0.090
1998 MON	NL East	0.521	84	78	0.401	65	97	-0.119
1998 PHI	NL East	0.520 F	84	78	0.463	75	87	-0.057
1998 NYM	NL East	0.472	77	85	0.543	88	74	0.071
1998 FLA	NL East	0.398 F	64	98	0.333	54	108	-0.064
1998 HOU	NL Central	0.530 D	86	76	0.630 D	102	60	0.100
1998 CHC	NL Central	0.523 w	85	77	0.552 w	90	73	0.030
1998 PIT	NL Central	0.522	85	77	0.426	69	93	0.096
1998 MIL	NL Central	0.513	83	79	0.457	74	88	-0.056
1998 CIN	NL Central	0.477 F	77	85	0.475	77	85	-0.002
1998 STL	NL Central	0.467	76	86	0.512	83	79	0.046
1998 SFG	NL West	0.539 D	87	75	0.546	89	74	0.007
1998 SDP	NL West	0.515	83	79	0.605 D	98	64	0.090
1998 LAD	NL West	0.510	83	79	0.512	83	79	0.003
1998 COL	NL West	0.433 F	70	92	0.475	77	85	0.043
1998 ARI	NL West	0.000 F	0	0	0.401	65	97	0.000
			1215	1215		1295	1299	
			2268	2268		2430	2430	

Franchise	League/Div.	OPW%	PW	PL	APW%	AW	AL	Diff(+/-)
1999 BOS	AL East	0.538 D	87	75	0.580 w	94	68	0.042
1999 BAL	AL East	0.496	80	82	0.481	78	84	-0.015
1999 TOR	AL East	0.492	80	82	0.519	84	78	0.026
1999 NYY	AL East	0.489	79	83	0.605 P	98	64	0.116
1999 TBD	AL East	0.000 F	0	0	0.426	69	93	0.000
1999 CLE	AL Central	0.555 P	90	72	0.599 D	97	65	0.043
1999 KCR	AL Central	0.508	82	80	0.398	64	97	-0.111
1999 CHW	AL Central	0.504	82	80	0.466	75	86	-0.038
1999 DET	AL Central	0.467	76	86	0.429	69	92	-0.038
1999 MIN	AL Central	0.453	73	89	0.394	63	97	-0.059
1999 SEA	AL West	0.549 D	89	73	0.488	79	83	-0.062
1999 TEX	AL West	0.512 w	83	79	0.586 D	95	67	0.074
1999 OAK	AL West	0.472 F	77	85	0.537	87	75	0.065
1999 ANA	AL West	0.458	74	88	0.432	70	92	-0.026
			1052	1054		1122	1141	
1999 ATL	NL East	0.540 D	87	75	0.636 P	103	59	0.096
1999 MON	NL East	0.500	81	81	0.420	68	94	-0.080
1999 NYM	NL East	0.481	78	84	0.595 w	97	66	0.114

Franchise	League/Div.	OPW%	PW	PL	APW%	AW	AL	Diff(+/-)
1999 PHI	NL East	0.476 F	77	85	0.475	77	85	-0.001
1999 FLA	NL East	0.408 F	66	96	0.395	64	98	-0.013
1999 HOU	NL Central	0.593 P	96	66	0.599 D	97	65	0.006
1999 PIT	NL Central	0.510	83	79	0.484	78	83	-0.025
1999 CHC	NL Central	0.496	80	82	0.414	67	95	-0.083
1999 CIN	NL Central	0.494 F	80	82	0.589	96	67	0.095
1999 STL	NL Central	0.487	79	83	0.466	75	86	-0.021
1999 MIL	NL Central	0.476	77	85	0.460	74	87	-0.017
1999 LAD	NL West	0.558 D	90	72	0.475	77	85	-0.083
1999 SFG	NL West	0.542 w	88	74	0.531	86	76	-0.011
1999 COL	NL West	0.482 F	78	84	0.444	72	90	-0.038
1999 SDP	NL West	0.467	76	86	0.457	74	88	-0.010
1999 ARI	NL West	0.000 F	0	0	0.617 D	100	62	0.000
			1217	1213		1305	1286	
			2269	2267		2427	2427	

Franchise	League/Div.	OPW%	PW	PL	APW%	AW	AL	Diff(+/-)
2000 BOS	AL East	0.576 P	93	69	0.525	85	77	-0.051
2000 BAL	AL East	0.515	83	79	0.457	74	88	-0.058
2000 TOR	AL East	0.485	79	83	0.512	83	79	0.028
2000 NYY	AL East	0.477	77	85	0.540 D	87	74	0.063
2000 TBD	AL East	0.000 F	0	0	0.429	69	92	0.000
2000 CLE	AL Central	0.525 D	85	77	0.556	90	72	0.031
2000 CHW	AL Central	0.520 w	84	78	0.586 P	95	67	0.067
2000 KCR	AL Central	0.507	82	80	0.475	77	85	-0.032
2000 MIN	AL Central	0.461	75	87	0.426	69	93	-0.035
2000 DET	AL Central	0.395	64	98	0.488	79	83	0.092
2000 SEA	AL West	0.551 D	89	73	0.562 w	91	71	0.011
2000 OAK	AL West	0.513	83	79	0.565 D	91	70	0.052
2000 ANA	AL West	0.503	81	81	0.506	82	80	0.003
2000 TEX	AL West	0.482	78	84	0.438	71	91	-0.043
			1055	1051		1143	1122	
2000 ATL	NL East	0.530 D	86	76	0.586 D	95	67	0.056
2000 MON	NL East	0.512	83	79	0.414	67	95	-0.099
2000 FLA	NL East	0.495 F	80	82	0.491	79	82	-0.004
2000 NYM	NL East	0.448	73	89	0.580 w	94	68	0.132
2000 PHI	NL East	0.435 F	71	91	0.401	65	97	-0.034
2000 HOU	NL Central	0.531 P	86	76	0.444	72	90	-0.087
2000 MIL	NL Central	0.519 w	84	78	0.451	73	89	-0.069
2000 STL	NL Central	0.503	81	81	0.586 D	95	67	0.083
2000 PIT	NL Central	0.495	80	82	0.426	69	93	-0.070 .
2000 CIN	NL Central	0.475 F	77	85	0.525	85	77	0.049
2000 CHC	NL Central	0.468	76	86	0.401	65	97	-0.067
2000 COL	NL West	0.583 F	94	68	0.506	82	80	-0.076
2000 SFG	NL West	0.520 D	84	78	0.599 P	97	65	0.079
2000 LAD	NL West	0.512	83	79	0.531	86	76	0.019
2000 SDP	NL West	0.461	75	87	0.469	76	86	0.008
2000 ARI	NL West	0.000 F	0	0	0.525	85	77	0.000
			1213	1217		1285	1306	
			2268	2268		2428	2428	

Franchise	League/Div.	OPW%	PW	PL	APW%	AW	AL	Diff(+/-)
2001 TOR	AL East	0.547 D	89	73	0.494	80	82	-0.053
2001 BOS	AL East	0.527	85	77	0.509	82	79	-0.017
2001 NYY	AL East	0.511	83	79	0.594 D	95	65	0.083
2001 BAL	AL East	0.436	71	91	0.391	63	98	-0.045
2001 TBD	AL East	0.000 F	0	0	0.383	62	100	0.000
2001 CLE	AL Central	0.527 D	85	77	0.562 D	91	71	0.035
2001 CHW	AL Central	0.493	80	82	0.512	83	79	0.019
2001 KCR	AL Central	0.475	77	85	0.401	65	97	-0.074
2001 MIN	AL Central	0.474	77	85	0.525	85	77	0.051
2001 DET	AL Central	0.422	68	94	0.407	66	96	-0.015
2001 SEA	AL West	0.567 P	92	70	0.716 P	116	46	0.149
2001 OAK	AL West	0.541 w	88	74	0.630 w	102	60	0.089
2001 TEX	AL West	0.513	83	79	0.451	73	89	-0.062
2001 ANA	AL West	0.467	76	86	0.463	75	87	-0.004
			1053	1053		1138	1126	
2001 MON	NL East	0.541 D	88	74	0.420	68	94	-0.121
2001 ATL	NL East	0.523	85	77	0.543 D	88	74	0.020
2001 PHI	NL East	0.500 F	81	81	0.531	86	76	0.031
2001 NYM	NL East	0.464	75	87	0.506	82	80	0.042
2001 FLA	NL East	0.400 F	65	97	0.469	76	86	0.070
2001 HOU	NL Central	0.591 P	96	66	0.574 P	93	69	-0.017
2001 STL	NL Central	0.546 w	88	74	0.574 w	93	69	0.029
2001 CIN	NL Central	0.534 F	87	75	0.407	66	96	-0.127
2001 CHC	NL Central	0.516 F	84	78	0.543	88	74	0.027
2001 PIT	NL Central	0.485	79	83	0.383	62	100	-0.103
2001 MIL	NL Central	0.463	75	87	0.420	68	94	-0.044
2001 COL	NL West	0.542 F	88	74	0.451	73	89	-0.092
2001 SFG	NL West	0.509 D	83	79	0.556	90	72	0.046
2001 LAD	NL West	0.502	81	81	0.531	86	76	0.029
2001 SDP	NL West	0.390	63	99	0.488	79	83	0.097
2001 ARI	NL West	0.000 F	0	0	0.568 D	92	70	0.000
			1216	1214		1290	1302	
			2269	2267		2428	2428	

Franchise	League/Div.	OPW%	PW	PL	APW%	AW	AL	Diff(+/-)
2002 TOR	AL East	0.572 D	93	69	0.481	78	84	-0.090
2002 NYY	AL East	0.518	84	78	0.640 P	103	58	0.121
2002 BOS	AL East	0.507	82	80	0.574	93	69	0.067
2002 BAL	AL East	0.440 F	71	91	0.414	67	95	-0.027
2002 TBD	AL East	0.419 F	68	94	0.342	55	106	-0.078
2002 CHW	AL Central	0.532 D	86	76	0.500	81	81	-0.032
2002 CLE	AL Central	0.495	80	82	0.457	74	88	-0.038
2002 MIN	AL Central	0.487	79	83	0.584 D	94	67	0.097
2002 KCR	AL Central	0.482	78	84	0.383	62	100	-0.100
2002 DET	AL Central	0.379 F	61	101	0.342	55	106	-0.037
2002 OAK	AL West	0.578 P	94	68	0.636 D	103	59	0.058
2002 ANA	AL West	0.548 w	89	73	0.611 w	99	63	0.063
2002 SEA	AL West	0.528	86	76	0.574	93	69	0.046
2002 TEX	AL West	0.521	84	78	0.444	72	90	-0.076
			1135	1133		1129	1135	

2002 MON	NL East	0.602 P	98	64	0.512	83	79	-0.090
2002 NYM	NL East	0.496	80	82	0.466	75	86	-0.030
2002 ATL	NL East	0.490	79	83	0.631 P	101	59	0.142
2002 PHI	NL East	0.485	79	83	0.497	80	81	0.012
2002 FLA	NL East	0.476 F	77	85	0.488	79	83	0.012
2002 HOU	NL Central	0.582 D	94	68	0.519	84	78	-0.064
2002 STL	NL Central	0.516 w	84	78	0.599 D	97	65	0.083
2002 CIN	NL Central	0.499 F	81	81	0.481	78	84	-0.018
2002 CHC	NL Central	0.483	78	84	0.414	67	95	-0.070
2002 PIT	NL Central	0.460	75	87	0.447	72	89	-0.013
2002 MIL	NL Central	0.350 F	57	105	0.346	56	106	-0.004
2002 ARI	NL West	0.609 F	99	63	0.605 D	98	64	-0.004
2002 SFG	NL West	0.519 D	84	78	0.590 w	95	66	0.071
2002 LAD	NL West	0.493	80	82	0.568	92	70	0.074
2002 SDP	NL West	0.485	79	83	0.407	66	96	-0.078
2002 COL	NL West	0.463 F	75	87	0.451	73	89	-0.012
			1297	1295		1296	1290	
			2432	2428		2425	2425	

Franchise	League/Div.	OPW%	PW	PL	APW%	AW	AL	Diff(+/-)
2003 TOR	AL East	0.557 D	90	72	0.531	86	76	-0.026
2003 NYY	AL East	0.556 w	90	72	0.623 P	101	61	0.068
2003 BOS	AL East	0.529	86	76	0.586 w	95	67	0.057
2003 BAL	AL East	0.488 F	79	83	0.438	71	91	-0.050
2003 TBD	AL East	0.382 F	62	100	0.389	63	99	0.006
2003 CHW	AL Central	0.506 D	82	80	0.531	86	76	0.025
2003 CLE	AL Central	0.502	81	81	0.420	68	94	-0.083
2003 MIN	AL Central	0.499	81	81	0.556 D	90	72	0.057
2003 KCR	AL Central	0.467	76	86	0.512	83	79	0.045
2003 DET	AL Central	0.400	65	97	0.265	43	119	-0.135
2003 SEA	AL West	0.594 P	96	66	0.574	93	69	-0.020
2003 ANA	AL West	0.529	86	76	0.475	77	85	-0.054
2003 OAK	AL West	0.527	85	77	0.593 D	96	66	0.065
2003 TEX	AL West	0.471	76	86	0.438	71	91	-0.032
			1135	1133		1123	1145	
2003 ATL	NL East	0.536 D	87	75	0.623 P	101	61	0.088
2003 FLA	NL East	0.522	85	77	0.562 w	91	71	0.040
2003 MON	NL East	0.522	85	77	0.512	83	79	-0.009
2003 PHI	NL East	0.475	77	85	0.531	86	76	0.056
2003 NYM	NL East	0.470	76	86	0.410	66	95	-0.061
2003 HOU	NL Central	0.566 P	92	70	0.537	87	75	-0.029
2003 STL	NL Central	0.540 w	88	74	0.525	85	77	-0.016
2003 CHC	NL Central	0.526 F	85	77	0.543 D	88	74	0.017
2003 PIT	NL Central	0.507	82	80	0.463	75	87	-0.044
2003 CIN	NL Central	0.500 F	81	81	0.426	69	93	-0.074
2003 MIL	NL Central	0.474 F	77	85	0.420	68	94	-0.055
2003 ARI	NL West	0.495 F	80	82	0.519	84	78	0.024
2003 LAD	NL West	0.471 D	76	86	0.525	85	77	0.054
2003 SFG	NL West	0.468 F	76	86	0.621 D	100	61	0.153
2003 SDP	NL West	0.467	76	86	0.395	64	98	-0.072
2003 COL	NL West	0.454	74	88	0.457	74	88	0.003

| | | | 1295 | 1297 | | 1306 | 1284 | |
| | | | 2430 | 2430 | | 2429 | 2429 | |

Franchise	League/Div.	OPW%	PW	PL	APW%	AW	AL	Diff(+/-)
2004 BOS	AL East	0.537 D	87	75	0.605 w	98	64	0.068
2004 TOR	AL East	0.519	84	78	0.416	67	94	-0.103
2004 BAL	AL East	0.519	84	78	0.481	78	84	-0.038
2004 NYY	AL East	0.513	83	79	0.623 P	101	61	0.111
2004 TBD	AL East	0.506 F	82	80	0.435	70	91	-0.071
2004 CLE	AL Central	0.553 P	90	72	0.494	80	82	-0.059
2004 CHW	AL Central	0.533 w	86	76	0.512	83	79	-0.020
2004 KCR	AL Central	0.483	78	84	0.358	58	104	-0.125
2004 DET	AL Central	0.467	76	86	0.444	72	90	-0.023
2004 MIN	AL Central	0.455	74	88	0.568 D	92	70	0.113
2004 TEX	AL West	0.526 D	85	77	0.549	89	73	0.023
2004 ANA	AL West	0.478	77	85	0.568 D	92	70	0.090
2004 OAK	AL West	0.474	77	85	0.562	91	71	0.088
2004 SEA	AL West	0.436	71	91	0.389	63	99	-0.047
			1133	1135		1134	1132	
2004 ATL	NL East	0.532 D	86	76	0.593 D	96	66	0.061
2004 PHI	NL East	0.515	83	79	0.531	86	76	0.016
2004 NYM	NL East	0.506	82	80	0.438	71	91	-0.068
2004 MON	NL East	0.495	80	82	0.414	67	95	-0.081
2004 FLA	NL East	0.465	75	87	0.512	83	79	0.047
2004 HOU	NL Central	0.601 P	97	65	0.568 w	92	70	-0.033
2004 STL	NL Central	0.532 F	86	76	0.648 P	105	57	0.116
2004 PIT	NL Central	0.512	83	79	0.447	72	89	-0.065
2004 MIL	NL Central	0.510 F	83	79	0.416	67	94	-0.094
2004 CIN	NL Central	0.492	80	82	0.469	76	86	-0.023
2004 CHC	NL Central	0.434 F	70	92	0.549	89	73	0.115
2004 SFG	NL West	0.543 F	88	74	0.562	91	71	0.019
2004 SDP	NL West	0.533 D	86	76	0.537	87	75	0.004
2004 COL	NL West	0.526 w	85	77	0.420	68	94	-0.106
2004 LAD	NL West	0.429	70	92	0.574 D	93	69	0.145
2004 ARI	NL West	0.364	59	103	0.315	51	111	-0.049
			1294	1298		1294	1296	
			2428	2432		2428	2428	

Franchise	League/Div.	OPW%	PW	PL	APW%	AW	AL	Diff(+/-)
2005 TOR	AL East	0.551 D	89	73	0.494	80	82	-0.057
2005 BAL	AL East	0.500	81	81	0.457	74	88	-0.043
2005 NYY	AL East	0.468	76	86	0.586 D	95	67	0.119
2005 BOS	AL East	0.462	75	87	0.586 w	95	67	0.125
2005 TBD	AL East	0.404 F	65	97	0.414	67	95	0.010
2005 CLE	AL Central	0.516 D	84	78	0.574	93	69	0.058
2005 MIN	AL Central	0.512	83	79	0.512	83	79	0.000
2005 CHW	AL Central	0.501	81	81	0.611 P	99	63	0.111
2005 KCR	AL Central	0.495	80	82	0.346	56	106	-0.150
2005 DET	AL Central	0.429	69	93	0.438	71	91	0.010
2005 OAK	AL West	0.567 P	92	70	0.543	88	74	-0.024
2005 LAA	AL West	0.560 w	91	71	0.586 D	95	67	0.027
2005 TEX	AL West	0.535	87	75	0.488	79	83	-0.047

Franchise	League/Div.	OPW%	PW	PL	APW%	AW	AL	Diff(+/-)
2005 SEA	AL West	0.514	83	79	0.426	69	93	-0.088
			1136	1132		1144	1124	
2005 NYM	NL East	0.564 D	91	71	0.512	83	79	-0.052
2005 WSN	NL East	0.539 w	87	75	0.500	81	81	-0.039
2005 ATL	NL East	0.528	86	76	0.556 D	90	72	0.027
2005 FLA	NL East	0.505	82	80	0.512	83	79	0.007
2005 PHI	NL East	0.488	79	83	0.543	88	74	0.055
2005 MIL	NL Central	0.572 F	93	69	0.500	81	81	-0.072
2005 HOU	NL Central	0.564 P	91	71	0.549 w	89	73	-0.015
2005 STL	NL Central	0.524 F	85	77	0.617 P	100	62	0.093
2005 PIT	NL Central	0.494	80	82	0.414	67	95	-0.081
2005 CIN	NL Central	0.489 F	79	83	0.451	73	89	-0.038
2005 CHC	NL Central	0.486 F	79	83	0.488	79	83	0.002
2005 COL	NL West	0.495 D	80	82	0.414	67	95	-0.081
2005 SFG	NL West	0.482	78	84	0.463	75	87	-0.019
2005 SDP	NL West	0.463 F	75	87	0.506 D	82	80	0.043
2005 ARI	NL West	0.444 F	72	90	0.475	77	85	0.031
2005 LAD	NL West	0.364	59	103	0.438	71	91	0.074
			1296	1296		1286	1306	
			2433	2427		2430	2430	

Franchise	League/Div.	OPW%	PW	PL	APW%	AW	AL	Diff(+/-)
2006 BOS	AL East	0.551 P	89	73	0.531	86	76	-0.020
2006 NYY	AL East	0.528 w	86	76	0.599 P	97	65	0.070
2006 TOR	AL East	0.527	85	77	0.537	87	75	0.010
2006 BAL	AL East	0.506 F	82	80	0.432	70	92	-0.074
2006 TBD	AL East	0.423 F	68	94	0.377	61	101	-0.046
2006 CHW	AL Central	0.533 D	86	76	0.556	90	72	0.022
2006 CLE	AL Central	0.501	81	81	0.481	78	84	-0.020
2006 DET	AL Central	0.485	79	83	0.586 w	95	67	0.102
2006 MIN	AL Central	0.470	76	86	0.593 D	96	66	0.122
2006 KCR	AL Central	0.435	70	92	0.383	62	100	-0.052
2006 SEA	AL West	0.524 D	85	77	0.481	78	84	-0.042
2006 TEX	AL West	0.522	85	77	0.494	80	82	-0.028
2006 LAA	AL West	0.503	82	80	0.549	89	73	0.046
2006 OAK	AL West	0.498	81	81	0.574 D	93	69	0.076
			1135	1133		1162	1106	
2006 ATL	NL East	0.525 D	85	77	0.488	79	83	-0.037
2006 FLA	NL East	0.502	81	81	0.481	78	84	-0.020
2006 WSN	NL East	0.500	81	81	0.438	71	91	-0.062
2006 NYM	NL East	0.495	80	82	0.599 P	97	65	0.104
2006 PHI	NL East	0.494	80	82	0.525	85	77	0.031
2006 HOU	NL Central	0.565 P	92	70	0.506	82	80	-0.059
2006 STL	NL Central	0.499 F	81	81	0.516 D	83	78	0.016
2006 CIN	NL Central	0.495 F	80	82	0.494	80	82	-0.001
2006 MIL	NL Central	0.492 F	80	82	0.463	75	87	-0.029
2006 PIT	NL Central	0.485	79	83	0.414	67	95	-0.071
2006 CHC	NL Central	0.442 F	72	90	0.407	66	96	-0.035
2006 LAD	NL West	0.546 D	88	74	0.543 w	88	74	-0.002
2006 ARI	NL West	0.523 w	85	77	0.469	76	86	-0.054
2006 COL	NL West	0.507	82	80	0.469	76	86	-0.038

Franchise	League/Div.							
2006 SDP	NL West	0.475 F	77	85	0.543 D	88	74	0.069
2006 SFG	NL West	0.447 F	72	90	0.472	76	85	0.025
			1295	1297		1267	1323	
			2430	2430		2429	2429	

Franchise	League/Div.	OPW%	PW	PL	APW%	AW	AL	Diff(+/-)
2007 NYY	AL East	0.518 D	84	78	0.580 w	94	68	0.063
2007 BOS	AL East	0.510 w	83	79	0.593 P	96	66	0.082
2007 TOR	AL East	0.497	81	81	0.512	83	79	0.015
2007 BAL	AL East	0.493 F	80	82	0.426	69	93	-0.067
2007 TBD	AL East	0.469	76	86	0.407	66	96	-0.062
2007 DET	AL Central	0.527 D	85	77	0.543	88	74	0.016
2007 CHW	AL Central	0.507	82	80	0.444	72	90	-0.063
2007 CLE	AL Central	0.504	82	80	0.593 D	96	66	0.089
2007 MIN	AL Central	0.475	77	85	0.488	79	83	0.012
2007 KCR	AL Central	0.457	74	88	0.426	69	93	-0.031
2007 SEA	AL West	0.591 P	96	66	0.543	88	74	-0.047
2007 TEX	AL West	0.496	80	82	0.463	75	87	-0.033
2007 LAA	AL West	0.480	78	84	0.580 D	94	68	0.100
2007 OAK	AL West	0.477	77	85	0.469	76	86	-0.008
			1134	1134		1145	1123	
2007 NYM	NL East	0.560 P	91	71	0.543	88	74	-0.017
2007 WSN	NL East	0.524 w	85	77	0.451	73	89	-0.073
2007 PHI	NL East	0.511	83	79	0.549 D	89	73	0.038
2007 FLA	NL East	0.455	74	88	0.438	71	91	-0.017
2007 ATL	NL East	0.424	69	93	0.519	84	78	0.095
2007 MIL	NL Central	0.616 F	100	62	0.512	83	79	-0.104
2007 HOU	NL Central	0.528 D	86	76	0.451	73	89	-0.077
2007 STL	NL Central	0.499	81	81	0.481	78	84	-0.017
2007 PIT	NL Central	0.489	79	83	0.420	68	94	-0.069
2007 CHC	NL Central	0.450 F	73	89	0.525 D	85	77	0.075
2007 CIN	NL Central	0.438 F	71	91	0.444	72	90	0.006
2007 COL	NL West	0.546 D	88	74	0.552 w	90	73	0.006
2007 SDP	NL West	0.538 F	87	75	0.546	89	74	0.008
2007 LAD	NL West	0.522	85	77	0.506	82	80	-0.016
2007 ARI	NL West	0.468	76	86	0.556 P	90	72	0.088
2007 SFG	NL West	0.429 F	70	92	0.438	71	91	0.009
			1296	1296		1286	1308	
			2430	2430		2431	2431	

Franchise	League/Div.	OPW%	PW	PL	APW%	AW	AL	Diff(+/-)
2008 BOS	AL East	0.560 P	91	71	0.586 w	95	67	0.026
2008 TBD	AL East	0.528 w	86	76	0.599 D	97	65	0.070
2008 BAL	AL East	0.512	83	79	0.422	68	93	-0.090
2008 TOR	AL East	0.499	81	81	0.531	86	76	0.032
2008 NYY	AL East	0.487	79	83	0.549	89	73	0.062
2008 MIN	AL Central	0.548 D	89	73	0.540	88	75	-0.008
2008 CLE	AL Central	0.504	82	80	0.500	81	81	-0.004
2008 KCR	AL Central	0.499	81	81	0.463	75	87	-0.036
2008 DET	AL Central	0.470	76	86	0.457	74	88	-0.014
2008 CHW	AL Central	0.378	61	101	0.546 D	89	74	0.168

397

Franchise	League/Div.	OPW%	PW	PL	APW%	AW	AL	Diff(+/-)
2008 OAK	AL West	0.519 D	84	78	0.466	75	86	-0.053
2008 SEA	AL West	0.519	84	78	0.377	61	101	-0.142
2008 LAA	AL West	0.504	82	80	0.617 P	100	62	0.113
2008 TEX	AL West	0.480	78	84	0.488	79	83	0.008
			1135	1133		1157	1111	
2008 NYM	NL East	0.526 D	85	77	0.549	89	73	0.024
2008 PHI	NL East	0.522	85	77	0.568 D	92	70	0.046
2008 ATL	NL East	0.503	81	81	0.444	72	90	-0.058
2008 WSN	NL East	0.503	81	81	0.366	59	102	-0.136
2008 FLA	NL East	0.467	76	86	0.522	84	77	0.055
2008 MIL	NL Central	0.560 F	91	71	0.556 w	90	72	-0.004
2008 HOU	NL Central	0.549 P	89	73	0.534	86	75	-0.015
2008 CHC	NL Central	0.532 w	86	76	0.602 P	97	64	0.071
2008 STL	NL Central	0.525 F	85	77	0.531	86	76	0.006
2008 PIT	NL Central	0.472	76	86	0.414	67	95	-0.058
2008 CIN	NL Central	0.425 F	69	93	0.457	74	88	0.032
2008 LAD	NL West	0.532 D	86	76	0.519 D	84	78	-0.014
2008 ARI	NL West	0.521	84	78	0.506	82	80	-0.015
2008 COL	NL West	0.462	75	87	0.457	74	88	-0.005
2008 SFG	NL West	0.461 F	75	87	0.444	72	90	-0.017
2008 SDP	NL West	0.447 F	72	90	0.389	63	99	-0.058
			1297	1295		1271	1317	
			2432	2428		2428	2428	

Franchise	League/Div.	OPW%	PW	PL	APW%	AW	AL	Diff(+/-)
2009 BOS	AL East	0.529 D	86	76	0.586 w	95	67	0.058
2009 TOR	AL East	0.508	82	80	0.463	75	87	-0.045
2009 NYY	AL East	0.507	82	80	0.636 P	103	59	0.128
2009 TBD	AL East	0.467	76	86	0.519	84	78	0.051
2009 BAL	AL East	0.451	73	89	0.395	64	98	-0.056
2009 KCR	AL Central	0.544 D	88	74	0.401	65	97	-0.143
2009 MIN	AL Central	0.540 w	87	75	0.534 D	87	76	-0.006
2009 DET	AL Central	0.506	82	80	0.528	86	77	0.021
2009 CHW	AL Central	0.451	73	89	0.488	79	83	0.037
2009 CLE	AL Central	0.439	71	91	0.401	65	97	-0.038
2009 TEX	AL West	0.571 P	93	69	0.537	87	75	-0.034
2009 SEA	AL West	0.527	85	77	0.525	85	77	-0.002
2009 OAK	AL West	0.507	82	80	0.463	75	87	-0.044
2009 LAA	AL West	0.460	75	87	0.599 D	97	65	0.139
			1135	1133		1147	1123	
2009 PHI	NL East	0.547 D	89	73	0.574 D	93	69	0.027
2009 ATL	NL East	0.526	85	77	0.531	86	76	0.004
2009 WSN	NL East	0.522	85	77	0.364	59	103	-0.158
2009 FLA	NL East	0.477	77	85	0.537	87	75	0.060
2009 NYM	NL East	0.460	75	87	0.432	70	92	-0.028
2009 MIL	NL Central	0.536 F	87	75	0.494	80	82	-0.042
2009 STL	NL Central	0.502 D	81	81	0.562 D	91	71	0.059
2009 PIT	NL Central	0.493	80	82	0.385	62	99	-0.108
2009 HOU	NL Central	0.488	79	83	0.457	74	88	-0.031
2009 CIN	NL Central	0.458 F	74	88	0.481	78	84	0.024
2009 CHC	NL Central	0.421	68	94	0.516	83	78	0.095

Franchise	League/Div.	OPW%	PW	PL	APW%	AW	AL	Diff(+/-)
2009 COL	NL West	0.561 P	91	71	0.568 w	92	70	0.007
2009 LAD	NL West	0.556 w	90	72	0.586 P	95	67	0.030
2009 ARI	NL West	0.503	82	80	0.432	70	92	-0.071
2009 SFG	NL West	0.483 F	78	84	0.543	88	74	0.060
2009 SDP	NL West	0.462 F	75	87	0.463	75	87	0.001
			1296	1296		1283	1307	
			2431	2429		2430	2430	

Franchise	League/Div.	OPW%	PW	PL	APW%	AW	AL	Diff(+/-)
2010 TBD	AL East	0.573 P	93	69	0.593 P	96	66	0.019
2010 NYY	AL East	0.564 w	91	71	0.586 w	95	67	0.022
2010 BOS	AL East	0.552	90	72	0.549	89	73	-0.003
2010 TOR	AL East	0.509	82	80	0.525	85	77	0.016
2010 BAL	AL East	0.456	74	88	0.407	66	96	-0.049
2010 CHW	AL Central	0.525 D	85	77	0.543	88	74	0.018
2010 MIN	AL Central	0.506	82	80	0.580 D	94	68	0.074
2010 CLE	AL Central	0.483	78	84	0.426	69	93	-0.057
2010 DET	AL Central	0.469	76	86	0.500	81	81	0.031
2010 KCR	AL Central	0.437 F	71	91	0.414	67	95	-0.023
2010 TEX	AL West	0.505 D	82	80	0.556 D	90	72	0.051
2010 OAK	AL West	0.483	78	84	0.500	81	81	0.017
2010 ANA	AL West	0.464	75	87	0.494	80	82	0.030
2010 SEA	AL West	0.462	75	87	0.377	61	101	-0.086
			1135	1133		1147	1123	
2010 PHI	NL East	0.543 D	88	74	0.599 P	97	65	0.056
2010 WSN	NL East	0.486	79	83	0.426	69	93	-0.060
2010 ATL	NL East	0.481	78	84	0.562 w	91	71	0.081
2010 NYM	NL East	0.470	76	86	0.488	79	83	0.017
2010 FLA	NL East	0.449	73	89	0.494	80	82	0.045
2010 MIL	NL Central	0.561 F	91	71	0.475	77	85	-0.086
2010 STL	NL Central	0.556 P	90	72	0.531	86	76	-0.025
2010 CIN	NL Central	0.526 w	85	77	0.562 D	91	71	0.036
2010 HOU	NL Central	0.485	79	83	0.469	76	86	-0.016
2010 CHC	NL Central	0.463	75	87	0.463	75	87	0.000
2010 PIT	NL Central	0.451	73	89	0.352	57	105	-0.099
2010 ARI	NL West	0.529 D	86	76	0.401	65	97	-0.128
2010 LAD	NL West	0.525	85	77	0.494	80	82	-0.032
2010 SFG	NL West	0.508 F	82	80	0.568 D	92	70	0.060
2010 SDP	NL West	0.496	80	82	0.556	90	72	0.060
2010 COL	NL West	0.476	77	85	0.512	83	79	0.037
			1296	1296		1283	1307	
			2431	2429		2430	2430	

Franchise	League/Div.	OPW%	PW	PL	APW%	AW	AL	Diff(+/-)
2011 NYY	AL East	0.573 P	93	69	0.599 P	97	65	0.025
2011 BOS	AL East	0.568 w	92	70	0.556	90	72	-0.012
2011 TOR	AL East	0.544	88	74	0.500	81	81	-0.044
2011 TBD	AL East	0.513	83	79	0.562 w	91	71	0.049
2011 BAL	AL East	0.399	65	97	0.426	69	93	0.027
2011 DET	AL Central	0.569 D	92	70	0.586 D	95	67	0.017
2011 KCR	AL Central	0.506	82	80	0.438	71	91	-0.068

Franchise	League/Div.	OPW%	PW	PL	APW%	AW	AL	Diff(+/-)
2011 CHW	AL Central	0.506	82	80	0.488	79	83	-0.018
2011 CLE	AL Central	0.450	73	89	0.494	80	82	0.044
2011 MIN	AL Central	0.428	69	93	0.389	63	99	-0.039
2011 TEX	AL West	0.511 D	83	79	0.593 D	96	66	0.082
2011 ANA	AL West	0.493	80	82	0.531	86	76	0.038
2011 OAK	AL West	0.479	78	84	0.457	74	88	-0.022
2011 SEA	AL West	0.466	76	86	0.414	67	95	-0.053
			1135	1133		1147	1123	
2011 WSN	NL East	0.538 D	87	75	0.497	80	81	-0.042
2011 FLA	NL East	0.510 w	83	79	0.444	72	90	-0.066
2011 ATL	NL East	0.498	81	81	0.549	89	73	0.051
2011 PHI	NL East	0.495	80	82	0.630 P	102	60	0.134
2011 NYM	NL East	0.484	78	84	0.475	77	85	-0.009
2011 MIL	NL Central	0.630 F	102	60	0.593 D	96	66	-0.038
2011 STL	NL Central	0.513 D	83	79	0.556 w	90	72	0.043
2011 CIN	NL Central	0.507	82	80	0.488	79	83	-0.019
2011 PIT	NL Central	0.473	77	85	0.444	72	90	-0.029
2011 HOU	NL Central	0.466	76	86	0.346	56	106	-0.121
2011 CHC	NL Central	0.454	74	88	0.438	71	91	-0.016
2011 LAD	NL West	0.572 P	93	69	0.509	82	79	-0.062
2011 SDP	NL West	0.479	78	84	0.438	71	91	-0.040
2011 ARI	NL West	0.478	77	85	0.580 D	94	68	0.103
2011 SFG	NL West	0.458 F	74	88	0.531	86	76	0.072
2011 COL	NL West	0.442	72	90	0.451	73	89	0.008
			1296	1296		1283	1307	
			2431	2429		2430	2430	

Franchise	League/Div.	OPW%	PW	PL	APW%	AW	AL	Diff(+/-)
2012 TBD	AL East	0.607 P	98	64	0.556	90	72	-0.051
2012 NYY	AL East	0.505 w	82	80	0.586 P	95	67	0.081
2012 BOS	AL East	0.472	77	85	0.426	69	93	-0.047
2012 TOR	AL East	0.465	75	87	0.451	73	89	-0.014
2012 BAL	AL East	0.448 F	73	89	0.574 w	93	69	0.126
2012 KCR	AL Central	0.552 D	89	73	0.444	72	90	-0.108
2012 DET	AL Central	0.510 w	83	79	0.543 D	88	74	0.033
2012 CHW	AL Central	0.492	80	82	0.525	85	77	0.033
2012 MIN	AL Central	0.487	79	83	0.407	66	96	-0.080
2012 CLE	AL Central	0.423 F	68	94	0.420	68	94	-0.003
2012 SEA	AL West	0.574 D	93	69	0.463	75	87	-0.111
2012 ANA	AL West	0.504	82	80	0.549	89	73	0.046
2012 TEX	AL West	0.493	80	82	0.574 w	93	69	0.081
2012 OAK	AL West	0.476	77	85	0.580 D	94	68	0.104
			1135	1133		1147	1123	
2012 WSN	NL East	0.578 D	94	68	0.605 P	98	64	0.027
2012 ATL	NL East	0.521 w	84	78	0.580 w	94	68	0.059
2012 NYM	NL East	0.492	80	82	0.457	74	88	-0.035
2012 FLA	NL East	0.478	77	85	0.426	69	93	-0.052
2012 PHI	NL East	0.465	75	87	0.500	81	81	0.035
2012 PIT	NL Central	0.597 P	97	65	0.488	79	83	-0.109
2012 MIL	NL Central	0.572 F	93	69	0.512	83	79	-0.059
2012 CIN	NL Central	0.515	83	79	0.599 D	97	65	0.084

Franchise	League/Div.	OPW%	PW	PL	APW%	AW	AL	Diff(+/-)
2012 STL	NL Central	0.498	81	81	0.543 w	88	74	0.045
2012 CHC	NL Central	0.471	76	86	0.377	61	101	-0.094
2012 HOU	NL Central	0.389	63	99	0.340	55	107	-0.049
2012 LAD	NL West	0.546 D	89	73	0.531	86	76	-0.016
2012 ARI	NL West	0.535 w	87	75	0.500	81	81	-0.035
2012 COL	NL West	0.466	76	86	0.395	64	98	-0.071
2012 SDP	NL West	0.458 F	74	88	0.469	76	86	0.012
2012 SFG	NL West	0.425	69	93	0.580 D	94	68	0.155
			1296	1296		1283	1307	
			2431	2429		2430	2430	

Franchise	League/Div.	OPW%	PW	PL	APW%	AW	AL	Diff(+/-)
2013 BOS	AL East	0.571 P	92	70	0.599 P	97	65	0.028
2013 TBD	AL East	0.541 w	88	74	0.564 w	92	71	0.024
2013 NYY	AL East	0.539 w	87	75	0.525	85	77	-0.014
2013 BAL	AL East	0.521	84	78	0.525	85	77	0.004
2013 TOR	AL East	0.401 F	65	97	0.457	74	88	0.056
2013 KCR	AL Central	0.677 F	110	52	0.531	86	76	-0.146
2013 DET	AL Central	0.504 D	82	80	0.574 D	93	69	0.070
2013 MIN	AL Central	0.472 F	76	86	0.407	66	96	-0.064
2013 CLE	AL Central	0.469 F	76	86	0.568 w	92	70	0.099
2013 CHW	AL Central	0.402	65	97	0.389	63	99	-0.013
2013 SEA	AL West	0.520 D	84	78	0.438	71	91	-0.081
2013 TEX	AL West	0.517	84	78	0.558	91	72	0.041
2013 ANA	AL West	0.514	83	79	0.481	78	84	-0.032
2013 OAK	AL West	0.439	71	91	0.593 D	96	66	0.154
2013 HOU	AL West	0.427	69	93	0.315	51	111	-0.112
			1217	1213		1220	1212	
2013 ATL	NL East	0.530 D	86	76	0.593 D	96	66	0.063
2013 WSN	NL East	0.524	85	77	0.531	86	76	0.007
2013 NYM	NL East	0.514	83	79	0.457	74	88	-0.057
2013 FLA	NL East	0.468	76	86	0.383	62	100	-0.085
2013 PHI	NL East	0.468	76	86	0.451	73	89	-0.017
2013 STL	NL Central	0.575 P	93	69	0.599 P	97	65	0.023
2013 CIN	NL Central	0.564 w	91	71	0.556 w	90	72	-0.008
2013 PIT	NL Central	0.552 w	89	73	0.580 w	94	68	0.028
2013 MIL	NL Central	0.477	77	85	0.457	74	88	-0.020
2013 CHC	NL Central	0.430	70	92	0.407	66	96	-0.023
2013 ARI	NL West	0.542 D	88	74	0.500	81	81	-0.042
2013 LAD	NL West	0.502	81	81	0.568 D	92	70	0.066
2013 COL	NL West	0.499	81	81	0.457	74	88	-0.042
2013 SFG	NL West	0.439	71	91	0.469	76	86	0.030
2013 SDP	NL West	0.412	67	95	0.469	76	86	0.057
			1296	1296		1283	1307	
			2431	2429		2430	2430	

P = "original" or "actual" pennant winner (best overall record)

D = "original" or "actual" division winner

w = "original" or "actual" wild card winner

F = failed to meet 4000 PA / BFP minimum requirements *

401

* adjusted PA/BFP minimum requirements:

- war-shortened seasons:	1918 = 3200, 1919 = 3400
- strike-shortened seasons:	1972 = 3800, 1981 = 2700, 1994 = 2700, 1995 = 3500
- 154-game schedule	1904-1912 NL, 1913-1917, 1920-1960 = 3800
- shorter schedule / misc.:	1901-1903 NL = 3400
	1901 AL = 500
	1902-1903 AL = 750
	1904 AL = 1500
	1905-1908 AL = 2000
	1909 AL = 2500
	1910 AL = 3000
	1911-1912 AL = 3400

Wins Above Replacement and Win Shares – Standings (1901-2013)

Franchise	OWAR	OWS	AWAR	AWS	WARdiff	WSdiff	P/D/W
1901 PHA	**7.359**	**50.964**	32.058	221.996	-24.699	-171.032	P
1901 DET	5.999	40.666	32.630	219.000	-26.630	-178.334	
1901 WS1	6.365	37.275	26.466	182.994	-20.100	-145.718	
1902 WS1	3.606	**40.708**	27.327	182.995	-23.722	-142.287	
1902 CLE	**6.219**	38.144	34.015	207.003	-27.796	-168.859	
1902 DET	4.850	32.148	17.116	156.001	-12.267	-123.853	P
1902 NYY	1.114	18.134	29.296	149.894	-28.183	-131.760	
1903 CLE	**9.901**	**55.197**	36.728	231.001	-26.827	-175.804	
1903 WS1	4.471	52.543	7.819	129.005	-3.348	-76.462	
1903 CHW	1.511	49.839	15.852	179.999	-14.342	-130.160	
1903 PHA	6.295	48.777	37.561	225.000	-31.266	-176.223	P
1903 DET	7.318	45.554	31.878	194.996	-24.560	-149.442	
1904 CHW	**16.337**	**108.010**	37.422	266.999	-21.084	-158.988	P
1904 PHA	13.129	76.025	41.955	243.006	-28.826	-166.982	
1904 BOS	6.354	75.513	41.874	**284.995**	-35.521	-209.483	
1904 CLE	9.129	70.634	**46.706**	257.997	-37.577	-187.363	
1904 WS1	5.695	62.486	5.058	113.998	0.637	-51.512	
1905 PHA	12.882	**102.132**	48.692	276.004	-35.810	-173.872	P
1905 CLE	**13.093**	100.522	33.477	228.003	-20.384	-127.481	
1905 BOS	10.993	98.662	33.893	233.999	-22.900	-135.337	
1905 SLB	11.968	96.628	21.016	161.997	-9.049	-65.369	
1905 DET	6.642	93.441	23.715	237.004	-17.073	-143.563	
1905 NYY	8.882	90.238	31.452	213.007	-22.570	-122.769	
1906 NYY	14.351	**151.869**	37.273	269.987	-22.922	-118.118	P
1906 PHA	15.285	114.550	38.923	234.002	-23.638	-119.451	
1906 DET	10.826	110.695	20.128	212.999	-9.302	-102.304	
1906 BOS	11.324	107.579	15.815	147.000	-4.492	-39.420	
1906 CLE	**15.855**	101.907	**52.350**	267.010	-36.495	-165.103	
1907 DET	19.362	**143.163**	38.710	**276.004**	-19.348	-132.842	P
1907 NYY	11.318	140.935	23.029	209.989	-11.711	-69.054	
1907 SLB	12.986	126.868	33.654	207.003	-20.668	-80.135	
1907 PHA	16.631	123.948	**45.341**	264.007	-28.711	-140.059	
1907 CLE	17.403	118.981	36.193	254.989	-18.790	-136.008	
1907 BOS	**20.054**	115.044	25.717	176.996	-5.662	-61.953	
1907 WS1	11.459	92.102	29.675	147.005	-18.217	-54.903	
1908 BOS	**24.902**	**174.278**	36.007	224.994	-11.105	-50.716	
1908 CLE	21.929	148.351	40.554	**269.997**	-18.625	-121.647	

1908 SLB	11.270	144.513	36.480	248.999	-25.210	-104.486	
1908 DET	23.317	144.321	**42.517**	269.997	-19.199	-125.676	
1908 PHA	20.908	141.547	28.316	204.003	-7.407	-62.456	P
1908 WS1	18.441	126.544	33.681	200.999	-15.240	-74.454	
1908 NYY	6.355	112.493	14.014	153.004	-7.659	-40.511	
1909 BOS	36.690	**244.326**	37.418	264.003	-0.728	-19.677	
1909 PHA	**43.552**	232.197	**55.227**	285.001	-11.675	-52.804	P
1909 DET	33.046	194.939	46.493	**293.955**	-13.447	-99.016	
1909 NYY	21.221	184.605	26.158	221.997	-4.937	-37.391	
1909 CLE	20.920	165.439	27.808	213.001	-6.888	-47.562	
1909 SLB	13.674	154.636	19.283	182.998	-5.608	-28.362	
1909 WS1	19.735	122.652	12.388	126.004	7.347	-3.352	
1910 PHA	**50.924**	**274.987**	**58.878**	**305.996**	-7.954	-31.010	P
1910 NYY	33.269	210.108	42.065	264.000	-8.796	-53.892	
1910 DET	30.267	193.061	35.661	257.995	-5.394	-64.933	
1910 CHW	27.779	183.292	25.057	204.006	2.722	-20.714	
1910 CLE	14.459	157.096	23.705	213.005	-9.245	-55.909	
1910 SLB	-1.479	133.499	1.329	141.003	-2.807	-7.504	
1911 PHA	**53.067**	**304.412**	52.339	303.002	0.728	1.410	P
1911 BOS	47.412	264.777	41.511	233.994	5.901	30.783	
1911 DET	33.347	215.667	35.596	267.006	-2.249	-51.339	
1911 NYY	34.227	209.515	37.263	227.999	-3.036	-18.483	
1911 CLE	17.434	189.332	31.451	239.998	-14.017	-50.666	
1911 SLB	2.893	129.202	4.497	135.000	-1.605	-5.798	
1912 BOS	**51.009**	**324.136**	52.304	**315.003**	-1.295	9.132	P
1912 PHA	46.395	289.380	42.452	269.994	3.942	19.386	
1912 CHW	33.069	226.974	33.250	234.005	-0.181	-7.031	
1912 DET	26.990	190.054	27.560	206.944	-0.570	-16.890	
1912 SLB	18.833	165.389	18.714	158.997	0.119	6.391	
1912 CLE	17.617	158.519	30.022	225.003	-12.405	-66.485	
1912 NYY	20.726	146.326	21.742	149.995	-1.016	-3.670	
1913 PHA	**46.882**	**282.386**	**48.880**	**287.995**	-1.998	-5.609	P
1913 BOS	43.290	257.050	42.955	237.005	0.335	20.045	
1913 CHW	28.726	249.052	29.462	234.006	-0.736	15.047	
1913 NYY	29.133	197.925	17.747	171.005	11.386	26.920	
1913 CLE	24.077	186.565	38.870	258.001	-14.793	-71.436	
1913 DET	25.629	181.958	28.376	197.999	-2.746	-16.040	
1913 SLB	17.456	173.239	17.219	170.998	0.237	2.241	
1914 BOS	**48.815**	**291.975**	41.049	272.999	7.767	18.976	
1914 PHA	47.288	276.718	**51.453**	**294.000**	-4.165	-17.282	P
1914 WS1	46.140	256.050	37.479	243.005	8.661	13.046	
1914 DET	36.928	241.550	34.876	239.997	2.052	1.553	
1914 NYY	29.601	231.667	30.461	210.001	-0.859	21.665	
1914 SLB	24.112	216.735	22.615	212.995	1.497	3.741	
1914 CHW	23.314	201.595	29.932	210.007	-6.618	-8.412	
1914 CLE	17.811	142.213	17.302	153.002	0.509	-10.789	
1915 BOS	**52.563**	**323.425**	46.533	**303.004**	6.031	20.421	P
1915 DET	52.451	299.013	50.256	300.005	2.195	-0.992	
1915 WS1	49.125	272.454	41.977	254.992	7.148	17.463	
1915 CHW	46.579	243.902	**59.484**	279.002	-12.905	-35.101	
1915 NYY	32.939	212.363	30.977	207.004	1.962	5.359	
1915 SLB	26.687	212.163	23.819	189.002	2.868	23.161	
1915 PHA	17.684	174.612	2.168	129.001	15.516	45.611	
1915 CLE	22.475	171.892	25.554	171.006	-3.079	0.886	

1916 BOS	**49.167**	**313.181**	38.423	**273.007**	10.743	40.174	
1916 DET	36.143	268.498	37.190	261.010	-1.048	7.489	P
1916 SLB	41.424	266.377	37.700	236.996	3.724	29.381	
1916 CHW	37.326	244.549	**48.783**	266.995	-11.457	-22.446	
1916 WS1	36.031	224.169	37.599	228.000	-1.568	-3.831	
1916 NYY	30.371	210.410	36.927	240.003	-6.556	-29.593	
1916 PHA	29.137	178.007	8.554	108.001	20.584	70.006	
1917 BOS	**54.197**	**326.662**	39.260	270.001	14.937	56.661	P
1917 CHW	45.546	284.106	**51.571**	**299.996**	-6.025	-15.890	
1917 DET	43.290	258.656	38.262	234.002	5.028	24.655	
1917 NYY	41.032	250.336	33.450	213.006	7.582	37.330	
1917 PHA	36.515	223.047	22.873	165.002	13.642	58.045	
1917 WS1	34.725	214.760	33.721	221.995	1.005	-7.234	
1917 SLB	21.997	189.141	20.483	170.998	1.514	18.143	
1918 CLE	31.761	**210.181**	**37.574**	218.997	-5.813	-8.816	
1918 CHW	32.263	209.873	31.114	171.003	1.150	38.870	
1918 SLB	29.783	203.787	27.868	174.001	1.915	29.787	
1918 DET	**33.063**	197.103	22.684	165.002	10.379	32.101	
1918 NYY	31.239	194.210	25.567	179.997	5.672	14.213	P
1918 WS1	26.160	188.581	35.366	215.999	-9.205	-27.418	
1918 PHA	23.361	181.710	10.491	155.999	12.869	25.711	
1919 DET	**48.731**	**282.396**	34.181	239.997	14.550	42.399	P
1919 CHW	39.769	276.482	**46.473**	**264.000**	-6.704	12.483	
1919 NYY	33.318	230.864	33.314	240.002	0.004	-9.138	
1919 PHA	33.314	224.448	9.061	107.996	24.253	116.451	
1919 SLB	28.950	209.189	27.448	200.996	1.502	8.193	
1919 WS1	33.616	194.938	31.056	168.000	2.559	26.937	
1920 DET	30.797	**236.583**	21.634	183.004	9.162	53.579	
1920 PHA	34.388	227.966	14.952	144.000	19.436	83.966	
1920 NYY	38.160	226.601	48.875	284.996	-10.714	-58.395	P
1920 SLB	**39.068**	223.288	39.640	227.996	-0.572	-4.708	
1920 WS1	27.020	215.647	29.048	204.006	-2.028	11.641	
1921 DET	**49.311**	**289.572**	40.443	212.999	8.868	76.573	
1921 CLE	41.138	279.636	**51.817**	282.001	-10.678	-2.365	P
1921 SLB	30.668	232.388	34.296	243.001	-3.628	-10.612	
1921 CHW	22.749	214.455	22.291	185.996	0.458	28.459	
1921 PHA	33.160	211.023	23.497	159.000	9.663	52.023	
1922 DET	39.393	**266.641**	39.064	237.001	0.330	29.639	
1922 CHW	31.744	251.772	30.662	230.997	1.082	20.775	P
1922 SLB	**45.836**	247.491	**55.191**	278.999	-9.355	-31.507	
1922 NYY	32.995	230.640	41.573	**282.002**	-8.578	-51.362	
1922 CLE	28.410	229.030	36.295	233.996	-7.885	-4.966	
1922 PHA	30.572	220.038	23.379	194.999	7.193	25.039	
1923 CLE	**42.432**	**248.258**	**47.113**	245.986	-4.681	2.271	
1923 DET	36.404	248.232	43.338	249.001	-6.934	-0.769	
1923 CHW	29.378	226.303	33.679	207.002	-4.301	19.301	
1923 PHA	31.242	225.553	24.395	206.996	6.847	18.558	P
1923 NYY	27.661	208.935	46.445	**293.999**	-18.784	-85.064	
1924 WS1	**43.125**	**287.500**	44.551	276.001	-1.426	11.500	P
1924 DET	42.051	259.036	42.773	257.997	-0.722	1.039	
1924 PHA	34.298	234.430	25.851	212.991	8.447	21.439	
1924 CLE	34.496	224.703	32.791	201.001	1.705	23.702	
1924 NYY	32.826	219.655	43.167	266.997	-10.341	-47.341	
1924 CHW	32.177	218.426	31.020	198.002	1.156	20.424	

404

1924 SLB	27.553	194.709	32.389	221.995	-4.836	-27.286	
1925 WS1	39.892	**267.134**	**45.091**	**287.995**	-5.199	-20.861	P
1925 CHW	37.130	266.510	36.812	237.000	0.318	29.510	
1925 PHA	**44.353**	263.705	44.802	264.000	-0.449	-0.295	
1925 DET	34.508	240.889	39.333	242.962	-4.825	-2.073	
1925 NYY	27.834	211.476	34.052	207.005	-6.218	4.471	
1925 CLE	27.772	211.130	32.860	210.002	-5.088	1.129	
1926 CLE	41.872	**273.967**	37.550	263.998	4.322	9.969	P
1926 WS1	34.200	269.441	34.610	243.001	-0.410	26.440	
1926 DET	40.341	263.185	36.348	237.005	3.993	26.180	
1926 CHW	**42.198**	262.706	42.683	242.997	-0.485	19.709	
1926 PHA	41.528	249.701	41.809	249.002	-0.281	0.699	
1926 NYY	35.214	243.379	**49.449**	**273.003**	-14.235	-29.624	
1926 SLB	30.067	231.559	18.892	185.999	11.175	45.560	
1927 NYY	**53.117**	**290.546**	**66.514**	**329.993**	-13.397	-39.447	P
1927 DET	41.210	281.465	36.906	246.000	4.304	35.465	
1927 PHA	41.194	273.945	48.349	273.000	-7.155	0.944	
1927 WS1	36.577	253.883	37.817	254.999	-1.241	-1.116	
1927 CLE	37.022	236.755	24.787	198.004	12.235	38.750	
1927 BOS	32.643	230.713	13.744	153.000	18.899	77.713	
1927 CHW	31.062	221.356	30.682	210.002	0.380	11.354	
1927 SLB	29.248	194.447	19.004	176.997	10.244	17.450	
1928 PHA	**48.115**	**296.547**	51.994	294.001	-3.880	2.545	P
1928 NYY	45.894	291.195	**52.421**	**303.002**	-6.527	-11.807	
1928 WS1	40.488	273.032	37.172	225.000	3.316	48.033	
1928 DET	39.168	259.372	28.379	203.999	10.789	55.373	
1928 SLB	33.171	223.656	34.443	246.001	-1.272	-22.345	
1928 CLE	36.038	220.311	22.578	186.004	13.460	34.307	
1928 BOS	29.777	218.346	19.138	171.000	10.638	47.346	
1928 CHW	25.277	216.797	23.707	216.003	1.570	0.794	
1929 NYY	48.765	**316.393**	46.521	264.002	2.244	52.391	
1929 PHA	**49.574**	300.264	**53.067**	**311.995**	-3.493	-11.732	P
1929 SLB	35.463	249.770	31.778	237.001	3.685	12.769	
1929 DET	40.425	248.055	34.500	210.000	5.925	38.056	
1929 WS1	30.760	245.104	30.379	212.997	0.381	32.106	
1929 CLE	41.574	239.153	32.608	243.003	8.966	-3.850	
1929 BOS	30.091	226.404	17.875	173.995	12.216	52.409	
1929 CHW	20.666	195.309	16.739	176.995	3.927	18.314	
1930 PHA	**51.987**	**311.741**	50.662	**306.005**	1.326	5.735	
1930 WS1	38.176	285.545	44.761	282.003	-6.585	3.542	P
1930 NYY	44.505	280.917	**52.064**	257.995	-7.559	22.921	
1930 DET	36.525	255.306	30.099	224.992	6.426	30.314	
1930 CLE	38.897	241.846	30.380	243.004	8.516	-1.159	
1930 CHW	31.388	233.382	25.122	186.000	6.266	47.382	
1930 SLB	28.246	212.334	20.780	192.006	7.465	20.327	
1930 BOS	33.762	209.073	13.794	155.997	19.968	53.075	
1931 PHA	**58.740**	**318.811**	53.495	**320.997**	5.245	-2.186	
1931 NYY	58.185	308.338	**65.642**	282.001	-7.456	26.337	P
1931 WS1	42.607	276.489	42.991	276.003	-0.384	0.486	
1931 CLE	43.344	245.205	37.082	233.999	6.262	11.206	
1931 BOS	32.501	230.903	19.105	185.996	13.396	44.907	
1931 DET	32.213	228.521	23.975	182.998	8.238	45.523	
1931 SLB	22.928	188.943	25.971	189.000	-3.043	-0.057	
1931 CHW	7.640	172.284	13.875	167.997	-6.235	4.288	

1932 NYY	**58.761**	**340.753**	**61.645**	**321.005**	-2.884	19.747	
1932 PHA	54.672	294.335	53.738	282.001	0.935	12.335	P
1932 WS1	36.755	265.995	40.665	279.004	-3.909	-13.009	
1932 CLE	43.291	257.027	41.130	261.002	2.161	-3.975	
1932 DET	44.729	255.911	31.314	228.005	13.416	27.906	
1932 CHW	21.515	205.372	17.043	146.998	4.472	58.374	
1932 BOS	28.555	204.367	11.482	129.001	17.074	75.366	
1932 SLB	24.577	191.088	27.328	188.995	-2.751	2.093	
1933 NYY	**53.321**	**286.581**	**56.655**	272.998	-3.334	13.583	
1933 PHA	40.046	265.775	40.812	237.002	-0.766	28.772	
1933 WS1	38.885	263.448	47.484	**297.000**	-8.599	-33.553	P
1933 DET	41.283	255.355	35.108	224.998	6.175	30.357	
1933 CLE	37.217	242.834	29.061	225.008	8.156	17.827	
1933 CHW	26.449	210.683	28.718	201.002	-2.269	9.681	
1933 SLB	17.589	172.835	23.509	165.001	-5.920	7.834	
1934 DET	**49.000**	**282.854**	52.440	**303.003**	-3.440	-20.149	P
1934 NYY	45.825	279.959	**53.273**	282.003	-7.449	-2.044	
1934 CLE	41.415	248.605	40.479	255.001	0.936	-6.395	
1934 PHA	35.992	231.672	29.518	204.003	6.474	27.669	
1934 WS1	28.616	206.555	29.897	197.996	-1.281	8.559	
1935 NYY	49.136	**294.364**	46.789	266.999	2.346	27.365	
1935 DET	**49.872**	272.301	**51.017**	**278.998**	-1.145	-6.697	P
1935 CLE	43.169	253.793	41.223	245.997	1.946	7.796	
1935 WS1	30.019	216.691	26.617	201.000	3.402	15.691	
1935 PHA	33.093	208.630	26.321	174.004	6.772	34.626	
1936 NYY	**55.536**	**305.509**	**59.685**	**306.007**	-4.149	-0.497	P
1936 DET	48.024	260.871	43.089	249.001	4.934	11.869	
1936 WS1	39.028	259.921	36.818	245.993	2.210	13.927	
1936 CLE	41.342	231.820	45.848	239.997	-4.506	-8.176	
1936 PHA	25.317	194.795	11.423	158.997	13.894	35.797	
1937 NYY	**57.614**	**339.863**	**57.223**	**305.995**	0.391	33.868	P
1937 DET	42.963	258.144	40.607	266.993	2.356	-8.849	
1937 CLE	42.012	243.905	41.760	249.005	0.252	-5.100	
1937 WS1	26.883	215.259	26.925	219.001	-0.042	-3.742	
1937 PHA	29.182	210.210	25.081	162.002	4.101	48.208	
1938 NYY	**50.287**	**310.104**	**52.768**	**297.000**	-2.481	13.104	P
1938 DET	37.906	255.920	34.791	252.001	3.116	3.919	
1938 WS1	37.530	246.722	34.704	225.006	2.826	21.716	
1938 CLE	38.163	242.928	40.880	257.996	-2.717	-15.068	
1938 PHA	33.276	225.507	22.078	159.000	11.198	66.507	
1938 BOS	32.805	222.853	43.252	263.995	-10.447	-41.142	
1939 NYY	**60.803**	**345.561**	**60.482**	**318.007**	0.321	27.555	P
1939 CLE	42.132	268.894	42.553	260.997	-0.421	7.897	
1939 DET	41.559	241.882	42.474	243.000	-0.915	-1.118	
1939 BOS	29.183	241.660	42.173	266.999	-12.990	-25.339	
1939 WS1	32.980	238.081	31.325	195.003	1.654	43.078	
1939 PHA	30.422	231.059	16.737	165.001	13.685	66.058	
1939 SLB	22.389	167.604	14.499	128.996	7.890	38.607	
1940 NYY	43.551	**298.437**	43.246	264.004	0.305	34.432	P
1940 CLE	42.932	268.698	42.376	266.996	0.555	1.702	
1940 DET	**45.539**	253.261	**51.904**	**269.997**	-6.365	-16.736	
1940 BOS	33.180	240.954	40.922	245.997	-7.742	-5.043	
1940 WS1	30.223	222.529	26.028	192.001	4.195	30.528	
1940 PHA	30.147	214.113	20.398	161.998	9.750	52.115	

1941 NYY	43.022	**287.700**	51.332	**303.000**	-8.311	-15.300	
1941 BOS	**52.304**	274.892	46.044	249.001	6.260	25.890	P
1941 CLE	43.074	267.373	34.966	225.004	8.108	42.369	
1941 WS1	32.188	255.613	29.697	210.006	2.492	45.607	
1941 DET	36.773	228.322	35.130	224.994	1.643	3.327	
1941 PHA	30.632	225.951	22.568	191.999	8.064	33.952	
1942 BOS	**52.133**	**302.712**	49.580	278.994	2.554	23.718	P
1942 NYY	48.896	296.661	**59.397**	**308.997**	-10.501	-12.336	
1942 DET	36.922	226.871	32.579	218.996	4.343	7.875	
1942 WS1	24.915	221.317	26.420	186.003	-1.505	35.313	
1942 CLE	34.444	218.837	29.097	224.999	5.347	-6.162	
1942 PHA	26.337	204.470	14.154	165.004	12.184	39.466	
1943 NYY	**49.706**	**284.756**	52.424	**293.995**	-2.719	-9.239	P
1943 DET	40.103	246.747	39.859	233.999	0.244	12.748	
1943 WS1	29.278	233.799	40.527	251.993	-11.249	-18.194	
1943 PHA	31.393	228.562	10.483	147.002	20.910	81.561	
1943 CLE	38.448	220.023	38.504	246.003	-0.056	-25.981	
1943 BOS	29.297	208.873	27.605	203.998	1.693	4.875	
1944 DET	42.123	**268.013**	40.320	**264.004**	1.804	4.008	P
1944 PHA	37.672	263.148	28.470	216.006	9.202	47.142	
1944 NYY	**42.402**	240.822	**41.007**	248.996	1.396	-8.174	
1944 BOS	41.309	231.744	38.218	230.999	3.091	0.745	
1944 CLE	41.191	229.366	36.507	216.003	4.684	13.363	
1945 DET	33.171	**249.397**	38.376	**264.000**	-5.204	-14.603	
1945 WS1	33.277	240.404	40.643	261.009	-7.366	-20.604	
1945 CLE	38.273	236.212	35.173	219.006	3.100	17.207	P
1945 NYY	**40.503**	223.617	**41.655**	242.996	-1.152	-19.379	
1945 PHA	30.228	221.741	18.276	156.006	11.952	65.735	
1945 BOS	26.376	186.551	26.968	212.997	-0.592	-26.446	
1946 BOS	56.132	**313.743**	51.043	**312.005**	5.089	1.738	P
1946 DET	**58.372**	303.604	49.857	275.999	8.514	27.605	
1946 NYY	47.289	267.259	46.596	260.995	0.694	6.263	
1946 CLE	39.276	235.470	31.320	203.996	7.957	31.474	
1946 WS1	17.150	208.480	27.373	227.993	-10.223	-19.513	
1946 PHA	22.270	178.905	20.877	146.999	1.393	31.906	
1947 NYY	**49.728**	**283.464**	51.027	**291.004**	-1.299	-7.539	
1947 BOS	46.452	269.194	39.982	248.996	6.470	20.199	
1947 DET	47.206	266.259	44.081	255.003	3.125	11.256	
1947 CLE	45.491	255.613	39.371	240.003	6.120	15.610	P
1947 CHW	27.216	250.449	24.598	210.006	2.618	40.443	
1947 PHA	27.895	226.057	29.981	233.998	-2.086	-7.942	
1947 WS1	20.055	217.685	18.222	192.002	1.833	25.683	
1948 CLE	**57.927**	**291.555**	59.662	**291.005**	-1.736	0.550	P
1948 NYY	48.516	281.574	50.714	282.010	-2.198	-0.436	
1948 DET	47.057	266.011	40.634	233.999	6.423	32.012	
1948 BOS	36.813	265.615	47.833	288.001	-11.020	-22.385	
1948 PHA	35.528	255.288	32.881	252.001	2.647	3.287	
1948 WS1	14.236	181.387	13.115	167.997	1.121	13.390	
1949 NYY	39.427	**269.388**	45.229	**291.003**	-5.802	-21.615	
1949 CLE	**43.503**	263.955	44.961	267.004	-1.458	-3.048	P
1949 PHA	34.672	253.725	31.233	243.003	3.439	10.722	
1949 BOS	39.556	248.411	**53.811**	287.999	-14.255	-39.588	
1949 DET	42.264	232.585	43.409	260.996	-1.145	-28.411	
1949 WS1	20.878	169.014	15.493	150.003	5.385	19.011	

1950 CLE	**46.822**	**268.999**	48.486	275.995	-1.664	-6.996	
1950 NYY	40.797	259.495	**51.444**	**294.000**	-10.647	-34.505	
1950 BOS	41.018	251.097	50.245	282.005	-9.226	-30.909	P
1950 DET	41.049	244.312	46.468	284.999	-5.418	-40.686	
1951 CLE	**51.200**	**287.005**	45.973	278.997	5.228	8.008	P
1951 NYY	36.856	247.643	**51.250**	**294.003**	-14.394	-46.360	
1951 BOS	34.692	214.744	43.569	260.998	-8.877	-46.254	
1951 DET	33.270	204.667	33.891	218.998	-0.621	-14.331	
1952 CLE	**54.950**	**295.508**	50.261	278.999	4.688	16.509	P
1952 NYY	42.349	256.725	**50.379**	**284.996**	-8.029	-28.271	
1952 BOS	25.934	198.868	31.688	227.997	-5.754	-29.129	
1952 DET	31.618	175.226	25.062	150.001	6.556	25.225	
1953 CLE	**48.460**	**277.574**	47.599	276.000	0.862	1.574	P
1953 NYY	34.622	240.927	**54.434**	**296.998**	-19.812	-56.071	
1953 BOS	28.482	210.886	36.350	251.994	-7.868	-41.108	
1953 DET	27.813	162.054	23.783	180.000	4.031	-17.946	
1954 CLE	**47.466**	**265.862**	52.132	279.005	-4.666	-13.143	P
1954 NYY	38.671	258.211	49.015	**288.006**	-10.344	-29.795	
1954 DET	41.703	226.462	42.884	237.002	-1.181	-10.540	
1954 BOS	34.099	205.846	42.691	252.008	-8.592	-46.162	
1954 CHW	16.096	171.747	47.132	273.011	-31.036	-101.264	
1955 NYY	38.749	**258.731**	49.015	**288.006**	-10.266	-29.275	
1955 CLE	**45.834**	256.721	**52.132**	279.005	-6.298	-22.284	
1955 DET	39.551	214.777	42.884	237.002	-3.333	-22.225	P
1955 BOS	32.030	193.357	42.691	252.008	-10.661	-58.651	
1955 MIN	28.329	189.083	18.605	159.001	9.724	30.082	
1956 CLE	**47.671**	**271.494**	44.193	264.005	3.478	7.488	P
1956 NYY	41.148	268.238	**50.279**	**290.998**	-9.131	-22.760	
1956 DET	36.684	214.645	45.575	246.003	-8.891	-31.357	
1956 BOS	35.502	211.091	42.353	252.003	-6.850	-40.912	
1957 NYY	**38.680**	**254.952**	49.789	**294.004**	-11.110	-39.052	
1957 CLE	36.296	245.826	32.486	227.996	3.810	17.830	
1957 DET	36.311	233.016	35.908	234.002	0.404	-0.985	P
1957 BOS	32.028	197.188	39.500	245.996	-7.472	-48.808	
1958 NYY	37.890	**258.351**	**48.268**	**275.992**	-10.378	-17.642	
1958 CLE	36.995	232.647	37.099	231.005	-0.104	1.642	
1958 DET	**37.965**	213.753	40.144	231.001	-2.179	-17.249	P
1958 BOS	25.029	187.489	36.942	236.998	-11.913	-49.509	
1959 NYY	36.328	**236.978**	**41.812**	237.002	-5.484	-0.024	
1959 CLE	**36.518**	235.532	35.962	266.999	0.556	-31.467	P
1959 DET	30.360	199.898	40.501	228.003	-10.142	-28.106	
1959 BOS	28.474	194.075	35.391	224.999	-6.917	-30.924	
1960 NYY	35.419	**250.073**	44.609	**291.000**	-9.190	-40.927	
1960 BAL	**37.594**	242.660	40.938	266.998	-3.344	-24.338	P
1960 CLE	34.718	218.614	32.272	227.997	2.446	-9.383	
1960 BOS	30.197	186.338	32.536	195.002	-2.340	-8.664	
1960 DET	27.895	175.296	39.013	213.003	-11.117	-37.707	
1961 NYY	**37.578**	**252.541**	53.194	**327.002**	-15.616	-74.461	P
1961 CLE	33.509	226.193	34.917	233.996	-1.408	-7.802	
1961 BAL	29.756	205.746	46.330	285.002	-16.574	-79.255	
1961 DET	27.520	192.803	**54.068**	303.002	-26.549	-110.199	
1961 BOS	24.428	171.555	28.900	227.997	-4.472	-56.441	
1962 NYY	33.679	**239.176**	50.207	**288.002**	-16.529	-48.826	
1962 CLE	34.594	233.486	28.135	239.996	6.459	-6.510	

1962 MIN	**42.312**	230.139	47.711	272.997	-5.398	-42.857	P
1962 CHW	34.570	222.079	40.869	254.998	-6.298	-32.920	
1962 DET	28.879	195.485	42.964	255.005	-14.085	-59.520	
1962 BAL	24.545	191.499	36.209	230.999	-11.664	-39.500	
1962 BOS	24.120	178.602	34.986	228.001	-10.866	-49.400	
1963 NYY	36.634	**256.435**	50.487	**311.992**	-13.853	-55.557	
1963 MIN	**44.352**	244.742	**51.410**	272.999	-7.057	-28.257	P
1963 CHW	42.954	243.678	50.803	281.998	-7.849	-38.320	
1963 CLE	29.427	213.039	34.846	236.997	-5.419	-23.959	
1963 BAL	27.538	201.025	39.713	257.999	-12.176	-56.974	
1963 DET	25.000	180.152	37.801	237.004	-12.800	-56.851	
1963 BOS	28.468	176.742	38.759	227.998	-10.290	-51.256	
1964 NYY	35.092	**259.430**	**46.265**	**296.999**	-11.173	-37.568	P
1964 BAL	42.061	256.550	44.621	291.003	-2.561	-34.454	
1964 CHW	36.570	235.552	45.469	293.998	-8.899	-58.446	
1964 MIN	**48.830**	221.533	46.238	236.996	2.592	-15.463	
1964 DET	33.526	216.343	40.803	254.998	-7.277	-38.655	
1964 CLE	28.137	198.466	38.647	237.001	-10.510	-38.535	
1964 BOS	32.144	179.511	35.222	216.001	-3.078	-36.490	
1965 MIN	**46.054**	**280.845**	45.782	**306.003**	0.273	-25.158	P
1965 CHW	38.075	246.201	44.551	284.992	-6.476	-38.791	
1965 NYY	31.036	228.496	36.648	230.989	-4.712	-2.493	
1965 CLE	39.404	215.290	**50.832**	260.996	-11.427	-45.706	
1965 BAL	28.616	211.004	39.876	282.005	-11.260	-71.001	
1965 DET	33.188	210.676	44.408	267.004	-11.220	-56.328	
1965 OAK	31.082	204.027	21.841	177.000	9.241	27.027	
1965 BOS	34.475	180.990	37.734	185.997	-3.259	-5.007	
1966 CHW	35.453	**243.456**	36.649	248.998	-1.195	-5.543	P
1966 DET	34.751	232.450	43.158	264.001	-8.407	-31.552	
1966 MIN	35.653	228.804	45.133	267.002	-9.480	-38.198	
1966 CLE	**37.665**	216.411	39.650	242.993	-1.985	-26.582	
1966 NYY	30.350	213.434	35.088	210.000	-4.737	3.434	
1966 BAL	30.935	203.484	**53.811**	290.992	-22.877	-87.509	
1966 BOS	25.955	195.249	31.628	216.000	-5.673	-20.750	
1967 BOS	43.455	**276.923**	46.157	**276.002**	-2.703	0.922	
1967 MIN	**43.867**	271.488	46.713	272.999	-2.846	-1.512	P
1967 DET	42.258	238.057	**49.030**	273.007	-6.772	-34.950	
1967 CHW	29.479	227.260	35.894	267.003	-6.415	-39.743	
1967 NYY	28.346	216.866	26.490	215.992	1.857	0.874	
1967 CLE	35.876	204.968	38.574	225.006	-2.698	-20.038	
1967 BAL	25.799	185.620	44.735	227.996	-18.936	-42.376	
1967 OAK	24.583	161.686	22.067	186.001	2.515	-24.315	
1968 DET	**37.928**	255.984	56.858	**309.004**	-18.930	-53.019	P
1968 BOS	30.128	235.410	37.550	257.999	-7.422	-22.589	
1968 MIN	34.833	234.130	41.742	237.001	-6.908	-2.871	
1968 NYY	26.009	226.954	32.135	249.002	-6.126	-22.048	
1968 CHW	36.093	222.081	26.098	201.000	9.995	21.080	
1968 OAK	34.888	221.355	39.514	246.001	-4.627	-24.646	
1968 CLE	34.962	209.212	41.936	257.998	-6.974	-48.787	
1968 BAL	35.685	208.923	47.742	273.001	-12.058	-64.078	
1969 BOS	31.375	**234.495**	40.808	260.997	-9.433	-26.502	D
1969 MIN	36.846	225.835	54.854	290.997	-18.008	-65.162	P
1969 OAK	33.091	225.229	38.925	263.993	-5.834	-38.764	
1969 DET	**37.464**	223.204	45.996	270.005	-8.532	-46.801	

409

1969 NYY	29.701	218.839	32.769	240.000	-3.068	-21.161	
1969 BAL	34.205	217.768	**61.183**	**327.006**	-26.978	-109.238	
1969 CHW	33.079	215.766	29.216	204.004	3.863	11.762	
1969 ANA	24.798	202.342	25.179	212.998	-0.381	-10.657	
1969 CLE	29.970	185.371	25.656	185.998	4.314	-0.628	
1970 BAL	37.545	**239.188**	**56.806**	**324.001**	-19.261	-84.813	
1970 NYY	34.403	238.748	38.483	279.000	-4.079	-40.252	P
1970 BOS	34.609	232.899	44.331	261.004	-9.722	-28.105	
1970 MIN	35.556	230.474	45.446	294.002	-9.890	-63.528	D
1970 CLE	**38.631**	211.289	37.323	228.000	1.308	-16.711	
1970 ANA	24.092	205.548	31.637	257.998	-7.545	-52.450	
1970 CHW	24.641	205.270	20.457	167.999	4.184	37.271	
1970 OAK	32.645	201.198	43.446	267.003	-10.801	-65.805	
1970 DET	25.231	186.338	35.209	237.001	-9.978	-50.663	
1971 BAL	38.820	**252.713**	**54.954**	303.005	-16.134	-50.293	
1971 MIN	**39.726**	243.341	33.626	222.002	6.100	21.339	D
1971 OAK	37.241	241.007	50.848	**303.006**	-13.607	-61.999	
1971 NYY	39.354	239.864	36.462	242.999	2.892	-3.135	P
1971 BOS	33.010	234.648	40.086	254.997	-7.076	-20.349	
1971 CHW	33.764	227.742	46.929	237.001	-13.165	-9.258	
1971 DET	36.201	222.732	47.530	272.999	-11.329	-50.267	
1971 ANA	32.267	206.240	25.913	228.006	6.355	-21.766	
1971 CLE	19.102	156.406	18.354	180.000	0.748	-23.594	
1972 BAL	**41.861**	249.587	40.264	240.000	1.597	9.587	P
1972 CHW	30.277	222.511	40.060	260.995	-9.783	-38.485	
1972 BOS	31.056	218.404	40.277	254.995	-9.221	-36.591	
1972 MIN	30.177	213.176	33.426	231.010	-3.249	-17.834	
1972 OAK	33.869	208.878	**48.453**	**278.999**	-14.584	-70.121	D
1972 NYY	31.281	199.461	37.095	236.994	-5.814	-37.533	
1972 DET	28.826	194.360	38.900	258.002	-10.074	-63.642	
1972 ANA	22.451	173.311	25.543	225.001	-3.093	-51.690	
1972 CLE	23.435	171.941	26.651	216.000	-3.216	-44.059	
1973 BAL	**41.123**	237.530	50.140	290.992	-9.017	-53.462	P
1973 OAK	37.876	234.422	46.999	281.993	-9.122	-47.571	D
1973 DET	33.657	215.707	36.853	254.999	-3.195	-39.292	
1973 MIN	41.045	215.089	43.992	243.001	-2.947	-27.912	
1973 NYY	28.647	202.511	35.980	239.998	-7.333	-37.487	
1973 BOS	30.668	198.097	42.057	267.008	-11.389	-68.911	
1973 CLE	26.441	176.806	27.440	213.007	-0.999	-36.201	
1973 ANA	12.910	148.814	32.309	236.997	-19.399	-88.183	
1974 OAK	**44.506**	253.925	45.484	269.998	-0.978	-16.073	P
1974 MIN	42.441	234.451	42.328	245.999	0.112	-11.548	
1974 BAL	32.479	219.207	40.396	**273.003**	-7.917	-53.796	
1974 BOS	33.062	217.914	37.555	252.008	-4.493	-34.094	D
1974 DET	30.728	207.677	20.604	215.997	10.124	-8.319	
1974 NYY	22.556	192.508	39.295	267.000	-16.739	-74.492	
1974 CLE	22.337	178.896	26.500	230.996	-4.163	-52.101	
1974 ANA	19.508	163.800	33.109	204.001	-13.601	-40.201	
1975 OAK	**42.604**	**262.242**	**50.476**	**294.001**	-7.872	-31.759	P
1975 BOS	34.424	233.886	41.970	285.004	-7.546	-51.118	D
1975 NYY	33.696	215.487	42.540	249.001	-8.844	-33.514	
1975 BAL	37.474	214.727	43.947	269.999	-6.472	-55.272	
1975 MIN	36.696	211.455	37.594	228.004	-0.898	-16.549	
1975 TEX	24.410	209.704	35.212	236.995	-10.802	-27.291	

410

1975 ANA	23.209	189.312	29.683	216.002	-6.474	-26.690	
1975 CLE	18.848	166.802	34.654	236.998	-15.807	-70.196	
1975 DET	22.415	166.157	19.161	170.999	3.254	-4.842	
1976 OAK	**43.024**	**246.956**	45.740	261.003	-2.716	-14.047	P
1976 BAL	30.292	232.697	37.037	264.004	-6.745	-31.307	D
1976 CLE	33.544	218.250	39.499	243.002	-5.955	-24.752	
1976 BOS	33.008	214.099	40.839	249.000	-7.831	-34.902	
1976 TEX	22.704	208.795	31.828	228.000	-9.124	-19.205	
1976 MIN	34.877	207.152	41.239	255.006	-6.362	-47.854	
1976 ANA	27.501	205.582	27.833	227.991	-0.332	-22.408	
1976 CHW	16.110	154.182	27.718	192.004	-11.608	-37.822	
1977 KCR	**40.323**	**246.708**	51.768	306.005	-11.445	-59.297	P
1977 MIN	40.288	242.466	40.670	251.998	-0.382	-9.532	
1977 OAK	33.610	222.023	19.591	189.007	14.018	33.016	
1977 BOS	32.757	219.701	50.158	291.000	-17.401	-71.299	D
1977 BAL	32.556	216.858	39.859	290.998	-7.303	-74.139	
1977 CLE	29.361	192.276	33.643	213.000	-4.282	-20.724	
1977 NYY	26.634	182.080	51.433	299.989	-24.798	-117.909	
1977 ANA	22.866	176.357	36.396	222.002	-13.531	-45.644	
1977 DET	22.017	170.257	33.612	221.997	-11.595	-51.741	
1978 OAK	**39.434**	**242.251**	22.344	206.997	17.090	35.254	
1978 BOS	33.630	217.214	46.258	296.996	-12.628	-79.782	
1978 CLE	29.497	209.596	32.046	207.004	-2.550	2.592	D
1978 TEX	34.576	209.338	45.303	260.997	-10.727	-51.659	
1978 ANA	22.980	204.310	36.192	260.998	-13.212	-56.689	
1978 DET	29.817	202.553	41.551	257.999	-11.735	-55.446	
1978 BAL	29.040	199.663	43.082	269.994	-14.041	-70.330	
1978 MIL	33.572	199.373	**49.491**	278.999	-15.919	-79.626	
1978 KCR	29.747	196.637	43.217	275.998	-13.469	-79.361	P
1978 NYY	25.370	195.075	49.358	**299.996**	-23.988	-104.921	
1978 MIN	31.127	191.576	39.679	218.999	-8.552	-27.423	
1979 MIL	**43.663**	**251.384**	45.505	284.998	-1.842	-33.614	D
1979 CLE	35.695	232.583	35.045	243.002	0.650	-10.419	
1979 KCR	34.956	224.194	37.276	254.994	-2.319	-30.801	P
1979 BOS	36.005	218.895	48.239	272.996	-12.235	-54.101	
1979 TEX	31.896	215.923	40.356	249.006	-8.460	-33.083	
1979 OAK	32.315	211.949	7.816	161.996	24.499	49.952	
1979 BAL	32.532	211.557	**50.233**	305.997	-17.701	-94.440	
1979 MIN	34.126	210.729	42.318	246.001	-8.192	-35.272	
1979 NYY	27.840	199.258	42.180	266.999	-14.340	-67.741	
1979 DET	30.641	197.924	40.810	251.995	-10.169	-54.071	
1980 KCR	42.677	**272.227**	44.396	291.003	-1.719	-18.776	P
1980 OAK	**45.955**	268.302	35.567	249.001	10.388	19.300	
1980 MIN	37.759	239.480	30.583	231.004	7.176	8.476	
1980 CLE	37.655	235.713	36.848	237.000	0.807	-1.286	
1980 BOS	35.088	224.029	43.376	249.004	-8.288	-24.975	
1980 MIL	38.754	218.546	47.629	258.000	-8.875	-39.454	D
1980 TEX	31.038	214.806	43.218	227.999	-12.180	-13.193	
1980 BAL	30.514	211.743	49.124	300.007	-18.610	-88.264	
1980 DET	30.161	201.799	41.188	252.001	-11.027	-50.202	
1980 ANA	22.076	197.221	29.433	195.000	-7.357	2.221	
1980 NYY	23.676	177.633	**55.899**	309.005	-32.224	-131.372	
1981 OAK	**30.334**	**186.902**	26.102	**192.002**	4.232	-5.101	P
1981 BOS	25.540	164.832	29.090	177.002	-3.550	-12.170	

411

1981 DET	24.179	151.177	26.300	180.004	-2.121	-28.826	D
1981 BAL	22.349	147.139	24.179	176.997	-1.830	-29.858	
1981 ANA	19.801	142.764	25.516	152.999	-5.715	-10.235	
1981 KCR	20.598	135.793	24.918	150.006	-4.320	-14.213	
1981 TEX	22.115	130.430	25.932	170.998	-3.816	-40.568	
1981 MIN	18.557	128.834	10.915	122.998	7.642	5.836	
1981 NYY	15.155	113.871	**36.293**	177.001	-21.138	-63.130	
1982 MIL	**46.034**	**252.422**	49.286	**284.992**	-3.252	-32.570	
1982 BOS	36.303	249.627	40.291	266.998	-3.988	-17.371	
1982 OAK	32.905	241.519	19.431	204.003	13.474	37.516	D
1982 CLE	38.464	231.523	38.359	233.994	0.105	-2.471	
1982 BAL	32.583	227.315	46.342	282.000	-13.759	-54.685	P
1982 DET	34.036	220.370	38.997	249.004	-4.961	-28.634	
1982 ANA	30.944	214.819	**52.356**	279.002	-21.412	-64.182	
1982 KCR	31.848	206.678	39.962	270.004	-8.115	-63.326	
1982 TEX	31.428	202.518	21.703	191.998	9.725	10.520	
1982 MIN	31.277	190.672	23.815	179.998	7.462	10.675	
1982 NYY	26.348	172.930	44.756	236.996	-18.408	-64.065	
1983 BAL	**42.650**	**255.462**	49.026	294.002	-6.376	-38.540	P
1983 BOS	39.809	254.070	33.581	233.992	6.228	20.078	
1983 MIL	40.591	238.376	41.141	261.000	-0.550	-22.624	
1983 ANA	30.298	224.473	29.511	209.999	0.787	14.474	
1983 OAK	31.885	220.328	29.133	222.001	2.752	-1.673	D
1983 NYY	34.238	215.460	48.379	273.001	-14.140	-57.541	
1983 DET	29.373	201.159	46.661	276.005	-17.288	-74.847	
1983 TEX	32.529	197.212	35.189	230.999	-2.659	-33.788	
1983 KCR	23.726	195.884	28.784	236.998	-5.058	-41.114	
1984 BAL	**39.426**	**256.693**	35.292	255.002	4.134	1.691	P
1984 DET	36.417	230.082	**57.261**	**311.996**	-20.844	-81.915	
1984 OAK	33.033	229.803	31.663	231.004	1.370	-1.201	D
1984 BOS	35.654	215.156	44.156	258.003	-8.503	-42.846	
1984 KCR	31.422	212.353	33.928	251.999	-2.506	-39.646	
1984 NYY	29.957	206.600	49.628	261.000	-19.671	-54.399	
1984 ANA	26.268	206.431	32.222	242.992	-5.954	-36.561	
1984 MIL	21.409	172.486	25.299	200.998	-3.891	-28.512	
1984 TEX	18.160	154.317	27.430	206.994	-9.270	-52.677	
1985 BOS	**48.209**	**242.836**	48.593	243.000	-0.384	-0.163	P
1985 ANA	32.144	220.726	36.589	270.004	-4.445	-49.278	D
1985 BAL	35.336	220.161	41.006	249.002	-5.670	-28.840	
1985 NYY	29.828	216.569	**53.440**	291.006	-23.612	-74.437	
1985 KCR	29.581	212.278	41.119	272.997	-11.538	-60.719	
1985 DET	33.241	202.995	45.574	252.006	-12.333	-49.010	
1985 MIL	22.978	193.422	24.653	212.999	-1.675	-19.577	
1985 TEX	22.857	172.387	28.825	185.995	-5.968	-13.609	
1986 BOS	38.999	**254.355**	45.466	**285.001**	-6.468	-30.645	
1986 OAK	40.097	246.255	29.324	228.000	10.773	18.255	
1986 MIN	38.870	237.987	33.149	212.999	5.720	24.988	
1986 DET	**42.418**	235.710	43.416	261.004	-0.998	-25.294	D
1986 KCR	37.454	219.020	34.879	228.006	2.574	-8.986	P
1986 TEX	33.124	208.917	39.312	260.999	-6.188	-52.082	
1986 NYY	24.318	196.435	46.716	269.996	-22.399	-73.561	
1986 MIL	28.939	196.411	32.568	231.000	-3.629	-34.590	
1986 ANA	28.575	195.154	**48.379**	276.001	-19.804	-80.847	
1986 BAL	30.213	195.004	34.104	219.002	-3.890	-23.997	

412

1986 SEA	26.876	181.218	28.997	200.997	-2.121	-19.779	
1987 MIL	**46.168**	**258.094**	44.628	272.999	1.540	-14.904	P
1987 SEA	33.942	219.881	38.105	234.001	-4.162	-14.121	
1987 BOS	36.456	217.811	42.394	234.002	-5.937	-16.191	
1987 KCR	32.823	210.175	37.157	249.002	-4.333	-38.827	
1987 BAL	29.051	191.144	26.449	201.000	2.602	-9.856	
1987 TEX	32.726	189.973	33.315	224.991	-0.589	-35.018	D
1987 ANA	26.666	187.249	33.491	224.998	-6.826	-37.749	
1988 MIN	42.407	**255.911**	47.802	273.000	-5.394	-17.089	
1988 MIL	38.508	251.227	36.548	261.002	1.961	-9.775	
1988 DET	34.271	248.159	36.186	263.999	-1.914	-15.840	
1988 CLE	37.134	246.097	32.913	233.996	4.221	12.101	
1988 BOS	**43.799**	235.592	**54.008**	266.998	-10.208	-31.406	P
1988 NYY	30.748	226.031	39.867	254.997	-9.120	-28.966	
1988 KCR	42.876	225.871	40.455	252.001	2.421	-26.130	D
1988 SEA	35.622	212.476	35.021	204.005	0.601	8.471	
1988 ANA	25.329	188.255	30.904	225.003	-5.575	-36.747	
1988 TEX	29.038	181.812	28.380	209.999	0.658	-28.187	
1988 BAL	19.457	179.413	16.728	162.000	2.729	17.413	
1989 MIL	41.332	**262.923**	34.979	243.006	6.353	19.917	D
1989 SEA	35.853	242.665	33.895	219.002	1.958	23.663	
1989 MIN	39.050	241.725	37.908	239.999	1.142	1.726	
1989 CLE	34.089	230.590	32.364	218.992	1.725	11.598	
1989 KCR	**42.328**	227.794	44.647	276.000	-2.319	-48.205	P
1989 NYY	30.832	220.214	30.760	221.997	0.073	-1.783	
1989 BOS	33.323	220.148	**47.563**	249.006	-14.240	-28.858	
1989 ANA	31.385	215.767	42.141	273.007	-10.756	-57.240	
1989 DET	33.361	205.719	17.397	177.000	15.964	28.719	
1989 TOR	32.373	204.830	44.546	267.005	-12.173	-62.176	
1989 TEX	30.314	181.952	39.048	248.969	-8.734	-67.017	
1990 OAK	**43.352**	**271.057**	**47.879**	**308.993**	-4.528	-37.935	
1990 BOS	40.059	245.962	45.283	263.997	-5.224	-18.035	
1990 NYY	29.759	239.472	21.664	200.999	8.096	38.473	
1990 SEA	40.816	236.478	38.781	231.004	2.035	5.474	D
1990 MIL	32.983	227.727	32.609	222.002	0.374	5.726	
1990 TOR	36.873	225.441	47.210	257.999	-10.337	-32.557	P
1990 DET	39.399	221.568	33.891	236.975	5.507	-15.407	
1990 MIN	33.021	218.050	31.903	222.000	1.119	-3.950	
1990 KCR	39.919	210.369	37.641	225.009	2.277	-14.640	
1990 BAL	32.888	209.199	30.513	228.001	2.374	-18.802	
1990 ANA	26.077	199.923	39.527	240.003	-13.450	-40.080	
1990 TEX	26.474	198.409	36.631	249.001	-10.158	-50.592	
1991 CHW	**45.646**	**278.919**	39.134	260.992	6.512	17.927	P
1991 OAK	43.815	272.896	31.063	252.000	12.752	20.897	
1991 MIL	39.784	258.992	37.216	248.995	2.568	9.996	D
1991 SEA	39.949	238.406	37.125	248.997	2.824	-10.590	
1991 DET	40.705	237.438	36.660	252.001	4.044	-14.563	
1991 MIN	32.542	233.610	**45.574**	**284.997**	-13.032	-51.387	
1991 BOS	35.894	233.589	41.720	251.998	-5.826	-18.409	
1991 ANA	30.107	224.031	32.524	242.997	-2.417	-18.966	
1991 TOR	29.419	219.330	43.965	273.003	-14.546	-53.673	
1991 NYY	26.503	213.467	33.247	213.000	-6.744	0.467	
1991 KCR	34.808	211.985	39.964	246.006	-5.156	-34.021	
1991 TEX	25.333	188.084	42.896	254.998	-17.564	-66.914	

1992 MIL	48.297	**290.782**	42.871	275.994	5.426	14.788	P
1992 OAK	47.853	280.475	43.856	287.995	3.998	-7.519	
1992 CHW	**48.770**	278.530	39.662	257.992	9.108	20.537	D
1992 BOS	38.359	245.402	30.645	219.005	7.715	26.397	
1992 ANA	30.106	245.010	20.027	215.995	10.079	29.015	
1992 NYY	33.018	236.673	37.612	227.996	-4.594	8.676	
1992 MIN	34.544	236.377	45.705	270.001	-11.160	-33.624	
1992 TOR	26.214	206.934	**47.687**	**287.996**	-21.473	-81.063	
1992 TEX	32.596	201.211	39.233	230.995	-6.637	-29.784	
1992 KCR	31.958	200.937	31.074	216.007	0.884	-15.069	
1992 SEA	32.057	181.962	30.889	192.002	1.168	-10.040	
1993 BOS	**46.725**	**281.952**	36.077	240.007	10.649	41.946	
1993 ANA	39.314	277.748	27.875	212.994	11.439	64.754	
1993 NYY	37.742	256.092	44.346	263.997	-6.604	-7.905	D
1993 OAK	35.233	254.003	27.663	204.002	7.570	50.001	
1993 DET	45.280	253.931	42.938	255.000	2.343	-1.069	
1993 TEX	39.806	250.862	39.051	258.001	0.755	-7.139	P
1993 MIL	33.806	247.255	24.253	206.999	9.553	40.257	
1993 KCR	42.799	244.449	34.952	252.003	7.848	-7.554	
1993 TOR	39.254	239.018	**49.403**	**285.003**	-10.149	-45.985	
1993 MIN	31.063	226.044	26.634	212.996	4.430	13.048	
1993 SEA	36.519	222.994	41.073	246.000	-4.554	-23.006	
1993 BAL	29.900	211.168	39.857	255.001	-9.957	-43.834	
1994 BOS	**40.667**	**239.370**	23.617	162.004	17.050	77.366	P
1994 KCR	37.410	193.905	28.105	192.006	9.305	1.899	D
1994 TOR	29.763	187.821	26.632	164.993	3.131	22.828	
1994 OAK	22.682	182.169	19.804	153.003	2.878	29.167	D
1994 NYY	26.781	178.909	37.190	**210.000**	-10.409	-31.091	
1994 TEX	26.011	172.528	22.144	156.000	3.866	16.528	
1994 BAL	28.300	172.223	32.438	189.004	-4.138	-16.781	W
1994 ANA	18.920	166.075	17.134	140.995	1.785	25.080	
1994 MIL	21.515	163.846	19.691	159.003	1.825	4.844	
1994 MIN	19.174	159.832	18.817	158.999	0.357	0.832	
1994 DET	19.304	153.096	22.971	158.998	-3.668	-5.903	
1994 SEA	18.498	141.031	24.646	147.002	-6.148	-5.971	
1995 CLE	**57.589**	**287.401**	52.841	**300.003**	4.748	-12.602	P
1995 ANA	38.897	263.948	39.515	234.005	-0.619	29.943	D
1995 NYY	32.132	241.346	37.550	237.005	-5.418	4.341	
1995 OAK	34.004	239.075	32.684	200.996	1.320	38.079	
1995 TEX	35.239	225.766	29.503	222.002	5.736	3.764	
1995 MIL	30.995	216.052	23.695	194.998	7.300	21.055	W
1995 BAL	35.396	211.505	38.339	213.000	-2.943	-1.495	D
1995 KCR	33.109	210.979	26.895	210.000	6.213	0.979	
1995 MIN	33.303	210.265	20.941	168.002	12.363	42.263	
1995 CHW	39.126	209.750	33.979	204.003	5.147	5.747	
1995 DET	29.385	209.395	19.417	180.003	9.968	29.392	
1995 SEA	37.665	209.269	41.265	237.003	-3.600	-27.734	
1995 TOR	27.167	208.686	25.408	168.001	1.760	40.685	
1996 BOS	**56.035**	**317.675**	40.848	254.999	15.187	62.676	D
1996 TEX	47.221	277.118	47.230	270.002	-0.009	7.116	P
1996 ANA	34.976	274.172	26.822	210.001	8.154	64.171	
1996 MIL	38.040	271.487	31.682	240.005	6.358	31.482	
1996 NYY	39.276	271.001	47.774	276.001	-8.498	-5.001	
1996 MIN	41.609	264.657	32.662	233.997	8.947	30.660	

1996 KCR	37.293	249.978	33.046	224.998	4.246	24.981	
1996 SEA	44.565	249.517	45.752	255.000	-1.187	-5.484	W
1996 CHW	48.492	246.680	46.145	255.001	2.347	-8.321	D
1996 TOR	36.934	244.077	34.660	222.002	2.273	22.076	
1996 OAK	29.079	241.483	32.565	233.997	-3.487	7.487	
1996 DET	38.156	216.911	12.101	159.003	26.055	57.909	
1996 BAL	25.557	201.104	43.166	264.002	-17.610	-62.898	
1997 BOS	**63.795**	**317.766**	41.418	234.001	22.377	83.765	P
1997 ANA	40.312	313.101	34.362	251.994	5.950	61.106	D
1997 MIL	34.358	271.020	28.555	234.005	5.802	37.015	
1997 NYY	39.112	270.519	**54.749**	287.996	-15.637	-17.477	W
1997 CLE	49.645	264.974	43.262	258.003	6.383	6.971	D
1997 SEA	42.600	262.799	49.551	269.995	-6.951	-7.196	
1997 TOR	37.701	251.125	33.269	227.997	4.432	23.128	
1997 MIN	42.301	250.472	30.106	203.998	12.195	46.473	
1997 CHW	32.783	241.113	30.577	240.003	2.206	1.110	
1997 BAL	36.941	240.550	46.903	**293.992**	-9.963	-53.442	
1997 DET	35.532	236.748	33.714	236.999	1.818	-0.250	
1997 TEX	35.874	228.851	32.603	231.003	3.271	-2.152	
1997 KCR	35.378	227.628	30.351	200.999	5.027	26.629	
1997 OAK	24.967	224.249	24.893	194.995	0.074	29.254	
1998 OAK	41.659	**306.850**	28.712	222.004	12.948	84.845	
1998 ANA	37.693	303.757	33.756	255.000	3.937	48.757	
1998 BOS	**58.555**	292.788	46.160	275.994	12.394	16.794	P
1998 CLE	49.122	289.082	42.317	267.003	6.805	22.079	D
1998 NYY	40.900	281.123	**57.949**	**342.010**	-17.049	-60.887	W
1998 TEX	46.336	278.847	43.402	264.002	2.934	14.845	D
1998 TOR	45.214	266.675	44.709	263.995	0.505	2.681	
1998 SEA	41.393	259.859	44.560	228.003	-3.167	31.856	
1998 MIN	39.972	257.042	25.960	210.003	14.011	47.038	
1998 KCR	36.016	244.294	23.842	216.001	12.174	28.293	
1998 DET	39.277	240.474	26.369	194.995	12.908	45.478	
1998 CHW	26.952	224.720	28.838	239.997	-1.886	-15.277	
1998 BAL	30.645	221.725	43.837	237.000	-13.192	-15.275	
1999 CLE	53.273	**308.505**	49.140	290.996	4.133	17.509	P
1999 BOS	**55.500**	298.980	49.180	282.008	6.321	16.972	D
1999 SEA	46.483	295.865	33.750	237.001	12.733	58.864	D
1999 CHW	45.117	289.088	28.552	225.001	16.566	64.088	
1999 TEX	50.446	284.386	46.675	284.996	3.771	-0.610	W
1999 NYY	42.592	283.117	**51.754**	**294.007**	-9.161	-10.890	
1999 BAL	39.025	256.085	39.434	234.003	-0.410	22.082	
1999 TOR	38.060	253.634	40.096	252.008	-2.036	1.626	
1999 ANA	25.270	247.865	20.918	209.996	4.352	37.869	
1999 KCR	38.882	244.390	27.273	191.997	11.608	52.393	
1999 MIN	27.978	226.534	21.881	189.008	6.097	37.526	
1999 DET	30.865	209.541	28.733	206.994	2.132	2.547	
2000 SEA	47.787	**296.644**	45.169	272.992	2.617	23.651	D
2000 CLE	49.110	289.713	**53.650**	270.002	-4.540	19.711	D
2000 CHW	41.715	284.283	44.747	**284.995**	-3.032	-0.712	W
2000 OAK	40.270	282.895	44.560	272.999	-4.290	9.897	
2000 ANA	43.944	279.669	34.732	246.003	9.212	33.666	
2000 BOS	**50.358**	278.596	41.134	254.994	9.224	23.602	P
2000 NYY	41.010	277.637	42.637	260.997	-1.628	16.640	
2000 TOR	46.780	272.402	37.825	249.000	8.955	23.402	

2000 TEX	45.009	266.731	28.246	212.999	16.763	53.732	
2000 BAL	35.175	241.342	30.223	222.007	4.952	19.334	
2000 KCR	34.920	235.243	26.839	231.001	8.081	4.242	
2000 MIN	32.744	235.115	28.959	206.999	3.785	28.116	
2000 DET	25.777	212.864	37.807	236.997	-12.030	-24.132	
2001 SEA	**59.116**	**326.214**	**60.246**	**348.002**	-1.130	-21.788	P
2001 TOR	51.500	297.261	38.727	239.998	12.774	57.264	D
2001 NYY	46.590	295.823	50.610	285.011	-4.020	10.812	
2001 OAK	44.124	287.895	53.715	306.003	-9.590	-18.108	W
2001 TEX	48.403	278.730	34.294	218.999	14.108	59.731	
2001 CLE	46.178	277.492	49.758	272.996	-3.580	4.496	D
2001 ANA	37.428	267.371	31.173	225.005	6.255	42.367	
2001 CHW	43.881	265.808	36.765	248.999	7.116	16.809	
2001 MIN	36.193	261.328	36.660	254.993	-0.467	6.335	
2001 DET	24.872	247.265	19.665	198.002	5.208	49.263	
2001 BOS	38.612	236.725	44.270	245.991	-5.659	-9.266	
2001 KCR	30.715	228.263	21.345	195.004	9.370	33.259	
2001 BAL	25.773	215.087	19.529	188.993	6.244	26.094	
2002 TOR	**51.472**	**312.267**	34.214	234.011	17.258	78.256	D
2002 OAK	45.802	304.820	48.601	**309.004**	-2.799	-4.185	P
2002 ANA	44.073	285.858	47.032	297.001	-2.959	-11.143	W
2002 NYY	43.916	281.132	**58.546**	308.996	-14.630	-27.864	
2002 SEA	49.153	280.615	48.516	278.998	0.637	1.616	
2002 MIN	40.867	272.649	42.066	281.995	-1.199	-9.346	
2002 CLE	43.406	259.196	29.503	221.997	13.904	37.199	
2002 CHW	41.990	253.545	40.629	243.003	1.361	10.542	D
2002 BOS	44.511	250.418	54.357	279.001	-9.846	-28.583	
2002 TEX	36.584	242.856	35.183	215.997	1.401	26.859	
2002 KCR	34.593	223.922	21.946	185.996	12.647	37.927	
2003 NYY	45.047	**301.904**	59.067	**303.002**	-14.020	-1.098	W
2003 SEA	**48.876**	290.442	45.808	279.006	3.068	11.436	P
2003 TOR	45.378	284.520	42.652	257.991	2.726	26.529	D
2003 CHW	42.527	283.164	44.264	257.997	-1.737	25.167	D
2003 OAK	44.382	280.236	42.729	287.995	1.653	-7.758	
2003 MIN	40.355	274.369	41.751	270.004	-1.396	4.365	
2003 ANA	39.926	266.117	33.515	231.010	6.411	35.107	
2003 CLE	41.685	262.595	26.747	203.998	14.938	58.597	
2003 KCR	26.189	234.273	28.871	249.002	-2.682	-14.729	
2003 BOS	42.195	229.434	**59.525**	284.997	-17.330	-55.563	
2003 TEX	25.846	229.399	31.584	213.000	-5.738	16.400	
2003 DET	14.806	195.132	7.174	129.001	7.631	66.132	
2004 CLE	**49.872**	**296.142**	40.332	240.000	9.540	56.142	P
2004 NYY	38.358	283.186	49.486	**303.008**	-11.129	-19.823	
2004 TEX	43.315	274.596	37.701	267.005	5.614	7.591	D
2004 TOR	38.084	268.643	27.112	200.993	10.972	67.649	
2004 ANA	44.596	267.174	45.309	276.002	-0.713	-8.828	
2004 CHW	39.604	265.983	36.515	248.997	3.089	16.986	W
2004 KCR	40.426	264.716	16.878	173.997	23.548	90.720	
2004 MIN	34.156	261.933	44.915	276.001	-10.760	-14.069	
2004 DET	27.453	238.621	36.609	215.995	-9.156	22.626	
2004 OAK	43.259	237.979	43.146	273.000	0.113	-35.021	
2004 SEA	36.569	234.024	28.142	188.995	8.428	45.029	
2004 BOS	39.572	225.448	**56.009**	294.000	-16.438	-68.552	D
2004 BAL	30.361	221.612	39.535	234.001	-9.175	-12.389	

2005 ANA	**48.236**	**309.898**	43.572	284.998	4.664	24.900	W
2005 CLE	47.764	300.279	**52.125**	279.009	-4.361	21.270	D
2005 TOR	43.422	279.321	37.516	239.999	5.905	39.322	D
2005 SEA	40.939	268.242	25.809	207.000	15.129	61.242	
2005 MIN	35.300	267.153	36.377	249.003	-1.077	18.150	
2005 OAK	38.892	265.707	41.031	264.000	-2.139	1.707	P
2005 CHW	35.927	256.555	43.287	**297.005**	-7.360	-40.450	
2005 TEX	39.219	246.558	40.624	237.003	-1.406	9.555	
2005 NYY	34.019	242.281	48.835	284.999	-14.815	-42.718	
2005 KCR	37.989	237.502	16.942	167.998	21.046	69.504	
2005 BAL	35.352	223.908	34.301	222.000	1.051	1.908	
2005 DET	30.181	221.187	30.858	213.002	-0.677	8.185	
2005 BOS	31.985	220.133	47.271	284.998	-15.286	-64.865	
2006 CHW	**45.039**	**293.984**	42.405	270.009	2.634	23.975	D
2006 NYY	43.791	274.115	**51.400**	290.996	-7.609	-16.881	W
2006 SEA	42.765	273.674	30.888	233.999	11.877	39.675	D
2006 CLE	44.020	272.579	42.751	234.003	1.269	38.576	
2006 MIN	38.149	269.287	45.923	288.001	-7.774	-18.714	
2006 BOS	43.300	268.792	39.188	258.014	4.112	10.778	P
2006 TOR	41.927	266.208	44.255	261.002	-2.328	5.207	
2006 OAK	38.488	263.016	35.690	279.001	2.798	-15.985	
2006 ANA	34.851	253.028	42.410	266.996	-7.559	-13.968	
2006 TEX	40.563	252.999	38.242	239.996	2.321	13.003	
2006 DET	35.092	241.979	39.790	285.006	-4.698	-43.027	
2006 KCR	32.386	234.758	17.022	185.999	15.364	48.759	
2007 SEA	**55.168**	**317.269**	33.710	263.995	21.458	53.273	P
2007 CLE	42.468	273.877	45.967	288.005	-3.499	-14.129	
2007 CHW	35.364	267.413	24.798	215.996	10.566	51.416	
2007 NYY	46.952	263.799	52.170	281.997	-5.218	-18.199	D
2007 BOS	38.511	262.704	**53.368**	**288.006**	-14.856	-25.302	W
2007 ANA	34.006	259.010	42.122	281.996	-8.116	-22.986	
2007 MIN	36.925	254.513	32.492	237.002	4.433	17.511	
2007 TEX	36.956	249.176	27.868	224.999	9.089	24.177	
2007 DET	39.992	242.749	41.585	264.000	-1.593	-21.250	D
2007 TOR	33.110	238.856	38.597	248.995	-5.487	-10.140	
2007 OAK	36.750	235.056	37.577	228.007	-0.827	7.049	
2007 KCR	30.035	223.043	23.780	206.999	6.255	16.044	
2007 TBD	34.993	221.479	32.138	197.999	2.855	23.480	
2008 ANA	39.517	**302.263**	38.328	**300.004**	1.189	2.259	
2008 TBD	39.490	276.109	46.519	291.006	-7.029	-14.897	W
2008 MIN	43.153	275.544	37.238	264.000	5.914	11.545	D
2008 BOS	**47.361**	264.550	**52.600**	284.999	-5.239	-20.449	P
2008 NYY	39.131	264.051	44.531	266.998	-5.400	-2.947	
2008 KCR	42.609	261.593	27.864	224.995	14.745	36.598	
2008 CLE	37.418	250.782	38.747	243.000	-1.329	7.782	
2008 SEA	40.994	250.537	21.313	182.999	19.682	67.539	
2008 OAK	35.378	250.244	28.574	225.003	6.804	25.241	D
2008 TOR	36.879	247.770	43.231	258.003	-6.351	-10.232	
2008 CHW	32.177	243.379	45.007	267.003	-12.830	-23.625	
2008 TEX	38.243	238.986	36.936	236.997	1.307	1.989	
2008 BAL	39.263	238.669	25.966	204.008	13.296	34.661	
2008 DET	33.982	223.819	32.577	222.002	1.404	1.816	
2009 SEA	43.873	**277.152**	29.030	255.003	14.844	22.148	
2009 MIN	**48.383**	275.684	39.601	260.997	8.783	14.687	W

2009 NYY	40.721	272.919	**56.210**	**309.006**	-15.489	-36.086	
2009 KCR	45.745	268.388	25.304	194.994	20.441	73.394	D
2009 BOS	41.133	263.647	48.796	285.004	-7.663	-21.358	D
2009 OAK	34.373	255.206	33.954	225.001	0.419	30.205	
2009 ANA	31.456	253.842	43.325	290.994	-11.869	-37.153	
2009 TOR	42.446	252.607	41.468	224.995	0.977	27.611	
2009 CHW	30.224	249.423	35.449	236.995	-5.225	12.428	
2009 TEX	35.867	247.794	36.833	261.004	-0.966	-13.210	P
2009 DET	39.307	244.018	33.423	257.997	5.885	-13.979	
2009 TBD	30.476	224.508	43.695	251.996	-13.219	-27.488	
2009 BAL	30.031	222.937	24.418	192.000	5.613	30.938	
2009 CLE	27.898	204.756	28.263	194.998	-0.364	9.758	
2010 TBD	**44.636**	**274.729**	46.465	**288.001**	-1.828	-13.272	P
2010 NYY	39.820	265.182	**49.391**	285.001	-9.571	-19.819	W
2010 MIN	38.260	252.950	44.243	282.002	-5.984	-29.053	
2010 TEX	36.142	216.585	42.410	270.009	-6.267	-53.423	D
2010 CHW	32.264	238.397	41.424	264.132	-9.160	-25.735	D
2010 TOR	31.410	223.208	43.434	255.002	-12.024	-31.794	
2010 BOS	42.852	234.380	42.248	247.459	0.604	-13.079	
2010 OAK	33.208	230.496	34.218	243.002	-1.010	-12.506	
2010 DET	36.613	238.643	38.512	242.999	-1.899	-4.356	
2010 ANA	26.313	215.354	29.193	240.246	-2.880	-24.892	
2010 CLE	31.141	222.767	24.465	206.959	6.675	15.808	
2010 BAL	39.126	252.836	21.630	197.996	17.495	54.840	
2010 SEA	33.060	244.855	18.030	182.998	15.030	61.857	
2011 DET	**47.774**	**285.458**	44.806	284.996	2.969	0.462	D
2011 NYY	40.410	268.450	**53.707**	**291.008**	-13.297	-22.557	P
2011 ANA	35.325	256.019	37.588	257.996	-2.263	-1.977	
2011 BOS	47.129	253.089	47.894	254.606	-0.765	-1.517	W
2011 OAK	34.718	238.618	31.320	222.001	3.398	16.618	
2011 KCR	38.420	237.947	33.435	213.003	4.985	24.944	
2011 CHW	32.429	237.946	37.136	237.002	-4.707	0.944	
2011 SEA	35.519	236.170	23.768	201.006	11.751	35.163	
2011 TOR	35.036	230.647	33.824	242.994	1.212	-12.347	
2011 CLE	36.358	224.834	31.018	239.994	5.341	-15.160	
2011 TBD	30.120	224.156	42.749	272.998	-12.629	-48.842	
2011 MIN	26.641	223.354	13.867	189.000	12.773	34.353	
2011 TEX	37.587	219.945	51.601	288.006	-14.014	-68.061	D
2011 BAL	29.646	217.103	24.918	206.998	4.727	10.105	
2012 SEA	37.047	**273.940**	32.319	224.998	4.728	48.942	D
2012 TBD	**46.470**	254.721	46.724	269.991	-0.254	-15.270	P
2012 KCR	39.112	246.344	30.128	215.993	8.984	30.350	D
2012 MIN	30.626	240.389	24.162	197.905	6.464	42.484	
2012 NYY	28.156	237.751	**52.429**	**284.997**	-24.273	-47.246	W
2012 ANA	41.245	237.644	44.717	267.004	-3.472	-29.360	
2012 DET	30.559	234.260	41.392	264.005	-10.834	-29.744	W
2012 OAK	26.109	223.381	48.411	282.000	-22.302	-58.619	
2012 BOS	32.425	213.861	26.245	204.236	6.180	9.625	
2012 TOR	17.566	213.055	29.220	219.001	-11.654	-5.946	
2012 CHW	34.667	210.753	43.002	246.094	-8.335	-35.340	
2012 TEX	29.155	201.006	47.890	278.998	-18.735	-77.992	
2013 SEA	37.416	**254.123**	23.136	213.005	14.279	41.118	D
2013 NYY	32.584	249.014	30.910	253.496	1.674	-4.482	W

2013 BOS	**42.852**	246.854	**56.132**	**290.998**	-13.280	-44.144	P
2013 BAL	28.712	243.411	34.892	247.856	-6.180	-4.446	
2013 ANA	41.353	237.737	34.451	234.005	6.902	3.732	
2013 TBD	29.548	226.227	41.110	276.000	-11.563	-49.773	W
2013 HOU	26.659	218.300	8.316	151.913	18.343	66.387	
2013 DET	24.898	216.833	55.027	278.996	-30.129	-62.163	D
2013 TEX	28.859	199.099	48.522	271.251	-19.663	-72.152	
2013 OAK	23.028	197.618	43.664	287.998	-20.636	-90.380	
2013 CHW	18.894	176.118	24.075	188.990	-5.181	-12.871	
1901 BRO	43.032	**277.511**	35.904	237.005	7.128	40.506	
1901 PHI	**46.276**	266.535	36.783	248.992	9.493	17.544	
1901 BSN	28.268	266.500	21.996	206.997	6.272	59.503	P
1901 PIT	33.704	237.138	**46.725**	**270.004**	-13.021	-32.866	
1901 CHC	28.319	227.465	21.502	158.998	6.817	68.467	
1901 CIN	30.263	220.830	13.892	155.997	16.371	64.834	
1902 BSN	44.124	**314.396**	27.911	219.007	16.213	95.389	
1902 CIN	**45.416**	282.225	30.749	210.008	14.667	72.217	P
1902 CHC	37.454	280.815	29.953	203.960	7.501	76.856	
1902 PIT	35.384	242.628	**57.030**	**305.997**	-21.647	-63.369	
1902 STL	20.500	230.700	12.561	167.977	7.939	62.723	
1902 PHI	37.859	224.506	13.518	167.995	24.341	56.511	
1902 BRO	25.294	220.407	29.107	224.999	-3.813	-4.592	
1903 CHC	48.042	**304.156**	39.349	246.008	8.693	58.147	
1903 CIN	**49.070**	298.541	37.800	222.001	11.270	76.540	
1903 PIT	32.829	256.224	43.391	**272.767**	-10.562	16.543	
1903 NYG	38.890	239.559	**45.983**	252.001	-7.094	-12.442	P
1903 PHI	39.253	232.401	18.439	147.005	20.814	85.396	
1903 BRO	26.875	228.569	35.208	210.005	-8.333	18.563	
1903 STL	22.025	198.780	10.346	128.995	11.679	69.785	
1904 NYG	**68.531**	**349.699**	**60.981**	**317.997**	7.550	31.702	P
1904 CIN	42.216	318.135	39.166	263.995	3.050	54.140	
1904 CHC	46.976	302.016	38.985	278.572	7.991	23.444	
1904 PHI	45.387	293.709	18.627	156.000	26.760	137.708	
1904 PIT	39.919	290.428	37.901	260.998	2.018	29.430	
1904 BSN	29.548	251.512	12.382	164.998	17.165	86.514	
1904 BRO	36.267	250.970	21.597	167.997	14.670	82.973	
1904 STL	27.305	246.083	38.618	222.010	-11.313	24.073	
1905 NYG	**69.916**	**348.165**	**66.630**	**315.008**	3.286	33.157	P
1905 PHI	51.374	329.655	35.937	248.996	15.437	80.658	
1905 CIN	36.974	284.589	33.972	237.005	3.001	47.584	
1905 BSN	30.130	261.326	11.379	152.984	18.750	108.343	
1905 PIT	34.797	257.436	40.228	287.995	-5.431	-30.560	
1905 CHC	40.997	256.416	45.824	275.921	-4.826	-19.505	
1905 STL	30.323	256.306	19.680	173.997	10.643	82.309	
1906 CHC	58.865	**362.820**	**59.017**	**344.999**	-0.152	17.821	
1906 NYG	**65.965**	361.065	50.899	287.986	15.066	73.079	P
1906 PHI	54.876	327.260	28.814	213.005	26.062	114.255	
1906 PIT	41.834	257.137	44.779	279.003	-2.945	-21.865	
1906 STL	27.066	244.970	16.363	155.993	10.703	88.977	
1907 PHI	**56.230**	**349.904**	31.087	249.009	25.143	100.895	
1907 BRO	42.515	276.763	20.755	194.999	21.760	81.764	
1907 CIN	39.991	275.331	30.384	198.001	9.607	77.330	
1907 CHC	40.745	271.726	48.625	**321.001**	-7.879	-49.275	P
1907 NYG	50.777	268.593	**48.654**	246.007	2.123	22.586	

1907 PIT	38.926	251.908	43.065	273.004	-4.139	-21.097	
1907 STL	21.339	230.221	14.184	152.999	7.155	77.222	
1908 CHC	47.751	**315.317**	49.838	**297.001**	-2.087	18.316	
1908 NYG	**61.831**	298.263	**61.849**	293.995	-0.018	4.268	P
1908 PHI	47.782	295.282	40.197	249.000	7.585	46.281	
1908 CIN	42.431	289.824	22.831	218.994	19.600	70.830	
1908 STL	29.224	247.717	13.512	146.996	15.712	100.720	
1908 BRO	28.520	234.364	15.716	158.998	12.804	75.366	
1908 PIT	28.729	228.405	42.756	294.009	-14.027	-65.605	
1909 CIN	42.932	**298.521**	38.388	230.995	4.544	67.526	
1909 NYG	**53.876**	288.436	53.928	275.997	-0.051	12.439	P
1909 PHI	39.034	258.197	34.392	222.004	4.642	36.193	
1909 CHC	33.640	253.822	53.230	311.999	-19.590	-58.177	
1909 PIT	29.711	239.907	**55.088**	**330.006**	-25.377	-90.099	
1909 STL	37.895	217.682	22.974	161.999	14.922	55.683	
1910 CIN	36.205	**282.007**	30.041	225.003	6.164	57.004	
1910 NYG	**53.090**	274.454	**59.493**	272.998	-6.404	1.457	P
1910 PHI	42.912	272.158	37.452	233.997	5.459	38.161	
1910 CHC	36.356	271.557	51.738	**311.997**	-15.381	-40.440	
1910 PIT	31.704	227.233	38.054	257.999	-6.350	-30.766	
1910 BRO	35.272	216.332	22.604	191.999	12.668	24.332	
1910 STL	30.481	207.693	25.713	188.995	4.768	18.698	
1911 NYG	**61.390**	**310.202**	**63.209**	**296.996**	-1.818	13.205	P
1911 PHI	39.944	243.527	32.707	236.974	7.237	6.553	
1911 CHC	25.443	233.121	43.514	276.004	-18.071	-42.883	
1911 PIT	31.318	223.246	46.182	254.998	-14.864	-31.752	
1911 BRO	32.991	222.703	17.935	191.995	15.055	30.708	
1911 STL	24.705	185.867	22.018	225.004	2.687	-39.137	
1912 NYG	**52.590**	290.540	56.783	308.997	-4.193	-18.457	
1912 PIT	39.622	275.570	47.749	279.009	-8.127	-3.439	P
1912 CHC	31.224	248.051	39.993	273.000	-8.768	-24.948	
1912 CIN	29.722	245.577	27.011	225.002	2.711	20.575	
1912 STL	27.132	180.909	21.509	189.002	5.623	-8.093	
1912 BSN	13.397	136.334	21.210	156.002	-7.813	-19.668	
1913 NYG	**48.369**	**276.217**	**55.195**	**302.999**	-6.826	-26.782	P
1913 CHC	32.278	247.783	37.644	264.001	-5.365	-16.217	
1913 PIT	31.156	244.095	38.092	233.997	-6.936	10.098	
1913 CIN	30.213	218.716	26.465	191.996	3.747	26.720	
1913 STL	20.762	158.351	13.069	152.992	7.693	5.358	
1914 NYG	**47.788**	**247.769**	**44.956**	251.997	2.832	-4.228	P
1914 PIT	23.691	224.191	25.030	206.998	-1.339	17.193	
1914 CIN	27.357	220.223	21.358	179.999	6.000	40.224	
1914 STL	24.442	202.183	37.310	243.005	-12.869	-40.822	
1914 CHC	22.278	199.687	31.076	233.996	-8.798	-34.309	
1915 NYG	**41.501**	**236.509**	31.122	207.002	10.379	29.507	P
1915 CHC	32.916	233.164	30.850	218.999	2.066	14.165	
1915 PIT	33.054	219.078	36.864	218.995	-3.810	0.082	
1915 CIN	26.052	211.040	29.968	213.001	-3.916	-1.961	
1915 STL	22.093	160.512	33.566	215.995	-11.473	-55.483	
1916 NYG	**47.491**	**251.460**	43.892	257.996	3.599	-6.536	P
1916 CIN	28.653	203.061	25.651	179.998	3.002	23.063	
1916 CHC	26.109	196.727	29.427	200.994	-3.317	-4.266	
1916 PIT	22.794	192.782	24.815	195.004	-2.021	-2.221	
1916 STL	20.665	187.843	17.845	179.999	2.820	7.844	

1917 NYG	**36.838**	**237.139**	**48.496**	**294.000**	-11.658	-56.861	P
1917 STL	29.083	231.070	30.145	245.999	-1.063	-14.929	
1917 CIN	22.431	174.580	34.339	234.000	-11.908	-59.421	
1917 PIT	20.523	161.169	21.708	153.004	-1.185	8.165	
1918 NYG	27.794	**185.667**	32.480	213.002	-4.686	-27.336	
1918 PIT	**30.867**	184.303	32.011	194.999	-1.143	-10.696	P
1918 BSN	26.696	177.942	21.287	158.999	5.409	18.943	
1918 STL	18.427	134.984	22.469	153.003	-4.042	-18.019	
1918 CIN	18.265	121.613	33.070	203.998	-14.805	-82.385	
1919 NYG	26.547	**186.135**	38.127	261.004	-11.580	-74.868	
1919 STL	23.626	169.531	19.850	162.003	3.776	7.528	
1919 BSN	**26.765**	164.982	23.987	171.002	2.778	-6.020	P
1919 PIT	16.261	138.119	30.694	213.003	-14.433	-74.884	
1920 STL	**36.534**	**230.095**	38.129	225.003	-1.595	5.091	
1920 NYG	26.918	208.020	40.193	258.001	-13.275	-49.981	
1920 PIT	30.899	195.640	31.825	237.006	-0.926	-41.366	
1920 BSN	26.118	180.631	18.155	185.997	7.963	-5.366	P
1920 CIN	24.295	169.501	34.758	245.998	-10.463	-76.496	
1921 PIT	**32.010**	**207.486**	40.525	269.999	-8.515	-62.513	P
1921 NYG	31.213	195.207	**45.104**	**282.002**	-13.892	-86.795	
1921 BSN	27.778	193.721	31.003	236.999	-3.225	-43.278	
1921 CIN	22.372	166.264	30.973	210.011	-8.601	-43.746	
1922 PIT	**37.420**	205.636	47.408	254.997	-9.988	-49.361	P
1922 BSN	27.071	195.413	12.018	158.999	15.052	36.414	
1922 NYG	27.104	186.919	**49.350**	**278.995**	-22.246	-92.075	
1922 CHC	24.954	184.576	32.276	239.993	-7.322	-55.418	
1923 STL	34.894	**232.805**	35.547	236.995	-0.653	-4.190	
1923 NYG	34.235	228.825	**45.912**	**285.002**	-11.677	-56.177	
1923 CHC	35.262	224.382	36.481	249.003	-1.219	-24.622	
1923 PIT	**39.133**	224.307	40.590	261.002	-1.457	-36.695	P
1923 BSN	29.462	196.552	20.555	162.000	8.907	34.552	
1924 NYG	**36.936**	**241.419**	**49.547**	**278.998**	-12.611	-37.579	
1924 CHC	25.490	223.234	26.800	242.996	-1.310	-19.762	
1924 STL	34.375	215.659	30.672	194.998	3.703	20.662	P
1924 PIT	34.920	207.780	40.634	270.004	-5.714	-62.224	
1924 BSN	14.795	151.181	11.249	158.999	3.546	-7.817	
1925 STL	38.468	**233.160**	37.569	231.000	0.899	2.160	
1925 NYG	30.190	221.282	36.199	258.001	-6.010	-36.719	
1925 PIT	**38.718**	218.545	**45.259**	**284.999**	-6.541	-66.453	P
1925 BSN	26.786	201.756	26.012	210.002	0.774	-8.246	
1925 CHC	27.551	200.357	25.690	204.002	1.861	-3.645	
1926 CHC	**33.302**	**219.413**	40.424	246.002	-7.122	-26.589	
1926 STL	30.104	209.987	41.431	267.006	-11.327	-57.019	
1926 NYG	31.332	208.779	31.707	222.009	-0.374	-13.230	
1926 PIT	29.142	202.565	33.772	252.004	-4.630	-49.439	P
1926 BSN	20.445	150.982	24.773	198.004	-4.329	-47.022	
1927 STL	32.484	**244.801**	39.630	276.002	-7.146	-31.201	P
1927 NYG	**39.276**	239.548	42.258	276.005	-2.981	-36.456	
1927 CHC	25.421	211.414	36.862	255.003	-11.441	-43.588	
1927 PIT	29.591	208.055	**42.460**	**281.996**	-12.870	-73.941	
1927 BSN	21.949	146.539	22.465	180.003	-0.516	-33.464	
1928 STL	**38.670**	**248.755**	46.151	**285.002**	-7.481	-36.247	
1928 PIT	33.218	226.424	37.904	254.994	-4.686	-28.570	P
1928 CHC	30.086	220.759	42.517	273.001	-12.431	-52.242	

421

Year	Team							
1928	NYG	32.036	219.356	**46.174**	279.002	-14.138	-59.646	
1928	BSN	29.002	191.260	16.160	149.999	12.842	41.260	
1928	PHI	17.030	134.655	13.923	129.001	3.106	5.654	
1929	NYG	**36.807**	**223.305**	43.666	251.999	-6.859	-28.693	P
1929	PIT	34.231	222.125	38.088	263.988	-3.857	-41.863	
1929	CHC	24.749	186.533	**49.043**	**294.000**	-24.294	-107.467	
1929	BSN	19.231	156.589	15.597	167.996	3.634	-11.408	
1930	NYG	**39.814**	**237.480**	44.431	261.001	-4.617	-23.520	
1930	STL	28.179	212.936	**48.243**	**275.993**	-20.064	-63.057	P
1930	PIT	32.024	212.384	29.239	239.998	2.784	-27.615	
1930	CHC	35.088	204.907	47.015	269.991	-11.926	-65.085	
1931	STL	**36.477**	**255.773**	45.436	**302.997**	-8.959	-47.224	
1931	NYG	36.084	225.026	**46.438**	260.997	-10.354	-35.971	P
1931	PIT	28.427	214.675	23.612	225.004	4.816	-10.329	
1931	CHC	22.867	180.641	44.120	252.002	-21.253	-71.361	
1932	PIT	**32.133**	**230.129**	30.524	257.999	1.609	-27.870	
1932	CHC	30.645	221.599	36.883	**270.000**	-6.237	-48.402	P
1932	STL	30.888	202.341	34.293	215.994	-3.405	-13.654	
1932	NYG	26.641	190.550	32.865	215.995	-6.224	-25.445	
1933	PIT	33.062	**222.972**	40.229	260.997	-7.168	-38.026	
1933	NYG	**33.980**	220.286	39.332	**273.006**	-5.353	-52.719	P
1933	STL	31.162	204.889	**40.460**	246.001	-9.298	-41.113	
1933	CHC	29.816	203.417	39.919	258.004	-10.103	-54.586	
1934	NYG	**38.340**	**245.403**	41.272	279.000	-2.933	-33.597	
1934	PIT	36.729	231.102	34.546	221.995	2.183	9.108	
1934	STL	34.690	226.310	**45.619**	**285.007**	-10.929	-58.697	P
1934	CHC	30.576	202.457	40.600	258.005	-10.024	-55.548	
1934	BRO	25.918	176.601	35.848	212.999	-9.929	-36.398	
1935	CHC	**42.070**	**271.574**	**49.918**	300.008	-7.848	-28.435	
1935	PIT	42.006	262.479	42.929	257.991	-0.923	4.488	P
1935	STL	33.079	233.527	45.410	287.999	-12.331	-54.471	
1935	NYG	31.569	214.401	42.258	273.001	-10.689	-58.600	
1935	BRO	28.741	174.195	29.771	210.001	-1.029	-35.806	
1936	PIT	**42.442**	**261.002**	40.548	252.003	1.893	8.999	
1936	STL	32.982	252.522	36.439	261.001	-3.456	-8.479	P
1936	CIN	32.901	218.356	29.092	222.002	3.809	-3.646	
1936	NYG	27.626	210.452	39.732	**275.997**	-12.107	-65.545	
1936	BRO	20.353	175.769	23.277	200.991	-2.924	-25.222	
1937	CHC	**41.323**	**261.522**	43.009	279.002	-1.686	-17.480	
1937	STL	32.572	234.433	34.561	240.004	-1.989	-5.571	P
1937	PIT	32.401	225.907	38.410	258.008	-6.009	-32.101	
1937	NYG	31.592	202.892	**44.875**	**284.995**	-13.283	-82.104	
1937	CIN	23.585	175.734	24.346	168.001	-0.761	7.733	
1938	PIT	**38.459**	**243.142**	41.532	258.002	-3.074	-14.859	
1938	STL	29.585	209.555	35.794	212.997	-6.209	-3.442	P
1938	NYG	28.659	192.618	39.562	249.001	-10.903	-56.383	
1938	BRO	27.983	181.973	31.001	206.998	-3.017	-25.025	
1938	PHI	12.342	146.160	8.811	134.998	3.531	11.163	
1939	CHC	31.455	**239.754**	37.154	252.002	-5.700	-12.248	
1939	PIT	**37.123**	226.598	31.347	204.005	5.776	22.593	P
1939	STL	34.068	210.151	**48.836**	275.995	-14.767	-65.844	
1939	BRO	26.298	182.190	37.386	252.000	-11.088	-69.810	
1940	BSN	31.529	**240.841**	15.628	195.001	15.901	45.840	
1940	NYG	**38.538**	231.041	33.334	216.000	5.204	15.041	P

Year/Team							
1940 CHC	36.215	222.380	38.531	224.995	-2.315	-2.615	
1940 STL	30.786	205.036	41.569	252.000	-10.782	-46.964	
1940 BRO	26.598	182.300	40.723	264.003	-14.125	-81.703	
1941 STL	**35.198**	**232.498**	45.232	290.994	-10.034	-58.496	
1941 CHC	32.236	231.306	35.155	209.997	-2.919	21.309	
1941 CIN	29.625	215.636	31.972	264.001	-2.347	-48.364	
1941 NYG	34.881	215.205	33.862	222.000	1.020	-6.795	P
1941 BSN	26.915	202.537	19.519	186.003	7.396	16.535	
1942 STL	**40.208**	**244.502**	**57.478**	**318.004**	-17.270	-73.501	P
1942 CHC	33.048	233.675	33.607	204.002	-0.560	29.673	
1942 BRO	29.596	179.437	50.107	311.994	-20.511	-132.557	
1942 BSN	20.852	173.491	20.634	174.005	0.219	-0.513	
1943 CHC	**40.157**	**243.068**	42.399	222.003	-2.242	21.064	P
1943 STL	35.928	218.532	**57.928**	**315.005**	-22.000	-96.473	
1943 BRO	25.668	194.441	37.118	243.000	-11.450	-48.559	
1943 NYG	15.553	156.958	22.368	164.998	-6.815	-8.040	
1944 STL	**44.903**	**239.168**	**61.646**	**315.002**	-16.743	-75.834	P
1944 CHC	32.541	237.074	37.140	224.995	-4.599	12.079	
1944 CIN	18.195	192.305	31.908	267.004	-13.713	-74.699	
1944 BRO	16.435	162.994	22.719	189.004	-6.284	-26.011	
1945 CHC	**50.436**	**307.150**	**53.177**	**293.996**	-2.742	13.154	P
1945 BRO	36.291	224.848	42.018	261.005	-5.727	-36.157	
1945 STL	37.231	219.564	45.847	285.008	-8.616	-65.444	
1945 CIN	24.339	207.038	19.725	182.999	4.614	24.039	
1946 CHC	37.312	**247.191**	37.752	245.996	-0.440	1.195	P
1946 STL	**39.184**	237.030	**47.547**	**293.994**	-8.362	-56.963	
1946 BRO	26.080	190.384	45.931	287.992	-19.851	-97.608	
1946 NYG	19.753	155.504	28.397	182.999	-8.644	-27.496	
1947 NYG	32.635	**218.004**	41.801	243.002	-9.165	-24.998	
1947 STL	**33.867**	210.701	**45.154**	266.996	-11.287	-56.294	P
1947 CHC	27.061	207.528	23.907	206.996	3.154	0.532	
1947 BRO	27.671	194.112	45.059	**281.999**	-17.388	-87.887	
1947 CIN	26.932	190.153	33.201	219.001	-6.269	-28.848	
1948 STL	**33.099**	**222.208**	39.266	255.005	-6.167	-32.797	P
1948 CHC	29.429	196.520	28.393	192.004	1.036	4.516	
1948 BRO	26.533	196.503	37.792	252.004	-11.260	-55.500	
1948 CIN	20.990	169.061	22.751	191.997	-1.761	-22.936	
1949 STL	37.309	**232.211**	45.970	288.001	-8.661	-55.790	
1949 BRO	35.279	216.043	**52.722**	**290.975**	-17.443	-74.932	P
1949 CHC	28.003	211.755	22.025	183.002	5.978	28.753	
1949 NYG	**38.625**	200.406	37.748	215.997	0.877	-15.592	
1949 CIN	23.640	183.118	21.298	186.001	2.342	-2.884	
1950 PHI	35.159	**249.729**	38.276	**273.002**	-3.117	-23.273	P
1950 STL	**36.474**	230.150	33.222	233.996	3.252	-3.846	
1950 NYG	26.021	228.482	40.573	258.001	-14.552	-29.520	
1950 BRO	35.649	225.273	**47.408**	266.997	-11.759	-41.724	
1950 CHC	27.964	197.132	23.591	191.997	4.374	5.135	
1950 CIN	27.684	189.999	26.440	197.998	1.244	-7.998	
1951 NYG	37.620	**261.045**	50.674	**294.001**	-13.054	-32.956	
1951 BRO	**38.743**	243.591	50.778	291.002	-12.035	-47.411	P
1951 STL	31.629	217.633	34.096	242.999	-2.467	-25.366	
1951 CIN	26.657	207.282	23.083	204.002	3.575	3.280	
1952 NYG	36.897	**261.146**	42.301	275.999	-5.404	-14.853	
1952 BRO	37.211	247.118	**51.051**	**287.996**	-13.840	-40.878	P

423

1952 PHI	**38.233**	245.301	45.778	261.004	-7.545	-15.703	
1952 CIN	30.096	217.824	26.235	207.002	3.862	10.822	
1952 STL	36.177	214.645	42.624	263.994	-6.447	-49.349	
1952 BSN	29.658	213.570	24.772	192.004	4.886	21.566	
1953 ML1	**52.223**	**300.727**	42.705	275.994	9.518	24.732	P
1953 BRO	41.891	278.094	**58.778**	**315.007**	-16.887	-36.913	
1953 PHI	38.820	238.795	40.090	249.000	-1.270	-10.205	
1953 CIN	31.293	226.158	24.867	204.001	6.427	22.157	
1953 CHC	30.197	219.018	24.535	195.002	5.661	24.016	
1953 STL	34.180	213.554	42.096	249.005	-7.917	-35.451	
1953 NYG	31.271	212.304	36.314	210.001	-5.043	2.303	
1954 ML1	**48.718**	**280.212**	38.423	255.000	10.296	25.213	P
1954 BRO	39.059	262.306	**52.865**	**293.997**	-13.806	-31.690	
1954 PHI	48.608	250.717	37.952	231.000	10.656	19.717	
1954 CIN	37.888	226.710	42.119	224.998	-4.231	1.712	
1954 NYG	30.198	226.520	37.956	239.999	-7.757	-13.478	
1954 CHC	27.472	225.463	26.338	215.994	1.134	9.469	
1954 STL	27.474	199.236	30.025	204.006	-2.551	-4.770	
1955 ML1	**46.507**	**267.495**	38.423	255.000	8.085	12.495	P
1955 BRO	36.807	247.185	**52.865**	**293.997**	-16.057	-46.811	
1955 CHC	29.661	243.424	26.338	215.994	3.323	27.430	
1955 STL	27.193	197.197	30.025	204.006	-2.832	-6.809	
1956 ML1	**47.512**	**266.896**	43.219	275.998	4.293	-9.102	P
1956 BRO	33.614	242.525	**45.666**	**278.996**	-12.052	-36.471	
1956 STL	34.739	218.923	33.894	228.002	0.846	-9.079	
1956 PIT	23.837	208.086	24.637	197.995	-0.799	10.091	
1956 PHI	34.030	206.364	30.278	213.000	3.752	-6.636	
1957 ML1	**46.812**	**271.879**	**45.814**	**284.999**	0.997	-13.121	P
1957 BRO	37.591	253.175	40.752	252.005	-3.160	1.170	
1957 STL	41.019	248.509	39.047	260.997	1.972	-12.487	
1957 PHI	37.985	239.009	35.818	230.998	2.167	8.011	
1957 NYG	25.608	209.830	31.782	207.001	-6.174	2.828	
1957 PIT	23.195	198.173	25.907	186.000	-2.712	12.174	
1957 CHC	29.240	172.910	26.175	186.000	3.065	-13.089	
1958 ML1	**43.641**	**266.553**	**45.571**	**275.992**	-1.930	-9.438	P
1958 SFG	36.484	261.799	38.306	240.001	-1.822	21.799	
1958 PIT	35.985	261.035	34.890	252.007	1.095	9.028	
1958 LAD	28.830	232.370	28.331	212.994	0.499	19.377	
1958 STL	37.177	229.334	27.734	215.989	9.443	13.345	
1958 PHI	37.503	197.283	37.132	207.004	0.372	-9.720	
1959 ML1	**45.484**	**260.696**	**44.340**	257.999	1.145	2.697	P
1959 LAD	32.582	254.305	41.404	**264.003**	-8.822	-9.697	
1959 STL	38.750	236.672	33.245	212.999	5.506	23.672	
1959 PIT	24.099	207.549	30.565	233.996	-6.466	-26.447	
1960 STL	39.965	**265.344**	36.209	258.004	3.755	7.340	
1960 LAD	**41.381**	259.591	41.799	245.995	-0.418	13.596	P
1960 ML1	36.808	237.896	39.515	264.002	-2.707	-26.107	
1960 PIT	29.772	222.696	**47.680**	**285.005**	-17.908	-62.309	
1961 SFG	**45.624**	**316.934**	42.139	255.001	3.484	61.932	
1961 LAD	42.733	291.622	**43.194**	266.999	-0.461	24.622	
1961 STL	44.906	285.162	32.852	239.997	12.054	45.165	
1961 ML1	41.939	279.200	35.297	248.998	6.642	30.202	P
1961 PIT	37.517	242.193	37.282	224.999	0.235	17.194	
1961 CHC	41.055	223.147	31.669	191.997	9.386	31.149	

1962 SFG	52.684	**355.041**	50.682	**308.992**	2.001	46.049	P
1962 CIN	**53.555**	322.783	43.913	293.995	9.642	28.788	
1962 LAD	41.594	296.147	50.567	306.000	-8.973	-9.852	
1962 ML1	48.550	287.384	41.171	258.000	7.379	29.383	
1962 PIT	39.789	260.351	39.890	278.994	-0.101	-18.643	
1962 STL	39.126	242.062	41.358	252.001	-2.232	-9.939	
1962 CHC	26.467	211.502	21.854	176.998	4.614	34.503	
1963 SFG	**54.073**	**333.547**	45.592	263.996	8.480	69.550	P
1963 CIN	53.319	316.922	42.754	257.995	10.565	58.927	
1963 LAD	34.863	284.812	43.996	**297.008**	-9.133	-12.195	
1963 STL	45.334	283.988	**48.967**	279.001	-3.633	4.987	
1963 CHC	38.586	276.742	34.959	245.995	3.627	30.747	
1963 ML1	45.629	275.551	37.294	251.997	8.335	23.554	
1963 PIT	35.158	234.173	34.704	222.007	0.455	12.167	
1964 SFG	**48.205**	**326.294**	43.622	270.005	4.583	56.288	P
1964 CIN	42.173	283.225	**46.861**	275.997	-4.687	7.227	
1964 LAD	40.366	278.446	40.865	240.000	-0.499	38.446	
1964 ML1	42.226	271.976	42.095	263.998	0.131	7.979	
1964 STL	41.600	269.263	39.719	**278.999**	1.881	-9.735	
1964 PIT	37.724	251.318	39.960	240.004	-2.236	11.314	
1964 CHC	34.562	251.188	32.489	228.001	2.074	23.187	
1965 SFG	**54.428**	**341.009**	44.556	284.992	9.872	56.017	P
1965 LAD	39.697	299.811	41.830	**291.001**	-2.132	8.810	
1965 CIN	53.538	296.110	**56.046**	266.991	-2.508	29.119	
1965 ML1	39.578	253.089	44.365	258.000	-4.787	-4.911	
1965 STL	33.860	234.385	35.564	240.002	-1.704	-5.618	
1965 PIT	32.128	226.133	44.062	269.999	-11.934	-43.866	
1965 PHI	34.899	213.797	42.473	254.992	-7.574	-41.195	
1966 SFG	**48.873**	**330.391**	40.445	279.000	8.428	51.391	P
1966 CIN	47.916	285.375	36.568	227.998	11.349	57.377	
1966 LAD	47.196	280.594	**51.701**	**284.995**	-4.504	-4.401	
1966 ATL	46.604	273.244	51.157	255.000	-4.553	18.244	
1966 STL	36.257	251.415	34.086	249.002	2.171	2.414	
1966 PIT	38.718	240.888	48.294	275.996	-9.576	-35.108	
1966 CHC	43.356	235.299	27.129	176.997	16.227	58.303	
1967 SFG	46.755	**326.669**	44.018	272.998	2.737	53.671	P
1967 CIN	**53.919**	316.075	39.885	261.014	14.034	55.061	
1967 CHC	41.962	279.000	39.193	260.997	2.769	18.003	
1967 LAD	45.481	274.573	32.579	218.995	12.903	55.578	
1967 ATL	38.267	260.727	37.326	230.994	0.941	29.733	
1967 PHI	38.066	242.386	42.614	245.995	-4.548	-3.609	
1967 STL	36.521	238.637	**48.581**	302.997	-12.060	-64.360	
1967 PIT	24.444	195.797	33.947	243.003	-9.503	-47.206	
1968 CIN	**51.138**	**326.679**	37.742	249.005	13.396	77.675	
1968 SFG	48.572	319.726	41.928	264.000	6.643	55.726	P
1968 ATL	46.236	281.801	39.505	242.995	6.730	38.806	
1968 CHC	39.275	269.331	34.477	251.998	4.798	17.333	
1968 LAD	37.884	256.222	34.472	227.999	3.412	28.223	
1968 STL	37.852	238.745	**46.289**	290.997	-8.437	-52.252	
1968 PHI	39.274	232.916	28.870	227.998	10.404	4.918	
1968 PIT	28.474	202.718	38.144	240.000	-9.670	-37.282	
1969 CIN	**58.167**	**352.671**	37.483	267.000	20.684	85.671	P
1969 SFG	41.571	306.293	42.520	270.001	-0.949	36.291	
1969 NYM	44.960	286.940	39.877	**300.006**	5.083	-13.066	D

1969 LAD	41.289	276.355	39.877	255.000	1.412	21.355	
1969 ATL	37.962	267.627	38.600	278.992	-0.638	-11.365	
1969 CHC	36.860	252.346	45.290	275.996	-8.430	-23.649	
1969 HOU	41.490	251.878	42.314	243.002	-0.825	8.877	
1969 PIT	40.944	248.355	**50.496**	264.002	-9.553	-15.647	
1969 STL	28.796	220.608	42.323	260.999	-13.526	-40.391	
1969 PHI	32.603	200.595	27.794	189.001	4.809	11.594	
1970 CIN	**48.671**	**329.778**	**46.745**	**306.002**	1.926	23.776	D
1970 ATL	47.259	298.953	37.993	227.990	9.266	70.964	
1970 LAD	44.826	294.111	37.956	261.004	6.871	33.107	
1970 PIT	39.505	278.954	42.125	266.996	-2.620	11.958	
1970 SFG	39.678	277.398	41.243	257.997	-1.565	19.401	
1970 HOU	36.446	273.539	36.786	236.999	-0.339	36.540	
1970 NYM	44.549	238.172	43.173	248.993	1.376	-10.820	
1970 CHC	39.722	234.366	46.068	252.005	-6.346	-17.639	P
1970 STL	35.151	230.316	36.509	228.000	-1.358	2.316	
1970 PHI	38.704	229.782	28.789	219.005	9.914	10.777	
1971 SFG	**44.975**	**302.926**	42.532	270.007	2.442	32.919	
1971 PIT	43.208	288.134	**50.994**	**291.003**	-7.787	-2.868	P
1971 ATL	43.878	287.444	34.069	246.008	9.809	41.436	
1971 HOU	38.261	278.753	38.152	237.002	0.109	41.751	
1971 CIN	36.703	275.798	31.722	237.001	4.982	38.797	D
1971 LAD	37.577	256.717	43.934	267.002	-6.357	-10.284	
1971 CHC	34.551	247.978	39.420	249.004	-4.870	-1.025	
1971 NYM	42.370	242.049	46.422	249.001	-4.052	-6.952	
1971 STL	39.319	241.771	41.001	270.001	-1.682	-28.229	
1971 PHI	32.675	210.713	25.457	201.002	7.217	9.711	
1972 CIN	46.007	**315.529**	47.317	284.995	-1.310	30.534	D
1972 HOU	**54.732**	298.004	44.367	251.993	10.365	46.011	
1972 PIT	44.672	287.420	**50.516**	**287.992**	-5.844	-0.572	
1972 LAD	44.327	279.939	44.037	255.002	0.290	24.937	
1972 SFG	38.653	269.669	31.847	206.995	6.805	62.674	
1972 ATL	36.834	260.926	29.182	209.992	7.652	50.933	
1972 CHC	38.799	255.152	43.683	255.006	-4.885	0.146	P
1972 STL	43.173	253.885	33.893	224.999	9.280	28.886	
1972 PHI	38.285	233.213	28.114	176.995	10.172	56.218	
1972 NYM	29.193	231.499	33.311	248.999	-4.118	-17.500	
1973 CIN	45.994	**345.449**	45.085	**297.003**	0.909	48.446	
1973 HOU	**54.877**	328.795	35.083	245.997	19.794	82.798	P
1973 LAD	45.996	308.907	**47.438**	284.993	-1.442	23.914	
1973 SFG	42.379	294.390	41.584	264.003	0.795	30.387	
1973 ATL	46.152	293.178	43.187	227.997	2.965	65.181	
1973 PIT	36.988	282.402	37.161	240.004	-0.173	42.398	
1973 CHC	43.278	271.195	33.151	231.006	10.127	40.189	
1973 PHI	33.855	252.322	29.642	213.005	4.213	39.317	
1973 NYM	43.292	250.624	35.368	246.004	7.924	4.620	D
1973 STL	31.532	225.330	37.372	242.999	-5.840	-17.669	
1974 CIN	**52.647**	336.816	52.734	294.003	-0.086	42.813	
1974 PIT	50.713	323.541	42.147	264.001	8.565	59.540	
1974 LAD	44.519	303.959	**59.790**	**305.993**	-15.272	-2.034	
1974 ATL	42.867	303.829	41.456	263.992	1.411	39.837	P
1974 PHI	43.854	285.523	32.543	240.008	11.310	45.515	D
1974 HOU	47.425	284.183	37.989	243.001	9.436	41.182	
1974 SFG	40.580	274.064	29.148	216.001	11.431	58.063	

Year Team							
1974 NYM	43.756	236.801	31.599	212.997	12.156	23.804	
1974 STL	33.482	236.118	38.345	258.002	-4.863	-21.884	
1974 CHC	29.593	207.937	30.551	198.001	-0.958	9.936	
1975 CIN	46.577	**312.470**	**55.267**	**324.004**	-8.690	-11.534	P
1975 PIT	45.238	302.351	44.462	275.996	0.777	26.355	
1975 SFG	49.460	300.759	36.212	239.998	13.248	60.761	
1975 HOU	**50.014**	291.176	28.737	192.002	21.277	99.175	
1975 PHI	47.410	289.900	47.902	258.004	-0.492	31.897	
1975 LAD	40.240	278.787	49.035	264.009	-8.795	14.778	
1975 ATL	35.123	265.447	22.405	201.001	12.719	64.447	
1975 STL	36.281	243.010	34.196	246.006	2.085	-2.996	
1975 CHC	38.738	237.698	31.189	225.000	7.550	12.698	D
1975 NYM	41.139	234.688	37.731	245.996	3.408	-11.308	
1976 HOU	**52.923**	**316.086**	31.137	240.002	21.786	76.084	
1976 PIT	46.124	306.920	42.357	276.005	3.767	30.915	P
1976 CIN	51.709	302.042	**65.283**	**306.001**	-13.575	-3.959	D
1976 LAD	35.320	299.517	37.509	275.995	-2.189	23.522	
1976 ATL	44.843	294.843	27.432	210.003	17.411	84.840	
1976 PHI	44.719	278.198	56.996	302.997	-12.276	-24.799	
1976 SFG	42.760	267.321	28.582	222.005	14.178	45.316	
1976 STL	34.626	246.647	30.576	215.999	4.051	30.647	
1976 NYM	40.806	241.444	45.354	258.002	-4.548	-16.558	
1976 CHC	32.805	219.223	29.896	225.005	2.909	-5.782	
1977 PIT	53.697	**347.737**	44.009	288.001	9.688	59.736	
1977 PHI	53.063	315.494	54.004	**303.003**	-0.941	12.491	
1977 HOU	**54.626**	306.086	38.910	242.996	15.716	63.090	P
1977 STL	43.799	305.041	30.841	248.992	12.959	56.049	D
1977 SFG	45.760	285.587	32.454	224.998	13.305	60.590	
1977 ATL	40.553	283.514	19.948	182.999	20.605	100.515	
1977 LAD	35.406	271.612	**55.285**	294.000	-19.878	-22.388	
1977 NYM	49.721	264.692	27.959	191.999	21.762	72.693	
1977 CIN	37.084	263.382	47.840	263.997	-10.755	-0.615	
1977 SDP	9.966	199.452	20.682	207.001	-10.717	-7.549	
1978 PIT	49.081	**345.711**	40.084	263.997	8.998	81.714	P
1978 PHI	**57.742**	320.607	47.194	270.003	10.548	50.604	
1978 SDP	46.670	307.174	36.294	251.999	10.376	55.175	
1978 SFG	45.951	298.934	41.001	266.996	4.950	31.937	
1978 LAD	40.828	297.693	**52.175**	**285.002**	-11.347	12.691	D
1978 CIN	34.727	285.888	42.093	276.002	-7.366	9.886	
1978 MON	47.071	282.663	28.719	228.006	18.352	54.656	
1978 STL	36.811	276.141	25.964	207.001	10.847	69.140	
1978 HOU	30.822	253.367	32.970	221.999	-2.148	31.368	
1978 ATL	28.293	252.046	24.654	207.000	3.639	45.046	
1978 NYM	37.731	225.124	26.719	197.996	11.012	27.127	
1979 MON	**53.985**	327.938	41.402	285.001	12.584	42.938	P
1979 HOU	46.949	314.221	33.128	266.996	13.821	47.225	D
1979 PHI	41.865	297.078	38.879	251.993	2.986	45.085	
1979 CIN	39.490	289.976	44.758	269.999	-5.268	19.977	
1979 STL	43.783	277.527	39.095	257.997	4.687	19.530	
1979 LAD	39.557	276.505	41.589	236.998	-2.033	39.507	
1979 PIT	34.469	271.808	**48.562**	**294.006**	-14.092	-22.197	
1979 NYM	50.780	262.505	24.827	188.998	25.954	73.506	
1979 SDP	35.982	260.449	24.457	203.995	11.525	56.454	
1979 SFG	26.028	243.120	23.609	213.003	2.419	30.117	

1979 ATL	28.880	231.889	27.716	198.002	1.164	33.887	
1980 HOU	**63.901**	**352.700**	**47.710**	**278.994**	16.191	73.706	P
1980 ATL	40.401	302.102	26.824	242.990	13.576	59.112	
1980 STL	49.024	291.693	35.271	222.003	13.752	69.691	D
1980 PIT	40.224	286.277	38.436	248.998	1.787	37.279	
1980 MON	45.032	285.414	42.283	270.004	2.749	15.410	
1980 PHI	44.548	279.951	44.014	272.995	0.534	6.956	
1980 LAD	33.748	263.362	44.319	275.999	-10.571	-12.638	
1980 CIN	34.474	260.424	42.016	267.000	-7.542	-6.576	
1980 NYM	41.185	242.012	25.220	200.999	15.966	41.013	
1980 SFG	28.052	221.883	25.256	224.990	2.797	-3.108	
1980 SDP	24.498	217.128	29.303	219.002	-4.806	-1.874	
1981 MON	**35.766**	**208.564**	28.952	179.998	6.814	28.567	
1981 ATL	31.196	206.536	20.112	150.007	11.084	56.529	
1981 STL	29.872	192.703	26.412	176.999	3.460	15.705	P
1981 HOU	30.229	189.276	**33.880**	183.005	-3.651	6.271	
1981 CIN	22.746	183.221	28.562	**197.998**	-5.816	-14.777	
1981 SFG	26.238	182.771	23.802	167.994	2.437	14.777	
1981 LAD	27.087	171.075	33.735	188.997	-6.647	-17.922	D
1981 PHI	20.779	169.888	28.277	177.001	-7.498	-7.113	
1981 NYM	28.375	166.164	17.426	123.002	10.949	43.163	
1981 PIT	21.633	162.733	21.834	138.006	-0.201	24.727	
1981 SDP	23.048	152.781	14.911	122.998	8.137	29.783	
1982 STL	**54.799**	**318.242**	37.231	**275.993**	17.568	42.248	
1982 PHI	44.347	304.436	42.252	266.996	2.095	37.441	
1982 ATL	46.472	298.663	37.173	266.998	9.299	31.665	D
1982 MON	52.837	297.169	46.740	257.998	6.097	39.171	P
1982 PIT	45.524	288.221	42.459	252.001	3.065	36.220	
1982 LAD	41.766	270.963	**50.335**	263.993	-8.569	6.970	
1982 SDP	29.177	250.747	27.933	242.999	1.244	7.747	
1982 SFG	25.211	246.855	36.020	260.999	-10.809	-14.144	
1982 CIN	35.598	243.755	29.841	182.997	5.757	60.758	
1982 NYM	28.742	229.650	19.318	195.001	9.424	34.649	
1983 STL	**54.815**	**310.452**	36.155	237.001	18.660	73.451	D
1983 LAD	43.768	299.690	42.637	**273.002**	1.131	26.688	
1983 ATL	51.061	293.661	**44.072**	264.000	6.989	29.661	P
1983 MON	49.209	277.497	41.451	245.996	7.757	31.501	
1983 PHI	44.543	275.280	43.623	269.994	0.920	5.286	
1983 CIN	33.260	266.013	24.826	222.005	8.434	44.007	
1983 SFG	24.989	250.192	32.110	237.006	-7.121	13.186	
1983 PIT	37.007	245.043	43.270	251.999	-6.263	-6.956	
1983 NYM	23.515	219.415	19.270	204.000	4.245	15.415	
1984 STL	42.319	**317.505**	33.549	252.007	8.770	65.498	D
1984 PHI	43.353	302.499	**46.988**	242.998	-3.634	59.501	
1984 SFG	42.939	294.610	27.794	198.000	15.145	96.610	
1984 LAD	43.762	280.742	34.368	236.997	9.393	43.746	
1984 MON	**45.679**	273.721	35.424	233.998	10.255	39.723	
1984 ATL	37.406	271.754	29.657	240.005	7.749	31.749	P
1984 NYM	41.814	267.114	36.755	270.001	5.059	-2.887	
1984 PIT	39.926	252.814	37.602	225.002	2.324	27.813	
1984 CIN	30.275	215.868	27.222	210.003	3.053	5.865	
1985 MON	**55.837**	**320.951**	37.539	252.000	18.299	68.951	D
1985 STL	39.416	306.622	**50.084**	**303.000**	-10.668	3.622	
1985 LAD	45.111	288.253	47.964	284.999	-2.853	3.253	P

428

1985 SDP	41.642	284.467	34.664	248.994	6.978	35.473	
1985 PHI	39.972	281.405	32.083	225.005	7.890	56.400	
1985 CIN	31.092	261.662	35.718	266.993	-4.626	-5.331	
1985 NYM	44.715	256.242	49.024	293.997	-4.309	-37.755	
1985 ATL	31.311	241.686	19.474	198.002	11.838	43.685	
1985 PIT	39.999	230.191	26.045	170.998	13.954	59.193	
1986 NYM	**59.311**	**299.730**	**56.605**	**323.994**	2.706	-24.264	P
1986 SDP	47.683	298.810	29.279	222.001	18.404	76.808	
1986 MON	44.176	293.454	36.582	234.001	7.594	59.453	
1986 PHI	38.650	288.979	37.409	258.009	1.241	30.969	
1986 STL	29.868	277.500	25.317	236.995	4.551	40.505	
1986 CIN	37.954	272.987	36.853	257.998	1.101	14.989	
1986 LAD	38.886	248.313	33.425	219.005	5.461	29.308	D
1986 PIT	36.003	238.900	29.207	192.000	6.796	46.901	
1986 ATL	27.798	214.969	28.756	215.993	-0.958	-1.024	
1987 SFG	**51.163**	**334.220**	44.647	270.002	6.517	64.217	
1987 MON	34.095	282.874	39.965	273.004	-5.869	9.870	
1987 STL	34.996	278.006	37.741	**284.998**	-2.745	-6.992	
1987 PHI	42.011	276.383	30.304	239.997	11.707	36.385	
1987 CIN	39.731	273.167	38.375	252.004	1.356	21.163	P
1987 SDP	40.580	269.373	26.810	195.001	13.770	74.371	
1987 NYM	47.001	267.430	**50.600**	275.997	-3.600	-8.567	D
1987 ATL	38.578	254.327	28.884	206.999	9.694	47.328	
1987 LAD	36.885	251.177	29.290	218.999	7.595	32.178	
1987 PIT	35.806	238.989	33.077	239.994	2.729	-1.005	
1987 CHC	37.153	212.135	35.931	228.002	1.223	-15.867	
1988 SDP	47.071	**291.467**	35.252	248.997	11.820	42.470	
1988 CIN	44.051	290.293	37.549	260.996	6.502	29.297	P
1988 NYM	**47.868**	276.796	**60.484**	**299.999**	-12.615	-23.203	
1988 PIT	45.187	269.015	35.713	255.004	9.475	14.011	
1988 CHC	39.673	268.668	33.919	231.000	5.754	37.667	D
1988 PHI	31.961	247.489	19.814	195.002	12.147	52.487	
1988 LAD	31.212	243.924	39.601	282.000	-8.389	-38.076	
1988 MON	26.006	239.071	36.069	242.988	-10.064	-3.917	
1988 STL	19.887	234.419	31.161	227.997	-11.274	6.422	
1988 ATL	32.285	230.910	16.230	162.001	16.055	68.909	
1989 CHC	40.642	**308.119**	41.222	**279.000**	-0.580	29.120	P
1989 SDP	46.434	303.790	37.508	266.997	8.926	36.794	
1989 CIN	44.505	298.096	31.601	225.006	12.904	73.090	D
1989 NYM	**47.808**	297.412	**46.509**	260.993	1.299	36.418	
1989 SFG	36.803	261.016	40.671	276.005	-3.868	-14.989	
1989 PIT	40.537	254.129	29.421	222.001	11.117	32.128	
1989 STL	25.967	240.401	39.801	257.993	-13.835	-17.592	
1989 PHI	32.402	238.474	26.586	200.999	5.816	37.475	
1989 MON	32.525	224.694	38.344	243.007	-5.819	-18.313	
1989 LAD	35.489	220.460	38.294	231.000	-2.805	-10.540	
1989 ATL	32.915	217.857	27.837	189.004	5.078	28.853	
1990 NYM	**49.233**	**294.815**	**53.587**	273.005	-4.354	21.811	
1990 CIN	47.512	288.853	45.960	273.007	1.552	15.846	P
1990 SDP	38.949	272.062	35.041	224.993	3.907	47.070	
1990 PIT	44.423	265.761	45.197	**284.999**	-0.774	-19.238	D
1990 CHC	33.630	263.740	29.853	231.002	3.777	32.738	
1990 SFG	34.936	259.692	34.957	255.005	-0.021	4.687	
1990 MON	34.967	247.710	41.564	255.012	-6.597	-7.302	

429

1990 LAD	34.545	243.882	39.568	257.999	-5.023	-14.117	
1990 PHI	33.256	237.206	27.565	231.003	5.690	6.203	
1990 ATL	34.684	231.313	26.791	194.999	7.893	36.314	
1991 SDP	40.679	**289.486**	33.040	252.003	7.640	37.482	
1991 ATL	**47.555**	279.209	44.433	282.002	3.122	-2.793	P
1991 CHC	41.111	274.306	34.774	231.002	6.337	43.304	D
1991 CIN	46.620	273.609	41.732	221.998	4.888	51.610	
1991 PHI	44.270	263.855	27.309	233.998	16.961	29.857	
1991 NYM	37.729	260.302	40.291	231.001	-2.561	29.301	
1991 PIT	36.714	259.512	**51.540**	**293.998**	-14.826	-34.486	
1991 SFG	36.613	254.544	29.686	224.997	6.927	29.546	
1991 MON	32.885	228.405	29.295	212.998	3.590	15.407	
1991 LAD	30.111	216.835	44.205	279.000	-14.094	-62.164	
1992 SDP	**52.682**	**324.283**	37.385	246.004	15.298	78.279	
1992 STL	47.819	286.817	40.029	248.998	7.791	37.819	D
1992 ATL	45.706	280.923	44.016	**294.002**	1.690	-13.079	P
1992 PIT	40.546	274.185	41.799	288.000	-1.254	-13.815	
1992 MON	37.385	255.975	39.882	260.999	-2.498	-5.024	
1992 CHC	28.797	253.484	28.823	233.997	-0.026	19.486	
1992 CIN	35.683	253.312	**45.485**	270.002	-9.802	-16.690	
1992 PHI	33.126	237.499	31.436	210.000	1.690	27.499	
1992 NYM	29.888	218.343	32.167	216.002	-2.278	2.341	
1992 LAD	30.120	216.503	28.605	188.997	1.515	27.506	
1992 SFG	25.640	213.983	26.794	216.002	-1.154	-2.018	
1993 ATL	**45.068**	**277.654**	50.596	**312.000**	-5.528	-34.346	P
1993 CHC	39.143	267.453	36.197	251.995	2.946	15.458	D
1993 SDP	34.824	252.479	28.381	183.001	6.444	69.478	
1993 SFG	37.418	247.671	48.221	308.992	-10.803	-61.322	
1993 STL	33.817	247.123	34.973	261.001	-1.156	-13.878	
1993 PHI	30.629	242.015	**51.695**	291.007	-21.066	-48.992	
1993 MON	36.075	233.252	38.158	281.991	-2.084	-48.739	
1993 PIT	33.302	232.975	30.144	224.994	3.159	7.982	
1993 CIN	28.236	213.147	33.301	219.000	-5.065	-5.853	
1993 LAD	27.208	210.831	38.805	242.995	-11.598	-32.165	
1993 NYM	33.221	194.518	26.184	177.005	7.037	17.513	
1994 CIN	27.366	**188.934**	36.184	198.002	-8.818	-9.068	P
1994 ATL	25.978	176.849	34.999	204.000	-9.021	-27.151	
1994 MON	25.933	170.041	**38.534**	**221.999**	-12.601	-51.958	
1994 STL	21.031	164.980	18.893	158.996	2.138	5.984	
1994 CHC	23.606	162.676	20.382	147.001	3.224	15.675	W
1994 SDP	28.589	161.208	27.159	140.998	1.430	20.210	D
1994 SFG	21.062	160.476	20.765	165.002	0.297	-4.525	
1994 PHI	**28.732**	159.720	23.349	162.000	5.384	-2.280	D
1994 PIT	19.341	154.784	14.434	159.007	4.908	-4.223	
1994 NYM	23.075	151.083	18.939	165.002	4.136	-13.919	
1994 LAD	20.296	147.340	28.131	174.002	-7.835	-26.662	
1995 CIN	**36.244**	**244.029**	44.132	255.004	-7.888	-10.975	D
1995 ATL	28.607	221.069	41.666	**269.998**	-13.059	-48.929	
1995 PIT	30.093	211.763	23.168	174.002	6.925	37.761	
1995 MON	29.960	209.983	29.201	197.990	0.759	11.993	P
1995 LAD	35.768	205.753	38.013	233.998	-2.244	-28.245	
1995 CHC	28.836	200.134	30.866	219.003	-2.031	-18.869	W
1995 NYM	27.536	199.041	32.753	207.001	-5.217	-7.960	
1995 STL	27.290	195.401	19.520	185.997	7.770	9.404	

1995 SDP	29.071	192.292	31.878	210.007	-2.807	-17.715	D
1995 SFG	21.020	184.260	19.875	200.997	1.146	-16.737	
1996 ATL	35.918	**254.357**	**52.504**	**287.997**	-16.586	-33.640	D
1996 MON	29.748	248.625	40.245	263.999	-10.497	-15.374	
1996 LAD	**41.068**	248.492	39.496	269.997	1.572	-21.505	P
1996 HOU	37.172	241.341	34.547	245.999	2.625	-4.657	
1996 PIT	32.696	233.456	31.043	218.992	1.653	14.463	
1996 STL	32.829	224.914	34.689	264.006	-1.860	-39.092	
1996 CHC	32.463	222.313	28.108	228.001	4.355	-5.688	D
1996 SDP	33.685	218.172	45.767	273.003	-12.082	-54.831	W
1996 NYM	27.288	202.324	30.533	213.001	-3.245	-10.677	
1996 SFG	25.229	184.350	22.707	203.999	2.522	-19.649	
1996 PHI	24.680	176.759	29.831	200.998	-5.150	-24.239	
1997 HOU	**40.182**	**257.771**	46.356	252.001	-6.174	5.771	P
1997 ATL	37.446	252.989	**55.402**	**303.001**	-17.956	-50.012	W
1997 MON	36.240	242.812	35.278	233.998	0.962	8.815	D
1997 PIT	35.086	241.115	33.921	237.001	1.166	4.115	
1997 NYM	26.425	237.865	33.318	264.004	-6.893	-26.139	
1997 LAD	38.197	232.754	42.876	263.996	-4.678	-31.242	D
1997 STL	36.372	221.177	37.217	219.009	-0.846	2.168	
1997 SDP	34.538	219.365	30.134	227.995	4.404	-8.631	
1997 PHI	33.085	206.658	25.057	204.001	8.028	2.657	
1997 CHC	22.555	194.311	25.186	204.000	-2.631	-9.689	
1997 SFG	23.977	190.622	35.954	270.000	-11.977	-79.379	
1998 HOU	**42.939**	**255.515**	57.266	305.996	-14.327	-50.480	D
1998 MIL	30.901	238.180	27.048	222.005	3.853	16.175	
1998 ATL	33.978	236.597	**60.187**	**318.002**	-26.209	-81.405	P
1998 PIT	33.673	230.719	30.282	206.995	3.391	23.723	
1998 SFG	34.893	223.852	45.067	266.993	-10.174	-43.140	D
1998 LAD	34.857	222.133	32.829	249.000	2.028	-26.867	
1998 NYM	24.652	222.086	36.776	264.001	-12.124	-41.915	
1998 MON	29.788	222.003	23.966	195.002	5.821	27.001	
1998 CHC	35.323	215.295	40.315	270.000	-4.992	-54.705	W
1998 SDP	27.229	199.889	47.499	294.004	-20.270	-94.115	
1998 STL	30.455	197.991	42.221	248.995	-11.765	-51.004	
1999 HOU	**50.391**	**269.030**	**52.636**	291.003	-2.245	-21.973	P
1999 SFG	36.880	247.166	38.981	258.002	-2.101	-10.836	W
1999 MIL	34.490	235.598	31.530	221.998	2.960	13.600	
1999 ATL	33.569	232.682	50.029	**308.999**	-16.460	-76.317	D
1999 NYM	32.959	230.352	49.322	290.997	-16.363	-60.645	
1999 LAD	37.573	220.504	36.594	230.997	0.979	-10.493	D
1999 MON	31.975	215.850	28.647	203.994	3.328	11.856	
1999 CHC	27.811	214.586	24.558	201.003	3.253	13.583	
1999 STL	24.419	191.161	34.315	225.001	-9.896	-33.841	
1999 PIT	27.902	189.514	34.682	233.999	-6.780	-44.485	
1999 SDP	29.469	188.222	30.280	221.999	-0.811	-33.778	
2000 ATL	**40.003**	**253.269**	44.532	285.009	-4.528	-31.739	D
2000 MIL	38.866	247.860	24.014	219.004	14.852	28.856	W
2000 NYM	33.008	236.691	43.210	281.997	-10.203	-45.306	
2000 MON	29.476	233.484	27.233	200.999	2.243	32.485	
2000 HOU	39.845	233.179	39.966	216.004	-0.121	17.175	P
2000 LAD	34.531	225.615	42.064	258.005	-7.533	-32.390	
2000 SFG	32.071	213.689	**52.354**	**290.995**	-20.283	-77.305	D
2000 STL	26.386	210.236	44.498	285.005	-18.112	-74.769	

431

2000 PIT	34.414	209.242	31.257	207.000	3.158	2.243	
2000 CHC	26.387	184.619	27.085	195.004	-0.698	-10.385	
2000 SDP	26.354	181.464	27.982	228.007	-1.627	-46.543	
2001 HOU	**42.408**	**263.649**	44.716	**279.003**	-2.308	-15.354	P
2001 STL	36.072	255.988	41.074	278.999	-5.002	-23.010	W
2001 MON	34.481	241.663	25.373	204.004	9.108	37.659	D
2001 ATL	32.643	238.317	39.905	263.994	-7.262	-25.677	
2001 PIT	32.770	220.991	15.728	185.995	17.042	34.996	
2001 NYM	28.125	210.622	34.251	245.997	-6.126	-35.375	
2001 MIL	28.448	205.359	27.355	204.003	1.094	1.356	
2001 LAD	28.545	203.976	38.827	258.007	-10.282	-54.030	
2001 SFG	29.281	192.083	46.994	270.000	-17.713	-77.917	D
2001 SDP	23.060	177.673	30.326	236.996	-7.266	-59.323	
2002 MON	**46.171**	**285.357**	38.361	249.002	7.811	36.355	P
2002 HOU	42.860	249.279	44.308	251.999	-1.448	-2.720	D
2002 STL	33.700	239.832	44.171	290.992	-10.471	-51.160	W
2002 ATL	30.779	227.685	44.087	**302.997**	-13.307	-75.311	
2002 NYM	29.754	222.595	30.149	225.001	-0.395	-2.406	
2002 LAD	28.454	214.597	38.054	275.997	-9.600	-61.400	
2002 PIT	27.253	212.359	22.395	216.001	4.858	-3.642	
2002 PHI	29.911	205.471	41.517	240.003	-11.606	-34.532	
2002 SFG	23.582	196.058	**51.809**	285.005	-28.227	-88.947	D
2002 SDP	34.447	192.559	22.416	197.997	12.031	-5.438	
2002 CHC	29.854	181.318	39.477	200.996	-9.623	-19.678	
2003 MON	41.074	**277.942**	33.613	248.998	7.461	28.944	
2003 HOU	**48.364**	260.850	44.142	261.000	4.222	-0.149	P
2003 FLA	43.871	260.130	46.076	272.991	-2.204	-12.861	
2003 STL	38.289	248.497	41.313	254.999	-3.023	-6.502	W
2003 PIT	40.560	244.534	33.173	225.000	7.387	19.535	
2003 ATL	34.595	230.432	**50.921**	**303.006**	-16.325	-72.574	D
2003 NYM	21.039	209.219	18.836	197.995	2.203	11.224	
2003 LAD	26.975	206.268	37.750	255.006	-10.776	-48.738	D
2003 SDP	25.366	200.134	24.412	192.004	0.953	8.129	
2003 PHI	31.878	196.917	44.343	257.999	-12.465	-61.082	
2003 COL	29.882	191.325	29.751	222.003	0.131	-30.678	
2004 HOU	**51.354**	**291.852**	47.327	276.000	4.026	15.852	P
2004 CIN	38.776	250.231	24.058	227.999	14.718	22.233	
2004 PIT	42.149	238.575	30.207	216.000	11.942	22.575	
2004 MON	36.386	237.834	23.554	201.000	12.832	36.834	
2004 SDP	39.964	233.695	41.507	261.004	-1.542	-27.309	D
2004 NYM	25.047	231.764	28.254	212.998	-3.208	18.766	
2004 ATL	35.366	231.270	45.166	287.999	-9.800	-56.728	D
2004 PHI	35.003	227.724	42.241	257.998	-7.237	-30.274	
2004 COL	33.545	225.731	27.524	204.002	6.021	21.728	W
2004 FLA	32.663	222.483	36.926	248.998	-4.263	-26.515	
2004 LAD	25.076	216.716	39.926	278.991	-14.850	-62.275	
2004 ARI	15.365	169.439	17.730	152.995	-2.365	16.444	
2005 WSN	**46.200**	**287.812**	30.011	242.997	16.189	44.815	W
2005 HOU	42.388	274.334	43.598	267.005	-1.211	7.329	P
2005 PHI	36.293	248.775	**45.094**	263.997	-8.801	-15.222	
2005 ATL	33.667	237.847	40.077	269.999	-6.410	-32.152	
2005 FLA	33.553	228.778	41.973	249.005	-8.420	-20.227	
2005 NYM	32.768	227.785	40.784	249.007	-8.015	-21.222	D
2005 COL	27.072	215.555	23.606	200.995	3.466	14.560	D

2005 SFG	30.008	207.194	25.098	224.999	4.910	-17.805	
2005 PIT	31.230	197.954	25.325	201.005	5.904	-3.051	
2005 LAD	21.797	173.179	28.449	212.998	-6.652	-39.819	
2006 HOU	**40.789**	**262.893**	41.155	245.999	-0.366	16.894	P
2006 WSN	36.609	249.632	25.934	212.995	10.675	36.637	
2006 NYM	29.348	241.738	44.481	**290.994**	-15.132	-49.255	
2006 LAD	33.667	238.472	**46.988**	265.823	-13.321	-27.351	D
2006 FLA	33.787	237.718	34.610	233.999	-0.822	3.719	
2006 ATL	34.181	237.605	38.254	237.002	-4.073	0.603	D
2006 PHI	37.716	227.599	44.858	254.996	-7.143	-27.397	
2006 ARI	40.435	213.324	38.753	228.002	1.682	-14.678	W
2006 PIT	33.081	211.008	26.193	201.002	6.888	10.006	
2006 COL	28.429	208.821	36.241	228.000	-7.812	-19.179	
2007 WSN	38.290	**277.790**	21.461	219.003	16.829	58.787	W
2007 STL	37.948	266.540	26.233	234.000	11.716	32.540	
2007 COL	**42.049**	264.226	43.781	**269.999**	-1.732	-5.774	D
2007 LAD	38.051	259.278	41.231	246.004	-3.180	13.273	
2007 NYM	39.772	247.256	42.786	264.001	-3.013	-16.745	P
2007 PHI	39.427	245.403	44.783	266.997	-5.356	-21.594	
2007 HOU	32.986	238.274	30.650	219.000	2.337	19.274	D
2007 FLA	29.720	232.508	34.075	213.001	-4.355	19.507	
2007 PIT	35.561	220.520	26.795	203.997	8.767	16.523	
2007 ARI	29.745	217.008	33.670	269.997	-3.925	-52.989	
2007 ATL	22.715	192.702	41.697	252.003	-18.982	-59.301	
2008 HOU	**42.147**	**273.666**	32.367	258.000	9.780	15.666	P
2008 WSN	37.239	243.311	18.384	177.003	18.856	66.308	
2008 NYM	36.966	243.258	42.656	267.000	-5.690	-23.742	D
2008 ARI	38.345	240.063	42.597	245.992	-4.252	-5.929	
2008 PHI	37.963	237.276	43.857	276.004	-5.894	-38.729	
2008 LAD	36.176	237.218	43.596	252.009	-7.420	-14.790	D
2008 COL	33.514	221.834	36.337	221.997	-2.823	-0.163	
2008 ATL	31.320	219.909	35.389	216.007	-4.069	3.902	
2008 CHC	35.965	218.507	**52.230**	290.994	-16.265	-72.487	W
2008 PIT	27.065	205.085	19.937	201.003	7.129	4.081	
2008 FLA	23.007	200.653	36.605	251.997	-13.598	-51.344	
2009 COL	**44.474**	**297.212**	45.891	275.998	-1.417	21.213	P
2009 STL	40.453	266.037	43.190	272.995	-2.737	6.958	D
2009 LAD	44.000	260.551	**50.921**	**285.002**	-6.922	-24.451	W
2009 PHI	43.028	259.568	45.546	279.003	-2.518	-19.435	D
2009 ATL	34.061	236.084	46.820	258.001	-12.760	-21.917	
2009 FLA	31.566	230.543	40.280	261.000	-8.714	-30.457	
2009 HOU	37.084	229.235	28.998	221.994	8.086	7.241	
2009 ARI	32.632	221.171	35.190	210.002	-2.557	11.169	
2009 WSN	35.246	214.390	22.151	177.002	13.095	37.388	
2009 PIT	26.851	208.307	22.048	186.000	4.803	22.307	
2009 NYM	28.639	194.226	27.318	209.994	1.321	-15.768	
2009 CHC	28.603	184.496	38.531	248.994	-9.928	-64.498	
2010 STL	45.873	**284.719**	40.837	257.999	5.036	26.720	P
2010 CIN	**46.226**	271.008	**46.808**	272.998	-0.581	-1.990	W
2010 PHI	43.749	270.102	46.480	**290.998**	-2.731	-20.896	D
2010 LAD	42.549	267.256	35.547	240.002	7.002	27.255	
2010 HOU	38.487	252.488	23.872	227.996	14.615	24.491	
2010 PIT	30.130	248.982	12.409	170.997	17.721	77.985	
2010 ATL	38.044	248.972	45.713	273.001	-7.668	-24.029	

2010 ARI	33.726	241.989	26.794	195.007	6.932	46.982	D
2010 FLA	36.261	237.115	36.767	239.995	-0.505	-2.881	
2010 COL	32.057	232.498	45.775	248.997	-13.717	-16.499	
2010 NYM	30.629	228.976	33.101	236.997	-2.472	-8.021	
2010 WSN	31.921	221.031	29.681	207.000	2.240	14.031	
2010 SDP	26.003	215.411	39.109	270.005	-13.107	-54.595	
2010 CHC	28.104	213.885	30.865	224.996	-2.761	-11.111	
2011 LAD	**46.168**	**285.889**	39.450	246.000	6.719	39.889	P
2011 STL	38.055	262.263	43.252	270.001	-5.197	-7.738	D
2011 PIT	35.142	260.608	20.514	215.997	14.627	44.611	
2011 ATL	36.586	259.492	41.130	266.995	-4.544	-7.503	
2011 ARI	32.428	258.582	38.388	282.001	-5.960	-23.419	
2011 FLA	39.805	254.047	35.685	215.998	4.120	38.050	W
2011 PHI	40.497	238.975	**52.996**	**305.997**	-12.499	-67.021	
2011 NYM	36.752	237.453	35.654	231.002	1.097	6.451	
2011 WSN	31.087	231.624	32.563	239.993	-1.476	-8.370	D
2011 HOU	33.892	229.775	21.302	167.975	12.589	61.800	
2011 CIN	30.929	215.269	35.702	236.997	-4.773	-21.728	
2011 SDP	34.102	210.664	29.603	212.996	4.499	-2.332	
2011 CHC	25.969	208.111	28.950	213.004	-2.981	-4.893	
2011 COL	22.713	193.280	33.880	218.992	-11.167	-25.712	
2012 PIT	46.182	**303.685**	24.273	236.997	21.909	66.688	P
2012 CIN	43.591	295.259	**45.480**	290.994	-1.889	4.265	
2012 LAD	47.171	289.726	34.519	257.993	12.651	31.733	D
2012 STL	34.043	268.103	43.159	264.002	-9.116	4.101	
2012 ARI	34.258	267.906	35.821	243.003	-1.563	24.903	W
2012 NYM	27.700	262.324	24.110	221.996	3.590	40.329	
2012 WSN	**47.859**	262.023	45.115	**294.004**	2.744	-31.981	D
2012 ATL	40.195	258.182	38.960	281.999	1.235	-23.817	W
2012 FLA	28.328	236.192	17.973	207.002	10.356	29.189	
2012 SFG	25.210	227.124	37.979	281.997	-12.769	-54.873	
2012 PHI	27.827	218.114	30.264	242.996	-2.437	-24.881	
2012 COL	27.808	217.691	23.697	191.997	4.111	25.694	
2012 CHC	25.228	208.638	13.628	182.998	11.600	25.640	
2012 HOU	19.018	194.890	10.308	164.995	8.710	29.895	
2013 PIT	43.887	**285.875**	42.840	281.993	1.047	3.882	W
2013 STL	37.277	284.324	41.891	**290.997**	-4.613	-6.672	P
2013 CIN	42.902	279.385	43.851	270.001	-0.949	9.384	W
2013 ARI	37.306	274.212	30.996	243.000	6.309	31.212	D
2013 LAD	38.454	263.085	**47.243**	276.002	-8.789	-12.917	D
2013 PHI	32.021	256.709	16.991	217.936	15.029	38.773	
2013 FLA	33.003	255.788	18.576	185.997	14.427	69.790	
2013 WSN	31.853	254.724	31.368	258.004	0.485	-3.280	
2013 ATL	**44.070**	254.324	44.993	283.361	-0.923	-29.037	
2013 MIL	38.416	254.089	28.310	222.004	10.106	32.085	
2013 NYM	36.890	251.612	20.944	221.997	15.945	29.615	
2013 COL	32.939	242.061	32.031	221.997	0.908	20.064	
2013 SFG	31.211	232.503	27.565	227.998	3.645	4.506	
2013 SDP	19.994	220.563	23.452	227.998	-3.458	-7.435	
2013 CHC	27.109	193.227	26.431	197.993	0.678	-4.766	

Highlighted row indicates League leader in oWAR, oWS and oPW%

Bibliography

Adler, Joseph. Baseball Hacks: Tips & Tools for Analyzing and Winning with Statistics. Sebastopol, CA: O'Reilly Media, 2006. Print.

Baseball America. Executive Database. Web. < http://www.baseballamerica.com/execdb/ >.

Baseball Prospectus Team of Experts. Baseball Between the Numbers: Why Everything You Know about the Game is Wrong. New York: Basic Books, 2006. Print.

Baseball-Reference. Web. < http://www.baseball-reference.com >.

Jaffe, Chris. Evaluating Baseball's Managers: A History and Analysis of Performance in the Major Leagues, 1876-2008. Kindle Edition.

James, Bill. The Bill James Baseball Abstract (1982-1987 Editions). New York: Ballantine Books, 1982-1987. Print.

James, Bill. The New Bill James Historical Baseball Abstract. New York: The Free Press, 2001. Print.

James, Bill, with Jim Henzler. Win Shares. Morton Grove, Ill.: STATS, 2002. Print.

MLB. First-Year Player Draft History – The Complete Draft History. Web. < http://mlb.mlb.com/mlb/history/draft/ >.

MLB. First-Year Player Draft History – Official Rules. Web. < http://mlb.mlb.com/mlb/draftday/rules.jsp >.

Palmer, Pete, and John Thorn. The Hidden Game of Baseball: A Revolutionary Approach to Baseball and Its Statistics. Garden City, N.Y.: Doubleday, 1984. Print.

Retrosheet. Web. < http://www.retrosheet.org >.
The information used here was obtained free of charge from and is copyrighted by Retrosheet. Interested parties may contact Retrosheet at "www.retrosheet.org".

Schwartz, Alan: The Numbers Game: Baseball's Lifelong Fascination with Statistics. New York: Thomas Dunne Books, 2004. Print.

Seamheads. Baseball Gauge. Web. < http://seamheads.com/baseballgauge/index.php >.
Win Shares and Wins Above Replacement data courtesy of Dan Hirsch

Sean Lahman. Lahman Database. Web. < http://seanlahman.com/baseball-archive/statistics >.
The information used here was obtained free of charge from and is copyrighted by Sean Lahman. Interested parties can download the database at www.SeanLahman.com.

Tango, Tom M., Mitchel G. Lichtman, and Andrew E. Dolphin. The Book: Playing the Percentages in Baseball. Washington: Potomac Books, 2007. Print

Wright, Craig R., and Tom House. The Diamond Appraised: A World Class Theorist & a Major-League Coach Square Off on Timeless Topics in the Game of Baseball. New York: Simon and Schuster, 1989. Print.

CPSIA information can be obtained at www.ICGtesting.com
Printed in the USA
LVOW09s0251040615

441126LV00015B/219/P